Roger Ebert's
Movie Yearbook
2006

Roger Ebert's Movie Yearbook 2006

**Andrews McMeel
Publishing**

Kansas City

Roger Ebert's Movie Yearbook 2006
copyright © 1999, 2000, 2001, 2002, 2003,
2004, 2005, 2006
by Roger Ebert

For information write
Andrews McMeel Publishing,
an Andrews McMeel Universal company,
4520 Main Street,
Kansas City, Missouri 64111.

ISBN-13: 978-0-7407-5538-5
ISBN-10: 0-7407-5538-2

www.andrewsmcmeel.com

All the reviews in this book originally appeared
in the *Chicago Sun-Times*.

This book is dedicated
to Robert Zonka, 1928–1985.
God love ya.

Contents

Introduction

The first collection in this series was published in October 1985, so this is the twentieth annual volume, under three different titles (*The Movie Home Companion, The Video Companion*, and, since 1999, the *Movie Yearbook*). The first two titles collected a cross-section of reviews since 1967, when I began at the *Chicago Sun-Times*. This became impractical, because more and more movies had to be culled for essentially the same space, and many new reviews had to be excluded. It seemed like a good idea to adopt a *Yearbook* format that would include every single one of my reviews from the most recent thirty months, as well as the most recent twelve months of interviews, film festival reports, Answer Man Q&As, and the invaluable Glossary entries. The book is often used as a guide to renting videos and DVDs, and most people rent fairly recent films. For classics, there are my books *The Great Movies* and *The Great Movies II*, and for the opposite of classics there are *I Hated, Hated, Hated This Movie* (2000) and a forthcoming volume tentatively titled *Your Movie Sucks*.

These books add up to a lot of reviews. When I began at the *Sun-Times*, I would review perhaps 130 movies in a typical year. Now I review at least twice as many. There are two reasons for that: The shelf life of the average Hollywood movie is much shorter, as even blockbusters go from their "record-setting" opening weekends to DVD in three or four months. And, despite the alleged demise of art houses, more foreign, independent, and documentary films open now than then.

Since 1967 I have been the principal film critic of the *Sun-Times*, although many other critics have also written for the paper; most papers our size have two or three full-time movie critics, but I have been at it for a long time now, reviewing as many films of interest (and without interest) as possible. As I commence the third screening of the day I tell myself it's not just for the paper, it's for the book and the Website.

There is also the matter that I love to write movie reviews almost as much as I love to watch movies—and in the case of some movies, even more. I've been reading some Edith Wharton lately and came across her discussion of the joy of losing herself in her writing; she quotes Charles Dickens, who claimed he was possessed by his books and characters. I am a newspaperman and not a Wharton or a Dickens, but I believe for all writers the effect is the same: When the game is afoot and the words are coming, I enter into a kind of joyful trance. I have experienced the same phenomenon when sketching. Time drops away, and the hands know what to do, what line to draw, what words to write. I sometimes speak to young writers and tell them I know one thing for sure: The Muse visits during the act of composition, not before. It is futile to wait for "inspiration." Start to write, and the inspiration will take care of itself.

Some of my reviews are not conventional in any sense. I receive e-mails from students who tell me I would fail the criticism classes they are taking. No doubt I would. Some of my reviews analyze the structure of a movie, others simply evoke the tone, and occasionally a review will jump the rails and turn out to be about something else altogether.

Other reviews seem strange to some readers, I suppose, because I do not seem to be doing criticism at all. My review of *Me and You and Everyone We Know*, for example, seeks to evoke rather than explain or analyze. Some reviews, like the ones for *The Honeymooners* and *Sahara*, read like an argument with hypothetical readers (in this case, most of them) who will not like the movie. Sometimes in a review I will find myself just discussing the plot. It was George Bernard Shaw who said description could be criticism, and I'm sure he was right: Sometimes to simply see what is in the movie, through your own eyes, is to comment on it. An example would be my review of *Downfall.*

There is the problem, too, of trying to tell great trash from ordinary trash. The sainted Pauline Kael told us, as I never tire of pointing out, that the movies are so rarely great art that if we cannot appreciate great trash, we might as well give up. *Mr. and Mrs. Smith*, for example, is a good movie of its kind, and *Son of the Mask*, while made with merciless energy, is not. This was a year when I stirred up some angry directors; the makers of *Chaos* bought a full-page ad in the *Sun-Times* to air their differences with me, and Tyler Perry was so unhappy with my review of *Diary of a Mad Black Woman* that he slipped an ad-lib attack on me into the dialogue of his stage alter ego, Madea. Discussions of both incidents are in this book.

On June 23, 2005, I got my own star on Hollywood's Walk of Fame. I was the "first film critic" to be honored with a star, or so it was said, and that brought up the reasonable question, did I deserve to be the first? I would have thought not. Names such as Pauline Kael, Stanley Kauffmann, David Bordwell, Jonathan Rosenbaum, and Andrew Sarris come to mind.

But the fact is, I was not honored for film criticism. The Walk of Fame does not honor film critics and my best guess is, they never will. I got the star for having been on television for thirty years. There is an irony here: The TV show has been a two-edged sword, responsible for my reviews and influence traveling outside Chicago, and responsible for many people dismissing me as the critic who reviews with thumbs.

On the other hand, being awarded the star was a great day for me, not least because so many friends and family shared it. The speakers at the ceremony included my wife, Chaz, and some of the film artists I have admired most over the years: Werner Herzog, Scott Wilson, Haskell Wexler, Anna Thomas, Virginia Madsen, and Joe Mantegna. The event was followed in July by the dedication of a plaque in front of the Chicago Theater, and the speakers included Mayor Richard M. Daley, Marlene Siskel, Harold Ramis, Tom Rosenberg, John Barron, Emily Barr, and my TV colleague Richard Roeper.

One reason I take my print reviews so seriously, and value books like this one, is that they allow me more depth, detail, and stylistic freedom than is possible on television. I value TV, on the other hand, for its impact, its influence, and the way it reaches people who do not and never will read a movie review. Our early reviews of *Monster* and *Million Dollar Baby* helped those films at a time when, as hard as it now is to believe, they were struggling to win a hearing in the tumult of holiday blockbusters. We make it a point on TV to include smaller films along with the big ones; there aren't many other shows where you hear about the new work by Werner Herzog, Takeshi Kitano, and Michael Winterbottom.

After I write a review, many brilliant and skillful editors are involved in its progress to print. They are thanked in the acknowledgments. I am also grateful to countless readers who write in with corrections, amendments, and useful observations. After writing about three-legged robots in my review of *War of the Worlds,* I was hearing from robot scientists for weeks.

I had long conversations with experts at MIT about the practicality of three-legged locomotion. It is stable for a stool, but is it stable for creatures that walk—and if it is, why has evolution sidestepped it? Many of these exchanges ended up in the Answer Man column, and this volume, as always, collects every Q&A of the last twelve months; a little pointing hand at the end of a review signals that there's a related Answer Man item.

*   *   *

At the Website RogerEbert.com, we are still adding new (i.e., old) reviews that have been scanned in from yellowing clippings, in an attempt to get everything since 1967 online. The site's editor is my friend and colleague Jim Emerson, himself a distinguished film critic and one of the editors of the late, lamented Microsoft Cinemania CD-ROM; he contributes a perceptive and contentious blog named Scanners. The *Sun-Times* people involved with RogerEbert.com have plans in motion to improve the speed and search functions of the site.

In bookstores right now: *The Great Movies II,* a collection of another one hundred essays about classic films. Coming in 2006: *Awake in the Dark,* a retrospective of my criticism and other writing from the University of Chicago Press.

ROGER EBERT

Acknowledgments

My editor is Dorothy O'Brien, tireless, cheerful, all-noticing. She is assisted by the equally invaluable Julie Roberts. My friend and longtime editor Donna Martin suggested this new approach to the annual volume. The design is by Cameron Poulter, the typographical genius of Hyde Park. My thanks to production editor Christi Clemons Hoffman, who renders Cameron's design into reality. I have been blessed with the expert and discriminating editing of John Barron, Laura Emerick, Miriam DiNunzio, Jeff Wisser, Darel Jevins, Avis Weathersbee, Jeff Johnson, Teresa Budasi, and John Grochowsky at the *Chicago Sun-Times;* Sue Roush at Universal Press Syndicate; and Michelle Daniel at Andrews McMeel Publishing. Many thanks are also due to the production staff at *Ebert & Roeper,* and to Marsha Jordan at WLS-TV. My gratitude goes to Carol Iwata, my expert personal assistant, and to Marlene Gelfond, at the *Sun-Times.* And special thanks and love to my wife, Chaz, for whom I can only say: If more film critics had a spouse just like her, the level of cheer in the field would rise dramatically.

ROGER EBERT

Key to Symbols

★★★★ A great film
★★★   A good film
★★   Fair
★   Poor

G, PG, PG-13, R, NC-17:
Ratings of the Motion Picture Association of America

G   Indicates that the movie is suitable for general audiences

PG   Suitable for general audiences but parental guidance is suggested

PG-13   Recommended for viewers 13 years or above; may contain material inappropriate for younger children

R   Recommended for viewers 17 or older

NC-17   Intended for adults only

141 m.   Running time

1999   Year of theatrical release

☞   Refers to "Questions for the Movie Answer Man"

Reviews

A

The Adventures of Sharkboy and Lavagirl in 3-D ★ ★
PG, 94 m., 2005

Cayden Boyd (Max), David Arquette (Dad), Kristin Davis (Mom), Taylor Dooley (Lavagirl), Taylor Lautner (Sharkboy), George Lopez (Mr. Electricidad), Sasha Pieterse (Ice Princess), Jacob Davich (Minus). Directed by Robert Rodriguez and produced by Elizabeth Avellan and Robert Rodriguez. Screenplay by Racer Rodriguez and Robert Rodriguez.

The Adventures of Sharkboy and Lavagirl in 3-D is an innocent and delightful children's tale that is spoiled by a disastrous decision to film most of it in lousy 3-D. Fully three-quarters of the movie is in "3"-D, which looks more like 1-D to me, removing the brightness and life of the movie's colors and replacing them with a drab, listless palette that is about as exciting as looking at a 3-D bowl of oatmeal.

The 3-D process subtracts instead of adding. Ordinary 2-D movies look perfectly real enough for audiences and have for years; if it's not broke, don't fix it. Paradoxically, since it allegedly resembles our real-world vision, 3-D is less real than standard flat movies; 3-D acts as a distraction from character and story, giving us something to think about that during a good movie we should not be thinking about.

To be sure, there is a new 3-D process that is pretty good. That would be the IMAX process that uses oversized glasses and creates a convincing 3-D effect, as in James Cameron's *Aliens of the Deep*. That is not the process used in *Sharkboy and Lavagirl*, which settles for those crummy old cardboard glasses where the left lens is such a dark red that the whole movie seems seen through a glass, darkly.

What a shame. I assume the unaltered original color footage of the movie exists, and no doubt will be used for the DVD. My suggestion to Robert Rodriguez, who directed the movie from a screenplay by one of his sons and uses three of them as actors, would be to make a non–3-D version available theatrically as soon as possible. This is a movie aimed at younger kids, who may be willing to sit through almost anything, but they're going to know something is wrong and they're not going to like it.

The origin of the film makes a good story. Rodriguez's son Racer, then seven, told him a story about a boy who grew gills and a fin and became half-shark, and a girl who incorporated fiery volcanic elements. He encouraged his son to keep working on the story, in which the young hero, Max (Cayden Boyd), is a daydreamer. Max is mocked by Linus, the school bully, because of his Dream Journal, where he documents the adventures of Sharkboy and Lavagirl. Then a tornado appears out of a clear sky, bringing with it Sharkboy (Taylor Lautner) and Lavagirl (Taylor Dooley), who explain they have been created by Max's dreams and now need his help; the world he created for them, Planet Drool, will be destroyed by darkness in forty-five minutes. I may not have followed these details with perfect fidelity, but you get the drift.

Max, SB, and LG go on a journey that takes them on the Stream of Consciousness to the Sea of Confusion; they ride a Train of Thought, and eventually arrive at a Dream Lair. There they find the nasty Minus, played by the same actor (Jacob Davich) who was the bully in Max's classroom. Many adventures result, some of them involving an Ice Princess and a robot named Tobor, as well as an all-knowing character named Mr. Electric, who looks exactly like Max's teacher Mr. Electricidad (George Lopez).

Mr. Electric appears as a big, round smiling face in a frame outfitted with spindly arms and legs. He reminded me of someone, which was odd, since he looked like nobody I've ever seen. Nobody, I realized, except the Man in the Moon in Georges Melies's *A Trip to the Moon* (1902). Mr. Electric floats about like a busybody commentator, offering advice, issuing warnings, and making a general nuisance of himself; one of his peculiarities is that he won't allow the kids on the planet to stop playing—ever. One group is trapped on a roller coaster that never stops.

Sharkboy and Lavagirl has the same upbeat charm as Rodriguez's *Spy Kids* movies, and it must be said that the screenplay by Racer Rodriguez involves the kind of free-wheeling invention that kids enjoy; this is a movie where dream logic prevails. Their movie also resembles *Spy Kids* in having roles for parents, including Max's dad and mom (David Arquette and Kristin Davis).

Because the real-world scenes are in 2-D and the dream and fantasy scenes are in 3-D, we get an idea of what the movie would have looked like without the unnecessary dimension. Signs flash on the screen to tell us when to put on and take off our polarizing glasses, and I felt regret every time I had to shut out those colorful images and return to the dim and dreary 3-D world. On DVD, this is going to be a great-looking movie.

After the Sunset ★ ★

PG-13, 100 m., 2004

Pierce Brosnan (Max Burdett), Salma Hayek (Lola Cirillo), Woody Harrelson (Stan Lloyd), Don Cheadle (Kingpin), Kate Walsh (Sheila), Naomie Harris (Sophie), Rachael Harris (June), Jeff Garlin (Ron). Directed by Brett Ratner and produced by Beau Flynn and Jay Stern. Screenplay by Paul Zbyszewski and Craig Rosenberg.

I am bemused by what a movie expects us to accept on faith. Consider the opening sequence of *After the Sunset,* a diamond heist movie. Woody Harrelson plays Stan, an FBI agent who is a passenger in an SUV; he holds a briefcase that contains a precious jewel. After the driver gets out of the SUV, the thief Max (Pierce Brosnan) uses a PDA to assume control of the vehicle, backs it up at high speed, and speeds away from the FBI security escort. On a side street, it halts in front of a garage door, and a semitruck pushes it sideways through the door, which slams shut behind it. Stan is relieved of the jewel and foiled again by his longtime arch-enemy.

Very good. But now think some more. Max's partner in the heist was Lola (Salma Hayek), who disguised herself as a bearded squeegee guy at a stoplight, using her squeegee to read the bar code on the SUV window so Max could key in the vehicle on his PDA. Very good. But why did he need to know the vehicle identification number when he manifestly had already customized the vehicle? After all, it contains the remote controls he is manipulating. Even the best-equipped SUVs don't come loaded with equipment allowing them to be driven automatically by PDAs. We're distracted from this logic by the obligatory scene in which Lola rips off her whiskers and wig, looking of course perfectly made up underneath.

All very well. But hold on: Did I say Max was on a rooftop? Yes, because that's how he can look down and see the SUV that he takes control of. Excellent. Except, what happens after the SUV turns the corner and races down the street and turns another corner? How can Max still see it? How does he know where to steer it? How come it doesn't run through a crosswalk containing a baby carriage, two nuns with six orphans, and a couple of guys carrying a sheet of plate glass? And how could they be sure the SUV would stop exactly in front of the open garage door, especially since Brosnan can't see what's happening? Maybe it was remote-controlled too.

The movies are never more mysterious than when they show us something that is completely preposterous, and get away with it. Not 1 viewer in 100 will ask the questions I've just asked, because in movies like this we go along with the flow. And this whole movie is flow.

After the Sunset is skillfully made, but it's not necessary. I can think of no compelling reason to see it during a time when your choices also include *Sideways, Ray, The Polar Express, The Incredibles, Primer, Vera Drake,* and *Undertow.* On the other hand, should you see it, the time will pass pleasantly.

The actors are good company. Pierce Brosnan and Salma Hayek hurl themselves into their roles—but gently, so nothing gets broken. She's in full plunging-neckline-in-the-sunset mode. Woody Harrelson has the necessary ambiguity to play the FBI agent's love-hate relationship with Max. Don Cheadle has fun as the American-born Bahamian gangster who wants to become Brosnan's partner in stealing a precious diamond from a cruise ship. Naomie Harris is intriguing as a local cop. The locations are sun-drenched, and there are enough plugs for the Atlantis resort hotel so that we know the cast enjoyed their stay on the island.

But what, really, is *After the Sunset* other than behavior-circling clichés? The heist itself, with its entrance through the ceiling, etc., is recycled from other films. However, the method by which Max establishes his alibi is clever. I can't describe it without giving away too much, but should you watch the film, ask yourself (1) if there's really enough time to do what he does, and (2) how likely it is that a nondiving FBI agent would agree to come along with a couple of thieves on a midnight scuba expedition to an old wreck?

The subplot is the old standby about the crooks who pull off one last job and plan to retire. Of course the woman is in favor of this, but the man grows restless and misses his old life. The same thing that happens to Max happened to Mr. Incredible. The female lead always gets the thankless task of trying to talk the hero out of doing what he obviously must do, or there would be no movie. "Now the challenge is to find joy in simple things," Lola tells Max. *After the Sunset* is a simple thing, so we could start there.

Against the Ropes ★ ★ ★
PG-13, 111 m., 2004

Meg Ryan (Jackie Kallen), Omar Epps (Luther Shaw), Charles S. Dutton (Felix Reynolds), Tony Shalhoub (Sam Larocca), Timothy Daly (Gavin Reese), Joseph Cortese (Irving Abel), Kerry Washington (Renee), Skye McCole Bartusiak (Young Jackie Kallen). Directed by Charles S. Dutton and produced by Robert W. Cort and David Madden. Screenplay by Cheryl Edwards.

You know the slow clap scene, where the key character walks into the room and it falls silent? And everybody is alert and tense and waiting to see what will happen? And then one person slowly starts to clap, and then two, three, four, and then suddenly the tension breaks and everyone is clapping, even the sourpuss holdouts? Can we agree that this scene is an ancient cliché? We can. And yet occasionally I am amazed when it works, all the same.

It works near the end of *Against the Ropes*, a biopic about Jackie Kallen, who was (and is) the first female fight promoter in the all-male world of professional boxing. It works, and another cliché works, too: the big fight scene, right out of *Rocky* and every other boxing movie, in which the hero gets pounded silly but then somehow, after becoming inspired between rounds, comes back and is filled with skill and fury.

Against the Ropes meanders until it gets to the final third of its running time, and then it catches fire. Its setup story is flat and lacks authenticity. Meg Ryan is barely adequate as Jackie Kallen, and Omar Epps, as her boxer, Luther Shaw, is convincing but underwritten. The film plays like a quick, shallow, made-for-TV biopic, but then it relies on those ancient conventions, and they pull it through.

When we meet Kallen, she is the assistant to Cleveland's top boxing promoter. She grew up in boxing; her dad ran a gym and when she was a little girl he sometimes had to chase her out of the ring. Now she knows as much about boxing as anyone, but of course as a woman isn't allowed to use that knowledge. Then, observing a fight in a ghetto drug apartment, she sees a (nondrug-related) guy waltz in and cream everyone, and she intuits that he could be a great fighter.

This is Luther Shaw, played by Epps as a man with psychic wounds from childhood that sometimes unleash a terrible fury. Kallen persuades him he can be a fighter, signs him, hires a trainer to prepare him, edges around the Cleveland boycott against her by convincing a Buffalo promoter it's time for him to return the favors he got from her dad. Many of the scenes in this stretch are routine, although the performance by Charles Dutton as a veteran trainer has a persuasive authenticity; he also directs.

Meg Ryan works hard at Jackie Kallen, but this is not a role she was born to play. Ryan is a gifted actress, best at comedy but with lots of *noir* in her; she's good in thrillers, too. But she's not naturally a brassy exhibitionist, and that's what this role calls for. Kallen, who seems to buy her wardrobe from Trashy Lingerie and Victoria's Secret, and who talks like a girl who grew up in a gym, might have better been cast with someone with rougher notes—Gina Gershon. Ryan seems to be pushing it.

There's also a problem with Renee (Kerry Washington), Kallen's best friend, who becomes

Luther's girlfriend, I think. I say "I think" because the role is so seriously underwritten that the movie would have been better off just not including it. Although Luther and Kallen are never romantically attracted, theirs is the movie's central relationship. Dutton (working from a screenplay by Cheryl Edwards) doesn't seem much interested in Luther's private emotional life, and so we get inexplicable scenes in which Luther and Renee seem to be best friends, or are hanging out together, or— what? The two of them have hardly any dialogue with each other, and although Renee is cheering during the big fight, there's no scene resolving her feelings for her man; the spotlight is on Kallen, which is all right, but it leaves a loose end.

Epps is always convincing, however, and by the last act of the movie we make our accommodation with Ryan because the character has grown more interesting. Intoxicated by the spotlight of publicity, she starts to think it's about her, not her boxer, and eventually she turns into a media caricature and finds herself forced outside the world she helped to create. Then comes the big fight, and the slow clap, and I'm damned if I wasn't really moved by the payoff.

Agent Cody Banks ★ ★ ½
PG, 110 m., 2003

Frankie Muniz (Cody Banks), Hilary Duff (Natalie Connors), Angie Harmon (Ronica Miles), Keith David (CIA Director), Cynthia Stevenson (Mrs. Banks), Daniel Roebuck (Mr. Banks), Arnold Vosloo (Molay), Ian McShane (Brinkman), Martin Donovan (Dr. Connors). Directed by Harald Zwart and produced by David Glasser, Andreas Klein, David Nicksay, Guy Oseary, and Dylan Sellers. Screenplay by Zack Stentz, Ashley Miller, Scott Alexander, and Larry Karaszewski.

Imagine James Bond as a suburban American fifteen-year-old, and you have *Agent Cody Banks*, a high-speed, high-tech kiddie thriller that's kinda cute but sorta relentless. Frankie Muniz stars as Cody, whose martial arts skills, skateboarding, ceiling-walking, and extreme snowboarding are all the more remarkable when you consider that he goes into action before the CIA has time to give him much more than what in the Bond pictures is the Q routine with the neat gizmos.

Frankie lives with his parents (Cynthia Stevenson and Daniel Roebuck), who mean well but are so inattentive they don't notice their son has become a spy with international missions. His CIA handler (Angie Harmon, low-cut and sexy) wants him to become friends with a classmate named Natalie Connors (Hilary Duff, from *Lizzie McGuire*). Frankie is, alas, so tongue-tied around girls that his grade-school brother boasts, "Cody's almost sixteen and I've had twice as many dates as he has." Cody fights back ("Sitting in a treehouse doesn't count"), but the kid is serene ("It does when you're playing Doctor").

Natalie attends the ultraexclusive William Donovan Prep School, no doubt named for the famous World War II spy "Wild Bill" Donovan, and Frankie transfers there, uses his karate skills to silence hecklers, and ends up on a mission to liberate Natalie's father, Dr. Connors (Martin Donovan), from the clutches of the evil masterminds Brinkman and Molay (Ian McShane and Arnold Vosloo), who want to (we know this part by heart) attain world domination by using the doctor's inventions—microscopic nanorobots that can eat through anything.

The movie imitates its Bond origins with a lot of neat toys. Cody is given a BMW skateboard that has unsuspected versatility, and a jet-powered snowboard, and a sports car, and X-ray glasses (Hello, Angie Harmon!), and a watch that will send electricity through your enemies, although I think (I'm not sure about this) you should not be wearing it yourself at the time.

The set design includes the scientist's laboratory in underground World Domination Headquarters—which includes, as students of *Ebert's Bigger Little Movie Glossary* will not be surprised to learn, commodious and well-lighted overhead air ducts so that Cody can position himself in comfort directly above all important conversations. There also is CIA regional headquarters, with a conference table that looks like it was designed by Captain Nemo in a nightmare. We learn that the CIA runs summer camps to train kids to become junior spies, although why Angie Harmon, who seems to be playing Young Mrs. Robinson, is their handler is hard to explain—maybe she's there for the dads, in the movie and in the audience.

The movie will be compared with the two *Spy Kids* pictures, and it looks more expensive and high-tech, but isn't as much fun. It has a lot of skill and energy, but its wit is more predictable and less delightful. It's a well-made movie, to be sure, and will probably entertain its target audience, but its target audience is probably not reading this review, and you (for whatever reason) are. The difference is, I could look you in the eye and recommend you go see the *Spy Kids* movies, but this one, if you're not a kid, I don't think so.

Agent Cody Banks 2: Destination London ★ ★ ½
PG, 93 m., 2004

Frankie Muniz (Cody Banks), Anthony Anderson (Derek), Hannah Spearritt (Emily), Daniel Roebuck (Mr. Banks), Keith Allen (Diaz), Keith David (CIA Director), Cynthia Stevenson (Mrs. Banks), Connor Widdows (Alex Banks). Directed by Kevin Allen and produced by David Glasser, Andreas Klein, David Nicksay, Guy Oseary, and Dylan Sellers. Screenplay Don Rhymer.

I've been trying to mind-control myself into the head of a kid the right age to enjoy *Agent Cody Banks 2: Destination London,* but either I was never that age, or I haven't reached it yet. I'm capable of enjoying the *Spy Kids* movies, so I know I'm not totally lacking in range, but the movie seems preassembled, like those kits where it takes more time to open the box than build the airplane.

The movie opens at a secret summer camp where the CIA trains teenagers to become junior James Bonds. The opening scene, in fact, is uncanny in the way it resembles the prologue of David Mamet's *Spartan.* In both movies, characters in combat uniforms with lots of camouflage paint on their faces creep through trees and try to cream one another. For Mamet, that is not the high point of his movie.

Cody Banks (Frankie Muniz) is a smart, resourceful kid who thinks there may be something fishy at the camp, which is run by Diaz (Keith Allen), love child of Patton and Rambo. After a secret plot is revealed, Cody finds himself on assignment in London, where his handler is Derek (Anthony Anderson) and his mission is to prevent the CIA's bad apples from gaining possession of a mind-control device that fits inside a tooth and turns its wearer into a zombie.

It's a pretty nifty device: At one point, its mad inventor fits it to a dog which then sits upright at a piano and plays a little tune, reminding me inevitably of Dr. Johnson's observation that when a dog walks on its hind legs, "it is not done well, but one is surprised to find it done at all." The dog is impressive but no pianist, and Derek, watching the demonstration on a spycam with Cody, decides he won't buy the CD.

The agency, as in the previous film, supplies Cody with various secret weapons, including a pack of Mentos that explode when moistened. Turns out the evil master plan is to subvert a conference of world leaders at Buckingham Palace; to infiltrate the palace, Cody must join a world-class youth orchestra—not easy, since he doesn't play an instrument, but easier than you might think, since his agency-supplied clarinet plays itself. It seems to know only "Flight of the Bumble Bee," unfortunately.

Hilary Duff, who played Cody's sidekick in the previous movie, is MIA this time, and her place is taken, sort of, by Emily (Hannah Spearritt), a British agent who looks in a certain light as if she might be a teenager, and in another as if she might be, oh, exactly twenty-three. You will recall from the previous film that Cody is too busy being an agent to date much, and his little brother sees more action. (That produced a good exchange: Cody says most of the brother's dating doesn't count because it's limited to a tree house, and the brother replies, "It does if you're playing Doctor.")

The big climax at Buckingham Palace features look-alikes for Tony Blair and the queen, and a scene that is supposed to be funny because the youth orchestra stalls for time by improvising a song with a funky rhythm and the queen boogies with the heads of state. Since I am enough of a realist to believe that a large part of the target audience for this movie doesn't know who the queen is or what she looks like, it's a good thing the action starts up again real soon.

There is a mind-controlled food fight that

begins promisingly but is awkwardly handled, and a chase through London that is (sigh) just one more chase through London, and apart from funny supporting work by the inventor of the mind control and the guy in the "Q" role, the movie is pretty routine. I wanted to be able to tell you the names of the actors in those two entertaining roles, but half an hour's research has not discovered them, although the movie's Website has signed me up for junior agent training.

The Agronomist ★ ★ ★ ½
NO MPAA RATING, 90 m., 2004

A documentary directed by Jonathan Demme and produced by Demme, Bevin McNamara, and Peter Saraf.

Jean Dominique was a brave man in a dangerous country, and Jonathan Demme's *The Agronomist* shows him telling the truth as he sees it, day after day, on the radio in Haiti. It is obvious that sooner or later he will be assassinated. Dissent cannot be tolerated in a nation that depends on secrecy to protect its powerful. What is remarkable is how long he survived, and how courageously he owned and operated Radio Haiti-Inter; it became the voice of the powerless in great part because it broadcast in Creole, the language they spoke, instead of in the French of their masters.

Jonathan Demme, who made the documentary, is a man who seems to lead parallel lives. In one, he is the successful director of such films as *The Silence of the Lambs, Philadelphia, Married to the Mob,* and *Melvin and Howard.* In the other, he has made documentaries about Haiti, has visited there countless times, has helped promote Haitian art and music, and has a heart that aches as he sees the country victimized by powerful interests both within and without.

In Jean Dominique and his wife, Michele Montas, Demme finds subjects who reflect the agony of Haiti's struggle. His documentary draws on hundreds of hours of filming and conversations from 1991 until Dominique's death in 2000. It begins at the moment when President Jean-Claude Aristide was overthrown in 1991, follows the Dominiques into exile in New York, watches as they return to Haiti and Aristide is restored to power, and observes how Dominique, originally a supporter of Aristide, became one of his critics.

Dominique is a man who seems to have come to heroism because it was the only choice for a man of his nature. His college education was in agriculture (which explains the movie's title), and he first came up against the ruling clique through his efforts for land reform. He was interested in the arts, started a cinema club in Port-au-Prince, and was shut down by the dictator "Papa Doc" Duvalier after showing Alain Resnais's *Night and Fog.* That was a film about the evil of Nazism; why Papa Doc found it unacceptable is easy to imagine.

At first it seemed that the rebel priest Aristide might force a change in his nation's destiny, but soon he, too, was employing the tactics of those he replaced. There is a sequence in the film where Dominique interviews Aristide and challenges him with pointed questions. The president responds with measured sound bites that repeat the same inanities again and again, as if he is incapable of understanding the actual meaning of the questions he has been asked.

Dominique and Montas are persons of great cheer and energy, leaping into each day with such zeal that they sometimes seem to forget the risks they are taking. Their problem in Haiti is that by honestly speaking to the ordinary people in their own language, they offend not only their obvious enemies but even those they do not know they have made. A nation built on lies cannot tolerate truth even when it agrees with it.

Radio Haiti-Inter comes under siege more than once, and Demme's camera does not overlook the bullet holes in the exterior walls. The station seems to be run informally, as a mixture of music, gossip, local news, and political opinion; at times of crisis, Dominique stays on the air as long as he can, until power outages or the government shut him down.

This is a couple who could have led the good life in Haiti. With the light complexions of the French-speaking Haitian establishment, with education and some wealth, they could have gone along with the ruling elite and earned a nice little fortune with their radio station or other enterprises. What fascinates us is Dominique's inability to do that. He is well enough connected to know what is going wrong, and too principled to ignore it.

Did he know he would be killed? Who can say? His country was in tumult, and the inconsistent policies of the United States did little to help. The country seemed almost to force its rulers into fearful and repressive policies. The wise course for Dominique would have been to return in exile to New York and use a dissenting magazine or Web site to spread his beliefs.

But no. When he could go back, he went back. Demme often followed him. We watch Dominique use humor and cynicism as well as anger, and we understand he is not a zealot but simply a reasonable man saying reasonable things in an unreasonable country. After his murder, Michele Montas goes on the air to insist that Jean Dominique is still alive, because his spirit lives on. But in this film Haiti seems to be a country that can kill the spirit, too.

Aileen: The Life and Death of a Serial Killer ★ ★ ★ ½
NO MPAA RATING, 89 m., 2004

A documentary directed by Nick Broomfield and Joan Churchill and produced by Jo Human.

Aileen Wuornos was trashed by life. That she committed seven murders is beyond dispute and unforgivable, but what can we expect from a child who was beaten by her grandfather, molested by a pedophile, abandoned by her mother, and raped by her brother and other neighborhood boys and men? A child who was selling sex for cigarettes at the age of nine, who had a baby at thirteen and was thrown out of the house, who lived for two years in the woods at the end of the street or, in cold weather, in the backseat of a car, wrapped in a single blanket? Society made Aileen into a weapon and turned her loose.

Aileen: The Life and Death of a Serial Killer is a documentary by Nick Broomfield, the guerrilla filmmaker who works with a crew of one (cinematographer and codirector Joan Churchill) and structures his films into the stories of how he made them. He met Aileen, invariably described as "America's first female serial killer," soon after her original arrest, and made the 1992 documentary *Aileen Wuornos: The Selling of a Serial Killer* about the media zoo and bidding war that surrounded her sudden notoriety. Florida police officers were fired after

it was disclosed they were negotiating for a Hollywood deal, and Aileen, meanwhile, was represented by "Dr. Legal," a bearded, pot-smoking ex-hippie who was incompetent and clueless. She saw his ad on late-night TV. She couldn't pay him, but he figured he could cash in, too.

As Wuornos's often-delayed execution date inexorably closed in, Broomfield returned to the story for this film, made in 2002. He had become friendly, if that is the word, with Aileen, and indeed she gave him her last interview. He also interviewed many people instrumental in her life, including childhood friends, former sexual partners, and even her long-lost mother. The portrait he builds of her life is one of cruel suffering and mistreatment. This was a young woman who hitchhiked to Florida when she was thirteen because she was tired of sleeping in the rough, and who became a roadside prostitute because, really, what else was open to her? Social services? Invisible in her case.

Wuornos herself is onscreen for much of the film. Charlize Theron has earned almost unanimous praise for her portrayal of Aileen in the film *Monster*, and her performance stands up to direct comparison with the real woman. There were times, indeed, when I perceived no significant difference between the woman in the documentary and the one in the feature film. Theron has internalized and empathized with Wuornos so successfully that to experience the real woman is only to understand more completely how remarkable her performance is.

Wuornos talks and talks and talks to Broomfield. She confesses and recants. She says at one point that her original defense (she was raped and attacked by her victims, and shot them in self-defense) was a lie—that she was in the "stealing biz" and killed them to cover her tracks. On another day she is likely to return to her original story. We hear her describing a man who tortured her with acid in a Visine bottle, and her vivid details make us feel we were there. Then she tells Broomfield she made it all up. What can we believe? Broomfield's theory is that after more than a decade on Death Row, Wuornos was insane, and that she used her last remaining shreds of reason to hasten the day of her execution. She said whatever she thought would speed her date with death.

Oh, yes, it's clear she was crazy on the day she died. She talks to Broomfield about secret signals and radio waves being beamed into her cell, about how the police knew she was the killer but let her keep on killing because it would make a better story for them to sell, about how she would be beamed up "like on *Star Trek*" to a spaceship waiting for her in Earth orbit.

Remarkably, three psychiatrists "examined" her right before her death and found her sane. No person who sees this film would agree with them. Florida Governor Jeb Bush was scarcely less enthusiastic about the death penalty than his brother George, who supported the notorious execution assembly line in Texas. Aileen died in October of an election year, just in time to send a law-and-order message to the voters. Should she have died? That depends on whether you support the death penalty. She was certainly guilty. The film makes it clear her imprisonment would simply have continued a lifelong sentence that began when she was born. No one should have to endure the life that Aileen Wuornos led, and we leave the movie believing that if someone, somehow, had been able to help that little girl, her seven victims would never have died.

The Alamo ★ ★ ★ ½
PG-13, 137 m., 2004

Dennis Quaid (Sam Houston), Billy Bob Thornton (Davy Crockett), Jason Patric (James Bowie), Patrick Wilson (William Barrett Travis), Emilio Echevarria (Santa Anna), Jordi Molla (Juan Seguin), Laura Clifton (Susanna Dickinson), Leon Rippy (Sergeant William Ward). Directed by John Lee Hancock and produced by Brian Grazer, Ron Howard, and Mark Johnson. Screenplay by Leslie Bohem, Stephen Gaghan, and Hancock.

The advance buzz on *The Alamo* was negative, and now I know why: This is a good movie. Conventional wisdom in Hollywood is that any movie named *The Alamo* must be simplistic and rousing, despite the fact that we already know all the defenders got killed. (If we don't know it, we find out in the first scene.) Here is a movie that captures the loneliness and dread of men waiting for two weeks for what they expect to be certain death, and it somehow succeeds in taking those pop culture brand names like Davy Crockett and James Bowie and giving them human form.

The arc of the Alamo story is a daunting one for any filmmaker: long days and nights of waiting, followed by a massacre. Even though the eventual defeat of Santa Anna by Sam Houston provides an upbeat coda, it's of little consolation to the dead defenders. This movie deals frankly with the long wait and the deadly conclusion by focusing on the characters of the leaders; it's about what they're made of, and how they face a bleak situation.

Davy Crockett, the man in the coonskin hat, surprisingly becomes the most three-dimensional of the Alamo heroes, in one of Billy Bob Thornton's best performances. We see him first in a theater box, attending a play inspired by his exploits. We learn of his legend; even Santa Anna's men whisper that he can leap rivers in a single bound and wrestle grizzly bears to death. And then we watch Crockett with a rueful smile as he patiently explains that he did not do and cannot do any of those things, and that his reputation has a life apart from his reality.

Crockett, who was a U.S. congressman before fate led him to the Alamo, has two scenes in particular that are extraordinary, and Thornton brings a poignant dignity to them. One is his memory of a U.S. Army massacre of Indians. The other occurs when the Mexicans, who have brought along a band, have their drummers put on a show. Crockett knows just what the percussion needs, climbs one of the battlements, takes out his violin and serenades both sides. It is one of those moments, like the Christmas Eve truce in World War I, when fighting men on both sides are reminded of the innocence they have lost. Crockett also has a line that somehow reminded me of the need, in *Jaws*, for a bigger boat: "We're going to need more men."

Leadership of the Alamo is contested between Colonel James Bowie (Jason Patric) and Lieutenant Colonel William Barrett Travis (Patrick Wilson). It involves a show of hands, a contest of wills, a truce, and then the inexorable weakening of Bowie, who is dying of tuberculosis and, it is murmured, other diseases. Travis is a humorless patriot who would rather, he tells us, have moments of glory than a lifetime of drudgery, and he strikes the men as over the top. But he is true to his principles, and at one point, although he has to be informed that the time has come to talk to his men, he delivers a speech filled with fire and resolve, reminding me of Henry V on the night before Agincourt.

Bowie faces the fact that he is a dying man, and it is agonizing to watch him attempt to button up his vest and climb from his deathbed to join in the battle. A revolver is placed in each of his hands, and when the Mexicans burst in, he takes two lives before they claim the few hours of life left in him. Both Travis and Bowie could have been caricatures; Wilson and Patric find their humanity.

The director and cowriter, John Lee Hancock, occupies more than an hour with scenes leading up to the final battle, as the Alamo defenders make their plans and wait for reinforcements that never arrive. As his troops surround them, General Santa Anna (Emilio Echevarria) struts and poses in front of his officers, who are appalled by his ignorance but intimidated by his temper. Ordering the final charge, he's told a twelve-pound cannon will arrive tomorrow that would breach the Alamo's walls without sacrifice of countless Mexican lives, but he disdains to wait, and dismisses the lives with a wave of his hand. (His own life was much more precious to him; he traded it for Texas.)

There are two scenes involving surrender that make an ironic contrast. Surrounded by dead bodies, himself gravely wounded, Davy Crockett is offered surrender terms by Santa Anna and replies by defiantly offering to accept Santa Anna's surrender. This is matched by the scene at the end where Houston (Dennis Quaid) has Santa Anna on his knees, and the general will agree to anything.

Much of the picture takes place at night, illuminated by campfires and candlelight, and Hancock's cinematographer, the gifted Dean Semler, finds color and texture in the shadows that evoke those hours between midnight and dawn that Fitzgerald called the dark night of the soul. Oddly enough, as Santa Anna's troops march up to within one hundred yards of the Alamo, there seem to be no watchmen to see them, and when they attack it is a surprise.

The battle scenes, when they come, are brutal and unforgiving; we reflect that the first Mexicans up the scaling ladders must have known they would certainly die, and yet they climbed them heedlessly. This intimate, hand-to-hand conflict is balanced by awesome long shots, combining the largest sets ever built by modern Hollywood with some special effects shots that are generally convincing.

Although the battle for the Alamo has taken its place as a sacred chapter in American history, the movie deals with the fact that it all came down to one thing: Mexico owned Texas, and ambitious Americans and Texans (or "Texians") wanted it. Many of the fighters had been promised 760 acres of land as a bonus for enlisting. For Bowie, Crockett, and Travis, the challenge was to rehabilitate reputations that had gone astray—to redeem themselves. For Sam Houston, who never sent reinforcements, it was an opportunity to apply Wellington's strategy in leading Napoleon on a chase until Napoleon's army was splintered and weakened. Houston was too wise to commit his army to the Alamo; that took foolishness, bravery, and a certain poetry of the soul.

Alex & Emma ★ ½
PG-13, 96 m., 2003

Kate Hudson (Emma, Eulva, Elsa, Eldora, and Anna), Luke Wilson (Alex, Adam), Sophie Marceau (Polina), David Paymer (John Shaw), Alexander Wauthier (Andre), Leili Kramer (Michele), Rip Taylor (The General), Gigi Birmingham (Madame Blanche), Jordan Lund (Claude). Directed by Rob Reiner and produced by Todd Black, Alan Greisman, Jeremy Leven, Reiner, and Elie Samaha. Screenplay by Reiner, Leven, Adam Scheinman, and Andrew Scheinman.

Alex & Emma is a movie about a guy who has to write a novel in thirty days in order to collect the money from his publisher to pay two gamblers who will otherwise kill him. So he hires a stenographer to take dictation, and they fall in love. But the thing is, it's a bad novel. Very bad. Every time the author started dictating, I was struck anew by how bad it was—so bad it's not even good romance fiction.

I guess I didn't expect him to write *The Gambler* by Dostoyevsky—although, come to think of it, Dostoyevsky dictated *The Gambler* in thirty days to pay off a gambling debt, and fell in love with his stenographer. I just expected him to write something presentable. You might reasonably ask why we even need to know what he's writing in the first place, since the movie involves the writer and the girl. But, alas, it involves much more: There are cutaways to the story he's writing, and its characters are played by Kate Hudson and Luke Wilson, the same two actors who star in the present-day story.

This other story takes place in 1924 and involves people who dress and act like the characters in *The Great Gatsby*. Not the central characters, but the characters who at*tend* Gatsby's parties and are in those long lists of funny names. It might have been a funny idea for the novelist to actually steal *The Great Gatsby*, confident that neither the gamblers nor his publisher would recognize it, but funny ideas are not easy to come by in *Alex & Emma*.

Alex is played by Luke Wilson. Emma is played by Kate Hudson. He also plays Adam, the young hero of the story within the story, and she plays four different nannies (Swedish, German, Latino, and American) who are employed by a rich French divorcée (Sophie Marceau) who plans to marry a rich guy (David Paymer) for his money, but is tempted by the handsome young Adam, who is a tutor to her children, who remain thoroughly untutored.

So the story is a bore. The act of writing the story is also a bore, because it consists mostly of trying out variations on the 1924 plot and then seeing how they look in the parallel story. Of course chemistry develops between Alex and Emma, who fall in love, and just as well: There is a Hollywood law requiring fictional characters in such a situation to fall in love, and the penalty for violating it is death at the box office. A lot of people don't know that.

Curious, the ease with which Alex is able to dictate his novel. Words flow in an uninterrupted stream, all perfectly punctuated. No false starts, wrong word choices, or despair. Emma writes everything down and then offers helpful suggestions, although she fails to supply the most useful observation of all, which would be to observe that the entire novel is complete crap.

Despite the deadly deadline, which looms ever closer, the young couple find time to get out of the apartment and enjoy a Semi-Obligatory Lyrical Interlude, that old standby where they walk through the park, eat hot dogs, etc., in a montage about a great day together. I do not remember if they literally walk through the park or eat hot dogs, but if they don't, then they engage in parklike and hot dog–like activities.

Now about his apartment. It's at the top of a classic brownstone, with balconies and tall windows, and should cost thousands of dollars a month, but he's flat broke, see, and just to prove it, there's a place where the plaster has fallen off the wall and you can see the bare slats underneath. He has art hanging all over his apartment, except in front of those slats. All Alex has to do is sublet, and his financial worries are over.

The movie has been directed by Rob Reiner and is not as bad as *The Story of Us* (1999), but this is a movie they'll want to hurry past during the AFI tribute. Reiner has made wonderful movies in the past (*Misery, The Princess Bride, Stand by Me*) and even wonderful romantic comedies (*The Sure Thing, When Harry Met Sally*). He will make wonderful movies in the future. He has not, however, made a wonderful movie in the present.

Alexander ★ ★
R, 175 m., 2004

Colin Farrell (Alexander), Angelina Jolie (Olympias), Val Kilmer (Philip), Rosario Dawson (Roxane), Jared Leto (Hephaistion), Anthony Hopkins (Ptolemy), Christopher Plummer (Aristotle). Directed by Oliver Stone and produced by Moritz Borman, Jon Kilik, Thomas Schuhly, Iain Smith, and Stone. Screenplay by Stone, Christopher Kyle, and Laeta Kalogridis.

When the mighty fall, it is from a greater height. So it was with Alexander the Great, and so it is with Oliver Stone's *Alexander*. Here is an ambitious and sincere film that fails to find a focus for its elusive subject. Stone is fascinated by two aspects of Alexander: his pannationalism, and his pansexualism. He shows him trying to unite many peoples under one throne while remaining equally inclusive with his choices of lovers.

But it remains unclear if Alexander has united those peoples or simply conquered them, and his sexuality is made murky by the film's shyness about gay sex and its ambiguity about Alexander's relationships with his "barbarian" bride and his tigress mother. We welcome the movie's scenes of battle, pomp, and circumstance because at least for a time we are free of sociopolitical concepts and the endless narration of Ptolemy the historian, who functions here like the Bill Kurtis of antiquity ("No tyrant ever gave back so much . . .").

The facts are quickly summarized. Alexander (Colin Farrell) is the son of Philip of Macedonia (Val Kilmer) and Queen Olympias (Angelina Jolie). As a boy, he sees his drunken father all but rape his mother, who for her part insists Alexander's actual father is Zeus, but doesn't give details. Young Alexander impresses his father by taming an intractable horse, but both mother and son are banished from the kingdom, Olympias advising her son to seize the throne before Philip has him murdered. In the event, Philip is murdered, and Alexander rules Macedonia.

Still a very young man, he sets out to conquer the known world. Told by Aristotle (Christopher Plummer) where the world ends, he finds it keeps on going, and so he keeps on conquering, defeating the other Greek city states, the Persians, and all the other peoples he confronts until he is finally defeated not so much by the rulers of India as by India itself. He dies at 32.

He is, in Stone's version, remarkably open-minded for a tyrant. There are many scenes in which he debates strategy and goals with the members of his army, something we cannot easily imagine Philip (or Patton) doing. He takes the Asian bride Roxane (Rosario Dawson) instead of choosing a nice Greek girl as his advisers recommend. He spends eight years in battle, taking with him his army, their wives and lovers, their servants and households, in a sort of movable empire. And always smoldering in the shadows is Hephaistion (Jared Leto), his closest friend since childhood.

In ancient times, we are told, powerful men often took men or boys as their lovers, reserving women for childbearing and suchlike. Alexander seems to be following that tradition to the extent that Stone (and perhaps the MPAA production code) will permit it. Hephaistion doesn't even go through the motions of taking a wife; he is always there for Alexander—but for what? They have what looks like the beginning of a love scene before it fades out, and the rest of the time, they hug a lot.

As for Alexander's sex life with Roxane, it is not surprising but nevertheless worthy of notice that we see a great deal more of her body than Hephaistion's, and observe them during a sex scene that begins with her fighting him off and ends with them engaged in the kind of unbridled passion where you hope nobody gets hurt. All right, so they have great sex—once. Then we learn that three years pass and she provides no male heir, although for all we see of them together, the fault may be Zeus's.

It's clear enough that Alexander loves Hephaistion and has married Roxane as a political gesture. In that case it is a miscalculation by Stone to make Hephaistion into a pouting sideline figure who specializes in significant glances, the significance of which the movie does not explore, while making Roxane into such an exciting hellion that we're disappointed Alexander doesn't let us spend more time with her, even if he doesn't want to. Dawson's Roxane is truly sexy, but Jared Leto's Hephaistion is not allowed to be seen as a male beauty; he looks like a drag queen, with more eye-liner than Elizabeth Taylor as Cleopatra. If Stone is not willing to make Hephaistion at least potentially as erotic a character as Roxane, he is not really engaging the logic of the story.

The ambiguities are not assisted by Colin Farrell's less-than-wholehearted embrace of his bisexuality. He goes after Roxane at first with the gusto of a rugby player, but approaches Hephaistion with a solemnity that borders on the doleful. Nor is he convincing as a conqueror. Farrell is a fine actor, but on a human scale; he's not cut out for philosopher-king. One needs to sense a certain madness in a colossus; George C. Scott brought it to Patton, Peter O'Toole brought it to Lawrence, Klaus Kinski to Fitzcarraldo, Mel Gibson had it as William Wallace, Willem Dafoe had it in Stone's *Platoon*, but Farrell seems too reasonable, too much of ordinary scale to drive men to the ends of the world with his unbending will. Of other actors Stone has worked with, perhaps Woody Harrelson has the strange light in his eyes that the role requires.

The running narration by Ptolemy (Anthony Hopkins) is a road map through three decades of history, but there are so many names, places, and dates that finally we want to ask, please, sir, will this be on the final? Perhaps the narration is supposed to bridge gaps in the disjointed narrative. Even so, at one late point the movie comes to a jarring halt with the title "Macedonia—Eight Years Earlier," and we get a flashback to scenes involving Philip that don't feel like a flashback at all, but more like material plucked from its place in the chronology and inserted later to clarify what the filmmakers fear we will not otherwise understand.

Alexander and Ptolemy both talk a lot about incorporating conquered peoples into the expanding empire. Their clothes, languages, foods, and customs are embraced, we hear, but the movie spends more energy telling us this than showing us. Even though the movie's battle scenes are impressive and sometimes brilliant, Alexander's opponents have the human dimension of video-game figures. They attack, are vanquished, are replaced by new foes. The battles in India are masterful, with Alexander's men and horses terrified by war elephants, and an earlier battle against the Persians at Gaugamela has scope and grandeur. It looks as if there might be real men on the ground, instead of the digital ants in *Troy*. But we don't get a sense of the humans on the other side.

To mention Wolfgang Petersen's *Troy*, the 2004 epic about Grecian myth, is to make a comparison necessary. *Alexander* far outreaches *Troy* in ambition, its action scenes seem at least conceivably plausible, and it is based on ideas, not formulas. Yet *Troy* tells a story that has some structure and clarity, and those are precisely the qualities that *Alexander* lacks. The parts don't fit together in *Alexander*. Transitions and segues are missing, and we seem to be looking at disconnected parts from a much larger whole—two wholes, perhaps, one involving Alexander's military and political careers, and the other his confused emotional life.

While we can at least process the problems in his marriage with Roxane (he lost interest), we are left baffled by his tangled relationship with his mother. Angelina Jolie seems so young and sexy as Olympias, especially in scenes involving Alexander, that we wonder if she will start raiding cradles instead of tombs. She hates Philip, and no wonder, for he is a drunken lout, but are her hopes for Alexander entirely geopolitical? She regards him in a way Roxane never does, and one of the reasons for the "Eight Years Earlier" flashback is to get her back into the film after a too-lengthy absence.

I have always admired Oliver Stone's courage in taking on big, challenging films, and his gift for marrying action and ideas. *Alexander* is not a success, but it is ambitious and risky, and incapable of the inanities of *Troy*. Fascinated by his subject, he has things he urgently wants to say about Alexander, but his urgency outraces his narrative; he gives us provocative notes and sketches but not a final draft. The film doesn't feel at ease with itself. It says too much, and yet leaves too much unsaid.

Alfie ★ ★ ★
R, 106 m., 2004

Jude Law (Alfie), Marisa Tomei (Julie), Omar Epps (Marlon), Nia Long (Lonette), Jane Krakowski (Dorie), Sienna Miller (Nikki), Susan Sarandon (Liz). Directed by Charles Shyer and produced by Shyer and Elaine Pope. Screenplay by Bill Naughton, Pope, and Shyer, based on the play by Naughton.

Strange, that *Alfie* (1966) is halfway remembered as a comedy, when it was actually about a man who attempted to live life as comedy despite the lowering gloom that he thoroughly deserved. Alfie, in 1966 and again in the 2004 version, desperately wants to keep smiling, have a great time, and be lover to a parade of women who are willing and friendly, and never complain, and make no demands, and understand his need to be unfaithful. Such a woman, if she exists, would not be worth having, but tell that to Alfie.

Michael Caine made *Alfie* and *The Ipcress File* (1965) back-to-back, and they made him a star. He had a brash Cockney self-confidence that suggested a hardness beneath the kidding around. Jude Law is already a movie star, currently one of the busiest, and in *Alfie* he is less a predator than Caine, more a needy hedonist who is wounded and even surprised when women won't put up with him.

Of course, he meets a different kind of

woman in 2004 than Caine met in 1966; the feminist revolution, the rise and fall of the one-night stand, and the specter of AIDS all happened between those two dates, and today a compulsively promiscuous man is more of a danger to himself and his partners than he was then. In 1966 the worst thing Alfie brings about is an abortion; in the 2004 version, his greatest crime is essentially to throw away the love of the only woman he really cares for.

That would be Julie (Marisa Tomei), who is honest and grounded and has a young son to care for, and absolutely will not share Alfie with other women. Of course, for a time she doesn't know about the other women. Alfie confesses, in one of his rueful speeches directly to the camera, that the tricky thing about dating a woman with a kid is that you get to really like the kid. It's also tricky, as Alfie discovers, when you get to like the woman.

Alfie is still British in this version, but more upmarket, and now living in Manhattan, where his job as a limo driver gives him access to a lot of women, and they to him. We meet them as he does: Dorie (Jane Krakowski), the lonely married woman; Liz (Susan Sarandon), a successful businesswoman with a no-nonsense approach to obtaining sex; and Nikki (Sienna Miller), a beautiful model who wanders into his life and seems to be the undemanding woman of his dreams. Then there's Lonette (Nia Long), the girlfriend of his best friend, Marlon (Omar Epps). She should be forbidden territory, but to Alfie borders are made to be crossed.

The first film, directed by Lewis Gilbert, closely followed the era of the British Angry Young Men movies, and contained echoes of the proletarian anger of characters played by such as Albert Finney and Tom Courtenay. The new film comes out of a lad-mag era, in which Alfie is better dressed, smoother, and smoldering not with anger but with a spoiled boy's desire to be indulged. Both 1966 and 2004 are probably getting the characters they deserve; narcissism has evolved in thirty-eight years from a character flaw to a male fashion attribute.

The women have evolved, too. Marisa Tomei's Julie might have felt helpless in 1966—felt she had to put up with Alfie because she had no choice. Now she has choices. The sexy businesswoman (Sarandon) is no longer seen as aging and needy (as Shelley Winters was in the original) but as desirable and independent; when Alfie finds her with another man, he asks, "What's he got better than me?" and her answer feels a little sorry for him: "He's younger than you." And when Lonette gets pregnant, abortion doesn't seem inevitable, even though the mixed race of her child will betray its father to her boyfriend. In 2004 it is possible for a woman to have a child outside the traditional rules; in 1966, that was not common.

But we don't go to see *Alfie* in order to make a sociological comparison of the two films; indeed, most of the audience members on opening night may not even know it's a remake. On its own terms, it's funny at times and finally sad and sweet. Alfie learns that to lie to women is to lie to himself about them. Jude Law's best scenes are when he doggedly tries to keep smiling as his lifestyle grows grim and depressing. He's sold himself on life as a ladies' man, and is beginning to realize he is his only customer.

Aliens of the Deep ★ ★ ★
G, 45 m., 2005

With James Cameron, Pamela Conrad, Djanna Figueroa, Kevin Hand, Loretta Hidalgo, and Maya Tolstoy. A documentary directed by James Cameron and Steven Quayle and produced by Cameron and Andrew Wight.

The timing of *Aliens of the Deep* couldn't be better. Days after a space probe landed successfully on Saturn's moon Titan and sent back spectacular photographs of its surface, here is a movie that explores the depths of the seas of Earth and then uses animation to imagine a probe that would fly to Jupiter's moon Europa and drill through its ice layer to the liquid water thought to be below. By finding living creatures on Earth that live under extreme conditions—no sunlight, no photosynthesis, incredible pressure, extremes of hot and cold—James Cameron convincingly argues that life could exist in the seas of Europa, or, for that matter, in any number of harrowing environments.

For Cameron, the film continues an obsession. When he wrote and directed *The Abyss* in 1989, his story involved scientists venturing into the deepest parts of the ocean. The movie was a box-office disappointment, not least because the director's cut reveals that the studio chopped crucial and amazing footage—and also, reportedly, because many potential ticket buyers did not know what an "abyss" is. For Cameron, it was an epiphany.

He returned to the sea bed for *Titanic* (1997), still the highest-grossing movie of all time, and essentially never came up for air. In 2002 his *Expedition: Bismarck,* made for the Discovery Channel, used deep-water submersibles to visit the grave of the doomed battleship, and in 2003 he made the 3-D IMAX movie *Ghosts of the Abyss,* which visited the wreck of the *Titanic* itself.

That was a movie with fascinating content, but I found the 3-D format unsatisfactory, and thought it might have been better to forget the gimmick and just give us the images. Now comes Cameron's *Aliens of the Deep,* also in IMAX 3-D, also fascinating, and with much-improved 3-D. After tinkering with the format for years, the IMAX technicians have devised oversized glasses that fit easily over existing eyeglasses and cover the entire field of vision. I saw the first 3-D movie, *Bwana Devil,* in 1952, and have been tired of the format ever since, but IMAX finally seems to be getting it right.

The movie is about expeditions to the deepest seas on Earth, where life is found to flourish under incredible conditions. We've read reports of some of these discoveries before—the worms that live around the sulphurous vents of hot water on the cold sea bottom, for example—but now we see them, photographed in lonely and splendid isolation, and the sights are magnificent.

What are these creatures? A good question, and one you might well still be asking after the movie, since it is high on amazement but low on information. His aquanauts, all real scientists or students, keep saying their discoveries are magnificent, beautiful, unbelievable, incredible, etc., and so they are, but only rudimentary facts are supplied about these life forms.

That didn't bother me as much as it might have, because *Aliens of the Deep* is not a scientific documentary so much as a journey to an alien world, and basically what we want to do is peer out the portholes along with the explorers. We see a vast, drifting, transparent creature, looking like nothing so much as a linen scarf, with a fragile network of vessels holding itself together. How does it feed? What does it know?

The tube worms are fascinating because they exist in symbiosis with bacteria that live inside of them. They have no digestive facility, and the bacteria have no food-gathering ability, but working together they both make a living. Astonishingly, we see shrimp, millions of them, darting endlessly through superheated vents of escaping lava-heated water, which is hundreds of degrees warmer than the icy water around it. How do these creatures move through such extremes of hot and cold so quickly, when either by itself would kill them?

Aliens of the Deep is a convincing demonstration of Darwin's theory of evolution because it shows creatures not only adapted perfectly to their environment but obviously generated by that environment. It drives me crazy when people say evolution is "only a theory," because that reveals they don't know what a scientific theory is. As *National Geographic* pointed out, a theory is a scientific hypothesis that is consistent with observed and experimental data, and the observations and experiments must be able to be repeated. Darwin passes that test. His rival, creationism, is not a theory, but a belief. There is a big difference.

Evolution aside, there are some wonderful images in *Aliens of the Deep,* even if the crew members say how much they love their jobs about six times too often. In a late segment of the film, Cameron uses special effects to imagine a visit to Europa, where a nuclear-heated probe would melt and drill its way down to the liquid seas thought to be three to fourteen miles below ice, and find there—well, life, perhaps. He even envisions an underwater city that belongs on the cover of *Amazing Stories,* circa 1940. It's not a million miles different from the one in the director's cut of *The Abyss.* That his city was astonishingly cut from the theatrical version of *The Abyss* to make more room for the love story is no doubt one of the several reasons Cameron has recently worked in documentary instead of fiction. It's tempting to say that Cameron should have stayed with the wonders of Earth and not created imaginary civilizations on Europa, but I was enthralled by those fictional sequences, unlikely as they are. I would suggest that if an advanced civilization has evolved on Europa, however, it is unlikely to have cities, since interior rooms and corridors would not occur naturally to swimming creatures. More likely, like dolphins, the Europans will fully exploit their given habitat. Or maybe they will all look like pond scum, which as discoveries go would also be quite amazing enough.

All the Real Girls ★ ★ ★ ★
R., 108 m., 2003

Paul Schneider (Paul), Zooey Deschanel (Noel), Shea Whigham (Tip), Danny McBride (Bust-Ass), Maurice Compte (Bo), Heather McComb (Mary-Margaret), Benjamin Mouton (Leland), Patricia Clarkson (Elvira). Directed by David Gordon Green and produced by Jean Doumanian and Lisa Muskat. Screenplay by Green.

We like to be in love because it allows us to feel idealistic about ourselves. The other person ennobles, inspires, redeems. Our lover deserves the most wonderful person alive, and that person is ourselves. Paul (Paul Schneider), the hero of All the Real Girls, has spent his young manhood having sex with any girl who would have sex with him and some who were still making up their minds, but when he meets Noel he doesn't want to rush things. He wants to wait, because this time is special.

Noel (Zooey Deschanel), who has spent the last several years in a girls' boarding school, is crazy in love with him and is a virgin. She is eighteen, an age when all the hormones in our bodies form ranks and hurl themselves against the ramparts of our inhibitions. That they can discuss these matters with romantic idealism does not entirely work as a substitute.

All the Real Girls, David Gordon Green's second film, is too subtle and perceptive, and knows too much about human nature, to treat their lack of sexual synchronicity as if it supplies a plot. Another kind of movie would be entirely about whether they have sex. But Green, who feels tenderly for his vulnerable characters, cares less about sex than about feelings and wild, youthful idealism. He comes

from North Carolina, the state where young Thomas Wolfe once prowled the midnight campus, so in love with life that he uttered wild goat cries at the moon.

Most movies about young love trivialize and cheapen it. Their cynical makers have not felt true love in many years, and mock it, perhaps out of jealousy. They find something funny in a twenty-year-old who still doesn't realize he is doomed to grow up to be as jaded as they are. Green is twenty-seven, old enough to be jaded, but he has the soul of a romantic poet. Wordsworth, after all, was thirty-six when he published:

The rainbow comes and goes,
And lovely is the rose;

How many guys that age would have that kind of nerve today? Green knows there are nights when lovers want simply to wrap their arms around each other and celebrate their glorious destinies.

He centers these feelings on characters who live in the same kind of rusty, overgrown southern mill town he used for his great first film, George Washington (2000). His characters grew up together. They look today on the faces of their first contemporaries. Paul's best friend, Tip (Shea Whigham), has been his best friend almost from birth. That he is Noel's brother is a complication, since Tip knows all about Paul's other girls. And more than a complication, because your best friend's sister embodies a history that includes your entire puberty, and may be the first person you noticed had turned into a girl.

Green likes to listen to his characters talk. They don't have much to do. Some of them work at the few remaining mill jobs, and we learn some details about their lives (an hourly sprinkler system washes the fibers out of the air). They stand around and sit around and idly discuss the mysteries of life, which often come down to whether someone did something, or what they were thinking of when they did it, or if they are ever going to do it. I had relatives who lived in towns like these, and I know that when you go to the salad bar it includes butterscotch pudding.

Paul's single mom, Elvira (Patricia Clarkson), works as a clown at parties and in the children's wards of hospitals. Some critics have mocked this occupation, but let me tell you something: A small-town woman with a family to feed can make better money with a Bozo wig and a putty nose than she can working unpaid overtime at Wal-Mart. People will pay you nothing to clean their houses, but they pay the going rate when their kids have birthdays. The fact that Green knows this and a lot of people don't is an indicator of his comfort with his characters.

Green's dialogue has a kind of unaffected, flat naturalism. ("You feel like waffles or French toast?" "No, the places I go are usually not that fancy.") That doesn't mean their speech is not poetic. His characters don't use big words, but they express big ideas. Their words show a familiarity with hard times, disappointment, wistfulness; they are familiar with all the concepts on television, but do not lead lives where they apply.

Two emotional upheavals strike at the narrative. One is inevitable; Tip is enraged to learn that Paul and Noel are dating. The other is not inevitable, and I will not even hint about it. There is a scene where it is discussed in a bowling alley, using only body language, in long shot.

The thing about real love is, if you lose it, you can also lose your ability to believe in it, and that hurts even more. Especially in a town where real love may be the only world-class thing that ever happens.

Almost Peaceful ★ ★ ★

NO MPAA RATING, 94 m., 2004

Simon Abkarian (Albert), Zabou Breitman (Lea), Denis Podalydes (Charles), Vincent Elbaz (Leon), Lubna Azabal (Jacqueline), Stanislas Merhar (Maurice), Clotilde Courau (Simone), Julie Gaynet (Mme. Andree), Malik Zidi (Joseph). Directed by Michel Deville and produced by Rosalinde Deville. Screenplay by Michel Deville and Rosalinde Deville, based on a novel by Robert Bober.

In a sunny upstairs room in Paris, eight or nine people gather daily to tailor clothes. The room is in a flat belonging to Albert and Lea, who run the business and have hired these people quite recently, for it is 1946 and all but one of them is Jewish and they have returned to their trade after the horror of the war. The atmosphere in the room is cozy and chatty, relaxed almost to a fault, as if these people have been holding their breath for years and are grateful for a day that passes without event.

Michel Deville's *Almost Peaceful* is unlike any other film I have seen about the Holocaust. Indeed, the abstract concept of a holocaust has not yet been formed as these people reassemble their ordinary lives. They speak about what happened, about "the camps" where their loved ones disappeared, about the war, but they do not go into detail because they lived through it firsthand and do not need to be reminded—none of them except the one gentile woman, who is puzzled when a new employee introduces himself and the others burst into laughter. What's so funny? What's funny, or at least what's able to be laughed about, is that he can say his Jewish name loudly and freely in Paris once again.

Albert (Simon Abkarian) and Lea (Zabou Breitman) own the business. Their children are away in the south of France, at summer camp, sending back letters and drawings that are eagerly awaited. Of the others, there is a man who returned to the neighborhood hoping any of his surviving relatives would find their way there, and an unemployed actor with a pregnant wife, and a new employee fit only to cut and trim, and a young man named Maurice (Stanislas Merhar), who visits the prostitutes at a nearby hotel. The gentile woman goes out to lunch one day with Albert to ask if he can find a job for her sister, who had a child by a German soldier and after the war had her head shaved and was made to run naked through the town. She tells it as a sad story. But Albert cannot help her. A lot of people had sad experiences in the war, he says, quietly.

The new employee, Joseph (Malik Zidi), goes around to the police station to have his papers put in order, and recognizes the cop behind the desk. He has seen this man before, through the crack in a wardrobe where his parents concealed him before the cop took them away, never to return. The cop is insolent. Joseph walks out, pauses on the pavement, goes back in and tells the man he knows who he is and what he did, and he wants to inform him that he, Joseph, is here and will remain here and has a right to be here. Then

Joseph walks out again and goes to a café and collapses at a table with a release of tension and a certain sad joy.

There are little plots involving the people, their children, their friends, their romantic intrigues (Maurice finds himself always returning to the same prostitute, Simone, who likes him well enough and prostitution not so much). Customers come and go. Albert must approve any garment that leaves the shop. He and Lea are happy beyond happiness. There is a woman who comes around twice a week with things to sell. Today she is selling scented soaps. She is also a matchmaker, and in her valise has letters and photographs of single people looking for a spouse. "Your marriageable people smell of soap," one of the tailors' kids her. "Was it better," she asks, "when soap smelled of marriageable people?"

In a line like that, which passes quickly and is not commented upon, an abyss of evil is glimpsed. These people live gently and embrace routine and love their jobs because they are still walking on ice, still aware of how fragile a life can be, how deceptive security can seem. The film ends with a picnic, and the sound of children playing. There is a new generation. There is the feeling that marriageable people should be married and having children. Maurice and Simone seem to be arriving at that conclusion. Life goes on, and that is what the movie is about, and all it is about, except for the unspeakable horrors it is not about.

Almost Salinas ★ ½
PG, 92 m., 2003

John Mahoney (Max Harris), Linda Emond (Nina Ellington), Lindsay Crouse (Allie), Virginia Madsen (Clare), Ian Gomez (Manny), Nathan Davis (Zelder Hill), Tom Groenwald (Leo Quinlan), Ray Wise (Jack Tynan). Directed by Terry Green and produced by Wade W. Danielson. Screenplay by Green.

Almost Salinas is a sweet and good-hearted portrait of an isolated crossroads and the people who live there, or are drawn into their lives. Shame about the plot. The people are real, but the story devices are clunkers from Fiction 101; the movie generates goodwill in its setup, but in the last act it goes haywire with revelations and

secrets and dramatic gestures. The movie takes place in Cholame, the California town where James Dean died in 1955, and maybe the only way to save it would have been to leave out everything involving James Dean.

John Mahoney stars as Max Harris, the proprietor of a diner in a sparsely populated backwater. He's thinking of reopening the old gas station. Virginia Madsen is Clare, his waitress, and other locals include Nathan Davis, as an old-timer who peddles James Dean souvenirs from a roadside table, and Ian Gomez, as the salt-of-the-earth cook.

The town experiences an unusual flurry of activity. A film crew arrives to shoot a movie about the death of James Dean. Max's ex-wife, Allie (Lindsay Crouse), turns up. And a magazine writer named Nina Ellington (Linda Emond) arrives to do a feature about the reopening of the gas station. If this seems like an unlikely subject for a story, reflect that she stays so long she could do the reporting on the reopening of a refinery. She gradually falls in love with Max, while one of the young members of the film crew falls for Clare's young assistant behind the counter.

The place and the people are sound. Mahoney has the gift of bringing quiet believability to a character; his Max seems dependable, kind, and loyal. Virginia Madsen is the spark of the place, not a stereotyped, gum-chewing hashslinger, but a woman who takes an interest in the people who come her way. If Emond is not very convincing as the visiting reporter, perhaps it's because her job is so unlikely. Better, perhaps, to make her a woman with no reason at all to be in Cholame. Let her stay because she has no place better to go, and then let her fall in love.

From the movie's opening moments, there are quick black-and-white shots of Dean's 1955 Porsche Spyder, racing along a rural highway toward its rendezvous with death. The arrival of the film crew, with its own model of the same car, introduces a series of parallels between past and present that it would be unfair to reveal.

Spoiler warning! Without spelling everything out, let us observe, however, that it is unlikely that a character who was locally famous in 1955 could stay in the same area and become anonymous just by changing his name. It is also unlikely that he would be moved, so many years later, to the actions he takes in the film. And cosmically unlikely that they would have the results that they do. Not to mention how pissed off the film company would be.

As the movie's great revelations started to slide into view, I slipped down in my seat, fearful that the simple and engaging story of these nice people would be upstaged by the grinding mechanics of plot contrivance. My fears were well grounded. *Almost Salinas* generates enormous goodwill and then loses it by betraying its characters to the needs of a plot that wants to inspire pathos and sympathy, but inspires instead, alas, groans and the rolling of eyes.

Along Came Polly ★ ★

PG-13, 90 m., 2004

Ben Stiller (Reuben Feffer), Jennifer Aniston (Polly Prince), Philip Seymour Hoffman (Sandy Lyle), Debra Messing (Lisa Kramer), Alec Baldwin (Stan Indursky), Hank Azaria (Claude), Bryan Brown (Leland Van Lew), Jsu Garcia (Javier). Directed by John Hamburg and produced by Danny DeVito, Michael Shamberg, and Stacey Sher. Screenplay by Hamburg.

I will never eat free nuts from the bowl on the bar again, having seen *Along Came Polly*. Not after hearing the expert risk-assessor Reuben Feffer (Ben Stiller) explain who has already handled them, what adventures they have had, and, for all we know, where they might have been. It's his job to know the risks of every situation, which is why his marriage seems like such a sure thing: His new bride, Lisa (Debra Messing), is like a computer printout of an ideal mate for life.

But it doesn't work out that way in *Along Came Polly*, a movie where a lot of things don't work out, including, alas, the movie itself. On the second day of their honeymoon in Saint Bart's, Lisa cheats on Reuben with a muscular scuba instructor (Hank Azaria), and he returns to New York crushed and betrayed. When he meets Polly (Jennifer Aniston), an old school chum, he doubts they can be happy together (assessing the risks, he sees the two of them as totally incompatible), but to his amazement they are soon involved in a neurotic but not boring relationship.

The problem is that their relationship, and indeed Reuben's entire array of friendships and business associations, are implausible not in a funny way but in a distracting way: We keep doubting that this person would be acting this way in this situation. What kind of a risk assessor is Reuben if he *knows* he has irritable bowel syndrome, and nevertheless goes on a first date with Polly to dinner at a North African spice palace? Yes, his dinner gives the movie the opportunity to launch one of those extended sequences involving spectacular digestive, eliminatory, and regurgitative adventures, but we're aware it's a setup. As Stiller himself classically demonstrated in *There's Something About Mary,* embarrassment is comic when it is thrust upon you by accident or bad luck, not when you go looking for it yourself.

Of the Polly character, it can be said that the risk of her ever falling in love with a man like Reuben is a very long shot. What attracts her? His constipated personality? Low self-esteem? Workaholism? Neurotic inability to engage spontaneously with fun? She's a free spirit who lives in one of those apartments that look like they were inspired by an old Sandy Dennis movie. Her favorite occupation is salsa dancing, which for her approaches virtual sex, especially with her favorite partner, Javier (Jsu Garcia). Reuben, uncoordinated and inhibited, is jealous of Javier until he signs up for salsa lessons, which could have been funny, but are not.

There isn't a lot in the movie that is funny. I did like Philip Seymour Hoffman as Sandy, Reuben's best man; he's a former child star, now reduced to having strangers tell him how amazed they are that he's still alive. How he responds to this in one early scene is a small masterpiece of facial melodrama, but how many times does he have to slip and fall on slick floors before we get tired of it? I grant him this: He knows exactly how a fat man looks in a red cummerbund from a tuxedo rental agency.

Alec Baldwin does a lot of good supporting work (notably in *The Cooler*), and he's Reuben's boss, the head of the agency, a slickster whose toast at the wedding skates artfully at the edge of crudeness and then pirouettes out of danger. He assigns Reuben to somehow make a case for insuring the high-risk Leland Van Lew (Bryan Brown), leading to still more fish-out-of-water material. Reuben's fish is so consistently out of water in this movie, indeed, that after a while we begin to wish it was smoked.

Amandla! ★ ★ ★
PG-13, 105 m., 2003

Featuring Hugh Masekela, Abdullah Ibrahim, Miriam Makeba, and Vusi Mahlasela. A documentary directed by Lee Hirsch and produced by Hirsch and Sherry Simpson.

"We'll catch the early staff boat and get there before the tourists arrive," A. M. Kathrada told my wife and me, in Cape Town in November 2001. We were going the next morning to visit Robben Island, where for twenty-seven years Nelson Mandela and others accused of treason, including Kathrada, were held by the South African apartheid government. We were having dinner with Kathrada, who is of Indian descent, and his friend Barbara Hogan, who won a place in history as the first South African white woman convicted as a traitor.

In those days it was easy to become a traitor. *Amandla!*, a new documentary about the role of music in the overthrow of apartheid, begins with the exhumation of the bones of Vuyisile Mini, who wrote a song named "Beware, Verwoerd! (The Black Man Is Coming!)," aimed at the chief architect of South Africa's racist politics of separation. Mini was executed in 1964 and buried in a pauper's grave.

Robben Island lies some twenty miles offshore from Cape Town, and the view back toward the slopes of Table Mountain is breathtaking. When I was a student at the University of Cape Town in 1965, friends pointed it out, a speck across the sea, and whispered that Mandela was imprisoned there. It would be almost twenty-five years until he was released and asked by F. W. DeKlerk, Verwoerd's last white successor, to run for president. No one in 1965 or for many years later believed there would be a regime change in South Africa without a bloody civil war, but there was, and Cranford's, my favorite used book shop, can now legally be owned by black South Africans; it still has a coffee pot and crooked stairs to the crowded upstairs room.

Kathrada, now in his early seventies, is known by everyone on the staff boat. At the Robben Island Store, where we buy our tickets, he introduces us to the manager—a white man who used to be one of his guards, and who smuggled forbidden letters ("and even the occasional visitor") on and off the island. On the island, we walk under a crude arch that welcomes us in Afrikaans and English, and enter the prison building, which is squat and unlovely, thick with glossy lime paint. The office is not yet open and Kathrada cannot find a key.

"First I am locked in, now I am locked out," he observes cheerfully. Eventually the key is discovered and we arrive at the object of our visit, the cell where Mandela lived. It is about long enough to lie down in. "For the first seven years," Kathrada said, "we didn't have cots. You got used to sleeping on the floor."

White political prisoners like Barbara Hogan were kept in a Pretoria prison. There were not a lot of Indian prisoners, and Kathrada was jailed with Mandela's African group.

"They issued us different uniforms," he observed dryly. "I was an Indian, and was issued with long pants. Mandela and the other Africans were given short pants. They called them 'boys,' and gave them boys' pants."

A crude nutritional chart hung on the wall, indicating that Indians were given a few hundred calories more to eat every day, because South African scientists had somehow determined their minimal caloric requirements were a little greater than those of blacks.

Weekdays, all of the men worked in a quarry, hammering rocks into gravel. No work was permitted on Sunday in the devoutly religious Afrikaans society. The prisoners were fed mostly whole grains, a few vegetables, a little fruit, very little animal protein. "As a result of this diet and exercise, plus all of the sunlight in the quarry," Kathrada smiled, "we were in good health and most of us still are. The sun on the white rocks and the quarry dust were bad for our eyes, however."

During the 1970s the apartheid government clamped such a tight lid on opposition that it seemed able to hold on forever. The uplifting film *Amandla!* argues that South Africa's music of protest played a crucial role in apartheid's eventual overthrow. Mandela's African National Congress was nonviolent from its birth until the final years of apartheid, when after an internal struggle one branch began to commit acts of bombing and sabotage (murder and torture had always been weapons of the whites). Music was the ANC's most dangerous weapon, and we see footage of streets lined with tens of thousands of marchers, singing and dancing, expressing an unquenchable spirit.

"We lost the country in the first place, to an extent, because before we fight, we sing," Hugh Masekela, the great South African jazzman, tells the filmmakers. "The Zulus would sing before they went into battle, so the British and Boers knew where they were and when they were coming."

There was a song about Nelson Mandela that was sung at every rally, even though mention of his name was banned, and toward the end of the film there is a rally to welcome him after his release from prison, and he sings along. It is one of those moments where words cannot do justice to the joy.

Amandla! (the Xhosa word means "power") was nine years in the making, directed by Lee Hirsch, produced with Sherry Simpson. It combines archival footage, news footage, reports from political exiles like Masekela and his former wife, Miriam Makeba, visits with famous local singers, an appearance by Archbishop Desmond Tutu, and a lot of music. The sound track CD could become popular like "The Buena Vista Social Club."

After the relatives of Vuyisile Mini disinter his bones, he is reburied in blessed ground under a proper memorial, and then his family holds a party. Among the songs they sing is "Beware, Verwoerd!" It is not a nostalgia piece, not dusty, not yet. They sing it not so much in celebration as in triumph and relief.

American Splendor ★ ★ ★ ★
R, 100 m., 2003

Paul Giamatti (Harvey Pekar), Harvey Pekar (Real Harvey), Hope Davis (Joyce Brabner), Joyce Brabner (Real Joyce), Shari Springer Berman (Interviewer), Earl Billings (Mr. Boats), James Urbaniak (Robert Crumb), Judah Friedlander (Toby Radloff), Robert Pulcini (Bob the Director), Toby Radloff (Real Toby), Madylin Sweeten (Danielle), Danielle Batone (Real Danielle). Directed by Shari Springer Berman and Robert Pulcini and produced by Ted Hope. Screenplay by Berman and Pulcini, based on the comic book series *American Splendor* by Harvey Pekar and *Our Cancer Year* by Joyce Brabner.

One of the closing shots of *American Splendor* shows a retirement party for Harvey Pekar, who is ending his career as a file clerk at a V.A. hospital in Cleveland. This is a real party, and it is a real retirement. Harvey Pekar, the star of comic books, the Letterman show, and now this movie, worked all of his life as a file clerk. When I met Harvey and his wife, Joyce Brabner, at Cannes 2003, she told me: "He's grade G-4. Grade G-2 is minimum wage. Isn't that something, after thirty years as a file clerk?"

Yes, but it got them to Cannes. Pekar is one of the heroes of graphic novels, which are comic books with a yearning toward the light. He had the good fortune to meet the legendary comic artist R. Crumb in the 1970s. He observed with his usual sour pessimism that comics were never written about people like him, and as he talked a lightbulb all but appeared above Crumb's head, and the comic book *American Splendor* was born, with Pekar as writer and Crumb as illustrator.

The books chronicle the life of a man very much indeed like Harvey Pekar. He works at a thankless job. He has friends at work, like the "world-class nerd" Toby Radloff, who share his complaints, although not at the Pekarian level of existential misery. The comic book brings him a visit from a fan named Joyce Brabner, who turns out improbably to be able to comprehend his existence while insisting on her own, and eventually they gain a daughter, Danielle Batone, sort of through osmosis (the daughter of a friend, she comes to visit, and decides to stay). The books follow Harvey, Joyce and Danielle as they sail through life, not omitting *Our Cancer Year*, a book retelling his travails after Harvey finds a lump on a testicle.

The comics are true, deep, and funny precisely because they see that we are all superheroes doing daily battle against twisted and perverted villains. We have secret powers others do not suspect. We have secret identities. Our enemies may not be as colorful as the Joker or Dr. Evil, but certainly they are malevolent— who could be more hateful, for example, than an anal-retentive supervisor, an incompetent medical orderly, a greedy landlord? When Harvey fills with rage, only the graphics set him aside from the Hulk.

The peculiarity and genius of *American Splendor* was always that true life and fiction marched hand in hand. There was a real Harvey Pekar, who looked very much like the one in the comic book, and whose own life was being described. Now comes this magnificently audacious movie, in which fact and fiction sometimes coexist in the same frame. We see and hear the real Harvey Pekar, and then his story is played by the actor Paul Giamatti, sometimes with Harvey commenting on "this guy who is playing me." We see the real Joyce Brabner, and we see Hope Davis playing her. We concede that Giamatti and Davis have mastered not only the looks but the feels and even the souls of these two people. And then there is Judah Friedlander to play Toby Radloff, who we might think could not be played by anybody, but there the two Tobys are, and we can see it's a match.

The movie deals not merely with real and fictional characters, but even with levels of presentation. There are documentary scenes, fictional scenes, and then scenes illustrated and developed as comic books, with the drawings sometimes segueing into reality or back again. The filmmakers have taken the challenge of filming a comic book based on a life and turned it into an advantage—the movie is mesmerizing in the way it lures us into the daily hopes and fears of this Cleveland family.

The personality of the real Harvey Pekar is central to the success of everything. Pekar's genius is to see his life from the outside, as a life like all lives, in which eventual tragedy is given a daily reprieve. He is brutally honest. The conversations he has with Joyce are conversations like those we really have. We don't fight over trivial things, because nothing worth fighting over is trivial. As Harvey might say, "Hey, it's important to me!"

The Letterman sequences have the fascination of an approaching train wreck. Pekar really was a regular on the program in the 1980s, where he did not change in the slightest degree from the real Harvey. He gave as good as he got, until his resentments, angers, and grudges led him to question the fundamental realities of the show itself, and then he was bounced. We see real Letterman footage, and then a fictional re-creation of Pekar's final show. Letterman is not a bad guy, but he has a show to do, and Pekar is a good guest following his own agenda up to a point, but then he goes far, far beyond that point. When I talked with Pekar at Cannes, he confided that after Letterman essentially fired him and went to a commercial break, Dave leaned over and whispered into Harvey's ear: "You blew a good thing."

Well, he did. But blowing a good thing is Harvey's fate in life, just as stumbling upon a good thing is his victory. What we get in both cases is the unmistakable sense that Pekar does nothing for effect, that all of his decisions and responses proceed from some limitless well of absolute certitude. What we also discover is that Harvey is not entirely a dyspeptic grump, but has sweetness and hope waving desperately from somewhere deep within his despair.

This film is delightful in the way it finds its own way to tell its own story. There was no model to draw on, but Shari Springer Berman and Robert Pulcini, who wrote and directed it, have made a great film by trusting to Pekar's artistic credo, which amounts to: What you see is what you get. The casting of Giamatti and Davis is perfect, but of course it had to be, or the whole enterprise would have collapsed. Giamatti is not a million miles away from other characters he has played, in movies such as *Storytelling*, *Private Parts*, and *Man on the Moon*, but Davis achieves an uncanny transformation. I saw her in *The Secret Lives of Dentists*, playing a dentist, wife, and mother with no points in common with Joyce Brabner—not in look, not in style, not in identity. Now here she is as Joyce. I've met Joyce Brabner, and she's Joyce Brabner.

Movies like this seem to come out of nowhere, like free-standing miracles. But *American Splendor* does have a source, and its source is Harvey Pekar himself—his life, and what he has made of it. The guy is the real thing. He found Joyce, who is also the real thing, and Danielle found them, and as I talked with her I could see she was the real thing, too. She wants to go into showbiz, she told me, but she doesn't want to be an actress, because then she might be unemployable after forty. She said she wants to work behind the scenes. More longevity that way. Harvey nodded approvingly. Go for the pension.

America's Heart & Soul ★ ★
PG, 84 m., 2004

A documentary directed and produced by Louis Schwartzberg.

America's Heart & Soul may be the first feature-length documentary filmed entirely in the style of a television commercial. It tells the stories of about twenty Americans who are colorful, eccentric, courageous, goofy, or musically talented—sometimes all five—and it uses the shorthand of TV spots, in which the point is that these people are wonderful and so, gosh darn it, are the good folks at (insert name of corporation). In this case, the sponsor is America, a nation where, in this film, poverty is an opportunity, racism doesn't exist, and (most miraculous of all) everyone is self-employed doing a job they love. Nobody grinds away for the minimum wage in this America.

Even though the method of the filmmaker, Louis Schwartzberg, is slick, superficial, and relentlessly upbeat, the people he finds are genuine treasures. I wanted to see a whole film about most of them, which means this film is a series of frustrations. Still, it underlines a point I like to make when students ask me about employment prospects: Figure out what you love and find a way to do it, no matter how badly it pays, because you will enjoy yourself and probably end up happy. Midcareer test: If retirement seems better than the job you're doing, you're doing the wrong job.

The first character we meet in *America's Heart & Soul* is Thomas "Roudy" Roudebush, a cowboy in Telluride, Colorado, whose life has much improved since he got sober, but who still rides his horse into a bar for a drink (water, straight up). Then we meet Marc and Ann Savoy, Cajun musicians, and watch them making gumbo, and visit a black gospel singer named Mosie Burks, and a weaver named Minnie Yancey ("If I've woven ten feet into the rug and it still doesn't say 'yes,' I'll cut it right off and start again"). As she weaves, she looks out the window at her husband, plowing a field on one of the few surviving family farms.

In Vermont, George Woodard, a dairy farmer, milks his cows, plays in a string band, and stars as Dracula in a local production. We say hello to Ben Cohen, of Ben & Jerry's, as he invents a new flavor. We meet a hat maker. A chair maker. A wine maker. Men who fight oil well fires. A New Orleans jazz band. Patty Wagstaff of Florida, who is a champion acrobatic pilot.

Also, people who dance on cliffs at the ends of ropes. A blind mountain climber. Rick Hoyt, a marathon runner with cerebral palsy whose father, Dick, pushes his wheelchair. Paul Stone of Creede, Colorado, who spends his winters blowing up stuff real good (one of his cannon shells is made of ham and cheese). And David Krakauer, a klezmer musician influenced by Jimi Hendrix.

An opera singer. Salsa dancers. Michael Bennett of Chicago, an armed robber who started boxing in the pen, became captain of the U.S. Olympic boxing team, and works to keep kids off the streets. Cecil Williams, the pastor of the progressive Glide Church in San Francisco, which supplies a million meals for the homeless every year. People who decorate their cars as works of art. A Manhattan bike messenger who loves racing through traffic. Dan Klennert, who makes art out of junk. The Indian elder Charles Jimmie Sr., who releases a healed eagle back into the skies.

All of these people are happy, productive, creative, and unconventional, and if there were more of them in our society the news would be a lot more cheerful. They live in a parallel universe where everyone is oddball and fascinating and has a story that can be neatly wrapped up in a few minutes. Surely there is more to all of these people, a lot more, but *America's Heart & Soul* has miles to go before it sleeps.

In the middle of a montage I saw one shot, a few seconds long, that was unmistakably of Howard Armstrong, the legendary African-American string musician who died in August 2003 at the age of ninety-three. At my Overlooked Film Festival, I showed two documentaries made fifteen years apart about this miraculous man, whose art was as distinctive as his music, and whose life was a work in progress. Because I know how much there was to say about him, I can guess how much there is to say about the others in *America's Heart & Soul*. But this movie doesn't pause to find out;

it's in such a hurry, it uses "&" because "and" would take too long. Working within the limitations of the star rating system, I give four stars to the subjects of this movie, and two stars to the way they have been boiled down into cute pictures and sound bites.

Anacondas: The Hunt for the Blood Orchid ★ ★

PG-13, 93 m., 2004

Johnny Messner (Bill Johnson), KaDee Strickland (Samantha Rogers), Matthew Marsden (Dr. Jack Byron), Morris Chestnut (Gordon Mitchell), Karl Yune (Tran), Salli Richardson-Whitfield (Gail Stern), Eugene Byrd (Cole Burris), Nicholas Gonzalez (Ben Douglas). Directed by Dwight H. Little and produced by Verna Harrah. Screenplay by John Claflin, Daniel Zelman, Michael Miner, and Edward Neumeier.

Deep in the jungles of Borneo lurks the blood orchid, which blooms only once in seven years, and whose red flowers contain a mysterious ingredient that extends the ability of living cells to reproduce themselves. A pill based on this substance would allow you to live forever, or at least long enough to feel like you had. "This is bigger than Viagra!" observes a drug company executive. Yes, and creates a whole new market for it. The notion of using Viagra when you're 150 is a little daunting, but at least, unlike George Burns, you could find plenty of girls your age.

Alas, there's a catch. The only existing samples of the blood orchid were "destroyed in testing," so it's necessary to return to Borneo for more blooms—and the blooming season ends in two weeks. There's barely time for an emergency expedition, and besides, it's the rainy season. We read a lot about how their profits allow drug companies to spend billions on research, but in the quest for eternal life this company is able to lease only the *Bloody Mary*, a river boat that looks hammered together out of spare parts from the tree house in *Benji: Off the Leash*.

The boat is commanded by Bill Johnson (Johnny Messner), who proves that even with the face of a Calvin Klein model he can earn a living piloting a leaky gutbucket into the jaws of hell. The scientific team includes four serious men, Dr. Jack Byron (Matthew Marsden), Gordon Mitchell (Morris Chestnut), Ben Douglas (Nicholas Gonzalez), and Tran (Karl Yune); two serious women, Gail Stern (Salli Richardson) and Samantha Rogers (KaDee Strickland); and a comic relief guy named Cole Burris (Eugene Byrd), who is always scared of everything. There is also a pet monkey that gets way, way too many reaction shots as it plays essentially the same role that Fred Willard filled in *Best in Show*.

It is dangerous to travel the rivers of Borneo even in the best of times, and treacherous in the rainy season, when the rivers overflow their banks, navigation is uncertain, alligators are hungry, submerged logs can rip the bottom out of your boat, and if you miss a turn you could go over a waterfall. Bill Johnson demands 50 grand to make the journey and later collects another 50 grand; looking at the *Bloody Mary*, we realize he's not so much charging for the trip as getting a good price on a used boat.

Ah, but there's a catch. The jungle where the blood orchid blooms is inhabited by giant anacondas. In fact, although they are solitary creatures, the snakes congregate in this very place during the rainy season, to form (or attend, perhaps) a "mating ball," so that the river and the jungle seem to be teeming with them. We have heard about salmon swimming upstream to mate and birds flying thousands of miles to their summer nesting homes, and perhaps that explains why the anaconda, which is a native of the South American rain forests and is unknown in Borneo, makes the arduous journey across the Pacific and up the river to the precise location of this movie.

No matter how they get there, they hang around a long while. That's because, of course, they eat the blood orchid and therefore do not die, but simply grow bigger and bigger. Perhaps they are immune to the bite of a local spider, which causes paralysis for forty-eight hours, although the cast of the movie certainly is not. You know when a spider paralyzes you and then you see an anaconda starting to eat you? I hate it when that happens.

There comes a point when we realize that *Anacondas: The Hunt for the Blood Orchid* is hunting not so much for orchids as for trouble.

The cast is so large because one must be eaten every so often, and the attrition rate grows after they fall into a cave. Bill Johnson keeps their spirits up: "There's a way in—there's a way out." True, but what if it's the way in?

Faithful readers will recall that I immensely enjoyed the original *Anaconda* (1997). It was a superb example of exactly what it was, and Jon Voight's final scene in the movie retains a sublime perfection. But I've seen *Anaconda*, and, senator, *Anacondas* is no *Anaconda*. The director, Dwight H. Little, has done a lot of TV and retains the annoying TV practice of the reaction-shot whip-round, in which A says something witty, B hears it and grins and looks at C, who smiles and shrugs, while D looks on, amused. With the monkey playing the E position, this can get monotonous.

The movie, however, is competent at a basic level, doing a good job of using its locations and a hardworking, fearless cast. The beautiful Salli Richardson-Whitfield continues the great tradition of the late Fay Wray as she struggles to escape the clutches of danger, and Matthew Marsden, obsessed with the millions to be made from the new drug, is suitably treacherous. The movie is competent formula entertainment, but doesn't make that leap into pure barminess that inspired *Anaconda*.

Anatomy of Hell ★

NO MPAA RATING, 77 m., 2004

Amira Casar (The Woman), Rocco Siffredi (The Man). Directed by Catherine Breillat and produced by Jean-Francois Lepetit. Screenplay by Breillat, based on her novel *Pornocratie*.

She is the only woman in a gay nightclub. She goes into the toilet and cuts her wrist. He follows her in, sees what she has done, and takes her to a drug store, where the wound is bandaged. If you cut your wrist and there's time to go to the drugstore, maybe you weren't really trying. He asks her why she did it. "Because I'm a woman," she says, although she might more accurately have replied, "Because I'm a woman in a Catherine Breillat movie."

Breillat is the bold French director whose specialty is female sexuality. Sometimes she is wise about it, as in *36 Fillette* (1989), the story of a troubled teenager who begins a series of risky flirtations with older men. Or in *Fat Girl* (2001), about the seething resentment of a pudgy twenty-year-old toward her sexpot older sister. Sometimes she is provocative about it, as in *Romance* (1999), which is about a frustrated woman's dogged search for orgasm. But sometimes she is just plain goofy, as in *Anatomy of Hell*, which plays like porn dubbed by bitter deconstructionist theoreticians.

The Woman makes an offer to The Man. She will pay him good money to watch her, simply watch her, for four nights. He keeps his end of the bargain, but there were times when I would have paid good money to not watch them, simply not watch them. I remember when hard-core first became commonplace, and there were discussions about what it would be like if a serious director ever made a porn movie. The answer, judging by *Anatomy of Hell*, is that the audience would decide they did not require such a serious director after all.

The Woman believes men hate women, and that gay men hate them even more than straight men, who, however, hate them quite enough. Men fear women, fear their menstrual secrets, fear their gynecological mysteries, fear that during sex they might disappear entirely within the woman and be imprisoned again by the womb. To demonstrate her beliefs, The Woman disrobes completely and displays herself on a bed, while The Man sits in a chair and watches her, occasionally rousing himself for a shot of Jack on the rocks.

They talk. They speak as only the French can speak, as if it is not enough for a concept to be difficult, it must be impenetrable. No two real people in the history of mankind have ever spoken like this, save perhaps for some of Catherine Breillat's friends that even she gets bored by. "Your words are inept reproaches," they say, and "I bless the day I was made immune to you and all your kind." After a few days of epigrams, they suddenly and sullenly have sex, and make a mess of the sheets.

Some events in this movie cannot be hinted at in a family newspaper. Objects emerge to the light of day that would distinguish target-practice in a Bangkok sex show. There are moments when you wish they'd lighten up a little by bringing in the guy who bites off chicken heads.

Of course we are expected to respond on a

visceral level to the movie's dirge about the crimes of men against women, which, it must be said, are hard to keep in mind given the crimes of The Woman against The Man, and the transgressions committed by The Director against Us. The poor guy is just as much a prop here as men usually are in porn films. He is played by Rocco Siffredi, an Italian porn star. The Woman is played by Amira Casar, who is completely nude most of the time, although the opening titles inform us that a body double will be playing her close-ups in the more action-packed scenes. "It's not her body," the titles explain, "it's an extension of a fictional character." Tell that to the double.

No doubt the truth can be unpleasant, but I am not sure that unpleasantness is the same as the truth. There are scenes here where Breillat deliberately disgusts us, not because we are disgusted by the natural life functions of women, as she implies, but simply because The Woman does things that would make any reasonable Man, or Woman, for that matter, throw up.

Anchorman ★ ★ ★
PG-13, 94 m., 2004

Will Ferrell (Ron Burgundy), Christina Applegate (Veronica Corningstone), David Koechner (Champ Kind), Steven Carell (Brick Tamland), Paul Rudd (Brian Fantana), Fred Willard (Ed Harken), Chris Parnell (Garth Holliday). Directed by Adam McKay and produced by Judd Apatow. Screenplay by Will Ferrell and McKay.

Sometimes the key to satire is to stay fairly close to the source. *Anchorman,* like *This Is Spinal Tap,* works best when it's only a degree or two removed from the excesses of the real thing. When the news director goes ape over stories about cute animals at the zoo, when the promos make the news "team" look like a happy family, the movie is right on target. But when rival local news teams engage in what looks like a free-for-all from a Roman arena, it doesn't work. Most of the time, though, *Anchorman* works, and a lot of the time it's very funny.

The movie centers on Ron Burgundy (Will Ferrell), the legendary top local anchor in San Diego in the early 1970s. Ron has bought into

his legend, believes his promos, and informs a blond at a pool party: "I have many very important leather-bound books, and my apartment smells of rich mahogany." His weakness is that he will read anything that is typed into his prompter. Anything. The words pass from his eyes into his mouth without passing through his brain.

There are viewers in every city who will think they know who this character is based on. Certainly anyone who was around Chicago TV news in the 1970s will instantly think of one name. I will not reveal the name here, but I will tell a story. A friend of mine was an assignment editor on this nameless anchor's station. One day he gave a juicy assignment to the man's coanchor and rival. The next day the nameless one leaned casually against my friend's door:

"Say, John, that was a great story you had for Maury yesterday. What do you have for me today?"

"Contempt."

True story. *Anchorman* also shows promotional spots in which Burgundy and his news teammates smile at each other lots and lots. Richard Roeper and I reviewed promos at PROMAX, the annual convention of TV promotion people. One spot showed the members of a news team doing magic tricks, performing with a hula hoop, playing a ukulele, etc. Yes, it was intended to be funny. And it was funny, especially if that's how you want to think of the people you trust for your news.

As *Anchorman* opens, Ron Burgundy faces a crisis. Ed Harken, the station's news director, played by the invaluable Fred Willard, wants to add "diversity" to the newsroom by hiring a woman—no, a *woman!*—as Burgundy's coanchor. This cannot be. It is not right. It is against nature. Burgundy is appalled. The new coanchor will be the efficiently named Veronica Corningstone (Christina Applegate), and, yes, reader, she was the blond Burgundy tried to pick up with the leather-and-mahogany line.

The other news team members include the wonderfully named Champ Kind (David Koechner), Brick Tamland (Steven Carell), and Brian Fantana (Paul Rudd). And yes, sometimes when they're together, they actually do sing "Afternoon Delight." They are united in their fear of adding a woman to the team. "I read somewhere," one of them ominously warns, "that their periods attract bears." Odors play an important role in the movie. Hoping to attract Corningstone, Brian Fantana splashes on a high-octane cologne that smells, the newsroom agrees, "like the time the raccoon got in the copier."

If the movie simply focused on making Ron and his team look ridiculous, it might grow tedious, because that would be such an easy thing to do. But it has a kind of sweetness to it. Despite his weaknesses, Ron is sort of a nice guy, darn it all, and Veronica Corningstone, despite her desire to project a serious image, kinda likes the guy—especially when he reveals an unsuspected musical talent in a lounge one night, after he's asked to "sit in on jazz flute."

The movie contains a lot of cameo appearances by other stars of the current comedy movie tour. Their names I will not reveal. Well, a character's name I will reveal: an anchorman named Wes Mantooth is Burgundy's archenemy. When the news teams clash in a free-for-all, it's over the top. But a lot of the quieter moments of rivalry are on target.

I have known and worked with a lot of anchorpersons, even female anchorpersons, over the years, and I can tell you that almost all of them are good people—smart professionals who don't take themselves too seriously. But every once in a while you get a Ron Burgundy, and you kind of treasure him, because you can dine out on the stories for years.

And Now Ladies and Gentlemen ★ ★ ½
PG-13, 126 m., 2003

Jeremy Irons (Valentin), Patricia Kaas (Jane Lester), Thierry Lhermitte (Thierry), Allesandra Martines (Françoise), Ticky Holgado (Boubou), Yvan Attal (David), Souad Amidou (Police Inspector), Claudia Cardinale (Countess Falconnetti). Directed by Claude Lelouch and produced by Lelouch. Screenplay by Lelouch, Pierre Leroux, and Pierre Uytterhoeven.

And Now Ladies and Gentlemen is a title that stopped me cold. What could it possibly have to do with this movie about jewel thieves, brain

tumors, sailing alone around the world, faith healers, adultery, cell-phone trickery, gigolos, police work, Paris, Morocco, and nightclub chantoosies? Suddenly I understood: The title refers not to the plot but to the performance by the director, Claude Lelouch, who pulls a new plot twist or exotic location out of his hat in every reel. The movie is so extravagant and outrageous in its storytelling that it resists criticism: It's self-satirizing.

For such a story you require an actor like Jeremy Irons, someone dour and inward and filled simultaneously with lust and with a conviction that the lust can never be satisfied. You would not want an extroverted actor, or a heroic one; if the story whirls, the actor must remain still, or the audience risks vertigo. For such a story, also, you require an audience in on the joke: The slightest shred of common sense would explode this movie. I fondly recall a conversation I had with Ken Turan of the *Los Angeles Times,* after we had seen *Gerry,* in which two guys get lost in the desert and walk for the rest of the movie. We agreed that the ordinary moviegoer would find it tedious beyond all reason, but that it could be appreciated by experienced and seasoned moviegoers—like ourselves, for example.

And Now Ladies and Gentlemen is not tedious, at least. It errs in the opposite direction. Like a sampler of Claude Lelouch's greatest hits, it has a score by Michel Legrand, and the technique of draining the color from some scenes, which reminds us that Lelouch alternated color and black-and-white in his first great hit, *A Man and a Woman* (1966). Oh, and it begins with a jewel robbery whose technique is inspired by *La Bonne Année* (1973), which itself inspired Peter Falk's astonishing performance in the remake, *Happy New Year* (1987). The theft depends on disguise and deception, and all one can say is that Falk (and Lino Ventura in the original) were a lot more deceptive than Jeremy Irons is this time. His disguise looks like something whipped up for a costume party.

No matter; one thing follows another, and soon Irons (whose character is the ominously named Valentin Valentin) falls in love with Françoise (Allesandra Martines), only to eventually kiss her farewell before setting off to sail single-handedly around the globe. (Thierry

Lhermitte, the Other Man du Jour of the French cinema, is poised to step in.) Valentin, alas, gets no further than the middle of the Mediterranean before passing out, and he is eventually found, rescued, and brought to Morocco, where friendly Dr. Lamy (Jean-Marie Bigard) diagnoses a brain tumor.

At this point, one hour into the movie, Valentin meets the other major character. Her name is Jane Lester, she is a nightclub singer played by the German singer Patricia Kaas, and, wouldn't you know, she has a brain tumor too. She knows because she starts blanking on lyrics, although since she sings with a handheld mike while strolling past the tables of oblivious diners, she is the first to notice.

The movie is episodic beyond all reason, as when Valentin Valentin and Jane Lester attend a faith healer, who suggests they go to the grave of a mighty saint who may be able to cure them—and, given the movie's happy ending, who is to say she did not? Meanwhile, in the hotel where Jane is performing, a faded countess (Claudia Cardinale—yes, Claudia Cardinale) loses some priceless jewels while her husband is out of town on business, and the police inspector (Amidou) at first suspects Valentin. This is a neat irony, when you come to think of it, since Valentin is in fact a jewel thief. The inspector is a cop of the world and observes, "I don't check alibis. Only the innocent don't have alibis."

Will the jewels be found, the thief arrested, Valentin cured and healed, Jane Lester healed and loved, Françoise comforted by Thierry, the journey resumed, the lyrics recalled? Oh, and I almost forgot the scam at the auction house. The answers to these questions are handed out at the end to the grateful audience. Did I dislike this movie? Not at all. Was it necessary for me to see it? No, but once it had my attention at least it labored sincerely to keep it. I can't quite recommend the movie, but I confess a certain fugitive affection for it.

Anger Management ★ ★
PG-13, 101 m., 2003

Jack Nicholson (Dr. Buddy Rydell), Adam Sandler (Dave Buznik), Marisa Tomei (Linda), Luis Guzman (Lou), Allen Covert (Andrew), Lynne Thigpen (Judge Daniels), Woody Harrelson (Galaxia), John Turturro (Chuck). Directed by Peter Segal and produced by Barry Bernardi, Derek Dauchy, Todd Garner, Jack Giarraputo, John Jacobs, and Joe Roth. Screenplay by David Dorfman.

The concept is inspired. The execution is lame. *Anger Management,* a film that might have been one of Adam Sandler's best, becomes one of Jack Nicholson's worst. Because Nicholson has a superb track record and a sure nose for trash, it's obvious the movie was a Sandler project with Nicholson as hired talent, not the other way around. The fact that four of the producers were involved in *The Master of Disguise* and *The Animal* indicates that quality control was not an issue.

Everything about the way the movie goes wrong—the dumbing down of plot developments, the fascination with Sandler's whiny one-note character, the celebrity cameos, the cringing sentimentality—indicates a product from the Sandler assembly line. No doubt Sandler's regular fans will love this movie, which is a return to form after the brilliant *Punch-Drunk Love.* Nicholson's fans will be appalled.

And yet there might really have been something here. When I heard the premise, I began to smile. Sandler plays a mild-mannered guy named Dave Buznik, who just got a promotion at work and is in love with his fiancée, Linda (Marisa Tomei). Through a series of bizarre misunderstandings on an airplane trip, he is misdiagnosed as a person filled with rage, and is assigned to therapy with the famed anger specialist Dr. Buddy Rydell (Jack Nicholson).

Nicholson's early scenes are his best because he brings an intrinsic interest to every character he plays, and we don't yet know how bad the movie is. He wears a beard making him look like a cross between Stanley Kubrick and Lenin, and works his eyebrows and sardonic grin with the zeal of a man who was denied them during the making of *About Schmidt.* He introduces Dave to a therapy group including the first of many guest stars in the movie, Luis Guzman and John Turturro. Both are clearly nuts—and so is Dr. Rydell, as Dave finds himself trapped in an escalating spiral of trouble, climaxing in a bar fight and a court appearance where he explains, "I was being attacked by someone while stealing a blind man's cane."

The blind man is played by Harry Dean Stanton. Also on display in the movie are Woody Harrelson (as a drag queen), John C. Reilly (as a Buddhist monk who gets a wedgie), Heather Graham, Mayor Rudolph Giuliani, and (ho, ho) the angry Bobby Knight. The use of celebrity walk-ons in a movie is often the sign of desperation, but rarely does one take over the movie and drive it to utter ruin, as Giuliani's role does. The closing scenes in Yankee Stadium, with the hero proposing to his girl over a loudspeaker, passed into the realm of exhausted cliché before Sandler was born.

Most good comedy has an undercurrent of truth. The genius of *Punch-Drunk Love* was that it identified and dealt with the buried rage that does indeed seem to exist in most of Sandler's characters. The falsity of *Anger Management* is based on the premise that Dave Buznik is not angry enough—that he needs to act out more and assert himself. That provides the explanation for the plot's "surprise," which will come as old news to most audiences.

I said that Nicholson brings an intrinsic interest to his characters. Sandler does not. His character is usually a blank slate waiting to be written on by the movie. While Nicholson has infinite variations and notes, Sandler is usually much the same. It's said the difference between character actors and stars is that the star is expected to deliver the same elements in every movie, while the character actor is supposed to change and surprise.

Nicholson, who has been a star character actor since he grinned triumphantly on the back of the motorcycle in *Easy Rider,* was part of a revolution that swept away old-model stars and replaced them with such character-stars as Dustin Hoffman, Robert De Niro, and, recently, Nicolas Cage, William H. Macy, or Steve Buscemi.

Sandler was wonderful in *Punch-Drunk Love* because, for once, he was in a smart movie that understood his screen persona. Paul Thomas Anderson, who wrote and directed that film, studied Sandler, appreciated his quality, and wrote a story for it. Most of Sandler's other movies have been controlled by Sandler himself (he is executive producer this time), and repeat the persona but do not seem willing to see

it very clearly. This is particularly true in the cloying romantic endings, in which we see what a very good fellow he is after all.

That there is a market for this I do not deny. But imagine, just imagine, a movie in which Dave Buznik truly was exploding with rage, and Dr. Buddy Rydell really was an anger therapist. This movie should be remade immediately, this time with Jack Nicholson as executive producer, and Adam Sandler as hired gun.

Anything but Love ★ ★ ★
PG-13, 99 m., 2003

Andrew McCarthy (Elliot Shepard), Isabel Rose (Billie Golden), Cameron Bancroft (Greg Ellenbogen), Alix Korey (Laney Golden), Ilana Levine (Marcy), Sean Arbuckle (TJ), Victor Argo (Sal), Eartha Kitt (Herself). Directed by Robert Cary and produced by Aimee Schoof and Isen Robbins. Screenplay by Cary and Isabel Rose.

Anything but Love is a new movie like those old musicals you watch on TV late at night. Filmed in the colors of newborn Technicolor, plotted as a tribute to the conventions of Hollywood romance, filled with standard songs, it's by and for people who love those kinds of movies. Others will find it clichéd and predictable, but they won't understand.

Remember the hapless guy Oscar Levant always played? The one who secretly loved the heroine but never won her? The one original element in *Anything but Love* is that Oscar Levant finally gets the girl. She is the flame-haired Billie Golden (Isabel Rose). I'm willing to bet my small change that she was named for Billie Holiday and the Golden Age of MGM musicals. She sings torchy standards in a tacky motel supper club at the "JFK Skytel," where the owner loves her work but has to change formats because business is bad.

That grizzled old Victor Argo plays the owner is almost too good to be true. That he is named Sal is inevitable. That he is the longtime boyfriend of Billie's mother, Laney (Alix Korey), shows that Rose and director Robert Cary have been studying the late show. And, of course, Billie has another job; she's a waitress at a high-class club headlining Eartha Kitt, playing herself. An early shot frames Billie's face in the round window of the door between the kitchen and the showroom, as she yearningly watches Kitt. This shot is obligatory in all movies about waitresses who want to be stars.

Times are hard for Billie and her mother, who hits the bottle. Sal doesn't want to fire her, and suggests a compromise: She might be able to keep working if she accompanies herself on the piano. Her playing is rusty, so she signs up for lessons, only to discover that her new teacher, Elliot (Andrew McCarthy), is the same jerk who sabotaged her at an audition by screwing up the accompaniment. Of course they hate each other. This is essential so that they can love each other later.

There is another possible path Billie could take. Greg Ellenbogen (Cameron Bancroft) has come back into her life. He was the high school hunk she had a crush on, now a thirty-ish success story who has lots of money and decides (as a logical exercise, I think) that he should get married. They court, they get engaged, she will be financially secure, and her dream of becoming a chanteuse can be forgotten (Greg suggests) as she raises their children and sings— oh, at parties and benefits and stuff like that.

Is there a person alive who doesn't know whether Billie chooses Greg or Elliot? But, of course, there must be enormous obstacles and pitfalls along the way, not to mention those kinds of overblown fantasy scenes much beloved of old musicals, where everything ratchets up six degrees into dreamy schmaltz before finally ending with a close-up of the heroine's face as she comes back to earth.

The Andrew McCarthy character inhabits a sparsely furnished walk-up studio, is dyspeptic and cynical, doesn't value his talent, and in general is a clone of the Oscar Levant character. He doesn't chain smoke, the cigarette dangling from his lips while he plays, and that's a missed opportunity. When it's announced that he may move to Paris, I thought—of course! He wants to be Gene Kelly's roommate in *An American in Paris*.

The movie is not perfect. It has been shot on a budget close to the minimum wage, and has the usual problem of crowd scenes without a large enough crowd. But it takes joy in its work, and that makes up for a lot. Eartha Kitt has a small but very functional role, singing a song (wonderfully) and offering the kind of advice that absolutely must be supplied in a plot of this kind. Was it Kitt's idea or the filmmakers' that after offering that advice she doesn't get all sentimental but stays tartly in character, reminding Billie that she is the star and Billie is the waitress? I liked that moment.

One obvious flaw: There is a wedding scene (I will not say who with, or even whether it is real or not—and no, don't think that's a hint). The scene bursts into fantasy and imaginings at precisely that moment when it should be played straight in order to exploit the emotions the movie has been building toward. But in general the movie works just as it wants to, and you will either enjoy it for that, or you will be the kind of person for whom the names Kathryn Grayson, Doris Day, Howard Keel, Dennis Morgan, Ann Miller, Jack Carson, Ann Blyth, and Gordon MacRae have no meaning.

Anything Else ★ ★ ★
R, 108 m., 2003

Woody Allen (David Dobel), Jason Biggs (Jerry Falk), Christina Ricci (Amanda), Stockard Channing (Paula), Danny DeVito (Harvey), Jimmy Fallon (Bob Styles). Directed by Woody Allen and produced by Letty Aronson. Screenplay by Allen.

The dialogue in Woody Allen's *Anything Else* is an exercise of neurotic bravery, a defense against fear and insecurity. His characters are doubtful about their prospects in life. Careers aren't going well, and romance works only through self-deception. To hold despair at bay they talk and talk, and because Allen is a master of comic dialogue, it is our pleasure to listen.

The new movie has both a mentor and a narrator, so one character gives insights about life, and the other gives insights about him. The hero is Jerry Falk (Jason Biggs), a would-be comedy writer whose career is going nowhere, and his adviser is David Dobel (Allen), a sixtyish New Jersey schoolteacher whose career has gone nowhere; he hasn't stopped hoping, but he keeps the day job. They meet in the park for long talks, Dobel doing most of the talking, Jerry grateful at first and then dubious: If Dobel knows so much, how come he's still stuck?

Jerry was once fully and happily in love with

Brooke (KaDee Strickland), a woman who presented no difficulties, which was perhaps the problem, since he left her for Amanda (Christina Ricci), a woman who consists of difficulties. Amanda is an actress who seems to keep Jerry around primarily as a foil for intimate improv scenes in which she explains the ways his life must be miserable if he is to continue enjoying her company. He asks if she doesn't love him. "Just because when you touch me I pull away?" she replies. At one point she declares a six-month moratorium on sex. When the ever-optimistic Jerry makes reservations at a fancy restaurant to celebrate their anniversary, she stands him up ("I already ate").

Jerry introduces Amanda to David. David's verdict is instantaneous: "She's cheating on you." He advises Jerry to spy on her, which he does by lurking in stairwells and skulking in doorways for hours at a time, until finally he thinks he has enough proof to confront her, not realizing that in matters of cheating the worst thing you can do is expose the other person—because then they have their excuse to leave. Better to suffer in silence, as the wise Charles Bukowski once advised, until they figure out which one they want.

Anything Else is not simply a comedy about Jerry's romance, Amanda's deceptions, and David's advice, however. There's a darker undercurrent. David has fears, not all of them revealed, and takes his young protégé to a gun shop to buy him a weapon. Everyone needs a gun, he explains, to feel safer, to protect themselves, and so on. Jerry is dubious, Amanda is appalled, and David seems to be revealing only the surface of his fears.

Amanda moves out, moves back in, and then her mother, Paula (Stockard Channing), moves in too, with a personality that overcrowds the apartment. Channing is a great original, an actress with the ability to make absurd statements as if anyone would agree with them. She wants to start over as a torch singer, she says, and has a young boyfriend she met at an AA meeting (apparently not a successful one, since they're soon doing coke together). With a girl who doesn't want to live with him and her mother who does, Jerry's almost ready to listen when David suggests he dump everything so that just the two of them can leave for Los Angeles, where all the jobs are anyway.

But that would mean leaving Harvey (Danny DeVito), Jerry's longtime agent, who charges him 25 percent, which is way above the industry standard, but then again, Jerry is his only client, and never works anyway. DeVito brings electric energy to his scenes, as an intense dynamo who feels so strongly about the agent-client relationship that when Jerry hints it may be ending, he pulls a scene in a restaurant that more or less defines the notion of a public spectacle.

The movie avoids the usual pitfalls of comedies about young romance, and gets jolts from the supporting work by Channing and DeVito. And Allen is inimitable, as the worrywart who backs into every decision, protesting and moaning about the pitfalls and certain disappointment sure to lie ahead. At a time when so many American movies keep dialogue at a minimum so they can play better overseas, what a delight to listen to smart people whose conversation is like a kind of comic music.

Note: Here's a strange thing. The studio, DreamWorks, seems to be trying to conceal Woody Allen's presence in the movie. He is the writer and director, and has top billing in the credits, but he is never seen in the trailer, the commercials, or the TV review clips. The trailer gives full-screen credits to Jason Biggs and Christina Ricci, but only belatedly adds "From Woody Allen," not mentioning that he also stars. It's as if they have the treasure of a Woody Allen movie and they're trying to package it for the American Pie *crowd.*

Après Vous ★ ★
R, 110 m., 2005

Daniel Auteuil (Antoine), José Garcia (Louis), Sandrine Kiberlain (Blanche), Marilyne Canto (Christine), Michèle Moretti (Martine), Garence Clavel (Karine), Fabio Zenoni (André). Directed by Pierre Salvadori and produced by Philippe Martin. Screenplay by Benoît Graffin, David Léotard, and Salvadori

Daniel Auteuil, who seems to be the busiest actor in France, has that look about him of a man worried about whether he is doing the right thing. In *Après Vous* he does the right thing and it results in nothing but trouble for him. He rescues a man in the act of committing suicide, and then, in an irony that is probably covered by several ancient proverbs, he feels responsible for the man's life.

Auteuil plays Antoine, the maître d' at a Paris brasserie that, if the customers typically endure as much incompetence as they experience during this movie, must have great food. Taking a shortcut through a park late one night, Antoine comes upon Louis (the sad-eyed, hangdog José Garcia) just as he kicks the suitcase out from under his feet to hang himself from a tree. Antoine saves him, brings him home, introduces him to his uneasy girlfriend, Christine (Marilyne Canto), and cares more about Louis than Louis does.

Louis, in fact, wishes he had committed suicide. He is heartbroken over the end of his romance with Blanche (Sandrine Kiberlain), and suddenly remembers he has written a letter bidding farewell from life and mailed it to the grandmother who raised him. Antoine promptly drives through the night with him to intercept the letter, and finds himself living Louis's life for him.

Après Vous is intended as a farce, but lacks farcical insanity and settles for being a sitcom, not a very good one. One problem is that neither Louis nor his dilemma is amusing. Another is that Antoine is too sincere and single-minded to suggest a man being driven buggy by the situation; he seems more earnest than beleaguered.

Farces often involve cases of mistaken or misunderstood identities, and that's what happens this time as Antoine seeks out Blanche, finds her in a florist shop, and falls in love with her. That would be a simple enough matter, since after all, she has already broken up with Louis, but Antoine is conscientious to a fault, and feels it is somehow his responsibility to deny himself romantic happiness and try to reconcile Louis and Blanche. Since there is nothing in the movie to suggest they would bring each other anything but misery, this compulsion seems more masochistic than generous.

Much of the action centers on the brasserie, Chez Jean, where I would like to eat the next time I am in Paris, always assuming Louis and Antoine no longer work there. Antoine gets Louis the wine steward's job, despite Louis's complete lack of knowledge about wine; he develops a neat trick of describing a wine by its results rather than its qualities, recommending expensive labels because they will make the customer feel cheery. This at least has the advantage of making him less boring than most wine stewards.

Blanche meanwhile doesn't realize the two men know each other, and that leads of course to a scene in which she finds that out and feels betrayed, as women always do in such situations, instead of being grateful that two men have gone to such pains to make her the center of their deceptions. There are also scenes that I guess are inevitable in romantic comedies of a certain sort, in which one character and then another scales a vine-covered trellis to Blanche's balcony, risking their lives in order to spy on her. I don't know about you, but when I see a guy climbing to a balcony and his name's not Romeo, I wish I'd brought along my iPod.

There is a kind of mental efficiency meter that ticks away during comedies, in which we keep an informal accounting: Is the movie providing enough laughter to justify its running time? If the movie falls below its recommended laughter saturation level, I begin to make use of the Indiglo feature on my Timex. Antoine and Louis and Blanche make two or three or even four too many trips around the maypole of comic misunderstandings, giving us time to realize that we don't really care how they end up anyway.

Are We There Yet? ★ ★
PG, 91 m., 2005

Ice Cube (Nick Persons), Nia Long (Suzanne Kingston), Aleisha Allen (Lindsey Kingston), Philip Bolden (Kevin Kingston), Jay Mohr (Marty). Directed by Brian Levant and produced by Matt Alvarez, Ice Cube, and Dan Kolsrud. Screenplay by Steven Gary Banks, Claudia Grazioso, J. David Stem, and David N. Weiss.

Ice Cube is an effortlessly likable actor, which presents two problems for *Are We There Yet?* Problem No. 1 is that he has to play a bachelor who hates kids, and No. 2 is that two kids make his life miserable in ways that are supposed to be funny but are mean and painful.

Mr. Cube plays Nick, owner of a sports memorabilia store, who one day is struck by the lightning bolt of love when he gazes upon Suzanne (Nia Long), who runs an event-management service across the street. There is a problem. She is the divorced mom of two kids. Nick hates kids. But one Dark and Stormy Night he passes Suzanne next to her stalled car and offers her a lift. There is chemistry, and it seems likely to lead to physics, but then she sadly observes that they can only be "good friends" because he doesn't really care for kids.

But . . . but . . . Nick cares so much for her that he's willing to learn. Suzanne is needed in Vancouver to coordinate a New Year's Eve party, her ex-husband breaks a promise to baby-sit the kids, and Nick agrees to bring the kids to Vancouver. That's when the trouble starts.

We've already seen what these kids are capable of. One of their mom's dates arrives on the front sidewalk, hits a trip wire, and is pelted with buckets of glue before losing his footing on dozens of marbles and falling hard to the ground. Hilarious, right?

Now it's Nick's turn. He attempts to take the kids north by plane and train before settling on automobile—in his case, a brand-new Lincoln Navigator, curiously enough the same vehicle that was used in *Johnson Family Vacation*. It's the SUV of choice for destruction in bizarre ways through family adventures.

Young Lindsey (Aleisha Allen) and younger Kevin (Philip Bolden) retain the delusion that their father will come back home someday, and have dedicated themselves to discouraging their mother's would-be boyfriends. This leads to such stunts as writing "Help us!" on a card and holding it to the car window so a trucker will think they're the captives of a child abuser. It also leads to several potentially fatal traffic adventures, a boxing match with a deer that stands on its hind legs and seems to think it's a kangaroo, and the complete destruction of the Navigator.

Nick displays the patience of a saint. Far from being the child-hater he thinks he is, he's gentle, understanding, forgiving, and empathetic. The kids are little monsters. What they do to him is so far over the top that it's sadistic, not funny, and it doesn't help when they finally get to Vancouver and Suzanne cruelly misreads the situation.

I would have loved to see a genuine love story involving Ice Cube, Nia Long, and the challenge of a lifelong bachelor dating a woman with children. Sad that a story like that couldn't get made, but this shrill "comedy" could. Maybe it's the filmmakers who don't like children. They certainly don't seem to know very much about them.

Around the Bend ★ ★ ½
R, 85 m., 2004

Michael Caine (Henry Lair), Christopher Walken (Turner Lair), Josh Lucas (Jason Lair), Jonah Bobo (Zach), Glenne Headly (Katrina). Directed by Jordan Roberts and produced by Elliott Lewitt and Julie Kirkham. Screenplay by Roberts.

Christopher Walken has become so expert at finely tuned walk-ons that he rarely stays around for a whole movie. His cameos are like the prize in a Cracker Jack box: You don't buy the ticket to see Walken, but you keep looking for him. In *Around the Bend* he has a role big enough to move around inside, and he reminds us what a very good actor he is. The movie, unfortunately, doesn't really work; it's one of those films where the characters always seem to be Behaving, as if ordinary life has to be jacked up into eccentricity.

The film opens with Michael Caine as old Henry, bedridden and being cared for by his adult grandson, Jason (Josh Lucas), his great-grandson, Zach (Jonah Bobo), and Katrina (Glenne Headly), the Danish live-in. He has one of those unspecified illnesses that permit grand gestures before the final exit. There is a generation missing from this picture, but the portrait is filled out when Turner (Christopher Walken) amazingly returns home for the first time in thirty years.

Jason doesn't much like his father, who abandoned him. Young Zach is impressed: You're not dead anymore! Turner says he must leave again the following day, but won't give his reasons (which turn out, in fact, to be excellent). Henry rouses himself for one last journey into the world with Zach, and the old man and the boy settle into a booth at the nearby Kentucky Fried Chicken restaurant, where Henry scribbles instructions on Post-it notes and stuffs them into KFC bags, one inside another, outlining a sort of scavenger hunt. Then he dies.

The opening of the KFC bags, which takes on the solemnity of the reading of a will, reveals Henry's plan. He wants to be cremated along with his dog, and he wants his son, grandson, and great-grandson to make a journey from Los Angeles to New Mexico, scattering ashes along the way. One specification: Every bag must be opened in a KFC restaurant, and the ashes scattered nearby.

Turner, the Walken character, decides he will go along with this plan. Of course, there are poignant reasons why he should not, even apart from the fact that he walked away from a prison, but one grand gesture deserves another.

The three men pilot a very old VW van down the desert highways from one chicken outlet to the next, faithfully consuming fried chicken at every meal, as if this were the sequel to *Super Size Me*. Why, we may ask, did Henry insist on KFC? Does it have anything to do with product placement? Is KFC trying to drum up postinterment business? I doubt it. I think they go to KFC because Jordan Roberts, the writer-director, wanted to make them into Characters and thought KFC would be quirky or funny or something.

But this is not exactly a comedy. It is, alas, a voyage of discovery, during which old secrets are revealed, new ones are shared, and the generations find peace with one another. These passages are well acted by Walken, Lucas, and young Bobo, but I always felt as if they were inhabiting a story, not their lives. Walken has some nice moments, though, and I love the way he releases dialogue as if first giving every word a friendly pat. There's a good scene where his son accuses him of stealing a spoon, and the explanation reveals important things about the way he lives now.

Around the Bend has the best will in the world, and its heart is in the right place. Walken is a pleasure to watch in a role he can stretch in, and there may be some audience members who get involved in these men trying to figure out how to talk to one another. But I dunno. It all seemed like a setup job to me. I know movie characters usually follow a script, but I don't like it when it feels like they are.

Around the World in 80 Days ★ ★ ★
PG, 120 m., 2004

Jackie Chan (Passepartout), Steve Coogan (Phileas Fogg), Cecile De France (Monique La Roche), Jim Broadbent (Lord Kelvin), Kathy Bates (Queen Victoria), Arnold Schwarzenegger (Prince Hapi), John Cleese (Grizzled Sergeant), Owen Wilson (Wilbur Wright), Luke Wilson (Orville Wright), Karen Mok (General Fang). Directed by Frank Coraci and produced by Bill Badalato and Hal Lieberman. Screenplay by David N. Titcher, David Benullo, and David Goldstein, based on the novel by Jules Verne.

Here against all probability is a jolly comedy made from that wheezy high concept, *Around the World in 80 Days*. I grew up with Phileas Fogg and his picaresque journey, plundered the Classics Illustrated comic, read the Jules Verne novel, and attended Michael Todd's 1956 film, but I never thought the story was much of a cliff-hanger. Even in its time, eighty days seemed doable. Verne's *20,000 Leagues Under the Sea* and *From the Earth to the Moon* were more like it.

But here's a film version that does some lateral thinking, that moves Fogg off dead center and makes Jackie Chan's Passepartout the real hero, and lingers for comic effect instead of always looking at its watch. The Todd production was famous for its wall-to-wall cameos ("Look! That piano player! Why, it's Frank Sinatra!"). And here we have Kathy Bates as Queen Victoria, Owen and Luke Wilson as the Wright brothers, John Cleese as a British sergeant, and, funniest of all, Arnold Schwarzenegger as a Turkish prince.

The setup is familiar. Phileas Fogg is much resented by the members of the fogbound Explorers' Club because of his crackpot inventions and fevered schemes. Lord Kelvin (Jim Broadbent), president of the club, is a mainstream scientist who no doubt gave his name to the scientific term "kelvin," which measures how many degrees of separation there are between you and Sir Kelvin Bacon, the inventor of gravity.

Fogg claims the world can be circled in eighty days. Kelvin is outraged by his presumption, and makes him dare: Either (a)

Fogg circles the globe by the deadline and Kelvin resigns from the club, or (b) Fogg resigns and discontinues his confounded experiments. Fogg (Steve Coogan) accepts the bet, and as he's preparing for his journey he hires a new valet, Passepartout (Jackie Chan).

This valet we have already met, making a sudden exit from the Bank of England after having stolen the priceless Jade Buddha, a relic much treasured by his native village in China, but nabbed by the Black Scorpions, hirelings of the evil warlord Fang. Passepartout's hidden motive for joining the journey is to elude the police, sneak out of England, and return the Buddha to China.

So off we go, by horse, train, ship, hot air balloon, and so on. There is a brief stop at an art fair in France, where the beautiful Monique (Cecile De France) insists on joining their expedition and cannot be dissuaded; we think at first she has a nefarious motive, but no, she's probably taken a class in screenplay construction and knows that the film requires a sexy female lead. This is not the first case in cinematic history of a character voluntarily entering a movie because of the objective fact that she is required.

Fogg is the straight man to Passepartout for much of the journey, allowing Chan to steal scenes with shameless mugging, astonished double-takes, and his remarkable physical agility. But all goes more or less as expected until the three arrive in Turkey and are made the guests of Prince Hapi (Arnold Schwarzenegger), whose hospitality is hard to distinguish from captivity. Smitten by the fragrant Monique, he invites all three to join him in the Turkish equivalent of a hot tub, observing ruefully, "I'm always embarrassing myself in front of visiting dignitaries." It may not be worth the price of admission, but it almost is, to hear Schwarzenegger proudly boast, "Guess who else was in this pool? U.S. president Rutherford B. Hayes!"

The director, Frank Coraci, takes advantage of Verne's structure to avoid the need for any real continuity. When one location runs out of gags, the three move on to the next, including an extended stay in Passepartout's native China, where Fang and the Black Scorpions do all they can to win back the Jade Buddha from the grateful village where it has exerted its benign charm for centuries.

Then across the Pacific and into the American desert, where the travelers encounter a couple of traveling bicycle salesmen, Wilbur and Orville Wright (Owen and Luke Wilson). They generously share their ideas for an airplane, and that comes in handy in the mid-Atlantic, when Fogg's chartered steamer runs out of fuel and the intrepid circumnavigators invent an airplane and fly to London. Oh, and before that there's an extended martial arts scene in the New York warehouse where the head of the Statue of Liberty provides a gigantic prop.

None of this amounts to anything more than goofy fun, but that's what the ads promise, and the movie delivers. It's light as a fly, but springs some genuinely funny moments, especially by Schwarzenegger, the Wilsons, and the irrepressible Chan.

The California governor's scenes were shot before he took office, and arguably represent his last appearance in a fiction film; if so, he leaves the movies as he entered, a man who shares our amusement at his improbability, and has a canny sense of his own image and possibilities. I met him when the documentary *Pumping Iron* was being released, and Mr. Universe was the first of the offices he would hold. I liked him then, I like him now, and I remember that when I introduced the film at the USA Film Festival in Dallas, he greeted the audience and then slipped off to the green room to study his business textbooks. He refused to be dismissed as muscles with an accent, but he got the joke.

The Assassination of Richard Nixon ★ ★ ★ ½
R, 95 m., 2005

Sean Penn (Samuel Bicke), Naomi Watts (Marie Bicke), Don Cheadle (Bonny Simmons), Jack Thompson (Jack Jones), Mykelti Williamson (Harold Mann), Michael Wincott (Julius Bicke). Directed by Niels Mueller and produced by Alfonso Cuaron and Jorge Vergara. Screenplay by Kevin Kennedy and Mueller.

Baltimore, 1974. Sam Bicke explains and explains and explains. He has it all worked out, why he is right and the world is wrong, and he has a fierce obsession with injustice. "My name is Sam Bicke," he says at the beginning of one of the tapes he mails to Leonard Bernstein, "and I consider myself a grain of sand." He sells office supplies, very badly. His marriage is at an end. The Small Business Administration is not acting on his loan application. Nixon is still in the White House. The Black Panthers are being persecuted. It is all part of the same rage coiling within him.

Sean Penn plays Bicke as a man who has always been socially inept and now, as his life comes apart, descends into madness. His own frustration and the evils in the world are all the same, all somehow someone else's fault, and in the opening scene of *The Assassination of Richard Nixon*, we see him in an airport parking garage, concealing a pistol in a leg brace. He mails one last tape to Leonard Bernstein. He plans to hijack a plane and fly it into the White House.

There was a real Sam Bicke (spelled Byck), whose plan of course failed. Niels Mueller's movie is based on his botched assassination scheme, but many of the other details, including some scenes of mordant humor, are the invention of Mueller and his cowriter, Kevin Kennedy. This is a character study of a marginal man who goes off the rails, and Penn is brilliant at evoking how daily life itself is filled, for Bicke, with countless challenges to his rigid sense of right and wrong.

Consider his job as an office supply salesman. He is selling chairs covered in Naugahyde. The client asks if they are leather. He says they are not. His boss, Jack Jones (Jack Thompson), steps in and smoothly explains they are "Naugahyde-covered leather." Uh-huh. When Sam offers a client a discount to close a sale, Jack calls him into his office and screams at him for selling the desk at a loss. The client overhears. Later Sam finds out the joke was on him. Jack wants to help him, and recommends reading *The Power of Positive Thinking* and *How to Win Friends and Influence People*.

His sense of honesty offended by his job, Sam becomes obsessed with Nixon: "He made us a promise—he didn't deliver. Then he sold us on the exact same promise and he got elected again." He visits the local Black Panther office to make a donation and, as a Panther official (Mykelti Williamson) listens incredulously, shares his ideas about renaming the Panthers the Zebras and admitting white members—like Sam Bicke, for example.

Sam is separated from his wife, Marie (Naomi Watts), and two daughters. He dreams of saving his marriage. She can't make him understand it's over. He is served with divorce papers and protests, "We're supposed to be working this out!" In one of the movie's most painful moments, he talks to the family dog: "You love me, don't you?" The dog seems indifferent.

Sam dreams of starting a limousine company with his closest friend, Bonny Simmons (Don Cheadle). This depends on a small business loan. Sam and Bonny are a poor risk, the bank drags out the paperwork, and Sam explains and explains and explains how important the loan is, and how urgent it is that it comes quickly.

Sean Penn conveys anger through small, contained details. He is one of our great actors, able to invest insignificant characters with importance because their lives are so urgent to themselves. Was it Penn or the filmmakers who thought of the touch where Sam puts on a false mustache in the airport parking lot. What for? Nobody knows who he is or what he looks like, and if his plan succeeds there will be no Sam Bicke left, mustache or not.

Penn shows him always on the outside. Kept out of his house. Turned away by the bank. Ineligible for the Black Panthers. The outsider at the office, listening to his boss and a coworker snickering about him. The only person he can confide in is Leonard Bernstein, whose music he admires. (The real Bernstein, who received tapes from the real Byck, was mystified to be attached however distantly to a hijacking plot.)

The Assassination of Richard Nixon is about a man on a collision course; given the stark terms in which he arranges right and wrong, he will sooner or later crack up. He hasn't a clue about appropriate behavior, about how others perceive him, about what may be right but is nevertheless impossible. The movie's title has one effect before we see it, and another afterward, when we can see the grandiosity and self-deceit that it implies. What really happens is that Sam Bicke assassinates himself.

Does the film have a message? I don't think it wants one. It is about the journey of a man going mad. A film can simply be a character study, as this one is. That is sufficient. A message might seem trundled in and gratuitous. Certainly our opinions of Nixon, Vietnam, and the Black Panthers are irrelevant; they enter the movie only as objects of Bicke's obsessions. We cannot help but sense a connection with another would-be assassin from the 1970s, another obsessed loner, Travis Bickle. Travis pours out his thoughts in journals; Sam uses tapes. They feel the need to justify themselves, and lack even a listener.

Assassination Tango ★ ★ ★
R, 114 m., 2003

Robert Duvall (John J. Anderson), Ruben Blades (Miguel), Kathy Baker (Maggie), Luciana Pedraza (Manuela), Julio Oscar Mechoso (Orlando), James Keane (Whitey), Frank Gio (Frankie), Katherine Micheaux Miller (Jenny). Directed by Robert Duvall and produced by Rob Carliner and Duvall. Screenplay by Duvall.

Robert Duvall's *Assassination Tango* is not entirely about crime or dance, and that will be a problem for some audiences. "More assassination, less tango!" demands the on-line critic Jon Popick. But I have seen countless movies about assassination and not a few about the tango, and while Duvall's movie doesn't entirely succeed, what it attempts is intriguing. It wants to lock itself inside the mind of a man whose obsessions distract him from the wider world.

John J. Anderson (Duvall) talks to himself a lot, carrying on a bemused commentary that may eventually descend into dementia, but not yet. No longer young, he is a professional hit man who plans to retire and devote his life to his woman, Maggie (Kathy Baker), and especially to her ten-year-old daughter, Jenny (Katherine Micheaux Miller). He likes Maggie but loves Jenny with a rather alarming intensity: "She is my soul, my life, my eyes, my everything."

Is he a suppressed child molester? Later in the film a hooker reports, "He wanted me to call him 'daddy.'" But no, I don't believe he represents a threat. He is not an actor-out but a holder-in, a brooder whose emotional weather is stormy but unseen. Most of the people he deals with, including Frankie (Frank Gio), the mobster who employs him, have no idea who he really is or what he really needs.

Sent to Buenos Aires on his final job, assassinating a wealthy general, Anderson meets with local contacts but keeps his own counsel. We realize this is not a conventional crime story; he rejects most of the advice of the local bad guys, drifts off by himself, seems preoccupied or distracted, and happens by chance into a dance club where he is entranced by one of the performers, Manuela (Luciana Pedraza). He returns. He asks her to dance. She has no idea what to make of him. He requests tango lessons. They begin a relationship impossible to define, and it seems for a time that the movie will deny us both of the usual payoffs: no murder, no romance.

Whether or not it delivers on those fronts I will leave for you to discover. Duvall, who wrote as well as directed, never makes them the point. His movie is not about a killer or a lover, but about a man who has been damaged in some unspecified way, and wanders through the world in an unorganized search for something to make him whole again. This could be love for a young girl, mastery of the tango, idealization of a dancer's skill, or exercise of his assassin's craft.

Audiences impatient for plot may miss Duvall's movie altogether. Yes, he spends a lot of time in cafés doing nothing. Yes, his conversation is limited. Yes, not even Manuela knows what he wants. Yes, he meanders toward assassination in maddening digressions. Yes, there are dance scenes that slow the progress—but if, and only if, the progress is the point.

The tango is a dance in which partners join in meticulously rehearsed passion, with such exact timing that no improvisation or error is possible. (You can tell a bad tango dancer by the bruises on the shins.) Why is Anderson so attracted to this dance? Obviously, because it provides a framework for his emotional turmoil—laces it in, gives it structure, allows him to show the world he is disciplined when he is not. For him it is about control, and it supplies rigid rules for how to interact with his partner.

What *Assassination Tango* is about, I think, is John J. Anderson's quiet and inward attempt to slow his descent toward incompetence. He has Maggie but cannot visualize their future. He meets Manuela but does not know whether to offer a future. He has a job but suspects it is a trap. People threaten him but his biggest threat is interior: He is falling to pieces, falling into confusion, losing his sense of himself. The tango is a fragment to shore up against his ruin.

The movie is not quite successful. It is too secretive about its heart. It seems unfocused unless we are quick to get the clues, to look at Anderson in a certain way, to realize it will not be about murder or love but about coping strategies. John J. Anderson has so many secrets from the world that even this movie preserves some of them. Duvall has created it from the inside out, seeing it not through the eyes of the audience but through the mind of Anderson. *Assassination Tango* is all the same a fascinating effort, and I am happy to have seen it. It taught me something about filmmaking strategy.

Assault on Precinct 13 ★ ★ ★
R, 109 m., 2005

Ethan Hawke (Jake Roenick), Laurence Fishburne (Marion Bishop), Drea de Matteo (Iris Ferry), Brian Dennehy (Jasper O'Shea), John Leguizamo (Beck), Jeffrey "Ja Rule" Atkins (Smiley), Maria Bello (Alex Sabian), Gabriel Byrne (Marcus Duvall). Directed by Jean-Francois Richet and produced by Pascal Caucheteux, Stephane Sperry, and Jeffrey Silver. Screenplay by James DeMonaco, based on the film by John Carpenter.

Assault on Precinct 13 is not so much a remake as a riff on an old familiar plot: The fort is surrounded, and the defenders have to fight off the attackers and deal with possible traitors in their midst. Howard Hawks did versions of this so often that after John Wayne starred for him in *Rio Bravo* (1959) and *El Dorado* (1966), he told Wayne he was sending over a script for *Rio Lobo*, and Wayne told him, "I'll make it, but I don't need to read it. We've already made it twice."

John Carpenter's 1976 film, made just before his famous *Halloween*, added some touches from George Romero's *Night of the Living Dead* and moved the action from a threatened sheriff's office in the Old West to a threatened police station in the inner city. Now French director Jean-Francois Richet takes essentially the same material and makes

it work with strong performances and a couple of new twists.

Precinct 13, in this version, is scheduled to close forever at midnight. Burnt-out desk sergeant Jake Roenick (Ethan Hawke), still traumatized by the death of two partners, is on the graveyard shift with old-timer Jasper O'Shea (Brian Dennehy), who in a revelation fraught with omens announces he will soon retire. Also in the station is the buxom secretary Iris (Drea de Matteo).

There's basically nothing for them to do except for Jake to pop some more painkillers and chase them with booze from the office bottle. Then everything changes. An ubercriminal named Bishop (Laurence Fishburne) has been arrested, and is being transported by police bus with some other detainees, including the motormouth Beck (John Leguizamo), a crew-cut girl crook (Aisha Hinds), and a counterfeiter named Smiley (Jeffrey Atkins, a.k.a Ja Rule). It's New Year's Eve, a Dark and Stormy Night, the highway is blocked by an accident, the officers on the bus decide to dump the prisoners at Precinct 13, and then things get dicey when it appears that Bishop's men are determined to break him free. It's up to Jake to pull himself together and command the defense of the surrounded station; he can't call for help because the phones, cell phones, and radios are all conveniently inoperable—all because of the Dark and Stormy, etc., I think.

Turns out the forces surrounding the station are not quite who they seem, ratcheting up the level of interest and danger, and providing Gabriel Byrne with one of his thankless roles in which he is hard, taciturn, and one-dimensional enough to qualify for Flatland. Never mind; an interesting dynamic develops inside the station, especially after Jake's psychiatrist, Alex Sabian (Maria Bello), comes to visit, leaves for home, has to return to the station because of the Dark, etc., and ends up as part of the defense team. Also recruited are the prisoners, who must fight for their own lives alongside the cops who have imprisoned them.

All classic and airtight, and handled by Richet with economy and a sturdy clarity of action; he doesn't go overboard with manic action scenes. There are, however, a few plot points that confused me. One is the way a forest seems to materialize near the station, which seemed in an overhead shot to be in an urban wasteland. My other problem is with a character who, in order to be who he is and what he is, would have to have known that Bishop would end up at Precinct 13, even though Bishop clearly ends up there by accident. Oh, and a tunnel turns up at a convenient moment, as tunnels so often do.

Problems like these amuse me with the nerve shown in trying to ignore them. Everybody is in a forest in the middle of downtown Detroit? Okay, then everybody can hide behind trees. They're running down a long-forgotten sewage tunnel? Okay, but not so forgotten that it doesn't have electric lights. There's no way for that particular character to have prior knowledge of where Bishop would be, and no way for him to communicate plans that are essential to the outcome? Okay, then just ignore those technicalities, and concentrate on such delightful synchronicities as that John Wayne played characters named both Ethan and Hawk.

The Aviator ★ ★ ★ ★
PG-13, 166 m., 2004

Leonardo DiCaprio (Howard Hughes), Cate Blanchett (Katharine Hepburn), Kate Beckinsale (Ava Gardner), Alec Baldwin (Juan Trippe), John C. Reilly (Noah Dietrich), Alan Alda (Senator Brewster), Gwen Stefani (Jean Harlow), Kelli Garner (Faith Domergue), Adam Scott (Johnny Meyer), Ian Holm (Professor Fitz), Danny Huston (Jack Frye), Jude Law (Errol Flynn), Matt Ross (Glenn Odekirk), Edward Herrmann (Joseph Breen). Directed by Martin Scorsese and produced by Michael Mann, Sandy Climan, Graham King, and Charles Evans Jr. Screenplay by John Logan.

Howard Hughes in his last two decades sealed himself away from the world. At first he haunted a penthouse in Las Vegas, and then he moved to a bungalow behind the Beverly Hills Hotel. He was the world's richest man, and with his billions bought himself a room he never left.

In a sense, his life was a journey to that lonely room. But he took the long way around: As a rich young man from Texas, the heir to his father's fortune, he made movies, bought airlines, was a playboy who dated Hollywood's famous beauties. If he had died in one of the airplane crashes he survived, he would have been remembered as a golden boy. Martin Scorsese's *The Aviator* wisely focuses on the glory years, although we can see the shadows falling, and so can Hughes. Some of the film's most harrowing moments show him fighting his demons; he knows what is normal and sometimes it seems almost within reach.

The Aviator celebrates Scorsese's zest for finding excitement in a period setting, re-creating the kind of glamour he heard about when he was growing up. It is possible to imagine him wanting to be Howard Hughes. Their lives, in fact, are even a little similar: heedless ambition and talent when young, great early success, tempestuous romances, and a dark period, although with Hughes it got darker and darker, while Scorsese has emerged into the full flower of his gifts.

The movie achieves the difficult feat of following two intersecting story arcs, one in which everything goes right for Hughes, and the other in which everything goes wrong. Scorsese chronicled similar life patterns in *GoodFellas, Raging Bull, The King of Comedy, Casino*, actually even *The Last Temptation of Christ*. Leonardo DiCaprio is convincing in his transitions between these emotional weathers; playing madness is a notorious invitation to overact, but he shows Hughes contained, even trapped, within his secrets, able to put on a public act even when his private moments are desperate.

His Howard Hughes arrives in Los Angeles as a good-looking young man with a lot of money, who plunges right in, directing a World War I aviation adventure named *Hell's Angels*, which was the most expensive movie ever made. The industry laughed at him, but he finished the movie and it made money, and so did most of his other films. As his attention drifted from movies to the airplanes in his films, he began designing and building aircraft, and eventually bought his own airline.

Women were his for the asking, but he didn't go for the easy kill. Jean Harlow was no pushover, Ava Gardner wouldn't take gifts of jewelry ("I am not for sale!"), and during his relationship with Katharine Hepburn, they both wore the pants in the family. Hepburn liked his sense of adventure, she was thrilled when he let her pilot his planes, she worried about him, she noted the growing signs of his eccentricity, and then she met Spencer Tracy and that was that. Hughes found Jane Russell and invented a pneumatic bra to make her bosom heave in *The Outlaw*, and by the end he had starlets on retainer in case he ever called them, but he never did.

DiCaprio is nobody's idea of what Hughes looked like (that would be a young Sam Shepard), but he vibrates with the reckless spirit of the man. John C. Reilly plays the hapless Noah Dietrich, his right-hand man and flunky, routinely ordered to mortgage everything for one of Hughes's sudden inspirations; Hughes apparently became the world's richest man by going bankrupt at higher and higher levels.

Scorsese shows a sure sense for the Hollywood of that time, as in a scene where Hughes, new in town, approaches the mogul L. B. Mayer at the Coconut Grove and asks to borrow two cameras for a big *Hell's Angels* scene. He already had twenty-four, but that was not enough. Mayer regards him as a child psychiatrist might have regarded the young Jim Carrey. Scorsese adds subtle continuity: Every time we see Mayer, he seems to be surrounded by the same flunkies.

The women in the film are wonderfully well cast. Cate Blanchett has the task of playing Katharine Hepburn, who was herself so close to caricature that to play her accurately involves some risk. Blanchett succeeds in a performance that is delightful and yet touching; mannered and tomboyish, delighting in saying exactly what she means, she shrewdly sizes up Hughes and is quick to be concerned about his eccentricities. Kate Beckinsale is Ava Gardner, aware of her power and self-protective; Gwen Stefani is Jean Harlow, whose stardom overshadows the unknown Texas rich boy; and Kelli Garner is Faith Domergue, "the next Jane Russell" at a time when Hughes became obsessed with bosoms. Jane Russell doesn't appear in the movie as a character, but her cleavage does, in a hilarious scene before the Breen office, which ran the Hollywood censorship system. Hughes brings his tame meteorology professor (Ian Holm) to the censorship hearing, introduces him as a systems analyst, and has him prove with calipers and mathematics that Russell displays no more cleavage than a control group of five other actresses.

Special effects can distract from a film or enhance it. Scorsese knows how to use them. There is a sensational sequence when Hughes crash-lands in Beverly Hills, his plane's wingtip slicing through living room walls seen from the inside. Much is made of the *Spruce Goose*, the largest airplane ever built, which inspires Senator Owen Brewster (Alan Alda) to charge in congressional hearings that Hughes was a war profiteer. Hughes, already in the spiral to madness, rises to the occasion, defeats Brewster on his own territory, and vows that the plane will fly—as indeed it does, in a CGI sequence that is convincing and kind of awesome.

By the end, darkness is gathering around Hughes. He gets stuck on words, and keeps repeating them. He walks into a men's room and then is too phobic about germs to touch the doorknob in order to leave; with all his power and wealth, he has to lurk next to the door until someone else walks in and he can sneak through without touching anything. His aides, especially the long-suffering Dietrich, try to protect him, but eventually he disappears into seclusion. What a sad man. What brief glory. What an enthralling film—166 minutes, and it races past. There's a match here between Scorsese and his subject, perhaps because the director's own life journey allows him to see Howard Hughes with insight, sympathy—and, up to a point, with admiration. This is one of the year's best films.

B

Baadasssss! ★ ★ ★ ★
R, 108 m., 2004

Mario Van Peebles (Melvin Van Peebles), Joy
Bryant (Priscilla), T. K. Carter (Bill Cosby), Terry
Crews (Big T), Khleo Thomas (Mario Van
Peebles), Ossie Davis (Grandad), David Alan
Grier (Clyde Houston), Nia Long (Sandra), Paul
Rodriguez (Jose Garcia), Saul Rubinek (Howie),
Len Lesser (Manny/Mort Goldberg). Directed by
Mario Van Peebles and produced by Bruce
Wayne Gillies, Dennis Haggerty, G. Marq
Roswell, and Van Peebles. Screenplay by Van
Peebles and Haggerty, based on the book by
Van Peebles.

*I want to show all the faces that Norman Rock-
well never painted.*
— Melvin Van Peebles

It would be nice if movies were always made
the way they are in Truffaut's *Day for Night,*
with idealism and romance, or Minnelli's *The
Bad and the Beautiful,* with glamour and intrigue. But sometimes they are made the way
they are in Mario Van Peebles's *Baadasssss!,*
with desperation, deception, and cunning.
Here is one of the best movies I've seen about
the making of a movie—a fictionalized eyewitness account by Mario of how and why his father, Melvin Van Peebles, made *Sweet
Sweetback's Baadasssss Song,* a landmark in the
birth of African-American cinema.

The original 1971 movie was scruffy and raw,
the story of a man born in a brothel and initiated to sex at the age of twelve, who grows up as
an urban survivor, attacks two racist cops, and
eludes capture. That Sweetback got away with it
electrified the movie's first audiences, who were
intrigued by ad lines like "Rated X by an All-
White Jury." Although it was not an exploitation
film, it was credited by *Variety* with creating
"blaxploitation," a genre that gave us Pam Grier,
Shaft, Superfly, and a generation of black filmmakers who moved into the mainstream.

That a big-budget action film is unthinkable today without a black costar is a direct
consequence of Melvin Van Peebles's $150,000
fly-by-night movie. *Sweet Sweetback* did astonishing business, proving that a viable market

existed for movies made by, for, and about
blacks. When the movie opened at the Oriental
Theater in Chicago, the marquee proclaimed:
"The Oriental Is Yo-riental Now!"

Mario Van Peebles was thirteen when the
movie was being made, and was pressed into
service by his father to play Sweetback as a boy.
That involved a scene with a hooker in the
brothel that still, today, Mario must feel resentment about, since in *Baadasssss!* he makes a
point of showing that some of the crew members and his father's girlfriend, Sandra (Nia
Long), objected to it. But Melvin was a force of
nature, a cigar-chewing Renaissance man who
got his own way. Only sheer willpower forced
the production ahead despite cash and personnel emergencies, and *Sweet Sweetback* is like a
textbook on guerrilla filmmaking.

Aware that he could not possibly afford to
pay union wages (there were days when he
could pay no wages at all), Melvin disguises the
production as a porn film to elude union rules.
The day the union reps visit the set is the day he
shoots a sex scene—a little more explicit, of
course, than the one he would use in the movie.
Determined to have a crew that included at least
50 percent minorities (in an industry where
most crews were all white), he trained some of
them on the job. At the end of *Baadasssss!,* a
white sound man has hired his assistant, a
tough black street guy who doubles as security,
to be his partner; that detail, like most of the
film, is based on fact. Surveying the set, he observes, "No crew has ever looked like this."

Mario plays his own father in the movie, and
Khleo Thomas plays Mario. It's clear that (the
real) Mario admires his father while at the same
time harbors some resentment against his old
man's strong-willed, single-minded treatment
of people. We see Melvin bouncing checks,
telling lies, roughing up a crew member who
wants to quit, and even getting a free shot courtesy of the Los Angeles Fire Department when
their trucks respond to an alarm for a car fire.
The car was blown up for a scene in the movie,
and Melvin kept the cameras rolling to get the
firemen for free.

As a director, Mario keeps the large cast alive,
from Melvin's alluring, exasperated assistant,
Priscilla (Joy Bryant), to his long-suffering

40

agent, Howie (Saul Rubinek), his hard-pressed producer, Clyde Houston (David Alan Grier), and Bill Cosby (T. K. Carter), whose $50,000 check bailed out Melvin at a crisis point. There is a double role for Len Lesser as Manny and Mort Goldberg, the dubious Detroit exhibitors who premiere *Sweetback* and are ready to close it after one screening, until they see the lines in front of the theater.

Mario could make another movie about the rest of his father's life, which has included being an officer in the U.S. Air Force, making art films in Paris, working as a trader on Wall Street, composing, painting, winning eleven Tony nominations for Broadway plays, and winning the French Legion of Honor. The last shot in the film is a wink and a cloud of cigar smoke from this living legend, now seventy-one.

What's fascinating is the way Mario, working from his father's autobiography and his own memories, has somehow used his firsthand experience without being cornered by it. He keeps a certain objectivity in considering the character of Melvin, seeing him as brave and gifted and determined, but also as a hustler who gets his movie made, in the words of Malcolm X, "by any means necessary." He steps on toes, hurts feelings, expects sacrifices, doesn't hesitate to use his own son in a scene that no professional child actor would have been allowed to touch.

To one degree or another, all low-budget films are like this one, with cast and crew members bludgeoned into hard work at low pay in the service of the director's ego. Mario Van Peebles captures the elusive sense of family that forms on a movie set, the moments of despair, the times when it seems impossible to continue, the sexual intrigue and (always) the bitching over the food. *Sweet Sweetback's Baadassssss Song* was historically a film of great importance, but in another sense it was just another low-rent, fly-by-night production. *Baadasssss!* manages to get both of those aspects just about right.

Note: This film's original title was How to Get the Man's Foot Outta Your Ass.

Bad Education ★ ★ ★ ½
NC-17, 104 m., 2004

Fele Martinez (Enrique Goded), Gael Garcia Bernal (Ignacio/Zahara), Daniel Gimenez Cacho (Father Manolo), Lluis Homar (Mr. Berenguer), Javier Camara (Paquito), Nacho Perez (Young Ignacio), Raul Garcia Forneiro (Young Enrique). Directed by Pedro Almodóvar and produced by Agustin Almodóvar and Pedro Almodóvar. Screenplay by Pedro Almodóvar.

I've just thrown out the first 500 words of my review and am starting again with a sense of joy and release. I was attempting to describe the plot of *Bad Education*. It was quicksand and I was sinking fast. You and I have less than 1,000 words to spend together discussing this fascinating film, and not only would the plot take up half of that, but if I were by some miracle to succeed in making it clear, that would only diminish your pleasure. This is a movie we are *intended* to wander around in. It begins in the present with a story about the past, presents that story as a film within the film, and then, if I am not mistaken, there is a paradoxical moment when the two categories leak into each other. It's like *Citizen Kane*, where the memories of one character curiously contain the memories of another.

So there's 152 words right there, and my guess is, you're thinking the hell with it, just tell us what it's about and if it's any good. Your instincts are sound. Pedro Almodóvar's new movie is like an ingenious toy that is a joy to behold, until you take it apart to see what makes it work, and then it never works again. While you're watching it you don't realize how confused you are, because it either makes sense from moment to moment or, when it doesn't, you're distracted by the sex. Life is like that.

The story, which I will not describe, involves a young movie director named Enrique (Fele Martinez) who is visited one day by Ignacio (Gael Garcia Bernal). Ignacio has written a story he wants Enrique to read. Enrique would ordinarily not be interested, but he learns that his visitor is *the* Ignacio—the boy who was his first adolescent love, back in school, and that the story is set in their school days and involves Ignacio being sexually abused by a priest at the school. Indeed, he permitted the abuse in order to get Enrique out of some trouble: "I sold myself for the first time that night in the sacristy."

That is all of the story you will hear from

me, although to fan your interest I will note that Gael Garcia Bernal, an actor who is turning out to be as versatile as Johnny Depp, portrays a drag queen in the movie, and does it so well that if he had played Hephaistion, Alexander would have stayed at home in Macedonia and they could have opened an antique shop, antiquities being dirt cheap at the time.

Almodóvar loves melodrama. So do I. "Lurid" for me is usually a word of praise. The film within the film allows Almodóvar to show transgressive sexual behavior at a time during Franco's fascist regime in Spain, when it was illegal and so twice as exciting. There is enough sex in the movie to earn it an NC-17 rating, although not enough to make it even distantly pornographic. You see hands and heads moving and it's up to you to figure out why.

Sex is a given in an Almodóvar movie, anyway. It's what his characters do. His movies are never about sex but about consequences and emotions. In *Bad Education*, he uses straight and gay (and for that matter, transvestite and transsexual) as categories that the "real" characters and the "fictional" characters use as roles, disguises, strategies, deceptions, or simply as a way to make a living. There's no doubt in my mind that Almodóvar screened Hitchcock's *Vertigo* before making the movie, and was fascinated by the idea of a man asking a woman to pretend to be the woman he loves, without knowing she actually *is* the woman he loves. When she's not playing that woman she's giving a performance—in his life, although it works the other way around in hers.

In Almodóvar's story, the Hitckcockian identity puzzle is even more labyrinthine, because the past depicted in Ignacio's screenplay is not quite the past either Ignacio or Enrique remembers, and, for that matter, although Enrique loved Ignacio only fifteen years ago, he doesn't think Ignacio looks much like Ignacio anymore. "Zahara," the drag queen, begins to take on a separate identity of his or her own, and then the guilty priest turns up with his own version of events.

Almodóvar wants to intrigue and entertain us, and he certainly does, proving along the way that Gael Garcia Bernal has the same kind of screen presence that Antonio Banderas brought to Almodóvar's earlier movies. For

that matter, as Zahara, he also has the kind of presence that Carmen Maura brought. Whether Almodóvar has a message, I am not quite sure. The movie is not an attack on sexually abusive priests, nor does it have a statement to make about homosexuality, which for Almodóvar is no more of a topic than heterosexuality is for Clint Eastwood. I think it's really more about erotic role-playing: about the roles we play, the roles other people play, and the roles we imagine them playing and they imagine us playing. If Almodóvar is right, some of our most exciting sexual experiences take place entirely within the minds of other people.

Bad Santa ★ ★ ★ ½
R, 93 m., 2003

Billy Bob Thornton (Willie T. Soke), Tony Cox (Marcus), Bernie Mac (Gin Slagel), Lauren Graham (Sue), John Ritter (Mall Manager), Brett Kelly (The Kid), Cloris Leachman (Grandma). Directed by Terry Zwigoff and produced by Sarah Aubrey, John Cameron, and Bob Weinstein. Screenplay by John Requa and Glenn Ficarra.

The kid gives Santa a carved wooden pickle as a Christmas present.

"How come it's brown?" Santa asks. "Why didn't you paint it green?"

"It isn't painted," the kid says. "That's blood from when I cut my hand while I was making it for you."

Santa is a depressed, alcoholic safecracker. The kid is not one of your cute movie kids, but an intense and needy stalker; think of Thomas the Tank Engine as a member of the Addams Family. Oh, and there's an elf, too, named Marcus. The elf is an angry dwarf who has been working with Santa for eight years, cracking the safe in a different department store every Christmas. The elf is fed up. Santa gets drunk on the job, he's screwing customers in the Plus Sizes dressing room, and whether the children throw up on Santa or he throws up on them is a toss-up, no pun intended.

Bad Santa is a demented, twisted, unreasonably funny work of comic kamikaze, starring Billy Bob Thornton as Santa in a performance that's defiantly uncouth. His character is named Willie T. Soke; W. C. Fields would have liked that. He's a foul-mouthed, unkempt, drunken louse at the beginning of the movie, and sticks to that theme all the way through. You expect a happy ending, but the ending is happy in the same sense that a man's doctors tell him he lost his legs but they were able to save his shoes.

There are certain unwritten parameters governing mainstream American movies, and *Bad Santa* violates all of them. When was the last time you saw a movie Santa kicking a department store reindeer to pieces? Or using the f-word more than Eddie Griffin? Or finding a girlfriend who makes him wear his little red hat in bed because she has a Santa fetish? And for that matter, when was the last movie where a loser Santa meets a little kid and the kid doesn't redeem the loser with his sweetness and simplicity, but attaches himself like those leeches on Bogart in *The African Queen*?

Movie critics have been accused of praising weirdo movies because we are bored by movies that seem the same. There is some justice in that. But I didn't like this movie merely because it was weird and different. I liked it because it makes no compromises and takes no prisoners. And because it is funny.

The director is Terry Zwigoff. He made the great documentary *Crumb*, about R. Crumb, the cartoonist who is a devoted misanthrope. (Crumb drew the *American Splendor* comic books about Harvey Pekar, his equal in misanthropy.) Zwigoff also directed the quirky *Ghost World*, with its unlikely romantic alliance between a teenage girl (Thora Birch) and a sour, fortyish recluse (Steve Buscemi). This is a director who makes a specialty of bitter antisocial oddballs. That he does it in comedy takes more guts than doing it in tragedy.

Zwigoff worked from an original screenplay by John Requa and Glenn Ficarra. And what is their track record, you are wondering? They cowrote *Cats & Dogs* (2001), with its parachuting Ninja cats, and their next movie is *Cats & Dogs 2: Tinkles' Revenge*. Maybe many screenwriters who do sweet, PG-rated movies like *Cats & Dogs* have a script like *Bad Santa* in the bottom desk drawer, perhaps in a lead-lined box.

When Billy Bob Thornton got the script, he must have read it and decided it would be career suicide. Then he put the script to his head and pulled the trigger. For him to play Hamlet would take nerve; for him to play Willie T. Soke took heroism. Wandering through the final stages of alcoholism, he functions only because of the determination of Marcus, who is played by Tony Cox as a crook who considers stealing to be a job, and straps on his elf ears every morning to go to work. Willie and Marcus always use the same MO: They use the Santa gig to get into the store, stay after closing, and crack the safe. Alas, this year the store's security chief (Bernie Mac, also pissed off most of the time) is wise to their plan and wants a cut. Because it's in his interest to keep Bad Santa in the store, he doesn't report little incidents like the reindeer-kicking to the store manager, played by the late John Ritter.

Willie becomes distracted by the arrival in his life of Sue (Lauren Graham), the Santa fetishist, who picks him up at a bar. Then there's the kid (Brett Kelly), who sits on his lap, tells him he isn't Santa Claus, and then doggedly insists on treating him as if he is. The kid is desperately lonely because his parents are away for reasons we understand better than he does, and he's being looked after by his comatose grandmother (Cloris Leachman). I know, I know—I disapproved of the cruel treatment of the comatose baby-sitter, Mrs. Kwan, in *The Cat in the Hat*, and here I am approving of the way they treat the kid's grandmother. The differences are: (1) This film is funny and that film was not, and (2) that one was intended for family audiences, and this one is not.

Is it ever not. I imagine a few unsuspecting families will wander into it despite the "R" rating, and I picture terrified kids running screaming down the aisles. What I can't picture is who *will* attend this movie. Anybody? Movies like this are a test of taste. If you understand why *Kill Bill* is a good movie and *The Texas Chainsaw Massacre* is not, and *Bad Santa* is a good movie and *The Cat in the Hat* is not, then you have freed yourself from the belief that a movie's quality is determined by its subject matter. You instinctively understand that a movie is not about what it is about, but about how it is about it. You qualify for *Bad Santa*.

The Ballad of Jack and Rose ★ ★ ★
R, 111 m., 2005

Daniel Day-Lewis (Jack), Camilla Belle (Rose), Catherine Keener (Kathleen), Paul Dano

(Thaddius), Ryan McDonald (Rodney), Jena Malone (Red Berry), Beau Bridges (Marty Rance). Directed by Rebecca Miller and produced by Lemore Syvan. Screenplay by Miller.

The Ballad of Jack and Rose is the last sad song of 1960s flower power. On an island off the East Coast, a craggy middle-aged hippie and his teenage daughter live alone in the remains of a commune. A generator is powered by wind. There is no television. Seaweed fertilizes the garden. They read. He homeschools her. They divide up the tasks. When Rose looks at Jack, her eyes glow with worship, and there is something wrong about that. When they lie side by side on the turf roof of their cottage, finding cloud patterns in the sky, they could be lovers. She is at an age when her hormones vibrate around men, and there is only one in her life.

Rebecca Miller's film is not about incest, but it is about incestuous feelings, and about the father's efforts, almost too late, to veer away from danger. Jack (Daniel Day-Lewis) is a fierce idealist who occasionally visits the other side of the island to fire shotgun blasts over the heads of workers building a housing development. Rose (Camilla Belle) admires him as her hero. "If you die, then I'm going to die," she tells him. "If you die," he says, "there will have been no point to my living."

This is not an academic discussion. He's had a heart attack, and he may die. She regularly takes away his home-rolled cigarettes, but out of her sight he's a chain-smoker, painfully thin, his idealistic serenity sometimes revealing a fierce anger just below the surface. He hates the developer (Beau Bridges) who is building the new homes on what Jack believes are wetlands: "That's not a house. It's a thing to keep the TV dry," he says, and, "They all want to live in places with people exactly like themselves, and have private police forces to keep their greedy little children safe."

Jack is being forced to think about the future. His daughter, he finally realizes, is too fixated on him. He visits the mainland, where for six months he has been dating Kathleen (Catherine Keener). He asks her to move with her two teenage boys out to the island and live with them: "It will be an experiment." Because

he has a trust fund, he can write her a handsome check to make the move more practical. Kathleen, who lives at home with her mother, needs the money and is realistic about that, while at the same time genuinely liking Jack. But how much does she know about him? She has never been to the island.

The film's best scenes involve the introduction of these three outsiders into the solitude of Jack and Rose. The sons, by different fathers, are different creatures. Rodney (Ryan McDonald) is an endomorphic sweetheart; Thaddius (Paul Dano) is a skinny pothead. "I'm studying to be a woman's hair dresser," Rodney tells Rose. "I wanted to be a barber, but men don't get enough pleasure out of their hair."

Having possibly fantasized herself as her father's lover, Rose reacts with anger to the newcomers and determines in revenge to lose her virginity as soon as possible. She asks Rodney to sleep with her, but he demurs ("I am sure my brother will be happy to oblige") and suggests a haircut instead. The short-haired Rose seems to have grown up overnight, and in reaction to her father's "experiment" offers him evidence of an experiment of her own.

The fundamental flaws in their idyllic island hideaway become obvious. As long as Jack and Rose lived in isolation, a certain continuity could be maintained. But the introduction of Kathleen as her father's lover, and the news that she is to start attending a school in town, cause Rose to rage against the loss of—what? Her innocence, or her ideas about her father's innocence?

Rebecca Miller, the writer and director, had a strong father of her own, the playwright Arthur Miller. She had a strong mother, too, the photographer Inge Morath. That she is now essentially the photographer (although the cinematography is by the visual poet Ellen Kuras) and her subject is a father and daughter may be less of a case of acting out her own childhood, as some writers have suggested, as identifying with her mother. It would be reckless and probably wrong to find literal parallels between Rebecca and Rose, but perhaps the film's emotional conflicts have an autobiographical engine.

Toward the end of the film, events pile up a little too quickly; there are poisonous snakes and sudden injuries, confrontations with the builder and medical concerns, and Jack resembles a lot of dying characters in the movies: His health closely mirrors the requirements of the story. By the end I had too much of a sense of story strands that had strayed too far to be neatly concluded, and there is an epilogue that could have been done without.

Despite these complaints, *The Ballad of Jack and Rose* is an absorbing experience. Consider the care with which Miller handles a confrontation between Jack and the homebuilder. Countless clichés are sidestepped when Jack finally sees their conflict for what it is, not right against wrong, but "a matter of taste." Is it idealistic to want a whole island to yourself, and venal to believe that other people might enjoy having homes there? The movie has a sly scene where Jack and Rose visit one of the model homes, which to Jack is an abomination and to Rose a dream.

The Barbarian Invasions ★ ★ ★ ★
R, 99 m., 2003

Rémy Girard (Rémy), Stéphane Rousseau (Sébastien), Marie-Josée Croze (Nathalie), Dorothée Berryman (Louise), Louise Portal (Diane), Dominique Michel (Dominique), Yves Jacques (Claude), Pierre Curzi (Pierre), Marina Hands (Gaëlle). Directed by Denys Arcand and produced by Daniel Louis and Denise Robert. Screenplay by Arcand.

Dying is not this cheerful, but we need to think it is. *The Barbarian Invasions* is a movie about a man who dies about as pleasantly as it's possible to imagine; the audience sheds happy tears. The man is a professor named Rémy, who has devoted his life to wine, women, and left-wing causes, and now faces death by cancer, certain and soon. His wife divorced him years ago because of his womanizing, his son is a millionaire who dislikes him and everything he stands for, many of his old friends are estranged, and the morphine is no longer controlling the pain. By the end of the story, miraculously, he will have gotten away with everything, and be forgiven and beloved.

The young embrace the fantasy that they will live forever. The old cling to the equally seductive fantasy that they will die a happy death.

This is a fantasy for adults. It is also a movie with brains, indignation, irony, and idealism— a film about people who think seriously and express themselves with passion. It comes from Denys Arcand of Quebec, whose *The Decline of the American Empire* (1986) involved many of the same characters during the fullness of their lives. At that time they either worked in the history department of a Montreal university or slept with somebody who did, and my review noted that "everybody talks about sex, but the real subject is wit ... their real passion comes in the area of verbal competition."

When people are building their careers, they need to prove they're better than their contemporaries. Those who win must then prove—to themselves—that they're as good as they used to be. Whether Rémy was a good history professor is an interesting point (his son has to bribe three students to visit his bedside, but one of them later refuses to take the money). He certainly excelled in his lifestyle, as the lustiest and most Falstaffian of his circle, but every new conquest meant leaving someone behind— and now, at the end, he seems to have left almost everyone behind.

We've all known someone like Rémy. Frequently their children don't love them as much as their friends do. We have a stake in their passions; they live at full tilt so we don't have to, and sometimes even their castaways come to admire the life force that drives them on to new conquests, more wine, later nights. His former wife, Louise (Dorothée Berryman), calls their son Sébastien (Stéphane Rousseau) in London, where he is a rich trader, to tell him his father is near death, and although he hasn't spoken to the old man in a long time, Sébastien flies home with his fiancée, Gaëlle (Marina Hands).

Their first meeting goes badly; it is a replay of Rémy's socialist rejection of Sébastien's values and his "worthless" job. But Sébastien has learned from the financial world how to get things done, and soon he has bribed a union official to prepare a private room for his father on a floor of the hospital no longer in use. He even wants to fly his father to America for treatment, but Rémy blusters that he fought for socialized medicine and he will stick with it. The movie is an indictment of overcrowded Canadian hospitals and absent-minded caregivers, but it also reveals a certain flexibility, as when the nun caring for Rémy tells his son that morphine no longer kills the pain . . . but heroin would.

How Sébastian responds to that information leads to one of the movie's most delightful sequences, and to the introduction of a drug addict named Nathalie (Marie-Josée Croze), who becomes another of Rémy's caregivers. Nathalie's story and her own problems are so involving that Croze won the best actress award at Cannes 2003.

Sébastian calls up his father's old friends. Some are Rémy's former lovers. Two are gay. One, Rémy's age, has started a new family. They gather at first rather gingerly around the deathbed of this person they had drifted away from, but eventually their reunion becomes a way to remember their younger days, their idealism, their defiant politics. Rémy is sometimes gray and shaking with pain, but the movie sidesteps the horrendous side effects of chemotherapy and uses heroin as the reason why he can play the graceful and even ebullient host at his own passing. There is a scene at a lakeside cottage that is so perfect and moving that only a churl would wonder how wise it is to leave a terminally ill man outside all night during the Quebec autumn, even with blankets wrapped around him.

The Barbarian Invasions, also written by Arcand, is manipulative without apology, and we want it to be. There's no market for a movie about a man dying a miserable death, wracked by the nausea of chemo. Indeed, Rémy is even allowed his taste for good wines and family feasts. And what a marvel the way his wife and his former (and current!) lovers gather around to celebrate what seems to have been the most remarkable case of priapism any of them have ever encountered. They are not so much forgiving him, I think, as envying his ability to live on his own terms and get away with it. His illusions are all he has, and although they were deceived by them, they don't want Rémy to die without them. As a good friend of mine once observed, nobody on his deathbed ever says, "I'm glad I always flew economy class."

Barbershop 2: Back in Business ★ ★ ½
PG-13, 118 m., 2004

Ice Cube (Calvin Palmer), Cedric the Entertainer (Eddie), Sean Patrick Thomas (Jimmy James), Eve (Terri Jones), Troy Garity (Isaac Rosenberg), Michael Ealy (Ricky Nash), Leonard Earl Howze (Dinka), Harry Lennix (Quentin Leroux), Kenan Thompson (Kenard), Queen Latifah (Gina). Directed by Kevin Rodney Sullivan and produced by Alex Gartner, Robert Teitel, and George Tillman Jr. Screenplay by Don D. Scott.

Calvin's Barbershop is still in business as *Barbershop 2* opens, and the same barbers are at the same chairs, dealing with the usual customers discussing the day's events, and providing free advice on each other's lives. Just like the first movie, the shop is a talk show where everybody is the host. The talk could go on forever, coiling from current events to current romances, but then danger strikes: Nappy Cutz, a slick franchise haircut emporium, is opening across the street, and it may put the little neighborhood shop out of business.

This would be a disaster for Calvin (Ice Cube), whose operation is not single-mindedly devoted to profit. If it were, why would he give a prized chair to Eddie (Cedric the Entertainer), who hardly ever seems to cut any hair? We learn the answer to that mystery in the course of this movie, along with a little of Eddie's background: We see him in a flashback, protecting the shop from rioters and winning the lifelong gratitude of Calvin's father.

Even back then, Eddie was on the conservative side, and again in this movie he delivers his trademark riffs against African-American icons. Although others in the shop cringed when they learned the D.C. sniper was black, for Eddie the contrarian that's something to be proud of: "He's the Jackie Robinson of crime." Alas, Eddie's I-Can't-Believe-He-Said-That act, which worked so well in the original *Barbershop,* seems a little perfunctory and obligatory this time, and it's often hard to understand what Cedric the E is saying; a little work in postproduction could have clarified his dialogue and allowed the zingers to land with more impact.

The plot, just like last time, involves a threat to the beloved neighborhood institution. An entrepreneur named Quentin Leroux (Harry Lennix) has purchased the property across the street and is erecting a huge Nappy Cutz emporium which, it is rumored, will even feature a basketball court. Calvin's could be doomed.

And there's a larger issue, because the Chicago City Council, in the pockets of developers, seems bent on tearing down all the little neighborhood stores and moving in giant franchisers.

This could have headed in an interesting direction if the movie wanted to be political, but it doesn't (the talkative crowd in Calvin's never mentions a name like, oh, say, "Daley"). There is an arm's-length recognition of city hall in the character of Jimmy (Sean Patrick Thomas), who used to work in the shop but now has the inside track to a powerful alderman.

Calvin struggles with the idea of new competition, and meanwhile Terri (Eve), the only female barber, tries to decide if there's any future with Ricky (Michael Ealy), and Eddie himself is flummoxed by the arrival of a flame from his torrid past. The only white barber, Isaac (Troy Garity), remains convinced he is the blackest man in the shop, and the African-born barber Dinka (Leonard Earl Howze) has a futile crush on Eve. Jimmy's empty chair is taken over by Calvin's cousin Kenard (Kenan Thompson), who doesn't seem to understand the fundamental purpose of a barbershop, which is to provide a refuge, affirmation, confirmation, entertainment, and occasionally haircuts.

Next door in a beauty salon, stylist Gina (Queen Latifah) stands by for several almost self-contained supporting scenes, including an insult contest with Eddie in which it sounds like Eddie has won, and we would be sure if we could understand him. The Queen has a high-energy presence in the film, and just as well, because she'll star in *Beauty Shop*.

Did I like the film? Yeah, kinda, but not enough to recommend. The first film arrived with freshness and an unexpected zing, but this one seems too content to follow in its footsteps. Maybe *Beauty Shop* is the one to wait for, if they can find half a dozen high-powered foils for the Queen. Prediction: Terri (Eve) will get tired of everyone stealing her apple juice and move next door.

Basic ★

R, 98 m., 2003

John Travolta (Agent Tom Hardy), Connie Nielsen (Lieutenant Julia Osborne), Samuel L. Jackson (Sergeant Nathan West), Giovanni Ribisi (Levi Kendall), Brian Van Holt (Raymond Dunbar), Taye Diggs (Pike), Timothy Daly (Colonel Bill Styles), Roselyn Sanchez (Nunez), Harry Connick Jr. (Pete Vilmer). Directed by John McTiernan and produced by Mike Medavoy, James Vanderbilt, Arnie Messer, and Michael Tadross. Screenplay by Vanderbilt.

I embarked on *Basic* with optimism and goodwill, confident that a military thriller starring John Travolta and Samuel L. Jackson, and directed by John McTiernan *(Die Hard)*, might be entertaining action and maybe more. As the plot unfolded, and unfolded, and unfolded, and unfolded, I leaned forward earnestly in my seat, trying to remember where we had been and what we had learned.

Reader, I gave it my best shot. But with a sinking heart I realized that my efforts were not going to be enough, because this was not a film that *could* be understood. With style and energy from the actors, with every sign of self-confidence from the director, with pictures that were in focus and dialogue that you could hear, the movie descended into a morass of narrative quicksand. By the end, I wanted to do cruel and vicious things to the screenplay.

There's a genre that we could call the Jerk-Around Movie, because what it does is jerk you around. It sets up a situation and then does a bait and switch. You never know which walnut the truth is under. You invest your trust and are betrayed.

I don't mind being jerked around if it's done well, as in *Memento*. I felt *The Usual Suspects* was a long ride for a short day at the beach, but at least as I traced back through it, I could see how it held together. But as nearly as I can tell, *Basic* exists with no respect for objective reality. It is all smoke and no mirrors. If I were to see it again and again, I might be able to extract an underlying logic from it, but the problem is, when a movie's not worth seeing twice, it had better get the job done the first time through.

The film is set in a rainy jungle in Panama. I suspect it rains so much as an irritant, to make everything harder to see and hear. Maybe it's intended as atmosphere. Or maybe the sky gods are angry at the film.

We are introduced to the hard-assed Sergeant Nathan West (Jackson), a sadistic perfectionist who is roundly hated by his unit. When various characters are killed during the confusion of the storm, there is the feeling the deaths may not have been accidental, may indeed have involved drug dealing. A former DEA agent named Tom Hardy (Travolta) is hauled back from alcoholism to join the investigation, teaming with Lieutenant Julia Osborne (Connie Nielsen).

The murders and the investigation are both told in untrustworthy flashbacks. We get versions of events from such differing points of view, indeed, that we yearn for a good old-fashioned omnipotent POV to come in and slap everybody around. There are so many different views of the same happenings that, hell, why not throw in a musical version?

Of course, there are moments that are engaging in themselves. With such actors (Giovanni Ribisi, Taye Diggs, Brian Van Holt, Roselyn Sanchez, and even Harry Connick Jr.), how could there not be? We listen and follow and take notes, and think we're getting somewhere, and then the next scene knocks down our theories and makes us start again. Finally we arrive at an ending that gives a final jerk to our chain and we realize we never had a chance.

What is the point of a movie like *Basic*? To make us feel cleverly deceived? To do that, the film would have to convince us of one reality and then give us another, equally valid (classics like *Laura* did that). This movie gives no indication even at the end that we have finally gotten to the bottom of things. There is a feeling that *Basic II* could carry right on, undoing the final shots, bringing a few characters back to life and sending the whole crowd off on another tango of gratuitous deception.

Batman Begins ★ ★ ★ ★
PG-13, 140 m., 2005

Christian Bale (Bruce Wayne/Batman), Michael Caine (Alfred Pennyworth), Liam Neeson (Henri Ducard), Katie Holmes (Rachel Dawes), Morgan Freeman (Lucius Fox), Gary Oldman (Lieutenant James Gordon), Cillian Murphy (Dr. Jonathan Crane), Tom Wilkinson (Carmine Falcone), Rutger Hauer (Richard Earle), Ken Watanabe (Ra's Al Ghul). Directed by Christopher Nolan and produced by Larry J. Franco, Charles Roven, and Emma Thomas. Screenplay by David S. Goyer and Nolan.

Batman Begins at last penetrates to the dark and troubled depths of the Batman legend, creating a superhero who, if not plausible, is at least persuasive as a man driven to dress like a bat and become a vigilante. The movie doesn't simply supply Batman's beginnings in the tradition of a comic book origin story, but explores the tortured path that led Bruce Wayne from a parentless childhood to a friendless adult existence. The movie is not realistic, because how could it be, but it acts as if it is.

Opening in a prison camp in an unnamed nation, *Batman Begins* shows Bruce Wayne (Christian Bale) enduring brutal treatment as a prisoner as part of his research into the nature of evil. He is rescued by the mysterious Henri Ducard (Liam Neeson), who appoints himself Wayne's mentor, teaches him sword-fighting and mind control, and tries to enlist him in his amoral League of Shadows ("We burned London to the ground"). When Wayne refuses to kill someone as a membership requirement, Ducard becomes his enemy; the reclusive millionaire returns to Gotham determined to fight evil, without realizing quite how much trouble he is in.

The story of why he identifies with bats (childhood trauma) and hates evildoers (he saw his parents killed by a mugger) has been referred to many times in the various incarnations of the Batman legend, including four previous films. This time it is given weight and depth.

Wayne discovers in Gotham that the family Wayne Corp. is run by a venal corporate monster (Rutger Hauer), but that in its depths labors the almost-forgotten scientific genius Lucius Fox (Morgan Freeman), who understands that Wayne wants to fight crime and offers him the weaponry. Lucius happens to have on hand a prototype Batmobile, which unlike the streamlined models in the earlier movies is a big, unlovely juggernaut that looks like a Humvee's wet dream. He also devises a Bat Cape with surprising properties.

These preparations, Gotham crime details, and the counsel of the faithful family servant Alfred (Michael Caine) delay the actual appearance of a Batman until the second act of the movie. We don't mind. Unlike the earlier films, which delighted in extravagant special-effects action, *Batman Begins* is shrouded in shadow; instead of high-detail, sharp-edged special effects, we get obscure developments in fog and smoke, their effect reinforced by a superb sound effects design. And Wayne himself is a slow learner, clumsy at times, taking foolish chances, inventing Batman as he goes along ("People need dramatic examples to shake them out of fear and apathy, and I can't do that as a human being").

This is at last the Batman movie I've been waiting for. The character resonates more deeply with me than the other comic super-heroes, perhaps because when I discovered him as a child he seemed darker and more grown-up than the cheerful Superman. He has secrets. As Alfred muses: "Strange injuries and a nonexistent social life. These things beg the question, what does Bruce Wayne do with his time?"

What he does is create a high profile as a millionaire playboy who gets drunk and causes scenes. This disappoints his friend since childhood, Rachel Dawes (Katie Holmes), who is now an assistant D.A. She and Lieutenant James Gordon (Gary Oldman), apparently Gotham's only honest cop, are faced with a local crime syndicate led by Carmine Falcone (Tom Wilkinson). But Falcone's gang is child's play compared to the deep scheme being hatched by the corrupt psychiatrist Dr. Jonathan Crane (Cillian Murphy), who in the tradition of Victorian alienists likes to declare his enemies insane and lock them up.

Crane's secret identity as the Scarecrow fits into a scheme to lace the Gotham water supply with a psychedelic drug. Then a super-weapon will be used to vaporize the water, citizens will inhale the drug, and it will drive them crazy, for reasons the Scarecrow and his confederates explain with more detail than clarity. Meanwhile, flashbacks establish Wayne's deepest traumas, including his special relationship with bats and his guilt because he thinks he is responsible for his parents' mugging.

I admire, among other things, the way the movie doesn't have the gloss of the earlier films. The Batman costume is an early design.

The Bat Cave is an actual cave beneath Wayne Manor. The Batmobile enters and leaves it by leaping across a chasm and through a waterfall. The early Bat Signal is crude and out of focus. The movie was shot on location in Chicago, making good use of the murky depths of Lower Wacker Drive (you may remember it from *Henry: Portrait of a Serial Killer*) and the Board of Trade building (now the Wayne Corp.). Special effects add a spectacular monorail straight down LaSalle Street, which derails in the best scene along those lines since *The Fugitive*.

Christian Bale is just right for this emerging version of Batman. It's strange to see him muscular and toned, after his cadaverous appearance in *The Machinist*, but he suggests an inward quality that suits the character. His old friend Rachel is at first fooled by his facade of playboy irresponsibility, but Lieutenant Gordon (destined to become in the fullness of time Commissioner Gordon) figures out fairly quickly what Batman is doing, and why. Instead of one villain as the headliner, *Batman Begins* has a whole population, including Falcone, the Scarecrow, the Asian League of Shadows leader Ra's Al Ghul (Ken Watanabe), and a surprise bonus pick.

The movie has been directed by Christopher Nolan, still only thirty-five, whose *Memento* (2000) took Sundance by storm and was followed by *Insomnia* (2002), a police procedural starring Al Pacino. What Warner Bros. saw in those pictures that inspired it to think of Nolan for Batman is hard to say, but the studio guessed correctly, and after an eight-year hiatus the Batman franchise has finally found its way.

I said this is the Batman movie I've been waiting for; more correctly, this is the movie I did not realize I was waiting for, because I didn't realize that more emphasis on story and character and less emphasis on high-tech action was just what was needed. The movie works dramatically in addition to being an entertainment. There's something to it.

The Battle of Shaker Heights ★ ★
PG-13, 85 m., 2003

Shia LaBeouf (Kelly Ernswiler), Elden Henson (Bart Bowland), Amy Smart (Tabby Bowland),

Kathleen Quinlan (Eve Ernswiler), William Sadler (Abe Ernswiler), Shiri Appleby (Sarah), Ray Wise (Harrison Bowland), Anson Mount (Miner Weber). Directed by Efram Potelle and Kyle Rankin and produced by Sean Bailey and Jeff Balis. Screenplay by Erica Beeney.

Gene Siskel liked to ask, "Is this film more interesting than a documentary of the same actors having lunch?" He would have been able to find out with Project Greenlight, the behind-the-scenes cable series. One winning screenplay a year is chosen to be produced by Miramax, and HBO airs a documentary series about the making of the movie, so that we can eavesdrop on the arguments, brainstorms, disagreements, and tantrums of the makers—and on their lunches.

Stolen Summer (2002), the first of the Greenlight movies, passed Siskel's test. It was a lovely coming-of-age story about a friendship between two Chicago kids during the last summer of one of their lives. *The Battle of Shaker Heights,* the second Greenlight movie, fails the test. I have actually had lunch with two of the actors—Elden Henson and Kathleen Quinlan—and that was a lot more interesting than the movie.

It's one of those stories where a formula is juiced up with stuff we don't expect, like the teenage hero's hobby of fighting in reenactments of famous battles. There's also a doomed infatuation with his best friend's college-age sister, which leads to him becoming a part-time honorary member of the friend's family. He finds it exquisitely painful to be in love with the sister, who likes to have him around because he's smart and cute, and doesn't take his puppy love seriously.

The hero is Kelly (Shia LaBeouf, the young lead of *Holes*), and he's the brightest kid in his high school, smart enough to correct his teacher during a class, but not smart enough to know that's a pretty dumb thing to do. His new friend is Bart (Elden Henson), and they meet when Kelly saves Bart's life, sort of, in a virtual kind of way.

Then Kelly meets Bart's sister Tabby (Amy Smart). I hope Tabby is a nickname. If it's a sin to give a pet a saint's name, unimaginable punishments must await anyone giving a daughter a pet's name. Because Kelly is obsessed with the unavailable Tabby, he ignores the hopeful friendliness of Sarah (Shiri Appleby), who shares the graveyard shift with him at a local store, one of those consumer temples where it's not too much of a stretch to imagine Robin Williams behind the photo counter. Sarah likes him, but represents the known, while Tabby is the unknown; for a boy of a certain age, it is a great deal easier (and more relaxing) to imagine sex with someone you don't know than with someone you do.

Bart and Tabby's dad, Harrison (Ray Wise), was once into war memorabilia but now obsesses over nesting dolls. You don't know if the characters in this movie are crazy, or simply the victims of bright ideas by Erica Beeney, the winning screenwriter. More examples of piling on at the story conference: Kelly's dad (William Sadler) is a former drug abuser, and his mom (Kathleen Quinlan) runs a fairly unusual home business involving immigrants who produce art on an assembly line—the kinds of paintings that come free with the bedroom suite.

It is important to note that imagining sex is the only way Kelly experiences it. His bond with Tabby comes through their mutual love of art, about which Kelly knows a surprising amount (this is a bright kid who apparently knows everything known to anyone who worked on the movie). Tabby, who has her own studio, produces paintings a step up from the assembly line at Kelly's house; her work is the kind that wins blue ribbons at fairs. She's heading to Yale in the fall, which means she has periods of ambivalence about her approaching marriage to her sometimes uncomprehending boyfriend Miner (Anson Mount)—which leads, somewhat unconvincingly, to a make-out session between Tabby and Kelly in which the movie focuses on Kelly's emotions, which we can easily imagine, instead of on Tabby's, which exist entirely at the convenience of the screenplay.

Shia LaBeouf makes his character a winning and charming kid, more believable than the movie deserves, and Elden Henson, who I've been monitoring since *The Mighty* (1998), is kind of a junior Vincent D'Onofrio, able to play almost anybody, as you could see when he went from the teenage Shakespearean tragedy *O* to *Dumb and Dumber*.

The Battle of Shaker Heights isn't bad so much as jumbled. One of the problems with Project Greenlight is that everybody tries to cross when the light turns green. You get the sense of too much input, too many bright ideas, too many scenes that don't belong in the same movie. Odd, how overcrowded it seems, for eighty-five minutes. Here's an idea: Next year, Miramax picks the winning screenplay, gives the filmmakers $1 million, and sends them off in total isolation to make a movie with absolutely no input from anybody. The HBO series could be about how the Miramax marketing department sees the result and figures out how to sell it.

Beauty Shop ★ ★ ★
PG-13, 105 m., 2005

Queen Latifah (Gina Norris), Alicia Silverstone (Lynn), Andie MacDowell (Terri Green), Alfre Woodard (Miss Josephine), Mena Suvari (Joanne Marcus), Djimon Hounsou (Joe), Kevin Bacon (Jorge Christophe), Keshia Knight Pulliam (Darnelle), Paige Hurd (Vanessa), Bryce Wilson (James). Directed by Bille Woodruff and produced by Robert Teitel, George Tillman Jr., Queen Latifah, David Hoberman, Shakim Compere, and Elizabeth Cantillon. Screenplay by Kate Lanier and Norman Vance Jr.

Early in *Beauty Shop*, Queen Latifah asks her daughter if her pants make her butt look big. When the answer is "yes," she slaps it and says, "Good!" And means it. Latifah is profoundly comfortable with herself, and *Beauty Shop* is comfortable with itself. It isn't simply trying to turn up the heat under a *Barber Shop* clone, but to be more plausible (not a lot, but a little) in the story of a woman starting her own business. It's more of a human comedy than stand-up or slapstick.

Queen Latifah stars as Gina, recently arrived in Atlanta from Chicago (where she appeared briefly in *Barber Shop 2*). She's already the top stylist in an upscale salon run by the improbable Jorge Christophe, a streaked blond self-promoter who keeps Latifah from being the only queen in the movie. Jorge is over the top in every possible way, and you have to blink a couple of times before you realize he's being played by—Kevin Bacon?

It's very funny work, and sets up Gina for a big showdown where she walks out on Jorge and starts her own beauty shop. There's nothing terrifically original in the way she finds an old salon, remodels and repaints it, and staffs it with a shampoo girl from Jorge's (Alicia Silverstone) and an array of expert and verbal hairdressers, most notably Miss Josephine (Alfre Woodard) and Darnelle (Keshia Knight Pulliam, from *Cosby*). But consider the scene where she applies for a bank loan, and gets it after she shows the loan officer what she should be doing with her hair.

It is a convention of these movies that the shop is under threat from a landlord, a developer, or another ominous menace. This time it is the jealous Jorge, bribing a corrupt city inspector to put Gina out of business, and later taking more drastic measures. The movie wisely doesn't treat the threats as the whole plot, and it's refreshing how most of the movie is essentially about the characters, their stories, their lives.

Gina, for example, is a widow raising her daughter, Vanessa (Paige Hurd), a promising pianist. The man who lives upstairs over the beauty shop is Joe (Djimon Hounsou), an African who is both an electrician and a pianist. That sets up a sweet romance that isn't the usual bawdiness, but kind of touching, especially since Hounsou has so much warmth as an actor.

Just as *Barber Shop* had one white barber (Troy Garrity), *Beauty Shop* has one white beautician (Silverstone, promoted from shampoo). Andie MacDowell plays a customer from Jorge's shop who makes a crucial trip across town to follow Gina, her favorite hairdresser, and Mena Suvari is another customer from the old shop, not so nice. Some of the other employees, including the outspoken Miss Josephine, came with the old shop; others walk in through the door, including Bryce Wilson as James, an ex-con truck driver who knows so much about braids that Gina hires him on the spot, setting off intense speculation in the shop about his sexuality.

The beauty of the *Beauty* movies is that they provide a stage for lively characters. Countless plays have been set in bars for the same reason. The format almost works like a variety show, allowing each character to get a solo, as when Woodard's Miss Josephine takes the floor for a passionate recital of Maya Angelou's "Still I Rise."

Presiding like a den mother and emcee, Queen Latifah exudes a quiet confidence that sort of hugs the movie, making it feel warmer than the *Barber Shop* films. *Beauty Shop* doesn't shout at us, not even when catastrophe strikes; it's more about choosing a goal, being confident you can get there, and having some fun along the way.

Because of Winn-Dixie ★ ★

PG, 105 m., 2005

AnnaSophia Robb (Opal), Jeff Daniels (Preacher), Cicely Tyson (Gloria Dump), Dave Matthews (Otis), Eva Marie Saint (Miss Franny). Directed by Wayne Wang and produced by Trevor Albert and Joan Singleton. Screenplay by Singleton, based on the novel by Kate DiCamillo.

Because of Winn-Dixie tells the story of a lonely girl with a distant father, who is adopted by a dog. The dog changes her life, helps her make friends, and gives her someone to confide in for the first time. All without doubt sweet and warmhearted, but there is another film with a similar story that is boundlessly better, and that is *My Dog Skip* (2000). Also with the lonely kid. Also with the dog who makes friends. Also with the dad who thinks the dog should go back to the pound.

The difference between the two films is that *My Dog Skip* is made with a complexity that appeals to adults as much as children, while *Because of Winn-Dixie* seems pretty firmly aimed at middle school and below. Its portrait of the adult world comes from storybooks, not life, and its small town is populated entirely by (1) eccentric characters, and (2) anonymous people seen from a distance.

The little girl is named Opal (AnnaSophia Robb). She is ten, and lives in a house trailer supplied rent-free to her dad, who preaches in a church that uses the corner convenience store. When Opal was three, her mother ran away from the family for reasons unknown. Preacher (apparently his only name) has been depressed ever since, and spends long hours gazing out the window and "working on a sermon."

He sends Opal to the Winn-Dixie supermarket, and while she's there a dog runs up and down the aisles and is chased by countless clerks, who skid into piles of cans and knock over pyramids of boxes; destruction during a supermarket chase is the indoor shopping equivalent of the Fruit Cart Scene. Opal rescues the dog, claims it is hers, and names it Winn-Dixie.

Although both her dad and Mr. Alfred, the mean old man who runs the trailer park, want the dog to go to the pound, Opal stubbornly bonds with Winn-Dixie, and together they meet (1) Otis, played by Dave Matthews, who is the temporary clerk at the local pet store; (2) Gloria Dump, played by Cicely Tyson, who is blind and very wise; (3) Miss Franny, played by Eva Marie Saint, who is a fading southern belle with genteel airs; and (4) various local kids.

Otis takes out his guitar and sings her his story one day, in a nice scene. But is he really the clerk in the pet shop? What happened to the owner? And why, for that matter, does this pet shop stock ducks, chickens, pigs, and pigeons in addition to cats and dogs and hamsters? Is this a pet store, or an ark? Another local business, now defunct, once made Luttmuss Lozenges; when you put one in your mouth, you think it tastes like emotions. No surprise to me; I've always thought M&Ms tasted like uncertainty, Peppermint Patties like sarcasm, and Tootsie Rolls like sweet revenge.

Although the movie has heartfelt conversations about the absence of Opal's mother, and scenes in which dog ownership is viewed as a great philosophical consolation, the picture mainly meanders until a big party scene at Miss Gloria's, to which all of the characters are invited—even Preacher, who, true to the ancient tradition of movie fathers, arrives late but then recognizes that his daughter has done a good thing.

It is one of those parties you see only in the movies, where the people may be poor, but they have an unlimited budget for candles. Hundreds of them. Thousands, maybe, all over the yard outside Miss Gloria's house. Covered dishes are uncovered, and meanwhile the stage has been set for drama.

"We have to be sure Winn-Dixie doesn't get out during a thunderstorm," Opal says. "He might run away." This makes it absolutely certain there will be a thunderstorm, right in the middle of the party, and that Winn-Dixie will run away, and have to be searched for all over town, with Opal's little voice piping, "Winn-Dixie! Winn-Dixie!" until . . . well, until the thunderstorm clears as quickly as it sprang up, and the party resumes, and so on.

Because of Winn-Dixie doesn't have a mean bone in its body, but it's dead in the water. It was directed by Wayne Wang, who usually (how can I put this?) makes films for grown-ups *(The Joy Luck Club, Smoke, The Center of the World, Maid in Manhattan)*. Why did he choose this project? Why did he feel it had to be made? Did he screen *My Dog Skip* and realize he'd been dealt a weak hand? I don't know, and maybe I don't want to know.

Be Cool ★ ½
PG-13, 112 m., 2005

John Travolta (Chili Palmer), Uma Thurman (Edie Athens), Vince Vaughn (Raji), Cedric the Entertainer (Sin LaSalle), Andre 3000 (Dabu), Steven Tyler (Himself), Christina Milian (Linda Moon), Harvey Keitel (Nicki Carr), Danny DeVito (Martin Weir), The Rock (Elliot Wilhelm). Directed by F. Gary Gray and produced by Danny DeVito, David Nicksay, Michael Shamberg, and Stacey Sher. Screenplay by Peter Steinfeld, based on the novel by Elmore Leonard.

John Travolta became a movie star by playing a Brooklyn kid who wins a dance contest in *Saturday Night Fever* (1977). He revived his career by dancing with Uma Thurman in *Pulp Fiction* (1994). In *Be Cool*, Uma Thurman asks if he dances. "I'm from Brooklyn," he says, and then they dance. So we get it: "Brooklyn" connects with *Fever*, Thurman connects with *Pulp*. That's the easy part. The hard part is, what do we do with it?

Be Cool is a movie that knows it is a movie. It knows it is a sequel, and contains disparaging references to sequels. All very cute at the screenplay stage, where everybody can sit around at story conferences and assume that a scene will work because the scene it refers to worked. But that's the case only when the new scene is also good as itself, apart from what it refers to.

Quentin Tarantino's *Pulp Fiction* knew that Travolta won the disco contest in *Saturday Night Fever*. But Tarantino's scene didn't de-

pend on that; it built from it. Travolta was graceful beyond compare in *Fever*, but in *Pulp Fiction* he's dancing with a gangster's girlfriend on orders from the gangster, and part of the point of the scene is that both Travolta and Thurman look like they're dancing not out of joy, but out of duty. So we remember *Fever* and then we forget it, because the new scene is working on its own.

Now look at the dance scene in *Be Cool*. Travolta and Thurman dance in a perfectly competent way that is neither good nor bad. Emotionally they are neither happy nor sad. The scene is not necessary to the story. The filmmakers have put them on the dance floor without a safety net. And so we watch them dancing and we think, yeah, *Saturday Night Fever* and *Pulp Fiction*, and when that thought has been exhausted, they're still dancing.

The whole movie has the same problem. It is a sequel to *Get Shorty* (1995), which was based on a novel by Elmore Leonard just as this is based on a sequel to that novel. Travolta once again plays Chili Palmer, onetime Miami loan shark, who in the first novel traveled to Los Angeles to collect a debt from a movie producer, and ended up pitching him on a movie based on the story of why he was in the producer's living room in the middle of the night threatening his life.

This time Chili has moved into the music business, which is less convincing because, while Chili was plausibly a fan of the producer's sleazy movies, he cannot be expected, ten years down the road, to know or care much about music. Funnier if he had advanced to the front ranks of movie producers and was making a movie with A-list stars when his past catches up with him.

Instead, he tries to take over the contract of a singer named Linda Moon (Christina Milian), whose agent (Vince Vaughn) acts as if he is black. He is not black, and that's the joke, I guess. But where do you go with it? Maybe by sinking him so deeply into dialect that he cannot make himself understood, and has to write notes. Chili also ventures into the hip-hop culture; he runs up against a Suge Knight type named Sin LaSalle (Cedric the Entertainer), who has a bodyguard named Elliot Wilhelm, played by The Rock.

I pause here long enough to note that Elliot

Wilhelm is the name of a friend of mine who runs the Detroit Film Theater, and that Elmore Leonard undoubtedly knows this because he also lives in Detroit. It's the kind of in-joke that doesn't hurt a movie unless you happen to know Elliot Wilhelm, in which case you can think of nothing else every second The Rock is on the screen.

The deal with The Rock's character is that he is manifestly gay, although he doesn't seem to realize it. He makes dire threats against Chili Palmer, who disarms him with flattery, telling him in the middle of a confrontation that he has all the right elements to be a movie star. Just as the sleazy producer in *Get Shorty* saved his own life by listening to Chili's pitch, now Chili saves his life by pitching The Rock.

There are other casting decisions that are intended to be hilarious. Sin LaSalle has a chief of staff played by Andre 3000, who is a famous music type, although I did not know that and neither, in my opinion, would Chili. There is also a gag involving Steven Tyler turning up as himself.

Be Cool becomes a classic species of bore: a self-referential movie with no self to refer to. One character after another, one scene after another, one cute line of dialogue after another, refers to another movie, a similar character, a contrasting image, or whatever. The movie is like a bureaucrat who keeps sending you to another office.

It doesn't take the in-joke satire to an additional level that might skew it funny. To have The Rock play a gay narcissist is not funny because all we can think about is that The Rock is not a gay narcissist. But if they had cast someone who was *also* not The Rock, but someone removed from The Rock at right angles, like Steve Buscemi or John Malkovich, then that might have worked, and The Rock could have played another character at right angles to himself—for example, the character played here by Harvey Keitel as your basic Harvey Keitel character. Think what The Rock could do with a Harvey Keitel character.

In other words: (1) Come up with an actual story, and (2) if you must have satire and self-reference, rotate it 90 degrees off the horizontal instead of making it ground-level. Also (3) go easy on the material that requires a familiarity with the earlier movie, as in the scenes with Danny DeVito, who can be the funniest man in a movie, but not when it has to be a movie other than the one he is appearing in.　　　　☞

Before Sunset ★ ★ ★ ½
R, 80 m., 2004

Ethan Hawke (Jesse), Julie Delpy (Celine). Directed by Richard Linklater and produced by Linklater and Anne Walker-McBay. Screenplay by Linklater, Julie Delpy, and Ethan Hawke.

Nine years have passed since Jesse and Celine met in Vienna and walked all over the city, talking as if there would be no tomorrow, and then promising to meet again in six months. "Were you there in Vienna, in December?" she asks him. Nine years have passed and they have met again in Paris. Jesse wrote a novel about their long night together, and at a book signing he looks up, and there she is. They begin to talk again, in a rush, before he must leave to catch his flight back to America.

Before Sunset continues the conversation that began in *Before Sunrise* (1995), but at a riskier level. Jesse (Ethan Hawke) and Celine (Julie Delpy) are over thirty now, have made commitments in life, no longer feel as they did in 1995 that everything was possible. One thing they have learned, although they are slow to reveal it, is how rare it is to meet someone you feel an instinctive connection with. They walk out of the bookstore and around the corner and walk, and talk, and director Richard Linklater films them in long, uninterrupted takes, so that the film feels like it exists in real time.

Before Sunset is a remarkable achievement in several ways, most obviously in its technical skill. It is not easy to shoot a take that is six or seven minutes long, not easy for actors to walk through a real city while dealing with dialogue that has been scripted but must sound natural and spontaneous. Yet we accept, almost at once, that this conversation is really happening. There's no sense of contrivance or technical difficulty.

Hawke and Delpy wrote the screenplay themselves, beginning from the characters and dialogue created the first time around by Linklater and Kim Krizan. They lead up to personal details very delicately; at the beginning they talk politely and in abstractions, edging around the topics we (and they) want answers to: Is either one married? Are they happy? Do they still feel that deep attraction? Were they intended to spend their lives together?

There is the feeling, as they discuss how their adult lives are unfolding, that sometimes the actors may be skirting autobiography. Certainly there is an unmistakable truth when Jesse, trying to describe what marriage is like, says, "I feel like I'm running a small nursery with someone I used to date." But the movie is not a confessional, and the characters don't rush into revelations. There is a patience at work, even a reticence, that reflects who they have become. They have responsibilities. They no longer have a quick instinctive trust. They are wary of revealing too much. They are grown-ups, although at least for this afternoon in Paris they are in touch with the open, spontaneous, hopeful kids they were nine years before.

Before Sunrise was a remarkable celebration of the fascination of good dialogue. But *Before Sunset* is better, perhaps because the characters are older and wiser, perhaps because they have more to lose (or win), and perhaps because Hawke and Delpy wrote the dialogue themselves. The film has the materials for a lifetime project; like the *7-Up* series, this is a conversation that could be returned to every ten years or so, as Celine and Jesse grow older.

Delpy worked often with Krzysztof Kieslowski, the Polish master of coincidence and synchronicity, and perhaps it's from that experience that *Before Sunset* draws its fascination with intersecting time lines. When Celine and Jesse parted, they didn't know each other's last names or addresses; they staked everything on that promise to meet again in six months. We find out what happened in Vienna in December, but we also find out that Celine studied for several years at New York University (just as Delpy did) while Jesse was living there (just as Hawke was). "In the months leading up to my wedding, I was thinking of you," he tells her. He even thought he saw her once, in the deli at 17th and Broadway. She knows the deli. Maybe he did.

What they are really discussing, as they trade these kinds of details, is the possibility that they missed a lifetime they were intended to spend together. Jesse eventually confesses that he wrote his book and came to Paris for a book signing because that was the only way he could think of to find her again. A little later, in a subtle moment of body language, she reaches out to touch him and then pulls back her hand before he sees it.

All this time they are walking and talking. Down streets, through gardens, past shops, into a café, out of the café, toward the courtyard where she has the flat she has lived in for four years. And it is getting later, and the time for his flight is approaching, just as he had to catch the train in Vienna. But what is free will for, if not to defy our plans? "Baby, you are gonna miss that plane," she says. ☞

Being Julia ★ ★ ½
R, 105 m., 2004

Annette Bening (Julia Lambert), Jeremy Irons (Michael Gosselyn), Michael Gambon (Jimmie Langton), Shaun Evans (Tom Fennel), Bruce Greenwood (Lord Charles), Juliet Stevenson (Evie), Rosemary Harris (Mrs. Lambert), Miriam Margolyes (Dolly de Vries), Lucy Punch (Avice Crichton), Thomas Sturridge (Roger Gosselyn). Directed by Istvan Szabo and produced by Robert Lantos. Screenplay by Ronald Harwood, based on the novel by W. Somerset Maugham.

Old Jimmie Langdon, the impresario who taught the young Julia Langdon much of what she knows about the world, refers at one point to "what civilians call the real world." Theater people know better. All the world's a stage, and Julia is but a player on it. At one point, when she's asked for a loan, she replies with the same speech she used earlier in a play. Her marriage is "in name only." Even her extramarital affair is a performance; her lover, Lord Charles, finally confesses, "I play for the other side." Her son, Roger, says: "You have a performance for everybody. I don't think you really exist."

In *Being Julia*, she departs from the playwright's lines and improvises a new closing act right there on the stage, and it's appropriate that her professional and personal problems should be resolved in front of an audience.

Like Margo Channing, the Bette Davis character in *All About Eve,* Julia draws little distinction between her public and private selves. She lives to be on the stage, and when, at forty-five, she perceives that her star is dimming, she fights back with theatrical strategies.

Annette Bening plays Julia in a performance that has great verve and energy, and just as well, because the basic material is wheezy melodrama. *All About Eve* breathed new life into it all those years ago, but now it's gasping again. The film is based on *Theater,* a 1937 novel by W. Somerset Maugham that was not one of his few great works, and has been adapted by a director and a writer who have separately created much more important fictions about the theater. Istvan Szabo directed *Mephisto,* with its brilliant performance by Klaus Maria Brandauer as an actor who sells out to the Nazis to protect his career, and Ronald Harwood wrote *The Dresser,* one of the most knowledgeable of backstage plays.

Here they all seem to have followed Maugham into a soap opera. Bening is fresh and alive (is there another actress who smiles and laughs so generously and naturally?), but she's surrounded by stock characters. Jeremy Irons plays her husband and producer, Michael, who turns a blind eye to her lover, Lord Charles (Bruce Greenwood), and why should he not, since Charles actually decides to break up with her because of all the gossip—and isn't gossip surely the best reason to have an affair with an actress?

They are all in the middle of an enormously successful play, but Julia has tired of it, complaining that the world is too much for her, she is weary and bored, she thinks she may retire. Circling her like moons, reflecting her light, are not only Michael and Charles but her loyal dresser Evie (Juliet Stevenson), her hopeful lesbian admirer Dolly (Miriam Margolyes), and the ghost of old Jimmie (Michael Gambon), who advises for practical reasons that she sleep with her young leading man: "If that doesn't improve your performance, then nothing will."

What happens instead is that she meets the callow young American theatrical accountant Tom Fennel (Shaun Evans), a man as exciting as the seed after which he is named. He's seen all of her plays—some of them three times!—and Julia is flattered, not so much by his praise as by sex with a man half her age. In a world with few secrets, Lord Charles frets: "I trust she doesn't tell the boy she loves him—that's always fatal."

She sort of does and it sort of is, especially after the arrival of the young ingenue Avice Crichton (Lucy Punch), in the Eve Harrington role. Not only does Avice feel warmly toward Tom, but she also sparks interest in old Michael, Julia's husband, whose genitals may be able to revive for a farewell tour.

All of this is fitfully entertaining, but it seems to be happening for the first time to only the Bening character. The others seem trapped in loops, as if they've traveled these clichés before. All comes to a head during rehearsals for a new play in which Avice seems to have better lines and staging than Julia. ("I'm going to give my all in this part!" she gushes to Julia, who replies, "Mustn't be a little spendthrift.") It's by departing from the staging and the lines, and improvising in an entirely different direction that Julia delivers Avice's comeuppance.

But it doesn't happen that way in the theater. An actor may improvise a line or two, or a bit of business, or communicate in an occult way with the audience, or if he's Groucho Marx or Alfie even address us directly, but is it possible to improvise an entire act with the other actors on stage, and somehow incorporate them in such a way that they're not left standing there and gawking at you? I don't think so. I think the movie leads up to a denouement that would work only if the improvisation (as it is here) were carefully scripted and rehearsed. There's never the feeling that poor Avice is really out to sea, because even her discomfiture seems carefully blocked.

I liked the movie in its own way, while it was cheerfully chugging along, but the ending let me down; the materials are past their sell-by date, and were when Maugham first retailed them. The pleasures are in the actual presence of the actors, Bening most of all, and the droll Irons, and Juliet Stevenson as the practical aide-de-camp, and Thomas Sturridge, so good as Julia's son that I wonder why he wasn't given the role of her young lover.

Bend It Like Beckham ★ ★ ★ ½
PG-13, 112 m., 2003

Parminder K. Nagra (Jesminder ["Jess"]
Bhamra), Keira Knightley (Juliette ["Jules"]),
Jonathan Rhys-Meyers (Joe), Anupam Kher (Mr.
Bhamra), Shaheen Khan (Mrs. Bhamra), Archie
Panjabi (Pinky Bhamra), Juliet Stevenson
(Paula). Directed by Gurinder Chadha and
produced by Chadha and Deepak Nayar.
Screenplay by Chadha, Paul Mayeda Berges,
and Guljit Bindra.

I saw more important films at Sundance 2003, but none more purely enjoyable than *Bend It Like Beckham*, which is just about perfect as a teenage coming-of-age comedy. It stars a young actress of luminous appeal, it involves sports, romance, and, of course, her older sister's wedding, and it has two misinformed soccer moms—one who doesn't know a thing about the game and another who doesn't even know her daughter plays it.

The movie, set in London, tells the story of Jesminder Bhamra, known as "Jess," who comes from a traditional Indian family. Her parents are Sikhs who fled from Uganda to England, where her dad works at Heathrow airport. They live in the middle-class suburb of Hounslow, under the flight path of arriving jets, where her mother believes that Jess has two great duties in life: to learn to prepare a complete Indian meal, and to marry a nice Indian boy, in exactly that order.

Jess plays soccer with boys in the park. In her family's living room is a large portrait of a Sikh spiritual leader, but above Jess's bed is her own inspiration—the British soccer superstar David Beckham, better known to some as Posh Spice's husband. To Beckham's portrait she confides her innermost dream, which is to play for England. Of course, a girl cannot hope to be a soccer star, and an Indian girl should not play soccer at all, since in her mother's mind the game consists of "displaying your bare legs to complete strangers."

Jess is seen in the park one day by Juliette (Keira Knightley), who plays for the Hounslow Harriers, a woman's team, and is recruited to join them. The coach is a young Irishman named Joe (Jonathan Rhys-Meyers), and it is love at second or third sight—complicated because Joe cannot date his players, and Juliette has a crush on him, too.

But all of these elements make the film sound routine, and what makes it special is the bubbling energy of the cast and the warm joy with which Gurinder Chadha, the director and cowriter, tells her story. I am the first to admit that Gurinder Chadha is not a name on everybody's lips, but this is her third film and I can promise you she has an unfailing instinct for human comedy that makes you feel good and laugh out loud.

Her previous film was the wonderful *What's Cooking*, about four American ethnic families (African-American, Latino, Jewish, and Vietnamese) all preparing a traditional Thanksgiving dinner, while their younger generations are connected in unsuspected ways. There is an emerging genre of comedies about second- and third-generation young people breaking loose from traditional parents (*My Big Fat Greek Wedding* is the most spectacular example), and I've seen these rite-of-entry comedies by directors with Filipino, Indian, Chinese, Mexican, Iranian, and Korean backgrounds, and even one, *Mississippi Masala*, where Denzel Washington and Sarita Choudhury played two such characters whose stories meet.

Bend It Like Beckham, which adds a British flavor to its London metroland masala, is good not because it is blindingly original but because it is flawless in executing what is, after all, a dependable formula. The parents must be strict and traditional, but also loving and funny, and Mr. and Mrs. Bhamra (Anupam Kher and Shaheen Khan) are classic examples of the type. So is Juliette's mother, Paula (the wry, funny British star Juliet Stevenson), who tries to talk her tomboy daughter into Wonderbras, and spends most of the movie fearing that a girl who doesn't want to wear one must be a lesbian ("There's a reason why Sporty Spice is the only one without a boyfriend"). The editing by Justin Krish gets laughs all on its own with the precision that it uses to cut to reaction shots as the parents absorb one surprise after another.

Jess, played by Parminder K. Nagra, is a physically exuberant girl whose love of soccer crosses over into a love of life. She runs onto the field as if simply at play, she does cartwheels after scoring goals, and although she deceives her parents about her soccer dreams, she loves them and understands their point of view. Her father, who played cricket in Uganda but was discriminated against by the local London club, still bears deep wounds, but "things are different now," Jess tells him, and there is the obligatory scene where he sneaks into the crowd at a match to see for himself.

Can there be an Indian comedy without a wedding? *Monsoon Wedding* is the great example, and here too we get the loving preparation of food, the exuberant explosion of music, and the backstage drama. All ethnic comedies feature scenes that make you want to leave the theater and immediately start eating, and *Bend It Like Beckham* may inspire some of its fans to make Indian friends simply so they can be invited over for dinner.

The movie's values run deep. It understands that for Jess's generation soccer is not about displaying bare legs (Jess has another reason to be shy about that), but it also understands the hopes and ambitions of parents—and, crucially, so does Jess, who handles the tentative romance with her coach in a way that combines tenderness with common sense. A closing scene at the airport, which in a lesser movie would have simply hammered out a happy ending, shows her tact and love.

Like all good movies, *Bend It Like Beckham* crosses over to wide audiences. It's being promoted in the magazines and on the cable channels that teenage girls follow, but recently we showed it on our Ebert & Roeper Film Festival at Sea to an audience that ranged in age from seven to eighty-one, with a fiftyish median, and it was a huge success. For that matter, the hip Sundance audience, dressed in black and clutching cell phones and cappuccinos, loved it, too. And why not, since its characters and sensibility are so abundantly lovable.

Benji: Off the Leash! ★ ★ ★
PG, 100 m., 2004

Benji (Puppy), Shaggy (Lizard Tongue), Nick Whitaker (Colby), Nate Bynum (Sheriff Ozzie), Chris Kendrick (Hatchett), Randall Newsome (Livingston), Duane Stephens (Sheldon), Christy Summerhays (Claire). Directed by Joe Camp and produced by Margaret Loesch and Camp. Screenplay by Camp.

Benji: Off the Leash! isn't one of the great dog movies, but it's a good one, abandoning wall-to-wall cuteness for a drama about a homeless puppy. And it sends a valuable message: Mongrels are just as lovable as pure breeds, or maybe in the case of Benji and Shaggy, the stars of this film, more so.

The movie resembles *Shiloh* in its story about a young boy who loves a dog and tries to protect it from the cruelty of an adult. Nick Whitaker stars as Colby, a fourteen-year-old whose stepfather, Hatchett (Chris Kendrick), breeds dogs in crowded kennels in the backyard. When one of his prize breeders gives birth to a white mongrel, he finds the dog useless and plans to put it to death. Colby steals it, names it Puppy, and successfully protects it for months, hiding it in a playhouse so interestingly designed he will no doubt grow up to become an architect. The playhouse is shared by a parrot named Merlin, who proves the point that parrots are not nearly as funny as they think they are.

The plot is not entirely about Colby and his mean stepfather, however. Its real costars are Benji and a dog named Shaggy, who was discovered in a Chicago animal shelter. Shaggy plays Lizard Tongue, a dog of the streets, who knows the ropes and provides invaluable help to Puppy in a world populated not only by cruel breeders but, inevitably, by dogcatchers.

The movie's PG-rated bad guys are carefully modulated to be evil but not too evil. The animal control wardens, named Livingston and Sheldon (Randall Newsome and Duane Stephens), are comic relief: bumbling flatfoots who actually kinda like dogs. Like all goofy characters in movies like this, they exhibit a genius for finding and falling facedown in mud puddles.

As for Hatchett, he is stern, heartless, and hateful, but never physically abuses Colby; his mom, Claire, played by Christy Summerhays, makes sure of that. There's a scene between Colby and his mother where she tries to explain to her son why she has stayed in her marriage; it's heartfelt and sincere, and could be useful to kids in the audience who are going through similar experiences in their families.

Joe Camp, who has directed a series of Benjis in six movies and a TV series, is a master at getting his animals to seem as smart as Lassie (who, as Dave Barry has pointed out, was smarter and possibly more articulate than any of the humans in her family). He has a winning character actor in Shaggy, a playful roughhouse type, and the latest Benji, of course, is cuteness squared.

The movie opens and closes with quasi-documentary footage about Camp's search for a new dog to play Benji. You might be tempted to wonder if being cast as Benji is something Puppy would prefer to life with Shaggy and Colby, but a paradox is involved, since the new Benji has already been discovered and is playing Puppy in this movie.

The drama continues. There have been recent medical bulletins about Benji's need for eye surgery; the movie's Web site says Benji underwent retinal reattachment. Dr. Sam Vainisi of Wheeling, Illinois, described as "the top veterinary ophthalmologist in the country," said the surgery was complicated because of inflammation from an earlier cataract operation, and an allergic reaction to an antibiotic. One wishes Benji a complete and speedy recovery, and prays that Shaggy doesn't have to go into training as Benji's Seeing Eye dog.

The Best of Youth ★ ★ ★ ★
R, 366 m., 2005

Luigi Lo Cascio (Nicola Carati), Alessio Boni (Matteo Carati), Adriana Asti (Adriana Carati), Sonia Bergamasco (Giulia Monfalco), Fabrizio Gifuni (Carlo Tommasi), Maya Sansa (Mirella Utano), Valentina Carnelutti (Francesca Carati), Jasmine Trinca (Giorgia), Andrea Tidona (Angelo Carati), Lidia Vitale (Giovanna Carati). Directed by Marco Tullio Giordana and produced by Angelo Barbagallo. Screenplay by Sandro Petraglia and Stefano Rulli.

Every review of *The Best of Youth* begins with the information that it is six hours long. No good movie is too long, just as no bad movie is short enough. I dropped outside of time and was carried along by the narrative flow; when the film was over, I had no particular desire to leave the theater, and would happily have stayed another three hours. The two-hour limit on most films makes them essentially short stories. *The Best of Youth* is a novel.

The film is ambitious. It wants no less than to follow two brothers and the people in their lives from 1963 to 2000, following them from Rome to Norway to Turin to Florence to Palermo and back to Rome again. The lives intersect with the politics and history of Italy during the period: the hippies, the ruinous flood in Florence, the Red Brigades, kidnappings, hard times and layoffs at Fiat, and finally a certain peace for some of the characters, and for their nation.

The brothers are Nicola and Matteo Carati (Luigi Lo Cascio and Alessio Boni). We meet their parents, Angelo (Andrea Tidona) and Adriana (Adriana Asti), their older sister, Giovanna (Lidia Vitale), and their kid sister, Francesca (Valentina Carnelutti). And we meet their friends, their lovers, and others who drift through, including a mental patient whose life seems to follow in parallel.

As the film opens, Nicola has qualified as a doctor and Matteo is still taking literature classes. Matteo, looking for a job, has been hired as a "logotherapist"—literally, a person who takes mental patients for walks. One of the women he walks with is Giorgia (Jasmine Trinca), who is beautiful, deeply wounded by electroshock therapy, and afraid of the world. On the spur of the moment, Matteo decides to spring her from the institution and take her along when he and Nicola take a summer trip to the "end of the world," the tip of Norway.

Giorgia is found by the police, but has the presence of mind to protect the brothers. Nicola continues on his journey and gets a job as a lumberjack, and Matteo returns to Rome and, impulsively, joins the army. They are to meet again in Florence, where catastrophic floods have drowned the city. Nicola is a volunteer, Matteo is a soldier assigned to the emergency effort, and in the middle of the mud and ruins Nicola hears a young woman playing a piano that has been left in the middle of the street.

This is Giulia (Sonia Bergamasco). Their

eyes meet and lock, and so do their destinies. They live together without marrying, and have a daughter, Sara. Giulia is drawn into a secret Red Brigade cell. She draws apart from her family. One night she packs to leave the house. He tries to block her way, then lets her go. She disappears into the terrorist underground.

Matteo meanwhile joins the police, takes an assignment in Sicily because no one else wants to go there, and meets a photographer in a café. This is Mirella (Maya Sansa). She wants to be a librarian, and he advises her to work at a beautiful library in Rome. Years later, he walks into the library and sees her for the second time in his life. They become lovers, but there is a great unexplained rage within Matteo, maybe also self-hatred, and he will not allow anyone very close.

Enough about the plot. These people, all of them, will meet again—even Giorgia, who is found by Nicola in the most extraordinary circumstances, and who will cause a meeting that no one in the movie could have anticipated, because neither person involved knows the other exists. Because of the length of the film, the director, Marco Tullio Giordana, has time and space to work with, and we get a tangible sense of the characters growing older, learning about themselves, dealing with hardship. The journey of Giulia, the radical, is the most difficult and in some ways the most touching. The way Nicola finally finds happiness is particularly satisfying because it takes him so long to realize that it is right there before him for the taking.

The film must have deep resonances for Italians, where it was made for national television; because of its politics, sexuality, and grown-up characters, it would be impossible on American networks. It is not easy on Italy. As he is graduating from medical school, Nicola is advised by his professor: "Do you have any ambition? Then leave Italy. Go to London, Paris, America if you can. Italy is a beautiful country. But it is a place to die, run by dinosaurs." Nicola asks the professor why he stays. "I'm one of the dinosaurs."

Nicola stays. Another who stays is his brother-in-law, who is marked for kidnapping and assassination but won't leave, "because then they will have won." There is a scene

where he stands in front of windows late at night and we feel real dread for him. With the politics and the personal drama there is also the sense of a nation that beneath the turbulent surface is deeply supportive of its citizens. Some of that is sensed through the lives of the parents of the Carati family: The father busies himself with optimistic schemes; the mother meets a grandchild who brings joy into her old age.

The film is being shown in two parts, three hours each, with separate admissions. You don't have to see both parts on the same day, but you may want to. It is a luxury to be enveloped in a good film, and to know there's a lot more of it—that it is not moving inexorably toward an ending you can anticipate, but moving indefinitely into a future that is free to be shaped in surprising ways. When you hear that it is six hours long, reflect that it is therefore also six hours deep.

Better Luck Tomorrow ★ ★ ★ ★
R, 98 m., 2003

Parry Shen (Ben), Jason Tobin (Virgil), Sung Kang (Han), Roger Fan (Daric), John Cho (Steve), Karin Anna Cheung (Stephanie). Directed by Justin Lin and produced by Lin, Ernesto M. Foronda, and Julie Asato. Screenplay by Lin, Foronda and Fabian Marquez.

Justin Lin's *Better Luck Tomorrow* has a hero named Benjamin, but depicts a chilling hidden side of suburban affluence that was unseen in *The Graduate*. Its heroes need no career advice; they're on the fast track to Ivy League schools and well-paying jobs, and their straight-A grades are joined on their résumés by an improbable array of extracurricular credits: Ben lists the basketball team, the academic decathlon team, and the food drive.

What he doesn't mention is the thriving business he and his friends have in selling cheat sheets. Or their drug sideline. Or the box hidden in his bedroom and filled with cash. Ben belongs to a group of overachieving Asian-American students in a wealthy Orange County suburb; they conform to the popular image of smart, well-behaved Asian kids, but although they have ambition they lack values, and step by step they move more deeply into crime. How deep is suggested by the film's opening scene, where Ben (Parry Shen) and his best friend, Virgil (Jason Tobin), are interrupted while sunbathing by the sound of a cell phone ringing on a body they have buried in Virgil's backyard.

Better Luck Tomorrow is a disturbing and skillfully told parable about growing up in today's America. These kids use money as a marker of success, are profoundly amoral, and project a wholesome, civic-minded attitude. They're on the right path to take jobs with the Enrons of tomorrow, in the dominant culture of corporate greed. Lin focuses on an ethnic group that is routinely praised for its industriousness, which deepens the irony, and also perhaps reveals a certain anger at the way white America patronizingly smiles on its successful Asian-American citizens.

Ben, Virgil, and their friends know how to use their ethnic identity to play both sides of the street in high school. "Our straight A's were our passports to freedom," Ben says in his narration. No parents are ever seen in the movie (there are very few adults, mostly played by white actors in roles reserved in most movies for minority groups). The kids get good grades, and their parents assume they are studying while they stay out late and get into very serious trouble.

Better Luck Tomorrow has all the obligatory elements of the conventional high school picture. Ben has a crush on the pretty cheerleader Stephanie Vandergosh (Karin Anna Cheung), but she dates Steve (John Cho), who plays the inevitable older teenager with a motorcycle and an attitude. Virgil is unlucky with girls, but thinks he once spotted Stephanie in a porno film (unlikely, but gee, it kinda looks like her). Han (Sung Kang) comes up with the scheme to sell homework for cash, and Daric (Roger Fan) is the overachiever who has, no doubt, the longest entry under his photo in the school yearbook.

These students never refer to, or are identified by, specific ethnic origin; they're known as the "Chinese Mafia" at school because of their low-key criminal activities, but that's not a name they give themselves. They may be Chinese, Japanese, Korean, Filipino, but their generation no longer obsesses with the nation before the hyphen; they are Orange County Americans, through and through, and although Stephanie's last name and Caucasian little brother indicate she was adopted, she brushes aside Ben's tentative question about her "real parents" by saying, "These are my real parents."

Better Luck Tomorrow is a coming-of-age film for Asian-Americans in American cinema. Like African-American films that take race for granted and get on with the characters and the story, Lin is making a movie where race is not the point but simply the given. After Ben joins the basketball team, a writer for the high school paper suggests he is the "token Asian" benchwarmer, and when students form a cheering section for him, he quits the team in disgust. He is not a token anything (and privately knows he has beaten the NBA record for free throws).

The story is insidious in the way it moves stealthily into darker waters, while maintaining the surface of a high school comedy. There are jokes and the usual romantic breakthroughs and reversals, and the progress of their criminal career seems unplanned and offhand, until it turns dangerous. I will not reveal the names of the key characters in the climactic scene, but note carefully what happens in terms of the story; perhaps the film is revealing that a bland exterior can hide seething resentment.

Justin Lin, who directed, cowrote, and co-produced, here reveals himself as a skilled and sure director, a rising star. His film looks as glossy and expensive as a mega-million studio production, and the fact that its budget was limited means that his cinematographer Patrice Lucien Cochet, his art director Yoo Jung Han, and the other members of his crew were very able and resourceful. It's one thing to get an expensive look with money, and another thing to get it with talent.

Lin keeps a sure hand on tricky material; he has obvious confidence about where he wants to go and how he wants to get there. His film is uncompromising, and doesn't chicken out with a U-turn ending. His actors expand and breathe as if they're captives just released from lesser roles (the audition reel of one actor, Lin recalls, showed him delivering pizzas in one movie after another). Parry Shen gives a watchful and wary undertone to his all-American boy, and Karin Anna Cheung finds the right note to deal with a boy she likes but finds a little too goody-goody. *Better Luck Tomorrow* is not just a thriller, not just a social commentary, not just a comedy or a romance, but all of those in a clearly seen, brilliantly made film.

Bewitched ★ ★ ½
PG-13, 100 m., 2005

Nicole Kidman (Isabel Bigelow), Will Ferrell (Jack Wyatt), Shirley MacLaine (Iris Smythson), Michael Caine (Nigel Bigelow), Jason Schwartzman (Richie), Kristin Chenoweth (Maria Kelly), Heather Burns (Nina), Steve Carell (Uncle Arthur), Stephen Colbert (Stu Robison). Directed by Nora Ephron and produced by Nora Ephron, Penny Marshall, Douglas Wick, and Lucy Fisher. Screenplay by Nora Ephron and Delia Ephron.

One of the many areas in which I am spectacularly ill-informed is prime-time television. You would be amazed at the numbers of sitcoms I have never seen, not even once. When you see 500 movies a year, you don't have a lot of leftover yearning for watching television. In the evenings, you involve yourself in more human pursuits. On TV you watch the news, talk shows, or old movies. You don't watch sports unless your team is in the finals. You can sense I am edging up to the admission that I have never seen a single episode of *Bewitched*. I knew it existed, however, because of my reading.

That makes me well prepared to review the movie *Bewitched*, since I have nothing to compare it with and have to take it on its own terms. It is tolerably entertaining. Many of its parts work, although not together. Will Ferrell and Nicole Kidman are funny and likable, but they're in a plot that doesn't allow them to aim for the same ending with the same reason. It's one of those movies where you smile and laugh and are reasonably entertained, but you get no sense of a mighty enterprise sweeping you along with its comedic force. There is not a movie here. Just scenes in search of one.

The joke is this: Will Ferrell plays Jack Wyatt, a movie star whose career has hit bottom. Sales of his last DVD: zero. In desperation he turns to television and finds himself considered for a starring role in a revival of *Bewitched*. He will play the Darrin role. At least that's what everyone says. I assume Darrin was a character on the original show. I know (from my reading) that the show's interest centered on Samantha, who was played by Elizabeth Montgomery. I know from the movie that Samantha had a way of twitching her nose that was very special, and that they can't find an actress with twitchability until Jack spots Isabel Bigelow (Nicole Kidman) in Book Soup on Sunset.

He insists on using her in the role because (a) he wants a complete unknown, so he'll get all the attention, (b) the twitch, and (c) already he is falling in love with her. What he doesn't realize, oh, delicious irony, is that Isabel is in fact a real witch. She has, however, just decided to move to the Valley, get a house with a VW bug in the garage, live a normal life, and find a guy who loves her for herself and not because she put a hex on him. Her father (Michael Caine) warns her that this dream is not possible, and indeed she has a lot of trouble giving up witchcraft. It's so tempting to charge your purchases on a Tarot card.

The movie has been directed by Nora Ephron *(Sleepless in Seattle, You've Got Mail)*, and written by her with her sister Delia. They have a lot of cute scenes. I like the way they make Jack Wyatt an egotistical monster who wants three trailers, star billing, and cake every Wednesday. He's hysterically in love with himself. His ego is, of course, no match for Samantha, who can make him act in Spanish if she wants to. Occasionally when things go wrong she rewinds the arrow of time, although even after a rewind, it's a funny thing: Something magical happens anyway.

The movie has fun with Ferrell on the star trip, and fun with Kidman's love-hate relationship with magic. It has a lot of good supporting work, including Jason Schwartzman as Jack's desperate agent, and Shirley MacLaine as Samantha's mother (her theory on actors: "Sometimes, deep down, there is no deep down"). If you watch *The Daily Show* you'll enjoy cameos by Stephen Colbert and Steve Carell. It might have been a good idea to bring in Samantha Bee, too, and have her interview Jack Wyatt ("You're staring at my boobs!").

Will Ferrell has become a major star in almost no time at all. One moment he was a

Saturday Night Live veteran who had played backup in a lot of movies, and the next moment he had made *Old School* and *Elf* and *Anchorman* and *Melinda and Melinda* and had *The Producers* on the way, and he was bigtime. One reason for that is, you like the guy. He has a brawny, take-no-prisoners style of comedy that suggests he's having a lot of fun.

Nicole Kidman, on the other hand, is an actor with more notes in her repertoire (maybe Ferrell could have played a role in *The Hours*, but that remains to be seen). Here, she is fetching and somehow more relaxed than usual as Samantha, and makes witchcraft seem like a bad habit rather than a cosmic force.

But what are they doing in the same movie? You have two immovable objects or two irresistible forces. Both characters are complete, right off the shelf. There's no room for them to move. Yes, Jack becomes a nicer guy after he falls in love, and yes, Samantha realizes that magic is sometimes just not fair. But they are separate at the beginning and essentially still self-contained at the end, and the movie never works them both into the same narrative logic. Still, that's a great moment when Jack shouts: "Guys! Make me 200 cappuccinos! Bring me the best one!"

Beyond Borders ★ ★

R, 127 m., 2003

Angelina Jolie (Sarah Jordan), Clive Owen (Nick Callahan), Linus Roache (Henry Bauford), Teri Polo (Charlotte), Yorick van Wageningen (Jan Steiger), Noah Emmerich (Elliot Hauser). Directed by Martin Campbell and produced by Dan Halsted and Lloyd Phillips. Screenplay by Caspian Tredwell-Owen.

Beyond Borders has good intentions and wants to call attention to the plight of refugees, but what a clueless vulgarization it makes of its worthy motives. Of course, there's more than one way to send a message, and maybe this movie will affect audiences that wouldn't see or understand a more truthful portrait of refugees, like Michael Winterbottom's *In This World*.

The movie stars Angelina Jolie, who is personally involved in efforts to help refugees and isn't simply dining out on a fashionable cause.

She plays Sarah Jordan, a London society woman whose bloodless husband will never understand the passion she feels for social causes—and for Nick Callahan (Clive Owen), the handsome doctor who flies from one trouble spot to another saving lives. Wherever Nick is in need, be it Cambodia, Ethiopia, or Chechnya, Sarah flies in with truckloads of supplies for the sexy, saturnine Nick.

I can understand a beautiful young woman getting a crush on a heroic and dedicated aid worker. Happens all the time in the movies. But could the doctor, just once, look like Giovanni Ribisi or Jack Black instead of like Clive Owen—so that we'd know she loved him for his good heart and didn't just have the hots for a potential James Bond?

Sarah first sees Nick at a charity ball in London, where he strides in carrying a starving Ethiopian boy and accuses the well-upholstered society people of letting kids like this one starve to death because he has the misfortune to be starving in an area controlled by Communist rebels. Good point. Sarah is married to Henry Bauford (Linus Roache), who doesn't understand why she can't just send a check instead of running off to Ethiopia to personally head a caravan of grain trucks. A professional would be better at the job, but wouldn't be so inspired by the need to be near Doctor Nick, in an area of the world where people may indeed be starving but where Sarah and Nick find an adequate supply of romantic vistas, while stirring music wells up behind them. They're serious about the starving masses, but they get *really* serious when they confront their mutual romantic destiny.

Sarah arrives wearing an all-white safari outfit that isn't even a little sweaty and dusty. Did she change right before driving into Nick's camp? She must have spent as much kitting herself out on Regent Street as she did buying the grain. She reminded me of the hero of Evelyn Waugh's *Scoop*, who also goes out to Ethiopia and takes along a trunk jammed with enough supplies to create a camp as cozy as a suite at the Savoy.

But perhaps that's to make a point: The rich woman wants to do well, and doesn't understand inappropriate gestures. Still, what are we to make of a scene where she stops the truck, gathers up a starving baby, and determines to save its life? The baby's mother, near death, reaches out a desperate arm and Sarah reassures her she will take care of the child. Too bad about the mother. Nick says the kid is too far gone to live, but Sarah clutches it to her reassuring bosom and feeds it high-energy fluids a drop at a time.

I know nothing at all about where they found the baby or what condition it was really in. Although it looks like a starving stick figure, I assume it was a healthy child. The point is that it *looks like* a child near death, and the use of the image is offensive in a movie that is essentially a romance. When the suffering of real children is used to enhance the image of movie stars who fall in love against the backdrop of their suffering, a certain decency is lacking. *Beyond Borders* wants it both ways — glamour up front, and human misery in the background to lend it poignancy.

The key shots revealing the movie's priorities are the close-ups right after Sarah meets Nick for the first time in Ethiopia. We've stayed in long and medium shot for most of the way, but then, after a line of dialogue in which it becomes clear Sarah has a romantic as well as a charitable motivation, we get close-ups of the two as they share this realization. Movie grammar suggests that we are being visually informed that their romance is the real subject of the movie. Another approach might show Sarah in long shot, moving through a field of suffering, and then a close-up of a starving child reaching out to her distant figure. You see the difference.

Now consider the climax of the movie. Something tragic happens, and before it does, the movie cuts back and forth between Nick and Sarah in close-ups that reminded me of Bonnie and Clyde in the instant before the shooting started. What is the message being conveyed here? What unspoken words are contained in the looks of these two lovers? It's curiously hard to answer this question; try it yourself if you see the movie. The story has insisted on Sarah's behavior and on the romance to such a degree that by the end no commonsense response is available. The movie has cut loose from real refugees, the real world, and real characters, and committed itself to the foreground romance, and now when implacable reality asserts itself, there is really nothing to be said.

Beyond the Sea ★ ★ ★

PG-13, 121 m., 2004

Kevin Spacey (Bobby Darin), Kate Bosworth (Sandra Dee), John Goodman (Steve Blauner), Bob Hoskins (Charlie Maffia), Brenda Blethyn (Polly Cassotto), Greta Scacchi (Mary Duvan), Caroline Aaron (Nina Cassotto Maffia), Peter Cincotti (Dick Behrke), William Ullrich (Young Bobby). Directed by Kevin Spacey and produced by Jan Fantl, Arthur Friedman, Andy Paterson, and Spacey. Screenplay by Spacey and Lewis Colick.

Kevin Spacey believes he was born to play Bobby Darin. I believe he was born to play more interesting characters, and has, and will, but I can see his point. He looks a little like Darin and sounds a lot like him, and apparently when he was growing up he formed one of those emotional connections with a performer where admiration is mixed with pity.

Darin's own emotional connection was apparently with Frank Sinatra, a pop singer he hoped to displace. That wasn't going to happen; there is a point beyond which talent cannot be extended into genius. He died young, at thirty-seven, having lived most of his life on borrowed time. After rheumatic fever at seven, he wasn't expected to live past fifteen. That he found twenty-two more years, had great success, and made recordings that are still popular today is an achievement, but not one that makes a biopic necessary, unless the filmmaker is moved by a personal obsession.

Kevin Spacey was, and *Beyond the Sea* is at least as much about Spacey playing Darin as about Darin himself. Is Spacey too old to be convincing as a singer in his teens, twenties, and thirties? Yes, but not too old to play an actor in his forties who feels driven to play such a role. Perhaps there are parallels. Spacey has struggled, been misunderstood, had triumphs and disasters, has recently been the target of malicious coverage in the British press (his sin was to presume to contribute to the London stage even though he is a Movie Star). In his own best work, Spacey has achieved genius; he is better as an actor than Darin ever was as a singer, but there must have been a time when Spacey identified strongly with Darin's disappointments and defeats, and *Beyond the Sea* is about those feelings.

It is also probably relevant that Spacey, in preparing the project, knew something we could not guess: He is a superb pop singer. In a rash ad lib on *Ebert and Roeper*, I said I thought he was probably even a better singer than Darin. A statement like that has an apples-and-oranges foolishness; Darin was himself and nobody else ever will be, and it's enough to observe that although many actors think they are wonderful singers, Spacey is correct.

He constructs the picture as a film within a film, to provide an explanation for the spectacle of an older man playing a much younger one. The film begins with Darin onstage at the Copacabana night club, and then pulls back to reveal that we're on a sound stage; the adult Darin is confronted by himself as a young boy, arguing that he's gotten it all wrong, and in a weird way the whole movie will be an argument among the various ages of Bobby Darin. There is a parallel with *De-Lovely*, in which the ancient Cole Porter reviews a musical about his life; in both cases, the POV is essentially posthumous.

Darin as a boy is the darling of his mother (Brenda Blethyn) and sister, Nina (Caroline Aaron), although his relationship with them is not quite what he believes. Nina's husband, Charlie (Bob Hoskins), helps start his career, a manager (John Goodman) signs aboard, and with big teeny-bopper hits like "Splish Splash," he becomes a star.

Darin hungers to grow, and moves into the mainstream of popular music with hits like "Mack the Knife" and "Beyond the Sea." On a movie set, he falls in love with Sandra Dee (Kate Bosworth) and marries her, at a time when their careers were both soaring. The marriage goes wrong for reasons that seem to have more to do with biopic conventions than real life; their careers keep them apart, etc., although there is a moment with the hard truth of *A Star Is Born* when Darin is nominated for an Oscar, loses, goes ballistic, and screams: "Warren Beatty is there with Leslie Caron and I'm there with Gidget!"

Darin's career collapse led at one point to exile in a house trailer, and then to a comeback in which he tried to cross over into polit-ically conscious acoustic folk singing, which was not a good fit for his talent. He was born to play Vegas, but not as an aging hippie. His Vegas debut flops, but he returns in triumph after restaging his show to include a black gospel choir, which brings a lot of energy onto the stage. He is advised of audiences, "remember—they hear what they see," and he nods at this wise insight, although I am not sure exactly what it means.

Bobby Darin's life provides a less-than-perfect template for a biopic, because he achieved success up to a certain point, then failed, then did not really have much of a comeback, then died young. Not precisely the inspirational ascent of a biographical Everest. But the movie possesses genuine feeling because Spacey is there with Darin during all the steps of this journey, up and down, all the way into death. Not all stories have happy endings. Not all lives have third acts. This was a life, too, and although it was a disappointment, it also contained more success and maybe even more happiness than Darin could have reasonably expected at age fifteen, his presumed cut-off date. What I sensed above all in *Beyond the Sea* was Spacey's sympathy with and for Bobby Darin. There have been biopics inspired by less worthy motivations. ☞

The Big Animal ★ ★ ★

NO MPAA RATING, 72 m., 2004

Jerzy Stuhr (Zygmunt Sawicki), Anna Dymna (Marysia Sawicki), Dominika Bednarczyk (Bank Clerk), Blazej Wojcik (Bank Clerk), Andrzej Franczyk (Bank Manager), Feliks Szajnert (Drunkard), Rublo from Zalewski Circus (Camel). Directed by Jerzy Stuhr and produced by Janusz Morgenstern and Slawomir Rogowski. Screenplay by Krzysztof Kieslowski, based on a novel by Kazimierz Orlos.

One day a camel appears in a Polish village. It must have been left behind by a circus. Bereft and abandoned, it seeks out the garden of the Sawicki family, Zygmunt and Marysia, and they are happy to give it a home. Not everyone has a camel, and Marysia feels as if there's another guest for dinner when the beast peers through their dining room window during meals.

So begins *The Big Animal*, a fable written by

Krzysztof Kieslowski, the Polish poet of serendipity and coincidence, who died in 1996, leaving behind such masterpieces as *The Double Life of Veronique* and the Three Colors Trilogy *(Blue, White,* and *Red).* He wrote this screenplay in 1973, adapted from a novel, six years before *Camera Buff* brought him his first wide attention. Now it has been filmed by his best friend, Jerzy Stuhr, who stars as Zygmunt and appeared in many Kieslowski films, including *White.*

This is not a major Kieslowski work, nor was it intended to be. Kieslowski sometimes liked to work in a minor key, and some of the ten-hour-long films in his masterful *Decalogue* (1988) occupy similar territory: They are small parables about trying to make moral choices in an indifferent universe. He finds unexpected connections between characters, and unexpected meetings, and unintended consequences. Surely, to acquire an orphaned camel is such an event.

At first the village is happy to have a camel in its midst. That may be because the villagers have never seen a camel molting in the spring, when for several weeks it resembles a sofa abandoned to the rain. The camel (played by Rublo the camel) is a docile creature who often seems to be trying to recapture a lost train of thought. Zygmunt takes it for strolls around the village, schoolchildren are delighted by it, and Marysia knits it a shawl that leaves holes for its two humps.

All is well until stirrings of discontent are heard. Even in the most hospitable of communities, there are always malcontents who don't want a camel hanging around. The camel smells, and is unlovely, and it relieves itself in the street. And the Sawickis begin to stand out from the crowd: They are the People Who Have the Camel. In 1973 when Kieslowski wrote his screenplay, perhaps he saw it as a parable about life under the sameness and regimentation of communism. But even in a democracy human nature is intolerant of those who are different, and to own a camel is to be different.

In a capitalist society, this film might not be made because the story is not commercial. In 1973, there were state sources in Poland for production funds, but I have no idea if *The Big Animal* was turned down by the authorities. It is the kind of story that could be seen as a satirical attack on the government, or on the other hand it might simply be the tale of a camel. You never know. It is whimsical, bittersweet, wise in a minor key.

I am reminded of a story Dusan Makavejev told me. When there was a Yugoslavia, it had a censor whose job was to approve film scripts. The censor was a friend of Makavejev's; they had gone to school together. Makavejev submitted a script, and the censor called him into his office. "Dusan, Dusan, Dusan," he said sorrowfully, "you know what this story is about, and I know what this story is about. Now go home and rewrite it so only the audience knows what it is about."

The Big Bounce ★ ★
PG-13, 89 m., 2004

Owen Wilson (Jack Ryan), Charlie Sheen (Bob Rogers Jr.), Vinnie Jones (Lou Harris), Sara Foster (Nancy Hayes), Morgan Freeman (Walter Crewes), Gary Sinise (Ray Ritchie), Willie Nelson (Joe Lurie), Harry Dean Stanton (Bob Rogers Sr.), Butch Helemano (Hawaiian Priest). Directed by George Armitage and produced by Jorge Saralegui and Steve Bing. Screenplay by Sebastian Gutierrez, based on a novel by Elmore Leonard.

Elmore Leonard is a writer you read with your fingers crossed, amazed at his high-wire act, reading dialogue that always sounds like Leonard even though the characters never quite sound the same. You love the jargon as they explain their criminal specialties. You savor the way he pulls oddballs and misfits out of the shrubbery and sets them to work at strange day jobs and illegal night jobs, and shows them wise to the heartbreaks of the world but vulnerable to them. Just today I bought Leonard's new novel, because I never miss one. Most of the time they're clear sailing right to the end, and you close the covers with a grin.

Such a distinctive voice translates only rarely to the movies. Although Leonard's plots are ingenious and delightful, they're not the reason we read the books; Agatha Christie, poor soul, has delightful and ingenious plots. It's not the what but the how with Leonard, and the movies (his work has generated thirty of them) are mostly distant echoes of the genius. Of those

I've seen, the ones that seem to channel him more or less successfully are John Frankenheimer's *52 Pick-Up*, Barry Sonnenfeld's *Get Shorty*, Quentin Tarantino's *Jackie Brown*, and Steven Soderbergh's *Out of Sight*, although all four cross the Leonard voice with the distinctive voices of their directors.

Now here is *The Big Bounce*, the second screen version of this Leonard novel, which was first filmed in California in 1969 with Ryan O'Neal and Leigh Taylor-Young and has now been transferred to Hawaii. There's a dream cast: Owen Wilson, Charlie Sheen, Vinnie Jones, Sara Foster, Morgan Freeman, Gary Sinise and, I am not kidding you, Willie Nelson and Harry Dean Stanton. And the location is well visualized: not the commercialized Hawaii of so many movies, but a more secluded area with colorful local characters, not least at the resort bungalows managed by Freeman (also the local lawman), where Wilson gets a job halfway between janitor and gigolo.

The area's bad guy is Ray Ritchie (Gary Sinise), a developer who wants to put up high-rise hotels and spoil the flavor of paradise. His foreman, Lou Harris (Vinnie Jones), gets into a televised fight with Jack Ryan (Wilson), a beach bum and sometime athlete. That brings in Ritchie's enforcer, Bob Jr. (Charlie Sheen). And then there's the lithesome Nancy Hayes (Sara Foster), who is Ritchie's mistress but has a jones for criminals and gets really turned on when Jack demonstrates his skills as a burglar.

The destinies of all of these characters intersect in a way it would be unfair to describe, except to say that Leonard has a gift for surprising us with the hidden motives of some of his characters, and their allegiances can shift in an instant. What they want and what they do are not the point, really; that's the excuse for providing them with a stage. The pleasure in the film comes from watching them and listening to them, and Owen Wilson is especially good with his dialogue, which masks hostility with sweet reason.

The movie doesn't work. It meanders and drifts and riffs. There is a part of me that enjoyed its leisurely celebration of its characters. I wanted more focus, and so will you, but on TV late some night you may stumble across it and find yourself bemused for a time by the way they live their lives as if there's nothing more

fun than being an Elmore Leonard character. Maybe they're right.

Big Fish ★ ★ ½
PG-13, 125 m., 2003

Ewan McGregor (Young Edward), Albert Finney (Old Edward), Billy Crudup (Will Bloom), Jessica Lange (Sandra Bloom), Helena Bonham Carter (Jenny/The Witch), Alison Lohman (Young Sandra), Robert Guillaume (Dr. Bennett), Marion Cotillard (Josephine), Steve Buscemi (Norther Winslow), Danny DeVito (Amos Calloway), Matthew McGrory (Karl the Giant). Directed by Tim Burton and produced by Bruce Cohen, Dan Jinks, and Richard D. Zanuck. Screenplay by John August, based on the novel by Daniel Wallace.

From his son's point of view, Edward Bloom's timing is off. He spent the years before his son's birth having amazing adventures and meeting unforgettable characters, and the years after the birth telling his stories to his son, over and over and over and over again. Albert Finney, who can be the most concise of actors, can also, when required, play a tireless blowhard, and in *Big Fish* his character repeats the same stories so relentlessly you expect the eyeballs of his listeners to roll up into their foreheads and be replaced by tic-tac-toe diagrams, like in the funnies.

Some, however, find old Edward heroic and charming, and his wife is one of them. Sandra (Jessica Lange) stands watch in the upper bedroom where her husband is leaving life as lugubriously as he lived it. She summons home their son, Will (Billy Crudup). Will, a journalist working in Paris, knows his father's stories by heart and has one final exasperated request: Could his father now finally tell him the truth? Old Edward harrumphs, shifts some phlegm, and starts recycling again.

Tim Burton directed the movie, and we sense his eagerness to plunge into the flashbacks, which show Young Edward (Ewan McGregor) and Young Sandra (Alison Lohman) actually having some of the adventures the old man tirelessly recounts. Those memories involve a witch (Helena Bonham Carter) whose glass eye reflects the way her visitors will die, and a circus run by Amos Calloway (Danny DeVito), where he makes friends with such as Karl the Giant (Matthew McGrory). One day as Edward walks under the Big Top, he becomes mesmerized by his first glimpse of Sandra, and time crawls into slo-mo as he knows immediately this is the woman he is destined to marry.

There are other adventures, one involving a catfish as big as a shark, but it would be hard to top the time he parachutes onto the stage of a Red Army talent show in China, and meets Ping and Jing, a conjoined vocal duo sharing two legs. Now surely all these stories are fevered fantasies, right? You will have to see the movie to be sure, although, of course, there is also the reliable theory that things are true if you believe them so; if it worked for Tinker Bell, maybe it will work for you.

Because Tim Burton is the director, *Big Fish* of course is a great-looking film, with a fantastical visual style that could be called Felliniesque if Burton had not by now earned the right to the adjective Burtonesque. Yet there is no denying that Will has a point: The old man is a blowhard. There is a point at which his stories stop working as entertainment and segue into sadism. As someone who has been known to tell the same jokes more than once, I find it wise to at least tell them quickly; old Edward, on the other hand, seems to be a member of Bob and Ray's Slow Talkers of America.

There's another movie about a dying blowhard who recycles youthful memories while his loved ones gather around his deathbed. His wife summons home their son from Europe. The son is tired of the old man's stories and just once would like to hear the truth from him. This movie, of course, is *The Barbarian Invasions,* by Denys Arcand, and it is one of the best movies of the year. The two films have the same premise and purpose. They show how, at the end, we depend on the legends of our lives to give us meaning. We have been telling these stories not only to others but to ourselves. There is some truth here.

The difference—apart from the wide variation in tone between Arcand's human comedy and Burton's flamboyant ringmastery—is that Arcand uses the past as a way to get to his character, and Burton uses it as a way to get to his special effects. We have the sensation that Burton values old Edward primarily as an entry point into a series of visual fantasies. He is able to show us a remarkable village named Spectre, which has streets paved with grass and may very well be heaven, and that catfish as big as Jumbo, and magicians and tumblers and clowns and haunted houses and on and on.

In a sense we are also at the bedside of Tim Burton, who, like Old Edward, has been recycling the same skills over and over again and desperately requires someone to walk in and demand that he get to the point. When Burton gives himself the guidance and anchor of a story, he can be remarkable (*Ed Wood, The Nightmare Before Christmas, Sleepy Hollow*). When he doesn't, we admire his visual imagination and technique, but isn't this doodling of a very high order, while he waits for a purpose to reveal itself?

Biker Boyz ★ ★
PG-13, 111 m., 2003

Laurence Fishburne (Smoke), Derek Luke (Kid), Orlando Jones (Soul Train), Djimon Hounsou (Motherland), Lisa Bonet (Queenie), Brendan Fehr (Stuntman), Larenz Tate (Wood), Kid Rock (Dogg), Vanessa Bell Calloway (Anita), Eriq La Salle (Slick Will). Directed by Reggie Rock Bythewood and produced by Stephanie Allain, Gina Prince-Bythewood, and Erwin Stoff. Screenplay by Bythewood.

Biker Boyz has an idea, but not an approach. The idea comes from an article in the *Los Angeles New Times* about motorcycle clubs that meet for scheduled but illegal road races. The members are affluent enough to maintain expensive bikes (even mechanics are on the payroll) and polite enough that the movie's language slipped in under the ropes at PG-13.

Many but not all of the boys are African American; some are still literally boys but others are men in their forties, and the (unexplored) subtext is that these are successful men who enjoy the excitement of street racing. Not much mention is made of jobs, but you can't buy and maintain these machines without a good one.

We meet Smoke (Laurence Fishburne), long-time undefeated champion of street racing, and his mechanic Slick Will (Eriq La Salle). Slick's son is Kid (Derek Luke). Smoke's longtime fierce competitor is Dogg (Kid Rock). Races involve money (bets to $5,000) and, even more significant, racing helmets: If you lose, you hand over your helmet to the guy who beat you.

All of this is intriguing material, but the movie doesn't do much with it. There are several races in the film, but they don't generate the kind of pulse-quickening suspense that the races did in *The Fast and the Furious*, a four-wheel street-racing picture. As a general rule the right people win for the right reasons, and during some of the races the spectators inexplicably cluster at the starting line, so there's time for soul-to-soul conversations at the finish line.

Some of those involve a secret revealed halfway through the film; stop reading now unless you want to learn that Kid's mother, Anita (Vanessa Bell Calloway), tells him, after the death of the man he thinks is his father, that Smoke is his real father. This leads to less trauma and more niceness than you might think, in a movie that is gentler and tamer than the ads might suggest. Even insults, when they are traded, seem more written than felt.

This is the third film I've seen Derek Luke in, after *Antwone Fisher* and the Sundance 2003 hit *Pieces of April*. It's his least significant role, and yet confirms his presence: He's a rising star, all right, with a particular way of holding back, as if sizing up a situation to find the best entry point. Like Denzel Washington, who cast him as Antwone, he'll spend most of his career playing nice guys. (Does he have a *Training Day* in him? I can't tell from here.)

Laurence Fishburne is a strong presence in the central role, but the character isn't very interesting; he's good at racing, he's not a bad man, he has few complexities. Vanessa Bell Calloway, a crucial woman in both men's lives, has a kind of sultry power that suggests if she ever got on a bike, she'd have all the helmets.

I think what happened here is that the filmmakers were fascinated by the original article, did some research that hooked them on this world, and then trusted the world would be enough to power the movie. It isn't. We need a stronger conflict, as we had in *The Fast and the Furious,* and better and more special effects (the crashes all seem to happen at a distance). The father–son scenes have an earnestness and sincerity that would be right in another kind of movie, but seem like sidebars to the main story.

Birth ★ ★ ★ ½
R, 100 m., 2004

Nicole Kidman (Anna), Cameron Bright (Sean), Danny Huston (Joseph), Lauren Bacall (Eleanor), Alison Elliott (Laura), Arliss Howard (Bob), Anne Heche (Clara), Peter Stormare (Clifford). Directed by Jonathan Glazer and produced by Jean-Louis Piel, Nick Morris, and Lizie Gower. Screenplay by Jean-Claude Carriere, Milo Addica, and Glazer.

Nobody sees the little boy come into the apartment, but suddenly there he is, a stranger in the room at a family birthday party. "I am Sean," he says. Sean is the name of Anna's husband, who died ten years ago. The boy's name is Sean, but that's not what he means. What he means is that he *is* Sean in that when Sean died while jogging in Central Park, he was reborn and now here he stands, aged ten.

Since the first two scenes of *Birth* show the death and the birth, we're prepared for the reincarnation. What I wasn't expecting was a film that treats it as intelligent, skeptical adults might. They don't believe in reincarnation. Neither did the original Sean; the movie opens with a black screen and we hear him giving a speech: "As a man of science, I just don't believe that mumbo jumbo."

Birth is an effective thriller precisely because it is true to the way sophisticated people might behave in this situation. Its characters are not movie creatures, gullible, emotional, and quickly moved to tears. They're realists, rich, a little jaded. At first they simply laugh at the boy (Cameron Bright). Even when he seems to know things that only her husband would know, Anna (Nicole Kidman) is slow to allow herself to be convinced. She loved Sean and mourned him a long time, but after ten years it is time to resume her life, and she has just announced her engagement to Joseph (Danny Huston).

Anna lives with her mother, Eleanor (Lauren Bacall), in a luxurious Manhattan duplex. The family includes her sister Laura (Alison Elliott), her brother-in-law Bob (Arliss Howard), and her close friends Clara (Anne Heche) and

Clifford (Peter Stormare). Since they're all present when Sean first appears, they're all involved in the dilemma of what to do about him. Sean's parents order him not to annoy Anna anymore, but he turns up anyway, an unsettling combination of a kid and a solemn, unblinking presence.

When Anna tells him she simply doesn't believe him, he says, "What if Bob comes to my house and asks me some questions?" "How do you know Bob?" "He was my brother-in-law." Bob comes and asks some questions, and as the family gathers to listen to a tape recording of Sean's answers, it's clear something exceedingly strange is going on.

Anna becomes convinced, reluctantly, but then firmly, that Sean really is her reincarnated husband. She arrives at this decision, I think, during an extraordinary shot: a close-up of her face for a full three minutes, during an opera performance. And then the film ventures into the delicate area of exactly how a woman in her thirties goes about relating to a ten-year-old boy who is or was or will again be her husband. In one mordantly funny scene, they eat ice cream while she asks him how they will live, and he says, "I'll get a job." And, "Have you ever made love to a girl?" Well, yes and no. Yes, as Sean One, and no, as Sean Two; one of the film's mysteries is that Sean seems to be simultaneously the dead husband and an actual little boy.

Much has been said about a scene where Sean boldly gets into the bathtub with her, but the movie handles it with such care and tact that it sidesteps controversy. Anna's mother, for her part, thinks the whole situation is dangerous nonsense, and could develop into a crime. As played by Bacall, Eleanor is tart and decisive. When it appears Anna is considering living with Sean, her mother says: "I will call his mother, and his mother will call the police." Anna's fiancé, Joseph, is the wild card, reacting first with disbelief and then with restraint, before . . .

Of course there's a lot I haven't described, including the role of Clara (Heche), Anna's best friend. The movie goes deep, and then it takes a turn and leaves us asking fundamental questions. There seem to be two possible explanations for what finally happens; neither one is consistent with all of the facts. At a point when the characters seem satisfied they have arrived at the truth, I believed them, but it wasn't truth enough for me.

Birth is a dark, brooding film, with lots of kettledrums and ominous violins on Alexandre Desplat's sound track. Harris Savides's cinematography avoids surprises and gimmicks and uses the same kind of level gaze that Sean employs. Echoes of *Rosemary's Baby* are inevitable, given the similarity of the apartment locations and Nicole Kidman's haircut, so similar to Mia Farrow's. But *Birth* is less sensational and more ominous, and also more intriguing, because instead of going for quick thrills it explores what might really happen if a ten-year-old turned up and said what Sean says. Because it is about adults who act like adults, who are skeptical and wary, it's all the creepier, especially since Cameron Bright is so effective as the uninflected and noncute Sean. Like M. Night Shyamalan's best work, *Birth* works less with action than with implication.

Blade: Trinity ★ ½
R, 105 m., 2004

Wesley Snipes (Blade), Kris Kristofferson (Whistler), Jessica Biel (Abigail Whistler), Ryan Reynolds (Hannibal King), Parker Posey (Danica Talos), Dominic Purcell (Dracula/Drake). Directed by David Goyer and produced by Goyer, Peter Frankfurt, and Lynn Harris. Screenplay by Goyer.

I liked the first two *Blade* movies, although my description of *Blade II* as "a really rather brilliant vomitorium of viscera" might have sounded like faint praise. The second film was directed by Guillermo del Toro, a gifted horror director with a sure feel for the quease-inducing, and was even better, I thought, than the first. Now comes *Blade: Trinity,* which is a mess. It lacks the sharp narrative line and crisp comic-book clarity of the earlier films, and descends too easily into shapeless fight scenes that are chopped into so many cuts that they lack all form or rhythm.

The setup is a continuation of the earlier films. Vampires are waging a war to infect humanity, and the most potent fighter against them is the half-human, half-vampire Blade

(Wesley Snipes). He has been raised from childhood by Whistler (Kris Kristofferson), who recognized his unique ability to move between two worlds, and is a fearsome warrior, but, despite some teammates, is seriously outnumbered.

As *Trinity* opens, the Vampire Nation and its leader, Danica (played by Parker Posey— yes, Parker Posey), convince the FBI that Blade is responsible for, if I heard correctly, 1,182 murders. "They're waging a goddamned publicity campaign," Whistler grumbles, in that great Kris Kristofferson seen-it-all voice.

Agents surround Blade headquarters, which is your basic action movie space combining the ambience of a warehouse with lots of catwalks and high places to fall from and stuff that blows up good. Whistler goes down fighting (although a shotgun seems retro given the sci-fi weapons elsewhere in the movie), and Blade is recruited by the Night Stalkers, who reach him through Whistler's daughter, Abigail (Jessica Biel). It would have been too much, I suppose, to hope for Whistler's mother.

The Night Stalkers have information that the Vampire Nation is seeking the original Dracula because, to spread the vampire virus, "they need better DNA; they need Dracula's blood." Dracula's superior DNA means he can operate by day, unlike his descendants, who must operate by night. The notion that DNA degrades or is somehow diluted over the centuries flies in the face of what we know about the double helix, but who needs science when you know what's right? "They found Dracula in Iraq about six months ago," we learn, and if that's not a straight line, I'm not Jon Stewart.

Dracula is some kinduva guy. Played by Dominic Purcell, he isn't your usual vampire in evening dress with overdeveloped canines, but a creature whose DNA seems to have been infected with the virus of Hollywood monster effects. His mouth and lower face unfold into a series of ever more horrifying fangs and suchlike, until he looks like a mug shot of the original *Alien*. He doesn't suck blood; he vacuums it.

Parker Posey is an actress I have always had affection for, and now it is mixed with increased admiration for the way she soldiers through an impossible role, sneering like the

good sport she is. Jessica Biel becomes the first heroine of a vampire movie to listen to her iPod during slayings. That's an excuse to get the sound track by Ramin Djawadi and RZA into the movie, I guess, although I hope she downloaded it from the iTunes Store and isn't a pirate on top of being a vampire.

Vampires in this movie look about as easy to kill as the ghouls in *Dawn of the Dead*. They have a way of suddenly fizzing up into electric sparks, and then collapsing in a pile of ash. One of the weapons used against them by the Night Stalkers is a light-saber device that is, and I'm sure I have this right, "half as hot as the sun." Switch on one of those babies and you'd zap not only the vampires but British Columbia and large parts of Alberta and Washington State.

Jessica Biel is the resident babe, wearing fetishistic costumes to match Blade's, and teaming up with Hannibal King (Ryan Reynolds), no relation to Hannibal Lecter, a former vampire who has come over to the good side. The vampire killers and their fellow Night Stalkers engage in an increasingly murky series of battles with the vampires, leading you to ask this simple strategic question: Why, since the whole world is theirs for the taking, do the vampires have to turn up and fight the Night Stalkers in the first place? Why not just figure out that since the Stalkers are in Vancouver, the vampires should concentrate on, say, Montreal?

Blue Car ★ ★ ★ ½
R, 96 m., 2003

David Strathairn (Auster), Agnes Bruckner (Meg), Margaret Colin (Diane), Regan Arnold (Lily), Frances Fisher (Delia). Directed by Karen Moncrieff and produced by Peer J. Oppenheimer, Amy Sommer, and David Waters. Screenplay by Moncrieff.

Blue Car watches with horror as a vulnerable teenage girl falls into the emotional trap set by her high school English teacher. The teacher watches with horror, too: He knows what he is doing is wrong, but he is weak, and pities himself more than the sad girl he is exploiting. Step by step, they move in a direction only he understands.

The girl is named Meg (Agnes Bruckner). She is beautiful, and her teacher knows that with a desperate urgency. He is Auster (David Strathairn), who poses in the classroom as a stern but inspiring romantic. Meg reads a poem one day about how her father left her family. Auster asks her to stay after class, tells her she can reach deeper, asks her to find more truth. "We need a map of your nerve centers," he says. He thinks maybe the poem is good enough to get her into a poetry competition in Florida.

Meg's home life is in turmoil. Her mother, Diane (Margaret Colin), is distant and over-worked, attending night school, complaining that her ex-husband is behind on his payments. Meg is baby-sitter and substitute mother for her kid sister, Lily (Regan Arnold), who is seriously disturbed and sometimes cuts herself.

Auster's approach to Meg is subtle and guarded. He flatters her with his attention. He maintains his authority and seems to keep his distance, but somehow she is sharing his sandwich at the noon hour and getting a ride home in his car. And then, when a family tragedy occurs, Auster comforts her a degree too eagerly.

This teacher is a piece of work. He knows that an open appeal to Meg would be rejected, that she would be creeped out by his lust. But by maintaining a position of power and then overpraising her work, he gets inside her defenses. Her poem is a good poem, but not that good. Sometimes he reads to her from his novel in progress, which sounds like subpar Thomas Wolfe but is as much a fraud as the rest of him. Notice the cruelty in the scene where he gives her a little speech about how we can't all be winners all of the time, and then, after she thinks she has lost the poetry competition, tells her she is a winner.

We see a bright, sad, lonely girl with absent parents, drifting into danger. She thinks she may be able to get a ride to Florida with a friend's family. That falls through. She takes the bus, sleeps on the beach, turns up for the competition, and even finds Auster on the beach, sunning with his wife (Frances Fisher) and son. Fisher has a brief scene, but it is played with acute observation. Watch the way she sizes up Meg and immediately reads her husband's intentions.

Blue Car, written and directed by Karen Moncrieff, is wise in the way it follows the progress of the story. Auster wants to have sex with Meg, but it must be within the twisted terms of his own compromised morality. She must in some sense seem to agree to it. I will leave it to you to witness how this scenario plays out, and to observe the sadness with which he pursues his pathetic goal.

The ending of the film is as calculated and cruel as a verbal assault by a Neil LaBute character. In a few merciless words and an unmistakable implication, Meg fights back. The story has its basis in everyday realism. The teacher is made not a stereotyped monster but a pathetic and weak one. The girl is not a sexpot nor childishly naive, but distracted and deceived. Moncrieff doesn't exploit the situation, but deplores it.

Bruckner, an eighteen-year-old veteran of soap opera and four smaller feature roles, negotiates this difficult script with complete conviction. Strathairn's role is even trickier, because Moncrieff doesn't want to make him into a stereotyped molester, but wants to show how he is about to manipulate himself into a situation where it seems, because he wants it to seem, that the girl accepts him. He is rotten in an everyday way, not in a horror movie way—and that makes him much more frightening.

Because the movie is an honest and forthright drama about a teenager in danger, of course the MPAA has rated it R. That despite the fact that it contains no nudity, no explicit sex, and only ordinary adolescent language. The theory of the ratings board, apparently, is that all manner of vulgarity and pop violence is suitable for those under seventeen, but any movie that addresses the actual conditions of teenage life must be off-limits. What the MPAA standards amount to is: Let students learn about sexual predators in their lives, not in the movies. *Blue Car* is a valuable cautionary tale.

Blue Collar Comedy Tour: The Movie ★ ★ ★
PG-13, 105 m., 2003

Featuring Jeff Foxworthy, Bill Engvall, Ron White, Larry the Cable Guy, Heidi Klum, and David Allen Grier. A documentary directed by C. B. Harding and produced by

Alan C. Blomquist, Casey LaScala, Joseph Williams, Hunt Lowry, and J. P. Williams.

Jeff Foxworthy, the "you know you're a redneck" guy, was ice-fishing in Minnesota once and started thinking of the experience from the point of view of the fish.

"Suppose you get caught and you're thrown back in. What do you tell your buddies? 'Man, I had an out-of-the-body experience. I was just minding my own business, living my life, when suddenly I felt myself under the control of a powerful force. I was drawn up toward the light. I went through a hole in the sky and found myself surrounded by all my dead relatives. And God was wearing a flannel shirt and a Budweiser hat.'"

The humor in that story is typical of all four performers in *Blue Collar Comedy Tour: The Movie*, a concert film starring Foxworthy, Bill Engvall, Ron White, and Larry the Cable Guy. I am informed that their national tour, just closing after four years, is the most successful in history, although whose history is not specified, and all tours say that. Certainly they're popular, and this film, which is kind of a redneck version of *The Original Kings of Comedy*, is the way to see them without having to find your car in the middle of all the pickups in the parking lot.

White and Cable Guy are the warm-ups, Foxworthy and Engvall are the stars, and then all four come on stage to share stories and listen to Foxworthy's redneck litany. ("If the wedding rehearsal dinner is at Hooter's—you know you're a redneck.") His uncle is such a NASCAR fan, he always gets into his car through the window.

But there I go, stealing his material. How do you review a movie like this without reprinting the jokes? The film consists of four concert segments, larded with "documentary" footage of the four buddies fishing, visiting Victoria's Secret, etc. The concert stuff is consistently funny, good-humored, and surprisingly clean; there's a lot more bathroom humor than sex or profanity, and the PG-13 rating is probably about right.

I do have some doubts about the other stuff. When they go shopping for underwear at Victoria's Secret, the sales clerk is played by supermodel Heidi Klum, which clues us that it's a setup and probably halfway scripted. What's the point? Why not let the boys walk into a real Victoria's Secret and start filming and see what happens? I was also a little puzzled by the role played by David Allen Grier, as the chauffeur and valet. Why have a recognizable star and not make any use of him?

These are minor quibbles. The underlying secret of the four comedians is the way they find humor in daily life, and in their families. In this they're a lot like the Kings of Comedy, and Engvall (the "here's your sign" guy) gets as much mileage out of his family as K of C's Bernie Mac.

Okay, I got a couple more. I liked the whole riff about leaf blowers being banned from airplanes. And I suppose it is thought-provoking that nobody ever has to stop to pee while tubing down a river.

Boat Trip ½ ★
R, 93 m., 2003

Cuba Gooding Jr. (Jerry), Horatio Sanz (Nick), Vivica A. Fox (Felicia), Roselyn Sanchez (Gabriela), Maurice Godin (Hector), Richard Roundtree (Malcolm), Roger Moore (Lloyd). Directed by Mort Nathan and produced by Frank Hübner, Brad Krevoy, Gerhard Schmidt, and Andrew Sugerman. Screenplay by Nathan and William Bigelow.

Boat Trip arrives preceded by publicity saying many homosexuals have been outraged by the film. Now that it's in theaters, everybody else has a chance to join them. Not that the film is outrageous. That would be asking too much. It is dim-witted, unfunny, too shallow to be offensive, and way too conventional to use all of those people standing around in the background wearing leather and chains and waiting hopefully for their cues. This is a movie made for nobody, about nothing.

The premise: Jerry (Cuba Gooding Jr.) is depressed after being dumped by his girl (Vivica A. Fox). His best buddy Nick (Horatio Sanz) cheers him up: They'll take a cruise together. Nick has heard that the ships are jammed with lonely women. But they offend a travel agent, who books them on a cruise of gay men, ho, ho.

Well, it could be funny. Different characters in a different story with more wit and insight might have done the trick. But *Boat Trip* requires its heroes to be so unobservant that it takes them hours to even figure out it's a gay cruise. And then they go into heterosexual panic mode, until the profoundly conventional screenplay supplies the only possible outcome: The sidekick discovers that he's gay, and the hero discovers a sexy woman on board and falls in love with her.

Her name is Gabriela (Roselyn Sanchez), and despite the fact that she's the choreographer on a gay cruise, she knows so little about gay men that she falls for Jerry's strategy: He will pretend to be gay, so that he can get close to her and then dramatically unveil his identity, or something. Uh-huh. Even Hector, the cross-dressing queen in the next stateroom, knows a straight when he sees one: "You want to convince people you are gay, and you don't know the words to 'I Will Survive'?"

The gays protesting the movie say it deals in stereotypes. So it does, but then again, so does the annual gay parade, and so do many gay nightclubs, where role-playing is part of the scene. Yes, there are transvestites and leather guys and muscle boys on the cruise, but there are also more conventional types, like Nick's poker-playing buddies. The one ray of wit in the entire film is provided by Roger Moore, as a homosexual man who calmly wanders through the plot dispensing sanity, as when, at the bar, he listens to the music and sighs, "Why do they always play Liza?"

One of the movie's problems is a disconnect between various levels of reality. Some of the scenes play as if they are intended to be realistic. Then Jerry or Nick goes into hysterics of overacting. Then Jerry attempts to signal a helicopter to rescue him, and shoots it down with a flare gun. Then it turns out to be carrying the Swedish suntanning team on its way to the Hawaiian Tropic finals. Then Jerry asks Gabriela to describe her oral sex technique, which she does with the accuracy and detail of a porn film, and then Jerry—but that pathetic moment you will have to witness for yourself. Or maybe you will not.

Note: The credit cookies weren't very funny, either, but at least they kept me in the theater long enough to notice the credits for the film's Greek support team.

Bobby Jones: Stroke of Genius ★ ★ ★
PG, 120 m., 2004

James Caviezel (Bobby Jones), Claire Forlani (Mary Jones), Jeremy Northam (Walter Hagen), Malcolm McDowell (O. B. Keeler), Connie Ray (Clara Jones), Brett Rice ("Big Bob" Jones), Aidan Quinn (Harry Vardon), Larry Thompson (John Malone). Directed by Rowdy Herrington and produced by Kim Dawson, Kim Moore, and John Shepherd. Screenplay by Herrington and Bill Pryor.

Bobby Jones (1902–1971) was perhaps the greatest golfer who ever lived. Not even Tiger Woods has equaled Jones's triumph in 1930, when he became the only player to win the U.S. Open, the British Open, the U.S. Amateur, and the British Amateur in the same year. Then he retired from competition—still only twenty-eight. Odds are good no golfer will ever equal that record—if only because no golfer good enough to do it will be an amateur. Jones also won seven U.S. titles in a row, an achievement that may be unmatchable.

Jones was not only an amateur, but an amateur who had to earn a living, so that he couldn't play golf every day and mostly played only in championship-level tournaments. This makes him sound like a man who played simply for love of the game, but *Bobby Jones: Stroke of Genius* shows us a man who seems driven to play, a man obsessed; there seems less joy than compulsion in his career, and the movie contrasts him with the era's top professional, Walter Hagen (Jeremy Northam), who seems to enjoy himself a lot more.

Jim Caviezel (*The Passion of the Christ*) plays Jones as an adult, after childhood scenes showing a young boy who becomes fascinated by the game and watches great players while hiding in the rough. He comes from a family dominated by a strict, puritanical grandfather, but Jones's father, "Big Bob" (Brett Rice), is supportive. Not so Jones's wife, Mary (Claire Forlani), who plays a role that has become standard in the biographies of great men—the woman who wishes her man would give up his dream and spend more time at home with her and the children.

Of course, Mary sees a side of Bobby that's invisible to the world. The man is tortured. He feels he must enter tournaments and win them to prove something he can never quite articulate, to show "them" without being sure who they are. And he is often in physical pain. After a sickly childhood, he grows up into a reed-thin man with a tense face, and doctors have only to look at him to prescribe rest. His stomach starts to hurt at about the same time he begins to drink and smoke, and although the movie does not portray him as an alcoholic, we hold that as a hypothesis until we find the pain is caused by syringomyelia, a spinal disease that would cripple him later in life.

Bobby Jones: Stroke of Genius tells this story in a straightforward, calm way that works ideally as the chronicle of a man's life but perhaps less ideally as drama. No doubt we should be grateful that Jones's story isn't churned up into soap opera and hyped with false crises and climaxes; it is the story of a golfer, and it contains a lot of golf. Much of the golf is photographed at the treacherous Old Course in St Andrews, Scotland, where the game began, and where we learn why there are eighteen holes: "A bottle of Scotch has eighteen shots," an old-timer explains, "and they reckoned that when it was empty, the game was over."

A major player in Jones' life is O. B. Keeler (Malcolm McDowell), his friend and "official biographer," and if Jones was an amateur golfer, Keeler seems to be an amateur biographer, with all day free, every day, to follow Jones around, carry his stomach medicine (and his whisky), and chronicle his exploits, sometimes typing while leaning against a stone wall on a course. Little wonder that although Jones retired in 1930, Keeler did not publish his "authorized biography" until 1953.

The director, Rowdy Herrington, has made more excited movies, including *Road House* (1989), legendary for its over-the-top performances by Patrick Swayze, Kelly Lynch, and Ben Gazzara. *Bobby Jones* is more solemn, more the kind of movie you're not surprised was financed by the Bobby Jones Film Co., and authorized by the Jones trustees, who also oversee lines of clothing and the like. It is also not astonishing, I suppose, that although the film mentions that Jones founded the Augusta National Golf Club and started the Masters tournament there, and although a photo over the end credits shows Jones with the course's favorite golfer, Dwight D. Eisenhower, there is no mention of the club's exclusion of blacks and women.

To be fair, the movie isn't really about Jones's entire life; it focuses on his youth and his championship golf. I am not a golfer, although I took the sport in P.E. class in college and have played a few rounds. There are too many movies to see, books to read, cities to explore, and conversations to hold for me to spend great parts of the day following that little ball around and around and around. I do concede that everyone I know who plays golf loves the game, and that most of them seem to derive more cheer from it than Bobby Jones does in this movie.

That Jones should obtain more pleasure than he does is all the more certain because the movie mostly shows him making impossible shots, at one point chipping the ball into the hole from close to the wall of a sand trap higher than his head. Walter Hagen spends a lot of the movie raising his eyebrows and grimacing in reaction shots, after Jones sinks another miracle.

Bon Voyage ★ ★ ★ ½
PG-13, 114 m., 2004

Isabelle Adjani (Viviane Denvers), Gerard Depardieu (Jean-Etienne Beaufort), Virginie Ledoyen (Camille), Yvan Attal (Raoul), Gregori Derangere (Frederic), Peter Coyote (Alex Winckler), Jean-Marc Stehle (Professeur Kopolski). Directed by Jean-Paul Rappeneau and produced by Laurent Petin and Michele Petin. Screenplay by Patrick Modiano, Gilles Marhand, Jean-Paul Rappeneau, Julien Rappeneau, and Jerome Tonnerre.

The Nazi occupation of France may seem like a strange backdrop for an adventure comedy, but consider how *Casablanca* found humor, irony, and courage in a related situation. Not that *Bon Voyage* is *Casablanca,* but it proceeds from the same cynicism, and unites the worlds of politics, science, and the movies. It also provides Isabelle Adjani with one of the best roles of her career, as a movie star who will do anything, say anything, and sleep with anybody, first to further her career and then to save her life.

The movie is a lavish, expensive period

production by Jean-Paul Rappeneau, who also made Gérard Depardieu's rabble-rousing *Cyrano de Bergerac* in 1990 and the exhilarating *The Horseman on the Roof* (1995). Depardieu returns in *Bon Voyage*, and he is an unmade bed no longer; he is astonishingly slimmed down, his hair trimmed and slicked back, wearing the tailored suits of a cabinet minister.

The movie opens in Paris, as the Nazis are moving into the city and many prudent citizens with the means or clout are moving to Bordeaux, which they think might be Nazi-free, at least for a while. Adjani plays Viviane Denvers, a great movie star and apparently an even greater lover. To say that she looks much younger than her forty-eight years is not flattery but the simple truth; Adjani was able to play a convincing teenager in *Camille Claudel* (1990). Here her character functions instinctively as a woman who is attracted to men who offer her money and safety. Her fatal flaw is that she is also attracted to men she loves. These tastes become thoroughly confused during the film, as she seeks money, safety, and love simultaneously, which means that no one man is going to be able to fill the bill.

Jean-Etienne Beaufort (Depardieu) is the harassed cabinet minister she's attached to as the movie opens. As some ministers urge collaboration with the Nazis, he commands a car and Viviane joins him on the exodus. But then she is astonished to see a childhood friend named Frederic (Gregori Derangere) on the streets—astonished because she thought he was in jail charged with murder. Such is her power over men that, some days earlier, after she murdered a blackmailer in her apartment, she called him up and because he had always been in love with her, he allowed the police to arrest him. He's free because his jailers helpfully released their prisoners ahead of the Nazi advance.

So now there is a man to care for her, and a man for her to care for. And not to forget Alex Winckler (Peter Coyote), a journalist who seems to have a lot of influence and is mesmerized by her. Can he be trusted? He speaks with an accent, and movie fans will know he has the same last name as one of the Nazi creeps in *The Third Man*. Viviane's strategy is to accept protection from the man of the moment, convince him she loves only him, and jump ship when

necessary. How does Adjani create the character? Not by vamping, not by flaunting sexuality, but by creating a kind of vacuum of need that draws men so close they cannot resist the lure of her large, liquid eyes—pools to drown in.

The film introduces a tributary that will eventually join with the mainstream, although at first we can't see how. This involves an emigré Jewish professor named Kopolski (Jean-Marc Stehle), an intellectual temperamentally unsuited to survive in an evil world. He is in possession of several very large bottles of heavy water, needed for nuclear experiments, and he wants to keep them away from the Nazis and somehow get them to England. (The heavy water bottles here, like the wine bottles filled with heavy earth in Hitchcock's *Notorious*, function essentially as a MacGuffin.) Professor Kopolski's only hope is a young assistant named Camille (Virginie Ledoyen), who rises to the occasion, saving both the professor and the heavy water from Nazi capture; she transports the bottles in the back of a station wagon, where we constantly expect them to break.

There are other characters, a lot of them, including a set of rich aristocrats and tourists who keep turning up in all of the hotels, demanding what cannot be had. But the underlying structure of the movie is farce crossed with action and oiled by romance, and Rappeneau and his four cowriters are virtuosos at keeping all of their balls in the air. The lives and fates of the characters crisscross, their motives are subject to sudden adjustments, and Viviane is like Eliza on the ice floes, leaping from one man to another.

The movie is funny, not in a ho-ho way, but in the way it surprises us with delights and blindsides us with hazards. There's a lot of contrivance involved—it is, after all, improbable that these characters would not only constantly cross paths, but always at moments of crisis. But once we accept the movie's method, it implicates us; the sudden separations and reunions are devices for testing Viviane's powers of romantic invention and Camille's desperate improvisations. There is also the amusement that men, especially powerful men, are powerless in the hands of a woman like Viviane. Their mistake is to love someone who loves only herself; their excuse is that she loves herself so much she loves them, too, or is able to make them believe she does, which comes to the same thing.

I haven't even mentioned the costumes, the sets, the ambience. If Rappeneau's *The Horseman on the Roof* was the most expensive French film to date, *Bon Voyage* must be in the same league. He uses the money not to manufacture a big, clunky entertainment, but to facilitate a world that seems real even into the farthest corners of Paris, Bordeaux, hotels, cabinet meetings, boudoirs, dark roads, and desperate rendezvous. This is a grand, confident entertainment, sure of the power of Adjani, Depardieu, and the others, and sure of itself.

Born into Brothels: Calcutta's Red Light Kids ★ ★ ★ ½
R, 85 m., 2005

A documentary directed and produced by Zana Briski and Ross Kauffman.

In a movie named *The Five Obstructions*, the Danish director Lars von Trier creates an ordeal for his mentor, Jorgen Leth. The older director will have to remake a short film in five different ways, involving five obstructions that von Trier will devise. One of the five involves making a film in "the most miserable place on Earth," which they decide is the red light district of Mumbai. The director is unable to deal with this assignment.

Now here is a documentary made in a place that is by definition as miserable: the red light district of Calcutta. I thought of the Danish film as I was watching this one, because the makers of *Born into Brothels: Calcutta's Red Light Kids* also find it almost impossible to make. They are shooting in an area where no one wants to be photographed, where lives are hidden behind doors or curtains, where with their Western features and cameras they are as obvious as the police, and indeed suspected of working for them.

Zana Briski, an American photographer, and Ross Kauffman, her collaborator, went to Calcutta to film prostitution and found that it melted out of sight as they appeared. It was all around them, it put them in danger, but it was invisible to their camera. What they did see were the children, because the kids of the

district followed the visitors, fascinated. Briski hit upon the idea of giving cameras to these children of prostitutes, and asking them to take photos of the world in which they lived.

It is a productive idea, and has a precedent of sorts in a 1993 project by National Public Radio in Chicago; two teenagers, LeAlan Jones and Lloyd Newman, were given tape recorders and asked to make an audio documentary of the Ida B. Wells public housing project, where they lived and where a young child had been thrown from a high window in a fight over candy. Their work won a Peabody Award.

The kids in *Born into Brothels* (which won the 2005 Oscar) take photos with zest and imagination, squint at the contact sheets to choose their favorite shots, and mark them with crayons. Their pictures capture life, and a kind of beauty and squalor that depend on each other. One child, Avijit, is so gifted he wins a week's trip to Amsterdam for an exhibition of photography by children.

Over a couple of years, Briski teaches photo classes and meets some of the parents of the children—made difficult because she must work through interpreters. Prostitution in this district is not a choice but a settled way of life. We meet a grandmother, mother, and daughter, the adults engaged in prostitution, and the granddaughter seems destined to join them. Curiously, the movie does not suggest that the boys will also be used as prostitutes, although it seems inevitable. The age of entry into prostitution seems to be puberty. There are no scenes that could be described as sexually explicit, partly because of the filmmakers' tact in not wanting to exploit their subjects, partly no doubt because the prostitutes refused to be filmed except in innocuous settings.

Briski becomes determined to get several of the children out of the district and into a boarding school, where they will have a chance at different lives. She encounters opposition from their parents and roadblocks from the Indian bureaucracy, which seems to create jobs by requiring the same piece of paper to be meaninglessly stamped, marked, read, or filed in countless different offices. She goes almost mad trying to get a passport for Avijit, the winner of the Amsterdam trip; of course with his background he lacks the "required" papers.

The film is narrated mostly by Briski, who is a good teacher and brings out the innate intelligence of the children as they use their cameras to see their world in a different way. The faces of the children are heartbreaking, because we reflect that in the time since the film was finished, most of them have lost childhood forever, some their lives. Far away offscreen is the prosperous India with middle-class enclaves, an executive class, and a booming economy. These wretched poor exist in a separate and parallel universe, without an exit.

The movie is a record by well-meaning people who try to make a difference for the better, and succeed to a small degree while all around them the horror continues unaffected. Yes, a few children stay in boarding schools. Others are taken out by their parents, drop out, or are asked to leave. The red light district has existed for centuries and will exist for centuries more. I was reminded of a scene in Buñuel's *Viridiana*. A man is disturbed by the sight of a dog tied to a wagon and being dragged along faster than it can run. The man buys the dog to free it, but does not notice, in the background, another cart pulling another dog.

The Bourne Supremacy ★ ★ ★

PG-13, 109 m., 2004

Matt Damon (Jason Bourne), Joan Allen (Agent Pamela Landy), Brian Cox (Ward Abbott), Karl Urban (Kirill), Franka Potente (Marie Helena Kreutz), Julia Stiles (Nicky). Directed by Paul Greengrass and produced by Patrick Crowley, Frank Marshall, and Paul Sandberg. Screenplay by Tony Gilroy, based on the novel by Robert Ludlum.

Jason Bourne obtained an identity in *The Bourne Identity* (2002), and the title of *The Bourne Supremacy* hints that he is not going to die—not with *The Bourne Ultimatum* still to go. He may not die even then, but live on like James Bond, caught in a time loop, repeating the same archetypal pattern again and again as his persona is inhabited by generations of actors.

Bourne may live forever, but the bad news is, people will always want to kill him; that is the defining reality of his life. The plot of *Supremacy*, like *Identity*, involves Bourne trying to survive the shadowy forces against him by using his awesome skills in spycraft, the martial arts, and running real fast. The movie works because he does these things well, and because Matt Damon embodies Bourne without adding any flashy heroism. A show-off would be deadly in this role.

The movie skillfully delivers a series of fights, stalkings, plottings, and chases, punctuated by a little brooding. The best word for Bourne is "dogged." After a brief illusion of happiness, he puts his head down and marches relentlessly ahead into the lairs of his enemies, not even bothering with disguises, because he's using himself as bait. He always wears the same black shirt, pants, and jacket, in scenes taking him from India to Italy to Germany to Russia (no one complains).

Bourne awakened from amnesia, we recall from the first movie, possessed of skills he did not even know he had, and with a cache of passports and other aids to survival, a cache left to him by—well, you remember. As *Supremacy* opens, he has gone as far away as he can go, dropping out with Marie (Franka Potente), the woman he met in the first adventure. They're living on the beach in Goa, in southern India, happy as clams until Bourne spots a stranger who is wearing the wrong clothes, driving the wrong car, and turning up in all the wrong places.

They're still after him, or someone is. What is it about Bourne that makes his enemies prepared to spend millions to wipe him out? Sometimes he seems tantalizingly close to remembering. He suffers from Manchurian Candidate's syndrome, a malady that fills your nightmares with disconnected flashes of something dreadful that may or may not have happened to you. I saw *The Bourne Supremacy* on the very same day I saw the new remake of *The Manchurian Candidate*, and I was able to compare the symptoms, which involve quick cuts of fragmentary images.

The movie is assembled from standard thriller ingredients, and hurtles from one action sequence to another in India and Europe, with cuts to parallel action in Washington and New York. What distinguishes it is Bourne's inventiveness. There's a scene where he takes about four seconds to disable an armed agent and steal his cell phone contact list, and you're thinking, this is a guy who knows what he's doing. And how about the innovative use he finds for a toaster? It's neat to see him read a situation and instantaneously improvise a response, often by using lateral thinking.

What Bourne doesn't know about his pursuers, we find out as the movie intercuts with a plot involving a CIA agent named Pamela Landy (Joan Allen) and her boss, Ward Abbott (Brian Cox). Julia Stiles plays a younger agent under Landy's direction. They've found Bourne's fingerprints at the scene of a murder in Berlin involving a CIA agent and his high-level criminal contact. But Bourne was in Goa at the time, so who's framing him?

We have a pretty good idea, long before anyone else does, because the movie observes the Law of Economy of Character Development, which teaches us that when an important actor is used in an apparently subordinate role, he's the villain. But the movie doesn't depend on its big revelations for its impact; the mystery is not why Bourne is targeted, but whether he will die. He survives one lethal trap or ambush after another, leaping off bridges, crashing cars, killing assailants, and finally limping a little after a chase that should have killed him.

I have the weakness of bringing logic to movies where it is not required. There's a chase scene where he commandeers a taxicab and leads a posse of squad cars through an urban version of a demo derby. Although the film does not linger over the victims, we assume dozens of cars were destroyed and dozens of people killed or maimed in this crash, and we have to ask ourselves: Is this cost in innocent victims justified in the cause of saving Jason Bourne's life? At the end of the film there is a heartfelt scene where he delivers an apology. If he ever goes back to Berlin, he'll have to apologize to hundreds if not thousands of people, assuming a lynch mob doesn't get to him first.

But I digress. Thrillers don't exist in a plausible universe. They consist of preposterous situations survived by skill, courage, craft, and luck. That Matt Damon is able to bring some poignancy to Jason Bourne makes the process more interesting, because we care more about the character. That the director, Paul Greengrass, treats the material with gravity and uses good actors in well-written supporting roles elevates the movie above its genre, but not quite out of it.

Breakin' All the Rules ★ ★ ★
PG-13, 85 m., 2004

Jamie Foxx (Quincy Watson), Gabrielle Union (Nicky Callas), Morris Chestnut (Evan Fields), Peter MacNicol (Philip Gascon), Jennifer Esposito (Rita Monroe), Bianca Lawson (Helen Sharp). Directed by Daniel Taplitz and produced by Lisa Tornell. Screenplay by Taplitz.

Breakin' All the Rules combines a romantic comedy, a little mistaken identity, and some satire about office politics into one of those genial movies where you know everything is going to turn out all right in the end. The movie depends for its success on the likability of Jamie Foxx, Morris Chestnut, and Gabrielle Union, and because they're funny and pleasant we enjoy the ride even though the destination is preordained.

Foxx plays Quincy Watson, a writer for *Spoils* magazine, one of those men's lifestyle books edited for readers who believe they can become rich, successful, and well groomed by studying a magazine. The magazine has fallen upon hard times, and the editor summons Quincy and gives him a list of people to fire. Quincy recoils; he hates the idea of firing anybody. So does Philip the editor (Peter MacNicol), who explains that one of the spoils of being the boss is that you can get other people to do your dirty work.

Rather than fire anyone, Quincy quits. He's depressed anyway; his fiancée, Helen Sharp (Bianca Lawson), has just broken up with him. He starts writing versions of a wounded, angry letter to her, and somehow the correspondence grows into a book titled *Break Up Handbook,* about how to break up with a girl before she can break up with you (danger signal: she says she "wants to have a talk").

Enter Quincy's cousin, Evan (Morris Chestnut), a moving target who prides himself on breaking up with girls as a preemptive strategy. His girl, Nicky (Gabrielle Union), says she wants to have a talk, and to deny her the opportunity of breaking up with him, Evan sends Quincy to a bar to meet her and tell her the relationship is over. Alas, Nicky has cut her hair and doesn't fit Evan's description; Quincy starts talking with her, and soon they're flirting with love. If the hair trick sounds contrived, recall that Shakespeare was not above mistaken identities even more absurd. Not that I hold it against him.

Gabrielle Union is one of those actresses whose smile is so warm you hope the other characters will say something just to make her happy. As a counterbalance, the movie supplies Rita (Jennifer Esposito), a mercenary mantrap who wants to get her hooks into Philip the editor. Quincy is called in as a consultant on this case, too, but Rita is too crafty to be easily fooled by tricks learned from a book.

There will, of course, be a scene of wounded betrayal, when Evan discovers that Quincy is dating Nicky and decides he loves her after all. And a titanic battle of the wills between Rita and Philip. And jokes about being the author of a best-seller; Quincy's book seems to hit the charts within days after he finishes it, having apparently been printed by magic.

Breakin' All the Rules is not a comic masterpiece, but it's entertaining and efficient and provides a showcase for its stars. It's on the level of a good sitcom. It's unusual in this way: Writer-director Daniel Taplitz has come up with a magazine title that would probably work on the newsstands, and a book idea that would probably sell. Most magazines in movies are completely implausible (in *13 Going on 30*, the heroine redesigned the magazine as a school yearbook). And most best-sellers in the movies sound way too good to ever sell many copies.

Bride and Prejudice ★ ★ ★
PG-13, 110 m., 2005

Aishwarya Rai (Lalita Bakshi), Martin Henderson (Will Darcy), Naveen Andrews (Balraj), Indira Varma (Kiran Bingley), Nitin Chandra Ganatra (Mr. Kholi), Daniel Gillies (Johnny Wickham), Anupam Kher (Mr. Bakshi), Nadira Babbar (Mrs. Bakshi), Namrata Shirodkar (Jaya Bakshi), Meghna Kothari (Maya Bakshi), Peeya Rai Chowdhary (Lucky Bakshi), Marsha Mason (Will's Mother). Directed by Gurinder Chadha and produced by Deepak Nayar and Chadha. Screenplay by Paul Mayeda Berges and Chadha, inspired by Jane Austen's *Pride and Prejudice*.

Bollywood musicals are the Swiss Army knives of the cinema, with a tool for every job: comedy, drama, song and dance, farce, pathos, adventure, great scenery, improbably handsome heroes, teeth-gnashing villains, marriage-obsessed mothers and their tragically unmarried daughters, who are invariably ethereal beauties. "You get everything in one film," my friend Uma da Cuhna told me, as she took me to see *Taal* in Hyderabad. "No need to run around here and there, looking for a musical or an action picture." The movie lasted more than three hours, including an intermission, which Uma employed by correctly predicting everything that would happen during the rest of the film.

Bollywood, is, of course, Bombay—or Mumbai, as it is now called, although there has been no movement to rename the genre Mumblywood. Although Western exhibitors aren't crazy about a movie they can show only twice a night, instead of three times, Bollywood has developed a healthy audience in London, where the Bollywood Oscars were held a year ago. Now comes *Bride and Prejudice*, which adds the BritLit genre to the mix.

Directed by Gurinder Chadha, whose *What's Cooking?* (2000) and *Bend It Like Beckham* (2002) make you smile just thinking about them, this is a free-spirited adaptation of the Jane Austen novel, in which Mr. Darcy and the unmarried sisters and their family are plugged into a modern plot that spans London, New York, Bombay, and Goa. Darcy is an American played by Martin Henderson, and Lizzie Bennett becomes Lalita Bakshi, second of four daughters in Amritsar, India—true to Austen, a country town.

Lalita is played by Aishwarya Rai, Miss World of 1994, recently described by at least one film critic (me) as not only the first but also the second most beautiful woman in the world. According to the Internet Movie Database, "The Queen of Bollywood" is so popular she was actually able to get away with appearing in ads for both Coke and Pepsi. I also learn she carried the Olympic Torch in 2004, has a puppy named Sunshine, and was listed by *Time* as one of the 100 most influential people in the world. If this review is not accompanied by a photograph of her, you have grounds for a lawsuit.

Aishwarya (ash-waar-e-ah) Rai exudes not the frightening seriousness of a woman who thinks she is being sexy, but the grace and ease of a woman who knows she is fun to look at and be around. What a smile. What eyes. Rai is not remotely overweight, but neither is she alarmingly skinny; having deliberately gained twenty pounds for this role, she is the flower of splendid nutrition.

Sorry, I got a little distracted there. Gurinder Chadha, who was born in Kenya, raised in London, and is married to a Japanese-American, seems attracted to ethnic multitasking. Her *What's Cooking?* is set in Los Angeles and tells parallel stories about families with Vietnamese, African-American, Mexican, and Jewish roots. *Bend it Like Beckham* was about a London girl from a Kenyan family with Punjabi roots, who wants to play soccer.

In *Bride and Prejudice* Chadha once again transcends boundaries. This is not a Bollywood movie, but a Hollywood musical comedy incorporating Bollywood elements. Her characters burst into song and dance at the slightest provocation, backed up by a dance corps that materializes with the second verse and disappears at the end of the scene. That's Bollywood. So is the emphasis on the mother and father; the lovers in most American romantic comedies seem to be orphans. And she employs the Bollywood strategy for using color, which comes down to: If it's a color, use it.

Will Darcy (Henderson) is a rich young New York hotel man, visiting India because his old friend from London, Balraj (Naveen Andrews), is the best man at a wedding. The Bakshi family is friendly with the family of the bride, and Mrs. Bakshi (Nadira Babbar) hopes her four daughters can meet eligible husbands at the event. That strategy works immediately for Balraj and Jaya Bakshi (Namrata Shirodkar), Lalita's older sister. For them, it's love at first sight. For Darcy and Lalita, it's not.

Darcy makes tactless remarks, disagrees with the custom of arranged marriages, seems stuck-up, is distracted by business, and creates the possibility that Lalita may have to follow her mother's instructions and marry the

creepy Hollywood mogul Mr. Kholi (Nitin Chandra Ganatra). Things could be worse; Harvey Weinstein is also visiting India. We know Lalita won't really marry Mr. Kholi, since he is never provided with a first name, but in stories of this sort it's necessary for Darcy and Lalita to rub each other the wrong way, so that later they can rub each other the right way.

This plot, recycled from Austen, is the clothesline for a series of dance numbers that, like Hong Kong action sequences, are set in unlikely locations and use props found there; how else to explain the sequence set in, yes, a Mexican restaurant? Even the most strenuous dances are intercut with perfectly composed close-ups of Aishwarya Rai, never sweaty, never short of breath. What a smile. Did I say that?

Bridget Jones: The Edge of Reason ★ ★ ★
R, 108 m., 2004

Renee Zellweger (Bridget Jones), Hugh Grant (Daniel Cleaver), Colin Firth (Mark Darcy), Gemma Jones (Mum), Jim Broadbent (Dad), Jacinda Barrett (Rebecca), Sally Phillips (Shazzer), James Callis (Tom), Shirley Henderson (Jude). Directed by Beeban Kidron and produced by Tim Bevan, Jonathan Cavendish, and Eric Fellner. Screenplay by Andrew Davies, Helen Fielding, Richard Curtis, and Adam Brooks, based on the novel by Fielding.

You ever have the kind of friend where for a long time you shake your head in admiration, and then gradually realize you're shaking your head in despair? Bridget Jones would be a friend like that. She's hopelessly lovable, and she's always going to be your friend no matter what, but really, who but Bridget, with her guilt-ridden diary entries for alcohol and nicotine units per day, would manage to get jailed in Thailand on drug-smuggling charges?

Bridget, of course, is not a drug smuggler, but being Bridget she did the one thing no tourist should *ever* do, and that is to carry in her luggage a souvenir given to her girlfriend by a guy. But Bridget has pluck. In no time at all, she's traded her pink bra for cigarettes, organized her prison inmates into a Madonna class, and they're rehearsing "Like a Virgin."

Bridget Jones: The Edge of Reason is a jolly movie, and I smiled pretty much all the way through, but it doesn't shift into high with a solid thunk, the way *Bridget Jones' Diary* (2001) did. In the first movie, things happened to Bridget. In the sequel, Bridget happens to things.

As the story opens, Bridget is happily involved with Mark Darcy (Colin Firth), who to her astonishment became her boyfriend in the earlier film. Plump Bridget, in love with a hunk! She's still working as an on-air personality for a TV show which seems to be running its private version of *Fear Factor* just for Bridget; surely this girl is not ready to sky dive? Or ski? Or manage a romance without getting unreasonably jealous of the quality time Mark seems to be spending with his colleague Rebecca (Jacinda Barrett). But she loves the guy. Who else could keep him standing outside her door while she finishes leaving a message for him on his answering machine? Especially when the message is, essentially, that he is standing outside even as she speaks?

Bridget depends as before on the wisdom of three friends whose advice is infallibly dangerous. They are Shazzer (Sally Phillips), Tom (James Callis), and Jude (Shirley Henderson), and they support her when she and Mark have a completely unreasonable fight. Bridget flies off to Thailand on assignment, and discovers that her former boyfriend Daniel (Hugh Grant) is already there. This is a man she should never, ever, have anything to do with, but because she is mad at Mark she allows herself to be maneuvered into a position where Daniel can cry with glee: "Please! Please be wearing the giant panties!"

Renée Zellweger is lovable to begin with, and combining her with Bridget Jones creates a critical mass of cuteness: You don't want to just watch her, you want to tickle her ears and scratch under her chin. She has that desperately hopeful smile, and the endearing optimism of a woman in a dress two sizes too small. When she embarrasses herself, it's bigtime, as when she single-handedly causes Mark's table to lose the annual quiz at the Law Society dinner.

The scenes in Thailand, it must be said, venture beyond contrivance. Bridget is the kind of woman who is more at home dealing with the sorts of things that could happen to anybody, like dropping a rock Cornish game hen down the front of her dress. She isn't made for cocaine busts. And it's a little mystifying why Daniel and Mark, two relatively important and successful men no longer in their first youth, have *another* brawl over her. Their motivation, I think, is that the fight in the first movie was so funny. Hugh Grant is so good at losing his dignity that we forget what skillful acting it requires to assure us he has any. Colin Firth plays the basically good guy, never a plum role; rascals always have more fun in comedies.

Standing back from *Bridget Jones: The Edge of Reason,* I can see that the perfection of the first film has been replaced here by a series of comic episodes that could as easily be about anything else. The movie doesn't have the dire necessity of Bridget One's quest for true love. If we didn't know better, we'd suspect that Bridget Two subtly engineers her way into pickles because she knows how cute she looks when she gets in trouble. Still, at the end of the day, I left hoping there will be a Bridget Three. Long may she squint and bravely smile and keep tugging her neckline up and believe in love.

Bright Leaves ★ ★ ★
NO MPAA RATING, 107 m., 2004

A documentary, directed and produced by **Ross McElwee**. Screenplay by McElwee.

Two scenes from *Bright Leaves*. In the first, Ross McElwee visits the fifty-two-room Duke mansion in Charlotte, North Carolina. In the second, he sits on the only bench in a threadbare little park in Charlotte—McElwee Park, named after his great-grandfather. If things had worked out differently, he would be living in the mansion and the Dukes would be sitting on the bench.

McElwee is a great-grandson of John McElwee, who patented the famous line of Bull Durham tobacco. John McElwee and Washington Duke, founder of the Duke dynasty, were rivals at the birth of the modern tobacco industry, and Duke essentially destroyed McElwee (whose warehouse was burned down three times by suspicious fires). The Dukes went on to found Duke University. Three generations of John McElwee's descendants became doctors, and Ross became a documentarian who films introspective essays about his life.

Bright Leaves is not a documentary about anything in particular. That is its charm. It's a meandering visit by a curious man with a quiet sense of humor, who pokes here and there in his family history and the history of tobacco. The title refers to the particular beauty of tobacco leaves, both in the fields and after they have been cured, and perhaps also to the leaves of his family's history.

McElwee's odyssey begins with a second cousin, a fanatic film buff who is convinced that *Bright Leaf*, a 1950 movie starring Gary Cooper and Patricia Neal, was inspired by the rivalry of Washington Duke and John McElwee. There do seem to be a lot of parallels in its story of the triumph of one family over another. McElwee interviews Patricia Neal, who knows nothing about the origins of the story, but does helpfully volunteer that Cooper was "the love of my life." Then he tracks down Marian Fitz-Simons, the widow of the writer, who assures him her husband did not have real people in mind.

Well, maybe not, but the parallels are uncanny. Unwilling to entirely let go of his notion, McElwee wanders about the area where he grew up, remembering that his childhood home, while large and comfortable, was known as the "Dukes' outhouse." He ruminates on the addiction of smoking, which he has given up while still understanding its appeal. He chats with five beauty-school students as they puff away on the sidewalk outside their classes, and with a couple who give him their deadlines for stopping smoking: When they get married, after the millennium, whenever. He also visits people who are dying of cigarette-related illnesses, but he doesn't preach about the evils of tobacco; it's more that he regrets that such a beautiful plant, which produces so much pleasure, should be lethal. Think how happy it would make so many people if smoking were good for you.

McElwee's lifework is his life. He has been making autobiographical films since 1976,

taking as his subjects his father, his southern heritage, his favorite teacher, his marriage, his son, his prospects. His most famous work is *Sherman's March* (1986), which traces the footsteps of the Civil War general while musing about southernness and whatever else occurs along the way.

In all of his films, McElwee runs into people by chance, and pauses to film them. In *Bright Leaves*, one of his discoveries is Vlada Petric, a film historian he consults for information about the Gary Cooper film. Almost immediately, the subject becomes not Gary Cooper, but Vlada Petric, who refuses to be interviewed in one of those boring shots where the camera looks at a guy sitting in a chair. Instead, Petric orders McElwee to sit in a wheelchair with his hand-held camera, while Petric looms over him, pushing the chair backward while being interviewed. Petric is right and the shot is interesting, but not as interesting as the shots of Petric insisting on it.

Others we meet along the way include Charleen Swansea, the inspirational teacher who has been in several of McElwee's films, and now talks about her dying sister, a smoker made ill by cigarettes. He talks with a civic booster about Charlotte's Tobacco Festival and its annual parade, only to discover that, starting next year, it will be renamed Farmer's Day. He finds that local residents have "mixed feelings" about tobacco, which has been so good to them financially and yet killed so many along the way.

McElwee's films are always, in a way, about why he makes them. He looks at faded home movies of his father, trying to recapture his memories of the man, and then he films his son and wonders how the son will feel, someday, seeing this film. Always at his back he hears time's winged chariot, hurrying near, and is fascinated by the way film seems to freeze time, or at least preserve it. He doesn't really much care that his family lost an incalculable fortune to the Dukes; he is content to be who he is, doing what he does, and his motivation for making the film is not to complain, but simply to meditate on how events in the past reverberate in our own lives. He goes back to the park, and sits on the bench again. McElwee Park. It's not much, but it's something.

Bright Young Things ★ ★ ★ ½
R, 106 m., 2004

Stephen Campbell Moore (Adam Symes), Emily Mortimer (Nina), Fenella Woolgar (Agatha Runcible), James McAvoy (Simon Balcairn), Dan Aykroyd (Lord Monomark), Peter O'Toole (Colonel Blount), David Tennant (Ginger Littlejohn), Jim Broadbent (Drunken Major), Stockard Channing (Mrs. Melrose Ape). Directed by Stephen Fry and produced by Gina Carter and Miranda Davis. Screenplay by Fry, based on the novel *Vile Bodies* by Evelyn Waugh.

If *Bright Young Things* were set today in Manhattan, it would be about Paris and Nicky Hilton and their circle, Rupert Murdoch, the gossip writers of Page Six, and bloggers for sites like defamer.com. That might make a good movie. Certainly it would if it were done in the spirit of Stephen Fry's new film, based on Evelyn Waugh's *Vile Bodies* (1930), which has been called the funniest English novel of the century. Five or six books by Wodehouse may outrank it, but never mind; what's striking about the Fry version is how clearly he sees the underlying sadness. Until a few years ago he was a Bright Young Thing himself, and there may be elements of autobiography lurking here somewhere. "What a lot of parties!" one of the exhausted young things sighs late one night.

The story takes place in London and English country houses between the two wars, and, like Anthony Powell's *A Dance to the Music of Time*, occupies the intersection of the aristocratic, the rich, the ambitious, the decadent, the fraudulent, and the bohemian. The most important requirement for BYT membership is never to be boring, although one can often be bored. Alcoholism is the recommended lifestyle.

The hero, as so often in comic novels, is an earnest young man who wants to get married but lacks the money. Adam Symes (Stephen Campbell Moore) has great hopes for his new novel, having already spent his publisher's advance, and when his only manuscript is seized as pornography at customs, he is in despair. How can he marry the fragrant Nina (Emily Mortimer) without the money to support her in the style to which she wants to become accustomed? Nina loves him, truly she does, but she hates poverty more.

Adam moves in circles that spin more quickly after midnight, and is a friend of the titled but impoverished Lord Simon Balcairn (James McAvoy), who attends all the best parties and then, as Mr. Chatterbox, writes anonymous scandal about them for a popular newspaper. His publisher is Lord Monomark (Dan Aykroyd), a Canadian press baron who seems to combine the worst (and, it must be said, the best) qualities of Murdoch and Conrad Black, although Monomark is of course the original. Simon has a crisis when his friends discover his double-dealing, and he is uninvited to a crucial party; he implores his friend Adam to cover for him, Adam produces a sensational (if libelous) scoop, and Lord Monomark (who likes to print tonight and call the lawyers in the morning) gives him the Chatterbox column.

This provides Adam with the money to marry Nina, but of course he will lose and regain his stake several times during the film; Waugh's novel, like so much of Wodehouse, is about characters who are realistic about romance but idealistic about money. Adam's rival for the hand of Nina is Ginger Littlejohn (David Tennant), who has money but is boring. Too bad, but to be poor like Adam is boring, too, and if she has to choose, Nina would rather be bored in comfort.

These friends are like sparrows in the springtime, all landing on a branch, chattering deliriously, and then at an invisible signal fluttering off together to perch on another tree. They move from restaurants to clubs to private parties, from town to the country, often awakening hungover to discover that their genitals have misbehaved during a spell of drunken inattention. The most desperate in their circle is the movie's manic party animal, Agatha Runcible (Fenella Woolgar). In a scene that transcends invention and moves into inspired lunacy, Agatha is invited back to spend the night at the house of a tipsy new girlfriend, blunders into the breakfast room in the morning, and as those around the table regard her with horror, reads in the morning paper about where she spent (and is still spending) the night.

Like *The Great Gatsby*, the works of Dawn

Powell, Jay McInerney, and all the other novels about heedless romance and debauchery, *Bright Young Things* is about people who think they can live forever, and discover that to live forever in the way they are living is not only impossible but would become exhausting and discouraging. Agatha is the poster girl for this discovery. Adam and Nina are luckier, redeemed by pluck and optimism and, it must be admitted, their real love for each other (this despite Adam's offer at one point to sell his share in her to Ginger for £100; later in the movie, after another setback, she asks bravely, "Oh, dear, have I been sold again?").

Fry, who as a younger actor was the obvious choice to play Bertie Wooster's butler Jeeves (and did), is also the obvious choice to direct this material. He has a feel for it; to spend a little time talking with him is to hear inherited echoes from characters just like those in the story. He supplies a roll call of supporting actors who turn up just long enough to convince us entire movies could be made about their characters. Among these are Peter O'Toole (who here, and in *Troy*, steals his scenes almost kindly from his fellow actors); he plays Nina's decaying old pater, Lord Blount, who has a gift for saying what he thinks while not seeming to know what he's saying. Jim Broadbent pops up regularly as a perpetually drunken army officer who makes extravagant promises to Adam, gives him tips on race horses ("Indian Runner at 37-to-1"), promises him money, disappears for months at a time, seems likely to be a fraud, and always remembers what he said when he was loaded, even though that may be of no help to Adam. The only character who doesn't really fit in is Mrs. Ape (Stockard Channing), a religious zealot whose appeal to bright young things is questionable, especially while she sings "Ain't No Flies on the Lamb of God."

As pure comedy, *Bright Young Things* would be funny up to a point, and then repetitive. Waugh's novel and Fry's movie wisely see that their characters live by spending their comic capital and ending up emotionally overdrawn. They begin by being awake when everyone else is asleep, and end by being asleep while everyone else is awake. The funniest person in a bar is rarely the happiest. The movie has a sweetness and tenderness for these characters, poor lambs, blissfully unaware that they're about to be flattened by World War II.

Bringing Down the House ★ ★
PG-13, 105 m., 2003

Steve Martin (Peter Sanderson), Queen Latifah (Charlene Morton), Eugene Levy (Howie Rosenthal), Jean Smart (Kate Sanderson), Michael Rosenbaum (Todd Gendler), Betty White (Mrs. Klein), Joan Plowright (Mrs. Arness). Directed by Adam Shankman and produced by Ashok Amritraj and David Hoberman. Screenplay by Jason Filardi.

I confess I expected Steve Martin and Queen Latifah to fall in love in *Bringing Down the House*. That they avoid it violates all the laws of economical screenplay construction, since they are constantly thrown together, they go from hate to affection, and they get drunk together one night and tear up the living room together, which in movies of this kind is usually the closer.

But, no, all they fall into is Newfound Respect, which, in a world of high-performance star vehicles, is the minivan. Eugene Levy is brought off the bench to console the Queen, and Martin ends up back with his divorced wife (Jean Smart), who exists only so that he can go back to her. These two couples had better never double-date, because under the table Queen and Steve are going to have their socks up each other's pants.

Why, I asked myself, is their mutual sexual attraction disguised as roughhousing when they are the stars, and movie convention demands that they get it on? There isn't a shred of chemistry between Latifah and Levy (who likes the Queen's wildness and is infatuated with her cleavage, which is understandable but shallow—his infatuation, not her cleavage). I think it's because the movie, coproduced by Latifah, was making a point, which is that the rich white lawyer had better learn to accept this bitch on her own terms instead of merely caving in to her sex appeal. This may be a point worth making, but not in a comedy.

I use the word "bitch" after some hesitation, to make a point: The movie is all about different ethnic styles of speech. It uses the B-word constantly (along, of course, with lots of "hos"), and I argue that since the MPAA rates the language PG-13, I can use it in a review. You kids under thirteen who are reading this better be getting parental guidance from a POS.

(Emergency definition: POS [n., slang]. Abbreviation used in teenage chat rooms, warning person at other end: "Parent over shoulder!")

Martin plays Peter Sanderson, a high-powered lawyer with a trophy ex-wife who lives in a posh Los Angeles neighborhood and speaks with meticulous precision he elevates to a kind of verbal constipation. Queen Latifah plays Charlene Morton, whom he meets in an Internet chat room, where she is LawyerGirl.

They both misrepresent their appearance—well, all right, she's guiltier than he is—and when they meet he's appalled to find, not a blond legal bimbo, but a trash-talking black ex-con who wants him to handle her case. Charlene *can* talk like a perfect middle-class lady, as she demonstrates, but the movie's point of pride is that she shouldn't have to. Peter can also talk like a black street dude, sort of. Maybe he learned it from his kids' rap records.

The movie's conceit is that Peter keeps throwing Charlene out and she keeps coming back because she's determined to prove her legal innocence. She breaks into his house, throws wild parties, embarrasses him at his club, and so on, until a magic night when she gets him drinking and dancing, plants his hands squarely on what Russ Meyer used to rhapsodically refer to as garbanzos, and breaks down his inhibitions. At this point—what? Wild nuzzling, rapturous caresses, shredded knickers, wild goat cries in the night? Peter takes her case, that's what, while Eugene Levy crawls out of his eyebrows and joins the tag team.

This is all wrong. It violates the immortal Stewart/Reagan principle: Steve Martin for Latifah, Eugene Levy for best friend. A comedy is not allowed to end with the couples incorrectly paired. It goes against the deeply traditional requirements of the audience. Here is a movie that ignores the Model Airplane Rule: First, make sure you have taken all of the pieces out of the box, then line them up in the order in which they will be needed. *Bringing Down the House* is glued together with one of the wings treated like a piece of tail.

Broken Lizard's Club Dread ★ ★ ½

R, 103 m., 2004

Jay Chandrasekhar (Putman), Steve Lemme (Juan), Paul Soter (Dave), Britanny Daniel (Jenny), Erik Stolhanske (Sam), Kevin Heffernan (Lars), M. C. Gainey (Hank), Greg Cipes (Trevor), Bill Paxton (Coconut Pete). Directed by Jay Chandrasekhar and produced by Richard Perello. Screenplay by Broken Lizard.

Broken Lizard's Club Dread is a definitive demonstration, if one is needed, that *The Real Cancun* was way too real. Filmed in Mexico but allegedly set on Coconut Pete's Pleasure Island off the coast of Costa Rica, it's a head-on smashup between spring break weekend and a machete-swinging slasher. Whether it works or not is a little hard to say; like *Super Troopers* (2001), the previous film by the Broken Lizard comedy troupe, it has lovable performances, very big laughs, and then some downtime while everybody (in the cast as well as the audience) waits to see what will happen next.

The leader of the troupe and director of both films is Jay Chandrasekhar, whose character in *Super Troopers* delighted in spreading confusing hints about his ethnic origin. Here he's the dreadlocked Indian (or perhaps British or Caribbean) tennis instructor, whose serve is so powerful that at one point he actually tries to kill the slasher by hitting balls at him.

Pleasure Island is run by Coconut Pete (Bill Paxton), who very briefly, a long time ago, had a record that was a hit for five minutes. It was called "Pina Colada-berg," and who knows what heights it might have reached on the charts had it not been for the treachery of "Margaritaville." Pete presides over an endless boozy sex-'n'-sand party that looks recycled out of every other movie ever made about beach blanket bingo, and if there is a babe (the film's preferred word) who ever wears anything other than a bikini, my memory fails me.

Alas, this island idyll is marred by the presence of a mad slasher, who stalks about garbed as if he (or she) once saw *I Know What You Did Last Summer* but either forgot how the fisherman dressed, or the costume supply store ran out of Groton's outfits. How a killer can roam a small tropical island dressed like Death in *The*

Seventh Seal and never be noticed is one of the many questions this movie answers by keeping the bar open twenty-four hours a day.

The cast includes a cop in charge of enforcing fun, a six-foot-one Swedish masseuse who turns out, to intense disappointment, to be a six-foot-two Swedish masseur, and an aerobics instructor whose best exercises are horizontal. Characters are periodically killed, and at one point a severed head turns up on the deejay's turntable, but the fun goes on because these characters, while admittedly brighter and more articulate than the real people in *The Real Cancun,* realize that the slightest insight would solve the mystery and terminate the movie right then and there, and if we paid for feature length, that's what we deserve.

Do I recommend this movie or not? I am at a loss to say. It is what it is. Criticism is irrelevant. Why are you even reading a review of *Club Dread?* You've seen the TV ads and you already know (a) you won't miss it or (b) not in a million years. There will be better movies playing in the same theater, even if it is a duplex, but on the other hand there is something to be said for goofiness without apology by broken lizards who just wanna have fun. I think I'll give it two and a half stars plus a nudge and a wink, as a signal to those who liked *Super Troopers* and know what they're in for. I gave *Super Troopers* two and a half stars, too, but I'd rather see it again than certain distinguished movies I could mention.

Brother Bear ★ ★ ★
G, 86 m., 2003

With the voices of: Joaquin Phoenix (Kenai), Jeremy Suarez (Koda), Jason Raize (Denahi), Rick Moranis (Rutt), Dave Thomas (Tuke), D. B. Sweeney (Sitka), Joan Copeland (Tanana), Michael Clarke Duncan (Tug), Harold Gould (Old Denahi). Directed by Aaron Blaise and Robert Walker and produced by Chuck Williams. Screenplay by Steve Bencich, Ron J. Friedman, Tab Murphy, Lorne Cameron, and David Hoselton.

Disney's *Brother Bear* is more mystical and New Age than your average animated movie about animals, although it does have a couple of talking moose and a cute cubby bear. It's ambitious in its artistry, incorporating images from prehistoric cave paintings and playing with the screen width. But it doesn't have the zowie factor of *The Lion King* or *Finding Nemo,* and is sweet rather than exciting. Children and their parents are likely to relate on completely different levels, the adults connecting with the transfer of souls from man to beast, while the kids are excited by the adventure stuff.

The story begins in a Native American tribe in the Pacific Northwest, thousands of years ago. We meet three brothers: brave older brother Sitka (D. B. Sweeney), strong-willed middle brother Denahi (Jason Raize), and the troublesome young Kenai (voice by Joaquin Phoenix). Each wears a totem around his neck, representing the animal spirit he is identified with. Sitka wears an eagle, Denahi a wolf, and Kenai—well, Kenai gets a bear, and considers himself shortchanged, especially when he's told that the bear represents the quality of love, which he considers pretty far down, so to speak, on the totem pole.

Kenai doesn't like bears, and picks a fight with one that tries to steal his fishing catch; he recklessly chases the bear, and when Sitka tries to protect him, the older brother is killed and is transformed into an eagle. Kenai is counseled by the tribe's wise man, Tanana (Joan Copeland), to accept this outcome as the will of the universe, but he determines to kill the bear. He succeeds, but the universe proves it has a sense of justice, or perhaps of humor, by transforming Kenai himself into a bear—so that Denahi assumes it was Bear Kenai who killed Kid Brother Kenai. Denahi continues the family tradition of vengeance by tracking down Bear Kenai, in an irony that is positively Shakespearean, and no wonder, since I learn that this story was originally inspired by *King Lear,* although the notion of three siblings seems to be all that survived.

The opening scenes are in a conventional screen ratio of 1:85 to 1, but after Kenai becomes a bear, the colors deepen and the screen widens to 2:35 to 1, so you'd better hope your projectionist is on his toes. Given Kenai's prejudices about bears, he is extremely unhappy to be one himself, but soon he's getting bear lessons from little Koda (Jeremy Suarez), a cub who shows him the ropes. Kenai discovers from the spirit of Tanana that he must seek Eagle Sitka on a mountain where light touches the Earth, and Koda leads him on the mission—perhaps because he really knows where the mountain is, perhaps for reasons of his own.

Their trek there involves many adventures, including a scary encounter with flowing lava from a volcano. Two Canadian moose named Rutt and Tuke turn up and have conversations that sound amazingly like the MacKenzie Brothers from SCTV, maybe because they are voiced by Rick Moranis and Dave Thomas. The outcome of the story, which I would not dream of revealing, has Kenai making a career choice that is far from practical but certainly shows he has learned to see things from a bear's point of view.

Note: The movie, a product of the same Orlando animation studio that produced Disney's Mulan *and* Lilo & Stitch, *is very good-looking, and sometimes seems to want to burst through the boundaries of conventional animation to present a more visionary portrait of its time and place; a sequence involving cave drawings comes impressively to life. There's also a curious early moment when the animators reproduce the effects of sunlight refracting through a lens, even though animation uses no lens and refracts no light.* Variety *says this will be the last 2-D animated film from Disney for the foreseeable future; the studio is switching to the 3-D style originally popularized by Pixar. Both formats have their strengths; one is not better than the other, simply different.*

Brothers ★ ★ ★ ½
R, 110 m., 2005

Connie Nielsen (Sarah), Ulrich Thomsen (Michael), Nikolaj Lie Kaas (Jannik), Bent Mejding (Henning), Solbjorg Hojfeldt (Else). Directed by Susanne Bier and produced by Sisse Graum Olsen. Screenplay by Anders Thomas Jensen, based on the story by Bier.

Jannik has always been the embarrassment of the family, an aimless younger brother who, as *Brothers* opens, is being released from prison after committing a crime hardly worth his time and effort. Was he breaking the law simply to play his usual role in the family drama?

Michael is the good brother, a loving husband, a responsible father, a man who does his duty. When his Danish military unit is sent to Afghanistan, he goes without complaint, because he sees it as the right thing to do. Within a shockingly short time, his helicopter is shot down, and his wife, Sarah, is told he was killed.

Jannik, with no better choice, tries to do what he sees as his duty: to be kind to Sarah, to be a good uncle to the children, to help around the house. In subtle ways that are never underlined, he starts acting from a different script in his life; with Michael gone, a vacancy has been created in the family, and Jannik steps into it. Now he is the person you can trust.

It is not a spoiler to reveal that Michael was not killed in the helicopter crash, but captured by Afghan enemies. This is made clear very early; the movie is not about mysteries and suspense, but about behavior. As a prisoner he is treated badly, but his real punishment comes when his captors force an impossible choice upon him. If he wants to save his own life, he will have to take the life of a fellow prisoner, a man he likes, who is counting on him.

Strangely enough, this parallels Paul Schrader's *Dominion*, in which a priest is told that if he doesn't choose some villagers to be killed, the whole village will die. Michael's choice is more direct: Either he will die, or the other prisoner will. In theory, Michael should choose death. Not so clear is what the priest should have done; theology certainly teaches him to do no evil, but does theology account for a world where good has been eliminated as a choice?

Michael saves his own life; let the first stones be cast by those who would choose to die. Eventually he is freed and returns home to find things somehow different. He is no longer able to subtly condescend to his screwed-up little brother because Jannik has changed. And Michael has changed too. Sarah senses it immediately. There is a torment in him that we know is an expression of guilt.

It shows itself in strange ways: in his anger, for example, about the new kitchen cabinets that Jannik installed in his absence, and at the love the children have for their uncle. And in Michael's own relentlessly growing jealousy. "It's all right if you did," he tells his brother, "since you both thought I was dead. But I have to know: Did you make love?"

The answer to the question is simple (and perhaps not the one you expect). The meaning of the answer is very tricky, because Michael is a time bomb, waiting to explode. He has lost his view of himself in Afghanistan, and back at home in Denmark he cannot find it again, perhaps because the way is blocked by Jannik.

The movie was directed by Susanne Bier, who wrote a story that was turned into a screenplay by Anders Thomas Jensen. They worked together once before, on *Open Hearts* (2003), the story of a couple engaged to be married when the young man is paralyzed from the neck down in a senseless accident. Will she still love him? Will she stay with him? How does he feel about that? Bier and Jensen are drawn to situations in which every answer leads to a question.

The central performance in *Brothers* is by Connie Nielsen, as Sarah, who is strong, deep, and true. You may remember her from *The Devil's Advocate* and *Gladiator*. What is she doing in a Danish movie? She is Danish, although this is her first Danish film.

The brothers are Ulrich Thomsen as Michael and Nikolaj Lie Kaas as Jannik. Both have to undergo fundamental transformations, and both must be grateful to Bier and Jensen for not getting all psychological on them. *Brothers* treats the situation as a real-life dilemma in which the characters behave according to how they are made and what they are capable of doing.

Like *Open Hearts,* this is the kind of movie that doesn't solve everything at the end—that observes some situations are capable not of solution but only of accommodation. That's more true to life than the countless movies with neat endings—happy endings, and even sad ones. In the world, sometimes the problem comes and stays forever, and the question with the hardest answer is, well, okay, how are you going to live with it?

The Brown Bunny ★ ★ ★
NO MPAA RATING, 92 m., 2004

Vincent Gallo (Bud Clay), Chloe Sevigny (Daisy), Cheryl Tiegs (Lilly), Elizabeth Blake (Rose), Anna Vareschi (Violet), Mary Morasky (Mrs. Lemon). Directed and produced by Vincent Gallo. Screenplay by Gallo.

In May 2003, I walked out of the press screening of Vincent Gallo's *The Brown Bunny* at the Cannes Film Festival and was asked by a camera crew what I thought of the film. I said I thought it was the worst film in the history of the festival. That was hyperbole—I hadn't seen every film in the history of the festival—but I was still vibrating from one of the most disastrous screenings I had ever attended.

The audience was loud and scornful in its dislike for the movie; hundreds walked out, and many of those who remained stayed only because they wanted to boo. Imagine, I wrote, a film so unendurably boring that when the hero changes into a clean shirt, there is applause. The panel of critics convened by *Screen International,* the British trade paper, gave the movie the lowest rating in the history of their annual voting.

But then a funny thing happened. Gallo went back into the editing room and cut 26 minutes of his 118-minute film, or almost a fourth of the running time. And in the process he transformed it. The film's form and purpose now emerge from the miasma of the original cut, and are quietly, sadly effective. It is said that editing is the soul of the cinema; in the case of *The Brown Bunny,* it is its salvation.

Critics who saw the film last autumn at the Venice and Toronto festivals walked in expecting the disaster they'd read about from Cannes. Here is Bill Chambers of Film Freak Central, writing from Toronto: "Ebert catalogued his mainstream biases (unbroken takes: bad; nonclassical structure: bad; name actresses being aggressively sexual: bad) . . . and then had a bigger delusion of grandeur than *The Brown Bunny*'s Gallo-centric credit assignations: 'I will one day be thin, but Vincent Gallo will always be the director of *The Brown Bunny*.'"

Faithful readers will know that I admire long takes, especially by Ozu, that I hunger for nonclassical structure, and that I have absolutely nothing against sex in the cinema. In quoting my line about one day being thin, Chambers might in fairness have explained that I was responding to Gallo calling me a "fat pig"—and, for that matter, since I made that statement I have lost eighty-six pounds and Gallo is indeed still the director of *The Brown Bunny*.

But he is not the director of the same *Brown Bunny* I saw at Cannes, and the film now plays so differently that I suggest the original Cannes cut be included as part of the eventual DVD, so that viewers can see for themselves how twenty-six minutes of aggressively pointless and empty footage can sink a potentially successful film. To cite but one cut: From Cannes, I wrote: "Imagine a long shot on the Bonneville Salt Flats where he races his motorcycle until it disappears as a speck in the distance, followed by another long shot in which a speck in the distance becomes his motorcycle." In the new version we see the motorcycle disappear, but the second half of the shot has been completely cut. That helps in two ways: (1) It saves the scene from an unintended laugh, and (2) it provides an emotional purpose, since to disappear into the distance is a much different thing than to ride away and then ride back again.

The movie stars Gallo as Bud Clay, a professional motorcycle racer who loses a race on the East Coast and then drives his van cross-country. (The race in the original film lasted 270 seconds longer than in the current version, and was all in one shot, of cycles going around and around a track.) Bud is a lonely, inward, needy man, who thinks much about a former lover whose name in American literature has come to embody idealized, inaccessible love: Daisy.

Gallo allows himself to be defenseless and unprotected in front of the camera, and that is a strength. Consider an early scene where he asks a girl behind the counter at a convenience store to join him on the trip to California. When she declines, he says "please" in a pleading tone of voice not one actor in a hundred would have the nerve to imitate. There's another scene not long after that has a sorrowful poetry. In a town somewhere in the middle of America, at a table in a park, a woman (Cheryl Tiegs) sits by herself. Bud Clay parks his van, walks over to her, senses her despair, asks her some questions, and wordlessly hugs and kisses her. She never says a word. After a time he leaves again. There is a kind of communication going on here that is complete and

heartbreaking, and needs not one word of explanation, and gets none.

In the original version, there was an endless, pointless sequence of Bud driving through Western states and collecting bug splats on his windshield; the eight and a half minutes Gallo has taken out of that sequence were as exciting as watching paint after it has already dried. Now he arrives sooner in California, and there is the now-famous scene in a motel room involving Daisy (Chloe Sevigny). Yes, it is explicit, and no, it is not gratuitous.

But to reveal how it works on a level more complex than the physical would be to undermine the way the scene pays off. The scene, and its dialogue, and a flashback to the Daisy character at a party, work together to illuminate complex things about Bud's sexuality, his guilt, and his feelings about women. Even at Cannes, even after unendurably superfluous footage, that scene worked, and I wrote: "It must be said that [Sevigny] brings a truth and vulnerability to her scene that exists on a level far above the movie it is in." Gallo takes the materials of pornography and repurposes them into a scene about control and need, fantasy, and perhaps even madness. That scene is many things, but erotic is not one of them. (A female friend of mine observed that Bud Clay, like many men, has a way of asking a woman questions just when she is least prepared to answer them.)

When movies were cut on Movieolas, there was a saying that they could be "saved on the green machine." Make no mistake: The Cannes version was a bad film, but now Gallo's editing has set free the good film inside. *The Brown Bunny* is still not a complete success—it is odd and off-putting when it doesn't want to be—but as a study of loneliness and need, it evokes a tender sadness. I will always be grateful I saw the movie at Cannes; you can't understand where Gallo has arrived unless you know where he started. ☞

Bruce Almighty ★ ★ ★
PG-13, 95 m., 2003

Jim Carrey (Bruce Nolan), Jennifer Aniston (Grace), Morgan Freeman (God), Lisa Ann Walter (Debbie), Philip Baker Hall (Jack Keller), Catherine Bell (Susan Ortega), Steven Carell

(Evan Baxter), Nora Dunn (Ally Loman), Sally Kirkland (Waitress). Directed by Tom Shadyac and produced by Michael Bostick, James Brubaker, and Shadyac. Screenplay by Steve Oedekerk, Steve Koren, and Mark O'Keefe.

There is about Jim Carrey a desperate urgency that can be very funny, as he plunges with manic intensity after his needs and desires. In *Bruce Almighty,* he plays a man for whom the most important thing on Earth is to become an anchor on the Buffalo TV station. When he fails to achieve this pinnacle, he vents his anger at the very heavens themselves, challenging God to show and explain himself.

One could argue that Bruce Nolan, Carrey's character, is not necessarily qualified to be anchor, on the basis of two remote reports we see him delivering, one from the scene of a chocolate chip cookie of record-breaking size, the other from onboard an anniversary cruise of the *Maid of the Mist,* the famous Niagara Falls tour boat. During the cruise he learns, while on the air live, that he will not be getting the coveted anchor job, and he goes ballistic, even uttering the dread f-word in his dismay.

Now that may argue that he is a loose cannon and not fit to anchor anyway (although he would be replacing a man whose primary skill seems to be smiling). Nevertheless, in anger and grief, and facing the loss of the love of his faithful girlfriend, Grace (Jennifer Aniston), he calls upon God, and God answers.

God is, in this case, a man in a white suit, played by Morgan Freeman with what can only be described as godlike patience with Bruce. Since Bruce is so dissatisfied with the job God is doing, God turns the controls of the universe over to him—or at least, the controls over his immediate neighborhood in Buffalo, although at one point this limited power seems to extend directly above Buffalo to such an extent that Bruce is able to change the distance of the moon, causing tidal waves in Japan.

Bruce Almighty, directed by Tom Shadyac and written by Steve Oedekerk, Steve Koren, and Mark O'Keefe, is a charmer, the kind of movie where Bruce learns that while he may not ever make a very good God, the experience may indeed make him a better television newsman.

The problem with playing God, the movie demonstrates, is that when such powers are entrusted to a human, short-term notions tend to be valued higher than long-term improvement plans. Consider, for example, the way Bruce deals with a dog that pees in the house (the payoff shot, showing the dog learning a new way to use the newspaper, had me laughing so loudly people were looking at me). And consider Bruce's methods for dealing with traffic jams, which work fine for Bruce but not so well for everyone else; when you're God, you can't think only of yourself.

Morgan Freeman plays God with a quality of warm detachment that is just about right, I think. You get the feeling that even while he's giving Bruce the free ride, he has a hand on the wheel, like a driver's training instructor. Jennifer Aniston, as a sweet kindergarten teacher and fiancée, shows again (after *The Good Girl*) that she really will have a movie career, despite the small-minded cavils of those who think she should have stayed on television. She can play comedy, which is not easy, and she can keep up with Carrey while not simply mirroring his zaniness; that's one of those gifts like being able to sing one song while typing the words to another.

Whether *Bruce Almighty* is theologically sound, I will leave to the better qualified. My own suspicion is that if you have God's power, even in a small area like Buffalo, it's likely to set things spinning weirdly everywhere. If a butterfly can flap its wings in Samoa and begin a chain of events leading to a tropical storm in the Caribbean, think what could happen when Bruce goes to work.

Bubba Ho-Tep ★ ★ ★
R, 92 m., 2003

Bruce Campbell (Elvis), Ossie Davis (Jack Kennedy), Ella Joyce (Nurse), Reggie Bannister (Administrator), Bob Ivy (Bubba Ho-Tep), Larry Pennell (Kemosabe), Heidi Marnhout (Callie), Harrison Young (Bull Thomas). Directed by Don Coscarelli and produced by Coscarelli and Jason R. Savage. Screenplay by Coscarelli, based on the short story by Joe R. Lansdale.

Elvis and JFK did not die, and today they're in an east Texas nursing home whose residents are being killed by an ancient Egyptian Soul Sucker named Bubba Ho-Tep. I want to get that on the table right at the get-go, so I can deal with the delightful wackiness of this movie, which is endearing and vulgar in about the right proportion. The movie doesn't exactly work, but sometimes when a car won't start it's still fun to look at the little honey gleaming in the driveway.

The movie's backstory: Elvis (Bruce Campbell) became sick of his lifestyle, his buddies, his groupies, his pills, his songs, his movies, and his Colonel Parker. He struck a deal with an Elvis impersonator to trade places. There's even a contract guaranteeing that Elvis can switch back if he changes his mind, but the contract is burned up in a barbecuing accident, and by then Elvis doesn't mind anyway, because he enjoys the freedom of performing just for the sheer joy, without the sideshow of fame.

The King explains all of this in a thoughtful, introspective voice-over narration that also deals with other matters on his mind, such as the alarming pustule on that part of his anatomy where it is least welcome. He talks about Priscilla and Lisa Marie, about his movies (not a single good one), about his decision to disappear, and about how he broke his hip falling off a stage. This narration is not broad comedy, but wicked, observant, and truthful. *Bubba Ho-Tep* has a lot of affection for Elvis, takes him seriously, and—this is crucial—isn't a camp horror movie but treats this loony situation as if it's really happening.

The man in the room down the hall is John F. Kennedy, played by Ossie Davis. "But, Jack . . . ," Elvis says hesitantly, "you're black." JFK nods in confirmation. When his assassination was faked by Lyndon B. Johnson, "they dyed me." Now the two old men wait for death in their hospital beds, Elvis on a stroller, JFK using a motorized wheelchair for longer trips, talking about what was and wasn't.

The rest home is almost a character in the movie, with its drab institutional corridors, its condescending nurse (Ella Joyce), its supercilious administrator (Reggie Bannister), its worn-out furniture, its flying cockroaches, its sense of being half-deserted. Pleasures here are hard to come by. "Let's get decadent," says JFK, opening his drawer and revealing a horde of Baby Ruth candy bars.

The cockroaches turn out to be giant scarab beetles worshiped by the ancient Egyptians, and that's a clue for JFK, who has been reading up on these matters and realizes that the nursing home is under attack by a Soul Sucker. He explains to Elvis that the soul can be sucked out of any orifice, but souls are small, so you need to suck a lot of them. The two men have a thoughtful conversation about whether a soul, after it is digested, leaves anything to be eliminated through the Soul Sucker's intestinal track. This sounds right: A lot of rest home conversations get around sooner or later to constipation.

The closing scenes of the movie show the two geezers in a fight to the finish with Bubba Ho-Tep (Bob Ivy), who looks like a threadbare version of the Mummy. Here the movie could get laughs by showing the old men with unexpected powers, but no: When Elvis tries out his old karate moves, it's disastrous. Assuming that elderly versions of Elvis and JFK ever really did do battle with an Egyptian Soul Sucker, this, I am forced to conclude, is more or less how it would look.

Of course there are laughs in the movie, which is a comedy, but an odd one. The movie was written and directed by Don Coscarelli, based on a short story by Joe R. Lansdale, the "mojo storyteller" from Nacogdoches, Texas. Coscarelli made the four *Phantasm* pictures, three unseen by me, the fourth unloved. What drew him to this material is not a mystery—the story sounds juicy enough—but what inspired him to tell it in this tone? *Bubba Ho-Tep* wants to be a *good* movie about Elvis, JFK, and the Soul Sucker. It doesn't sneer, it's not about cheap shots, it is perfectly sincere.

You never catch Campbell or Davis winking at the audience or patronizing the material. They approach their characters with all the curiosity and respect they'd deserve in a serious film. Campbell sounds uncannily like Elvis might sound by now, and looks more like Elvis than anyone else I've seen in the role. Davis, of course, looks not at all like JFK, but I don't think we're really supposed to think he is JFK; one of the movie's sweet touches is the way Elvis just takes him at his word and proceeds from there.

I said the movie doesn't work. And so it doesn't. How *could* it work? It doesn't work as a horror movie because a Bubba Ho-Tep monster would make Ed Wood's monsters look slick by comparison. It doesn't work as a cult movie because it challenges the cleverness of the audience instead of congratulating it. It doesn't work as a traditional story arc because the story jumps the rails when Bubba Ho-Tep turns up.

But it does sort of work in one way: It has the damnedest ingratiating way of making us sit there and grin at its harebrained audacity, laugh at its outhouse humor, and be somewhat moved (not deeply, but somewhat) at the poignancy of these two old men and their situation. Elvis asks himself how in the world the King of Rock 'n' Roll ended up in a run-down east Texas nursing home with a boil on the family treasure, and by the end of the movie he has answered this excellent question more amusingly than any reasonable moviegoer could have expected.

Buffalo Soldiers ★ ★ ★

R, 98 m., 2003

Joaquin Phoenix (Ray Elwood), Anna Paquin (Robyn Lee), Ed Harris (Colonel Wallace Berman), Scott Glenn (Sergeant Robert Lee), Dean Stockwell (General Lancaster), Elizabeth McGovern (Mrs. Berman), Gabriel Mann (Knoll). Directed by Gregor Jordan and produced by Rainer Grupe and Ariane Moody. Screenplay by Eric Weiss, Nora MacCoby, and Jordan, based on the book by Robert O'Connor.

Buffalo Soldiers is a black comedy about larceny, theft, drug dealing, adultery, and a cheerful dereliction of duty among U.S. Army troops stationed in Germany in 1989. Although they know how to cook drugs and sell missile launchers on the black market, when the Berlin Wall falls there is a discussion about where Berlin is, and whether they are currently in East or West Germany.

This strain of irreverent Army misbehavior runs in various forms from *Catch-22* to *Apocalypse Now* to *M*A*S*H* to *Beetle Bailey* and in happier times the movie might have opened without controversy. But it premiered three days before 9/11 at the 2001 Toronto Film Festival, and as *Variety*'s critic Todd McCarthy wrote a day or two later, "All of a sudden, this looks like the wrong film at the wrong time."

Is now the right time? Maybe it's time to observe that *Buffalo Soldiers* is not about all soldiers at all times, but about those soldiers at

that time—some of them, like company clerk Ray Elwood (Joaquin Phoenix), in uniform because the judge gave them a choice between jail and enlisting. Elwood is a crafty, high-living hustler who steals everything from Mop-n-Glo to missiles, whose men process drugs on the base, who drives a Mercedes, and who has his commander completely buffaloed. In an early scene, Colonel Berman (Ed Harris) and Elwood discuss a letter home to the parents of a soldier whose actual death was not exactly as in-the-line-of-duty as their description of it.

This seems to be the wackiest base in the army. During a session of tank maneuvers, the crew of one tank, zonked out of their minds, steer their tank away from the training field and through a nearby village market before causing a gas station explosion. Elwood and his men, who come upon the scene and find the unlucky drivers of two army trucks burned dead, think quickly and steal the trucks.

Here and elsewhere, Elwood is cold, amoral, and not very likable. We're used to rogues in uniform whom we like because they give the finger to authority, but Phoenix makes Elwood a calculating schemer who isn't a rebel for fun, but for profit. Consider his sex life. He is the secret lover of Colonel Berman's wife (Elizabeth McGovern), and later starts dating Robyn (Anna Paquin), the teenage daughter of the company's new top sergeant, Robert Lee (Scott Glenn).

This sergeant is a piece of work. Lean and unforgiving as only Glenn can make him, the new top is a Vietnam veteran who quickly figures out Elwood is a thief (the Mercedes is a clue), and methodically sets out to make life miserable for him. Elwood tries to bribe him, but to say that doesn't work is an understatement. And when he starts dating the top's daughter, it's war between the two men—made more complicated because, to his astonishment, Elwood actually starts to like Robyn.

The dark climax of the movie, involving an enormous amount of drugs and money, leads to an ending that is a little too melodramatic— and then to an epilogue that some find too upbeat, although the more you consider it, the more downbeat it becomes. The film is filled with spot-on performances, by Harris, Glenn, and Phoenix, and by Anna Paquin, who has grown up after her debut in *The Piano* to become one of the most gifted actresses of her generation—particularly in tricky, emotion-straddling roles like this one.

To be sure, the movie is not a patriotic hymn to our fighting forces. It illustrates an ancient tradition best summarized in that classic army acronym SNAFU. At a time when the idea of patriotism is sometimes used to stifle dissent, it is important to remember that gripes and disgruntlement and antiauthoritarian gestures are part of our national heritage. I do not approve of Elwood or even much like him, but I think he represents a type, and Gregor Jordan's film is dark enough to suggest that sometimes such types prevail.

Bukowski: Born Into This ★ ★ ★ ½
NO MPAA RATING, 130 m., 2004

A documentary directed and produced by John Dullaghan.

Charles Bukowski was blessed, as if to compensate for everything else, with the most beautiful smile. It was, as more than one woman probably told him, his best feature. When he was not smiling he was craggy at best; when he was angry he was unlovely. His early years, punctuated by regular beatings from his father, were scarred by acne so disfiguring it left him with a face pitted like the surface of the moon. He told a friend about standing outside his school prom—he didn't dare to ask a girl to be his date—with his pimply face wrapped in toilet paper, holes cut for the eyes, blood seeping through.

He was twenty-four when he had sex for the first time. She was a 300-pound prostitute. He remembers her name. As he tells the story, he does an extraordinary thing. He blushes. Here was a man who made a living and became a legend by being hard-boiled, and he blushes, and in that moment we glimpse the lonely, wounded little boy inside.

John Dullaghan's *Bukowski: Born Into This* is a documentary about the poet and novelist who died in 1994. It draws from many interviews, from footage of poetry readings and from the testimony of his friends, who include Sean Penn, Harry Dean Stanton, Bono, and the publisher John Martin, who started Black Sparrow Press specifically to publish

Bukowski's work. There are also the memories of his wife, Linda Lee Bukowski, who loved him and cared for him, despite scenes like one in the film where he kicks her and curses at her.

That was the booze talking, you could say, except when precisely was Bukowski sober? He drank with dedication and abandon for most of his adult years, slowed only by illness toward the end. And he chain-smoked little cigarettes named Mangalore Ganesh Beedies. "You can get them in any Indian or Pakistani store," he told me in 1987. "They're what the poor, poor people smoke in India. I like them because they contain no chemicals and no nicotine, and they go very well with red wine."

Linda Lee Bukowski, it must be said, possessed extraordinary patience to put up with him, but then she understood him, and his life was often as simple as that: a plea for understanding. I sense from his work and from a long day spent with him that even when he was drunk and angry, obscene and hurtful, he was not the aggressor; he was fighting back.

The movie opens with Bukowski on a stage for a reading, very drunk, threatening to come down into the audience and kick some ass. There is another reading where, backstage, he asks the organizer, "You got a little pot on the stage I can vomit in?" He drank most every day, red wine his preference, and his routine usually included a visit to the track, a return home, and long hours at his typewriter with classical music on the radio. For all of his boozing, he was, like the prodigious Thomas Wolfe, amazingly productive.

He wrote poems as if the words were bricks to be laid. He cut through the labyrinthine, indulgent difficulty of much modern verse, and wrote poems anyone could understand. Yet they *were* poems, real poems, and the film director Taylor Hackford remembers the first time he heard Bukowski reading; he was presented by Lawrence Ferlinghetti, one of the founding Beats, at Ferlinghetti's City Lights Bookstore in San Francisco—where to this day you can find a shelf of Bukowski, most of it with the bold Black Sparrow lettering on the spine.

John Martin, the publisher, says he offered Bukowski a monthly stipend to live on, with the condition that he quit his job at the post office. One of his first novels was *Post Office*, a snarl at the daily torture of hard work under stupid bureaucrats. It snarled, yes, but it also sang, and was romantic and funny. It came directly from Bukowski's life, as did such autobiographical novels as *Women* and *Hollywood.*

The Hollywood book was inspired by his experiences when his *Barfly* was adapted into a movie starring Mickey Rourke and Faye Dunaway. He didn't like the movie much—he thought Rourke was a "showoff." I thought it was a good movie, and wondered if part of his dislike was because he was played by a handsome man who had never suffered the agonies of being Charles Bukowski. It is probably also true that in his barfly days he was rarely fortunate enough to be the lover of a woman who looked like Faye Dunaway.

On the set one day, Dunaway turned up to question him, doing research on the character she would play.

"This woman," she asked him, "what would she put under her pillow?"

"A rosary."

"What sort of perfume did she wear?"

He looked at her incredulously.

"Perfume?"

I can testify to the way his life became his fiction because the day I spent on the set of the movie became part of *Hollywood,* and the movie critic in the book is a fair enough portrait of me. Central to his fiction and poetry was his lifelong love-hate relationship with women; by the time his fame began to attract groupies, he complains, "it was too late."

The movie is valuable because it provides a face and a voice to go with the work. Ten years have passed since Bukowski's death, and he seems likely to last, if not forever, then longer than many of his contemporaries. He outsells Kerouac and Kesey, and his poems, it almost goes without saying, outsell any other modern poet on the shelf.

How much was legend, how much was pose, how much was real? I think it was all real, and the documentary suggests as much. There were no shields separating the real Bukowski, the public Bukowski, and the autobiographical hero of his work. They were all the same man. Maybe that's why his work remains so immediate and affecting: The wounded man is the man who writes, and the wounds he writes about are his own.

Bulletproof Monk ★ ★
PG-13, 103 m., 2003

Chow Yun-Fat (Monk with No Name), Seann William Scott (Kar), Jamie King (Jade/Bad Girl), Karel Roden (Struker), Victoria Smurfit (Nina), Patrick Hagarty (Mr. Funktastic). Directed by Paul Hunter and produced by Terence Chang, Charles Roven, John Woo, and Douglas Segal. Screenplay by Ethan Reiff and Cyrus Voris, based on the comic book by Brett Lewis and RA Jones.

Let us first consider the Scroll of the Ultimate. "Whoever reads it aloud in its entirety," an ancient monk explains to his young acolyte, "will gain the power to control the world." It is Tibet in 1943. The Nazis are there to capture the Scroll of the Ultimate. We recall from *Raiders of the Lost Ark* that the Third Reich was also trying to capture the Ark of the Covenant, perhaps so that Leni Riefenstahl, Hitler's favorite filmmaker, could direct *The Scroll of the Ultimate vs. the Ark of the Covenant,* a title I have just registered with the Writers Guild.

The young acolyte accepts responsibility for the Scroll and renounces his name, becoming the Monk with No Name, a name Clint Eastwood should have registered with the Writers Guild. No sooner does the Monk (Chow Yun-Fat) take possession than the sky churns with sensational visual effects, high winds blow, and the Nazis attack the temple. The Monk escapes by jumping off a high cliff, after first taking a Nazi bullet, which hits him right in the Scroll. He survives the jump, as he later explains, because gravity exists only if you think it does.

Since he walks around on the ground a lot, apparently he thinks it does, most of the time. The knack is to learn how to turn your belief on and off. Sixty years later, which is how long any one monk can guard the Scroll, the Monk is in New York City when he happens upon a pickpocket named Kar (Seann William Scott). Kar is working the subway, and has indeed just picked the Scroll from the Monk's briefcase, when he is forced into the subterranean lair of a gang of young toughs who look as dangerous as the crowd in a leather bar on date night. This gang is led by Mr. Funktastic (Patrick Hagarty), who has his name tattooed across his chest, and also

95

includes the beautiful Bad Girl (Jamie King), who turns out to be a good girl. Kar engages in a violent martial arts struggle with the gang for a long time, after which they stop, because the scene is over, and Mr. Funktastic issues a dire warning should Kar ever stray their way again. Like he wants to hang out down there in the subterranean lair.

The Monk with No Name has secretly observed the fight, perhaps because Mr. Funktastic's men failed to notice the arrival of an unexpected monk, and he becomes friends with Kar, who seems to fit the Three Prophecies made about the one who will be chosen to guard the Scroll for the next sixty years. Of course, Kar is a reckless youth and must learn much about life, and meanwhile the Nazis turn up again and at one point have the Monk with No Name strapped to a torture machine crucifix-style, and are about to screw things into his brain.

Bulletproof Monk is a cross between a traditional Hong Kong martial arts movie and various American genres, incorporating the dubious notion that the wisest and most skilled practitioners of the ancient Asian arts have nothing better to do than tutor young Americans. To be sure, Kar has been studying on his own. "Where do you study fighting?" the Monk asks him. "The Golden Palace," he says. This is the broken-down movie palace where he is the projectionist, and he copies the moves from old karate movies.

The fight scenes in *Bulletproof Monk* are not as inventive as some I've seen (although the opening fight on a rope bridge is so well done that it raises expectations it cannot fulfill). The film demonstrates, *Matrix*-style, that a well-trained fighter can leap into the air and levitate while spinning dozens of times, although why anyone would want to do this is never explained. Chow Yun-Fat and Seann William Scott do as much with the material as they can, although it's always a little awkward trying to shoehorn a romance into a movie like this, especially when you have to clear time for Bad Girl and Nina (Victoria Smurfit), who is a third-generation Nazi and the real bad girl, to have their obligatory hand-to-hand combat.

Bulletproof Monk was written by Ethan Reiff and Cyrus Voris, based on the comic book by Brett Lewis and RA Jones, and will appeal to more or less the same audience as the comic book. The ads and trailer hope we confuse it with *Crouching Tiger, Hidden Dragon,* but this is more like the Young Readers' version.

Bus 174 ★ ★ ★ ½
NO MPAA RATING, 122 m., 2003

A documentary directed by Felipe Lacerda and José Padilha and produced by Padilha and Marcos Prado.

On June 12, 2000, a man named Sandro do Nascimento tried to rob the passengers on a bus in Rio de Janeiro, eventually took them hostage, and initiated a crisis that was televised live and ended in tragedy. *Bus 174* re-creates that crime with TV news footage, interviews with survivors and police, memories of those who knew the young man, and insights into the million or more homeless who live on the streets of Rio.

Sandro do Nascimento is not merely poor, or hungry, or doomed to poverty, but suffers from the agonizing psychic distress of being invisible. Yes, says the movie, literally invisible: Brazilians with homes and jobs go about their lives while unable to see people like Sandro, who exists in a parallel universe. In North America we have similar blindness. One of the blessings of the *Streetwise* paper in Chicago is that it provides not only income for its vendors, but also visibility; by giving them a role, it gives us a way to relate to them—to see them, to nod, to say a word or two, whether or not we buy the paper.

Bus 174 opens with a news bulletin about the attempted robbery on the bus and then, as the bus is surrounded by police and the robber takes hostages, provides details about do Nascimento's early life. He saw his mother shot dead in a robbery. His father was not in the picture. He lived on the streets, and survived an infamous police massacre of homeless who used a downtown square as a sleeping area. He had been in jail. We listen to a social worker who talks of the boy's dreams—of how he wanted to find a job and have a home.

Meanwhile, negotiations continue in the hostage situation. Several of the police who were involved (one hooded and his voice disguised) talk about their decisions and mistakes. After do Nascimento threatened to kill hostages—and after police for a time thought he had killed one—there were many opportunities for a sniper to take him out with one shot. He walked around in plain view, sometimes not close to his hostages, but the police didn't act until the crisis reached a climax in the evening.

By that point in the film we know a lot about the human refuse of Rio's streets. And we have seen one of the most horrifying sequences I've witnessed in a movie. The camera goes inside a crowded jail, where the prisoners press their faces against the bars and shout out their urgent protests against the inhuman conditions they endure. Cells are so crowded that the prisoners must live in shifts, half lying down while the other half stand. The temperature is over 100 degrees. The food is rotten, the water is dirty, disease runs quickly through the cells, and some prisoners are left for months or years without charges being filed; they have been forgotten.

The director, José Padilha, films this scene with a digital camera, using the negative mode that switches black with white. The faces behind the bars cry out to us like souls in hell; nothing in the work of Bosch or the most abysmal horror films prepares us for these images. A nation that could permit these conditions dare not call itself civilized. Since prisoners are the lowest inhabitants of any society, how the society treats them establishes the bottom line of how it regards human beings. That prisons like this exist in Brazil makes it less surprising that the streets are filled with the lost and forgotten.

The conclusion of *Bus 174* is both surprising and inevitable. The bus hijacking captured the public's attention in a way that dramatized the plight of the homeless, and the film, by documenting the conditions of Sandro do Nascimento and countless others, shows that the journey began long before the passengers boarded the bus.

If you have seen the masterful 2002 Brazilian film *City of God* or the 1981 film *Pixote*, both about the culture of Rio's street people, then *Bus 174* plays like a sad and angry real-life sequel. Fernando Ramos Da Silva, the young orphan who played Pixote, died on the streets some years after the film was made, and do Nascimento in a sense stands for him—and for countless others.

The Butterfly Effect ★ ★ ½
R, 113 m., 2004

Ashton Kutcher (Evan Treborn), Amy Smart (Kayleigh Miller), William Lee Scott (Tommy Miller), Elden Henson (Lenny), Eric Stoltz (George Miller), Kevin Schmidt (Lenny at Thirteen), Melora Walters (Andrea Treborn), John Patrick Amedori (Evan at Thirteen), Cameron Bright (Tommy at Eight). Directed by Eric Bress and J. Mackye Gruber and produced by Chris Bender, A. J. Dix, Anthony Rhulen, Lisa Richardson, and J. C. Spink. Screenplay by Bress and Gruber.

Chaos theory teaches us that small events can have enormous consequences. An opening title informs us that a butterfly flapping its wings in Asia could result in a hurricane halfway around the world. Yes, although given the number of butterflies and the determination with which they flap their little wings, isn't it extraordinary how rarely that happens? *The Butterfly Effect* applies this theory to the lives of four children whose early lives are marred by tragedy. When one of them finds he can go back in time and make changes, he tries to improve the present by altering the past.

The characters as young adults are played by Ashton Kutcher, as Evan, a college psych major; Amy Smart and William Lee Scott as Kayleigh and Tommy, a brother and sister with a pedophile father; and Elden Henson as Lenny, their friend. The story opens in childhood, with little Evan seriously weird. His drawings in kindergarten are sick and twisted (and also, although nobody ever mentions it, improbably good for a child). He has blackouts, grabs kitchen knives, frightens his mother (Melora Walters), becomes a suitable case for treatment.

A shrink suggests that he keep a daily journal. This he does, although apparently neither the shrink nor the mother ever read it, or their attention might have been snagged by entries about how Mr. Miller (Eric Stoltz), father of Kayleigh and Tommy, forced them all to act in kiddie porn movies. Evan hangs onto the

97

journals, and one day while reading an old one at school he's jerked back into the past and experiences a previously buried memory.

One thing he'd always done, after moving from the old neighborhood, was to promise Kayleigh "I'll come back for you." (This promise is made with handwriting as precocious as his drawing skills.) The flashbacks give him a chance to do that, and eventually he figures out that by reading a journal entry, he can return to that page in his life and relive it. The only problem is, he then returns to a present that is different than the one he departed from—because his actions have changed everything that happened since.

This is a premise not unknown to science fiction, where one famous story by Ray Bradbury has a time traveler stepping on a butterfly millions of years ago and wiping out humanity. The remarkable thing about the changes in *The Butterfly Effect* is that they're so precisely aimed: They apparently affect only the characters in the movie. From one reality to the next, Kayleigh goes from sorority girl to hooker, Evan zaps from intellectual to frat boy to prisoner, and poor Lenny spends some time as Kayleigh's boyfriend and more time as a hopeless mental patient.

Do their lives have no effect on the wider world? Apparently not. External reality remains the same, apart from minute adjustments to college and prison enrollment statistics. But it's unfair to bring such logic to bear on the story, which doesn't want to *really* study the butterfly effect, but simply to exploit a device to jerk the characters through a series of startling life changes. Strange, that Evan can remember everything that happened in the alternate lifetimes, even though by the theory of

the movie, once he changes something, they didn't happen.

Ashton Kutcher has become a target lately; the gossip press can't forgive him for dating Demi Moore, although that is a thing many sensible young men dream of doing. He was allegedly fired from a recent film after the director told him he needed acting lessons. Can he act? He can certainly do everything that's required in *The Butterfly Effect*. He plays a convincing kid in his early twenties, treating each new reality with a straightforward realism when most actors would be tempted to hyperventilate under the circumstances.

The plot provides a showcase for acting talent, since the actors have to play characters who go through wild swings (even Evan's mom has a wild ride between good health and death's door). And there's a certain grim humor in the way the movie illustrates the truth that you can make plans, but you can't make results. Some of the futures Evan returns to are so seriously wrong from his point of view that he's lucky he doesn't just disappear from the picture, having been killed at fifteen, say, because of his meddling.

I enjoyed *The Butterfly Effect*, up to a point. That point was reached too long before the end of the movie. There's so much flashing forward and backward, so many spins of fate, so many chapters in the journals, that after a while I felt that I, as well as time, was being jerked around. Eric Bress and J. Mackye Gruber, the cowriters and directors, also collaborated on *Final Destination 2* (2003), another film in which fate works in mysterious ways, its ironies to reveal. I gave that one half a star, so *The Butterfly Effect* is five times better. And outside, the wind is rising . . .

C

Cabin Fever ★ ½
R, 94 m., 2003

Rider Strong (Paul), Jordan Ladd (Karen), Joey Kern (Jeff), Cerina Vincent (Marcy), James DeBello (Bert), Arie Verveen (The Hermit), Giuseppe Andrews (Deputy Winston). Directed by Eli Roth and produced by Roth, Lauren Moews, Sam Froelich, and Evan Astrowsky. Screenplay by Randy Pearlstein and Roth.

Unsure of whether it wants to be a horror film, a comedy, an homage, a satire, or a parable, *Cabin Fever* tries to cover every base; it jumps around like kids on those arcade games where the target lights up and you have to stomp on it. It assembles the standard package of horror heroes and heroines (sexy girl, nice girl, stalwart guy, uncertain guy, drunk guy) and takes them off for a postexam holiday in the woods where things get off to a bad start when a man covered with blood comes staggering out of the trees.

What they eventually figure out is that the man has some kind of disease—for which we could, I suppose, read AIDS or SARS—and it may be catching. When the nice girl (Jordan Ladd) comes down with the symptoms, they lock her in a shed, but before long they're all threatened, and there is a scene where the sexy girl (Cerina Vincent) is shaving her legs in the bathtub and finds, eek, that she's shaving a scab.

The film could develop its plague story in a serious way, like a George Romero picture or *28 Days Later*, but it keeps breaking the mood with weird humor involving the locals. Everyone at the corner general store seems seriously demented, and the bearded old coot behind the counter seems like a racist (when at the end we discover that he isn't, the payoff is more offensive than his original offense). There's a deputy sheriff named Winston (Giuseppe Andrews) who is a seriously counterproductive character; the movie grinds to an incredulous halt every time he's onscreen.

The drama mostly involves the characters locking the door against dogs, the locals, and each other; running into the woods in search of escape or help; trying to start the truck (which, like all vehicles in horror films, runs only when the plot requires it to), and having sex, lots of sex. The nature of the disease is inexplicable; it seems to involve enormous quantities of blood appearing on the surface of the skin without visible wounds, and then spreading in wholesale amounts to every nearby surface.

If some of this material had been harnessed and channeled into a disciplined screenplay with a goal in mind, the movie might have worked. But the director and coauthor, Eli Roth, is too clever for his own good, and impatiently switches between genres, tones, and intentions. There are truly horrible scenes (guy finds corpse in reservoir, falls onto it), over-the-top horrible scenes (dogs have eaten skin off good girl's face, but she is still alive), and just plain inexplicable scenes (Dennis, the little boy at the general store, bites people). By the end, we've lost all interest. The movie adds up to a few good ideas and a lot of bad ones, wandering around in search of an organizing principle.

Calendar Girls ★ ★ ★
PG-13, 108 m., 2003

Helen Mirren (Chris Harper), Julie Walters (Annie Clark), John Alderton (John Clark), Linda Bassett (Cora), Annette Crosbie (Jessie), Philip Glenister (Lawrence), Ciaran Hinds (Rod Harper), Celia Imrie (Celia), Geraldine James (Marie), Penelope Wilton (Ruth). Directed by Nigel Cole and produced by Nick Barton and Suzanne Mackie. Screenplay by Tim Firth and Juliette Towhidi.

You may have read about it at the time. A British woman's club, trying to raise money for charity, hit on the idea of having its members pose nude for a pinup calendar. The women were eminently respectable and of a certain age, the photographs were modest if not chaste, and the calendar was an enormous hit, raising something like $1 million for the local hospital.

Calendar Girls retells the story in a very slightly risqué comedy. Every press mention makes the inevitable reference to *The Full Monty*, but this movie is not as bawdy and only about 10 percent as monty. It's the kind of sweet, good-humored comedy that used to star Margaret Rutherford, although Helen Mirren and Julie Walters, its daring top-liners, would have curled Dame Margaret's eyebrows.

People sometimes ask me whether I see the movies in "real theaters" or screening rooms—"or do the studios send them to your home?" (Fat chance of that with the piracy paranoia.) I usually say it doesn't much matter; once the movie starts, if it works, it upstages the venue. But I cannot resist telling you that I saw *Calendar Girls* at the Locarno (Switzerland) Film Festival, under the stars in the Piazza Grande, with 12,000 other people, including the presidents of Switzerland and Germany.

A setting like that might have overwhelmed *The Lord of the Rings*, and here was a modest little British comedy. Interesting, how the story was so straightforward and universal that it played perfectly well, got laughs in all the right places, and left maybe 10,000 of us pleased, if not overwhelmed.

The movie begins at a Yorkshire village chapter of the Women's Institute, a community organization widespread in the UK and Canada, where we watch the members nodding through lectures on, if I recall correctly, the private life of the broccoli. Mirren plays Chris Harper, a high-spirited woman who finds a porno magazine in her son's bedroom, sees a girlie calendar on the wall at the local garage, puts two and two together, and gets her big idea.

Some of the women are appalled and others are titillated, but all of them have the first thought any reasonable person over forty would have: How will I look nude? Luckily the W.I.'s long tradition of flower arranging, trellis construction, and greenhouse repair suggests an endless number of foreground items that can obscure the naughty bits, in the tradition of Austin Powers.

Walters plays Chris's best pal Annie, whose husband, John (John Alderton), dies of leukemia early in the film, supplying a cause for the fund-raising. There is, of course, opposition, supplied by reactionary elements in the local and national W.I., and Mirren makes a speech to the national convention that Winston Churchill would have been proud of. (In real life, apparently, everyone thought the calendar was a great idea, but a movie, as Robert McKee teaches us, needs obstacles to overcome.)

After the calendar becomes a best-seller, the calendar girls promote a North American version with a trip to Los Angeles and an appearance on the Jay Leno show; of course fame goes to their heads a little, for a while, but that plot point also suggests the strong hand of McKee. Actually, this is a very simple story: A cute idea caught the fancy of a lot of people, and raised a bundle for charity.

That the movie works, and it does, is mostly because of the charm of Mirren and Walters, who show their characters having so much fun that it becomes infectious. *Calendar Girls* was directed by Nigel Cole, who also made *Saving Grace* (2000), the comedy starring Brenda Blethyn as a new widow who supports herself by growing marijuana in her cottage garden. That one also went for laughs with some naked middle-aged ladies dashing around, but this one is gentler to the ladies, and thank God for the flower arrangements.

Callas Forever ★ ★ ½
NO MPAA RATING, 108 m., 2004

Fanny Ardant (Maria Callas), Jeremy Irons (Larry Kelly), Joan Plowright (Sarah Keller), Jay Rodan (Michael), Gabriel Garko (Marco), Manuel de Blas (Esteban Gomez), Justino Diaz (Scarpia), Jean Dalric (Gerard). Directed by Franco Zeffirelli and produced by Riccardo Tozzi and Giovannella Zannoni. Screenplay by Zeffirelli and Martin Sherman.

In 1977, when she is fifty-three and near the end of her life, the great diva Maria Callas is approached by a man who directed some of her greatest performances. He wants to film her in *Carmen*. Impossible! she says, playing him a tape of her final concert, in Tokyo, where the great voice was in ruins. His idea: Use the Callas of today and the voice of Callas in her prime. "But—it's dishonest!" she says. Still, since almost all European movies until recent years were lip-synched anyway, it is not such a transgression as it seems, and it would at least make possible the great opera film that Callas never made.

This fictional story, told in *Callas Forever*, has parallels with real life. Franco Zeffirelli, who directed and cowrote the film, directed Callas on stage in *Norma*, *La Traviata*, and *Tosca*. In 1964, he directed her TV special

"Maria Callas at Covent Garden," and he remained a friend of the singer until the end. In addition to his famous feature work like *Romeo and Juliet* (1967), he directed several films of operas, notably *La Traviata* (1982) and *Pagliacci* (1982) with Placido Domingo and Teresa Stratas, and *Cavalleria Rusticana* (1982) and *Otello* (1986) with Domingo. He must have dreamed of one grand final film for Callas, and might even have spoken with her about it.

What else in the movie is based on fact, we cannot know. Terrence McNally's play *Master Class*, which shows Callas teaching opera students, shows her at a similar time in her life, but the story structure of *Callas Forever* is original, and pointed in another direction. It is perhaps Zeffirelli's consolation for the film he was never able to make. (It is small consolation, however, for Faye Dunaway, who starred powerfully in *Master Class* for a year and dreamed of making a film version of the play.)

Callas is played in *Callas Forever* by Fanny Ardant, that tall, grave French actress with the facial structure of a Greek heroine (one thinks of Irene Papas in *Electra*). Ardant (who starred in Paris in *Master Class*) cannot sing, but then neither could Callas at the time. What she does have is the fiery passion needed for *Carmen*, and Zeffirelli stages several scenes from the opera in the style, we can only assume, that he would have used had he made the actual film. These show Callas in her impetuous, imperious, man-scorning pride, physically dominating the production. And the voice is . . . Callas.

The visual style is all Zeffirelli, and it is interesting that the opera-within-the-film is not skimped on, as is usually the case in films containing scenes from other productions. Indeed, most of the budget seems to have gone to the moments of *Carmen* that we see; they look sumptuous and robust, and the surrounding film looks, well, like a low-budget art movie.

Callas shares the story with Larry Kelly (Jeremy Irons), probably meant to be Zeffirelli, a hardworking professional director, gay, whose infatuation with a young man named Michael (Jay Rodan) seems like a slight embarrassment, and seems meant to be; he drags Callas over to the youth's studio to look at his paintings, and Callas praises him because she knows that at some level Larry has to deliver her as part of his romantic bargain with Michael. These scenes are a distraction, and slow down the main line of the movie.

Ardant excels at playing a temperamental diva, whose entrances transform a room, who is instantly the center of attention, who gives orders and expects to be obeyed. This is all true to life. Callas was famous in a way no other twentieth-century opera singer was famous, and she deserved her fame, not only for the toll she paid through her celebrated liaison with Aristotle Onassis, but also because her voice was called the voice of the century, and that may have been true.

Her problems with *Carmen* involve more than the dubbed sound track. She is concerned about how she looks. Half-persuaded she should let her fans remember her as she was. Uncertain about a flirtation with a young man on the set. And, for that matter, just generally flighty on principle, as a diva has a right to be.

The Larry Kelly character is patient, flattering, persuasive, insidious. To his credit, he seems to want to make the film not so much for himself as to collaborate with Callas on a film she should have made and never did. But there is a crucial moment when he visits her apartment late at night and sees her singing along with her recordings and then sobbing, and he realizes that anyone who sang as Callas did must always live with the pain of having lost her gift.

Callas Forever reminded me a little of two documentaries by Maximilian Schell, *Marlene* (1984) and *My Sister Maria* (2002). Both were about great beauties, now reclusive. His friend Marlene Dietrich refused to be seen on camera. His sister Maria did not. Dietrich made the wiser decision, and in *Callas Forever* we are asked to decide if Callas does too.

Note: It is amusing, in a movie where dubbing is one of the subjects, that the opening airport scene is so poorly dubbed.

Capturing the Friedmans ★ ★ ★ ½
NO MPAA RATING, 107 m., 2003

Featuring Arnold Friedman, David Friedman, Elaine Friedman, and Jesse Friedman.

A documentary directed by Andrew Jarecki and produced by Jarecki and Marc Smerling.

After the Sundance screenings of *Capturing the Friedmans*, its director, Andrew Jarecki, was asked point-blank if he thought Arnold Friedman was guilty of child molestation. He said he didn't know. Neither does the viewer of this film. It seems clear that Friedman is guilty in some ways and innocent in others, but the truth may never be known—may not, indeed, be known to Friedman himself, who lives within such a bizarre personality that truth seems to change for him from moment to moment.

The film, which won the Grand Jury Prize at Sundance 2003, is disturbing and haunting, a documentary about a middle-class family in Great Neck, Long Island, that was torn apart on Thanksgiving 1987 when police raided their home and found child pornography belonging to the father. Arnold was a popular high school science teacher who gave computer classes in his basement den, which is where the porn was found—and also where, police alleged, he and his eighteen-year-old son, Jesse, molested dozens of young boys.

Of the porn possession there is no doubt, and in the film Arnold admits to having molested the son of a family friend. But about the multiple molestation charges there is some doubt, and it seems unlikely that Jesse was involved in any crimes.

As Jarecki's film shows the Friedmans and the law authorities who investigated their case, a strange parallel develops: We can't believe either side. Arnold seems incapable of leveling with his family, his lawyers, or the law. And the law seems mesmerized by the specter of child abuse to such an extent that witnesses and victims are coached, led, and cajoled into their testimony; some victims tell us nothing happened, others provide confused and contradictory testimony, and the parents seem sometimes almost too eager to believe their children were abused. By the end of the film there is little we can hang onto, except for our conviction that the Friedmans are a deeply wounded family, that Arnold seems capable of the crimes he is charged with, and that the police seem capable of framing him.

Our confusion about the facts is increased, not relieved, by another extraordinary fact: All during the history of the Friedmans, and even during the period of legal investigations, charges, and court trials, the family was video-taped by another son, David. A third son, Seth, is visible in some of this footage, but does not otherwise participate in the film. At the very time when Arnold is charged with possession of child porn, when the abuse charges make national headlines, when his legal strategy is being mapped and his and Jesse's trials are under way, David is there, filming with the privileged position of a family insider. We even witness the last family council on the night before Arnold goes to prison.

This access should answer most of our questions, but does not. It particularly clouds the issue of Jesse's defense. It would appear—but we cannot be sure—that he was innocent but pled guilty under pressure from the police and his own lawyer, who threaten him with dire consequences and urge him to make a deal. Given the hysteria of the community at the time, it seems possible he was an innocent bystander caught up in the moment.

The dynamics within the family are there to see. The mother, Elaine, who later divorced and remarried, seems in shock at times within a family where perception and reality have only a nodding acquaintance. She withdraws, is passive-aggressive; it's hard to know what she's thinking.

Arnold is so vague about his sexual conduct that sometimes we can't figure out exactly what he's saying. He neither confirms nor denies. Jesse is too young and shell-shocked to be reliable. The witnesses contradict themselves. The lawyers seem incompetent. The police seem more interested in a conviction than in finding the truth. By the end of *Capturing the Friedmans*, we have more information, from both inside and outside the family, than we dreamed would be possible. We have many people telling us exactly what happened. And we have no idea of the truth. None.

The film is an instructive lesson about the elusiveness of facts, especially in a legal context. Sometimes guilt and innocence are discovered in court, but sometimes, we gather, only truths about the law are demonstrated. I am reminded of the documentaries *Paradise Lost* and *Paradise Lost 2: Revelations*, which involve the trials of three teenage boys charged with the murders of three children. Because the boys were outsiders, dressed in black, listened to heavy metal, they were perfect suspects—and were convicted amid hysterical allegations of "satanic rituals," even while the obvious prime suspect appears in both films doing his best to give himself away. Those boys are still behind bars. Their case was much easier to read than the Friedman proceedings, but viewers of the films are forced to the conclusion that the law and the courts failed them.

Carandiru ★ ★ ★
R, 148 m., 2004

Luiz Carlos Vasconcelos (Doctor), Milton Goncalves (Chico), Ivan de Almeida (Ebony), Ailton Graca (Majestade), Maria Luisa Mendonca (Dalva), Aide Leiner (Rosirene), Rodrigo Santoro (Lady Di), Gero Camilo (No Way). Directed by Hector Babenco and produced by Babenco and Oscar Kramer. Screenplay by Babenco, Fernando Bonassi, and Victor Navas, based on the book *Estacao Carandiru* by Dr. Drauzio Varella.

In the Brazilian documentary *Bus 174*, there is a scene that could have been shot in hell. Using the night-vision capability of a digital camera, the film ventures into an unlit Brazilian prison to show desperate souls reaching through the bars. Jammed so closely they have to sit down in shifts, with temperatures above 100 degrees Fahrenheit, with rotten food and dirty water, many jailed without any charges being filed, they cry out for rescue.

Hector Babenco's *Carandiru* is a drama that adds a human dimension to that Dantean vision. Shot on location inside a notorious prison in São Paolo, it shows 8,000 men jammed into space meant for 4,000, and enforcing their own laws in a place their society has abandoned. The film, based on life, climaxes with a 1992 police attack on the prison during which 111 inmates were killed.

How this film came to be made is also a story. Babenco is the gifted director of *Pixote, Kiss of the Spider Woman,* and *At Play in the Fields of the Lord.* An illness put him out of action for several years, and he credits his doctor, Drauzio Varella, with saving his life. As it hap-

pens, Varella was for years the physician on duty inside the prison, and his memoir *Carandiru Station* inspired Babenco to make this film, with Varella as his guide.

What we see at first looks like lawless anarchy. But as characters develop and social rules become clear, we see that the prisoners have imposed their own order in the absence of outside authority. The prison is run more or less by the prisoners, with the warden and guards looking on helplessly; stronger or more powerful prisoners decorate their cells like private rooms, while the weak are crammed in head to toe. Respected prisoners act as judges when crimes are committed. A code permits homosexuality but forbids rape. And the prison has such a liberal policy involving conjugal visits that a prisoner with two wives has to deal with both of them on the same day. Some prisoners continue to function as the heads of their families, advising their children, counseling their wives, approving marriages, managing the finances.

Dr. Varella, played in the film by Luiz Carlos Vasconcelos, originally went to Carandiru when AIDS was still a new disease; he lectures on the use of condoms, advises against sharing needles, but is in a society where one of his self-taught assistants sews up wounds without anesthetic or sanitation. The prisoners come to trust the doctor and confide in him, and as some of them tell their stories, the movie flashes back to show what they did to earn their sentences.

In a prison filled with vivid, Dickensian characters, several stand out. There is, for example, the unlikely couple of Lady Di (Rodrigo Santoro), tall and muscular, and No Way (Gero Camilo), a stunted little man. They are the great loves of each other's lives. Their marriage scene is an occasion for celebration in the prison, and later, when the police murder squads arrive, it is No Way, the husband, who fearlessly uses his little body to protect the great hulk of his frightened bride. Their story and several others are memorably told, although the film is a little too episodic and meandering.

Although there are weapons everywhere in the prison, the doctor walks unarmed and without fear, because he is known and valued. The warden is not so trusted, and with good reason. After a prison soccer match ends in a fight that escalates into a protest, he stands in the courtyard, begs for a truce, and asks the inmates to throw down their weapons. In an astonishing scene, hundreds or even thousands of knives rain down from the cell windows. And then, when the prisoners are unarmed, the police attack.

The movie observes laconically that the police were "defending themselves," even though 111 prisoners and no police were killed. The prison was finally closed in 2002, and the film's last shot shows it being leveled by dynamite. Strange, how by then we have grown to respect some of the inmates and at least understand others. *Bus 174* is a reminder that although Carandiru has disappeared, prison conditions in Brazil continue to be inhuman.

Casa de los Babys ★ ★ ★
R, 95 m., 2003

Daryl Hannah (Skipper), Marcia Gay Harden (Nan), Mary Steenburgen (Gayle), Rita Moreno (Señora Muñoz), Lili Taylor (Leslie), Maggie Gyllenhaal (Jennifer), Susan Lynch (Eileen), Vanessa Martinez (Asunción). Directed by John Sayles and produced by Hunt Lowry, Alejandro Springall, and Lemore Syvan. Screenplay by Sayles.

Casa de los Babys gets its title from a motel in an unnamed South American country where American women wait while the local adoption process slowly matches them with babies. "They're making us pay for our babies with the balance of trade," complains the always-critical Nan (Marcia Gay Harden), as the days and weeks go by. The women shop, sunbathe, go out to lunch, and gossip about each other, and we eavesdrop on conversations that are sometimes cynical, sometimes heartbreaking.

The movie was written and directed by John Sayles, the conscience of American independent filmmaking, who doesn't package it with a neat message because there is nothing easy to be said about the adoption industry. We meet local mothers who have given up their babies for adoption, and local radicals who oppose adoption for ideological reasons, but we also see young children living on the streets.

In one of the movie's most effective passages, two women, one Irish, one Latino, tell the stories of their own longings in monologues. Neither one can understand a word of the other's language, but somehow the emotion comes through. Eileen (Susan Lynch, from Sayles's *The Secret of Roan Inish*) and Asunción (Vanessa Martinez, from his *Lone Star*) speak quietly, inwardly, and we feel the deep pools of emotion they draw from.

Another extraordinary scene is by Daryl Hannah, as Skipper, an athletic woman who is forever running on the beach while the others look on from behind sunglasses and margaritas. One day, as she is giving another woman a massage, she begins to talk about her three miscarriages, and as she names her babies (Cody, Joshua, and Gabriel) we feel how deeply and personally she misses each one.

Nan, the Marcia Gay Harden character, is less sentimental. She won't pay local prices ("bargaining is an accepted part of the culture"), uses pressure to move herself to the head of the line, and steals handfuls of toiletries from the maids' carts. "We don't like her," agree Gayle and Leslie (Mary Steenburgen and Lili Taylor). They even wonder, with her character flaws, if she should be adopting.

Each woman has a story. Gayle isn't a mother because of years of alcoholism. Leslie can't stay with the same man long enough to make parenthood an option. Jennifer (Maggie Gyllenhaal) can't conceive. Señora Muñoz (Rita Moreno), who owns the Casa, has seen hundreds of these women come and go. Her brother is the lawyer who handles the adoptions. Her son thinks of the women as capitalist exploiters, but for that matter, his mother is exploiting them.

John Sayles handles this material with gentle delicacy, as if aware that the issues are too fraught to be approached with simple messages. He shows both sides; the maid Asunción gave up her baby and now imagines her happy life in "el norte," but we feel how much she misses her. The squeegee kids on the corner have been abandoned by their parents and might happily go home with one of these rich Americanos. Sayles sees like a documentarian, showing us the women, listening to their stories, inviting us to share their hopes and fears, and speculate about their motives. There are no answers here, just the experiences of waiting for a few weeks in the Casa de los Babys.

Catch That Kid ★ ★ ★
PG, 92 m., 2004

Kristen Stewart (Maddy Phillips), Corbin Bleu (Austin), Max Thieriot (Gus), Jennifer Beals (Molly), Sam Robards (Tom), Michael Des Barres (Brisbane). Directed by Bart Freundlich and produced by Andrew Lazar and Uwe Schott. Screenplay by Nicolai Arcel, Hans Fabian Wullenweber, Erlend Loe, Michael Brandt, and Derek Haas.

Now here's something you don't see every day: a heist movie involving twelve-year-old kids. *Catch That Kid* respects all of the requirements of the genre, and the heist itself is worthy of *Ocean's Eleven* (either one; take your pick). Kristen Stewart's plucky heroine will win the hearts of the same young audiences who liked *Bend It Like Beckham* and *Whale Rider*.

This is not, to be sure, a movie as good as those two wonderful titles. But it's plenty good, and it has the same buried theme: Anything a guy can do, a girl can do too. It stars Stewart as Maddy Phillips, an athletic young girl whose father, Tom (Sam Robards), once climbed Mount Everest. He had a nasty fall on the way down, which is why he discourages Maddy from climbing, while her mother, Molly (Jennifer Beals), forbids it. But as the movie opens, she's scaling the local water tower.

Maddy has two best friends. Austin (Corbin Bleu) is a computer geek. Gus (Max Thieriot) is a mechanic at the go-kart track operated by her father. They both have crushes on her, although at one point, when she's hanging in danger high in the air during the heist, Gus complains that he never even got a chance to kiss her once.

A crisis comes into her life with all the melodrama of a silent movie. One night while her dad and mom are dancing in the living room, he falls to the floor and says, "I can't feel my legs!" It's paralysis—whether from the neck or waist down, we don't learn, but in any event the condition is incurable, except for an experimental procedure offered in Europe; it costs $250,000 the family doesn't have.

Common sense at this point steps in and suggests that if such an operation really existed, Christopher Reeve would already be on site with a charity to help the Toms of the world, but no: Molly the mother is turned down for a loan at the bank where she has installed the security system. The bank president, named Brisbane (Michael Des Barres), is a teeth-gnashing, scenery-chewing villain whose origins go back even before silent films—back to Horatio Alger, if anybody remembers who that was. Been a while since we've had a banker this evil in the movies.

So the kids take things into their own hands. With Maddy's climbing skills, Austin to hack into the bank's security system, and Gus to devise mechanical devices and the getaway, they'll break into the bank vault and steal the $250,000. This is not so easy, since the vault is suspended in midair, surrounded by motion detectors, protected by savage rottweilers, etc.

The movie is a remake of a Danish film, unseen by me, named *Klatretøsen*, which was hailed at the Berlin Film Festival. This version, directed by Bart Freundlich and sporting five writing credits, is well made, straightforward, and entertaining. It doesn't bog down in a lot of cute kid stuff, but gets on with telling the story, and has some unexpected touches. For example, the getaway scene with the kids in go-karts. Yes, and the police chase them, shouting on loudspeakers: "You kids in the go-karts! Pull over! You're leaving the scene of a crime." Sure, because any cop seeing kids on a city street in go-karts is instinctively going to link them to a bank robbery.

Kristen Stewart is at the center of the movie, stalwart and sure. You may remember her as Jodie Foster's daughter in a more harrowing thriller, *Panic Room* (2002). Corbin Bleu and Max Thieriot, as her two pals, are just plain likable, and the attraction between Bleu and Stewart may be the screen's first example of interracial puppy love. For that matter, Jennifer Beals is cast as a possibly mixed-race mother, and I would not bother to make this point except to observe that all of a sudden racial categories are evaporating in mainstream movies, and for the first time in history actors are being cast because they're right for a role, not because they passed an identity check.

Catch That Kid doesn't have the flash of *Spy Kids*, but it's solid entertainment—better than *Agent Cody Banks*. Faithful readers know that my definition of a good family film is one the parents can enjoy, and you know what? In the middle of the heist scene, we're just about as involved as if the movie starred George Clooney and Julia Roberts. A heist is a heist, and a good one works no matter what.

Catwoman ★
PG-13, 91m., 2004

Halle Berry (Patience Philips), Benjamin Bratt (Detective Tom Lone), Lambert Wilson (George Hedare), Frances Conroy (Ophelia Powers), Sharon Stone (Laurel Hedare). Directed by Pitof and produced by Denise Di Novi and Edward McDonnell. Screenplay by John Rogers, John Brancato, and Michael Ferris.

Catwoman is a movie about Halle Berry's beauty, sex appeal, figure, eyes, lips, and costume design. It gets those right. Everything else is secondary, except for the plot, which is tertiary. What a letdown. The filmmakers have given great thought to photographing Berry, who looks fabulous, and little thought to providing her with a strong character, story, supporting characters, or action sequences. When *Spider-Man 2* represents the state of the art, *Catwoman* is tired and dated.

Although the movie's faults are many, the crucial one is that we never get any sense of what it feels like to turn into a catwoman. The strength of *Spider-Man 2* is in the ambivalence that Peter Parker has about being part nerdy student, part superhero. In *Catwoman,* where are the scenes where a woman comes to grips with the fact that her entire nature and even her species seems to have changed?

Berry plays Patience Philips, a designer for an ad agency, who dies and is reborn after Midnight, a cat with ties to ancient Egypt, breathes new life into her. She becomes Catwoman, but what is a catwoman? She can leap like a cat, strut around on top of her furniture, survive great falls, and hiss. Halle Berry looks great doing these things, and spends a lot of time on all fours, inspiring our almost unseemly gratitude for her cleavage.

She gobbles down tuna and sushi. Her eyes have vertical pupils instead of horizontal ones. She sleeps on a shelf. The movie doesn't get into the litter box situation. What does she *think* about all of this? Why isn't she more astonished that it has happened to her? How does it affect her relationship with that cute cop, Tom Lone (Benjamin Bratt)?

The movie makes it clear that they make love at least once, but we don't see that happening because *Catwoman,* a film that was born to be rated R, has been squeezed into the PG-13 category to rake in every last teenage dollar. From what we know about Catwoman, her style in bed has probably changed along with everything else, and sure enough the next day Tom notices a claw mark on his shoulder. Given the MPAA's preference for violence over sex, this might have been one sex scene that could have sneaked in under the PG-13.

Catwoman dresses like a dominatrix, with the high heels and the leather skirt, brassiere, mask, and whip. But why? Because the costume sketches looked great, is my opinion. The film gives her a plot that could have been phoned in from the 1960s: She works for a corporation that's introducing a new beauty product that gives women eternal youth, unless they stop taking it, in which case they look like burn victims. When Patience stumbles over this unfortunate side effect, she is attacked by security guards, flushed out of a waste pipe, and is dead when Midnight finds her.

Soon she has a dual identity: Patience by day, Catwoman by night. She already knows Tom Lone. They met when she crawled out of her window and balanced on an air conditioner to rescue Midnight, and Tom thought she was committing suicide and saved her after she slipped. Uh, huh. That meeting begins a romance between Patience and Tom that is remarkable for its complete lack of energy, passion, and chemistry. If the movie had been ten minutes longer it would have needed a scene where they sigh and sadly agree their relationship is just not working out. One of those things. Not meant to be.

The villains are Laurel and George Hedare (Sharon Stone and Lambert Wilson). He runs the cosmetics company and fires his wife as its model when she turns forty. She is not to be trifled with, especially not in a movie where the big fight scene is a real catfight, so to speak, between the two women. Stone's character is laughably one-dimensional, but then that's a good fit for this movie, in which none of the characters suggest any human dimensions and seem to be posing more than relating. Take George, for example, whose obnoxious mannerisms are so grotesque he's like the *Saturday Night Live* version of Vincent Price.

Among many silly scenes, the silliest has to be the Ferris wheel sequence, which isn't even as thrilling as the one in *The Notebook*. Wouldn't you just know that after the wheel stalls, the operator would recklessly strip the gears, and the little boy riding alone would be in a chair where the guard rail falls off, and then the seat comes loose, and then the wheel tries to shake him loose and no doubt would try to electrocute him if it could.

The score by Klaus Badelt is particularly annoying; it faithfully mirrors every action with what occasionally sounds like a karaoke rhythm section. The director, whose name is given as Pitof, was probably issued with two names at birth, and would be wise to use the other one on his next project.   ☞

Cellular ★ ★ ★ ½
PG-13, 94 m., 2004

Kim Basinger (Jessica Martin), Chris Evans (Ryan), Eric Christian Olsen (Chad), William H. Macy (Mooney), Jason Statham (Greer), Adam Taylor Gordon (Ricky Martin), Rick Hoffman (Porsche Owner), Richard Burgi (Craig Martin). Directed by David R. Ellis and produced by Dean Devlin and Lauren Lloyd. Screenplay by Larry Cohen and Chris Morgan.

Cellular stands *Phone Booth* on its head. The 2003 thriller was about a psychopath who threatens Colin Farrell with death if he leaves a Manhattan phone booth. The new one has Chris Evans racing desperately all over Los Angeles as he tries to stay on his cell phone with a woman who says she's been kidnapped. The same writer, Larry Cohen, collaborated on both projects and is no doubt currently involved in a thriller about chat rooms.

The plot of *Cellular* sounds like a gimmick, and no wonder: It *is* a gimmick. What's surprising is how convincing it is, under the circumstances, and how willingly we accept the premise and get involved in it. The movie is skillfully plotted, halfway plausible, and well acted; the craftsmanship is in the details, including the astonishing number of different ways in which a cell phone

can be made to function—both as a telephone and as a plot device.

Kim Basinger stars as Jessica, a high school science teacher who is kidnapped by violent home invaders and held prisoner in an attic. The men who have taken her want something from her husband—something she knows nothing about. They know where her young son, Ricky (Adam Taylor Gordon), attends school and plan to kidnap him too. The kidnappers are hard men, especially their cold, intense leader, Greer, played by Jason Statham. Because they've allowed Jessica to see them, she assumes they will eventually kill her.

The attic has a wall phone, which a kidnapper smashes to bits. But Jessica the science teacher is able to fit some of the parts back together and click on the wires to make a call—at random. She reaches Ryan (Chris Evans), a twenty-something kid who at first doesn't believe her when she says she has been kidnapped. At one point, he even puts her on hold; that's part of the movie's strategy of building our frustration by creating one believable obstacle after another. Jessica pleads with him not to hang up: to trust her enough to hand his cell phone to a cop. Something in her voice convinces him. He walks into a police station and hands the phone to a desk cop named Mooney (William H. Macy), who gets sidetracked and advises him to go to homicide, up on the fourth floor. Uh-huh. But Mooney, too, hears something in her voice, and later in the day it still resonates. He's not your typical hot-dog movie cop, but a quiet, thoughtful professional with unexpected resources.

The movie's surprises, when they come, mostly seem to make sense. When we find out who the kidnappers are and what it is they want from Jessica's husband, it doesn't seem like too much of a reach. But the real fun of the movie comes from the hoops Ryan has to jump through in order to somehow stay on the line with Jessica, convince people he's not crazy, and get personally involved in the deadly climax. Yes, the action scenes are over the top, and yes, the chase scenes involve unthinkable carnage on the freeways, but, yes, we go along because the motivations and strategies of the characters are strong and clear.

About the crime and the criminals I will say

no more. What's ingenious about the movie is the way it uses telephones—and the people who use them. At one point Ryan gets a "low battery" warning and desperately needs a charger, so of course he finds himself in a cell phone store where he is instructed with maddening condescension to take a number and wait his place in line. At another point he comes into the life of a spectacularly obnoxious lawyer (Rick Hoffman), and steals his Porsche not once but twice.

And then there are the ways phones can be used for things other than making calls. Ways they can preserve evidence, maintain callback records, function as an emergency alarm system, convey unintended information, or even betray themselves. Larry Cohen and his cowriter, Chris Morgan, must have spent days with their yellow pads, jotting down every use they could think of for a cell phone.

The director, David R. Ellis, does have the usual chases and shoot-outs, but he doesn't depend on them to make his movie work. He's attentive to how and why the characters behave, he makes it clear what they're thinking, and he has a good feel for situations in which everything depends on human nature. Kim Basinger, who for such a healthy-looking woman has always been so good at seeming vulnerable, is ideally cast here, and young Chris Evans (from *Not Another Teen Movie*) has a star-making role. But the real juice comes from the old pros William H. Macy, as a dogged cop who might surprise you in a tight spot, and Jason Statham as the leader of the kidnappers. By occupying their roles believably, by acting as we think their characters probably would, they save the movie from feeling like basic Hollywood action (even when it probably is). This is one of the year's best thrillers. Better than *Phone Booth*, for my money, and I liked that too.

Charlie's Angels: Full Throttle ★ ★ ½
PG-13, 105 m., 2003

Cameron Diaz (Natalie Cook), Drew Barrymore (Dylan Sanders), Lucy Liu (Alex Munday), Demi Moore (Madison Lee), Bernie Mac (Jimmy Bosley). Directed by McG and produced by Drew Barrymore, Leonard Goldberg, and Nancy Juvonen. Screenplay by John August, Cormac Wibberley, and Marianne Wibberley, based on the television series by Ivan Goff and Ben Roberts.

Sometimes it has more to do with mood than with what's on the screen. *Charlie's Angels: Full Throttle* is more or less the same movie as the original *Charlie's Angels* (2000), and yet I feel more forgiving this time. Wow, did I hate the first one: "a movie without a brain in its three pretty little heads." I awarded it one-half of a star.

But what, really, was so reprehensible about that high-tech bimbo eruption? Imagine a swimsuit issue crossed with an explosion at the special-effects lab, and you've got it. Maybe I was indignant because people were going to spend their money on this instead of going to better movies that were undoubtedly more edifying for them. But if people wanted to be edified every time they went to the movies, Hollywood would be out of business.

Charlie's Angels: Full Throttle is not a funny movie, despite a few good one-liners, as when Bernie Mac explains that the Black Irish invented the McRib. It is not an exciting movie, because there is no way to genuinely care about what's happening, and it doesn't make much sense, anyway. It is not a sexy movie, even though it stars four sexy women, because you just can't get aroused by the sight of three babes running toward you in slow motion with an explosion in the background. I've tried it.

So what is it? Harmless, brainless, good-natured fun. Leaving *Full Throttle*, I realized I did not hate or despise the movie, and so during a long and thoughtful walk along the Chicago River, I decided that I sort of liked it because of the high spirits of the women involved.

Say what you will, Drew Barrymore, Cameron Diaz, Lucy Liu, and Demi Moore were manifestly having fun while they made this movie. They're given outrageous characters to play, an astonishing wardrobe (especially considering the fact that they go everywhere without suitcases), remarkable superpowers, and lots of close-ups in which they are just gorgeous when they smile.

It's a form of play for them, to be female James Bonds, just as male actors all like to be in Westerns because you get to ride a horse and shoot up saloons. There is a scene where the three angels discuss what Dylan Sanders (Drew Barrymore) was named before she went into the witness protection program. It turns out she was named Helen Zas. Now there's a name to go in the books with Norma Stitz. Natalie (Cameron Diaz) and Alex (Lucy Liu) kid her mercilessly about her name, and as Lucy Liu comes up with wicked puns, you almost get the impression she's thinking them up herself.

The plot . . . but why should I describe the plot? It is an arbitrary and senseless fiction designed to provide a weak excuse for a series of scenes in which the angels almost get killed, in Mongolia and elsewhere, mostly elsewhere, while blowing up stuff, shooting people, being shot at, almost getting killed, and modeling their PG-13-rated outfits.

Two new faces this time: Demi Moore, as Madison Lee, a fallen angel, and Bernie Mac, taking over for Bill Murray in the Bosley role, as Bosley's brother, who I think is also called Bosley. The Angels confront Madison high atop Los Angeles at the Griffith Observatory, which for mysterious reasons is completely deserted during their showdown and shoot-out.

So. I give the movie 2½ stars, partially in expiation for the half-star I gave the first one. But if you want to see a movie where big stars trade witty one-liners with one another in the midst of high-tech chase scenes and all sorts of explosive special effects, the movie for you is *Hollywood Homicide*.

Charlotte Sometimes ★ ★ ★ ½
NO MPAA RATING, 85 m., 2003

Michael Idemoto (Michael), Jacqueline Kim (Darcy), Eugenia Yuan (Lori), Matt Westmore (Justin), Shizuko Hoshi (Auntie Margie), Kimberly Rose (Annie). Directed by Eric Byler and produced by Marc Ambrose and Byler. Screenplay by Byler.

The man lives alone in his apartment, sometimes reading, sometimes standing quietly in the dark. Through the walls he can hear passionate lovemaking. After a time there is a knock on his door. It is, we know, the young woman who lives next door. She can't sleep, she says. The man and his neighbor sit on his couch to watch television, and in the morning she is still asleep in his arms.

This simply, Eric Byler's *Charlotte Sometimes* draws us into its mysterious, erotic story. The man is named Michael (Michael Idemoto). His neighbor—actually his tenant in a two-unit building—is Lori (Eugenia Yuan). Her lover is Justin (Matt Westmore), and while their sex life is apparently spectacular she seems to have a deep, if platonic, love for Michael. What is their relationship, exactly? Michael is so quiet, so reserved, we cannot know for sure, although it seems clear in his eyes that he does not enjoy what he hears through the wall.

Lori asks Michael if he would like to meet a girl—she knows someone she could introduce him to. Before that can happen, one night in a neighborhood bar, he sees a young woman sitting alone across the room. He looks at her; she looks at him. He leaves, but comes back just as she is leaving—clearly to find her, although he claims he forgot something.

This is Darcy (Jacqueline Kim). She is tall and grave, the opposite of the pretty, cuddly Lori. "Men don't want me," she says. "They only think they want me." She reveals little about herself. As they talk into the night, they develop that kind of strange intimacy two people can have when they know nothing about each other but feel a deep connection. Eventually she offers to have sex with him, but Michael doesn't want that. It's too soon. Sex may be a shortcut to intimacy, but he values something more: perhaps his privacy, perhaps his growing attraction for her, which he doesn't want to reduce to the physical just yet.

Byler's screenplay never says too much, never asks the actors to explain or reveal in words what we sense in their presence and guarded, even coded, conversations. Jacqueline Kim, an experienced classical stage actress (from the Goodman in Chicago and the Guthrie in Minneapolis), brings a quality to Darcy that is intriguing and unsettling at the same time. She leaves and returns unpredictably. There is something she is not saying. Michael feels attracted, and yet warned.

This story, which is almost Gothic in its undertones, is filmed in an ordinary Los Angeles neighborhood. The house is on a winding road on a hillside. Michael owns a garage. "You're a mechanic—and you read," Darcy muses. He took over the family garage, but lives inside his ideas and his loneliness. How does he feel that Lori has sex with Justin but prefers to spend her nights with him? That Darcy is willing to have sex with him but then disappears, and withholds herself and her secrets?

The film has been photographed by Rob Humphreys in dark colors and shadows, sometimes with backlighting that will catch part of a face or an expression and leave the rest hidden. Then there are ordinary daytime scenes, such as a double date when the two couples have lunch. There is subtle verbal fencing; Michael, Darcy, and Lori are Asian, Justin is half-Asian, and when Darcy asks which of his parents taught him to use chopsticks, there is an undercurrent they all feel, and when he says he cannot remember the time when he could not use chopsticks, he is answering more than her question.

The movie has revelations I must not reveal, but let it be said that Byler conceals nothing from us except what is concealed from the characters, and what they learn, we learn. It becomes clear that Darcy came into Michael's life in the wrong way and cannot undo that, and that Lori is deeply disturbed that her platonic friend may become this other woman's lover. Little is actually said about any of this; it is all there in the air between these guarded and wounded characters.

Charlotte Sometimes drew me in from the opening shots. Byler reveals his characters in a way that intrigues and even fascinates us, and he never reduces the situation to simple melodrama, which would release the tension. This is like a psychological thriller, in which the climax has to do with feelings, not actions.

Idemoto brings such a loneliness to his role, such a feeling of the character's long hours of solitary thought, that we care for him right from the start, and feel his pain about this woman who might be the right one for him, but remains elusive and hidden. Kim has a way of being detached and observant in her scenes, as if Darcy is seeing it all happen within a context only she understands. At the end, when we know everything, the movie has not cheated; we sense the deep life currents that have brought these people to this place. There is sad-

ness and tenderness here, and the knowledge that to find true love is not always to possess it.

Chasing Liberty ★ ★
PG-13, 111 m., 2004

Mandy Moore (Anna Foster), Matthew Goode (Ben Calder), Jeremy Piven (Alan Weiss), Annabella Sciorra (Cynthia Morales), Mark Harmon (James Foster), Caroline Goodall (Michelle Foster). Directed by Andy Cadiff and produced by Broderick Johnson, Andrew A. Kosove, and David Parfitt. Screenplay by Derek Guiley and David Schneiderman.

Chasing Liberty is surprisingly good in areas where it doesn't need to be good at all, and pretty awful in areas where it has to succeed. It centers on a couple of engaging performances in impossible roles, and involves a madcap romp through a Europe where 9/11 never happened and *Roman Holiday* was never made. The movie is ideal for audiences who kinda know that we have a president, and he could have a teenage daughter, and she might be protected by the Secret Service, but don't know a whole lot else.

The movie has a view of reality, danger, romance, foreigners, sex, and impulsive behavior that would have made ideal honeymoon viewing for Britney and Jason, had their marriage not tragically ended before the movie could open. It reflects precisely the prudence and forethought of two people who could get married at 5:30 A.M. in a Vegas chapel after seeing *The Texas Chainsaw Massacre* and then file for an annulment after belatedly realizing they hadn't discussed having children, where they want to live, community property, religious affiliation, and whether the toilet paper should roll out or in.

You may protest that I'm hauling Britney and Jason into a review of a movie they have nothing to do with, but you would be wrong. There are going to be people who say that no one could possibly be as glamorous and yet as stupid as the characters in this film, and I give you Jason and Britney, case closed.

The movie stars Mandy Moore, a singer-actress of precisely Britney's generation, who has undeniable screen presence and inspires instant affection. Britney used to inspire instant affection herself, but now inspires instant alarm and concern. Mandy Moore is just plain likable, a Slurpee blended from scoops of Mary Tyler Moore, Sally Field, and Doris Day.

In *Chasing Liberty* she plays Anna Foster, code-named Liberty, who is the only daughter of U.S. president James Foster (Mark Harmon) and his first lady (Caroline Goodall). Her dating life is impossible. A hapless kid from her class arrives at the White House to take her out on a date, and the Secret Service strips the petals from the sweet little bouquet he brought her, seeking tiny and fragrant weapons of mass destruction.

The president is planning a state visit to Prague, and she wants to go along. What's more, she wants to hook up (in the old-fashioned sense, let us pray) with the daughter of the French ambassador, so they can skip over to Berlin for the annual Love Parade. And she demands freedom from the omnipresent Secret Service.

Her father nixes the Love Parade, promises to assign only two Secret Service agents, and is alarmed when Anna pulls a fast one, slips out of a nightclub, and is able to escape her agents by hitching a ride on the back of a motorcycle driven by Ben Calder (Matthew Goode). Ben is a saturnine Brit of about thirty, very dry and mysterious, and she knows absolutely nothing about him as she entrusts her life to him by embarking on a tour of Berlin, Venice, London, and other popular tourist destinations. Life on the road is easier when, by pure charm, for example, you can find a gondolier in Venice who not only waives his fee but invites you home so his mother can cook dinner for you and you can spend the night. Why does this gondolier remind me of the joke about the housewife who invites the mailman in for breakfast?

Anna doesn't know who Ben is, but she knows who she is, and it's fairly inconsiderate of her to run away and inspire a vast Euro hunt involving the Secret Service, Interpol, countless black helicopters, and millions of the taxpayers' dollars; this is one child who could have been left behind. Ben, however, does know who he is, and so do we—he's working for the Secret Service, and has been assigned by the president to keep an eye on Anna while letting her think she's getting away with something.

Mandy Moore and Matthew Goode have a quirky and appealing chemistry, based on her confusion over whether she wants to have sex or not, or maybe over whether she's had sex or not, and his confusion when his private emotions begin to interfere with his job. There's a scene where Anna goes bungee-jumping and you want to explain to Ben that his job is to *prevent* her from bungee-jumping, not to tie himself to her bungee so they can die together. That would be a job for the Last Samurai.

I liked Goode's dry way of sardonically holding his distance, and Moore's unforced charm. It was a useful contrast to the movie's parallel romance between two agents named Weiss and Morales (Jeremy Piven and Annabella Sciorra), who grumble their way into love in dialogue that seems recycled from a shelved sitcom. Harmon is singularly unconvincing as the president, not only because he recklessly endangers his daughter's life and his country's fortune, but also because he reads the newspaper, and there's no telling where that could lead.

Chasing Papi ★ ★ ½
PG, 92 m., 2003

Roselyn Sanchez (Lorena), Sofia Vergara (Cici), Jaci Velasquez (Patricia), Eduardo Verastegui (Papi), Lisa Vidal (Carmen), D. L. Hughley (Rodrigo), Freddy Rodriguez (Victor), Maria Conchita Alonso (Maria), Paul Rodriguez (Costas Delgado). Directed by Linda Mendoza and produced by Tracey Trench and Forest Whitaker. Screenplay by Laura Angelica Simon, Steven Antin, Alison Balian, and Liz Sarnoff.

Chasing Papi is a feature-length jiggle show with Charlie's Angels transformed into Latina bimbos. Well, not entirely bimbos: The movie's three heroines are smart and capable, except when they're in pursuit of the man they love, an occupation that requires them to run through a lot of scenes wearing high heels and squealing with passion or fear or delight, while a stupendous amount of jiggling goes on.

These are great-looking women. Forgive me if I sound like a lecher, but, hey, the entire purpose and rationale of this film is to display Roselyn Sanchez, Sofia Vergara, and Jaci Velasquez in a way that would make your average *Maxim* reader feel right at home. So high are the movie's standards of beauty that even two supporting roles feature the ravishing Lisa Vidal and the immortal Maria Conchita Alonso.

The three stars are veterans of Spanish-language TV soap operas, a genre that celebrates cleavage with single-minded dedication. In the story, they are the three girlfriends of Thomas Fuentes (Eduardo Verastegui), aka Papi, an advertising executive whose travels require him to visit Lorena (Sanchez) in Chicago, Cici (Vergara) in Miami, and Patricia (Velasquez) in New York. He does not intend to be a three-timer and sincerely loves them all, but asks: "How can you choose between the colors of nature's beautiful flowers?"

All three women happen to be watching the same astrologer on TV, and take the seer's advice to drop everything and race to the side of their man. This leads to an improbable scene when all three burst through doors leading into Papi's bedroom while wearing his gift of identical red lingerie. Papi is not home at the time, supplying an opportunity for the women to discover his betrayal and decide to gang up and have what is described as revenge but looks more like a fashion show by Victoria's Secret.

Meanwhile, let's see, there's a plot about a bag of money, and an FBI agent (Vidal) trails the women to Los Angeles while some tough guys, led by Paul Rodriguez, also are on the trail of the money, and this all leads inevitably to the girls making their onstage dancing debut at a festival headlining Sheila E.

Chasing Papi is as light as a feather, as fresh as spring, and as lubricious as a centerfold. Its three heroines are seen in one way or another as liberated women, especially Lorena, who is said to be a lawyer, but their hearts go a-flutter in the presence of Papi. The movie's purpose is to photograph them as attractively as possible, while covering up the slightness of the plot with wall-to-wall Latin music, infectiously upbeat scenes, and animated sequences that introduce New York, Miami, Chicago, and Los Angeles. (The use of these cartoon intervals is an inspired solution to the problem that the movie was shot entirely in Canada.)

I cannot recommend *Chasing Papi*, but I cannot dislike it. It commits no offense except the puppylike desire to please. It celebrates a vibrant and lively Latino world in which everyone speaks English with a charming accent, switching to Spanish only in moments of intense drama. There is something extroverted and refreshing in the way these women enjoy their beauty and their sexiness. They've got it, and they flaunt it.

The movie could have been smarter and wittier. The plot could have made a slight attempt to be original. There are better ways to pass your time. But it will make you smile, and that is a virtue not to be ignored.

Cheaper by the Dozen ★ ★ ★
PG, 98 m., 2003

Steve Martin (Tom Baker), Bonnie Hunt (Kate Baker), Tom Welling (Charlie Baker), Piper Perabo (Nora Baker), Ashton Kutcher (Hank), Hilary Duff (Lorraine Baker), Forrest Landis (Mark Baker). Directed by Shawn Levy and produced by Michael Barnathan, Ben Myron, and Robert Simonds. Screenplay by Craig Titley, Joel Cohen, Sam Harper, and Alec Sokolow, based on the book by Frank B. Gilbreth Jr. and Ernestine Gilbreth Carey.

Here's my old copy of *Cheaper by the Dozen* right here. The bright orange binding is worn through to the cardboard, there are grape juice stains all through Chapter 3, and a couple of pages are stuck together with what still, incredibly, smells like peanut butter. God, I loved that book. I read it over and over again as pure escapism. I was an only child curled up at the end of the sofa, imagining what it would be like to have eleven brothers and sisters.

Cheaper by the Dozen was a best-seller in the 1940s, and inspired a 1950 movie starring Clifton Webb and Myrna Loy as Frank and Lillian Gilbreth, who raised twelve kids with ingenuity and precision. Now here is the 2003 version, with Steve Martin and Bonnie Hunt. It isn't my purpose to use the old movie to hammer the new one, because they're both sweet and zany, but to notice how much our ideas have changed in fifty-three years; especially our ideas about fathers.

Frank Gilbreth was a real man, and the original book was cowritten by two of his children. He was, they explained, a time-and-motion expert, who broke down every task into its essential elements and then studied them to see how they could be done more quickly and easily. At work he improved assembly lines. At home he applied his theories to his family, believing that twelve children were as easy to raise as two, if you analyzed the daily family routine and assigned part of it to every kid—even very small parts for very small kids. The unspoken assumption was that the father was the center of authority, he knew best, and his wife was his loyal copilot.

We know now that this model is a case of sexist chauvinism. Gilbreth's view of fathers is long out of date, and American men survive in the movies only as examples of incompetence, unrealistic ambition, and foolish pride. Gene Siskel once started a list of movies with fathers in them, to demonstrate that Hollywood preferred whenever possible to have single mothers and avoid fathers altogether. If there had to be a father, he was (a) in a comedy, the butt of the joke, and (b) in a drama, a child abuser, an alcoholic, an adulterer, an abandoner of families, or preferably all of the above. At some point during a half-century of Hollywood fathering, "father knows best" was replaced by "shut your pie hole."

Tom Baker, the Steve Martin character in *Cheaper by the Dozen,* has a good heart and loves his wife and children, but that leaves him with a few promising character flaws. He is incapable of inspiring discipline, for example, and would sacrifice his family to his ambition. He's a football coach for a cow college in Midland, Illinois, but is offered the head coaching job at Lincoln University in Evanston. We're supposed to think of Northwestern.

Well, of course, fool that Tom is, he takes the job and steps up to national prominence and a big salary, even though this means his kids will have to switch schools and find new boyfriends and girlfriends, and they will have to move out of the overcrowded bungalow where they all lived in each other's pockets, and into a sprawling two-story corner home in a $1 million neighborhood. One of those houses with a circular drive and balconies and garrets and a garden.

Worse, the move is scheduled to coincide with the national tour to promote the new book about the family by Tom's wife, Kate (Bonnie Hunt). This is quite a publishing coup. Her book is submitted, accepted, edited, printed, in the stores, and on the best-seller lists within a week. Forget the coach; make us a

movie about the publisher. The book's success means Tom has to run team practices and steer his new team through a couple of big games while Kate is on the road, and although his oldest daughter Nora (Piper Perabo) agrees to come home and baby-sit, she brings along her boyfriend, Hank (Ashton Kutcher), causing a family crisis about where Hank will sleep. This in a family where everybody was sharing two and a half beds until a month ago.

The movie is lighthearted fun, providing little character bits for all of the family members, from young Forrest Landis, whose life centers on his pet frog, all the way up to older sister Hilary Duff, whose romantic adventures involve the usual PG-rated heartbreak. The neighbors complain that they're living next door to Animal House, the alums complain that the small-time coach is not ready for big-time football, the kids complain that they miss home—and of course only evil, stupid, reactionary, ambitious, greedy Dad is standing in the way of a return to Midland, a town so friendly they don't say, "Attention, Shoppers!" at Wal-Mart, but call you by name (only kidding).

Hey, I liked the movie. These actors are skilled at being nice. It's just that the movie settles when it ought to push. Consider the Bonnie Hunt character. Here she's reasonable, exasperated, and loves that lunk of a husband. But compare her work here with what she did in *Stolen Summer* (you remember, that 2002 Operation Greenlight movie I recommended, but you ignored my review and went to see *Sorority Boys* instead). In that one she was the mother of a large Irish Catholic family in Chicago, where she had edge and sass and was not afraid to smack a potty-mouth up alongside the head. *Cheaper by the Dozen* doesn't understand that kind of family; it's based on sitcom families, where the most essential family value is not stepping on anybody's lines.

The Chorus ★ ★ ½
PG-13, 95 m., 2005

Gerard Jugnot (Clement Mathieu), Jean-Baptiste Maunier (Pierre Morhange [young]), Jacques Perrin (Pierre Morhange [adult]), Francois Berleand (Rachin), Kad Merad (Chabert), Marie Bunel (Violette Morhange). Directed by Christophe Barratier and produced by Arthur Cohn, Nicolas Mauvernay, and Jacques Perrin. Screenplay by Barratier and Philippe Lopes-Curval.

This time the teacher is named Clement Mathieu. In earlier films it was Mr. Chips, Miss Jean Brodie, Mr. Holland, Mr. Crocker-Harris (in *The Browning Version*), John Keating (in *Dead Poets Society*), Joe Clark (in *Lean on Me*), Katherine Ann Watson (in *Mona Lisa Smile*), Jaime A. Escalante (in *Stand and Deliver*), and Roberta Guaspari (in *Music of the Heart*). In theaters right now, his name is Coach Carter. The actors have included Morgan Freeman, Meryl Streep, Edward James Olmos, Albert Finney, Robin Williams, Samuel L. Jackson, Julia Roberts, Maggie Smith, Richard Dreyfuss, and even, in one version of *Chips*, Peter O'Toole. They all have two things in common: Their influence will forever change the lives of their students, and we can see that coming from the opening frame.

I have nothing against the formula. Done well, it can be moving, as it was in *Mr. Holland's Opus*. But *The Chorus*, the film France selected as its Oscar candidate this year, does it by the numbers, so efficiently this feels more like a Hollywood wannabe than a French film. Where's the quirkiness, the nuance, the deeper levels?

The movie begins with a middle-aged man named Pierre (Jacques Perrin) being awakened from his slumber by the news of a death. That night he conducts an orchestra, and we learn that he is the world's greatest conductor. I would have been better pleased if he had merely been a really good conductor. Then Pierre makes a journey to the country to attend the funeral of the teacher who found him as a juvenile delinquent and instilled a love of music and learning in him.

All of this is quickly known, and more details are easy to come by because in the town, he meets his old classmate Pepinot, who produces the diary kept fifty years ago by Mr. Mathieu. It is the kind of helpful journal that seems to have been written as the treatment for a film.

But perhaps I am too cynical about a perfectly sincere sentimental exercise. We flash back to 1949 and the Fond de d'Etang boarding school; the name means (not its official

title, I believe) something like the bottom of the pond. Here the students are considered pond scum, too impossible to reach in ordinary schools, and the headmaster maintains an iron discipline. Young Pierre (now played by young Jean-Baptiste Maunier) is a handful, sent to the school by a single mom who despairs for him.

Also new to the school this term is Clement Mathieu (Gerard Jugnot), a pudgy and somewhat unfocused middle-aged man who is hired as a teacher's assistant. He loves music, and one day when he hears the boys singing, a light glows in his eye and he decides to begin a boys' choir in the school. This, of course, is frowned upon by the headmaster, who disapproves of anything even remotely educational, as such headmasters always do, and hates even more the idea of students having fun. But Mr. Mathieu holds rehearsals anyway, secretly, in sort of a boarding school parallel of the Resistance.

We know without having to see the movie that there will be vignettes establishing how troubled the kids are, and scenes in which Mr. Mathieu loses all hope, and a scene where the kids surprise him, and a scene of triumph, and a glorious performance at the end. All done competently. What is disconcerting, however, is how well these boys sing. After a few months of secret lessons, they sing as well as—well, as well as Les Petits Chanteurs de Saint-Marc Choir, the professional boys' choir that does the actual singing. Every time those little rascals open their mouths, somebody seems to have slipped a CD into the stereo.

Wouldn't it work better for the movie if they were simply a really good choir? The choice of a real choir makes for a better sound track album, no doubt, but causes a disconnect in the film's reality. I guess we have to accept this, along with the cruel fate that inevitably awaits any teacher who dares to break the mold, defy the establishment, and challenge his students with the wonders of the world.

The Great Teacher Who Forever Changes Lives is not as rare as these movies would suggest.

As it happens, I have had several such teachers, none more lovably eccentric than Mrs. Seward of Urbana High School, who taught senior rhetoric by gazing out the window and rhapsodizing about the worms on her farm, who came up after heavy rains and glistened in their wormy perfection. She also taught us to write. I had been working for two years as a sportswriter on the local daily, but she disabused me of the notion that a sentence equaled a paragraph, and gently suggested that the day would come when I would no longer find Thomas Wolfe readable.

The Chorus is only a fair example of its genre. I would rank it below *Mr. Holland's Opus* and *Music of the Heart.* Am I wearied because I have seen too many movies telling similar stories? No, it is just that since I know the story and so does everybody else in the theater, it should have added something new and unexpected, and by that I do not mean hiring Les Petits Chanteurs de Saint-Marc.

Christmas with the Kranks ★
PG, 98 m., 2004

Tim Allen (Luther Krank), Jamie Lee Curtis (Nora Krank), Dan Aykroyd (Vic Frohmeyer), Erik Per Sullivan (Spike Frohmeyer), Cheech Marin (Officer Salino), Jake Busey (Officer Treen), M. Emmet Walsh (Walt Scheel), Julie Gonzalo (Blair Krank). Directed by Joe Roth and produced by Michael Barnathan, Chris Columbus, and Mark Radcliffe. Screenplay by Columbus, based on a novel by John Grisham.

Christmas with the Kranks doesn't have anything wrong with it that couldn't be fixed by adding Ebenezer Scrooge and Bad Santa to the cast. It's a holiday movie of stunning awfulness that gets even worse when it turns gooey at the end. And what is it finally so happy about? Why, that the Kranks's neighbors succeed in enforcing their lockstep conformity upon them. They form a herd mentality, without the mentality.

The movie is not funny, ever, in any way, beginning to end. It's a colossal miscalculation. Tim Allen and Jamie Lee Curtis star, as Luther and Nora Krank, who live in a Chicago suburb with their daughter, Blair (Julie Gonzalo). Julie is going to Peru in the Peace Corps, so this will be their first Christmas without her, and Luther suggests that instead of spending $6,000 on Christmas, he and Nora spend $3,000 on a Caribbean cruise.

Sounds reasonable to me. But perhaps you're wondering how a couple with one child and no other apparent relatives on either side of the family spends $6,000 on Christmas. The answer is, they decorate. Their street coordinates a Christmas display every year in which neighbors compete to hang the most lights from their eaves and clutter the lawn with secular symbolism. Everyone has Frosty on their rooftop.

When the word gets around that the Kranks are taking a year off, the neighborhood posse gets alarmed. Their leader is Vic Frohmeyer (Dan Aykroyd), who leads a delegation to berate them. Before long, pickets are on the front lawn, chanting "Free Frosty!" and the local paper writes a story about "The only house on the block that's keeping Frosty in the basement."

As a satire against neighborhood conformity, *Christmas with the Kranks* might have found a way to be entertaining. But no. The reasonable Kranks are pounded down by the neighbors, and then their daughter decides, after having been away only about two weeks, to fly home for Christmas with her new Peruvian fiancé. So the Kranks of course must have their traditional Christmas Eve party after all, and the third act consists of all the neighbors pitching in to decorate the house, prepare the food and decorations, etc., in a display of self-righteous cooperation that is supposed to be merry but frankly is a little scary. Here's an idea: Why don't the Kranks meet Blair and her fiance in Miami and go on the cruise together?

The movie's complete lack of a sense of humor is proven by its inability to see that the Kranks are reasonable people and their neighbors are monstrous. What it affirms is not the Christmas spirit but the Kranks caving in. What is the movie really about? I think it may play as a veiled threat against non-conformists who don't want to go along with the majority opinion in their community. What used to be known as American individualism is now interpreted as ominous. We're supposed to think there's something wrong with the Kranks. The buried message is: Go along, and follow the lead of the most obnoxious loudmouth on the block.

Christmas, some of my older readers may recall, was once a religious holiday. Not in this movie. Not a single crucifix, not a single creche, not a single mention of the J-name. It's not that I want *Christmas with the Kranks* to get all religious, but that I think it's secular as a cop-out, to avoid any implication of religious intolerance. No matter what your beliefs or lack of them, you can celebrate Christmas in this neighborhood, because it's not about beliefs; it's about a shopping season.

So distant are the spiritual origins of the holiday, indeed, that on Christmas Eve one of the guests at the Kranks's big party is the local priest (Tom Poston), who hangs around gratefully with a benevolent smile. You don't have to be raised Catholic to know that priests do not have time off on Christmas Eve. Why isn't he preparing for Midnight Mass? Apparently because no one in the Kranks's neighborhood is going to attend—they're too busy falling off ladders while stringing decorations on rooftops.

There is, however, one supernatural creature in the movie, and I hope I'm not giving away any secrets by revealing that it is Santa Claus. The beauty of this approach is that Santa is a nonsectarian saint, a supernatural being who exists free of theology. Frosty, on the other hand, is apparently only a snowman.

The Chronicles of Riddick ★ ★
PG-13, 118 m., 2004

Vin Diesel (Richard B. Riddick), Colm Feore (Lord Marshal), Alexa Davalos (Kyra), Karl Urban (Vaako), Thandie Newton (Dame Vaako), Judi Dench (Aereon), Keith David (Abu "Imam" al-Walid), Alexis Llewellyn (Ziza). Directed by David Twohy and produced by Vin Diesel and Scott Kroopf. Screenplay by Twohy.

"In normal times, evil should be fought by good, but in times like this, well, it should be fought by another kind of evil."

So says a character named Aereon in the opening moments of *The Chronicles of Riddick,* a futuristic battle between a fascist misfit and a fascist master race. The opening shot shows a gargantuan steel face that looks like Mussolini after a face-lift, and when the evil Necromongers rally to hail their Lord Marshal, it looks like they've been studying *The Triumph of the Will.*

Against this intergalactic tribe stands one man, a man with the somewhat anticlimactic name of Richard B. Riddick. He is one of the few surviving Furions, fierce warriors who have, alas, mostly been captured and turned into Necromongers. Such is his prowess that with merely his flesh and blood he can defeat and capture a Necromonger fighter ship. What a guy. Riddick, played by Vin Diesel, is a character we first encountered in *Pitch Black,* the 2000 film by the same director, David Twohy. Although a few other characters repeat from that film, notably Abu "Imam" al-Walid (Keith David), there's no real connection between them, apart from Riddick's knack of finding himself on absurdly inhospitable planets. Here he fights for life on Crematoria, a planet whose blazing sun rockets over the horizon every fifteeen minutes or so and bakes everything beneath it. That you can shield yourself from it behind rocks is helpful, although it begs the question of why, since the atmosphere is breathable, the air is not superheated.

But never mind. The Necromongers want everybody to be a Necromonger, and they line up behind the Lord Marshal (Colm Feore), who alone among his race has visited the Underverse. Aereon tells us he returned "half alive and half . . . something else." This Aereon, she's awfully well informed, and has a way of materializing out of thin air. She's a member of the race of Elementals, a fact I share with you since I have no idea what an Elemental is, or was, or wants to be.

Her character is one of several who are introduced with great fanfare and then misplaced. There's also a big-eyed, beautiful little girl named Ziza (Alexis Llewellyn), who keeps asking Riddick if he will fight the monsters, and Riddick keeps looking like he may have a heart of stone but this little girl melts it, and we're all set up for a big scene of monster-bashing and little-girl-saving that somehow never comes. (In this movie, a setup is as good as a payoff, since the last shot clearly establishes that there will be a sequel, and we can find out about all the missing stuff then.)

The Chronicles of Riddick is above all an exercise in computer-generated effects, and indeed the project represents the direction action movies are taking, as its human actors (or their digital clones) are inserted into manifestly artificial scenes that look like frames from the darkest of superhero comic books. The jolly reds, yellows, and blues of the classic Superman and Spiderman have been replaced in these grim days with black and gunmetal gray. *Chronicles* doesn't pause for much character development, and is in such a hurry that even the fight scenes are abbreviated chop-chop sessions. There are a lot of violent fights (the movie is made of them, which explains the PG-13 rating), but never do we get a clear idea of the spatial locations of the characters or their complete physical movements. Twohy breaks the fights down into disconnected flashes of extreme action in close-up, just as a comic book would, and maybe this is a style. It's certainly no more boring than most conventional CGI fight scenes.

I think the Lord Marshal wants to conquer all planets colonized by humans and make them Necromongers, but I was never sure that Richard B. Riddick didn't approve of that. Riddick seems more angered that there is a bounty on his head, and when he wreaks vengeance against the Necromongers, it's personal. His travails are intercut with the story of Vaako and Dame Vaako (Karl Urban and Thandie Newton), who want to overthrow the Lord Marshal, although whether they constitute a movement or just a coterie, I cannot say.

Vin Diesel was born to play a character like Riddick, and he growls and scowls impressively. I like Diesel as an actor and trust he was born to play other, better characters, in movies that make sense. None of the other actors do anything we couldn't do if we looked like them. Films like *The Chronicles of Riddick* gather about them cadres of fans who obsess about every smallest detail, but somehow I don't think *Riddick* will make as many converts as *The Matrix*. In fact, I owe an apology to fans of *The Lord of the Rings* trilogy.

When Richard Roeper reviewed the current two-disc DVD of *The Lord of the Rings: The Return of the King* on TV, I noted that a four-disc set of the movie was coming out later. He observed that the complete trilogy will come out on "an accordion-size set that will take up the next six years of your life." I observed that *LOTR* fans should "get a life." I meant this as an affectionate, ironic throwaway, but have received dozens of wounded e-mails from *Ring* devotees who believe *LOTR* has, indeed, given them a life, and after seeing *The Chronicles of*

Riddick, I agree. They have a life. The prospect of becoming an expert on *Riddick,* in contrast, is too depressing to contemplate.

Cinderella Man ★ ★ ★ ½
PG-13, 144 m., 2005

Russell Crowe (Jim Braddock), Renée Zellweger (Mae Braddock), Paul Giamatti (Joe Gould), Craig Bierko (Max Baer), Bruce McGill (Jimmy Johnston), Paddy Considine (Mike Wilson), Ron Canada (Joe Jeanette), Connor Price (Jay Braddock). Directed by Ron Howard and produced by Brian Grazer, Howard, and Penny Marshall. Screenplay by Cliff Hollingsworth and Akiva Goldsman.

There is a moment early in *Cinderella Man* when we see Russell Crowe in the boxing ring, filled with cocky self-confidence, and I thought I knew what direction the story would take. I could not have been more mistaken. I walked in knowing nothing about Jim Braddock, "The Bulldog of Bergen," whose riches-to-rags-to-riches career inspired the movie. My friend Bill Nack of *Sports Illustrated,* who just won the A.J. Liebling Award, the highest honor a boxing writer can attain, could have told me all about Braddock, but I am just as happy to have gone in cold, so that I could be astonished by Crowe's performance.

I think of Crowe as a tough customer, known to get in the occasional brawl. Yes, he plays men who are inward and complex, as in *The Insider* and *A Beautiful Mind,* or men who are tempered and wise, as in *Master and Commander.* But neither he nor anyone else in a long time has played such a *nice* man as the boxer Jim Braddock. You'd have to go back to actors like James Stewart and Spencer Tracy to find such goodness and gentleness. Tom Hanks could handle the assignment, but do you see any one of them as a prize-fighter? Tracy, maybe.

As the film opens, Braddock is riding high with a series of victories that buy a comfortable, but not opulent, lifestyle for his wife, Mae (Renée Zellweger), and their children, Jay, Rosemarie, and Howard. Also doing okay is Braddock's loyal manager, Joe Gould (Paul Giamatti, in a third home run after *American Splendor* and *Sideways*). Then Braddock breaks his right hand, loses some matches so badly his license is taken away, and descends with his family to grim poverty in the early days of the Great Depression.

What is remarkable during both the highs and the lows is that Jim Braddock, as Crowe plays him, remains level-headed, sweet-tempered, and concerned about his family above all. Perhaps it takes a tough guy like Crowe to make Braddock's goodness believable. Mae is just the wife he deserves, filled with love and loyalty, and so terrified he will be hurt that she refuses to attend his fights and won't even listen on the radio.

Their poverty takes them from a nice family house to a cramped little apartment where there is no heat and hardly anything to eat. Braddock gets a job on the docks in Hoboken, slinging sacks of grain and coal, using his left arm because of his injured right hand, and although that job is a low point, it is also the secret to the left hook that will eventually get him named "Cinderella Man" by Damon Runyon.

The movie teams Crowe once again with director Ron Howard; they made *A Beautiful Mind* together, and the screenwriter of that film, Akiva Goldsman, cowrote this one with Cliff Hollingsworth. They find human ways to mirror the descent into despair; the Braddock family's poverty, for example, seems to weigh most heavily on the oldest son, Jay (Connor Price), who fears above all being sent away to live with "rich" relatives—rich here meaning those with something to eat. He steals a sausage from a butcher shop, is caught, and then, in a scene typical of Braddock's gentle wisdom, is not punished by his father, but talked to, softly and earnestly, because his father instinctively knows why his son stole the sausage, and that the kid's daring was almost noble.

Up to this point, there would not be a comeback, and no occasion for Damon Runyon nicknames. Jim Braddock gets one more chance at a fight, as Gould edges him past the doubts of promoter Jimmy Johnston (Bruce McGill). Without much time to train, he takes on a leading contender and to everyone's amazement wins the fight. One victory leads to another, and finally Gould is able to broker a title fight with the heavyweight champion Max Baer (Craig Bierko), who has killed two of his opponents and seems likely to kill the outweighed and outclassed Braddock.

What happens in the fight you will see. Ron Howard, Russell Crowe, Craig Bierko, the cinematographer Salvatore Totino, and the editors Daniel P. Hanley and Mike Hill step into a ring already populated by the ghosts of countless movie fights, most memorably those in *Raging Bull*, *Million Dollar Baby*, and the *Rocky* movies. They don't try to outfight those movies, but to outmaneuver them emotionally. The closest connection is with *Million Dollar Baby*, also a film about a fighter whose deepest motivation is the fear of poverty (at a press conference, Braddock says he fights in order to be able to buy milk for his family). The visual strategy of the big fight is direct and brutal, but depends not so much on the technical depiction of boxing as on the development of the emotional duel going on in the ring. When an underdog fights from "heart" after his strength and skill are not enough, the result is almost always unconvincing—but not always.

Cinderella Man is a terrific boxing picture, but there's no great need for another one. The need it fills is for a full-length portrait of a good man. Most serious movies live in a world of cynicism and irony, and most good-hearted movie characters live in bad movies. Here is a movie where a good man prevails in a world where every day is an invitation to despair, where resentment would seem fully justified, where doing the right thing seems almost gratuitous, because nobody is looking and nobody cares. Jim Braddock is almost transparent in the simple goodness of his character; that must have made him almost impossible to play. Russell Crowe makes him fascinating, and it takes a moment or two of thought to appreciate how difficult that must have been.

A Cinderella Story ★
PG, 96 m., 2004

Hilary Duff (Sam), Jennifer Coolidge (Fiona), Chad Michael Murray (Austin), Dan Byrd (Carter), Regina King (Rhonda), Julie Gonzalo (Shelby), Lin Shaye (Mrs. Wells), Madeline Zima (Brianna), Andrea Avery (Gabriella). Directed by Mark Rosman and produced by Ilyssa Goodman, Casey La Scala, Hunt Lowry, Dylan Sellers, and Clifford Werber. Screenplay by Leigh Dunlap.

Ernest Madison says he swore off movie critics when they panned Dragonslayer, *one of the favorites of his childhood. "I stopped paying attention to critics because they kept giving bad reviews to good movies," says Madison, now thirty-five.*

Fourteen-year-old Byron Turner feels the same way. He turns to the Web for movie information and trailers, then shares what he's discovered with his friends, his sister, Jasmine, even his mother, Toni.

"I used to watch Roger Ebert, but now I get most of my information from Byron," Toni Turner says. "I don't really pay attention to critics anymore."

—story by Bob Curtright
in the *Wichita Eagle*

Dear Byron,

I know what your mother means because when I was fourteen I was also pummeling my parents with information about new movies and singing stars. I didn't have the Internet, but I grabbed information anywhere I could—mostly from other kids, Hollywood newspaper columnists, and what disk jockeys said. Of course, that was a more innocent time, when movies slowly crept around the country and there was time to get advance warning of a turkey.

Your task is harder than mine was because the typical multiplex movie is heralded by an ad campaign costing anywhere from $20 million to $50 million. Fast-food restaurants now have tie-ins with everyone from Shrek to Spider-Man; when I was a kid we were lucky to get ketchup with the fries. Enormous pressure is put on the target audience to turn out on opening weekends. And Hollywood's most valued target audience, Byron, is teenage males. In other words, you.

So I am writing you in the hope of saving your friends, your sister, Jasmine, and your mother, Toni, from going to see a truly dismal new movie. It is called *A Cinderella Story,* and they may think they'll like it because it stars Hilary Duff. I liked her in *Cheaper by the*

Dozen, and said she was "beautiful and skilled" in *The Lizzie McGuire Movie,* but wrote:

"As a role model, Lizzie functions essentially as a spokeswoman for the teen retail fashion industry, and the most-quoted line in the movie is likely to be when the catty Kate accuses her of being an 'outfit repeater.' Since many of the kids in the audience will not be millionaires and do indeed wear the same outfit more than once, this is a little cruel, but there you go." That's probably something your mother might agree with.

In *A Cinderella Story,* Hilary plays Sam, a Valley Girl whose happy adolescence ends when her dad is killed in an earthquake. That puts her in the clutches of an evil stepmother (Jennifer Coolidge, whom you may remember fondly as Stifler's mom in the *American Pie* movies, although since they were rated R, of course you haven't seen them). Sam also naturally has two evil stepsisters. Half the girls in school have a crush on Austin (Chad Michael Murray), a handsome football star, but Sam never guesses that Austin is secretly kind of poetic—and is, in fact, her best chatroom buddy. She agrees to meet him at the big Halloween dance, wearing a mask to preserve her anonymity; as a disguise, the mask makes her look uncannily like Hilary Duff wearing a mask.

Anyway, this is a lame, stupid movie, but Warner Bros. is spending a fortune, Byron, to convince you to see it and recommend it to your mom and Jasmine. So you must be strong and wise, and do your research. Even though your mother no longer watches my TV show, you use the Internet as a resource and no doubt know about movie review sources like rottentomatoes.com, metacritic.com, and even (pardon me while I wipe away a tear) rogerebert.com. Even when a critic dislikes a movie, if it's a good review, it has enough information so you can figure out whether you'd like it anyway.

For example, this review is a splendid review because it lets you know you'd hate *A Cinderella Story,* and I am pretty much 100 percent sure that you would. So I offer the following advice. Urgently counsel your mom and sister to forget about going out to the movies this week, and instead rent *Ella Enchanted.* This is a movie that sank without a trace, despite the fact that it was magical, funny, intelligent, romantic, and charming. It stars the beautiful Anne Hathaway (from *The Princess Diaries*) as a young girl whose fairy godmother (Vivica A. Fox) puts a spell on her that makes her life extremely complicated. She has the usual evil stepmother and two jealous stepsisters. Will she win the love of Prince Charmont (Hugh Dancy)? *A Cinderella Story* is a terrible movie, sappy and dead in the water, but *Ella Enchanted* is a wonderful movie, and if Jasmine and your mom insist on *Cinderella* you can casually point out what "Ella" is short for.

As for that guy Ernest Madison, he was about eleven when *Dragonslayer* came out. He must have been a child prodigy, to swear off movie critics at an age when most kids don't even know they exist. If he still feels the same way, I hope he goes to see *A Cinderella Story.* That'll teach him.

Your fellow critic,
Roger

Cinemania ★ ★ ★

NO MPAA RATING, 80 m., 2003

Featuring Jack Angstreich, Eric Chadbourne, Harvey Schwartz, Roberta Hill, and Bill Heidbreder. A documentary directed by Angela Christlieb and Stephen Kijak and produced by Gunter Hanfgarn. Screenplay by Christlieb and Kijak.

Cinemania tells the story of five New Yorkers who spend as much of their life as possible going to the movies. They go to a whole lot of movies. It's my job to attend movies, and in a year I probably see only about 450. If I were one of these cinephiles, I would have seen 700 to 1,000, would know the exact count, and would also have the programs, ticket stubs, press kits, and promotional coffee mugs.

These are not crazy people. Maladjusted and obsessed, yes, but who's to say what normal is? I think it makes more sense to see movies all day than to golf, play video games, or gamble. Not everyone agrees. I know people like these, and I understand their desire to be absorbed in the darkness and fantasy. As a professional moviegoer, my life is even a little nuttier than theirs, because they at least choose which titles

to see, and spend a lot of time seeing revivals and classics; I have to monitor whatever is opening every week.

The five cinephiles are Jack Angstreich, Eric Chadbourne, Harvey Schwartz, Roberta Hill, and Bill Heidbreder. They agree that New York ranks with Paris as the best place to see a lot of movies. They have the screening times and subway schedules coordinated to maximize the number of movies they can see in a day, and Jack deliberately eats a constipating diet (no fruits or vegetables) to minimize trips to the rest room. None of them is married (duh), and some talk about their nonexistent sex lives. Bill says he wouldn't want to make love with Rita Hayworth because he couldn't do it in black-and-white, and her dark lips in old b&w movies are crucial to her appeal. Bill was disappointed, too, during a trip to Europe. He loves French movies about people sitting in cafés, but when he went to Paris and sat in a café, he discovered it was—only a café. Not as good as in the movies.

They have their specialties. Bill likes European movies since the French New Wave. Harvey obsesses on running times. Eric will go to see almost anything, including *The Amazing Crab Monster*. Roberta gets in fights with ushers who impede her single-minded determination to see movies. Jack wants to get a cell phone so he can call the booth and complain about the projection without having to walk out to the lobby. For key screenings, they arrive early and save their favorite seats, and they are willing to take direct measures against anyone interfering with their enjoyment of a movie.

They really, really like movies. They cry during them. One stumbled out of *Umbrellas of Cherbourg* and walked for blocks in the rain, weeping. "A commitment to cinema means one must have a technically deviant lifestyle," Jack acknowledges. That includes being able to avoid the tiresome necessity of earning a living. Jack has inheritance ("If I don't blow it all on hookers, I will never have to work"). Bill is on unemployment. Harvey, Eric, and Roberta are on disability, and at one point discuss the possibility that having to go to the movies should qualify them for disability.

They talk warmly and with enthusiasm about certain titles, but I have the eerie feeling that they must be at a movie whether they enjoy it or not. And only a real movie will do. Except for Eric, who also watches a lot of videos, they insist on movies and hate TV. Sometimes their dreams are movies, they say, perhaps in black-and-white or Cinemascope. But only the night-mares are in video. Or is it that anything on video is a nightmare? To be asleep at all is to lose moviegoing time. "I'm so far behind in the cin-ema," Jack sighs, "that it's just a hopeless Sisyphean struggle." As the movie ends, Jack and the other four subjects have gathered to watch another movie: This one.

City of Ghosts ★ ★ ★
R, 116 m., 2003

Matt Dillon (Jimmy Cremming), James Caan (Marvin), Natascha McElhone (Sophie), Gérard Depardieu (Emile), Kem Sereyvuth (Sok), Stellan Skarsgard (Casper), Rose Byrne (Sabrina). Directed by Matt Dillon and produced by Willi Bar, Michael Cerenzie, and Deepak Nayar. Screenplay by Dillon and Barry Gifford.

When a hurricane wipes out large parts of the East Coast, many homeowners are understand-ably alarmed to learn that their insurer, the Ca-pable Trust Co., is incapable of paying their claims because it has no money in the bank. Jimmy Cremming is also upset, or so he tells the cops. Played by Matt Dillon, he runs the U.S. office of the company, which is owned by a shady figure named Marvin, who when last heard from was in Cambodia. When federal agents start asking difficult questions, Jimmy leaves for Phnom Penh to find Marvin.

This is, you will agree, a preposterous setup for a movie. And the rest of the plot of *City of Ghosts* is no more believable. But believability is not everything, as I have to keep reminding myself in these days of *The Matrix Reloaded*. Character and mood also count for some-thing—and so does location, since Matt Dillon shot his movie mostly on location in Cambo-dia; it's the first picture primarily filmed there since *Lord Jim* in 1965.

Dillon and his cinematographer, Jim De-nault, find locations that don't look like loca-tions; they have the untidiness and random details of real places, as indeed they are, and I particularly liked the hotel and bar run by Gérard Depardieu, who shambles around with a big shirt hanging over his belly and breaks up fights while casually holding a baby in his arms. Although such bars, and such exiles as propri-etors, are standard in all *film noir* set in exotic locations, this one had a funky reality that made me muse about a sequel in which we'd find out more about Depardieu, the baby, and a mon-key he seems to have trained as a pickpocket.

In such movies, all visitors to Asia from the West quickly find a local helper who is instantly ready to risk his life to help the foreigner. Mel Gibson's character found Billy Kwan in *The Year of Living Dangerously*, and Dillon's char-acter finds Sok (Kem Sereyvuth), a pedicab dri-ver who serves as chauffeur, spy, and adviser to the outsider. Also hanging around the bar is Casper (Stellan Skarsgard), who says he works with the mysterious Marvin and conveys enig-matic messages. The one character who seems unlikely, although obligatory, is the beautiful woman Sophie (Natascha McElhone), who is an art historian but finds time to get tender with Jimmy. (I wonder if movie Americans who land in Asia are supplied with a list, so they can check off Friendly Bartender, Local Helper, Sinister Insider, Beautiful Girl, Monkey . . .)

Marvin is kept offscreen so long that he be-gins to take on the psychic heft of Harry Lime in *The Third Man*. Such a concealed character needs to have presence when he is revealed, and James Caan rises to the occasion, as a financial hustler who not only stiffed the policyholders of Capable Trust but now seems to be in bed with the Russian Mafia in a scheme to build a luxury hotel and casino.

When and how Jimmy finds Marvin, and what happens then, are surprises for the plot to reveal. What can be said is that the details of Marvin's scheme, and the plans of his enemies, seem more than a little muddled, and yet Dil-lon, as director, handles them in a way that makes the moments convincing, even if they don't add up.

City of Ghosts reminded me of *The Quiet American*, which likewise has visiting Western-ers, beautiful women, sinister local figures, etc. It lacks a monkey, but has a more sharply told story, one with a message. *The Quiet American* was based on Graham Greene's novel about America's illegal activities, circa 1960, in Viet-nam. The screenplay for *City of Ghosts*, by Dil-lon and sometime David Lynch collaborator

Barry Gifford, avoids a rich vein of true Cambodian stories and recycles the kind of generic financial crimes that Hollywood perfected in the 1940s.

Still, sometimes the very texture of the film, and the information that surrounds the characters on the screen, make it worth seeing. I didn't believe in James Caan's cons, but I believed him, and at times like that it's helpful to stop keeping score and live in the moment. Between the Caan and Dillon characters there are atmosphere, desperation, and romance, and, at the end, something approaching true pathos. Enough.

City of God ★ ★ ★ ★
R, 135 m., 2003

Matheus Nachtergaele (Sandro Cenoura), Seu Jorge (Knockout Ned), Alexandre Rodrigues (Rocket), Leandro Firmino da Hora (L'il Zé), Phellipe Haagensen (Bené [Benny]), Jonathan Haagensen (Cabeleira [Shaggy]), Douglas Silva (Dadinho), Roberta Rodriguez Silvia (Berenice), Graziela Moretto (Marina), Renato de Souza (Goose). Directed by Fernando Meirelles and produced by Andrea Barata Ribeiro and Mauricio Andrade Ramos. Screenplay by Bráulio Mantovani, based on the novel by Paulo Lins. In Portuguese with English subtitles.

City of God churns with furious energy as it plunges into the story of the slum gangs of Rio de Janeiro. Breathtaking and terrifying, urgently involved with its characters, it announces a new director of great gifts and passions. Fernando Meirelles. Remember the name. The film has been compared with Martin Scorsese's *Good-Fellas*, and it deserves the comparison. Scorsese's film began with a narrator who said that for as long as he could remember he wanted to be a gangster. The narrator of this film seems to have had no other choice.

The movie takes place in slums constructed by Rio to isolate the poor people from the city center. They have grown into places teeming with life, color, music, and excitement—and also with danger, for the law is absent and violent gangs rule the streets. In the virtuoso sequence opening the picture, a gang is holding a picnic for its members when a chicken escapes. Among those chasing it is Rocket (Alexandre Rodrigues), the narrator. He suddenly finds himself between two armed lines: the gang on one side, the cops on the other.

As the camera whirls around him, the background changes and Rocket shrinks from a teenager into a small boy, playing soccer in a housing development outside Rio. To understand his story, he says, we have to go back to the beginning, when he and his friends formed the Tender Trio and began their lives of what some would call crime and others would call survival.

The technique of that shot—the whirling camera, the flashback, the change in colors from the dark brightness of the slum to the dusty, sunny browns of the soccer field—alert us to a movie that is visually alive and inventive as few films are. Meirelles began as a director of TV commercials, which gave him a command of technique—and, he says, trained him to work quickly, to size up a shot, and get it and move on. Working with the cinematographer César Charlone, he uses quick-cutting and a mobile, handheld camera to tell his story with the haste and detail it deserves. Sometimes those devices can create a film that is merely busy, but *City of God* feels like sight itself, as we look here and then there, with danger or opportunity everywhere.

The gangs have money and guns because they sell drugs and commit robberies. But they are not very rich because their activities are limited to the City of God, where no one has much money. In an early crime, we see the stickup of a truck carrying cans of propane gas, which the crooks sell to homeowners. Later there is a raid on a bordello, where the customers are deprived of their wallets. (In a flashback, we see that raid a second time, and understand in a chilling moment why there were dead bodies at a site where there was not supposed to be any killing.)

As Rocket narrates the lore of the district he knows so well, we understand that poverty has undermined all social structures in the City of God, including the family. The gangs provide structure and status. Because the gang death rate is so high, even the leaders tend to be surprisingly young, and life has no value except when you are taking it. There is an astonishing sequence when a victorious gang leader is killed in a way he least expects, by the last person he would have expected, and we see that essentially he has been killed not by a person but by the culture of crime.

Yet the film is not all grim and violent. Rocket also captures some of the Dickensian flavor of the City of God, where a riot of life provides ready-made characters with nicknames, personas, and trademarks. Some, like Benny (Phellipe Haagensen), are so charismatic they almost seem to transcend the usual rules. Others, like Knockout Ned and L'il Ze, grow from kids into fearsome leaders, their words enforced by death.

The movie is based on a novel by Paulo Lins, who grew up in the City of God, somehow escaped it, and spent eight years writing his book. A note at the end says it is partly based on the life of Wilson Rodriguez, a Brazilian photographer. We watch as Rocket obtains a (stolen) camera that he treasures, and takes pictures from his privileged position as a kid on the streets. He gets a job as an assistant on a newspaper delivery truck, asks a photographer to develop his film, and is startled to see his portrait of an armed gang leader on the front page of the paper.

"This is my death sentence," he thinks, but no: The gangs are delighted by the publicity, and pose for him with their guns and girls. And during a vicious gang war, he is able to photograph the cops killing a gangster—a murder they plan to pass off as gang-related. That these events throb with immediate truth is indicated by the fact that Luiz Inacio Lula da Silva, the president of Brazil, actually reviewed and praised *City of God* as a needful call for change.

In its actual level of violence, *City of God* is less extreme than Scorsese's *Gangs of New York*, but the two films have certain parallels. In both films, there are really two cities: the city of the employed and secure, who are served by law and municipal services, and the city of the castaways, whose alliances are born of opportunity and desperation. Those who live beneath rarely have their stories told. *City of God* does not exploit or condescend, does not pump up its stories for contrived effect, does not contain silly and reassuring romantic sidebars, but simply looks, with a passionately knowing eye, at what it knows.

The Clearing ★ ★ ★
R, 91 m., 2004

Robert Redford (Wayne Hayes), Helen Mirren (Eileen Hayes), Willem Dafoe (Arnold Mack), Alessandro Nivola (Tim Hayes), Matt Craven (Agent Ray Fuller), Melissa Sagemiller (Jill Hayes), Wendy Crewson (Louise Miller). Directed by Pieter Jan Brugge and produced by Brugge, Jonah Smith, and Palmer West. Screenplay by Justin Haythe and Brugge.

A movie that begins with a pleasant morning in an ordinary marriage is never about mornings or marriages. As *The Clearing* opens, we meet Wayne and Eileen Hayes, long and apparently happily married, in their elegant stone-walled mansion in a woodsy suburb. Wayne (Robert Redford) gets in his car, at the end of his driveway stops for a man who seems to know him, and finds himself kidnapped at gunpoint. Eileen (Helen Mirren) has a cup of coffee at the side of their pool.

We've already met the kidnapper, a man named Arnold Mack (Willem Dafoe). He lives with his perpetually disappointed wife and her father in a row house in a nearby city. We see him paste on a mustache in the mirror, which seems odd, and we follow him as he travels to his work (kidnapping) on a commuter train. Arnold approaches Wayne with such easy familiarity, waving a manila envelope as if it contained important papers, that Wayne automatically stops and puts down the car window for him. Perhaps he even sort of remembers him, or feels that good manners require him to say that he does.

The movie intercuts between two story lines: Wayne, his hands tied, led by Arnold on a long trek at gunpoint through a wooded area; and Eileen, concerned when he doesn't return home and eventually calling in the FBI. These time lines are not parallel, a fact that eventually occurs to us, along with its implications.

We learn a lot about Wayne as he and Arnold talk. Arnold has studied up on him, knows he's a self-made millionaire who bought and sold a car rental company at the right time. Wayne is rich, lives surrounded by luxury, and is expensively dressed, but he has the tough instincts of a negotiator, and tries to talk Arnold out of the kidnapping. Arnold says the men who hired him are waiting in a cottage at the end of their walk, and Wayne asks him why those men should honor their deal with him. Arnold, who is not a professional criminal, listens politely and perhaps agrees with some of what Wayne says.

In the mansion, Eileen deals with an FBI agent (Matt Craven) who is all business, too much business. Her children, Tim and Jill (Alessandro Nivola and Melissa Sagemiller), join the vigil with their mother, and privately share an interesting insight: At first, their mother was afraid Wayne might simply have run away from the marriage. The FBI man finds out about an affair Wayne had, and discusses it in front of the children. That angers Eileen, who knew about it but didn't want them to know. And it sets up one of the most extraordinary scenes in the movie, a meeting between Eileen and Louise Miller (Wendy Crewson), who was her husband's mistress. This scene is written so precisely and acted so well that it sidesteps all the hazards of jealousy and sensation, and becomes simply a discussion of emotional realities.

What happens, of course, I cannot reveal, nor will it be what you expect. Indeed, the events in a late scene are so unexpected and yet so logical that we are nodding with agreement as we react with surprise. And there is another scene, after that, indirectly dealing with psychological truth, with why people do the things they do, although I must say no more.

The Clearing is the first film directed by the successful producer Pieter Jan Brugge *(The Insider, The Pelican Brief, Heat)*. The screenplay is by Brugge and Justin Haythe, a British novelist. They know how to make a conventional thriller, but are not interested in making one. Instead, they use the crime here as the engine to drive their parallel psychological portraits. While Eileen has the reality of her marriage made uncomfortably clear, Wayne and Arnold engage in a little subtle class warfare. Wayne acts as if he was born to lead, and Arnold thinks of himself as a born loser with one last chance to hit a jackpot. Certainly, kidnapping offers enormous penalties and uncertain rewards, and Wayne thinks maybe Arnold doesn't really have the stomach for it.

What finally happens, and how, has a certain inevitable rightness to it, but you can't say you see it coming, especially since *The Clearing* doesn't feel bound by the usual formulas of crime movies. What eventually happens will emerge from the personalities of the characters, not from the requirements of Hollywood endings. Sensing that, we grow absorbed in the story, knowing that what happens along the way will decide what happens at the end.

Closer ★ ★ ★ ★
R, 101 m., 2004

Julia Roberts (Anna), Jude Law (Dan), Natalie Portman (Alice), Clive Owen (Larry). Directed by Mike Nichols and produced by Cary Brokaw, John Calley, and Nichols. Screenplay by Patrick Marber, based on his play.

Mike Nichols's *Closer* is a movie about four people who richly deserve one another. Fascinated by the game of love, seduced by seduction itself, they play at sincere, truthful relationships that are lies in almost every respect except their desire to sleep with each other. All four are smart and ferociously articulate, adept at seeming forthright and sincere even in their most shameless deceptions.

"The truth," one says. "Without it, we're animals." Actually, truth causes them more trouble than it saves, because they seem compelled to be most truthful about the ways in which they have been untruthful. There is a difference between confessing you've cheated because you feel guilt and seek forgiveness, and confessing merely to cause pain.

The movie stars, in order of appearance, Jude Law, Natalie Portman, Julia Roberts, and Clive Owen. Law plays Dan, who writes obituaries for his London newspaper; Portman is Alice, an American who says she was a stripper and fled New York to end a relationship; Roberts is Anna, an American photographer; and Owen is Larry, a dermatologist. The characters connect in a series of Meet Cutes that are perhaps no more contrived than in real life.

In the opening sequence, the eyes of Alice and Dan (Portman and Law) meet as they approach each other on a London street. Eye contact leads to an amused flirtation, and then Alice, distracted, steps into the path of a taxicab. Knocked on her back, she opens her eyes, sees Dan, and says "Hello, stranger."

Time passes. Dan writes a novel based on his relationship with Alice, and has his book jacket photo taken by Anna, whom he immediately desires. More time passes. Dan, who has been with Anna, impersonates a woman named "Anna" on a chat line, and sets up a date with Larry, a stranger. When Larry turns up as planned at the Aquarium, Anna is there, but when he describes "their" chat, she disillusions him: "I think you were talking with Daniel Wolf."

Eventually both men will have sex with both women, occasionally as a round trip back to the woman they started with. There is no constancy in this crowd: When they're not with the one they love, they love the one they're with. It is a good question, actually, whether any of them are ever in love at all, although they do a good job of saying they are.

They are all so very articulate, which is refreshing in a time when literate and evocative speech has been devalued in the movies. Their words are by Patrick Marber, based on his award-winning play. Consider Dan as he explains to Alice his job writing obituaries. There is a kind of shorthand, he tells her: "If you say someone was 'convivial,' that means he was an alcoholic. 'He was a private person' means he was gay. 'Enjoyed his privacy' means he was a raging queen."

Forced to rank the four characters in order of their nastiness, I would place Dr. Larry at the top of the list. He seems to derive genuine enjoyment from the verbal lacerations he administers, pointing out the hypocrisies and evasions of the others. Dan is an innocent by comparison; he wants to be bad, but isn't good at it. Anna, the photographer, is accurately sniffed out by Alice as a possible lover of Dan. "I'm not a thief, Alice," she says, but she is. Alice seems the most innocent and blameless of the four until the very end of the movie, when we are forced to ask if everything she did was a form of stripping, in which much is revealed, but little is surrendered. "Lying is the most fun a girl can have without taking her clothes off," she tells Dr. Larry, "but it's more fun if you do."

There's a creepy fascination in the way these four characters stage their affairs while occupying impeccable lifestyles. They dress and present themselves handsomely. They fit right in at the opening of Anna's photography exhibition. (One of the photos shows Alice with tears on her face as she discerns that Dan was unfaithful with Anna; that's the stuff that art is made of, isn't it?) They move in that London tourists never quite see, the London of trendy restaurants on dodgy streets, and flats that are a compromise between affluence and the exorbitant price of housing. There is the sense that their trusts and betrayals are not fundamentally important to them; "You've ruined my life," one says, and is told, "You'll get over it."

Yes, unless, fatally, true love does strike at just that point when all the lies have made it impossible. Is there anything more pathetic than a lover who realizes he (or she) really is in love, after all the trust has been lost, all the bridges burnt, and all the reconciliations used up?

Mike Nichols has been through the gender wars before, in films like *Carnal Knowledge* and *Who's Afraid of Virginia Woolf?* Those films, especially *Woolf,* were about people who knew and understood each other with a fearsome intimacy, and knew all the right buttons to push. What is unique about *Closer,* making it seem right for these insincere times, is that the characters do not understand each other, or themselves. They know how to go through the motions of pushing the right buttons, and how to pretend their buttons have been pushed, but do they truly experience anything at all except their own pleasure?

Coach Carter ★ ★ ★
PG-13, 140 m., 2005

Samuel L. Jackson (Coach Ken Carter), Robert Ri'chard (Damien Carter), Rob Brown (Kenyon Stone), Debbi Morgan (Tonya Carter), Ashanti (Kyra), Rick Gonzalez (Timo Cruz). Directed by Thomas Carter and produced by David Gale, Brian Robbins, and Michael Tollin. Screenplay by Mark Schwahn and John Gatins.

Samuel L. Jackson made news by refusing to costar with 50 Cent in a movie based on the rapper's life. He not only refused, but did it publicly, even though the film is to be directed by six-time Oscar nominee Jim Sheridan (*In America*). A clue to Jackson's thinking may be found in his film, *Coach Carter,* based on the true story of a California high school basketball coach who placed grades ahead of sports. Like Bill Cosby, Jackson is arguing against the antiintellectual message that success for young black males is better sought in the worlds of rap and sports than in the classroom.

There is, however, another aspect to Jackson's refusal: He said he thought Sheridan wanted him to "lend legitimacy" to 50 Cent's acting debut. He might have something there. Jackson has an authority on the screen; he occupies a character with compelling force, commanding attention, and can bring class to a movie. He might, he said, be interested in working with 50 Cent after the rapper makes another five movies or so, and earns his chops.

This reasoning may not be fair. Consider the work that Ice Cube did in *Boyz N the Hood* (1991), his first movie and the beginning of a successful acting career. Or look at the promise that Tupac Shakur showed, especially in his last feature, *Gridlock'd* (1997), holding his own with the veteran Tim Roth. Maybe 50 Cent has the stuff to be an actor. Maybe not. Jackson's decision may have more to do with the underlying values of the rapper's life; he may not consider 50 Cent's career, so often involving violent episodes, to be much of a role model.

Role models are what *Coach Carter*, Jackson's film, is all about. He plays Ken Carter, who began as a sports star at Richmond (California) High School, setting records that still stand, and then had success in the military and as a small businessman. He's asked to take over as basketball coach, an unpaid volunteer position; the former coach tells him, "I can't get them to show up for school." Ken Carter thinks he can fix that.

The movie was directed by Thomas Carter (*Save the Last Dance*), no relation to the coach. It follows long-established genre patterns; it's not only a sports movie with the usual big games and important shots, but also a coach movie, with inspiring locker-room speeches and difficult moral decisions. There are certain parallels with *Friday Night Lights*, although there it's the movie itself, and not the coach, that underlines the futility of high school stars planning on pro sports as a career.

Certainly both movies give full weight to public opinion in the communities where they're set—places where the public's interest in secondary education seems entirely focused on sports, where coaches are more important than teachers, where scores are more important than grades.

Coach Carter wants to change all that. He walks into a gymnasium ruled by loud, arrogant, disrespectful student jocks, and commands attention with the fierceness of his attitude. He makes rules. He requires the students to sign a contract, promising to maintain a decent grade-point average as the price of being on the team. He deals with the usual personnel problems; a star player named Kenyon Stone (Ron Brown) has a pregnant girlfriend named Kyra (Ashanti, in her, a-hem, first role), and she sees a threat to her future in Carter's determination to get his players into college.

Ken Carter's most dramatic decision, which got news coverage in 1999, was to lock the gymnasium, forfeit games, and endanger the team's title chances after some of his players refused to live up to the terms of the contract. The community, of course, is outraged that a coach would put grades above winning games; for them, the future for the student athletes lies in the NBA, not education. Given the odds against making it in the NBA (dramatically demonstrated in the great documentary *Hoop Dreams*), this reasoning is like considering the lottery a better bet than working for a living.

Jackson has the usual big speeches assigned to all coaches in all sports movies, and delivers on them, big time. His passion makes familiar scenes feel new. "I see a system that's designed for you to fail," he tells his players, pointing out that young black men are 80 percent more likely to go to prison than to go to college. The movie's closing credits indicate that six of the team members did go on to college, five with scholarships. Lives, not games, were won.

Code 46 ★ ★ ½
R, 92 m., 2004

Tim Robbins (William), Samantha Morton (Maria), Om Puri (Backland), Jeanne Balibar (Sylvie). Directed by Michael Winterbottom and produced by Andrew Eaton. Screenplay by Frank Cottrell Boyce.

Michael Winterbottom's *Code 46* reminds me of a William Gibson novel; the values and mood of *film noir* are linked with modern alienation and futuristic newspeak. The film takes place in cities named Seattle and Shanghai, although they may not be the cities of today, and the hero ventures from one to the other to track down traffickers in stolen or forged "papelles"—papers necessary to travel from one zone of this world to another.

The papelles function not like passports but like genetic ID codes. In this future, couples are forbidden to reproduce unless their DNA is a good match: no more first cousins or recessive negative traits in the bedroom. This positive breeding strategy is not racist but a form of quality control, and indeed, races and cultures seem mingled in Winterbottom's new world, and words from many languages are mixed into everyday speech. Samantha Morton, who plays the heroine, looks as British as the queen but is named Maria Gonzalez, perhaps suggesting ethnic distinctions have been lost in generations of government-supervised DNA matchups.

The hero, played by Tim Robbins, has a name well suited to this context: William Geld. He's on assignment to Shanghai to investigate Maria, a suspect in the papelle operation, but is thunderstruck by love the moment he sets eyes on her. This may be because romance in science fiction is more often a plot convenience than an emotional process. Or it may be because William has been injected with an "empathy virus" that allows him powerful intuitive powers. He investigates in the Dr. Phil style, by feeling your pain. He sees into souls. And in the case of Maria, to know, know, know her is to love, love, love her.

The viruses are an ingenious idea, one of many enriching the screenplay by Frank Cottrell Boyce, who undoubtedly contracted the empathy virus himself before writing *Hilary and Jackie,* and whose intelligence and imagination are well suited for collaboration with the restless, eclectic, never predictable Winterbottom. If you're familiar with the titles *Butterfly Kiss, Welcome to Sarajevo, The Claim,* and *24 Hour Party People,* ask yourself how these films and *Code 46* could possibly have been created by the same two people. Their luncheon conversations must resemble a season of Charlie Rose.

Viruses, of course, carry information. That's what they do, and zoologist Richard Dawkins points out that from their point of view, they are the life form and we are simply the carriers to get them from one generation to the next. Boyce indirectly but amusingly suggests how they work when Maria mentions she once tried a virus that allowed her to speak Mandarin: "Chinese people could understand what I was saying, but I couldn't." Why does that line make me think of Groucho Marx?

Maria and William engage in a daring, forbidden romance and exchange information that's subversive under the new laws. Her crime was to help a friend get papelles in order to travel to India to study a rare breed of bats. India, apparently, is not part of the DNA-protected zone, and indeed there are "freeports" throughout the world where the rules don't apply. That raises the question of why anybody would go to the trouble of living under these rules: It's like moving all the way to Singapore just in case you're ever seized with the need to chew gum or spit on the sidewalk. The love scenes between Maria and William are enlivened by his empathy virus, as you might imagine; I assume it makes him a rare male who knows *and* cares how his partner is feeling. Such science fiction aids to romance have been insufficiently explored. If Lois Lane gets Clark Kent into the sack, I hope she shares with us about the Man of Steel.

But I digress. The problem with *Code 46* is that the movie, filled with ideas and imagination, is murky in its rules and intentions. I cannot say I understand the hows and whys of this future world, nor do I much care, since it's mostly a clever backdrop to a love affair that would easily teleport to many other genres: Investigator falls in love with mystery woman, helps her commit crime, risks being left hanging out to dry. *Double Indemnity.*

William knows she's guilty, frames someone else, leaves after their affair to go home to his wife and family, then returns to Maria because his wife offers less to empathize with, or perhaps because neither one of them understands when he speaks Mandarin. But back in Shanghai, he finds that Maria's memory of him has been erased, indicating that the future didn't learn its lesson from *Eternal Sunshine of the Spotless Mind*. And then the freeport business at the end isn't so much like lovers leaving paradise to live in hell, as like suburbanites moving to San Francisco.

Code 46 is filled with ideas. Robbins and Morton in their scenes together suggest the same kind of lonely sharing of needs I responded to in *Lost in Translation* (a movie about people trying to catch the empathy virus but ending up with its antibody, jet lag). There's nice control of moods in the intimate dialogue scenes, but the movie is more successful at introducing the slang and science of the future than incorporating it into a story.

Coffee and Cigarettes ★ ★ ★

R, 96 m., 2004

With Roberto Benigni, Steven Wright, Joie Lee, Cinque Lee, Steve Buscemi, Iggy Pop, Tom Waits, Joe Rigano, Vinny Vella, Vinny Vella Jr., Renee French, E. J. Rodriguez, Alex Descas, Isaach De Bankole, Cate Blanchett, Meg White, Jack White, Alfred Molina, Steve Coogan, GZA, RZA, Bill Murray, Bill Rice, and Taylor Mead. Directed by Jim Jarmusch and produced by Joana Vicente and Jason Kliot. Screenplay by Jarmusch.

Jim Jarmusch has been working on *Coffee and Cigarettes* for so long that when he started the project, you could still smoke in a coffee shop. The idea was to gather unexpected combinations of actors and, well, let them talk over coffee and cigarettes. He began with the short film *Coffee and Cigarettes I*, filmed in 1986, before we knew who Roberto Benigni was (unless we'd seen Jarmusch's *Down by Law*). Benigni the verbal hurricane strikes the withdrawn Steven Wright, and is so eager to do him a favor that he eventually goes to the dentist for him.

There's no more to it than that, but how much more do you need? A few minutes, and the skit is over. None of these eleven vignettes overstays its welcome, although a few seem to lose their way. And although Jarmusch has the writing credit, we have the feeling at various moments (as when Bill Murray walks in on a conversation between RZA and GZA of Wu-Tang Clan and exchanges herbal remedies with them) that improvisation plays a part.

My favorite among the segments is one of the longest, starring the actors Alfred Molina and Steve Coogan. Molina has asked for the meeting. Coogan is not sure why, and grows more condescending as Molina, all politeness and charm, explains that his genealogical researchers have discovered that the two men are related through a common Italian ancestor centuries ago. Molina hopes perhaps this connection might lead to them becoming friends and "doing things together." Coogan is distinctly unenthusiastic, until Molina says something that impresses him, and then he becomes ingratiating. In its compact way, this segment contains a lot of human nature.

The structure—smoking and drinking—provides all the explanation we need for the meetings, although sometimes the actors seem to smoke a little too self-consciously, and Murray drinks his coffee straight from the pot. The prize for virtuosity goes to Cate Blanchett, who plays a dual role: herself and her cousin. As herself, she is the movie star Cate Blanchett. As her cousin, she is quietly jealous of Cate's success, and feels patronized when Cate gives her some perfume—a bottle, she correctly guesses, that the star just received as a freebie.

The third of the segments to be filmed, "Somewhere in California," won the award for best short at Cannes and is a little masterpiece of observation about two musicians acutely aware of who they are and who the other one is, while trying to appear unimpressed. Tom Waits and Iggy Pop star, in a subtle bout of one-upmanship. Agreeing that they have given up smoking, they smoke—which is okay, they agree, as long as they've given it up. They're sitting next to a jukebox, which leads to a little understated competition over who does, or doesn't, have songs on the machine.

Sometimes a segment depends largely on the screen persona of an actor. That's the case with a conversation between Cinque and Joie Lee and Steve Buscemi, who confides incredible facts to them in an all-knowing style, so confident they are powerless to penetrate it. Elvis was replaced by his twin brother, Buscemi explains, but it's not the theory that's amusing so much as his determination to force it upon two listeners manifestly not eager to hear it.

Sometimes movies tire us by trying too relentlessly to pound us with their brilliance and energy. Here is a movie pitched at about the energy level of a coffee break. That the people are oddly assorted and sometimes very strange is not so very unusual, considering some of the conversations you overhear in Starbucks.

Cold Creek Manor ★ ½
R, 118 m., 2003

Dennis Quaid (Cooper Tilson), Sharon Stone (Leah Tilson), Stephen Dorff (Dale Massie), Juliette Lewis (Ruby), Kristen Stewart (Kristen Tilson), Ryan Wilson (Jesse Tilson), Dana Eskelson (Sheriff Annie Ferguson), Christopher Plummer (Mr. Massie). Directed by Mike Figgis and produced by Figgis and Annie Stewart. Screenplay by Richard Jefferies.

Cold Creek Manor is another one of those movies where a demented fiend devotes an extraordinary amount of energy to setting up scenes for the camera. Think of the trouble it would be for one man, working alone, to kill a horse and dump it into a swimming pool. The movie is an anthology of clichés, not neglecting both the Talking Killer, who talks when he should be at work, and the reliable climax where both the villain and his victims go to a great deal of inconvenience to climb to a high place so that one of them can fall off.

The movie stars Dennis Quaid and Sharon Stone as Cooper and Leah Tilson, who get fed up with the city and move to the country, purchasing a property that looks like *The House of the Seven Gables* crossed with *The Amityville Horror*. This house is going to need a lot of work. In *Under the Tuscan Sun*, Diane Lane is able to find some cheerful Polish workers to rehab her Tuscan villa, but the Tilsons have the extraordinarily bad judgment to hire the former owner of the house, Dale Massie (Stephen Dorff), an ex-con with a missing family. "Do you know what you're getting yourselves into?" asks a helpful local. No, but everybody in the audience does.

The movie of course issues two small children to the Tilsons, so that their little screams can pipe up on cue, as when the beloved horse is found in the pool. And both Cooper and Leah are tinged with the suggestion of adultery, because in American movies, as we all know, sexual misconduct leads to bad real estate choices.

In all movies involving city people who move to the country, there is an unwritten rule that everybody down at the diner knows all about the history of the new property and the secrets of its former owners. The locals act as a kind of Greek chorus, living permanently at the diner and prepared on a moment's notice to issue portentous warnings or gratuitous insults. The key player this time is Ruby (Juliette Lewis), Dale's battered girlfriend, whose sister is Sheriff Annie Ferguson (Dana Eskelson). Ruby smokes a lot, always an ominous sign, and is ambiguous about Dale—she loves the lug, but gee, does he always have to be pounding on her? The scene where she claims she wasn't hit, she only fell, is the most perfunctory demonstration possible of the battered woman in denial.

No one in this movie has a shred of common sense. The Tilsons are always leaving doors open even though they know terrible dangers lurk outside, and they are agonizingly slow to realize that Dale Massie is not only the wrong person to rehab their house, but the wrong person to be in the same state with.

Various clues, accompanied by portentous music, ominous winds, gathering clouds, etc., lead to the possibility that clues to Dale's crimes can be found at the bottom of an old well, and we are not disappointed in our expectation that Sharon Stone will sooner or later find herself at the bottom of that well. But answer me this: If you were a vicious mad-dog killer and wanted to get rid of the Tilsons and had just pushed Leah down the well, and Cooper was all alone in the woods leaning over the well and trying to pull his wife back to the surface, would you just go ahead and push him in? Or what?

But no. The audience has to undergo an extended scene in which Cooper is not pushed down the well, in order for everyone to hurry back to the house, climb up to the roof, fall off, etc. Dale Massie is not a villain in this movie, but an enabler, a character who doesn't want to kill but exists only to expedite the plot. Everything he does is after a look at the script, so that he appears, disappears, threatens, seems nice, looms, fades, pushes, doesn't push, all so that we in the audience can be frightened or, in my case, amused.

Cold Creek Manor was directed by Mike Figgis, a superb director of drama *(Leaving Las Vegas)*, digital experimentation *(Timecode)*, adaptations of the classics *(Miss Julie)*, and atmospheric *film noir (Stormy Monday)*. But he has made a thriller that thrills us only if we abandon all common sense. Of course, preposterous things happen in all thrillers, but there must be at least a gesture in the direction of plausibility, or we lose patience. When evil Dale Massie just stands there in the woods and doesn't push Cooper Tilson down the well, he stops being a killer and becomes an excuse for the movie to toy with us—and it's always better when a thriller toys with the victims instead of the audience.

Cold Mountain ★ ★ ★

R, 150 m., 2003

Jude Law (Inman), Nicole Kidman (Ada Monroe), Renée Zellweger (Ruby Thewes), Donald Sutherland (Reverend Monroe), Ray Winstone (Teague), Brendan Gleeson (Stobrod Thewes), Philip Seymour Hoffman (Reverend Veasey), Natalie Portman (Sara), Eileen Atkins (Maddy), Giovanni Ribisi (Junior), Kathy Baker (Sally Swanger). Directed by Anthony Minghella and produced by Albert Berger, William Horberg, Sydney Pollack, and Ron Yerxa. Screenplay by Minghella, based on the book by Charles Frazier.

Cold Mountain has the same structural flaw as *The Mexican* (2001), a movie you've forgotten all about. Both stories establish a torrid romantic magnetism between two big stars, and then keep them far apart for almost the entire movie. Filling the gap in both films is a quirky supporting character who makes us unreasonably grateful, because the leads take themselves very seriously indeed, and speak as if being charged by the word. Hardly anybody but me gave *The Mexican* a favorable review, and I'm sort of in favor of *Cold Mountain,* too—not because of the noble and portentous reasons you will read about in the ads, but because it evokes a backwater of the Civil War with beauty, and lights up with an assortment of colorful supporting characters.

The movie stars Nicole Kidman as Ada Monroe, the daughter of a Charleston preacher man (Donald Sutherland) who has moved to the district for his health. The first time she meets Inman (Jude Law), their eyes lock and a deep, unspoken communication takes place. Inman, as shy and awkward as a ploughboy in a ballet, contrives excuses to be standing about slack-jawed when she comes into view, but she has mercy on him, and after he has joined the Confederates and gone off to fight the war, she observes, "I count the number of words that have passed between us, Inman and me—not very many. But I think about it." So few are their meetings, indeed, that later in the story they're able to count off on their fingers every time they have seen each other, and it doesn't take long enough to make us restless.

Ada's father dies, leaving her as a poor city girl to farm the land, something she is ill-equipped to do. A sensible neighbor lady dispatches an energetic young woman named Ruby (Renée Zellweger) to help out, and Ruby sets to work splitting rails, milking cows, wringing turkey necks, and expressing herself of opinions so colorful Garrison Keillor would blush with envy. Ruby and Ada are also prepared to stand in their doorway with a rifle when necessary, and just as well, since the home guard is captained by Teague (Ray Winstone), who figures Inman isn't going to come home, and that Ada will need a man to protect her—against Teague, for that matter.

Inman witnesses one of the most horrible battles of the war, in a set-piece that director Anthony Minghella and production designer Dante Ferratti can be proud of. After Union troops tunnel under Confederate lines and set off powerful explosives, the position caves in—but not with the expected results. The Union men, pushed forward by those behind them, are hurled down into the vast bomb crater, and it's a "turkey shoot" as the Confederates pick them off. That Inman jumps down to save a friend is unwise, that he survives is unlikely, and that he decides to heed the latest letter from Ada and walk away from the war and back to her is unsurprising.

His long trek back to Cold Mountain has been compared with some justice to Homer's *Odyssey,* since he meets fabled characters and seductresses along the way, but in a movie that begins with the two heroes barely meeting each other, this long sequence becomes alarming: Will their reunion take place in old age?

To return to the comparison with *The Mexican*—it too went to extraordinary lengths to tell parallel stories that separated Brad Pitt and Julia Roberts, despite the manifest fact that the audience had purchased tickets in order to see them together. It was only the fortuitous appearance of a colorful crook played by James Gandolfini that saved the film and brought life to Roberts's scenes—just as, this time, Renée Zellweger saves the day.

There is so much to enjoy about *Cold Mountain* that I can praise it for its parts, even though it lacks a whole. I admire the characters played by Kidman and Law, even though each one is an island, entire to himself. I loved Renée Zellweger's gumption, and the way she treats a dress like a dishrag. The battle scenes and the Civil War landscapes (shot in Romania) had beauty and majesty. But Ray Winstone's villain turns up so faithfully when required that he ought to be checking his clock like Captain Hook, and although there is true poignancy in Inman's encounter with the desperate widow Sara (Natalie Portman), it is poignancy that belongs in another movie. Nothing takes the suspense out of Boy Meets Girl like your knowledge that Boy Has Already Met Star.

By the end of the film you admire the artistry and the care, you know that the actors worked hard and are grateful for their labors, but you wonder who in God's name thought this was a promising scenario for a movie. It's not a story; it's an idea. Consider even the letters that Ada and Inman write each other. You can have a perfectly good love story based on correspondence—but only, I think, if the letters arrive, are read, and are replied to. There are times when we feel less like the audience than like the post office.

Collateral ★ ★ ★ ½
R, 119 m., 2004

Tom Cruise (Vincent), Jamie Foxx (Max), Jada Pinkett Smith (Annie), Mark Ruffalo (Fanning), Peter Berg (Weidner), Bruce McGill (Pedrosea), Barry Shabaka Henley (Daniel), Irma P. Hall (Ida). Directed by Michael Mann and produced by Mann and Julie Richardson. Screenplay by Stuart Beattie.

Collateral opens with Tom Cruise exchanging briefcases with a stranger in an airport. Then, intriguingly, it seems to turn into another movie. We meet a cab driver named Max (Jamie Foxx), who picks up a ride named Annie (Jada Pinkett Smith). She's all business. She rattles off the streets he should take to get her to downtown Los Angeles. He says he knows a faster route. They end up making a bet: The ride will be free if he doesn't get them downtown faster.

The scene continues. It's not about flirtation. Sometimes you need to have only a few words with a person to know you would like to have many more. They open up. She's a federal prosecutor who confesses she's so nervous the night before a big case that she cries. He says he plans to own his own limousine service. They like each other. He lets her get out of the cab and knows he should have asked for her number. Then she taps on the window and gives him her card.

This is a long scene to come at the beginning of a thriller, but a good one, establishing two important characters. It is also good on its own terms, like a self-contained short film. It allows us to learn things about Max we could not possibly learn in the scenes to follow, and adds a subtext after the next customer into his cab is Tom Cruise.

Cruise plays a man named Vincent, who seems certain, centered, and nice. He needs a driver to spend all night with him, driving to five destinations, and offers Max six crisp $100 bills as persuasion. First stop, an apartment building. No parking in front. Vincent tells Max to wait for him in the alley. If you know nothing about the film, save this review until after.

A body lands on top of the cab. "You threw him out of the window and killed him?" Max asks incredulously. No, says Vincent, the bullets killed him, *then* he went out the window. So now we know more about Vincent. The movie is structured to make his occupation a surprise, but how much of a surprise can it be when the movie's Web site cheerfully blurts out: "Vincent is a contract killer." Never mind. The surprise about Vincent's occupation is the least of the movie's pleasures.

Collateral is essentially a long conversation between a killer and a man who fears for his life. Director Michael Mann punctuates the conversation with what happens at each of the five stops, where he uses detailed character roles and convincing dialogue by writer Stuart

Beattie to create, essentially, more short films that could be freestanding. Look at the heartbreaking scene where Vincent takes Max along with him into a nightclub, where they have a late-night talk with Daniel (Barry Shabaka Henley), the owner. Daniel remembers a night Miles Davis came into the club, recalling it with such warmth and wonder, such regret for his own missed opportunities as a musician, that we're looking into the window of his life.

Mann is working in a genre with *Collateral*, as he was in *Heat* (1995), but he deepens the genre through the kind of specific detail that would grace a straight drama. Consider a scene where Vincent asks (or orders) Max to take him to the hospital where Max's mother is a patient. The mother is played by Irma P. Hall (the old lady in the Coens' *The Ladykillers*), and she makes an instant impression, as a woman who looks at this man with her son, intuits that everything might not be right, and keeps that to herself.

These scenes are so much more interesting than the standard approach of the shifty club owner or the comic-relief Big Mama. Mann allows dialogue into the kind of movie that many directors now approach as wall-to-wall action. Action gains a lot when it happens to convincing individuals, instead of to off-the-shelf action figures.

What's particularly interesting is the way he, and Cruise, modulate the development of Vincent as a character. Vincent is not what he seems, but his secret is not that he's a killer; that's merely his occupation. His secret is his hidden psychological life going back to childhood, and in the way he thinks all the time about what life means, even as he takes it. When Max tells him the taxi job is "temporary" and talks about his business plans, Vincent finds out how long he's been driving a cab (twelve years) and quotes John Lennon: "Life is what happens while you're making other plans." Max tells Vincent something, too: "You lack standard parts that are supposed to be there in most people."

I would have preferred for the movie to end in something other than a chase scene, particularly one involving a subway train, but Mann directs it well. And he sets it up with a cat-and-mouse situation in a darkened office, which is very effective; it opens with a touch of *Rear Window* as Max watches what's happening on different floors of an office building.

Cruise and the filmmakers bring a great deal more to his character than we expect in a thriller. What he reveals about Vincent, deliberately and unintentionally, leads up to a final line that is worthy of one of those nihilistic French crime movies from the 1950s. Jamie Foxx's work is a revelation. I've thought of him in terms of comedy *(Booty Call, Breakin' All the Rules)*, but here he steps into a dramatic lead and is always convincing and involving. Now I'm looking forward to him playing Ray Charles; before, I wasn't so sure. And observe the way Jada Pinkett Smith sidesteps the conventions of the Meet Cute and brings everyday plausibility to every moment of Annie's first meeting with Max. This is a rare thriller that's as much character study as sound and fury.

The Company ★ ★ ★ ½
PG-13, 112 m., 2003

Neve Campbell (Ry), Malcolm McDowell (Alberto Antonelli), James Franco (Josh), Barbara E. Robertson (Harriet), William Dick (Edouard), Susie Cusack (Susie). Directed by Robert Altman and produced by Joshua Astrachan and David Levy. Screenplay by Barbara Turner.

"You have to fiddle on the corner where the quarters are."

—Robert Altman

Why did it take me so long to see what was right there in front of my face—that *The Company* is the closest Robert Altman has come to making an autobiographical film? I've known him since 1970, have been on the sets of many of his films, had more than a drink with him in the old days, and know that this movie reflects exactly the way he works—how he assembles cast, story, and location and plunges in up to his elbows, stirring the pot. With Altman, a screenplay is not only a game plan but a diversionary tactic, to distract the actors (and characters) while Altman sees what they've got.

The Company involves a year in the life of the Joffrey Ballet of Chicago, during which some careers are born, others die, romance glows uncertainly, a new project begins as a mess and improbably starts to work, and there is never enough money. The central characters are Ry (Neve Campbell), a promising young dancer; Harriet (Barbara E. Robertson), a veteran who has paid her dues and keeps on paying; Josh (James Franco), a young chef who becomes Ry's lover; and Alberto Antonelli (Malcolm McDowell), the company's artistic director. It is said that "Mr. A" is based on Gerald Arpino, the Joffrey's legendary director and choreographer, and that no doubt is true. But there's another Mr. A standing right there in full view, and his name is Robert Altman.

The Player (1992) was Altman's film about the movie industry, an insider's look at the venality, ambition, romance, and genius of Hollywood. But *The Company* is his film about the creative process itself, and we see that ballet, like the movies, is a collaborative art form in which muddle and magic conspire, and everything depends on that most fragile of instruments, the human body.

There is a moment early in the film when a French-Canadian choreographer named Robert Desrosiers pitches a project named *Blue Snake* to Mr. A and he confesses himself baffled by the work and frightened by the budget. When Altman himself was pitched this screenplay by Neve Campbell and the writer Barbara Turner, he remembers saying: "Barbara, I read your script and I don't get it. I don't understand. I don't know what it is. I'm just the wrong guy for this." But in *The Company* Mr. A finds a glimmer of something in the new ballet, a nugget of authenticity, and begins to play with it. For a long stretch in the middle of the film, we may suspect that *Blue Snake* is a satiric target—a work so absurd that Altman wants it for target practice. The dancers seem to disdain it. Desrosiers can be insufferable. And then somehow, inexplicably, the work falls into place and is actually very good.

The *process* by which both Mr. As transform the material is the subject of the movie. At preview screenings of *The Company,* some Joffrey supporters in the audience were disappointed by the choice of *Blue Snake* and wondered why Altman hadn't closed with one of the pieces for which the company has become famous (several of those works are seen in the movie, including Arpino's *Trinity*). But that would have missed the point. This is a movie, not a dance concert documentary—the record not of a performance but of a process.

Altman is known for the way his camera tries to capture elusive moments as they happen. He uses overlapping dialogue, incomplete thoughts, and unresolved actions, showing us life in development. This time, using the flexibility of a digital camera, he takes what he can use from a fusion of fiction and real life. The love story between Ry and Josh doesn't take the foreground, as it might in a conventional film, but is part of the mix in the exhausting lives of the characters. They like each other and the sex is great, but they're ambitious young professionals with crazy schedules, and there's a scene where Josh cooks an elaborate dinner for Ry but she turns up very late and he has already fallen asleep, and yes, that's about right: He had to cook, she had to be late, because of who they are.

The movie almost offhandedly shows us how hard dancers work. To be a dancer in the Joffrey, one of the most respected companies in the world, is itself back-breaking. But then see how Ry rushes out to her second job, as a waitress in a beer and burger joint. And see the second-floor flat she lives in, with the El trains roaring right outside the window. This is a different reality than the glamorous Monte Carlo existence in a ballet classic like *The Red Shoes.* Altman observes the exhausting lifestyle, and then shows us the older dancer Harriet (Robertson), who is nearing the end of her professional life, and has made such sacrifices for years because—well, because she is one of the very few people in the world who can dance as she dances, and so she must.

There is a moment during rehearsal when a dancer's Achilles' tendon snaps. It is an audible pop, heard all over the stage, and everybody knows exactly what it means. It means she will not ever dance again. Altman handles this moment with cold-blooded realism. Instead of grief and violins and fraught drama, he shows the company almost frightening in its detachment. This could happen to any of them, they know it, there is nothing to be done about it, and the rehearsal must go on.

McDowell's performance as Mr. A is a case study in human management. He has strategies for playing the role of leader, for being inspirational, for being a disciplinarian, for remaining a mystery. He teaches obliquely ("You know how I hate pretty"). He has an assistant named Edouard (William Dick) whose primary duty seems to consist of signaling urgently so Mr. A can escape a situation by being needed elsewhere. Antonelli has a way of praising on the run ("You *are* a genius") and then hurrying out of the room. His style, which is similar to the style of Altman, is to lavish praise while always leaving everyone a little uncertain about whether he really means it.

Neve Campbell trained with the National Ballet of Canada before turning to acting as a career. She has been very good in movies like *Wild Things* and *Panic,* and good in a different way in the *Scream* movies, but she had to initiate this project herself, and bring Turner on board as the writer. She plays the role with complete knowledge of Ry (maybe it's as much her autobiography as Altman's), and her dancing is always convincing. The movie comes out at the same time as *Monster,* with its remarkable performance by Charlize Theron; two actresses of about the same age, who have had success in the commercial mainstream, placed bets on themselves that they could do great work, and they were right.

As for Robert Altman, I imagine some of the most heartfelt scenes in the movie for him are the ones involving Mr. A's attempt to create art while always having to think about money. Altman has rarely had big box-office hits (his most popular film was one of his earliest, *M*A*S*H,* and yet he has found a way to work steadily—to be prolific despite almost always choosing projects he wants to work on. How does he do it? *The Company* offers some clues.

Confidence ★ ★
R, 98 m., 2003

Edward Burns (Jake Vig), Rachel Weisz (Lily), Andy Garcia (Gunther Butan), Dustin Hoffman (King), Paul Giamatti (Gordo), Donal Logue (Whitworth), Luis Guzman (Manzano), Franky G. (Lupus), Brian Van Holt (Miles). Directed by James Foley and produced by Michael Burns, Marc Butan, Michael Ohoven, and Michael Paseornek. Screenplay by Doug Jung.

Confidence is a flawless exercise about con games, and that is precisely its failing: It is an exercise. It fails to make us care, even a little, about the characters and what happens to them. There is nothing at stake. The screenplay gives away the game by having the entire story narrated in flashback by the hero, who treats it not as an adventure but as a series of devious deceptions that he can patiently explain to the man holding a gun on him—and to us. At the end, we can see how smart he is and how everybody was fooled, but we don't care.

The obvious contrast is with David Mamet's *House of Games,* which also told a story of cons within cons, but which had stakes so high that at the end the victim called the con man's bluff by—well, by shooting him dead, after which he didn't have any twists left. We cared about those characters. *Confidence* lacks that passion and urgency; there are times when the narration sounds like the filmmakers at a pitch meeting, explaining how tricky their plot is and unable to keep the enthusiasm out of their voices.

That's not to say the movie, directed by James Foley, is badly made. It's great-looking, with its *film noir* reds and greens and blues, its neon Bud Ice signs, its shadows and mean streets, its sleazy strip clubs, and its use of wipes and swish-pans (sideways, up, down, sometimes two at a time). You know this is a crime movie, which is nice to be reminded of, except that every reminder also tells us it's only a movie, so that there is no possibility that we can commit to the characters, worry about them, want them to succeed or fail.

The movie stars Edward Burns as Jake Vig, a confidence mastermind, who has a crew of regulars and uses them to stage fake murders in order to scare marks into running away without their money. One day he makes the mistake of stealing $150,000 from the bagman for a nasty crimelord, the King (Dustin Hoffman). He confronts the King in his strip club and tells him he'll get the money back, but first he wants the King to supply an additional $200,000 as seed money for a $5 million scam Jake has in mind.

Jake's last name, Vig, is possibly short for "vigorish," the word gamblers use to describe the money the house takes off the top. If I were looking for someone to play with $200,000 of my money, I don't think I would choose a con man named Vig. But the King is confident that no one would even dream of cheating him, because he has such a fearsome reputation. And to keep an eye on Jake, he sends along his henchman Lupus (Frankie G.) to watch Jake's every move.

Dustin Hoffman's performance as the King is the best thing in the movie—indeed, the only element that comes to life on the screen. The King runs a strip club as a front, launders money for the mob, and suffers from attention deficit disorder—or, as he meticulously specifies, "attention deficit hyperactivity disorder." To control his condition, he takes pills that slow him way down. "Feel my heart," he says to one of the strippers in his club, to prove that it is hardly beating. Hoffman, chewing gum, wearing a beard and glasses, looks like the gnome from hell, and fast-talks his way into a brilliant supporting performance.

So brilliant, I couldn't help wondering how much energy the film would have gained if Hoffman, say, had played the lead instead of Burns. With Hoffman, you look at him and try to figure out what he's thinking. With Burns, you look at him and either you already know, or he doesn't make you care. Burns is the right actor for a lot of roles, especially young men tortured by the pangs of romance, but as a con man he lacks the shadings and edges. Once again, the comparison is with Joe Mantegna in *House of Games*.

Jake Vig's crew includes fellow hoods Gordo (Paul Giamatti) and Miles (Brian Van Holt). He has recently enlisted Lily (Rachel Weisz), who is very pretty and whom he likes—two ominous signs for a con man. And when he needs two guys to turn up and pretend to be L.A. cops, he has two real cops (Donal Logue and Luis Guzman) to play the roles. There is also the enigmatic federal agent Gunther Butan (Andy Garcia), whose name means "butane" in German, and who spends a great deal of time relighting his cigar. Garcia has been on Jake's tail for years, we learn, although he may simply represent a higher level in the game.

Confidence is a jerk-around movie, a film that works by jerking us around. I don't mind being misled and fooled in a clever way, especially when the movie makes me care about the characters before pulling the rug out from under them, or me. But there is no sense of risk here. No real stakes. It's all an entertainment, even

for the characters, and at the end of the movie, as one surprise after another is revealed, there is no sense that these amazing revelations are really happening; no, they're simply the screenplay going through its final paces so the audience will appreciate the full extent to which it has been duped. What a shame that such a well-made movie is never able to convince us it is anything more than merely well made.

Connie and Carla ★ ½
PG-13, 98 m., 2004

Nia Vardalos (Connie), Toni Collette (Carla), David Duchovny (Jeff), Stephen Spinella (Robert/Peaches), Alec Mapa (Lee/N'Cream), Chris Logan (Brian/Brianna), Robert Kaiser (Paul), Debbie Reynolds (Herself). Directed by Michael Lembeck and produced by Gary Barber, Roger Birnbaum, Jonathan Glickman, Tom Hanks, and Rita Wilson. Screenplay by Nia Vardalos.

Connie and Carla plays like a genial amateur theatrical, the kind of production where you'd like it more if you were friends with the cast. The plot is creaky, the jokes are laborious, and total implausibility is not considered the slightest problem. Written by and starring Nia Vardalos, it's a disappointment after her hilarious *My Big Fat Greek Wedding*.

This time, in a retread of *Some Like It Hot*, Vardalos and Toni Collette play Connie and Carla, two friends who have been a singing duo since schooldays. Now they're in their thirties, stardom has definitively passed them by, and they perform a medley of musical comedy hits in an airport lounge that resembles no airport lounge in history, but does look a lot like somebody's rec room with some tables and chairs and a cheesy stage.

The guys they date beg them to face facts: They'll never really be any good. But they still dream the dream, and then, in a direct lift from *Some Like It Hot*, they witness a mob murder and have to go on the lam. The way this scene is handled is typical of the film's ham-handed approach: They're hiding in a parking garage when their boss is rubbed out, so what do they do? Stay hidden? Nope, they both stand up, scream, and wave their hands. They have to: Otherwise, there wouldn't be any movie.

135

Connie and Carla hit the road, head for Los Angeles, happen into a drag bar, and inspiration strikes: They can pretend to be female impersonators! That way no one will find them, or even know where to look. One of the running gags in *Some Like It Hot* was that Jack Lemmon and Tony Curtis did not make very plausible women, but the movie handled that by surrounding them with dim bulbs like the characters played by Marilyn Monroe and Joe E. Brown. *Connie and Carla* is set in today's Los Angeles gay community, where the other characters are supposed to be real, I guess, and where never in a million years could they pass as boys passing as girls.

Their danger from the mob is put on hold as the movie switches to another reliable formula, the showbiz rags-to-riches epic. Their act, of course, is an immediate hit, they make lots of buddies among the other drag queens, and there are many close calls as they're almost discovered out of drag, or would that be not out of drag? The time scheme of the movie is sufficiently forgiving for them to suggest that their little club remodel itself and double in size; and there is actually a scene where the show goes on while plastic sheeting separates the old club from the new addition. Next scene, the construction work is finished. Forget the drag queens, get the names of those contractors.

Nia Vardalos was of course wonderful in *My Big Fat Greek Wedding*, and Toni Collette has proven she can do about anything—but she can't do this. The movie masks desperation with frenzied slapstick and forced laughs. And when Connie meets a straight guy she likes (David Duchovny), we groan as the plot manufactures Meet Cutes by having them repeatedly run into each other and knock each other down. Uh-huh. I think maybe the point in *Some Like It Hot* was that Joe E. Brown fell in love with Jack Lemmon, not Marilyn Monroe. I'm not saying *Connie and Carla* would have been better if Connie had attracted a gay guy, or maybe a lesbian who saw through the drag, but at least that would have supplied a comic problem, not a romantic one.

My Big Fat Greek Wedding was such a huge success that it gave Vardalos a free ticket for her next movie. Someone should have advised her this wasn't the right screenplay to cash in the pass. Nor does director Michael Lembeck save

the day. He's done a lot of TV sitcoms, including many episodes of *Friends*, and his only other feature film, *The Santa Clause 2*, was funny enough, but here he took on an unfilmable premise and goes down with it. By the end, as the gangsters, the midwestern boyfriends, Duchovny, various drag queens, and Debbie Reynolds (herself) all descend on the finale, we're not watching a comedy, we're watching a traffic jam.

Constantine ★ ½
R, 120 m., 2005

Keanu Reeves (John Constantine), Rachel Weisz (Angela and Isabel Dodson), Shia LeBeouf (Chas), Djimon Hounsou (Midnite), Max Baker (Beeman), Pruitt Taylor Vince (Father Hennessy), Gavin Rossdale (Balthazar), Tilda Swinton (Gabriel), Peter Stormare (Satan). Directed by Francis Lawrence and produced by Lauren Shuler Donner, Benjamin Melniker, Michael E. Uslan, Erwin Stoff, Lorenzo di Bonaventura, and Akiva Goldsman. Screenplay by Kevin Brodbin and Frank Cappello, based on the comic book *Hellblazer* by Jamie Delano and Garth Ennis.

No, *Constantine* is not part of a trilogy including *Troy* and *Alexander*. It's not about the emperor at all, but about a man who can see the world behind the world, and is waging war against the scavengers of the damned. There was a nice documentary about emperor penguins, however, at Sundance. The males sit on the eggs all winter long in, like, 60 degrees below zero.

Keanu Reeves plays Constantine as a chain-smoking, depressed demon-hunter who lives above a bowling alley in Los Angeles. Since he was a child, he has been able to see that not all who walk among us are human. Some are penguins. Sorry about that. Some are half-angels and half-devils. Constantine knows he is doomed to hell because he once tried to kill himself, and is trying to rack up enough frames against the demons to earn his way into heaven.

There is a scene early in the movie where Constantine and his doctor look at his X-rays, never a good sign in a superhero movie. He has lung cancer. The angel Gabriel (Tilda

Swinton) tells him, "You are going to die young because you've smoked thirty cigarettes a day since you were thirteen." Gabriel has made more interesting announcements. Constantine has already spent some time in hell, which looks like a postnuclear Los Angeles created by animators with a hangover. No doubt it is filled with carcinogens.

The half-angels and half-devils are earthly proxies in the war between God and Satan. You would think that God would be the New England Patriots of this contest, but apparently there is a chance that Satan could win. Constantine's lonely mission is to track down half-demons and cast them back to the fires below. Like Blade, the vampire-killer, he is surprisingly optimistic, considering he is one guy in one city dealing on a case-by-case basis, and the enemy is global.

Constantine has a technical adviser named Beeman (Max Baker), who lives in the ceiling of the bowling alley among the pin-spotting machines, and functions like Q in the James Bond movies. Here he is loading Constantine with the latest weaponry: "Bullet shavings from the assassination attempt on the pope, holy water from the river of Jordan, and, you'll love this, screech beetles." The screech beetles come in a little matchbox. "To the fallen," Beeman explains, "the sound is like nails on a blackboard." Later there is a scene where Constantine is inundated by the creatures of hell, and desperately tries to reach the matchbox and *get* those beetles to *screeching*.

Rachel Weisz plays Angela Dodson, an L.A. police detective whose twin sister, Isabel, has apparently committed suicide. Isabel reported seeing demons, so Angela consults Constantine, who nods wisely and wonders if Isabel jumped, or was metaphysically pushed. Later in the film, to show Angela that she also has the gift of seeing the world behind the world, Constantine holds her underwater in a bathtub until she passes out and sees the torments of hell. No bright white corridors and old friends and Yanni for her. You wonder what kind of an L.A. cop would allow herself to be experimentally drowned in a bathtub by a guy who lives over a bowling alley.

Together, they prowl the nighttime streets. At one point, Constantine needs to consult Midnite (Djimon Hounsou), a former witch doctor who runs a private nightclub where half-angels and half-demons can get half-loaded and talk shop. There is a doorman. To gain admittance, you have to read his mind and tell him what's on the other side of the card he's holding up. "Two frogs on a bench," Constantine says. Could have been a lucky guess.

There is a priest in the film, the alcoholic Father Hennessy (Pruitt Taylor Vince), whose name, I guess, is product placement. Strange that there is a priest, since that opens the door to Catholicism and therefore to the news that Constantine is not doomed unless he wages a lifelong war against demons, but needs merely go to confession; three Our Fathers, three Hail Marys, and he's outta there. Strange that movies about Satan always require Catholics. You never see your Presbyterians or Episcopalians hurling down demons.

The forces of hell manifest themselves in many ways. One victim is eaten by flies. A young girl is possessed by a devil, and Constantine shouts, "I need a mirror! Now! At least three feet high!" He can capture the demon in the mirror and throw it out the window, see, although you wonder why supernatural beings would have such low-tech security holes.

Keanu Reeves has a deliberately morose energy level in the movie, as befits one who has seen hell, walks among half-demons, and is dying. He keeps on smoking. Eventually he confronts Satan (Peter Stormare), who wears a white suit. (Satan to tailor: "I want a suit just like God's.") Oh, and the plot also involves the Spear of Destiny, which is the spear that killed Christ, and which has been missing since World War II, which seems to open a window to the possibility of Nazi villains, but no.

Control Room ★ ★ ★

NO MPAA RATING, 84 m., 2004

With Sameer Khader, Lieutenant Josh Rushing, Tom Mintier, Hassan Ibrahim, David Shuster, and Deema Khatib. A documentary directed by Jehane Noujaim and produced by Hani Salama and Rosadel Varela. Screenplay by Noujaim.

The final film I saw at Cannes 2004 came from Egypt and contained a surprise. It was *Alexandrie . . . New York*, by the veteran director Youssef Chahine, and it told the autobiographical story of an Egyptian who comes to America in 1950 to study at the Pasadena Playhouse, and returns again in 1975 and 2000. There is a lot more to it than that, but what struck me was when the student joined his classmates in singing "God Bless America" at the graduation. I hadn't heard that in an American film since *The Deer Hunter* in 1978. The character in 1950, and apparently the seventy-eight-year-old Egyptian who told his story, loved America.

I thought of them as I watched *Control Room,* an enlightening documentary about how the U.S. networks and the Arab satellite news channel Al Jazeera covered the early days of the war in Iraq. If Americans are familiar with Al Jazeera at all, it is because, as Donald Rumsfeld charges in the film, it is a source of anti-American propaganda, "willing to lie to the world to make their case." Yet there is an extraordinary moment in the film when Sameer Khadar, an engaging and articulate producer for Al Jazeera, confides that if he were offered a job with Fox News, he would take it. He wants his children to seek their futures in the United States, he says, and I carefully wrote down his next words: "to exchange the Arab nightmare for the American dream." These are the words of a man Rumsfeld calls a liar. That many American news organizations, including the *New York Times,* have had to apologize for errors in their coverage of Iraq may indicate that Rumsfeld and his teammates may also have supplied them with . . . inaccuracies.

Khadar is seen in action, interviewing an American "analyst" named Jeffrey Steinberg who attacks U.S. policy. Afterward, Khadar is angry that his network arranged the interview: "He's just a crazy activist. He wasn't an analyst. He was just against America." We also see correspondents from CNN, Fox, and the networks attempting to stay objective, although they collectively lose it when a military spokesman holds up the famous deck of cards with the faces of Iraq's "most wanted" on it, announces the decks will be distributed by the thousands throughout the country, and then refuses to let the journalists see the cards.

The documentary is low-key for the most part, just watching and listening. Many of its scenes take place in and around CentCom, the temporary media center in Qatar where the world's journalists gathered during the run-up to the invasion of Iraq. Here Americans have long conversations with their counterparts at Al Jazeera, which is privately owned and heavily watched in Arab countries because viewers trust it more than their own government channels.

I have not seen Al Jazeera and am in no position to comment on its accuracy. I have seen this film, however, which contains enlightening moments. Remember the TV scene when joyous Iraqis toppled the statue of Saddam Hussein after the capture of Baghdad? TV pictures on the monitors at CentCom clearly see something American audiences were not shown: The square was not filled with cheering citizens, but was completely empty except for the small band of young men who toppled the statue. Al Jazeera producers watch the footage with their U.S. counterparts and observe that those who are interviewed "do not have Baghdad accents." They wonder why one "happened to have the old Iraqi flag in his pocket." The implication: This was a staged event, initiated by the U.S. occupation and bought into by the U.S. media.

The movie listens in on many philosophical bull sessions between a U.S. marine press spokesman, Lieutenant Josh Rushing, and an Al Jazeera producer named Hassan Ibrahim, who once worked for the BBC. Rushing defends the American line, but is willing to listen to Ibrahim, who deconstructs some of the American claims (his version: "Democratize or we'll shoot you"). Some of Rushing's statements ring a little hollow, as when he says, "The American POWs expect to be treated humanely, just like we are treating our prisoners humanely."

The correspondents are saddened when three journalists are killed in Baghdad by U.S. strikes. We see one of them, working for Al Jazeera, sitting sadly behind sandbags on the roof of a building, looking like a man who has had his last meal. The network carefully informed American authorities of the location of their bureau, it's noted, and American rockets struck that location not long after Rumsfeld and others complained about Al Jazeera's coverage. An accident of war.

Control Room was directed by Jehane Noujaim, an Arab-American documentarian who made *Startup.com*, the absorbing 2001 doc about an ambitious Web site that got caught in the collapse of the Internet bubble. In this film, she seems content to watch and listen as journalists do their jobs and talk about them. She doesn't take sides, but in insisting that there is something to be said for both sides she offends those who want to hear only one side.

What is clear is that the Al Jazeera journalists feel more disappointment than hatred for America. During one of those bull sessions, there's a rhetorical question: "Who's going to stop the United States?" And an Arab replies: "The United States is going to stop the United States. I have absolute confidence in the U.S. Constitution and the U.S. people." The film's buried message is that there is a reservoir of admiration and affection for America, at least among the educated classes in the Arab world, and they do not equate the current administration with America.

Note: Salon.com reported June 6 that Lieutenant Josh Rushing was ordered by the Pentagon not to comment on this film, "and as a result, the fourteen-year career military man, recently promoted to captain, plans to leave the Marines."

The Cooler ★ ★ ★ ½
R, 101 m., 2003

William H. Macy (Bernie Lootz), Alec Baldwin (Shelly Kaplow), Maria Bello (Natalie Belisario), Shawn Hatosy (Mikey), Ron Livingston (Larry Sokolov), Paul Sorvino (Buddy Stafford), Estella Warren (Charlene), Joey Fatone (Johnny Capella). Directed by Wayne Kramer and produced by Sean Furst and Michael A. Pierce. Screenplay by Frank Hannah and Kramer.

Bernie Lootz's sad eyes scan the casino floor, and he shuffles into action. A high roller is having a winning streak at a craps table. Bernie walks near him, maybe just only brushes his sleeve, and the guy's luck sours. For Bernie there is no joy in this, only the confirmation of something he has known for a long time: "People get next to me—their luck turns. It's been like that my whole life." How does he do it? "I do it by being myself."

Bernie, played by William H. Macy as another of his gloomy everymen, is a professional loser: A "cooler," is what his boss Shelly (Alec Baldwin) calls him. He is employed by the Shangri-La casino to wander the floor, bringing an end to winning streaks. But now modern Las Vegas is catching up with Bernie and Shelly. A group of investors have brought in a hotshot from business school to update the Shangri-La, which is the last of the old-style casinos. Shelly hates this idea; taking a dig at Steve Wynn's vision for the new Vegas and saying his place is "not for the stroller crowd" but for old-timers with real money.

Bernie and Shelly go back a long way, to when Shelly had Bernie kneecapped because of a bad debt, then paid to have him patched up, then put him on the payroll, because anyone with his bad luck was worth a lot of money. But now Bernie wants out. He's saved some money and plans to leave town in a week. That's his exit strategy, anyway, until he uses his influence to get a better job for a waitress named Natalie (Maria Bello), and she repays him with the first sex he's had in a long time—and the best sex ever.

The Cooler may sound as if it's a dark sitcom, with broad characters and an easy payoff. But the movie, directed by first-timer Wayne Kramer and written by him with Frank Hannah, has a strange way of being broad and twisted at the same time, so that while we surf the surface of the story, unexpected developments are stirring beneath. There's more to the movie than at first it seems, and what happens to Bernie, Natalie, and Shelly has a rough but poignant justice.

Consider Shelly. This is one of Alec Baldwin's best performances, as a character who contains vast contradictions. He can be kind and brutal simultaneously; affection and cruelty are handmaidens. Look at the way he breaks Bernie's knee and then gives him a job. Or the way he treats Buddy Stafford (Paul Sorvino), the broken-down, smack-addicted lounge singer. Shelly is fiercely loyal to Buddy, and doesn't even want to listen to the new guys with their plans to replace him with a sexy revue. What eventually happens to Buddy has a kind of poetic justice to it, yes, but in a hard, cold way: Shelly is capable of sentimental gestures that make your skin crawl.

Macy and Bello succeed in creating characters who seem to be having a real, actual, physical relationship right there before our eyes. I don't mean anything like hard-core; I mean like the kind of stuff that happens when the bodies involved are made of flesh rather than cinema. One of their sex scenes reminds me of the heedless joy of Jack Nicholson in *Five Easy Pieces*, when he strutted around the room wearing a "Triumph" T-shirt. Macy, who is fifty-three, says he spent thirty years staying in shape in case he was ever asked to be in a sex scene, and he finally got his chance. After a battle with the MPAA we get to see it substantially intact in an R-rated version; it's not porn or anything close, but life—messy, energetic, and sweaty.

Bernie's life at this time seems blessed, except for the detail that Mikey (Shawn Hatosy), his son, turns up unexpectedly with a pregnant wife named Charlene (Estella Warren). Bernie's history with Mikey's mother is complicated, his relationship with his son is fraught, and Mikey is not a nice boy. But because Bernie has always been a loser and is now feeling great about himself, he projects his benevolence onto Mikey, and that turns out to be a mistake. Hatosy is superb in evoking the kind of person who uses lying as a life strategy.

Bernie and Natalie remind us a little of the characters in *Leaving Las Vegas*, although their situation is not as desperate. They fall in love. That turns out to be a problem, because Bernie's luck changes, and he's no longer a cooler, but quite the opposite. Shelly's attempt to deal with this is ingenious—not just for Shelly, but also for the script, which finds drama and tension in a resolution that could have seemed facile, but doesn't. The story's strength is all in the telling; no synopsis will prepare you for the emotional charge that's eventually delivered. And it's unusual to find a screenplay that gives weight to parallel stories; Shelly isn't simply an element in Bernie's life, but is a free-standing character with a dilemma of his own.

The Cooler is old-fashioned in the way the Shangri-La is old-fashioned, and I mean that as a compliment. This is a movie without gimmicks, hooks, or flashy slickness. It gives us characters who are worn and real, who inhabit a world that is seen with unforgiving perception, whose fates have more to do with their personalities than with the requirements of the plot. The acting is on the money, the writing

has substance, the direction knows when to evoke *film noir* and when (in a trick shot involving loaded dice) to get fancy.

There is a crucial scene that takes place on the roof of the casino, and while it is happening, I want you to watch the eyes of the two bodyguards who are standing in the background. They're minor characters, and I don't have any idea what the director told them to do, but what their eyes reflect feels like pain and uneasiness, and it seems absolutely real. Not many movies have foregrounds that can inspire backgrounds like that.

The Core ★ ★ ½
PG-13, 135 m., 2003

Aaron Eckhart (Josh Keyes), Hilary Swank (Major Rebecca Childs), Delroy Lindo (Dr. Edward Brazzleton), Stanley Tucci (Dr. Conrad Zimsky), Tchéky Karyo (Serge Leveque), Bruce Greenwood (Colonel Robert Iverson), DJ Qualls (Taz "Rat" Finch), Richard Jenkins (General Thomas Purcell), Alfre Woodard (Talma Stickley). Directed by Jon Amiel and produced by Sean Bailey, David Foster, and Cooper Layne. Screenplay by Layne and John Rogers.

Hot on the heels of *Far from Heaven*, which looked exactly like a 1957 melodrama, here is *The Core*, which wants to be a 1957 science fiction movie. Its special effects are a little too good for that (not a lot), but the plot is out of something by Roger Corman, and you can't improve on dialogue like this:

"The Earth's core has stopped spinning!"

"How could that happen?"

Yes, the Earth's core has stopped spinning, and in less than a year the Earth will lose its electromagnetic shield and we'll all be toast—fried by solar microwaves. To make that concept clear to a panel of U.S. military men, professor Josh Keyes of the University of Chicago (Aaron Eckhart) borrows a can of room freshener, sets the propellant alight with his Bic, and incinerates a peach.

To watch Josh Keyes and the generals contemplate that burnt peach is to witness a scene that cries out from its very vitals to be cut from the movie and made into ukulele picks. Such goofiness amuses me.

I have such an unreasonable affection for

this movie, indeed, that it is only by slapping myself alongside the head and drinking black coffee that I can restrain myself from recommending it. It is only a notch down from *Congo, Anaconda, Lara Croft, Tomb Raider,* and other films that those with too little taste think they have too much taste to enjoy.

To be sure, *The Core* starts out in an unsettling manner, with the crash landing of the space shuttle. Considering that *Phone Booth,* scheduled for release in October 2002, was shelved for six months because it echoed the Beltway Sniper, to put a shuttle crash in a March 2003 movie is pushing the limits of decorum, wouldn't you say?

And yet the scene is a humdinger. Earth's disturbed magnetic field has confused the shuttle's guidance system, causing it to aim for downtown Los Angeles. Pilot Richard Jenkins insists, "It's Mission Control's call," but copilot Hilary Swank has an idea, which she explains *after* the shuttle passes over Dodger Stadium at an altitude of about 800 feet.

If the shuttle glided over Wrigley Field at that altitude, I'm thinking, it would have crashed into the 23d Precinct Police Station by now, or at the very least a Vienna Red Hot stand. But no, there's time for a conversation with Mission Control, and then for the shuttle to change course and make one of those emergency landings where wings get sheared off and everybody holds on real tight.

Other portents show something is wrong with Gaia. Birds go crazy in Trafalgar Square, people with pacemakers drop dead, and then Josh Keyes and fellow scientist Conrad Zimsky (Stanley Tucci) decide that Earth's core has stopped spinning. To bring such an unimaginable mass shuddering to a halt would result, one assumes, in more than confused pigeons, but science is not this film's strong point. Besides, do pigeons need their innate magnetic direction-sensing navigational instincts for such everyday jobs as flying from the top of Nelson's column to the bottom?

Dr. Zimsky leads the emergency team to the Utah salt flats, where eccentric scientist Edward Brazzleton (Delroy Lindo) has devised a laser device that can cut through solid rock. He has also invented a new metal named, I am not making this up, Unobtainium. (So rare is this substance that a Google search reveals only

8,060 sites selling Unobtainium ski gear, jackets, etc.) Combining the metal and the laser device into a snaky craft that looks like a BMW Roto-Rooter, the United States launches a $50 billion probe to Earth's core, in scenes that will have colonoscopy survivors shifting uneasily in their seats.

Their mission: Set off a couple of nuclear explosions that (they hope) will set the core a-spinnin' again. Earth's innards are depicted in special effects resembling a 1960s underground movie seen on acid, and it is marvelous that the crew have a video monitor so they can see out as they drill through dense matter in total darkness. Eventually they reach a depth where the pressure is 800,000 pounds per square inch—and then they put on suits to walk around outside. Their suits are obviously made of something stronger and more flexible than Unobtainium. Probably corduroy.

The music is perfect for this enterprise: ominous horns and soaring strings. The cast includes some beloved oddballs, most notably DJ Qualls *(The New Guy),* who plays Rat, a computer hacker who can talk to the animals, or at least sing to the dolphins. The only wasted cast member is Alfre Woodard, relegated to one of those Mission Control roles where she has to look worried and then relieved.

The Core is not exactly good, but it knows what a movie is. It has energy and daring and isn't afraid to make fun of itself, and it thinks big, as when the Golden Gate Bridge collapses and a scientist tersely reports, "The West Coast is out." If you are at the video store late on Saturday night and they don't have *Anaconda,* this will do.

The Corporation ★ ★ ★
NO MPAA RATING, 145 m., 2004

A documentary directed by Jennifer Abbott and Mark Achbar and produced by Achbar and Bart Simpson. Screenplay by Joel Bakan and Harold Crooks.

Muley: *Who's the Shawnee Land and Cattle Co.?*
Land agent: *It ain't anybody. It's a company.*
—*The Grapes of Wrath*

I was at a health ranch last week, where the idea is to clear your mind for serene thoughts.

At dinner one night, a woman at the table referred to Arizona as a "right to work state." Unwisely, I replied: "Yeah—the right to work cheap." She said, "I think you'll find the nonunion workers are quite well paid." Exercising a supreme effort of will to avoid pronouncing the syllables "Wal-Mart," I replied: "If so, that's because unions have helped raise salaries for everybody." She replied: "The unions steal their members' dues." I replied, "How much money would you guess the unions have stolen compared to corporations like Enron?" At this point our exchange was punctuated by a kick under the table from my wife, and we went back to positive thinking.

The Corporation is not a film my dinner companion would enjoy. It begins with the unsettling information that, under the law, a corporation is not a thing but a person. The U.S. Supreme Court so ruled, in a decision based, bizarrely, on the 14th Amendment to the Constitution. That was the one that guaranteed former slaves equal rights. The court ruling meant corporations were given the rights of individuals in our society. They are free at last.

If Monsanto and WorldCom and Enron are indeed people, what kind of people are they?

The movie asks Robert Hare, a consultant who helps the FBI profile its suspects. His diagnosis: Corporations by definition have a personality disorder and can be categorized as psychopathic. That is because they single-mindedly pursue their own wills and desires without any consideration for other people (or corporations) and without reference to conventional morality. They don't act that way to be evil; it's just, as the scorpion explained to the frog, that it's in their nature.

Having more or less avoided the corporate world by living in my little movie critic corner, I've been struck by the way classmates and friends identify with their corporations. They are loyal to an entity that exists only to perpetuate itself. Any job that requires you to wear a corporate lapel pin is taking more precious things from you than display space. Although I was greatly cheered to see Ken Lay in handcuffs, I can believe he thinks he's innocent. In corporate terms, he is: He was only doing his job in reflecting Enron's psychopathic nature.

The movie assembles a laundry list of corporate sins: bovine growth hormone, Agent Orange, marketing research on how to inspire children to nag their parents to buy products. It is in the interest of corporations to sell products, and therefore in their interest to have those products certified as safe, desirable, and good for us. No one who knows anything about the assembly-line production of chickens would eat a nonorganic chicken. Cows, which are vegetarians, have been fed processed animal protein, leading to the charming possibility that they can pass along mad cow disease. Farm-raised salmon contains mercury. And so on.

If corporations are maximizing profits by feeding Strangelovian chemicals to unsuspecting animals, what are we to make of the U.S. Supreme Court decision that living organisms can be patented? Yes, strains of laboratory mice, cultures of bacteria, even bits of DNA, can now be privately owned.

Fascinated as I am by the labyrinthine reasoning by which stem-cell research somehow violates the right to life, I have been waiting for opponents of stem cell to attack the private ownership and patenting of actual living organisms, but I wait in vain. If there is one thing more sacred than the right to life, it is the corporation's right to patent, market, and exploit life.

If I seem to have strayed from the abstract idea of a corporation, *The Corporation* does some straying itself. It produces saintly figures like Ray Anderson, chairman of Interface, the largest rug manufacturer in the world, who tells his fellow executives they are all "plundering" the globe, and tries to move his corporation toward sustainable production. All living organisms on Earth are in decline, the documentary argues, mostly because corporations are stealing from the future to enrich themselves in the present.

The Corporation is an impassioned polemic, filled with information sure to break up any dinner-table conversation. Its fault is that of the dinner guest who tells you something fascinating, and then tells you again, and then a third time. At 145 minutes, it overstays its welcome. The wise documentarian should treat film stock as a nonrenewable commodity.

Cradle 2 the Grave ★ ★
R, 100 m., 2003

Jet Li (Su), DMX (Fait), Anthony Anderson (Tommy), Kelly Hu (Sona), Tom Arnold (Archie), Mark Dacascos (Ling), Gabrielle Union (Daria). Directed by Andrzej Bartkowiak and produced by Joel Silver. Screenplay by John O'Brien and Channing Gibson.

The funniest scene in *Cradle 2 the Grave* comes over the end credits, as supporting actors Tom Arnold and Anthony Anderson debate how the story should be filmed. This scene, which feels ad-libbed, is smart and self-aware in a way the movie never is. The film itself is on autopilot and overdrive at the same time: It does nothing original, but does it very rapidly.

Jet Li and DMX are the stars, both ready for better scripts, playing enemies who become buddies when it turns out they have a common antagonist. DMX plays a character pronounced "fate" but spelled "Fait," which would give you a neat pun you could use in French class, if the spelling of his name were ever seen. Jet Li plays a boy named Su. After Fait and his accomplices break into a Los Angeles diamond vault, their caper is interrupted by Su, who is working for the Taiwanese police.

Bad guys end up with the diamonds and kidnap Fait's beloved little daughter, in a plot that started out as a remake of Fritz Lang's *M* (1931). The journey from *M* to *2* was downhill all the way. The result is a Joel Silver nonstop action thriller, well produced, slickly directed, sure to please slackjaws who are not tired to death of this kind of material recycled again and again and again.

It makes at least a sincere attempt to one-up previous cop-crook-buddy-sex-chase-caper-martial-arts thrillers. Jet Li doesn't merely take on a lot of opponents at the same time, he gets in a fight with all of the competitors in an illegal extreme fighting club. He doesn't merely do stunts, but drops in free-fall from one high-rise balcony to the next. Tom Arnold doesn't merely play a black market arms dealer, he supplies a tank. The black diamonds are not merely black diamonds, but are actually a superweapon that would bring down the cost of weapons of mass destruction into the price range of a nice private jet. There is not merely a hood who has special privileges in jail, but one with a private cell where the prison guards melt butter for his fresh lobster while he waits impatiently. There is not merely a chase, but one involving an all-terrain vehicle, which is driven up the stairs of a store and then jumps from one rooftop to another more or less for the hell of it. And the girl is not merely sexy but Gabrielle Union.

I can see that this movie fills a need. I have stopped feeling the need. The problem with action movies is how quickly state of the art becomes off-the-shelf. We yearn for wit and intelligence, and a movie like *Shanghai Knights* looks sophisticated by comparison.

Cradle 2 the Grave will, however, be a box-office hit, I imagine, and that will be demographically interesting because it demonstrates that a savvy producer like Silver now believes a white star is completely unnecessary in a mega-budget action picture. At one point, there were only white stars. Then they got to have black buddies. Then they got to have Asian buddies. Then *Rush Hour* proved that black and Asian buddies could haul in the mass audience. Long ago a movie like this used a black character for comic relief. Then an Asian character. Now the white character is the comic relief. May the circle be unbroken.

Not only is Gabrielle Union the female lead, but Kelly Hu is the second female lead, slapping the kid around and engaging in a catfight with Union. Lots of mild sex in the movie, although an opening scene assumes a security guard is a very slow study. First Gabrielle Union goes in to flirt with him so he won't look at the TV security monitors. When he turns out to be gay, she sends in the second team, Anthony Anderson, to flirt with him. When two people try to pick you up in ten minutes and you're a security guard on duty, do you suspect anything?

It's a common complaint that the cops are never around during sensational movie chase scenes and shoot-outs. Dozens of squad cars turn up twice in *Cradle 2 the Grave*, however— once when they're told a robbery is in progress, and again at the end, when a battle involving guns, rockets, explosives, and a tank blowing a helicopter out of the sky inspires an alert response after only twenty minutes.

Crash ★ ★ ★ ★
R, 100 m., 2005

Sandra Bullock (Jean), Don Cheadle (Graham), Matt Dillon (Officer Ryan), Jennifer Esposito (Ria), William Fichtner (Flanagan), Brendan Fraser (Rick), Terrence Dashon Howard (Cameron), Ludacris (Anthony), Thandie Newton (Christine), Ryan Phillippe (Officer Hansen), Larenz Tate (Peter), Shaun Toub (Farhad), Michael Pena (Daniel). Directed by Paul Haggis and produced by Haggis, Mark R. Harris, Robert Moresco, Cathy Schulman, and Tom Nunan. Screenplay by Haggis and Moresco.

Crash tells interlocking stories of whites, blacks, Latinos, Koreans, Iranians, cops and criminals, the rich and the poor, the powerful and powerless, all defined in one way or another by racism. All are victims of it, and all are guilty of it. Sometimes, yes, they rise above it, although it is never that simple. Their negative impulses may be instinctive, their positive impulses may be dangerous, and who knows what the other person is thinking?

The result is a movie of intense fascination; we understand quickly enough who the characters are and what their lives are like, but we have no idea how they will behave because so much depends on accident. Most movies enact rituals; we know the form and watch for variations. *Crash* is a movie with free will, and anything can happen. Because we care about the characters, the movie is uncanny in its ability to rope us in and get us involved.

Crash was directed by Paul Haggis, whose screenplay for *Million Dollar Baby* led to Academy Awards. It connects stories based on coincidence, serendipity, and luck, as the lives of the characters crash against each other like pinballs. The movie presumes that most people feel prejudice and resentment against members of other groups, and observes the consequences of those feelings.

One thing that happens, again and again, is that peoples' assumptions prevent them from seeing the actual person standing before them. An Iranian (Shaun Toub) is thought to be an Arab, although Iranians are Persian. Both the Iranian and the white wife of the district attorney (Sandra Bullock) believe a Mexican-American locksmith (Michael Pena) is a gang member and a crook, but he is a family man.

A black cop (Don Cheadle) is having an affair with his Latino partner (Jennifer Esposito), but never gets it straight which country she's from. A cop (Matt Dillon) thinks a light-skinned black woman (Thandie Newton) is white. When a white producer tells a black TV director (Terrence Dashon Howard) that a black character "doesn't sound black enough," it never occurs to him that the director doesn't "sound black," either. For that matter, neither do two young black men (Larenz Tate and Ludacris), who dress and act like college students, but have a surprise for us.

You see how it goes. Along the way, these people say exactly what they are thinking, without the filters of political correctness. The district attorney's wife is so frightened by a street encounter that she has the locks changed, then assumes the locksmith will be back with his "homies" to attack them. The white cop can't get medical care for his dying father, and accuses a black woman at his HMO of taking advantage of preferential racial treatment. The Iranian can't understand what the locksmith is trying to tell him, freaks out, and buys a gun to protect himself. The gun dealer and the Iranian get into a shouting match.

I make this sound almost like episodic TV, but Haggis writes with such directness and such a good ear for everyday speech that the characters seem real and plausible after only a few words. His cast is uniformly strong; the actors sidestep clichés and make their characters particular.

For me, the strongest performance is by Matt Dillon, as the racist cop in anguish over his father. He makes an unnecessary traffic stop when he thinks he sees the black TV director and his light-skinned wife doing something they really shouldn't be doing at the same time they're driving. True enough, but he wouldn't have stopped a black couple or a white couple. He humiliates the woman with an invasive body search, while her husband is forced to stand by powerless, because the cops have the guns—Dillon, and also a unseasoned rookie (Ryan Phillippe), who hates what he's seeing but has to back up his partner.

That traffic stop shows Dillon's cop as vile and hateful. But later we see him trying to care for his sick father, and we understand why he explodes at the HMO worker (whose race is only an excuse for his anger). He victimizes others by exercising his power, and is impotent when it comes to helping his father.

Then the plot turns ironically on itself, and both of the cops find themselves, in very different ways, saving the lives of the very same TV director and his wife. Is this just manipulative storytelling? It didn't feel that way to me because it serves a deeper purpose than mere irony: Haggis is telling parables, in which the characters learn the lessons they have earned by their behavior.

Other cross-cutting Los Angeles stories come to mind, especially Lawrence Kasdan's more optimistic *Grand Canyon* and Robert Altman's more humanistic *Short Cuts*. But *Crash* finds a way of its own. It shows the way we all leap to conclusions based on race—yes, all of us, of all races, and however fair-minded we may try to be—and we pay a price for that.

If there is hope in the story, it comes because as the characters crash into one another, they learn things, mostly about themselves. Almost all of them are still alive at the end, and are better people because of what has happened to them. Not happier, not calmer, not even wiser, but better. Then there are those few who kill or get killed; racism has tragedy built in.

Not many films have the possibility of making their audiences better people. I don't expect *Crash* to work any miracles, but I believe anyone seeing it is likely to be moved to have a little more sympathy for people not like themselves. The movie contains hurt, coldness, and cruelty, but is it without hope? Not at all.

Stand back and consider. All of these people, superficially so different, share the city and learn that they share similar fears and hopes. Until several hundred years ago, most people everywhere on Earth never saw anybody who didn't look like them. They were not racist because, as far as they knew, there was only one race. You may have to look hard to see it, but *Crash* is a film about progress.

Criminal ★ ★ ½
R, 87 m., 2004

John C. Reilly (Richard Gaddis), Diego Luna (Rodrigo), Maggie Gyllenhaal (Valerie Gaddis), Jonathan Tucker (Michael Gaddis), Peter Mullan (William Hannigan), Zitto Kazann (Ochoa). Directed by Gregory Jacobs and produced by George Clooney, Steven Soderbergh, and Jacobs. Screenplay by Jacobs and Soderbergh, based on the screenplay by Fabian Bielinsky.

It comes down to this: *Criminal* is an English-language remake of *Nine Queens*, an Argentinean film I saw in 2002 and remember well. *Criminal* follows the original fairly closely, and because I already knew the plot secrets, it couldn't work on me in its intended way. As the recycled characters, dialogue, and events turned up, there seemed to be an echo in the room.

The film may work for you. *Nine Queens* worked for me and I gave it three stars. Much depends on whether you enjoy films that deliberately set out to mislead you. This one is a con about a con, and occupies the territory staked out so perfectly by such as David Mamet's *House of Games* and Ridley Scott's *Matchstick Men*. Odds are you'll have an inkling of what's going on under the surface, but the ending is likely to surprise you—not in what it reveals, but in how it forces you to think again about parts you thought were on the level.

John C. Reilly and Diego Luna costar, as Richard and Rodrigo, who meet in a casino when Richard, a veteran con man, observes Rodrigo clumsily trying to trick waitresses into giving him his change twice. Richard steps in, tells casino security he's a cop, and leads Rodrigo away in handcuffs he conveniently carries in his pocket. Then he explains that he went to all this trouble because he needs a partner for a few days, and Rodrigo looks promising.

They warm up slowly, conning waiters and little old ladies, and then a larger quarry swims into view. Richard's sister Valerie (Maggie Gyllenhaal), who works in a hotel, calls him to say an old forger pal of his (Zitto Kazann) is sick in the men's room, and needs help. That leads to Richard and Rodrigo's involvement in the forger's scheme to sell a counterfeit bank note to a wealthy collector named Hannigan (Peter Mullan), who is staying in the hotel.

The plot as it uncoils is indeed ingenious. Like many such plots, it depends on outrageous coincidence, lucky timing, and the ability to think through the con and come out on the other side. I'm convinced there's a logical flaw in the story structure, having to do with why Richard thinks he needs Rodrigo before he finds out what makes Rodrigo of interest to him. And no, that's not giving anything away, as you will discover when you see the film.

The actors do a good job of giving edge and momentum to the material: John C. Reilly is always in character (as his character, if you see what I mean), and Diego Luna, from *Y Tu Mama Tambien,* walks a fine line between being a novice con man and being a very quick study. It's all done well. The director is Gregory Jacobs, who has worked as an assistant director for Stephen Soderbergh (the film's producer) and no doubt learned a thing or two about cons on *Ocean's 11* and *Out of Sight.* His decision to remake this recent film is defensible, since the plot of *Nine Queens* was what distinguished it, and plots translate better than intangibles like, oh, say, artistry.

Because I had an excellent idea of what was really happening and why, however, the film couldn't work on me in its intended way. Some con-game films have such great dialogue *(House of Games)* or such intense acting *(Matchstick Men)* that they work entirely apart from the con. But *Criminal* needs the element of puzzlement and surprise. Since you have probably not seen *Nine Queens* (which grossed less than $2 million at the North American box office), *Criminal* will be new to you, and I predict you'll like the remake about as much as I liked the original—three stars' worth. If, however, you've seen *Nine Queens,* you may agree that some journeys, however entertaining, need only be taken once.

Crimson Gold ★ ★ ★
NO MPAA RATING, 97 m., 2004

Hussein Emadeddin (Hussein), Kamyar Sheissi (Ali), Azita Rayeji (Bride), Shahram Vaziri (Jeweler), Ehsan Amani (Man in the Tea House), Pourang Nakhayi (Rich Man), Kavey Najmabadi (Seller), Saber Safael (Soldier). Directed by Jafar Panahi and produced by Panahi. Screenplay by Abbas Kiarostami.

The success of *Crimson Gold* depends to an intriguing degree on the performance of its leading actor, a large, phlegmatic man who embodies the rule that an object at rest will stay at rest until some other force sets it into motion. The character, named Hussein and played by Hussein Emadeddin, is a pizza deliveryman in Tehran, heavy-set, tall, undemonstrative. He sits where he sits as if planted there, and when he rides his scooter around the city streets he doesn't lean and dart like most scooter drivers, but seems at one with his machine in implacable motion. When he smokes, he is like an automaton programmed to move the cigarette toward and away from his lips.

He has a friend named Ali (Kamyar Sheissi). We meet Ali for the first time in a teahouse, where he produces a purse he has just found. Its contents are disappointing—a broken gold ring. Another man overhears their conversation, assumes they stole the purse, and delivers a little lecture on the morality of theft. He believes the rewards should suit the crime; you should not put your targets through a great deal of suffering just to relieve them of pocket change.

Hussein, who is engaged to Ali's sister, seems an unlikely candidate for marriage. We learn indirectly that he was wounded in the Iraq-Iran War, and Ali refers to his "medication." Perhaps that accounts for his sphinxlike detachment; he acts as little as it is possible to act and yet, paradoxically, we can't take our eyes off of him.

The film uses Hussein and his life as a lens to look at Tehran today. The director, Jafar Panahi, also made *The Circle* (2000), a film showing the impossibility of being a single woman in modern Iran without having a man to explain your status. *Crimson Gold* was written by Abbas Kiarostami, the best-known Iranian director, and includes his trademark: long, unbroken shots of a character driving somewhere. In this case, it is Hussein on his scooter, sometimes with Ali as a passenger.

Hussein lives a solitary existence in an untidy little flat, venturing out at night to deliver pizzas. One night he delivers a stack of pizzas to the penthouse of an apartment building in a wealthy neighborhood. He is greeted at the door by the occupant (Pourang Nakhayi), who complains that "the women have gone" and he doesn't need the pizza. But he invites Hussein in, asks him to eat the pizza, and talks obsessively about himself: How his parents only lived in the apartment for a month before moving overseas, how he has just returned to Iran and finds it not organized to his liking, how women are crazy and unpredictable.

Hussein eats steadily and regards him. Later, as the man is on the telephone, he walks around the apartment (he has never been so high up in his life), looks at the skyline, visits a bathroom more luxurious than any he could imagine, dives fully clothed into the swimming pool, and is seen later wrapped in towels.

When he leaves the apartment he goes directly to a jewelry store that he and Ali had visited twice before. The first time, they wanted to get a price on the gold ring, and were treated rudely and with suspicion by the store owner and guard. Returning, wearing ties and with Ali's sister along, they said they were shopping for a wedding ring—but were treated rudely again; it is a high-end store and they look like low-end people.

After he leaves the high-rise apartment, Hussein returns to the store. We already know much of what will happen now, because *Crimson Gold* opens with a version of the same scene it closes with. But I will not discuss the opening (and closing) because they proceed with a kind of implacable logic. What seems impulsive and reckless at the beginning of the film takes on a certain logic after we have spent some time in Hussein's company. In his case, still waters run deep and cold. He has been still and implacable for the entire film, but now we understand he was not frozen, but waiting.

Note: In real life, Hussein Emadeddin, a nonactor, is a paranoid schizophrenic. Having learned this information, I felt obliged to share it with you, but the film does not refer to the disease; perhaps Jafar Panahi found that Emadeddin's demeanor, whatever its source, provided the kind of detachment he needed for his character. Hussein (the character) is doubly effective because he does not seem to be an active participant in the story, but an observer carried along by the currents of chance.

D

Daddy Day Care ★
PG, 93 m., 2003

Eddie Murphy (Charlie Hinton), Jeff Garlin (Phil), Anjelica Huston (Miss Harridan), Steve Zahn (Marvin), Khamani Griffin (Ben Hinton), Regina King (Kim Hinton). Directed by Steve Carr and produced by John Davis, Matt Berenson, and Wyck Godfrey. Screenplay by Geoff Rodkey.

Daddy Day Care is a woeful miscalculation, a film so wrongheaded audiences will be more appalled than amused. It imagines Eddie Murphy and sidekick Jeff Garlin in charge of a daycare center that could only terrify parents in the audience, although it may look like fun for their children. The center's philosophy apparently consists of letting kids do whatever they feel like, while the amateur staff delivers one-liners.

I realize that the movie is not intended as a serious work about day-care centers. It is a comedy (in genre, not in effect). But at some point we might expect it to benefit from real life, real experiences, real kids. Not a chance. It's all simply a prop for the Eddie Murphy character. Aggressively simpleminded, it's fueled by the delusion that it has a brilliant premise: Eddie Murphy plus cute kids equals success. But a premise should be the starting point for a screenplay, not its finish line.

In the film, Murphy plays Charlie Hinton, an advertising executive assigned to the account of a breakfast cereal based on vegetables. This leads eventually to desperate scenes involving Murphy dressed in a broccoli suit, maybe on the grounds that once, long ago, he was funny in a Gumby suit. The cereal fails, and he's fired along with his best pal, Phil (Garlin). Charlie's wife, Kim (Regina King), goes to work as a lawyer, leaving her husband at home to take care of their son, Ben (Khamani Griffin). Next thing you know, Charlie has the idea of opening a day-care center.

Enter the villainess, Miss Harridan (Anjelica Huston), whose own day-care center is so expensive that Charlie can no longer afford to send Ben there. Huston plays the role as your standard dominatrix, ruling her school with an iron hand, but you know what? It looks to me like a pretty good school, with the kids speaking foreign languages and discussing advanced science projects. Obviously, in the terms of this movie, any school where the kids have to study is bad, just as a school where the kids can run around and raise hell is good. This bias is disguised as Charlie's insight into child psychology.

The new school is successful almost from the outset, and empty seats begin to turn up in Miss Harridan's school as parents switch their kids to the cheaper alternative. No sane parent would trust a child to Charlie and Phil's chaotic operation, but never mind. Soon the partners hire an assistant, Marvin, played by Steve Zahn as a case of arrested development. Miss Harridan, facing the failure of her school, mounts a counterattack and of course is vanquished. She appears in the movie's final shot in a pathetically unfunny attempt to force humor long after the cause has been lost.

What the movie lacks is any attempt to place Murphy and his costars in a world of real kids and real day care. This entire world looks like it exists only on a studio lot. A few kids are given identifiable attributes (one won't take off his superhero costume), but basically they're just a crowd of rug rats in the background of the desperately forced comedy. Even the movie's poop joke fails, and if you can't make a poop joke work in a movie about kids, you're in trouble.

The movie's miscalculation, I suspect, is the same one that has misled Murphy in such other recent bombs as *I Spy* and *The Adventures of Pluto Nash* (which was unseen by me and most of the rest of the world). That's the delusion that Murphy's presence will somehow lend magic to an undistinguished screenplay. A film should begin with a story and characters, not with a concept and a star package.

The Dancer Upstairs ★ ★ ★
R, 128 m., 2003

Javier Bardem (Augustin Rejas), Laura Morante (Yolanda), Juan Diego Botto (Sucre), Elvira Minguez (Llosa), Alexandra Lencastre (Sylvina), Oliver Cotton (General Merino), Luis Miguel Cintra (Calderon), Abel Folk (Ezequiel/Duran). Directed by John Malkovich and produced by

Malkovich and Andrés Vicente Gómez.
Screenplay by Nicholas Shakespeare, based on
his novel.

John Malkovich's *The Dancer Upstairs* was
filmed before 9/11 and is based on a novel published in 1997, but has an eerie timeliness in its
treatment of a terrorist movement that works
as much through fear as through violence.

Filmed in Ecuador, it stars Javier Bardem as
Augustin, an inward, troubled man who left the
practice of law to join the police force because
he wanted to be one step closer to justice. Now
he has been assigned to track down a shadowy
terrorist named Ezequiel, who is everywhere
and nowhere, and strikes at random to sow fear
in the population. His trademark is to leave
dead dogs hanging in public view. In China, a
dead dog is symbolic of a tyrant executed by
the people, we learn.

The movie's story, based on a novel by
Nicholas Shakespeare, is inspired by the Shining
Path, a terrorist group in Peru. But this is not a
docudrama; it is more concerned with noticing
the ways in which terrorism takes its real toll in
a nation's self-confidence. Ezequiel commits
bold and shocking but small-scale public executions, many of helpless civilians in remote districts, but the central government is paralyzed
by fear, martial law is declared, and the army
steps into Augustin's investigation. The cure
may be more damaging than the crime.

Augustin is a very private man. He seems to
be happily married and to dote on his daughter, but he is happy to spend long periods away
from home, and doesn't really seem to focus on
his wife's obsession with getting herself an improved nose. He never gives a convincing explanation of why he left the law. His approach
to the Ezequiel crimes is largely intuitive; faced
with an enemy who works through rumor and
legend, he looks more for vibes than clues, and
at one point revisits the rural district where his
family owned a coffee farm, since confiscated.
There he will find—well, whatever he will find.

The movie is contemplative for a police procedural; more like Georges Simenon or Nicolas
Freeling than like Ed McBain. Bardem, who
was so demonstrative as the flamboyant writer
in *Before Night Falls*, now turns as subtle and
guarded as—well, as John Malkovich. It is typical that when he falls in love with Yolanda

(Laura Morante), his daughter's ballet teacher,
both he and she are slow to realize what has
happened, and reluctant to act on it.

When Ezequiel is finally discovered, it is
through a coincidence that I will not reveal
here, although his location is made clear to the
audience long before Augustin discovers it. I
cannot resist, however, quoting one of the
film's most cutting lines. We have heard that
Ezequiel represents what Marx called "the
fourth stage of communism," and when the
terrorist is finally dragged into the light of day,
Augustin says, "The fourth stage of communism is just a big fat man in a cardigan."

Malkovich has not set out to make a thriller
here, so much as a meditation about a man
caught in a muddle of his own thinking. By
rights, Augustin says at one point, he should be
a coffee farmer. The government's confiscation
of his family's farm paradoxically did him a
favor, by pushing him off the land and into law
school, and he is caught between a yearning for
the land and a confused desire to make a difference in his society.

As a cop he is trusted by his superiors with
great responsibility, but we see him more as a
dreamy idealist who doesn't have a firm program for his life and is pushed along by events.
He hates the cruelty of Ezequiel, but is baffled,
as the whole nation is, by Ezequiel's lack of a
program, focus, or identity. His violent acts
function as classic anarchism, seeking the
downfall of the state with the hope that a new
society will somehow arise from the wreckage.

The Dancer Upstairs is elegantly, even languorously, photographed by Jose Luis Alcaine,
who doesn't punch into things but regards
them, so that we are invited to think about
them. That doesn't mean the movie is slow; it
moves with a compelling intensity toward its
conclusion, which is not a "climax" or a "solution" in the usual police-movie mode, but a
small moral victory that Augustin rescues from
his general confusion.

When he finally gets to the end of his five-
year search for the figure who has distracted
and terrorized the country all of that time, his
quarry turns out to be a little like the Wizard of
Oz. And having pulled aside the curtain, Augustin now has to return to Kansas, or in this
case to his wife, who will soon be talking once
again about plastic surgery.

Danny Deckchair ★ ★
PG-13, 100 m., 2004

Rhys Ifans (Danny Morgan), Miranda Otto (Glenda Lake), Justine Clarke (Trudy Dunphy), Rhys Muldoon (Sandy Upman). Directed by Jeff Balsmeyer and produced by Andrew Mason. Screenplay by Balsmeyer.

You don't have to be a bigwig to be a somebody.
—Danny

There really was a Danny Deckchair. His name was Larry Walters, and the Web site snopes.com reports that on July 2, 1982, he "filled 45 weather balloons with helium and tethered them in four tiers to an aluminum lawn chair he purchased at Sears for $110, loading his makeshift aircraft with a large bottle of soda, milk jugs full of water for ballast, a pellet gun, a portable CB radio, an altimeter and a camera." The pellet gun was to shoot at balloons when he wanted to come down. That worked fine until he dropped the gun.

His flight was all too successful, the site says; he was seen by commercial airline pilots at 16,000 feet above Long Beach, California, was a guest of the Carson and Letterman shows, received an award from the Bonehead Club of Dallas, and was fined by the FAA for, among other transgressions, "operating a civil aircraft for which there is not currently in effect an air-worthiness certificate."

Danny Deckchair is a splendid movie while its hero is preparing for his flight and actually experiencing it, but it's not nearly as interesting once he descends to Earth. The hero is Danny Morgan, played by Rhys Ifans, that guy you see in a lot of movies and you always think, "I've seen that guy in a lot of movies." Ifans is a splendid actor in both serious and comic roles, but once he lands after his flight, the movie provides him with a role neither serious nor comic but, I fear, uplifting.

Danny is unhappily married to a Realtor named Trudy (Justine Clarke), who doesn't understand him, as indeed who could. He makes his escape from his backyard, lands in a small town, and more or less falls in love with Glenda, the town cop (Miranda Otto). Although his flight and disappearance have received national publicity, no one in the small town watches TV or reads the papers, I guess, and so they buy his story that he's Glenda's former teacher. Soon he's been promoted to the town's wise guru, this being one of those movie towns where the citizens have nothing better to do than congregate for speeches at which Danny informs them of truths like the one that prefaces this review.

Every single shred of the movie's plot after Danny ends his flight is unnecessary, contrived, unlikely, or simply not interesting. Even when a man has done an amazing thing, that doesn't make him an authority on anything except his amazing thing, if that. Here is a man who knows more than anyone alive about manned flight using a lawn chair and helium balloons, and that is the one thing he never gets to talk about.

The movie is sweet enough in its barmy way, partly because of the charm of Ifans and Otto, partly because the writer-director, Jeff Balsmeyer, must have a certain hopefulness about things. To have made this movie at all probably shows he has a good heart; it is not the work of a cynic. But if only the people in that small town had known Danny Deckchair's real identity, the movie might have been rescued from smarminess. It is human nature to believe whatever an expert tells you if the expert has descended from the clouds, but it is prudent to determine whether you're dealing with a "deus ex machina" or only a "doofus ex deckchair."

Daredevil ★ ★ ★
PG-13, 97 m., 2003

Ben Affleck (Matt Murdock/Daredevil), Jennifer Garner (Elektra Natchios), Michael Clarke Duncan (Kingpin), Colin Farrell (Bullseye), Jon Favreau (Franklin "Foggy" Nelson), Joe Pantoliano (Ben Urich), David Keith (Jack Murdock), Scott Terra (Young Matt Murdock). Directed by Mark Steven Johnson and produced by Avi Arad, Gary Foster, and Arnon Milchan. Screenplay by Johnson, based on the comic by Stan Lee, Bill Everett, and Frank Miller.

The origin is usually similar: A traumatic event in childhood, often involving the loss of parents, leaves the future superhero scarred in some ways but with preternatural powers in others. Daredevil came out of the Marvel Comics stable in the same period as Spider-Man, and both were altered by accidents, which gave Peter Parker his spidey-sense, and blinded Matt Murdock but made his other four senses hypersensitive. They grew up together in Marvel Comics, sometimes sharing the same adventures, but you won't see them fraternizing in the movies because their rights are owned by different studios.

Daredevil stars Ben Affleck as the superhero, wearing one of those molded body suits that defines his six-packs but, unlike Batman's, doesn't give him dime-size nipples. His mask extends over his eyes, which are not needed, since his other senses fan out in a kind of radar, allowing him to visualize his surroundings and "see" things even in darkness.

By day (I love that "by day") he is a lawyer in the Hell's Kitchen area of Manhattan. By night, he tells us, he prowls the alleys and rooftops, seeking out evildoers. Of these there is no shortage, although most of the city's more lucrative crime is controlled by the Kingpin (Michael Clarke Duncan) and his chief minister, Bullseye (Colin Farrell).

There must be a woman, and in *Daredevil* there is one (only one, among all those major male characters), although the fragrant Ellen Pompeo has a slink-on. She is Elektra Natchios (Jennifer Garner), who, like her classical namesake, wants to avenge the death of her father. By day she is, well, pretty much as she is by night. She and Daredevil are powerfully attracted and even share some PG-13 sex, which is a relief, because when superheroes have sex at the R level I am always afraid someone will get hurt. There is a rather beautiful scene where he asks her to stand in the rain because his ears are so sensitive they can create an image of her face from the sound of the raindrops.

Matt Murdock's law partner is Franklin "Foggy" Nelson (Jon Favreau). He has little suspicion of whom he is sharing an office with, although he is a quick study. Another key character is Ben Urich (Joe Pantoliano), who works for the *New York Post,* the newspaper of choice for superheroes.

Daredevil has the ability to dive off tall buildings, swoop thorough the air, bounce off stuff, land lightly, and so forth. There is an explanation for this ability, but I tend to tune out such

explanations because, after all, what do they really explain? I don't care what you say, it's Superman's cape that makes him fly. Comic fans, however, study the mythology and methodology with the intensity of academics. It is reassuring, in this world of inexplicabilities, to master a limited subject within a self-contained universe. Understand, truly understand, why Daredevil defies gravity, and the location of the missing matter making up 90 percent of the universe can wait for another day.

But these are just the kinds of idle thoughts I entertain during a movie like *Daredevil,* which may have been what the Vatican had in mind when it issued that statement giving its limited approval of Harry Potter, as long as you don't start believing in him. Daredevil describes himself as a "guardian devil," and that means there are guardian angels, and that means God exists and, by a process of logical deduction, that Matt Murdock is a Catholic. Please address your correspondence to Rome.

The movie is actually pretty good. Affleck and Garner probe for the believable corners of their characters, do not overact, are given semi-particular dialogue, and are in a very good-looking movie. Most of the tension takes place between the characters, not the props. There is, of course, a fancy formal ball to which everyone is invited (Commissioner Gordon must have been at the rival affair across town).

Affleck is at home in plots of this size, having just recently tried to save Baltimore from nuclear annihilation and the world from *Armageddon,* but Garner, Farrell, and Duncan are relatively newer to action epics, although Garner did see Affleck off at the station when he took the train from Pearl Harbor to New York, and Duncan was Balthazar in *The Scorpion King.* They play their roles more or less as if they were real, which is a novelty in a movie like this, and Duncan in particular has a presence that makes the camera want to take a step back and protect its groin.

The movie is, in short, your money's worth, better than we expect, more fun than we deserve. I am getting a little worn-out describing the origin stories and powers of superheroes, and their relationships to archvillains, gnashing henchmen, and brave, muscular female pals. They weep, they grow, they astonish, they overcome, they remain vulnerable, and their enemies spend inordinate time on wardrobe, grooming, and props, and behaving as if their milk of human kindness has turned to cottage cheese. Some of their movies, like this one, are better than others.

Dark Blue ★ ★ ★
R, 116 m., 2003

Kurt Russell (Eldon Perry Jr.), Scott Speedman (Bobby Keough), Ving Rhames (Arthur Holland), Brendan Gleeson (Jack Van Meter), Michael Michele (Beth Williamson), Lolita Davidovich (Sally Perry). Directed by Ron Shelton and produced by David Blocker, Caldecot Chubb, Sean Daniel, and James Jacks. Screenplay by David Ayer, based on a story by James Ellroy.

Two cops. One a veteran, one a rookie. One corrupt, the other still learning. Two sets of bad guys. One pair guilty of a heartless crime, the other pair guilty, but not of this crime. Two women, one a disillusioned wife, the other a disillusioned girlfriend. Two superior officers, one rotten, the other determined to bring him down. All the action takes place in the final days before the Rodney King verdict was announced in April 1992, and in the immediate aftermath, when the LAPD abandoned some neighborhoods to looters and arsonists.

Dark Blue is a formula picture in its broad outlines, but a very particular film in its characters and details. It doesn't redeem the formula or even tinker with it very much, but in a performance by Kurt Russell and in some location work on the angry streets, it has something to say and an urgent way of saying it.

The movie is based on a story by James Ellroy, a novelist who knows Los Angeles like the back of his hand, just after it has been stepped on. The screenplay for *L.A. Confidential* came from him, and a lot of hard-boiled fiction, punched out in short paragraphs, as if he has to keep ducking. He's been trying to get this story made into a movie for so long it was originally set during the Watts riots. The update works better, because the King verdict fits more neatly with his police department ripe for reform.

Kurt Russell and Scott Speedman star as Perry and Keough, two detectives who prowl the streets like freelance buccaneers; we know this type and even the veteran–rookie relationship from *Training Day, Narc,* and many other movies. The older cop explains you have to play tough to get things done, and the younger one tries to go along, even though he keeps failing the Hemingway test (it's immoral if you feel bad after you do it). They're the street agents, in a sense, of top cop Jack Van Meter (Brendan Gleeson). He has a couple of snitches he's protecting, and after they murder four people in a convenience store robbery, he orders Perry and Keough to frame and kill a couple of sex criminals for the crimes. Now young Keough, having balked at his first chance to execute a perp in the streets, gets a second chance.

The movie surrounds this situation with a lot of other material—too much, so that it sometimes feels hurried. Perry is married to one of those cop wives (Lolita Davidovich) who is stuck with the thankless task of telling him he just doesn't see her anymore ("You care more about the people you hate"). Keough is dating a young black woman (Michael Michele) who insists they not tell each other their last names. A man who sleeps with a woman who will not reveal her last name is marginally to be preferred, I suppose, to a man who will sleep with a woman who tells him her name but he forgets it in the morning.

The good cop, Deputy Chief Arthur Holland, played by Ving Rhames, knows Van Meter is crooked and has to decide whether to stay and prove it, or take an offer to become police chief of Cleveland. Meanwhile, the clock ticks toward an "innocent" verdict for the cops who were videotaped while beating Rodney King. (This does not stop the police academy from scheduling a promotion ceremony at the very same time, so that everyone will be in the same room when they are required for the big scene.)

I'm making the film sound too obvious. It follows well-worn pathways, but it has a literate, colloquial screenplay by David Ayer (*Training Day, The Fast and the Furious*), whose dialogue sounds as if someone might actually say it, and the direction is by Ron Shelton (*White Men Can't Jump, Bull Durham*), who marches us right up to clichés and then pulls them out from under us.

Above all, the movie has the Kurt Russell

performance going for it. Every time I see Russell or Val Kilmer in a role, I'm reminded of their *Tombstone* (1993), which got lost in the year-end holiday shuffle and never got the recognition it deserved. Russell has reserves he can draw on when he needs them, and he needs them here, as Perry descends into self-disgust and then, finally, understands the world and the role he has chosen. There is a late shot in which we look over his character's shoulder as Los Angeles burns all the way to the horizon. It takes a lot of setup to get away with a payoff like that, but Shelton and Russell earn it.

Dark Blue is not a great movie, but it has moments that go off the meter and find visceral impact. The characters driving through the riot-torn streets of Los Angeles provide some of them, and the savage, self-hating irony of Russell's late dialogue provides the rest. It is a clanging coincidence that the LAPD would be indicted just at the moment it was being exonerated, but then that's what the movies are for sometimes: to provide the outcomes that history overlooked.

Dawn of the Dead ★ ★ ★
R, 100 m., 2004

Sarah Polley (Ana), Ving Rhames (Kenneth), Jake Weber (Michael), Mekhi Phifer (Andre), Inna Korobkina (Luda), Michael Kelly (CJ). Directed by Zack Snyder and produced by Marc Abraham, Eric Newman, and Richard P. Rubinstein. Screenplay by James Gunn, based on the original by George A. Romero.

The contrast between this new version of *Dawn of the Dead* and the 1979 George Romero original is instructive in the ways that Hollywood has grown more skillful and less daring over the years. From a technical point of view, the new *Dawn* is slicker and more polished, and the acting is better, too. But it lacks the mordant humor of the Romero version, and although both films are mostly set inside a shopping mall, only Romero uses that as an occasion for satirical jabs at a consumer society. The 1979 film dug deeper in another way, by showing two groups of healthy humans fighting each other; the new version draws a line between the healthy and the zombies and maintains it. Since the zombies cannot be blamed for their behavior, there is no

real conflict between good and evil in Zack Snyder's new version; just humans fighting ghouls. The conflict between the two healthy groups in the Romero film does have a pale shadow in the new one; a hard-nosed security guard (Michael Kelly) likes to wave his gun and order people around, and is set up as the bad guy, but his character undergoes an inexplicable change just for the convenience of the plot.

All of which is not to say that the new *Dawn of the Dead* doesn't do an efficient job of delivering the goods. The screenplay, credited to James Gunn (based on Romero's original screenplay), has been coproduced by Richard P. Rubinstein, who produced the original. They use the same premise: An unexplained disease or virus, spread by human bites, kills its victims and then resurrects them as zombies. The creatures then run berserk, attacking healthy humans, infecting them, and so on. The only way to kill them is to shoot them in the head. True to the general speed-up in modern Hollywood, these new-issue zombies run fast, unlike the earlier ones, who lurched along. They also seem smarter and make decisions faster, unlike the 1979 models, who were likely to lurch up the down escalator.

The story begins with Ana (Sarah Polley) greeting a young girl who lives in the neighborhood. As the girl skates away on her in-lines, the shot is held just a little longer than seems natural, informing us that Something Bad Will Happen to Her. And does, as the next morning she attacks Ana's boyfriend, and Ana barely escapes with her life. After zombies roam the streets, newscasters fight hysteria, and neighborhoods burn, Ana eventually finds herself part of a small group in the local shopping mall.

Well, not such a small group. Unlike the tight little group of survivors in *28 Days Later*, this one expands to the point where we don't much care about some of the characters (the blond with the red lipstick, for example). But we do care about Kenneth (Ving Rhames), a gravel-voiced cop with hard-edged authority. We care about Michael (Jake Weber), a decent guy who tries to make the right decisions. And we care about Andre (Mekhi Phifer), whose wife, Luda (Inna Korobkina), is great with child and will give birth at any moment; the way that plot plays out is touching and horrifying. We even work up some feeling for the guy marooned on the roof of the gun shop across the street, who communicates with Kenneth by holding up signs.

For the rest, the movie consists mostly of dialogue and character scenes, alternating with violent attacks by zombies. The movie wisely doesn't give us too many of those scenes where one guy wanders off by himself when we're mentally screaming, "Stick together!" And although there is a cute dog, at least it's made useful in the plot. Of course, the movie makes full use of the shock shot where a zombie suddenly appears in the foreground from out of nowhere.

Of gore and blood there is a sufficiency. When the survivors devise a risky way to escape from the mall (which I will not reveal), a chain saw plays a key role. The survivors take chances that are probably unwise; maybe they should stay in a safe place, since the zombies will presumably sooner or later run out of gas. But taking chances makes for good action scenes, and exploding propane is always useful.

So, yes, *Dawn of the Dead* works, and it delivers just about what you expect when you buy your ticket. My only complaint is that its plot flat-lines compared to the 1979 version, which was trickier, wittier, and smarter. Romero was not above finding parallels between zombies and mall shoppers; in the new version, the mall is just a useful location, although at least there are still a few jokes about the Muzak.

The Day After Tomorrow ★ ★ ★
PG-13, 124 m., 2004

Dennis Quaid (Jack Hall), Jake Gyllenhaal (Sam Hall), Ian Holm (Terry Rapson), Emmy Rossum (Laura Chapman), Sela Ward (Dr. Lucy Hall), Dash Mihok (Jason Evans), Kenneth Welsh (Vice President Becker), Jay O. Sanders (Frank Harris), Austin Nichols (J.D.), Perry King (President), Arjay Smith (Brian Parks). Directed by Roland Emmerich and produced by Emmerich and Mark Gordon. Screenplay by Emmerich and Jeffrey Nachmanoff.

It is such a relief to hear the music swell up at the end of a Roland Emmerich movie, its restorative power giving us new hope. Billions of people may have died, but at least the major characters have survived. Los Angeles was wiped out by flying saucers in Emmerich's *Independence Day*,

New York was assaulted in his *Godzilla*, and now, in *The Day After Tomorrow*, Emmerich outdoes himself: Los Angeles is leveled by multiple tornadoes, New York is buried under ice and snow, the United Kingdom is flash-frozen, and lots of the Northern Hemisphere is wiped out for good measure. Thank God that Jack, Sam, Laura, Jason, and Dr. Lucy Hall survive, along with Dr. Hall's little cancer patient.

So, yes, the movie is profoundly silly. What surprised me is that it's also very scary. The special effects are on such an awesome scale that the movie works in spite of its cornball plotting. When tornadoes rip apart Los Angeles (not sparing the Hollywood sign), when a wall of water roars into New York, when a Russian tanker floats down a Manhattan street, when snow buries skyscrapers, when the crew of a space station can see nothing but violent storm systems—well, you pay attention.

No doubt some readers are already angry with me for revealing that Jack, Sam, Laura, Jason, Dr. Lucy Hall, and the little cancer patient survive. Have I given away the plot? This plot gives itself away. When cataclysmic events shred uncounted lives but the movie zeroes in on only a few people, of *course* they survive, although some supporting characters may have to be sacrificed. What's amusing in movies like *The Day After Tomorrow* is the way the screenplay veers from the annihilation of subcontinents to whether Sam should tell Laura he loves her.

The movie stars Dennis Quaid as the paleo-climatologist Jack Hall, whose computer models predict that global warming will lead to a new ice age. He issues a warning at a New Delhi conference, but is sarcastically dismissed by the American vice president (Kenneth Welsh), whom the movie doesn't even try to pretend doesn't look just like Dick Cheney. "Our economy is every bit as fragile as the environment," the vice president says, dismissing Jack's "sensational claims."

Before long, however, it is snowing in India, and hailstones the size of softballs are ripping into Tokyo. Birds, which are always wise in matters of global disaster, fly south double-time. Turbulence tears airplanes from the sky. The president (Perry King) learns the FAA wants to ground all flights, and asks the vice president, "What do you think we should do?"

Meanwhile, young Sam Hall (Jake Gyllenhaal)

goes to New York with an academic decathlon team, which includes Laura (Emmy Rossum of *Mystic River*) and Brian (Arjay Smith). They're stranded there. Ominous portents abound and Jack finally gets his message through to the administration ("This time," says a friend within the White House, "it will be different. You've got to brief the president directly.")

Jack draws a slash across a map of the United States and writes off everybody north of it. He issues a warning that supercooled air will kill anybody exposed to it, advises those in its path to stay inside, and then ... well, then he sets off to walk from Washington to New York to get to his son. Two of his buddies, also veterans of Arctic treks, come along.

We are wondering (a) why walk to New York when his expertise is desperately needed to save millions, (b) won't his son be either dead or alive whether or not he makes the trek? And (c) how quickly *can* you walk from Washington to New York over ice sheets and through a howling blizzard? As nearly as I can calculate, this movie believes it can be done in two nights and most of three days. Oh, I forgot; they drive part of the way, on highways that are gridlocked and buried in snow, except for where they're driving. How they get gas is not discussed in any detail.

As for the answer to (a), anyone familiar with the formula will know it is because he Feels Guilty About Neglecting His Son by spending all that time being a paleoclimatologist. It took him a lot of that time just to spell it. So okay, the human subplots are nonsense—all except for the quiet scenes anchored by Ian Holm, as a sad, wise Scottish meteorologist. Just like Peter O'Toole in *Troy*, Holm proves that a British-trained actor can walk into almost any scene and make it seem like it means something.

Quaid and Gyllenhaal and the small band of New York survivors do what can be done with impossible dialogue in an unlikely situation. And Dr. Lucy Hall (Sela Ward), Jack's wife and Sam's mother, struggles nobly in her subplot, which involves the little cancer patient named Peter. She stays by his side after the hospital is evacuated, calling for an ambulance, which we think is a tad optimistic, since Manhattan has been flooded up to about the eighth floor, the water has frozen, and it's snowing. But does the ambulance arrive? Here's another one for you:

Remember those wolves that escaped from the zoo? Think we'll see them again?

Of the science in this movie I have no opinion. I am sure global warming is real, and I regret that the Bush administration rejected the Kyoto treaty, but I doubt that the cataclysm, if it comes, will come like this. It makes for a fun movie, though. Especially the parts where Americans become illegal immigrants in Mexico, and the vice president addresses the world via the Weather Channel. *The Day After Tomorrow* is ridiculous, yes, but sublimely ridiculous—and the special effects are stupendous.

Deadline ★ ★ ★
NO MPAA RATING, 93 m., 2004

A documentary directed by Katy Chevigny and Kirsten Johnson and produced by Dallas Brennan and Chevigny.

If there were one hundred condemned prisoners on death row and one of them was innocent, would it be defensible to kill all one hundred on the grounds that the other ninety-nine deserved to die? Most reasonable people would answer that it would be wrong. Yet evidence has been gathering for years that far more than 1 percent of the inhabitants of death row are innocent. In the Illinois penal system, for example, a study following twenty-five condemned men ended after twelve of them had been executed, and the other thirteen had been exonerated of their crimes after new evidence was produced.

Deadline is a sober, even low-key documentary about how the American death penalty system is broken and probably can't be fixed. It climaxes with the extraordinary January 2003 press conference at which Republican Governor George Ryan commuted the death sentences of all 167 prisoners awaiting execution in Illinois. His action followed a long, anguished, public process scrutinizing the death penalty in Illinois—a penalty here, as throughout the United States, administered overwhelmingly upon defendants who are poor and/or belong to minority groups.

The film opens with Ryan speaking to students at Northwestern University, where students in an investigative journalism class had been successful in proving the innocence of three men on death row. That was a tribute not only to their skills as student journalists but also to the ease with which the evidence against the prisoners could be disproved. Many thoughtful observations in the doc come from Scott Turow, the Chicago lawyer and crime novelist who was appointed by Ryan to a commission to consider clemency for Illinois's condemned. He is not against the death penalty itself, he says, and was completely comfortable with the execution of John Wayne Gacy, killer of thirty-three young men. "But can we construct a system that *only* executes the John Wayne Gacys, without executing the innocent?" Turow doubts it.

Murder cases have high profiles, and the police are under pressure for arrests and charges. They don't precisely frame innocent people, the movie argues, but when they find someone who looks like a plausible perpetrator they tend to zero in with high-pressure tactics, willing their prisoner to be guilty. Confessions were tortured out of some of the Illinois prisoners in *Deadline,* including one who was dangled out of a high window by his handcuffs, and another who signed a confession in English even though he could not speak it.

The death penalty was briefly outlawed by the U.S. Supreme Court in 1972, and then reinstated in 1976 after the justices were persuaded the system's flaws had been repaired. It was during that time, the movie says, that Richard M. Nixon "discovered crime as a national issue." Before then, it had been thought of as a local problem and did not enter into presidential campaigns. After Nixon's law-and-order rhetoric, politicians of both parties followed his lead. "All politicians want to be seen as tough on crime," observes Illinois GOP house leader Tom Cross.

Since 1976 there has been a startling rise in executions in America, one of the few Western countries that still allow the death penalty. The movie cites statistics for American prisoners put to death:

1976–1980: 3 executions.
1981–1990: 140 executions.
1991–2000: 540 executions.

That latest figure was enhanced by just one governor, George W. Bush of Texas; 152 prisoners were executed under his watch between 1995 and 2000, as Texas in five years out-stripped the entire nation in the previous decade. In a speech, Bush says he is absolutely certain they were all guilty. For that matter, Bill Clinton must have known one of his Arkansas prisoners was so brain-damaged he asked the warden after his last meal, "Save my dessert so I can have it after the execution." But Clinton was running for president and dared not pardon this man, lest he be seen as soft on crime.

Some of the movie's most dramatic moments take place during hearings before Ryan's clemency commission, which reheard all 167 pending cases. The relatives of many victims say they will not be able to rest until the guilty have been put to death. But then we hear testimony from a group called Murder Victims' Families Against the Death Penalty. Among their witnesses are the father of a woman killed in the Oklahoma City terror attack, and the mother of the Chicago youth Emmett Till, murdered by southern racists fifty years ago. They say they do not want revenge and are opposed to the death penalty.

Deadline is all the more effective because it is calm, factual and unsensational. There are times when we are confused by its chronology and by how its story threads fit together, but it makes an irrefutable argument: Our criminal justice system is so flawed, especially when it deals with the poor and the nonwhite, that we cannot be sure of the guilt of many of those we put to death. George Ryan, not running for reelection, faced that truth and commuted those sentences, and said he could live with his decision. George Bush was absolutely confident he was right to allow 152 prisoners to die. He could live with his decision too.

The Deal ★ ★ ½
R, 107 m., 2005

Christian Slater (Tom Hanson), Selma Blair (Abbey Gallagher), Robert Loggia (Jared Tolson), John Heard (Professor Roseman), Colm Feore (Hank Weiss), Angie Harmon (Anna), Kevin Tighe (John Cortland), Françoise Yip (Janice Long). Directed by Harvey Kahn and produced by Chris Dorr, Ruth Epstein, Kahn, and Robert Lee. Screenplay by Epstein.

The Deal is a thriller about Wall Street insiders, set during an oil crisis a few years in the future. The United States is at war with the "Confederation of Arab States," gas is $6 a gallon and getting more expensive, and there's enormous pressure to find new sources for oil.

More than most thrillers, this one seems to be based on expert insights; its author, Ruth Epstein, wrote the screenplay against a background of Wall Street experience, and its view of boardroom politics has a convincing level of detail. It's not in every thriller that you hear someone say, "Oil is a fungible commodity."

Christian Slater stars as Tom Hanson, an associate with an old-line Wall Street investment firm that has kept its reputation during a period of corporate scandals. That's why the firm is attractive to the giant Condor Corp. and its sleek president, Jared Tolson (Robert Loggia, never scarier than when he smiles).

Condor wants to merge with Black Star, a privately held Russian oil company that controls massive oil reserves. We know from the start that the deal is fishy because at the top of the film a lawyer tells Tolson he can't continue to work on the deal; a few hours later the lawyer is shot dead. Hanson, the Slater character, is brought in as his replacement. His assignment: Perform due diligence to be sure Black Star is sound and the merger is in the best interests of Condor's shareholders.

The movie surrounds this main story line with several other intersecting strands, of which the most interesting involves young Abbey Gallagher (Selma Blair), a graduate student and "tree hugger" from Harvard who is recruited by Hanson to join his firm on the grounds that she can get a better hearing for her environmental concerns from inside the establishment.

Blair does specific things with her character that are interesting; she makes Abbey not one of those Harvard superhumans but a sincere, sometimes naive young woman who could use some social polish. Soon she is working with Hanson, and although they are indeed attracted to each other, romance is not the focus of this movie.

The Deal appreciates how big institutions like Slater's have factions and infighting; when he lands the Condor account, there's jealousy from Hank Weiss (a leaner, meaner Colm Feore), who is supposed to be the firm's oil expert.

There is also a middle-aged woman in research who knows all sorts of things that nobody ever asks her about: for example, that there is no oil in the "oil fields" controlled by Black Star. What's going on? "Oil may have been shipped from there," Hanson is told by a cryptic insider, "but I can't tell you where it came out of the ground."

The movie is a little too laden with details for its own good, and it has more characters than it needs, but sometimes that complexity works; like the hero, we're feeling our way through a maze of motives and possibilities, and although it's fairly clear who cannot be trusted, it's not always clear who can be. "He's my only friend at the firm," Hanson says of one associate, "and he'd stab me in the back in a second."

The pressure to close the deal is enormous; Hanson's firm alone expects to bank $25 million in commissions. But would it be worth it if Black Star were phony and Condor's shareholders were buying a worthless company? More to the point, what if Black Star is the front for an oil-laundering scheme?

Plots like this once seemed paranoid, but no one who has seen the documentary Enron: The Smartest Guys in the Room will find the lies and deceit in this film surprising. It expresses a system of moral values that keeps running into the discovery that "in the real world," as they say, "things don't work that way." The last scenes of the movie are deeply cynical and yet, we have a sinking feeling, not a million miles from the way Wall Street and the federal government actually do business.

There is of course always the Ethics Task Force, set up by the SEC and the FBI to guard against Wall Street fraud. One of the movie's continuing puzzles involves the possibility that several characters may be working undercover for the task force or Black Star. Secret information has a way of getting around, and the seriousness of the people behind the deal is made fairly clear when Hanson finds a bleeding heart in his refrigerator. "Not a human heart," the cops quickly reassure him.

I admire the film's anger and intelligence, and the generally persuasive level of the performances; Robert Loggia really seems like a

CEO, and Selma Blair really seems like an idealistic college graduate. Françoise Yip, for that matter, seems like the sort of best corporate friend who always seems to know more than she should, and to be trying to tell you more than she can say.

But the problem is, *The Deal*, like a lot of real-life Wall Street deals, is a labyrinth into which the plot tends to disappear. The ideas in the film are challenging, the level of expertise is high, the performances are convincing, and it's only at the level of story construction and dramatic clarity that the film doesn't succeed. One more rewrite might have been a good idea. I can't quite recommend it purely as a film, but as a double feature with *Enron: The Smartest Guys in the Room*, it's a slam dunk.

Dear Frankie ★ ★ ★ ½
PG-13, 102 m., 2005

Emily Mortimer (Lizzie Morrison), Gerard Butler (The Stranger), Sharon Small (Marie), Jack McElhone (Frankie Morrison), Mary Riggans (Nell Morrison). Directed by Shona Auerbach and produced by Caroline Wood. Screenplay by Andrea Gibb.

There is a shot toward the end of *Dear Frankie* when a man and a woman stand on either side of a doorway and look at each other, just simply look at each other. During this time they say nothing, and yet everything they need to say is communicated: their doubts, cautions, hopes. The woman is named Lizzie (Emily Mortimer), and the man, known in the movie only as "The Stranger," is played by Gerard Butler. Here is how they meet.

Lizzie has fled from her abusive husband, and is raising her deaf son, Frankie (Jack McElhone) with the help of her mother (Mary Riggans). Instead of telling Frankie the truth about his father, Lizzie creates the fiction that he is away at sea—a crew member on a freighter named the *Accra*. Frankie writes to his dad, and his mother intercepts the letters and answers them herself. Frankie's letters are important to her "because it's the only way I can hear his voice."

The deception works until, one day, a ship named the *Accra* actually docks in Glasgow.

Frankie assumes his father is on board, but a schoolmate bets his dad doesn't care enough to come and see him. After all, Frankie is nine and his father has never visited once.

Lizzie decides to find a man who will pretend, for one day, to be Frankie's father. Her friend Marie (Sharon Small), who runs the fish and chips shop downstairs, says she can supply a man, and introduces The Stranger, who Lizzie pays to pretend to be Frankie's dad for one day.

This sounds, I know, like the plot of a melodramatic tearjerker, but the filmmakers work close to the bone, finding emotional truth in hard, lonely lives. The missing father was brutal; Lizzie reveals to The Stranger, "Frankie wasn't born deaf. It was a gift from his dad." But Frankie has been shielded from this reality in his life and is a sunny, smart boy, who helps people deal with his deafness by acting in a gently funny way. When the kid at the next desk in school writes "Def Boy" on Frankie's desk, Frankie grins and corrects his spelling.

"Call me Davey," The Stranger says, since that is the name of Frankie's dad. So we will call him Davey, too. He is a man who reveals nothing about himself, who holds himself behind a wall of reserve, who makes the arrangement strictly business. We follow Frankie and his "dad" through a day that includes a soccer game, and the inevitable visit to an ice-cream shop. At the end of the day, Davey tells Lizzie and Frankie that his ship isn't sailing tomorrow after all—he'll be able to spend another day with his son. This wasn't part of the deal. But then Davey didn't guess how much he would grow to care about the boy, and his mother.

A movie like this is all in the details. The director, Shona Auerbach, and her writer, Andrea Gibb, see Lizzie, Frankie, and his grandmother not as archetypes in a formula, but as very particular, cautious, wounded people, living just a step above poverty, precariously shielding themselves from a violent past. The grandmother gives every sign of having grown up on the wrong side of town, a chain-smoker who moved in with her daughter "to make sure" she didn't go back to the husband.

Davey, or whatever his name is, comes into

the picture as a man who wants to have his exit strategy nailed down. He insists money is his only motive. It is quietly impressive how the young actor Jack McElhone as Frankie understands the task of his character, which is to encourage this man to release his better nature. There is also the matter of how much Frankie knows, or intuits, about his father's long absence.

What eventually happens, while not entirely unpredictable, benefits from close observation, understated emotions, unspoken feelings, and the movie's tact; it doesn't require its characters to speak about their feelings simply so that we can hear them. That tact is embodied in the shot I started out by describing: Lizzie and The Stranger looking at each other.

"We shot several takes," Emily Mortimer told me after the film's premiere. "Shona knew it had to be long, but she didn't know how long, and she had to go into the edit and find out which length worked. She is a very brave director in that way, allowing space around the action."

Every once in a long while, a director and actors will discover, or rediscover, the dramatic power of silence and time. They are moving pictures, but that doesn't mean they always have to be moving. In Miranda July's *You and Me and Everyone We Know,* there is a scene where a man and a woman who don't really know each other walk down a sidewalk and engage in a kind of casual word play that leads to a defining moment in their lives. The scene is infinitely more effective than all the countless conventional ways of obtaining the same result. In the same way, the bold long shot near the end of *Dear Frankie* allows the film to move straight as an arrow toward its emotional truth, without a single word or plot manipulation to distract us. While they are looking at each other, we are looking at them, and for a breathless, true moment, we are all looking at exactly the same fact.

D.E.B.S. ★ ½
PG-13, 91 m., 2005

Sara Foster (Amy), Meagan Good (Max), Jill Ritchie (Janet), Devon Aoki (Dominique), Jordana Brewster (Lucy), Jessica Cauffiel (Ninotchka), Michael Clarke Duncan (Academy President), Holland Taylor (Mrs. Peatree). Directed by Angela Robinson and produced by Jasmine Kosovic and Andrea Sperling. Screenplay by Robinson.

At some point during the pitch meetings for *D.E.B.S.* someone must certainly have used the words "Charlie's Lesbians." The formula is perfectly obvious: Four sexy young women work for a secret agency as a team that is gifted at lying, cheating, stealing, and killing. How do we know they have these gifts? Because of the movie's funniest moment, during the opening narration, when we learn that trick questions on SAT exams allow an agency to select high school graduates who can and will lie, cheat, steal, kill.

Amy (Sara Foster), the leader of the group, is a latent lesbian. Lucy Diamond (Jordana Brewster), a thief and master criminal, goes on a blind date with a semi-retired Russian assassin named Ninotchka (Jessica Cauffiel). When the D.E.B.S. monitor the date on a surveillance assignment, Amy is attracted to the smiling, seductive Lucy, which causes security complications. Pause for a moment to ask with me, would this movie be as interesting if the blind date had been with a guy? I submit it would not, because the lesbian material is all that separates *D.E.B.S.* from the standard teenage Insta-Flick.

The character traits of the "D.E.B.S." are only slightly more useful than the color-coded uniforms of the Teenage Mutant Ninja Turtles. In such movies, taxonomy is personality; once you've got the label straight, you know all you're ever going to know about the character. In addition to Amy, who is a lesbian, we meet Max (Meagan Good), who is black, Janet (Jill Ritchie), who is white, and Dominique (Devon Aoki), who corners the market on character attributes by being an Asian with a French accent who smokes all the time. I would not identify the characters by race, but the movie leaves us with no other way to differentiate them.

Dominique's smoking fascinates me. She never lights a cigarette, extinguishes one, or taps an ash. She simply exists with a freshly lit filter tip in her mouth, occasionally removing it to emit a perky little puff of uninhaled smoke. I wish I had stayed through the credits to see if there was a cigarette wrangler. Dominique's very presence on the screen inspires me to imagine an excited pitch meeting during which the writer-director, Angela Robinson, said with enthusiasm: "And Dominique, the Asian chick, smokes all the time!" At which the studio executives no doubt thanked the gods for blessing them with such richness and originality in character formation.

I have mentioned the pitch more than once because this movie is all pitch. It began as a popular short subject at Sundance, where audiences were reportedly amused by a send-up of the *Charlie's Angels* formula in which the angels were teenagers and one was a lesbian. The problem is, a short subject need only delight while a feature must deliver.

At one point in *D.E.B.S.* a team member uses the term "supervillain," not ironically but descriptively, leading to a new rule for *Ebert's Little Movie Glossary:* "Movies that refer to supervillains not ironically but descriptively reveal an insufficient disconnect between the pitch and the story." The rule has countless subsets, such as characters referring to themselves or others as heroes. Best friends who say, "I'm only comic relief" are given a provisional pass.

The Charlie figure in the movie is the president of the D.E.B.S. Academy, played by Michael Clarke Duncan, who looks spiffy in a tailored suit and rimless glasses. He gives them their orders, while never asking himself, I guess, how goes the homeland security when bimbos are minding the front lines. For that matter, Lucy Diamond, whose middle name I hope is Intheskywith, would rather make love than war, which leads to some PG-13 smooching.

Mrs. Peatree (Holland Taylor), headmistress of the D.E.B.S. Academy, asks Amy to turn the situation to her advantage by using herself as bait ("like Jodie did in that movie— you know the one, what was its name?"). I confess at this point I was less interested in Jodie's filmography than in the news that the D.E.B.S. Academy has a headmistress. I found myself wanting to know more about the academy's school song, lunchroom menu, student council, and parents' day. ("Janet has perfect scores in lying and cheating, but needs work on her stealing, and is flunking murder.") The uniform is cute little plaid skirts and white blouses, with matching plaid ties.

Other notes: I think I heard correctly, but may not have, that one character's "Freudian analysis" is that she suffers from a "dangerous Jungian symbiosis." Now there's a Freudian analysis you don't hear every day. I know I heard correctly when two of the girls share their dream: "Let's pretend we're in Barcelona, and you're at art school and I'm renting boats to tourists." The young people today, send them on junior year abroad, they go nuts. I note in passing that the movie quotes accurately from the famous shot in *Citizen Kane* where the camera moves straight up past the catwalks, drops, ropes, and pulleys above a stage. For me, that shot was like the toy in a box of Cracker-Jacks: not worth much, but you're glad they put it in there.

Deliver Us from Eva ★ ★

R, 105 m., 2003

Gabrielle Union (Eva), LL Cool J (Ray), Essence Atkins (Kareenah), Mel Jackson (Tim), Meagan Good (Jacqui), Dartanyan Edmonds (Darrell), Robinne Lee (Bethany), Duane Martin (Mike). Directed by Gary Hardwick and produced by Len Amato and Paddy Cullen. Screenplay by Hardwick, James Iver Mattson, and B. E. Brauner.

Deliver Us from Eva is the second movie of the same weekend based on a romantic bet. See my review of *How to Lose a Guy in 10 Days* for my general comments on this unhappy genre. *Eva* has the advantage of being about one bet, not two, preserving at least one of the protagonists as a person we can safely like. But it proceeds so deliberately from one plot point to the next that we want to stand next to the camera, holding up cards upon which we have lettered clues and suggestions.

The movie stars two tall and striking actors, Gabrielle Union and LL Cool J, who have every reason to like each other anyway, even if Union's brothers-in-law were not paying him $5,000 to take her out, make her fall in love, and move with her to a town far, far away. They can't stand the woman. Well, hardly can we.

Union plays Eva, oldest of the four Dandridge sisters. After the untimely death of their parents, Eva took on the task of raising the girls, and has never been able to stop giving the orders—no, not even now that they're grown up. The sisters are Kareenah (Essence Atkins), who won't get pregnant, on Eva's orders; Bethany (Robinne Lee), whom Eva won't let live with her cop boyfriend; and Jacqui (Meagan Good), who is married to a mailman who always feels like there's postage due.

The Dandridge sisters like their local fame and kind of enjoy being under Eva's motherly thumb. The director, Gary Hardwick, often films them cresting a hill, four abreast, hair and skirts flying, arms linked, while straggling after them are their luckless men, left in the rear. Much of the action centers on a beauty parlor, serving, like the title location in *Barbershop*, as the stage upon which daily soap operas are played out to loud acclaim or criticism.

The Dandridge family logjam is broken, as we can easily foresee, when Eva actually begins to fall for that big lug Ray (played by LL Cool J, who says after this movie he is changing his name back to James Todd Smith, a victory for punctuationists everywhere). He wins her over by admiring her spicy beans, which are too hot for the wimps she usually dates. If the way to a man's heart is through his stomach, the way to a woman's heart is through adoring a recipe that only she thinks is edible.

But let's back up. The problem with their love affair, of course, is that although Eva loves Ray and Ray loves Eva, Eva is certain to find out about the bet, causing a scene of heartbreak and betrayal that would be moving if I hadn't also seen it in *How to Lose a Guy in 10 Days* and every other movie in history where lovers begin with secret deception and arrive at the truth.

Any two lovers with the slightest instinct for each other, with the most perfunctory ability to see true romance glowing in the eyes of the beloved, would not have the fight because they would not need the fight. They would know their love was true. I live to see the following scene:

> She: You mean . . . you only went out with me on a bet!?!
> He: That's right, baby.
> She: Well, you won, you dumb lug. Now haul your lying ass over here and make me forget it.

De-Lovely ★ ★ ★ ½

PG-13, 125 m., 2004

Kevin Kline (Cole Porter), Ashley Judd (Linda Lee Porter), Jonathan Pryce (Gabe), Kevin MacNally (Gerald Murphy), Sandra Nelson (Sara Murphy), Allan Corduner (Monty Woolley), Peter Polycarpou (Louis B. Mayer), Keith Allen (Irving Berlin). Directed by Irwin Winkler and produced by Rob Cowan, Charles Winkler, and Irwin Winkler. Screenplay by Jay Cocks.

I wanted every kind of love that was available, but I could never find them in the same person, or the same sex.

—Cole Porter

Porter floated effortlessly for a time between worlds: gay and straight, Europe and America, Broadway and Hollywood, showbiz and high society. He had a lifelong love affair with his wife, and lifelong love affairs without his wife. He thrived, it seemed, on a lifestyle that would have destroyed other men (and was, in fact, illegal in most of the places that he lived), and all the time he wrote those magical songs. Then a horse fell down and crushed his legs, and he spent twenty-seven years in pain. And *still* he wrote those magical songs.

De-Lovely is a musical and a biography, and brings to both of those genres a worldly sophistication that is rare in the movies. (If you seek to find how rare, compare this film with *Night and Day*, the 1946 biopic that stars Cary Grant as a resolutely straight Porter, even sending him off to World War I). *De-Lovely* not only accepts Porter's complications, but bases the movie on them; his lyrics take on a tantalizing ambiguity once you understand that they are not necessarily written about love with a woman:

> It's the wrong game, with the wrong chips
> Though your lips are tempting, they're
> the wrong lips
> They're not her lips, but they're such
> tempting lips
> That, if some night, you're free
> Then it's all right, yes, it's all right with me.

It would appear from *De-Lovely* that on many nights Porter was free, and yet Linda Lee Porter was the love and solace of his life, and she accepted him as he was. One night in Paris they put their cards on the table.

"You know then, that I have other interests," he says.

"Like men."

"Yes, men."

"You like them more than I do. Nothing is cruel if it fulfills your promise."

Dialogue like this requires a certain wistful detachment, and Kevin Kline is ideally cast as Cole Porter: elegant, witty, always onstage, brave in the face of society and his own pain. Kline plays the piano, too, which allows the character to spend a lot of convincing time at the keyboard, writing the sound track of his life. But who might have known Ashley Judd would be so nuanced as Linda Lee? In those early scenes she lets Porter know she wants him and yet allows him his freedom, and she speaks with such tact that she is perfectly understood without really having said anything at all. Yet their relationship was by definition painful for her, because it was really all on his terms. Many of his lyrics are fair enough to reflect that from her point of view:

> Every time we say goodbye, I die a little,
> Every time we say goodbye, I wonder why
> a little,
> Why the gods above me, who must be in
> the know.
> Think so little of me, they allow you to go.

Cole and Linda met in Paris at that time in the twenties when expatriate Americans were creating a new kind of lifestyle. Scott and Zelda were there, too, and Hemingway, and the movie supplies as the Porters' best friends the famous American exile couple Sara and Gerald Murphy (the originals for Fitzgerald's *Tender Is the Night*). Porter was born

with money, made piles more, and spent it fabulously, on parties in Venice and traveling in high style. Linda's sense of style suited his own: They always looked freshly pressed, always seemed at home, always had the last word, even if beneath the surface there was too much drinking and too many compromises. The chain smoking that eventually killed Linda was at first an expression of freedom, at the end perhaps a kind of defense.

The movie, directed by Irwin Winkler *(Life as a House)* and written by Jay Cocks *(The Age of Innocence)*, is told as a series of flashbacks from a ghostly rehearsal for a stage musical based on Porter's life. Porter and a producer (Jonathan Pryce) sit in the theater, watching scenes run past, but the actors cannot see or hear Porter, and the producer may in a sense be a recording angel.

This structure allows the old, tired, widowed, wounded Porter to revisit the days of his joy, and at the same time explains the presence of many musical stars who appear, both on stage and in dramatic flashbacks, to perform Porter's songs. Porter has famously been interpreted by every modern pop singer of significance, most memorably by Ella Fitzgerald in *The Cole Porter Songbook*, but here we get a new generation trying on his lyrics: Elvis Costello, Alanis Morissette, Sheryl Crow, Natalie Cole, Robbie Williams, Diana Krall.

The movie contains more music than most musicals, yet is not a concert film because the songs seem to rise so naturally out of the material and illuminate it. We're reminded how exhilarating the classic American songbook is, and how inarticulate so much modern music sounds by contrast. Kevin Kline plays Porter as a man apparently able to write a perfect song more or less on demand, which would be preposterous if it were not more or less true. One of Porter's friends was Irving Berlin, who labored to bring forth his songs and must have given long thought to how easy it seemed for Porter.

If the film has a weakness, it is that neither Cole nor Linda ever found full, complete, passionate, satisfying romance. They couldn't find it with each other, almost by the terms of their arrangement, but there is no evidence that Porter found it in serial promiscuity, and although Linda Lee did have affairs, they are not made a significant part of this story. They were a good fit not because they were a great love story, but because they were able to provide each other consolation in its absence.

Strange, dear, but true, dear, he began a
song that confessed:
Even without you,
My arms fold about you,
You know, darling why,
So in love with you am I.

Demonlover ★ ★
NO MPAA RATING, 129 m., 2003

Connie Nielsen (Diane de Monx), Charles Berling (Hervé Le Millinec), Chloë Sevigny (Elise Lipsky), Gina Gershon (Elaine Si Gibril), Jean-Baptiste Malartre (Henri-Pierre Volf), Dominique Reymond (Karen), Edwin Gerard (Edward Gomez). Directed by Olivier Assayas and produced by Xavier Giannoli and Edouard Weil. Screenplay by Assayas.

Demonlover begins in the cutthroat world of big business, and descends as quickly as it can to just plain cutting throats. It's a high-gloss corporate thriller that watches a group of vicious women executives as they battle for control of lucrative new 3-D Internet porn technology. One of the sites in question offers real-time torture and death, leading us to wonder: (1) Can such a dangerously illegal site actually generate the fortune that seems to be involved? and (2) Are any of these women queasy about selling human suffering at retail? The movie's answers are apparently yes, and no.

My description makes the movie sound like a sleazy bottom-feeder, but this is an ambitious production by director Olivier Assayas, whose last film, *Les Destinees* (2000), was about a struggle for control of a family firm that manufactures Limoges china. Yes. Now we have another corporate struggle, but in a corporation with no values, no scruples, and apparently no employees, since all we see are executives.

The movie is set in the chilly world of high-gloss offices, international hotels, and private jets. French, English, and Japanese are spoken interchangeably. The story opens with Henri-Pierre Volf (Jean-Baptiste Malartre), Internet millionaire, flying to Tokyo to close a deal with TokyoAnime to buy new 3-D imaging software, which will make online porn unbelievably

profitable. Also on board is his ruthless assistant Diane (Connie Nielsen), who slips drugs into the Evian of her rival, Karen (Dominique Reymond). Karen passes out in the airport, her briefcase is stolen, and Diane is promoted to her job.

Until this point the movie has had the look and feel of your average corporate thriller; Michael Douglas could turn up at any moment. Then it takes a sudden drop into some really nasty business. We see demos of cutting-edge Internet porn (not graphic, but close), and we glimpse the first hints that beneath the surface an even more demented level lurks, at which users in real time are able to suggest tortures for the women they see on the screen.

Let's assume we all agree this is depraved and evil. Let's move on to the logic of the story. Would it be cost-effective to torture people online? How would you advertise this site and bill for it? How much would it cost? Who would be reckless enough to pay? An international corporation like Henri-Pierre's would obviously be wiser to sell soft porn instead of this illegal material with a tiny audience.

But never mind. The movie is confused about this and many other things, in a scenario that grows steadily murkier. Back home in Paris, Diane's scheme has paid off in the big job with the big salary, but Elise (Chloë Sevigny), who is loyal to Karen, suspects what she did to get the job, and Elise is a dangerous customer. So is Elaine (Gina Gershon), who works for the American firm Demonlover and is bidding against Magnatronics for the rights owned by Henri-Pierre. Their rivalry is further complicated (or is it made unnecessary?) by the fact that Diane is actually a corporate spy.

If that seems like a secret I should not have revealed, be assured that it is irrelevant to the progress of the movie, which exists largely in content-free visuals of beautiful women, ripped lingerie, luscious suites, sexual jousting, and lots and lots of people coming down all manner of corridors and going into one door after another in order to capture, threaten, ravish, seduce, blackmail, or murder one another.

By the end of the movie, I frankly didn't give a damn. There's an ironic twist, but the movie doesn't pay for it and doesn't deserve it. And I was struck by the complete lack of morality in *Demonlover*. No one seems to question the fact that they all plan to make money by torturing people. It's all just business. As a metaphor for certain tendencies in modern commerce, this may be intended, but somehow I don't think so. I think *Demonlover* is so in love with its visuals and cockeyed plot that it forgets to think about the implications.

Diary of a Mad Black Woman ★
PG-13, 116 m., 2005

Kimberly Elise (Helen McCarter), Shemar Moore (Orlando), Cicely Tyson (Myrtle), Steve Harris (Charles McCarter), Tyler Perry (Grandma Madea), Lisa Marcos (Brenda), Tamara Taylor (Debrah). Directed by Darren Grant and produced by Reuben Cannon and Tyler Perry. Screenplay by Perry, based on his play.

Diary of a Mad Black Woman begins as the drama of a wife of eighteen years, dumped by her cruel husband and forced to begin a new life. Then this touching story is invaded by the Grandma from Hell, who takes a chainsaw to the plot, the mood, everything. A real chainsaw, not a metaphorical one. The Grandma is not merely wrong for the movie, but fatal to it—a writing and casting disaster. And since the screenplay is by the man who plays Grandma in drag, all blame returns to Tyler Perry. What was he *thinking*?

There's a good movie buried beneath the bad one. Kimberly Elise stars as Helen, wife of Atlanta's attorney of the year. She lives with her husband, Charles (Steve Harris), in a house big enough to be the suburban headquarters of an insurance company. Their marriage seems ideal, but he cheats on her and assaults her with verbal brutality. When Helen comes home the next day, her clothes are being loaded into a U-Haul. That's how she finds out Charles is dumping her and moving in his mistress, Brenda (Lisa Marcos). Oh, and he has two children by Brenda.

Luckily for Helen, the U-Haul is driven by Orlando (Shemar Moore, from *The Young and the Restless*), who is handsome and kind and everything Charles is not. Helen weepingly flees to the house of her grandmother, and that's when everything goes spectacularly wrong.

Grandma Madea, who is built along the lines of a linebacker, is a tall, lantern-jawed, smooth-skinned, balloon-breasted gargoyle with a bad wig, who likes to wave a loaded gun and shoot test rounds into the ceiling. This person is not remotely plausible; her dialogue is so offensively vulgar that it's impossible to believe that the intelligent, sweet, soft-spoken Helen doesn't seem to notice. Madea at one point invades Charles's mansion, tells his mistress she is a ho (which is correct), and destroys all the furniture in his living room with a chainsaw she is able to find and employ within seconds. What's with this bizarre grandmother? She's like Moms Mabley at a church social. Did nobody realize that Grandma Madea comes from Planet X, would seem loud at the Johnson Family Picnic, is playing by different rules than anyone else in the cast, and fatally sabotages Kimberly Elise's valiant attempt to create a character we can care about?

The director is Darren Grant. Did he approve as Grandma took a chainsaw to his movie? Did he see Kimberly Elise in *Beloved* and *Woman, Thou Art Loosed* and realize what she was capable of in a Grandma-free movie? I can imagine this movie working perfectly well with Grandma played as a sympathetic human being, perhaps by Irma P. Hall.

For that matter, Helen has an aunt as well as a grandmother, and her aunt, Myrtle, is played with taste and sympathy by Cicely Tyson. It is impossible that Grandma the harridan could have given life to such gentle and civilized women as Myrtle and Helen. The math doesn't work, either. We learn that Myrtle was thirty-nine when Helen was born, and that makes Grandma about eighty-five, which is too old to operate a chainsaw.

Without the interruptions by Grandma Madea, the movie would be about Helen as a shattered woman who (1) tells the judge Charles can keep all his assets, because she doesn't want a penny; (2) goes to work as a waitress; and (3) is courted by the handsome Orlando, who is kind, understanding, sincere, and knows how to listen to women. No. 1 is impossible, because no judge is going to let a wife abandoned by an adulterer after eighteen years walk away without a penny, but never mind. Does Helen find happiness with Orlando?

Not so fast. The movie has a Christian agenda, which is fine with me, if only it had been applied in a believable way. After melodramatic events occur in the life of the evil Charles, Helen gets the opportunity to practice the virtues of forgiveness and redemption, at the apparent cost of her own happiness. We hate Charles so much that it's impossible to feel sorry for him, or believe in his miraculous recovery in body or reformation of character. It just doesn't play—especially while Helen keeps poor Orlando in the dark about her true feelings, for no better reason than to generate phony romantic suspense.

At the end of the film, Orlando makes a comeback that demonstrates he has carefully studied *An Officer and Gentleman,* but before then we have had one emotionally implausible scene after another involving Charles and Helen, interrupted by periodic raids by the Grandma Madea action figure, who brings the movie to a halt every time she appears. She seems like an invasion from another movie. A very bad another movie. I've been reviewing movies for a long time, and I can't think of one that more dramatically shoots itself in the foot.

Dickie Roberts: Former Child Star ★ ★
PG-13, 99 m., 2003

David Spade (Dickie Roberts), Mary McCormack (Grace Finney), Jon Lovitz (Sidney), Craig Bierko (George Finney), Jenna Boyd (Sally Finney), Scott Tessa (Sam Finney), Alyssa Milano (Cyndi), Rob Reiner (Himself). Directed by Sam Weisman and produced by Jack Giarraputo. Screenplay by Fred Wolf and David Spade.

Here is an inspired idea for a comedy, but why have they made it into a dirge? *Dickie Roberts: Former Child Star* has a premise that would be catnip for Steve Martin or Jim Carrey, but David Spade (who, to be fair, came up with the premise) casts a pall of smarmy sincerity over the material. There are laughs, to be sure, and some gleeful supporting performances, but after a promising start the movie sinks in a bog of sentiment.

Spade plays Dickie Roberts, now about thirty-five, who has been struggling ever since the end of his career as a child TV star. As fame and fortune disappeared, so did his mother; a biographical mockumentary about Dickie says

he was orphaned after she "moved out of the area." Now he's a car valet and plays poker with other former child stars, including (playing themselves) Danny Bonaduce, Dustin Diamond, Barry Williams, Leif Garrett, and Corey Feldman. His desperate agent Sidney (Jon Lovitz, pitch perfect) can't find him work, and when Dickie hears about the lead in the new Rob Reiner movie, Sidney sighs, "That's out of our league."

But Dickie runs into Brendan Fraser (the movie is like a reality TV version of *Hollywood Squares*), who gets him a meeting with Reiner. And Reiner drops some bad news: "I don't think you can play the part because you're not a real person." Dickie never had a real childhood, he explains, and so he grew up to be—Dickie.

That sets into motion the second, soapy, half of the movie. Dickie advertises for a "real family" where he can spend a month recapturing his lost childhood, and hooks up with the self-promoting ad man George Finney (Craig Bierko) and his nice family: the mother, Grace (Mary McCormack), and the kids, Sally (Jenna Boyd) and Sam (Scott Tessa). And right there a nice, sharp-edged satire gets traded in for a sappy sitcom.

Spade's comic persona is essentially not sweet and lovable, and his attempt to force Dickie into that mode is never convincing. The best moments in the sitcom half of the movie come when he plays against type, as when he throws a wine cork at a sometime girlfriend, Cyndi (Alyssa Milano), or phones in a false alarm so that Grace can follow the fire trucks to the address she's looking for. Funny, but not so funny are the staged docudramas in which his loving family stages a Christmas in the summertime so he can recapture his lost youth.

The Grace character is played by Mary McCormack with her usual true-blue charm, and for a long time the movie wisely sidesteps any suggestion of romance between Grace and Dickie. When at the end we learn they get married, we give the nuptials about as much of a chance as Liza Minnelli's next matrimony. George, Grace's husband, is an underwritten figure who pops up from time to time in oddly written scenes, and then runs off with Cyndi, so we're told, since by then we haven't seen either one of them for some time.

David Spade has a peculiar but definite

165

screen persona, and in the right role he could be effective. In the old days of the studio system, he could have worked as a supporting player at Warner's, pinch-hitting for Elisha Cook Jr. He is too recessive, narcissistic, and dreamy-voiced to be a star, although he could play the lead in a story that hated his character. As the guy we're supposed to love here, the little lost boy who finally grows up, not a chance.

Note: One of the pleasures of the movie is its population of former child stars. The end credits include a gathering of all those who appeared in the movie and a lot more, singing a song with lyrics that seem to come straight from the heart.

Die, Mommie, Die ★ ★

R, 90 m., 2003

Charles Busch (Angela Arden), Natasha Lyonne (Edith Sussman), Jason Priestley (Tony Parker), Frances Conroy (Bootsie Carp), Philip Baker Hall (Sol Sussman), Stark Sands (Lance Sussman), Victor Raider-Wexler (Sam Fishbein), Nora Dunn (Shatzi Van Allen). Directed by Mark Rucker and produced by Dante Di Loreto, Anthony Edwards, and Bill Kenwright. Screenplay by Charles Busch.

There's a 1950s genre of films that asked to be decoded through a gay lens. They undermined the conventional view of straight, middle-class American life, inviting the irony of outsiders (homosexual or not). Their glamorous, overwrought heroines were role models for the emerging camp sensibility. Douglas Sirk's melodramas (among them *Imitation of Life*, *Written on the Wind*, and *All That Heaven Allows*) are at the head of this category, and Todd Haynes's *Far from Heaven* (2002) was a film that moved Sirk's buried themes into the foreground. What made Sirk a great director is that his stories were sappy in a way that was subversive to the restrictive values of the time.

The whole point, though, was that Sirk's movies never copped to what they were doing. They didn't wink or nudge or engage in Wildean double entendres (well, maybe sometimes, as when Rock Hudson is told it's time to get married and says, "I have trouble enough just finding oil"). Sirk was as sincere about his surface story as he was about his subtext, and that's why his movies still function as real melodrama and not as camp. The strength of *Far from Heaven* is its complete earnestness; it isn't a 2002 satire of Sirk, but wants to be the 1957 movie he couldn't make. We can smile at the story's hysteria about homosexual and interracial romance, but those were not laughing matters in the 1950s, and the movie honors that.

The problem with *Die, Mommie, Die*, a drag send-up of the genre, is that it spoils the fun by making it obvious. While it is true that late in their careers Joan Crawford or Bette Davis sometimes seemed like drag queens, they were not, and would have been offended by the suggestion. The lead in *Die, Mommie, Die* is Charles Busch, a professional drag queen, and the whole point of the movie is precisely that he is a drag queen.

There is a crucial difference between a drag queen and a female impersonator. Impersonators want to be "read" as women, and may sincerely think of themselves as women. That would seem to be the case with Jaye Davidson's character in *The Crying Game*. The drag queen, on the other hand, wants you to know he is a man. Charles Busch is in that category; he looks like a man in drag, and that's the point. The performance consists of a send-up by a gay man of a straight woman, and the story is a lampoon of cherished heterosexual conventions.

It is also, of course, a comedy, and I know I'm getting awfully serious about something that intends to be silly and trashy. But I'm trying to explain to myself why it didn't work, and I think it's because drag queens are no longer funny just because they're drag queens; we've lost the nervousness about gender that once made us need to laugh at a man in drag. The material started out as a play, and probably worked better then because a simpatico audience could make it an event.

The story stars Busch as Angela Arden, a failed singer married to a failing Hollywood producer named Sol Sussman (Philip Baker Hall). He makes bad movies but has lost the touch of making a profit on them. During his latest debacle in Europe, she's had an affair with the young stud Tony Parker (Jason Priestley). Now she wants a divorce from Sol, but nothing doing: "We're a famous couple, Angela, and we're going to stay together." Completing the Sussman household are their maid, Bootsie Carp (Frances Conroy), their slutty daughter, Edith (Natasha Lyonne), and their gay pothead son, Lance (played by an actor whose name may really be Stark Sands, although that sounds like a retro product of the Rock-Troy-Tab name generator).

Angela has a singing engagement in a third-rate resort. Sol cancels it in a fit of rage. Angela strikes back. Sol has been complaining loudly (and, because this is the great Philip Baker Hall, convincingly) about his constipation, and so she poisons his suppository, ho, ho. Many complications ensue, all provoking Angela to run amok through the gamut of emotions.

Some of the dialogue and many of the gags are in fact funny. But the movie's reason for being is Busch's drag performance, and I didn't find anything funny because he was a man in drag. What was funny worked despite that fact. A woman in the role might have been funnier, because then we wouldn't have had to be thinking about two things at once: the gag, and the drag. Imagine a very good actor who is also a very good juggler. You admire his versatility, but during *Hamlet* you'd want him to put down his balls during the soliloquies.

Dirty Dancing: Havana Nights ★ ★
PG-13, 87 m., 2004

Diego Luna (Javier Suarez), Romola Garai (Katey Miller), Sela Ward (Jeannie Miller), John Slattery (Bert Miller), Jonathan Jackson (James Phelps), January Jones (Eve), Rene Lavan (Carlos Suarez), Mika Boorem (Susie Miller), Mya Harrison (Lola Martinez). Directed by Guy Ferland and produced by Lawrence Bender and Sarah Green. Screenplay by Boaz Yakin and Victoria Arch.

I was not a fan of *Dirty Dancing*, although $150 million in 1987 box-office dollars attempted, unsuccessfully, to convince me I was wrong. I thought Patrick Swayze and Jennifer Grey were terrific dancers, and I thought the plot was a clunker assembled from surplus parts at the Broken Plots Store. The actions of the characters (especially her parents) were so foreordained they played like closing night of a run that had gone on way too long.

Now here is *Dirty Dancing: Havana Nights*. Same characters, new names, same plot, new location. The wealthy Miller family from St. Louis arrives in 1958 Havana with their teenage daughter, Katey (Romola Garai). She is courted by young James Phelps (Jonathan Jackson), son of a wealthier family. Has anybody in the movies named Phelps ever been poor? She meets Javier Suarez (Diego Luna), a nice Cuban waiter about her age, and by her clumsiness gets him fired. But . . .

Well, of course she finds Phelps a bore and Javier a nice and considerate friend, not nearly as sexually vibrant, by the way, as Swayze. Except when he's dancing. She has to choose between the godawful official balls and the excitement at La Rosa Negra, the club where Javier and his friends hang out—a club not a million miles distant in function from the disco in *Saturday Night Fever*.

Can this white-bread American princess learn rhythm? Of course she can, with Javier wading with her into the ocean and teaching her to feel the motion of the waves and allow her body to sway with them, and to listen to the music as if it is the waves, and meanwhile perfecting choreography so complex and demanding that it would have had Rita Moreno, in her heyday, pleading for the Sloan's Liniment.

Is it not clear to all of us that sooner or later Katey and Javier will have to defy social convention and enter the dance contest, and that Mr. and Mrs. Miller will find themselves at the big contest but astonished to discover their own daughter out there on the floor? Of course they will be shocked, but then they will be proud, and Mrs. Miller (Sela Ward), who was a heck of a dancer in her day, will realize that the fruit has not fallen far from the tree, and that Katey must follow her dream, realize her talent, go with the flow, sway with the waves, and bring home the bacon.

Meanwhile, in the hills, Fidel Castro readies his assault on the corrupt Batista regime. All very well, and his revolution could have supplied some good scenes, as we know from *Havana* and the *Godfather* saga. But is Fidel really needed in a retread of *Dirty Dancing*? And do the inevitable scenes of upheaval, people separated from each other, confusion in the streets, etc., create tension, or only tedium? How can we get excited about action that the movie isn't even about? Couldn't Castro at least have crashed the dance contest in disguise, like Douglas Fairbanks would have done?

Why, then, do I give this movie two stars and the original only one? Because I have grown mellow and forgiving? Perhaps, but perhaps too because we go to the movies to look at the pretty pictures on the screen, like infants who like bright toys dangled before us. And *Dirty Dancing: Havana Nights* is a great movie to look at, with its period Havana (actually San Juan, Puerto Rico, with lots of 1950s cars). The dancing is well done, the music will sell a lot of sound tracks, and . . .

Romola Garai and Diego Luna. He you remember from *Y Tu Mama Tambien*, and here again he has that quirky, winning charm. She is a beauty and a gifted comedienne, who played Kate in *Nicholas Nickleby* and was the younger sister, Cassandra, in the wonderful 2003 film *I Capture the Castle*. They must be given credit for their presence and charisma in *Dirty Dancing: Havana Nights*, and together with the film's general ambience they do a lot to make amends for the lockstep plot. But here's an idea. Rent *Y Tu Mama También*, *Nicholas Nickleby*, and *I Capture the Castle*, and eliminate the middleman.

Dirty Pretty Things ★ ★ ★ ½
R, 107 m., 2003

Chiwetel Ejiofor (Okwe), Audrey Tautou (Senay), Sergi López (Sneaky [Juan]), Sophie Okonedo (Juliette), Benedict Wong (Guo Yi), Zlatko Buric (Ivan). Directed by Stephen Frears and produced by Robert Jones and Tracey Seaward. Screenplay by Steve Knight.

The hall porter is sent upstairs to repair a blocked toilet and finds the source of the trouble: a human heart stuck in the pipes. He asks about the recent occupants of the room, but nobody seems to know anything, not even the helpful hooker who acts like an unofficial member of the staff. The porter, a Nigerian named Okwe, takes it up with his boss, Sneaky, and is advised to mind his own business.

This is a splendid opening for a thriller, but *Dirty Pretty Things* is more than a genre picture. It uses the secret and malevolent activities at the hotel as the engine to drive a story about a London of immigrants, some illegal, who do the city's dirty work. Okwe (Chiwetel Ejiofor) was a doctor in Nigeria, is here as a political exile, has a past that haunts him. He rents couch space in the tiny flat of a chambermaid named Senay (Audrey Tautou, from *Amelie*), who is from Turkey and fled an arranged marriage. His best friend, Guo Yi (Benedict Wong), presides over poker games at the mortuary where he works. His circle also includes the doorman Ivan (Zlatko Buric) and the hooker Juliette (Sophie Okonedo). These characters and the vile night manager Sneaky are the major characters in the story, immigrants all, while white Londoners exist only as customers or immigration officials.

Okwe works hard at two jobs. He drives a minicab during the day, works all night at the hotel, buys illegal herbs at a local café to keep himself more or less awake. He is aware that Senay likes him and would not object if he moved from her couch to her bed, but he must be true to a wife in Nigeria; his faithfulness becomes more poignant the more we learn about the wife ("It is an African story," he says simply).

The heart of the movie, directed by Stephen Frears, is in the lives of these people. How they are always alert to make a little money on the side (as when Okwe and Ivan supply their own cash-only room-service sandwiches after the hotel kitchen closes). How they live in constant fear of immigration officials, who want to deport them even though a modern Western economy could not function without these shadow workers. How there is a network of contact and support in this hidden world, whose residents come from so many places and speak so many languages that they stop keeping score and simply accept each other as citizens of the land of exile.

We get to know these people and something of their lives, as Okwe stubbornly persists in trying to find out where that heart came from. He discovers that Sneaky is the key, and that the hotel is the center of a cruel enterprise that I will not reveal. The movie takes us into dark places in its closing scenes. But this is not a horror movie, not a shocker (although it is shocking). It is a story of desperation, of people who cannot live where they were born and cannot find a safe haven elsewhere.

This is familiar territory for Stephen Frears, an uncommonly intelligent director whose strength comes from his ability to empathize with his characters. They are not markers in a plot, but people he cares about. Two of his early films, *My Beautiful Launderette* (1985) and *Sammy and Rosie Get Laid* (1987), deal with the London of immigrants from India and Pakistan. He's fascinated by people who survive in cracks in the economy, as in two of his American films, *The Grifters* (1990) and *High Fidelity* (2000), one about con artists, the other set in a used-record store.

Crucial to the success of *Dirty Pretty Things* is the performance by Chiwetel Ejiofor—who, I learn, was born in England and copied his Nigerian accent from his parents. A natural actor with leading-man presence, he has the rare ability to seem good without seeming sappy, and his quiet intensity here is deepened by the sense that his character carries great sadness from his past. Audrey Tautou isn't the first actress you'd think of to play the Turkish girl, but her wide-eyed sincerity is right for the role, and Sergi López brings such crafty venality to his night manager that we suspect people must actually work in vile trades such as his.

The strength of the thriller genre is that it provides stories with built-in energy and structure. The weakness is that thrillers often seem to follow foreseeable formulas. Frears and his writer, Steve Knight, use the power of the thriller and avoid the weaknesses in giving us, really, two movies for the price of one.

A Dirty Shame ★
NC-17, 89 m., 2004

Tracey Ullman (Sylvia Stickles), Johnny Knoxville (Ray-Ray Perkins), Chris Isaak (Vaughn Stickles), Selma Blair (Caprice Stickles), Suzanne Shepherd (Big Ethel), Mink Stole (Marge the Neuter), Patricia Hearst (Paige). Directed by John Waters and produced by Ted Hope and Christine Vachon. Screenplay by Waters.

There is in showbiz something known as "a bad laugh." That's the laugh you don't want to get, because it indicates not amusement but incredulity, nervousness, or disapproval. John Waters's *A Dirty Shame* is the only comedy I can think of that gets more bad laughs than good ones.

Waters is the poet of bad taste, and labors mightily here to be in the worst taste he can manage. That's not the problem—no, not even when Tracey Ullman picks up a water bottle using a method usually employed only in Bangkok sex shows. We go to a Waters film expecting bad taste, but we also expect to laugh, and *A Dirty Shame* is monotonous, repetitive, and sometimes wildly wrong in what it hopes is funny.

The movie takes place in Baltimore, as most Waters films do. Stockholm got Bergman, Rome got Fellini, and Baltimore—well, it also has Barry Levinson. Ullman plays Sylvia Stickles, the owner of a 7-Eleven–type store. Chris Isaak plays Vaughn, her husband. Locked in an upstairs room is their daughter, Caprice (Selma Blair), who was a legend at the local go-go bar until her parents grounded and padlocked her. She worked under the name of Ursula Udders, a name inspired by breasts so large they are obviously produced by technology, not surgery.

Sylvia has no interest in sex until a strange thing happens. She suffers a concussion in a car crash, and it turns her into a sex maniac. Not only can't she get enough of it, she doesn't even pause to inquire what it is before she tries to get it. This attracts the attention of a local auto mechanic named Ray-Ray Perkins, played by Johnny Knoxville, who no longer has to consider *Jackass* his worst movie. Ray-Ray has a following of sex addicts who joyfully proclaim their special tastes and gourmet leanings.

A digression. In 1996, David Cronenberg made a movie named *Crash*, about a group of people who had a sexual fetish for car crashes, wounds, broken bones, crutches, and so on. It was a good movie, but as I wrote at the time, it's about "a sexual fetish that, in fact, no one has." I didn't get a lot of letters disagreeing with me.

John Waters also goes fetish-shopping in *A Dirty Shame,* treating us to such specialties as infantilism (a cop who likes to wear diapers), bear lovers (those who lust after fat, hairy men), and Mr. Pay Day, whose fetish does not involve the candy bar of the same name. We also learn about such curious pastimes as shelf-humping, mallet whacking, and tickling. As the movie introduced one sex addiction after another, I sensed a curious current running through the screening room. How can I describe it? Not disgust, not horror, not shock, but more of a sincere wish that Waters had found a way to make his movie without being quite so encyclopedic.

The plot, such as it is, centers on Sylvia and other characters zapping in and out of sex addiction every time they hit their heads, which they do with a frequency approaching the kill rate in *Crash*. This is not really very funny the first time, and grows steadily less funny until it becomes a form of monomania.

I think the problem is fundamental: Waters hopes to get laughs because of what the characters are, not because of what they do. He works at the level of preadolescent fart jokes, hoping, as the French say, to *"epater les bourgeois."* The problem may be that Waters has grown more bourgeois than his audience, which is so epatered that he actually thinks he is being shocking.

To truly deal with a strange sexual fetish can indeed be shocking, as *Kissed* (1996) demonstrated with its quiet, observant portrait of Molly Parker playing a necrophiliac. It can also be funny, as James Spader and Maggie Gyllenhaal demonstrated in *Secretary* (2002). Tracey Ullman is a great comic actress, but for her to make this movie funny would have required not just a performance but a rewrite and a miracle.

Fetishes are neither funny nor shocking simply because they exist. You have to do more with them than have characters gleefully celebrate them on the screen. Waters's weakness is to expect laughs because the *idea* of a moment is funny. But the idea of a moment exists only for the pitch; the movie has to develop it into a reality, a process, a payoff. An illustration of this is his persisting conviction that it is funny by definition to have Patty Hearst in his movies. It is only funny when he gives Ms. Hearst, who is a good sport, something amusing to do. She won't find it in this movie.

Distant ★ ★ ★

NO MPAA RATING, 110 m., 2004

Muzaffer Ozdemir (Mahmut), Mehmet Emin Toprak (Yusuf), Zuhal Gencer Erkaya (Nazan), Nazan Kirilmis (Lover), Feridun Koc (Janitor), Fatma Ceylan (Mother), Ebru Ceylan (Young Girl). Directed by Nuri Bilge Ceylan and produced by Ceylan. Screenplay by Ceylan.

How is it that the same movie can seem tedious on first viewing and absorbing on the second? Why doesn't it grow even more tedious? In the case of *Distant*, which I first saw at Cannes in 2003, perhaps it helped that I knew what the story offered and what it did not offer, and was able to see it again without expecting what would not come.

The film takes place in Turkey, but its dynamic could be transplanted anywhere—maybe to our own families. It is about a cousin from the country who comes to the big city searching for work, and asks to stay "for a few days" with his relative, who is a divorced photographer with walls filled with books and an apartment filled with sad memories.

Mahmut (Muzaffer Ozdemir) is the photographer, whose wife has divorced him and is marrying another man; the couple will move to Canada. What went wrong is not hard to guess: Mahmut is a man of habit, silent, introspective, exhausted by life. Yusuf (Mehmet Emin Toprak) comes from a small town where the factory has failed and there are no jobs; he foolishly thinks he can get hired on one of the ships in the port, but there are no jobs, and an old sailor informs him that the wages are so bad he'll never have anything left over to send home.

It is the dead of winter. Yusuf tramps through the snow with no gloves and inadequate shoes, and his job search starts unpromisingly when the first ship he finds is listing and sinking. He haunts the coffee bars of the sailors, who smoke and wait. Mahmut, meanwhile, says good-bye to his wife and then secretly and sadly watches her leaving from the airport. He has a shabby affair with a woman who lives nearby, and who will not make eye contact in a restaurant. He watches art videos (Tarkovsky, I think) to drive Yusuf from the room, and then switches to porno.

For both men, smoking is a consolation, and they spend a lot of time standing alone, doing nothing, maybe thinking nothing, smoking as if it is a task that provides them with purpose. Mahmut has rules (smoking only in the kitchen or on the balcony), but Yusuf sits in his favorite chair and smokes and drinks beer when Mahmut is away, and Mahmut grows gradually furious at the disorder that has come into his life. "Close the door," he says, as Yusuf goes to the guest bedroom, because he wants to shut him away from his privacy.

A photographic expedition to the countryside, with Yusuf hired as his assistant, turns out badly for Mahmut; sharing rented rooms, they invade each other's space. Finally Mahmut has had enough and asks Yusuf, "What are your plans?" But Yusuf has none. He does not even have an opening for plans. He is trapped in unemployment, has no money, no skills, no choices.

The film, directed by Nuri Bilge Ceylan, is shot with a frequently motionless camera that regards the men as they, frequently, regard nothing in particular. It permits silences to grow. Perhaps in the hurry of Cannes, with four or five films a day, I could not slow down to occupy those silences, but seeing the film a second time I understood they were crucial: There is little these men have to say to each other and—more to the point—no one else for them to talk with. Women are a problem for them both. Yusuf shadows attractive women, but is too shy to approach them before they inevitably meet a man and walk off arm-in-arm. A man without funds is in a double bind: He has no way to attract good women, or to hire bad ones. The one sex scene we witness with Mahmut, which is out of focus at the far end of a room, is so joyless that solitude seems preferable.

A movie like this touches everyday life in a way that we can recognize as if Turkey were Peoria. I can imagine a similar film being made in America, although Americans might talk more. What do you say to a relative who is out of work and seems unlikely to ever work again? He is family, and so there is a sense of responsibility embedded in childhood, but there are no jobs and he has no skills, and your own comfort, which seems enviable to him, is little consolation to you. To have joyless work means you have employment but not an occupation. At the end, one of the men is sitting on a bench on a gray, cold day, staring at nothing, and if we could see the other man we could probably see another bench. *Distant* is a good title for this movie.

Note: At Cannes, the movie won the Jury Grand Prize, and Muzaffer Ozdemir and Mehmet Emin Toprak shared the prize as best actors. The previous December, Toprak died in a traffic accident. He was twenty-eight.

Divine Intervention ★ ★ ★
NO MPAA RATING, 89 m., 2003

Elia Suleiman (E. S.), Manal Khader (The Woman), Nayef Fahoum Daher (The Father), Amer Daher (Auni), Jamel Daher (Jamel). Directed by Elia Suleiman and produced by Humbert Balsan. Screenplay by Suleiman.

Divine Intervention is a mordant and bleak comedy, almost without dialogue, about Palestinians under Israeli occupation. Its characters live their daily lives in ways that are fundamentally defined by the divisions between them, and the scene with the most tension simply involves two drivers, one Israeli, one Palestinian, who lock eyes at a traffic light. Neither will look away. In their paralysis, while the light turns green and motorists behind them start to honk, the film sums up the situation in a nutshell.

The movie stars Elia Suleiman, who also wrote and directed it, and who has probably included more political references than an outsider is likely to understand. Most of his ideas are conveyed in scenes that would be right at home in a silent comedy, and on the few occasions when the characters talk, they say nothing more than what could be handled in a title card.

One running gag, for example, involves a household that throws its daily bag of garbage into the neighbor's yard. When the neighbor one day angrily throws it back, the original litterer complains. The neighbor responds: "The garbage we threw in your yard is the same garbage you threw in our garden." Nevertheless, the offender says, it is bad manners to throw it back.

This is the sort of parable that can cut both ways, and I get the sense that, for Suleiman, it doesn't matter at this point which neighbor represents an Israeli and which a Palestinian. The same simmering hostility is reflected in other scenes, as in one where a man takes a sledgehammer to a driveway so that his neighbor's car will get stuck in a hole.

There is a romance in the movie, involving the Suleiman character and a woman played by Manal Khader. Because they live in different districts and cannot easily pass from one to another, they meet in the parking lot of a checkpoint and sit in his car, holding hands and staring with hostility at the Israeli guards. In one stunning shot, she boldly walks across the border and right past the guards, who level their rifles at her but are unwilling to act.

Later, marksmen do shoot at her, in a weird scene involving special effects. After taking target practice at cardboard dummies that resemble her, the riflemen are amazed to see the woman herself materialize before them. She whirls and levitates. They shoot at her, but the bullets pause in midair and form themselves in a crown around her head, an image not impossible to decipher.

The film has been compared to the comedies of Jacques Tati, in which everyday actions build up to an unexpected comic revelation. I was reminded also of the Swedish film *Songs from the Second Floor,* set in a city where all seems normal but the inhabitants are seized with a strange apocalyptic madness. Suleiman's argument seems to be that the situation between Palestinians and Israelis has settled into a hopeless stalemate, in which everyday life incorporates elements of paranoia, resentment, and craziness.

The film was so well received around the world that it seemed likely to get an Oscar nomination but was rejected by the Motion Picture Academy because entries must be nominated by their nation of origin, and Palestine is not a nation. That's the sort of catch-22 that Suleiman might appreciate.

Dodgeball:
A True Underdog Story ★ ★ ★
PG-13, 97 m., 2004

Vince Vaughn (Peter La Fleur), Ben Stiller (White Goodman), Christine Taylor (Kate Veatch), Rip Torn (Patches O'Houlihan), Justin Long (Justin), Stephen Root (Gordon), Joel Moore (Owen), Chris Williams (Dwight), Alan Tudyk (Steve the Pirate). Directed by Rawson Marshall Thurber and produced by Stuart Cornfeld and Ben Stiller. Screenplay by Thurber.

Dodgeball: A True Underdog Story is a title that rewards close study. It does not say it is a true story. It says it is about a true underdog. That is true. This is a movie about a spectacularly incompetent health club owner (Vince Vaughn) who tries to save his club from foreclosure by entering a team in the $50,000 world series of dodgeball in Las Vegas. Proof that the team is an underdog: One of the team members believes he is a pirate, and another team member hasn't noticed that.

Vaughn's club, Average Joe's Gym, is run-down and shabby, but has a loyal if nutty clientele. Across the street is a multimillion-dollar muscle emporium known as Globa Gym (there is no "l" in the title because it fell off). Globa is owned by Ben Stiller, overacting to the point of apoplexy as White Goodman; his manic performance is consistently funny, especially when he protects against Small Man Complex by surrounding himself with enormous bodybuilders and building an inflatable crotch into his training pants.

Vaughn, playing the absentminded Peter La Fleur, acts as a steadying influence; he plays it more or less straight, which is wise, since someone has to keep the plot on track. He's visited by the lithesome Kate Veatch (Christine Taylor), who works for the bank and explains that Average Joe's needs $50,000 in thirty days or the bank will foreclose. Standing by to turn Joe's into a parking lot: White Goodman. Among other questionable business practices, La Fleur has neglected to collect membership dues for several months.

Kate hates Globa's White Goodman, not least because at their last meeting he rudely drew attention to his extremely well-inflated crotch. One of the Average Joe staff members comes up with the idea of the dodgeball tournament, and for reasons unnecessary to explain, Kate becomes a member of the team, along with the pirate and four others.

None of them know anything about dodgeball. This may not be a handicap. My own experiences with dodgeball have led me to conclude that it is basically a game of luck; the only skill you need is to pick bigger kids for your side. But I learn that Extreme Dodgeball is actually a real sport, with its own cable TV show.

Dodgeball explains the sport by pausing for a grade-school educational documentary from 1938. It is a very short documentary, because all you need to know about the game are the Five Ds, of which both D No. 1 and D No. 5 are "Dodge!" The film is hosted by dodgeball legend Patches O'Houlihan, who must therefore be in his eighties when he appears at Average Joe's in his motorized wheelchair, and announces that he will coach them to victory. Patches is played by Rip Torn, whose training methods get enormous laughs.

The Las Vegas tournament itself follows the time-honored formulas of all sports movies, but is considerably enhanced by the weird teams in the finals. Weirdest is Globa Gym, captained by White Goodman and including four gigantic musclemen and a very hairy woman from an obscure former Soviet republic. The finals are telecast on ESPN8 ("If it's almost a sport, we have it here!").

I dare not say much more without giving away jokes; in a miraculous gift to the audience, 20th Century Fox does *not* reveal all of the best gags in its trailer. Therefore, let me just gently say that late in the movie a famous man approaches Peter La Fleur at the airport and gets laughs almost as big as the Patches O'Houlihan training technique.

Dog Days ★ ★
NO MPAA RATING, 120 m., 2003

Maria Hofstatter (Hitchhiker), Christine Jirku (Teacher), Victor Hennemann (Teacher's Lover), Georg Friedrich (Lucky), Alfred Mrva (Alarm Salesman), Erich Finsches (Old Man), Gerti Lehner (Housekeeper), Franziska Weiss (Klaudia). Directed by Ulrich Seidl and produced by Helmut Grasser and Philippe Bober. Screenplay by Seidl and Veronika Franz.

In a suburb of Vienna, during the hottest days of the summer, in a row of cookie-cutter houses facing a river, unhappy people make themselves still more miserable as they indulge in lust, avarice, jealousy, gluttony, anger, and sloth. Pride is not much of a problem with them. *Dog Days* is an unblinking look at what passes in some minds as everyday life and in others as human misery.

The movie has been made by Ulrich Seidl, known for his documentaries, who shot it over a period of three years in order to be able to work only on the very hottest days. He was able to get his actors to cooperate because most of them were amateurs. Considering that many of them are seen nude and some engage in degrading sexual behavior, it might seem strange that he was able to persuade nonprofessionals to take these roles, but reality television has shown that there are people willing to do almost anything if a camera is recording it. Odd, isn't it? Not too long ago people would do these things only if nobody was watching.

There are nine or ten characters, including a stripper whose boyfriend hangs around the clubs where she performs, beating up anybody who looks at her; a divorced couple who still share the same house and devote themselves to making each other miserable; a fat man who wants his middle-aged housekeeper to do a harem dance in honor of the fiftieth anniversary of his marriage to his long-dead wife; a teacher so desperate for dates that she'll maybe even sleep with the sadistic friend of her latest boyfriend; and so on. Oh, and there's a mentally retarded woman who hitches rides and sits in the backseat asking annoying questions.

The physical action in the movie has been constructed with meticulous care and timing. Sometimes (not often) we almost feel as if we're involved in a sight gag from a Jacques Tati movie—as, for example, when the couple next door won't stop their loud quarrel, and so the fat man simply starts up his power mower and lets it run next to their fence. More often we simply watch sad people degrade each other, as when a man is forced to apologize at gunpoint for his behavior to a woman who is no happier because she is forced to make him do so.

The movie won the Grand Jury Prize at Venice 2001 and arrives festooned with other awards. It is admirable and well made, but unutterably depressing and unredeemed by any glimmer of hope. In that it reminded me a little of the wonderful Swedish film *Songs from* the *Second Floor,* but that one used style and mordant humor to elevate itself into a kind of joyous dirge. *Dog Days* is a long slog through the slough of despond.

Dogville ★ ★
R, 177 m., 2004

Nicole Kidman (Grace), Paul Bettany (Tom Edison), James Caan (The Big Man), Patricia Clarkson (Vera), Jeremy Davies (Bill Henson), Ben Gazzara (Jack McKay), Philip Baker Hall (Tom Edison Sr.), John Hurt (Narrator), Chloe Sevigny (Liz Henson), Stellan Skarsgård (Chuck), Lauren Bacall (Ma Ginger), Blair Brown (Mrs. Henson), Bill Raymond (Mr. Henson). Directed by Lars von Trier and produced by Vibeke Windelov. Screenplay by von Trier.

Lars von Trier exhibits the imagination of an artist and the pedantry of a crank in *Dogville,* a film that works as a demonstration of how a good idea can go wrong. There is potential in the concept of the film, but the execution had me tapping my wristwatch to see if it had stopped. Few people will enjoy seeing it once and, take it from one who knows, even fewer will want to see it a second time.

The underlying vision of the production has the audacity we expect from von Trier, a daring and inventive filmmaker. He sets his story in a small Rocky Mountain town during the Great Depression, but doesn't provide a real town (or a real mountain). The first shot looks straight down on the floor of a large sound stage, where the houses of the residents are marked out with chalk outlines, and there are only a few props—some doors, desks, chairs, beds. We will never leave this set and never see beyond it; on all sides in the background there is only blankness.

The idea reminds us of *Our Town,* but von Trier's version could be titled *Our Hell.* In his town, which I fear works as a parable of America, the citizens are xenophobic, vindictive, jealous, suspicious, and capable of rape and murder. His dislike of the United States (which he has never visited, since he is afraid of airplanes) is so palpable that it flies beyond criticism into the realm of derangement. When the film premiered at Cannes 2003, he was accused of not portraying America accurately, but how many movies do? Anything by David Spade come to mind? Von Trier could justifiably make a fantasy about America, even an anti-American fantasy, and produce a good film, but here he approaches the ideological subtlety of a raving prophet on a street corner.

The movie stars Nicole Kidman in a rather brave performance: Like all the actors, she has to act within a narrow range of tone, in an allegory that has no reference to realism. She plays a young woman named Grace who arrives in Dogville being pursued by gangsters (who here, as in Brecht, I fear, represent native American fascism). She is greeted by Tom Edison (Paul Bettany), an earnest young man, who persuades his neighbors to give her a two-week trial run before deciding whether to allow her to stay in town.

Grace meets the townspeople, played by such a large cast of stars that we suspect the original running time must have been even longer than 177 minutes. Tom's dad is the town doctor (Philip Baker Hall); Stellan Skarsgård grows apples and, crucially, owns a truck; Patricia Clarkson is his wife; Ben Gazzara is the all-seeing blind man; Lauren Bacall runs the general store; Bill Raymond and Blair Brown are the parents of Jeremy Davies and Chloe Sevigny. There are assorted other citizens and various children, and James Caan turns up at the end in a long black limousine. He's the gangster.

What von Trier is determined to show is that Americans are not friendly, we are suspicious of outsiders, we cave in to authority, we are inherently violent, etc. All of these things are true, and all of these things are untrue. It's a big country, and it has a lot of different kinds of people. Without stepping too far out on a limb, however, I doubt that we have any villages where the helpless visitor would eventually be chained to a bed and raped by every man in town.

The actors (or maybe it's the characters) seem to be in a kind of trance much of the time. They talk in monotones, they seem to be reciting truisms rather than speaking spontaneously, they seem to sense the film's inevitable end. To say that the film ends in violence is not to give away the ending so much as to wonder how else it could have ended. In the apocalyptic mind-set of von Trier, no less than general destruction could conclude his fable; life in Dogville clearly cannot continue for a number of reasons, one of them perhaps that the Dogvillians would go mad.

Lars von Trier has made some of the best films of recent years *(Europa, Breaking the Waves, Dancer in the Dark)*. He was a guiding force behind the Dogma movement, which has generated much heat and some light. He takes chances, and that's rare in a world where most films seem to have been banged together out of other films. But at some point his fierce determination has to confront the reality that a film does not exist without an audience. *Dogville* can be defended and even praised on pure ideological grounds, but most moviegoers, even those who are sophisticated and have open minds, are going to find it a very dry and unsatisfactory slog through conceits masquerading as ideas.

Note No. 1: Although Lars von Trier has never been to the United States, he does have one thing right: In a small town, the smashing of a collection of Hummel figurines would count as an atrocity.

Note No. 2: I learn from Variety *that Dogville* Confessions, *a making-of documentary, was filmed using a soundproof "confession box" near the soundstage where actors could unburden themselves. In it, Stellan Skarsgård describes von Trier, whom he has worked with many times, as "a hyperintelligent child who is slightly disturbed, playing with dolls in a dollhouse, cutting their heads off with nail clippers." Von Trier himself testifies that the cast is conspiring against him.* Variety *thinks this doc would make a great bell and/or whistle on the eventual DVD.*

Note No. 3: We should not be too quick to condemn von Trier, a Dane, for not filming in the United States when The Prince and Me, *a new Hollywood film about a Wisconsin farm girl who falls in love with the prince of Denmark, was filmed in Toronto and Prague.*

Dolls ★ ★ ★
NO MPAA RATING, 113 m., 2005

Miho Kanno (Sawako), Hidetoshi Nishijima (Matsumoto), Tatsuya Mihashi (Hiro, the Boss), Chieko Matsubara (Woman in the Park), Kyoko Fukada (Haruna, the Pop Star), Tsutomu Takeshige (Nukui, the Fan). Directed by Takeshi Kitano and produced by Masayuki Mori and Takio Yoshida. Screenplay by Kitano.

Takeshi Kitano is known for directing pictures in which flashes of violence are punctuated by periods of waiting, reflection, and loneliness. Using the name of Beat Takeshi, he stars in them. He is a distinctive, original director; his *The Blind Swordsman: Zatoichi* (2004) took a durable Japanese series character and transformed him into a philosophical wanderer. In his film, *Dolls,* he makes his longest journey from his action-film roots, into a land of three tragic relationships.

The title is taken from the Japanese tradition of Bunraku, or puppet plays. Elaborate dolls are moved about the stage, each one with two or three artists to manipulate their eyes, heads, arms. One artist is visible, the others hooded in black. A reader recites all of the dialogue, and there is music.

Kitano's film opens with a Bunraku performance, and then segues into the first of three live-action stories in which the characters seem moved about the stages of their own lives without wills of their own. We are reminded of Gloucester's line in *King Lear:* "As flies to wanton boys, are we to the gods; they kill us for their sport."

The first story involves Matsumoto (Hidetoshi Nishijima), who is engaged to Sawako (Miho Kanno). His parents insist he break off the engagement and marry his boss's daughter. Sawako attempts suicide, is brain-damaged, and is spirited out of a nursing home by Matsumoto, who devotes his life to being with her. They live in a hotel room, in a car, and finally in the wild; because she wanders away, he joins them with a length of rope, and as they walk through the countryside they become known as the Bound Beggars.

The second story involves a gangster boss named Hiro (Tatsuya Mihashi). As a young man he is in love with a woman (Chieko Matsubara), who meets him on a park bench every Saturday with two box lunches. One Saturday he breaks up with her; a woman would be a complication now that he has decided to become a yakuza. She says she will come every Saturday no matter what. Years later, old and disillusioned, he returns to the park to look for her.

The third story is about a pop idol named

Haruna (Kyoko Fukada). A fan named Nukui (Tsutomu Takeshige) is obsessed with her. His job is to wave a warning light at a highway construction zone; Haruna is disfigured in a traffic accident that may have been caused (the movie is a little vague) by Nukui being distracted from his job by thoughts of her. After her injury she refuses to be seen by any of her fans; Nukui's determination to meet her leads to a gruesome decision.

Dolls moves with a deliberate pace. I have seen Bunraku performances in Japan, and found them long, slow, and stylized; the same can be said of the film. Kitano is not content to simply tell his stories, but wants to leave us time to contemplate them, to experience the passage of time for these characters and the way their choices will define them for the rest of their lives. The three active lovers in the film—Matsumoto, the woman, and the fan—willingly sacrifice their freedom and happiness in acts of romantic abnegation. Such gestures seem odd in the modern world, but not in classical tragedy, not in Bunraku, and not in the Japanese tradition of dramatic personal gestures.

The film has moments of great loveliness. Some of the landscapes, filled with autumn leaves of astonishing shades of red, are beautiful and lonely. The film is about three people who have unhappiness forced upon them, and three others who choose it. *Dolls* isn't a film for everybody, especially the impatient, but Kitano does succeed, I think, in drawing us into his tempo and his world, and slowing us down into the sadness of his characters.

Dominion: Prequel to the Exorcist ★ ★ ★

R, 111 m., 2005

Stellan Skarsgard (Father Merrin), Gabriel Mann (Father Francis), Clara Bellar (Rachel), Billy Crawford (Cheche), Antonie Kamerling (Lieutenant Kessel), Ralph Brown (Sergeant-Major), Julian Wadham (Major Granville), Eddie Osei (Emekwi). Directed by Paul Schrader and produced by James G. Robinson. Screenplay by Caleb Carr and William Wisher Jr.

Paul Schrader's *Dominion: Prequel to the Exorcist* does something risky and daring in this time of jaded horror movies: It takes evil seriously. There really are dark Satanic forces in the Schrader version, which takes a priest forever scarred by the Holocaust and asks if he can ever again believe in the grace of God. The movie is drenched in atmosphere and dread, as we'd expect from Schrader, but it also has spiritual weight and texture, boldly confronting the possibility that Satan may be active in the world. Instead of cheap thrills, Schrader gives us a frightening vision of a good priest who fears goodness may not be enough.

The film's hero, Merrin (Stellan Skarsgard), considers himself an ex-priest; during World War II he was forced by Nazis to choose some villagers for death in order that a whole village not be killed. This is seen by a Nazi officer as an efficient way to undermine Merrin's belief in his own goodness, and indeed forces the priest to commit evil to avoid greater evil. This is not theologically sound; the idea is to do no evil and leave it to God to sort out the consequences.

His trauma from this experience hurls Merrin out of the priesthood and into an archeological dig in Africa, where he is helping to excavate a remarkably well-preserved church buried in the sand. Why this church, in this place? It doesn't fit in architectural, historical, or religious terms, and seems intended not so much to celebrate God as to trap something unspeakably evil that lies beneath it.

Schrader is famously a director of moral values crossed with dangerous choices; his own movies *(Hardcore, Light Sleeper, The Comfort of Strangers)* and those he has written for Martin Scorsese *(Taxi Driver, Raging Bull)* deal with men obsessed with guilt and sin. His *Dominion* is not content to simply raise the curtain on William Friedkin's classic *The Exorcist* (1974), but is more ambitious: It wants to observe the ways Satan seduces man.

The film's battle between good and evil involves everyone on the dig, notably the young priest Father Francis (Gabriel Mann), who has been assigned by Rome to keep an eye on Merrin. Then there is the doctor Rachel (Clara Bellar), whose special concern is a deformed young man named Cheche (Billy Crawford). Curiously, Cheche seems to improve beyond all expectations of medicine, as if something supernatural were going on. Also on the site, in "British East Africa," is the Sergeant-Major (Ralph Brown), a racist who assigns the devil's doings to the local Africans.

In a lesser movie, there would be humid goings-on at the camp, and a spectacular showdown between the humans and special effects. Not in the Schrader version, which trusts evil to be intrinsically fascinating and not in need of f/x enhancement. His vision, however, was not the one the powers at Morgan Creek were looking for (although Schrader was filming a script by Caleb Carr and William Wisher Jr. that the producers presumably approved). After Schrader delivered his version, a scenario developed that is, I think, unprecedented in modern movie history. The studio, having spent millions on the Schrader version, hired the director Renny Harlin to spend more millions remaking it in a presumably more commercial fashion.

Harlin kept some of the actors, including Skarsgard, and substituted others (Gabriel Mann was replaced by James D'Arcy, Clara Bellar by Izabella Scorupco). The same cinematographer, the great Vittorio Storaro, filmed for both directors. After Harlin's version, *Exorcist: The Beginning*, did a break-even $82 million at the box office but drew negative reviews, Schrader succeeded in getting his version screened at a film festival in Brussels, where the positive reception inspired this theatrical release, a resurrection fully in keeping with the film's theme.

I've seen both versions and much prefer Schrader's, and yet it must be said that Harlin did not prostitute himself in his version. Indeed, oddly, it opens with more talk and less excitement than the Schrader version (Harlin dissipates the power of the Nazi sequence by fragmenting it into flashbacks).

What is fascinating from a movie buff's point of view is that the movie has been filmed twice in different ways by different directors. Maybe this is what Gus Van Sant was getting at when he inexplicably did his (almost) shot-by-shot remake of Hitchcock's *Psycho*. Film students are often given a series of shots and assigned to edit them to tell a story. They can fit together in countless ways, to greater or less effect. Here we have the experiment conducted with $80 million.

It's eerie, to see the same locations occupied by different actors speaking similar dialogue. Odd to see the young priest and the doctor occupying the same rooms but played by different people. Strange to see Skarsgard in both versions, some shots and dialogue exactly the same, others not. Curious how the subplot about the British shrinks in the Harlin version, while the horror is ramped up. I prefer the Schrader version, certainly, but you know what? Now that two versions exist and are available, each one makes the other more interesting. ☞

Donnie Darko: The Director's Cut ★ ★ ★
R, 142 m., 2004

Jake Gyllenhaal (Donnie Darko), Mary McDonnell (Rose Darko), Holmes Osborne (Eddie Darko), Jena Malone (Gretchen Ross), Drew Barrymore (Ms. Pomeroy), Daveigh Chase (Samantha Darko), Patrick Swayze (Jim Cunningham), Katharine Ross (Dr. Thurman), Noah Wyle (Dr. Monnitoff). Directed by Richard Kelly and produced by Adam Fields and Sean McKittrick. Screenplay by Kelly.

"Pay close attention," warns the Web site for *Donnie Darko: The Director's Cut*, because "you could miss something." Damn, I missed it. I'm no closer to being able to explain the film's events than I was after seeing the 2001 version, which was about twenty minutes shorter. The difference is, that doesn't bother me so much. The movie remains impenetrable to logical analysis, but now I ask myself: What logical analysis would explain the presence of a six-foot-tall rabbit with what looks like the head of a science-fiction insect?

The director's cut adds footage that enriches and extends the material, but doesn't alter its tone. It adds footnotes that count down to a deadline, but without explaining the nature of the deadline or the usefulness of the countdown (I think it comes from an omniscient narrator who, despite his omniscience, sure does keep a lot to himself). What we have, in both versions, is a film of paradox that seems to involve either time travel or parallel universes. Having seen in *The Butterfly Effect* (2004) how a film might try to explain literally the effects of temporal travel, I am more content to accept this version of the Darko backward and abysm of time.

Let it be said that writer-director Richard Kelly's first film engages us so intriguingly that we *desire* an explanation. It opens with Donnie Darko (Jake Gyllenhaal) sprawled at dawn in the middle of a remote road next to his bicycle. Just sleeping, he explains. He's out of his house a lot at night, apparently on the advice of the rabbit, which is named Frank. It's good advice, since Donnie returns home to find that the engine of a jet airliner has fallen from the skies into his bedroom. The strange thing is, the government has no record of a plane losing its engine.

Given the eerie national mood after 9/11, this detail did not much recommend the film to audiences when it opened on October 26, 2001. The film, a success at Sundance 2001, opened and closed in a wink, grossing only about $500,000 and inspiring some negative reviews ("Insufferable, lumpy and dolorous . . . infatuated with an aura of hand-me-down gloom."—Elvis Mitchell, *New York Times*). But it gathered a band of admirers, became a hit on DVD and at midnight shows, and is returning to theaters.

More than one critic said the movie was set in "John Hughes country," that 1980s suburban land of teenage angst and awkward love. Certainly, Jake Gyllenhaal is convincing in his convoluted relationship with Gretchen (Jena Malone), the new girl in town—who walks into the English class of Ms. Pomeroy (Drew Barrymore), asks where she should sit, and is told as only Drew Barrymore could tell her, "Sit next to the boy you think is the cutest." When she chooses Donnie, we can see why Gyllenhaal was once considered to play Spider-Man; he's got the look of a guy whose inner demons wall him off from girlfriends.

Donnie's suburb is green and leafy, and his home life happy. His mother (Mary McDonnell) is filled with warmth and love, and his father (Holmes Osborne) is not the standard monster of dad-hating Hollywood formulas. At school, Ms. Pomeroy is a good enough teacher to get herself fired. And the parent-teacher conference involving Donnie's run-in with the gym teacher is one of those scenes where parents try to look properly appalled at

their son's behavior while it's all they can do to keep from laughing.

Then there's Frank, who is definitely not from Hughesland. He shows Donnie how to look into the future, and even gives him the power to visualize other people as they follow their time lines (a time line resembles a rope of coiling water, like the effect in *The Abyss*). And there is the case of the wizened old lady known as Grandma Death, who lives down the street and once wrote a book titled *The Philosophy of Time Travel*, which hinted or warned or predicted or intuited something ominous, I think, although I have no idea what it might have been.

The details of daily life are exactly right. We believe Donnie as a teenager who did not ask to be haunted by doubts and demons and is bearing up as best he can. He lives in a real world; apart, to be sure, from the rabbit and the time lines. Richard Kelly shows that he could make a straightforward movie about these characters, but *Donnie Darko* has no desire to be straightforward. I wrote in my original review: "The movie builds twists on top of turns until the plot wheel revolves one time too many and we're left scratching our heads. We don't demand answers at the end, but we want some kind of closure; Keyser Soze may not explain everything in *The Usual Suspects*, but it *feels* like he does."

In that 2001 review, I found a lot to admire and enjoy in *Donnie Darko*, including the director's control of tone and the freshness of the characters. My objection was that you couldn't understand the movie, which seemed to have parts on order. With the director's cut, I knew going in that I wouldn't understand it, so perhaps I was able to accept it in a different way. I ignored logic and responded to tone, and liked it more. There may have been another factor at work: As I grow weary of films like *The Princess Diaries II*, which follow their formulas with relentless fidelity to cliché and stereotype, I feel gratitude to directors who make something new.

Donnie Darko: The Director's Cut is alive, original, and intriguing. It's about a character who has no explanation for what is happening in his life, and is set in a world that cannot account for prescient rabbits named Frank. I think, after all, I am happier that the movie *doesn't* have closure. What kind of closure could there be? Frank takes off the insect head and reveals Drew Barrymore, who in a classroom flashback explains the plot and brings in Grandma Death as a resource person?

The Door in the Floor ★ ★ ★
R, 111 m., 2004

Jeff Bridges (Ted Cole), Kim Basinger (Marion Cole), Jon Foster (Eddie O'Hare), Mimi Rogers (Eleanor Vaughn), Bijou Phillips (Alice), Elle Fanning (Ruth). Directed by Tod Williams and produced by Anne Carey, Michael Corrente, and Ted Hope. Screenplay by Williams, and based on the novel *A Widow for One Year* by John Irving.

What is it about Jeff Bridges, the way he can say something nice in a way that doesn't sound so nice? How does he find that balance between the sunny optimism and the buried agenda? Early in *The Door in the Floor,* playing an author named Ted Cole, he suggests to his wife, Marion (Kim Basinger), that they add a swimming pool to the lawn of their home in the East Hamptons. How do we know his proposal is like turning a knife in his wife's ribs?

I saw the movie after rewatching Bridges' first performance, in *The Last Picture Show* (1971). More than thirty years later, he still has the same open face, the same placid smile, the same level voice that never seems to try very hard for emotion, and the same ability to suggest the depths and secrets of his character. In this story of a wounded marriage, Kim Basinger is well chosen as his target in an emotional duel. There can be something hurt and vulnerable about her, a fear around the eyes, a hopeful sweetness that doesn't seem to expect much. Here she transgresses moral boundaries by deliberately seducing a sixteen-year-old boy, and yet still seems to be the victim.

The movie is about a marriage between two smart people who are too afraid, or perhaps too cruel, to fight out in the open. They play a deep game of psychological chicken, all the more hurtful because they know so well what buttons to push. We learn eventually that their two sons were killed in a car crash, that Marion in some ways blames Cole, that in middle life they've had a daughter, Ruth (Elle Fan-

ning), to try to heal the loss, and that the loss was not healed. Now Cole proposes to hire a young student as their assistant for the summer. This is Eddie (Jon Foster). Because we have already visited the upstairs corridor lined with photographs of their two dead boys, we notice immediately that Eddie looks a lot like the older boy. Marion notices too, as she is intended to.

The movie is based on an early section of John Irving's 1998 novel *A Widow for One Year,* which is mostly about Ruth growing up and developing problems of her own. This story focuses on the relationship of her parents. Ted Cole is a womanizer, a failed serious novelist who has found success with children's books that he illustrates himself; his illustrations require female models, whom he recruits from the neighborhood, and who only gradually discover that they are to be nude and to have sex with Cole. Marion, meanwhile, is stuck in a sad blankness, unable to stir herself back into life.

The boy Eddie is smart, serious, ambitious, headed for a good school, and very impressed to be working for a famous writer. Cole has little for him to do, except to drive him to and from liaisons with Mrs. Vaughn (Mimi Rogers), one of his current mistresses. Cole can't drive himself because his license is suspended.

During the course of the summer Cole says he has been "thinking," which in a marriage usually means trouble, and he suggests a "trial separation," which usually means the trial will be successful. He times this suggestion for soon after Eddie comes to work for them, and Eddie finds himself dividing his time between the beach house and the house in town. That this is part of Cole's plan to passively urge his wife into adultery is obvious to Marion if not to Eddie, who becomes sexually obsessed with the older woman. She catches him one day masturbating with the inspiration of her bra and panties.

I don't know what I think—or what I'm supposed to think—about the sex they eventually have. Certainly Basinger is perfectly modulated in the way she talks with Eddie, soothes his guilt over the masturbation scene, asks him to dinner and eventually to bed. Young men have daydreams about older women like this, just as older women have nightmares about the young men. But the director, Tod Williams, pays unseemly attention to their sex itself. The film should be about their transgression, not their technique. The relationship between Marion and Eddie is the least satisfactory in the movie, because the movie isn't really about it—it's about how Cole and Marion use it.

Cole is a thoroughgoing SOB. Marion may be evil too, but she's nicer about it. The way Cole treats the Mimi Rogers character ventures beyond cruelty into sadism, and Williams makes a mistake by allowing its tension to be released in a quasi-slapstick scene where she tries to run him over in her SUV. That's letting him off too easy. But Williams handles the main line of the story, the war between Cole and Marion, clearly and strongly; you may not always hurt the one you love, but you certainly know how to.

Bridges plays his role with an untidy beard, wild hair, and a wardrobe that ranges from ratty bathrobes to casual nudity in front of strangers. He's doing something with his lower jaw, as if he's talking with a mouthful of water, and it makes him seem more like a predator. Basinger has to internalize more. Jon Foster, the young actor, is given a good character but the screenplay denies him either an objective or a release; all he can do is escape. Ruth, the little girl, meanwhile, watches disturbing sights with big eyes, screams at the top of her lungs, and will grow up to be the heroine of a John Irving novel, not something you would wish lightly upon a child.

Dopamine ★ ★ ★ ½
R, 79 m., 2003

John Livingston (Rand), Sabrina Lloyd (Sarah), William Windom (Rand's Father), Bruno Campos (Winston), Reuben Grundy (Johnson), Kathleen Antonia (Tammy), Nicole Wilder (Machiko). Directed by Mark Decena and produced by Debbie Brubaker and Ted Fettig. Screenplay by Decena and Timothy Breitbach.

People really do have jobs and they work all day at them and sometimes all night, and have to work so hard at them that their romantic life suffers. Those would be real people. People in

the movies have so much free time that their lives are available for the requirements of movie formulas. They get crazy in love. Real people, on the other hand, look at a potential lover and decide they'd have to be crazy to take a chance on someone like that. Start with two people who think that way and you're describing most of the relationships we really do have. In one way or another, *Dopamine* is about us.

You may not be Rand, trapped in a room with two other guys twenty hours a day, living on coffee and creating a digital pet named Koy Koy. You may not be Sarah, a preschool teacher who sometimes goes to a bar simply because she wants to get laid, and the next morning, when she looks at her prize, she just wants to get out of there and go home. But such details will seem more realistic to you than the romantic comedies of Meg Ryan, which is why Meg Ryan's adventures are so popular: They're about what you're looking for the night before, not what you end up with the morning after.

Dopamine, written and directed by Mark Decena, is about imperfect people who talk a lot, are smart, have big defenses, and have been burned more than once by love. Since Sarah sleeps with a guy on the first date, it may not seem like she has such big defenses, but she does; her defenses are against having the second date. And Rand is so wounded he invests his own emotions in a pathetic little animated bird who is programmed to get to know him. It's all right to be pleased that the bird recognizes you, but sad to feel good because the bird likes you. The bird doesn't really like you. The bird is just some code.

Rand is renting his life to people who want to buy a corrupt version of what he loves to do. He loves artificial intelligence. They want Koy Koy, which they can sell to the children of the world, robbing them of trees and dogs. Rand hates the people but loves the work. The people want to test-market his program in a preschool. What's this? He's spent three years in a room writing this code, and now five-year-olds are going to *criticize* it?

Rand (John Livingston) goes to the classroom and meets the teacher, Sarah (Sabrina Lloyd). Oh, there's no doubt they're meant for each other. They look at each other and each person's empty spaces are the same size as the other person's full spaces. But Rand has issues with women. That's why he's so hung up on programming a girlfriend for Koy Koy: safer to fix up Koy Koy than get fixed up himself. Loneliness is so much less troublesome than this emotional minefield.

Complicating the process is Rand's father (William Windon), who was in perfect love with his wife for fifty years before Alzheimer's replaced her with a space holder. If even a perfect love like his dad's betrays you in the end, what's the sense in beginning? Rand's father is a scientist, and believes love is basically chemical. Endorphins explain it. His father lectures on the scent code, we see visuals of molecules at work, and then there is the most extraordinary shot of Sarah walking near to Rand while he smells her hair.

What's alluring is the way the characters played by John Livingston and Sabrina Lloyd savor each other in between their troubles. Movies are too quick to interrupt romance with sex. Sarah and Rand fascinate us with their dance of dread and desire because they try to discuss their situation in abstractions, and they should let their fingers do the talking.

The movie is one of the Sundance Film Series, movies that were successful at Sundance and are being opened around the country as a package. Perhaps it didn't get picked up for solo distribution because it was too intellectual and talky. You use a word like *endorphin* and you're in trouble in some theaters. *Intolerable Cruelty* is also about two people who are meant to be in love and keep talking themselves out of it. It has big stars and a big budget and it's smart, too, but it lacks the one thing *Dopamine* guards as its treasure: a belief in the possibility of love.

Dot the I ★ ★ ★
R, 92 m., 2005

Gael Garcia Bernal (Kit), Natalia Verbeke (Carmen), James D'Arcy (Barnaby), Tom Hardy (Tom), Charlie Cox (Theo). Directed by Matthew Parkhill and produced by George Duffield and Meg Thomson. Screenplay by Parkhill.

There is an ancient French tradition that on the night before her marriage, the bride-to-be can choose a handsome stranger and share

with him one last kiss. If you have never heard of this tradition, neither have I, because it, along with a great deal else, was invented for this movie. *Dot the I* is like one of those nests of Chinese boxes within boxes. The outer box is a love story. There are times when we despair of ever reaching the innermost box.

An opening scene is set in a French restaurant in London, where Carmen (Natalia Verbeke), a Spanish dancer, is having a dinner with her girlfriends on the eve of her wedding. The maitre d' explains the ancient tradition, Carmen believes him, looks around the restaurant, and her eyes settle on Kit (Gael Garcia Bernal). She kisses him. This is interesting: The kiss continues longer than we would expect. They seem to want it to go on forever. They have so much chemistry it threatens to trespass upon biology.

Kit is from Brazil, an out-of-work actor. Since Bernal is in fact from Mexico, he could perfectly well speak Spanish, which is why he is made Brazilian and would speak Portuguese, so that he and his Spanish friend will have to talk for our convenience in English. Sometimes it is jolly, this neocolonialism. As for the title, we are told that "a kiss dots the 'I' on the word 'love,'" but not in English, obviously, or Spanish or Portuguese, either (they both use "amor"). Maybe in German ("liebe"). Or maybe, we eventually realize, not in this movie.

Although Carmen and Kit are obviously made for each other, Carmen persists in her plan to marry the rich but odious Barnaby (James D'Arcy). As *Dot the I* moves along, it becomes clear that there is very little, however, that this Barnaby would not do.

The opening hour of the movie is a wonderfully complicated love story, during which Carmen goes ahead with her plans to marry Barnaby, and Kit fails in his attempt to emulate Benjamin in *The Graduate* and interrupt the ceremony with a wild goat cry of love. But Kit is not easily discouraged. He finds out Carmen's name from her friends in the restaurant, and contacts her to ask if they can meet: "Just once! Just one glass of water! In a brightly lit public place! We don't even have to speak!" She has mercy on him.

What happens next it would be unfair to reveal, and perhaps impossible. The movie not only scatters undotted I's and uncrossed T's in its wake, but unsquared circles, unfactored primes, unrisen soufflés, and unconsummated consummations. Matthew Parkhill, who wrote and directed it, is not a man to deny us the fruits of his boundless, some would say excessive, invention.

Watching the movie, I went through several stages. I liked the first half perfectly well as a love story involving sympathetic people. I hoped they would find happiness out from under the cloud of the snarfy Barnaby. Then—well, there was a surprise, and I rather liked the surprise, too, because it put things in a new light and made everyone just that much more interesting. And then another surprise, and another, until . . .

The last ten or fifteen minutes are going to require a great deal of patience with the filmmakers, as they riffle through the plot like a riverboat gambler with aces up his wazoo. I suppose that in a logical way it all makes sense—except that there is no logical way that it would happen in the first place. Having been tricked into accepting the characters as people we can trust in and care for, we now discover their world is but a stage, and they but players on it. Psychological realism and emotional continuity be damned!

Am I unhappy because the concluding scenes in the movie rob me of my feelings about the characters, or because the earlier scenes created those feelings? Certainly the film would not be better if the first hour had been given over to game-playing. The ingenuity of the film is admirable, I suppose, although we walk out of the theater with perplexing questions about motives, means, access, and techniques.

So let us observe that good work is performed here by all three of the leading actors—Bernal, who is so likable he had better play a villain soon just to add some Tabasco; Verbeke, who is so touchingly torn between love and loyalty, and then between loyalty and love; and D'Arcy, who creates a truly scary two-faced personality. To keep their emotional bearings in this plot is no small achievement. And let us concede that Matthew Parkhill has at least not taken the easy way out. Yes, we'd prefer a straightforward love triangle without the bells and whistles, but that might turn out boring, while *Dot the I* keeps our attention even while stomping on it.

Downfall ★ ★ ★ ★
R, 155 m., 2005

Bruno Ganz (Adolf Hitler), Alexandra Maria Lara (Traudl Junge), Juliane Kohler (Eva Braun), Corinna Harfouch (Magda Goebbels), Thomas Kretschmann (Hermann Fegelein), Ulrich Matthes (Joseph Goebbels), Heino Ferch (Albert Speer), Christian Berkel (Dr. Schenck), Ulrich Noethen (Heinrich Himmler). Directed by Oliver Hirschbiegel and produced by Bernd Eichinger. Screenplay by Eichinger, based on the book *Inside Hitler's Bunker* by Joachim Fest and the book *Bis zur letzten Stunde* by Traudl Junge and Melissa Muller.

Downfall takes place almost entirely inside the bunker beneath Berlin where Adolf Hitler and his inner circle spent their final days, and died. It ventures outside only to show the collapse of the Nazi defense of Berlin, the misery of the civilian population, and the burning of the bodies of Hitler, Eva Braun, and Joseph and Magda Goebbels. For the rest, it occupies a labyrinth of concrete corridors, harshly lighted, with a constant passage back and forth of aides, servants, guards, family members, and Hitler's dog, Blondi. I was reminded, oddly, of the claustrophobic sets built for *Das Boot*, which took place mostly inside a Nazi submarine.

Our entry to this sealed world is Traudl Junge (Alexandra Maria Lara), hired by Hitler as a secretary in 1942 and eyewitness to Hitler's decay in body and mind. She wrote a memoir about her experiences, which is one of the sources of this film, and *Blind Spot* (2002) was a documentary about her memories. In a clip at the end of *Downfall*, filmed shortly before her death, she says she now feels she should have known more than she did about the crimes of the Nazis. But like many secretaries the world over, she was awed by the power of her employer and not included in the information loop. Yet she could see, as anyone could see, that Hitler was a lunatic. Sometimes kind, sometimes considerate, sometimes screaming in fits of rage, but certainly cut loose from reality.

Against the overarching facts of his personal magnetism and the blind loyalty of his lieutenants, the movie observes the workings of the world within the bunker. All power flowed from Hitler. He was evil, mad, ill, but long after Hitler's war was lost he continued to wage it in fantasy. Pounding on maps, screaming ultimatums, he moved troops that no longer existed, issued orders to commanders who were dead, counted on rescue from imaginary armies.

That he was unhinged did not much affect the decisions of acolytes like Joseph and Magda Goebbels, who decided to stay with him and commit suicide as he would. "I do not want to live in a world without National Socialism," says Frau Goebbels, and she doesn't want her six children to live in one, either. In a sad, sickening scene, she gives them all a sleeping potion and then, one by one, inserts a cyanide capsule in their mouths and forces their jaws closed with a soft but audible crunch. Her oldest daughter, Helga, senses there is something wrong; senses, possibly, she is being murdered. Then Magda sits down to a game of solitaire before she and Joseph kill themselves. (By contrast, Heinrich Himmler wonders aloud, "When I meet Eisenhower, should I give the Nazi salute, or shake his hand?")

Hitler is played by Bruno Ganz, the gentle soul of *Wings of Desire*, the sad-eyed romantic or weary idealist of many roles over thirty years. Here we do not recognize him at first, hunched over, shrunken, his injured left hand fluttering behind his back like a trapped bird. If it were not for the 1942 scenes in which he hires Frau Junge as a secretary, we would not be able to picture him standing upright. He uses his hands as claws that crawl over battlefield maps, as he assures his generals that this or that impossible event will save them. And if not, well: "If the war is lost, it is immaterial if the German people survive. I will shed not one tear for them." It was his war, and they had let him down, he screams: betrayed him, lied to him, turned traitor.

Frau Junge and two other secretaries bunk in a small concrete room, and sneak away to smoke cigarettes, which Hitler cannot abide. Acting as a hostess to the death watch, his mistress, Eva Braun (Juliane Köhler), presides over meals set with fine china and crystal. She hardly seems to engage Hitler except as a social companion. Although we have heard his rants and ravings about the Jews, the Russians, his own treacherous generals, and his paranoid delusions, Braun is actually able to confide to Junge, toward the end: "He only talks about dogs and vegetarian meals. He doesn't want anyone to see deep inside of him." Seeing inside of him is no trick at all: He is flayed bare by his own rage.

Downfall was one of 2005's Oscar nominees for Best Foreign Film. It has inspired much debate about the nature of the Hitler it presents. Is it a mistake to see him, after all, not as a monster standing outside the human race, but as just another human being?

David Denby, *The New Yorker*: "Considered as biography, the achievement (if that's the right word) of *Downfall* is to insist that the monster was not invariably monstrous—that he was kind to his cook and his young female secretaries, loved his German shepherd, Blondi, and was surrounded by loyal subordinates. We get the point: Hitler was not a supernatural being; he was common clay raised to power by the desire of his followers. But is this observation a sufficient response to what Hitler actually did?"

Stanley Kauffman, *The New Republic*: "Ever since World War II, it has been clear that a fiction film could deal with the finish of Hitler and his group in one of two ways: either as ravening beasts finally getting the fate they deserved or as consecrated idealists who believed in what they had done and were willing to pay with their lives for their actions. The historical evidence of the behavior in the bunker supports the latter view . . . . *Downfall*, apparently faithful to the facts, evokes—torments us with—a discomfiting species of sympathy or admiration."

Admiration I did not feel. Sympathy I felt in the sense that I would feel it for a rabid dog, while accepting that it must be destroyed. I do not feel the film provides "a sufficient response to what Hitler actually did," because I feel no film can, and no response would be sufficient. All we can learn from a film like this is that millions of people can be led, and millions more killed, by madness leashed to racism and the barbaric instincts of tribalism.

What I also felt, however, was the reality of the Nazi sickness, which has been distanced and diluted by so many movies with so many Nazi villains that it has become more like a plot device than a reality. As we regard this broken and pathetic Hitler, we realize that he did not alone create the Third Reich, but was the focus for a spontaneous uprising by many of the German people, fueled by racism, xenophobia, grandiosity, and fear. He was skilled in the ways he exploited that feeling, and surrounded himself with gifted strategists and propagandists, but he was not a great man, simply one armed by fate to unleash unimaginable evil. It is useful to reflect that racism, xenophobia, grandiosity, and fear are still with us, and the defeat of one of their manifestations does not inoculate us against others.

Down with Love ★ ★ ★

PG-13, 94 m., 2003

Renée Zellweger (Barbara Novak), Ewan McGregor (Catcher Block), David Hyde Pierce (Peter MacMannus), Sarah Paulson (Vikki Hiller), Tony Randall (Theodore Banner). Directed by Peyton Reed and produced by Bruce Cohen and Dan Jinks. Screenplay by Eve Ahlert and Dennis Drake.

Down with Love opens with the big Cinema-Scope logo that once announced 20th Century Fox mass-market entertainments. The titles show animated letters bouncing each other off the screen, and the music is chirpy. The movie's opening scenes confirm these clues: This is a movie set in 1962, and filmed in the style of those Doris Day–Rock Hudson classics about the battle of the sexes. That it adds an unexpected twist is part of the fun.

Maybe the filmmakers believe that movies lost something when they added irony. *Far from Heaven* was in the style of a 1957 Universal melodrama, and now this wide-screen comedy, with bright colors and enormous sets filled with postwar modern furniture, wants to remember a time before the sexual revolution.

Well, just barely before. Its heroine is determined to usher it in. She is Barbara Novak (Renée Zellweger), a New Englander whose new best-seller, *Down with Love,* has just pushed John F. Kennedy's *Profiles in Courage* off the charts (and about time, too, since JFK's book was published in 1956). Novak's book announces a new woman who will not be subservient to men in the workplace, and will call her own shots in the bedroom.

This attracts the attention of Catcher Block (Ewan McGregor), a womanizing male chauvinist pig who works as a magazine writer, specializing in exposés. He bets his boss Peter MacMannus (David Hyde Pierce) that he can seduce Barbara, prove she's an old-fashioned woman at heart, and write a sensational article about it. Meanwhile, Barbara's publisher, Vikki Hiller (Sarah Paulson), announces a publicity coup: She's arranged an interview with . . . well, Catcher Block, of course.

Any movie fan can figure out the 1962 casting of these characters. Barbara and Catcher are Doris Day and Rock Hudson, Vikki is Lauren Bacall, and Peter is Tony Randall; Randall himself, in fact, is in this movie, as chairman of the board. And the plot resembles Doris Day's movies in the sex department: Barbara Novak talks a lot about sex and gets in precarious positions, but never quite compromises her principles.

The movie has a lot of fun with the split-screen techniques of the 1960s, which exploited the extra-wide screen. If you remember the split-screen phone calls in *Pillow Talk,* you'll enjoy the same technique here, in a series of calls where Catcher stands up Barbara on a series of dinner dates. *Down with Love* borrows a technique from the Austin Powers series (itself a throwback to the 1960s) with scenes in which the split screen is used to suggest strenuous sexual activity that is, in fact, quite innocently nonsexual.

I don't believe anyone will equal whatever it was that Doris Day had; she was one of a kind. But Renée Zellweger comes closest, with her wide eyes, naive innocence, and almost aggressive sincerity. She has a speech toward the end of the movie where the camera simply remains still and regards her, as a torrent of words pours out from her character's innermost soul.

Down with Love is no better or worse than the movies that inspired it, but that is a compliment, I think. It recalls a time when society had more rigid rules for the genders, and thus more adventure in transcending them. And it relishes the big scene where a hypocrite gets his comeuppance. The very concept of "comeuppance" is obsolete in these permissive modern times, when few movie characters have a sense of shame and behavior is justified in terms of pure selfishness. Barbara Novak's outrage at sneaky behavior is one of the movie's most refreshing elements from the 1960s—not to say she isn't above a few neat tricks herself.

Dracula:
Pages from a Virgin's Diary ★ ★ ★ ½
NO MPAA RATING, 75 m., 2003

Zhang Wei-Qiang (Dracula), Tara Birtwhistle (Lucy Westernra), David Moroni (Dr. Van Helsing), CindyMarie Small (Mina Murray), Johnny Wright (Jonathon Harker), Stephane Leonard (Arthur Holmwood), Matthew Johnson (Jack Seward), Keir Knight (Quincy Morris). Directed by Guy Maddin and produced by Vonnie Von Helmolt. Screenplay by Mark Godden.

The ballet as a silent movie with an orchestra. I'd never thought of it that way before. The dancers embody the characters, express emotion with their bodies and faces, try to translate feeling and speech into physical movement. They are borne up on the wings of the music. *Dracula: Pages from a Virgin's Diary* uses (and improvises on and kids and abuses) the style of silent films to record a production of *Dracula* by the Royal Winnipeg Ballet. The film is poetic and erotic, creepy and melodramatic, overwrought and sometimes mocking, as if F. W. Murnau's *Nosferatu* (1922) had a long-lost musical version.

The director is Guy Maddin, who lives in Winnipeg and is Canada's poet laureate of cinematic weirdness. His films often look as if the silent era had continued right on into today's ironic stylistic drolleries; he made a 2000 short named *The Heart of the World* that got more applause than most of the films it preceded at the Toronto film festival. Imagine *Metropolis* in hyderdrive.

In *Dracula: Pages from a Virgin's Diary* he begins with the Royal Winnipeg Ballet's stage production of *Dracula,* choreographed and produced by Mark Godden, and takes it through a series of transformations into something that looks a lot like a silent film but feels like avant-garde theater. The music is by Mahler (the first and second symphonies), the visuals include all the favorite devices of the silent period (wipes, iris shots, soft framing, intertitles, tinting), and the effect is—well, surprisingly effective. The emphasis is on the erotic mystery surrounding Dracula, and the film underlines the curious impression we sometimes have in vampire films that the victims experience orgasm as the fangs sink in.

The Dracula story is so easily mocked and satirized that it is good to be reminded of the unsettling erotic horror that it possesses in the hands of a Murnau or Werner Herzog (1979) or now Maddin. Not that Maddin is above poking it in the ribs (sample titles: "Why can't a woman marry two men? Or as many as want her?" and "She's filled with polluted blood!").

It deals primarily with Count Dracula's seduction, if that is the word, of Lucy Westernra (Tara Birtwhistle), whose name in Bram Stoker's novel was Westerna. The "westernization" is no doubt to underline Dracula's own relocation from Transylvania to the mysterious East; he is played here by the ballet's Zhang Wei-Qiang, whose stock melodramatic Asian characteristics are made not much more subtle than D. W. Griffith's Cheng Haun in *Broken Blossoms* (1919).

Jonathon Harker (Johnny Wright), the hapless estate agent, and his fiancée, Mina (Cindy-Marie Small), who both played major roles in the Stoker novel and most of the resulting films, have been somewhat downgraded in importance here, but Van Helsing (David Moroni), the vampire expert and hater, is well employed, and there are the usual crowds of townspeople to exhume coffins and perform other useful tasks. The story is less a narrative than an evocation of the vampire's world. Maddin shoots on sets and locations that resemble silent films in their overwrought and bold imagery, and he combines a number of low-tech filming formats, including 16 mm and Super 8; among the evocative stills on the movie's Website (www.zeitgeistfilms.com) is one in which Maddin is seen photographing with a tiny camera.

For the purposes of this film, the original

images are only a starting point. Madden manipulates them with filters, adds grain, softens focus, moves through them with wipes, and takes the silent technique of tinting to a jolly extreme with blood and capes that suddenly flood the screen with red.

Dracula: Pages from a Virgin's Diary is not concerned with the story mechanics of moving from A to B. At times it feels almost like one of those old silent films where scenes have gone missing and there are jumps in the chronology. This is not a problem but an enhancement, creating for us the sensation of glimpsing snatches of a dream. So many films are more or less alike that it's jolting to see a film that deals with a familiar story but looks like no other.

Dreamcatcher ★ ½

R, 134 m., 2003

Morgan Freeman (Colonel Abraham Curtis), Thomas Jane (Dr. Henry Devlin), Jason Lee (Joe "Beaver" Clarendon), Damian Lewis (Gary "Jonesy" Jones), Timothy Olyphant (Pete Moore), Donnie Wahlberg (Douglas "Duddits" Cavell), Tom Sizemore (Captain Owen Underhill). Directed by Lawrence Kasdan and produced by Kasdan and Charles Okun. Screenplay by William Goldman and Kasdan, based on the novel by Stephen King.

Dreamcatcher begins as the intriguing story of friends who share a telepathic gift, and ends as a monster movie of stunning awfulness. What went wrong? How could director Lawrence Kasdan and writer William Goldman be responsible for a film that goes so awesomely cuckoo? How could even Morgan Freeman, an actor all but impervious to bad material, be brought down by the awfulness? Goldman, who has written insightfully about the screenwriter's trade, may get a long, sad book out of this one.

The movie is based on a novel by Stephen King, unread by me, apparently much altered for the screen version, especially in the appalling closing sequences. I have just finished the audiobook of King's *From a Buick 8*, was a fan of his *Hearts in Atlantis*, and like the way his heart tugs him away from horror ingredients and into the human element in his stories.

Here the story begins so promisingly that I hoped, or assumed, it would continue on the same track: Childhood friends, united in a form of telepathy by a mentally retarded kid they protect, grow up to share psychic gifts and to deal with the consequences. The problem of *really* being telepathic is a favorite science-fiction theme. If you could read minds, would you be undone by the despair and anguish being broadcast all around you? This is unfortunately not the problem explored by *Dreamcatcher*.

The movie does have a visualization of the memory process that is brilliant filmmaking; after the character Gary "Jonesy" Jones (Damian Lewis) has his mind occupied by an alien intelligence, he is able to survive hidden within it by concealing his presence inside a vast memory warehouse, visualized by Kasdan as an infinitely unfolding series of rooms containing Jonesy's memories. This idea is like a smaller, personal version of Jorge Luis Borges's *The Library of Babel*, the imaginary library that contains all possible editions of all possible books. I can imagine many scenes set in the warehouse—it's such a good idea it could support an entire movie—but the film proceeds relentlessly to abandon this earlier inspiration in its quest for the barfable.

But let me back up. We meet at the outset childhood friends Henry Devlin, Joe "Beaver" Clarendon, Jonesy Jones, and Pete Moore. They happen upon Douglas "Duddits" Cavell, a retarded boy being bullied by older kids, and they defend him with wit and imagination. He's grateful, and in some way he serves as a nexus for all of them to form a precognitive, psychic network. It isn't high-level or controllable, but it's there.

Then we meet them as adults, played by (in order) Thomas Jane, Jason Lee, Lewis, and Timothy Olyphant (Duddits is now Donnie Wahlberg). When Jonesy has an accident of startling suddenness, that serves as the catalyst for a trip to the woods, where the hunters turn into the hunted as alien beings attack.

It would be well not to linger on plot details, since if you are going to see the movie, you will want them to be surprises. Let me just say that the aliens, who look like a cross between the creature in *Alien* and the things that crawled out of the drains in that David Cronenberg movie, exhibit the same problem I often have with such beings: How can an alien that consists primarily of teeth and an appetite, that apparently has no limbs, tools, or language, travel to Earth in the first place? Are they little clone creatures for a superior race? Perhaps; an alien nicknamed Mr. Gray turns up, who looks and behaves quite differently, for a while.

For these aliens, space travel is a prologue for trips taking them where few have gone before; they explode from the business end of the intestinal tract, through that orifice we would be least willing to lend them for their activities. The movie, perhaps as a result, has as many farts as the worst teenage comedy—which is to say, too many farts for a movie that keeps insisting, with mounting implausibility, that it is intended to be good. These creatures are given a name by the characters that translates in a family newspaper as Crap Weasels.

When Morgan Freeman turns up belatedly in a movie, that is usually a good sign, because no matter what has gone before, he is likely to import more wit and interest. Not this time. He plays Colonel Abraham Curtis, a hard-line military man dedicated to doing what the military always does in alien movies, which is to blast the aliens to pieces and ask questions later. This is infinitely less interesting than a scene in King's *Buick 8* where a curious state trooper dissects a batlike thing that seems to have popped through a portal from another world. King's description of the autopsy of weird alien organs is scarier than all the gnashings and disembowelments in *Dreamcatcher*.

When the filmmakers are capable of the first half of *Dreamcatcher,* what came over them in the second half? What inspired their descent into the absurd? On the evidence here, we can say what we already knew: Lawrence Kasdan is a wonderful director of personal dramas (*Grand Canyon, The Accidental Tourist, Mumford*). When it comes to Crap Weasels, his heart just doesn't seem to be in it.

The Dreamers ★ ★ ★ ★
NC-17, 115 m., 2004

Michael Pitt (Matthew), Eva Green (Isabelle), Louis Garrel (Theo), Robin Renucci (Father), Anna Chancellor (Mother). Directed by Bernardo Bertolucci. and produced by Jeremy Thomas. Screenplay by Gilbert Adair, based on his novel.

In the spring of 1968, three planets—Sex, Politics, and the Cinema—came into alignment and exerted a gravitational pull on the status quo. In Paris, what began as a protest over the ouster of Henri Langlois, the legendary founder of the Cinématheque Français, grew into a popular revolt that threatened to topple the government. There were barricades in the streets, firebombs, clashes with the police, a crisis of confidence. In a way that seems inexplicable today, the director Jean-Luc Godard and his films were at the center of the maelstrom. Other New Wave directors and the cinema in general seemed to act as the agitprop arm of the revolution.

Here are two memories from that time. In the spring of 1968, I was on vacation in Paris. Demonstrators had barricaded one end of the street where my cheap Left Bank hotel was located. Police were massed at the other end. I was in the middle, standing outside my hotel, taking it all in. The police charged, I was pushed out in front of them, and rubber truncheons pounded on my legs. "Tourist!" I shouted, trying to make myself into a neutral. Later I realized they might have thought I was saying "tourista!" which is slang for diarrhea. Unwise.

The second memory is more pleasant. In April 1969, driving past the Three Penny Cinema on Lincoln Avenue in Chicago, I saw a crowd lined up under umbrellas on the sidewalk, waiting in the rain to get into the next screening of Godard's *Weekend.* Today you couldn't pay most Chicago moviegoers to see a film by Godard, but at that moment, the year after the Battle of Grant Park, at the height of opposition to the Vietnam War, it was all part of the same alignment.

Oh, and sex. By the summer of 1969, I was in Hollywood, writing the screenplay for Russ Meyer's *Beyond the Valley of the Dolls.* It would be an X-rated movie from 20th Century-Fox, and although it seems tame today (R-rated, probably), it was part of a moment when sex had entered the mainstream and was part of a whole sense of society in flux.

I indulge in this autobiography because I have just seen Bernardo Bertolucci's *The*

Dreamers and am filled with poignant and powerful nostalgia. To be sixteen in 1968 is to be fifty today, and so most younger moviegoers will find this film as historical as *Cold Mountain*. For me, it is yesterday; above all, it evokes a time when the movies—good movies, both classic and newborn—were at the center of youth culture. "The Movie Generation," *Time* magazine called us in a cover story. I got my job at the *Sun-Times* because of it; they looked around the feature department and appointed the longhaired new kid who had written a story about the underground films on Monday nights at Second City.

Bertolucci is two years older than I am, an Italian who made his first important film, *Before the Revolution*, when he was only twenty-four. He would, in 1972, make *Last Tango in Paris*, a film starring Marlon Brando and the unknown Maria Schneider in a tragedy about loss, grief, and sudden sex between two strangers who find it a form of urgent communication. Pauline Kael said, "Bertolucci and Brando have altered the face of an art form." Well, in those days we talked about movies that way.

It is important to have this background in mind when you go to see *The Dreamers* because Bertolucci certainly does. His film, like *Last Tango*, takes place largely in a vast Parisian apartment. It is about transgressive sex. Outside the windows, there are riots in the streets, and indeed, in a moment of obvious symbolism, a stone thrown through a window saves the lives of the characters, the revolution interrupting their introverted triangle.

The three characters are Matthew (Michael Pitt), a young American from San Diego who is in Paris to study for a year, but actually spends all of his time at the Cinémathèque, and the twins Isabelle (Eva Green) and Theo (Louis Garrel), children of a famous French poet and his British wife. They also spend all of their time at the movies. Almost the first thing Isabelle tells Matthew is, "You're awfully clean for someone who goes to the cinema so much." He's clean in more ways than one; he's a naive, idealistic American, and the movie treats him to these strange Europeans in the same way Henry James sacrifices his Yankee innocents on the altar of continental decadence.

These are the children of the cinema. Isabelle tells Matthew, "I entered this world on the Champs Élysées in 1959, and my very first words were *New York Herald Tribune!*" Bertolucci cuts to the opening scene in Godard's *Breathless* (1959), one of the founding moments of the New Wave, as Jean Seberg shouts out those words on the boulevard. In other words, the New Wave, not her parents, gave birth to Isabelle. There are many moments when the characters quiz each other about the movies, or reenact scenes they remember; a particularly lovely scene has Isabelle moving around a room, touching surfaces, in a perfect imitation of Garbo in *Queen Christina*. And there's a bitter argument between Matthew and Theo about who is greater—Keaton or Chaplin? Matthew, the American, of course, knows that the answer is Keaton. Only a Frenchman could think it was Chaplin.

But *The Dreamers* is not Bertolucci's version of Trivial Pursuit. Within the apartment, sex becomes the proving ground and then the battleground for the revolutionary ideas in the air. Matthew meets the twins at the Cinémathèque during a demonstration in favor of Langlois (Bertolucci intercuts newsreel footage of Jean-Pierre Leaud in 1968 with new footage of Leaud today, and we also get glimpses of Truffaut, Godard, and Nicholas Ray). They invite him back to their parents' apartment. The parents are going to the seaside for a month, and the twins invite him to stay.

At first it is delightful. "I have at last met some real Parisians!" Matthew writes his parents. Enclosed in the claustrophobic world of the apartment, he finds himself absorbed in the sexual obsessions of the twins. He glimpses one night that they sleep together, naked. Isabelle defeats Theo in a movie quiz and orders him to masturbate (on his knees, in front of a photo of Garbo). Theo wins a quiz and orders Matthew to make love to his sister. Matthew is sometimes a little drunk, sometimes high, sometimes driven by lust, but at the bottom he knows this is wrong, and his more conventional values set up the ending of the film, in which sex and the cinema are engines, but politics is the train.

The film is extraordinarily beautiful. Bertolucci is one of the great painters of the screen. He has a voluptuous way here of bathing his characters in scenes from great movies, and referring to others. Sometimes his movie references are subtle, and you should look for a lovely one. Matthew looks out a window as rain falls on the glass, and the light through the window makes it seem that the drops are running down his face. This is a quote from a famous shot by Conrad L. Hall in Richard Brooks's *In Cold Blood* (1967). And although Michael Pitt usually looks a little like Leonardo DiCaprio, in this shot, at that angle, with that lighting, he embodies for a moment the young Marlon Brando. Another quotation: As the three young people run down an outdoor staircase, they are pursued by their own giant shadows, in a nod to *The Third Man*.

The movie is rated NC-17, for adults only, because of the themes and because of some frontal nudity. So discredited is the NC-17 rating that Fox Searchlight at first thought to edit the film for an R, but why bother to distribute a Bertolucci film except in the form he made it? The sexual content evokes that time and place. The movie is like a classic argument for an A rating, between the R and NC-17, which would identify movies intended for adults but not actually pornographic. What has happened in our society to make us embrace violence and shy away from sexuality?

Bertolucci titles his film *The Dreamers*, I think, because his characters are dreaming, until the brick through the window shatters their cocoon and the real world of tear gas and Molotov cocktails enters their lives. It is clear now that Godard and sexual liberation were never going to change the world. It only seemed that way for a time. The people who really run things do not go much to the movies, or perhaps think much about sex. They are driven by money and power. Matthew finds he cannot follow the twins into whatever fantasy the times have inspired in them. He turns away and disappears into the crowd of rioters, walking in the opposite direction. Walking into a future in which, perhaps, he will become the director of this movie.

Dr. Seuss' the Cat in the Hat ★ ★
PG, 81 m., 2003

Mike Myers (The Cat), Alec Baldwin (Lawrence Quinn), Kelly Preston (Joan Walden), Dakota Fanning (Sally Walden), Spencer Breslin (Conrad Walden), Sean Hayes (The Fish [voice]), Amy Hill (Mrs. Kwan), Sean Hayes (Mr. Humberfloob). Directed by Bo Welch and produced by Brian Grazer. Screenplay by Alec Berg, David Mandel, and Jeff Schaffer, based on the book by Dr. Seuss.

Dr. Seuss' the Cat in the Hat is a triumph above all of production design. That's partly because the production design is so good, partly because the movie is so disappointing. It's another overwrought clunker like *How the Grinch Stole Christmas*, all effects and stunts and CGI and prosthetics, with no room for lightness and joy. Poor Dr. Seuss, whose fragile wonderments have been crushed under a mountain of technology.

Mike Myers stars as The Cat, in the ritual sacrifice of a big star to a high concept. Like Jim Carrey as The Grinch, he's imprisoned beneath layers of makeup. There is a reason why Myers and Carrey are stars, and that reason is not because they look like cats or grinches. Nor does it much help that The Cat sometimes lapses uncannily into the voice of Linda Richman, Myers's classic *SNL* character. The Cat is a nudge, a scold, a card, an instigator, a tease— oh, lots of things, but one of them isn't lovable. It's been said you should never marry anyone you wouldn't want to take along on a three-day bus trip. I have another insight: Never make a movie about a character you can't stand.

The movie follows the book, sort of, if you can imagine a cute balloon inflated into a zeppelin. The two kids, Conrad and Sally, are played by Spencer Breslin and Dakota Fanning; he's seemingly compelled to mess things up, she's so compulsive that the to do list on her Palm includes: "Make out tomorrow's to do list."

Their mom, Joan (Kelly Preston), is a real estate agent who works for the germophobic Mr. Humberfloob (Sean Hayes); everything depends on her house being spic and span for a big reception, and so, of course, the moment she entrusts the kids into the hands of Mrs. Kwan the baby-sitter (Amy Hill), who should show up but The Cat, and the house is eventually in ruins. What happens then? Is Joan fired? Is the house perhaps magically repaired? I would be happy to tell you, but I had better not

189

give away the ending; there may be unfortunate readers who have not read *The Cat in the Hat*, or had it read to them, or even had it summarized for them by a trusted adviser.

The movie consists of wall-to-wall action, sort of like *The Fast and the Furious* for the third-grade hyperactive set. The Cat's catmobile sprouts three steering wheels, and The Cat leads them on a fantasy tour of the town in search of their runaway dog. The theory is that Mrs. Kwan, apparently a narcoleptic, will never notice their absence since she has fallen asleep immediately after arriving to baby-sit.

But Mrs. Kwan does turn up later, during their visit to an imaginary amusement park, where the dumpy old Chinese lady, still insensate, her body stiff as a board, functions admirably as a raft for the water slide. The cat and the kids mount her and down they go, with a close-up of water splashing over Mrs. Kwan's prow, or brow. To use the unconscious Mrs. Kwan in this way is creepy and offensive. Now I'm not getting P.C. and decrying the movie for making fun of Chinese. I'm glad an Asian-American actress got the job. No, I think it's making fun of old people in general, in a cruel way, and I don't think it's funny.

Other stuff is a little funnier, including the story of what is in the muffins Joan serves at her reception, and how it all got there. And, of course, the movie has the obligatory smart-aleck sidekick, a fish (voice by Sean Hayes) that adds approximately nothing.

Similarly wasted is Alec Baldwin, as the marriage-minded neighbor Lawrence. He wants to marry Joan. The kids rightly suspect him of smarmy nefariousness, and wow, is this the same actor I saw starring on Broadway in *Cat on a Hot Tin Roof*? Baldwin gave an interview recently talking about his fall from stardom and grace, but he is gifted and will make a comeback when the time is right (for advice, he could turn to Joan, played by Mrs. John Travolta). Baldwin is electrifying as a hard-boiled but old-fashioned casino boss in *The Cooler*; pity about this role.

What went wrong here? Well, the producer is Brian Grazer, who also produced *The Grinch*, and apparently learned little from it, although since it grossed north of $300 million maybe he didn't want to. Grazer is a nice guy and has produced some wonderful movies,

often with Ron Howard; this time, he's working with first-timer Bo Welch, a famous and gifted production designer *(Batman Returns, Edward Scissorhands, Beetlejuice, Men in Black)*. I should mention this movie's production designer, Alex McDowell, as well as art directors Alec Hammon and Sean Haworth, Anne Kuljian's sets, Rita Ryack's costumes, and all the makeup artists. But this is where we came in.

Duplex ★ ★
PG-13, 88 m., 2003

Ben Stiller (Alex), Drew Barrymore (Nancy), Eileen Essel (Mrs. Connell), Harvey Fierstein (Realtor), Justin Theroux (Cooper Sinclair), Michelle Krusiec (Dr. Kang), Swoosie Kurtz (Alex's Editor), Wallace Shawn (Nancy's Editor). Directed by Danny DeVito and produced by Drew Barrymore, Stuart Cornfeld, Richard N. Gladstein, Nancy Juvonen, Meryl Poster, and Ben Stiller. Screenplay by Larry Doyle and John Hamburg.

When all the world was agog over the butter scene between Marlon Brando and Maria Schneider in *Last Tango in Paris*, it took Art Buchwald to explain the movie. It was not about sex at all, he said, but about what people are willing to do for a rent-controlled apartment in Paris. *Duplex* is about a yuppie couple who eventually get to the point where they are contemplating murder.

Drew Barrymore and Ben Stiller play Nancy and Alex, young professionals fleeing a Manhattan flat "the size of a small child." In Brooklyn they buy a perfect apartment, with three fireplaces and original stained-glass windows, on a quiet street; there are even shelves for his collection of first editions. Here he'll be able to finish his second novel, while she commutes to her job as a magazine editor. The apartment is even a duplex, but there's a hitch: The upstairs is occupied by a sweet little old rent-controlled lady who pays only $88 a month.

"She hasn't been feeling too well lately," their real estate agent (Harvey Fierstein) optimistically informs them. So it's perfect. They'll move in, the sweet little old lady will die, and then they can take over the upstairs and start their family. The problem is that the sweet little old lady is annoying and obnoxious on a truly alarming scale.

Her name is Mrs. Connell, and she's played by the actress Eileen Essel, who is eighty-one, but skips around the apartment like a cheerleader. Maybe they used doubles for some of the movement, but Essel is filled with energy, aggressively cheerful despite their raids on her sanity, and keeps them guessing: She mentions at one point that her husband died in 1963, after they had been married fifty-eight years. Barrymore's eyes almost cross as she tries to do the math.

Essel's energy and timing are delightful. Stiller and Barrymore are fun, too; few actors have a better slow burn than Stiller, who eventually realizes that he will never finish his novel or have a life as long as Mrs. Connell lives upstairs. But the movie becomes an elaboration on one joke: Mrs. Connell, in her passive-aggressive and sometimes plain aggressive way, makes life miserable for them, and they take it as long as they can, and then snap.

Mrs. Connell, for example, plays her TV at top volume all night long. She wants Alex to run errands for her all day. He helps her go shopping, and she meticulously counts out everything: blueberries, pennies. One day when he is working against the deadline for his novel, she invites some friends over to visit—little old ladies like herself, who turn out to be members of a brass ensemble.

Eventually it becomes possible to contemplate murdering her, and at one point Alex is cruising the subway system hoping to pick up a killer flu bug, so he can sneeze on popcorn and send it upstairs. But murder schemes aimed at Mrs. Connell don't generate the laughter they should, maybe because no matter what she does, she still seems, irremediably, unredeemably, a sweet little old lady.

The movie was directed by Danny DeVito, who brings some of the same dark comedy he used in his great *The War of the Roses* (1989). But that one was about equals (Michael Douglas and Kathleen Turner) whose hate turns homicidal, and it had psychological depth to justify their extremes. *Duplex* is all about plotting; it tries to impose emotions that we don't really feel. We can't identify with Mrs. Connell, that's for sure, but we can't identify with Alex and Nancy either, because we don't share their frustration—and the reason we don't is because we don't believe it. There's too much contrivance and not enough plausibility, and so finally we're just enjoying the performances and wishing they'd been in a more persuasive movie.

Dust to Glory ★ ★ ★
PG, 97 m., 2005

With appearances by Mario Andretti, Sal Fish, James Garner, Ricky Johnson, Chad McQueen, Steve McQueen, Jimmy N. Roberts, and Malcolm Smith. A documentary directed by Dana Brown and produced by Mike "Mouse" McCoy and Scott Waugh.

Let's be sure we have this right. The Baja 1000 is the world's longest nonstop point-to-point race. It has more than a dozen categories of vehicles, from $2 million racing cars to motorcycles to unmodified pre-1972 VW Beetles. The course changes every year. You can leave the course and take a shortcut, but that way you might miss one of the secret checkpoints. The race includes both dirt back roads and Mexican highways. The highways are not blocked to civilian traffic during the event, and the racers have to weave in and out of ordinary traffic. Oh, and they could get stopped by the highway police.

Dust to Glory tells the story of the 2003 running of this legendary race, which offers glory but not much money; they can't even sell tickets, since the fans essentially just walk over to the edge of the road and watch the cars go by. And yet the Baja 1000 attracts stars like Mario Andretti and Parnelli Jones, and in years past, celebrities like James Garner and Steve McQueen.

The documentary was directed by Dana Brown, son of Bruce (*The Endless Summer*) Brown, who uses some fifty cameras, including lightweight digital cameras mounted on cars and motorcycles. That's helpful because there is no one place to stand in order to get a good idea of the entire race, especially since each category of vehicle is dispatched separately—the fastest cars, trucks, and motorcycles first, the Beetles last. There is a ham radio operator who keeps in touch with the checkpoints, provides weather reports, reports accidents, and communicates with the drivers' support teams, but he looks less like Command Central than like a guy in a hut on a hill with some stuff from Radio Shack.

The record time for the race is sixteen hours. There is a winner in every category. You have to finish in thirty-two hours, and in this race, to finish at all is a victory. Most of the teams have two or three drivers, but the movie's star (maybe because he is also the co-producer) is Mike "Mouse" McCoy, a motorcycle racing legend who plans to drive solo, nonstop, for all 1,000 miles.

Since the race runs through the night and passes areas where fine silt makes a dust cloud that limits visibility, this is a dangerous thing to do, but then the Baja 1000 is dangerous anyway: not least for the spectators, who seem to stand awfully close to hairpin turns where vehicles can spin out. Miraculously, only one person was killed in 2003—a spectator hit by a motorcycle belonging not to a racer, but to another spectator, who was driving the wrong way on the course.

There is a kind of madness involved in a race like this, and that's apparently its appeal. Car companies like Porsche invest big money in their teams, despite the lack of a purse or even much TV coverage (how could ESPN spot cameras along all 1,000 miles, and how would it make sense of the countless categories?). The race is more like a private poker game held upstairs in somebody's suite during the World Series of Poker.

Does Mouse make it? I would not dream of telling you. I will, however, tell you that he has a camera on his motorcycle that records with a sickening thud an accident he has sixty miles from the finish line, during which he injures or breaks (he isn't sure) some ribs, a shoulder, and a finger.

DysFunKtional Family ★ ★ ★
R, 83 m., 2003

A concert documentary by Eddie Griffin. Directed by George Gallo and produced by Griffin, David Permut, and Paul Brooks.

Eddie Griffin uses the N-word 382 times in his new concert film, *DysFunKtional Family*. I know this because David Plummer of the Ebert & Roeper staff counted them. It isn't uncommon for speakers to use placeholders, such as "you know" or "uh" or "like," but in Griffin's case the N-word functions more as a lubricant. It speeds his sentences ahead, provides timing, delays punch words until the right moment. The N-word in his act is so omnipresent that it becomes invisible, like air to a bird or water to a fish. It's his rhythm section.

Much has been written about how African-American musicians, comedians, and writers began to use the N-word in order, they said, to rob it of its poison. When Dick Gregory titled his 1963 autobiography *Nigger,* it was shocking and controversial, but he was making a bold gesture to strip the word of its hurtful power. ("Also," he told his mother, "whenever you hear it, they're advertising my book.")

The N-word is now spoken mostly by those who mean it as a sign of affection and bonding. The rules are: Blacks can say it, but whites should be very sure how, where, when, and why they are using it. (Not all agree. The black scholar Randall Kennedy's new book, *Nigger: The Strange Career of a Troublesome Word,* argues that the word is always wrong.)

I mention this because on a single day recently I received a curiously large number of e-mails criticizing my use of the word "redneck." I've used the word in several reviews over the years, but the occasion this time was a review of *Blue Collar Comedy Tour,* another new comedy concert film. It stars Jeff Foxworthy, who is famous for his litany ending ". . . you may be a redneck." (Example: If the wedding rehearsal dinner is at Hooter's, you may be a redneck.)

Whether these e-mails were all inspired by the same source, I cannot say. Odd that they came in a cluster. They made the same point: "Redneck" is as offensive to white Americans as the N-word is to African Americans. I doubt that this is the case, and suspect some of my correspondents may have even laughed at a Jeff Foxworthy concert.

One correspondent writes: "I notice that as a liberal you are highly sensitive to the rights of minority groups and would never apply a derogatory adjective to an African-American, a Hispanic-American or a Jew. However, when it comes to White Americans, it seems that you apply a different standard."

The implication is that a conservative would not be so "highly sensitive," I guess, although every true conservative would be. The reasoning behind this message derives from David Duke's European-American Unity and Rights Organization, and it's pretty obvious what they're getting at.

Is "redneck" an offensive term? Yes and no. It does not refer to all white people (as the N-word refers to all blacks, or certain terms refer to all Jews or all Mexicans). It is a term for a specific character type. The dictionary says it is "disparaging," but it is often used affectionately, as Foxworthy does. It is in wide usage. A Google search turns up 524,000 sites using "redneck"—amazingly, two and a half times as many as those using the N-word. Among "redneck" sites, Foxworthy's places second and Redneck World is sixth. I doubt that my correspondents have complained to Redneck World.

Of course, "redneck" would be an insult if used against a given person in a particular situation. Most of the time, it is not used in that way. Everything depends on who you are, how you use a word, who you use it to, and in what spirit. Words are not neutral. My use of "redneck" was not intended to offend, but by taking offense at it, my correspondents have made a not very subtle equation of civil rights in general and their own specialized version of white civil rights, which in Duke's case slides smoothly into white supremacy.

Foxworthy's act is genial, not hurtful, and his definitions of "redneck" include so much basic human nature that we often laugh in recognition. Griffin is also not hurtful (the word "genial" does not occur in connection with his sharp-edged material), but his N-word usage creates uncertainty among whites, who are unsure how to respond. It may limit his crossover appeal to general audiences. As he grows and deepens he may find he can live without it, as Bill Cosby, the greatest of all standup comedians, has always been able to.

I haven't said much about Eddie Griffin's film itself, perhaps because it made me think more about the N-word than about his comedy. Griffin is quick, smart, and funny, and presents the critics with the usual challenge in reviewing a comedy concert: What do you write about, apart from quoting his funniest lines? I have a few quibbles about the way he ropes in his actual family members, especially two uncles, one a pimp, the other addicted to porn; although they seem cheerful enough about going along with the joke, is the joke on them? Still, Griffin made me laugh.

As for "redneck," well, as someone who comes from a part of Illinois where the salad bar includes butterscotch pudding, I can use it, but don't you call me that.

E

Elektra ★ ½
PG-13, 97 m., 2005

Jennifer Garner (Elektra), Goran Visnjic (Mark Miller), Will Yun Lee (Kirigi), Cary-Hiroyuki Tagawa (Roshi), Terence Stamp (Stick), Kirsten Prout (Abby Miller). Directed by Rob Bowman and produced by Arnon Milchan, Avi Arad, and Gary Foster. Screenplay by Zak Penn, Stuart Zicherman, and Raven Metzner.

Elektra plays like a collision between leftover bits and pieces of Marvel superhero stories. It can't decide what tone to strike. It goes for satire by giving its heroine an agent who suggests mutual funds for her murder-for-hire fees, and sends her a fruit basket before her next killing. And then it goes for melancholy, by making Elektra a lonely, unfulfilled overachiever who was bullied as a child and suffers from obsessive-compulsive disorder. It goes for cheap sentiment by having her bond with a thirteen-year-old girl, and then . . . but see for yourself. The movie's a muddle in search of a rationale.

Elektra, you may recall, first appeared on screen in *Daredevil* (2003), the Marvel saga starring Ben Affleck as a blind superhero. Jennifer Garner, she of the wonderful lips, returns in the role as a killer for hire, which seems kind of sad, considering that in the earlier movie she figured in the beautiful scene where he imagines her face by listening to raindrops falling on it.

Now someone has offered her $2 million for her next assassination, requiring only that she turn up two days early for the job—on Christmas Eve, as it works out. She arrives in a luxurious lakeside vacation home and soon meets the young girl named Abby (Kirsten Prout), who lives next door. Abby's father is played by Goran Visnjic with a three-day beard, which tells you all you need to know: Powerful sexual attraction will compel them to share two PG-13-rated kisses.

The back story, which makes absolutely no mention of Daredevil, involves Elektra's training under the stern blind martial arts master Stick (Terence Stamp), who can restore people to life and apparently materialize at will, yet is reduced to martial arts when he does battle. Her enemies are assassins hired by the Order of the Hand, which is a secret Japanese society that seeks the Treasure, and the Treasure is . . . well, see for yourself.

As for the troops of the Hand, they have contracted Movie Zombie's Syndrome, which means that they are fearsome and deadly until killed, at which point they dissolve into a cloud of yellow powder. I don't have a clue whether they're real or imaginary. Neither do they, I'll bet. Eagles and wolves and snakes can materialize out of their tattoos and attack people, but they, too, disappear in clouds. Maybe this is simply to save Elektra the inconvenience of stepping over her victims in the middle of a fight.

The Order of the Hand is not very well defined. Its office is a pagoda on top of a Tokyo skyscraper, which is promising, but inside all we get is the standard scene of a bunch of suits sitting around a conference table giving orders to paid killers. Their instructions: Kill Elektra, grab the Treasure, etc. Who are they and what is their master plan? Maybe you have to study up on the comic books.

As for Elektra, she's a case study. Flashbacks show her tortured youth, in which her father made her tread water in the family's luxury indoor pool until she was afraid she'd drown. (Her mother, on balcony overlooking pool: "She's only a girl!" Her father, at poolside: "Only using your legs! Not your hands!" Elektra: "Glub.")

Whether this caused her OCD or not, I cannot say. It manifests itself not as an extreme case, like poor Howard Hughes, but fairly mildly: She counts her steps in groups of five. This has absolutely nothing to do with anything else. A superheroine with a bad case of OCD could be interesting, perhaps; maybe she would be compelled to leap tall buildings with bound after bound after bound.

The movie's fight scenes suffer from another condition, attention deficit disorder. None of their shots are more than a few seconds long, saving the actors from doing much in the way of stunts and the director from having to worry overmuch about choreography. There's one showdown between Elektra and the head killer of the Hand that involves a lot of white sheets, but all they do is flap around; we're expecting maybe an elegant Zhang Yimou sequence, and it's more like they're fighting with the laundry.

Jennifer Garner is understandably unable to make a lot of sense out of this. We get a lot of close-ups in which we would identify with what she was thinking, if we had any clue what that might be. Does she wonder why she became a paid killer instead of a virtuous superheroine? Does she wonder why her agent is a bozo? Does she clearly understand that the Order of the Hand is the group trying to kill her? At the end of the movie, having reduced her enemies to yellow poofs, she tells Goran Visnjic to "take good care" of his daughter. Does she even know those guys in suits are still up there in the pagoda, sitting around the table?

Elephant ★ ★ ★
R, 81 m., 2003

Alex Frost (Alex), Eric Deulen (Eric), John Robinson (John), Elias McConnell (Elias), Jordan Taylor (Jordan), Carrie Finklea (Carrie), Nicole George (Nicole), Brittany Mountain (Brittany). Directed by Gus Van Sant and produced by Dany Wolf. Screenplay by Van Sant.

Gus Van Sant's *Elephant* is a record of a day at a high school like Columbine, on the day of a massacre much like the one that left thirteen dead. It offers no explanation for the tragedy, no insights into the psyches of the killers, no theories about teenagers or society or guns or psychopathic behavior. It simply looks at the day as it unfolds, and that is a brave and radical act; it refuses to supply reasons and assign cures so that we can close the case and move on.

Van Sant seems to believe there are no reasons for Columbine and no remedies to prevent senseless violence from happening again. Many viewers will leave this film as unsatisfied and angry as *Variety*'s Todd McCarthy, who wrote after it won the Golden Palm at Cannes 2003 that it was "pointless at best and irresponsible at worst." I think its responsibility comes precisely in its refusal to provide a point.

Let me tell you a story. The day after Columbine, I was interviewed for the Tom Brokaw news program. The reporter had been assigned a theory and was seeking sound bites to support it.

"Wouldn't you say," she asked, "that killings like this are influenced by violent movies?"

No, I said, I wouldn't say that.

"But what about *The Basketball Diaries*?" she asked. "Doesn't that have a scene of a boy walking into a school with a machine gun?"

The obscure 1995 Leonardo DiCaprio movie did indeed have a brief fantasy scene of that nature, I said, but the movie failed at the box office (it grossed only $2.5 million), and it's unlikely the Columbine killers saw it.

The reporter looked disappointed, so I offered her my theory.

"Events like this," I said, "if they are influenced by anything, are influenced by news programs like your own. When an unbalanced kid walks into a school and starts shooting, it becomes a major media event. Cable news drops ordinary programming and goes around the clock with it. The story is assigned a logo and a theme song; these two kids were packaged as the Trench Coat Mafia.

"The message is clear to other disturbed kids around the country: 'If I shoot up my school, I can be famous. The TV will talk about nothing else but me. Experts will try to figure out what I was thinking. The kids and teachers at school will see they shouldn't have messed with me. I'll go out in a blaze of glory.'"

In short, I said, events like Columbine are influenced far less by violent movies than by *CNN*, the *NBC Nightly News*, and all the other news media who glorify the killers in the guise of "explaining" them. I commended the policy at the *Sun-Times*, where our editor said the paper would no longer feature school killings on Page One.

The reporter thanked me and turned off the camera. Of course, the interview was never used. They found plenty of talking heads to condemn violent movies, and everybody was happy.

Van Sant's *Elephant* is a violent movie in the sense that many innocent people are shot dead. But it isn't violent in the way it presents those deaths. There is no pumped-up style, no lingering, no release, no climax. Just implacable, poker-faced, flat, uninflected death.

Truffaut said it was hard to make an antiwar film because war was exciting even if you were against it. Van Sant has made an antiviolence film by draining violence of energy, purpose, glamour, reward, and social context. It just happens.

I doubt that *Elephant* will ever inspire anyone to copy what they see on the screen. Much more than the insipid message movies shown in social studies classes, it might inspire useful discussion and soul-searching among high school students.

Van Sant simply follows a number of students and teachers as they arrive at the school and go about their daily routines. Some of them intersect with the killers, and many of those die. Others escape for no particular reason.

The movie is told mostly in long tracking shots; by avoiding cuts between close-ups and medium shots, Van Sant also avoids the film grammar that goes along with such cuts, and so his visual strategy doesn't load the dice or try to tell us anything. It simply watches.

At one point he follows a tall, confident African-American student in a very long tracking shot as he walks into the school and down the corridors, and all of our experience as filmgoers leads us to believe this action will have definitive consequences; the kid embodies all those movie heroes who walk into hostage situations and talk the bad guy out of his gun. But it doesn't happen like that, and Van Sant sidesteps all the conventional modes of movie behavior and simply shows us sad, sudden death without purpose.

"I want the audience to make its own observations and draw its own conclusions," Van Sant told me at Cannes. "Who knows why those boys acted as they did?"

He is honest enough to admit that he does not. Of course a movie about a tragedy that does not explain the tragedy—that provides no personal or social "reasons" and offers no "solutions"—is almost against the law in the American entertainment industry. When it comes to tragedy, Hollywood is in the catharsis business.

Van Sant would have found it difficult to find financing for any version of this story (Columbine isn't "commercial"), but to tell it on a small budget, without stars or a formula screenplay, is unthinkable. He found the freedom to make the film, he said, because of the success of his *Good Will Hunting*, which gave him financial independence: "I came to realize since I had no need to make a lot of money, I should make films I find interesting, regardless of their outcome and audience."

Elf ★ ★ ★
PG, 95 m., 2003

Will Ferrell (Buddy), James Caan (Walter), Zooey Deschanel (Jovie), Mary Steenburgen (Emily), Edward Asner (Santa Claus), Bob Newhart (Papa Elf), Daniel Tay (Michael), Faizon Love (Elf Manager). Directed by Jon Favreau and produced by Jon Berg, Todd Komarnicki, and Shauna Weinberg. Screenplay by David Berenbaum.

If I were to tell you *Elf* stars Will Ferrell as a human named Buddy who thinks he is an elf and Ed Asner as Santa Claus, would you feel an urgent desire to see this film? Neither did I. I thought it would be clunky, stupid, and obvious, like *The Santa Clause* or *How the Grinch Stole Christmas*. It would have grotesque special effects and lumber about in the wreckage of holiday cheer, foisting upon us a chaste romance involving the only girl in America who doesn't know that a man who thinks he is an elf is by definition a pervert.

That's what I thought it would be. It took me about ten seconds of seeing Will Ferrell in the elf costume to realize how very wrong I was. This is one of those rare Christmas comedies that has a heart, a brain, and a wicked sense of humor, and it charms the socks right off the mantelpiece.

Even the unexpected casting is on the money. James Caan as the elf's biological father. Yes! Bob Newhart as his adoptive elf father. Yes! Mary Steenburgen as Caan's wife, who welcomes an adult son into her family. Yes! Zooey Deschanel as the girl who works in a department store and falls for his elfin charm. Yes! Faizon Love as Santa's elf manager—does it get any better than this? Yes, it does. Peter Dinklage, who played the dwarf in *The Station Agent*, has a brief but sublime scene in which he cuts right to the bottom line of elfhood.

Elf, directed by Jon Favreau and written by David Berenbaum, begins with a tragic misunderstanding on a Christmas long ago. As Santa is making his rounds, a human orphan crawls into his sack and accidentally hitches a ride to the North Pole. Raised as an elf by Papa Elf (Newhart), he knows he's at least four feet taller than most of the other elves, and eventually he decides to go to New York and seek out his birth father.

This is Walter (Caan), a hard-bitten publisher whose heart does not instantly melt at the prospect of a six-foot man in a green tunic and yellow stretch tights who says he is his son. But when Buddy drops the name of Walter's long-lost girlfriend, a faraway look appears in the old man's eyes, and soon Buddy is invited home, where Mary Steenburgen proves she is the only actress in America who could welcome her husband's out-of-wedlock elf into her family and make us believe she means it.

The plot is pretty standard stuff, involving a crisis at the old man's publishing company and a need for a best-selling children's book, but there are sweet subplots involving Buddy's new little brother, Michael (Daniel Tay), and Buddy's awkward but heartfelt little romance with the department store girl (Deschanel). Plus heart-tugging unfinished business at the North Pole.

Of course there's a big scene involving Buddy's confrontation with the department store Santa Claus, who (clever elf that he is) Buddy instantly spots as an imposter. "You sit on a throne of lies!" he tells this Santa. Indeed, the whole world has grown too cynical, which is why Santa is facing an energy crisis this year. His sleigh is powered by faith, and if enough people don't believe in Santa Claus, it can't fly. That leads to one of those scenes where a flying machine (in this case, oddly enough, the very sleigh we were just discussing) tries to fly and doesn't seem to be able to achieve takeoff velocity, and . . . well, it would be a terrible thing if Santa were to go down in flames, so let's hope Buddy convinces enough people to believe. It should be easy. He convinced me this was a good movie, and that's a miracle on 34th Street right there.

Ella Enchanted ★ ★ ★ ½
PG, 95 m., 2004

Anne Hathaway (Ella), Hugh Dancy (Prince Charmont), Cary Elwes (Prince Regent Edgar), Minnie Driver (Mandy), Vivica A. Fox (Fairy Lucinda), Joanna Lumley (Dame Olga), Patrick Bergin (Sir Peter), Jimi Mistry (Benny the Book), Aiden McArdle (Slannen the Elf), Lucy Punch (Hattie), Jennifer Higham (Olive), Eric Idle (Narrator), Parminder K. Nagra (Areida). Directed by Tommy O'Haver and produced by Jane Startz. Screenplay by Laurie Craig, Karen McCullah Lutz, and Kirsten Smith, based on the novel by Gail Carson Levine.

Ella Enchanted is enchanted, all right. Based on the beloved novel by Gail Carson Levine, it's a high-spirited charmer, a fantasy that sparkles with delights. A lot of the fun is generated because it takes place in a world that is one part *Cinderella,* one part *Shrek,* and one part *The Princess Bride.* It even stars the hero from *The Princess Bride,* Cary Elwes, who has grown up to become evil Prince Regent Edgar, who killed his brother the king and now has his sights on the king's son, who will inherit the throne. So make that one part *Hamlet* crossed with one part *Macbeth.*

Anne Hathaway, that improbably beautiful young woman from *The Princess Diaries,* stars as Ella, who at her birth is burdened with a spell from her fairy godmother, Lucinda (Vivica A. Fox). In this kingdom, everyone gets a fairy spell, but Ella's is a real inconvenience: She is given the spell of obedience, which means she has to do whatever she's told. As she grows older this becomes a real problem, especially after her widowed father, Sir Peter (Patrick Bergin), provides her with an evil stepmother named Dame Olga (Joanna Lumley) and two jealous stepsisters, Hattie and Olive (Lucy Punch and Jennifer Higham).

So we get the Cinderella story, but with a twist, because Ella is sort of a medieval civil rights crusader and thinks it's wrong that Prince Edgar has condemned all the nonhumans in the kingdom to leave the city and live in the forest. That would include the giants, the ogres, and the elves. Ella is in the forest one day when she is captured by ogres, who suspend her above a boiling cauldron and prepare to boil her for lunch. An ogre asks her, "How do you like to be eaten? Baked? Boiled?" I like her answer: "Free range." Ella explains she's on their side, and as she sets out to end discrimination, she takes along a talking book named Benny; the front cover is a hologram showing Benny (Jimi Mistry), whose body was unfortunately lost in a wayward spell. Open the book and he can show you anyone you want to see, although Benny's powers are limited and he can't tell you where to find these people.

She has a Meet Cute (three, actually) with Prince Charmont (Hugh Dancy), and it's love at first, second, and third sight, plunging Ella into the middle of palace intrigue. Edgar plans to murder his nephew and assume the throne, and although Ella discovers this danger, her stepsisters know the secret of the curse and use it to alienate her from Charmont.

The look of the movie is delightful. Special effects create a picture-book kingdom in which the medieval mixes with the suburban (there is a mall). I like the casual way that computer-animated graphics are used with real fore-grounds; sure, it doesn't look as convincing as it did (sometimes) in *The Lord of the Rings*, but a certain artifice adds to the style. The cast is ap-propriately goofy, including the household fairy, Mandy (Minnie Driver), who is not good for much in the spell department; Slannen the Elf (Aiden McArdle), Ella's plucky sidekick; a narrator played by Eric Idle, who sings a few songs; and a slithering snake named Heston, who is Edgar's chief adviser. The role of Ella's best friend, played by Parminder K. Nagra of *Bend It Like Beckham*, seems to have been much abbreviated, alas; we lose track of her for an hour, until she turns up waving happily at the end.

One of the charms of the movie is its goofiness, which extends to the songs, which verge on sing-along chestnuts; what else would the elves sing, after all, but "Let Us En-tertain You"?

And Anne Hathaway is, well, kind of lumi-nous. She has that big smile and open face, and here she's working with a witty and wicked plot, instead of with the wheezy contrivances of *The Princess Diaries*. She looks like she's having fun. So does everyone, even the snake. This is the best family film so far this year.

The Embalmer ★ ★ ★

NO MPAA RATING, 101 m., 2003

Ernesto Mahieux (Peppino), Valerio Foglia Manzillo (Valerio), Elisabetta Rocchetti (Deborah), Lina Bernardi (Deborah's Mother), Pietro Biondi (Deborah's Father), Bernardino Terracciano (Boss), Marcella Granito (Manuela).

Directed by Matteo Garrone and produced by Domenico Procacci. Screenplay by Ugo Chiti, Garrone, and Massimo Gaudioso.

The little man joins the big man at the zoo, where he is admiring a vulture. The little guy, named Peppino, is a charmer. He's about fifty, balding, under five feet tall. The big guy, named Valerio, is a looker, about twenty, handsome, over six feet tall. As they try to remember where they've met before, the point of view some-times switches from the humans to the vulture; the image is distorted, the sound is muffled, and we get an inside-out view of the bird blink-ing its eyes. Valerio says animals are his passion. Funny, says Peppino, they're also his. Peppino is a taxidermist.

Matteo Garrone's *The Embalmer* was origi-nally titled *The Taxidermist*, and while the re-vised title may be more commercial, it may send the wrong message about this profoundly creepy psychological study from Italy. The movie is an acute study of two personalities, and then a third that acts as a catalyst. Peppino, with a bright personality and a friendly smile, is a predator who likes to court young men with his money and favors. Valerio, who is told he "looks like a god," is not very bright, and likes to be courted. Peppino acts by indirection, tak-ing Valerio to clubs and hiring hookers for par-ties; the two friends end up in bed with the girls, and Valerio doesn't understand that for Peppino the girls are bait and he is the fish.

This Peppino (Ernesto Mahieux) is a piece of work, with the same electric self-confidence of Danny DeVito, but with undertones that only gradually reveal themselves. He tracks Valerio (Valerio Foglia Manzillo) down to his job as a cook, and offers him a big raise to become a trainee taxidermist. Like a kid displaying his treasures, he shows Valerio some jobs he's proud of: a turtle, a boa constrictor, a tiny shrew. Soon Valerio is learning the right way to sharpen a knife.

Peppino suggests Valerio save rent by mov-ing in with him. Valerio's girlfriend objects, as well she might. This is Manuela (Marcella Granito), who says she's heard the "dwarf" is connected to the Mafia. She walks out, but not long after, in a gas station, Valerio is picked up by the girl behind the counter, who attaches herself to him. This is the sexy, confident brunette Deborah (Elisabetta Rocchetti), who comes from a rich family that is puzzled but hospitable when she turns up with Valerio and . . . Peppino.

The Embalmer is masterful at concealing its true nature and surprising us with the turns of the story. Among the movie's mysteries are: (1) Does Peppino think of himself as a homosexual, or as a swinger who likes good buddies and is open-minded in bed? (2) Does Valerio know Peppino is hot for his bod? (3) Does Valerio prefer Peppino's money and partying to Deborah's considerable sexual prowess? I am tempted to add: (4) Is Valerio completely clueless? Twice he enrages Deborah by standing her up; he keeps falling for Peppino's urging to have "just one more."

Oh, and we should also ask: (5) In that scene where Peppino sends the hookers home and slips in next to Valerio in bed, what goes on? "Something happened between you, didn't it?" screams Deborah at a moment when things are going badly. Is it a weakness or a strength of the film that we don't know what happened? A little of both, as we puzzle over Valerio, an ingenue who, when he's not with the one he loves, loves the one he's with—if he loves anybody.

The movie is set mostly in Italian beach towns, but in a gray season, against cold concrete skies. The sea is distant and cheerless, and Garrone's visuals drain the life out of some scenes. This is not a comedy or a sex romp, but a curious business involving two single-minded hunters (Peppino and Deborah) and their quarry, whose good looks may have made life so easy for him that he never got the knack of living it.

Elisabetta Rocchetti is ideally cast as Deborah, because she has such a palpable, acquisitive sexuality. But the movie's center of energy is Ernesto Mahieux as Peppino. I mentioned Danny DeVito earlier not for the obvious reason that he's short like Mahieux is, but because both men dominate every scene they're in, and convince us they can impose their will on any situation. It may seem unlikely that a balding, middle-aged midget could lure a theoretically straight young male out of the arms of a sexual tigress, but after Deborah sizes up Peppino she knows she has to take him seriously. What the little man wants, he goes after with craft, cunning, and enormous need, and it's fascinating to watch him operate.

And why was that opening scene viewed partly through the vulture's eyes? The vulture is a bird that makes a living by spotting dead meat.

Enduring Love ★ ★ ★
R, 97 m., 2004

Daniel Craig (Joe Rose), Rhys Ifans (Jed), Samantha Morton (Claire), Bill Nighy (Robin), Andrew Lincoln (TV Producer), Helen McCrory(Mrs. Logan), Susan Lynch (Rachel). Directed by Roger Michell and produced by Kevin Loader. Screenplay by Joe Penhall, based on the novel by Ian McEwan.

In a grassy, sunlit field, the lovers Joe and Claire spread out their picnic lunch and open a bottle of champagne. Just then a hot-air balloon appears in the sky. It drifts down and lands, and a man jumps out, leaving a small boy inside. A gust of wind catches the balloon. The man tries to hold it down with a rope, but it is away. Joe runs to grab at another rope. Other men appear and grab ropes, but the balloon inexorably rises. One by one, the men let go and fall safely to Earth. One hangs on too long, past the point of no return. As the others stare silently at the long, quiet ascent of the balloon, this man hangs on as long as he can, and then he falls to Earth and is shattered.

This opening scene in *Enduring Love* is implacable in its simplicity. It literally shows death appearing from out of a clear blue sky. The others run through fields to the body of the dead man, and then one of the other survivors kneels down and asks Joe (Daniel Craig) to join him in prayer. This is Jed (Rhys Ifans), stringy-haired, skin and bones, with an intensity that is off-putting. Joe explains that he does not much believe in prayer. Jed implores him.

We follow Joe home, where he is a university lecturer and his girlfriend, Claire (Samantha Morton), is a sculptor. He is haunted by what happened in the field. The man who held on too long, he learns, was a doctor who happened on the scene entirely by fate. The balloon landed safely; the small boy was safe. The doctor died unnecessarily. Joe becomes obsessed by which of the men was first to let go of a rope. Was he the one? When one let go, all had to let go; if all had held on, he believes, the balloon would have returned to Earth and the doctor would not have died. "We let him down," Joe tells Claire.

Joe teaches a university class on love and ethics, and asks his students if love is real and ethics have meaning. His experience in the field undermines all he thinks he knows about such matters, and his classroom manner grows odd and tortured. There is another problem. Jed starts to stalk him. He stands in the park across from Joe's home. He is there when Joe visits the Tate Modern. He feels it is urgent that they know each other better. "You know what passed between us," he tells Joe. "Love—God's love. It was a sign."

Jed is clearly mad. He exists at the intersection of religious hysteria and erotomania, and confuses God's love with his own sudden love for Joe. But what can Joe do? He warns him away, he tries to elude him, he changes his daily patterns. And meanwhile the specter of Jed's and Joe's haunting doubts about the death of the doctor create a tortured space between Joe and Claire.

The movie, directed by Roger Michell, has been adapted by Joe Penhall from a novel by Ian McEwan; it begins with ethical issues and then gradually descends into thriller material. The character of Jed is nicely modulated by Rhys Ifans; in the early scenes, he's the kind of man you instinctively know you want to get away from, but you nod and are polite and agree in a perfunctory way to whatever he's saying, while edging away and hoping never to see him again. Such people take such small talk literally, and convince themselves you have made promises or, worse, sent them a coded message.

The movie's questions about love take a turn when Joe goes to visit Mrs. Logan (Helen McCrory), widow of the dead doctor. She doesn't seem as grief-stricken as she should. "He was bound to die saving someone," she says. Then she asks questions about that day that must not be revealed here, but that cast the doctor's participation in a different light.

Most movies remain at the top level of action: They are about what happens. A few consider the meaning of what happened, and even fewer deal with the fact that we have a

choice, some of the time, about what happens and what we do about it. It's impossible not to imagine ourselves in that field, seeing the father struggling with the rope as his son cries in the gondola. Would we run and grab a rope? Probably. Would we hang on too long? Not me. Rapid situational calculations dictate our decisions: The boy will not necessarily die if the balloon drifts away, but I will die if I lose my grip at a great height.

Joe is obsessed with the question of who let go first, but from another point of view, the doctor held on for too long. Now why did he do that? Is his widow correct in the way she imagines the scenario? Certainly the doctor did nothing to save the boy, and everything to bring Joe and Jed together. Joe thinks of ethical questions in an objective, logical way. Jed responds emotionally to his own demons. No one thinks to blame the boy's father for getting out of the balloon too soon. ☞

Enron: The Smartest Guys in the Room ★ ★ ★ ½
NO MPAA RATING, 110 m., 2005

Narrated by Peter Coyote. Featuring Kenneth Lay, Jeff Skilling, Lou Pai, Mike Muckleroy, Sherron Watkins, Reverend James Nutter, Bethany McLean, Peter Elkind, and others. A documentary directed by Alex Gibney and produced by Gibney, Jason Kliot, and Susan Motamed, based on the book *The Smartest Guys in the Room: The Amazing Rise and Scandalous Fall of Enron* by Bethany McLean and Peter Elkind.

This is not a political documentary. It is a crime story. No matter what your politics, *Enron: The Smartest Guys in the Room* will make you mad. It tells the story of how Enron rose to become the seventh-largest corporation in America with what was essentially a Ponzi scheme, and in its last days looted the retirement funds of its employees to buy a little more time.

There is a general impression that Enron was a good corporation that went bad. The movie argues that it was a con game almost from the start. It was "the best energy company in the world," according to its top executives, Kenneth Lay and Jeffrey Skilling. At the time they made that claim, they must have known that the company was bankrupt, had been worthless for years, had inflated its profits and concealed its losses through bookkeeping practices so corrupt that the venerable Arthur Andersen accounting firm was destroyed in the aftermath.

The film shows how it happened. To keep its stock price climbing, Enron created good quarterly returns out of thin air. One accounting tactic was called "mark to market," which meant if Enron began a venture that might make $50 million ten years from now, it could claim the $50 million as current income. In an astonishing in-house video made for employees, Skilling stars in a skit that satirizes "HFV" accounting, which he explains stands for "Hypothetical Future Value."

Little did employees suspect that was more or less what the company was counting on.

Skilling and Lay were less than circumspect at times. When a New York market analyst questions Enron's profit-and-loss statements during a conference call, Skilling can't answer and calls him an "asshole"; that causes bad buzz on the street. During a Q&A session with employees, Lay actually reads this question from the floor: "Are you on crack? If you are, that might explain a lot of things. If you aren't, maybe you should be."

One Enron tactic was to create phony offshore corporate shells and move their losses to those companies, which were off the books. We're shown a schematic diagram tracing the movement of debt to such Enron entities. Two of the companies are named "M. Smart" and "M. Yass." These "companies" were named with a reckless hubris: One stood for "Maxwell Smart" and the other one . . . well, take out the period and put a space between "y" and "a."

What did Enron buy and sell, actually? Electricity? Natural gas? It was hard to say. The corporation basically created a market in energy, gambled in it, and manipulated it. It moved on into other futures markets, even seriously considering "trading weather." At one point, we learn, its gambling traders lost the entire company in bad trades, and covered their losses by hiding the news and producing phony profit reports that drove the share price even higher. In hindsight, Enron was a corporation devoted to maintaining a high share price at any cost. That was its real product.

The documentary is based on the best-selling book of the same title, cowritten by *Fortune* magazine's Bethany McLean and Peter Elkind. It is assembled out of a wealth of documentary and video footage, narrated by Peter Coyote, from testimony at congressional hearings, and from interviews with such figures as disillusioned Enron exec Mike Muckleroy and whistle-blower Sherron Watkins. It is best when it sticks to fact, shakier when it goes for visual effects and heavy irony.

It was McLean who started the house of cards tumbling down with an innocent question about Enron's quarterly statements, which did not ever seem to add up. The movie uses in-house video made by Enron itself to show Lay and Skilling optimistically addressing employees and shareholders at a time when Skilling in particular was coming apart at the seams. Toward the end, he sells $200 million in his own Enron stock while encouraging Enron employees to invest their 401(k) retirement plans in the company. Then he suddenly resigns, but not quickly enough to escape Enron's collapse not long after. Televised taking the perp walk in handcuffs, both he and Lay face criminal trials in Texas.

The most shocking material in the film involves the fact that Enron cynically and knowingly created the phony California energy crisis. There was never a shortage of power in California. Using tape recordings of Enron traders on the phone with California power plants, the film chillingly overhears them asking plant managers to "get a little creative" in shutting down plants for "repairs." Between 30 percent and 50 percent of California's energy industry was shut down by Enron a great deal of the time, and up to 76 percent at one point, as the company drove the price of electricity higher by nine times.

We hear Enron traders laughing about "Grandma Millie," a hypothetical victim of the rolling blackouts, and boasting about the millions they made for Enron. As the company goes belly-up, 20,000 employees are fired. Their pensions are gone, their stock worthless. The usual widows and orphans are victimized. A power company lineman in

Portland, who worked for the same utility all his life, observes that his retirement fund was worth $248,000 before Enron bought the utility and looted it, investing its retirement funds in Enron stock. Now, he says, his retirement fund is worth about $1,200.

Strange that there has not been more anger over the Enron scandals. The cost was incalculable, not only in lives lost during the power crisis, but in treasure: The state of California is suing for $6 billion in refunds for energy overcharges collected during the phony crisis. If the crisis had been created by al-Qaida, if terrorists had shut down half of California's power plants, consider how we would regard these same events. Yet the crisis, made possible because of legislation engineered by Enron's lobbyists, is still being blamed on "too much regulation." If there was ever a corporation that needed more regulation, that corporation was Enron.

Early in the film, there's a striking image. We see a vast, empty room, with rows of what look like abandoned lunchroom tables. Then we see the room when it was Enron's main trading floor, with countless computer monitors on the tables and hundreds of traders on the phones. Two vast staircases sweep up from either side of the trading floor to the aeries of Lay and Skilling, whose palatial offices overlook the traders. They look like the stairway to heaven in that old David Niven movie, but at the end they only led down, down, down.

Envy ★ ★
PG-13, 99 m., 2004

Ben Stiller (Tim Dingman), Jack Black (Nick Vanderpark), Rachel Weisz (Debbie Dingman), Amy Poehler (Natalie Vanderpark), Christopher Walken (J-Man), Ariel Gade (Lula Dingman), Lily Jackson (Nellie Vanderpark). Directed by Barry Levinson and produced by Levinson and Paula Weinstein. Screenplay by Steve Adams.

Jack Black becomes a zillionaire named Nick Vanderpark in *Envy*, who gets rich by inventing a product named Vapoorize. Yes, with a double O. It makes doggy-do into doggy-didn't. Spray some on your dog's morning gift and it disappears. His best friend, Tim Dingman, played by Ben Stiller, lives across the street. They share the commute every day to the sandpaper factory. When Vanderpark comes up with the idea for Vapoorize, he offers Dingman a 50 percent share, but Dingman turns it down. He can't figure out how it could possibly work. Soon, of course, he is being eaten alive by envy. My memory for some reason dredged up an ancient science fiction story in which a child's toy would zap little metal objects like paper clips into the fourth dimension. Great, until they started leaking back into our three. When you walk through a speck of paper clip, you can do serious damage. I wondered if maybe the same phenomenon would happen in *Envy*, causing, say, five years of dog poop to reappear all at once. Not a pretty picture.

The plot idea resembles that classic British comedy *The Man in the White Suit*, with Alec Guinness, who invented a fabric that never gets dirty. Of course, Guinness underplayed the comedy, a concept alien to Black and Stiller. Not that we want them to dial down; they're gifted comedians, and it's fun to watch Dingman gnashing while Vanderpark celebrates his untold riches. Vanderpark doesn't lord it over his neighbor; he builds an enormous mansion, yes, but right across the street from his best buddy because he doesn't want to leave the neighborhood. So that every time Dingman looks out the window, he has to witness Vanderpark's latest acquisition: ancient statuary, a proud white stallion, a merry-go-round, whatever.

Because Stiller and Black are in the movie, it contains laughs, and because Christopher Walken is in the movie, it contains more laughs. Walken is becoming Hollywood's version of a relief pitcher who comes on in the seventh and saves the game. You can sense the audience smiling when he appears onscreen.

Here he plays a stumblebum who calls himself J-Man, perhaps in homage to that immortal movie character Z-Man, perhaps not. After Dingman's life melts down, he turns to a saloon for consolation, and finds J-Man standing at the bar ready to provide advice and inspiration. J-Man's dialogue is Walkenized; he says strange things in strange, oracular ways.

So the movie is funny, yes, but not really funny enough. The screenplay, by Steve Adams, reportedly with uncredited input by Larry David, is best at showing a friendship being destroyed by envy, but weak at exploiting the comic potential of the invention itself. It gets sidetracked into the story of how Dingman hits Vanderpark's white horse with a bow and arrow, and we are reminded of the dog set on fire in *There's Something About Mary*. Dingman also hits J-Man with an arrow, although J-Man reacts to this development almost indifferently.

Dingman is married to Debbie (Rachel Weisz) and Vanderpark to Natalie (Amy Poehler), and there is a certain tension when the two families, plus kids, gather for dinner at Vanderpark's palatial mansion. There is also the matter of the fountain that Vanderpark gives to Dingman; it's a nice thought, but it does look a little out of scale with his little suburban home. Meanwhile, there is a certain tension between Dingman and his wife, since Stiller was, after all, *offered* 50 percent of the invention and *refused* it. (That's not the end of it, but I dare not spoil a plot point.)

Toward the end of the film, but not before the final revelations, Dingman has a speech that Stiller delivers with manic comic zeal. Allowing all of his pent-up feelings to explode, he tells Vanderpark what he really thinks about horses and offices and houses and dog poop and having flan for dessert, and his entire being quakes with Stillerian angst. Well done.

But the film, directed by Barry Levinson, doesn't generate heedless glee. Jack Black somehow feels reined in; shaved and barbered, he's lost his anarchic passion and is merely playing a comic role instead of transforming it into a personal mission. Walken, good as he is, isn't used enough by the plot, and Stiller's envy is replaced by plot logistics involving the dead horse, the merry-go-round, and so on, until the characters get mired in the requirements of the screenplay, which lumbers on its way, telling a story that increasingly strays from what was funny to begin with.

Eros
R, 104 m., 2005

The Hand ★ ★ ★ ★

Gong Li (Miss Hua), Chang Chen (Zhang). Directed by Wong Kar Wai and produced by Jacky Pang Yee Wah.

Equilibrium ★ ★ ★

Robert Downey Jr. (Nick Penrose), Alan Arkin (Dr. Pearl). Directed by Steven Soderbergh and produced by Jacques Bar, Raphael Berdugo, Gregory Jacobs, and Stephane Tchal Gadjieff.

The Dangerous Thread of Things ★

Christopher Buchholz (Christopher), Regina Nemni (Cloe), Luisa Ranieri (La Ragazza). Directed by Michelangelo Antonioni and produced by Marcantonio Borghese and Domenico Procacci. Screenplay by Antonioni and Tonino Guerra.

Are the three films in *Eros* intended to be (a) erotic, (b) about eroticism, or (c) both? The directors respond in three different ways. Wong Kar Wai chooses (c), Steven Soderbergh chooses (b), and Michelangelo Antonioni, alas, arrives at None of the Above.

Wong Kar Wai's film, named *The Hand*, stars Gong Li as Miss Hua, a prostitute who is at the top of her game the first time the shy tailor Zhang (Chang Chen) meets her. He has been sent by his boss to design her clothes, and as he waits in her living room he clearly hears the sounds of sex on the other side of the wall. Her client leaves, she summons him, and curtly interrogates him. He passes muster. To be sure he will think about her while designing her clothes, she says, she will supply him with an aid to his memory. This she does; the film's title is a clue.

Steven Soderbergh's film, *Equilibrium,* is a sketch starring Robert Downey Jr. as the neurotic client of Dr. Pearl (Alan Arkin), his psychiatrist. Downey goes through verbal riffs as only Downey can do, moping about a recurring dream. Because the doctor is not in his line of sight, he is unaware that Dr. Pearl, between cursory responses, has seen someone through the window and is eagerly trying to mime the suggestion that they meet later.

Michelangelo Antonioni's film, *The Dangerous Thread of Things,* takes place near a resort on a lake, out of season. A man named Christopher (Christopher Buchholz) and his wife, Cloe (Regina Nemni), stroll and talk and discuss their problems, and then he sees a sexy young woman (Luisa Ranieri), and his wife tells him where she lives.

He goes to visit her, in improbable quarters inside a crumbling medieval tower, and they have sex. She laughs a lot. After he leaves, she does the kind of dance on the beach that hippies used to perform at dawn in Chicago's Lincoln Park back when the world was young and dance standards were more relaxed.

The Wong Kar Wai film is erotic. At least I found it so, and in matters of eroticism one is always the only judge who matters. It has no nudity, no explicit sex, no lingering shots of Gong Li's beauty. It is about situation and personality. She sees him, understands him, creates his obsession with her almost casually. Later, when the tailor comes to measure her again, he uses his hands instead of a tape measure. She allows him. There is an extraordinary scene in his tailor shop where his hands and arms venture inside her dress as if she were wearing it. Time passes. There is a sad and poetic closure.

The Soderbergh film makes the point that few things are more boring than what arouses someone else—unless it also arouses you, of course, in which case you can forget the other person and just get on with it. Downey's dream is all he can think of, but the psychiatrist cannot force himself to listen, and neither can we; it's much more exciting to speculate on the (unseen) object of his hoped-for tryst.

The Antonioni film is an embarrassment. Regina Nemni acts all of her scenes wearing a perfectly transparent blouse for no other reason, I am afraid, than so we can see her breasts. Luisa Ranieri acts mostly in the nude. The result is soft-core porn of the most banal variety, and when the second woman begins to gambol on the beach one yearns for Russ Meyer to come to the rescue. When a woman gambols in the nude in a Meyer film, you stay gamboled with.

I return to Wong Kar Wai's *The Hand*. It stays with me. The characters expand in my memory and imagination. I feel empathy for both of them: Miss Hua, sadly accepting the fading of her beauty, the disappearance of her clients, the loss of her health, and Mr. Zhang, who will always be in her thrall. "I became a tailor because of you," he says. It is the greatest compliment it is within his power to give, and

she knows it. Knows it, and is touched by it as none of the countless words of her countless clients have ever, could ever, touch her.

Eternal Sunshine of the Spotless Mind ★ ★ ★ ½

R, 106 m., 2004

Jim Carrey (Joel Barish), Kate Winslet (Clementine Kruczynski), Kirsten Dunst (Mary), Mark Ruffalo (Stan), Elijah Wood (Patrick), Tom Wilkinson (Dr. Howard Mierzwiak). Directed by Michel Gondry and produced by Anthony Bregman and Steve Golin. Screenplay by Charlie Kaufman.

How happy is the blameless vestal's lot! The world forgetting, by the world forgot. Eternal sunshine of the spotless mind! Each pray'r accepted, and each wish resign'd.
    —Alexander Pope, "Eloisa to Abelard"

It's one thing to wash that man right outta your hair, and another to erase him from your mind. *Eternal Sunshine of the Spotless Mind* imagines a scientific procedure that can obliterate whole fields of memory—so that, for example, Clementine can forget that she ever met Joel, let alone fell in love with him. "Is there any danger of brain damage?" the inventor of the process is asked. "Well," he allows, in his most kindly voice, "technically speaking, the procedure *is* brain damage."

The movie is a labyrinth created by the screenwriter Charlie Kaufman, whose *Being John Malkovich* and *Adaptation* were neorealism compared to this. Jim Carrey and Kate Winslet play Joel and Clementine, in a movie that sometimes feels like an endless series of aborted Meet Cutes. That they lose their minds while all about them are keeping theirs is a tribute to their skill; they center their characters so that we can actually care about them even when they're constantly losing track of their own lives. ("My journal . . . ," Joel observes oddly, "is . . . just blank.")

The movie is a radical example of maze cinema, that style in which the story coils back upon itself, redefining everything and then throwing it up in the air and redefining it again. To reconstruct it in chronological order would be cheating, but I will cheat: At some point before the technical beginning of the movie, Joel and Clementine were in love, and their affair ended badly, and Clementine went to Dr. Howard Mierzwiak (Tom Wilkinson) at Lacuna Inc., to have Joel erased from her mind.

Discovering this, Joel in revenge applies to have *his* memories of her erased. But the funny thing about love is, it can survive the circumstances of its ending; we remember good times better than bad ones, and Joel decides in midprocess that maybe he would like to remember Clementine after all. He tries to squirrel away some of his memories in hidden corners of his mind, but the process is implacable.

If you think this makes the movie sound penetrable, you have no idea. As the movie opens, Joel is seized with an inexplicable compulsion to ditch work and take the train to Montauk, and on the train he meets Clementine. For all they know they have never seen each other before, but somehow there's a connection, a distant shadow of déjà vu. During the course of the film, which moves freely, dizzyingly, forward and backward in time, they will each experience fragmentary versions of relationships they had, might have had, or might be having.

Meanwhile, back at the Lacuna head office, there are more complications. Lacuna (www. lacunainc.com) seems to be a prosperous and growing firm (it advertises a Valentine's Day special), but in reality it consists only of the avuncular Dr. Mierzwiak and his team of assistants: Stan (Mark Ruffalo), Patrick (Elijah Wood), and Mary (Kirsten Dunst). There are innumerable complications involving them, which I will not describe because it would not only be unfair to reveal the plot but probably impossible.

Eternal Sunshine has been directed by Michel Gondry, a music video veteran whose first feature, *Human Nature* (2002), also written by Kaufman, had a lunacy that approached genius and then veered away. Tim Robbins starred as an overtrained child who devotes his adult life to teaching table manners to white mice. The scene where the male mouse politely pulls out the chair for the female to sit down is without doubt in a category of its own.

Despite jumping through the deliberately disorienting hoops of its story, *Eternal Sunshine* has an emotional center, and that's what makes it work. Although Joel and Clementine ping-

pong through various stages of romance and reality, what remains constant is the human need for love and companionship, and the human compulsion to keep seeking it despite all odds. It may also be true that Joel and Clementine, who seem to be such opposites (he is shy and compulsive; she is extroverted and even wild), might be a good match for each other, and so if they keep on meeting they will keep on falling in love, and Lacuna Inc. may have to be replaced with the Witness Protection Program.

For Jim Carrey, this is another successful attempt, like *The Truman Show* and the underrated *The Majestic*, to extend himself beyond screwball comedy. He has an everyman appeal, and here he dials down his natural energy to give us a man who is so lonely and needy that a fragment of memory is better than none at all. Kate Winslet is the right foil for him, exasperated by Joel's peculiarities while paradoxically fond of them. The shenanigans back at Lacuna belong on a different level of reality, but even there, secrets are revealed that are oddly touching.

Charlie Kaufman's mission seems to be the penetration of the human mind. His characters journeyed into the skull of John Malkovich, and there is a good possibility that two of them were inhabiting the same body in *Adaptation*. But both of those movies were about characters trying to achieve something outside themselves. The insight of *Eternal Sunshine* is that, at the end of the day, our memories are all we really have, and when they're gone, we're gone.

Everybody Says I'm Fine ★ ★
NO MPAA RATING, 103 m., 2004

Rehaan Engineer (Xen), Koel Purie (Nikita), Rahul Bose (Rage), Pooja Bhatt (Tanya), Anahita Oberoi (Misha), Boman Irani (Mr. Mittal), Sharokh Bharucha (Bobby), Juneli Aguiar (Tina). Directed by Rahul Bose and produced by Viveck Vaswani. Screenplay by Bose.

The English-language Indian film *Everybody Says I'm Fine* is too cluttered and busy, but as a glimpse into the affluent culture of a country with economic extremes, it's intriguing. Occasionally, it's funny and moving, too. The movie was shot in English not for the export market, but for India's domestic English speakers, who tend to be toward the top of the economic scale and are beginning to tire of endless Bollywood megaproductions. This film, at 103 minutes, almost qualifies in its market as a short subject, although true to Bollywood tradition it does include one completely arbitrary and inexplicable song-and-dance sequence.

Rehaan Engineer stars as Xen, a hairdresser whose parents died tragically when the sound board short-circuited in their recording studio. The trauma has left him with a psychic gift: When he cuts a person's hair, he can read the person's thoughts. He learns of adulteries, deceptions, and hypocrisies, and keeps them all to himself, going upstairs after work to his lonely room, where the shades are never opened and the TV sound is muted.

One day a pretty woman named Nikita (Koel Purie) arrives in his chair, and he picks up nothing. No thoughts. Is her mind a blank? He has acted as a matchmaker for some of his other customers whom he learns are attracted to one another, but now here is a challenge for him.

If the story had stayed more or less focused on Xen and his adventures, it might have been more involving, but it strays outside the salon to tell other stories, including one about a beautiful wife who has been left abandoned and penniless by her faithless husband, and a snoopy friend who has secrets of her own. There is also a flamboyant actor named Rage, played by director Rahul Bose, whose desperate attempts to find work are reflected by his bizarre hairstyles.

Movies like this are intrinsically interesting for the way they regard the culture they are immersed in, one where a Domino's pizza across the street coexists with crowds of desperate beggars. I enjoyed watching it just for the information and attitudes it contained, but as a story, it's too disorganized to really involve us.

The Eye ★ ★ ½
NO MPAA RATING, 99 m., 2003

Lee Sin-Je (Mun), Lawrence Chou (Dr. Wah), Chutcha Rujinanon (Ling), Yut Lai So (Yingying), Candy Lo (Yee), Yin Ping Ko (Mun's Grandmother), Pierre Png (Dr. Eak), Edmund Chen (Dr. Lo). Directed by Oxide Pang Chun

and Danny Pang and produced by Lawrence Cheng. Screenplay by Jo Jo Yuet-chun Hui, Pang Chun, and Pang.

The Eye is a thriller about a blind young violinist from Hong Kong whose sight is restored through surgery, but who can then see a little too well, so that she observes the grim reaper leading the doomed in solemn procession to the other side, and shares the anguish of the donor of her eyes. What's more, she's thrown out of the blind orchestra now that she can see.

All I know about restored sight I learned in the books of Oliver Sacks, who writes about a patient whose sight was miraculously restored. The problem turns out to be knowing what you're looking at. Babies do all the hard work in the first months after birth, learning to interpret shapes and colors, dimension and distance. For an adult who relates to the world through the other four senses, the addition of sight is not always a blessing.

The movie touches on that, in a scene where the blind girl, named Mun (Lee Sin-Je) is shown a stapler and asked what it is. She can tell by feeling it. But she's a quick study, and in no time is moving independently through the world and falling in love with Dr. Wah, her handsome young therapist (Lawrence Chou).

Lee has an expressive face, which is crucial to the success of the film, because she has an extraordinary number of reaction shots, and no wonder: The movie is about what Mun sees and how she reacts to it. Unlike the overwrought heroines of most women-in-danger films, Mun is quiet, introspective, reasonable, and persuasive.

Perhaps that's why Dr. Wah believes her. She becomes convinced that she can see the dead leaving this Earth and anticipate tragedies before they happen. She thinks this may be connected in some way with the donor of her new eyes, and Dr. Wah begins to believe her, not least because he falls in love with her. His uncle, Dr. Lo (Edmund Chen), takes a jaundiced view of this development, which violates medical ethics and perhaps common sense, and refuses to divulge the name of the donor.

But Wah and Mun eventually do figure out that the corneas came from a girl in Thailand, and journey there for a conclusion that includes a startling scene of carnage that's all the more unexpected because it comes at the end of a relatively quiet and inward movie.

The Eye is better than it might have been, especially in moments of terror involving Mun's ability to see what no one else can see, and in her relationship with a little girl at the hospital who seems to be dying, and becomes her special friend. But the notion that body parts retain the memories of their owners is an outworn horror cliché, as in *The Beast with Five Fingers* and Oliver Stone's early screenplay, *The Hand*. This is the kind of movie you happen across on TV, and linger to watch out of curiosity, but its inspired moments serve only to point out how routine, and occasionally how slow and wordy, the rest of it is.

Eyes Without a Face ★ ★ ★ ½
NO MPAA RATING, 88 m., 1960 (rereleased 2003)

Pierre Brasseur (Professor Génessier), Alida Valli (Louise), Edith Scob (Christiane Génessier), Juliette Mayniel (Edna Gruberg), François Guérin (Jacques Vernon), Alexandre Rignault (Detective Parot), Béatrice Altariba (Paulette Merodon). Directed by Georges Franju and produced by Jules Borkon. Screenplay by Pierre Boileau, Pierre Gascar, Thomas Narcejac, Jean Redon, and Claude Sautet, based on the novel by Redon.

"I've done so much wrong to perform this miracle."

Professor Génessier has good reason for remorse. He is a Parisian plastic surgeon, respected in the profession, a lecturer on the subject of "heterografting," which involves transferring living tissue from one person to another. The downside to this procedure is that it requires both persons to be alive. Having destroyed the face of his daughter in a reckless car accident, he now wants to repair the damage by transplanting the face of another woman. The "miracle" he refers to involves the face of his lover, nurse, and assistant, Louise. He has restored her face so successfully that she now looks just like Alida Valli, who played Harry Lime's lover in *The Third Man*. Valli's characters have bad luck on dates.

Génessier (Pierre Brasseur) is the mad scientist at the heart of *Eyes without a Face* (1960), Georges Franju's merciless horror classic, now being revived in a new 35-mm print. The professor was presumably at one time a reputable plastic surgeon, but now, in his isolated suburban mansion, he experiments on dogs, birds, and helpless young women who are supplied to him by the faithful Louise. One of the startling elements of the film is how graphic it is about his procedures; we see bloody incisions being made all around a victim's face, and when one transplant is interrupted by a visit with the police, he leaves the skin flaps open and waiting, secured by surgical implements.

The film opens with Louise on a nocturnal mission for the doctor, driving a corpse to the Seine and dumping it in. This is the latest victim of a failed procedure. Since Génessier's great success with Louise, his work has not gone well, and soon he sends her out to kidnap another woman. His daughter, Christiane (Edith Scob), waits sedated in a locked room, her flayed face concealed by a mask so that only her eyes move. Having reported Christiane missing after the accident, Génessier identifies the dead woman in the river as his daughter, and prepares to remove the face of the new victim, Paulette (Béatrice Altariba).

The film is done in a sober, muted style, with stark black-and-whites and the bizarre camera angles much loved by *film noir*. Notice a scene in the cemetery, where the doctor has gone to conceal a body in his own family tomb. At the cemetery gate, a shriek of dead branches against the sky dominates the composition, so that humans seem diminished beneath their stark outline. There is surrealism here, and in the oddly shaped cages that contain his experimental dogs, and the way his mansion seems at once enormous (with limitless corridors) and so small we can hear the dogs from the garage. The matter-of-fact way he presents the outrageous is in the tradition of Buñuel, who felt that the only response to the shocking was to refuse to be shocked by it.

Franju (1912–1987) was a cofounder of the Cinematheque Francaise, worked during the war to hide its treasures from the Nazis, and began making features only in 1949. He worked mostly in the horror genre (*Eyes without a Face* was originally released in North America as *The Horror Chamber of Dr. Faustus,* although it contained no chamber and no Faust). He is concerned with mood, not story, and so this

207

film ends not with a conventional resolution but with an image that could have come from a painting by Dali: The faceless daughter wanders into the wood, surrounded by doves.

One of the tasks faced by serious filmgoers is to distinguish good films in disreputable genres. It is insufferable to claim you "never" see horror movies (or Westerns, musicals, war movies, teenage romances, or slasher pictures). You're presenting ignorance as taste. The trick is to find the good ones. The French auteur critics did a lot of helpful spadework, resurrecting genres and rehabilitating reputations, but they were not always right—and besides, you have to feel it for yourself. If a film holds my attention, it is in one way or another a good one. If it moves or delights me, it may be great. If I am distracted by its conventions, obligatory scenes and carelessness, or lack of ambition, it deserves to be tossed back into the genre.

Eyes without a Face passes my test. It riveted me with its story—or rather, with its lack of one. There is no sense of a conclusion on the way, but more of a sense that the professor may remain forever in his operating theater, slicing off faces while his daughter goes mad. It moved me because the daughter, once she understands what is happening, is more heartbroken over her father's victims than over her own fate. On this foundation Franju constructs an elegant visual work; here is a horror movie in which the shrieks are not by the characters but by the images.

F

Fahrenheit 9/11 ★ ★ ★ ½
R, 110 m., 2004

A documentary directed and produced by
Michael Moore.

Michael Moore's *Fahrenheit 9/11* is less an exposé of George W. Bush than a dramatization
of what Moore sees as a failed and dangerous
presidency. The charges in the film will not
come as news to those who pay attention to
politics, but Moore illustrates them with dramatic images and a relentless commentary
track that essentially concludes Bush is incompetent, dishonest, failing in the war on terrorism, and has bad taste in friends.

Although Moore's narration ranges from
outrage to sarcasm, the most devastating passage in the film speaks for itself. That's when
Bush, who was reading *My Pet Goat* to a classroom of Florida children, is notified of the second attack on the World Trade Center, and yet
lingers with the kids for almost seven minutes
before finally leaving the room. His inexplicable paralysis wasn't underlined in news reports
at the time, and only Moore thought to contact
the teacher in that schoolroom—who, as it
turned out, had made her own video of the
visit. The expression on Bush's face as he sits
there is odd indeed.

Bush, here and elsewhere in the film, is characterized as a man who owes a lot to his friends,
including those who helped bail him out of
business ventures. Moore places particular emphasis on what he sees as a long-term friendship between the Bush family (including both
presidents) and powerful Saudi Arabians. More
than $1.4 billion in Saudi money has flowed
into the coffers of Bush family enterprises, he
says, and after 9/11 the White House helped expedite flights out of the country carrying,
among others, members of the Bin Laden family (which disowns its most famous member).

Moore examines the military records released by Bush to explain his disappearance
from the Texas Air National Guard, and finds
that the name of another pilot has been blacked
out. This pilot, he learns, was Bush's close
friend James R. Bath, who became Texas money
manager for the billionaire Bin Ladens. An-

other indication of the closeness of the Bushes
and the Saudis: The law firm of James Baker, the
secretary of state for Bush's father, was hired by
the Saudis to defend them against a suit by a
group of 9/11 victims and survivors, who
charged that the Saudis had financed al-Qaida.

To Moore, this is more evidence that Bush
has an unhealthy relationship with the Saudis,
and that it may have influenced his decision to
go to war against Iraq at least partially on their
behalf. The war itself Moore considers un-
justified (no WMDs, no Hussein–Bin Laden
link), and he talks with American soldiers, including amputees, who complain bitterly about
Bush's proposed cuts of military salaries at the
same time he was sending them into a war that
they (at least, the ones Moore spoke to) hated.
Moore also shows American military personnel
who are apparently enjoying the war; he has
footage of soldiers who use torture techniques
not in a prison but in the field, where they hood
an Iraqi prisoner, call him "Ali Baba," and pose
for videos while touching his genitals.

Moore brings a fresh impact to familiar material by the way he marshals his images. We are
all familiar with the controversy over the 2000
election, which was settled by the U.S. Supreme
Court. What I hadn't seen before was footage of
the ratification of Bush's election by the U.S.
Congress. An election can be debated at the request of one senator and one representative;
ten representatives rise to challenge it, but not a
single senator. As Moore shows the challengers,
one after another, we cannot help noting that
they are eight black women, one Asian woman,
and one black man. They are all gaveled into silence by the chairman of the joint congressional session—Vice President Al Gore. The
urgency and futility of the scene reawaken old
feelings for those who believe Bush is an illegitimate president.

Fahrenheit 9/11 opens on a note not unlike
Moore's earlier films, such as *Roger & Me* and
Bowling for Columbine. Moore, as narrator,
brings humor and sarcasm to his comments,
and occasionally appears onscreen in a gadfly
role. It's vintage Moore, for example, when he
brings along a marine who refused to return to
Iraq; together, they confront congressmen, urging them to have their children enlist in the

service. And he makes good use of candid footage, including eerie video showing Bush practicing facial expressions before going live with his address to the nation about 9/11.

Apparently Bush and other members of his administration don't know what every TV reporter knows—that a satellite image can be live before they get the cue to start talking. That accounts for the quease-inducing footage of Deputy Defense Secretary Paul Wolfowitz wetting his pocket comb in his mouth before slicking back his hair. When that doesn't do it, he spits in his hand and wipes it down. If his mother is alive, I hope for his sake she doesn't see this film.

Such scenes are typical of vintage Moore, catching his subjects off-guard. But his film grows steadily darker, and Moore largely disappears from it, as he focuses on people such as Lila Lipscomb, from Moore's hometown of Flint, Michigan; she reads a letter from her son, written days before he was killed in Iraq. It urges his family to work for Bush's defeat.

Fahrenheit 9/11 is unashamedly partisan: Moore dislikes and distrusts Bush, and wants to motivate his viewers to vote against him. Whether his film will make a big difference is debatable, since it's likely most of the audience members will be in agreement with Moore. We tend to choose films that support our decisions, not those that challenge them. Moore's complaints are familiar to those who share his opinion of Bush; they seem to have had little effect on Bush's supporters. If the film does have an effect on the election, as Moore fervently hopes, it will be because it energizes and motivates those who already plan to vote against the president.

Fahrenheit 9/11 is a compelling and persuasive film, at odds with the White House effort to present Bush as a strong leader. He comes across as a shallow, inarticulate man, simplistic in speech and inauthentic in manner. If the film is not quite as electrifying as Moore's *Bowling for Columbine,* that may be because Moore has toned down his usual exuberance and was sobered by attacks on the factual accuracy of elements of *Columbine;* playing with larger stakes, he is more cautious here, and we get an op-ed piece, not a stand-up routine. But he remains one of the most valuable figures on the

political landscape, a populist rabble-rouser, humorous and effective; the outrage and incredulity in his film are exhilarating responses to Bush's determined repetition of the same stubborn sound bites. ☞

Fat Albert ★ ★
PG, 93 m., 2004

Kenan Thompson (Fat Albert), Kyla Pratt (Doris Roberts), Dania Ramirez (Lauri), Shedrack Anderson III (Rudy), Jermaine Williams (Mushmouth), Keith Robinson (Bill), Alphonso McAuley (Bucky), Aaron Frazier (Old Weird Harold), Marques Houston (Dumb Donald). Directed by Joel Zwick and produced by John Davis. Screenplay by Bill Cosby and Charles Kipps.

Now here is a movie for which the words "good-hearted" come straight into mind. It takes the characters of Bill Cosby's *Fat Albert* TV cartoon show from the 1970s, and sends them popping magically out of the TV screen and into the life of a teenage girl—where, hey-hey-hey, they give her advice that has always worked for them in Toonland.

It's ingenious in the way it shows the cartoon characters amazed by the real world (hey-hey-hey, they learn from a poster in a video store that they're on a "de-ved," or however you say "DVD"). But in a season where the standards have been set for animated entertainment by *The Polar Express* and *The Incredibles,* I don't think *Fat Albert* is up to speed; in its meandering, low-key way, it seems destined more for a future on de-ved, returning to the video world where the characters say they feel more at home.

Kyla Pratt plays Doris, a high school student who is pretty and smart but lacks self-confidence and feels left out of things. There's a big party tonight (a rich kid's father is blocking off the street), but she's not invited. Oh, she was kinda included in an invitation to her popular foster sister, Lauri (Dania Ramirez), but that's not the same thing.

Doris comes home, turns on the TV, and sheds a single tear, which falls onto the TV screen and creates a portal in space, time, and reality. On the *Fat Albert* TV show, in a

Philadelphia junk yard, the characters see this glistening sphere floating in midair, take a reckless chance by jumping through it, and find themselves in Doris's living room.

Many movies have inserted cartoon characters into the real world, but usually while still representing them as cartoons, as in *Roger Rabbit, Space Jam,* and *Garfield.* In *Fat Albert,* the toons become real humans, played by actors who look amazingly like their TV counterparts, including Kenan Thompson of *Saturday Night Live,* who wears a padded costume that makes him look not like an actual fat kid, but like a cartoon fat kid who is round in all the right places and has a belt around the equator that looks drawn on. (In a poignant sequence at the very end of the film, we discover that the toons also look like Bill Cosby's real-life childhood friends, who inspired *Fat Albert and the Cosby Kids.*)

Doris, who is worried about her popularity, isn't thrilled to be joined by cartoonish caricatures like Fat Albert, Mushmouth (Jermaine Williams), Bucky (Alphonso McAuley), Old Weird Harold (Aaron Frazier), Dumb Donald (Marques Houston), and Rudy (Shedrack Anderson III). Nor are they exactly thrilled to be in the real world, where things work different than in a cartoon. They try to jump back into the screen, but the *Fat Albert* show is over, and they deduce that the magic portal opens only while they're on the air; that means they have to stick around for twenty-four hours. Alas, the bright colors of their costumes seem to be slowly fading away, as if they're losing their unreality.

There's an awkward little subplot in which Fat Albert gets a crush on Lauri, a strange moment when Dumb Donald reveals that he wears a hood "because I haven't got a face," and lots of scenes in which Doris's low self-esteem is boosted by the Cosby Kids' hey-hey-hey style of positive thinking.

The movie is sweet and gentle, but not very compelling. All but its younger viewers will be expecting a little more excitement along with Fat Albert's genial encouragement of Doris. And I was wondering, as I always do with plot devices like this, why the human characters deal so calmly with the appearance of toons. Yes, Doris is surprised when the Fat Albert

gang pops through her TV set, but isn't that event more than just . . . surprising? Isn't it *incredibly amazing?* When the laws of the physical universe as we know them are fundamentally violated, shouldn't it be for more earth-shaking purposes than to cheer up Doris?

Fear and Trembling ★ ★ ★
NO MPAA RATING, 107 m., 2005

Sylvie Testud (Amelie), Kaori Tsuji (Fubuki), Taro Suwa (Monsieur Saito), Bison Katayama (Monsieur Omochi), Yasunari Kondo (Monsieur Tenshi), Sokyu Fujita (Monsieur Haneda), Gen Shimaoka (Monsieur Unaji). Directed by Alain Corneau and produced by Alain Sarde and based on the novel by Amelie Nothomb.

The opening shot of *Fear and Trembling* shows the heroine at the age of five, sitting at the edge of the ancient rock garden at the Ryoanji Zen temple in Kyoto. This is an elegant arrangement of rocks on a surface of smooth pebbles. They are so placed that no matter where you sit, you can't see all of them at the same time. Some see the garden as a metaphor for Japanese society, intricately arranged so that it looks harmonious from every viewpoint, but is never all visible at once.

The heroine, whose name is Amelie, returns with her parents to her native Belgium. But she has fallen in love with Japan, and at the age of twenty, she returns to take a job with a vast corporation and "become a real Japanese." Now played by Sylvie Testud as a college graduate who speaks perfect Japanese, she is hired as a translator and assigned to work under the beautiful Fubuki (Kaori Tsuji). She idolizes this woman, so beautiful, so flawless, so tall—too tall, probably, to ever marry, Amelie reflects.

The story of her year at the Yumimoto Corp., based on a semiautobiographical novel by Amelie Nothomb, is the story of a Westerner who speaks flawless Japanese but in another sense does not understand Japanese at all. In one way after another she commits social errors, misreads signals, violates taboos, and has her fellow workers wondering, she is told, "how the nice white geisha became a rude Yankee." That she is Belgian makes her no less a Yankee from the Japanese point of view; what is important is that she is not Japanese.

Consider her first blunder. She is ordered to serve coffee to visiting executives in a conference room. As she passes around the cups, she quietly says, "Enjoy your coffee." Soon after she leaves the room, the visitors walk out in anger, and Omochi (Bison Katayama), the boss of the boss of her boss, screams, "Who is this girl? Why does she speak Japanese?" But, she says, she was *hired* because she speaks Japanese. "How could they discuss secret matters in front of a foreigner who speaks Japanese?" the boss of her boss screams. "You no longer speak Japanese!"

She argues that it is impossible for her to forget how to speak Japanese, but this is taken as an example of her inability to understand Japan. She learns quickly that the corporate hierarchy is unbending: "You may only address your immediate superior, me," says Fubuki. Eager to find a role, Amelie begins to distribute the mail, only to find she is taking the job of the mailman. She assigns herself to updating every calendar in the office, but is told to stop because it is a distraction. That's a shame, because she finds she enjoys her simple tasks. "How silly I was to get a college degree," she says in the narration, "when my mind was satisfied by mindless repetition. How nice it was to live without pride or brains!" Eventually she is assigned to clean the toilets.

This is indeed a woman who is lost in translation. But how accurate is this portrait of Japanese corporate life? I searched for a review from Japan, but wasn't able to find one. My guess is that an actual Japanese corporation has been transformed here through a satirical filter into an exaggeration of basic truths: There is a hierarchy, there is suspicion of foreigners, no one who is not Japanese can ever possibly understand the Japanese, etc. Donald Richie has lived in Japan for most of the last fifty-six years and written invaluable books about its society and films; he was able to relax and adjust, he writes in his recently published journals, only when he realized that he would always be an invisible outsider, exempt from social laws because he was not expected to be able to understand them.

Fear and Trembling, directed by Alain Corneau, may be a sardonic view of Japanese corporate culture, but that's not all it is. The movie is also subtly sexual and erotic, despite the fact that almost every scene takes place in the office and there is not a single overt sexual act or word or gesture or reference. Sexuality in the movie's terms is transferred into the power of one person over another; Amelie begins by adoring Fubuki, but eventually realizes that the other woman hates her and is jealous of her as a competitor. Fubuki finds her one demeaning task after another, and Amelie responds simply by—doing them. By submitting.

This response has a quietly stimulating result for Fubuki, who is aroused by the other woman's submission. The brilliance of the movie is to suppress all expression of this arousal; we have to sense it in small moments of body language, in almost imperceptible pauses or reactions, in the rhythm set up between command and obedience. Understanding Fubuki better than she understands herself, Amelie is eventually able to win the game by becoming so submissive, so much in fear of the taller, more powerful woman, that a kind of erotic release takes place. She exaggerates the "fear and trembling" that, it is said, one should exhibit when addressing the emperor.

The movie that comes to mind is *Secretary*, the 2002 film with James Spader as a lawyer whose new secretary, played by Maggie Gyllenhaal, gradually enters with him in an S&M relationship that she, as the submissive one, finds a source of power (and amusement). Much the same thing happens in *Fear and Trembling*; that it happens below the level of what is said and done and acknowledged makes it doubly erotic because it cannot be admitted or acknowledged. The film ends again in the Kyoto rock garden, whose message is perhaps: If you could see all the rocks at once, what would be the point of the garden?

Fellini: I'm a Born Liar ★ ★ ½
NO MPAA RATING, 105 m., 2003

With Roberto Benigni, Italo Calvino, Federico Fellini, Donald Sutherland, Terence Stamp, and Giuseppe Rotunno. A documentary directed by

Damian Pettigrew and produced by Olivier Gal. Screenplay by Pettigrew and Gal.

Federico Fellini created a world that was gloriously his own, and there is scarcely a shot—certainly not a scene—in his work that doesn't announce its maker. That's also true of Hitchcock, Ozu, Tati, and a few other filmmakers; their work gives us the impression, somehow, of being in their presence.

Fellini: I'm a Born Liar is a documentary centering on a lengthy interview Fellini gave to the filmmakers in 1993, shortly before his death. As a source of information about his life and work, this interview is almost worthless, but as an insight into his style, it is priceless. Having interviewed the master twice, once on the location of his *Fellini Satyricon*, I was reminded of his gift for spinning fables that pretend to be about his work but are actually fabricated from thin air.

Consider, for example, the way he confides to the camera that he gets on very well with actors, because he loves them and understands them. Then listen to two of the actors he worked with, Donald Sutherland and Terence Stamp, who recall the experience as if their skins are still crawling.

Fellini, we learn, sometimes gave no direction at all, expecting his actors to intuit his desires. At other times (seen in footage of the director at work) he stood next to the camera and verbally instructed his actors on every move and nuance. This was possible because he often didn't record sound, preferring to dub the dialogue later, and some of his actors simply counted, "one, two, three," knowing the words would be supplied. It is clear that Stamp and Sutherland did not enjoy the experience, and so much did Fellini treat them like his puppets that at one point Sutherland says "Fellini" when he means his own character.

The actor he worked with most often and successfully, Marcello Mastroianni, was the most cooperative: "He would turn up tired in the morning, sleep between takes, and do whatever Fellini told him to do without complaining." That this approach created the two best male performances in Fellini's work (in *La Dolce Vita* and *8½*) argues that Mastroianni may have been onto something.

The documentary includes many clips from Fellini's work, none of them identified, although his admirers will recognize them immediately. And we revisit some of the original locations, including a vast field with strange concrete walls (or are they crypts?) where Fellini's hero helped his father climb down into a grave in *8½*.

The movie does not do justice to Fellini's love of sensuous excess, both in his films and in his life, although when he says he "married the right woman . . . for a man like me" he may be telling us something. The film assumes such familiarity with Fellini that although that woman, the actress Giulietta Masina, is seen more than once, she is never identified.

No doubt the existence of the extended Fellini interview is the movie's reason for existing, and yet it is less than helpful. Fellini is maddeningly nonspecific, weaves abstractions into clouds of fancy, rarely talks about specific films, actors, or locations. When he mentions his childhood home of Rimini, it is to observe that the Rimini in his films is more real to him. And so it should be, but why not even a word about his youthful days as a cartoonist, hustling on the Via Veneto for assignments? Why no mention of his apprenticeship in neorealism? Why not a word about the collapse and death of the Rome studio system?

I love Fellini, and so I was happy to see this film, and able to add it to my idea of his charming but elusive personality. But if you know little about Fellini, this is not the place to start. Begin with the films. They are filled with joy, abundance, and creativity. You cannot call yourself a serious filmgoer and not know them.

Fever Pitch ★ ★ ★ ½
PG-13, 98 m., 2005

Drew Barrymore (Lindsey Meeks), Jimmy Fallon (Ben Wrightman). Directed by Bobby Farrelly and Peter Farrelly and produced by Drew Barrymore, Alan Greenspan, Nancy Juvonen, Gil Netter, Amanda Posey, and Bradley Thomas. Screenplay by Lowell Ganz and Babaloo Mandel, based on the book by Nick Hornby.

It must be Nick Hornby who understands men so well, and how they think about women, and how women think about them. His books have been the starting point for three wonderful movies about the truce of the sexes: *High Fidelity* (2000), *About a Boy* (2002), and now *Fever Pitch*. Their humor all begins in the same place, with truth and close observation. We know these people. We dated these people. We are these people.

Because *Fever Pitch* involves a Boston Red Sox fan and takes place during the miraculous 2004 season, do not make the mistake of thinking it is a baseball movie. It is a movie about how men and women, filled with love and motivated by the best will in the world, simply do not speak the same emotional language. She cannot understand why he would rather go to spring training camp in Florida than meet her parents. He cannot understand why this is even an issue.

Drew Barrymore and Jimmy Fallon star, as Lindsey and Ben, both around thirty. She thinks it may be time to get married. He already seems married, to the Red Sox. His love for the team, he confesses to her, "has been a problem with me . . . and women." She is a high-paid business executive. He is a high school teacher.

Should she date below her income level? She has a strategy meeting with her girlfriends. When men have these meetings, they talk about how a woman really understands them. Women talk about how a man doesn't really understand them. Men talk about how a woman looks. Women ask questions like: "Where has he been?" Ben is thirty and single. Lindsey at least *knows* why she's still single: She works all the time.

Their first date begins unpromisingly, with food poisoning and Lindsey hurling into a garbage can. But Ben is a nice guy and cleans up, puts her to bed, sleeps on the couch. In no time at all, they're in love. What she doesn't understand is, she's in love with Winter Guy.

Summer Guy is a Red Sox fan. She is from Venus; he is from Fenway Park. He has season tickets. The people in the nearby seats are his "summer family." When they talk Red Sox lore, it sounds like they know what they're talking about. When he considers selling his season tickets, they observe that "technically" he's supposed to return them to the team. His apartment looks like a sports memorabilia store. Even the telephone is made out of a baseball mitt. She looks at the T-shirts and

warm-up jackets in his closet, and says, "This is not a man's closet."

Jimmy Fallon is perfectly cast in the role. *Saturday Night Live* veterans tend to disappear into the fourth dimension of "*SNL* comedies" that are usually pretty bad. Only occasionally does someone like Bill Murray find a wider range of roles. Fallon was recently in the awful *Taxi*, but here it must be said (as it could be said about John Cusack in *High Fidelity* and Hugh Grant in *About a Boy*) that you cannot imagine anyone else in the role. He achieves a kind of perfection in his high spirits, his boyish enthusiasm, his dependence on the Sox for a purpose in his life, and his bafflement about romance. He doesn't know that Freud's dying words were allegedly, "Women! What do they want?" But he would have understood them.

Drew Barrymore is also perfectly cast, in part because in real life, as in the movie, she's not only adorable but also a high-powered businesswoman (she is listed first among the film's producers). Her Lindsey likes Ben because he is a good and nice man, funny, considerate, and sexy. That's the Winter Guy. The Summer Guy is also all of those things, when his busy schedule as a Red Sox fan permits him. "All those things you feel for that team," she tells him in despair, "I feel them too, for you."

Well, come on. Think how the guy feels. The Sox are down 0-3 to the Yankees in the AL playoffs and behind in the fourth and apparently final game. He's at a party she wanted him to attend. He has a great time at the party, until he finds out *the Red Sox tied it up and won 6–4 in the 12th inning!* That will be a moment that he will always, always regret missing. Is he a fool? I would like to say that he is, but if I hadn't seen the final four minutes of the Illinois game against Arizona, *when they came from 15 behind to tie it up and win in overtime!* I would have been . . . discontented.

Yes, it's only a game. There's a bright little boy in the movie who says to Ben: "Let me just leave you with this thought. You love the Sox, but have they ever loved you back?" Lindsey loves him back. But one transgression follows another. Consider her thoughts as she watches the TV news, which shows her being hit by a foul ball and knocked out, while next to her Ben jumps up and down in excitement and hasn't noticed his girl is unconscious. Women remember things like that.

The movie has been directed by the Farrelly brothers, Peter and Bobby, who tend to make a different kind of movie (*Dumb and Dumber, Kingpin, There's Something About Mary, Stuck on You*). Here, they're sensitive and warm-hearted, never push too hard, empathize with the characters, allow Lindsey and Ben to become people we care about. What's going on? first Danny (*Trainspotting*) Boyle makes *Millions*, and now this. Maybe the Farrellys were helped by the script by Lowell Ganz and Babaloo Mandel, who have nine children between them, and whose writing collaborations include *Parenthood, Forget Paris*, and *A League of Their Own*, which knew a lot about baseball.

What's really touching is the way Lindsey works and works to try to understand Ben. When he tries to tell her why he loves the Red Sox even though they always, always let him down, she says: "You have a lyrical soul. You can live under the best and worst conditions." What she doesn't understand is that the girlfriend of a Red Sox fan must also endure the best and the worst, and have a soul not only lyrical but forgiving. How does it feel when his Sox tickets are *always* more important than *anything* she suggests? "Here's a tip, Ben," she says. "When your girlfriend says let's go to Paris for the weekend—you go." ☞

50 First Dates ★ ★ ★
PG-13, 96 m., 2004

Adam Sandler (Henry Roth), Drew Barrymore (Lucy Whitmore), Rob Schneider (Ula), Lusia Strus (Assistant Alexa), Blake Clark (Marlin Whitmore), Sean Astin (Doug Whitmore), Dan Aykroyd (Dr. Keats). Directed by Peter Segal and produced by Jack Giarraputo, Steve Golin, Nancy Juvonen, Larry Kennar, and Adam Sandler. Screenplay by George Wing.

50 First Dates is a spin on the *Groundhog Day* notion of a day that keeps repeating itself. This time, though, the recycling takes place entirely inside the mind of Lucy Whitmore (Drew Barrymore), who was in an accident that caused short-term memory loss. Every night while she sleeps, the slate of her memory is wiped clean, and when she wakes up in the morning she remembers everything that happened up to the moment of the accident, but nothing that happened afterward.

Is this possible? I'd like to bring in Oliver Sacks for a second opinion. Seems to me that short-term memory loss doesn't work on a daily timetable, but is more like the affliction of Ten-Second Tom, a character in the movie who reboots every ten seconds. Still, this isn't a psychiatric docudrama but a lighthearted romantic comedy, and the premise works to provide Adam Sandler and Barrymore with a sweet story. They work well together, as they showed in *The Wedding Singer*. They have the same tone of smiling, coy sincerity.

The movie is sort of an experiment for Sandler. He reveals the warm side of his personality, and leaves behind the hostility, anger, and gross-out humor. To be sure, there's projectile vomiting on a vast scale in an opening scene of the movie, but it's performed by a sea lion, not one of the human characters, and the sea lion feels a lot better afterward. This is a kinder and gentler Adam Sandler.

He plays Henry Roth, a marine biologist at a Hawaiian sea world, healing walruses, sea lions, and dolphins, and moonlighting as an expert in one-night stands. He romances babes who are in Hawaii on vacation, and then forgets them when they go home, so imagine his amazement when he meets Lucy and finds that she forgets him every night. Lucy is surrounded by a lot of support (her loving dad and the staff at the local diner), and they're dubious about the motives of this guy who says he's so much in love he's willing to start over with this girl every morning.

You'd think it would be hard to construct an arc for a story that starts fresh every day, but George Wing's screenplay ingeniously uses videotape to solve that problem—so that Lucy gets a briefing every morning on what she has missed, and makes daily notes in a journal about her strange romance with Henry. Eventually this leads her to conclude that it's unfair to Henry to have to endure her daily memory losses, and she says she wants to break up. Of course, the formula requires this, but how the movie solves it is kind of charming.

The movie doesn't have the complexity and depth of *Groundhog Day* (which I recently saw described as "the most spiritual film of our time"), but as entertainment it's ingratiating and lovable. And it suggests that Adam Sandler, whose movies are so often based on hostility, has another speed, another tone, that plays very nicely.

The Fighting Temptations ★ ★ ★
PG-13, 123 m., 2003

Cuba Gooding Jr. (Darrin Hill), Beyonce Knowles (Lilly), Mike Epps (Lucius), Steve Harvey (Miles Smoke), LaTanya Richardson (Paulina Pritchett), T-Bone (Bee-Z Briggs), Mickey Jones (Scooter), Faizon Love (Warden). Directed by Jonathan Lynn and produced by David Gale, Loretha C. Jones, Benny Medina, and Jeff Pollack. Screenplay by Elizabeth Hunter and Saladin K. Patterson.

The Fighting Temptations follows a formula in a kind of easygoing way, and you know it, but it generates so much goodwill and so many laughs that you don't really care. It's sort of a musical and sort of a first cousin of *Barbershop,* and you can feel the audience just plain liking it. Although it represents Beyonce Knowles's first starring role, it's not in awe of her; it uses her in the story instead of just pushing her to the front of every shot, and she comes across as warm and sympathetic.

Cuba Gooding Jr. stars as Darrin, a New York ad executive with roots in the small town of Montecarlo, Georgia. His Aunt Sally dies just as he's fired for falsifying his résumé, and he returns home for a reading of the will, which leaves him $150,000 if he'll direct the church choir and get it into the annual Gospel Explosion contest. With his credit cards maxed out and creditors on his trail, he stays in Georgia—and gets involved in church politics involving Paulina (LaTanya Richardson), the church treasurer. She drove Darrin and his mother out of town twenty years ago by accusing the mother of being immoral because she sang in the local juke joint. Now she's Darrin's enemy, opposed to him leading the choir or perhaps even staying in town.

But he has good reasons to stay. Not just because his creditors are looking for him in New York, but because he's moonstruck by a local singer named Lilly (Beyonce Knowles). She was his childhood sweetheart, and now she may hold the key to the gospel competition—and to his heart.

Darrin has his work cut out for him. The church choir is small and untalented, and his recruiting efforts are not successful. Steve Harvey plays the local disc jockey who reads his recruiting announcements—which start out by specifying that no one need apply who smokes or drinks, and end by saying pretty much anyone, even a heathen, is welcome. There's a funny sequence involving a concert in the nearby prison; when the warden (Faizon Love) says he's got prisoners who can sing better than the choir, Darrin perks up, and before long three prisoners are singing in the choir, wearing their handcuffs and their Sunday best orange convict suits.

Does the choir get into the Gospel Explosion? Do Darrin and Lilly find love and happiness? These are not really questions in a movie like this, which of course supplies the obligatory sequence of temporary defeat before ultimate victory. But the movie doesn't depend on an original story, it simply rides in on one before it starts being funny.

The humor in *The Fighting Temptations,* like the humor in *Barbershop,* isn't based on one-liners or insults, but on human nature. When the characters say something funny, it's usually funny because it's true. A lot of the laughs come when characters who don't like each other say so, out loud, right there in front of everybody.

Although most of the actors in *The Fighting Temptations* are experienced pros, a funny thing happens: In this story, they all seem like real people, maybe because they're playing characters like those they knew, or were, when they were younger. LaTanya Richardson, for example, has been in more than twenty movies (in private life she's Mrs. Samuel L. Jackson), but here, as Paulina, we don't sense a performance, we sense a woman—stubborn, unbending, envious, yet curious to see what happens next. There's lovely body language in the scene where she begins to stalk out of church, and then changes her mind and takes a seat in a back pew.

Another nice, quiet thing about the movie

is that white people turn up here and there, without much notion being taken of them. There are some whites in the choir, which is often the case in real life, and when Darrin recruits a new organist named Scooter (Mickey Jones), he's white, bearded, and a mountain man type, but he sure can play.

There's music all through the movie, a lot of it high-energy gospel music, some of it quieter. Beyonce is singing "Fever" the first time we see her, and later does a wonderful job with spirituals. There's no attempt to force her own music into the movie, and that works well, I think; after some supporting work (including the most recent Austin Powers movie), here we get to see her in a lead and sense that she can play dramatic parts and need not always be a version of herself.

I saw the movie, as it happens, at a public preview. A real one, with an audience that bought tickets because they wanted to see this movie, not because they won passes from a radio station. It was a pleasure to be surrounded by so much good feeling. *The Fighting Temptations* is not brilliant and it has some clunky moments where we see the plot wheels grinding, but it has its heart and its grin in the right places.

The Final Cut ★ ★ ★
PG-13, 105 m., 2004

Robin Williams (Alan Hackman), Mira Sorvino (Delila), James Caviezel (Fletcher), Thom Bishops (Hasan), Mimi Kuzyk (Thelma), Stephanie Romanov (Jennifer Bannister). Directed by Omar Naim and produced by Nick Wechsler. Screenplay by Naim.

There is another Robin Williams, a lonely recluse hiding inside the extrovert. Williams is able to channel this furtive, secretive persona for roles that are far removed from Mork, Mrs. Doubtfire, and *Aladdin*'s Genie. As early as *Seize the Day* (1986), a little-seen adaptation of Saul Bellow's novel about a man who loses everything of importance, Williams was accepting roles in which he would be inward, withdrawn, obsessive, peculiar. Consider his work in *The Secret Agent* (1996), as a man who prowls Edwardian London with explosives strapped to his body; *One Hour Photo* (2002), where he plays a

loner who lives vicariously through the photographs he develops; and *Insomnia* (2002), where he plays a killer who forgives himself because, well, these things happen.

Williams brings this oddball outsider to a kind of perfection in Omar Naim's *The Final Cut*, a moody science fiction drama. He plays a cutter, a man who edits memories. In an unspecified time that looks like the present, it is possible to acquire "Zoe implants"—chips in the brain that record everything you see, hear, and say. After your death, a cutter can edit highlights of your memories into a two-hour video called a "rememory" for your friends and family to watch.

Of course, a cutter sees *everything*. He knows every secret, witnesses every sin, observes every lie. But a good cutter, like a good mortician, puts the best possible face on things. Alan Hackman, Williams's character, is the best: "The dead mean nothing to me," he says. "I took this job out of respect for the living." A rival cutter puts it more clearly: "If you can't bear to look at it, he will." And another says: "He's first on the list for cutting scumbags and lowlifes." He is, they say behind his back, a sin eater.

He lives alone, spending most of his time in a room with his cutting machines. A woman friend despairs of tearing him away from his work, and says, "You're like a magician—or a priest—or a taxidermist." He is especially like a taxidermist, removing the rotting parts hidden inside his subjects while preserving the external covering in its ideal form. What does he think about the horrors he witnesses, the terrible things he edits from his rememories? We don't know. We don't even know if he enjoys his voyeurism.

He looks sad and weary much of the time, like the angels in *Wings of Desire*, who also see and know all. They pity and envy their humans—pity them for the frailties, and envy them because they live in time, not eternity. It is impossible to say how Alan feels. Certainly he has no life of his own, apart from his job, which consists of rememories of other lives. I was reminded of the documentary *Cinemania*, about five or six people who plan their days in order to spend every waking moment watching a movie. Their entire lives, and Alan's, are vicarious.

There is a thriller plot of sorts, which doesn't add much to the movie, since Alan's peculiar relationship to his job is at the heart of everything. A rich, evil man, probably a child abuser, has died, and his wealthy widow (Stephanie Romanov) hires Hackman to create a rememory of her husband. She knows, or suspects, Zoe may have recorded images of their daughter being molested. She knows Hackman (what a precise name) can be trusted.

Jim Caviezel plays the leader of a group opposed to rememories. Their slogan: "Remember for yourself!" Characters argue against the Zoe implant because of its inhibiting influence on human lives: If you know everything you do is being recorded, or if you suspect you are with a person with a Zoe implant, can you behave naturally? In Catholic school we learned that God was always watching us, but God forgave, and didn't maintain digital files.

The movie is bookended with the story of a childhood tragedy that may have twisted Alan into the cutter he is today. The tragedy is well handled, but its aftermath in his adult life seems unfinished and unsatisfying. Indeed, the movie never really finds its way out of the dilemmas it has created. But Robin Williams stands apart from the problems of *The Final Cut*, just as he stands apart from the other characters. It's been said that inside every comedian is a sad man refusing to weep. Williams has extraordinary success in channeling this other person. How strange that the same actor can play some of the most uninhibited of all characters, and some of the most morose.

Final Desination 2 ★ ½

R, 100 m., 2003

Ali Larter (Clear Rivers), A. J. Cook (Kimberly Corman), Michael Landes (Thomas Burke), David Paetkau (Evan Lewis), James Kirk (Tim Carpenter), Lynda Boyd (Nora Carpenter), Keegan Connor Tracy (Kat), Jonathan Cherry (Rory). Directed by David Ellis and produced by Warren Zide and Craig Perry. Screenplay by J. Mackye Gruber and Eric Bress.

"Look, we drove a long way to get here, so if you know how to beat death, we'd like to know."

So say pending victims to a morgue attendant in *Final Destination 2,* which takes a good idea from the first film and pounds it into the ground, not to mention decapitating, electrocuting, skewering, blowing up, incinerating, drowning, and gassing it. Perhaps movies are like history, and repeat themselves, first as tragedy, then as farce.

The earlier film involved a group of friends who got off an airplane after one of them had a vivid precognition of disaster. The plane crashed on takeoff. But then, one by one, most of the survivors died, as if fate had to balance its books.

That movie depends on all the horror clichés of the Dead Teenager Movie (formula: Teenagers are alive at beginning, dead at end). But it is well made and thoughtful. As I wrote in my review: "The film in its own way is biblical in its dilemma, although the students use the code word 'fate' when what they are really talking about is God. In their own terms, in their own way, using teenage vernacular, the students have existential discussions."

That was then; this is now. Faithful to its genre, *Final Destination 2* allows one of its original characters, Clear Rivers (Ali Larter), to survive, so she can be a link to the earlier film. In the new film, Clear is called upon by Kimberly Corman (A. J. Cook), a twenty-something, who is driving three friends in her SUV when she suddenly has a vision of a horrendous traffic accident. Kimberly blocks the on-ramp, saving the drivers behind her when logs roll off a timber truck, gas tanks explode, etc.

But is it the same old scenario? Are the people she saved all doomed to die? "There is a sort of force—an unseen malevolent presence around us every day," a character muses. "I prefer to call it death."

The malevolent presence doesn't remain unseen for long. Soon bad things are happening to good people, in a series of accidents that Rube Goldberg would have considered implausible. In one ingenious sequence, we see a character who almost trips over a lot of toys while carrying a big Macintosh iMac box. In his house, he starts the microwave and lights a fire under a frying pan, then drops his ring down the garbage disposal, then gets his hand trapped in the disposal while the microwave explodes and the frying pan starts a fire, then gets his hand loose, breaks a window that mysteriously slams shut, climbs down a fire escape, falls to the ground, and finally, when it seems he is safe . . . well, everything that could possibly go wrong does, except that he didn't get a Windows machine.

Other characters die in equally improbable ways. One is ironically killed by an air bag, another almost chokes in a dentist's chair, a third is severed from his respirator, and so on, although strange things do happen in real life. I came home from seeing this movie to read the story about the teenager who was thrown twenty-five feet in the air after a car crash, only to save himself by grabbing some telephone lines. If that had happened in *Final Destination 2*, his car would have exploded, blowing him off the lines with a flying cow.

There is a kind of dumb level on which a movie like this works, once we understand the premise. People will insist on dying oddly. Remember the story of the woman whose husband left her, so she jumped out the window and landed on him as he was leaving the building?

The thing about *FD2* is that the characters make the mistake of trying to figure things out. Their reasoning? If you were meant to die, then you owe death a life. But a new life can cancel out an old one. So if the woman in the white van can safely deliver her baby, then that means that someone else will be saved, or will have to die, I forget which. This is the kind of bookkeeping that makes you wish Arthur Andersen were still around.

Note: The first Final Destination *(2000) had characters named after famous horror-film figures, including Browning, Horton, Lewton, Weine, Schreck, Hitchcock, and Chaney. The sequel has just two that I can identify: Corman and Carpenter.*

Finding Nemo ★ ★ ★ ★
G, 101 m., 2003

With the voices of: Albert Brooks (Marlin), Ellen DeGeneres (Dory), Alexander Gould (Nemo), Willem Dafoe (Gill), Geoffrey Rush (Nigel), Brad Garrett (Bloat), Barry Humphries (Bruce), Allison Janney (Peach). Directed by Andrew Stanton and produced by Graham Walters. Screenplay by Stanton.

Finding Nemo has all of the usual pleasures of the Pixar animation style—the comedy and wackiness of *Toy Story* or *Monsters Inc.* or *A Bug's Life*. And it adds an unexpected beauty, a use of color and form that makes it one of those rare movies where I wanted to sit in the front row and let the images wash out to the edges of my field of vision. The movie takes place almost entirely under the sea, in the world of colorful tropical fish—the flora and fauna of a shallow warm-water shelf not far from Australia. The use of color, form, and movement make the film a delight even apart from its story.

There is a story, though, one of those Pixar inventions that involves kids on the action level while adults are amused because of the satire and human (or fishy) comedy. The movie involves the adventures of little Nemo, a clownfish born with an undersized fin and an oversized curiosity. His father, Marlin, worries obsessively over him because Nemo is all he has left: Nemo's mother and all of her other eggs were lost to barracudas. When Nemo goes off on his first day of school, Marlin warns him to stay with the class and avoid the dangers of the drop-off to deep water, but Nemo forgets and ends up as a captive in the saltwater aquarium of a dentist in Sydney. Marlin swims off bravely to find his missing boy, aided by Dory, a bright blue Regal Tang fish with enormous eyes whom he meets along the way.

These characters are voiced by actors whose own personal mannerisms are well known to us; I recognized most of the voices, but even the unidentified ones carried buried associations from movie roles, and so somehow the fish take on qualities of human personalities. Marlin, for example, is played by Albert Brooks as an overprotective, neurotic worrywart, and Dory is played by Ellen DeGeneres as helpful, cheerful, and scatterbrained (she has a problem with short-term memory).

The Pixar computer animators, led by writer-director Andrew Stanton, create an undersea world that is just a shade murky, as it should be; we can't see as far or as sharply in sea water, and so threats materialize more quickly, and everything has a softness of focus. There is something dreamlike about *Finding Nemo's* visuals, something that evokes the reverie of scuba diving.

The picture's great inspiration is to leave the

sea by transporting Nemo to that big tank in the dentist's office. In it we meet other captives, including the Moorish Idol fish Gill (voice by Willem Dafoe), who are planning an escape. Now it might seem to us that there is no possible way a fish can escape from an aquarium in an office and get out of the window and across the highway and into the sea, but there is no accounting for the ingenuity of these creatures, especially since they have help from a conspirator on the outside—a pelican with the voice of Geoffrey Rush.

It may occur to you that many pelicans make a living by eating fish, not rescuing them, but some of the characters in this movie have evolved admirably into vegetarians. As Marlin and Dory conduct their odyssey, for example, they encounter three carnivores who have formed a chapter of Fish-Eaters Anonymous and chant slogans to remind themselves that they abstain from fin-based meals.

The first scenes in *Finding Nemo* are a little unsettling, as we realize the movie is going to be about fish, not people (or people-based characters like toys and monsters). But of course animation has long since learned to enlist all other species in the human race, and to care about fish quickly becomes as easy as caring about mice or ducks or Bambi.

When I review a movie like *Finding Nemo*, I am aware that most members of its primary audience do not read reviews. Their parents do, and to them and adults who do not have children as an excuse, I can say that *Finding Nemo* is a pleasure for grown-ups. There are jokes we get that the kids don't, and the complexity of Albert Brooks's neuroses, and that enormous canvas filled with creatures that have some of the same hypnotic beauty as—well, fish in an aquarium. They may appreciate another novelty: This time the dad is the hero of the story, although in most animation it is almost always the mother.

Finding Neverland ★ ★ ★ ½
PG, 101 m., 2004

Johnny Depp (J. M. Barrie), Kate Winslet (Sylvia Llewelyn Davies), Julie Christie (Mrs. Emma du Maurier), Dustin Hoffman (Charles Frohman), Radha Mitchell (Mary Ansell Barrie), Freddie Highmore (Peter Llewelyn Davies), Nick Roud (George Llewelyn Davies), Joe Prospero (Jack Llewelyn Davies), Luke Spill (Michael Llewelyn Davies). Directed by Marc Forster and produced by Nellie Bellflower and Richard N. Gladstein. Screenplay by David Magee, based on a play by Allan Knee.

Finding Neverland is the story of a man who doesn't want to grow up, and writes the story of a boy who never does. The boy is Peter Pan, and the man is Sir J. M. Barrie, who wrote his famous play after falling under the spell of a widow and her four young boys. That Barrie was married at the time, that he all but ignored his wife, that he all but moved into the widow's home, that his interest in the boys raised little suspicion, would make this story play very differently today. Johnny Depp's performance makes Barrie not only believable, but acceptable. And he does it without evading the implications of his behavior: The movie doesn't inoculate Barrie as a "family friend," but shows him truly and deeply in love with the widow and her boys, although in an asexual way; we wonder, indeed, if this man has ever had sex, or ever wants to.

The movie opens in 1903 in a London theater where Barrie, a Scottish playwright, has seen his latest play turn into a disaster. He needs something new, and quickly, because his impresario (Dustin Hoffman) has a lease on the house and needs to keep it filled. In Kensington Gardens, Barrie happens upon the Davies family: the mother, Sylvia (Kate Winslet), and her boys Peter, George, Jack, and Michael. As he watches them at play, a kind of spiritual hunger begins to glow in his eyes. They represent an innocence and purity that strikes him so powerfully he's unable to think of anything else.

He becomes friendly with the family. Sylvia has recently become widowed and is not interested in a new romance, but then, curiously, nothing about Barrie's behavior suggests he's attracted to her in that way. He idealizes her, he obsesses about her boys, and when he talks about his own unhappy childhood we get a glimpse of his motivation; when his older brother died, his parents started calling him by the brother's name, and perhaps he felt he lived his brother's childhood and never had his own.

He plays games with the boys. He wrestles with a big stuffed bear. He leads them in games involving pirates and cowboys and Indians. He dresses in funny costumes. The children like him, and Sylvia is grateful for his attention, especially since she has developed an alarming cough and he helps take care of the boys. The only holdout is Peter, the oldest, played by Freddie Highmore in a remarkable performance; if Barrie never grew up, Peter was perhaps never a child. He is wise and solemn, feels the loss of his father more sharply than his younger brothers, and boldly tells Barrie: "You're not my father." Nor does Barrie want to be; he wants to be his brother. Sylvia's condition worsens, and when Barrie stages a play in the family garden, it's cut short by her coughing. The boys are reassured that nothing serious is wrong, but Peter is sure they're lying to him about her illness: "I won't be made a fool!"

Two other women regard this situation with alarm. Barrie's wife, Mary (Radha Mitchell), rarely sees him at home and is understandably disturbed about his relationship with the Davies family, although she is not as angry as she might be; there is the implication that she has long since given up on expecting rational behavior from her husband. He lives in a dream world, and to some degree she understands that. Not as sympathetic is Emma du Maurier (Julie Christie), Sylvia's mother, who as the widow of the famous George du Maurier moved in sophisticated circles and is not amused by a forty-three-year-old man who wants to become the best playmate of her grandchildren.

It is Barrie's innocence, or naïveté, or perhaps even a kind of rapture, impervious to common sense, that steers him past all obstacles as he begins to form the idea of *Peter Pan* in his mind. The boys are his muses. He tries to explain his new play to his impresario, who has just closed one flop, doesn't want to open another, and is less than thrilled about a play involving fairies, pirates, and children who can fly. Depp in his scenes shows Barrie in the grip of a holy zeal, his mind operating on a private, almost trancelike level, as the play comes into focus for him. He knows, if nobody else does, that he is creating a myth that will powerfully involve children. His masterstroke is to invite twenty-five orphans to the play's opening night and scatter them through the audience, where their laugher and delight stirs the adults to see the magic in the play.

For Johnny Depp, *Finding Neverland* is the latest in an extraordinary series of performances. After his Oscar nomination for *Pirates of the Caribbean* (2003), here is another role that seems destined for nomination. And then think of his work in *Secret Window* (2004), the Stephen King story about the author caught in a nightmare, and his demented CIA agent in *Once Upon a Time in Mexico* (2003), and *The Libertine*, as the depraved and shameless Earl of Rochester. That the flamboyance of his pirate and the debauchery of the earl could exist in the same actor as the soft-spoken, gentle, inward J. M. Barrie is remarkable. It is commonplace for actors to play widely differing roles, but Depp never makes it feel like a reach; all of these notes seem well within his range.

Finding Neverland is, finally, surprisingly moving. The screenplay by David Magee and the direction of Marc Forster *(Monster's Ball)* manipulate the facts to get their effect; Sylvia's husband was still alive in the original story, for example, and her illness had not taken hold. But by compressing events, the movie creates for the Barrie character an opportunity for unconditional love. What he feels for the Davies family is disinterested and pure, despite all the appearances. What he feels for his wife remains a mystery, not least to her.

First Daughter ★ ★
PG, 104 m., 2004

Katie Holmes (Samantha Mackenzie), Marc Blucas (James Lansome), Amerie Rogers (Mia Thompson), Michael Keaton (President Mackenzie), Margaret Colin (Melanie Mackenzie), Lela Rochon (Liz Pappas). Directed by Forest Whitaker and produced by John Davis, Wyck Godfrey, Mike Karz, and Arnon Milcan. Screenplay by Jessica Bendinger and Kate Kondell.

First Daughter is all heart and has the best intentions in the world, but what a bore. It's a beat slower than it should be, it makes its points laboriously, and the plot surprise would be obvious even if I hadn't seen the same device used in exactly the same way in *Chasing Liberty*. Even the ending isn't as happy as it thinks it is.

Katie Holmes, so fetching in *Wonder Boys* and *Pieces of April*, stars as Samantha Mackenzie, daughter of a U.S. president whose party is carefully not mentioned even though when we learn the United Auto Workers support him, the secret is out. She has spent her entire life as a good, sweet, dutiful daughter, smiling loyally at the side of her parents (Michael Keaton and Margaret Colin) as they campaign for office. Now it is time for her to go to college, and she yearns to be treated as a normal kid. Her definition of this is that she would get to drive herself there in her little Volkswagen, with a cooler in the front seat that has a can of beer hidden under the bologna sandwiches. What is wrong with this picture? (1) As we find out at the end of the movie, it's a classic VW bug, not one of the new models, and the kids who dreamed of driving off to college in one of those are now closer in age to, oh, say, the filmmakers. (2) Today's progressive modern parents, spotting the beer and the bologna, would gasp in horror, "Bologna?" Samantha enrolls at the University of Redmond, where to her horror the school band plays "Hail to the Chief" while she walks into her dorm with the chief and first lady. Her new roomie Mia (Amerie Rogers) is a cutey-pie who's used to getting all the attention herself, and doesn't want to play second banana to the F.D. Samantha wears clothes that inspire Joan Rivers monologues on TV, she sits in a roped-off section of lecture classes, flanked by Secret Service agents, and she is thoroughly miserable.

So she stages a revolt that is painfully awkward in its conception and execution, pretending to be a bad girl, so the president will hear her cry for help. Her first transgression is to slide down a hill on a wet tarp at a frat party, which gets her on the front page of the *New York Post,* a paper more easily shocked in this movie than in life. Her slide seems to me like a plus (first daughter is real kid, has harmless fun), but no: She gets a scolding, and then she gets a *severe* scolding when Mia talks her into attending another party dressed, so help me, like a go-go dancer in the days when the words "go-go" were being used (high white lace-up boots, denim miniskirt, pink fur pimp hat, the works). Realizing Samantha is serious about wanting more privacy, or maybe fearing that she will in desperation pose for *Playboy* if he doesn't relent, the president agrees to pull back her Secret Service detail. Half of her agents disappear. Joyous with her new freedom, she has a Meet Cute with James Lansome (Marc Blucas), the handsome resident adviser who just happens to be the resident on her floor of the dorm. Soon true love blooms between them. No, really.

The stages by which the movie arrives at this point and travels onward are so deliberate the movie seems reluctant to proceed. It keeps pausing and looking back to make sure we're keeping up. Katie Holmes plays Samantha with wide-eyed wonder, underlining every point. Her normal kid is a strange anachronism, like the 1940s music that plays at all of the dances; she'd be right at home as a freshman in, say, *The Glenn Miller Story.* No first daughter in recent memory has been this square. She doesn't even seem to have met Paris and Nicky Hilton.

The surprise, when it comes, is sadly unsurprising. It leads to a formula in which Samantha must first be depressed, then be resolute, then be joyous again. All fine, except that the movie makes her be depressed again and resolute again, and ends with muted joy, and then with more resolution. Girls have renounced thrones and entered convents with less trouble. Even worse, everyone in the movie, but surely no one in the audience, believes it arrives at the correct ending. Having tortured us with clichés for more than 100 minutes, the movie denies us the final upbeat cliché that we have paid our dues for. Who wants a movie about a first daughter who finds, loses, refinds, reloses, sort of refinds, and probably loses perfect love, only to end up alone and responsible?

The Five Obstructions ★ ★ ★
NO MPAA RATING, 90 m., 2004

As themselves: Jorgen Leth, Lars von Trier, Daniel Hernandez Rodriguez, Patrick Bauchau, Jacqueline Arenal, and Bob Sabiston. A documentary directed by Jorgen Leth and Lars von Trier and produced by Carsten Holst. Screenplay by Sophie Destin, Asger Leth, Leth, and von Trier, inspired by *The Perfect Human* by Leth.

The Five Obstructions is a perverse game of one-upmanship between the Danish director Lars von Trier and his mentor, Jorgen Leth. In 1967, we learn, Leth made a twelve-minute film named *The Perfect Human*. Von Trier admired it so much he saw it twenty times in a single year. Now he summons the sixty-seven-year-old Leth from retirement in Haiti and commands him to remake the film in five different ways, despite obstructions that von Trier will supply.

The first obstruction seems almost insurmountable: Von Trier commands Leth to go to Cuba (and bring back some cigars while he's at it) and remake the film in shots no more than twelve frames, or half a second, in length. "That will be totally destructive!" Leth complains. "It will be a spastic film." But when he returns after facing the first obstruction, he is all smiles, and tells von Trier: "The twelve frames were like a gift."

Von Trier accepts this news while lounging behind his desk like a headmaster. The joke seems to be that Leth, nineteen years his senior and once von Trier's teacher, is to be ordered around like an unruly schoolboy. There is an additional element in play: Leth's style is clean, spare, and classical, while von Trier is the architect of the Dogma movement, which is essentially a series of obstructions (use natural light and sound, no music except that found at the source, etc.). "I want to banalize you," von Trier cheerfully informs him.

Von Trier sends Leth out again, this time to "the most miserable place on Earth." They settle on the Falkland Road red-light district in Mumbai. Leth journeys there and films himself eating an elegant meal. "This is not the film I asked for!" growls von Trier, and offers him a choice: (1) go back to India and do it again, or (2) make a completely freestyle film, which would be against all of Leth's stylistic instincts.

Leth, who in his cool and amused way seems impervious to von Trier's challenges, emerges intact from this third obstruction with a film shot in his native Brussels. For obstruction No. 4, von Trier has a real zinger in mind. "I hate animation," he observes. "So do I," says Leth. "Make an animated film," von Trier says. Leth protests: "I can't be bothered to invent the technology, or to learn it. No stupid drawing board!" His solution is as brilliant as it is elegant. I will not reveal it, except to say the result will speak loudly to anyone who has seen Richard Linklater's *Waking Life*.

At this point Leth seems ahead 4-0, but von Trier has one more twist up his sleeve. See for yourself. A film like this has a limited audience, I suppose, but for that audience it offers a rare fascination. Von Trier has deliberately set up a contest between two generations and styles of filmmaking, and in the pose of honoring *The Perfect Human* he tries to force Leth to demolish and reinvent it. Leth is more than his equal, and the entire enterprise is infected with a spirit of mischievous play. *The Five Obstructions* clearly calls for a sequel, in which Leth requires von Trier to remake *Dogville* despite Obstructions Six through Ten.

Flight of the Phoenix ★ ★
PG-13, 112 m., 2004

Dennis Quaid (Frank Towns), Giovanni Ribisi (Elliott), Tyrese Gibson (A.J.), Mirando Otto (Kelly), Hugh Laurie (Ian). Directed by John Moore and produced by William Aldrich, Alex Blum, John Davis, and Wyck Godfrey. Screenplay by Scott Frank and Edward Burns, based on the screenplay by Lukas Heller.

Flight of the Phoenix is a fairly faithful remake of the 1965 adventure classic, with no big surprises. But it uses special effects to create scenes unavailable to the earlier film, including sensational sandstorms, a detailed crash sequence, and a convincing takeoff. If effects had been available in 1965, a life would have been saved; the older movie used a real plane, flown by legendary stunt pilot Paul Mantz, who crashed and was killed. The knowledge of that real event shadowed the 1965 film, giving it an eerie reality.

The remake follows the same story pattern: An oil company crew in the middle of a desert is picked up by a hotshot pilot. The return flight runs into a violent sandstorm and crashes. The survivors are without a radio, and grimly add up their water and food supplies while a last-minute passenger stands aside, thinking deep thoughts to himself. He eventually announces that a new plane can be made from the wreckage of the old, and they can fly themselves to safety.

The pilot this time is Dennis Quaid, who shares with the 1965 pilot, James Stewart, the ability to be abrupt at the beginning and mellow toward the end. A woman is added to the cast: Kelly, an oil engineer played by Miranda Otto. The key role of the would-be aircraft designer is taken by Giovanni Ribisi, who has a fierce but defensive pride that is explained when more details emerge about his background.

My memory of the 1965 film, somewhat obscured by the sands of time, is that there was less sand. Yes, they crashed in the desert, but the 2004 version can whip up unlimited sandstorms on a moment's notice, and more than once the plane is completely buried except for part of its tail. This leads to a moment when the characters determine to dig it out one last time, and then a shot of the plane ready to take off, without so much as a single shot of a shovel or a bucket. Why bother to bury it if you're not going to show it being dug out? So Quaid can give his inspirational speech, I think.

When it comes to movies about people trying to return alive after catastrophic accidents, nothing else for a long time is going to be more riveting than *Touching the Void,* the film about a man climbing down from a mountain with a shattered leg. *Flight of the Phoenix* is more in the old-fashioned mold of heroes who fight among themselves but eventually decide to cooperate, depending on pluck and

luck. There is also a half-realized subplot about local "nomads" or "bandits"—nobody seems quite sure—who seem to survive quite comfortably in large numbers in the desert, and whose comings and goings bear an uncanny relationship to exactly when they are required by the plot.

Because I had, in a sense, already seen this movie, it didn't have surprises or suspense for me, and the actors on their own aren't enough to save it. I'm not recommending it for those who know the original, but it might work nicely enough for those who have not.

The Flower of Evil ★ ★ ★
NO MPAA RATING, 105 m., 2003

Benoit Magimel (Francois Vasseur), Nathalie Baye (Anne Charpin-Vasseur), Melanie Doutey (Michele Charpin-Vasseur), Suzanne Flon (Aunt Line), Bernard Lecoq (Gerard Vasseur), Thomas Chabrol (Matthieu Lartigue). Directed by Claude Chabrol and produced by Marin Karmitz. Screenplay by Caroline Eliacheff, Louise L. Lambrichs, and Chabrol.

A country house and a corpse. Yes. We are comfortable already. It is a big house, with a sweeping staircase and doorways through which we glimpse life continuing just as if the owner were not dead upstairs. That must be the cook setting the table. But wait. The camera, having climbed the stairs and regarded the dead body, slides on down the corridor and looks through another door, where a young woman sits on the floor, distraught. We have come up these stairs just a few seconds too late to be eyewitnesses to murder.

Claude Chabrol has been climbing these stairs all of his life, and discovering the secrets of the French bourgeois. Many of his murderers have the easy manners of good old families. Before we go back downstairs and join the story of *The Flower of Evil,* which is his fiftieth film, we should pause for a moment to honor this milestone. Chabrol was one of the founders of the French New Wave, so early he did not know it was the New Wave and he was founding it. As a character says in *Citizen Kane,* he was there before the beginning and now here he is, after the end. "He began directing in

1958," Stanley Kauffman writes in the *New Republic*, "and has never committed an ill-made film, has rarely made a dull one, and has occasionally created a gem."

I shared an enormous sea bass once with Chabrol in a New York Chinese restaurant, and on another night we did some drinking and talked about his latest film. That was in 1972, at the New York Film Festival. Five years earlier Andrew Sarris had already been able to write about Chabrol in the past tense: "He quickly became one of the forgotten figures of the nouvelle vague." Now it is 2003 and Chabrol still has his hand in. So does Sarris. "With respect to Mr. Chabrol's *The Flower of Evil*," he writes tactfully in the *New York Observer*, "I would prefer to think of it as a masterly work of the artist's late period rather than as the tired product of his old age."

And so we beat on, boats against the current. I feel such an affection for Chabrol and his work that I probably can't see *The Flower of Evil* as it would be experienced by a first-time viewer. Would that newcomer note the elegance, the confidence, the sheer joy in the way he treasures the banalities of bourgeois life on his way to the bloodshed? And would they understand the truly savage quality that lurks just under the surface—the contempt he feels for these characters who move in such style between their jobs and homes, their political campaigns and love affairs? Here is a movie in which the one romance that nearly everyone approves of is between a brother and a sister.

Their incest requires footnotes: Francois (Benoit Magimel) is the son of Gerard Vasseur (Bernard Lecoq); his mother was killed in an accident, and so his father married Anne Charpin-Vasseur (Nathalie Baye), who brought a daughter into the marriage. This is Michele (Melanie Doutey). So Francois and Michele aren't technically siblings—but they are cousins, because this family has been intermarrying for generations. Francois flew off to Chicago to study law for four years ("The Americans are not as stupid as they like to pretend"), but he couldn't outgrow his infatuation with Michele, and soon after his return they borrow the holiday cottage of old Aunt Line (Suzanne Flon) and consummate what they have so long imagined.

The family is remarkably unruffled. There are other plots afoot. Gerard has made a fortune with his semilegal pharmaceutical factory. His wife is using his money to run for local office, and Gerard has had enough of the way she drags her political adviser Matthieu (Thomas Chabrol) to family gatherings and dinners. Matthieu tries to make his excuses and slip away, but Gerard insists he stay, the better to make him feel uncomfortable.

Someone in the town has sent around an anonymous letter libeling three generations of the family for collaboration with the Nazis, profiteering, corruption, adultery, incest, and not being nice. Most of these charges are true, as old Aunt Line has reason to know, and after Chabrol's elegant establishing scenes and hints of buried shame there is, all of a sudden, a shocking revelation, a dead body, a woman sitting on the floor, and this time the police are coming up the stairs.

Chabrol's buried theme, as frequently, involves the rotten French monied class. He attacks the rich not as a leftist but simply because he is fastidious and cannot stand them. He has also found time for murderers of the middle and lower classes, but his heart quickens when he finds death in corrupt suburban villas. A boxed set of six classic Chabrol DVDs has just been issued, and if you want to see him among the working classes, rent *Le Boucher*, one of his two or three best films, which is about an elegant schoolmistress who falls in love with a charming butcher, only to be faced with the possibility that she is about to be filleted.

The Fog of War ★ ★ ★ ★
PG-13, 106 m., 2004

A documentary directed by Errol Morris and produced by Morris, Michael Williams, and Julie Ahlberg. Screenplay by Morris.

How strange the fate that brought together Robert McNamara and Errol Morris to make *The Fog of War*. McNamara, considered the architect of the Vietnam War, an Establishment figure who came to Washington after heading the Ford Motor Company and left to become the president of the World Bank. And Morris, the brilliant and eccentric documentarian who has chronicled pet cemeteries, Death Row, lion tamers, robots, naked mole rats, a designer of electric chairs, people who cut off their legs for the insurance money, and Stephen Hawking's *A Brief History of Time.*

McNamara agreed to talk with Morris for an hour or so, supposedly for a TV special. He eventually spent twenty hours peering into Morris's "Interrotron," a video device that allows Morris and his subjects to look into each other's eyes while also looking directly into the camera lens. Whether this invention results in better interviews is impossible to say, but it does have the uncanny result that the person on the screen never breaks eye contact with the audience.

McNamara was eighty-five when the interviews were conducted—a fit and alert eighty-five, still skiing the slopes at Aspen. Guided sometimes by Morris, sometimes taking the lead, he talks introspectively about his life, his thoughts about Vietnam, and, taking Morris where he would never have thought to go, his role in planning the firebombing of Japan, including a raid on Tokyo that claimed 100,000 lives. He speaks concisely and forcibly, rarely searching for a word, and he is not reciting boilerplate and old sound bites; there is the uncanny sensation that he is thinking as he speaks.

His thoughts are organized as *Eleven Lessons from the Life of Robert S. McNamara,* as extrapolated by Morris, and one wonders how the planners of the war in Iraq would respond to lesson Nos. 1 and 2 ("Empathize with your enemy" and "Rationality will not save us"), or for that matter, No. 6 ("Get the data"), No. 7 ("Belief and seeing are both often wrong"), and No. 8 ("Be prepared to reexamine your reasoning"). I cannot imagine the circumstances under which Donald Rumsfeld, the current secretary of defense, would not want to see this film about his predecessor, having recycled and even improved upon McNamara's mistakes.

McNamara recalls the days of the Cuban missile crisis, when the world came to the brink of nuclear war (he holds up two fingers, almost touching, to show how close—"this close"). He recalls a meeting, years later, with Fidel Castro, who told him he was prepared to accept the destruction of Cuba if that's what the war would mean. He recalls two telegrams to Kennedy from Khrushchev, one more conciliatory, one

perhaps dictated by Kremlin hard-liners, and says that JFK decided to answer the first and ignore the second. (Not quite true, as Fred Kaplan documents in an article at Slate.com.) The movie makes it clear that no one was thinking very clearly, and that the world avoided war as much by luck as by wisdom.

And then he remembers the years of the Vietnam War, inherited from JFK and greatly expanded by Lyndon Johnson. He began to realize the war could never be won, he says, and wrote a memo to the president to that effect. The result was that he resigned as secretary. (He had dinner with Kay Graham, publisher of the *Washington Post,* and told her, "Kay, I don't know if I resigned or was fired." "Oh, Bob," she told him, "of course you were fired.") He didn't resign as a matter of principle, as a British cabinet minister might; it is worth remembering that a few months later Johnson, saying he would not stand for reelection, did effectively resign.

McNamara begins by remembering how, at the age of two, he witnessed a victory parade after World War I, and engages in painful soul-searching about his role in World War II. He was a key aide to General Curtis LeMay, the hard-nosed warrior whose strategy for war was simplicity itself: kill them until they give up. Together, they planned the bombing raids before the atomic bomb ended the war, and Morris supplies a chart showing the American cities equivalent in size to the ones they targeted. After the war, McNamara says, in one of the film's most astonishing moments, LeMay observed to him that if America had lost, they would have been tried as war criminals. Thinking of the 100,000 burned alive in Tokyo, McNamara finds lesson No. 5: "Proportionality should be a guideline in war." In other words, I suppose, kill enough of the enemy but don't go overboard. Lesson No. 9: "In order to do good, you may have to engage in evil."

McNamara is both forthright and elusive. He talks about a Quaker who burned himself to death below the windows of his office in the Pentagon, and finds his sacrifice somehow in the same spirit as his own thinking—but it is true he could have done more to try to end the war and did not, and will not say why he did not, although now he clearly wishes he had. He will also not say he is sorry, even though Morris prompts him; maybe he's too proud, but I get the feeling it's more a case of not wanting to make a useless gesture that could seem hypocritical. His final words in the film make it clear there are some places he is simply not prepared to go.

Although McNamara is photographed through the Interrotron, the movie is far from offering only a talking head. Morris is uncanny in his ability to bring life to the abstract, and here he uses graphics, charts, moving titles, and visual effects in counterpoint to what McNamara is saying. There's also a lot of historical footage, including some shots of Curtis LeMay with his cigar clenched between his teeth—images that describe whatever McNamara neglected to say about him. There are tape recordings of Oval Office discussions involving McNamara, Kennedy, and Johnson. And archival footage of McNamara's years at Ford (he is proud of introducing seat belts). Underneath all of them, uneasily urging the movie along, is the Philip Glass score, which sounds—what? Mournful, urgent, melancholy, driven?

The effect of *The Fog of War* is to impress upon us the frailty and uncertainty of our leaders. They are sometimes so certain of actions that do not deserve such certitude. The farce of the missing weapons of mass destruction is no less complete than the confusion in the Kennedy White House over whether there were really nuclear warheads in Cuba. Some commentators on the film, notably Kaplan in his informative Slate essay, question McNamara's facts. What cannot be questioned is his ability to question them himself. At eighty-five, he knows what he knows, and what he does not know, and what cannot be known. Lesson No. 11: "You can't change human nature."

A Foreign Affair ★ ★ ★
PG-13, 94 m., 2004

David Arquette (Josh), Tim Blake Nelson (Jake), Emily Mortimer (Angela), Larry Pine (Tour Guide), Lois Smith (Ma), Megan Follows (Lena), Redmond Gleeson (Funeral Director), Allyce Beasley (Librarian). Directed by Helmut Schleppi and produced by David-Jan Bijker, Esli Bijker, Geert Heetebrij, and Schleppi. Screenplay by Heetebrij.

When their mother dies, Josh and Jake are saddened, yes, but they are also frightened, because Ma took care of everything. She cooked, she washed, she darned, she remembered where things were. Now there is no one to perform those tasks, and the boys are helpless. A farm they can manage, but a house is beyond them.

A Foreign Affair shows them taking matters into their own hands. With the help of the friendly town librarian, they find a Web site that features young women from Russia who want to marry Americans and are apparently packed and ready to go. They sign up for the package tour, and find themselves in St. Petersburg, where they never expected to be, and considered very desirable, which they have never been before.

Their task is simpler because they are seeking only one wife. That isn't because they plan to practice reverse polygamy, or because one of them is gay, but because they do not think of this as a true marriage. Jake (Tim Blake Nelson), the serious one, is up-front with the women he interviews: no sex, but you keep house for us for a few years, and you get your citizenship.

His brother, Josh (David Arquette), agreed to this plan back on the farm, but now, attending the nightly parties arranged by the tour group, he finds delightful women throwing themselves at him, and this is a new experience he begins to enjoy. He falls in love more or less nightly, using an ancient formula: When he's not with the one he loves, he loves the one he's with.

The movie, directed by Helmut Schleppi and written by Geert Heetebrij, could have gone several ways. I can imagine it as a sex comedy, as a romance, as a bittersweet exploration of lonely people. Schleppi has a little of all three elements at work here, but it's Tim Blake Nelson's character who keeps the plot from spinning out of control, because he has a natural and unforced respect for these women that yanks his brother's chain and keeps their mission on course.

Watching Josh and Jake as they negotiate this process, Emily Mortimer plays a British documentary-maker named Angela. She's been assigned to make a film about the whole phenomenon of Internet brides, but becomes fascinated by Jake because he is not really looking for a bride in the traditional sense, and is up-front about it. As she shoots his interviews with prospective partners, we see her footage, and we sense that we are close to the line between fiction and reality. Maybe closer than we think: I was talking about the movie with Mortimer at Cannes, and she said the filmmakers and the two actors actually took the real tour to do their research.

Mortimer's character provides a subtle subtext. As she watches Jake, listens to him and films him, she begins to be moved by his honesty and his good heart. He is a simple, forthright man, unlike most of those she meets, and we begin to sense he may find a bride in the last place he's looking. Or maybe that's too easy; maybe there's no way their worlds can meet, and yet she has a way of looking at him . . .

Do marriages like this work? Many Americans find mail-order brides or arranged marriages bizarre, but think how bizarre it is to seek your spouse in a singles bar or on a blind date. There are countless possible partners out there somewhere, but we never meet most of them, and most of those we meet are impossible. Maybe it helps to use a system. If you're interested, the actual Web site is at www.aforeignaffair.com.

The Forgotten ★ ★
PG-13, 89 m., 2004

Julianne Moore (Telly Paretta), Dominic West (Ash Correll), Gary Sinise (Dr. Munce), Alfre Woodard (Detective Ann Pope), Linus Roache (Friendly Man), Anthony Edwards (Jim Paretta). Directed by Joseph Ruben and produced by Bruce Cohen, Dan Jinks, and Joe Roth. Screenplay by Gerald DiPego.

Warning: This review contains spoilers. If it didn't, I can think of no way to review it at all, short of summarizing the first three minutes and then telling you some very strange stuff happens. My advice: If you plan to see the film (which I do not recommend), hold the review until afterward.

Whenever I hear about aliens who abduct human subjects and carry them off in spaceships and conduct weird experiments on them and shove scientific probes where the sun don't shine, I ask myself this question: Why do these alien visitations always seem to be aimed at just those kinds of people who are most likely to believe in them? Why do the

aliens always pick people who summer at Roswell, New Mexico, instead of choosing someone like Stephen Hawking, Howard Stern, or Dick Cheney?

The Forgotten is not a good movie, but at least it supplies a credible victim. Julianne Moore plays Telly Paretta, a mother who for fourteen months has mourned her nine-year-old son, Sam. He died in a plane crash along with nine other kids. Her psychiatrist (Gary Sinise) wonders if perhaps she is . . . enhancing . . . her memories of Sam. She tries to limit her daily visits to photo albums and home videos, and then, one horrifying day, she finds that all her photos and videos of Sam have vanished!

She blames her husband (Anthony Edwards), but then she gets the bad news: She never had a son. She had a miscarriage. All of her memories of Sam have been fabricated in some kind of posttraumatic-syndrome scenario. The shrink and her husband agree: no Sam. In desperation she turns to a neighbor (Dominic West) whose daughter also died in the same crash. He tells her he never had a daughter.

How can this be? She remembers Sam so clearly. So do we, because the director, Joseph Ruben, supplies repeated reruns of her memories, or home movies, I'm not sure which, and there's Sam, smiling at the camera and playing in the park and looking defiantly pre-traumatic.

But how, and why, would her husband, and her shrink, and her neighbor, and her *other* neighbor, and even the *New York Times*, completely forget about Sam and the crash and all those little kids? The most likely hypothesis is that Telly is crazy and everybody else is right. But who would make a movie about a mother discovering her beloved child was imaginary? That would be too sad, too tragic, and, for that matter, too thought-provoking and artistically challenging, and might even make a good movie.

So we determine that Telly is not crazy. Therefore, she had a son, and she is the only person whose memory of Sam has not been erased. The whole world is arrayed against her. Even the federal government is her enemy. She's trailed by agents for the National Security Agency, who are sinister but astonishingly incompetent. A local cop (Alfre Woodard) wonders why the feds are involved: "They don't chase missing children." Being a woman, she of course intuitively believes Telly while all of the logical males diagnose her as a hysteric. She is a great help to Telly until she is suddenly pulled off the case, so to speak.

I will not spoil details of the last act, except to say that it is preposterous, and undoes a good deal of sympathy that Moore's performance has built up in the earlier scenes. There comes a point at which even the most patient moviegoer wearies of chases in which frantic female book editors outrun trained male agents. In which there is a large empty warehouse/hangar space for a dramatic confrontation. In which the Talking Killer Syndrome, by which the villain explains his misdeeds, is not a flaw but is desperately necessary if the plot is ever to be explained at all.

I will content myself with the very final scenes. You know, the ones in the playground. How are they possible? What repairs were necessary to the fabric of the physical world and remembered events? Who keeps track of this stuff? How come such stupid experiments are carried out by beings so superbly intelligent as to be able to conduct them?

The movie begins with a premise: A mother remembers her lost son, and everyone she trusts tells her she only imagines she had a son. That's a great story idea. But it's all downhill from there. *The Forgotten* is best left.

Freaky Friday ★ ★ ★
PG, 93 m., 2003

Jamie Lee Curtis (Tess Coleman), Lindsay Lohan (Anna Coleman), Mark Harmon (Ryan), Chad Murray (Jake), Ryan Malgarini (Harry), Harold Gould (Grandpa), Lucille Soong (Chinese Grandma). Directed by Mark S. Waters and produced by Andrew Gunn. Screenplay by Heather Hach and Leslie Dixon, based on the novel by Mary Rodgers.

Actors must love to make body-switch movies. Look at the fun Jamie Lee Curtis and Lindsay Lohan have in *Freaky Friday*. Each one gets to imitate the body language and inner nature of the other, while firing salvos across the generation gap. Body-switch plots are a license for adults to act like kids; probably nobody has had more fun at it than Tom Hanks did in *Big*, but Curtis comes close.

The movie is a remake of the 1976 film starring Barbara Harris and Jodie Foster, and also connects with the mid-1980s body-switch craze, when three or four switcheroos were released more or less simultaneously. Curtis plays Tess Coleman, a widowed psychiatrist soon to be remarried, and Lohan is Anna, her fifteen-year-old daughter, who is certainly the most clean-cut garage band guitarist in history. There is a kid brother named Harry (Ryan Malgarini), who, like all kid brothers, thinks his older sister is picking on him.

Anna believes Tess is remarrying with unseemly haste; she's going through what in a Disney movie passes for a rebellious phase, and in real life would be exemplary teenage behavior. Mother and daughter join the future husband, Ryan (Mark Harmon), for dinner in a Chinese restaurant, where they get into a fight. The restaurant family's grandmother (Lucille Soong) zaps them with a fortune-cookie curse, and the next morning when they wake up Tess and Anna are in each other's bodies. (There was an article not long ago about how angels and God always seem to be played by African-Americans in the movies. Another could be written on the usefulness of movie Asian Americans, who can always be counted on to supply magic potions, exotic elixirs, ancient charms, and handy supernatural plot points.)

Anna looks in the mirror and is shocked to see her mother's body: "I look like the crypt-keeper!" Tess oversleeps just like her daughter always does. They go through the obligatory scene of horrified disbelief, although, like all body-switch movie characters, they are not simply paralyzed by astonishment and dread, but quickly decide to lead each other's lives for a while, so that there can be a story.

The movie, directed by Mark S. Waters and written by Heather Hach and Leslie Dixon, delivers scenes we can anticipate, but with more charm and wit than we expect. There is, for example, the case of Anna's flirtation with a slightly older boy named Jake (Chad Murray). He rides a motorcycle, so of course Tess disapproves of him, but now Tess, in Anna's body, is inexplicably cold to the kid, while Anna, in Tess's body, is so delighted to see him that before long she's on the back of the bike and Jake is telling her he feels like they really understand each other and maybe the age gap can be overcome.

Other entertaining scenes: The mother discovers her daughter's body has a pierced navel. The daughter buys her mother's body new clothes and a new haircut and gets her ears pierced. Tess attends a class Anna has been having trouble with, and realizes the teacher has been picking on her daughter because she (the mother) turned him down for a prom date. Everything comes down to a conflict between a rehearsal dinner and the garage band's big chance at the House of Blues, and when Anna, in Tess's body, makes her little speech at the dinner, we hear the daughter's resentments: "It's great we're getting married—even though my husband died. How quickly I've been able to get over it!"

The outlines of body-switch movies almost write themselves, although I'd like to see what would happen with an R-rated version. The clever writing here helps, but the actors help even more, with Lohan and Curtis taking big physical chances. Curtis, channeling the daughter inside her, has a hilarious scene on a talk show; she's supposed to be a serious psychiatrist discussing her new book, but sits cross-legged in her chair and leads the audience in routines that seem vaguely inspired by summer camp.

Lindsay Lohan, who starred in the recycled *The Parent Trap* (1998), has that Jodie Foster sort of seriousness and intent focus beneath her teenage persona, and Jamie Lee Curtis has always had an undercurrent of playfulness; they're right for these roles not only because of talent, but because of their essential natures. We're always sure who is occupying each body, even if sometimes they seem to forget. Now if only their Chinese enabler doesn't run out of fortune cookies.

Friday Night Lights ★ ★ ★ ½
PG-13, 115 m., 2004

Billy Bob Thornton (Coach Gary Gaines), Tim McGraw (Charles Billingsley), Derek Luke (Boobie Miles), Jay Hernandez (Brian Chavez), Lucas Black (Mike Winchell), Garrett Hedlund (Don Billingsley), Lee Thompson Young (Chris Comer), Lee Jackson (Ivory Christian), Grover Coulson (L. V. Miles). Directed by Peter Berg

and produced by Brian Grazer. Screenplay by David Aaron Cohen and Berg, based on the book *Friday Night Lights* by H. G. Bissinger.

You have the responsibility of protecting this team and this school and this town.
—Coach Gary Gaines

Protecting them against what? We're not talking about war here, we're talking about high school football. And yet as *Friday Night Lights* unfolds, we begin to understand: The role of the team is to protect against the idea that the town is inconsequential and its citizens insignificant. If Gaines can lead the Odessa-Permian team to a state championship, that will prove that Odessa is a place of consequence, a center of power and glory. Well, won't it?

Certainly there are countless citizens in Odessa who lead happy and productive lives, and are fulfilled without depending on high school football. We just don't meet any of them in the movie, which focuses on the team, the coach, and the local boosters—adults who define themselves in terms of their relationship to the team.

These people are obsessed beyond all reason with winning and losing, and the pressure they put on the kids and their coach is relentless. "Take us to State, coach," one booster tells Gaines in a supermarket parking lot. "Or what?" asks Gaines. Or else. "Are we going to be moving again?" the coach's young daughter asks after a defeat. "No, honey," says her mother, but Gaines answers: "Possibly."

Gaines is played by Billy Bob Thornton in another great performance: He played the drunken title character in *Bad Santa,* and Davy Crockett in *The Alamo.* The man has range, and he has a command of tone, too. Santa was over the top, but his Coach Gaines is a private man, inward, who finds it wise to keep his thoughts to himself. Consider the scene where he's told that his star player's injury won't prevent him from playing. Look at his eyes. He has reason to believe he is being lied to. He has reason to hope he is not.

The player is Boobie Miles (Derek Luke), a motormouth with a giant talent that comes wrapped in ego. When one of his teammates accused him of not working out in the weight room, he explains that his gift is "God-given."

But in the first game of the season he injures his knee. He pretends it's nothing. Eventually the uncle who is raising him (Grover Coulson) takes him to Midland for an MRI, which reveals a badly torn ligament. Boobie dismisses the doctor as a Midland fan "jealous of Odessa," and he and his uncle tell the coach he's ready to play. He isn't. Because he depended on sports for his future, because he doesn't read very well, there is a moment when he sits on the porch and watches some garbage men at work, and contemplates his future.

The movie is based on real life, described in the best-seller *Friday Night Lights: A Town, a Team, and a Dream*, by H. G. Bissinger. It depicts Odessa as a town consumed by high school football; its stadium is larger than those at many colleges. Local talk radio keeps up a steady drumbeat of criticism against Gaines. "They're doing too much learning in the schools," one caller complains.

The movie has been directed by Peter Berg not as character studies, but as emotional snapshots. We catch on who the key characters are. Others are never identified. Gaines has enormous focus, and can deliver a powerful message at halftime, but he understands better than anyone else that football is only a game. Unfortunately, his job is not only a game, and so he must take football very seriously; his job is not to protect the town and the school, but to protect his family. At dinner parties, in restaurants, everywhere he goes, he undergoes an endless stream of comments, criticism, suggestions, threats masked as praise. The way Thornton plays him, Gaines reminds me of Hemingway's definition of courage: grace under pressure.

There is something pathetic about a grown man still living his life in terms of high school, and that's the case with Charles Billingsley (played with great power by the country singer Tim McGraw). He still wears his ring from Odessa's championship team of twenty years earlier, and bullies his son, Don (Garrett Hedlund), who is a receiver on the team. When Don fumbles early in the season, his dad actually walks onto the field to chew him out. He slaps his son around, trash-talks him, gets drunk, and directs a withering stream of sarcasm at the kid—and has a revealing moment when he tells Don that high school football will be the high point of his life.

I started in journalism at fifteen, as a sportswriter covering high school football. I thought it was the most important thing on Earth. But it was more innocent in those days. At what point in American history did the phrase "It's not whether you win or lose, but how you play the game" get replaced by "Winning is the only thing"? Today's teams are like surrogate nations for their fans. When your team wins, it enhances you.

Oddly enough, despite all these undertones, *Friday Night Lights* does also work like a traditional sports movie, and there's enormous tension and excitement at the end, when everything comes down to the last play in the State finals. The movie demonstrates the power of sports to involve us; we don't live in Odessa and are watching a game played sixteen years ago, and we get all wound up.

Friday Night Lights reminded me of another movie filmed in Texas: *The Last Picture Show*, set fifty years ago. In that one, after the local team loses another game, the players catch flak everywhere they go. It's gotten worse. I'll bet if you phoned talk radio in Odessa and argued that high school football is only a game, you'd make a lot of people mad at you. The poor kids who play it are under cruel pressure. One of the team members tells a friend, midway through the season: "I just don't feel like I'm seventeen." ☞

G

The Game of Their Lives ★ ½
PG, 95 m., 2005

Gerard Butler (Frank Borghi), Wes Bentley (Walter Bahr), Gavin Rossdale (Stanley Mortensen), Jay Rodan (Pee Wee), Zachery Bryan (Harry Keough), Jimmy Jean-Louis (Joe Gatjaens), Richard Jenik (Joe Maca), Craig Hawksley (Walter Giesler), John Rhys-Davis (Coach Bill Jeffrey). Directed by David Anspaugh and produced by Howard Baldwin, Karen Elise Baldwin, Peter Newman, and Ginger T. Perkins. Screenplay by Angelo Pizzo, based on the book by Geoffrey Douglas.

The Game of Their Lives tells the story of an astonishing soccer match in 1950, when an unsung team of Americans went to Brazil to compete in the World Cup, and defeated England, the best team in the world. So extraordinary was the upset, I learn on the Internet Movie Database, that "London bookmakers offered odds of 500-1 against such a preposterous event," and "The *New York Times* refused to run the score when it was first reported, deeming it a hoax."

So it was a hell of an upset. Pity about the movie. Obviously made with all of the best will in the world, its heart in the right place, this is a sluggish and dutiful film that plays more like a eulogy than an adventure. Strange, how it follows the form of a sports movie, but has the feeling of an educational film. And all the stranger because the director, David Anspaugh, has made two exhilarating movies about underdogs in sports, *Hoosiers* (1986) and *Rudy* (1993).

In those films he knew how to crank up the suspense and dramatize the supporting characters. Here it feels more like a group of Calvin Klein models have gathered to pose as soccer players from St. Louis. Shouldn't there be at least one player not favored by nature with improbably good looks? And at least a couple who look like they're around twenty, instead of thirty-five? And a goalie who doesn't look exactly like Gerard Butler, who played *The Phantom of the Opera*? True, Frank Borghi, the goalie, is played by Gerard Butler, but that's no excuse: In *Dear Frankie,* Butler

played a perfectly believable character who didn't look like he was posing for publicity photos.

The one personal subplot involves a player who thinks he can't go to Brazil because it conflicts with his wedding day. Instead of milking this for personal conflict, Anspaugh solves it all in one perfunctory scene: The coach talks to the future father-in-law, the father-in-law talks to his daughter, she agrees to move up the wedding, and so no problem-o.

This team is so lackluster, when they go out to get drunk, they don't get drunk. It's 1950, but there's only one cigarette and three cigars in the whole movie. The sound track could have used big band hits from the period, but William Ross's score is so inspirational it belongs on a commercial.

As the movie opens, we see a St. Louis soccer club from a mostly Italian-American neighborhood, and hear a narration that sounds uncannily like an audiobook. Word comes that soccer players from New York will travel to Missouri, an American team will be chosen, and they'll travel to Brazil. The players get this information from their coach, Bill Jeffrey (John Rhys-Davis), who is so uncoach-like that at no point during the entire movie does he give them one single word of advice about the game of soccer. Both Rhys-Davis and the general manager, Walter Giesler (Craig Hawksley), are perfectly convincing in their roles, but the screenplay gives them no dialogue to suggest their characters know much about soccer.

As for the big game itself, the game was allegedly shot on location in Brazil, but never do we get a sense that the fans in the long shots are actually watching the match. The tempo of the game is monotonous, coming down to one would-be British goal after another, all of them blocked by Borghi. This was obviously an amazing athletic feat, but you don't get that sense in the movie. You don't get the sense of soccer much at all; *Bend It Like Beckham* had better soccer—*lots* better soccer, and you could follow it and get involved.

At the end of the film, before a big modern

soccer match, the surviving members of that 1950 team are called out onto the field and introduced. That should provide us with a big emotional boost, as we see the real men next to insets of their characters in the movie. But it doesn't, because we never got to know the characters in the movie. *The Game of Their Lives* covers its story like an assignment, not like a mission.

Games People Play: New York ★ ★
NO MPAA RATING, 100 m., 2004

As themselves, more or less: Joshua Coleman, Sarah Smith, Scott Ryan, Dani Marco, David Maynard, Elisha Imani Wilson, Dr. Gilda Carle, and Jim Caruso. Directed by James Ronald Whitney and produced by Whitney and Neil Stephens. Screenplay by Whitney.

Games People Play: New York plays most of its games with the audience. It pretends to be a documentary about the filming of a pilot for a TV reality program, but it contains so much full frontal nudity, semi-explicit sex, and general raunchiness that it's impossible to imagine it anywhere on TV except pay-for-view adult cable. As viewers, we intuit that it is more, or less, than it seems: That in some sense the whole project is a scam. Yes, but a scam that involves real actors doing real things while they're really in front of the camera.

The premise: Auditions are held to select six finalists for a game-show pilot. The winner of the contest will be paid $10,000. The actors are asked to be attractive and "completely uninhibited," and so they are. They're awarded points for their success at such events as: (1) asking complete strangers for a urine sample; (2) the men: enacting casting-couch seductions with would-be actresses not in on the gag; (3) the women: seducing delivery men by dropping a towel and standing there naked; (4) persuading strangers to join a man and woman in a "naked trio" in a nearby hotel room, and (5) persuading a stranger in the next toilet stall to join them in the reading of a scene they're rehearsing.

Amazingly (or maybe not, given the times we live in), the movie not only finds actors willing to play these roles, but men and women

off the street who volunteer (in the case of the urine and naked trio gags) or are at least good sports (as in the dropped towel routine). After having been tricked into appearing in the film, they actually sign releases allowing their footage to be used.

These episodes are intercut with sessions where a psychologist named Dr. Gilda Carle and a publicist named Jim Caruso interview the finalists. I have no idea if these people are real, but their cross-examinations elicit harrowing confessions: One woman was raped at four and then beaten by her father, another saw her father murdered, a third is bulimic, a man is a male prostitute, and so on. The uncanny thing about the revelations at the end of the movie is that we cannot be absolutely sure if this is all fiction, or only some of it.

The film was made by James Ronald Whitney, whose *Just, Melvin* is one of the most powerful documentaries I've seen, about a man who abused and molested many members of Whitney's extended family and is finally confronted on screen. What's odd about *Games People Play* is that Whitney seems to have set up the film and offered the $10,000 prize in order to manipulate his actors and their victims into abusing themselves.

Although acting is a noble profession, there is little nobility in being an out-of-work actor, and the ambience at a lot of auditions resembles the desperation of a soup line. *Games People Play* proves, if nothing else, that there are actors who will do almost anything to get in a movie. The actors here (Joshua Coleman, Sarah Smith, Scott Ryan, Dani Marco, David Maynard, Elisha Imani Wilson) are all effective in their scenes, sometimes moving, sometimes more convincing than they have a right to be. But we cringe at how the movie uses them.

How do you rate a movie like this? Star ratings seem irrelevant. It is either a brilliant example of an experiment in psychological manipulation (four stars) or a reprehensible exploitation of the ambitions and vulnerabilities of actors and others who did the director no harm (zero stars). Because it evokes a strange and horrible fascination, I suppose the stars must fall in the middle (two), but your reaction will swing all the way to one side or the other. I felt creepy afterward.

Garage Days ★ ★ ★
R, 105 m., 2003

Kick Gurry (Freddy), Maya Stange (Kate), Pia Miranda (Tanya), Russell Dykstra (Bruno), Brett Stiller (Joe), Chris Sadrinna (Lucy), Andy Anderson (Kevin), Marton Csokas (Shad Kern). Directed by Alex Proyas and produced by Topher Dow and Proyas. Screenplay by Proyas, Dave Warner, and Michael Udesky.

Garage Days is about an Australian rock band that's a little too old and a little too untalented to make the big time, but kids itself that stardom is on the way—maybe because the alternative is a boring job and no dreams. The movie is set in the Sydney suburb of Newtown, which is a little like Chicago's New Town or Rogers Park, a mixture of clubs, bars, and (relatively) affordable housing. Sleeping in each other's beds and living in each other's pockets, the band members pick up a gig here or there, no thanks to a helpless manager.

Kick Gurry stars as Freddy, the Val Kilmer-ish lead singer, and the band also includes his girlfriend, Tanya (Pia Miranda), the guitarist, Joe (Brett Stiller), and the usually zonked Lucy (Chris Sadrinna) on drums. Freddy and Joe's girlfriend, Kate (Maya Stange), have a conversation one day that leads to an unexpected kiss, and to all sorts of warfare within the band, leading to a lot of anguished changing of partners.

Meanwhile, the band hangs out in a hotel bar where the owner does everything he can to make them feel unwelcome, and they track down an elusive rock impresario (Marton Csokas) who may or may not give them the big break they may or may not deserve. Always around as an omen of what could happen is Kevin (Andy Anderson), Joe's dad, who was sort of a rock star in the 1970s, and now looks exactly like someone who might have once been sort of a rock star in the 1970s and never got over it.

Garage Days is more about style than plot, and the director, Alex Proyas *(The Crow, Dark City),* hurtles into scenes with gleeful energy, sends words careening into space, uses whammo titles to introduce "Fun with Drugs" segments, and edits some sequences like a music video on fast-forward. We eventually catch on that the purpose of the movie is not to portray these lives, but the scene itself, a bohemian quarter where would-be musicians, well past their sell-by dates, hold onto the lifestyle because, well, it's fun.

The movie has a lot of affection for these scruffy wannabes, and I liked the fact that they were not arrogant, aggressive types, but sort of average, with reasonable values and ambitions. At the end, when the love of Freddy's life seems to be moving out of town and he desperately pursues her in a taxi, the scene is purely and simply about romance, and Freddy is perfectly prepared to seem uncool.

The movie is not in any sense a musical featuring this band (which, as nearly as I could tell, does not have a name). The sound track has a lot of music, freely selected from pop hits old and new, but the running gag is that the band never gets to play, and so we never get to hear it. When we finally do, at a big annual rock concert, it provides a suitably affectionate ending for this whimsical and kind of lovable story.

Garden State ★ ★ ★
R, 109 m., 2004

Zach Braff (Andrew Largeman), Natalie Portman (Sam), Peter Sarsgaard (Mark), Ian Holm (Gideon Largeman), Method Man (Diego), Jean Smart (Carol). Directed by Zach Braff and produced by Pamela Abdy, Gary Gilbert, Dan Halsted, and Richard Klubeck. Screenplay by Braff.

Andrew Largeman, the hero of *Garden State,* is almost catatonic when first we see him. He's flat on his back under an unwrinkled white sheet on a white bed in a white room with no other furnishings except for an answering machine, which is recording a message from his father informing him that his mother has drowned in the bathtub. Andrew gets up and looks into his medicine cabinet, where every shelf is filled with neatly arranged rows of prescription drugs.

We learn in the following scenes that Andrew is a would-be actor (he played a retarded quarterback on a made-for-cable movie), works in a Vietnamese restaurant, has not been home to New Jersey in nine years, and is overmedicated. When he leaves all the pills behind before flying home for the funeral, his life begins to budge again.

Garden State was written and directed by Zach Braff, who stars as Andrew. He has one of those faces, like David Schwimmer's, that seem congenitally dubious. He returns home to his father, Gideon (Ian Holm), who is very dry and distant, masking anger: Gideon is a psychiatrist who believes Andrew will never be well "until you forgive yourself for what you did to your mother." What Andrew did, in Gideon's mind, was to make the woman into a paraplegic by pushing her so that she fell over the door of a dishwasher. What Andrew believes is that he was a very small boy, the dishwasher had a broken latch, and his father is full of it.

Andrew's new life begins when he recognizes the gravediggers at his mother's funeral. These are high school buddies he left behind. Soon he's high on Ecstasy and playing spin-the-bottle at a party, and not long after that he's unexpectedly in love. She is Sam (Natalie Portman), a local girl who is one of those creatures you sometimes find in the movies, a girl who is completely available, absolutely desirable, and really likes you. Portman's success in creating this character is all the more impressive because we learn almost nothing about her except that she's great to look at and has those positive attributes.

The movie joins Andrew, Sam, and his high school buddy Mark (Peter Sarsgaard) on an odyssey through the wilds of New Jersey, which contains stranger denizens than Oz. Mark is a stoner with a wide range of interesting friends, including a couple who live in a boat at the bottom of a stone quarry, and a high school classmate who's made millions with the invention of silent Velcro ("it doesn't make that noise when you pull it apart").

Andrew is awakening gradually from a long, sedated nothingness. He tries to communicate with his father, he tries to reconnect with his feelings, and mostly he tries to deal with the enormous puzzle that Sam represents. What is he to do about her? His romantic instincts have been on hold for so long he's like a kid with his first girlfriend.

Garden State inspires obvious comparisons with *The Graduate*, not least in the similarity of the two heroes; both Benjamin and Andrew are passive, puzzled, and quizzical in the face of incoming exhortations. The presence of Simon and Garfunkel on the sound track must not be entirely coincidental. But *The Graduate* is a critique of the world Benjamin finds himself in, and *Garden State* is the world's critique of Andrew. All of the people he meets are urging him, in one way or another, to wake up and smell the coffee. All except for his father, whose anger is so deep he prefers his son medicated into a kind of walking sleep. Ian Holm plays the role with perfect pitch, making small emotional adjustments instead of big dramatic moves.

This is not a perfect movie; it meanders and ambles and makes puzzling detours. But it's smart and unconventional, with a good eye for the perfect detail, as when Andrew arrives at work in Los Angeles and notices that the spigot from a gas pump, ripped from its hose when he drove away from a gas station, is still stuck in his gas tank. Something like that tells you a lot about a person's state of mind.

Garfield: The Movie ★ ★ ★
PG, 85 m., 2004

Voice of Bill Murray (Garfield), Breckin Meyer (Jon Arbuckle), Jennifer Love Hewitt (Dr. Liz Wilson), Stephen Tobolowsky (Happy Chapman), Eve Brent (Mrs. Baker), Voice of Debra Messing (Arlene), Voice of David Eigenberg (Nermal), Voice of Brad Garrett (Luca), Voice of Alan Cumming (Persnikitty), Voice of Jimmy Kimmel (Spanky). Directed by Peter Hewitt and produced by John Davis. Screenplay by Joel Cohen and Alec Sokolow, based on the comic strip by Jim Davis.

Yep, this is Garfield, all right. *Garfield: The Movie* captures the elusive charm of the most egotistical character on the funny pages, and drops him into a story that allows him to bask in his character flaws. That Garfield is revealed to be brave and conscientious after all will not surprise anyone, although it might embarrass him.

I don't know who had the idea that Bill Murray would be the right actor to do Garfield's voice, but the casting is inspired.

Murray's voice-over work finds the right balance for Garfield—between smugness and uncertainty, between affection and detachment, between jealousy and a grudging ability to see the other point of view.

In this case, the other POV belongs to Odie, a dog that is given to Jon (Breckin Meyer), Garfield's owner, by his sexy veterinarian, Dr. Liz (Jennifer Love Hewitt). Garfield is shocked and astonished to have to share pillow space with a dog, not to mention quality time with Jon ("You're not just my owner—you're my primary caregiver"). Being Garfield, he expresses his displeasure not with a humiliating public display, but by subtle subterfuge. He steers the dog outdoors, and, dogs being dogs, Odie chases a car and then another one, and gets lost, and is picked up by a little old lady who advertises him.

There's a parallel plot involving the talentless Happy Chapman (Stephen Tobolowsky), who hosts a TV show with a pet cat. He thinks maybe using a dog might bring him national exposure, tells the little old lady he is Odie's owner, and as a training strategy gives him electrical shocks from a cruel collar. Whether Garfield is able to break into and out of the pound, save Odie, expose Chapman, and reunite Jon with both the dog and Garfield's own noble presence, I will leave for you to discover.

The movie, based on the comic strip by Jim Davis, has been directed by Peter Hewitt and written by Joel Cohen and Alec Sokolow. The filmmakers obviously understand and love Garfield, and their movie lacks that sense of smarmy slumming you sometimes get when Hollywood brings comic strips to the screen. Although Garfield claims "I don't do chases," the movie does have a big chase scene and other standard plot ingredients, but it understands that Garfield's personality, his behavior, his glorious self-absorption, are what we're really interested in. The Davis strip is not about a story but about an attitude.

If they hadn't gotten Garfield right, nothing else would have mattered. But they did. And they've also solved the perplexing problem of how to integrate a cartoon cat into a world of real humans and animals. Garfield talks all through the movie (this is one of Murray's most talkative roles), but only we can hear him; that's the equivalent of his

thought bubbles in the strip. Garfield is animated, the other animals and the humans are real, and the movie does a convincing job of combining the two levels. Garfield looks like neither a cartoon nor a real cat, but like something in between—plump, squinty, and satisfied. Uncanny how when he talks his mouth looks like Murray's.

In a film mostly involved with plot, there are two scenes that are irrelevant but charming. In one of them, Garfield and Odie perform in sort of a music video, and in the other, at the end, Garfield has a solo, singing "I Feel Good" and dancing along. Oh, and Jon and Dr. Liz fall in love, although Garfield is no doubt confident he will remain the center of their attention.

George A. Romero's Land of the Dead ★ ★ ★
R, 93 m., 2005

Simon Baker (Riley), John Leguizamo (Cholo), Asia Argento (Slack), Robert Joy (Charlie), Dennis Hopper (Kaufman), Eugene Clark (Big Daddy). Directed by George Romero and produced by Romero, Mark Canton, Bernie Goldmann, and Peter Grunwald. Screenplay by Romero.

In a world where the dead are returning to life, the word trouble has lost its meaning.
—Dennis Hopper in *Land of the Dead*

Now this is interesting. In the future world of *George A. Romero's Land of the Dead,* both zombies and their victims have started to evolve. The zombies don't simply shuffle around mindlessly, eating people. And the healthy humans don't simply shoot them. The zombies have learned to communicate on a rudimentary level, to make plans, however murky, and to learn from their tormenters. When the zombie named Big Daddy picks up a machine gun in this movie, that is an ominous sign.

The healthy humans, on the other hand, have evolved a class system. Those with money and clout live in Fiddler's Green, a luxury high-rise where all their needs are catered to under one roof—and just as well, because they are not eager to go outside. Other survivors cluster in the city at the foot of the tower, in a city barricaded against the zombie hordes outside. Mercenaries stage raids outside the safe zone in Dead Reckoning, a gigantic armored truck, and bring back canned food, gasoline, and booze.

The most intriguing single shot in *Land of the Dead* is a commercial for Fiddler's Green, showing tanned and smiling residents, dressed in elegant leisure wear, living the good life. They look like the white-haired eternally youthful golfers in ads for retirement paradises. The shot is intriguing for two reasons: (1) Why does Fiddler's Green need to advertise, when it is full and people are literally dying to get in? And (2) What is going through the minds of its residents as they relax in luxury, sip drinks, shop in designer stores, and live the good life? Don't they know the world outside is one of unremitting conflict and misery?

Well, yes, they probably do, and one of the reasons George A. Romero's zombie movies have remained fresh is that he suggests such questions. The residents of Fiddler's Green and the zombies have much the same relationship as citizens of rich nations have with starving orphans and refugees. The lesson is clear: It's good to live in Fiddler's Green.

That's why Cholo (John Leguizamo) wants to move in. He's one of the best mercenaries in the hire of Kaufman (Dennis Hopper), who is the Donald Trump of Fiddler's Green. Kaufman sits in his penthouse, smokes good cigars, sips brandy, and gets rich, although the movie never explains how money works in this economy, where possessions are acquired by looting and retained by force. How, for that matter, do the residents of Fiddler's Green earn a living? Do they spend all day in their casual wear, flashing those white teeth as they perch on the arms of each other's lounge chairs? The thing that bothers me about ads for retirement communities is that the residents seem condemned to leisure.

Cholo works under Riley (Simon Baker), the leader of Kaufman's hired force and the movie's hero. Riley is responsible, calm, and sane. Cholo is not, and Leguizamo plays another one of his off-the-wall loose cannons. He has added an unreasonable amount of interest to any number of recent movies. Also important to the plot is Slack (Asia Argento), a sometime hooker who is beautiful and

heroic and intended for better things, and is thrown into a pit of zombies to fend for herself. For that matter, zombies themselves are occasionally hung by the heels with bull's-eyes painted on them for target practice. And Romero finds still new and entertaining ways for unspeakably disgusting things to happen to the zombies and their victims.

The balance of power in this ordered little world is upset when Kaufman refuses Cholo's request to move into Fiddler's Green. There is a long waiting list, etc. Cholo steals Dead Reckoning, he is pursued, the zombies get (somewhat) organized, and Big Daddy (Eugene Clark) begins to develop a gleam of intelligence in his dead blue eyes.

The puzzle in all the zombie movies is why any zombies are still—I was about to write "alive," but I guess the word is "moving." Shooting them in the head or decapitating them seems simple enough, and dozens are mowed down with machine guns by the troops in Dead Reckoning. Guards at the city barriers kill countless more. Since they are obviously zombies and no diagnosis is necessary before execution on sight, why do they seem to be winning?

This and other questions may await Romero's next movie. It's good to see him back in the genre he invented with *Night of the Living Dead*, and still using zombies not simply for target practice but as a device for social satire. It's probably not practical from a box office point of view, but I would love to see a movie set entirely inside a thriving Fiddler's Green. There would be zombies outside but we'd never see them or deal with them. We would simply regard the Good Life as it is lived by those who have walled the zombies out. Do they relax? Have they peace of mind? Do the miseries of others weigh upon them? The parallels with the real world are tantalizing.

Gerry ★ ★ ★
R, 103 m., 2003

Casey Affleck (Gerry), Matt Damon (Gerry). Directed by Gus Van Sant and produced by Dany Wolf. Screenplay by Casey Affleck, Matt Damon, and Van Sant.

Not long after Gus Van Sant got the bright idea of doing a shot-by-shot remake of Hitchcock's

Psycho in color, I ran into him at the Calcutta Film Festival, and asked him why in the hell he'd come up with that bright idea. "So that no one else would have to," he replied serenely. With his new film, *Gerry*, he has removed another project from the future of the cinema and stored it prudently in the past. He is like an adult removing dangerous toys from the reach of reckless kids.

Gerry stars Casey Affleck and Matt Damon as two friends named Gerry who go for a walk in the desert and get lost. There, I've gone and given away the plot. They walk and walk and walk. For a while they talk, and then they walk in silence, and then they stagger, and then they look like those *New Yorker* cartoons of guys lost in the desert who reach out a desperate hand toward a distant mirage of Jiffy-Lube. It would have been too cruel for Van Sant to add Walter Brennan on the sound track, listenin' to the age-old story of the shiftin', whisperin' sands.

A movie like this doesn't come along every day. I am glad I saw it. I saw it at the 2002 Sundance Film Festival, where a fair number of people walked out. I would say half. I was reminded of advice once given me by the veteran Chicago movie exhibitor Oscar Brotman: "Roger, if nothing has happened by the end of the first reel, nothing is going to happen." If I were to advise you to see *Gerry*, you might have a good case on your hands for a class-action suit.

And yet, and yet—the movie is so gloriously bloody-minded, so perverse in its obstinacy, that it rises to a kind of mad purity. The longer the movie ran, the less I liked it and the more I admired it. The Gerrys are stuck out there, and it looks like no plot device is going to come along and save them. The horizon is barren for 360 degrees of flat wasteland. We have lost most of the original eight hours of *Greed* (1925), Erich von Stroheim's film that also ends with its heroes lost in Death Valley, but after seeing *Gerry* I think we can call off the search for the missing footage.

The screenplay for *Gerry*, by Affleck, Damon, and Van Sant, is not without humor. Before they realize the enormity of their predicament, the two Gerrys discuss this dumb contestant they saw on *Jeopardy*, and Affleck expresses frustration about a video game he has been playing (he

conquered Thebes, only to discover he needed twelve horses and had but eleven).

One morning one of the characters finds himself standing on top of a tall rock, and is not sure how he got there, or whether he should risk breaking an ankle by jumping down. If I ever get lost in Death Valley, it will be more or less exactly like this.

After seeing the film at Sundance, as I reported at the time, I got in a conversation with three women who said they thought it was "existential."

"Existential?" I asked.

"Like, we have to choose whether to live or die."

"They do not have a choice to make," I said. "They're lost and they can't find their car. They have no water and no food."

"What I think," said one of the women, "is that it's like Samuel Beckett's *Waiting for Godot*, except without the dialogue."

"It has dialogue," her friend said.

"But not serious dialogue."

"The dialogue in *Godot* is not serious," I said. "At least, it is not intended by the speakers to be serious."

"In *Godot*," the woman said, "they wait and wait and Godot never comes. In *Gerry*, they walk and walk and they never get anywhere."

"There you have it," I said.

I arrive at the end of this review having done my duty as a critic. I have described the movie accurately, and you have a good idea what you are in for, if you go to see it. Most of you will not. I cannot argue with you. Some of you will—the brave and the curious. You embody the spirit of the man who first wondered what it would taste like to eat an oyster.

Ghosts of the Abyss ★ ★ ★

G, 59 m., 2003

Narrated by Bill Paxton, and featuring Lewis Abernathy, Dr. Lori Johnston, Don Lynch, Ken Marschall, Dr. Charles Pellegrino, and Tava Smiley. A documentary directed and written by James Cameron. Produced by Cameron, Chuck Comisky, and Andrew Wight.

The wreck of *Titanic*, which for decades seemed forever out of reach, has in recent years been visited by documentaries that bring back ghostly images of a party that ended in midsong. These films have an undeniable fascination, and none has penetrated more completely and evocatively than James Cameron's *Ghosts of the Abyss.*

The earliest films about *Titanic* were marvelous just because they existed at all. Cameron mounts a much more ambitious expedition to the bottom of the sea, involving a powerful light "chandelier" that hangs above the wreck and illuminates it, and two remote-controlled cameras named Jake and Elwood that propel themselves into tight corners and explore the inside of the ship.

Guiding them are expedition members in deep-diving exploration subs, including Bill Paxton, who starred in Cameron's *Titanic* and now narrates this documentary and shoots some of it himself. The result is often spellbinding, and to mention some of the sights we see is to praise the film's ambition.

The agile little camera-bots are able, for example, to snake their way into the ship's grand ballroom, and to discover that the Tiffany cut-glass windows are, astonishingly, still intact. Later, Cameron is able to position one of the minisubs outside the ship to shine its light through the windows for the camera inside, and we see the colors brought alive by light for the first time since the ship hit the fatal iceberg.

Other scenes actually discover the brass bed in the suite occupied by the "unsinkable" Molly Brown, who was such a famous survivor she had a Broadway musical named after her, and who always insisted her bed was brass, not wood. We also see a bowler hat, still waiting atop a dresser, and glasses and a carafe, left where they were put down after a final drink.

Cameron, who achieved so much with digital effects in *Titanic,* here uses similar technology to animate his haunted undersea scenes. He shoots the *Titanic* today—its empty corridors, its deserted grand staircase, its abandoned decks—and then populates the ship with a ghostly overlay showing the restored ship with its elegant passengers on their cruise to doom.

The movie is an impressive achievement, but that is not because of its trumpeted selling-point, the fact that it was shot in 3-D. I saw the first 3-D movie *(Bwana Devil)* and I have seen most of them since, as the technology has been improved and perfected, and I have arrived at the conclusion that 3-D will never be ready for prime time: It is an unnecessary and distracting redundancy. It can be done very well (as with the custom-made $200 glasses supplied with some IMAX features) and we can admire its quality and yet doubt its usefulness. Old-fashioned 2-D provides an illusion of reality that has convinced moviegoers for one hundred years. We accept it and do not think about it. The 3-D process is a mistake because it distracts attention away from the content and toward the process.

Ghosts of the Abyss is being shown around the country in 3-D on IMAX screens and also in some regular theaters. Do not feel deprived if your theater does not have 3-D. You won't be missing a thing.

Note: I learn that Cameron's next fiction film, his first since Titanic, *will be a feature shot in 3-D. "People are looking for a new way to be stimulated," industry analyst Paul Dergarabedian said in the announcement story.*

He is correct about people, but wrong that 3-D is a new way to be stimulated. It is an old way that has never lived up to its promise. If Cameron wants to be a pioneer instead of a retro hobbyist, he should obviously use Maxivision 48, which provides a picture of such startling clarity that it appears to be 3-D in the sense that the screen seems to open a transparent window on reality. Ghosts of the Abyss *would have been incomparably more powerful in the process.*

Maxivision 48 would be cheaper than 3-D, would look dramatically better, would not require those silly glasses, would be backward-compatible for standard theaters, and would allow Cameron to introduce the next step forward in movie projection, rather than returning to the obsolete past. Cameron has the clout and the imagination to make this leap forward, not just for his next film but for an industry that needs something dramatic and new and realizes it isn't going to be digital projection. This is his chance to explore the future of cinema as bravely as he ventured to the ocean floor.

Gigli ★★½
R, 124 m., 2003

Ben Affleck (Larry), Jennifer Lopez (Ricki), Justin Bartha (Brian), Christopher Walken (Det.

Jacobellis), Lenny Venito (Louis), Lainie Kazan (Mother). Directed and produced by Martin Brest. Screenplay by Brest.

Jennifer Lopez and Ben Affleck are in love and plan to get married, as you already know unless you are sealed off from all media, in which case you are not reading this review, so put it down. Because they are a famous couple, starring in a movie romance, we expect something conventional and predictable, and that is not what we get from *Gigli*. The movie tries to do something different, thoughtful, and a little daring with their relationship, and although it doesn't quite work, maybe the movie is worth seeing for some scenes that are really very good.

Consider the matching monologues. They've gotten into an argument over the necessity of the penis, which she, as a lesbian, feels is an inferior device for delivering sexual pleasure. He delivers an extended lecture on the use, necessity, and perfect design of the appendage. It is a rather amazing speech, the sort of thing some moviegoers are probably going to want to memorize. Then she responds. She is backlit, dressed in skintight workout clothes, doing yoga, and she continues to stretch and extend and bend and pose as she responds with her speech in praise of the vagina. When she is finished, Reader, the vagina has won, hands down. It is so rare to find dialogue of such originality and wit, so well written, that even though we know the exchange basically involves actors showing off, they do it so well, we let them.

Affleck plays Larry Gigli (rhymes with "Geely") and one wonders, learning that they rejected several earlier titles for the movie, which ones could have been worse than this. He's an errand boy for a tough-talking Los Angeles mobster named Louis (Lenny Venito). Louis wants to do a favor for a New York mob boss, and orders Gigli to kidnap the mentally disabled brother of a federal prosecutor. Gigli does, walking out of a care facility with Brian (Justin Bartha), who has Rain Man's syndrome. He takes him home, there is a knock on the door, and he meets Ricki (Lopez), who is also a mob enforcer. Louis is taking no chances and has assigned both of them to guard the boy.

This is the setup for an obvious plot that the movie, written by director Martin Brest, wisely avoids. Instead of falling in love and psychically

adopting Brian, or (alternate cliché) fighting all the time, Gigli and Ricki get to like each other very, very much, even though she makes it perfectly clear that she is a lesbian. So resolute is the movie in its idea of her character that she doesn't even cave in and have a conversion experience, which is what we're expecting, but remains a lesbian—as indeed, as a good lesbian, she should.

Their conversations take on a rather desperate quality, since Gigli feels lust and love, and she feels strong affection. What transpires between them, and whether they ever put their theories about genitalia through a field test, I will not reveal. Meanwhile, Brian behaves like a well-rehearsed Movie Retarded Person, does or doesn't do whatever the script requires, and conveniently disappears into his room when he is not needed.

Lopez and Affleck are sweet and appealing in their performances; the buzz said they didn't have chemistry, but the buzz was wrong. What they don't have is conviction. There is no way these two are killers for the mob. They don't have the disposition for it. And consider this: If you had kidnapped the highly recognizable Rain Man brother of a top federal prosecutor, would you drive him all over Los Angeles in a convertible with the top down, and take him to restaurants and malls? So the crime plot is completely unconvincing. It does, however, open the door for the movie's collection of inspired supporting performances. Christopher Walken, as a cop who knows Gigli, walks into his apartment and does five minutes of Walkenizing and the audience eats up every second. Lainie Kazan, as Gigli's mother, sizes up Ricky instantly, likes her, learns she is a lesbian, chucks her under the chin, and says, "But you've been with guys, right?" Then she talks about her own Highly Experimental youth, while solidifying her position as the ethnic mother of choice in modern American movies. And then toward the end, Starkman, the mob boss from New York, arrives, and is played in a cameo by Al Pacino—who makes the journey from extravagant dopiness to chilling intimidation faster and better than anyone else I can think of.

So the movie doesn't work. The ending especially doesn't work, and what's worse, it doesn't work for a long time, because it fails to work for minute after minute, and includes dialogue that is almost entirely unnecessary. But there is good stuff here. Affleck and Lopez create lovely characters, even if they're not the ones they're allegedly playing, and the supporting performances and a lot of the dialogue is wonderful. It's just that there's too much time between the good scenes. Too much repetitive dialogue. Too many soulful looks. Behavior we can't believe. I wonder what would happen if you sweated 15 minutes out of this movie. Maybe it would work. The materials are there.

The Girl Next Door ½ ★
R, 110 m., 2004

Emile Hirsch (Matthew Kidman), Elisha Cuthbert (Danielle), Timothy Olyphant (Kelly), James Remar (Hugo Posh), Chris Marquette (Eli), Paul Dano (Klitz). Directed by Luke Greenfield and produced by Harry Gittes, Charles Gordon, and Marc Sternberg. Screenplay by Stuart Blumberg, David Wagner, and Brent Goldberg.

The studio should be ashamed of itself for advertising *The Girl Next Door* as a teenage comedy. It's a nasty piece of business, involving a romance between a teenage porn actress and a high school senior. A good movie could presumably be made from this premise—a good movie can be made from anything, in the right hands and way—but this is a dishonest, quease-inducing "comedy" that had me feeling uneasy and then unclean. Who in the world read this script and thought it was acceptable?

The film stars Emile Hirsch as Matthew Kidman. (Please tell me the "Kidman" is not an oblique reference to Nicole Kidman and therefore to Tom Cruise and therefore to *Risky Business,* the film this one so desperately wants to resemble.) One day he sees a sexy girl moving in next door, and soon he's watching through his bedroom window as she undresses as girls undress only in his dreams. Then she sees him, snaps off the light, and a few minutes later rings the doorbell.

Has she come to complain? No, she says nothing about the incident and introduces herself to Matthew's parents: Her aunt is on vacation, and she is house-sitting. Soon they're in her car together and Danielle is coming on to Matthew: "Did you like what you saw?" He did. She says now it's her turn to see him naked, and makes him strip and stand in the middle of the road while she shines the headlights on him. Then she scoops up his underpants and drives away, leaving him to walk home naked, ho, ho. (It is not easy to reach out of a car and scoop up underpants from the pavement while continuing to drive. Try it sometime.)

Danielle (Elisha Cuthbert) has two personalities: In one, she's a sweet, misunderstood kid who has never been loved, and in the other she's a twisted emotional sadist who amuses herself by toying with the feelings of the naive Matthew. The movie alternates between these personalities at its convenience, making her quite the most unpleasant character I have seen in some time.

They have a romance going before one of Matthew's buddies identifies her, correctly, as a porn star. The movie seems to think, along with Matthew's friends, that this information is in her favor. Matthew goes through the standard formula: first he's angry with her, then she gets through his defenses, then he believes she really loves him and that she wants to leave the life she's been leading. Problem is, her producer is angry because he wants her to keep working. This character, named Kelly, is played by Timothy Olyphant with a skill that would have distinguished a better movie, but it doesn't work here, because the movie never levels with us. When a guy his age (thirty-six, according to IMDB) "used to be the boyfriend" of a girl her age (nineteen, according to the plot description) and she is already, at nineteen, a famous porn star, there is a good chance the creep corrupted her at an early age; think Traci Lords. That he is now her "producer" under an "exclusive contract" is an elevated form of pimping. To act in porn as a teenager is not a decision freely taken by many teenage girls, and not a life to envy.

There's worse. The movie produces a basically nice guy, named Hugo Posh (James Remar), also a porn king, who is Kelly's rival. That a porn king saves the day gives you an idea of the movie's limited moral horizons. Oh, and not to forget Matthew's best friends, named Eli and Klitz (Chris Marquette and Paul Dano). Klitz? "Spelled with a *K*," he explains.

Kelly steals the money that Matthew has raised to bring a foreign exchange student from Cambodia, and to replace the funds, the resourceful Danielle flies in two porn star friends (played by Amanda Swisten and Sung Hi Lee), so that Matthew, Eli, and Klitz can produce a sex film during the senior prom. The nature of their film is yet another bait-and-switch, in a movie that wants to seem dirtier than it is. Like a strip show at a carnival, it lures you in with promises of sleaze, and after you have committed yourself for the filthy-minded punter you are, it professes innocence.

Risky Business (1983), you will recall, starred Tom Cruise as a young man left home alone by his parents, who wrecks the family Porsche and ends up enlisting a call girl (Rebecca De Mornay) to run a brothel out of his house to raise money to replace the car. The movie is the obvious model for *The Girl Next Door*, but it completely misses the tone and wit of the earlier film, which proved you can get away with that plot, but you have to know what you're doing and how to do it, two pieces of knowledge conspicuously absent here.

One necessary element is to distance the heroine from the seamier side of her life. *The Girl Next Door* does the opposite, actually taking Danielle and her "producer" Kelly to an adult film convention in Las Vegas, and even into a dimly lit room where adult stars apparently pleasure the clients. (There is another scene where Kelly, pretending to be Matthew's friend, takes him to a lap dance emporium and treats him.) We can deal with porn stars, lap dances, and whatever else in a movie that declares itself and plays fair, but to insert this material into something with the look and feel of a teen comedy makes it unsettling. The TV ads will attract audiences expecting something like *American Pie*; they'll be shocked by the squalid content of this film.

Girl with a Pearl Earring ★ ★ ★ ★
PG-13, 95 m., 2003

Scarlett Johansson (Griet), Colin Firth (Johannes Vermeer), Tom Wilkinson (Van Ruijven), Judy Parfitt (Maria Thins), Essie Davis (Catharina), Cillian Murphy (Pieter), Joanna Scanlan (Tanneke), Alakina Mann (Cornelia). Directed by Peter Webber and produced by Andy Paterson and Anand Tucker. Screenplay by Olivia Hetreed, based on the novel by Tracy Chevalier.

Girl with a Pearl Earring is a quiet movie, shaken from time to time by ripples of emotional turbulence far beneath the surface. It is about things not said, opportunities not taken, potentials not realized, lips unkissed. All of these elements are guessed at by the filmmakers as they regard a painting made in about 1665 by Johannes Vermeer. The painting shows a young woman regarding us over her left shoulder. She wears a simple blue headband and a modest smock. Her red lips are slightly parted. Is she smiling? She seems to be glancing back at the moment she was leaving the room. She wears a pearl earring.

Not much is known about Vermeer, who left about thirty-five paintings. Nothing is known about his model. You can hear that it was his daughter, a neighbor, a tradeswoman. You will not hear that she was his lover, because Vermeer's household was under the iron rule of his mother-in-law, who was vigilant as a hawk. The painting has become as intriguing in its modest way as the *Mona Lisa*. The girl's face turned toward us from centuries ago demands that we ask, who was she? What was she thinking? What was the artist thinking about her?

Tracy Chevalier's novel speculating about the painting has now been filmed by Peter Webber, who casts Scarlett Johansson as the girl and Colin Firth as Vermeer. I can think of many ways the film could have gone wrong, but it goes right because it doesn't cook up melodrama and romantic intrigue but tells a story that's content with its simplicity. The painting is contemplative, reflective, subdued, and the film must be too: We don't want lurid revelations breaking into its mood.

Sometimes two people will regard each other over a gulf too wide to ever be bridged and know immediately what could have happened, and that it never will. That is essentially the message of *Girl with a Pearl Earring*. The girl's name is Griet, according to this story. She lives nearby. She is sent by her blind father to work in Vermeer's house, where several small children are about to be joined by a new arrival. The household is run like a factory with the mother-in-law, Maria Thins (Judy Parfitt), as foreman. She has set her daughter to work producing babies while her son-in-law produces paintings. Both have an output of about one a year, which is good if you are a mother, but not if you are a painter.

Nobody ever says what they think in this house except for Maria, whose thoughts are all too obvious anyway. Catharina (Essie Davis), Vermeer's wife, sometimes seems to be standing where she hopes nobody will see her. It becomes clear that Griet is intelligent in a natural way, but has no idea what to do with her ideas. Of course she attracts Vermeer's attention; she's a hard worker and responds instinctively to the manual labor of painting—to the craft, the technique, the strategy, even the chemistry (did you know that the color named Indian Yellow is distilled from the urine of cows fed on mango leaves?).

In one flawless sequence, Griet is alone in Vermeer's studio and looks at the canvas he is working on, looks at what he is painting, looks back, looks forth, and then moves a chair away from a window. When he returns and sees what she has done, he studies the composition carefully and removes the chair from his painting. Eventually he has her move up to the attic, closer to his studio, where she can mix his paints, which she does very well.

And then of course they start sleeping together? Not in this movie. Vermeer has a rich patron named Van Ruijven (Tom Wilkinson). If Vermeer is too shy to reveal feelings for his maid, Van Ruijven is not. He wants a painting of the girl. This, of course, would be unacceptable to Catharina Vermeer, whose best-developed quality is her insecurity—but it is not unacceptable to her mother, who must keep a rich patron happy. Thus Griet becomes a model.

There is a young man in the town, Pieter (Cillian Murphy), a butcher's apprentice, who is attracted to Griet. He would make her a good husband, in this world where status and opportunity are assigned by caste. Griet likes him. It's not that she likes Vermeer more; indeed, she's so intimidated she barely speaks to the artist. It's that—well, Griet could never be a butcher, but she could be a painter.

Mankind has Shakespeares who were illiterate, Mozarts who never heard a note, Picassos who never touched a brush. Griet *could* be a painter. Whether a good or bad one, she will never know. Vermeer senses it. The moments of greatest intimacy between the simple peasant girl and the famous artist come when they sit side by side in wordless communication, mixing paints, both doing the same job, both understanding it.

Do not believe those who think this movie is about the "mystery" of the model, or Vermeer's sources of inspiration, or medieval gender roles, or whether the mother-in-law was the man in the family. A movie about those things would have been a bad movie. *Girl with a Pearl Earring* is about how they share a professional understanding that neither one has in any way with anyone else alive. I look at the painting and I realize that Griet is telling Vermeer, without using any words, "Well, if it were *my* painting, I'd have her stand like this."

Gloomy Sunday ★ ★ ★
NO MPAA RATING, 114 m., 2003

Erika Marozsán (Ilona Varnai), Joachim Król (László Szabo), Ben Becker (Hans Wieck), Stefano Dionisi (András Aradi). Directed by Rolf Schübel and produced by Michael André and Richard Schöps. Screenplay by Schübel and Ruth Toma, based on the novel by Nick Barkow.

Odd, how affecting this imperfect film becomes. It's a broad romantic melodrama set in Budapest before and during the Holocaust, and that is not, you will agree, an ideal time to set a love story. And if it is true that the title song drove hundreds to commit suicide, some of them may have merely been very tired of hearing it.

And yet *Gloomy Sunday* held my attention, and there were times when I was surprisingly involved. It's an old-fashioned romantic triangle, told with schmaltzy music on the sound track and a heroine with a smoky singing voice, and then the Nazis turn up and it gets very complicated and heartbreaking.

The movie opened Friday in Chicago. So far as I can tell, this is its first American theatrical booking. But listen to this: In New Zealand, it ran for more than a year and became a local phenomenon.

The story begins in Budapest in the 1930s, where László Szabo (Joachim Król) runs a restaurant celebrated for its beef rolls. His hostess is the young and fetching Ilona (Erika Marozsán), and he is in love with her. Together they hire a piano player named András (Stefano Dionisi), and András falls in love with Ilona, and she with him, but she still loves László, and since they all like one another, they arrive at a cozy accommodation.

A regular customer in the 1930s is a German named Hans Wieck (Ben Becker), who also falls in love with Ilona, and says if she will marry him, he will build Germany's largest import-export business, just for her. But as she already has her hands full, she turns him down.

András meanwhile composes a song named "Gloomy Sunday" that sweeps the world and which he has to play every night at the restaurant. Soon a legend grows up around the song, that people who hear it commit suicide. Strangely enough, this detail is based on fact; it was written in 1933 by Rezsó Seress, became an international hit, was recorded by such as Artie Shaw and Billie Holiday (and later Bjork and Elvis Costello), and was banned by the BBC because of its allegedly depressing effect. On the night that Ilona rejects Hans, indeed, he casts himself into the Danube and is hauled out by László. You see what I mean about melodrama.

The war comes. It is well known what the Nazis are doing to the Jews, but László, who is Jewish, has never given much thought to religion and believes such things will never happen in Hungary. He has more than one chance to escape, but remains, and his restaurant becomes even more popular in wartime. A regular customer is none other than Hans Wieck, now in charge of the Hungarian final solution, and he gives László an exemption; his beef rolls are a contribution to the war effort. Wieck, too, is said to be based on a historical figure, a Nazi named Kurt Becher who held a similar job in Budapest.

The movie, which has been fanciful and romantic, now descends into tragedy and betrayal. The carefree days of romance and denial are over, and the closing scenes of the film have an urgency that blindsides us, given the movie's earlier innocence. Then there is an epilogue, which is gratuitous and overlong; we could have done without it.

But the main story has the strength of its characters, who feel deeply and are brave and foolish in equal measure. András is a basket case who wears his emotions on his sleeve, but Ilona loves him for his vulnerability, and László is one of those good souls who find the calm in every situation, think the best of people, are generous and not jealous, and trusting—too trusting. The actors give the characters a touching presence and reality.

The movie will play for a week or two and disappear from Chicago and, for all I know, from North America. Maybe not. Maybe it will play for eighty weeks, like in Auckland.

Note: My information about the legend of Gloomy Sunday *was obtained at www.phespirit. info/gloomysunday, which includes several sets of lyrics.* ☞

Gods and Generals ★ ½
PG-13, 216 m., 2003

Jeff Daniels (Lieutenant Colonel Joshua Chamberlain), Stephen Lang (General "Stonewall" Jackson), Robert Duvall (General Robert E. Lee), Chris Conner (John Wilkes Booth), C. Thomas Howell (Tom Chamberlain), Kevin Conway (Sergeant "Buster" Kilrain), Patrick Gorman (Brigadier General John Bell Hood), Brian Mallon (Brigadier General Winfield Scott Hancock). Directed and produced by Ronald F. Maxwell. Screenplay by Maxwell, based on the book by Jeff M. Shaara.

Here is a Civil War movie that Trent Lott might enjoy. Less enlightened than *Gone with the Wind*, obsessed with military strategy, impartial between South and North, religiously devout, it waits seventy minutes before introducing the first of its two speaking roles for African-Americans; Stonewall Jackson assures his black cook that the South will free him, and the cook looks cautiously optimistic. If World War II were handled this way, there'd be hell to pay.

The movie is essentially about brave men on both sides who fought and died so that . . . well, so that they could fight and die. They are led by generals of blinding brilliance and nobility, although one Northern general makes a stupid error and the movie shows hundreds of his men being slaughtered at great length as the result of it.

The Northerners, one Southerner explains, are mostly Republican profiteers who can go home to their businesses and families if they're voted out of office after the conflict, while the Southerners are fighting for their homes. Slavery is not the issue, in this view, because it would have withered away anyway, although a liberal professor from Maine (Jeff Daniels) makes a speech explaining it is wrong. So we get that cleared up right there, or for sure at Strom Thurmond's birthday party.

The conflict is handled with solemnity worthy of a memorial service. The music, when it is not funereal, sounds like the band playing during the commencement exercises at a sad university. Countless extras line up, march forward, and shoot at each other. They die like flies. That part is accurate, although the stench, the blood, and the cries of pain are tastefully held to the PG-13 standard. What we know about the war from the photographs of Mathew Brady, the poems of Walt Whitman, and the documentaries of Ken Burns is not duplicated here.

Oh, it is a competently made film. Civil War buffs may love it. Every group of fighting men is identified by subtitles, to such a degree that I wondered, fleetingly, if they were being played by Civil War reenactment hobbyists who would want to nudge their friends when their group appeared on the screen. Much is made of the film's total and obsessive historical accuracy; the costumes, flags, battle plans, and ordnance are all doubtless flawless, although there could have been no Sergeant "Buster" Kilrain in the 20th Maine, for the unavoidable reason that "Buster" was never used as a name until Buster Keaton used it.

The actors do what they can, although you can sense them winding up to deliver pithy quotations. Robert Duvall, playing General Robert E. Lee, learns of Stonewall Jackson's battlefield amputation and reflects sadly, "He has lost his left arm, and I have lost my right." His eyes almost twinkle as he envisions that one ending up in *Bartlett's*. Stephen Lang, playing Jackson, has a deathbed scene so wordy, as he issues commands to imaginary subordinates and then prepares himself to cross over the river, that he seems to be stalling. Except for Lee, a nonbeliever, both sides trust in God, just like at the Super Bowl.

Donzaleigh Abernathy plays the other African-American speaking role, that of a maid named Martha who attempts to jump the gun

on Reconstruction by staying behind when her white employers evacuate, and telling the arriving Union troops it is her own house. Later, when they commandeer it as a hospital, she looks a little resentful. This episode, like many others, is kept so resolutely at the cameo level that we realize material of such scope and breadth can be shoehorned into three and a half hours only by sacrificing depth.

Gods and Generals is the kind of movie beloved by people who never go to the movies, because they are primarily interested in something else—the Civil War, for example—and think historical accuracy is a virtue instead of an attribute. The film plays like a special issue of *American Heritage*. Ted Turner is one of its prime movers, and gives himself an instantly recognizable cameo appearance. Since sneak previews must already have informed him that his sudden appearance draws a laugh, apparently he can live with that.

Note: The same director, Ron Maxwell, made the much superior Gettysburg *(1993) and at the end informs us that the third title in the trilogy will be* The Last Full Measure. *Another line from the same source may serve as a warning: "The world will little note, nor long remember, what we say here."*

Godsend ★ ★
PG-13, 102 m., 2004

Greg Kinnear (Paul Duncan), Rebecca Romijn-Stamos (Jessie Duncan), Robert De Niro (Dr. Richard Wells), Cameron Bright (Adam Duncan). Directed by Nick Hamm and produced by Marc Butan, Sean O'Keefe, and Cathy Schulman. Screenplay by Mark Bomback.

Godsend tells the story of parents whose only son is killed in an accident, and who are offered the opportunity to clone him. If all goes well, the grieving mother will bear a child genetically identical to the dead boy. I would find that unspeakably sad, but the movie isn't interested in really considering the implications; it's a thriller, a bad thriller, completely lacking in psychological or emotional truth.

Greg Kinnear and Rebecca Romijn-Stamos star, as Paul and Jessie Duncan; he's an inner-city high school teacher, and she's a photographer.

Immediately after their son, Adam, is killed, they're approached by Dr. Richard Wells (Robert De Niro), who offers them an illegal opportunity to retrieve one of Adam's cells and implant it in Jessie's womb so that she can bear another Adam. At first they resist, but then they agree, and soon they have another son named Adam. Both boys are played by Cameron Bright.

Dr. Wells, who made millions earlier in his career, operates out of a vast medical laboratory in Vermont, and persuades the Duncans to move up there; they must cut all ties with former friends and family, he explains, because of course the Adam clone will raise difficult questions. To help them settle in, he provides a waterfront house that will have every real-estate agent in the audience thinking in the millions. Adam Two is born (in a particularly unconvincing live childbirth scene) and quickly reaches the same birthday that Adam One celebrated just before he was killed. Until then he has been an ideal child, but now he begins to get weird. "Dad," he tells his father, "I've been thinking. I don't think I like you so much any more." As Kinnear recoils in pain, the kid grins and says he was only kidding. Ho, ho. "There was always the possibility," Dr. Wells intones, "that things could change once he passed the age when he died."

I dare not reveal the secret around which the plot revolves, but I can say that Adam Two has visions and night terrors, and in them sees a little boy whose experiences seem to intersect with his own. At school, Adam Two is not popular, perhaps because he spits on playmates and a teacher, perhaps because he is just plain weird; the movie *Omenizes* him with big close-ups, his face pinched and ominous. At home, he has a habit of hanging around in the woodshed with sharp instruments or invading his mother's darkroom, where a lot of photos of Adam One are kept in a box that really should have been locked.

The movie's premise is fascinating, and has stirred up a lot of interest. Some opponents of cloning reportedly confused its Web site (godsendinstitute.org) for the real thing, although that "confusion" has the aroma of a publicity stunt. No matter; *Godsend* isn't about cloning so much as about shock, horror, evil, deception, and the peculiar appeal that demonic children seem to possess for movie audiences.

The performances are ineffective. I would say they are bad, but I suppose they're as good as the material permits. Kinnear and Romijn-Stamos are required to play a couple whose entire relationship is formed and defined by plot gimmicks, and as for De Niro, there are times when he seems positively embarrassed to be seen as that character, saying those things. His final conversation with Kinnear must be the most absurd scene he has ever been asked to play seriously. The movie is so impossible that even the child actor is left stranded. He seems lovable as Adam One, but as Adam Two he seems to have been programmed, not by genetics, but by sub-"Omen" potboilers.

For a brief time, however, I thought director Nick Hamm was using at least one original strategy. During certain tense scenes, I heard a low, ominous, scraping noise, and I thought it was some kind of audible flash-forward to terrors still to come. Then I realized I was hearing carpenters at work on the floor below the screening room. I recommend they be added to an optional sound track on the DVD.

Note: That's going to be one crowded DVD. My fellow critic Joe Leydon points me to a story at scififx.com reporting that director Hamm shot at least seven alternate endings to the movie, including those in which two different characters are killed two different ways, and little Adam kills everybody. Nothing like covering your bases.

Godzilla ★ ½
NO MPAA RATING, 98 m., 2004

Takashi Shimura (Dr. Kyohei Yamane), Momoko Kochi (Emiko Yamane), Akira Takarada (Hideto Ogata), Akihiko Hirata (Dr. Serizawa), Sachio Sakai (Reporter Hagiwara), Fuyuki Murakami (Dr. Tabata), Toranosuke Ogawa (CEO of Shipping Company), Ren Yamamoto (Masaji). The fiftieth-anniversary release of a film directed by Ishiro Honda and produced by Tomoyuki Tanaka. Screenplay by Takeo Murata and Honda, based on the original story by Shigeru Kayama.

Regaled for fifty years by the stupendous idiocy of the American version of *Godzilla*, audiences can now see the original 1954 Japanese version, which is equally idiotic, but, properly decoded, was the *Fahrenheit 9/11* of its time. Both films come after fearsome attacks on their nations, embody urgent warnings, and even incorporate similar dialogue, such as, "The report is of such dire importance it must not be made public." Is that from 1954 Tokyo or 2004 Washington?

The first *Godzilla* set box-office records in Japan and inspired countless sequels, remakes, and rip-offs. It was made shortly after an American H-bomb test in the Pacific contaminated a large area of ocean and gave radiation sickness to a boatload of Japanese fishermen. It refers repeatedly to Nagasaki, H-bombs, and civilian casualties, and obviously embodies Japanese fears about American nuclear tests.

But that is not the movie you have seen. For one thing, it doesn't star Raymond Burr as Steve Martin, intrepid American journalist, who helpfully explains, "I was headed for an assignment in Cairo when I dropped off for a social call in Tokyo." The American producer Joseph E. Levine bought the Japanese film, cut it by forty minutes, removed all of the political content, and awkwardly inserted Burr into scenes where he clearly did not fit. The hapless actor gives us reaction shots where he's looking in the wrong direction, listens to Japanese actors dubbed into the American idiom (they always call him "Steve Martin" or even "the famous Steve Martin"), and provides a reassuring conclusion in which Godzilla is seen as some kind of public health problem, or maybe just a malcontent.

The Japanese version, now in general U.S. release to mark the film's fiftieth anniversary, is a bad film, but with an undeniable urgency. I learn from helpful notes by Mike Flores of the Psychotronic Film Society that the opening scenes, showing fishing boats disappearing as the sea boils up, would have been read by Japanese audiences as a coded version of U.S. underwater H-bomb tests. Much is made of a scientist named Dr. Serizawa (Akihiko Hirata), who could destroy Godzilla with his secret weapon, the Oxygen Destroyer, but hesitates because he is afraid the weapon might fall into the wrong hands, just as H-bombs might, and have. The film's ending warns that atomic tests may lead to more Godzillas. All cut from the U.S. version.

In these days of flawless special effects, Godzilla and the city he destroys are equally crude. Godzilla at times looks uncannily like a man in a lizard suit, stomping on cardboard sets, as indeed he was, and did. Other scenes show him as a stiff, awkward animatronic model. This was not state-of-the-art even at the time; *King Kong* (1933) was much more convincing.

When Dr. Serizawa demonstrates the Oxygen Destroyer to the fiancée of his son, the superweapon is somewhat anticlimactic. He drops a pill into a tank of tropical fish, the tank lights up, he shouts "Stand back!" The fiancée screams, and the fish go belly-up. Yeah, that'll stop Godzilla in his tracks.

Reporters covering Godzilla's advance are rarely seen in the same shot with the monster. Instead, they look offscreen with horror; a TV reporter, broadcasting for some reason from his station's tower, sees Godzilla looming nearby and signs off, "Sayonara, everyone!" Meanwhile, searchlights sweep the sky, in case Godzilla learns to fly.

The movie's original Japanese dialogue, subtitled, is as harebrained as Burr's dubbed lines. When the Japanese Parliament meets (in what looks like a high school home room), the dialogue is portentous but circular:

"The professor raises an interesting question! We need scientific research!"

"Yes, but at what cost?"

"Yes, that's the question!"

Is there a reason to see the original *Godzilla*? Not because of its artistic stature, but perhaps because of the feeling we can sense in its parable about the monstrous threats unleashed by the atomic age. There are shots of Godzilla's victims in hospitals, and they reminded me of documentaries of Japanese A-bomb victims. The incompetence of scientists, politicians, and the military will ring a bell. This is a bad movie, but it has earned its place in history, and the enduring popularity of Godzilla and other monsters shows that it struck a chord. Can it be a coincidence, in these years of trauma after 9/11, that in a 2005 remake, King Kong will march once again on New York? ☞

Going Upriver: The Long War of John Kerry ★ ★ ★
PG-13, 89 m., 2004

Directed by George Butler and produced by Butler and Mark Hopkins. Screenplay by Joseph

Dorman, based on the book *Tour of Duty* by Douglas Brinkley.

Of all the dirty tricks in the unhappy 2004 presidential campaign, the most outrageous was the ad campaign by the Swift Boat Veterans for Truth, attempting to discredit John Kerry's service in Vietnam. Supporters of the malingering Bush shamelessly challenged the war record of a wounded and decorated veteran. Their campaign illustrated the tactic of the Big Lie, as defined by Hitler and perfected by Goebbels: Although a little lie is laughed at, a Big Lie somehow takes on a reality of its own through its sheer effrontery.

Going Upriver: The Long War of John Kerry is a matter-of-fact documentary that describes Kerry's war service and his later role as a leader of the Vietnam Veterans Against the War. It's not an in-your-face Michael Moore–style doc, but an attempt to rationally respond to the damaging TV ads. The most remarkable connection it makes is that John O'Neill, mastermind of the Swift Boat Veterans for Truth and coauthor of the current book *Unfit for Command,* was originally recruited by the dirty tricksters in the Nixon White House to play precisely the same role!

The movie documents this with tapes of Oval Office conversations showing Richard Nixon discussing John Kerry with his aides H. R. Haldeman and Charles Colson. Kerry had made a strong impression as a spokesman for Vietnam vets who now felt the war was immoral and ill-advised. Senator J. William Fulbright, head of the Senate Foreign Relations Committee, visited the veterans' bivouac on the Mall and asked Kerry to testify before the committee. Kerry's testimony, sampled in the film, is forceful and yet not radical; essentially he was early with what has become the consensus about that war.

In the Oval Office, it is noted that Kerry made a good impression, especially on the network news programs. "He's a Kennedy-type guy. He looks like a Kennedy and sounds like a Kennedy," says Haldeman. "We have to destroy the young demagogue before he becomes another Nader," Colson tells the president. Asked to get some dirt on Kerry, Colson reports, "We couldn't find anything on him." Then he comes up with the idea of recruiting Vietnam vets who would be coached to smear Kerry. Colson enlists O'Neill, who thirty years later has revived his old role.

The film argues that Kerry has truthfully described his role in the war. This is testified to by those in the boat with him, those on the same river at the time, and a man whose life he saved. What's interesting is to learn more about the Swift Boats themselves. Since the Viet Cong blended with the civilian population, anybody could be the enemy, and the Swift Boats were sent upriver in the hopes they would be fired on by Cong troops who would then reveal their positions.

Patrols like those led by Kerry had casualty rates above 75 percent; no wonder he was wounded. Yet some of his opponents have questioned if Kerry actually shed blood in Vietnam. Since Kerry carries shrapnel in his leg, it must have been a neat trick to get it in there without puncturing the skin. A case for the Amazing Randi.

Going Upriver has been directed by George Butler, a longtime Kerry friend who is a veteran documentarian (he made *Pumping Iron* about young Arnold Schwarzenegger, and *Endurance,* the documentary about Ernest Shackleton's expedition to the Antarctic). His film is pro-Kerry, yes, but the focus is on history, not polemics, and provides a record of the crucial role of the Vietnam Veterans Against the War, who because of their credentials could not be dismissed as peaceniks. Kerry comes across even then not as a hot-headed young radical, but as a centered, thoughtful man whose appearance before the Foreign Relations Committee draws respectful reviews even from its Republican members.

The Nixon instinct to smear him finds an echo today in the "Veterans for Truth" ads. It is Kerry's great misfortune that Dan Rather and CBS News deflected attention from Bush's inexplicable (or at least unexplained) absence from guard duty. If the polls can be believed, many American voters are inattentive, credulous, and unable to think critically about political claims. The Swift Boat ads reportedly lost votes for Kerry, but the Rather debacle gained votes for Bush; some voters apparently believed that if Rather was wrong, then somehow Bush's military irregularities have been vindicated.

Did this film change any votes? Doubtful, since most members of the audience were Kerry supporters. It is sad but true that a thirty-second commercial, which any literate person should instinctively question, can shift votes, but the truth cannot. Not that the Swift Boat Veterans for Truth know much about truth.

Good Boy! ★
PG, 89 m., 2003

Liam Aiken (Owen Baker), Kevin Nealon (Owen's Dad), Molly Shannon (Owen's Mom), Matthew Broderick (Hubble [voice]), Brittany Moldowan (Connie Flemming [voice]), Hunter Elliott (Franky [voice]), Donald Faison (Wilson [voice]), Brittany Murphy (Nelly [voice]), Carl Reiner (Shep [voice]), Delta Burke (Barbara Ann [voice]). Directed by John Robert Hoffman and produced by Kristine Belson and Lisa Henson. Screenplay by Zeke Richardson and Hoffman.

Millions of Dog Owners Demand to Know: "Who's a Good Boy?"
— headline in the *Onion*

If a child and a dog love each other, the relationship is one of mutual wonder. Making the dog an alien from outer space is not an improvement. Giving it the ability to speak is a disaster. My dog Blackie used his eyes to say things so eloquent that Churchill would have been stuck for a comeback. Among my favorite movie dogs are Skip, in *My Dog Skip*, who teaches a boy how to be a boy, and Shiloh, in *Shiloh*, who teaches a boy that life is filled with hard choices. Hubble, the dog in *Good Boy!* teaches that dogs will be pulled off Earth and returned to their home planet in a "global recall."

I've told you all you really need to know about the movie's plot. Owen Baker (Liam Aiken), the young hero, adopts a terrier who turns out to have arrived in a flying saucer to investigate why dogs on Earth are our pets, instead of the other way around. This will be a no-brainer for anyone who has watched a dog operating a pooper scooper, nor do dogs look like the master race when they go after your pants leg. But I am willing to accept this premise if anything clever is done with it. Nothing is.

Having seen talking and/or audible dogs in many movies (how the years hurry by!), I have arrived at the conclusion that the best way to present animal speech is by letting us hear their thoughts in voice-over. Sometimes it works to show their lips moving (it certainly did in *Babe*), but in *Good Boy!* the jaw movements are so mechanical it doesn't look like speech, it looks like a film loop. Look at *Babe* again and you'll appreciate the superior way in which the head movements and body language of the animals supplement their speech.

But speech is not the real problem with *Good Boy!* What they talk about is. The movie asks us to consider a race of superior beings who are built a few feet off the ground, lack opposable thumbs, and walk around nude all the time. Compared to them, the aliens in *Signs* are a model of plausibility. The dogs live within a few blocks of one another in Vancouver, and we meet their owners. I kept hoping maybe Jim Belushi had moved to the neighborhood with Jerry Lee from *K-9*, or that I'd spot Jack Nicholson walking Jill. (Jack and Jill: I just got it.)

But no. The humans are along the lines of Kevin Nealon and Molly Shannon, as Owen's parents. The dogs are voiced by Matthew Broderick (as Hubble), Brittany Moldowan, Brittany Murphy, Donald Faison, Carl Reiner, and Delta Burke. Voicing one of the dogs in this movie is the career move of people who like to keep working no matter what. At least when you do the voice of an *animated* animal, they make it look a little like you, and your character can be the star. But when you voice a real dog, do you have to stand around all day between shots talking to the trainer about what a good dog it is?

Good Bye, Lenin! ★ ★ ★
R, 121 m., 2004

Katrin Sass (Christiane Kerner), Daniel Bruhl (Alex Kerner), Maria Simon (Ariane Kerner), Chulpan Khamatova (Lara), Florian Lukas (Denis). Directed by Wolfgang Becker and produced by Stefan Arndt. Screenplay by Bernd Lichtenberg, Becker, Hendrik Handloegten, and Achim von Borries.

East Berlin, 1989. In the final days before the fall of the Berlin Wall, there are riots against the regime. A loyal Communist named Christiane (Katrin Sass) sees her son Alex (Daniel Bruhl)

249

beaten by the police on television, suffers an attack of some sort, and lapses into a coma. During the months she is unconscious, the Wall falls, Germany is reunified, and the world as she knew it disappears. When she miraculously regains consciousness, the doctors advise, as doctors always do in the movies, "the slightest shock could kill her."

What to do? After her husband abandoned her (for another woman, she told her children), the German Democratic Republic became her life. To learn that it has failed ignominiously would surely kill her, and so Alex decides to create a fictional world for her, in which Erich Honecker is still in office, consumer shortages are still the rule, and the state television still sings the praises of the regime.

Good Bye, Lenin! is a movie that must have resonated loudly in Germany when it was released; it is no doubt filled with references and in-jokes we do not quite understand. But the central idea travels well: Imagine an American Rip Van Winkle who is told that President Gore has led a United Nations coalition in liberating Afghanistan, while cutting taxes for working people, attacking polluters, and forcing the drug companies to cut their bloated profits. Sorry, something came over me for a second.

Change, when it comes to East Germany, arrives in a torrent. Alex is reduced to plundering Dumpsters for discarded cans and boxes that contained GDR consumer products, which were swept away by the arrival of competition. In his day job, he sells satellite systems with his friend Denis (Florian Lukas), and together the two of them produce phony news broadcasts to show his mom—even enlisting a former East German astronaut for plausibility.

This works fine until one day Christiane ventures outside, finds the streets awash with Westerners, and is confused by all the ads for Coke. Improvising desperately, Alex and Denis produce newscasts reporting that the West is in collapse, Westerners are fleeing to the East, and the rights to Coke reverted to the Communist nation after it was revealed that its famous formula was devised, not in Atlanta, but in East Germany.

Good Bye, Lenin! is a comedy, but a peculiar one. Peculiar, because it never quite addresses the self-deception that causes Christiane to support the Communist regime in the first place. Many people backed it through fear, ambition, or prudence, but did anyone actually love it and believe in it? The scenes of joyous East Berliners pouring across the fallen Wall are still fresh in our minds. Toward the end of the movie we get a surprise plot point that suggests Christiane may have replaced her husband with the party in an act of emotional compensation, but that seems to be a stretch.

We all feel nostalgia for the environs of our past, of course, which is why someone like me once treasured a 1957 Studebaker Golden Hawk even though new cars are incomparably better made (they aren't as sexy, though). There are fan clubs in Germany for the Trabant, the singularly ugly and poorly made official auto of the GDR, and great is Christiane's delight when Alex tells her the family now owns one. Our pasts may be flawed, but they are ours, and we are attached to them. What *Good Bye, Lenin!* never quite deals with is the wrongheadedness of its heroine. Imagine a film named *Good Bye, Hitler!* in which a loving son tries to protect his cherished mother from news of the fall of the Third Reich.

Well, maybe that's too harsh. *Good Bye, Lenin!* is not a defense of the GDR, which Alex and his sister Ariane are happy to see gone (she's proud of her new job at Burger King). The underlying poignancy in this comedy is perhaps psychological more than political: How many of us lie to our parents, pretending a world still exists that they believe in but we have long since moved away from? And are those lies based on love or cowardice? Sometimes, despite doctors' warnings, parents have to take their chances with the truth.

The Good Thief ★ ★ ★ ½
R, 109 m., 2003

Nick Nolte (Bob), Tchéky Karyo (Roger), Nutsa Kukhianidze (Anne), Saïd Taghmaoui (Paulo), Gérard Darmon (Raoul), Ralph Fiennes (Tony), Marc Lavoine (Remi). Directed by Neil Jordan and produced by Steven Woolley, John Wells, and Seaton McLean. Screenplay by Jordan, based on the film by Jean-Pierre Melville.

Nick Nolte plays a great shambling wreck of a wounded Hemingway hero in *The Good Thief*, a film that's like a descent into the funkiest dive on the wrong side of the wrong town. He's Bob, the child of an American father and a French mother, so he claims—but he seems to change his story every time he tells it. He lives in Nice, on the French Riviera, moving easily through the lower depths of crime and drugs, and—this is the tricky part—liked by everyone. When it's rumored he is up to a new heist, the policeman Roger (Tchéky Karyo) tells his partner, "Find out before he does it!" He doesn't want to arrest Bob; he wants to save him from himself.

Bob is a thief and a heroin addict. "Heroin is his lady," his friend Raoul observes. "I thought luck was his lady," says another friend. "When one runs out he turns to the other," says Raoul. Bob is intimately familiar with the language of AA, talking about the Twelve Steps and "one day at a time" and even at one point citing the Serenity Prayer. But his only visit to a Narcotics Anonymous meeting involves walking in one door and out the other to elude pursuit ("I'm Bob, and I'm an addict," he says on the way through).

Bob is a good man, a good thief, to the bottom of his soul, a gentleman who rescues a teenage Bosnian hooker (Nutsa Kukhianidze) from a vicious pimp and then becomes her protector, although to be sure he introduces her to bad company. He is headed toward some kind of showdown with his fate. Down to his last 70,000 francs, he goes to the races. "What if you lose?" asks his friend. "I'll have hit rock bottom. I'll have to change my ways."

He hits rock bottom. He changes his ways. "I feel a confinement coming on," he says in that deep gravel voice. He chains himself to a bed, eats ice cream, goes through an agonizing detox, and is ready to consider an ingenious plan to steal the treasures of a Monte Carlo casino. No, not the money. The paintings.

The Good Thief, directed by Neil Jordan *(Mona Lisa, The Crying Game),* is a remake of a famous 1955 French film named *Bob le Flambeur* by Jean-Pierre Melville. *The Good Thief* is drawn to the affectionate study of a character who is admirable in every way except that he cannot bring himself to stop breaking the law. But it is juicier, jazzier, with a more charismatic hero.

Bob le Flambeur was filmed in elegant black and white, with Roger Duchesne playing Bob as a trim, self-contained, sleek operator. Nolte, on the other hand, has such a bulldog look that

even his clothes have jowls. He told a press conference at the Toronto Film Festival that he used "a little heroin" every day while making the movie, just to get in the mood. Not long ago, it is well known, he was arrested while driving under the influence, and his mug shot, widely circulated, showed a man who had made dissipation his life's work. Nolte recently said he was on his way to an AA meeting when something made him turn away and led eventually to his arrest. Maybe he wanted to be arrested, he speculated, so he could get help. *The Good Thief* looks like the direction he took when he turned away.

Whether or not Nolte topped up every day on the set, it is clear that he was born to play Bob. It is one of those performances that flows unhindered from an actor's deepest instincts. Jordan and his cinematographer, Chris Menges, place him in a world of smoke, shadows, and midnight blues, where cops and robbers supply work for each other. Into this world drift occasional outsiders like the kinky art dealer (Ralph Fiennes), who talks like a Batman villain: "If I don't get my money back by Monday, what I do to your faces will definitely be Cubist."

The plot I will not breathe a word about, since it is so elegantly ironic in the way Bob outflanks the cops, his partners, the casino, and ourselves. It leads up to a deeply satisfying conclusion, but along the way what we enjoy is the portrait of this man who is engaged in some kind of lifelong showdown between his goodness and his weakness. This is a struggle Nolte seems to know a great deal about.

Gothika ★ ★ ★
R, 95 m., 2003

Halle Berry (Miranda Grey), Robert Downey Jr. (Pete Graham), Penelope Cruz (Chloe Sava), Charles S. Dutton (Dr. Douglas Grey), John Carroll Lynch (Sheriff Ryan), Bernard Hill (Phil Parsons), Dorian Harewood (Teddy Howard), Bronwen Mantel (Irene). Directed by Mathieu Kassovitz and produced by L. Levin, Susan Levin, Joel Silver, and Robert Zemeckis. Screenplay by Sebastian Gutierrez.

The sainted Pauline Kael taught us: The movies are so rarely great art that if we cannot appreciate great trash, we might as well stop going. I don't know if she would have defined *Gothika* as great trash, but in trash as in art there is no accounting for taste, and reader, I cherished this movie in all of its lurid glory.

Yes, the plot is preposterous. No, I do not understand for sure how the murder was plotted. True, the function of the ghost is terrifically murky. Yes, the ghost should have communicated more clearly, instead of in cryptic hints like "Not alone." No, I don't know why a man who entertains himself by torturing victims in a hidden video studio would suddenly desire, in middle age, to add a conventional marriage to his mix. Yes, I agree that a prison psychiatrist accused of murder would hardly be locked up in her own prison among her former patients.

But those are all bothersome details of plausibility and logic, and those are the last two qualities you should seek in *Gothika*. This is a psychothriller with the plausibility of a nightmare—which is to say, it doesn't make sense, but it keeps your attention. The movie is by Mathieu Kassovitz, the thirty-five-year-old French director and actor who in *Crimson Rivers* (2001) made one of the most original and stylish of recent thrillers. He's worked with stars before (Jean Reno and Vincent Cassel in that one), but here, with the Oscar winner Halle Berry at the center of the story, he depends on star power to involve us in the classic Hitchcock formula of the innocent character wrongly accused. Hitch explained that if you cast the right star—Jimmy Stewart or Cary Grant, for example—the audience *knew* they didn't do it, and so you moved on from there.

Berry's character is Miranda Grey, a psychiatrist in a prison straight out of Dickens. She works with fellow shrink Pete Graham (Robert Downey Jr.) and is newly wed to her boss, Dr. Douglas Grey (Charles S. Dutton). I'm thinking, hey, this is refreshing: The beautiful woman is married to an overweight guy for a change. But, no, fat equals fate.

On the obligatory dark and stormy night, Miranda takes a detour and swerves to avoid a ghostly, ghastly girl standing in the middle of the road, who bursts into flames. When she wakes up, she's a prisoner in her own institution and Pete breaks the news to her: She's accused of the brutal murder of her husband. How can this be? She tries to remember, but there's a blank. Chloe (Penelope Cruz), a former patient, now a fellow inmate, explains the rules: Now that Miranda is officially insane, it doesn't matter what she says, since it will be dismissed as her illness talking.

The movie introduces several intriguing characters, including Sheriff Ryan (John Carroll Lynch) and Phil Parsons (Bernard Hill), the prison warden. And it teases us with the possibility that any of them—or Pete, of course—could be behind the monstrous misunderstanding. Miranda tries to reason her way free. "Did we have an affair?" she asks Pete. "Did you want to?" Downey and Berry have a lot of fun in a scene where both characters realize they are heading toward a dangerous possibility.

All is finally explained in an appropriately overwrought series of climaxes, which left me wondering how (1) the ghost of the girl triggered Miranda's blackout, (2) whether the murderer(s) of Dr. Grey could have controlled, evoked, or summoned the ghost, (3) how, assuming he/she/they could not have, they could have predicted or triggered Miranda's blackout and timed the murder to match.

But this sort of wondering is not a bad thing, because it keeps you guessing all through the movie and supplies so many possible answers that the heroine seems surrounded by threats. And after the movie ends the questions don't bother you, because *Gothika* is in a genre with the specific duty of involving, scaring, and absorbing us for its precise running time, after which it is over and we can go home. Some plots have to do with life, and must be pondered. Others are engines to cause emotions in the audience, and if they succeed, they have discharged their duty.

The casting of Halle Berry is useful to the movie, because she evokes a vulnerable quality that triggers our concern. Hitchcock might have wanted to work with her. He didn't cast so much for acting ability as for an innate quality. Berry can act, all right (see *Monster's Ball*) but she can also simply evoke, and here, where she's required to fight her way out of a nightmare, that quality is crucial. She carries us along with her, while logic and plausibility (see above) simply become irrelevant.

Any criticism of this movie that says it doesn't make sense is missing the point. Any review that faults it for going over the top into lurid overkill is criticizing its most entertaining quality. Any critic who mocks the line "I'm not deluded, Pete—I'm possessed!" should be honest enough to admit that, in the moment, he liked it. It takes nerve to make a movie like this in the face of the taste police, but Kassovitz and Berry have the right stuff.

The Grey Automobile ★ ★ ★ ★
NO MPAA RATING, 90 m., 1919 (rereleased 2003)

In the film: Juan Manuel Cabrera (Himself), Gang Members (Themselves). On the stage: Irene Akiko Iida (Japanese Benshi), Enrique Arreola (Spanish Dialogue), Thomasi McDonald (English Dialogue), Ernesto Gomez Santana (Pianist). A live performance with a 1919 Mexican silent film. Film originally directed by Enrique Rosas; interpreted, augmented, and staged by Claudio Valdes-Kuri.

A little-known 1919 Mexican silent film . . . and already your attention is drifting, right? You've been meaning to catch up on the Mexican silent cinema, but somehow the time is never right. Now the time has come. *The Grey Automobile* provides the inspiration for an astonishing theatrical experience.

By the Marx Brothers out of Gilbert and Sullivan and incorporating an early Japanese film tradition, the event devised by director Claudio Valdes-Kuri is slapstick, surrealist, charming, and lighthearted, especially considering that an actual automobile gang is literally executed during the course of the film. A Japanese benshi, a Mexican actor, and an English "interpreter" join the film on the stage, as a pianist supplies the score.

To begin with benshis. During the silent film era, Japanese exhibitors supplied a benshi, or interpreting actor, to stand next to the screen and explain films. The benshis might or might not understand the Western stories and characters any more than the audience did, but that didn't matter, because benshis evolved a performance tradition of their own—not only explaining, but praising, criticizing, sympathizing, and applauding, in parallel with the film. Benshis became so popular that their names were billed above the stars, they had theaters of their own, and silent films survived in Japan for almost a decade after the introduction of sound—because audiences could not do without their beloved benshis.

Claudio Valdes-Kuri, an avant-garde theatrical director from Mexico City, discovered the benshi tradition during a visit to Japan, where benshis still flourish, many of them trained in a line going back to the original artists. Back home in Mexico, he decided to adapt the tradition to *The Grey Automobile*, said to be Mexico's finest silent film, which is about the real-life Grey Automobile Gang.

This film, originally a serial, has existed in many forms over the years, but it is safe to say that no one associated with it could have imagined the ninety-minute version now presented by Valdes-Kuri and his Certain Inhabitants Theater. The film stars Juan Manuel Cabrera, the actual detective who apprehended the gang, playing himself. The real gang members also appear, briefly to be sure, in a startling scene where they are (really) executed. Other scenes are fiction.

It is impossible to say, on the basis of this presentation, whether *The Grey Automobile* is a good film or not—my four-star rating refers to the entire theatrical experience. As the performance opens, Irene Akiko Iida, a Japanese-Mexican actress dressed in a traditional kimono, joins the pianist, Ernesto Gomez Santana, by the side of the screen and provides a traditional benshi commentary in Japanese. Then she is joined by Enrique Arreola, who begins a Spanish commentary. Then they are joined by Thomasi McDonald, who supplies commentary and translation in English.

But that sounds straightforward, and the performance quickly jumps the rails into sublime zaniness. Other languages—German, French, and Russian—creep into the commentary. The film seems to have no subtitles, but suddenly generates them, and then the titles leave the bottom of the screen and begin to emerge from the mouths of the movie actors in a variety of typefaces; the words coil around the screen and take on lives of their own. Then the actors begin to interpret the on-screen dialogue so freely that at times they have the characters barking at one another. At one point the action stops for a little song-and-dance number, and at another Ms. Iida performs a tap dance.

But this description fails to do justice to the technical virtuosity of the verbal performers.

253

For long stretches, they create perfect lip-synch with the actors on-screen while talking at breakneck speed, never missing a cue or a beat; what they do is so difficult, and done so effortlessly, that it suggests a Zenlike identification with the material. I avoid clichés such as "You've never seen anything like this before," but the fact is, you haven't.

Grind ★ ★
PG-13, 100 m., 2003

Mike Vogel (Eric Rivers), Vince Vieluf (Matt Jensen), Adam Brody (Dustin Knight), Joey Kern (Sweet Lou), Jennifer Morrison (Jamie). Directed by Casey La Scala and produced by La Scala, Bill Gerber, and Hunt Lowry. Screenplay by Ralph Sall.

Grind has a tone like *The Endless Summer*, that dreamy surfing movie in which a bunch of buddies devote their lives to hanging out together and searching for the perfect wave. This time it's skateboards, not surfboards, and the goal is not the perfect wave but sponsorship for their team and a chance to tour with the champion they admire. But the ethic is about the same: Skateboarding is forever, and things like college and girls only ruin an endlessly savored adolescence.

The buddies live in that southern California which is a state of mind, where life centers on the skateboard store and famous skateboarders are mobbed the way rock stars are in another universe. They dream of turning professional, but can't get the pros to look at their demo tapes, and can't win the sponsorship necessary to get into the big tournaments. So they hit the road, stalking the tour of the famous champion Jimmy Wilson, hoping they can get his attention, or somebody's attention; they have T-shirts printed advertising a fake company that they claim is their sponsor.

That's the plot, more or less. The guys are only vaguely differentiated; the lead is Eric (Mike Vogel), but the one who stands out is Sweet Lou (Joey Kern), who fancies himself a ladies' man and sidles up to a potential conquest with a soft-voiced come-on, as if to notice him is to surrender to him. Two women do actually enter their orbit: one who seems too good to be true, and is, and another who likes them and gets them into a tournament.

There is also an interlude with Matt's (Vince Vieluf) parents. They ran away from home to join the circus, and so they should have no complaints about his skateboarding tour. Matt and the guys visit them at a clown college (or Klown Kollege, I suppose), where Matt is embarrassed to find his folks in putty noses, but where the possibility of becoming skateboarding clowns briefly beckons.

That leaves the skateboarding itself. I am no expert on the sport, but I have seen the 2001 documentary *Dogtown and Z-Boys*, which chronicles the birth of skateboarding in Santa Monica, circa 1975. Based on the performances in that movie, the guys in *Grind*, if they were golfers, might shoot par on a few holes, but never for a whole game. The skateboarding footage is underwhelming compared to *Dogtown*. They seem to be repeating the same limited moves over and over again; I was astonished by some of the things I saw in *Dogtown*, but the moves here made me wonder what the crowd was applauding.

The movie is nevertheless sweet, in its meandering way. It has no meanness in it, no cynicism, no desire to be anything other than what it is, an evocation of the fun of living your life as a skateboarder. While there are few things more poignant than an ancient skateboarder (as *Dogtown and Z-Boys* also suggests), these guys are still in their endless summer and don't yet understand that.

Neither this movie nor *Dogtown*, by the way, answers the question I have every time I see high-level skateboarding: In order to learn to fly free, high into the air, and go through body twists, and land again on your board, you presumably must fail a lot of times before you succeed. It looks to me as if that would involve a drop of ten or twenty feet to a hard surface. How many skateboarders are killed? Maimed? Paralyzed? What about that first guy who thought about flying free beyond the lip of his skating surface—how did he think he would get down again?

The Grudge ★
PG-13, 96 m., 2004

Sarah Michelle Gellar (Karen), Jason Behr (Doug), Clea DuVall (Jennifer Williams), William Mapother (Matthew Williams), KaDee

Strickland (Susan Williams), Bill Pullman (Peter), Rosa Blasi (Maria), Grace Zabriskie (Emma). Directed by Takashi Shimizu and produced by Doug Davison, Roy Lee, and Robert G. Tapert. Screenplay by Shimizu and Stephen Susco.

The Grudge has a great opening scene, I'll grant you that. Bill Pullman wakes up next to his wife, greets the day from the balcony of their bedroom, and then—well, I, for one, was gob-smacked. I'm not sure how this scene fits into the rest of the movie, but then I'm not sure how most of the scenes fit into the movie. I do, however, understand the underlying premise: There is a haunted house, and everybody who enters it will have unspeakable things happen to them.

These are not just any old unspeakable things. They rigidly follow the age-old formula of horror movies, in which characters who hear alarming sounds go to investigate, unwisely sticking their heads/hands/body parts into places where they quickly become forensic evidence. Something attacks them in a shot so brief and murky it could be a fearsome beast, a savage ghost—or, of course, Only A Cat.

The movie, set in Japan but starring mostly American actors, has been remade by Takashi Shimizu from his original Japanese version. It loses intriguing opportunities to contrast American and Japanese cultures, alas, by allowing everyone to speak English; I was hoping it would exploit its locations and become *Lost, Eviscerated and Devoured in Translation*.

An opening title informs us that when an event causes violent rage, a curse is born that inhabits that place and is visited on others who come there. We are eventually given a murky, black-and-white, tilt-shot flashback glimpse of the original violent rage, during which we can indistinctly spot some of the presences who haunt the house, including a small child with a big mouth and a catlike scream.

The house shelters at various times the mother of one of the characters, who spends most of her time in bed or staring vacantly into space, and a young couple who move in, and a real estate agent who sees that the bathtub is filled up and sticks his hand into the water to pull the plug, and is attacked by a woman with long hair who leaps out of the water. This woman's hair, which sometimes looks like seaweed, appears in many scenes, hanging down into the frame as if it dreams of becoming a boom mike.

Various cops and social workers enter the house, some never to emerge, but the news of its malevolence doesn't get around. You'd think that after a house has been associated with gruesome calamities on a daily basis, the neighbors could at least post an old-timer outside to opine that some mighty strange things have been a-happening in there.

I eventually lost all patience. The movie may have some subterranean level on which the story strands connect and make sense, but it eluded me. The fragmented time structure is a nuisance, not a style. The house is not particularly creepy from an architectural point of view, and if it didn't have a crawl space under the eaves, the ghosts would have to jump out from behind sofas.

Sarah Michelle Gellar, the nominal star, has been in her share of horror movies, and all by herself could have written and directed a better one than this. As for Bill Pullman, the more I think about his opening scene, the more I think it represents his state of mind after he signed up for the movie, flew all the way to Japan, and read the screenplay.

Guess Who? ★ ★ ★
PG-13, 105 m., 2005

Bernie Mac (Percy Jones), Ashton Kutcher (Simon Green), Zoe Saldana (Theresa Jones), Judith Scott (Marilyn Jones), Kellee Stewart (Keisha Jones). Directed by Kevin Rodney Sullivan and produced by Jason Goldberg, Erwin Stoff, and Jenno Topping. Screenplay by David Ronn, Jay Scherick, and Peter Tolan.

Thirty-eight years after Katharine Houghton brought Sidney Poitier home to meet her parents in *Guess Who's Coming to Dinner*, it's time for an African-American woman to bring her white fiancé home in *Guess Who*. Not much has changed over the years, or in the parents, who go through various forms of discomfort and disapproval before finally caving in when they realize the fiancé is, after all, a heck of a nice guy with a great future ahead of him.

Although racially mixed marriages are more frequent than they were in 1967, it is still probably true that no parents of any race have ever said to a child: "You're marrying someone of another race, and that's it!" When a child chooses a spouse from another group, it is usually because they have more things in common than the bits of DNA that separate them. Most parents—not all—eventually conclude that the happiness of their child is the most important factor of all.

Parents did not come quite so willingly to that conclusion in 1967, which is why Stanley Kramer's film, now often dismissed as liberal piety, took some courage to make. No doubt it worked better because the African-American who came to dinner was played by Sidney Poitier as a famous doctor who lived in Switzerland. And it was crucial that the parents were played not merely by white actors, but by the icons Spencer Tracy and Katharine Hepburn, whose screen presence carried great authority.

In *Guess Who,* the white fiancé is not quite the world-class catch that Poitier was. Named Simon and played by Ashton Kutcher, who must have had an interesting evening when he came home for dinner with Demi Moore, he is a Wall Street trader with a bright future, who has suddenly quit his job. He's in love with Theresa (Zoe Saldana), an artist. Her parents are Percy (Bernie Mac), a bank loan officer, and Marilyn (Judith Scott). Like Tracy and Hepburn, they live in an expensive home in an upscale suburb.

"You didn't tell me your parents were black!" Simon says when he meets them, in a lame attempt at humor. The fact is, Theresa didn't tell them he was white. Simon discovers this during the cab ride to the suburbs. "I didn't tell them because it doesn't matter," she says. The black cab driver (Mike Epps) looks in the rearview mirror and says, "It's gonna matter."

It does, and the movie is a little uneasy about how to deal with that fact. Percy has already run a credit check on Simon and discovered (a) that he has an impressive net worth, but (b) is newly unemployed. When he finds out Simon hasn't told Theresa about his joblessness, Percy decides that the young man is not to be trusted. He is also not to be trusted with Theresa's body,

at least not under Percy's roof; her father insists that Simon sleep on the sofa-bed in the basement, and to be sure he stays there, Percy sleeps in the same bed with him. This leads to several scenes that are intended to be funny, but sit there uncomfortably on the screen because the humor comes from a different place than the real center of the film.

Simon and Theresa are indeed in love, indeed seem compatible, indeed have us hoping things will work out for them. But Percy is smart and suspicious, with a way of setting traps for the unsuspecting younger man. One of the film's best scenes, because it reflects fundamental truths, comes at dinner, when Simon says he doesn't approve of the "ethnic jokes" that "some people" tell at work. Percy asks him to provide a sample. Simon refuses, but then he decides, in a fatal spasm of political correctness, that it "empowers" the joke if he *doesn't* tell it.

So he does. ("How do we know Adam and Eve weren't black? Ever try to get a rib away from a black man?") Not everyone around the table may think this is funny, but they all laugh—except Theresa, who senses the danger. Percy asks for another joke, and Simon obliges. And a third. Encouraged by Percy, Simon inevitably tells one joke too many—one that isn't funny, but racist. A terrible silence falls. Percy leaves the table. Simon is aghast. "I should never have told that joke," he says to Theresa. "You should never have started," she says. His mistake was to tell the first one. But she forgives him his mistake: "He dared you."

He did. And if the movie had spent more time walking that tightrope between the acceptable and the offensive, between what we have in common and what divides us, it would have been more daring. Instead, it uses sitcom and soap opera formulas that allow the characters easy ways out. (The scene where Percy finds Simon wearing Theresa's negligee is painfully awkward.) No one in the audience of any race is going to feel uncomfortable about much of anything on the screen.

That said, *Guess Who?* works efficiently on its chosen level. Bernie Mac, who often cheerfully goes over the top in his roles, here provides a focused and effective performance as a father who would subject a boyfriend of any race to merciless scrutiny. He has a moment of sudden intuition about Simon that is perfectly realized and timed. Ashton Kutcher is not the actor Sidney Poitier was, but the movie doesn't require him to be; his assignment is to be acceptable and sympathetic in a situation where he is coached through the hazards by his girlfriend.

The movie focuses primarily on the two men. If we heard a lot about strong black women after *Diary of a Mad Black Woman,* here we have a movie about a strong black man and about male bonding that has more to do with corporate than racial politics. Zoe Saldana, a true beauty, is lovable and charming as Theresa, but in her home she's upstaged by her father. As her mother, Marilyn, Judith Scott has a much smaller role than Katharine Hepburn had in the earlier movie, and although we meet Theresa's feisty sister, Keisha (Kellee Stewart), not much is done with the character.

Interracial relationships may be an area where the daily experience of many people is better-informed and more comfortable than the movies are ready to admit. Certainly after the first few dates any relationship is based more on love, respect, and mutual care than it is on appearances. I think the couple in *Guess Who?* has figured that out, but if they haven't, I predict they'll have a wonderful starter marriage.

Gunner Palace ★ ★ ★ ½
PG-13, 85 m., 2005

A documentary directed by Michael Tucker and Petra Epperlein and produced by Epperlein.

Gunner Palace is a ground-level documentary, messy and immediate, about the daily life of a combat soldier in Iraq. It is not prowar or antiwar. It is about American soldiers, mostly young, who are strangers in a strange land, trying to do their jobs and stay alive.

It has become dangerous to be a news correspondent in Iraq. As I write this, the front-page story is about an Italian journalist who was freed from her kidnappers, only to be wounded by friendly fire while trying to cross to safety at an American checkpoint. The man who negotiated her freedom was killed. In recent months many news organizations have pulled out their reporters; even the supposedly safe Green Zone inside Baghdad has become dangerous.

That's why this film is so valuable. Not because it argues a position about the war and occupation, but because it simply goes and observes as soldiers work and play, talk and write letters home and, on a daily basis, risk their lives in sudden bursts of violence. Sometimes they translate their experiences into songs. The African-American soldiers, in particular, use hip-hop as an outlet, and their lyrics are sometimes angry, more often lonely and poetic; all wars seem to create poets, and so has this one.

The movie was directed, produced, written, and edited by Michael Tucker and Petra Epperlein, a married American couple who live in Germany and visited Iraq twice, in late 2003 and 2004. They followed the 2/3 Field Artillery Division (the "gunners") of the army's 1st Armored Division. As it happens, a platoon from that division was also being followed by *Time* magazine, which picked "The American Soldier" as its 2003 Person of the Year. The woman on the cover, SPC Billie Grimes, is the only woman seen in the film. SPC Stuart Wilf, much seen in the film, "is the centerfold" in *Time,* according to an online journal kept by Tucker, who notes that two *Time* reporters were wounded while reporting the article.

The cover story takes a large view: "About 40 percent of the troops are Southern, 60 percent are white, 22 percent are black, and a disproportionate number come from empty states like Montana and Wyoming. When they arrive at the recruiter's door, Defense Secretary Donald Rumsfeld told *Time,* 'They have purple hair and an earring, and they've never walked with another person in step in their life. And suddenly they get this training, in a matter of weeks, and they become part of a unit, a team.'"

Gunner Palace plays like the deleted scenes from the *Time* cover story. The self-proclaimed gunners of the title live in the half-destroyed ruins of a palace once occupied by Saddam's son Uday. What's left of the furnishings make it look like a cross between a bordello and a casino, and some rooms end abruptly with bomb craters, but there is still a functioning swimming pool, and the soldiers' own rock band blasts Smokey Robinson's *My Girl* from loudspeakers during their party time. We're reminded that songs by The Doors provided a sound track for *Apocalypse Now,* with the difference that the soldiers in that film were often stoned, and these young men (and one woman) seem more sober and serious.

Their job is impossible to define, which is one of their frustrations. At some times they are peacekeepers, at other times targets; they may be overseeing a community meeting, acting like paramedics as they handle a stoned street kid, breaking down doors during raids, engaging in firefights in the midnight streets. Eight of them were killed during this period of time; one of them, known as "Super Cop," was an Iraqi attached to their unit who was famous for capturing wanted fugitives. Another trusted Iraqi, an interpreter, was charged with passing intelligence to insurgents. "If it is true," Tucker writes in his journal, "he is responsible for at least four deaths."

The filmmakers go along with the gunners on their nighttime patrols, and the camera follows them into houses harboring suspected terrorists. Gunfire breaks out at unexpected moments. You don't see this on TV. Tucker, who photographed his own movie, was willing to take risks, and the gunners were willing to have him come along with them; you can sense by the way they relax in front of the camera and confide their thoughts that they were comfortable with him, accustomed to him. What's working here is the technique Frederick Wiseman uses in his documentaries: He hangs around for so long that he disappears into the scene, and his subjects forget that they're on camera.

That doesn't mean Tucker catches them off guard, or finds them cynical or disloyal. It's a truism of war that a combat soldier of any nation is motivated in action not by his flag, his country, his cause, or his leaders, but by his buddies. He has trained with them, fought with them, seen some of them die and others take risks for him, and he doesn't want to let them down. That's what we feel here, along with the constant awareness that death can come suddenly in the middle of a routine action. We hear about "IEDs," which are Improvised Explosive Devices, easy to place, hard to spot, likely to be almost anywhere. A sequence involves the investigation of a carrier bag on a city street, a bag that turns out to contain— nothing.

It's clear the soldiers don't think their logistical support amounts to much. Long before Rumsfeld was asked the famous question about the lack of armor for military vehicles, we see these men improvising homemade armor for their trucks and joking about it. There is a serious side: The flimsy junkyard shields they add are as likely to create deadly shrapnel as to protect them.

I wondered during the movie whether a sound track album exists. Apparently not. There should be one, or perhaps the original lyrics could be covered by established artists. The lyrics composed by the soldiers provide a view of the war that is simply missing in the middle of all the political rhetoric and gaseous briefings.

On May 23, 2004, after he had finished his principal photography, director Tucker made a last entry in his online journal: "I've asked soldiers what they think about the war and their answers are surprisingly simple. After a year, the war isn't about WMDs, democracy, Donald Rumsfeld, or oil. It's about them. Simple. They just want to finish the job they were sent to do so they can go home."

H

The Hard Word ★ ★ ½
R, 102 m., 2003

Guy Pearce (Dale), Rachel Griffiths (Carol),
Robert Taylor (Frank), Joel Edgerton (Shane),
Damien Richardson (Mal), Rhondda Findleton
(Jane), Kate Atkinson (Pamela). Directed by
Scott Roberts and produced by Al Clark.
Screenplay by Roberts.

The Twentyman brothers—Dale, Shane, and
Mal—are stickup men with the motto "Nobody
gets hurt." Despite their benevolence, they end
up in prison, where Mal practices the butcher's
trade and Dale works as a librarian. Then their
lawyer, Frank, springs them for one last brilliant
job. The job is much complicated by the fact
that Dale's wife has become Frank's mistress.

The wife-slash-mistress is Carol, played by
Rachel Griffiths with her intriguing ability to
combine the qualities of a tomboy and a sex
kitten. She's married to Dale Twentyman (Guy
Pearce), insists she loves him, yet is having an
affair with the crooked lawyer Frank (Robert
Taylor). Which one does she really love? Sometimes she seems to be smiling to herself with
the evil contentment of a woman whose bread
is buttered on both sides.

It is good to hear Pearce (*L.A. Confidential,
Memento*) and Griffiths (a star of HBO's *Six
Feet Under*) speaking in their native Australian
accents in *The Hard Word*, a movie that exists
halfway between Tarantinoland and those old
black-and-white British crime comedies. The
characters seem to have devised themselves as
living works of art, as if personal style and
being "colorful" is the real point of being a
criminal, and the money is only a bothersome
technicality.

Consider Shane Twentyman (Joel Edgerton), the brother with a big-time problem with
anger. A big guy who looks a little like young
Albert Finney, he's assigned a prison counselor
named Jane (Rhondda Findleton), and they fall
in love with startling speed. Mal Twentyman
(Damien Richardson) also has a magnetic attraction for women, which comes as a surprise
to him, since he is usually much abashed around
them. After the gang steals a getaway car, its
owner and driver, Pamela (Kate Atkinson),
comes down with a critical case of Stockholm
Syndrome and falls in love with Mal.

These scenes have a charm that works all the
better considering that they are surrounded by
a good deal of startling violence. Frank's big
plan involves the brothers stealing the bookies'
money after the running of the Melbourne
Cup, but an outsider, brought in to keep an eye
on them, opens fire and there is blood and carnage as the brothers flee on foot.

The foot chase has a quality missing in a lot
of modern action movies, and that is the sensation of physical effort. William Friedken
achieved it, too, in the underrated *The Hunted*.
The robbers run through malls and down stairs
and across pedestrian overpasses and are hauling the money and panting and sweating, and
we realize belatedly that one of the things wrong
with Spiderman was that he never seemed to go
to any effort.

Griffiths is at the center of both of the movie's
key relationships, with her husband the crook
and her lover the lawyer. Robert Taylor's lawyer is
one of those devious creatures from 1940s
movies who seem more interested in taking the
woman away from a man than in actually having
her. If he were a fisherman he would throw her
back in. Does Griffiths's character know this?
There is the suggestion that she does and is in
love with Dale the whole time, but she is so good
at looking a guy straight in the eye and telling
him she loves him that her actions are eventually
going to have to speak louder than her words.

The movie has room for quirky little side
trips, as when the loot is hidden in a peculiar
place, and for classic *film noir* moments, as
when several key characters gather for a showdown that is not quite what some of them had
in mind, but they get to engage in a lot of high-
style crime dialogue before they find that out.

And then there's more. Too much more. *The
Hard Word* feels like it should be more or less
over after the Melbourne Cup heist, but it's
barely getting started, as writer-director Scott
Roberts supplies twists and double crosses and
startling developments and surprise revelations and unexpected appearances and disappearances, until finally we give up. This movie
could obviously go on fooling us forever, but
we are good sports only up to a point, and then

259

our attention drifts. Shame, since there's so much good stuff in it, like how effortlessly Rachel Griffiths keeps two tough guys completely at her mercy.

Harold and Kumar
Go to White Castle ★ ★ ★

R, 96 m., 2004

John Cho (Harold), Kal Penn (Kumar), Paula Garces (Maria), Neil Patrick Harris (Himself), Eddie Kaye Thomas (Rosenberg), Christopher Meloni (Freakshow), Fred Willard (Dr. Woodruff), Sandy Jobin-Bevans (Officer Palumbo). Directed by Danny Leiner and produced by Nathan Kahane and Greg Shapiro. Screenplay by Jon Hurwitz and Hayden Schlossberg.

One secret of fiction is the creation of unique characters who are precisely defined. The secret of comedy is the same, with the difference that the characters must be obsessed with unwholesome but understandable human desires. Many comedies have the same starting place: a hero who *must* obtain his dream, which should if possible be difficult, impractical, eccentric, or immoral. As he marches toward his goal, scattering conventional citizens behind him, we laugh because of his selfishness, and because secretly that's how we'd like to behave, if we thought we could get away with it.

I realize this is a lofty beginning for a review about a stoner road comedy, but there you are. The summer has been filled with comedies that failed because they provided formula characters, mostly nice teenagers who wanted to be loved and popular. *Harold and Kumar Go to White Castle,* on the other hand, is about two very specific roommates who want to smoke pot, meet chicks, and eat sliders in the middle of the night. Because this column is read in Turkey, Botswana, Japan, and California, I should explain that "sliders" are what fans of the White Castle chain call their hamburgers, which are small and cheap and slide right down. We buy 'em by the bag.

Is a slider worth the trouble of leaving home and journeying through two states? If you're stoned and have the munchies, as Harold and Kumar are, and if you're in the grip of a White Castle obsession, the answer is clearly yes. The only hamburger worth that much trouble when you're clean and sober is at Steak 'n Shake. Californians believe the burgers at In 'n Out are better, but that is because they do not appreciate the secret of Steak 'n Shake, expressed in its profound credo, "In Sight, It Must Be Right." (Many people believe the names of In 'n Out and Steak 'n Shake perfectly describe the contrast in bedroom techniques between the coast and the heartland.)

Harold Lee (John Cho) is a serious, bookish, shy Korean-American accountant. Kumar Patel (Kal Penn), an Indian American, is a party animal whose parents think he's about to enroll in med school. That the dean is played by the benevolent but obscurely disturbed Fred Willard lets you know this process will not be without setbacks. Harold and Kumar are getting stoned one night when a White Castle commercial plays on TV and fixates them with a slider fixation.

Kumar seems to remember that there is a White Castle near where they live in New Jersey. There is not. If there were, it's questionable whether they could find it, as they careen through the night on a journey that makes the travels of Cheech and Chong look like outings in the popemobile.

It is an item of faith in comedies that if you leave the main road, you will instantly be in a land inhabited by people who did not learn all they know about chain-saw massacres from the movies. Consider Freakshow (Christopher Meloni), an auto mechanic who comes to their rescue after they run off the road while wearing what John Prine calls illegal smiles. Freakshow has a complexion so bad it upstages sausage pizza. Alarming fluids erupt from its protuberances; volcanic activity on the Jovian moon Io comes to mind.

Harold and Kumar eventually find themselves, inexplicably as far as they are concerned, on the campus at Princeton, where the students may be Ivy Leaguers but, like students everywhere, occasionally unwind with ear-shattering demonstrations of flatulence. This is the kind of movie where they pick up a hitchhiker and ask him, "Are you Neil Patrick Harris?" and find out that he is. Later he steals Harold's car. Harold is incredulous: "Did

Doogie Howser just steal my car?" Yes, but he did it for a good reason. He did it so that when they finally get to a White Castle and find him there ahead of them, Harold can ask, "Dude, where's my car?"

Danny Leiner, who directed this film, began his career with *Dude, Where's My Car?* I inexplicably missed that movie, but I laughed often enough during the screening of *Harold and Kumar* that afterward I told Dann Gire, distinguished president of the Chicago film Critics' Association, that I thought maybe I should rent *Dude* and check it out. Dann cautioned me that he did not think it was all that urgent. Still another reason our leader's photograph should be displayed in every government office and classroom.

Harry Potter and the Prisoner of Azkaban ★ ★ ★ ½
PG, 136 m., 2004

Daniel Radcliffe (Harry Potter), Rupert Grint (Ron Weasley), Emma Watson (Hermione Granger), Gary Oldman (Sirius Black), David Thewlis (Professor Lupin), Michael Gambon (Albus Dumbledore), Alan Rickman (Professor Severus Snape), Maggie Smith (Professor Minerva McGonagall), Robbie Coltrane (Rubeus Hagrid), Tom Felton (Draco Malfoy), Emma Thompson (Professor Sybil Trelawney), Julie Walters (Mrs. Weasley), Timothy Spall (Peter Pettigrew), Julie Christie (Madame Rosmerta), Richard Griffiths (Uncle Vernon), Pam Ferris (Aunt Marge). Directed by Alfonso Cuaron and produced by Chris Columbus, David Heyman, and Mark Radcliffe. Screenplay by Steven Kloves, based on the novel by J. K. Rowling.

I've just returned from London, where Daniel Radcliffe created a stir by speculating that his famous character, Harry Potter, might have to die at the end of the series. Certainly that seems like more of a possibility in *Harry Potter and the Prisoner of Azkaban,* the third Potter film, than it did in the first two. It's not that Harry, Ron, and Hermione are faced with any really gruesome dangers (there's nothing here on the order of the spider that wrapped up Frodo for his dinner in the *Ring* trilogy), but that Harry's world has grown a little darker and more menacing.

The film centers on the escape of the sinister Sirius Black (Gary Oldman) from Azkaban Prison; Sirius was convicted in Voldemort's plot to murder Harry's parents, and now it's suspected he must finish the job by killing Harry. As Harry returns for his third year at Hogwarts, grim wraiths named Dementors are stationed at every entrance to the school to ward off Sirius, but the Dementors are hardly reassuring, with their trick of sucking away the soul essence of their victims.

Harry, too, has developed an edge. We first met him as the poor adopted relative of a suburban family who mistreated him mercilessly; this time, Harry is no longer the long-suffering victim but zaps an unpleasant dinner guest with a magical revenge that would be truly cruel if it were not, well, truly funny. Harry is no longer someone you can mess with.

Harry and his friends Ron and Hermione (Radcliffe, Rupert Grint, and Emma Watson) return to a Hogwarts that boasts, as it does every school year, peculiar new faculty members (this school policy promises years of employment for British character actors). New this year are Professor Lupin (David Thewlis), who tutors Harry in a tricky incantation said to provide protection against the dark magic of the Dementors; and Professor Sybil Trelawney (Emma Thompson), whose tea readings don't pull punches—not when she gazes into the bottom of Harry's cup and sees death in the leaves.

To distract Harry from his presumed fate, his friend the gamekeeper Hagrid (Robbie Coltrane) introduces the three friends to a wondrous new beast named Buck Beak, which is a hippogriff, half-bird, half-horse, wholly misunderstood. When a werewolf begins to prowl the grounds, a battle between the two creatures is inevitable. Who could the werewolf be by day? Does no one at Hogwarts find the Latin root of Lupus suggestive?

Among the movie's many special effects, I especially admired the gnarled tree that figures in the third act. The tree is introduced with a wink to the viewer who knows it is CGI: It shakes melting snow from its branches, and some of the snow seems to plop on the camera lens. Beneath this tree is a warren that shelters unimaginable terrors for Ron, when he is dragged into it as part of a longer climactic sequence that plays tricks with time. First the

261

three heroes witness one version of events, and then, after reversing the flow of time, they try to alter them. The ingenuity of the time-tricks worked for me, but may puzzle some of the film's youngest viewers.

Chris Columbus, the director of the first two Potter films, remains as producer but replaces himself as director with Alfonso Cuaron, director of the wonderful *A Little Princess* (1995), as well as the brilliant *Y Tu Mama También*. Cuaron continues the process, already under way in *Harry Potter and the Chamber of Secrets*, of darkening the palate. The world of the first film, with its postal owls and Quidditch matches, seems innocent now, and although there is indeed a Quidditch match in this film, it's played in a storm that seems to have blown in from *The Day After Tomorrow*. I like what Cuaron does with the look of the picture, but found the plotting a little murky; just when we should be focusing on exactly who Sirius Black is and why he killed Harry's parents, there is the sudden appearance of a more interesting, if less important character, Peter Pettigrew (Timothy Spall), a real rat who undergoes a change of purpose.

The actors playing Harry, Ron, and Hermione have outgrown their childhoods in this movie, and by the next film will have to be dealt with as teenagers, or replaced by younger actors. If they continue to grow up, I'm afraid the series may begin to tilt toward less whimsical forms of special-effects violence, but on the other hand I like Radcliffe, Grint, and Watson, and especially the way Watson's Hermione has of shouldering herself into the center of scenes and taking charge. Although the series is named for Harry, he's often an onlooker, and it's Hermione who delivers a long-delayed uppercut to the jaw of Draco Malfoy.

Unlike American movies such as *Spy Kids* where the young actors dominate most of their scenes, the Harry Potter movies weave the three heroes into a rich tapestry of character performances. Here I savored David Thewlis as a teacher too clever by half, Emma Thompson as the embodiment of daffy enthusiasm, Alan Rickman as the meticulously snippy Snape, Robbie Coltrane as the increasingly lovable Hagrid, and Michael Gambon, stepping into the robes and beard of the late Richard Harris as Dumbledore.

Is *Harry Potter and the Prisoner of Azkaban* as good as the first two films? Not quite. It doesn't have that sense of joyously leaping through a clockwork plot, and it needs to explain more than it should. But the world of Harry Potter remains delightful, amusing, and sophisticated; the challenge in the films ahead will be to protect its fragile innocence and not descend into the world of conventional teen thrillers. ☞

The Haunted Mansion ★ ★ ½
PG, 99 m., 2003

Eddie Murphy (Jim Evers), Marsha Thomason (Sara Evers), Nathaniel Parker (Master Gracey), Jennifer Tilly (Madame Leota), Terence Stamp (Ramsley), Wallace Shawn (Ezra), Dina Waters (Emma), Marc John Jefferies (Michael), Aree Davis (Megan). Directed by Rob Minkoff and produced by Andrew Gunn and Don Hahn. Screenplay by David Berenbaum.

The surprising thing about *The Haunted Mansion* isn't that it's based on a Disney theme park ride, but that it has ambition. It wants to be more than a movie version of the ride. I expected an inane series of nonstop action sequences, but what I got was a fairly intriguing story and an actual plot that is actually resolved. That doesn't make the movie good enough to recommend, but it makes it better than the ads suggest.

The movie stars Eddie Murphy as Jim Evers, workaholic real estate agent, who is headed for a weekend vacation with his family when they get sidetracked by the chance to put a vast old mansion on the market. His wife, Sara (Marsha Thomason), is his business partner, but complains, as all movie wives always complain, that her husband is spending too much time at work. Their kids are Michael and Megan (Marc John Jefferies and Aree Davis).

Evers (or more accurately his wife, whose photo appears on their fliers) is invited to visit the Gracey Mansion, isolated behind a forbidding iron gate and surrounded by a jungle of sinister vegetation. It's a triumph of art direction, inspired by the Disney World attraction and by every haunted house ever crept through by Bela Lugosi, Lon Chaney, Christopher Lee, Peter Cushing, Abbott, Costello, et al. Doors bulge, curtains sway, and there's a scenic graveyard behind the house, complete with four marble busts that perform as a barbershop quartet.

The visitors are greeted by the butler, Ramsley (Terence Stamp), gaunt, cadaverous, with a voice that coils up from unimaginable inner caverns. Also on staff are servants Ezra (Wallace Shawn, looking his most homuncular) and Emma (Dina Waters, simpering over). On the premises, but not exactly in residence, is Madame Leota (Jennifer Tilly), whose disembodied head floats in a crystal ball and offers timely if disturbing advice.

The lord of the manor is Master Gracey (Nathaniel Parker), who seems obsessed with Sara Evers. Flashbacks explain why. In antebellum New Orleans, Gracey was in love with a young woman who looked exactly like Sara, and when they could not marry, they both killed themselves. Which means Gracey is a ghost, of course, but leaves unanswered the question of why he could not marry the ghost of his original lover and stop haunting respectable married real estate agents.

The most intriguing element of the movie is the way it does and doesn't deal with the buried racial theme. We learn that the sinister Ramsley sabotaged his master's romance because if he married, the family would be destroyed. Presumably that would be because an interracial romance was dangerous in old New Orleans, but the movie never says so and indeed never refers to the races of any of its characters. That is either (a) refreshing and admirable, or (b) puzzling, since the whole plot is motivated by race.

The story, in any event, gives the characters a lot to deal with, which means we are not relegated to a movie full of banging doors, swinging chandeliers, and other ghostly effects. There are a lot of those, of course, especially as the kids make their own way around the gloomy pile, but there is a certain poignancy about the central dilemma, and the Gracey character reflects it well, eventually answering one of the questions posed above, although I will not say which one.

The movie doesn't quite work, maybe because the underlying theme is an uneasy fit with the silly surface. Murphy is not given much to do; he's the straight man, in a story involving his wife and ghosts. If anyone steals the movie, it's Stamp, who must have been studying Hammer horror films for years, and puts the ham back into Hammer. *The Haunted Mansion* won't much entertain older family members, but it might be fun for kids, and seems headed for a long run on home video.

Head in the Clouds ★ ★ ★
R, 132 m., 2004

Charlize Theron (Gilda Besse), Penelope Cruz (Mia), Stuart Townsend (Guy), Thomas Kretschmann (Major Thomas Bietrich), Steven Berkhoff (Charles Besse), David La Haye (Lucien), Karine Vanasse (Lisette). Directed by John Duigan and produced by Michael Cowan, Bertil Ohlsson, Jonathan Olsberg, Jason Piette, Andre Rouleau, and Maxime Remillard. Screenplay by Duigan.

Head in the Clouds uses World War II as the backdrop for a romantic triangle. Well, so did *Pearl Harbor*, but I liked this one more, perhaps because it isn't so serious about itself. Oh, it keeps a straight face, but the plot has been rigged so the heroine can be seen in every possible light from the noble to the sinister, occasionally at the same time. She's Gilda Besse (Charlize Theron), one of those women who is so rebellious, daring, sexy, scandalous, shocking, and brave that it's a good thing the war came around to give her a context. A woman like this in peacetime would have a terrifying volume of unreleased energy and would be driven to find a channel to vent it. Maybe that explains Martha Stewart.

The movie begins with a fortune-teller who predicts amazing things in Gilda's thirty-fourth year. This is a device to tip off the audience that it's not going to be entirely about the school days of a young woman who pops up in the rooms of an Oxford undergraduate one night. He is Guy (Stuart Townsend), and he offers Gilda refuge from the campus scouts; he knows she's having an affair with one of the dons (who at Oxford are professors, not gangsters, with occasional exceptions, especially in earlier centuries).

Gilda is already a legend. Her father, played by the alarming British actor Steven Berkhoff, is a French millionaire. Her mother is an American. Her affairs are legion, her behavior notorious. Although Guy should be beneath her radar, she kind of likes him, and he of course is smitten. One thing leads to another, and a few years later he's invited to join her in Paris, where she is now a famous photographer and lives with her model Mia (Penelope Cruz). Mia is quite a character herself: former apache dancer and stripper, probably once a hooker, also a committed political idealist who is taking nursing classes in order to volunteer against the fascists in her native Spain.

Of course Mia and Gilda are lovers, sort of; they're the kind of movie lesbians whose relationships exist primarily to accommodate the men in their lives and excite the men in their audience. Mia's reaction to Gilda's uncertain but real affection for Guy is to look pensive in quiet little shots, as if she is thinking, "I wish that was me."

Eventually, Guy gets to look pensive, too, after the war breaks out and he returns to Paris as a British spy, only to find that Gilda is now the mistress of a powerful Nazi officer. The Nazis had excellent taste in mistresses, if we can judge by the two best recent movies on the theme, *Bon Voyage* and *Gloomy Sunday.* Their mistresses, of course, had lousy taste in men, which is why Guy can't understand what Gilda has done. Surely this great free spirit is not sleeping with a man just to get nylons, cigarettes, and champagne?

Whether she is or not, I will leave for you to determine. What is certain is that Gilda is a considerable movie character, as Gildas so often are in the movies. The function of poor Guy is to follow her from one continent to another, gaze at her in admiration, lust, shock, horror, and dismay, and then in admiration and lust again. Wonderful as Gilda is, it must be exhausting to be fascinated by her.

Charlize Theron is one of the few actresses equal to the role, bringing to it beauty, steel-edged repose, and mystery. Gilda will be compared unfavorably to her great work in *Monster,* but I find it fascinating that the two films come so close together, underlining what magic really is involved in being an actor. Penelope Cruz is given a character who seems to combine the attributes of several other people who must have been written out of the script, so that she's busy being jealous, heroic, political, seductive, and studious; she

walks with a limp, except in her lesbo tango with Gilda, where we don't much miss it.

The screenplay, by director John Duigan, seems constructed to put Gilda through the paces of most of the activities that would later be described in the little green paperbacks of the Traveler's Companion series published by Olympia in postwar Paris. When Mia's date leaves her black and blue with welts from a beating, for example, Gilda calls him up, hints that she's really interested in finding out more about his techniques, and then ties him to a bed and whips him, not entirely to his disliking. What she does with her Nazi is not entirely clear, but he seems content.

All the same, what *does* she think about Guy? Does she see him as a lover, a pet, a mascot, a dupe, a friend, an enemy? That's the movie's central puzzle, and no one is more baffled than Guy. By the time he (and we) get it all figured out, the war's about over, and so is the movie. I know *Head in the Clouds* is silly and the plot is preposterous, but it labors under no delusions otherwise. It wants to be a hard-panting melodrama, with spies and sex and love and death, and there are times when a movie like this is exactly what you feel like indulging.

Head of State ★ ★ ★
PG-13, 95 m., 2003

Chris Rock (Mays Gilliam), Bernie Mac (Mitch Gilliam), Dylan Baker (Martin Geller), Nick Searcy (Brian Lewis), Lynn Whitfield (Debra Lassiter), Robin Givens (Kim), Tamala Jones (Lisa Clark), James Rebhorn (Senator Bill Arnot), Stephanie March (Nikki). Directed by Chris Rock and produced by Ali LeRoi, Rock, and Michael Rotenberg. Screenplay by Rock and LeRoi.

Head of State is an imperfect movie, but not a boring one, and not lacking in intelligence. What it does wrong is hard to miss, but what it does right is hard to find: It makes an angry and fairly timely comic attack on an electoral system where candidates don't say what they really think, but simply repeat safe centrist banalities.

In *Head of State,* the presidential and vice presidential candidates of an unnamed party, obviously the Democrats, are killed when their campaign planes crash into each other less than two months before the election. Seeking a replacement candidate, the party settles on Mays Gilliam, an obscure Washington, D.C., alderman (Chris Rock), who has saved a woman and her cat from a burning building. He seems to have no chance of victory, but of course party boss Senator Bill Arnot (James Rebhorn) doesn't want him to win—he wants to exploit him as a token black candidate who will lose, but win painless points for the party.

If Mays can't win, then he has nothing to lose, and his strategy is obvious: Instead of trying to please everyone, he should say the unsayable. We've seen this strategy before from movie candidates, notably Kevin Kline in *Dave,* Warren Beatty in *Bulworth,* and Eddie Murphy in *Distinguished Gentleman,* and the notion runs back to Frank Capra. What Chris Rock brings to it is brashness—zingers that hurt. "What kind of a drug policy," he wants to know, "makes crack cheaper than asthma medicine?"

The movie, directed and cowritten by Rock, is wickedly cynical about the American electoral system. It shows Mays being supplied with a prostitute named Nikki (Stephanie March) because, campaign manager Martin Geller (Dylan Baker) explains, "We got tired of getting caught up in sex scandals, so we commissioned our own team of superwhores." And it gives him an opponent, the incumbent vice president (Nick Searcy), whose claim to fame is he's Sharon Stone's cousin, and whose motto has a certain resonance: "God bless America—and no place else."

Mays bumbles through the first weeks of his campaign, following the instructions of his profoundly conventional campaign advisers, Geller and Debra Lassiter (Lynn Whitfield), until his brother, a Chicago bail bondsman named Mitch (Bernie Mac), asks him when he's going to start speaking his mind. When he does, the first thing he says is that he wants Mitch as his running mate.

This is one of the areas that doesn't work. Bernie Mac could be a funny veep candidate, but not as a bondsman whose peculiar personal quirk is to hit people as hard as he can as a sign of friendship. The character should have been redefined, and a scene where Mays and Mitch batter each other should have been edited out; it works only as an awkward puzzlement for the audience.

Another element that doesn't work is the character of Kim (Robin Givens), who begins the movie as Mays's fiancée, is dumped, and then turns into a crazy stalker who follows him everywhere, overacting on a distressingly shrill note until she exits in a particularly nasty way. This character could have been dumped, especially since Mays meets a cute caterer named Lisa (Tamala Jones), who looks like first lady material.

Chris Rock is a smart, fast-talking comedian with an edge; I keep wondering when the Academy will figure out he could host the Oscars. Here he plays his usual persona, more or less, in a movie where some of the edges are rough and others are serrated. We keep getting these movie fantasies where political candidates say what they think, are not afraid to offend, cut through the crap, and take stands. Must be wish fulfillment.

Head-On ★ ★ ★
NO MPAA RATING, 118 m., 2005

Birol Unel (Cahit), Sibel Kekilli (Sibel), Catrin Striebeck (Maren), Guven Kirac (Seref), Meltem Cumbul (Selma). Directed by Fatih Akin and produced by Ralph Schwingel and Stefan Schubert. Screenplay by Akin.

"Are you Turkish? Will you marry me?" This may not be the shortest marriage proposal in movie history, but it is certainly one of the most sincere. It comes early in *Head-On,* a film about two people who would deserve each other, except that no one deserves either one of them. Sibel is a Turkish woman of about twenty-two, living in Germany with her parents. Cahit, who is at least twenty years older, is also a Turk living in Germany, which is all Sibel needs to know, because what she needs is a Turkish husband (any Turkish husband will do) who can take her out of her home and the domination of her father and brother and the threat of being married off to a loathsome man of their choosing.

Not that Sibel is a prize. Her wrists are scarred after suicide attempts, and she meets Cahit in a mental institution, where he has been taken after driving his car into a wall at full speed. Not a promising couple. She explains the deal: She will cook and keep house for him, do his laundry and stay out of the way. He doesn't have to have sex with her, and she gets to have sex with anybody she wants. This sounds like a good enough deal to Cahit, who desperately needs a housecleaner (and a bath and a haircut) and is getting all the sex he needs from a buxom hairdresser who hangs out with him at the sleaziest saloon since *Barfly*.

Cahit (Birol Unel) and Sibel (Sibel Kekilli) are played with a deadpan self-destructiveness that sometimes tilts toward comedy, sometimes toward tragedy, sometimes simply toward grossing us out. Cahit picks up the empty bottles in a bar in return for free drinks, uses cocaine when he can get it, is morose about the unexplained loss of his first wife (maybe he misplaced her), and is a sight to behold when he is brought home by Sibel to meet her family. Her father, a bearded patriarch, looks on incredulously. Her brother whispers to the old man that at least Cahit will take her off their hands. To Cahit, he says: "Your Turkish sucks. What did you do with it?" Cahit: "I threw it away."

It is not that he hates Turkish or Turkey; it is that he hates himself. He prefers to speak German because that is the language of the society he moves in, one of garish bars and sudden fights and desperate bloody hangovers. Everyone in his world is a realist with no delusions. I treasured the scene where Cahit's new brother-in-law suggests they all make a trip to a brothel and is enraged when Cahit suggests that the man return home and sleep with his wife instead.

In a conventional movie, the formula would be: They put up with each other out of necessity, she starts to care for him, he begins to like her but she draws away, he grows angry and distant, she sees that he needs her, and they end by discovering that, what do you know, they actually love each other. *Head-On* goes through these stages in five minutes, on its way to much more desperate and harrowing adventures, which you will discover for yourself.

The film won the Berlin Film Festival and a lot of European Film Awards, and was praised partly, I imagine, because it provides a portrait (however dire) of Germany's large population of Turks and other immigrants—who,

like undocumented Mexicans in America, are made to feel unwelcome while at the same time being essential to the functioning of the economy. The most memorable film I've seen about immigrants in Germany was *Ali—Fear Eats the Soul* (1974), by Rainer Werner Fassbinder, a director with an uncanny resemblance to Cahit, especially in the categories of personal hygiene, barbering, and drug abuse. In *Ali*, a middle-aged cleaning woman marries a much younger Moroccan man, and when she announces this fact to her family, a son (played by Fassbinder) stares at her for a second, stands up, and kicks out the screen of her television set.

Head-On not only includes a car crash, but has the fascination of one. It is possible that no good can come to these characters, no matter what changes they make or what they can do for each other. Their marriage functions primarily to yank both parties out of their personal spirals of self-destruction and allow them to join in a double helix of personal misfortune.

From time to time, the movie cuts to a band performing on a stage of Turkish carpets on a bank of the Bosphorus strait, with Istanbul in the background. These musical interludes suggest that we may be seeing a version of a ballad or folk-legend, which has been processed through generations of urban grunge. What I can say for the film is what I could also say of *Barfly*, *Last Exit to Brooklyn*, and *Sid & Nancy*, which is that the characters in these movies are making their mistakes so we don't have to.

I can also observe that I watched with fascination. The movie is well and fearlessly acted, and the writer-director (Fatih Akin) is determined to follow the story to a logical and believable conclusion, rather than letting everyone off the hook with a conventional ending.

The Heart of Me ★ ★ ★
R, 96 m., 2003

Helena Bonham Carter (Dinah), Olivia Williams (Madeleine), Paul Bettany (Rickie), Eleanor Bron (Mrs. Burkett), Luke Newberry (Anthony), Alison Reid (Bridie), Tom Ward (Jack), Gillian Hanna (Betty), Andrew Havill (Charles).

Directed by Thaddeus O'Sullivan and produced by Martin Pope. Screenplay by Lucinda Coxon, based on the novel *The Echoing Grove* by Rosamond Lehmann.

The lovers in *The Heart of Me* have a line of poetry by William Blake as their touchstone: "And throughout all eternity, I forgive you and you forgive me." This implies much to forgive, and the movie involves a decade of suffering, punctuated by occasional bliss, and inspired by their misfortune in falling in love with one another. For theirs is not an ordinary adultery, but one complicated by the inconvenience that he is married to her sister.

The film is a soapy melodrama set from about 1936 to 1946 and done with style—Jerry Springer crossed with *Masterpiece Theater*. Helena Bonham Carter stars as Dinah, a raffish bohemian who is the despair of her sister, Madeleine (Olivia Williams), and their mother (Eleanor Bron). Madeleine at last contrives to get Dinah engaged to a presentable man, but when the intended nuptials are announced at a family dinner, we notice that Madeleine's husband, Rickie, winces. We notice, and so does Dinah, who sends him a barely perceptible shrug. Later that night Rickie (Paul Bettany) opens her bedroom door and announces, "You are not going through with this. Break it off."

She agrees. His statement clarifies what has been vibrating in the air between them, a romantic love of the abandoned, hopeless variety that is most irresistible when surrounded by the codes of a society that places great value on appearances. The family maintains "the smartest house in London," Rickie has one of those jobs in the city that provides a large income for tasks hard to define, and while there is no love between him and his wife, it is simply not done to cheat with your sister-in-law.

The movie is based on a 1953 novel by Rosamond Lehmann, and while it is hard to say it was inspired by her affair with C. Day Lewis, they had an affair, and she wrote a novel about an affair, and there you are. No doubt the facts are different, but the feelings are similar. Helena Bonham Carter does suggest a woman with something of Lehmann's flair for romantic drama; her Dinah is the kind of person it is easy to criticize until you look into her heart and see with what fierce integrity she opposes

the strictures of society. It is really Dinah, and not Rickie, who is taking the big chances, because no matter what sins Rickie commits he will always be required to remain on display as Madeleine's husband, while the punishment for Dinah must be exile. "I love you!" Madeleine cries at a crucial moment, and Rickie's reply is dry and exact: "Madeleine, I think if that were true, you would have said it sooner."

Madeleine is not a bad person either, really; she is the aggrieved party, after all, and has good reason to be cross with her sister and her husband. But it never occurs to her to cut loose from Ricky; this man who has betrayed her remains necessary for her to keep up appearances, and she and her mother tell appalling lies to both Dinah and Rickie in trying to force the relationship to an end. The great sadness in the movie is the waste of love, which is a rare commodity and must be consumed in season.

An intriguing supporting character in the movie is Bridie (Alison Reid), who serves as Dinah's confidante and companion in exile, and who, like many privileged insiders, cannot resist sharing what she knows with just those people who least should know it. As Dinah waits sadly in lovers' nests and French hideaways, it is Bridie who harbors resentments.

There are major developments in the story that I will not reveal, but, oh! how sad these people are by the end. And how pathetic. There is a certain nobility in the way Rickie, a wrecked man, displays what is left of himself to Madeleine and bitterly tells her, "This is what you fought so hard to hold onto." If they only had attended to the entire poem by Blake ("My spectre around me night and day") they would not have taken such comfort from its promise of forgiveness.

The movie has won only a mixed reception. Many of the complaints have to do with the fact that the characters are wealthy and upper-class and speak English elegantly. The names of Merchant and Ivory are used like clubs to beat the film. This is the same kind of thinking that led Jack Warner to tell his producers, "Don't give me any more pictures where they write with feathers." The movie is *about* the punishment of being trapped in a system where appearances are more important than reality. After she breaks her engagement at the beginning of the movie, Dinah has lunch with Madeleine, who says, "You've put us all in a very awkward position." Dinah said, "I thought that preferable to marrying a man I didn't love." Madeleine, on the other hand, believes it is better to marry a man you do not love than be put in an awkward position. And just as well, as that turns out to be the story of her marriage.

Heights ★ ★ ★

R, 93 m., 2005

Glenn Close (Diana), Elizabeth Banks (Isabel), James Marsden (Jonathan), Jesse Bradford (Alec), Eric Bogosian (Henry), John Light (Peter), Andrew Howard (Ian), George Segal (Rabbi Mendel). Directed by Chris Terrio and produced by Ismail Merchant and Richard Hawley. Screenplay by Amy Fox, based on her stage play.

The most thankless task in Shakespeare may not be playing Lady Macbeth, but playing an actress who is playing Lady Macbeth. She can't even name the play she's in, referring instead to "the Scottish play," so that most people think they missed the first half of her sentence, while the rest of us reflect on what a long time has passed since we learned why she says that. In *Heights,* Glenn Close plays Diana, the actress who is playing Lady Macbeth and interrupts a rehearsal to declare, "We have forgotten passion." Yes, but in this movie they'll remember it soon enough.

The film is one of those interlocking dramas where all of the characters are involved in one another's lives, if only they knew it. We know, and one of our pleasures is waiting for the pennies to drop. Diana is the mother of Isabel (Elizabeth Banks), a photographer who is engaged to Jonathan (James Marsden). Meanwhile, Jonathan has been contacted by Peter (John Light), who is interviewing the subjects of a British photo exhibition in which a photograph of Jonathan suggests that Isabel should think twice, or three times, before marrying him.

At an audition, Diana meets Alec (Jesse Bradford), a young actor. He leaves his jacket behind. Diana discovers that Alex lives in the same building as Isabel and Jonathan, and gives the jacket to her daughter to return to the actor. The astonishing thing about this is that an unemployed actor could afford to live in the same building as two well-employed people who are sharing the rent.

Diana's husband is having an affair with a young actress, which Diana pretends to accept, while meanwhile she seems to audition young lovers everywhere she goes; she doesn't want to sleep with them so much as see if she's still famous enough that they think they have to sleep with her. Other characters include George Segal as a rabbi who is counseling the Jewish Jonathan and the Christian Isabel before their marriage; his experiment with flash cards is not successful.

That the threads of all of these lives intersect in about twenty-four hours is the movie's reality. That they are interesting is the movie's success. There is a sense in which this movie could simply play as a puzzle, but the acting is good enough to carry the contrivance. Glenn Close, hovering over the characters like a malevolent succubus, is wonderful here; her character must have had to dial down to play Lady Macbeth.

Much in the plot depends on the discovery of a secret that is not much of a secret to us at any point during the film. Oddly enough, that's not a problem, since the drama is based not on our surprise, but on the reaction of characters in the film. Suspecting, and then knowing, what they do not suspect and do not want to know allows us a kind of superiority that is one of the pleasures of being in the audience. After everything has been revealed, we do have a question, though: Why exactly did the character with a secret make the choices that are made? What would be proven? What would be accomplished? How would happiness come that way?

Apart from the movie's mysteries and revelations, its chief pleasure comes through simple voyeurism. It is entertaining to see the lives of complex people become brutally simple all of a sudden. They build elaborate facades of belief and image, they think they know who they are and what people think of them, and suddenly they're back at the beginning. That can be a disaster, or a relief. We start with nothing, we slowly construct this person we call ourselves, and eventually we live inside that person and it is too late to bring in another architect. Idea for a movie: A character takes a year's leave of absence from his life in order to go where he is unknown, and experience the adventure of starting from scratch.

But I digress. Let me just say that another of the movie's pleasures is the way it introduces characters for brief scenes in which it's suggested that another movie could be made by following them out of this one. One of those characters is Ian (Andrew Howard), a Welsh artist whom Isabel meets, and whose life takes a sudden turn. One of the other pleasures of narrative is when elaborate fictional scenes are built up, only to be smacked down.

Heights is not a great movie, and makes no great point, unless it is "To thine own self be true." But director Chris Terrio, working from a screenplay by Amy Fox (based on her play), sees the characters clearly and watches them with accuracy as they occupy their delusions, or lose them. The movie is one of the last produced by Ismail Merchant, who as always was attracted to stories and characters, not to genres, concepts, or marketing plans.

Hellboy ★ ★ ★ ½
PG-13, 132 m., 2004

Ron Perlman (Hellboy) John Hurt (Professor Bruttenholm), Selma Blair (Liz Sherman), Jeffrey Tambor (Tom Manning), Karel Roden (Grigori Rasputin), Rupert Evans (John Myers), Corey Johnson (Agent Clay), Doug Jones (Abe Sapien), Bridget Hodson (Ilsa), Ladislav Beran (Kroenen). Directed by Guillermo del Toro and produced by Lawrence Gordon, Lloyd Levin, and Mike Richardson. Screenplay by Guillermo del Toro, based on the comic by Mike Mignola.

Hellboy is one of those rare movies that's not only based on a comic book, but feels like a comic book. It's vibrating with energy, and you can sense the zeal and joy in its making. Of course it's constructed of nonstop special effects, bizarre makeup, and a preposterous story line, but it carries that baggage lightly; unlike some CGI movies that lumber from one set piece to another, this one skips lightheartedly through the action. And in Ron Perlman

it has found an actor who is not just playing a superhero, but enjoying it; although he no doubt had to endure hours in makeup every day, he chomps his cigar, twitches his tail, and battles his demons with something approaching glee. You can see an actor in the process of making an impossible character really work.

The movie, based on comics by Mike Mignola and directed by the Mexican-born horror master Guillermo del Toro *(Cronos, Blade II)*, opens with a scene involving Nazis, those most durable of comic book villains. In a desperate scheme late in World War II, they open a portal to the dark side and summon forth the Seven Gods of Chaos—or almost do, before they are thwarted by U.S. soldiers and Professor Bruttenholm (John Hurt), who is President Roosevelt's personal psychic adviser. Nothing slips through the portal but a little red baby with horns and a tail; he spits and hisses at the professor, who calms him with a Baby Ruth bar, cradles him in his arms, and raises him to become mankind's chief warrior against the forces of hell.

Meanwhile, the psychic practitioner Grigori Rasputin (Karel Roden), who is working for the Nazis, is sucked through a portal and disappears. Yes, he's *that* Rasputin. We flash-forward to the present. The professor, now in his eighties, is told he will die soon. Two of his old enemies have inexplicably not grown older, however: a Nazi named Ilsa (Bridget Hodson) and a weirdo named Kroenen (Ladislav Beran), who is addicted to surgical modifications on his body. In an icy pass in Mondavia they perform ceremonies to bring Rasputin back from the other side, and they're ready to rumble.

Cut to a secret FBI headquarters where Hellboy lives with the professor and an aquatic creature named Abe Sapien (Doug Jones)—a fishboy who got his name because he was born the day Abraham Lincoln was assassinated. The professor is showing the ropes to young FBI agent Myers (Rupert Evans) when the Nazis attack a museum and liberate a creature imprisoned inside an ancient statue. This creature, a writhing, repellant, oozing mass of tentacles and teeth, reproduces by dividing, and will soon conquer the Earth, unless Hellboy can come to the rescue.

Which he does, of course, in action sequences that seem storyboarded straight off the pages of a comic book. Hellboy gets banged up a lot, but is somehow able to pick himself up off the mat and repair himself with a little self-applied chiropractic; a crunch of his spine, a pop of his shoulders, and he's back in action. Abe the fishboy, who wears a breathing apparatus out of the water, is more of a dreamer than a fighter, with a personality that makes him a distant relative of Jar Jar Binks.

Hellboy's life is a lonely one. When you are seven feet tall and bright red, with a tail, you don't exactly fit in, even though HB tries to make himself look more normal by sawing his horns down to stumps, which he sands every morning. He is in love with another paranormal: Liz Sherman (Selma Blair), a pyrokineticist who feels guilty because she starts fires when she gets excited. There is a terrific scene where Hellboy kisses her and she bursts into flames, and we realize they were made for each other, because Hellboy, of course, is fireproof.

The FBI, which is occasionally accused of not sharing its information with other agencies, keeps Hellboy as its own deep secret; that droll actor Jeffrey Tambor plays the FBI chief, a bureaucrat who is just not cut out for battling the hounds of hell. He has some funny setup scenes, and indeed the movie is best when it's establishing all of these characters and before it descends to its apocalyptic battles.

Hellboy battles the monsters in subway tunnels and subterranean caverns, as Liz, Myers, and Abe the fishboy tag along. I know, of course, that one must accept the action in a movie like this on faith, but there was one transition I was utterly unable to follow. Liz has saved them all from the monsters by filling a cave with fire, which shrivels them and their eggs into crispy s'mores, and then— well, the movie cuts directly to another cave in which they are held captive by the evil Nazis, and Hellboy is immobilized in gigantic custom-made stocks that have an extra-large hole for his oversized left hand. How did that happen?

Never mind. Doesn't matter. Despite his sheltered upbringing, Hellboy has somehow obtained the tough-talking personality of a Brooklyn stevedore, but he has a tender side, not only for Liz but for cats and kittens. He has one scene with the FBI director that reminded me of the moment when Frankenstein enjoys a cigar with the blind man. He always lights his stogies with a lighter, and Tambor explains that cigars must always be ignited with a wooden match. Good to know when Liz isn't around.

Herbie: Fully Loaded ★ ★
G, 101 m., 2005

Lindsay Lohan (Maggie Peyton), Justin Long (Kevin), Breckin Meyer (Ray Peyton Jr.), Matt Dillon (Trip Murphy), Michael Keaton (Ray Peyton Sr.), Cheryl Hines (Sally). Directed by Angela Robinson and produced by Robert Simonds. Screenplay by Thomas Lennon, Ben Garant, Alfred Gough, and Miles Millar.

The question that haunted me during *Herbie: Fully Loaded* involved the degree of Herbie's intelligence. Is the car alive? Can it think? Does it have feelings? Can it really fall in love, or is its romance with that cute little yellow VW bug just a cynical ploy to get publicity, since it has a new movie coming out?

To the dim degree that I recall the premise of the earlier *Herbie* movies, none of which I seem to have reviewed or indeed seen, Herbie was essentially just a car. A car with a personality, a car that feelings and emotions could be projected upon, a car that sometimes seemed to have a mind of its own, but nevertheless a car existing in the world as we know it. In *Herbie: Fully Loaded*, Herbie can blink his headlights and roll them from side to side, he can let his front bumper droop when he's depressed, and he can suddenly open his doors to cause trouble for people he doesn't like.

I see I have subconsciously stopped calling Herbie "it" and am now calling Herbie "he." Maybe I've answered my own question. If Herbie is alive, or able to seem alive, isn't this an astonishing breakthrough in the realm of Artificial Intelligence? That's if computer scientists, working secretly, programmed Herbie to act the way he does. On the other hand, if Herbie just sort of became Herbie on his own, then that would be the best argument yet for Intelligent Design.

Either way, a thinking car is a big story. It is

an incredible, amazing thing. In *Herbie: Fully Loaded,* Herbie becomes the possession of a young woman named Maggie (Lindsay Lohan), who is the daughter of a famous racing family headed by her dad, Ray (Michael Keaton). The family dynasty falls on hard times after her brother Ray Jr. (Breckin Meyer) gets caught in a slump. She rescues Herbie from a junkyard, a friendly mechanic (Justin Long) rebuilds the car, and then Herbie offends the sensibilities of a hotshot racing champion (Matt Dillon). The champ challenges Herbie and Maggie, the bug is entered in a NASCAR race, and I would not dream of telling you who wins.

The movie is pretty cornball. Little kids would probably enjoy it, but their older brothers and sisters will be rolling their eyes, and their parents will be using their iPods. The story is formula from beginning to end: the plucky girl and her plucky car, both disregarded by the dominant male culture, but gritting their teeth, or radiators, for a chance to prove themselves. The ineffectual dad. The teeth-gnashing villain. The racing footage. There is a moment when Herbie narrowly escapes being crushed into scrap metal in the junkyard, and his escape is sort of ingenious, but for the most part, this movie, like Herbie, seems to have been assembled from spare parts.

But let's rewind a little. *Herbie: Fully Loaded* opens with a montage of headlines and TV coverage from Herbie's original burst of fame, as chronicled in three earlier movies. That leads me to wonder (a) why Herbie ended up in a junkyard, when such a famous car should obviously be in a classic automobile museum in Las Vegas, and (b) why, when Maggie appears with the rebuilt and customized Herbie, no one in the racing media realizes this is the same car.

Never mind. The real story is Herbie's intelligence. The car seems to be self-aware, able to make decisions on its own, and able to communicate with Maggie on an emotional level, and sometimes with pantomime or example. Why then is everyone, including Lohan, so fixated on how fast the car can go? The car could be up on blocks and be just as astonishing.

It goes to show you how we in the press so often miss the big stories that are right under our noses. There is a famous journalistic legend about the time a young reporter covered the Johnstown flood of 1889. The kid wrote: "God sat on a hillside overlooking Johnstown today and looked at the destruction He had wrought." His editor cabled back: "Forget flood. Interview God."

Her Majesty ★ ★ ½
PG, 105 m., 2005

Sally Andrews (Elizabeth Wakefield), Vicky Haughton (Hira Mata), Liddy Holloway (Virginia Hobson), Mark Clare (John Wakefield), Craig Elliott (Stuart Wakefield), Alison Routledge (Victoria Wakefield), Anna Sheridan (Annabel Leach). Directed by Mark J. Gordon and produced by Walter Coblenz. Screenplay by Gordon.

Her Majesty has all the makings of a perfectly charming family picture, and then the plot runs off the rails. At some point during the writing process, a clear-headed realist should have stepped in and restored sanity. This hypothetical person would have realized (1) that the heroine's brother is not just a nasty young boy, but a psychopath, (2) that it is not necessary for the rhododendron lady to be having an affair with the mayor in order to be reprehensible, and (3) it is not very likely that Queen Elizabeth, on a state visit to New Zealand, would go out of her way to visit the village of Middleton and call on an old Maori lady in order to return a spear stolen from her grandfather.

I realize it is (3) where I'm asking for trouble. The notes for the movie say it is "inspired by real events." I learn that Queen Elizabeth did indeed visit New Zealand in 1953, and even the hamlet of Cambridge, which plays Middleton in the film. Now I will no doubt be informed that she also tracked down the old Maori woman on the porch of her humble shack, and gave her the spear. In that case, the scene in question will not be inaccurate, but merely unbelievable.

Her Majesty is the kind of movie where you start out smiling, and then smile more broadly, and then really smile, and then realize with a sinking heart that the filmmakers are losing it. It stars a sunny-faced twelve-year-old named

Sally Andrews as Elizabeth Wakefield, who is obsessed with the young Queen Elizabeth. A panning shot across her bedroom reveals enough QEII mementoes to bring a fortune on eBay. When she learns that the queen plans to visit her subjects in New Zealand, Elizabeth (the heroine, not the II) writes her more than fifty letters, suggesting Middleton as a destination. Apparently they work.

Elizabeth the Heroine has meanwhile made fast friends with Hira Mata (Vicky Haughton), the old Maori woman whose unpainted shack is an eyesore on the road into town. Hira takes Elizabeth the Heroine to a mountaintop and shows her that all she surveys—and land, the sea, and the sky—once belonged to the Maori, but now all that is left is her little patch of land. She reveals that Elizabeth II's ancestor once gave her grandfather a brace of dueling pistols in admiration of his bravery, but that two weeks later her grandfather was murdered and the pistols and his spear were stolen.

The pistols turn up as a family heirloom of the loathsome Mrs. Hobson (Liddy Holloway), busybody and head of the Rhododendron Trust, who plans to present them to the queen during her inspection, of course, of the rhododendrons. This Hobson creature is a powdery-faced screecher whose sex life with the mayor involves unspeakable games based on bee-keeping. She is insufferable, but consider Elizabeth the H's brother, Stuart (Craig Elliott), who, if he survives his adolescence, has a good chance of developing into New Zealand's most alarming criminal case study.

Stuart throws a brick through the Maori woman's window. He steals his sister's QEII collection and burns it. He gets fired for laziness and lies about it. He sneaks out to the Maori woman's house, douses it with gasoline, and prepares to burn it down, which is not a youthful prank but a crime for which I would throw the little bastard behind bars. And he locks up Elizabeth the H on the day when Elizabeth II is coming to town.

This is going too far. Stuart's depredations break through the veneer of small-town comedy and turn into some kind of sick weirdness. Elizabeth the H keeps smiling, preserves her pluck, and dutifully rehearses with the girls' drill team, and we would like to relax and

smile with her and wish her the best, but we are distracted by the vile little desperado and his band of degenerate buddies.

I agree with the Maori woman that the land was her tribe's, and was taken from them. I agree that treatment of the Maoris was a crime against humanity. I have seen *Rabbit-Proof Fence*, which is about the treatment of aboriginal orphans in Australia as recently as 1970. That a neighboring commonwealth nation engaged in such practices until 1970 argues that in 1953, Queen Elizabeth was not rummaging through the attic at Buckingham Palace looking for a Maori spear her relative might have stolen, so that she could return it to the friend of the nice young woman who has been writing her from Middleton. It's a feel-good scene for white viewers, but Maoris may view it a little more ironically.

There is a sense in which all of my logic is wasted. *Her Majesty*, directed by Mark J. Gordon, will work perfectly well for its intended audience of girls about Elizabeth the H's age, which is twelve; they will like her pluck and spirit, and won't ask themselves if her brother is a little over the top, since at that age they consider most brothers to be monsters. I do not want to discourage this audience, because entertaining family movies are hard enough to find, and maybe only a curmudgeon like me would ask the questions that distract me.

There's another movie from Down Under that is also about a small town and an important visit. That would be *The Dish* (2001), about a little Australian town where a radio telescope has been installed that will track man's first moon landing. The U.S. ambassador and the Australian prime minister are scheduled to visit, and when things go very wrong, the way in which they are made to seem right is hilarious and inspired. I thought of *The Dish*, which found the perfect notes, and regretted that *Her Majesty*, which has all the right ingredients for its story, also has so many wrong ones.

Hero ★ ★ ★ ½
PG-13, 96 m., 2004

Jet Li (Nameless), Tony Leung (Broken Sword), Maggie Cheung (Flying Snow), Zhang Ziyi

(Moon), Chen Dao Ming (King of Qin), Donnie Yen (Long Sky). Directed by Zhang Yimou and produced by Bill Kong and Yimou. Screenplay by Li Feng, Wang Bin, and Yimou.

Zhang Yimou's *Hero* is beautiful and beguiling, a martial arts extravaganza defining the styles and lives of its fighters within Chinese tradition. It is also, like *Rashomon*, a mystery told from more than one point of view; we hear several stories, which all could be true, or false. The movie opens, like many folk legends, with a storyteller before the throne of an imperious ruler, counting on his wits to protect his life.

The storyteller is Nameless (Jet Li), who comes to the imperial court of the dreaded king of Qin (Chen Dao Ming). Qin dreams of uniting all of China's warring kingdoms under his rule; his plans to end war, the opening narration observes, "were soaked in the blood of his enemies." Three assassins have vowed to kill him: Broken Sword (Tony Leung), Flying Snow (Maggie Cheung), and Long Sky (Donnie Yen). Now comes Nameless to claim he has killed all three of them. He wishes to become the king's valued retainer, and collect a reward.

These opening scenes are visually spectacular. Nameless approaches the royal residence past ranks of countless thousands of soldiers, passes through entrance rooms of great depth and richness, and is allowed to kneel within 100 paces of the king—which is closer than anyone has been allowed to approach in many years. One pace closer, he is warned, and he will be killed.

The king asks to hear his stories. Nameless explains that his martial arts skill by itself was not enough to defeat such formidable enemies. Instead, he used psychological methods to discover their weak points. The style of Broken Sword's swordplay, for example, was betrayed by the style of his calligraphy. Sword and Snow were lovers, so jealousy could be used. Perhaps Snow could discover Sword making love with the beautiful Moon (Zhang Ziyi), which would sunder their alliance. As Nameless talks, there are flashbacks to the scenes he describes.

Hero is the most expensive film in Chinese history, a frank attempt to surpass Ang Lee's *Crouching Tiger, Hidden Dragon,* and the sets, costumes, and special effects are of astonishing beauty. Consider a scene where Nameless and Long Sky fight to the death during a torrential rainstorm that pierces the ceiling of the room where they fight, while a blind musician plucks his harp in counterpoint; they pause sometimes to urge the musician to continue. At one point Nameless launches himself across the room in slow motion, through a cloud of suspended raindrops that scatter like jewels at his passage.

Consider another scene where Nameless and Broken Sword do battle while floating above the vast mirror of a lake, sometimes drawing patterns in the water with their blades; Zhang even seems to film them from below the surface of the water they're walking on. Or another scene that takes place in a rain of bright red leaves. Or another where an imperturbable master of calligraphy continues his instruction, and his students sit obediently around him, while a rain of arrows slices through the roof of their school. Never have more archers and more arrows been seen in a movie; although I knew special effects were being used, I was not particularly aware of them.

These stories are of great fascination to the king of Qin, and after each is finished he allows Nameless to approach the throne a little closer, until finally only ten paces separate them. But the king has not survived years of assassination attempts by being a fool, and after the stories, he speaks, providing his own interpretation of what must have happened. His version is also visualized by Zhang, creating the *Rashomon* effect.

We can easily imagine the king being correct in his rewriting of Nameless's stories, and we wonder if Nameless has invented them as a strategy to get closer to the throne and murder the king himself. This idea occurs not only to us but, obviously, to the king, who may have a strategic reason in permitting Nameless to come so close. The two are playing an elaborate game of truth or consequences, in which it hardly matters what really happened to Sword, Sky, and Snow, because everything has finally come down to these two men in the throne room.

A film like *Hero* demonstrates how the

martial arts genre transcends action and violence and moves into poetry, ballet, and philosophy. It is violent only incidentally. What matters is not the manner of death, but the manner of dying: In a society that takes a Zen approach to swordplay and death, one might win by losing. There is an ancient martial arts strategy in which one lures the opponent closer to throw him off balance, and yields to his thrusts in order to mislead him. This strategy works with words as well as swords. One might even defeat an opponent by dying—not in the act of killing him, but as a move in a larger game.

Every genre has its cadre of moviegoers who think they dislike it. Sometimes a movie comes along that they should see nevertheless. If you've avoided every superhero movie, for example, *Spider-Man 2* is the one to see. If you dislike martial arts even after *Crouching Tiger*, then *Hero* may be the right film. Is it better than *Crouching Tiger*? Perhaps not, because the *Rashomon* structure undermines the resonance and even the reality of the emotional relationships. But Zhang Yimou, whose *Raise the Red Lantern* was so beautiful, once again creates a visual poem of extraordinary beauty.

Herod's Law ★ ★

R, 120 m., 2003

Damián Alcázar (Juan Vargas), Leticia Huijara (Gloria), Pedro Armendáriz Jr. (López), Delia Casanova (Rosa), Juan Carlos Colombo (Ramírez), Alex Cox (Gringo), Guillermo Gil (Padre), Eduardo López Rojas (Doctor), Salvador Sánchez (Pek), Isele Vega (Doña Lupe). Directed and produced by Luis Estrada. Screenplay by Estrada, Jaime Sampietro, Fernando León, and Vicente Leñero.

Juan Vargas is a simple man with unswerving loyalty to the party, and that is why he is chosen to be the mayor of San Pedro. There is an election coming up, three mayors have been killed in the last five years, and López, the regional party leader, hopes Vargas can keep the lid on and not cause much trouble. As Juan (Damián Alcázar) and his wife, Gloria (Leticia Huijara), drive to San Pedro in the dusty Packard supplied by the party, they dream of his assignment

to bring "Modernity, Peace, and Progress" to the little town, little suspecting how little it is.

"Where is San Pedro?" Juan asks a man. "This is it," the man replies. "I am Pek, your secretary." Vargas and his wife look around in dismay at the pathetic hamlet he is to lead. Pek (Salvador Sánchez) will be invaluable, because he speaks the Indian language, and few of the residents speak Spanish. Vargas quickly meets other important local figures, including the doctor (Eduardo López Rojas), the priest (Guillermo Gil), and Doña Lupe (Isele Vega), the madam of the local brothel.

All of the trouble in San Pedro comes from the brothel, the doctor bitterly tells Vargas. It is responsible for disease, corruption, murder. The padre is more forgiving: "San Pedro lacks many things, and Doña Lupe performs an important social function." The priest advises Vargas to accept Doña Lupe's bribes so that village life will continue as before. This is a mercenary padre: In the confessional, he charges one peso per sin and pointedly informs Vargas he would like a car: "A Ford . . . or perhaps a Packard, like yours."

Herod's Law uses Vargas and his backwater town to form a parable about political corruption in Mexico in 1949—and before and since, we have no doubt. It is a savage attack on the Institutional Revolutionary Party (PRI), which ruled Mexico from the days of revolution until the recent rise of President Vicente Fox and his National Action Party. In the figure of Juan Vargas, it sees a humble working-class man with high ideals, who caves in to the temptations of high office, even in so low a town, and is soon demanding bribes, making himself mayor for life, and paying free visits to Doña Lupe's girls. He justifies his actions with a motto learned from his party leader, who quotes Herod's Law, which is (somewhat reworded), "Either you screw them or you get screwed."

His wife, who is not blind to Juan's visits to the brothel, finds consolation from a visiting American (Alex Cox). The gringo's function in the parable is not difficult to decipher: He repairs Juan's car, demands an exorbitant payment, moves into Juan's house, and has sex with his wife. I think (I am pretty sure, actually) this is intended to suggest the helpful role of American advisers in Mexico.

The film is bold and passionate, but not

subtle, and that is its downfall. Luis Estrada, the writer and director, uses his characters so clearly as symbols that he neglects to give them the complexity of human beings. Juan Vargas begins as a simple and honest idealist and then converts to corruption so instantly at the sight of money that we have little idea of who he really was before or after. His escalation into a madman and murderer is laying it on a little thick; the recent Mexican film *The Crime of Father Amaro* made a similar critique of Mexican society and the church without such heavy-handed, almost comic, melodrama.

There are a couple of scenes that suggest a more moderate approach Estrada might have taken. One involves a dinner in the midst of all the chaos, at which the principal characters sit down to discuss their nation. The American is asked his opinion, and refers to Mexico as a "dictatorship," which makes the others, except the doctor, laugh. The doctor observes, "In Mexico if there were true democracy, the president would be a priest."

Note: Isele Vega, who plays Doña Lupe, starred as a prostitute in Sam Peckinpah's Bring Me the Head of Alfredo Garcia. *It must be a nod to that movie that this one has a character named Alfredo Garcia.*

Hidalgo ★ ★ ★
PG-13, 135 m., 2004

Viggo Mortensen (Frank Hopkins), Omar Sharif (Sheikh Riyadh), Zuleikha Robinson (Jazira), Adam Alexi-Malle (Aziz), Louise Lombard (Lady Anne Davenport), Said Taghmaoui (Prince Bin al Reeh). Directed by Joe Johnston and produced by Casey Silver. Screenplay by John Fusco.

Hidalgo is the kind of movie Hollywood has almost become too jaundiced to make anymore. Bold, exuberant, and swashbuckling, it has the purity and simplicity of something Douglas Fairbanks or Errol Flynn might have bounded through. Modern movies that attempt the adventure genre usually feel they have to tart it up, so in *Pirates of the Caribbean,* which once would have been played straight, we get animated cadavers and Johnny Depp channeling Keith Richards. Well, okay, *Pirates* was fun, but *Hidalgo* is a throwback to a more innocent time when heroes and their horses risked everything

just because life was so damned boring in the slow lane.

The movie is a completely fictionalized version of the life of a real cowboy named Frank Hopkins; a moment's research on the Web will suggest that an accurate portrait of his life would have been much briefer and very depressing. But never mind. Let us assume, as the movie does, that Hopkins was a half-Indian cowboy who bonded with an uncommonly talented mustang pony named Hidalgo. And that after he grew drunk and morose while laboring in Buffalo Bill's Wild West Show, he risked everything to travel to the Saudi Desert and enter the Ocean of Fire, a legendary race across the sands with a $10,000 prize.

Hopkins is played by Viggo Mortensen, fresh from *The Lord of the Rings,* as a bronzed, lean loner who (if I guess right) enters the race as much for the sake of his horse as for the prize. He respects and loves Hidalgo, especially after the scornful Arab riders scoff at the notion that a mixed-breed mustang could challenge their desert stallions with their ancient lineages. Of course, Hopkins is a half-breed, too, and so we're dealing with issues here.

The race is so grueling that many men and horses die, and some are murdered by their rivals. Hopkins functions in this world like a duck in a shooting gallery. When he is discovered in the tent of the beautiful princess Jazira (Zuleikha Robinson), he is brought before her father, powerful Sheikh Riyadh (Omar Sharif), and threatened with the loss of that possession he would least like to part with, even more than his horse. But then, in the kind of development that sophisticates will deplore but true children of the movies will treasure, his manhood is spared when the sheikh discovers that Hopkins knew—actually worked with, and spoke with, and could tell stories about!—that greatest of all men, that paragon of the sheikh's favorite pulp magazines, Buffalo Bill!

Hopkins is quite a babe magnet for an ex-drunk cowpoke who bunks with his horse. Not only does the lovely Jazira hope he will rescue her from capture by her father's lustful rival, but there's a rich woman named Lady Anne Davenport (Louise Lombard), who throws herself at him in an attempt to influence the outcome of the race, or maybe just because her husband is fifty years older.

275

Hopkins passes up so many of these opportunities that we're forced to speculate that his life might have gone on much as before if the sheikh had carried out his plans for the cowboy's netherlands.

This is a movie that has concealed pits in the sand with sharpened stakes at the bottom; exotic sprawling villas made with corridors and staircases and balconies and rooftops where countless swordsmen can leap forward to their doom; sandstorms that can be outrun by a horse like Hidalgo; tents as large and elaborately furnished as a Malcolm Forbes birthday party; blazing close-ups of the pitiless sun; poisoned oases; tantalizing mirages; parched lips; six-shooters, whips, daggers, and . . . no, I don't think there were any asps. Some will complain that Hidalgo magically arrives on the scene whenever Hopkins whistles, but Hidalgo knows that if he could whistle, Hopkins would be right there for him, too.

I have done my duty. Not a moviegoer alive will be able to attend *Hidalgo* and claim that I have not painted an accurate portrait of the film. Whether you like movies like this, only you can say. But if you do not have some secret place in your soul that still responds even a little to brave cowboys, beautiful princesses, and noble horses, then you are way too grown up and need to cut back on cable news.

Hide and Seek ★ ★

R, 100 m., 2005

Robert De Niro (Dr. David Callaway), Dakota Fanning (Emily Callaway), Famke Janssen (Dr. Katherine Carson), Elisabeth Shue (Elizabeth Young), Amy Irving (Alison Callaway), Dylan Baker (Sheriff Hafferty). Directed by John Polson and produced by Barry Josephson. Screenplay by Ari Schlossberg.

A small girl is haunted by fears after her mother's suicide. Her father, a psychiatrist, feels powerless to console her, and thinks perhaps if they move out of the apartment where the death took place, that might help. Since John Polson's *Hide and Seek* is a thriller, he finds the ideal new home: a vast summer home, with lots of attics and basements and crannies and staircases, on a lakeside that must be jolly enough in the summertime, but is deserted now, in the wintertime. All except for some friendly but peculiar neighbors.

This is a setup for a typical horror film, but for the first hour, at least, *Hide and Seek* feels more like M. Night Shyamalan and less like formula. Robert De Niro and Dakota Fanning, as Dr. David Callaway, the father, and Emily, his preadolescent daughter, create characters that seem, within the extremes of their situation, convincing and sympathetic. De Niro's Dr. David Callaway is a patient and reasonable man, who treats his daughter with kindness, but there's something else going on . . .

Consider, for example, the night when Callaway brings home a neighbor woman, Elizabeth (Elisabeth Shue), for dinner. "Did Daddy tell you that my mommy died?" little Emily asks, volunteering: "She killed herself in our bathtub. Slit her wrists with a razor." Callaway gently tells his daughter he doesn't think their guest needs to hear that right now, at dinner, but there is a way Emily has of staring out of her big round eyes and seeming to look into darker spheres than the rest of us can see.

Then there is the matter of her imaginary friend, Charlie. Dr. Callaway knows kids have imaginary friends, and that troubled kids often invent confidants to share their fears. He consults a colleague (Famke Janssen), who specializes in children, meets Emily, and agrees. But then strange things begin to happen. Callaway is awakened in the middle of the night and finds a bloody message written on the bathroom walls. Something unpleasant happens to the family cat. Either Emily is acting out, or . . . well, perhaps Charlie is not imaginary at all.

This possibility is enhanced by the presence in the cast of Dylan Baker as the local sheriff, a nosy type who carries the keys to all the summer homes on a big ring on his belt. Baker is so reliable playing clean-cut but creepy types that once, when I saw him in a simply likable role, I was caught off guard. Here he hangs around way too much, and always seems about to ask a question and then deciding not to. There is also some oddness going on with the neighbors.

Up until about that point, the movie has played convincingly, within the terms of its premise. Dakota Fanning does an accomplished job of making us wonder what she knows and what she imagines. When she produces those scary drawings, for example, of people dying, are they prescient? Troubled? Or just a form of release?

To find out the answer to these and other more unexpected questions, you will have to see the movie. I found the third act to be a disappointment. There was a point in the movie when suddenly everything clicked, and the Law of Economy of Characters began to apply. That is the law that says no actor is in a movie unless his character is necessary. A corollary is that if a minor actor is set up as a suspect, he's a decoy. I began to suspect I knew the answer to Emily's nightmares and the nature of her imaginary friend, and I was right.

I would have been content, however, if the movie had found a way to make its solution more psychologically probable, or at least less contrived. In the best Shyamalan movies, everything fits, and you can go back and see them again and understand how all the parts worked. With *Hide and Seek,* directed by Polson from a screenplay by Ari Schlossberg, you don't get that satisfaction. It's not technically true to say the movie cheats, but let's say it abandons the truth and depth of its earlier scenes.

At Sundance, I saw Rebecca Miller's *The Ballad of Jack and Rose,* also a movie where the mother is killed. Also a movie where the father and daughter live together in isolation, on the far side of an island. Also a movie where the father brings home a woman for dinner, and the daughter resents her role in her father's life. But the Miller picture is interested in the dramatic developments in the situation—in character, and how it forms in one situation and tries to adapt to another.

Hide and Seek is not really interested in its situation, except as a way to get to the horror ending. I like horror films, but I don't like to feel jerked around by them. They're best when they play straight and don't spring arbitrary surprises. At the beginning of *Hide and Seek,* I thought I was going to be interested in the characters all the way to the end, but then the plot went on autopilot. In a movie like *The Ballad of Jack and Rose,* the characters keep on

living and learning and hurting and hungering, and there's no surprise at the end to let them off the hook.

High Tension ★
R, 91 m., 2005

Cecile De France (Marie), Maiwenn Le Besco (Alex), Philippe Nahon (The Killer), Franck Khalfoun (Jimmy), Andrei Finti (Alex's Father), Oana Pellea (Alex's Mother). Directed by Alexandre Aja and produced by Alexandre Arcady and Robert Benmussa. Screenplay by Aja and Gregory Levasseur.

The philosopher Thomas Hobbes tells us life can be "poor, nasty, brutish and short." So is this movie. Alexandre Aja's *High Tension* is a slasher film about a madman prowling a rural area of France, chopping, slicing, and crunching his way through, let's see, a body count of five or six people, including a small child that the film does not neglect to show crumpled and dead in a cornfield. That's what it's about, anyway, until we discover it actually consists of something else altogether, something I think is not possible, given our current understanding of the laws of physics.

The movie premiered at Toronto 2003 in a version that would clearly have received an NC-17 rating. It has been edited down to an R, perhaps the hardest R for violence the MPAA has ever awarded, and into the bargain Lions Gate has dubbed great parts of it into English. Not all: There are inexplicable sections where the characters swear in French, which is helpfully subtitled.

I had forgotten how much I hate dubbing, especially when it's done as badly as in *High Tension.* It's lip-flap on parade. The movie was originally shot in French, but for purposes of dubbing, one of the characters, Alex (Maiwenn Le Besco), has been given an American accent. As she and her friend Marie (Cecile De France) arrive at the country home of Alex's family, Alex warns her: "Their French is even worse than mine." Since the parents hardly speak except to scream bilingually, this is not a problem.

The story: Alex and Marie are driving out to a country weekend with Alex's parents. Alex seems normal, but Marie is one of those goofy sorts who wanders into a cornfield for no better reason than for Alex to follow her, shouting "Marie! Marie!" while the wind sighs on the sound track—a track that beavers away with Ominous Noises throughout the movie; is there a technical term like Ominoise?

The girls are followed into the deep, dark woods by a large man in blood-soaked coveralls, who drives a battered old truck that must have been purchased used from a 1940s French crime movie. We know he's up to no good the first time we see him. We know this because he drops a woman's severed head out the window of his truck.

At the isolated country home, Marie gets the guest room in the attic, and goes out into the Ominoise night to have a smoke. There is a swing hanging from a tree limb, and she sways back and forth on it while she smokes, so that later we can get the standard thriller shot of the swing seat still swinging, but now suddenly empty. This is not because Marie has been shortened by the decapitator, but because she has gone back into the house. Soon it's lights out, although there is enough in the way of moonglow and night lights for us to see Marie masturbate, perhaps so that we can see if it makes her lose her mind or anything.

The killer (Philippe Nahon) breaks into the house, stomps around heavily, and slaughters everyone except Alex, whom he takes prisoner, and Marie, who hides under the bed— yes, *hides under the bed*. The killer lifts up the mattress to check, but looks under the wrong end. Uh-huh. Marie should then remain still as a church mouse until the killer leaves, but no, she follows him downstairs and eventually ends up locked in the back of the truck with the kidnapped and chained Alex.

From the point when Marie crawls out from under the bed and follows the killer downstairs, she persists in making one wrong decision after another and ignoring obvious opportunities to escape. Perhaps she feels her presence is needed for the movie to continue, a likely possibility as the list of living characters shrinks steadily. She does have wit enough to pick up a big kitchen knife, so that we can enjoy the slasher movie cliché where such knives make the noise of steel-against-steel all by themselves, just by existing, and without having to scrape against anything.

After the truck leaves the deserted house and stops at a gas station, Marie has another opportunity to get help, but blows it. Reader, take my advice and never hang up on a 911 operator just because you get mad at him because he's so stupid he wants to know where you're calling from, especially not if the slasher has picked up an ax.

The rest of the movie you will have to see for yourself—or not, which would be my recommendation. I am tempted at this point to issue a Spoiler Warning and engage in discussion of several crucial events in the movie that would seem to be physically, logically, and dramatically impossible, but clever viewers will be able to see for themselves that the movie's plot has a hole that is not only large enough to drive a truck through, but in fact does have a truck driven right through it.

Note: The film's British title is Switchblade Romance, *which, if you see the film, will seem curiouser and curiouser.*

Hijacking Catastrophe: 9/11, Fear and the Selling of American Empire ★ ★ ★
NO MPAA RATING, 68 m., 2004

Narrated by Julian Bond. With Daniel Ellsberg, Karen Kwiatkowski, Noam Chomsky, and Norman Mailer. A documentary directed and produced by Sut Jhally and Jeremy Earp.

I have here a commentary by John Eisenhower, son of the late president, who states in the *Union Leader* of Manchester, New Hampshire, that for the first time in fifty years he plans to vote for the Democratic candidate for president. "The fact is that today's 'Republican' Party is one with which I am totally unfamiliar," he writes, citing its $440 billion budget deficit and unilateral foreign policy. The current administration, he says, "has confused confident leadership with hubris and arrogance."

That is essentially the same argument made in *Hijacking Catastrophe: 9/11, Fear and the Selling of American Empire,* the most outspoken and yet in some ways the calmest of the new documentaries opposing the Bush presidency. It charges that America is in the hands of radicals at the right-wing extreme of the Republican Party. This view has some backing among traditional conservatives; none other than Patrick Buchanan has founded a magazine, the *American Conservative,* to argue against Bush and the war in Iraq.

For the neocons, the movie says, the invasion of Iraq has been a goal since the early 1990s, and deputy secretary of defense Paul Wolfowitz, called the "intellectual force" of the group, chillingly wrote in a 2000 report that it would be hard to sell a preemptive strike to the American people, unless a "catastrophic event—like a new Pearl Harbor" made it seem necessary. Immediately after 9/11, he and his associates argued for an attack on Iraq, making a connection between Saddam Hussein and Osama bin Laden that has now been proven false, and claiming Saddam had weapons of mass destruction, which we now know he did not.

Hijacking Catastrophe essentially consists of a parade of talking heads, all of them arguing that the Bush administration is more radical than most Americans realize. To be sure, the movie tells only one side. There are no defenders of the administration, and some of the speakers are well-known left-wing critics such as Noam Chomsky, Norman Mailer, and Daniel Ellsberg. Others are more centrist, including Lieutenant Colonel Karen Kwiatkowski (retired), an Air Force staff officer at the Pentagon, retired Army Special Forces master sergeant Stan Goff, weapons inspector Scott Ritter, and Nobel laureate Jody Williams.

What they do is look at the camera and talk. Although the film is only sixty-eight minutes long, it's so intense that it seems longer, and a point comes when I half-wished the filmmakers would relent and give us some of that goofy Michael Moore stuff. In urgent sound bites of mounting alarm, they charge that the neocon insurgents envision an "American colossus" that stands "astride the world," makes its own policies, and disdains cooperation with the family of nations. We went into Iraq without UN backing not because we had to, the movie argues, but because we wanted to; it was a good way to weaken the organization. By the same token, budget deficits are useful because they will bankrupt programs such as Social Security and Medicare that the neocons oppose but cannot destroy through conventional legislation.

Well, that's what the movie says, and a lot more. As your correspondent, I report it. And I will receive e-mails from readers who will protest this review and tell me a movie critic has no business getting involved in politics. But here is the movie, and here is what it says.

The most difficult aspect of *Hijacking Catastrophe* is to accept the argument that the neocons have wanted to invade Iraq for years, as part of a plan to conquer and occupy the Middle East, and that is why 9/11 inspired their curious decision to deflect American power from bin Laden to Saddam, an uninvolved bystander. Why does this make me think of Larry punching Curly, who retaliates by punching Moe? Fear of terrorists provided their cover, and Norman Solomon of the Institute for Public Accuracy says Roosevelt's statement "the only thing we have to fear is fear itself" has been rewritten by the neocons and their Orange Alerts into "the only thing we have to fear is not enough fear."

It is an ancient debating technique to identify your opponent's ideas with similar statements by evildoers. Nevertheless, this movie opens with a quote that seems eerie in its relevance:

The people can always be brought to the bidding of the leaders. That is easy. All you have to do is tell them they are being attacked, and denounce the peacemakers for lack of patriotism and exposing the country to danger. It works the same in any country.

Hermann Goering said that at the Nuremberg trials.

Hitch ★ ★ ½
PG-13, 120 m., 2005

Will Smith (Hitch), Kevin James (Albert), Eva Mendes (Sara), Amber Valletta (Allegra), Michael Rapaport (Ben), Adam Arkin (Max). Directed by Andy Tennant and produced by James Lassiter, Will Smith, and Teddy Zee. Screenplay by Kevin Bisch.

"Ninety percent of what you're saying isn't coming out of your mouth."

So says the Date Doctor. You communicate with your body language, your posture, your mood, your attitude about yourself. Nothing a guy can say will impress a woman nearly as much as the nonverbal messages she receives. So stand up straight, Fat Albert, and stop slumping around as if your tummy can be hidden in the shadows.

Hitch is a romantic comedy, timed for Valentine's Day, starring Will Smith as Alex "Hitch" Hitchens, professional dating consultant. In the cutthroat world of New York romance, where fates are decided in an instant, your average Lonely Guy needs skilled counseling. Hitch is your man. He understands women: how to get their attention, how to seem heroic in their eyes, what to tell them, and what definitely not to tell them.

Some of his strategies would be right at home in a silent comedy, such as an opening Meet Cute in which a babe's beloved pet dog is apparently saved from instant death by a guy who wants to get to know her. Others are more subtle, involving inside intelligence so that you seem able to read her mind. Then there are the grand dramatic gestures.

For Hitch's client Albert (Kevin James), the romantic quarry seems forever beyond his reach. He is in love with the rich, powerful, and beautiful Allegra (Amber Valletta), and surely she would not date a shy and pudgy accountant—would she? But at a board meeting he is outraged by investment advice she is being given, and in a Grand Dramatic, etc., he resigns. That gets her attention. She's touched that the guy would care so much.

Yes, but how can Albert follow up? He's one of those guys whose shirts seem to come back from the laundry with the mustard already on them. Hitch works desperately to smooth him out, clean him up, and give him some class. Meanwhile, his own romantic life is in a shambles. He's fallen in love with a really hot babe who is also smart and cynical. This is Sara (Eva Mendes), who writes for a gossip column not a million miles apart from Page Six. None of his advice seems to work for Hitch, maybe because in the game of romantic chess, Sara can see more moves ahead, maybe because—can this be possible?—he is losing his cool by trying too hard.

Hitch, you will have perceived, is not a great cinematic breakthrough. It depends for its appeal on the performances, and gets a certain undeserved mileage because of the likability of

Will Smith and Kevin James, who are both seen with sympathy. Allegra (Valletta) is a sweetheart, too, and not as unapproachable as she seems. But Sara is a real challenge, played by Eva Mendes as the kind of woman who seems more desirable the more she seems unattainable.

There is a purpose for a movie like *Hitch*, and that purpose is to supply a pleasant and undemanding romantic comedy that you can rent next Valentine's Day. It's not a first-run destination, especially with *Bride and Prejudice* and *The Wedding Date* playing in the same multiplex. It's not that I dislike it; it's that it just doesn't seem entirely necessary. The premise is intriguing, and for a time it seems that the Date Doctor may indeed know things about women that most men in the movies are not allowed to know, but the third act goes on autopilot just when the doctor should be in.

The Hitchhiker's Guide to the Galaxy ★ ★
PG, 110 m., 2005

Martin Freeman (Arthur Dent), Sam Rockwell (President Zaphod Beeblebrox), Mos Def (Ford Prefect), Zooey Deschanel (Trillian), Bill Nighy (Slartibartfast), Anna Chancellor (Questular Rontok), John Malkovich (Humma Kavula), Warwick Davis (Marvin the Paranoid Android), Alan Rickman (Marvin the Paranoid Android). Directed by Garth Jennings and produced by Gary Barber, Roger Birnbaum, Jonathan Glickman, Nick Goldsmith, and Jay Roach. Screenplay by Douglas Adams and Karey Kirkpatrick, based on the book by Adams.

It is possible that *The Hitchhiker's Guide to the Galaxy* should be reviewed by, and perhaps seen by, only people who are familiar with the original material to the point of obsession. My good friend Andy Ihnatko is such a person, and considered the late Douglas Adams to be one of only three or four people worthy to be mentioned in the same breath as P. G. Wodehouse. Adams may in fact have been the only worthy person.

Such a Hitchhiker Master would be able to review this movie in terms of its in-jokes, its references to various generations of the Guide universe, its earlier manifestations as books, radio shows, a TV series, and the center of a matrix of Websites. He would understand what the filmmakers have done with Adams's material, and how, and why, and whether the film is faithful to the spirit of the original.

I cannot address any of those issues, and I would rather plead ignorance than pretend to knowledge. If you're familiar with the Adams material, I suggest you stop reading right now before I disappoint or even anger you. All I can do is speak to others like myself, who will be arriving at the movie innocent of *Hitchhiker* knowledge. To such a person, two things are possible if you see the movie:

1. You will become intrigued by its whimsical and quirky sense of humor, understand that a familiarity with the books is necessary, read one or more of the *Hitchhiker* books, return to the movie, appreciate it more, and eventually be absorbed into the legion of Adams admirers.

2. You will find the movie tiresomely twee, and notice that it obviously thinks it is being funny at times when you do not have the slightest clue why that should be. You will sense a certain desperation as actors try to sustain a tone that belongs on the page and not on the screen. And you will hear dialogue that preserves the content of written humor at the cost of sounding as if the characters are holding a Douglas Adams reading.

I take the second choice. The movie does not inspire me to learn lots more about *The Hitchhiker's Guide to the Galaxy, The Ultimate Hitchhiker's Guide, The Salmon of Doubt,* and so on. Like *The Life Aquatic With Steve Zissou,* but with less visual charm, it is a conceit with little to be conceited about.

The story involves Arthur Dent (Martin Freeman), for whom one day there is bad news and good news. The bad news is that Earth is being destroyed to build an intergalactic freeway, which will run right through his house. The good news is that his best friend, Ford Prefect (Mos Def), is an alien temporarily visiting Earth to do research for a series of *Hitchhiker's Guides,* and can use his magic ring to beam both of them up to a vast spaceship operated by the Vogons, an alien race that looks like a cross between Jabba the Hutt and Harold Bloom. The Vogons are not a cruel race, apart from the fact that they insist

on reading their poetry, which is so bad it has driven people to catatonia.

Once aboard this ship, Arthur and Ford are hitchhikers themselves, and quickly transfer to another ship named the *Heart of Gold,* commanded by the galaxy's president, Zaphod Beeblebrox (Sam Rockwell), who has a third arm that keeps emerging from his tunic like the concealed arm of a samurai warrior, with the proviso that a samurai conceals two arms at the most. Zaphod is two-faced in a most intriguing way. Also on the ship are Trillian (Zooey Deschanel), an earthling, and Marvin the Android (body by Warwick Davis, voice by Alan Rickman), who is a terminal kvetcher. There is also a role for John Malkovich, who has a human trunk and a lower body apparently made from spindly robotic cranes' legs; this makes him a wonder to behold, up to a point.

What these characters do is not as important as what they say, how they say it, and what it will mean to Douglas Adams fans. To me, it got old fairly quickly. The movie was more of a revue than a narrative, more about moments than an organizing purpose, and cute to the point that I yearned for some corrosive wit from its second cousin, the Monty Python universe. But of course I do not get the joke. I do not much want to get the joke, but maybe you will. It is not an evil movie. It wants only to be loved, but movies that want to be loved are like puppies in the pound: No matter how earnestly they wag their little tails, you can only adopt one at a time.

Holes ★ ★ ★ ½
PG, 111 m., 2003

Sigourney Weaver (The Warden), Jon Voight (Mr. Sir), Patricia Arquette (Kissin' Kate), Tim Blake Nelson (Mr. Pendanski), Dule Hill (Sam), Shia LaBeouf (Stanley IV), Henry Winkler (Stanley III), Nathan Davis (Stanley II), Khleo Thomas (Hector Zero), Eartha Kitt (Madame Zeroni). Directed by Andrew Davis and produced by Davis, Lowell D. Blank, Mike Medavoy, and Teresa Tucker-Davies. Screenplay by Louis Sachar, based on his novel.

"You take a bad boy, make him dig holes all day long in the hot sun, it makes him a good boy. That's our philosophy here at Camp Green Lake."

So says Mr. Sir, the overseer of a bizarre juvenile correction center that sits in the middle of the desert, surrounded by countless holes, each one five feet deep and five feet wide. It is the fate of the boys sentenced there to dig one hole a day, day after day; like Sisyphus, who was condemned to forever roll a rock to the top of a hill so that it could roll back down again, they are caught in a tragic loop.

Holes, which tells their story, is a movie so strange that it escapes entirely from the family genre and moves into fantasy. Like *Willy Wonka and the Chocolate Factory*, it has fearsome depths and secrets. Based on the much-honored young adult's novel by Louis Sachar, it has been given the top-shelf treatment: The director is Andrew Davis *(The Fugitive)* and the cast includes not only talented young stars but also weirdness from such adults as Jon Voight, Sigourney Weaver, Tim Blake Nelson, and Patricia Arquette.

In a time when mainstream action is rigidly contained within formulas, maybe there's more freedom to be found in a young people's adventure. *Holes* jumps the rails, leaves all expectations behind, and tells a story that's not funny ha-ha but funny peculiar. I found it original and intriguing. It'll be a change after dumbed-down, one-level family stories, but a lot of kids in the upper grades will have read the book, and no doubt their younger brothers and sisters have had it explained to them. (If you doubt the novel's Harry Potter–like penetration into the youth culture, ask a seventh-grader who Armpit is.)

The story involves Stanley Yelnats IV (Shia LaBeouf), a good kid who gets charged with a crime through no fault of his own, and is shipped off to Camp Green Lake, which is little more than a desert bunkhouse surrounded by holes. There he meets his fellow prisoners and the ominous supervisory staff: Mr. Sir (Jon Voight) and Mr. Pendanski (Tim Blake Nelson) report to the Warden (Sigourney Weaver), and both men are thoroughly intimidated by her. All three adult actors take their work seriously; they don't relax because this is a family movie, but create characters of dark comic menace. Voight's work is especially detailed; watch him spit in his hand to slick back his hair.

Holes involves no less than two flashback stories. We learn that young Stanley comes from a long line of Yelnatses (all named Stanley, because it is the last name spelled backward). From his father (Henry Winkler) and grandfather (Nathan Davis) he learns of an ancient family curse, traced back many generations to an angry fortune-teller (Eartha Kitt; yes, Eartha Kitt). The other flashback explains the real reason the Warden wants the boys to dig holes; it involves the buried treasure of a legendary bandit queen named Kissin' Kate Barlow (Arquette).

There is a link between these two back stories, supplied by Zero (Khleo Thomas), who becomes Stanley's best friend and shares a harrowing adventure with him. Zero runs away despite Mr. Sir's warning that there is no water for miles around, and when Stanley joins him they stumble upon ancient clues and modern astonishments.

Shia LaBeouf and Khleo Thomas are both new to me, although LaBeouf is the star of a cable series, *Even Stevens*. They carry the movie with an unforced conviction, and successfully avoid playing cute. As they wander in the desert and discover the keys to their past and present destinies, they develop a partnership which, despite the fantastical material, seems like the real thing.

The whole movie generates a surprising conviction. No wonder young viewers have embraced it so eagerly: It doesn't condescend, and it founds its story on recognizable human nature. There are all sorts of undercurrents, such as the edgy tension between the Warden and Mr. Sir that add depth and intrigue; Voight and Weaver don't simply play caricatures.

Davis has always been a director with a strong visual sense, and the look of *Holes* has a noble, dusty loneliness. We feel we are actually in a limitless desert. The cinematographer, Stephen St. John, thinks big, and frames his shots for an epic feel that adds weight to the story. I walked in expecting a movie for thirteen-somethings, and walked out feeling challenged and satisfied. Curious, how much more grown-up and sophisticated *Holes* is than *Anger Management*.

Hollywood Homicide ★ ★ ★
PG-13, 111 m., 2003

Harrison Ford (Joe Gavilan), Josh Hartnett (K. C. Calden), Lena Olin (Ruby), Lolita

Davidovich (Cleo), Bruce Greenwood (Bennie Macko), Keith David (Lieutenant Fuqua). Directed by Ron Shelton and produced by Lou Pitt and Shelton. Screenplay by Robert Souza and Shelton.

The most popular occupations in movies about Hollywood are cops, crooks, hookers, psychics, and actors, and to this list we must add the people they are all terrified of, real estate brokers.

Hollywood Homicide covers these bases with a murderer, a cop who is a realtor, a cop who wants to be an actor, and a psychic who can visualize that the murderer will be in an SUV on Rodeo Drive in half an hour. There are also two hookers, although one scarcely counts, being an undercover cop in drag. Still, in Hollywood, maybe that does count.

The movie stars Harrison Ford and Josh Hartnett as the two cops, named Joe Gavilan and K. C. Calden, who are detectives assigned to Hollywood. Gavilan is so preoccupied with his real estate business that he tries to sell a house to the owner of a club where four rappers have just been killed, and later negotiates the purchase price during a police chase. Calden has decided he wants to be an actor, and makes Gavilan run lines for him from *A Streetcar Named Desire*. Gavilan is not impressed: "Who wrote this stuff?"

The movie was directed by Ron Shelton, who cowrote with Robert Souza. Shelton also made *Bull Durham* and *White Men Can't Jump* and specializes in funny dialogue for guy characters who would rather talk than do just about anything else. One of the pleasures of *Hollywood Homicide* is that it's more interested in its two goofy cops than in the murder plot; their dialogue redeems otherwise standard scenes. It's kind of a double act, between a man who has seen everything and a man who's seen too much.

Consider a scene where K. C. commandeers a vehicle containing a mother and her two small children. He needs it to chase a bad guy. "We're gonna die!" whines one of the kids. "Yes," agrees K. C., who moonlights as a yoga instructor, "we *are* all going to die someday, but . . ." His philosophical observations are cut short by a crash.

The movie opens with a hit on a rap group in a music club. Four people are dead when Joe

and K.C. turn up to investigate. Joe immediately sends out for food. K.C. tells the club owner he is an actor. Their investigation is hampered by an inconvenient development: They are under investigation by Bennie Macko (Bruce Greenwood), the Internal Affairs guy who hates Joe, and who reminds us once again that movie villains usually have a hard C or K in their names.

Joe is suspected of "mingling funds," which is to say, he confuses his personal debts and the debts of his real estate business. He has been seen with Cleo (Lolita Davidovich), who is a known hooker. No wonder; you do not get to be an unknown hooker by being chauffeured around town in your own stretch limousine. Internal Affairs thinks he is fooling around with Cleo, but he isn't; he's fooling around with Ruby the psychic (Lena Olin). She's yet another in the baffling legion of Los Angeles women who believe it is fun to make love on a blanket on the hardwood floor of an empty house while surrounded by a lot of candles.

At Harrison Ford's age, this qualifies as a dangerous stunt. But Ford just gets better, more distilled, more laconic, and more gruffly likable year after year. It is hard to catch him doing anything at all while he's acting, and yet whatever it is he isn't doing, it works. You don't feel he's going for laughs when he tries to sell the club owner a house while the two of them are standing in fresh pools of blood, metaphorically speaking; you feel he desperately needs to unload the house.

Hartnett makes an able partner for Ford, trading deadpan dialogue and telling everyone he's really an actor. He's given one of Shelton's nicest little scenes, when he goes to the morgue and looks at the dead bodies of the murder victims (he hates looking at dead bodies), and then notices some other dead bodies that have just arrived at the morgue, checks their shoe sizes, and says, "Hey . . . those guys shot these guys."

There is a chase and a half near the end of the movie, a lot of it near the Kodak Theatre at Hollywood and Highland. That gives the movie a chance to interrupt Robert Wagner as he's leaving his handprints in front of Graumann's Chinese Theater, and indeed the movie is filled with cameos and walk-bys, including Frank Sinatra Jr. as a showbiz lawyer, Martin Landau very funny as a fading producer who needs to unload his mansion, Lou Diamond Phillips as Wanda the cop in drag, Gladys Knight, Dwight Yoakam, Isaiah Washington, Master P, Kurupt, Eric Idle, Dr. Dre, and just plain Dre.

Much of the closing excitement depends on the Fallacy of the Climbing Killer, that dependable chase cliché in which the killer climbs to a high place, from which he cannot escape unless he can fly. *Hollywood Homicide* uses this as an excuse to show police helicopters and TV news helicopters crowding each other out of the skies. It's a skillful chase, well done, but the dialogue is the reason to see the movie. This may be the most exciting film ever made about real estate.

A Home at the End of the World ★ ★ ★ ½
R, 120 m., 2004

Colin Farrell (Bobby Morrow), Dallas Roberts (Jonathan Glover), Robin Wright Penn (Clare), Sissy Spacek (Alice Glover). Directed by Michael Mayer and produced by John Hart, Tom Hulce, Pamela Koffler, Hunt Lowry, Katie Roumel, Jeff Sharp, Christine Vachon, and John Wells. Screenplay by Michael Cunningham, based on his novel.

A Home at the End of the World tells the story of Bobby Morrow, who at seven sees his adored older brother walk into a glass door and die, who lost his mother even earlier, who finds his father dead in bed, who solemnly announces to his best friend, "I'm the last of my kind." Soon he is living with the friend's family, so comfortably that the mother eventually has to tell him, "You can't just live with us forever." By then he is twenty-four.

Bobby is played as an adult by Colin Farrell in a performance that comes as an astonishment. Farrell is a star who has appeared mostly in action pictures that reflect his bad-boy offscreen image. Here he plays a quiet, complex, unconventional character, a young man who has been deeply hurt, who fears abandonment, and whose guiding principle has become, "I just want everybody to be happy."

Bobby is sweet. Everybody likes him. But does anybody know him? He has such a need to please, to reassure, to comfort, to heal, that it is hard to say what might comfort and heal

him. We attend to this character more than to most, because we like him but find him a mystery.

His best friend is Jonathan (played as an adult by Dallas Roberts), an outsider in high school until Bobby befriends him, gives him pot for the first time, and shares his dead brother's philosophy, which is basically that all is good, life is wonderful, so chill. Jonathan is clearly gay from an early age, and as the two boys share a bed, they eventually share a shy sexual experience. Jonathan moves to New York and Bobby eventually follows, joining a household that also includes Clare (Robin Wright Penn). She is older, experiments with bizarre hair-coloring strategies, embraces the unconventional, and eventually embraces Bobby. He confesses he is a virgin and may not be "adept"; she calls him "junior" and takes charge.

So is Bobby actually straight? "Bobby's not gay," Jonathan muses. "It's hard to say what Bobby is." Hard, because Bobby is much less interested in sex than in helping other people to feel better. That's why the filmmakers were correct in their well-publicized decision to leave out Farrell's scene of full frontal nudity; the movie is not about the size or function of Bobby's penis but about its friendliness. Consider his muted flirtation with Jonathan's mother, Alice (Sissy Spacek). He gives her pot, dances with her, turns her on to Laura Nyro, frees her to accept Jonathan's lifestyle, and to wonder what directions her own life might have taken, if she had not been so conventional, suburban, and married.

A Home at the End of the World, directed by Michael Mayer, is based on a novel and screenplay by Michael Cunningham, author of *The Hours.* Once again he is fascinated by very particular kinds of unconventional households, by nontraditional family groups that do not even fall into the usual nontraditional categories. One might think Bobby, Jonathan, and Clare were all gay, but no: Jonathan has an active homosexual life, but Clare is straight, and so concerned with remaining free that sex is approached warily. When she and Bobby have a daughter, their household makes a move toward a more conventional arrangement, and then backs off.

There is also the question of how Jonathan feels about their little family. He loves Bobby, and his many sexual partners are a way to escape that inescapable fact. Bobby loves him, but in the same way he loves everybody. Jonathan sometimes feels Bobby is elbowing him out of his own life: "You can be the son and I'll be the best friend." Clare studies Bobby and is baffled: "You can live in the suburbs, the East Village, the country—it just doesn't make any difference to you, does it?" By now they have moved to Woodstock, bought a little frame house, and opened a café in town.

The movie exists outside our expectations for such stories. Nothing about it is conventional. The three-member household is puzzling not only to us but to its members. We expect conflict, resolution, an ending happy or sad, but what we get is mostly life, muddling through. Some days are good and other days are bad. When Bobby makes the most important decision of the film, we know why he makes it, but Clare doesn't and it's hard to say about Jonathan. Bobby doesn't explain. He makes it because one of them needs him more than the other; there is really no thought of himself.

Plots in fiction are usually based on need, greed, fear, and guilt. Even love plays out in that context. All Bobby has is the need to please, in order to assure himself of a place where he belongs. A home. Colin Farrell is astonishing in the movie, not least because the character is such a departure from everything he has done before. Charlize Theron's leap of faith in *Monster* comes to mind, although Farrell's work here is less risky and lower-key. Rare, in a movie that sidesteps melodrama, for a character to fascinate us with his elusiveness.

"Is there anything you can't do?" one of them asks him.

"I couldn't be alone," he says.

Home on the Range ★ ★ ½

PG, 76 m., 2004

With the voices of: Roseanne Barr (Maggie), Judi Dench (Mrs. Caloway), Jennifer Tilly (Grace), Cuba Gooding Jr. (Buck), Randy Quaid (Alameda Slim), Richard Riehle (Sheriff Brown), Charles Dennis (Rico), Steve Buscemi (Wesley), Charles Haid (Lucky Jack), Estelle Harris (Audrey). Directed by Will Finn and John Sanford and produced by Alice Dewey Goldstone. Screenplay by Finn and Sanford.

Home on the Range, Disney's new animated feature, has the genial friendliness of a 1940s singing cowboy movie, and the plot could have been borrowed from Hopalong Cassidy or Roy Rogers, apart from the slight detail that they aren't cows. The new songs by Alan Menken ("The Little Mermaid," "Beauty and the Beast") are in the tradition of western swing; I can easily imagine Gene Autry performing any of them, including the yodeling number, and wasn't too surprised to find that the Sons of the Pioneers starred in a 1946 movie with the same name.

The pace is up-to-date, though. Gene Autry and Roy Rogers always had time to relax next to a campfire and sing a tune, but *Home on the Range* jumps with the energy of a cartoon short subject. The movie is said to be Disney's last release in the traditional 2-D animation style; its feature cartoons in the future will have the rounded 3-D look of *Finding Nemo.* Whether that is a loss or not depends on how you relate to animation; there are audiences even for those dreadful Saturday morning cartoon adventures that are so stingy on animation they're more like 1.5-D.

The story takes place on the Patch of Heaven ranch, which faces foreclosure because of the depredations of the vile cattle rustler Alameda Slim (voice by Randy Quaid). Pearl, the owner, could raise money by selling her cows—but they're family, you see, and so presumably they'll all be homeless soon. But then the cows get a bright idea: Why not track down Slim, collect the $750 reward, pay off the bank, and save the ranch?

Each of the cows has unique qualities to contribute to this effort. Mrs. Caloway (Judi Dench) is the voice of prudence. Grace (Jennifer Tilly) is the New Age cow, who makes observations like, "This is an organic problem and needs a holistic solution." Their catalyst is a newcomer to the farm, Maggie (Roseanne Barr), who quickly becomes the aggressive, in-your-face leader. Rounding out the team is Buck (Cuba Gooding Jr.), the stallion, who is a master of the martial arts.

The voices are all quickly recognizable, especially Barr's; the idea of using the voices of familiar stars instead of anonymous dubbing artists has added an intriguing dimension to recent animated features. Listen, for example, to Randy Quaid as the dastardly Slim. It's traditional in Disney animation to fill the edges of the screen with hyperactive little supporting characters, and we get Lucky Jack the jackrabbit (Charles Haid) and Audrey the chicken, who is chicken (Estelle Harris). There are also three very busy little pigs, and Steve Buscemi almost seems to be playing himself as a critter named Wesley.

Buck, by the way, has delusions of grandeur; he thinks maybe he can capture Slim and collect the reward, especially after he becomes the horse of the famed bounty hunter Rico (Charles Dennis), which leads to a fierce competition with the cows. The plot makes pit stops at all the obligatory Western sights: saloons, mine shafts, main streets, deserts with Monument Valley landscapes, and trains. All of these locations become the backdrops of chases in a movie that seldom stands still.

The songs are performed by k.d. lang, Bonnie Raitt, Tim McGraw, and the Bleu Sisters. None of the songs is likely to be requested by fans at future concerts. They sound generic and don't have the zest of Menken's earlier work.

A movie like this is fun for kids: bright, quick-paced, with broad, outrageous characters. But *Home on the Range* doesn't have the crossover quality of the great Disney films like *Beauty and the Beast* and *The Lion King*. And it doesn't have the freshness and originality of a more traditional movie like *Lilo & Stitch*. Its real future, I suspect, lies in home video. It's only seventy-six minutes long, but although kids will like it, their parents will be sneaking looks at their watches.

Honey ★ ★ ½
PG-13, 89 m., 2003

Jessica Alba (Honey Daniels), Mekhi Phifer (Chaz), Lil' Romeo (Benny), Joy Bryant (Gina), David Moscow (Michael Ellis), Lonette McKee (Darlene Daniels), Zachary Isaiah Williams (Raymond). Directed by Bille Woodruff and produced by Marc Platt and Andre Harrell. Screenplay by Alonzo Brown and Kim Watson.

"Hey, kids! Let's rent the old barn and put on a show!"

These words are so familiar that surely I must have actually heard them in a movie at one time or another, but I confess I cannot remember when. They summarize one of the most persistent of all movie formulas, pioneered in the days of Mickey Rooney and Judy Garland, reborn in the era of Frankie Avalon and Annette Funicello, and now finding new life with Jessica Alba and Lil' Romeo.

If I were to tell you (a) that Jessica Alba works as a dance instructor in a neighborhood center, (b) that she discovers Lil' Romeo and his friends break-dancing in the streets, (c) that city inspectors shut down the center because of leaks and unsafe construction, and (d) that there is an empty church nearby that could be borrowed for an evening, what would you say the chances are that Alba will hit on the notion of using the old church to put on a show with the kids, to raise money for the community center?

It's amazing that this formula still survives, but it does, right down to the crucial moment when the doors open and her parents (who disapprove of her hip-hop dance style) join the audience, are moved by the performance, and have maybe a few tears in their eyes, having seen the light and understood their daughter's dream at last. *Honey* crosses this formula with another: the talented girl from the neighborhood who is discovered by a big producer, who lures her away from her old friends. Will she be dazzled by the bright lights and the big city? Will the slickster's limousine and champagne lifestyle make her forget the honest and dependable neighborhood barber who truly loves her? Will she let the kids down?

There is not a lot of suspense behind these questions, because Jessica Alba doesn't have the face and smile of the kind of creep who would sell out to a crass big-shot producer and dump the dear hearts and gentle people back in the neighborhood. She plays Honey Daniels, who teaches a dance class at the center run by her mother (Lonette McKee). She hangs out with her best friend, Gina (Joy Bryant), and dreams of someday surviving an audition and being selected to dance in a music video. Meanwhile, Honey and Gina dance at clubs on weekends, and a scout supplies a video of her style to Michael (David Moscow), a famous video producer. He bypasses the auditions, gives her a role in his new video, hires her to choreograph three more, and takes her to fancy parties and opening nights. It takes her just a little too long to figure out what's perfectly obvious to us: He wants to be her lover.

Honey has been inspired by the free dance styles of Benny (Lil' Romeo) and his buddies, borrows some of them for her choreography, and convinces Michael to let her use the kids in a new video starring Ginuwine. Meanwhile, Chaz (Mekhi Phifer), the faithful barber, wonders if Honey is lost to him—even though she likes him a lot and likes Michael less and less.

A movie like *Honey* is aimed at younger teenagers, who may not precisely be students of Mickey and Judy; scenes that have unfolded in a thousand other movies can seem new if you're seeing them for the first time. I wasn't seeing them for the first or even the fiftieth time, but the warmth of Jessica Alba and likability of Mekhi Phifer were real enough—a consolation even when their characters were repeating all the old moves. *Honey* doesn't have a shred of originality (except for the high-energy choreography), but there's something fundamentally reassuring about a movie that respects ancient formulas; it's like a landmark preservation program.

The Honeymooners ★ ★ ★
PG-13, 85 m., 2005

Cedric the Entertainer (Ralph Kramden), Mike Epps (Ed Norton), Gabrielle Union (Alice Kramden), Regina Hall (Trixie Norton), Eric Stoltz (William Davis), John Leguizamo (Dodge), Jon Polito (Kirby), Carol Woods (Alice's Mom), Anne Pitoniak (Miss Benvenuti). Directed by John Schultz and produced by Julie Durk, David T. Friendly, Eric Rhone, and Marc Turtletaub. Screenplay by Barry W. Blaustein, Danny Jacobson, Saladin K. Patterson, Don Rhymer, and David Sheffield.

The Honeymooners is a surprise and a delight, a movie that escapes the fate of weary TV re-treads and creates characters that remember the originals, yes, but also stand on their own. Playing Ralph Kramden and Ed Norton, Cedric the Entertainer and Mike Epps don't even try to imitate Jackie Gleason and Art Carney; they borrow a few notes, just to show us they've seen the program, and build from there. And Gabrielle Union and Regina Hall, as Alice and Trixie, flower as the two long-suffering wives, who in this version get more story time and do not ever, even once, get offered a one-way ticket to the moon. Instead, Ralph even sweetly promises Alice he will "take her to the moon," although, to be sure, that's when he proposes marriage.

The externals of the movie resemble the broad outlines of the TV classic. The Kramdens live downstairs, the Nortons live upstairs, Ralph drives a bus, Ed is proud of his command of the sewer system's scenic routes. Ralph is a dreamer who falls for one get-rich-quick scheme after another, and the closet is filled with his failed dreams: the pet cactus, the Y2K survival kit. His wife, Alice, is the realist. All she wanted when she got married was to live in a home of their own. They're still renting.

Cedric the Entertainer is funny in the role, yes, but he's also sweet. He understands the underlying goodness and pathos of Ralph Kramden, who is all bluff. Mike Epps makes Norton into a sidekick like Sancho Panza, who realizes his friend is nutty, but can't bear to see him lose his illusions.

The plot: Alice and Trixie, who work as waitresses at a diner, meet a sweet little old lady (Anne Pitoniak) who wants to sell her duplex at a reasonable price. They're up against a wily real estate king (Eric Stoltz) who wants to turn the whole block into condos, but if they can come up with a $20,000 down payment, the house is theirs. That means $10,000 from the Kramdens, who have $5,000 in the bank; Alice thinks maybe she can borrow the rest from her mother (Carol Woods), a fearsome force of nature who served in Vietnam, was a Golden Gloves champ, and despises her son-in-law (her advice to Ralph on eating his dinner: "When you get to the plate, stop").

There is a problem with Alice's financial plan. The problem is that Ralph has spent all the money on a series of failed dreams. Desperate to raise cash, Ralph and Ed try hip-hop dancing in the park, at which they are very bad, and begging as blind men, at which they are worse. Then they find a greyhound dog in a trash bin, and decide to race it at the dog track.

Enter John Leguizamo as Dodge, a "trainer" recommended by the track's shady owner (Jon Polito). Leguizamo is optimistic ("I started with nothing and still have most of it left") and fancies himself a Dog Whisperer, but Izzy the dog doesn't seem to understand the principle behind racing, which is that he has to leave the gate and run around the track. Ralph, however, believes in the "homeless Dumpster dog," and in a big scene describes him as "a survivor . . . like Seabiscuit, Rocky, and Destiny's Child."

All of this is handled by the director John Schultz (Like Mike) with an easygoing confidence in the material. There's nothing frantic about the performances, nothing forced about the plot; the emphasis is on Ralph's underlying motive, which is to prove to Alice that he is not invariably a failure and can buy her a house one way or another. That was the secret of Gleason's Honeymooners—Ralph lost his temper and ranted and raved, but he had a good heart, and Alice knew it.

The supporting performances bring the movie one comic boost after another. Leguizamo's con-man dog trainer is an invention in flim-flammery, Polito's track owner is an opportunist, Stoltz finds just the right slick charm as the real estate sharpie, and Carol Woods is the mother-in-law Ralph Kramden deserves for his sins. Regina Hall and Gabrielle Union spend a lot of their scenes with each other, while the boys are out getting in trouble. They provide the engine that drives the movie's emotions: They want that house, they have a deadline to meet, and Ralph grows increasingly desperate because he doesn't want to let Alice down yet once again.

I was afraid Cedric the Entertainer and Mike Epps would try to imitate Gleason and Carney. Not at all. What they do is work a subtle tribute to the earlier actors into new inventions of their own. Cedric has that way of moving his neck around inside his collar that reminds us of Gleason, and the slow burn, and

the wistful enthusiasm as he outlines plans that even he knows are doomed. Epps has the hat always hanging on at an angle, the pride in the sewer system, the willingness to go along with his goofy pal. And the movie's story actually does work as a story and not simply as a wheezy Hollywood formula. Sometimes you walk into a movie with quiet dread, and walk out with quiet delight.

Horns and Halos ★ ★ ★
NO MPAA RATING, 79 m., 2003

A documentary featuring Sander Hicks, J. H. Hatfield, Peter Slover, and Mark Crispin Miller. Directed by Suki Hawley and Michael Galinsky and produced by Hawley, Galinsky, and David Beilinson.

It is forgotten now that a book published in 1999 charged, among other things, that George W. Bush was arrested for cocaine possession in the early 1970s, and the bust was covered up through the influence of his father. The charge was made in Fortunate Son, which briefly made the best-seller lists and sparked a flurry of press interest before lawyers for Bush threatened a lawsuit, and it was revealed that the book's author, James Howard Hatfield, had served five years in prison after being convicted of attempted murder.

Bush never precisely denied the charge, nor did he need to: "Obviously," he said, "if he's a convicted felon, his credibility's nothing." A discredited author amounted to a discredited story, and Hatfield's actual past trumped Bush's alleged past. St. Martin's Press, which published the book, withdrew its edition and destroyed all copies. Then a fly-by-night publisher named Soft Skull reprinted Fortunate Son, and Hatfield, who had refused to reveal the source of his information about the alleged cocaine arrest, now dropped a bombshell: His source, he said, was Karl Rove, Bush's closest political adviser.

All sensational stuff, very questionable, and there was even a 60 Minutes segment on the would-be scandal, but Hatfield was a loose cannon, and his personal life was coming apart at the seams. Eventually he was found dead in a motel room after an overdose of prescription pills, in what appeared to be a genuine suicide.

In a sense, his book was a service to the Bush campaign, because the cocaine story and its author, generally seen to be discredited, drew attention away from the roughly simultaneous charges that the future commander in chief had been AWOL for a year from the Air National Guard.

Horns and Halos, a documentary that resurrects this political footnote, begins with Hatfield and his book, but the attention keeps getting stolen by a mercurial eccentric named Sander Hicks, the owner, operator, and sole employee of the Soft Skull Press. He works from his home, and his home is a tiny apartment in a New York apartment building where he is the janitor. Hicks is a splendid argument for diversity in media ownership, since with almost no capital he was able to print and distribute the book.

The filmmakers, Suki Hawley and Michael Galinsky, focus on Hicks's passion for the book, which easily outstrips Hatfield's. "Not a day goes by that I don't regret writing this book," Hatfield says at one point, and there are signs toward the end that, despite his joy over the birth of a baby daughter, he is coming unhinged.

The movie suggests that the Dallas story identifying Hatfield as a convicted felon was planted by the Bush campaign, and indeed there is a dubious conspiracy theory that Rove *did* give Hatfield information, because he knew of Hatfield's past and thought it was best that the scandal come to light through an easily discredited source. Hatfield hardly needed outside help to undermine his book; his introduction to the Soft Skull edition included comments about his conviction that inspired a lawsuit by a former associate.

Although Hicks shepherds Hatfield to Book Expo and other book shows, the book, once dismissed, is no longer news. And after Hatfield's death the entire episode disappears from our collective memory. *Horns and Halos* is effective in presenting its portraits of these two men, Hatfield so depressed, Hicks so optimistic, but it's not successful at getting to the bottom of the cocaine charges. It commits the same mistake it charges the mainstream press with: It allows Hatfield's story to upstage his allegations. The adventures of Hicks in taking on the media establishment from his janitor's quarters make a great human-interest story, but it too has nothing to do with the underlying charges.

All that can be said at this late date is that the cocaine use, if any, is a dead issue, and Bush covered himself during the campaign by saying he had not used drugs since 1974. (He did not say if he had used drugs before 1974, and his campaign quickly called his original words a misstatement.) In today's political climate, this movie and its people all seem to come from a very long time ago.

Hostage ★ ★ ★
R, 113 m., 2005

Bruce Willis (Jeff Talley), Kevin Pollak (Mr. Smith), Jonathan Tucker (Dennis Kelly), Ben Foster (Mars), Jimmy Bennett (Tommy Smith), Michelle Horn (Jennifer Smith), Jimmy "Jax" Pinchak (Sean Mack), Marshall Allman (Kevin Kelly), Serena Scott Thomas (Jane Talley). Directed by Florent Emilio Siri and produced by Mark Gordon, Arnold Rifkin, and Bob Yari. Screenplay by Doug Richardson, based on a novel by Robert Crais.

The opening titles of *Hostage* are shot in saturated blacks and reds with a raw, graphic feel, and the movie's color photography tilts toward dark high-contrast. That matches the mood, which is hard-boiled and gloomy. Bruce Willis, who feels like a resident of action thrillers, not a visitor, dials down here into a man of fierce focus and private motives; for the second half of the movie, no one except for (some of) the bad guys knows what really motivates him.

There's also an interesting use of the movie's three original villains, who are joined later by evildoers from an entirely different sphere. As the film opens, three gormless teenagers in a pickup truck follow a rich girl being driven "in her daddy's Escalade" to a mountaintop mansion with fearsome security safeguards. Their motive: Steal the Cadillac. These characters are Mars (Ben Foster), a mean customer with a record, and two brothers: Dennis and Kevin Kelly (Jonathan Tucker and Marshall Allman). Kevin is the kid brother along for the ride, appalled by the lawbreaking Mars leads his brother into.

Trapped inside the house when police respond to an alarm, they take hostages: Smith, the rich man (Kevin Pollak), his teenage daughter, Jennifer (Michelle Horn), and his young son, Tommy (Jimmy Bennett). Bruce Willis plays the police chief who leads the first response team, but after a bad hostage experience in Los Angeles, he has retired to Ventura County to avoid just such adventures, and hands over authority to the sheriff's department. Then, inexplicably, he returns and demands to take command again.

Moderate spoiler warning: What motivates him is that unknown kidnappers have captured Willis's own wife and child, and are holding them hostage. They want Willis to obtain a DVD in the Smith house, which (we gather) contains crucial information about illegal financial dealings. So we have a hostage crisis within a hostage crisis, and Willis is trying to free two sets of hostages, only one known to his fellow lawmen.

This is ingenious, and adds an intriguing complexity to what could have been a one-level story. Some other adornments, however, seem unlikely. Little Tommy is able to grab his sister's cell phone and move secretly throughout the house, using his secret knowledge of air ducts and obscure construction details. This development takes full advantage of the Air Duct Rule, which teaches us that all air ducts are large enough to crawl through, and lead directly to vantage points above crucial events in the action. Left unanswered is why the three hostage takers aren't concerned that the kid is missing for long periods of time.

Some elements exist entirely for the convenience of the plot. For example, the Kevin Pollack character functions long enough to establish his role and importance, then is conveniently unconscious when not needed, then is on the brink of death when Willis desperately wants to revive him, then miraculously recovers and is able to act with admirable timing at a crucial moment. I would love to examine his medical charts during these transitions.

But I am not much concerned about such logical flaws, because the main line of the movie is emotional, driven by the Bruce Willis character, who is able to project more intensity with less overacting than most of his rivals. He brings credibility to movies that can use some, and that will be invaluable in *Die Hard 4*. The mechanics of the final showdown are unexpected and yet show an undeniable logic, and are sold by the acting skills of Willis and Pollak.

The movie was directed by Florent Emilio Siri, creator of two Tom Clancy–written video games, which may explain why some of my colleagues were chortling when the Willis character uses his knowledge of Captain Woobah and Planet Xenon (persons and places unknown to me) to reassure Little Tommy. I say, if you know it, flaunt it. If he had been quoting Nietzsche, now that would have been a red flag.

What Siri brings to the show is an intimate visual style that keeps us claustrophobically close to the action, an ability to make action sequences clear enough to follow, and a dark sensibility that leads to at least two deaths we do not really expect. In scenes where a hero must outgun four or five armed opponents, however, *Hostage* does use the reliable action movie technique of cutting from one target to the next, so that we never see what the others are doing while the first ones are being shot. Waiting for their close-ups, I suppose.

Hotel ★ ★ ★
NO MPAA RATING, 119 m., 2003

Rhys Ifans (Trent Stoken), David Schwimmer (Jonathan Danderfine), Salma Hayek (Charlee Boux), Andrea Di Stefano (Assassin), John Malkovich (Omar Jonnson), Valeria Golino (Italian Actress), Saffron Burrows (Duchess of Malfi), Lucy Liu (Kawika), Chiara Mastroianni (Nurse), Julian Sands (Tour Guide), Danny Huston (Hotel Manager). Directed by Mike Figgis and produced by Andrea Calderwood, Figgis, Annie Stewart, Lesley Stewart, and Ernst Etchie Stroh. Screenplay by Figgis and John Webster.

Here's a strange case. *Hotel* is a movie that works in no conventional sense, and succeeds in several unconventional ones. Most audiences will find it baffling and unsatisfactory. Those who are open to its flywheel peculiarities may find it bold, funny, peculiar, and delightful.

The movie is told like three stories running in a circle, snapping at one anothers' tails. One story involves a self-important movie director named Trent Stoken (Rhys Ifans), who is in Venice shooting a version of John Webster's *The Duchess of Malfi* in the Dogma style. The second involves a documentary crew led by Charlee Boux (Salma Hayek) that is making one of those "making of" films about the production. The third involves the workings of the hotel itself, which is run by and for cannibal vampires. All of this is much in the spirit of Webster, Shakespeare's contemporary, whose plays dripped with violence, melodrama, conspiracy, and sexual intrigue.

Figgis is a bold experimenter whose films often leave conventional pathways to achieve their effect. His *Leaving Las Vegas* (1995) was shot on Super 16-mm so that the cast and crew could work quickly on locations without clearances or permits. His *Timecode* (2000) was shot on digital video that used a four-way split screen to tell the story with four simultaneous and unbroken shots (*Russian Ark* had only one ninety-minute take). In *Hotel* he shows the film-within-a-film on digital video, goes outside it with conventional celluloid, and sometimes presents the same scene with messy location sound and then polished postproduction sound.

Now imagine all this stylistic freedom with an all-star cast of actors invited to play broadly, wryly, erotically. There is a feud between the Ifans character and his producer (David Schwimmer), and a stunning moment when the director is shot, only to linger in a long, eyes-open coma that inspires an extraordinary erotic monologue by his nurse (Chiara Mastroianni). Saffron Burrows plays the Duchess of Malfi and is involved first with Ifans, then with Schwimmer.

Familiar faces are everywhere: Lucy Liu as an instinctive enemy of Hayek; Danny Huston as the helpful, sinister hotel manager; Julian Sands as the tour guide, whose explanations of Venice and the Webster play provide a road map, Valeria Golina as another of the actresses, and Burt Reynolds, who convincingly occupies what seems to be a completely superfluous role. Used most oddly of all is John Malkovich, in an opening sequence where he is taken down into the catacombs of the hotel and participates in a formal feast where, it becomes clear, the main dish is human flesh. Malkovich's seat at the table, ominously, is behind bars separating it from the others.

The movie does a fair job of satirizing the conceits of the Dogma movement—showing the hapless Burrows trying to perform period costume scenes in the middle of a Piazza San Marco filled with rubbernecking tourists. It shows the competition for power, money, and sex that can take place when gigantic egos are assembled. It has more than one unusually erotic scene, including a monologue as evocative as the one in Bergman's *Persona*. Salma Hayek finds more than a documentarian could hope for when she wanders into hidden passages and discovers dismembered body parts. The treatment of the comatose director is cruel, funny, sad, and creepy. The fact that all of these characters are being preyed on by vampires may be a metaphor for the megacorporations that own the movie industry. Or maybe not.

Many critics have agreed that *Hotel* is not successful, but I would ask: Not successful at what? Before you conclude that a movie doesn't work, you have to determine what it intends to do. This is not a horror movie, a behind-the-scenes movie, a sexual intrigue, or a travelogue, but all four at once, elbowing each other for screen time. It reminds me above all of a competitive series of jazz improvisations, in which the musicians quote from many sources and the joy comes in the way they're able to keep their many styles alive in the same song. Figgis is a musician (he composed for the film, in addition to cowriting, cophotographing, and coproducing). Maybe that occurred to him. There is a heady freedom in his riffs here that might appeal to you, if you don't doggedly insist that everything reduce itself to the mundane. The movie has to be pointless in order to make any sense.

Hotel Rwanda ★ ★ ★ ★
PG-13, 110m., 2004

Don Cheadle (Paul Rusesabagina), Sophie Okonedo (Tatiana), Nick Nolte (Colonel Oliver), Joaquin Phoenix (Jack). Directed by Terry George and produced by Terry George and A.

Kitman Ho. Screenplay by Keir Pearson and
George.

You do not believe you can kill them all?
Why not? Why not? We are halfway there already.

In 1994 in Rwanda, a million members of the
Tutsi tribe were killed by members of the Hutu
tribe, in a massacre that took place while the
world looked away. *Hotel Rwanda* is not the
story of that massacre. It is the story of a hotel
manager who saved the lives of 1,200 people by
being, essentially, a very good hotel manager.

The man is named Paul Rusesabagina, and
he is played by Don Cheadle as a man of quiet,
steady competence in a time of chaos. This is
not the kind of man the camera silhouettes
against mountaintops, but the kind of man
who knows how things work in the real world,
and uses his skills of bribery, flattery, apology,
and deception to save these lives who have
come into his care.

I have known a few hotel managers fairly
well, and I think if I were hiring diplomats
they would make excellent candidates. They
speak several languages. They are discreet.
They know how to function appropriately in
different cultures. They know when a bottle
of Scotch will repay itself six times over. They
know how to handle complaints. And they
know everything that happens under their
roof, from the millionaire in the penthouse
to the bellboy who can get you a girl (the wise
manager fires such bellboys, except perhaps
for one who is prudent and trustworthy and
a useful resource on certain occasions).

Paul is such a hotel manager. He is a Hutu,
married to a Tutsi named Tatiana (Sophie
Okonedo). He has been trained in Belgium
and runs the four-star Hotel Des Milles
Collines in the capital city of Kigali. He does
his job very well. He understands that when a
general's briefcase is taken for safekeeping, it
contains bottles of good Scotch when it is returned. He understands that to get the imported beer he needs, a bribe must take place.
He understands that his guests are accustomed to luxury, which must be supplied even
here in a tiny central African nation wedged
against Tanzania, Uganda, and the Congo. Do
these understandings make him a bad man?
Just the opposite. They make him an expert

on situational ethics. The result of all the
things he knows is that the hotel runs well and
everyone is happy.

Then the genocide begins, suddenly, but
after a long history. Rwanda's troubles began,
as so many African troubles began, when European colonial powers established nations
that ignored traditional tribal boundaries.
Enemy tribes were forced into the same land.
For years in Rwanda under the Belgians, the
Tutsis ruled, and killed not a few Hutu. Now
the Hutus are in control, and armed troops
prowl the nation, killing Tutsis.

There is a United Nations "presence" in
Rwanda, represented by Colonel Oliver (Nick
Nolte). He sees what is happening, informs his
superiors, asks for help and intervention, and
is ignored. Paul Rusesabagina informs corporate headquarters in Brussels of the growing
tragedy, but the hotel in Kigali is not the
chain's greatest concern. Finally it comes
down to these two men acting as freelancers to
save more than a thousand lives they have
somehow become responsible for.

When *Hotel Rwanda* premiered at Toronto
2004, two or three reviews criticized the film
for focusing on Rusesabagina and the
colonel, and making little effort to "depict"
the genocide as a whole. But director Terry
George and writer Keir Pearson have made
exactly the correct decision. A film cannot be
about a million murders, but it can be about
how a few people respond. Paul Rusesabagina, as it happens, is a real person, and
Colonel Oliver is based on one, and *Hotel
Rwanda* is about what they really did. The
story took shape after Pearson visited
Rwanda and heard of a group of people who
were saved from massacre.

Don Cheadle's performance is always held
resolutely at the human level. His character
intuitively understands that only by continuing to act as a hotel manager can he achieve
anything. His hotel is hardly functioning, the
economy has broken down, the country is
ruled by anarchy, but he puts on his suit and
tie every morning and fakes business as
usual—even on a day he is so frightened he
cannot tie his tie.

He deals with a murderous Hutu general,
for example, not as an enemy or an outlaw,
but as a longtime client who knows that the

value of a good cigar cannot be measured in cash. Paul has trained powerful people in Kigali to consider the Hotel Des Milles Collines an oasis of sophistication and decorum, and now he pretends that is still the case. It isn't, but it works as a strategy because it cues a different kind of behavior; a man who has yesterday directed a mass murder might today want to show that he knows how to behave appropriately in the hotel lobby.

Nolte's performance is also in a precise key. He came to Rwanda as a peace-keeper, and now there is no peace to keep. The nations are united in their indifference toward Rwanda. Nolte's bad-boy headlines distract from his acting gifts; here his character is steady, wise, cynical, and a master of the possible. He makes a considered choice in ignoring his orders and doing what he can do, right now, right here, to save lives.

How the 1,200 people come to be "guests" in the hotel is a chance of war. Some turn left, some right, some live, some die. Paul is concerned above all with his own family. As a Hutu he is safe, but his wife is Tutsi, his children are at threat, and in any event he is far beyond thinking in tribal terms. He has spent years storing up goodwill, and now he calls in favors. He moves the bribery up another level. He hides people in his hotel. He lies. He knows how to use a little blackmail: Sooner or later, he tells a powerful general, the world will take a reckoning of what happened in Kigali, and if Paul is not alive to testify for him, who else will be believed?

This all succeeds as riveting drama. *Hotel Rwanda* is not about hotel management, but about heroism and survival. Rusesabagina rises to the challenge. The film works not because the screen is filled with meaningless special effects, formless action, and vast digital armies, but because Don Cheadle, Nick Nolte, and the filmmakers are interested in how two men choose to function in an impossible situation. Because we sympathize with these men, we are moved by the film. Deep movie emotions for me usually come not when the characters are sad, but when they are good. You will see what I mean.

Note: The character of Colonel Oliver is based on Lieutenant General Romeo Dallaire, a Canadian who was the UN force commander in *Rwanda. His autobiography,* Shake Hands with the Devil, *was published in October 2004.*

The Housekeeper ★ ★ ★
NO MPAA RATING, 90 m., 2003

Jean-Pierre Bacri (Jacques), Émilie Dequenne (Laura), Brigitte Catillon (Claire), Jacques Frantz (Ralph), Axelle Abbadie (Helene), Catherine Breillat (Constance). Directed by Claude Berri and produced by Berri. Screenplay by Berri, based on the novel by Christian Oster.

Claude Berri's *The Housekeeper* opens with a leisurely survey of a Paris apartment. The place is a mess. Dirty laundry, unmade beds, clothes thrown anywhere, the man sleeping on a couch and then stumbling to his bed in the middle of the night. His wife has walked out and he needs a housekeeper. He finds a notice in a store, calls the number on the little tag of paper, and finds himself in a café having coffee with a young woman who says she will be happy to take the job.

She is young, sexy in a certain light, says she has not worked as a housekeeper before, but needs the job and will work hard. He hires her. We might cynically assume he has erotic thoughts in the back of his mind, but apparently not: He scarcely seems to notice her, and at first arranges for her to work during hours when he is not at home.

He is Jacques (Jean-Pierre Bacri), a serious man in his fifties, balding, good-looking, masculine, preoccupied, busy. She is Laura (Émilie Dequenne), has two-tone hair, the roots growing out, and seems a little sloppy, but she does a capable job of cleaning the apartment and very slowly, with instinctive craft, she expands her role in his life, insinuating herself, being useful in unexpected ways, doing some of the domestic things a wife might do—and eventually, all of the things a wife might do. That he sleeps with her is more a result of his capitulation than his lust. Soon he hears the momentous words "I love you," and the crucial question, "Do you love me?" and the camera is looking directly at his face as he agrees, not with enthusiasm, that he does.

He doesn't love her, of course; his emotions are a mixture of pity, gratitude, fondness, and lust, but men have ineffective defenses against tears and sex. With the same application she brings to the housework, she elevates herself from housekeeper to that undefined sort of female companion that his friends think they understand, even though they do not.

There is a vacation trip to visit an old friend of his. She comes along. She is soon wearing a ring, and there is a story behind the ring, which I will not reveal, but which helps to define the gulf between his adult life and this accidental liaison that is almost certainly going to be more trouble than it's worth. A confrontation with his friend reveals how much more important his wife is, even absent and despite his resentment, than the girl who shares his bed. (We get a few glimpses of the wife, played by Catherine Breillat, the director of such more harrowing examinations of sex as *Fat Girl* and *Romance*.)

Many movies celebrate romances between older men and younger women. That is because most movie directors are older men, and they find such stories congenial and plausible. In their eyes older men are more attractive, irresistible, fascinating than the callow boys the same age as their young partners. What these movies often fail to observe is that their young lovers are callow, too. When you are forty or fifty or sixty, to sleep with a girl of twenty might indeed be delightful, but to live with her day in and day out might be an ordeal beyond all imagining.

There is, first of all, the business of dancing. Young girls want to stay out very late and dance endlessly to barbaric music. Mature men are amused to spend a little time on the dance floor—but not hours and hours and hours, surrounded by inexhaustible youth, the music so loud they can make no use of their treasured conversational abilities. They do not understand, or have forgotten, that the whole point of loud music is to make it possible to date without talking. There are other problems. Girls want to swim when the water is too cold. They want to sunbathe far beyond any reasonable period that a person with an active mind can abide remaining prone on the sand. They have limited interest in spending hours listening to the older man and his old friends remembering times and people they will never, ever know for themselves.

The Housekeeper is wise and subtle in the way it presents its older man. A less interesting movie would make him lustful and self-deceiving, a man who believes his is the secret of eternal youth and virility. In the case of Jacques, however, he goes along, up to a point, indulges his weakness and his curiosity, up to a point, and then he finds that point—or, more poignantly, has it pointed out for him. The closing shots of the movie, which use Jean-Pierre Bacri's face as their primary canvas, say all that needs to be said about what he has learned, and with what wry acceptance he has received the message.

House Of D ★ ½
PG-13, 96 m., 2005

Anton Yelchin (Tommy), Tea Leoni (Mrs. Warshaw), David Duchovny (Tom Warshaw), Robin Williams (Pappass), Erykah Badu (Lady Bernadette), Magali Amadei (Coralie Warshaw), Harold Cartier (Odell Warshaw), Mark Margolis (Mr. Pappass), Zelda Williams (Melissa). Directed by David Duchovny and produced by Richard Barton Lewis, Jane Rosenthal, and Bob Yari. Screenplay by Duchovny.

Yes, I take notes during the movies. I can't always read them, but I persist in hoping that I can. During a movie like *House of D*, I jot down words I think might be useful in the review. Peering now at my three-by-five cards, I read *sappy, inane, cornball, shameless* and, my favorite, *doofusoid*. I sigh. The film has not even inspired interesting adjectives, except for the one I made up myself. I have been reading Dr. Johnson's invaluable *Dictionary of the English Language,* and propose for the next edition:

doofusoid, adj. Possessing the qualities of a doofus; sappy, inane, cornball, shameless. "The plot is composed of doofusoid elements."

You know a movie is not working for you when you sit in the dark inventing new words. *House of D* is the kind of movie that particularly makes me cringe, because it has such a shameless desire to please; like Uriah Heep, it bows and scrapes and wipes its sweaty palm on its trouser-leg, and also like Uriah Heep it privately thinks it is superior.

I make free with a reference to Uriah Heep because I assume if you got past Dr. Johnson and did not turn back, Uriah Heep will be like an old friend. You may be asking yourself, however, why I am engaging in wordplay, and the answer is: I am trying to entertain myself before I must get down to the dreary business of this review. Think of me as switching off my iPod just before going into traffic court.

So. *House of D.* Written and directed by David Duchovny, who I am quite sure created it with all of the sincerity at his command, and believed in it so earnestly that it did not occur to him that no one else would believe in it at all. It opens in Paris with an artist (Duchovny) who feels he must return to the Greenwich Village of his youth, there to revisit the scenes and people who were responsible, I guess, for him becoming an artist in Paris, so maybe a thank-you card would have done.

But, no, we return to Greenwich Village in 1973, soon concluding Duchovny would more wisely have returned to the Greenwich Village of 1873, in which the clichés of Victorian fiction, while just as agonizing, would at least not have been dated. We meet the hero's younger self, Tommy (Anton Yelchin). Tommy lives with his mother, Mrs. Warshaw (Tea Leoni), who sits at the kitchen table smoking and agonizing and smoking and agonizing. (Spoiler warning!) She seems deeply depressed, and although Tommy carefully counts the remaining pills in her medicine cabinet to be sure his mother is still alive, she nevertheless takes an overdose and, so help me, goes into what the doctor tells Tommy is a "persistent vegetative state." How could Duchovny have guessed when he was writing his movie that such a line, of all lines, would get a laugh?

Tommy's best friend is Pappass, played by Robin Williams. Pappass is retarded. He is retarded in 1973, that is; when Tommy returns many years later, Pappass is proud to report that he has been upgraded to "challenged." In either case, he is one of those characters whose shortcomings do not prevent him from being clever like a fox as he (oops!) blurts out the truth, underlines sentiments, says things that are more significant than he realizes, is insightful in the guise of innocence, and always appears exactly when and where the plot requires.

Tommy has another confidant, named Lady Bernadette (Erykah Badu), who is an inmate in the Women's House of Detention. She is on an upper floor with a high window in her cell, but by using a mirror she can see Tommy below, and they have many conversations, in which their speaking voices easily carry through the Village traffic noise and can be heard across, oh, fifty yards. Lady Bernadette is a repository of ancient female wisdom, and advises Tommy on his career path and the feelings of Pappass, who "can't go where you're going"—no, not even though he steals Tommy's bicycle.

The whole business of the bicycle being stolen and returned, and Pappass and Tommy trading responsibility for the theft, and the cross-examination by the headmaster of Tommy's private school (Frank Langella) is tendentious beyond all reason. (Tendentious, adj. Tending toward the dentious, as in having one's teeth drilled.) The bicycle is actually an innocent bystander, merely serving the purpose of creating an artificial crisis which can cause a misunderstanding, so that the crisis can be resolved and the misunderstanding healed. What a relief it is that Pappass and Tommy can hug at the end of the movie.

Damn! I didn't even get to the part about Tommy's girlfriend, and my case is being called. ☞

House of Flying Daggers ★ ★ ★ ★
PG-13, 119 m., 2004

Zhang Ziyi (Mei), Takeshi Kaneshiro (Jin), Andy Lau (Leo), Song Dandan (Yee). Directed by Zhang Yimou and produced by William Kong and Yimou. Screenplay by Feng Li, Bin Wang, and Yimou.

Movie imagery, which has grown brutal and ugly in many of the new high-tech action pictures, may yet be redeemed by the elegance of martial arts pictures from the East. Zhang Yimou's *House of Flying Daggers*, like his *Hero* (2004) and Ang Lee's *Crouching Tiger, Hidden Dragon* (2000), combines excitement, romance, and astonishing physical beauty; to Pauline Kael's formula of "kiss kiss bang bang" we can now add "pretty pretty."

Forget about the plot, the characters, the intrigue, which are all splendid in *House of Flying Daggers*, and focus just on the visuals. There are interiors of ornate, elaborate richness, costumes of bizarre beauty, landscapes of mountain ranges and meadows, fields of snow, banks of autumn leaves, and a bamboo grove that functions like a kinetic art installation.

The action scenes set in these places are not broken down into jagged short cuts and incomprehensible foreground action. Zhang stands back and lets his camera regard the whole composition, wisely following Fred Astaire's belief that to appreciate choreography you must be able to see the entire body in motion. Tony Scott of the *New York Times* is on to something when he says the film's two most accomplished action scenes are likely to be "cherished like favorite numbers from *Singin' in the Rain* and *An American in Paris*." Try making that claim about anything in *The Matrix* or *Blade: Trinity*.

The scenes in question are the Echo Game and a battle in a tall bamboo grove. The Echo Game takes place inside the Peony Pavilion, a luxurious brothel that flourishes in the dying days of the Tang Dynasty, A.D. 859. An undercover policeman named Jin (Takeshi Kaneshiro) goes there on reports that the new dancer may be a member of the House of Flying Daggers, an underground resistance movement. The dancer is Mei (Zhang Ziyi, also in *Hero* and *Crouching Tiger*), and she is blind; martial arts pictures have always had a special fondness for blind warriors, from the old *Zatoichi* series about a blind swordsman to Takeshi Kitano's *Zatoichi* remake (2004).

After Mei dances for Jin, his fellow cop Leo (Andy Lau) challenges her to the Echo Game, in which the floor is surrounded by drums on poles, and he throws a nut at one of the drums. She is to hit the same drum with the weighted end of her long sleeve. First one nut, then three, then countless nuts are thrown, as Mei whirls in midair to follow the sounds with beats of her own; like the house-building sequence in the Kitano picture, this becomes a ballet of movement and percussion.

Jin and Mei form an alliance to escape from the emperor's soldiers, Mei not suspecting (or does she?) that Jin is her undercover enemy. On their journey, supposedly to the secret headquarters of the House of Flying Daggers, they fall in love; but Jin sneaks off to confer with Leo, who is following them with a contingent of warriors, hoping to be led to the hideout. Which side is Jin betraying?

Still other warriors, apparently not aware of the undercover operation, attack the two lovers, and there are scenes of improbable delight, as when four arrows from one bow strike four targets simultaneously. Indeed most of the action in the movie is designed not to produce death, but the pleasure of elegant ingenuity. The impossible is cheerfully welcome here.

The fight in the bamboo grove inspires comparison with the treetop swordfight in *Crouching Tiger*, but is magnificent in its own way. Warriors attack from above, hurling sharpened bamboo shafts that surround the lovers, and then swoop down on tall, supple bamboo trees to attack at close range. The sounds of the whooshing bamboo spears and the click of dueling swords and sticks have a musical effect; if these scenes are not part of the sound track album, they should be.

The plot is almost secondary to the glorious action, until the last act, which reminded me a little of the love triangle in Hitchcock's *Notorious*. In that film, a spy sends the woman he loves into danger, assigning her to seduce an enemy of the state, which she does for patriotism and her love of her controller. Then the spy grows jealous, suspecting the woman really loves the man she was assigned to deceive. In *House of the Flying Daggers* the relationships contain additional levels of discovery and betrayal, so that the closing scenes in the snowfield are operatic in their romantic tragedy.

Zhang Yimou has made some of the most visually stunning films I've seen (*Raise the Red Lantern*) and others of dramatic everyday realism (*To Live*). Here, and with *Hero*, he wins for mainland China a share of the martial arts glory long claimed by Hong Kong and its acolytes like Ang Lee and Quentin Tarantino. The film is so good to look at and listen to that, as with some operas, the story is almost beside the point, serving primarily to get us from one spectacular scene to another. ☞

House of Fools ★ ★ ★
R, 104 m., 2003

Julia Vysotsky (Janna), Sultan Islamov (Akhmed), Bryan Adams (Himself), Vladas Bagdonas (Doctor), Stanislav Varkki (Ali). Directed by Andrei Konchalovsky and produced by Konchalovsky and Felix Kleiman. Screenplay by Sergei Kozlov.

Why are madhouses seen as such useful microcosms of human society? Why are their inhabitants invariably seen, in the movies anyway, as saner than the rest of us? The inmates are invariably choreographed as a group, acting like a Greek chorus. These groups I like to describe as the Baked Potato People, a name suggested by my old friend Billy ("Silver Dollar") Baxter, who once found a flag stuck into his baked potato, which read: "I've been tubbed, I've been rubbed, I've been scrubbed! I'm lovable, hugable, and eatable!"

Andrei Konchalovsky's *House of Fools* begins with ominous signs that it will be yet another recycling of simple fools, angelic heroines, and Baked Potatoes, with the familiar moral that it's the outside world that's crazy. It doesn't help that the movie is "based on a true story." But Konchalovsky was not born yesterday, has no doubt seen *King of Hearts, One Flew Over the Cuckoo's Nest,* and all the others, and shows courage in pressing ahead into this fraught territory. To my amazement, he salvages a good film from the genre—a film that succeeds not by arguing that the world is crazier than the asylum, but by arriving at the melancholy possibility that both are equally insane.

His true story: In 1996, during the Chechen war, the staff of a mental institution abandoned their posts as Russian and Chechen troops approached, and the inmates ran the place by themselves. Konchalovsky, a Russian who has worked for Hollywood (and made two admirable pictures there, *Shy People* and *Runaway Train*), not only shot in a real mental asylum, but used its actual inmates, who are blended with actors in the leads. This lends an authenticity and a certain unpredictability to the story.

We meet Janna (Julia Vysotsky), blonde and cheerful, in her twenties, an inmate who cheers the others with her accordion; so effective is her music that the image, usually a gray-green-blue, brightens up and admits yellow tones when she plays. In charge is the doctor (Vladas Bagdonas), who goes in search of a bus to evacuate his charges, and Ali (Stanislav Varkki), a poet who never goes anywhere without his knapsack, and even sleeps with it.

For the inmates, the daily high point comes right before bedtime, when they cluster around a window to watch a train roll past. Improbably bedecked with glittering lights like a Christmas tree, it still more improbably has an engineer who not only looks like the Canadian singer Bryan Adams but *is* the Canadian singer Bryan Adams, who sings "Have You Ever Really Loved a Woman?" while he guides the train.

A later shot of a passing train shows that it carries Russian tanks, and there is a good possibility, I think, that so does the Bryan Adams train. But Janna believes Adams is her fiancé and will come to marry her, and has a giant poster of him over her bed, like the poster of David Beckham in *Bend It Like Beckham*. She is all primed for love, and so when Chechen troops arrive it is only a matter of time until she transfers her affections to an Adamesque blond soldier named Akhmed (Sultan Islamov), who goes along with the joke and agrees to be engaged to her.

The early scenes in the asylum are conventionally in Baked Potato land, but the arrival of the troops nudges the film into new and riskier territory, and there are frightening moments when the inmates wander oblivious in the face of danger. One shot shows Janna completely unaware that a helicopter has crashed and exploded behind her. Intriguingly, the soldiers are shown, not as violent outsiders, but as essentially confused and alarmed creatures who are as surprised to find themselves in this situation as the inmates are. One adroit bit of plotting even allows a soldier to enlist in the ranks of the mad.

House of Fools doesn't take sides in the Chechen conflict but offers us two groups of soldiers equally uncomfortable with the situation. The masterstroke is the use of Bryan Adams, who seems like a joke when he first appears (the movie knows this), but is used by Konchalovsky in such a way that eventually he becomes the embodiment of the ability to imagine and dream—an ability, the movie implies, that's the only thing keeping these crazy people sane.

House of Sand and Fog ★ ★ ★ ★
R, 126 m., 2003

Jennifer Connelly (Kathy Nicolo), Ben Kingsley (Massoud Amir Behrani), Ron Eldard (Lester

Burdon), Shohreh Aghdashloo (Nadi Behrani), Jonathan Ahdout (Esmail Behrani), Frances Fisher (Connie Walsh). Directed by Vadim Perelman and produced by Michael London and Perelman. Screenplay by Perelman and Shawn Lawrence Otto, based on the novel by Andre Dubus III.

It's so rare to find a movie that doesn't take sides. Conflict is said to be the basis of popular fiction, and yet here is a film that seizes us with its first scene and never lets go, and we feel sympathy all the way through for everyone in it. To be sure, they sometimes do bad things, but the movie *understands* them and their flaws. Like great fiction, *House of Sand and Fog* sees into the hearts of its characters, and loves and pities them. It is based on a novel by Andre Dubus III, and there must have been pressure to cheapen and simplify it into a formula of good and evil. But no. It stands with integrity, and breaks our hearts.

The story is simply told. Kathy Nicolo (Jennifer Connelly), a recovering alcoholic, has been living alone since her husband walked out eight months ago. She has fallen behind on the taxes for her modest split-level home that has a view, however distant, of the California shore. She neglects warnings from the county, the house is put up for auction, and it is purchased by Massoud Amir Behrani (Ben Kingsley), an Iranian immigrant who was a colonel in the Shah's air force but now works two jobs to support his family, and dreams that this house is the first step in rebuilding the lives of his wife and son.

The director and cowriter, Vadim Perelman, doesn't lay out the plot like bricks on a wall, but allows it to reveal itself. We see Massoud working on a highway construction gang, washing himself in a rest room, getting into a Mercedes, and driving to his other job, as an all-night clerk in a roadside convenience store. When the wealthy have a fall, the luxury car is often the last treasure to go; better an expensive old car than a cheap new one. And they are a reminder. Yes, Massoud has memories of the good life they led and their shore cottage in Iran.

Kathy has memories, too. The house was left to her and her brother when their father died. The brother lives in the East, sometimes loans her money, is not sure he believes she is clean and sober. She hasn't had a drink in three years, but is depressed by the departure of her husband, has started smoking again, has needed this shock to blast her out of her lethargy. After she is evicted, she drives past her house in disbelief, seeing this foreigner with his family and his furniture, and one night she sleeps in her car, right outside the gate.

Both of these people desperately need this house. Both have a moral claim to it. Neither can afford to let go of it. Yes, Kathy should have opened her mail and paid her taxes. Yes, perhaps, Massoud should agree with Kathy's public defender (Frances Fisher) and sell the house back for what he paid. But we know, from looking into his books (where every Snickers bar is accounted for), that he is almost broke. This is his last chance to keep up appearances for his wife and son, and to look substantial in the eyes of his daughter's new Iranian husband and her in-laws.

Into the lives of these two blameless parties comes a third, Lester Burdon (Ron Eldard), the deputy sheriff who evicts Kathy but is touched by her grief, then stirred by her beauty. If we are keeping a moral accounting, then his is the blame for what eventually happens. It is fair enough to fight for your home and family, but not fair to misuse your uniform—not even if your excuse is love, or what is spoken of as love. Lester says he will leave his wife and family for Kathy, and although maybe he will, he certainly shouldn't. There is a moment when they start sharing an empty cottage in the woods, and as he leaves she asks if he'll come back, and then quickly adds, "I'll understand if you don't." But he holds himself to a bargain he should not have made and cannot fulfill, and because he is not a moral man he brings unimaginable suffering into the lives of Kathy and the Behrani family, who in all of their dealings after all acted only as good people would from strong motives.

There is much more that the movie will unfold to you, but although I will not reveal it, it isn't in the nature of a surprise plot development. At every step, we feel we are seeing what could and would naturally happen next—not because of coincidence or contrivance, but because of the natures of the people involved.

Not much is said about Massoud Amir Behrani's background in Iran; he has nightmares, he lived in a bad time, but now has pulled back to the simplest things: to find a house for his wife and a wife for his son. Kingsley is such an unbending actor when he needs to be, has such reserves of dignity, that when the deputy attempts to intimidate him with the uniform and the badge, Massoud stands his ground and says, "I don't know who you think you're talking to," and we see at once that he is the man and the deputy is the boy.

As for Kathy, misfortune and injury follow her. Even new love is bad luck. There are scenes involving her being taken back into her old house. And a crisis when the Behranis, whose family is threatened by this woman, simplify everything with one simple sentence: "We have a guest in the house." And a subtle subtext in the way Nadi Behrani (Shohreh Aghdashloo), Massoud's wife, treats the sad girl as a mother would, while hardly understanding a word she says.

I have not read the novel by Andre Dubus III, and no doubt changes have been made in the adaptation—they always are. But I sense that the essential integrity has been defended. *House of Sand and Fog* relates not a plot with its contrived ups and downs, but a story. A plot is about things that happen. A story is about people who behave. To admire a story you must be willing to listen to the people and observe them, and at the end of *House of Sand and Fog* we have seen good people with good intentions who have their lives destroyed because they had the bad luck to come across a weak person with shabby desires. And finally there is a kind of love and loyalty, however strange to us, that reveals itself in the marriage of Massoud and Nadi, and must be respected.

House of Wax ★ ★

R, 113 m., 2005

Elisha Cuthbert (Carly Jones), Chad Michael Murray (Nick Jones), Brian Van Holt (Bo), Paris Hilton (Paige Edwards), Jared Padalecki (Wade), Jon Abrahams (Dalton), Robert Ri'chard (Blake). Directed by Jaume Collet-Sera and produced by Susan Levin, Joel Silver, and Robert Zemeckis. Screenplay by Chad Hayes and Carey Hayes.

The Dead Teenager Movie has grown up. The characters in *House of Wax* are in their twen-

ties and yet still repeat the fatal errors of all the *Friday the 13th* kids who checked into Camp Crystal Lake and didn't check out. ("Since all the other campers have been beheaded, eviscerated, or skewered, Marcie, obviously there's only one thing for us to do: Go skinny-dipping at midnight in the haunted lake.")

In *House of Wax,* two carloads of college students leave Gainesville for a big football game in Baton Rouge, and take an ominous detour along the way, leading them into what looks like the Texas Chainsaw Theme Park. "This town is not even on the GPS!" says one of the future Dead Post-Teenagers.

Some will complain that the movie begins slowly, despite a steamy sex scene involving Paris Hilton, and an ominous confrontation with a slack-jawed local man who drives a pickup truck, an innocent and utilitarian vehicle that in horror movies is invariably the choice of the depraved. I didn't mind the slow start, since it gave me time to contemplate the exemplary stupidity of these students, who surely represent the bottom of the academic barrel at the University of Florida.

Consider. They decide to camp overnight in a clearing in the dark, brooding woods. There is a terrible smell. The guy in the pickup truck drives up and shines his brights on them until Carly's ex-con brother, Nick (Chad Michael Murray), breaks one of the headlights. You do not get away with headlight-breaking in Chainsaw Country. The kids should flee immediately, but no: They settle down for the night.

In the morning, a fan belt is found to be mysteriously broken. An ominous sign: Fan belts do not often break in parked cars. Wade (Jared Padalecki) and girlfriend Carly (Elisha Cuthbert) unwisely take a ride into town for a replacement fan belt—from a guy they meet when they discover the source of the smell: a charnel pit of rotting road-kill. The guy is dumping a carcass into the pit at the time. Not the kind of person you want to ask for a lift. Is that a human hand sticking up from the middle of the pile? "This is weird," observes Paige. That night, when they are alone at the camp (not prudent), she treats her boyfriend, Blake (Robert Ri'chard), to a sexy dance that perhaps reminds him of a video he once saw on the Web.

299

The nearby town seems stuck in a time warp from the 1960s. The movie theater is playing *Whatever Happened to Baby Jane?* Yes, and for that matter, what happened to everybody else? No citizens prowl the streets, although some seem to be attending a funeral. Carly and Wade are attracted to a mysterious House of Wax that dominates the town, much as the Bates's home towered above *Psycho*. Wade scratches a wall of the house and says, "It *is* wax—literally!" This is either an omen, or the homeowners were victimized by siding salesmen. Had Wade and Carly only seen the 1953 Vincent Price thriller, they might have saved themselves, but no. They haven't even seen *Scream* and don't know they're in a horror movie.

The progress of the plot is predictable: One Post-Teenager after another becomes Dead, usually while making a stupid mistake like getting into a pickup or entering the House of Wax ("Hello? Anyone home?"). Knowing that at least one and preferably two of the Post-Teenagers will survive for the sequel, along with possibly one of the Local Depraved, we keep count: We know Paris Hilton is likely to die, but are grateful that the producers first allow her to run in red underwear through an old shed filled with things you don't want to know about.

The early reviewers have been harsh with Miss Hilton ("so bad she steals the show," says the *Hollywood Reporter*), but actually she is no better or worse than the typical Dead Post-Teenager, and does exactly what she is required to do in a movie like this, with all the skill, admittedly finite, that is required. *House of Wax* is not a good movie, but it is an efficient one, and will deliver most of what anyone attending *House of Wax* could reasonably expect, assuming it would be unreasonable to expect very much.

Where the movie excels is in its special effects and set design. Graham "Grace" Walker masterminds a spectacular closing sequence in which the House of Wax literally melts down, and characters sink into stairs, fall through floors, and claw through walls. There is also an eerie sequence in which a living victim is sprayed with hot wax and ends up with a finish you'd have to pay an extra four bucks for at the car wash.

Howl's Moving Castle ★ ★ ½
PG, 120 m., 2005

With the voices of: Emily Mortimer (Young Sophie), Jean Simmons (Old Sophie), Christian Bale (Howl), Lauren Bacall (Witch of the Waste), Billy Crystal (Calcifer), Blythe Danner (Madame Suliman), Crispin Freeman (Prince Turnip), Josh Hutcherson (Markl). An animated film directed by Hayao Miyazaki and produced by Toshio Suzuki. Screenplay by Miyazaki, based on the novel by Diana Wynne Jones.

Almost the first sight we see in *Howl's Moving Castle* is the castle itself, which looks as if it were hammered together in shop class by wizards inspired by the lumbering, elephantine war machines in *The Empire Strikes Back*. The castle is an amazing visual invention, a vast collection of turrets and annexes, protuberances and afterthoughts, which makes its way across the landscape like a turtle in search of a rumble.

I settled back in my seat, confident that Japan's Hayao Miyazaki had once again created his particular kind of animated magic, and that the movie would deserve comparison with *Spirited Away, Princess Mononoke, My Neighbor Totoro, Kiki's Delivery Service,* and the other treasures of the most creative animator in the history of the art form.

But it was not to be. While the movie contains delights and inventions without pause and has undeniable charm, while it is always wonderful to watch, while it has the Miyazaki visual wonderment, it's a disappointment compared to his recent work. Adapted from a British novel by Diana Wynne Jones, it resides halfway between the Brothers Grimm and *The Wizard of Oz*, with shape-shifting that includes not merely beings but also objects and places.

Chief among the shape-shifters is the castle itself, which can swell with power and then shrivel in defeat. Inside the castle are spaces that can change on a whim, and a room with a door that opens to—well, wherever it needs to open. The castle roams the Waste Lands outside two warring kingdoms, which seem vaguely nineteenth-century European; it is controlled by Howl himself, a young wizard much in demand but bedeviled with personal issues.

The story opens with Sophie (voice by Emily Mortimer), a hat maker who sits patiently at her workbench while smoke-belching trains roar past her window. When she ventures out, she's attacked by obnoxious soldiers but saved by Howl (voice by Christian Bale), who is himself being chased by inky globs of shapeless hostility. This event calls Sophie's existence to the attention of Howl's enemy, the Witch of the Waste (Lauren Bacall), who fancies Howl for herself and in a fit of jealousy turns Sophie into a wrinkled old woman, bent double and voiced now by Jean Simmons. For most of the rest of the movie, the heroine will be this ancient crone; we can remind ourselves that young Sophie is trapped inside, but the shape-switch slows things down, as if Grandmother were creeping through the woods to Red Riding Hood's house.

Sophie meets a scarecrow (Crispin Freeman) who bounces around on his single wooden leg and leads her to Howl's castle. Sophie names the scarecrow Turniphead, and we think perhaps a lion and a tin man will be turning up before long, but no. Nor is the castle run by a fraudulent wizard behind a curtain. Howl is the real thing, a shape-shifter who sometimes becomes a winged bird of prey. So is his key assistant, Calcifer (Billy Crystal), a fiery being whose job is to supply the castle's energy. Sophie also meets Markl (Josh Hutcherson), Howl's aide-de-camp, and sets about appointing herself the castle's housekeeper and maid of all work.

The plot deepens. Howl is summoned to serve both of the warring kingdoms, which presents him with a problem, complicated by the intervention of Madame Suliman, a sorceress voiced by Blythe Danner, who reminds us of Yubaba, the sorceress who ran the floating bathhouse in *Spirited Away*. These bloated old madame types seem to exert a fascination for Miyazaki scarcely less powerful than his fondness for young heroines. Howl cravenly sends old Sophie to represent him before King Sariman, and on her way there she gets into a race with the Witch of the Waste, who haunts the hinterlands where the castle roams. Sophie is obviously trapped in a web of schemes that's too old and too deep for her to penetrate, and there comes a moment when defeat seems certain and even Calcifer despairs.

All of this is presented, as only Miyazaki can, in animation of astonishing invention and detail. The castle itself threatens to upstage everything else that happens in the movie, and notice the way its protuberances move in time with its lumbering progress, not neglecting the sphincteresque gun turret at the rear. Sophie, old or young, never quite seems to understand and inhabit this world; unlike Kiki of the delivery service or Chihiro, the heroine of *Spirited Away*, she seems more witness than heroine. A parade of weird characters comes onstage to do their turns, but the underlying plot grows murky and, amazingly for a Miyazaki film, we grow impatient at spectacle without meaning.

I can't recommend the film, and yet I know if you admire Miyazaki as much I do you'll want to see it anyway. When his movies are working and on those rare occasions when they are not, Miyazaki nevertheless is a master who, frame by frame, creates animated compositions of wonderment. Pete Doctor (writer of *Toy Story*) and John Lasseter (director of *Toy Story*), his great American supporters, have supervised the English dubbing; online anime sites say, however, that the Japanese voices are more in character (we'll be able to compare on the DVD). In the meantime, the big screen is the only way to appreciate the remarkable detail of the castle, which becomes one of the great unique places in the movies.

How to Lose a Guy in 10 Days ★ ½
PG-13, 116 m., 2003

Kate Hudson (Andie), Matthew McConaughey (Ben), Adam Goldberg (Tony), Michael Michele (Spears), Shalom Harlow (Green), Bebe Neuwirth (Lana), Robert Klein (Phillip). Directed by Donald Petrie and produced by Christine Forsyth-Peters, Lynda Obst, and Robert Evans. Screenplay by Kristen Buckley, Brian Regan, and Burr Steers, based on the book by Michele Alexander and Jeannie Long.

I am just about ready to write off movies in which people make bets about whether they will, or will not, fall in love. The premise is fundamentally unsound, since it subverts every love scene with a lying subtext. Characters are nice when they want to be mean, or mean when they want to be nice. The easiest thing at the movies is to sympathize with two people who are falling in love. The hardest thing is to sympathize with two people who are denying their feelings, misleading each other, and causing pain to a trusting heart. This is comedy only by dictionary definition. In life, it is unpleasant and makes the audience sad.

Unless, of course, the characters are thoroughgoing rotters in the first place, as in *Dirty Rotten Scoundrels* (1988), in which Steve Martin and Michael Caine make a $50,000 bet on who will be the first to con the rich American Glenne Headly. They deserve their comeuppance, and we enjoy it. *How to Lose a Guy in 10 Days* is not, alas, pitched at that modest level of sophistication, and provides us with two young people who are like pawns in a sex game for the developmentally short-changed.

He works at an ad agency. She works for a magazine that is *Cosmopolitan,* spelled a different way. She pitches her editor on an article about how to seduce a guy and then drive him away in ten days. He pitches his boss on an idea that involves him being able to get a woman to fall in love with him in ten days. They don't even Meet Cute, but are shuffled together by a treacherous conspirator.

Now, of course, they will fall in love. That goes without saying. They will fall in love even though she deliberately creates scenes no man could abide, such as nicknaming his penis Princess Sophia. She allows her disgusting miniature dog to pee on his pool table. She even puts a plate of sandwiches down on top of the pot in their poker game, something Nancy would be too sophisticated to do to Sluggo.

He puts up with this mistreatment because he has his own bet to win, and also because, doggone it, he has fallen in love with this vaporous fluffball of narcissistic cluelessness. That leaves only one big scene for us to anticipate, or dread: the inevitable moment when they both find out the other made a bet. At a moment like that, a reasonably intelligent couple would take a beat, start laughing, and head for the nearest hot-sheets haven. But no. These characters descend from the moribund fictional ideas of earlier decades and must react in horror, run away in grief, prepare to leave town,

etc., while we in the audience make our own bets about their IQs.

Matthew McConaughey and Kate Hudson star. I neglected to mention that, maybe because I was trying to place them in this review's version of the Witness Protection Program. If I were taken off the movie beat and assigned to cover the interior design of bowling alleys, I would have some idea of how they must have felt as they made this film.

Hukkle ★ ★ ★
NO MPAA RATING, 75 m., 2003

Ferenc Bandi (Uncle Cseklik), Józsefné Rácz (Midwife), József Forkas (Police Officer), Ferenc Nagy (Beekeeper), Ferencné Virag (Beekeeper's wife), Jánosné Nagy (Boske), Milhalyne Kiraly (Grandmother), Mihaly Kiraly (Grandfather). Directed by György Pálfi and produced by Csaba Bereczki and András Bohm. Screenplay by Pálfi.

An old man hiccups. He shuffles slowly about his morning ritual and then takes his place on a bench outside his cottage beside the road, still hiccupping. A goose goes about its business. flies buzz. A cat earns its living. A runaway cart causes a stir in the village. The old man hiccups.

These opening shots announce György Pálfi's *Hukkle* as a film that will proceed in its own way to its own destination, without regard to convention. The title, a Hungarian word that sounds like a hiccup, is not much help. The film is told almost entirely without dialogue, but is alive to sound; we spend observant, introspective time in a Hungarian hamlet where nothing much seems to happen—oh, except that there's a suspicious death.

The murder enters the film like another chapter in *Hukkle*'s natural history. We have already seen the violence of nature: a frog, to its astonishment, suddenly eaten whole; a bee crushed; a cat dead; bees shaken from their hives; the very firmament shaken by what seems to be an earthquake but is only a low-flying jet. These omens are portents of trouble, in a film that finds a new tone: ominous pastoral.

The film is photographed with loving care, and seems at first to be merely a slice of life from a village day; in its attention to the smallest details of life (animal, vegetable, insect) it has been compared to *Microcosmos*. But there is a macro level, too, almost too large in scale to be seen, and the ingenuity of the film is in suggesting a larger reality—a forest it almost cannot see because it clings so closely to the trees.

This reality involves the dead body, pale and cold at the bottom of a stream, and the investigation of a local policeman, who takes photos of the riverbank where the victim was fishing before his—accident? Murder? Later, in a scene that's a quiet nudge to *Blowup*, the policeman studies the photos and notices a missing bottle. Still later, in another wordless scene, a woman who is brewing illegal spirits in a cave looks up from her still and sees the policeman standing in the cave opening, regarding her.

Can this murder mystery be extracted from *Hukkle* and explained with the clarity of a newspaper account? I doubt it. I think the murder is part of the whole warp and woof of the movie, which studies the events in this village with the attention and yet the random choices of an alien observer who is very interested but doesn't know quite what to look for.

Given its odd choices of perspective and subject, the movie's point of view is almost a character. *Hukkle* doesn't suggest, but I will, as a possible approach to the film, that the opening shot of the old man could be the first glimpse of Earth life by this objective observer, which pokes here and there in the village, so that we—who know what to look for and pick up on the clues—know a murder has been committed, but to the observer all the images are equal. We have the knowledge to find meaning in a pattern that the observer doesn't perceive. Since the hypothetical observer doesn't speak a human language, of course the movie doesn't much notice such sounds.

That may, of course, simply be my fancy. On another level, *Hukkle* is a lovingly photographed natural history of a day of village life. Some audience members will find it maddening. It requires patience and attention. It is not soothing, like a nature study, but disturbing, seeing life as an arena for deadly struggles in which most creatures earn a living by eating each other. To my imaginary alien, perhaps the fisherman was not murdered at all, but simply drowned while attempting to asphyxiate a fish.

Maybe, like hunters who shoot themselves, he found a certain justice.

And still the old man hiccups.

Hulk ★ ★ ★
PG-13, 138 m., 2003

Eric Bana (Bruce Banner), Jennifer Connelly (Betty Ross), Sam Elliott (Ross), Josh Lucas (Talbot), Nick Nolte (Father), Paul Kersey (Young David Banner), Cara Buono (Edith Banner), Todd Tesen (Young Ross). Directed by Ang Lee and produced by Avi Arad, Larry J. Franco, Gale Anne Hurd, and James Schamus. Screenplay by John Turman, Michael France, Schamus, Jack Kirby, and Stan Lee, based on the story by Schamus.

The Hulk is rare among Marvel superheroes in that his powers are a curse, not an advantage. When rage overcomes Dr. Bruce Banner and he turns into a green monster many times his original size, it is not to fight evil or defend the American way, but simply to lash out at his tormentors. Like the Frankenstein stories that are its predecessors, *Hulk* is a warning about the folly of those who would toy with the secrets of life. It is about the anguish of having powers you did not seek and do not desire. "What scares me the most," Banner tells his only friend, Betty Ross, "is that when it happens, when it comes over me, when I totally lose control, I like it."

Ang Lee's *Hulk* (the movie's title drops "the") is the most talkative and thoughtful recent comic book adaptation. It is not so much about a green monster as about two wounded adult children of egomaniacs. Banner (Eric Bana) was fathered by a scientist (Nick Nolte) who has experimented on his own DNA code and passed along genes that are transformed by a lab accident into his son's hulkhood. Betty Ross (Jennifer Connelly) is his research partner; they were almost lovers, but it didn't work out, and she speaks wryly of "my inexplicable fascination with emotionally distant men." Her cold father is General Ross (Sam Elliott), filled with military bluster and determined to destroy the Hulk.

These two dueling Oedipal conflicts are at the heart of *Hulk,* and it's touching how in many scenes we are essentially looking at damaged children. When the Hulk's amazing powers become known, the military of course tries to kill him (that's the routine solution in most movies about aliens and monsters), but there's another villain who has a more devious scheme. That's Talbot (Josh Lucas), a venal entrepreneur who wants to use Banner's secret to manufacture a race of self-repairing soldiers. Lots of money there.

The movie brings up issues about genetic experimentation, the misuse of scientific research, and our instinctive dislike of misfits, and actually talks about them. Remember that Ang Lee is the director of such films as *The Ice Storm* and *Sense and Sensibility*, as well as *Crouching Tiger, Hidden Dragon;* he is trying here to actually deal with the issues in the story of the Hulk, instead of simply cutting to brainless special effects.

Just as well, too, because the Hulk himself is the least successful element in the film. He's convincing in close-up but sort of jerky in long shot—oddly, just like his spiritual cousin, King Kong. There are times when his movements subtly resemble the stop-frame animation used to create Kong, and I wonder if that's deliberate; there was a kind of eerie oddness about Kong's movement that was creepier than the slick smoothness of modern computer-generated creatures.

King Kong is of course one of Lee's inspirations, in a movie with an unusual number of references to film classics. *Bride of Frankenstein* is another, as in a scene where Hulk sees his reflection in a pond. No prizes for identifying *Dr. Jekyll and Mr. Hyde* as the source of the original comics. Other references include *Citizen Kane* (the Hulk tears apart a laboratory) and *The Right Stuff* (a jet airplane flies so high the stars are visible). There is also a shade of General Jack D. Ripper in General Ross, who is played by Sam Elliott in a masterful demonstration of controlled and focused almost-overacting.

The film has its share of large-scale action sequences, as rockets are fired at the Hulk and he responds by bringing down helicopters. And there are the obligatory famous landmarks, real and unreal, we expect in a superhero movie: the Golden Gate Bridge, Monument Valley, and of course an elaborate secret laboratory where Hulk can be trapped in an immersion chamber while his DNA is extracted.

But these scenes are secondary in interest to the movie's central dramas, which involve the two sets of fathers and children. Banner has a repressed memory of a traumatic childhood event, and it is finally jarred loose after he meets his father again after many years. Nolte, looking like a man in desperate need of a barber and flea powder, plays Banner's dad as a man who works in the same laboratory, as a janitor. He uses DNA testing to be sure this is indeed his son, and in one clandestine conversation tells him, "You're going to have to watch that temper of yours."

Connelly's character also has big issues with her father—she trusts him when she shouldn't—and it's amusing how much the dilemma of this character resembles the situation of the woman she played in *A Beautiful Mind*. Both times she's in love with a brilliant scientist who's a sweetheart until he goes haywire, and who thinks he's being pursued by the government.

The movie has an elegant visual strategy; after countless directors have failed, Ang Lee figures out how split-screen techniques can be made to work. Usually they're an annoying gimmick, but here he uses moving frame-lines and pictures within pictures to suggest the dynamic storytelling techniques of comic books. Some shots are astonishing, as foreground and background interact and reveal one another. There is another technique, more subtle, that reminds me of comics: He often cuts between different angles in the same close-up—not cutting away, but cutting from one view of a face to another, as graphic artists do when they need another frame to deal with extended dialogue.

Whether *Hulk* will appeal to its primary audience—teenage science fiction fans—is hard to say. No doubt it will set the usual box office records over the weekend, but will it reach audiences who will respond to its dramatic ambition? Ang Lee has boldly taken the broad outlines of a comic book story and transformed them to his own purposes; this is a comic book movie for people who wouldn't be caught dead at a comic book movie.

The Human Stain ★ ★ ★ ½
R, 106 m., 2003

Anthony Hopkins (Coleman Silk), Nicole Kidman (Faunia Farley), Ed Harris (Lester Farley), Gary Sinise (Nathan Zuckerman), Wentworth Miller (Young Coleman Silk),

Jacinda Barrett (Steena Paulsson), Phyliss
Newman (Iris Silk), Ann Deavere Smith (Mrs.
Silk). Directed by Robert Benton and produced
by Gary Lucchesi, Tom Rosenberg, and Scott
Steindorff. Screenplay by Nicholas Meyer,
based on the novel by Philip Roth.

The Human Stain contains a significant secret
about one of the characters. This review discusses it. "There's no way we can contain the
secret, and we're not even trying to," the producer, Tom Rosenberg, told me at the Toronto
Film Festival. "It's out there already with the
Philip Roth novel. And this isn't a movie like
The Crying Game, which is really about its
secret."

That's because the secret belongs to the character, not the movie. It is one he has lived with
all of his adult life. Coleman Silk is a professor
of classics at a university whose stature he has
enhanced. One day he notes that two students
have not attended class. "What are they,
spooks?" he asks his students. Because they are
African-Americans, his wisecrack is interpreted
as a racist remark, and he is called before a faculty tribunal. Rather than defend himself, he
resigns in a rage. His rage is fueled by his secret:
He is an African-American himself.

The world thinks Coleman Silk (Anthony
Hopkins) is Jewish. His family knows otherwise. In flashbacks, we see a bright young man,
light-skinned enough to pass, who sees two career paths ahead of him, one as a white, the
other as a black. He decides the choice is clear,
enlists in the navy as a white man, and severs
his links with his past. There are heartbreaking
scenes involving his mother (Anna Deavere
Smith), whom he treats with cool disregard.
Early in the film, dating a white girl, he takes
her home to meet his mother having not made
it clear he is black; his revelation is made
through the fact of her appearance, which
seems cowardly and cruel.

Passing for white is not as uncommon as
some of the reviewers of *The Human Stain*
seem to think. Many black family trees have
branches that drifted over the color line. One
problem with *The Human Stain*, however, is
that Anthony Hopkins doesn't look anything at
all like Wentworth Miller, who plays him as a
young man. We simply have to accept the mis-
match as a given, and move on. (Does Hopkins

look as if he "could" have been black? How can
you answer that question about a man who
successfully passes for white? The racist white
man on the train who berates the porter is
played by Allison Davis, a Chicago attorney
who is black.)

Hopkins makes our acceptance easier
because he is a fine actor and involves us so
directly in the character's life that we forget
about the technical details. After his resignation, unexpectedly, in middle age, he begins a
passionate affair with Faunia Farley (Nicole
Kidman), an unlettered school janitor half his
age. Whether Kidman convinces us she is a
working-class woman with a wife-beating ex-
husband (Ed Harris) is another hurdle the
movie sets for itself. I think she clears it. Harris
is frighteningly effective as the ex-husband;
hard to believe this is the same man who plays
the kind football coach in *Radio*.

The movie's narrator is Nathan Zuckerman
(Gary Sinise), a recurring character in Roth's
later novels. Silk must have someone to confide
in, and Zuckerman provides a listener. Eventually there is Faunia, but his talks with her are
more confessional; with Zuckerman, he expresses his rage at the P.C. extremism that cost
him his job because of an innocent verbal slip,
and asks him to write about it. (It's tempting to
say the response to his slip is exaggerated, but
every campus has a story or two about P.C. fascism; what's harder to believe is the self-abasing
apology delivered late in the movie by one of
Silk's tormentors.)

The story involves two different kinds of
passing: crossing the race line, and the class
line. Which is more difficult? Consider that
Coleman and Faunia must deal with each other
despite their lack of common references, education, background, assumptions, manners of
speech, tastes, and instincts. To cross the race
line involves deep psychological anguish, as
you betray yourself and your past, but in the
routine of daily existence it is perhaps easier
than crossing the class line. You can talk and
think just the way you do now. It was different
50 or 100 years ago, but today most of us find it
more difficult to deal in depth with someone of
another class than with someone of another
race. (I am not forgetting that to cross from
white to black would be much more difficult,
because you'd take on the impact of racism.)

What makes *The Human Stain* ambitious and fascinating is how it considers both of these journeys. Once he decides to pass, Coleman Silk finds it relatively easy to exist as a white navy officer, college student, and professor; he must have had problems, but we don't see them. I wish the movie had told us more about how he handled his new Jewish identity (by claiming to be completely secularized, I imagine). But when he becomes the lover of a night-shift janitor who is younger and semi-literate, who has an ex-husband from the world of *Deliverance*, who looks to strangers as if she is too pretty and tall for this balding sixtyish guy, he has his work cut out for him.

They do, of course, communicate through sex, the universal language, although we may have some doubt about how well Coleman speaks it. And this is crucial: They can communicate through revelation, confession, and empathy. Anyone who works a twelve-step program knows how strangers from different backgrounds become friends because they identify with similar experiences. Coleman and Faunia have been cruelly devalued by life, and find in each other a spark of identification that can cross any barrier. And there's the lifeboat factor; since they're both under extreme pressure, they're not looking for a "match" but need bailing out—they respond to each other as rescuers.

The Human Stain has been directed by Robert Benton with a sure feel for the human values involved. Yes, we have to suspend disbelief over the casting, but that's easier since we can believe the stories of these people. Not many movies probe into matters of identity or adaptation. Most movie characters are like Greek gods and comic-book heroes: We learn their roles and powers at the beginning of the story, and they never change. Here are complex, troubled, flawed people, brave enough to breathe deeply and take one more risk with their lives.

The Hunted ★ ★ ★ ½

R, 94 m., 2003

Tommy Lee Jones (L. T. Bonham), Benicio Del Toro (Aaron Hallam), Connie Nielsen (Abby Durrell), Jenna Boyd (Loretta Kravitz), Leslie Stefanson (Irene Kravitz), Robert Blanche (Crumley), Aaron Brounstein (Stokes), Ron Canada (Van Zandt). Directed by William Friedkin and produced by James Jacks and Ricardo Mestres. Screenplay by David Griffiths, Peter Griffiths, and Art Monterastelli.

The Hunted is a pure and rather inspired example of the one-on-one chase movie. Like *The Fugitive,* which also starred Tommy Lee Jones, it's about one man pursuing another more or less nonstop for the entire film. Walking in, I thought I knew what to expect, but I didn't anticipate how William Friedkin would jolt me with the immediate urgency of the action. This is not an arm's-length chase picture, but a close, physical duel between its two main characters.

Jones plays L.T. Bonham, a civilian employee of the U.S. Army who trains elite forces to stalk, track, hunt, and kill. His men learn how to make weapons out of shards of rock, and forge knives from scrap metal. In a sequence proving we haven't seen everything yet, they learn how to kill an enemy by the numbers—leg artery, heart, neck, lung. That Jones can make this training seem real goes without saying; he has an understated, minimalist acting style that implies he's been teaching the class for a long time.

One of his students is Aaron Hallam (Benicio Del Toro), who fought in Kosovo in 1999 and had experiences there that warped him ("his battle stress has gone so deep it is part of his personality"). Back home in Oregon, offended by hunters using telescopic sights, he claims four victims—"those hunters were filleted like deer." Bonham recognizes the style and goes into the woods after him ("If I'm not back in two days that will mean I'm dead").

Hallam's stress syndrome has made him into a radical defender of animal rights; he talks about chickens on assembly lines, and asks one cop how he'd feel if a higher life form were harvesting mankind. Of course, in killing the hunters, he has promoted himself to that superior life form, but this is not a movie about debate points. It is a chase.

No modern director is more identified with chases than Friedkin, whose *The French Connection* and *To Live and Die in L.A.* set the standard. Here the whole movie is a chase, sometimes at a crawl, as when Hallam drives a stolen car directly into a traffic jam. What makes the movie fresh is that it doesn't stand back and regard its pursuit as an exercise, but stays very close to the characters and focuses on the actual physical reality of their experience.

Consider an early hand-to-hand combat between Bonham and Hallam. We've seen so many fancy, high-tech, computer-assisted fight scenes in recent movies that we assume the fighters can fly. They live in a world of gravity-free speedup. Not Friedkin's characters. Their fight is gravity-based. Their arms and legs are heavy. Their blows land solidly, with pain on both sides. They gasp and grunt with effort. They can be awkward and desperate. They both know the techniques of hand-to-hand combat, but in real life it isn't scripted, and you know what? It isn't so easy. We are involved in the immediate, exhausting, draining physical work of fighting.

The chase sequences—through Oregon forests and city streets, on highways and bridges—are also reality-oriented. The cinematography, by the great Caleb Deschanel *(The Right Stuff)*, buries itself in the reality of the locations. The forests are wet and green, muddy and detailed. The leaves are not scenery but right in front of our faces, to be brushed aside. Running, hiding, stalking, the two men get dirty and tired and gasp for breath. We feel their physical effort; this isn't one of those movies where shirts are dry again in the next scene and the hero has the breath for long speeches.

The Hunted requires its skilled actors. Ordi-nary action stars would not do. The screenplay, by David Griffiths, Peter Griffiths, and Art Monterastelli, has a kind of minimalist clarity, in which nobody talks too much and every-thing depends on tone. Notice scenes where Del Toro is interrogated by other law officials. He doesn't give us the usual hostile, aggressive clichés, but seems to be trying to explain him-self from a place so deep he can't make it real to outsiders. This man doesn't kill out of rage but out of sorrow.

There are moments when Friedkin lays it on a little thick. The early how-to sequence, where Bonham's trainees learn how to make weapons from scratch, implies there will be a later se-quence where they need to. Fair enough. But would Hallam, in the heat of a chase, have the time to build a fire from shavings, heat an iron rod and hammer it into a knife? Even if Bon-ham cooperates by meanwhile pausing to chip his own flint weapon? Maybe not, or maybe the two hunters are ritualistically agreeing to face each other using only these tools of their trade. The resulting knife fight, which benefits from the earlier knife training sequence, is physical action of a high order.

There are other characters in the movie, other relationships. A woman with a child, whom Hallam visits (she likes him but is a little afraid). A woman who is an FBI field officer. Various cops. They add background and at-mosphere, but *The Hunted* is about two hard-working men who are good at their jobs, although only one can be the best.

I

I, Robot ★ ★
PG-13, 114 m., 2004

Will Smith (Del Spooner), Bridget Moynahan (Susan Calvin), Bruce Greenwood (Lance Robertson), James Cromwell (Dr. Alfred Lanning), Chi McBride (Lieutenant John Bergin), Alan Tudyk (Sonny). Directed by Alex Proyas and produced by John Davis, Topher Dow, and Laurence Mark. Screenplay by Jeff Vintar and Akiva Goldsman, based on the book by Isaac Asimov.

1. *A robot may not injure a human being or, through inaction, allow a human being to come to harm.*
2. *A robot must obey orders given it by human beings except where such orders would conflict with the First Law.*
3. *A robot must protect its own existence as long as such protection does not conflict with the First or Second Law.*
                        —*Isaac Asimov's I, Robot*

I, Robot takes place in Chicago circa 2035, a city where spectacular new skyscrapers share the skyline with landmarks like the Sears (but not the Trump) Tower. The tallest of the buildings belongs to U.S. Robotics, and on the floor of its atrium lobby lies the dead body of its chief robot designer, apparently a suicide.

Detective Del Spooner is on the case. Will Smith plays Spooner, a Chicago Police Department detective, who doesn't think it's suicide. He has a deep-seated mistrust of robots, despite the famous Three Laws of Robotics, which declare above all that a robot must not harm a human being.

The dead man is Dr. Alfred Lanning (James Cromwell), who, we are told, wrote the Three Laws. Every schoolchild knows the laws were set down by the good doctor Isaac Asimov, after a conversation he had on December 23, 1940, with John W. Campbell, the legendary editor of *Astounding Science Fiction*. It is peculiar that no one in the film knows that, especially since the film is "based on the book by Isaac Asimov." Would it have killed the filmmakers to credit Asimov?

Asimov's robot stories were often based on robots that got themselves hopelessly entangled in logical contradictions involving the laws. According to the invaluable *Wikipedia* encyclopedia on the Web, Harlan Ellison and Asimov collaborated in the 1970s on an *I, Robot* screenplay that, the good doctor said, would produce "the first really adult, complex, worthwhile science fiction movie ever made."

While that does not speak highly for *2001: A Space Odyssey* (1968), it is certain that the screenplay for this film, by Jeff Vintar and Akiva Goldsman, is not adult, complex, or worthwhile, although it is indeed science fiction. The director is Alex Proyas, whose great *Dark City* (1998) was also about a hero trying to make sense of the deceptive natures of the beings around him.

The movie makes Spooner into another one of those movie cops who insult the powerful, race recklessly around town, get their badges pulled by their captains, solve the crime, and survive incredible physical adventures. In many of these exploits he is accompanied by Dr. Susan Calvin (Bridget Moynahan), whose job at U.S. Robotics is "to make the robots seem more human."

At this she is not very successful. The movie's robots are curiously uninvolving as individuals, and when seen by the hundreds or thousands look like shiny chromium ants. True, a robot need not have much of a personality, but there is one robot, named Sonny and voiced by Alan Tudyk, who is more advanced than the standard robot, more "human," and capable of questions like "What am I?"—a question many movie characters might profitably ask themselves.

If Sonny doesn't have real feelings, he comes as close to them as any of the humans in the movie. Both Spooner and Calvin are kept in motion so relentlessly that their human sides get overlooked, except for a touching story Spooner tells about how a little girl dies because a robot was too logical. Sonny doesn't seem as "human" as, say, Andrew, the robot played by Robin Williams in *Bicentennial Man* (1999), based on a robot story by Asimov and Robert Silverberg. But his voice has a certain poignancy, and suggests some of the chilly chumminess of HAL 9000.

I Am David

The plot I will not detail, except to note that you already know from the ads that the robots are up to no good, and Spooner could write a lot of tickets for Three Laws violations. The plot is simple-minded and disappointing, and the chase and action scenes are pretty much routine for movies in the sci-fi CGI genre. The robots never seem to have the heft and weight of actual metallic machines, and make boring villains.

Dr. Susan Calvin is one of those handy movie characters who know all the secrets, can get through all the doors, and can solve all the problems. She helps Spooner move almost at will through the Robotics skyscraper, which seems curiously ill-guarded. When they team up against the eventual villain, it's an obvious ploy to create yet another space where characters can fall for hundreds of feet and somehow save themselves.

As for the robots, they function like the giant insects in *Starship Troopers*, as video game targets. You can't even be mad at them, since they're only programs. Although, come to think of it, you *can* be mad at programs; Microsoft Word has inspired me to rage far beyond anything these robots engender. ☞

I Am David ★ ½
PG, 95 m., 2004

Ben Tibber (David), James Caviezel (Johannes), Joan Plowright (Sophie). Directed by Paul Feig and produced by Davina Belling, Lauren Levine, and Clive Parsons. Screenplay by Feig, based on a novel by Anne Holm.

I Am David tells the story of a twelve-year-old orphan boy who escapes from a Bulgarian forced labor camp and travels alone through Greece, Italy, and Switzerland to his eventual destiny in Denmark. He has awfully good luck: Along the way, he meets mostly nice people who do what they can to help him, and there's an enormous coincidence just when it's most needed. Benji encounters more hazards on his travels than this kid.

I know, I know, I'm supposed to get sentimental about this heartwarming tale. But I couldn't believe a moment of it, and never identified with little David, who is played by young Ben Tibber as if he was lectured to mind

his manners. In an era with one effective child performance after another, here is a bad one.

The premise: In the cold war, enemies of the Bulgarian state are sent to forced labor camps, where they break up rocks into gravel under the merciless prodding of sadistic guards. I am sure the movie explains how David became an enemy of the state at his tender age, but the detail escaped me; maybe he inherited his status from his dead parents. Certainly he's lucky in his choice of friends, starting with Johannes (James Caviezel), a fellow inmate who gives him encouragement and dreams before—well, see for yourself.

A mysterious voice on the sound track advises David to escape. He is supplied with a bar of soap, half a loaf of bread, a compass, and an envelope not to be opened until he gets to Denmark, or finds Carmen Sandiego, whichever comes first. Sorry about that. The power is conveniently turned off for thirty seconds on the camp's electrified fences so that David can run across an open field and begin his long odyssey.

How, you may wonder, will the lad communicate in the many lands he must traverse? "You've picked up many languages from the others in the camp," the voice reminds him, and indeed David apparently speaks Bulgarian, Greek, Italian, and English, all with a wee perfect British accent. He lucks into rides on trucks, gets over the border to Greece through an unlikely series of events, stows away on a ship for Italy with astonishing ease, and fetches up in an Italian bakery where, please, sir, may I have a loaf? When the baker calls the cops, the kid is able to escape, although not with any bread.

Then something happens that would seem far-fetched even in a silent melodrama. He comes upon a burning cabin, hears screams, breaks in, and rescues a young girl who is tied to a chair. This girl, as it happens, is the victim of a prank by her younger siblings, who didn't mean to set the fire. The girl's rich parents embrace the lad and feed him, but ask too many questions, so he moves on to Switzerland and happens into friendship with a grandmotherly painter (Joan Plowright), who brings his story to a happy ending through a spectacularly unlikely coincidence.

As it turns out, the papers in his envelope

309

could probably have been read by anyone in Greece or Italy and solved David's dilemma, and the advice to travel all the way to Denmark was not necessarily sound. But we forget that when we discover the secret of the mysterious voice that advised David—a secret I found distinctly underwhelming, although the movie makes much of it. The lesson, I guess, is that if you are a twelve-year-old orphan in a Bulgarian forced labor camp, you need not despair, because the world is filled with good luck and helpful people, and besides, you speak all those languages.

Note: In stark contrast to the fairy-tale events of I Am David, *the 2003 film* In This World, *by Michael Winterbottom, tells the story of a sixteen-year-old Afghan boy who journeys to London from a refugee camp in Pakistan. The film follows a real boy on a real journey, and includes scenes of documentary reality; it helps underline the unreal storytelling of* David.

I Capture the Castle ★ ★ ★ ½
R, 113 m., 2003

Romola Garai (Cassandra Mortmain), Rose Byrne (Rose Mortmain), Henry Thomas (Simon Cotton), Marc Blucas (Neil Cotton), Bill Nighy (James Mortmain), Tara Fitzgerald (Topaz Mortmain), Sinead Cusack (Mrs. Cotton), Henry Cavill (Stephen). Directed by Tim Fywell and produced by David Parfitt, Anant Singh, and David M. Thompson. Screenplay by Heidi Thomas, based on the novel by Dodie Smith.

I Capture the Castle is the kind of novel dreamy adolescents curl up with on rainy Saturdays, imagining themselves as members of a poor but brilliantly eccentric family living in a decrepit English castle. It's that kind of movie, too, about a sublimely impractical family given to sudden dramatic outbursts. It's a romance ever so much more inspiring for teenage girls than the materialist propaganda they get from Hollywood, teaching them to value genius above accessories. And there's a serious undercurrent; this story was close to the heart of the author Dodie Smith, whose other novel, *101 Dalmatians,* was more lighthearted and aimed at younger readers.

As the movie opens, the Mortmain family on a country outing finds a castle—small and run-down, it is true, but undeniably a castle—and the father, James, stands on the battlements and declares, "I will write masterpieces here!" He is given to such pronouncements, often followed by a sideways glance to see if anyone believes him. He did write one well-regarded book, it is true, but now he descends into a long barren period, and in 1936, when the story takes place, the Mortmains are behind on the rent, short on food money, and increasingly desperate.

The Mortmains are: James (Bill Nighy), the father, who seems to be going around the bend; his wife, Topaz (Tara Fitzgerald), a long-tressed artist; younger sister Cassandra (Romola Garai), who is the narrator; and the official family beauty, Rose (Rose Byrne), who is so impatient with poverty that at one point she runs out into the rain and announces she plans to sell herself on the streets and will borrow the train fare to the city from the vicar.

The girls' mother died some years earlier, and Topaz does her best with two ungrateful girls and a husband who seems on the edge of madness. Then one day all changes when two young Americans arrive in the district. They are Simon and Neil Cotton (Henry Thomas and Marc Blucas), the sons and heirs of the owner of the property, and rather than collect the back-due rent they proceed to fall in love with Rose—Simon obviously, Neil quietly. Their British mother (Sinead Cusack) is both appalled and amused by the family, and invites them over to dinner, an event that has to be seen to be believed.

"Why are you all dressed in green?" the brothers ask on their first meeting with this family. It has to do with a surfeit of dye and too much time on their hands. The family is educated, literate, creative, but alarmingly unworldly; what the brothers take for artful naïveté is artless lack of sophistication. Rose, however, knows that she will marry anyone to get out of the leaky, drafty castle, and that leads to a complicated romantic melodrama that also involves Cassandra's and Neil's secret feelings, not necessarily for each other.

The film is shot with that green British palette that makes everything look damp and makes us imagine the sheets will be clammy. The countryside is unspeakably picturesque, and the girls flourish here; it is sad to see the wild-haired Rose in town, after her engagement and after the hairdressers have styled her into a copy of everyone else. The father meanwhile sinks into despond, and the family finds a way to treat his writer's block that is heartless but effective.

The first-time director, Tim Fywell, handles his material with an excusable fondness for the eccentricities of his characters, but generates touching emotion through the plight of Cassandra, who is honest and true, and finds her way almost blindly through the labyrinth of love, trusting to her best instincts. Romola Garai, who was Kate in *Nicholas Nickleby,* is heartwinning in the role.

We like these people, which is important, and we are amused by them, which is helpful, but most of all we envy them, because they negotiate their romantic perplexities with such dash and style. It would be fun to be a member of the Mortmain family—maybe the younger brother, who shows every sign of growing up to be Harry Potter.

Note: The R rating ("for brief nudity") is another attempt by the MPAA to steer teenagers away from useful and sophisticated entertainments, and toward vulgarity and violence. If this movie is R and Charlie's Angels: Full Throttle *is PG-13, then the rating board has no shame. Better the Angels as strippers than an innocent nipple during a swim in the castle moat.*

Ice Princess ★ ★ ★
G, 92 m., 2005

Joan Cusack (Mrs. Carlyle), Kim Cattrall (Tina Harwood), Michelle Trachtenberg (Casey Carlyle), Hayden Panettiere (Gen Harwood), Kirsten Olson (Nikki), Jocelyn Lai (Tiffany), Juliana Cannarozzo (Zoe). Directed by Tim Fywell and produced by Bridget Johnson. Screenplay by Hadley Davis.

The computer doesn't make the jumps. You do.
—Casey to Gen

Yes, *Ice Princess* is a formula movie. Yes, it makes all the stops and hits all the beats and, yes, it ends exactly as we expect it will. It even has the inevitable scene where the gifted young heroine is in the middle of her performance and she looks up into the audience—and there she is! Her mother! Who disapproves of figure skating but came to the semifinals without telling her, and now nods and smiles like dozens of other parents in dozens of other movies, recognizing at last that their child has the real stuff.

Yes, yes, and yes. And yet the movie works. I started by clicking off the obligatory scenes, and then somehow the film started to get to me, and I was surprised how entertained I was. Like *Shall We Dance* or *Saturday Night Fever,* it escapes its genre. That's partly because the screenplay avoids the usual rigid division of good and evil and gives us characters who actually change during the movie. Partly because the acting is so convincing. And partly because the actresses in the movie really can skate—or seem to. Well, no wonder, since two of them are figure skaters, but the surprise is that Michelle Trachtenberg seems able to skate too. That didn't look like a double on the ice, although *Variety,* the showbiz bible, reports, "Four different skaters sub for Trachtenberg in the more difficult performances."

Trachtenberg plays Casey Carlyle, a brilliant high school science student, who hopes to win a Harvard scholarship with a physics project. Her teacher advises her to find an original subject, and she gets a brainstorm: What if she films figure skaters, analyzes their movements on her computer, and comes up with a set of physics equations describing what they do and suggesting how they might improve?

Casey has always been a science nerd. She's pretty but doesn't know it, and so shy "I can't talk to anyone I haven't known since kindergarten." She goes to the ice rink in her Connecticut town run by Tina Harwood (Kim Cattrall), herself an Olympic figure skating contender until a disqualification at Saravejo. Now Tina coaches her daughter, Gen (Hayden Panettiere), toward championship status.

Casey's computer program works. She breaks down the moves, analyzes the physics, and advises Gen and other skaters on what they can change to improve their performance. Along the way, a funny thing happens;

311

Casey has always enjoyed skating on the pond near her home, and now she grows fascinated by figure skating, and wants to start training.

This is horrifying news for her mom (Joan Cusack), a feminist and teacher who is pointing Casey toward Harvard and sniffs, "Figure skaters have no shelf life." Meanwhile, Gen confesses she envies Casey: "I hate to train all the time. I'd love to have a real life, like you." To her mom, Gen says, "I'm fed up with being a dunce in math class because I don't have time to do the homework."

The movie, written by Hadley Davis and directed by Tim Fywell, starts with a formula and then takes it to the next level. We have two obsessive stage mothers and two driven overachievers, and the girls want to trade places, to the despair of their moms (no dads are in sight, except for a proud Korean-American father). This leads to more substance than we're expecting, and more acting, too, since the central characters don't follow the well-worn routines supplied by the GCFDDPO formula (Gifted Child Follows Dream Despite Parental Opposition). They strike out with opinions and surprises of their own.

I am informed that every actress in the movie does all of her own skating, but the movie's publicity is coy on the point, apart from pointing out that actresses Kirsten Olson (Nikki) and Juliana Cannarozzo (Zoe) are figure skaters making their first movie. All I know, as I said above, is that they look as if they do. What's important is not whether all the actors do their own skating, but that they play figure skaters so convincingly, and also bring a realistic dimension into their lives as high school students. Gen's first scene seems to set her up as the popular blond snob who's a fixture in all high school movies, but no: She makes a friend of Casey, and together the girls help each other figure out what they really want to do.

At one point, when a skater makes a really nice move on the ice, someone sniffs that it's because of Casey's computer. That's when she says the computer doesn't make the jumps. *Ice Princess* starts out with something like a computer formula too. But the formula doesn't make the moves. You can take it to another level, and that's what *Ice Princess* does. This movie is just about perfect for teenagers, and it's a surprise that even their parents are allowed to have minds of their own. ☞

Identity ★ ★ ★
R, 90 m., 2003

John Cusack (Ed), Ray Liotta (Rhodes), Amanda Peet (Paris), Alfred Molina (Doctor), Clea DuVall (Ginny), Rebecca De Mornay (Caroline), John C. McGinley (George York), John Hawkes (Larry), William Lee Scott (Lou), Jake Busey (Robert Maine), Pruitt Taylor Vince (Man), Leila Kenzle (Alice York), Bret Loehr (Timothy York). Directed by James Mangold and produced by Cathy Konrad. Screenplay by Michael Cooney.

It is a dark and stormy night. A violent thunderstorm howls down on a lonely Nevada road. A family of three is stopped by a blowout. While the father tries to change the tire, his wife is struck by a passing limousine. Despite the protests of the limo's passenger, a spoiled movie star, the driver takes them all to a nearby motel. The roads are washed out in both directions. The phone lines are down. Others seek shelter in the motel, which is run by a weirdo clerk.

Altogether, there are ten guests. One by one, they die. Agatha Christie fans will assume that one of them is the murderer—or maybe it's the clerk. Meanwhile, the story intercuts an eleventh-hour hearing for a man (Pruitt Taylor Vince) convicted of several savage murders. A grumpy judge has been awakened for this appeal, and unless he overturns his own ruling, the man will die. His psychiatrist (Alfred Molina) comes to his defense.

We don't know yet how these two stories will intersect, although they eventually must, but meanwhile events at the motel take our attention. We know the formula is familiar, and yet the treatment owes more to horror movies than to the classic whodunit. The group gathered at the motel includes the limousine driver (John Cusack), who says he is a former cop and seems kind of competent. There's another cop (Ray Liotta), who is transporting a killer (Jake Busey) in leg irons. The driver with the blowout (John C. McGinley) tenderly cares for his gravely injured wife (Leila Kenzle) while his solemn little son (Bret Loehr) looks on.

Also at the rain-swept rendezvous are the movie star (Rebecca De Mornay) that Cusack was driving, a hooker (Amanda Peet) on her way out of Nevada, and a young couple (William Lee Scott and Clea DuVall) who recently got married, for reasons still in dispute. The motel manager (John Hawkes) finds them all rooms—numbered from 1 to 10, of course.

While lightning rips through the sky and the electricity flickers, gruesome events start to occur. I will not describe them in detail, of course, since you will want to be horrified on your own. Although many in the group fear a mad killer is in their midst, and the Busey character is a prime suspect, some of the deaths are so peculiar it is hard to explain them—or to know whether they are murders, or a case of being in the wrong place at the wrong time.

That there is an explanation goes without saying. That I must not hint at it also goes without saying. I think it is possible that some audience members, employing the Law of Economy of Characters, so usefully described in my *Bigger Little Movie Glossary,* might be able to arrive at the solution slightly before the movie does, but this isn't the kind of movie where all is revealed in a sensational final moment. The director, James Mangold, and the writer, Michael Cooney, play fair, sort of, and once you understand their thinking you can trace back through the movie and see that they never cheated, exactly, although they were happy enough to point to the wrong conclusions.

A movie like this is an acid test for actors. Can they keep their self-respect while jammed in a room while grisly murders take place, everybody is screaming and blaming one another, heads turn up without bodies, bodies disappear—and, of course, it is a dark and stormy night?

John Cusack does the best job of surviving. His character is a competent and responsible person, while all about him are losing their heads (sometimes literally) and blaming it on him. I also liked Amanda Peet's hooker, who suggests she's seen so much trouble that all of this is simply more of the same. And there is something to be said for the performance of John Hawkes as the motel manager, although I can't say what it is without revealing a secret (no, it's not the secret you think).

I've seen a lot of movies that are intriguing for the first two acts and then go on autopilot with a formula ending. *Identity* is a rarity, a movie that seems to be on autopilot for the first two acts and then reveals that it was not, with a third act that causes us to rethink everything that has gone before. Ingenious, how simple and yet how devious the solution is.

I Heart Huckabees ★ ★
R, 105 m., 2004

Jason Schwartzman (Albert Markovski), Dustin Hoffman (Bernard Jaffe), Isabelle Huppert (Caterine Vauban), Jude Law (Brad Stand), Lily Tomlin (Vivian Jaffe), Mark Wahlberg (Tommy Corn), Naomi Watts (Dawn Campbell). Directed by David O. Russell and produced by Russell, Gregory Goodman, and Scott Rudin. Screenplay by Russell and Jeff Baena.

I went to see *I Heart Huckabees* at the Toronto Film Festival. It was on the screen, and I was in my chair, and nothing was happening between us. There was clearly a movie being shown, but what was its purpose and why were the characters so inexplicable? To help myself focus, I found the pressure point that is said by the master Wudang Weng Shun Kuen to increase mental alertness. Then I dashed out for a cup of coffee. Then I fell into the yoga sutra of "yatha abhimata dhyanat va," literally clearing the mind by meditating on a single object until I become tranquil. I meditated on the theater exit door.

At festivals, the moment a movie is over everybody asks you what you thought about it. I said, "I didn't know what I thought." Then how did it make you feel? "It made me feel like seeing it again." You mean you liked it so much you want to see it twice? "No, I'm still working on seeing it the first time."

Now I have seen it twice. The movie is like an infernal machine that consumes all of the energy it generates, saving the last watt of power to turn itself off. It functions perfectly within its constraints, but it leaves the viewer out of the loop. This may be the first movie that can exist without an audience between the projector and the screen. It falls in its own forest, and hears itself. It's the kind of movie that would inspire a Charlie Kaufman screenplay about how it couldn't be made. The director and cowriter is David O. Russell, who made the brilliant *Three Kings* and the quirky *Flirting with Disaster*, and now . . . well, he has made this. God knows he's courageous.

I am about to commence a description. Not a plot description, as I am not sure it has a plot in a meaningful way, but an account of what transpires. Jason Schwartzman plays Albert, an environmentalist who wants to save nature, and begins by saving a large rock that is all that remains from a despoiled swamp (he reads a poem beginning, "You rock, Rock"). Albert makes a deal with Huckabees, a chain store, to underwrite his Open Space Coalition. Huckabees doesn't care about the environment, but cares deeply about seeming to care. Albert turns out to be a wild card for them, doing things like planting trees in the middle of parking lots to reclaim them for nature right then and there.

We meet Brad Stand (Jude Law), a Huckabees spokesman, and Dawn (Naomi Watts), a Huckabees spokesperson. They are in what in their limited way they interpret as love. Brad's plan is to use Albert as a cover for a scheme to turn virgin marshland into a shopping mall. Albert meanwhile constantly crosses paths with a towering African exchange student, and knows this must Mean Something, so he hires two Existential Detectives to sort it out for him. These are Bernard and Vivian Jaffe (Dustin Hoffman and Lily Tomlin).

Their method is to follow a client everywhere, taking notes on all that he does. "Even into the bathroom?" Yes, even into the bathroom. Bernard and Vivian now begin to be seen in the backgrounds of many shots, or outside the windows, or behind the door, or under the furniture, taking notes. They need to see everything in his life because they believe that everything is connected, and so to know everything is to know all the connections. Perhaps they are followers of E. M. Forster, who wrote "Only connect!" in the novel *A Passage to India*, which was about a cave where, no matter what words you said, the echo always sounded like "boum." Curiously enough, a lot of Bernard and Vivian's dialogue has the same effect.

Brad, the double-crossing executive, decides to undercut Albert by hiring the detectives to also follow him and Dawn around. Albert meanwhile meets a fireman named Tommy (Mark Wahlberg). Tommy is so eco-conscious that he refuses to ride the fire truck to fires, pedaling alongside on his bike. (He usually gets there first.) Tommy for reasons unclear to me knows about another Existential Detective named Caterine Vauban (Isabelle Huppert), who is from France. She is an old enemy of the Jaffes, and no wonder: French existentialists define themselves by being old enemies. Caterine has a peculiar sex scene in a mud puddle.

Everybody talks a lot, the Jaffes in particular. They do a kind of double act, finishing or repeating each other's sentences. They seem to believe quantum physics is somehow involved in their theories, and talk about how two objects can be in different places at the same time—no, hold on, that's the easy part. They talk about how the *same* object can be in two places at once.

Their discussions about this quantum phenomenon reminded me wonderfully of the explanations of the same topic in *What the #$*! Do We Know?* a "documentary" in which one of the "expert physicists" has been unmasked as a chiropractor, and the filmmakers are all followers of Ramtha, a 35,000-year-old spirit guide from Atlantis. Because nobody knows #$*! about quantum physics, this doc actually got respectful reviews from gullible critics like me, because it made about as much sense as most of what I've read on the subject.

Individual moments and lines and events in *I Heart Huckabees* are funny in and of themselves. Viewers may be mystified but will occasionally be amused. It took boundless optimism and energy for Russell to make the film, but it reminds me of the Buster Keaton short where he builds a boat but doesn't know how to get it out of the basement. The actors soldier away like the professionals they are, saying the words as if they mean something. Only Wahlberg is canny enough to play his role completely straight, as if he has no idea the movie might be funny. The others all seem to be trying to get in on the joke, which is a neat trick. I will award a shiny new dime to anyone who can figure out what the joke is.

I'll Sleep When I'm Dead ★ ★ ★ ½
R, 103 m., 2004

Malcolm McDowell (Boad), Jonathan Rhys-Meyers (Davey Graham), Clive Owen (Will Graham), Jamie Foreman (Mickser), Charlotte Rampling (Helen), Ken Stott (Turner). Directed by Mike Hodges and produced by Michael Corrente and Mike Kaplan. Screenplay by Trevor Preston.

Mike Hodges's gritty new *film noir*, *I'll Sleep When I'm Dead*, begins in enigma and snakes its way into stark clarity. At the beginning we don't even know who the characters are or why they matter to one another. For Hodges, this isn't a matter of keeping us in the dark, but follows simple logic: The characters know who they are and don't have to tell one another, and we are outsiders who will need to fit it together.

Some of the reviews have complained that *I'll Sleep When I'm Dead* is needlessly convoluted—that we're asked to spend too much time trying to identify the characters and become oriented within the plot. That assumes we want a simple story, simply told, and indeed many mainstream movies and TV shows treat audiences as simpletons. But there is a tangible pleasure in following enigmatic characters through the shadows of their lives; deprived for a time of a plot, given characters who are not clearly labeled and assigned moral categories, we're allowed to make judgments based on their manner and speech.

Hodges begins with parallel stories. In South London, an ingratiating charmer named Davey (Jonathan Rhys-Meyers) delivers drugs to parties, is popular on the circuit, picks up girls for a night, will steal anything not nailed down. Somewhere in a remote area, a man named Will (Clive Owen) lives alone in a van, is a manual laborer, finds a man who has been beaten, and helps him. In a third story, a car cruises through London with a hard man in the backseat, surrounded by hired muscle.

These stories will converge. Davey is dragged off the street and raped, he apparently kills himself, and when Will learns of this he returns to London. They are brothers. Whatever Will Graham did in the old days, whoever he was, there are a lot of people in South London who remember and fear him, even though he's been off the scene for years. In Clive Owen, Hodges has an actor who suggests the buried mystery and menace the role requires.

Hodges is a hard-boiled director who began with *Get Carter* (1971), with Michael Caine in one of his best performances, also as a gangster seeking vengeance for a dead brother. Hodges made a comeback in 1998 with *Croupier*, a sleeper hit starring Owen, who was not then widely known but was launched toward stardom by that film; you can currently see him in the title role of *King Arthur*, where he creates a harder, darker Arthur than the movies usually give us. In *I'll Sleep When I'm Dead*, he plays a familiar type, the retired killer forced to return to his old skills.

Will Graham still looms large in the memories of those he left behind when he chose to, or had to, disappear. He was a crime boss, we gather, and apparently he walked away from the life because he could no longer stomach it. Back on the scene but unrecognizable at first, because of his full beard and unshorn hair, he reconnects with his onetime lover Helen (Charlotte Rampling) and his former lieutenant Mickser (Jamie Foreman), who was Davey's friend. Word travels through the underworld that Will is back in London, and all sorts of people stir uneasily at the news.

The movie's main line involves Will's methodical investigation as he traces a series of contacts and witnesses back to the name of the man who raped his brother. At the same time, Hodges and Owen, working with a screenplay by Trevor Preston, suggest other dimensions of Will Graham's life. There is, for example, the nature of his relationship with Helen, who is not a typical gangster's girl but an independent woman, wise and sad. That Will loved her—that he still has feelings for her—suggests he's a more complicated and thoughtful person than his fearsome reputation suggests. Indeed, his whole present life—

315

his bare-bones lifestyle, his unkempt appearance—indicate a kind of self-chosen exile, as if he has not merely left the scene but is trying to purge himself of it.

More of the plot I must not reveal, although *film noir* exists more in detail, behavior, and mood than in what happens. But listen during a conversation Will has late in the film with a man named Boad, played by Malcolm McDowell in his most sneering and contemptuous mode, and you will sense all of the threads of the story coming together. "I wanted to show him what he was—nothing," says Boad. Then Will Graham shows Boad what he is, and gives him some time, not too much, to reflect upon it.

Imaginary Heroes ★ ★ ★

R, 112 m., 2005

Sigourney Weaver (Sandy Travis), Emile Hirsch (Tim Travis), Jeff Daniels (Ben Travis), Michelle Williams (Penny Travis), Kip Pardue (Matt Travis), Deirdre O'Connell (Marge Dwyer), Ryan Donowho (Kyle Dwyer), Suzanne Santo (Steph Connors). Directed by Dan Harris and produced by Ilana Diamant, Moshe Diamant, Frank Hubner, Art Linson, Gina Resnick, and Denise Shaw. Screenplay by Harris.

Imaginary Heroes gives us yet one more troubled suburban family, with suicide and drugs and a chill at the dinner table. But it gives us something else: a heroine with a buried but real sense of humor, and an ability to look at life from the outside instead of only through her own needs. That this person is the mother in the family, and that the father is cold and distant, goes without saying; fathers in the movies, as a group, supply only a few more heroes than Nazis. But the mother is worth having, and makes the movie work despite its overcrowded plot.

Her name is Sandy Travis, and she is played by Sigourney Weaver as someone whose teenage years were spent in the 1970s, which means that in a sense she will always be younger, or at least more unpredictable, than her children. When she makes it clear in early scenes how much she hates Marge, her neighbor, we feel a certain self-satire under the anger. When she talks to her son, Tim

(Emile Hirsch), she's the kind of adult kids need to talk to when they can't communicate with their parents. Unusual to find that in a parent.

The film is narrated by Tim, who tells us about his older brother, Matt (Kip Pardue). Matt is the best swimmer anyone has ever seen. He holds all the records and is headed for the Olympics. Then, only a minute or two into the film, he shoots himself in the head. Tim knows something about Matt that few people were allowed to find out: Matt hated swimming. Mostly he hated it because of the way he was driven by his father, Ben (Jeff Daniels), a cold perfectionist who made Matt's life a daily final exam.

That's all prologue. *Imaginary Heroes* starts with the family trying to recover emotionally. Ben insists that a plate be served for Matt at every meal, on the table in front of his empty chair. "That creeps me out," says Penny (Michelle Williams), the older sister home from college. Sandy says: "I won't be making all this food for every meal. It's a waste." That's what she does, speaking her mind in front of the family, coming across as the one who may not be beloved but at least sees clearly.

Tim is going through unsettled times at school. He is smaller than Matt was, has no athletic gifts, looks young for his age, is assumed at the funeral to be headed for high school when in fact he is already a senior. He seems to have no communication with his father, who takes a leave of absence at work and drifts off into shapeless days of sad park benches.

But Sandy sees him and senses his needs, and talks with him. They have one extraordinary conversation on the front porch swing in which she observes that they may be the only mother and son in town who can talk openly about masturbation. She tells Tim: "You may never know how really good I am for you until I die. I never loved my parents until they died."

Tim, who looks uncannily like Leonardo DiCaprio's younger brother, is dating a girl at school named Steph. She thinks they may be ready for sex.

"Steph told me she loves me," he tells his mother.

"Well, do you love her?" she asks.

"I don't know."

"Then you don't."

The relationship between Sandy and her son is the heart of the movie, and works, and Sandy's character on her own is an unfolding fascination. Who else could get busted for pot quite the way she does? And who else would say to her would-be drug dealer, "Your parents should be ashamed of you." It was a wise decision for Dan Harris, the writer-director, to avoid getting bogged down in the legal aftermath of the arrest; the point, for the story the movie wants to tell, is that she felt an urgent need to get high, and behaved more like a kid than like a prudent adult.

Dan Harris is a kid himself, only twenty-two when he sent this screenplay to Bryan Singer, director of *X-Men* and (more to the point) *Apt Pupil* and *The Usual Suspects.* Singer liked it, hired Harris to work on the screenplay for *X-2*, and then the new *Superman* movie Singer is directing, and after that *Logan's Run.* Then Harris came back at twenty-four to direct his own screenplay.

I can see what Singer saw in it: a sensitivity to characters, an instinct for the revealing, unpredictable gesture, and good dialogue. I think I see a little too much more besides. The film might have been stronger as simply the story of the family trying to heal itself after its tragedy, with the focus on Sandy and Tim. But Harris feels a need to explain everything in terms of melodramatic revelations and surprise developments, right up until the closing scenes. The emotional power of the last act is weakened by the flood of new information. The key revelation right at the end explains a lot, yes, but it comes so late that all it can do is explain. If it had come earlier, it would have had to be dealt with, and those scenes might have been considerable.

I haven't gone into detail about Marge (Deirdre O'Connell), the neighbor, or her son, Kyle Dwyer (Ryan Donowho), who is Tim's best friend. Marge never really worked for me except as a plot convenience, and Tim's friendship with Kyle, while it produces some risky and effective scenes, is best left for you to discover. What remains when the movie is over is the memory of Sandy and Tim talking, and of a mother who loves her son, understands him, and understands herself in a wry

but realistic way. The characters deserve a better movie, but they get a pretty good one.

I'm Not Scared ★ ★ ★ ½
R, 108 m., 2004

Guiseppe Cristiano (Michele), Aitana Sanchez-Gijon (Anna), Dino Abbrescia (Pino), Diego Abatantuono (Sergio), Giorgio Careccia (Felice), Mattia Di Pierro (Filippo). Directed by Gabriele Salvatores and produced by Marco Chimenz, Giovanni Stabilini, Maurizio Totti, and Riccardo Tozzi. Screenplay by Niccolo Ammaniti (based on his novel) and Francesca Marciano.

Michele is a ten-year-old boy whose summer is unfolding as one perfect day after another. He lives in a rural district in southern Italy, and spends his days exploring the countryside with his friends. One day they go poking about an old abandoned house, and later he returns alone to look for his sister's lost glasses. In the yard he finds a slab of sheet metal, and when he lifts it up he sees, at the bottom of a pit, a leg sticking out from under a blanket.

Michele (Guiseppe Cristiano) lets the covering slam down and races for home. He doesn't tell anyone what he has seen. Returning again, he discovers that the pit holds a small boy named Filippo (Mattia Di Pierro), who is chained. On the television news Michele will learn that Filippo has been kidnapped.

I'm Not Scared tells its story mostly through Michele's eyes. He is just at that age when he has glimmers of understanding about adult life, but still lives within the strange logic of childhood. A year or two older, and he might have known to call the police. But no. Filippo becomes his secret, and he visits him frequently, bringing him bread to eat. It is almost as if he takes pride of possession.

We learn that Michele's father, Pino (Dino Abbrescia), is involved in the kidnapping, along with a friend named Sergio (Diego Abatantuono). Sergio has recently returned from Brazil, is clearly a criminal, is capable of violence. But Michele comes to understand this only gradually. His father is a figure of awe to him, a truck driver whose visits home are great occasions for Michele, his sister, and his mother, Anna (Aitana Sanchez-Gijon). The father is tall and strong and enveloped in a cloud of cigarette smoke, and his conversations with Sergio contain hints of menace.

This story unfolds surrounded by an almost improbable pastoral beauty. The children race their bicycles down country lanes, explore caves and ravines, roll down hillsides through boundless fields of golden wheat. Life at the farmhouse centers around dinners and much conversation, and later, when the children are asleep, the drinking and the talk continue. Michele pieces the clues together and understands that Filippo has been kidnapped by his father and Sergio, and when a police helicopter is seen in the neighborhood, he understands enough to realize that Filippo could be murdered—unless he saves him.

The film has been directed by Gabriele Salvatores, whose *Mediterraneo* won an Oscar for Best Foreign Film in 1992. The screenplay is by Niccolo Ammaniti and Francesca Marciano, based on Ammaniti's novel. The plot is essentially a thriller, but the film surrounds those elements with details of everyday life, with ambiguities and mysteries seen through a child's eyes, and a puzzle about the nature of the agreement between Pino and Sergio. Certainly the family is poor, and at one crucial moment, his mother asks Michele to promise, when he grows up, to "get away from here." The ransom money represents a hope for a new beginning.

Salvatores is not in a hurry to get to the climax. He allows summer days to follow one upon another, as Michele's secret grows in the boy's mind. There are details that enrich the portrait, as when he longs for a blue toy truck that belongs to a friend, and strikes a bargain to get it. We are acutely conscious of Filippo, chained in the hole, but for Michele, there are other things to think about, and the urgency of the situation only gradually grows upon him.

The film reminds us that, in childhood, days and weeks seemed to last forever. Summer was not a season but a lifetime. Parents represented a law that stood above our own best thinking, because they had demonstrated time and again that they knew best, that we were only children. The coming-of-age experience, which *I'm Not Scared* incorporates, involves that moment or season when we realize that we can see outside

the box of childhood, that it is time to trust our own decisions.

Hollywood movies give us children who are miniature adults, secret agents like Cody Banks and the Spy Kids, who control technology and save the world. *I'm Not Scared* is a reminder of true childhood, of its fears and speculations, of the way a conversation can be overheard but not understood, of the way that the shape of the adult world forms slowly through the mist.

In America ★ ★ ★ ★
PG-13, 103 m., 2003

Paddy Considine (Johnny), Samantha Morton (Sarah), Sarah Bolger (Christy), Emma Bolger (Ariel), Djimon Hounsou (Mateo). Directed by Jim Sheridan and produced by Arthur Lappin and Jim Sheridan. Screenplay by Jim Sheridan, Naomi Sheridan, and Kirsten Sheridan.

In America has a moment when everything shifts, when two characters face each other in anger and there is an unexpected insight into the nature of their relationship. It is a moment sudden and true; we realize how sluggish many movies are in making their points, and how quickly life can blindside us.

The moment takes place between Johnny (Paddy Considine), the father of an Irish immigrant family recently arrived in New York, and Mateo (Djimon Hounsou), the angry Nigerian painter who lives below them in a shabby tenement. Mateo is known as "the man who screams" because his anguish sometimes echoes up the stairs. But when Johnny's young daughters knock on his door for trick-or-treating, he is unexpectedly gentle with them. Johnny's wife, Sarah (Samantha Morton), invites Mateo to dinner, he becomes friendly with the family during a time when Paddy is feeling hard-pressed and inadequate, and slowly Paddy begins to suspect that romantic feelings are developing between his wife and the man downstairs.

All of that grows slowly in the movie, in the midst of other events, some funny, some sad, all rich with life. It is a suspicion rustling beneath the surface, in Paddy's mind and ours. Finally Paddy confronts Mateo: "Do you want to be in my place?"

"I might," says Mateo.

"Do you love my wife?"

"I love your wife. And I love you. And I love your children," Mateo says, barking the words ferociously.

There is a silence, during which Paddy's understanding of the situation changes entirely. I will not reveal what he believes he has discovered (it may not be what you are thinking). The rest of the film will be guided by that moment, and what impressed me was the way the dialogue uses the techniques of short fiction to trigger the emotional shift. This is not a "surprise" in the sense of a plot twist, but a different way of seeing—it's the kind of shift you find in the sudden insight of the young husband at the end of Joyce's *The Dead*. It's not about plot at all. It's about how you look at someone and realize you have never really known them.

The screenplay is by Jim Sheridan, the director, and his daughters Naomi and Kirsten. It is dedicated "to Frankie," and in the movie the family has two young daughters, and there was a son named Frankie who died of a brain tumor after a fall down the stairs. *In America* is not literally autobiographical (the real Frankie was Sheridan's brother, who died at ten), but it is intensely personal. It's not the typical story of turn-of-the-century immigrants facing prejudice and struggle, but a modern story, set in the 1980s and involving new sets of problems, such as racism and drug addiction in the building and the neighborhood.

It is also about the way poverty humiliates those who have always prided themselves on being able to cope. It is a very hot summer in New York, the apartment is sweltering, and there is a sequence involving the purchase of a cheap air conditioner that is handled perfectly: We see a father trying to provide for his family and finding shame, in his own eyes, because he does not do as well as he wants to.

The film is also about the stupid things we do because we are human and flawed. Consider the scene at the street carnival, where Johnny gets involved in a "game of skill"—throwing balls at a target, hoping to win a prize for his daughters. The film knows exactly how we try to dig ourselves out, and only dig ourselves deeper.

The mother is played by Samantha Morton, who in film after film (as the mute in *Sweet and Lowdown* and one of the psychics in *Minority Report*) reveals the power of her silences, her quiet, her presence. The two young girls are played by real sisters, Sarah and Emma Bolger, who are sounding boards and unforgiving judges as the family's troubles grow. "Don't 'little girl' me," Sarah says. "I've been carrying this family on my back for over a year."

Paddy Considine is new to me; I saw him in *24 Hour Party People*, I guess, but here he makes an impression: He plays Johnny as determined, insecure, easily wounded, a man who wants to be an actor but fears his spirit has been broken by the death of his son. Djimon Hounsou, given his first big role by Steven Spielberg in *Amistad*, often plays strong and uncomplicated types (as in *Gladiator*). Here, as an artist despairing for his art and his future, he reveals true and deep gifts.

From Ireland and Nigeria, from China, the Philippines, Poland, India, Mexico, and Vietnam, we get the best and the brightest. I am astonished by the will and faith of the recent immigrants I meet. Think what it takes to leave home, family, and even language, to try for a better life in another country. *In America* is not unsentimental about its new arrivals (the movie has a warm heart and frankly wants to move us), but it is perceptive about the countless ways in which it is hard to be poor and a stranger in a new land.

Incident at Loch Ness ★ ★ ★
PG-13, 94 m., 2004

Playing themselves, more or less: Werner Herzog, Zak Penn, Kitana Baker, Gabriel Beristain, Michael Karnow, Robert O'Meara, John Bailey, and David A. Davidson. Directed by Zak Penn and produced by Werner Herzog and Penn. Screenplay by Penn.

The story goes like this. Werner Herzog, the holy genius of the German New Wave, decides to make a documentary about the Loch Ness Monster. At the same time, a documentary is being made about Herzog by John Bailey, the famous cinematographer. Bailey and his crew follow Herzog and his crew to Loch Ness, where Herzog's producer turns out to be a jerk who hires his girlfriend as the "sonar expert" and expects everyone to wear official matching jumpsuits "so it will look like a real expedition." On the suits, he spells it "expediition."

Herzog realizes he is in the hands of a charlatan. The "sonar expert" (Kitana Baker) explains that her professional experience includes modeling for *Playboy* and appearing in the Miller Lite cat-fight commercials. The producer (Zak Penn) also springs a "cryptozoologist" on Herzog, and we learn that cryptozoology is "the study of undiscovered animals." The crypto guy produces a test tube containing a "mysterious" tentacle of which it can be said that it is definitely small. The sonar expert appears in an American flag bikini. Herzog is enraged that the producer has hired these people; the director should make such decisions.

They are all meanwhile on a boat named the *Discovery IV;* the producer liked the sound of that, despite the fact that there was no Discovery I, II, or III. The captain, a grizzled old sea dog (or loch dog) named David A. Davidson, mutters darkly about it being bad luck to change the name of a boat. A miniature fake Loch Ness monster is produced, and Herzog, asked to photograph it, says it is "stupid" and tells Bailey's doc camera: "I became aware that there was something seriously wrong." But then something attacks the boat, a crew member is eaten, the producer makes off in the only lifeboat, the sonar expert reveals, "I did study up a little," and tries to summon help on the radio, and Herzog dons a wet suit and announces plans to swim to shore for help.

This material falls somewhere between *This Is Spinal Tap* and *Burden of Dreams,* Les Blank's (real) documentary about the filming of Herzog's *Fitzcarraldo,* a movie shot deep in the Amazon jungles. There is even a moment when the producer pulls a gun on Herzog, echoing the story (inaccurate, Herzog says) that Herzog forced Klaus Kinski to act at gunpoint.

Is the film what it claims to be, or is it a contrivance from beginning to end? It must be said that Herzog himself is always completely convincing, and everything he says and does seems authentic. But was he really going to make a documentary? Or is that merely the pretext for this film? Or is this film what emerged from the collision of Herzog's failed film and Bailey's documentary? Is there a point at which reality becomes fiction and everybody redefines what they are really doing?

It's intriguing to puzzle out such questions, while looking like a hawk for shots that betray themselves. There's one where two characters go upstairs to have a secret conference, and Bailey's camera sneaks up after them, and peeks through an open bedroom door and sees a crucial chart reflected in a mirror, and you know this shot didn't just happen; it was a setup.

On the other hand, an opening scene at Herzog's home in Los Angeles seems manifestly real, as Herzog and his wife, Lena, throw a dinner party for the crew of the film and some friends, including Jeff Goldblum and the magician Ricky Jay. It's at this party that the producer wants to discuss the "lighting package" that the cinematographer, Gabriel Beristain, will be using, and Herzog declares that a documentary needs no lights. Beristain is a real figure, who photographed *K2* and *S.W.A.T.,* and indeed everyone we see is who they say they are (in one way or another). Zak Penn, for example, is a writer of *Last Action Hero.*

Rather than say exactly what I think about the veracity of *Incident at Loch Ness,* let me tell you a story. A few years ago at the Telluride Film Festival, Herzog invited me to his hotel room to see videos of two of his new documentaries. One was about the Jesus figures of Russia, men who dress, act, and speak like Jesus and walk through the land being supported by their disciples. The other was about a town whose citizens believe that a city of angels exists on the bottom of a deep lake and can be seen through the ice at the beginning of winter. Wait too long, and the ice is too thick to see through. Crawl onto the ice too soon, and you fall in.

Herzog has made many great documentaries in his career, and I was enthralled by both of these. He's a master of the cinema, with an instinct for the bizarre and unexpected. After I saw the films, he said he only had one more thing to tell me: Both of the documentaries were complete fiction.

To what degree *Incident at Loch Ness* is truthful is something you will have to decide. Indeed, that's part of the fun, since some scenes are either clearly real, or exactly the same as if they were. Watching the movie is an entertaining exercise in forensic viewing, and the insidious thing is, even if it is a con, who is the conner and who is the connee?

Note: The Website www.truthaboutlochness. com supplies a lot of information, speculation, and gossip about the film, not all of it necessarily trustworthy.

The Incredibles ★ ★ ★ ½
PG, 115 m., 2004

With the voices of: Craig T. Nelson (Bob Parr/Mr. Incredible), Holly Hunter (Helen Parr/Elastigirl), Samuel L. Jackson (Lucius Best/Frozone), Jason Lee (Buddy Pine/Syndrome), Sarah Vowell (Violet Parr), Elizabeth Pena (Mirage), Spencer Fox (Dashiell Parr), Eli Fucile (Jack Jack), Brad Bird (Edna "E" Mode). Directed by Brad Bird and produced by John Walker. Screenplay by Bird.

The Pixar Studio, which cannot seem to take a wrong step, steps right again with *The Incredibles,* a superhero spoof that alternates breakneck action with satire of suburban sitcom life. After the *Toy Story* movies, *A Bug's Life, Monsters, Inc.,* and *Finding Nemo,* here's another example of Pixar's mastery of popular animation. If it's not quite as magical as *Nemo,* how many movies are? That may be because it's about human beings who have some connection, however tenuous, with reality; it loses the fantastical freedom of the fish fable.

The story follows the universal fondness for finding the chinks in superhero armor; if Superman hadn't had kryptonite, he would have been perfect and therefore boring, and all the superheroes since him have spent most of their time compensating for weaknesses. Think about it: Every story begins with a superhero who is invincible, but who soon faces total defeat.

Mr. Incredible, the hero of *The Incredibles,* is a superhero in the traditional 1950s mold, dashing about town fighting crime and saving the lives of endangered civilians. Alas, the populace is not unanimously grateful, and he's faced with so many lawsuits for unlawful rescue and inadvertent side effects that he's forced to retire. Under the government's Superhero Relocation Program, Mr. Incredible (voice by Craig T. Nelson) moves to the suburbs, joined by his wife, Elastigirl (Holly Hunter), and their children, Violet (Sarah Vowell), Dashiell (Spencer Fox), and little Jack Jack (Eli Fucile).

They are now officially the Parr family, Bob and Helen. Bob works at an insurance agency, where his muscle-bound supertorso barely squeezes into a cubicle. Helen raises the kids, and there's a lot of raising to do: The world is occasionally too much for the teenager Violet, whose superpowers allow her to turn invisible and create force fields out of (I think) impregnable bubbles. Dashiell, called "Dash," can run at the speed of light, but has to slow down considerably in school track meets (if they can't see you running around the track, they assume you never left the finish line, instead of that you're back to it already). Jack Jack's powers are still limited, not yet encompassing the uses of the potty.

Bob Parr hates the insurance business. Joining him in the suburb is another relocated superhero, Frozone (Samuel L. Jackson), who can freeze stuff. Claiming they belong to a bowling league, they sneak out nights to remember the good old days and do a little low-profile superheroing. Then the old life beckons, in the form of a challenge from Mirage (Elizabeth Pena), who lures Mr. Incredible to a Pacific island where, overweight and slowed down, he battles a robot named Omnidroid 7.

This robot, we learn, is one of a race of fearsome new machines created by the evil mastermind Syndrome (Jason Lee), who once admired Mr. Incredible as a kid but became bitter when Incredible refused to let him become his boy wonder. He now wants to set up as a superpower by unleashing his robots on an unsuspecting world. That sets up the final climactic conclusion, which ranges from near-apocalyptic on the one hand to slapstick on the other (Elastigirl, whose body can stretch almost to infinity, gets trapped in two doors at once).

On the surface, *The Incredibles* is a goof on superhero comics. Underneath, it's a critique of modern American uniformity. Mr. Incredible is forced to retire not because of age or obsolescence, but because of trial lawyers seeking damages for his unsolicited good deeds; he's in the same position as the Boy Scout who helps the little old lady across the street when she doesn't want to go. What his society needs is not superdeeds but tort reform. "They keep finding new ways," he sighs, "to celebrate mediocrity."

Anyone who has seen a Bond movie will make the connection between Syndrome's island hideout and the headquarters of various Bond villains. *The Incredibles* also has a character inspired by Q, Bond's gadget-master. This is Edna Mode, known as "E" and voiced by Brad Bird, who also wrote and directed. She's a horn-rimmed little genius who delivers a hilarious lecture on the reasons why Mr. Incredible does not want a cape on his new uniform; capes can be as treacherous as Isadora Duncan's scarf, and if you don't know what happened to Isadora Duncan, Google the poor woman and shed a tear.

Brad Bird's previous film was *The Iron Giant* (1999), about a misunderstood robot from outer space and the little boy who becomes his friend. It had a charm and delicacy that was unique in the genre, and *The Incredibles*, too, has special qualities, especially in the subtle ways it observes its gifted characters trying to dumb down and join the crowd. Kids in the audience will likely miss that level, but will like the exuberance of characters like Dash. Grown-ups are likely to be surprised by how smart the movie is, and how sneakily perceptive.

Infernal Affairs ★ ★ ★
R, 100 m., 2004

Tony Leung (Chan Wing-yan), Andy Lau (Inspector Lau Kin-ming), Anthony Wong (Superintendant Wong), Eric Tsang (Hon Sam). Directed by Alan Mak and Andrew Lau and produced by Lau. Screenplay by Mak and Felix Chong.

Infernal Affairs is about a cop who is actually a gangster, and a gangster who is actually a cop. Early scenes show them being put into deep cover: A young gangster is assigned by a crime boss to enter the police academy, and a young academy graduate is spun off from the force and assigned to undercover work as a criminal. In each case, the strategy is to leave them in place for years, doing their jobs as well as possible, so they can rise in the ranks and become invaluable as moles.

This idea, made into the most successful Hong Kong production of recent years, is such a good one that a Hollywood remake is planned, perhaps by Martin Scorsese. What makes it so intriguing is that as the story grows more tangled, the lives of the two characters take on a hidden desperation. Both of them have spent so long pretending to be someone else that their performances have become the reality.

Andy Lau plays Lau, the young mobster who is assigned by his triad boss (Eric Tsang) to infiltrate the police force. He becomes a good cop, skilled at his job, smooth at departmental politics, cool as a cucumber.

Tony Leung, who won as best actor at Cannes for *In the Mood for Love*, plays Chan, the young police recruit who is assigned to infiltrate the mob. At first only two members of the force know his true identity, and eventually there is only one: Police Superintendent Wong (Anthony Wong), to whom he turns with increasing desperation. He is tired of being a criminal, the work is depressing, he is the only person besides Wong who knows he's not a bad guy, and he wants to come in out of the cold.

These two characters come into full play ten years after the opening scenes, when both of them are brought in by their original employers, and both sides realize they have a traitor in their ranks. In a kind of symmetry that is unlikely and yet poetically appropriate, each one is assigned to find the mole—to find himself, that is.

There's another level of irony since Lau and Chan actually graduated in the same academy class, and knew each other if only by sight; Chan has no way of knowing Lau is a sleeper for the mob, but Lau knew at the time that Chan was a cop, and possibly knew he disappeared to go undercover. The two meet by chance years later in a stereo store, but don't recognize each other—a possibility easier for us to accept because they were played by other actors as younger men.

It's a long, tense buildup, with Lau prospering professionally while Chan begs with Wong to leave undercover work. Wong refuses; the department has invested years in putting him into place. Eventually, in a sustained virtuoso sequence, the two moles are in play at once, aware of each other's existence but not identity, and the plot ingeniously plays them against each other.

A lot of the action here has to do with cell phone strategy, brought to a level of complexity that would impress a logician. Each character is on the edge of discovering who the other is, and of being discovered himself, as a long-prepared police sting comes down on a long-planned criminal operation.

But this plot, clever and complex, is not the reason to see the movie. What makes it special is the inner turmoil caused by living a lie. If everyone you know and everything you do for ten years indicates you are one kind of person, and you know you are another, how do you live with that?

The movie pays off in a kind of emotional complexity rarely seen in crime movies. I cannot reveal what happens, but will urge you to consider the thoughts of two men who finally confront their own real identities—in the person of the other character. The crook has been the good cop. The cop has been the good crook. It's as if they have impersonated each other. All very lonely, ironic, and sad, and without satisfaction—especially if your superiors, the people you did it for, do not or cannot appreciate it. You might as well just forge ahead undercover for the rest of your life, a mole forever unawakened, and let the false life become the one you have lived.

In Good Company ★ ★ ★
PG-13, 131 m., 2005

Dennis Quaid (Dan Foreman), Topher Grace (Carter Duryea), Scarlett Johansson (Alex Foreman), Marg Helgenberger (Ann Foreman), David Paymer (Morty), Philip Baker Hall (Eugene Kalb). Directed by Paul Weitz and produced by Chris Weitz and Paul Weitz. Screenplay by Paul Weitz.

Corporations have replaced Nazis as the politically correct villains of the age—and just in time, because it was getting increasingly difficult to produce Nazis who survived into the twenty-first century (*Hellboy* had to use a portal in time). *The Manchurian Candidate* used a corporation instead of the Chinese Communists, and thrillers like *Resident Evil* give us corporations whose recklessness turn the population into zombies. *In Good Company* is a rare species: a feel-good movie about big business. It's about a corporate culture that tries to be evil and fails.

It doesn't start out that way. We meet Dan Foreman (Dennis Quaid), head of advertising sales at a sports magazine, who has the corner office and the big salary and is close to landing a big account from a dubious client (Philip Baker Hall). Then disaster strikes. The magazine is purchased by Teddy K (an unbilled Malcolm McDowell), a media conglomerator in the Murdoch mode, who takes sudden notice of a twenty-six-year-old hotshot named Carter Duryea (Topher Grace) and sends him in to replace Dan. Carter takes Dan's job and corner office, but instinctively keeps Dan as his "assistant," perhaps sensing that someone in the department will have to know more than Carter knows.

Dan accepts the demotion. He needs his job to keep up the mortgage payments and support his family. But Carter, known as a "ninja assassin" for his firing practices, fires Morty (David Paymer), an old-timer at the magazine. As we learn more about Morty's home life, we realize this only confirms the suspicions of his wife, who thinks he's a loser.

Developments up to this point have followed the template of standard corporate ruthlessness, with lives made redundant by corporate theories that are essentially management versions of a pyramid scheme: Plundering victims and looting assets can be made to look, on the books, like growth.

Dan has a wife named Ann (Marg Helgenberger) and a pretty college-age daughter named Alex (Scarlett Johansson). He is concerned about Alex, especially after finding a pregnancy-testing kit in the garbage, but doesn't know how concerned he should be until he discovers that Carter, the rat, has not only demoted him but is dating his daughter.

In Good Company so far has been the usual corporate slasher movie, in which good people have bad things happen to them because of the evil and greedy system. Then it takes a curious turn, which I will suggest without describing, in which goodness prevails and unexpected humility surfaces. The movie was directed by Paul Weitz, who with his brother Chris made *American Pie* and the Hugh Grant charmer *About a Boy*, and with those upbeat works behind him I didn't expect *In Good Company* to attain the savagery of Neil LaBute's *In the Company of Men*, but I was surprised all the same when the sun came out.

Dennis Quaid has a comfort level in roles like this that makes him effortlessly convincing; as he tries to land the account from the big client, we see how Dan uses psychology and his own personality to sell the magazine. Young Carter is years away from that ease. Topher Grace plays him as a kid who doesn't know which Christmas present he wants to play with first; he has achieved success more quickly than the experience to deal with it. Like a pro sports rookie, he can think of no more imaginative way to celebrate his wealth than to buy a new Porsche; he finds that such joys do not last forever.

Scarlett Johansson continues to employ the gravitational pull of quiet fascination. As in *Lost in Translation* and *Girl with a Pearl Earring* (both much better films), she creates a zone of her own importance into which men are drawn not so much by lust as by the feeling that she knows something about life that they might be able to learn. That turns the Alex-Carter affair into something more interesting than the sub-*American Pie* adventure we might have expected.

David Paymer's character provides the movie with emotional ballast; he is not only out of work, but probably unemployable, at his age and salary level, and unsuited to survive at a lower level. His story is common enough. It is a corporate strategy to create narratives for employees to imagine, in which they begin as junior executives and ascend to the boardroom. Countless college graduates enter this dream world every year, without reflecting (a) that there are many fewer positions at the top than at the bottom, and (b) that therefore, if the corporations are still hiring at the bottom, it is because there are fatalities at the top. You can always get someone younger and cheaper to do the job of the older and more experienced.

There's one scene in the movie that works well even though it's less than convincing. The conglomerator Teddy K jets in for a meeting with the staff, at which he recites various corporate platitudes to an adoring audience (one of the keys to success in business is the ability to endure the gaseous inanities of Management-Speak as if they meant anything). Then Dan stands up and, with everything to lose, explains clearly and mercilessly just why Teddy K is full of it. Whenever anyone speaks the plain truth on such an occasion, there is a palpable shock; how can such enterprises survive realism? Consider the soldier who asked Donald Rumsfeld, please, sir, may we have some more armor?

I don't believe the real Dan would have made quite that speech, but then I don't believe the third act of *In Good Company*. I'd like to, but I just can't. I don't think corporate struggles turn out that way. Still, the movie is smart enough, the performances strong, and the subplots involving Johansson and Paymer have their moments. If nothing else, *In Good Company* shows that Paul Weitz has the stuff to tell a ruthless story—and he does, until he loses his nerve. Since most audiences no doubt will prefer his version to the one I imagine, who is to say he is wrong?

The In-Laws ★ ★
PG-13, 98 m., 2003

Michael Douglas (Steve Tobias), Albert Brooks (Jerry Peyser), Robin Tunney (Angela Harris), Ryan Reynolds (Mark Tobias), Candice Bergen (Judy), David Suchet (Jean-Pierre Thibodoux), Lindsay Sloane (Melissa Peyser), Maria Ricossa (Katherine Peyser). Directed by Andrew Fleming and produced by Bill Gerber, Elie Samaha, Joel Simon, and Bill Todman Jr. Screenplay by Nat Mauldin and Ed Solomon, based on a screenplay by Andrew Bergman.

The In-Laws is an accomplished but not inspired remake of a 1979 comedy that was inspired and so did not need to be accomplished. The earlier movie was slapdash and at times seemed to be making itself up as it went along, but it had big laughs and a kind of lunacy. The remake knows the moves but lacks the recklessness.

Both movies begin with the preparations for a wedding. The father of the bride is a dentist in 1979, a podiatrist this time. The father of the groom is a secret agent, deeply involved in dubious international schemes. The spy takes the doctor along on a dangerous mission, and they encounter a loony foreign leader who cheerfully proposes to kill them.

Now consider the casting: Peter Falk and Alan Arkin in the earlier film, versus Michael Douglas and Albert Brooks this time. Splendid choices, you would agree, and yet the chemistry is better in the earlier film. Falk goes into his deadpan lecturer mode, slowly and patiently explaining things that sound like utter nonsense. Arkin develops good reasons for suspecting he is in the hands of a madman.

Michael Douglas makes his character more reassuring and insouciant, as if he's inviting his new in-law along on a lark, and that's not as funny because he seems to be trying to make it fun, instead of trying to conceal the truth of a deadly situation. Albert Brooks is portrayed as neurotic and fearful by nature, and so his reactions are not so much inspired by the pickle he's in as by the way he always reacts to everything.

These are small adjustments in the natures of the two characters, but crucial to the success of the films. Comedy works better when the characters seem utterly unaware that they are being funny. And something else is missing, too: the unexpected craziness of the foreign leader, who in the 1979 film brought the movie almost to a halt (I wrote that I laughed so hard, I laughed at myself laughing). The new film plows much more familiar comic terrain.

Richard Libertini was the South American dictator in the earlier film, a sublime nutcase who had an intimate relationship with a sock puppet he addresses as Señor Wences. His two North American visitors desperately try to play along with the gag, without being sure whether the guy really believes the sock puppet is alive or is only testing them.

In the new version, the foreign madman is an international arms dealer named Thibodoux. He's played by David Suchet with sublime comic timing, and is very funny in a scene where he explains that he was once ruthless, but after studying under Depak Chopra has become more gentle, and now allows his victims a running start before shooting at them. All very well, but where is the sock puppet? Why remake a movie and leave out its funniest element—a

sequence so funny, it's all a lot of people can remember about the movie? My guess is that David Suchet could have risen to the occasion with a masterful sock puppet performance.

There are moments when the movie seems perverse in the way it avoids laughs. Consider a scene where Douglas is at the controls of a private jet and Brooks is terrified not simply because he hates flying, but also because they are flying so low—"to come in under the radar," Douglas explains. Why, oh why, isn't there an exterior shot showing the jet ten feet above the ground?

Another missed opportunity: Since the arms dealer develops a crush on the podiatrist, why no sex scenes involving toes? Or not toes necessarily, but anything involving the bad guy discovering a new kind of bliss while the podiatrist improvises desperately with nail clippers and corn removal techniques? True, the podiatrist defends himself by pressing on the dealer's painful foot nerve. But that's level one. The sock puppet was level three.

I'm suggesting such notions not because I want to rewrite the screenplay, but because I miss a certain kind of zany invention. *The In-Laws* seems conventional in its ideas about where it can go and what it can accomplish. You don't get the idea anyone laughed out loud while writing the screenplay. It lacks a strange light in its eyes. It is too easily satisfied. The one moment when it suggests the lunacy of the earlier film is when the Brooks character refuses to get into the water because, he explains, he was born with an unusual condition; his skin is not waterproof.

Now consider the character of Douglas's ex-wife, played by Candice Bergen, who has a lot of fun with it. She hates the guy, but confides that at least the sex was great. "Great, great, great." This is the setup for a scene of potential comic genius, but the movie uses it only for a weak curtain line. The notion of Michael Douglas and Candice Bergen having great sex while she continues to hate him is, I submit, a scene this movie should not be lacking. Think how mad you'd be at someone who could arouse you as no one else before or since, but who is such a complete jerk you can't stand to have him around. Bergen could have an orgasm while screaming passionate vituperations. Now that's a scene I'd like to see.

In My Country ★ ★ ½
R, 100 m., 2005

Samuel L. Jackson (Langston Whitfield), Juliette Binoche (Anna Malan), Brendan Gleeson (de Jager), Menzi Ngubane (Dumi Mkhalipi), Sam Ngakane (Anderson), Aletta Bezuidenhout (Elsa), Lionel Newton (Edward Morgan), Langley Kirkwood (Boetie). Directed by John Boorman and produced by Robert Chartoff, Mike Medavoy, Kieran Corrigan, and Lynn Hendee. Screenplay by Ann Peacock, based on a book by Antjie Krog.

In the final decades of apartheid in South Africa, few observers thought power would change hands in the country without a bloody war. But white rule gave way peacefully to the Nelson Mandela government, and Mandela and F. W. de Klerk, the departing prime minister, shared the Nobel Peace Prize.

That miracle nevertheless left a nation scarred by decades of violence—not only of whites against blacks, although that predominated. The Truth and Reconciliation Commission, the inspiration of Mandela, Archbishop Desmond Tutu, and other leaders in the new society, found a way to deal with those wounds without resorting to the endless cycle of bloody revenge seen in Northern Ireland, Bosnia, and elsewhere. The commission made a simple offer: Appear before a public tribunal, confess exactly what you did, convince us you were acting under orders, make an apology we can believe, and we will move on from there.

John Boorman's *In My Country* is set at the time of the commission's hearings, and stars Samuel L. Jackson as Langston Whitfield, a *Washington Post* reporter covering the story, and Juliette Binoche as Anna Malan, a white Afrikaner, who is doing daily broadcasts for the South African Broadcasting Company. As the commission and its caravan of press and support staff travel rural areas, Whitfield and Malan find themselves in disagreement about the commission, but strongly attracted to each other.

I confess I walked into the film with strong feelings. I've spent a good deal of time in South Africa, including a year at the University of Cape Town. I had the opportunity to discuss the commission with Archbishop Tutu. I believe the transitional period in South Africa is a model for an enlightened and humane reconciliation with past evils. *In My Country* shows the process at work and argues in its favor, and I tended to approve of it just on that basis.

Yet there is something not quite right about the film itself. The affair between Whitfield and Malan seems arbitrary, more like two writers having sex on the campaign trail than like two people involved in a romance that would be important to them. Both are married, and neither wants to leave their marriage, although perhaps in the grip of infatuation they waver. Although apartheid imposed criminal penalties for interracial sex under its "Immorality Act," that does not necessarily mean that interracial sex has to be in the foreground of a movie about Truth and Reconciliation—particularly if it's an affair involving a visiting foreigner. There seems something too calculated about the movie's pairing up of the political and the personal.

There is another unconvincing aspect: Whitfield, the *Washington Post* reporter, is not convinced that the commission hearings are useful or just. He thinks the wrongdoers are getting off too easy, and says so at press conferences, becoming an advocate and making no attempt to seem objective. It is up to Anna Malan (and the plot) to convince him otherwise. There is a certain poetic irony in an Afrikaner convincing an African-American that Mandela's new South Africa is on the right track, but isn't it more of a fictional device than a likely scenario?

A scene where Malan brings Whitfield home to her family farm seems contrived because we are not sure what Anna hopes to accomplish with it, and at the end of the scene, that is still unclear. True, during the visit we are able to see white unease about the transfer of power. ("They're not our police anymore. It's not our country anymore.") But the romance adds complications that are essentially a distraction from the main line of the story.

The movie, written by Ann Peacock, is based on a book by Antjie Krog, whose own radio and newspaper reports of the hearings inspired the character of Anna Malan. It has scenes of undeniable power. Many of them involve a character named de Jager (Brendan Gleeson), a South African cop with a zeal for torture and murder that went far beyond his job requirements. Whitfield's encounter with de Jager is tense and strongly played. There are also moments of real emotion during the testimony from a parade of whites (and one black) seeking forgiveness.

As it happens, I've seen another film on the same subject. That is *Red Dust*, a selection at Toronto 2004, starring Hilary Swank as a New York attorney who returns to her native South Africa to represent a political activist (Chiwetel Ejiofor) in the amnesty hearing for his torturer (Jamie Bartlett). Bartlett's character serves something of the same function as Gleeson's in the other film, but all of the characters and their stories are more complex and contradictory, reflecting their turbulent times.

Inside Deep Throat ★ ★ ★
NC-17, 90 m., 2005

A documentary directed by Fenton Bailey and Randy Barbato and produced by Brian Grazer, Bailey, and Barbato. Screenplay by Bailey and Barbato.

In the beginning, Gerard Damiano was a hairdresser. Listening to his clients talk about sex, which in his salon was apparently all they talked about, he realized that pornography had cross-over appeal. All you had to do was advertise a movie in such a way that couples would come, instead of only the raincoat brigade. With a budget of $25,000 and an actress named Linda Lovelace, he made *Deep Throat* (1972), which inspired a national censorship battle, did indeed attract couples, and allegedly grossed $600 million, making it the most profitable movie of all time.

Deep Throat was made on the far fringes of the movie industry; Damiano later complained that most of the profits went to people he prudently refused to name as the mob. Since the mob owned most of the porn theaters in the prevideo days and inflated box office receipts as a way of laundering income from drugs and prostitution, it is likely, in fact, that *Deep Throat* did not really gross $600 million, although that might have been the box office tally.

Inside Deep Throat, a documentary that premiered at Sundance and is now going into national release, was made not on the fringes but by the very establishment itself. The studio is Universal, a producer is Brian Grazer *(A Beautiful Mind, How the Grinch Stole Christmas)* and the directors are Fenton Bailey and Randy Barbato *(Party Monster, The Eyes of Tammy Faye).* The rating, of course, is NC-17. It is a commentary on the limitations of the rating system that Universal would release a documentary about an NC-17 film, but would be reluctant to make one.

The movie uses new and old interviews and newsreel footage to remember a time when porn was brand-new. In my 1973 review of *Deep Throat,* written three days after a police raid on the Chicago theater showing it, I wrote: "The movie became 'pornographic chic' in New York before it was busted. Mike Nichols told Truman Capote he shouldn't miss it, and then the word just sort of got around: This is the first stag film to see with a date."

A year or two earlier, porn audiences darted furtively into shabby little theaters on the wrong side of town; now they lined up for *Deep Throat* and talked cheerfully to news cameras about wanting to see it because, well, everybody else seemed to be going. The movie was not very good (even its director, Gerard Damiano, would tell you that), but it was explicit in a way that was acceptable to its audiences, and it leavened the sex with humor. Not very funny humor, to be sure, but it worked in the giddy, forbidden atmosphere of a mixed-gender porn theater.

The modern era of skin flicks began in 1960 with Russ Meyer's *The Immoral Mr. Teas,* which inspired Meyer and others to make a decade of films featuring nudity but no explicit sex. Then a Supreme Court ruling seemed to permit the hard-core stuff, and *Deep Throat* was the first film to take it to a mass audience. (Meyer himself never made hard-core, explaining (1) he didn't like to share his profits with the mob, and (2) he didn't think what went on below the waist was nearly as visually interesting as the bosoms of his supervixens.) The movie was raided in city after city, it was prosecuted for obscenity, it was seized and banned, and the publicity only made it more popular. There were predictions that explicit sex would migrate into mainstream films, even rumors that Stanley Kubrick wanted to make a porn film.

But by 1974 the boomlet was pretty much over, and the genre had gone back into the hands of the raincoat rangers. When I interviewed Damiano that year, he said porn would soon be a thing of the past: "The only thing that's kept it going this long is the FBI and the Nixon administration. Without censorship to encourage people's curiosity, the whole thing would have been over six months ago." And that was pretty much the story until home video came onto the market, creating a new and much larger audience, but destroying what shreds of artistic ambition lurked in the styles of the film-based pornographers (see *Boogie Nights* for the story of that transition).

Inside Deep Throat has some headlines that go against popular wisdom:

—While everybody remembers that Linda Lovelace later said she had virtually been raped on screen, the movie suggests that her troubles were the doing of her sadistic lover at the time, not Damiano. By the time she was fifty, she was posing for *Leg Show* magazine and saying she thought she looked pretty good for her age.

—While everyone remembers the report of a presidential commission that found pornography to be harmful, not many people remember that was the *second* commission to report on the subject, not the first. The 1970 commission, headed by former Illinois Governor Otto Kerner, found that pornography was not particularly linked to antisocial behavior, and that indeed sex criminals as a group tended to have less exposure to pornography than nonsex criminals. This report, based on scientific research and findings, was deemed unacceptable by the Reagan White House, which created a 1986 commission headed by Attorney General Edwin Meese, which did no research, relied on anecdotal testimony from the witnesses it called, and found pornography harmful.

—Charles Keating Jr. and his Citizens for Decent Literature got a lot of publicity for leading the charge against *Deep Throat* and Larry Flynt. Keating got less publicity when he

was charged with racketeering in the Lincoln Savings and Loan scandal, and eventually served four years in prison.

As for *Inside Deep Throat*, it remembers a time before pornography was boring, and a climate in which nonpornographic films might consider bolder sexual content. It has some colorful characters, including a retired Florida exhibitor whose wife provides a running commentary on everything he says. And it tells us where they are now: Damiano is comfortably retired, Linda Lovelace died in a traffic accident, and her costar, Harry Reems, is a recovering substance abuser who now works as a Realtor in Park City, Utah, home of the Sundance Film Festival. 👉

Intacto ★ ★ ½
R, 108 m., 2003

Leonardo Sbaraglia (Tomás), Eusebio Poncela (Federico), Max von Sydow (Sam), Mónica López (Sara), Antonio Dechent (Alejandro). Directed by Juan Carlos Fresnadillo and produced by Sebastián Álvarez. Screenplay by Fresnadillo and Andrés M. Koppel.

The Spanish film *Intacto*, like the recent Sundance entry *The Cooler*, believes that luck is a commodity that can be given and received, won or lost, or traded away. Most people have ordinary luck, some have unusually good or bad luck, and then there is a character like Tomás, who is the only survivor of an airplane crash, beating the odds of 237 million to 1. (I am not the statistician here, only the reporter.)

The movie involves a man named Sam (Max von Sydow), who survived the Holocaust and now operates a remote casino at which rich people bet against his luck, usually unsuccessfully. So unshakable is his confidence that he will remove one bullet from a gun holding six and then bet that he will not die. That he is alive to be a character in the movie speaks for itself.

Von Sydow, who in *The Seventh Seal* played a game of chess with Death, believes that he will lose his luck if the wrong person looks on his face at the wrong time, or takes his photograph. To guard himself, he must often sit in a closed room with a hood over his face. We wonder, but he does not tell us, if he thinks this is a high price to pay for good fortune. He has a young man named Federico (Eusebio Poncela) as his confederate; Federico also has good luck, and searches for others who have his gift. When Sam steals his luck from him, he goes searching for a protégé of his own, and finds Tomás.

The single-mindedness of these men assumes that winning at gambling is the most important thing in the world. Certainly there are gamblers who think so. Another of the Sundance entries, *Owning Mahowny*, starred Philip Seymour Hoffman as a Toronto bank clerk who steals millions in order to fund his weekend getaways to Atlantic City and Las Vegas. He has a winning streak at roulette that in its intensity of focus has a kind of awesome power. In *The Cooler*, William H. Macy plays a man whose luck is so bad that he is employed by a casino to merely rub up against someone in a winning streak; then his luck changes.

The two North American films are pretty straightforward in telling their stories. *The Cooler* involves an element of fantasy, but it involves the story, not the visual approach. *Intacto*, directed by the talented young Juan Carlos Fresnadillo, is wilder visually, using the fractured narrative and attention-deficit camera style that can be effective or not, but often betrays a lack of confidence on the simple story level.

The story involves another more human element, centered on Sara (Mónica López), a cop who is chasing Tomás while grieving a tragic loss of her own. Will his luck protect him? What happens when it's luck versus luck?

I admired *Intacto* more than I liked it, for its ingenious construction and the way it keeps a certain chilly distance between its story and the dangers of popular entertainment. It's a Hollywood premise, rotated into the world of the art film through mannerism and oblique storytelling. The same ideas could be remade into a straightforward entertainment, and perhaps they already have been.

There's a fashion right now among new writers and directors to create stories of labyrinthine complexity, so that watching them is like solving a puzzle. I still haven't seen Alejandro Amenabar's *Open Your Eyes*, which a lot of people admire, but when I saw Cameron Crowe's American remake, *Vanilla Sky*, I knew as I walked out of the theater that I would

need to see it again. I did, and got a different kind of overview, and liked the film. I liked it the first time, too, but through instinct, not understanding.

When you solve a film like this, have you learned anything you wouldn't have learned in a straight narrative, or have you simply had to pay some dues to arrive at the same place? Depends. *Pulp Fiction*, which jump-started the trend, depends crucially on its structure for its effect. *Intacto*, which is not as complex as the other films I've mentioned, may be adding the layer of style just for fun. That is permitted, but somewhere within that style there may be a hell of a thriller winking at us.

Intermission ★ ★ ★ ½
R, 105 m., 2004

Cillian Murphy (John), Kelly Macdonald (Deirdre), Colin Farrell (Lehiff), Colm Meaney (Detective Jerry Lynch), David Wilmot (Oscar), Brian F. O'Byrne (Mick), Shirley Henderson (Sally), Michael McElhatton (Sam), Deirdre O'Kane (Noeleen). Directed by John Crowley and produced by Neil Jordan, Alan Moloney, and Stephen Woolley. Screenplay by Mark O'Rowe.

Here is a movie where the characters discover that brown steak sauce tastes great in coffee, where a TV producer wants "more reality" after filming a rabbit race, where a cop's car is stolen while he's carrying out a drug bust, where . . . but *Intermission* goes on and on, in a tireless series of inventions, like a plot-generating machine in overdrive. That it succeeds is some kind of miracle; there's enough material here for three bad films, and somehow it becomes one good one.

The movie is a dark comedy—no, make that a dark, dark, *dark* comedy—set in Dublin and starring more or less everyone in town. That its cast includes Colin Farrell, now a big movie star, is less remarkable than the fact that the cast is so large and colorful that we sometimes lose track of him. Here is yet more evidence that *Pulp Fiction* was the most influential movie of recent years, as eccentric characters with distinctive verbal styles coil around a plot involving romance, betrayal, kidnapping, bank robbery, and a lot of brown sauce. Whether the sauce is Daddy's or HP, the two favorite brands in Ireland, is impossible to say, perhaps because both sauce manufacturers preferred to keep their labels out of this movie.

Like *Pulp Fiction*, the movie begins with sweet talk that suddenly turns violent, as Lehiff (Farrell) betrays a hard side. We meet his mates, including John (Cillian Murphy), who hates his job in a supermarket, and Oscar (David Wilmot), who despairs of finding a girlfriend and is advised to target older ladies who will be grateful for his attention. Meanwhile, John breaks up with his girlfriend, Deirdre (Kelly Macdonald), who begins dating a married bank manager, Sam (Michael McElhatton), while Sam's abandoned wife, Noeleen (Deirdre O'Kane, not to be confused with the character Deirdre), goes to a lonely-hearts dance and meets, of course, Oscar.

But to summarize the plot is insanity. There are a dozen major characters whose lives intersect in romance, crime, and farce; the screenplay by Mark O'Rowe is so ingenious and energetic that we almost don't feel like we're being jerked around. The other character who must be introduced is Jerry Lynch (Colm Meaney), who has watched too many cop reality shows and thinks he should star in one himself. Oh, and I should mention Sally (Shirley Henderson), who after a tragic disappointment in love has become a recluse and doesn't seem to realize she has enough of a mustache to be referred to occasionally as Burt Reynolds. Her character brings a new dimension to the classic movie scene in which a plain girl is told she would be beautiful if she got rid of the glasses/braces/bangs, etc.

Director John Crowley, a first-timer with enormous promise, seems to know his way through this maze even if we don't, and eventually with a sigh and a smile we give up and let him take us where he will. That will include a kidnapping that combines the motives of bank robbery and cuckold's revenge, and a bus crash caused by a particularly vile little boy in a red coat, who has no connection with the other characters except that he occasionally turns up and causes horrible things to happen to them.

The movie is astonishing in the way it shifts gears, again like Tarantino. There are scenes of sudden, brutal violence. Scenes of broad comedy (especially involving the detective's attempts to be *C.S.I.* when he was born to be *Starsky and Hutch*). Moments of raw truth, as when an older woman at a pickup bar tells a younger man exactly how she feels. Moments of poignancy, as when John tries to win back Deirdre by saying all the things he should have told her in the first place. And moments of exquisitely bad timing, as when the bank manager unzips his pants in the living room just as Deirdre's mother walks in.

It's interesting how the stars fit right into the ensemble. Not only Farrell but Colm Meaney have famous faces for American audiences, and devoted moviegoers will recognize Kelly Macdonald from *Trainspotting* and Shirley Henderson from the wonderful *Wilbur Wants to Kill Himself*. What all of these actors do is fit seamlessly into the large cast, returning in some cases to the accents and body language of their preacting days. *Intermission* is a virtuoso act from beginning to end, juggling violence and farce, coincidence and luck, characters with good hearts and others evil to the core. In a movie filled with incredulities, the only detail I was absolutely unable to accept is that brown sauce tastes good in coffee.

The Interpreter ★ ★ ★
PG-13, 128 m., 2005

Nicole Kidman (Silvia Broome), Sean Penn (Tobin Keller), Catherine Keener (Dot Woods), Jesper Christensen (Nils Lud), Yvan Attal (Philippe), Earl Cameron (Zuwanie). Directed by Sydney Pollack and produced by Tim Bevan, Eric Fellner, and Kevin Misher. Screenplay by Charles Randolph, Scott Frank, and Steven Zaillian.

Sydney Pollack's *The Interpreter* is a taut and intelligent thriller, centering on Nicole Kidman as an interpreter at the United Nations, and Sean Penn as a Secret Service agent. And, no, they don't have romantic chemistry: For once, the players in a dangerous game are too busy for sex—too busy staying alive and preventing murder. They do, however, develop an intriguing closeness, based on shared loss and a sympathy for the other person as a human being. There's a moment when she rests her head on his shoulder, and he puts a protective arm around her, and we admire the movie for being open to those feelings.

The story was filmed largely on location in and around the United Nations, including the General Assembly Room; it's the first film given permission to do that. I mention the location because it adds an unstated level of authenticity to everything that happens. There's a scene where a security detail sweeps the building, and it feels like a documentary. Like when Drew Barrymore runs onto the field at Fenway Park in *Fever Pitch,* the U.N. scenes provide what Werner Herzog calls "the voodoo of location"—the feeling of the real thing instead of the artifice of sets and special effects.

The movie has a realism of tone, too. This isn't a pumped-up techno-thriller, but a procedural, in which Secret Service agents Keller (Penn) and Woods (Catherine Keener) are assigned to the U.N. after an interpreter named Silvia Broome (Kidman) overhears a death threat. The threat is against an African dictator named Zuwanie (Earl Cameron), once respected, now accused of genocide. He announces that he will address the General Assembly to defend his policies. The head of the Secret Service (played by Pollack himself) says the last thing the United States needs, at this point in history, is the assassination of a foreign leader on American soil.

Zuwanie is clearly intended to represent Robert Mugabe of Zimbabwe, also once hailed as a liberator, now using starvation as a political tool. Silvia, we learn, grew up in Zuwanie's country, was a supporter of Zuwanie, saw her parents killed, became disillusioned. She speaks many languages, including Ku, the tongue of the (fictional) country of Matobo, and five years ago became a U.N. interpreter.

After she reports the death threat, she expects to be believed. But Keller draws an instant conclusion: "She's lying." A polygraph indicates "she's under stress, but not lying." Is she, or isn't she? We meet a gallery of suspects, including Zuwanie's white security chief and two of his political opponents. Keller looks into Silvia's background, convinced she has reasons for wanting Zuwanie dead, although she says she joined the U.N. because she supports peaceful change.

"Vengeance is a lazy form of grief," she tells the agent, who has some grief and vengeance issues of his own. She also tells him of a custom from Matobo: When a man kills a member of your family and is captured, he is tied up and thrown into the river, and it is up to your family to save him or let him drown. If he drowns, you will have vengeance, but you will grieve all of your days. If you save him, you will be released from your lament. This is not a practice I was familiar with, and seems even to have escaped the attention of the Discovery Channel; I'd like to see a family debating whether to save the killer or drown him. Maybe a family like the Sopranos.

What I admire most about the film is the way it enters the terms of this world—of international politics, security procedures, shifting motives—and observes the details of all-night stakeouts, shop talk, and interlocking motives and strategies. More than one person wants Zuwanie dead, and more than one person wants an assassination attempt, which is not precisely the same thing.

Nicole Kidman is a star who consistently finds dramatic challenges and takes chances. Consider her in *Birth, The Human Stain, Dogville, The Hours, The Others,* and *Moulin Rouge.* Here, with a vaguely South African accent and a little-girl fear peering out from behind her big-girl occupation, she sidesteps her glamour and is convincing as a person of strong convictions. Sean Penn matches her with a weary professionalism, a way of sitting there and just looking at her, as if she will finally break down and tell him what he thinks she knows. It's intriguing the way his character keeps several possibilities in his mind at once, instead of just signing on with the theory that has the most sympathy from the audience.

The final scene is perhaps not necessary; it has "obligatory closure" written all over it. But at least we are spared romantic clichés, and I was reminded of Robert Forster and Pam Grier in Tarantino's *Jackie Brown,* playing two adults with so much emotional baggage that for them romance is like a custom in another country.

Note: I don't want to get Politically Correct; I know there are many white Africans, and I admire Kidman's performance. But I couldn't help wondering why her character had to be white. I imagined someone like Angela Bassett in the role, and wondered how that would have played. If you see the movie, run that through your mind. ☞

In the Cut ★ ★ ½
R, 113 m., 2003

Meg Ryan (Frannie Avery), Mark Ruffalo (Detective James Malloy), Jennifer Jason Leigh (Pauline), Kevin Bacon (John Graham), Nick Damici (Detective Richard Rodriguez), Sharrieff Pugh (Cornelius), Nancy La Scala (Tabu). Directed by Jane Campion and produced by Nicole Kidman and Laurie Parker. Screenplay by Campion and Susanna Moore, based on the novel by Moore.

Jane Campion's *In the Cut* has ornaments of a thriller about sexually bold women, but ticking away underneath is the familiar slasher genre in which women are the victims. What makes it stranger, and a little scarier than it might have been, is the way its heroine willfully sleepwalks into danger, dreaming of orgasm.

Frannie Avery (Meg Ryan, reshaping her image with a bad-girl role) is a high school English teacher who likes sex and wishes she got more of it, but not from the guys she's been getting it from, who tend to be obsessed weirdos. Her half-sister Pauline (Jennifer Jason Leigh) is also sex-deprived; at one point, as they're discussing a man that Frannie has every reason to be wary of, Pauline advises her sister to sleep with the guy "if only for the exercise."

This man is James Malloy (Mark Ruffalo), a homicide detective, who meets Frannie while investigating the murder and "de-articulation" of a woman whose severed limb was found beneath Frannie's window. James is the kind of man who talks about sex in a way that would be offensive if he didn't deliver so skillfully what he describes so crudely. "How did you make me feel like that?" Frannie asks him after their first encounter. He must have made her feel really good, because later, even after she begins to suspect he is the de-articulator, she goes on another date. This is a new variety of high-risk sex: Get as much action as you can before being de-articulated.

James wanders in a musky daze, too, in a movie where the sex is so good they both keep getting distracted by their duties as potential vic-tim and possible killer. Campion's screenplay, cowritten with Susanna Moore and based on Moore's novel, locates these characters close to street level in a hard-bitten New York neighborhood where people act on their needs without apology. The story has fun playing against certain conventions of the slasher genre, and the dialogue has a nice way of sidestepping clichés. Listen to the words and watch the body language as James responds when Frannie asks him, "Did you kill her?" Without for a moment revealing if he did or didn't, I can promise you that Ruffalo's choices here are true to this character and do not come from the pool of slasher clichés.

The movie is leisurely, as thrillers go, but I liked that, especially in the intimate conversations of the two sisters, who sound and behave like two women who have understood each other very well for a long time. Ryan and Leigh have a verbal and emotional shorthand that creates a kind of conspiracy against the mechanics of the plot: Sometimes, even when you're in danger you can still feel horny. And James's introductory pitch to Frannie, when he tells her who he can be and what he can do, shows that he knows who he is and who she is; that's why she lets him talk that way—even though she walks out when his partner (Nick Damici) tries for the same crude note.

So all of this is well done, and yet the movie is kind of a shambles. The key supporting characters are awkwardly used, as if the movie thinks it ought to have them but doesn't know why. Sharrieff Pugh plays Cornelius, a muscular African-American who is Frannie's student; she meets him for tutoring in a pool hall with sex in the shadows, and the movie keeps trying to suggest something about them but never knows what it is. Kevin Bacon turns up as John Graham, an intern who works eighteen hours a day, needs someone to walk his dog, and takes it very badly when Frannie breaks up with him—but in such an odd way that when Bacon went home that night he must have told someone that Campion didn't know what the hell to do with him. And Damici, as James Malloy's partner, is so obviously the deus ex machina that you can almost hear the gears grinding as he's lowered into play.

The most intriguing element in the movie is the way Frannie is made so heedless of danger. She's drunk sometimes, but she acts like she's on other stuff too, like maybe hog tranquilizers. She's smart enough to make sure James is really a cop before letting him into her apartment, but why does she get into various cars, go to various meetings, trust various situations, and arrive at obvious conclusions, but then act as if she's forgotten them?

And what kind of eyesight does she have that she can see a three of spades tattooed on the hand of a man whose face she looks right at but isn't sure about? For that matter, what kind of coincidence is involved in that whole scene in the basement of the bar? Incredible that she would just happen to see the de-articulator and the de-articulatee together—and, no, I'm not giving something away.

In the Cut reminds me a little of the Coen brothers' film *Intolerable Cruelty*. Here are two genre movies, a slasher thriller and a screwball comedy, made by assuredly great directors, but both movies are too hip for the room. It is possible to transcend genres, but I think you have to go through them, not around them. Both films are concerned with being good (and are good) in ways that are irrelevant to whether they arrive at their goals. In the case of *In the Cut*, Meg Ryan does such an effective job of evoking her sexually hungry lonely girl that it might have been better to just follow that line and not distract her and the audience with a crime plot that becomes transparent the moment you recall the Rule of Economy of Characters ("no unnecessary character is unnecessary").

And what the *hell* was the point of those ice-skating flashbacks?

In This World ★ ★ ★
R, 88 m., 2003

Jamal Udin Torabi (Himself), Enayatullah (Himself), Imran Paracha (Travel Agent), Hiddayatullah (Enayat's Brother), Jamau (Enayat's Father), Mirwais Torabi (Jamal's Older Brother). Directed by Michael Winterbottom and produced by Andrew Eaton and Anita Overland. Screenplay by Tony Grisoni.

In This World tells the story of a sixteen-year-old Afghan boy who journeys by land and sea to London from a refugee camp in Pakistan. What makes the film astonishing is that it follows a real boy on a real journey, and the boy is

in England at this moment. What's real and what's fiction in the film is hard to say, but we trust that the images are informed by truth, and there is a scene at night in the mountains of Turkey where it looks as if real gunfire is being aimed at the travelers.

The film's hero is Jamal Udin Torabi, playing himself. He lives with his family in a refugee camp in Pakistan. His uncle, Wakeel, wants to send his son Enayat to London; Jamal speaks English and is allowed to go along as a translator and companion. The two make a deal with a professional smuggler of humans, who starts them off on a long journey through Iran, Turkey, Italy, and France.

The film is not a documentary, although many scenes might as well be. Director Michael Winterbottom and his cinematographer, Marcel Zyskind, shot with a small digital camera, and many shots were apparently taken without the knowledge of the people in them. I learn that the film's producer, Anita Overland, worked as an advance scout, staying a day or two ahead of Winterbottom and his actors and arranging scenes—up to a point, we gather. Most of the dialogue is improvised, based on a script by Tony Grisoni, who interviewed others who had made the journey.

We read all the time of ships, trucks, and containers filled with human beings desperate to live in another land. Sometimes this illegal cargo arrives dead, and there is an agonizing scene in *In This World* where Jamal, his cousin, and many others are locked inside a shipping container where the air is running out and their desperate cries and bangings cannot be heard. Jamal survives this and other harrowing experiences with a resilience, adaptability, and defiant wit that is impossible to fake: The real Jamal, like the Jamal he plays in the movie, must be both a heroic survivor and quite a character.

The film's politics are muddled. Winterbottom wants us to identify with Jamal because of the risks he has taken and the excruciating experiences he has survived during the long months of his journey. The movie ends with the information that the real Jamal, who actually made this journey, was ordered by a court to leave England by the day before his eighteenth birthday. We are, I guess, supposed to find this heartless, and of course we sympathize with Jamal and his ordeal. But immigrants are not allowed into countries on the basis of the trouble they endured to get there, and Jamal doesn't qualify as a political rufugee.

The movie strikes a curious note right at the beginning, as it shows us the Shamshatoo refugee camp in Pakistan. Here live more than 50,000 Afghans, we're told, who fled from the 1979 Soviet invasion of their land, and again because of the "U.S. bombing" in 2001. But surely many of these people fled the Taliban in the years in between, and although it is true that the United States bombed Afghanistan, it is also true that there was a reason for that.

Winterbottom surely does not expect his audiences to be so simple-minded that these observations do not occur to them, so why does he allow that alienating glitch right at the outset? The unspoken subtext of his movie is that his characters, and millions more, are willing to undergo unimaginable danger and hardship in order to live in the West instead of where they are.

But the movie never brings that notion to the surface, and indeed is not an overtly political film anyway. It is more the story of these people—or, more exactly, of their journey, for which we can read the journeys of exiles all over the world. The dilemma is that the planet has more undesirable societies to live in than desirable ones. The answer is perhaps not for the discontented and visionaries to leave, but for them to stay and try to bring about change. Yet I instinctively identify with Jamal's desire, and suspect that in his shoes I would want to do what he has done. The next time I read about desperate immigrants trying to sneak into another land, the images in this film will inform me.

Intimate Strangers ★ ★ ★ ½
R, 104 m., 2004

Sandrine Bonnaire (Anna Delambre), Fabrice Luchini (William Faber), Michel Duchaussoy (Docteur Monnier), Anne Brochet (Jeanne), Gilbert Melki (Marc), Laurent Gamelon (Luc), Helene Surgere (Madame Mulon), Urbain Cancelier (Chatel). Directed by Patrice Leconte and produced by Alain Sarde. Screenplay by Jerome Tonnerre.

Men in the films of Patrice Leconte sometimes find themselves in a kind of paralysis of admiration for women. Consider the hero of *The Hairdresser's Husband,* who as a child developed an erotic obsession involving female hairdressers and their rituals and powders, their scents and tools, and now operates a beauty shop simply so that he can gaze in admiration as his wife cuts hair. Or consider *Monsieur Hire,* about a mousy little man who becomes aware that he can see into a seductive woman's bedroom across the air shaft from his flat. When she makes it clear she knows he is watching her and doesn't mind, his distance from her is threatened and he is profoundly shaken.

Now here is William Faber (Fabrice Luchini), a quiet, precise, middle-aged man who still lives in the flat where he was raised, and carries on the accounting business his father established there. He hasn't gone far from home. Even his father's secretary, Madame Mulon, still works for him. He is a man for whom probity is a cardinal virtue, and revealing passion is unthinkable.

One day a nervous young woman named Anna Delambre (Sandrine Bonnaire) walks into his office, lights a cigarette, and begins to spill the beans. She is so nervous that the camera becomes uneasy, regarding her with jerky little noticing shots. She talks frankly of problems in her marriage. William remains almost motionless behind his desk, his face a study in astonishment and alarm. The few words that he speaks are noncommittal and open-ended.

She thinks he is a psychiatrist. He is not, but doesn't tell her that, and as she continues her visits he ignores the withering stares of Madame Mulon and sits sphinxlike behind his desk, hardly moving a muscle, listening to her story as it grows steadily more strange and, it must be said, more erotic—so much so you would almost think Anna was trying to arouse him.

You may think I have revealed a great secret by explaining the mistaken identity. If Leconte were a lesser filmmaker, that would be true. But Leconte and his writer, Jerome Tonnerre, present her error and his deception only to prepare their canvas. We find we cannot take anything at face value in this story, that the motives of this woman and her husband are so deeply masked that even at the end of the film we are still uncertain about exactly what to believe, and why.

What is real is William's fascination. He doesn't move a muscle, say an unnecessary word, reveal in any way how transfixed he is by Anna and her story. But certainly she knows. There's something deeply sexual in a woman's discovery that she has ultimate power over a man, and one possibility is that she continues her visits to the wrong office because they excite her. There is also the possibility that her original motive changes in response to new developments. There is the mystery of her relationship with her husband, whom she seems to have accidentally crippled with the car, so that he walks with a cane. And the matter of what her husband wants her to do. And the way in which this is made known to William.

Bubbling away beneath most of Leconte's films is a stream of wicked humor. He is incapable of a film that exists on one level, for one purpose. He is quite capable, as in *Intimate Strangers*, of telling a story that has completely different meanings for the major characters, so that although they occupy the same rooms and hear the same words, they don't perceive the same scenario. And then with what delight he surprises us—not with anything so vulgar as a twist, but with a revelation of character so sudden it's like a psychic blow.

His camera is a coconspirator in *Intimate Strangers*. We are invited to become voyeurs as we follow the progress of the perverse therapy sessions—sessions that may be doing Anna as much good as if William really were a psychiatrist, although what would be good for Anna becomes increasingly hard to say. William watches this woman as she does small but closely observed things, like tipping the ash of her cigarette into a wastepaper basket. No, that doesn't start a fire—not in a Leconte film—but functions simply to make her seem reckless.

Consider a high-angle shot late in the film, which establishes that Anna is wearing a dress displaying noticeable cleavage. Now watch as Leconte cuts to William, whose gaze begins to waver as he tries resolutely not to look, and then notice the reaction shot (now our point of view as well as William's), as the camera hovers almost unsteadily, begins to dip to regard her neckline, and then subtly refuses to. William has not looked, but Leconte has demonstrated that we wanted him to. No big point is made of this, but some members of the audience actually crane their necks, trying to get a better angle through the camera lens.

Leconte is not famous, but he is addictive. You could do worse than hole up for a weekend with half a dozen of his films, also including *Ridicule*, *The Girl on the Bridge*, *The Widow of Saint-Pierre*, and *The Man on the Train*. His characters are fascinated by other lives, and by missed opportunities in their own. They think they know their motives, and then life reveals their real motives to them. They are presented with feelings that may be shameful, but are undeniable, and are theirs. It is up to them to decide if they would become more miserable through the realization of their desires or through the tantalizing denial of them.

Intolerable Cruelty ★ ★ ½
PG-13, 100 m., 2003

George Clooney (Miles Massey), Catherine Zeta-Jones (Marylin Rexroth), Geoffrey Rush (Donovan Donaly), Cedric the Entertainer (Gus Petch), Edward Herrmann (Rex Rexroth), Paul Adelstein (Wrigley), Richard Jenkins (Freddy Bender), Billy Bob Thornton (Howard D. Doyle). Directed by Joel Coen and Ethan Coen and produced by Ethan Coen and Brian Grazer. Screenplay by Robert Ramsey, Matthew Stone, Ethan Coen, and Joel Coen.

The camera just stands there and gawks at Catherine Zeta-Jones, and so does George Clooney, and so do we. She goes on the list with Ava Gardner and Deborah Kerr. It's not a long list. She has the kind of beauty that could melt a divorce lawyer's heart and soften his brain, which is what happens in *Intolerable Cruelty*, a comedy by the Coen brothers.

Clooney plays Miles Massey, the millionaire author of the Massey Pre-Nup, a prenuptial agreement so tightly written that it has, we learn, never been cracked. "They spend an entire semester on it at Harvard Law." We meet him in divorce court, representing an outraged husband (Geoffrey Rush) who discovered his wife with the pool man and found that odd, since they didn't have a pool.

Massey is hired by Rex Rexroth (Edward Herrmann), who has been briefly married to Marylin (Zeta-Jones). She has a video, taken by her detective Gus (Cedric the Entertainer) exposing Rex as a cheater, and wants to win his millions in the settlement. Miles wins the case, so it's curious that Marylin wants to hire him to draft a Massey Pre-Nup for her next marriage, which will be to a gulping, blushing Texas oil billionaire named Howard (Billy Bob Thornton in full display). Miles, who is already gobsmacked with Marylin's bewitching sex appeal, can't understand why she wants to marry a yahoo like Howard. Or, actually, he can: She wants Howard's money. In that case, why does she want the Massey Pre-Nup? To prove she really loves him, she says. Since she really doesn't, Miles can only look on in wonderment and admiration. He's fascinated by the brilliance with which she violates conventional morality.

The Coens start with nothing but ducks in this movie, and for a long time it looks like they're all in a row. Clooney and Zeta-Jones are both great-looking people, both smart, both able to play comedy, both able to handle the kind of dialogue fondly described in our nation's literate past as witty repartee. Both characters are sharks, but both are human, too, and their mutual sexual attraction is so palpable you could cook with it. Miles is moved with the profound admiration only one slickster can have for another; when Marylin actually inspires Howard to eat the uncrackable Massey Pre-Nup (with barbecue sauce), Miles realizes he is witnessing not just beauty and genius, but a will to challenge his own.

Plots like this have fueled lovely screwball comedies, and *Intolerable Cruelty* is in the genre, but somehow not of it. The Coens sometimes have a way of standing to one side of their work: It's the puppet and they're the ventriloquists. The puppet is sincere, but the puppet master is wagging his eyebrows at the audience and asking, can you believe this stuff? Joel and Ethan are bounteously gifted filmmakers, but sometimes you just want them to lay off the irony and climb down here with the groundlings. Their *Fargo* was a movie that loved its characters, and it's one of the best movies I've ever seen.

It is hard to show the Coens' distancing process at work without revealing the movie's secrets, but let me try. The film is told from Massey's point of view. There is something that he wants: Marylin. He desires her so badly that in order to get her, he would balance the Massey Pre-Nup on his own head and crack it himself, with a hammer. We sympathize with this desire, because we share it. We *want* him to win her. The question is, does she want him? Of course she wants his money; that goes with the territory. But does she want to marry a millionaire, or simply become one herself?

I was reminded of Ernst Lubitsch's great *Trouble in Paradise*, which is about a con man, a con woman who loves him but can't afford him, and a rich widow who thinks she can buy him but would be happy enough to rent him for the season. By the end of that movie, everyone knows all about each other, and they accept the situation; if we cannot have what we want, they agree, let us at least be able to admire the way we behaved.

Miles and Marylin acknowledge their mutual chicanery. Neither one is very nice. But, aw, come on, when she walks across the room and his heart leaps up, or when she looks at him in a close-up that undresses itself, what makes the Coens pull back from this emotion? Why won't they give us the payoff their setup demands? We enjoy many turns of the screw in this movie, but there comes a time when the screw is seated and they keep turning until they strip the groove. We poor saps, who invested our emotions in the movie, are hung out to dry. The materials are available in *Intolerable Cruelty* to create a movie with an irresistible comic payload, so why must they skew it into a warning against itself?

That said: The movie has scenes of delicious comedy, Clooney and Zeta-Jones play their characters perfectly in an imperfect screenplay, and the man with the asthma puffer gets the biggest single laugh since the hair gel in *There's Something About Mary*.

Irreversible ★ ★ ★
NO MPAA RATING, 99 m., 2003

Monica Bellucci (Alex), Vincent Cassel (Marcus), Albert Dupontel (Pierre), Philippe Nahon (Philippe), Jo Prestia (Le Tenia), Stéphane

Drouot (Stéphane), Mourad Khima (Mourad). Directed by Gaspar Noé and produced by Christophe Rossignon and Richard Grandpierre. Screenplay by Noé.

Irreversible is a movie so violent and cruel that most people will find it unwatchable. The camera looks on unflinchingly as a woman is raped and beaten for several long, unrelenting minutes, and as a man has his face pounded in with a fire extinguisher, in an attack that continues until after he is apparently dead. That the movie has a serious purpose is to its credit, but makes it no more bearable. Some of the critics at the screening walked out, but I stayed, sometimes closing my eyes, and now I will try to tell you why I think the writer and director, Gaspar Noé, made the film in this way.

First, above all, and crucially, the story is told backward. Two other films have famously used that chronology: Harold Pinter's *Betrayal* (1983), the story of a love affair that ends (begins) in treachery, and Christopher Nolan's *Memento* (2001), which begins with the solution to a murder and tracks backward to its origin. Of *Betrayal,* I wrote that a sad love story would be even more tragic if you could see into the future, so that even this joyous moment, this kiss, was in the shadow of eventual despair.

Now consider *Irreversible.* If it were told in chronological order, we would meet a couple very much in love: Alex (Monica Bellucci) and Marcus (Vincent Cassel). In a movie that is frank and free about nudity and sex, we see them relaxed and playful in bed, having sex and sharing time. Bellucci and Cassel were lovers at the time the film was made, and are at ease with each other.

Then we would see them at a party, Alex wearing a dress that makes little mystery of her perfect breasts. We would see a man hitting on her. We would hear it asked how a man could let his lover go out in public dressed like that: Does he like to watch as men grow interested? We would meet Marcus's best friend, Pierre (Albert Dupontel), who himself was once a lover of Alex.

Then we would follow Alex as she walks alone into a subway tunnel, on a quick errand that turns tragic when she is accosted by Le Tenia (Jo Prestia), a pimp who brutally and mercilessly rapes and beats her for what seems like an eternity, in a stationary-camera shot that goes on and on and never cuts away.

And then we would follow Marcus and Pierre in a search for Le Tenia, which leads to an S&M club named the Rectum, where a man mistaken for Le Tenia is finally discovered and beaten brutally, again in a shot that continues mercilessly, this time with a handheld camera that seems to participate in the beating.

As I said, for most people, unwatchable. Now consider what happens if you reverse the chronology, so that the film begins with shots of the body being removed from the nightclub and tracks back through time to the warm and playful romance of the bedroom scenes. There are several ways in which this technique produces a fundamentally different film:

1. The film doesn't build up to violence and sex as its payoff, as pornography would. It begins with its two violent scenes, showing us the very worst immediately, and then tracking back into lives that are about to be forever altered.

2. It creates a different kind of interest in those earlier scenes, which are foreshadowed for us but not for the characters. When Alex and Marcus caress and talk, we realize what a slender thread all happiness depends from. To know the future would not be a blessing but a curse. Life would be unlivable without the innocence of our ignorance.

3. Revenge precedes violation. The rapist is savagely punished before he commits his crime. At the same time, and this is significant, Marcus is the violent monster of the opening scenes, and Le Tenia is a victim whose crime has not yet been seen (although we already know Alex has been assaulted).

4. The party scenes, and the revealing dress, are seen in hindsight as a risk that should not have been taken. Instead of making Alex look sexy and attractive, they make her look vulnerable and in danger. While it is true that a woman should be able to dress as she pleases, it is not always wise.

5. We know by the time we see Alex at the party, and earlier in bed, that she is not simply a sex object or a romantic partner, but a fierce woman who fights the rapist for every second of the rape. Who uses every tactic at her command to stop him. Who loses, but does not surrender. It makes her sweetness and warmth

337

much richer when we realize what darker weathers she harbors. This woman is not simply a sensuous being, as women so often simply are in the movies, but a fighter with a fierce survival instinct.

The fact is, the reverse chronology makes *Irreversible* a film that structurally argues against rape and violence, while ordinary chronology would lead us down a seductive narrative path toward a shocking, exploitative payoff. By placing the ugliness at the beginning, Gaspar Noé forces us to think seriously about the sexual violence involved. The movie does not end with rape as its climax and send us out of the theater as if something had been communicated. It starts with it, and asks us to sit there for another hour and process our thoughts. It is therefore moral at a structural level.

As I said twice and will repeat again, most people will not want to see the film at all. It is so violent, it shows such cruelty, that it is a test most people will not want to endure. But it is unflinchingly honest about the crime of rape. It does not exploit. It does not pander. It has been said that no matter what it pretends, pornography argues for what it shows. *Irreversible* is not pornography.

The Isle ★ ★ ★
NO MPAA RATING, 89 m., 2003

Suh Jung (Hee-Jin), Yoosuk Kim (Hyun-Shik), Sung-hee Park (Eun-A), Jae-Hyun Cho (Mang-Chee), Hang-Seon Jang (Middle-aged Man). Directed by Ki-duk Kim, and produced by Eun Lee. Screenplay by Kim.

The audiences at Sundance are hardened and sophisticated, but when the South Korean film *The Isle* played there in 2001, there were gasps and walkouts. People covered their eyes, peeked out, and slammed their palms back again. I report that because I want you to know: This is the most gruesome and queasiness-inducing film you are likely to have seen. You may not even want to read the descriptions in this review. Yet it is also beautiful, angry, and sad, with a curious sick poetry, as if the Marquis de Sade had gone in for pastel landscapes.

The film involves a lake where fishermen rent tiny cottages, each on its own raft, and bob with the waves as they catch and cook their dinners. It is the ultimate getaway. Once they have been delivered to their rafts by Hee-Jin, a woman who lives in a shack on the bank and operates a motorboat, they depend on her for all of their supplies and for the return to shore. She also sometimes brings them prostitutes, or services them herself.

Hee-Jin (Suh Jung) does not speak throughout the film, and is thought to be a mute, until she utters one piercing scream. She is like the heroine of *Woman of the Dunes,* ruling a domain in which men, once lured, can be kept captive. Most of the time she simply operates her business, ferrying the fishermen back and forth to their floating retreats. The men treat Hee-Jin and the prostitutes with brutality and contempt, even making them dive into the water to get their payments; that these women are willing to work in this way is a measure of their desperation.

Hee-Jin is indifferent to most of the men, but becomes interested in Hyun-Shik (Yoosuk Kim). Because we share his nightmares, we know that he was a policeman, killed his girlfriend, and has come to the floating hut to hide and perhaps to die. Watching him one day, she sees that he is about to commit suicide and interrupts his chain of thought with sudden violence, swimming under his raft and stabbing him through the slats of the floor. They develop what on this lake passes for a relationship, but then he tries suicide again (you might want to stop reading now) by swallowing a line knotted with fishhooks and pulling it up again. This leads to a sex scene I will not describe here, and later to an equally painful sequence involving Hee-Jin's use of fishhooks.

It is not uncommon for South Korean films to involve sadomasochism, as indeed do many films from Japan, where bondage is a common subject of popular adult comic books. The material doesn't reflect common behavior in those countries, but is intended to evoke extremes of violent emotion. It also dramatizes hostility toward women, although in *The Isle* the tables are turned. Between these two people who have nothing in common, one of them mute, sex is a form of communication—and pain, this movie argues, is even more sincere and complete.

Why would you want to see this film? Most people would not. I was recently at a health resort where a movie was shown every night, and one of the selections was Pedro Almodóvar's *All About My Mother*, which involves transgendered characters. "Why," a woman asked me, "would they show a movie with things I do not want to see?" She is not unusual. Most people choose movies that provide exactly what they expect, and tell them things they already know. Others are more curious. We are put on this planet only once, and to limit ourselves to the familiar is a crime against our minds.

The way I read *The Isle*, it is not about fishhooks and sex at all. It is a cry of pain. The man on the raft, as we have seen in flashbacks, is violent and cruel, and he killed his girlfriend because he was jealous. Of course, jealousy is the face of low self-esteem. The woman sells her body and dives into the water for her payment. Her power is that she can leave these hateful men stranded on their rafts. I believe that Hee-Jin comes to "like" Hyun-Shik, although that is the wrong word. Maybe she feels possessive because she saved his life. His second attempt, with the fishhooks, reveals the depth of his sad self-loathing. When she employs the fishhooks on herself, what is she saying? That she understands? That she feels the same way too? That even in agony we need someone to witness and share?

The film, as I said, is beautiful to look at. The little huts are each a different color. The mist over the water diffuses the light. What a lovely postcard this scene would make, if we did not know the economy it reflects, and the suffering it conceals. Now there's a subject for meditation.

The Italian Job ★ ★ ★
PG-13, 105 m., 2003

Mark Wahlberg (Charlie Croker), Charlize Theron (Stella Bridger), Edward Norton (Steve Frezelli), Seth Green (Lyle), Jason Statham (Handsome Rob), Mos Def (Left-Ear), Donald Sutherland (John Bridger). Directed by F. Gary Gray and produced by Donald De Line. Screenplay by Donna Powers and Wayne Powers.

I saw *The Italian Job* in a Chicago screening room, in the midst of a rush of new summer releases. I recollect it now from the Cannes Film Festival, which has assembled one unendurable film after another for its worst year in memory. That doesn't make *The Italian Job* a better film, but it provides a reminder that we do, after all, sometimes go to the movies just to have a good time, and not to be mired in a slough of existential despond. Don't get me wrong. I like a good mire in despond now and again; it's just that the despond at Cannes has been so unadmirable.

F. Gary Gray's *The Italian Job*, on the other hand, is nothing more, or less, than a slick caper movie with stupendous chase scenes and a truly ingenious way to steal $35 million in gold bars from a safe in a Venetian palazzo.

The safe is stolen by a gang led by Donald Sutherland, who must be relieved to note that Venice has no dwarfs in red raincoats this season. His confederates include Charlie (Mark Wahlberg), a strategic mastermind; second-in-command Steve (Edward Norton); the computer whiz Lyle (Seth Green); the getaway driver Handsome Rob (Jason Statham); and Left-Ear (Mos Def), who can blow up stuff real good.

After a chase through the canals of Venice, which in real life would have led to the loss of six tourist gondolas and the drowning of an accordion player, the confederates go to an extraordinary amount of trouble to meet, with the gold, in a high Alpine pass apparently undisturbed since Hannibal. I have no idea how hard it is to move $35 million in gold from Venice to the Alps with Interpol looking for you, or for that matter how hard it would be to move it back down again, but golly, it's a pretty location.

After betrayal and murder, the action shifts to Los Angeles. Think of the overweight baggage charges. Wahlberg and company, who have lost the gold, are determined to get it back again, and enlist Sutherland's daughter, Stella (Charlize Theron), who is a safecracker. A legal one, until they enlist her.

Stella drives a bright red Mini Cooper, which is terrifically important to the plot. Eventually there is a fleet of three. That the crooks in the original *Italian Job* (1968) also drove Mini Coopers is one of the few points of similarity between the two movies. Good job that the Mini Cooper was reintroduced in time for product placement in this movie.

Actually, that's unfair; they need Mini Coopers because their size allows them to drive through very narrow spaces, although they have no idea how handy the little cars will become when they drive down the stairs and onto the tracks of the Los Angeles subway system. They're also handy in traffic jams, and there are nice sequences in which traffic lights are manipulated by the Seth Green character, who hilariously insists he is the real inventor of Napster, which was stolen by his roommate while he was taking a nap, thus the name.

There are a couple of nice dialogue touches; Edward Norton is not the first actor to say, "I liked him right up until the moment I shot him," but he is certainly the latest. The ending is suitably ironic. This is just the movie for two hours of mindless escapism on a relatively skilled, professional level. If I had seen it instead of the Cannes entry *The Brown Bunny*, I would have wept with gratitude.

It Runs in the Family ★ ★ ½
PG-13, 101 m., 2003

Michael Douglas (Alex Gromberg), Kirk Douglas (Mitchell Gromberg), Cameron Douglas (Asher Gromberg), Diana Douglas (Evelyn Gromberg), Bernadette Peters (Rebecca Gromberg), Rory Culkin (Eli Gromberg), Sarita Choudhury (Peg Maloney), Irene Gorovaia (Abigail Staley). Directed by Fred Schepisi and produced by Michael Douglas. Screenplay by Jesse Wigutow.

I have no idea how accurately the story of *It Runs in the Family* parallels the actual story of the Douglas family, whose members play four of the characters. My guess is that most of the facts are different and a lot of the emotions are the same. Like *On Golden Pond,* which dealt obliquely with the real-life tensions between Jane Fonda and her father Henry, this new film seems like a way for the Douglases to test and resolve assorted family issues—to reach closure, that most elusive of psychobabble goals.

The film is certainly courageous in the way it deals with Kirk Douglas's stroke, Michael Douglas's infidelity, and the drug problems of a son played by Cameron Douglas. Even if the movie doesn't reflect real life, any attentive reader of the supermarket sleaze sheets will guess that it comes close. In a way, just by making the film, the Douglases have opened themselves up to that.

My wish is that they'd opened up a little more. The movie deals with these touchy subjects, and others, but in a plot so jammed with events, disputes, tragedies, and revelations that the most serious matters don't seem to receive enough attention. The film seems too much in a hurry.

It introduces us to the Grombergs. Alex (Michael Douglas) is a prosperous attorney whose father, Mitchell (Kirk Douglas), was a founder of the firm. Not a bad man, Alex volunteers in a soup kitchen, where a sexy fellow volunteer (Sarita Choudhury) finds him so attractive that she all but forces them to have sex, which they do—almost. Their scenes are stunningly unconvincing, except as a convenience to the plot.

At home, Alex is married to Rebecca (Bernadette Peters) and his father is married to Evelyn (Diana Douglas, who was, in an intriguing casting choice, Kirk's real-life first wife). Alex and Rebecca have two sons, the college student Asher (Cameron Douglas, Michael's son by his first marriage) and the eleven-year-old Eli (Rory Culkin, whose family could also inspire a movie). Mitchell also has a brother who is senile and lives in a care facility.

During the course of the movie, there will be two deaths, Alex's marriage will almost break up because of suspected infidelity, Asher will get in trouble with the law, Eli will go on a walk on the wild side with a nose-ringed eleven-year-old girlfriend, and Alex and Mitchell will seem incapable of having a conversation that doesn't descend into criticism and resentment. Only the old folks, Mitchell and Evelyn, seem to have found happiness, perhaps out of sheer exhaustion with the alternatives.

The film, directed by Fred Schepisi, has moments I fear are intended to be more serious than they play. One involves a midnight mission by Alex and Mitchell to set a rowboat adrift with an illegal cargo. I did not for a moment believe this scene, at least not in an ostensibly serious movie. Would two high-powered lawyers collaborate on such an act? When it is clear they can be traced? Really?

The scenes between Michael and Kirk Douglas, which are intended as the heart of the movie, seem inadequately realized in Jesse Wigutow's screenplay. They fret, fence, and feud, but without the sense of risk and hurt we felt between the two Fondas. Even less satisfying are the marital arguments between Alex and Rebecca, who has found a pair of panties in her husband's pocket. How they got there and what they mean, or don't mean, could be easily explained by the defensive husband—but he can never quite get the words out, and his dialogue remains infuriatingly inconclusive. As a result, all of the tension between them feels like a plot contrivance.

There are some good moments. I liked Kirk Douglas's fierce force of personality, and I liked moments, almost asides, in which Michael Douglas finds simple humanity amid the emotional chaos. There is a lovely scene involving Rory Culkin and his first date (Irene Gorovaia), in which their dialogue feels just about right for those two in that time and place. Their first kiss is a reminder that few first kisses are exactly wonderful. And a scene where Kirk and Diana Douglas dance has a simple warmth and truth.

But the movie is simply not clear about where it wants to go and what it wants to do. It is heavy on episode and light on insight, and although it takes courage to bring up touchy topics it would have taken more to treat them frankly.

What about a movie in which a great actor, now somewhat slowed by a stroke, collaborates with his successful son in a movie that will involve other family members and even the great actor's first wife? What does the great actor's second wife (who has been married to him for almost fifty years) think of that? What about a movie in which the son divorces his first wife to marry a famous beauty, who then wins an Oscar? These musings may seem unfair, but *It Runs in the Family* makes them inevitable. The Douglas family would have to make one hell of a movie to do justice to their real lives.

It's All Gone Pete Tong ★ ★ ★
R, 90 m., 2005

Paul Kaye (Frankie Wilde), Mike Wilmot (Max Haggar), Beatriz Batarda (Penelope), Kate Magowan (Sonja), Pete Tong (Himself).
Directed by Michael Dowse and produced by Allan Niblo and James Richardson. Screenplay by Dowse.

Frankie Wilde is the king of the club scene in Ibiza, a Mediterranean island where jumbo jets ferry in party animals on package tours. He stands like a colossus above the dance floor, vibrating in sympathy with his audience. Lately he's even started to produce a few records. He has a big house, a beautiful wife, and a manager who worships him. What could go wrong?

Frankie goes deaf. Maybe it was the decibel level in his earphones, night after night. Maybe it's a side effect from his nonprescription drugs; given enough cocaine, he makes Al Pacino's Scarface look laid-back. Frankie (Paul Kaye) tries to fake it, but his sets become exercises in incompatible noise.

He and his manager, Max (Mike Wilmot), share a painful truth: "Generally, the field of music, other than the obvious example, has been dominated by people who can hear." (When I hear a line like that, I am divided between admiration for the writing, and concern for audience members who will be asking each other who the obvious example is.) Frankie goes berserk one night, and is carried out of his club and out of his world.

It's All Gone Pete Tong presents Frankie's story in mockumentary form. Like Werner Herzog and Zak Penn's *Incident at Loch Ness*, it goes to some effort to blur the line between fact and fiction. It insists Frankie Wilde was an actual disc jockey and interviews "real" witnesses to his rise and fall; there are fake Websites discussing his legend, but the movie is fiction. There really is a Pete Tong, however; he's a British disc jockey who is seen interviewing Frankie in a doc-within-the-mock.

The title is real, too. *It's All Gone Pete Tong* is Cockney rhyming slang for "It's all gone wrong," and that's what it's gone, all right, for Frankie Wilde. His wife and her son bail out, his manager despairs, and Frankie descends into a slough of despond, drink, and cocaine. Occasionally he is attacked by a large, hallucinatory stuffed bear, reminding me of the bats that attacked Hunter S. Thompson on the road to Vegas. There is a time when he has sticks of dynamite strapped like a crown to his head, but the movie was a little manic just at that moment and I am not completely sure if the dynamite was real or a fantasy. Real, I think.

The downward arc of the first two acts of

the movie is made harrowing and yet perversely amusing by the performance of Paul Kaye, a British comedian who sees Frankie as a clown who overacts even in despair. Then comes salvation in the form of a speech therapist named Penelope (Beatriz Batarda), who begins by teaching Frankie to lip-read and ends by saving his life and restoring him to happiness. Much of the solution involves Frankie's discovery that he can feel the vibes of the music through the soles of his feet; the discovery comes because, as he claims at one point, he is "the Imelda Marcos of flip-flops."

The movie works because of its heedless comic intensity; Kaye and his writer-director, a first-timer named Michael Dowse, chronicle the rise and fall of Frankie Wilde as other directors have dealt with emperors and kings.

Frankie may not be living the most significant life of our times, but tell that to Frankie. There is a kind of desperation in any club scene (as *24-Hour Party People* memorably demonstrated); it can be exhausting, having a good time, and the relentless pursuit of happiness becomes an effort to recapture remembered bliss from the past.

Note: For me, a bonus was the island of Ibiza itself. It became famous in America in the early 1970s as the home of an author named Clifford Irving, who forged the memoirs of Howard Hughes and almost got away with it. In his defense, let it be said that Irving probably did a better job on the book than Hughes would have, and that he gave to the world his mistress, Nina Van Pallandt, who starred in Robert Altman's The Long Goodbye *(1973) as a woman one would gladly forge for, and with.*

J

The Jacket ★ ★
R, 102 m., 2005

Adrien Brody (Jack Starks), Keira Knightley (Jackie), Kris Kristofferson (Dr. Becker), Jennifer Jason Leigh (Dr. Lorenson), Daniel Craig (Mackenzie), Kelly Lynch (Jean), Brad Renfro (Stranger). Directed by John Maybury and produced by George Clooney, Peter Guber, and Steven Soderbergh. Screenplay by Massy Tadjedin.

In Iraq in 1991, an American soldier momentarily trusts a small boy, who has a gun and shoots him in the head. "That was the first time I died," says Jack Starks, the soldier, played by Adrien Brody as if he's not quite sure he didn't. That's not a criticism, but a description: The metaphysical and real horrors undergone by Jack in this movie include dying, not dying, feeling like he's dead, wishing he were dead, and being locked alive for long periods in a morgue drawer. No way to treat a returning hero.

Adrien Brody is an ideal actor for such a role, since his face can reflect such dread and suffering. He also has a cocky, upbeat speed (see *Bread and Roses*), but since *The Pianist* directors have used him for mournfulness. He has a lot to mourn this time.

After being declared dead in Iraq, it's discovered he's alive after all, and Jack is returned to the States and treated for amnesia. Out on his own, he's hitching through Vermont when he comes upon a spaced-out mother (Kelly Lynch) and her worried young daughter; their car has broken down. After helping them, he gets a lift with a passing motorist, who soon enough kills a cop. Jack passes out and wakes up to find himself a convicted cop killer, sent to a mental asylum. If only he could find that woman and daughter, he could establish an alibi. But the woman was zoned out, and the daughter was only a child.

The asylum is not one of your modern and enlightened asylums. Edgar Allan Poe would raise his eyebrows. It's run by Dr. Becker (Kris Kristofferson), whose theories are a cover for his sadism, or maybe it's the other way around. He believes that locking cold, wet patients in morgue drawers for long hours will help them—I dunno, get in touch with their feelings, or remember why they're there. Who knows.

The movie now begins to play with time. In a gas station, Jack, forlorn and homeless, is befriended by a woman named Jackie (Keira Knightley, from *Bend It Like Beckham*). She takes him home, cares for him, and here's where we have to get crafty to preserve plot points. To make a long plot short, when he is in the morgue drawer, Jack's brain, traumatized by a head wound, amnesia, and shock treatments, is able to time travel. Or maybe Jack himself physically time travels; the people who meet him on his journeys certainly think he's really there.

It's up to Jackie to believe this story and act on it, so that Jack can use his knowledge of the future to make important decisions in the present. Or maybe it's in the future that he makes the decisions, and in the past that he carried them out. Take notes. Able to assist him, if she believes his story, is Dr. Lorenson (Jennifer Jason Leigh) and even the evil, retired Dr. Becker himself. Lorenson always looked askance at Becker's barbaric methods. Try it yourself sometime, looking askance. Can be fun.

Meanwhile, the movie, taking its cue from Jack's deep weariness and depression, trudges through its paces as if it were deep and meaningful, which I am afraid it is not. It involves two or three time-paradox tricks too many to take seriously as anything other than a plot crafted to jump through all the temporal hoops. I was reminded of *Jacob's Ladder* (1990), also about a traumatized vet who descends into the abyss between the real and the imagined. I admired it at the time, but have been meaning to view it again after Fr. Andrew Greeley told me he thinks it's one of the most spiritual films of our time.

The Jacket will probably not make Andy's list. It has some touching moments between Jack and Jackie, whose curious willingness to trust him is explained in reasonable terms. But Dr. Becker comes intact from an old Hammer horror film, and would be right at home in *Scream and Scream Again* (1969), which involves a character who keeps waking up to find his inventory of body parts is shrinking. Becker's torturous "treatments" of Jack are so bizarre that the gentler and more philosophical possibilities in the story go astray.

The director, John Maybury, made *Love Is the Devil* (1998), a film about the British artist Francis Bacon, whose portraits of his subjects often seemed to catch them in their post–*Scream and Scream Again* periods. It was a perceptive, good film. In *The Jacket* you can sense an impulse toward a better film, and Adrien Brody and Keira Knightley certainly take it seriously, but the time-travel whiplash effect sets in, and it becomes, as so many time-travel movies do, an exercise in early entrances, late exits, futile regrets. If there is anything worse than time creeping at its petty pace from day to day, it would be if time jumped around. Better to die at the end, don't you think, than randomly, from time to time?

Japanese Story ★ ★ ★ ½
R, 110 m., 2004

Toni Collette (Sandy Edwards), Gotaro Tsunashima (Tachibana Hiromitsu), Matthew Dyktynski (Bill Baird), Lynette Curran (Mum), Yumiko Tanaka (Yukiko Hiromitsu), Kate Atkinson (Jackie), John Howard (Richards), Bill Young (Jimmy Smithers). Directed by Sue Brooks and produced by Sue Maslin. Screenplay by Alison Tilson.

Toni Collette can have an angular presence on the screen; she can look hard and tough, and is well cast in *Japanese Story* as an unmarried geologist whose idea of dinner is a can of baked beans poured over two slices of toast. But then there comes another side that is tender and dreamy. Her body becomes sensuous instead of distant, and her eyes are seeing from a different part of her soul.

Both of those identities are used in Sue Brooks's *Japanese Story*, a film in which her character journeys into the Australian desert with a Japanese businessman she begins by hating, and then begins to . . . not love, but cherish. She plays Sandy, an expert on the mining of minerals. She's assigned to baby-sit Tachibana (Gotaro Tsunashima), who has flown in from Kyoto and whose father owns 9 percent of the company.

Sandy flies with him to a dorp town in the interior, rents a Jeep, and shows him the mine: a massive hole in the ground whose terraces remind him of a Mayan temple. Then he wants to drive on, further, into the vastness. She protests. There's only a one-track dirt road, and "People die in this desert. Frequently." Their Jeep gets mired in the fine powder of the red earth, they can't drive it out or dig it out, they spend a cold night around a campfire, and she is very, very angry, because Tachibana got them into this mess, and it looks as if they may die, and he refuses to use his cell phone because of shame: Having caused their trouble, he refuses to admit it to his colleagues.

This sounds like some sort of survival adventure, but even in the moments of despair in the desert, *Japanese Story* is about characters, not plot. The Japanese man is not fluent in English, but he knows a great many more words than he first reveals. He doesn't know she's a geologist, and treats her like his driver (he lets her wrestle his heavy suitcase into the Jeep). But during the long, cold night (at one point she shifts to put her back against his, for warmth), something rotates in his consciousness, and the next day there are scenes in which each looks at the other for a long time, thinking, sensing, beginning to like. That night in a motel, they make love; undressing, she puts on his pants before walking over to the bed.

And now you must put the review aside, if you plan to see the movie. There is something I want you to experience for yourself.

What future do they have? None, really, even before she sees the photograph of his wife and family in his billfold. They're strangers with a thousand words between them, in the middle of a limitless empty place. What they have is not merely sex, yet not love; it is more like a means of communication to show relief and acceptance. Then, in a moment of heedless fun, he has an absurd accident and dies. Snap, the movie breaks in two. She must wrestle his body into the Jeep, take it to a small town, find Smithers the undertaker

("We'll put it in the cold room so it doesn't go off"), and deal with the police, the report, her colleagues . . . and the widow, who is flying in from Japan.

It's here that the movie demonstrates what it's been trying to say all along. Alison Tilson's screenplay follows its logic into deep feelings. What does another person mean to us, really, if they are not available to share our lives, and we cannot really know them—but we cherish them for the transient joy they have shared with us? Who was he, really? She had to ask which was his first and which his family name. Did he ever know her surname? After surviving death in the desert, after saving each other's lives, after making love and looking at the belittling landscape and becoming a team of two in an ocean of emptiness, they have come to this: His corpse, its head lolling from side to side, as she cleans off the sand and mud with a cloth.

Japanese Story never steps wrong in its crucial closing passages, especially in the precise and exact way that Sandy and the widow have a limited but bottomless communication. The mundane details of the undertaker, the coroner, the police, and the funeral are like a series of events that are—wrong. Wrong, all wrong, because Tachibana should not be dead. There is no sense in it. He lost his life in a senseless instant, and brought a horrible finality to a relationship not real enough to support it; it should have ended with a kiss and some tears and a rueful smile at an airport. It imposed enormous significance on their time together, which did not deserve and cannot support such significance. What she feels at the end, I think, is not love for him or sorrow, but a great pity that his whole life should have been wiped away and lost for no reason at all, just like that, carelessly, thoughtlessly, in the middle of things.

The movie wants to record how such things happen, and how they present the survivor with an insoluble challenge: What does Sandy think, how does she behave, what should she feel, what should she do now? Patiently, observantly, it takes her through all of these questions and shows her clumsy, but honest attempt to answer them. And gradually the full arc of Toni Collette's performance reveals itself, and we see that the end was there even in the beginning. This is that rare sort of film that is not about what happens, but about what happens then.

Jeepers Creepers 2 ★
R, 103 m., 2003

Ray Wise (Jack Taggart), Jonathan Breck (The Creeper), Travis Schiffner (Izzy Bohen), Eric Nenninger (Scott Braddock), Al Santos (Dante Belasco), Nicki Lynn Aycox (Minxie Hayes). Directed by Victor Salva and produced by Tom Luse. Screenplay by Salva.

Every 23rd spring, for 23 days, it gets to eat.
—opening title of Jeepers Creepers 2

The next shot is ominously subtitled: *Day 22.* A young boy is installing scarecrows in a field when he notices that one of them looks—not right. He approaches, sees the claws, and then becomes the first of many characters in this movie to fortify the Creeper for his next twenty-three-year hibernation. Cut to a school bus filled with a team returning from an out-of-town game along a highway where there is not one single other vehicle. The team and cheerleaders are singing a song, which is more or less required, I think, on buses where the passengers will soon be faced with unspeakable horrors.

Victor Salva's *Jeepers Creepers 2* supplies us with a first-class creature, a fourth-rate story, and dialogue possibly created by feeding the screenplay into a pasta maker. The movie basically consists of a half-man, half-bat that whooshes down out of the sky and snatches its prey. Sometimes it rips the tops off of old Rambler station wagons, and it opens up a pretty good hole in the top of the school bus. Meanwhile local farmer Jack Taggart (Ray Wise) tears himself away from his post-hole puncher, narrows his eyes, and stares intently at the edge of the screen while remembering that this all happened twenty-three years ago (maybe) or that the creature has eaten his youngest son (certainly).

The most notable character on the bus is Scott Braddock (Eric Nenninger), a virulent homophobe who doth, I think, protest too much as he accuses fellow team members of being gay. Later he tries to clear the bus of everyone the Creeper looked at, because then the ones who aren't his targets will be safe. This sidesteps the fact that the Creeper looked at Scott. One of the pom-pom girls has a hallucination or vision or something, and is able to explain that the creature chooses his victims according to body parts he requires, both as nutrition and as replacements. (Think through the lyrics of the song "Jeepers Creepers," and you'll get the idea.)

To call the characters on the bus paper thin would be a kindness. Too bad, then, that we spend so much time on the bus, listening to their wretched dialogue and watching as they race from one window to another to see what foul deeds are occurring outside. Speaking of outside, Scott is the obligatory obstreperous jerk who is forever speculating that the creature has gone and won't return; he keeps suggesting they leave the bus to trek to a hypothetical nearby farmhouse. He's a direct throwback to the standard character in Dead Teenager Movies who's always saying, "Hmmm . . . all of the other campers have been found dead and eviscerated, Mimsy, so this would be an ideal time to walk out into the dark woods and go skinny-dipping in the pond where dozens of kids have died in the previous movies in this series."

Despite Scott's homophobia, the movie has a healthy interest in the male physique, and it's amazing how many of the guys walk around bare-chested. The critic John Fallon writes, "At a certain point, I thought I was watching soft gay erotica," and observes that when four of the guys go outside to pee, they line up shoulder to shoulder, which strikes him as unlikely since they are in a very large field. True in another movie, but in a film where the Creeper is likely to swoop down at any second and carry someone away, I would pick the tallest guy and stand next to him, on the theory that lightning will strike the tree and not you.

It is futile to bring logic to a film like this, but here goes: At one point, we hear local newscasters discussing the shocking discovery of 300 corpses knit together into a tapestry in the basement of an old church—all of them with one body part missing. So obviously the Creeper has been operating in the area for years. Would anyone notice 300 disappearances in a county so small that the main road has no

traffic? Maybe that's what Jack Taggart is thinking about as he studies the side of the screen: "Hmmm . . . wonder if the disappearance of my son is connected to the carnage that occurs every twenty-three years hereabouts?"

The movie wants to work at the level of scaring us every so often with unexpected sudden attacks of the Creeper, although in this genre you expect sudden unexpected attacks, so you end up evaluating the craftsmanship instead of being scared. On that level, praise for the makeup and costume departments, including Richard Redlefsen, credited for "Creeper makeup and lead suit." Why the creature is called the Creeper when he leaps and flies, I am not sure. Why Francis Ford Coppola decided to produce this movie, I am also not sure.

Jersey Girl ★ ★ ★ ½
PG-13, 103 m., 2004

Ben Affleck (Ollie Trinke), Liv Tyler (Maya Harding), George Carlin (Bart Trinke), Raquel Castro (Gertie Trinke), Jason Biggs (Arthur Brickman), Jennifer Lopez (Gertrude). Directed by Kevin Smith and produced by Scott Mosier. Screenplay by Smith.

Jersey Girl is a romantic comedy written and directed by a kinder, gentler Kevin Smith. It's the kind of movie Hugh Grant might make, except for the way Smith has with his dialogue, which is truer and more direct than we expect. There are a couple of scenes here where a video store clerk cuts directly to the bottom line, and it feels like all sorts of romantic rules and regulations are being rewritten.

The movie stars Ben Affleck as Ollie Trinke, a hotshot Manhattan publicist whose beloved wife, Gertrude (Jennifer Lopez), is great with child. I would hesitate to reveal that she dies in childbirth if I had not already read and heard this information, oh, like 500 times, so obsessed is the nation with Ben and J-Lo. Lopez is luminous in her few scenes, helping to explain why Ollie remains so true to her memory that he remains celibate for many years.

His career meanwhile goes to pieces. Under pressure to hold a job while raising a daughter, he loses it one day, fatally offending his employers by causing a scene at the opening of a Hard Rock Café; he fails to understand why he should take Will Smith seriously ("Yeah, like the Fresh Prince of Bel Air is ever gonna have a movie career"). By the time the story resumes, he has moved back to New Jersey and is living in the same house with his father, Bart (George Carlin), and his beloved daughter, Gertie (Raquel Castro), who is now about seven. He's not in public relations anymore; he works with his dad in the public works department.

Because Ben Affleck is a movie star and looks like one, you might expect him to start dating eventually, but no. You might expect that he could find another high-paying PR job, but no. He doesn't because *then there wouldn't be a movie.* When a movie isn't working, we get all logical about things like this, but when it works, we relax.

Several times a week, Ollie and Gertie go to the local video store, where she plunders the kiddie section while he makes a quick dash through the bamboo curtain to grab a porno. One night he's confronted by Maya (Liv Tyler), the clerk, who claims she's taking a survey about pornography usage and asks Ollie how many times a week he masturbates. She is seriously disturbed by his reply, alarmed to learn he has had no sex in seven years, and informs him, "We're gonna have some sex."

And it's in a scene like this that Kevin Smith shows why he's such a good comedy writer. There is a bedrock of truth in the scene, which is based on embarrassment and shyness and Maya's disconcerting ability to say exactly what she's thinking, and when Ollie tries to explain why he has remained celibate (except for his relationship with countless porno titles), she patiently explains about sex: "It's the same thing only you're saving the $2 rental fee."

Inarguable logic, but he demurs, finally breaking down and agreeing to a lunch date. And thus does love reenter Ollie's life. For Maya may be bold about sex, but she is serious about love, and soon Gertie is saying, "Hey, you're the lady from the video store" at a moment when it would be much, much better had she not walked into the room.

Liv Tyler is a very particular talent who has sometimes been misused by directors more in love with her beauty than with her appropriateness for their story. Here she is perfectly cast as the naive and sincere Maya, whose boldness is *not* a seduction technique but an act of generosity, almost of mercy. It takes a special tone for a woman to convince us she wants to sleep with a man out of the goodness of her heart, but Tyler finds it, and it brings a sweetness to the relationship.

Kevin Smith, I believe, has spent almost as much time in video stores as Quentin Tarantino, and his study of ancient clichés is put to good use in the closing act of his movie, which depends on not one but three off-the-shelf formulas: (1) the choice between the big city and staying with your family in a small town; (2) the parent who arrives at a school play just at the moment when the child onstage is in despair because that parent seems to be missing; and (3) the slow clap syndrome. Smith is a gifted writer and I believe he knew exactly what he was doing by assembling these old reliables. I'm not sure he couldn't have done better, but by then we like the characters so much that we give the school play a pass.

Besides—without the school play, we wouldn't get a chance to see the set constructed for little Gertie by two of the guys who work with Bart and Ollie in the public works department. Let it be said that the Lyric Opera's set for *Madame Butterfly* was only slightly more elaborate.

Jet Lag ★ ★
R, 85 m., 2003

Jean Reno (Felix), Juliette Binoche (Rose), Sergi Lopez (Sergio), Scali Delpeyrat (Doctor), Karine Belly (Air France Hostess), Raoul Billerey (Felix's father). Directed by Daniele Thompson and produced by Alain Sarde. Screenplay by Christopher Thompson and Daniele Thompson.

Jet Lag is sort of a grown-up version of *Before Sunrise.* In both films two travelers Meet Cute by chance and spend a long night in a strange city, talking and eating and flirting and concealing and revealing. The difference between the two films is sort of depressing.

In *Before Sunrise* (1995), Ethan Hawke and Julie Delpy were young students, and they wandered all over Vienna, encountering fortune-tellers, street poets, and friendly bartenders. In *Jet Lag,* Jean Reno and Juliette Binoche are meant to be twenty years older, and although they are in Paris they do not wander the streets or meet fascinating people, but huddle in airport lounges, hotel rooms, and tourist restaurants. The younger people talk about reincarnation, dreams, death, etc. The older people talk about abusive boyfriends, parental alienation, and cuisine.

That's the whole story, right there: The young people have their lives ahead of them and are filled with hope. The older ones are stuck with responsibilities, relationships, careers, and fears. Although *Jet Lag* has a certain morose appeal, we cannot help thinking that this night they've spent together is the most interesting time either character has had in years, and if they get married, they will look back on it as if they were out of their minds.

There are, however, moments of intrigue. Some of them involve Juliette Binoche's makeup. If you know her from her many movies (she won the Oscar for *The English Patient*), you know she has a fresh, natural complexion. As we first see her in *Jet Lag*, she is wearing too much makeup of the wrong kind, and it doesn't flatter her. Makeup is her business, in a vague way. At one point she wipes it all off, and looks younger and more beautiful. Because the director, Daniele Thompson, devotes a lot of the movie to the close-up scrutiny of her actors, this transformation has a fascination entirely apart from the character Binoche plays.

Jean Reno is a rough-hewn French star, always with what looks like a two-week-old beard, often seen in action movies (*La Femme Nikita*). Here he shows gentleness and humor, and we believe him as a celebrity chef who was once great but is now merely rich. When the Binoche character mixes a vinaigrette for him and he likes it, their fate seems possibly sealed.

The plot is based on contrivance. They meet because she needs to borrow his cell phone. When their flights are canceled, he offers to let her stay in his hotel room, the last one available at the airport. We meet her current, former, and perhaps future boyfriend, a jealous creep. We hear about how the Reno character walked out of the life of his father, also a famous chef. They keep getting calls on the wrong phone.

But somehow none of this really matters. The movie is set up as if it should matter—as if much depends on whether they fall in love. The beauty of *Before Sunrise* was that nothing was supposed to matter. They talked, they walked, and the movie (directed by Richard Linklater) was content to let them do that, without forcing false obstacles and goals upon them.

I don't know if the distance between the two films is because of the difference in filmmakers or the difference in ages. It may be that we have a heedlessness around twenty that we have lost, perhaps prudently, around forty. One thing I know for sure: When you're twenty you know that one night could change your life forever, and when you're forty, not only do you doubt that, but you're sort of relieved.

Jiminy Glick in La La Wood ★ ½
R, 90 m., 2005

Martin Short (Jiminy Glick/David Lynch), Jan Hooks (Dixie Glick), Elizabeth Perkins (Miranda Coolidge), Linda Cardellini (Natalie Coolidge), Janeane Garofalo (Dee Dee), Corey Pearson (Ben DiCarlo), Carlos Jacott (Barry King), John Michael Higgins (Andre Divine). Directed by Vadim Jean and produced by Bernie Brillstein, Paul Brooks, Peter Safran, and Martin Short. Screenplay by Martin Short, Paul Flaherty, and Michael Short.

The problem with Jiminy Glick is that he doesn't know who he is. Or, more precisely, Martin Short doesn't know who he is. Jiminy is allegedly a chubby TV news entertainment reporter from Butte, Montana, who alternates between fawning over celebrities, insulting them, and not quite knowing who they are. I can sympathize. When I ran into Jiminy at the Toronto Film Festival, I didn't know he was Martin Short; the makeup job was masterful, and I hadn't seen the character in his earlier TV manifestations. One of the side effects of seeing 500 movies a year is that you miss a lot of TV.

Martin Short himself is one of the funniest men alive, or can be, and has been. But Jiminy Glick needs definition if he's to work as a character. We have to sense a consistent comic personality, and we don't; Short changes gears and redefines the character whenever he needs a laugh. That means Jiminy is sometimes clueless, sometimes uses knowledgeable in-jokes, sometimes is a closeted gay, sometimes merely neuter, sometimes an inane talk show host, and at other times essentially just

Martin Short having fun with his celebrity friends.

Jiminy Glick in La La Wood takes the character to the Toronto Film Festival, where he confronts celebrities in situations that are sometimes spontaneous, sometimes scripted. He stays in a hotel from hell with his wife, Dixie (Jan Hooks), and their twin sons, Matthew and Modine. He is obsessed with getting an interview with the reclusive Ben DiCarlo (Corey Pearson), director of *Growing Up Gandhi,* in which the young Mahatma is seen as a prizefighter. He is also entranced by the presence of the legendary star Miranda Coolidge (Elizabeth Perkins).

The movie combines two story lines: Jiminy interviewing celebs, and Jiminy trapped in a nightmarish murder scenario narrated by David Lynch (played by Short himself, uncannily well). Lynch lights his already-lit cigarette and intones ominous insights about the lonely highway of doom, and Miranda's blood-drenched handkerchief turns up in Jiminy's possession; perhaps he did not merely dream that he murdered her.

The murder plot is a nonstarter (not funny, not necessary), and although Short does a good David Lynch, he stops at imitation and doesn't go for satire. He's at his best in a couple of sit-down interviews with cooperative movie stars (Kurt Russell and Steve Martin), in what feel like improvised Q&A sessions; he asks Martin, for example, if it's true that the commies still run Hollywood, and Martin refuses to name names—except for Meg Ryan and Tom Hanks. There is also an intriguing discussion of Martin's theory of tabletops and testicles, which put me in mind of his famous magic trick where eggs and lighted cigarettes emerge from his fly.

A comedy could be made about inane celebrity interviewers, yes, but it would have to be more reality-oriented. When a real person like Joe Franklin exists, how can Jiminy Glick outflank him? A comedy could be made about the Toronto Film Festival, but it would need to know more about festivals; interviewers from Butte, Montana, do not ordinarily have their private festival publicity person to knock on the hotel room every morning with a list of the day's interviews, and Glick (or Short) misses a chance to skewer publicists,

junkets, and the hissy fits of critics afraid they'll miss a big movie.

Some stand-alone moments are funny. Jiminy thinks Whoopi Goldberg is Oprah Winfrey ("Remember, my name is spelled O-p-e-r-a," she advises him). Rappers in a hotel corridor try to teach an African how to sound like an American hip-hopper, but try as he will, "Y'allknowhaimean" comes out as "Yao Ming." And Jiminy and Kurt Russell begin a discussion about Elvis Presley, whom Russell starred with as a child actor and later, as an adult, played in a movie. Where this discussion eventually leads is hard to believe, and impossible to describe. And when David Lynch says, "My name is David Lynch. I'm a director," I like Jiminy's reply: "Well who isn't, dear?"

Johnny English ★ ½
PG, 87 m., 2003

Rowan Atkinson (Johnny English), John Malkovich (Pascal Sauvage), Natalie Imbruglia (Lorna Campbell), Ben Miller (Bough), Douglas McFerran (Klaus Vendetta), Tim Pigott-Smith (Pegasus), Kevin McNally (Prime Minister). Directed by Peter Howitt. and produced by Tim Bevan, Eric Fellner, and Mark Huffam. Screenplay by Neal Purvis, Robert Wade, and William Davies.

Can we all pretty much agree that the spy genre has been spoofed to death? The James Bond movies have supplied the target for more than forty years, and generations of Bond parodies have come and gone, from Dean Martin's Matt Helm to Mike Myers's Austin Powers. If *Austin Powers* is the funniest of the Bondian parodies, *Johnny English* is the least necessary, a mild-mannered ramble down familiar paths.

The movie stars Rowan Atkinson, best known in America as Mr. Bean, star of *Bean* (1997), and as the star of the PBS reruns of *The Black Adder,* where he played countless medieval schemers and bumblers in "the most gripping sitcom since 1380." He's the master of looking thoughtful after having committed a grievous breach of manners, logic, the law, personal hygiene, or common sense.

In *Johnny English,* he plays a character who became famous in Britain as the star of a long-running series of credit-card commercials. Johnny English is a low-level functionary in the British Secret Service pressed into active duty when a bomb destroys all of the other agents. His assignment: Foil a plot to steal the crown jewels.

The evil mastermind is Pascal Sauvage (John Malkovich), a French billionaire who believes his family was robbed of the crown two centuries ago. Now the head of a mega-billion-dollar international chain of prisons, he poses as a benefactor who pays to protect the jewels in new theft-proof quarters in the Tower of London—but actually plans to steal them and co-opt the archbishop of Canterbury to crown him king. And how does Queen Elizabeth II feel about this? The film's funniest moment has her signing an abdication form after a gun is pointed at the head of one of her beloved corgis.

The movie is a series of scenes demonstrating how dangerously incompetent Johnny English is, as when he lectures on how the thieves got into the tower without noticing he is standing on the edge of a tunnel opening. He can't even be trusted to drive during a chase scene, and spends most of one in a car suspended from a moving wrecker's crane. Meanwhile the beautiful Lorna Campbell (Natalie Imbruglia) turns up coincidentally wherever he goes, performing a variety of functions, of which the only explicable one is to be the beautiful Lorna Campbell.

John Malkovich does what can be done with Pascal Sauvage, I suppose, including the French accent we assume is deliberately bad, since Malkovich lives in France and no doubt has a better one. The character is such a stick and a stooge, however, that all Malkovich can do is stand there and be mugged by the script. Funnier work is done by Ben Miller, as Johnny's sidekick Bough (pronounced "Boff"). After Johnny breaks up the wrong funeral, Bough saves the day by passing him off as an escaped lunatic.

And so on. Rowan Atkinson is terrifically popular in Britain, less so here, because as a nation we do not find understatement hilarious. *Johnny English* plays like a tired exercise, a spy spoof with no burning desire to be that, or anything else. The thing you have to credit Mike Myers for is that he loves to play Austin Powers

and is willing to try anything for a laugh. Atkinson seems to have had Johnny English imposed upon him. And thus upon us.

Johnson Family Vacation ★ ★
PG-13, 95 m., 2004

Cedric the Entertainer (Nate Johnson), Vanessa L. Williams (Dorothy Johnson), Bow Wow (DJ Johnson), Solange Knowles (Nikki Johnson), Shannon Elizabeth (Chrishelle), Gabby Soleil (Destiny), Steve Harvey (Max Johnson), Shari Headley (Jackie Johnson), Tanjareen Martin (Tangerine), Lorna Scott (Gladys), Aloma Wright (Glorietta). Directed by Christopher Erskin and produced by Cedric the Entertainer, Paul Hall, Wendy Park, and Eric Rhone. Screenplay by Todd R. Jones and Earl Richey Jones.

Cedric the Entertainer can be a break-out comic force if given the least opportunity, but *Johnson Family Vacation* tames him in a routine cross-country comedy that feels exactly like a series of adventures recycled out of every other cross-country comedy. There's even a semi that tries to run them off the road.

The movie begins in a California suburb, where the Johnson family is on thin ice. Nate (Cedric) lives in the family house with his son, DJ (Bow Wow), while his wife, Dorothy (Vanessa L. Williams), teenage daughter, Nikki (Solange Knowles), and preschooler Destiny (Gabby Soleil) have moved into a second house nearby. Dorothy agrees to go along on the trip in a last-gasp attempt to save the marriage. So off they go in Nate's new Lincoln Navigator, which has been pimped out by the overeager car dealer (hard to explain, however, the Burberry pattern on the head rests). It will be a running gag that Nate has to return the car unscratched in order to get a replacement, which of course means the car will be scratched, dented, crashed, and covered in concrete before the trip is over. To repair the car, Cedric turns up in a dual role as Uncle Earl, a wizard mechanic.

Many of their adventures along the way involve Nate's decision to pick up a sexy but obviously flaky hitchhiker named Chrishelle (Shannon Elizabeth), who for fairly obscure reasons sneaks a Gila monster into their hotel room, but this subplot just doesn't work; better to stick with family dynamics than have Nate pick up a hitchhiker his wife obviously wants nothing to do with. Dorothy's idea of revenge—luring her husband into a hot tub and stealing his clothes, so that he has to tip-toe through the "Four Seasonings" hotel in the nude—is meant to be funny, but is cringe-inducing. Nothing about Dorothy's character makes us believe she would do that.

The family reunion, when they finally arrive, is all too brief, considering its comic possibilities. We meet Nate's older brother and lifetime rival, Max (Steve Harvey), who always wins the reunion trophy, and his mother, Glorietta (Aloma Wright), whose comic possibilities aren't developed. The rest of the family consists mostly of extras, and the Johnsons seem to be on their way home again after only a few hours.

The success of a movie like this depends on comic invention. The general outline is already clear: During the trip, the Johnsons will endure many misadventures, but the broken marriage will be mended. Whether we laugh or not depends on what happens to them along the way. Cedric, whose character is channeling Chevy Chase from *National Lampoon's Summer Vacation,* is a gifted comedian who could have brought the movie to life, but the screenplay by Todd R. Jones and Earl Richey Jones is paint-by-numbers, and one-time music video director Christopher Erskin films in a style without zing.

There's one funny scene where Nate bans his son from playing rap music by "anyone who got shot"—like Tupac or Biggie. He throws those CDs out the window. Then the son goes to work on his dad's CD collection, also with singers who got shot, like Marvin Gaye. This is such a neat turnaround that you wonder why the movie doesn't have more inspirations like that. It deals with specifics, but the movie itself is genial and unfocused and tired.

The Jungle Book 2 ★ ½
G, 72 m., 2003

With the voices of: Haley Joel Osment (Mowgli), John Goodman (Baloo), Mae Whitman (Shanti), Connor Funk (Ranjan), Tony Jay (Shere Khan), Bob Joles (Bagheera), Jim Cummings (Kaa/Colonel Hathi), Phil Collins (Lucky). An animated film directed by Steve Trenbirth and produced by Christopher Chase and Mary Thorne. Screenplay by Karl Geurs.

The Jungle Book 2 is so thin and unsatisfying it seems like a made-for-DVD version, not a theatrical release. Clocking in at seventy-two minutes and repeating the recycled song "The Bare Necessities" three if not four times, it offers a bare-bones plot in which Mowgli wanders off into the jungle, is threatened by a tiger and a snake, is protected by a bear, takes care of his little girlfriend, and sings and dances with Baloo.

There's none of the complexity here, in story or style, we expect in this new golden age of animation. It's a throwback in which cute animals of no depth or nuance play with the hero or threaten him in not very scary ways.

As the film opens, Mowgli (who once, long ago and at another level of literacy, was the hero of stories by Rudyard Kipling) lives in a village and is forbidden to cross the river. But "you can take boy out of the jungle, but you can't take the jungle out of boy," we learn. Whoever wrote that dialogue must have gone home weary after a hard day's work.

Mowgli (voice by Haley Joel Osment) and his little village playmate Shanti (voice by Mae Whitman) do, however, venture into the forest, where Mowgli's old friend Baloo the Bear (John Goodman) is delighted to see him, although a little jealous of all the attention he is paying to Shanti. Maybe Baloo should discuss this problem with a counselor. They dance and sing and peel mangos, and then Mowgli and/or Shanti wander off alone to be threatened by the tiger and the snake (whose coils are cleverly animated), and to be rescued by Baloo, with a reprise or two of "The Bare Necessities."

In a time that has given us Miyazaki's great animated film *Spirited Away* (also a Disney release), parents have some kind of duty to take a close look at the films offered. I got in an argument at Sundance with a Salt Lake City man who sells software that automatically censors DVDs in order to remove offending scenes and language. (Theoretically, there could be a version of *Fight Club* suitable for grade-schoolers, although it would be very short.) By this yardstick, *The Jungle Book 2* is inoffensive and harmless.

But it is not nutritious. A new book argues

that the average American child spends twice as much time watching television than interacting with his parents, and movies like *The Jungle Book 2* are dim-witted baby-sitters, not growth experiences. If kids grow up on the movie equivalent of fast food, they will form an addiction to that instant action high and will never develop the attention span they need to love worthwhile fiction.

Disney can do better, will do better, usually does better. To release this film theatrically is a compromise of its traditions and standards. If you have children in the target age range, keep them at home, rent an animated classic or Miyazaki's great *My Neighbor Totoro*, and do them a favor.

Just Married ★ ½
PG-13, 94 m., 2003

Ashton Kutcher (Tom Leezak), Brittany Murphy (Sarah McNerney), Christian Kane (Peter Prentis), Monet Mazur (Lauren McNerney), David Moscow (Kyle), Valeria (Wendy), David Rasche (Mr. McNerney), Veronica Cartwright (Mrs. McNerney), Raymond Barry (Mr. Leezak). Directed by Shawn Levy and produced by Robert Simonds. Screenplay by Sam Harper.

Just Married is an ungainly and witless comedy, made more poignant because its star, Brittany Murphy, made such a strong impression as Eminem's sometime girlfriend in *8 Mile*. With her fraught eyes and husky voice, she has a rare and particular quality (I think of Jennifer Jason Leigh), and yet here she's stuck in a dumb sitcom.

She and Ashton Kutcher play newlyweds in a plot that proves that opposites repel. She's a rich kid named Sarah, expensively raised and educated. He's Tom, an example of the emerging subspecies Sports Bar Man. They have a perfect relationship, spoiled by marriage (I think that may even be one of the lines in the movie). They're too tired for sex on their wedding night, but make up for it on their honeymoon flight to Europe with a quickie in the toilet of the airplane. There is perhaps the potential for a glimmer of comedy there, but not in Sam Harper's overwritten and Shawn Levy's overdirected movie, which underlines and emphasizes like a Power Point presentation for half-wits.

Consider. It may be possible to find humor in a scene involving sex in an airplane rest room, but not by pushing the situation so far that Tom's foot gets caught in the toilet and the bitchy flight attendant suffers a broken nose. Later, in their honeymoon hotel in Venice, it may be possible that energetic sex could break a bed frame—but can it actually destroy the wall to the adjoining room? And it may be possible for an improper electrical device to cause a short in a hotel's electrical system, but need the offending device be a vibrator? And for that matter, isn't it an alarming sign of incipient pessimism to take a vibrator along on your honeymoon?

Europe was not the right choice for this honeymoon. He should have gone to Vegas, and she should have stayed single. Sarah wants to visit every church and museum, but Tom abandons her in the middle of Venice when he finds a bar that's showing an American baseball game. This is as likely as a sports bar in Brooklyn televising *boules* in French.

Sarah and Tom have nothing to talk about. They are a pathetic, stupid couple and deserve each other. What they do not deserve, perhaps, is a screenplay that alternates between motivation and slapstick. Either it's character-driven or it isn't. If it is, then you can't take your plausible characters and dump them into Laurel and Hardy. Their rental car, for example, gets a cheap laugh, but makes them seem silly in the wrong way. And earlier in the film, Tom is responsible for the death of Sarah's dog in a scenario recycled directly from an urban legend everyone has heard.

Would it have been that much more difficult to make a movie in which Tom and Sarah were plausible, reasonably articulate newlyweds with the humor on their honeymoon growing out of situations we could believe? Apparently.

K

Kicking and Screaming ★ ★ ★
PG, 95 m., 2005

Will Ferrell (Phil Weston), Robert Duvall (Buck Weston), Kate Walsh (Barbara Weston), Mike Ditka (Himself), Dylan McLaughlin (Sam Weston), Josh Hutcherson (Bucky Weston), Musette Vander (Janice Weston), Elliott Cho (Byong Sun). Directed by Jesse Dylan and produced by Jimmy Miller. Screenplay by Leo Benvenuti and Steve Rudnick.

The problem with team sports involving kids is that the coaches are parents. The parents become too competitive and demanding, and put an unwholesome emphasis on winning. One simple reform would enormously improve childhood sports: The coaches should be kids, too. Parents could be around in supervisory roles, sort of like the major league commissioner, but kids should run their own teams. Sure, they'd make mistakes and the level of play would suffer and, in fact, the whole activity would look a lot more like a Game and less like a Sporting Event. Kids become so co-opted by the adult obsession with winning that they can't just mess around and have fun.

This insight came to me midway through *Kicking and Screaming*, which illustrates my theory by giving us a father-and-son coaching team who will haunt the nightmares of their players for decades to come. The movie is actually sweet and pretty funny, so don't get scared away: It's just that when a kid hears an adult say, "I eat quitters for breakfast and I spit out their bones," that kid is not going to rest easier tonight.

Will Ferrell stars as Phil Weston, an adult who still feels like a kid when his dad, Buck (Robert Duvall), is around. Buck is a version of Bull Meechum, the character Duvall played in *The Great Santini* (1979), where he was trying to run his family like a Marine unit. Buck coaches in the local kids' soccer league, and as the movie opens, he trades his grandson—*his own grandson*—because the kid is no good. That makes Phil mad: He was always told he was a loser, and now his own kid is getting the same treatment from Buck.

So Phil decides to become a coach himself. But he's just as obsessed with winning as his dad. He makes three key recruits. Two of them are the kids of the local Italian butcher; they're great players. The third is Mike Ditka, as himself; he's Buck's neighbor, the two men hate each other, and Ditka agrees to become Phil's assistant coach.

Phil's basic coaching strategy is simple: Get the ball to the Italians. The movie could have taken better advantage of Ditka by really focusing on his personality, but that would have shouldered aside the father-son rivalry, and so I guess they have it about right, with Ditka supplying advice and one-liners from the sidelines. He makes one crucial contribution to the plot: He introduces Phil to coffee. Phil has never been a coffee drinker, but from the first sip he finds it addictive, and then maddening. "What is that fascinating aroma?" he asks, before going on a caffeine binge that actually leads to him being barred for life from a coffee shop.

With Ferrell in the movie, we might expect a raucous comedy like *Old School*, or maybe *Dodgeball*, a movie I have to keep reminding myself Ferrell was not in. But no, *Kicking and Screaming* is more like *The Bad News Bears* or *The Mighty Ducks*, with the underdogs coming from the bottom of the league standings to eventually—but I dare not reveal the ending, even though it will be obvious to every sentient being in the theater.

Will Ferrell is now a major movie star. I learn of his status from the industry analyst David Poland, who has crunched the numbers and come up with the "real" list of box-office heavyweights. He says the top ten stars in terms of actual ticket sales are, in order: Will Smith, Tom Cruise, Adam Sandler, Jim Carrey, Russell Crowe, Tom Hanks, Eddie Murphy, Ben Stiller, Will Ferrell, and Denzel Washington. The highest-ranking woman on the list is Reese Witherspoon, at No. 12.

The list is fascinating because it sets Ferrell apart from several other recent *Saturday Night Live* alums cycling through hapless comedies; he has broken loose from the *SNL* curse that, for example, haunts Martin Short in *Jiminy Glick*. Ferrell plays actual characters, as he did in *Elf,* rather than recycled *SNL* skit creatures. In *Kicking and Screaming,* he understands that the role requires a certain vulnerability and poignancy, and although he goes berserk with all the coffee, it is kept within character. His soccer coach has an emotional arc and is not simply a cartoon. Duvall, of course, is superb. No one has a meaner laugh. He even begins to smile and you wish you were armed. He goes head-to-head with Ditka and you wait for them to spit out the bones.

The movie is pure formula from beginning to end, and it doesn't pay as much attention to the individual kids as it might have—especially to Byong Sun (Elliott Cho), the smallest member of the team, who seems to have something really going on down there among the knees of his opponents. There is also the usual thankless role of the hero's wife, played here by Kate Walsh; her job is to talk sense to Phil, which is never much fun. Buck's wife is a sexy bombshell played by Musette Vander, but she turns out to be sensible and sane, which is a disappointment. Still, *Kicking and Screaming* is an entertaining family movie, and may serve a useful purpose if it inspires kids to overthrow their coaches and take over their own sports.

Kill Bill: Volume 1 ★ ★ ★ ★
R, 93 m., 2003

Uma Thurman (The Bride), Lucy Liu (O-Ren Ishii), Daryl Hannah (Elle Driver), Vivica A. Fox (Vernita Green), Michael Parks (Sheriff), Sonny Chiba (Hattori Hanzo), Chiaki Kuriyama (Go Go Yubari), Julie Dreyfus (Sofie Fatale), David Carradine (Bill), Michael Madsen (Budd). Directed by Quentin Tarantino and produced by Lawrence Bender and Tarantino. Screenplay by Tarantino.

Kill Bill: Volume 1 shows Quentin Tarantino so effortlessly and brilliantly in command of his technique that he reminds me of a virtuoso violinist racing through "Flight of the Bumble Bee"—or maybe an accordion prodigy setting a speed record for "Lady of Spain." I mean that as a sincere compliment. The movie is not about anything at all except the skill and humor of its making. It's kind of brilliant.

His story is a distillation of the universe of martial arts movies, elevated to a trancelike mastery of the material. Tarantino is in the Zone. His story engine is revenge. In the opening scene, Bill kills all of the other members of a bridal party, and leaves The Bride (Uma Thurman) for dead. She survives for years in a coma, and is awakened by a mosquito's buzz. (Is QT thinking of Emily Dickinson, who heard a fly buzz when she died? I am reminded of Manny Farber's definition of the auteur theory: "A bunch of guys standing around trying to catch someone shoving art up into the crevices of dreck.")

The Bride is no Emily Dickinson. She reverses the paralysis in her legs by "focusing." Then she vows vengeance on the Deadly Viper Assassination Squad, and as *Volume 1* concludes she is about half-finished. She has wiped out Vernita Green (Vivica A. Fox) and O-Ren Ishii (Lucy Liu), and in *Volume 2* will presumably kill Elle Driver (Daryl Hannah), Budd (Michael Madsen), and, of course, Bill (David Carradine). If you think I have given away plot details, you think there can be doubt about whether the heroine survives the first half of a two-part action movie, and should seek help.

The movie is all storytelling and no story. The motivations have no psychological depth or resonance, but are simply plot markers. The characters consist of their characteristics. Lurking beneath everything, as it did with *Pulp Fiction,* is the suggestion of a parallel universe in which all of this makes sense in the same way that a superhero's origin story makes sense. There is a sequence here (well, it's more like a third of the movie) where The Bride singlehandedly wipes out O-Ren Ishii and her entire team, including the Crazy 88 Fighters, and we are reminded of Neo fighting the clones of Agent Smith in *The Matrix Reloaded,* except the Crazy 88 Fighters are individual human beings, I think. Do they get their name from the Crazy 88 blackjack games on the Web, or from Episode 88 of the action anime *Tokyo Crazy Paradise,* or should I seek help?

The Bride defeats the eighty-eight superb fighters (plus various bodyguards and specialists) despite her weakened state and recently paralyzed legs because she is a better fighter than all of the others put together. Is that because of the level of her skill, the power of her focus, or the depth of her need for vengeance?

Skill, focus, and need have nothing to do with it: She wins because she kills everybody without getting killed herself. You can sense Tarantino grinning a little as each fresh victim, filled with foolish bravado, steps forward to be slaughtered. Someone has to win in a fight to the finish, and as far as the martial arts genre is concerned, it might as well be the heroine. (All of the major characters except Bill are women, the men having been emasculated right out of the picture.)

Kill Bill: Volume 1 is not the kind of movie that inspires discussion of the acting, but what Thurman, Fox, and Liu accomplish here is arguably more difficult than playing the nuanced heroine of a Sundance thumb-sucker. There must be presence, physical grace, strength, personality, and the ability to look serious while doing ridiculous things. The tone is set in an opening scene, where The Bride lies near death and a hand rubs at the blood on her cheek, which will not come off because it is clearly congealed makeup. This scene further benefits from being shot in black and white; for QT, all shots in a sense are references to other shots—not particular shots from other movies, but archetypal shots in our collective moviegoing memories.

There's b&w in the movie, and slo-mo, and a name that's bleeped entirely for effect, and even an extended sequence in anime. The animated sequence, which gets us to Tokyo and supplies the backstory of O-Ren Ishii, is sneaky in the way it allows Tarantino to deal with material that might, in live action, seem too real for his stylized universe. It deals with a Mafia kingpin's pedophilia. The scene works in animated long shot; in live action close-up it would get the movie an NC-17.

Before she arrives in Tokyo, The Bride stops off to obtain a sword from Hattori Hanzo ("special guest star" Sonny Chiba). He has been retired for years, and is done with killing. But she persuades him, and he manufactures a sword that does not inspire his modesty: "This my finest sword. If in your journey you should encounter God, God will be cut." Later the sword must face the skill of Go Go Yubari (Chiaki Kuriyama), O-Ren's teenage bodyguard and perhaps a major in medieval studies, since her weapon of choice is the mace and chain. This is in the comic-book tradition by which charac-

ters are defined by their weapons. To see The Bride's God-slicer and Go Go's mace clashing in a field of dead and dying men is to understand how women have taken over from men in action movies. Strange, since women are not nearly as good at killing as men are. Maybe they're cast because the liberal media wants to see them succeed. The movie's women warriors remind me of Ruby Rich's defense of Russ Meyer as a feminist filmmaker (his women initiate all the sex and do all the killing).

There is a sequence in which O-Ren Ishii takes command of the Japanese Mafia and beheads a guy for criticizing her as half-Chinese, female, and American. O-Ren talks Japanese through a translator, but when the guy's head rolls on the table everyone seems to understand her. Soon comes the deadly battle with The Bride, on a two-level set representing a Japanese restaurant. Tarantino has the wit to pace this battle with exterior shots of snowfall in an exquisite formal garden. Why must the garden be in the movie? Because gardens with snow are iconic Japanese images, and Tarantino is acting as the instrument of his received influences.

By the same token, Thurman wears a costume identical to one Bruce Lee wore in his last film. Is this intended as coincidence, homage, impersonation? Not at all. It can be explained by quantum physics: The suit can be in two movies at the same time. And when the Daryl Hannah character whistles the theme from *Twisted Nerve* (1968), it's not meant to suggest she is a Hayley Mills fan but that leakage can occur between parallel universes in the movies. Will *Volume 2* reveal that Mr. Bill used to be known as Mr. Blond?

Kill Bill: Vol. 2 ★ ★ ★ ★
R, 137 m., 2004

Uma Thurman (The Bride), David Carradine (Bill), Daryl Hannah (Elle Driver), Michael Madsen (Budd), Gordon Liu (Pei Mei). Directed by Quentin Tarantino and produced by Lawrence Bender and Tarantino. Screenplay by Tarantino and Uma Thurman.

Quentin Tarantino's *Kill Bill: Vol. 2* is an exuberant celebration of moviemaking, coasting with heedless joy from one audacious chapter to another, working as irony, working as satire, working as drama, working as pure action. I liked it even more than *Kill Bill* (2003). It's not a sequel but a continuation and completion, filmed at the same time; now that we know the whole story, the first part takes on another dimension. *Vol. 2* stands on its own, although it has deeper resonance if you've seen *Kill Bill*.

The movie is a distillation of the countless grind house kung-fu movies Tarantino has absorbed, and which he loves beyond all reason. Web sites have already enumerated his inspirations—how a sunset came from this movie, and a sword from that. He isn't copying, but transcending; there's a kind of urgency in the film, as if he's turning up the heat under his memories.

The movie opens with a long close-up of the Bride (Uma Thurman) behind the wheel of a car, explaining her mission, which is to kill Bill. There is a lot of explaining in the film; Tarantino writes dialogue with quirky details that suggest the obsessions of his people. That's one of the ways he gives his movies a mythical quality; the characters don't talk in mundane, everyday dialogue, but in a kind of elevated geekspeak that lovingly burnishes the details of their legends, methods, beliefs, and arcane lore.

Flashbacks remind us that the pregnant Bride and her entire wedding party were targeted by the Deadly Viper Assassination Squad in a massacre at the Two Pines Wedding Chapel. Bill was responsible—Bill, whom she confronts on the porch of the chapel for a conversation that suggests the depth and weirdness of their association. He's played by David Carradine in a performance that somehow, improbably, suggests that Bill and the Bride had a real relationship despite the preposterous details surrounding it. (Bill is deeply offended that she plans to marry a used record store owner and lead a normal life.)

The Bride, of course, improbably survived the massacre, awakened after a long coma, and in the first film set to avenge herself against the Deadly Vipers and Bill. That involved extended action sequences as she battled Vernita Green (Vivica A. Fox) and O-Ren Ishii (Lucy Liu), not to mention O-Ren's teenage bodyguard Go Go Yubari (Chiaki Kuriyama) and the martial arts team known as the Crazy 88.

Much of her success came because she was able to persuade the legendary sword maker Hattori Hanzo (Sonny Chiba) to come out of retirement and make her a weapon. He presented it without modesty: "This my finest sword. If in your journey you should encounter God, God will be cut."

In *Vol. 2*, she meets another Asian legend, the warrior master Pei Mei, played by Gordon Liu. Pei Mei, who lives on the top of a high, lonely hill reached by climbing many stairs, was Bill's master, and in a flashback, Bill delivers his protégé for training. Pei Mei is a harsh and uncompromising teacher, and the Bride sheds blood during their unrelenting sessions.

Pei Mei, whose hair and beard are long and white and flowing, like a character from the pages of a comic book, is another example of Tarantino's method, which is to create lovingly structured episodes that play on their own while contributing to the legend. Like a distillation of all wise, ancient, and deadly martial arts masters in countless earlier movies, Pei Mei waits patiently for eons on his hilltop until he is needed for a movie.

The training with Pei Mei, we learn, prepared the Bride to begin her career with Bill ("jetting around the world making vast sums of money and killing for hire"), and is inserted in this movie at a time and place that makes it function like a classic cliff-hanger. In setting up this scene, Tarantino once again pauses for colorful dialogue; the Bride is informed by Bill that Pei Mei hates women, whites, and Americans, and much of his legend is described. Such speeches function in Tarantino not as long-winded detours, but as a way of setting up characters and situations with dimensions it would be difficult to establish dramatically.

In the action that takes place "now," the Bride has to fight her way past formidable opponents, including Elle Driver (Daryl Hannah), the one-eyed master of martial arts, and Budd (Michael Madsen), Bill's beer-swilling brother, who works as a bouncer in a strip joint and lives in a mobile home surrounded by desolation. Neither one is a pushover for the Bride—Elle because of her skills (also learned from Pei Mei), Budd because of his canny instincts.

The showdown with Budd involves a sequence where it seems the Bride must surely die after being buried alive. (That she does not is a given, considering the movie is not over and

Bill is not dead, but she sure looks doomed.) Tarantino, who began the film in black and white before switching to color, plays with formats here, too; to suggest the claustrophobia of being buried, he shows the Bride inside her wooden casket, and as clods of earth rain down on the lid, he switches from wide-screen to the classic 4x3-screen ratio.

The fight with Elle Driver is a virtuoso celebration of fight choreography; although we are aware that all is not as it seems in movie action sequences, Thurman and Hannah must have trained long and hard to even seem to do what they do. Their battle takes place inside Bill's trailer home, which is pretty much demolished in the process, and provides a contrast to the elegant nightclub setting of the fight with O-Ren Ishii; it ends in a squishy way that would be unsettling in another kind of movie, but here all the action is so ironically heightened that we may cringe and laugh at the same time.

These sequences involve their own Tarantinian dialogue of explanation and scene-setting. Budd has an extended monologue in which he offers the Bride the choice of Mace or a flashlight, and the details of his speech allow us to visualize horrors worse than any we could possibly see. Later, Elle Driver produces a black mamba, and in a sublime touch reads from a Web page that describes the snake's deadly powers.

Of the original *Kill Bill*, I wrote: "The movie is all storytelling and no story. The motivations have no psychological depth or resonance, but are simply plot markers. The characters consist of their characteristics." True, but one of the achievements of *Vol. 2* is that the story is filled in, the characters are developed, and they do begin to resonate, especially during the extraordinary final meeting between the Bride and Bill—which consists not of nonstop action but of more hypnotic dialogue, and ends in an event that is like a quiet, deadly punch line.

Put the two parts together, and Tarantino has made a masterful saga that celebrates the martial arts genre while kidding it, loving it, and transcending it. I confess I feared that *Vol. 2* would be like those sequels that lack the intensity of the original. But this is all one film, and now that we see it whole, it's greater than its two parts; Tarantino remains the most brilliantly oddball filmmaker of his generation, and this is one of the best films of the year. ☞

King Arthur ★ ★ ★
PG-13, 130 m., 2004

Clive Owen (Arthur), Keira Knightley (Guinevere), Stellan Skarsgard (Cerdic), Stephen Dillane (Merlin), Ray Winstone (Bors), Hugh Dancy (Galahad), Til Schweiger (Cynric), Ioan Gruffudd (Lancelot), Joel Edgerton (Gawain). Directed by Antoine Fuqua and produced by Jerry Bruckheimer. Screenplay by David Franzoni.

For centuries, countless tales have been told of the legend of King Arthur. But the only story you've never heard . . . is the true story that inspired the legend.

—trailer for *King Arthur*

Uh, huh. And in the true story, Arthur traveled to Rome, became a Christian and a soldier, and was assigned to lead a group of yurt-dwelling warriors from Sarmatia on a fifteen-year tour of duty in England, where Guinevere is a fierce woman warrior of the Woads. His knights team up with the Woads to battle the Saxons. In this version, Guinevere and Lancelot are not lovers, although they exchange significant glances; Arthur is Guinevere's lover. So much for all those legends we learned from Thomas Malory's immortal *Le Morte d'Arthur* (1470), and the less immortal *Knights of the Round Table* (1953).

This new *King Arthur* tells a story with uncanny parallels to current events in Iraq. The imperialists from Rome enter England intent on overthrowing the tyrannical Saxons, and find allies in the brave Woads. "You—all of you—were free from your first breath!" Arthur informs his charges and future subjects, anticipating by a millennium or so the notion that all men are born free and overlooking the detail that his knights have been pressed into involuntary servitude.

The movie is darker and the weather chillier than in the usual Arthurian movie. There is a round table, but the knights scarcely find time to sit down at it. Guinevere is not a damsel in potential distress, but seems to have been cloned from Brigitte Nielsen in *Red Sonja*. And everybody speaks idiomatic English—even the knights, who as natives of Sarmatia might be expected to converse in an early version of Uzbek, and the Woads, whose accents get a free pass because not even the Oxford English Dictionary has heard of a Woad. To the line "Last night was a mistake" in *Troy*, we can now add, in our anthology of unlikely statements in history, Arthur's line to Guinevere as his seven warriors prepare to do battle on a frozen lake with hundreds if not thousands of Saxons: "There are a lot of lonely men over there."

Despite these objections, *King Arthur* is not a bad movie, although it could have been better. It isn't flat-out silly like *Troy*, its actors look at home as their characters, and director Antoine Fuqua curtails the use of CGI in the battle scenes, which involve mostly real people. There is a sense of place here, and although the costumes bespeak a thriving trade in tailoring somewhere beyond the mead, the film's locations look rough, ready, and green, (it was filmed in Ireland).

Clive Owen, who has been on the edge of stardom for a decade, makes an Arthur who seems more like a drill instructor, less like a fairy-tale prince, than most of the Arthurs we've seen. Lean, dark, and angular, he takes the character to the edge of antihero status. Keira Knightley, who was the best friend in *Bend It Like Beckham*, here looks simultaneously sexy and muddy, which is a necessity in this movie, and fits right into the current appetite for women action heroes who are essentially honorary men, all except for the squishy parts. The cast is filled with dependable actors with great faces, such as Ray Winstone as a tough-as-nails knight who inexplicably but perhaps appropriately anticipates the Cockney accent, and Stephen Dillane as Merlin, leader of the Woads and more of a psychic and sorcerer than a magician who does David Copperfield material.

The plot involves Rome's desire to defend its English colony against the invading Saxons, and its decision to back the local Woads in their long struggle against the barbarians. But Rome, declining and falling right on schedule, is losing its territorial ambitions and beginning to withdraw from the far corners of its empire. That leaves Arthur risking his neck

without much support from the folks at home, and perhaps he will cast his lot with England. In the traditional legends he became king at fifteen, and went on to conquer Scotland, Ireland, Iceland—and Orkney, which was flattered to find itself in such company.

The movie ends with a pitched battle that's heavy on swords and maces and stabbings and skewerings, and in which countless enemies fall while nobody we know ever dies except for those whose deaths are prefigured by prescient dialogue or the requirements of fate. I have at this point seen about enough swashbuckling, I think, although producer Jerry Bruckheimer hasn't, since this project follows right on the heels of his *Pirates of the Caribbean*. I would have liked to see deeper characterizations and more complex dialogue, as in movies like *Braveheart* or *Rob Roy*, but today's multiplex audience, once it has digested a word like *Sarmatia*, feels its day's work is done.

That the movie works is because of the considerable production qualities and the charisma of the actors, who bring more interest to the characters than they deserve. There is a kind of direct, unadorned conviction to the acting of Clive Owen and the others; raised on Shakespeare, trained for swordfights, with an idea of Arthurian legend in their heads since childhood, they don't seem out of time and place like the cast of *Troy*. They get on with it.

Kingdom of Heaven ★ ★ ★ ½
R, 145 m., 2005

Orlando Bloom (Balian of Ibelin), Eva Green (Sibylla), Liam Neeson (Godfrey of Ibelin), David Thewlis (Hospitaler), Marton Csokas (Guy de Lusignan), Brendan Gleeson (Reynald), Jeremy Irons (Tiberias), Ghassan Massoud (Saladin), Edward Norton (King Baldwin). Directed by Ridley Scott and produced by Scott. Screenplay by William Monahan.

The first thing to be said for Ridley Scott's *Kingdom of Heaven* is that Scott knows how to direct a historical epic. I might have been kinder to his *Gladiator* had I known that *Troy* and *Alexander* were in my future, but *Kingdom of Heaven* is better than *Gladiator*— deeper, more thoughtful, more about human motivation, and less about action.

The second thing is that Scott is a brave man to release a movie at this time about the wars between Christians and Muslims for control of Jerusalem. Few people will be capable of looking at *Kingdom of Heaven* objectively. I have been invited by both Muslims and Christians to view the movie with them so they can point out its shortcomings. When you've made both sides angry, you may have done something right.

The Muslim scholar Hamid Dabashi, however, after being asked to consult on the movie, writes in the new issue of *Sight & Sound:* "It was neither pro- nor anti-Islamic, neither pro- nor anti-Christian. It was, in fact, not even about the Crusades. And yet I consider the film to be a profound act of faith." It is an act of faith, he thinks, because for its hero, Balian (Orlando Bloom), who is a nonbeliever, "All religious affiliations fade in the light of his melancholic quest to find a noble purpose in life."

That's an insight that helps me understand my own initial question about the film, which was: Why don't they talk more about religion? Weren't the Crusades seen by Christians as a holy war to gain control of Jerusalem from the Muslims? I wondered if perhaps Scott was evading the issue. But not really: He shows characters more concerned with personal power and advancement than with theological issues.

Balian, a village blacksmith in France, discovers he is the illegitimate son of Sir Godfrey (Liam Neeson). Godfrey is a knight returning from the Middle East, who paints Jerusalem not in terms of a holy war but in terms of its opportunities for an ambitious young man; it has a healthy economy at a time when medieval Europe is stagnant. "A man who in France has not a house is in the Holy Land the master of a city," Godfrey promises. "There at the end of the world you are not what you were born, but what you have it in yourself to be." He makes Jerusalem sound like a medieval Atlanta, a city too busy to hate.

For the 100 years leading up to the action, both Christians and Muslims were content to see each other worship in the Holy City. It was only when Christian zealots determined to control the Holy Land more rigidly that things went wrong. The movie takes place circa 1184, as the city is ruled by the young King Baldwin (Edward Norton), who has leprosy and conceals his disfigured face behind a silver mask. Balian takes control of the city after the death of its young king. Then the Knights Templar, well known from *The Da Vinci Code,* wage war on the Muslims. Saladin (Ghassan Massoud) leads a Muslim army against them, and Balian eventually surrenders the city to him. Much bloodshed and battle are avoided.

What Scott seems to be suggesting, I think, is that most Christians and Muslims might be able to coexist peacefully if it were not for the extremists on both sides. This may explain why the movie has displeased the very sorts of Muslims and Christians who will take moderation as an affront. Most ordinary moviegoers, I suspect, will not care much about the movie's reasonable politics, and will be absorbed in those staples of all historical epics, battle and romance.

The romance here is between Balian and Sibylla (Eva Green), sister of King Baldwin. You might wonder how a blacksmith could woo a princess, but reflect that Sir Godfrey was correct, and there are indeed opportunities for an ambitious young man in Jerusalem, especially after his newly discovered father makes him a knight, and Tiberias (Jeremy Irons) enlists him as an aide to Baldwin.

One spectacular battle scene involves the attack of Saladin's forces on Christian-controlled Jerusalem, and it's one of those spectacular set-pieces with giant balls of flame that hurtle through the air and land close, but not too close, to the key characters. There is a certain scale that's inevitable in films of this sort, and Scott does it better than anybody.

Even so, I enjoyed the dialogue and plot more than the action. I've seen one or two vast desert cities too many. Nor do thousands of charging horses look brand-new to me, and the hand-to-hand combat looks uncannily like all other hand-to-hand combat. Godfrey gives Balian a lesson in swordsmanship (chop from above), but apparently the important thing to remember is that if you're an anonymous enemy, you die, and if you're a hero, you live unless a glorious death is required. You'd think people would be killed almost by accident in the middle of a thousand sword-swinging madmen, but every encounter is broken down into a confrontation between a victor and a vanquished. It's well done, but it's been done.

What's more interesting is Ridley Scott's visual style, assisted by John Mathieson's cinematography and the production design of Arthur Max. A vast set of ancient Jerusalem was constructed to provide realistic foregrounds and locations, which were then enhanced by CGI backgrounds, additional horses and troops, and so on. There is also exhilarating footage as young Balian makes his way to Jerusalem, using the twelfth-century equivalent of a GPS: "Go to where they speak Italian, and then keep going."

The movie is above all about the personal codes of its heroes, both Christian and Muslim. They are men of honor: Gentlemen, we would say, if they were only a little gentle. They've seen enough bloodshed and lost enough comrades to look with a jaundiced eye at the zealots who urge them into battle. There is a scene where Baldwin and Saladin meet on a vast plain between their massed troops, and agree, man-to-man, to end the battle right then and there. Later, one of Balian's prebattle speeches to his troops sounds strangely regretful: "We fight over an offense we did not give, against those who were not alive to be offended." Time for a Truth and Reconciliation Commission?

King of the Corner ★ ★ ★ ½
R, 93 m., 2005

Peter Riegert (Leo Spivak), Eli Wallach (Sol Spivak), Isabella Rossellini (Rachel Spivak), Eric Bogosian (Rabbi Evelyn Fink), Beverly D'Angelo (Betsy Ingraham), Jake Hoffman (Ed Shifman), Rita Moreno (Inez), Harris Yulin (Pete Hargrove), Ashley Johnson (Elena Spivak). Directed by Peter Riegert and produced by Lemore Syvan. Screenplay by Riegert and Gerald Shapiro.

Leo Spivak is trapped in the Bermuda Triangle of middle age: He hates his job, his father is dying, his teenage daughter is rebelling. He'd rather be the father, the child, or the boss—anything but Leo, the man in the middle, well paid and with a corner office, but devoting his days to market research. When he subjects instant stew to a blind taste-testing and the consumers say it tastes like dog food, they know how he feels most of the time.

King of the Corner is Peter Riegert's movie. He directed it, he cowrote it, and he stars as Leo. It's a well-chosen project for one of his particular talents, which is to play intelligent, sardonic losers. One of Leo's problems is that he knows his goals are worthless: If his market-research firm makes its money testing lousy products on dim-witted consumers, why would he even want to be the vice president?

One reason might be that Ed Shifman also wants the job. Ed (Jake Hoffman) is Leo's young protégé, or "management trainee," and scores points by stealing Leo's ideas and taking them directly to the boss (Harris Yulin). Ed will work for half the money, and won't be borderline depressive all the time. Together, they test products such as the Flaxman Voice-Altering Telephone, which answers the phones of timid widows with sturdy male voices, including Gregory Peck's.

At home, Leo is worried about his daughter, Elena (Ashley Johnson), who is staying out too late with an elusive lout named Todd who would rather honk for her than come to the door. He's worried, but not as worried as his despairing wife, Rachel (Isabella Rossellini), who seems borderline hysterical. Leo tries one of those excruciating conversations where he simultaneously advises Elena against sex and in favor of precautions. "Dad," she whines, "we're not doing anything." Uh-huh.

Every other weekend Leo flies out to Arizona, where his father, Sol (Eli Wallach), is in a retirement home. Sol was a salesman like Leo, always on the road, dragging his samples around like Willy Loman. When his wife died he moved to Arizona, found a girlfriend (Rita Moreno), and did a lot of fox-trotting before age caught up with him. Now he wants to die: "Why is it so hard for me to die? Other people do it every day." Leo has had an uneasy relationship with his father, but Leo, we begin to understand, is a good man who desperately wants to be seen as a good man: by his wife, his daughter, his father, even by Ed.

King of the Corner is not plot-driven. It's like life: just one damn thing after another. It's based on a collection of short stories named

Bad Jews and Other Stories by Gerald Shapiro, who cowrote the screenplay with Riegert. Leo and his father were both bad Jews in the sense that they were not believers, although to a certain degree they were observant, if only because of family tradition. What it means to be a good Jew, or a good son or a good man, is discovered by Leo only after his father dies.

The whole movie has been leading up to this moment, and I don't want to describe it in detail because it needs to happen to you, to unfold as the logical answer to the question of why the movie exists and where it thinks it is going. I will say a brief word about a freelance rabbi named Evelyn Fink (Eric Bogosian), who begins every conversation by specifying there be no jokes about his names.

Other rabbis from his class have nice jobs with good congregations, but Rabbi Fink is still picking up a living from funeral homes that need a rabbi in a hurry. He begins to question Leo about his father at the funeral home, but when sobbing from the next room becomes a nuisance, he suggests they go somewhere else to talk. Where they go tells you a lot about the freelance rabbi.

Bogosian's role is brief, but perfectly realized. His eulogy at the funeral does what no eulogy should dare; it tells the truth. And then Leo discovers what he thinks about his father, his life, and himself. It is a scene that brings the whole movie into a poignant focus. In the "kaddish," the prayer for the dead, he becomes a good Jew at last.

A movie like this depends on the close observation of behavior. It is not so much about what the characters do as who they are, who they fear they are, and who they want to be. Leo, as played by Riegert, has reached an accommodation with life by keeping a certain dry distance from it. That's why a midmovie meeting seems so odd. He accidentally runs into the girl he lusted after in high school (Beverly D'Angelo), and that sets into motion a peculiar chain of events.

I am not sure I believe them, especially when he visits her home and meets her husband, but observe Riegert's body language. There are times, here and in his boss's office, when he does things that are completely inexplicable. He falls to his knees, or invites a fight, or behaves with sudden recklessness. Why does he do these things? Is he crazy? No, not at all; he is reminding himself he is alive by stepping right outside the ordained limits of his life. At times like these he reminds me of the line in the Stevie Smith poem about the swimmer who is "not waving, but drowning."

Kings and Queen ★ ★ ★
NO MPAA RATING, 150 m., 2005

Emmanuelle Devos (Nora Cotterelle), Mathieu Amalric (Ismael Vuillard), Maurice Garrel (Louis Jenssens), Catherine Deneuve (Mme. Vasset), Magalie Woch (Arielle), Elsa Wolliaston (Dr. Devereux), Nathalie Boutefeu (Chloe Jenssens), Jean-Paul Roussillon (Abel Vuillard). Directed by Arnaud Desplechin and produced by Pascal Caucheteux. Screenplay by Roger Bohbot and Desplechin.

When you ask someone for the truth about themselves, you may get the truth, or part of the truth, or none of the truth, but you will certainly get what they would like you to think is the truth. This is a useful principle to keep in mind during *Kings and Queen*, a film that unfolds like a court case in which all of the testimony sounds like the simple truth, and none of it agrees.

We begin with a character named Nora (Emmanuelle Devos), smart, chic, an art gallery owner who buys a rare illustrated edition of *Leda and the Swan* as a present for her father, a famous author. We learn she has been divorced twice, will soon marry a very rich man, and has an eleven-year-old son named Elias. She visits her father, Louis (Maurice Garrel), who is in great pain; it is revealed he's dying of stomach cancer. What does he think about his daughter, and she of him? We think we know.

We meet another character, a violinist named Ismael (Mathieu Amalric). He was Nora's most recent lover. He is functional enough in a strange way, but behaves so unwisely that he finds himself in a mental institution. We sit in on his consultations with the hospital administrator (Catherine Deneuve), who is onscreen just about long enough for him to tell her, "You're very beautiful," and for her to reply, "I've been told." There is also his French-African psychiatrist (Elsa Wolliaston).

Neither is much charmed by his theory that women lack souls. Ismael makes a friend at the hospital, a young woman named Arielle (Magalie Woch), who is so fond of attempting suicide that it would be a shame if she should succeed and thus bring her pastime to an end.

Nora has seemed like a decent enough woman, but what kind of a mother would not want to raise her own child? The boy's father is out of the picture (in more ways than one), and she strikes on the notion that Ismael, the former lover, is just the person to adopt Elias. Ismael loves the little boy, who loves him, and if this were a different sort of a movie such an arrangement might work.

Kings and Queen is, however, a *very* different sort of movie, in which it will not work for reasons that are explained by Ismael in a way both insightful and peculiar. Nora's father meanwhile leaves a journal entry that completely redefines everything we thought we knew about their relationship, and Ismael has an encounter with the leader of the string quartet where he thinks he is a valued member, but is mistaken. Sometimes you don't really want to know what people really think about you.

I have revealed nothing crucial, except that there are crucial revelations. The point of the movie is to call into question our personal versions of our own lives, and the emphasis on *Leda and the Swan* may be a nudge to suggest we construct myths to give a shape and meaning to lives we have lived with untidy carelessness.

The movie, directed by Arnaud Desplechin and written by him with Roger Bohbot, begins as such a straightforward portrait of ordinary life that it's unsettling to find layer after layer of reality peeled away. It opens with what seems like a conventional array of emotions, and then shows that they're like the bandages on Arielle's wrists, concealing deep desperation. The feelings of the dying father are particularly painful because of the way he has chosen to reveal them.

By the end of the film, we're a little stunned; everything seemed to be going so nicely, to be sure with the ordinary setbacks and tragedies of life, but nothing approaching mythic, tragic, chaotic, emotional decay. You think you know someone, you think they know

themselves, and suddenly you're both dealing with a complete stranger. Meanwhile, "Moon River" is playing on the sound track, but is far from a comfort.

Kinsey ★ ★ ★ ★
R, 118 m., 2004

Liam Neeson (Alfred Kinsey), Laura Linney (Clara McMillen), Chris O'Donnell (Wardell Pomeroy), Peter Sarsgaard (Clyde Martin), Timothy Hutton (Paul Gebhard), John Lithgow (Alfred Sequine Kinsey), Tim Curry (Thurman Rice), Oliver Platt (Herman Wells), Dylan Baker (Alan Gregg). Directed by Bill Condon and produced by Gail Mutrux. Screenplay by Condon.

"Everybody's sin is nobody's sin. And everybody's crime is no crime at all."

Talk like that made people really mad at Dr. Alfred C. Kinsey. When his first study of human sexual behavior was published in 1947, it was more or less universally agreed that masturbation would make you go blind or insane, that homosexuality was an extremely rare deviation, that most sex was within marriage, and most married couples limited themselves to the missionary position.

Kinsey interviewed thousands of Americans over a period of years, and concluded: Just about everybody masturbates, 37 percent of men have had at least one homosexual experience, there is a lot of premarital and extramarital sex, and the techniques of many couples venture well beyond the traditional male-superior position.

It is ironic that Kinsey's critics insist to this day that he brought about this behavior by his report, when in fact all he did was discover that the behavior was already a reality. There's controversy about his sample, his methods, and his statistics, but ongoing studies have confirmed his basic findings. The decriminalization of homosexuality was a direct result of Kinsey's work, although there are still nine states where oral sex is against the law, even within a heterosexual marriage.

Kinsey, a fascinating biography of the Indiana University professor, centers on a Liam Neeson performance that makes one thing clear: Kinsey was an impossible man. He studied human behavior but knew almost nothing about human nature, and was often not aware that he was hurting feelings, offending people, making enemies, or behaving strangely. He had tunnel vision, and it led him heedlessly toward his research goals without prudent regard for his image, his family and associates, and even the sources of his funding.

Neeson plays Kinsey as a man goaded by inner drives. He began his scientific career by collecting and studying 1 million gall wasps, and when he switched to human sexuality he seemed to regard people with much the same objectivity that he brought to insects. Maybe that made him a good interviewer; he was so manifestly lacking in prurient interest that his subjects must have felt they were talking to a confessor imported from another planet. Only occasionally is he personally involved, as when he interviews his strict and difficult father (John Lithgow) about his sex life, and gains a new understanding of the man and his unhappiness.

The movie shows Kinsey arriving at sex research more or less by accident, after a young couple come to him for advice. Kinsey and his wife, Clara McMillen (Laura Linney), were both virgins on their wedding night (he was twenty-six, she twenty-three) and awkwardly unsure about what to do, but they worked things out, as couples had to do in those days. Current sexual thinking was summarized in a book named *Ideal Marriage: Its Physiology and Technique,* by Theodoor Hendrik van de Velde, a volume whose title I did not need to double-check because I remember so vividly finding it hidden in the basement rafters of my childhood home. Van de Velde was so cautious in his advice that many of those using the book must have succeeded in reproducing only by skipping a few pages.

One of the movie's best scenes shows Kinsey giving the introductory lecture for a new class on human sexuality, and making bold assertions about sexual behavior that were shocking in 1947. His book became a bestseller, Kinsey was for a decade one of the most famous men in the world, and he became the target of congressional witch-hunters who were convinced his theories were somehow linked with the Communist conspiracy. That patriotic middle Americans had contributed to Kinsey's statistics did not seem to impress them, as they pressured the Rockefeller Foundation to withdraw its funding. One of the quiet amusements in the film is the way the foundation's Herman Wells (Oliver Platt) wearily tries to prevent Kinsey from becoming his own worst enemy through tactless and provocative statements.

The movie has been written and directed by Bill Condon, who shows us a Kinsey who is a better scientist than a social animal. Kinsey objectified sex to such an extent that he actually encouraged his staff to have sex with one another and record their findings; this is not, as anyone could have advised him, an ideal way to run a harmonious office. Kinsey didn't believe in secrets, and he brings his wife to tears by fearlessly and tactlessly telling her all of his. Laura Linney's performance as Clara McMillen is a model of warmth and understanding in the face of daily impossibilities; she loved Kinsey and understood him, acted as a buffer for him, and has an explosively funny line: "I think I might like that."

Kinsey evolved from lecturing to hectoring as he grew older, insisting on his theories in statements of unwavering certainty. His behavior may have been influenced by unwise use of barbiturates, at a time when their danger was not fully understood; he slept little, drove himself too hard, alienated colleagues. And having found that people are rarely exclusively homosexual or heterosexual but exist somewhere between zero and six on the straight-to-gay scale, he found himself settling somewhere around three or four. Condon, who is homosexual, regards Kinsey's bisexuality with the kind of objectivity that Kinsey would have approved; the film, like Kinsey, is more interested in what people do than why.

The strength of *Kinsey* is finally in the clarity it brings to its title character. It is fascinating to meet a complete original, a person of intelligence and extremes. I was reminded of Russell Crowe's work in *A Beautiful Mind* (2001), also the story of a man whose brilliance was contained within narrow channels. *Kinsey* also captures its times, and a political and moral climate of fear and repression; it is instructive to remember that as recently as

1959, the University of Illinois fired a professor for daring to suggest, in a letter to the student paper, that students consider sleeping with each other before deciding to get married. Now universities routinely dispense advice on safe sex and contraception. Of course there is opposition, now as then, but the difference is that Kinsey redefined what has to be considered normal sexual behavior.

Kontroll ★ ★ ★ ½
R, 105 m., 2005

Sandor Csanyi (Bulcsu), Zoltan Mucsi (Professor), Csaba Pindroch (Muki), Sandor Badar (Lecso), Zsolt Nagy (Tibi), Bence Matyassy (Bootsie), Gyozo Szabo (Shadow), Eszter Balla (Szofi). Directed by Nimrod Antal and produced by Tamas Hutlassa. Screenplay by Jim Adler and Antal.

On the London underground you sometimes realize the train has roared through an abandoned station, past a ghost platform illuminated only from the train windows; you get a murky glimpse of advertising posters from decades ago. In *Kontroll*, which takes place entirely within the Budapest subway system, such a subterranean world has a permanent population.

The trains are run on an honor system, and inspectors with red-and-black armbands prowl the underground, asking riders to show their tickets. The passengers descend from the sunshine to be accosted by kontrollers who are slovenly, unkempt, sallow-faced, with a certain madness in their eyes. Many riders consider the trains to be free and treat the inspectors like vagrants asking for a handout.

It is strange to work entirely under the ground in noisy, hostile, rat-infested caverns, and even stranger for those like the kontroller Bulcsu (Sandor Csanyi), who never ever returns to the surface. Once he was an architect who dreamed of buildings that would reach to the sky, but now he has retreated to a waking grave, sleeps on benches, eats the indescribable food vended in the system, and heads a crew of three other inspectors as haunted as he is.

Theirs is a miserable job, made more unbearable by the periodic visits of their boss, who descends from light and comfort to urge greater vigilance. The kontrollers don't really care if people are riding free; what they care about is meeting a daily quota of deadbeats in a duel of wills. They risk their lives, they engage in reckless chases and fights, not because they care about the fares, but because it is the price they pay to continue their melancholy existence.

There is a killer in the system, a hooded figure who emerges from the shadows to push passengers in front of trains. He seems to know the underground as well as the kontrollers, and, like the Phantom of the Opera, to occupy his own hidden world. The security cameras see only his hood. Bulcsu and his crew are faced with daily train delays because of jumpers, and while they can't blame those who were pushed, they wonder why suicides don't have the decency to kill themselves with less inconvenience to others.

Kontroll is the first feature by Nimrod Antal, born of Hungarian parents, raised in Los Angeles, returning to Budapest for this haunting film shot during the five hours every night when the subway shuts down. His film opens with a statement read by a self-conscious spokesman for the subway system, explaining that Antal was granted permission to film with some reluctance, and with the hope that audiences will realize the film is only symbolic. Is this spokesman real or fictional? Certainly the symbolism is more Kafkaesque than political, as the kontrollers apply logic (you must have a ticket) to an illogical situation (riders know they will rarely be asked to show one). We feel we've entered one of those postnuclear science-fiction societies where the surface has become uninhabitable, and a few survivors cling to subterranean life.

Bulcsu's colleagues include a new recruit named Tibi (Zsolt Nagy), who is trying to learn a job he has not yet realized is his doom. There is the Professor (Zoltan Mucsi), who seems to consider kontrolling a holy vocation, and Muki (Csaba Pindroch), who is a narcoleptic, a dangerous condition when you work next to subway tracks.

One day a bear wanders into the system. This is a young woman named Szofi (Eszter Balla), who always wears a bear suit, perhaps because she is employed as a bear, or more likely because it is her fashion choice. She keeps an eye out for her father, an alcoholic train driver who possibly thinks he sees bears and is occasionally comforted to find out he is correct. Bulcsu begins to have feelings for the bear.

In a world denied respect by society, the inhabitants seek it from each other. Bulcsu's crew stages competitions with other crews, most dangerously at the end of the day, when they challenge each other to foot races down the tracks between stations, just before the last train of the day. The point is not so much to win as to survive. That is also perhaps the point of the film.

Kontroll is the first work by a director who is clearly gifted, and who has found a way to make a full-bore action movie on a limited budget; there are no special effects in the movie, all of the trains are real, and I gather that at one point when we see Bulcsu barely crawling onto a platform ahead of a moving train, he is really doing exactly that.

Nimrod Antal has a feeling for action, but what distinguishes *Kontroll* is his control of characters and mood. He could have given us a standard group of misfits, but his characters are all peculiar in inward, secretive ways, suggesting needs they would rather not reveal. His visuals create a haunted house where the lights are off in most of the rooms, and there may indeed be a monster in the closet.

Kung Fu Hustle ★ ★ ★
R, 99 m., 2005

Stephen Chow (Sing), Yuen Wah (Landlord), Yuen Qiu (Landlady), Leung Siu Lung (The Beast), Huang Sheng Yi (Fong), Chan Kwok Kwan (Brother Sum), Lam Tze Chung (Sing's Sidekick), Dong Zhi Hua (Doughnut), Chiu Chi Ling (Tailor). Directed by Stephen Chow and produced by Chow, Po Chu Chui, and Jeffrey Lau. Screenplay by Tsang Kan Cheong, Chow, Lola Huo, and Chan Man Keung.

There is an opinion in some quarters that martial arts movies are violent. Many are, to be sure, but the best ones have the same relationship to violence that Astaire and Rogers have to romance: Nobody believes they take it seriously, but it gives them an excuse for some wonderful choreography.

Lurking beneath the surface of most good martial arts movies is a comedy. Sometimes it bubbles up to the top, as in Stephen Chow's *Kung Fu Hustle*. The joke is based not so much on humor as on delight: The characters have overcome the laws of gravity and physics. To be able to leap into the air, spin in a circle, and kick six, seven, eight, nine enemies before landing in a graceful crouch is enormously gratifying.

Realists grumble that such things are impossible. Well, of course they are. The thing about Astaire and Rogers is that they were really doing it, in long unbroken takes, and we could see that they were. Stephen Chow uses concealed wires, special effects, trick camera angles, trampolines, and anything else he can think of. We know it, and he knows we know it. But the trickery doesn't diminish his skill, because despite all the wires and effects in the world, a martial arts actor must be a superb athlete. Hang your average movie star on the end of a wire and he'll look like he's just been reeled in by the Pequod.

Kung Fu Hustle is Chow's seventh film as a director and sixty-first job as an actor, counting TV. He is forty-two years old, and has been busy. His only other film seen by me is *Shaolin Soccer* (2002), the top-grossing action comedy in Hong Kong history. Purchased by Miramax, it was held off the market for two years, cut by thirty minutes, and undubbed: Yes, Harvey Weinstein replaced the English sound track with subtitles. The movie opened a year ago, inspiring a review in which I gave my most rational defense of the relativity theory of star ratings.

Now comes *Kung Fu Hustle*. This is the kind of movie where you laugh occasionally and have a silly grin most of the rest of the time. It must have taken Chow a superhuman effort to avoid singing a subtitled version of *Let Me Entertain You*—or, no, I've got a better example—of *Make 'em Laugh*, the Donald O'Connor number in *Singin' in the Rain*. In that one, O'Connor crashed into boards and bricks, wrestled with a dummy, ran up one wall and through another one, and sang the whole time. Stephen Chow doesn't sing, but he's channeling the same spirit.

The movie is centered in a Shanghai slum named Pig Sty Alley. It's ruled by a dumpy

365

landlady (Yuen Qiu) who marches around in slippers and has one of those cartoon cigarettes that always stays in her mouth no matter what happens. Shanghai is terrorized by the Axe Gang, which mostly leaves Pig Sty Alley alone because the pickings are too slim. But when counterfeit gang members are confronted by neighborhood kung fu fighters, the real gang moves in to take revenge. The Axe Gang doesn't exactly blend in: They all wear black suits and top hats, and carry axes. That'll make you stand out. I am reminded of Jack Lemmon's story about the time he saw Klaus Kinski buying a hatchet at Ace Hardware.

The war between the Pig Stygians and the Axe Gang is an excuse for a series of sequences in which the stylized violence reaches a kind of ecstasy. Of course nothing we see is possible, but the movie doesn't even pretend it's possible: Maybe everyone is having matching hallucinations. One of the jokes is that completely unlikely characters, including the landlady and local middle-aged tradesmen, turn out to be better warriors than the professionals.

Chow not only stars and directs, but cowrote and coproduced. We get the sense that his comedies are generated in the Buster Keaton spirit, with gags being worked out on the spot and everybody in orbit around the star, who is physically skilled, courageous, and funny. Chow plays Sing, also the name of his character in *Shaolin Soccer* and at least six other movies. This time he's an imposter, pretending to be an Axe Gang member in order to run a shakedown racket in Pig Sty Alley. Imagine how inconvenient it is when the real Axe Gang shows up and he's in trouble with everyone. By the end of the movie, he's going one-on-one with The Beast (Leung Siu Lung), in a kung fu extravaganza. The joke is that most of what Sing knows about kung fu he learned by reading a useless booklet sold to him by a con man when he was a child.

It's possible you don't like martial arts movies, whether funny or not. Then why have you read this far? Or, you prefer the elegant and poetic epics like *Crouching Tiger, Hidden Dragon* or *House of Flying Daggers*. Those are not qualities you will find in *Kung Fu Hustle*. When I saw it at Sundance, I wrote that it was "like Jackie Chan and Buster Keaton meet Quentin Tarantino and Bugs Bunny." You see how worked up you can get, watching a movie like this. ☞

L

Ladder 49 ★ ★ ★ ½
PG-13, 120 m., 2004

Joaquin Phoenix (Jack Morrison), John Travolta (Mike Kennedy), Morris Chestnut (Tommy Drake), Jacinda Barrett (Linda Morrison), Robert Patrick (Lenny Richter), Jay Hernandez (Keith Perez), Kevin Daniels (Don Miller), Kevin Chapman (Frank McKinny), Balthazar Getty (Ray Gauquin). Directed by Jay Russell and produced by Casey Silver. Screenplay by Lewis Colick.

The best compliment I can pay *Ladder 49* is to say that it left me feeling thoughtful and sad. I was surprised it had such an effect. I walked in expecting an action picture with heroic firemen charging into burning buildings for last-minute rescues. *Ladder 49* has the heroes and the fires and the rescues, but it's not really about them. It's about character, and about the kind of man who risks his life for a living. And it's about work, about what kind of a job it is to be a fireman.

The movie stars Joaquin Phoenix as Jack Morrison, a fireman assigned to search and rescue. John Travolta plays Kennedy, his chief. The other guys at the firehouse include Tommy (Morris Chestnut), Don (Kevin Daniels), Lenny (Robert Patrick), and Frank (Kevin Chapman).

We see them in action before we really meet them. A warehouse is on fire, and people are trapped on the twelfth floor. There's grain dust in the building that could explode at any moment. Jack and his team charge into the building, and Jack finds a survivor on the twelfth floor—which is too high for the cherry pickers or ladders to reach. "Stick with me. I'll take care of you," he tells the guy, and lowers him out a window on a rope until firemen below can grab him, calm his panic, and return him safe to earth.

The grain dust blows. Jack falls through a hole in the center of the building and lands a few floors below, stunned, half-buried by debris. Eventually he regains consciousness and is able to radio Travolta, who coordinates the rescue effort. It is clear that there's a limited window of opportunity to save Jack before the building kills him.

The movie flashes back to Jack's first day as a rookie in the fire department, and we understand what the structure will be: His present danger will be intercut with the story of his life as a fireman. So far, everything in *Ladder 49* has been basic and predictable, by the numbers, although the special effects and stunt work inside the burning building were convincing. But as the movie explores Jack's life, it shows an attention and sensitivity that elevates the flashbacks from the usual biographical stops along the way.

Yes, he's the victim of practical jokes. Yes, he does a lot of after-hours drinking with his firehouse buddies, chugging beer competitively. Yes, he and a buddy pick up two girls in the supermarket, and the one named Linda (Jacinda Barrett) becomes his wife. And they have kids. And some of his friends have bad things happen to them during fires. And he volunteers for search and rescue. And Linda worries about him, and dreads the day a red fire chief's car may pull up in front of her house to deliver a man with dreadful news.

As I list these scenes, you may think you can guess what they contain and how they play, but you would be wrong. The director, Jay Russell, working from Lewis Colick's screenplay, brings a particular humanity to the scenes; I am reminded of how his movie *My Dog Skip* transcended the basic elements of a boy and his dog. The marriage of Jack and Linda is not a movie marriage, but a convincing one with troubles and problems and love that endures. Linda is not one more of those tiresome wives in action movies, who appear only to complain that the hero should spend more time with his family. She is Jack's partner in their family, and a source of his pride and courage at work. And Jack's relationship with Chief Kennedy (Travolta) is complex, too, because Kennedy worries about him, and is not at all sure he should allow him to volunteer for search and rescue.

After Jack has lost one friend and another has been badly burned, Kennedy offers him a transfer to a safe job downtown. Jack stays where he is, not because he is a fearless hero, but because it is his job, and he is faithful to it. There is the sense that the men of Ladder 49 go into danger and take risks largely out of loyalty to their comrades. Soldiers in battle, it is said, fight not so much for the flag or for a cause as for their buddies, to not let them down. Russell allows small details to accumulate into the subtle but crucial fact that the camaraderie of the firehouse is what motivates these men above all.

The effort to rescue Jack is desperate but skilled. Diagrams are used to figure out where he must be inside the building. He gives them clues based on what he can see. Kennedy asks if he can get to a brick wall, knock a hole in it, and crawl through it to a room they think they can reach. He thinks he can.

The movie is not about a dying man whose life passes before his eyes, but about a man who saved a life and put himself in danger, and how he got to that place in his life, and what his life and family mean to him. Because it is attentive to these human elements, *Ladder 49* draws from the action scenes instead of depending on them. Phoenix, Travolta, Jacinda Barrett, and the others are given characters with dimension, so that what happens depends on their decisions, not on the plot.

As I said, I was surprisingly affected by the film. After I left the screening, I walked a while by the river, and sat and thought, and was happy not to have anything that had to be done right away.

Ladies in Lavender ★ ★

PG-13, 103 m., 2005

Judi Dench (Ursula Widdington), Maggie Smith (Janet Widdington), Daniel Bruhl (Andrea Marowski), Miriam Margolyes (Dorcas), Natascha McElhone (Olga Danilof), David Warner (Dr. Francis Mead). Directed by Charles Dance and produced by Nicolas Brown, Elizabeth Karlsen, and Nik Powell. Screenplay by Dance.

Ladies in Lavender assembles those two great dames, Judi Dench and Maggie Smith, and sends them off to play sisters sharing a cozy little cottage on the Cornwall coast. That is an inspiration. What they do there is a disappoint-

ment. Their days are spent gardening and having tea, their evenings with knitting and the wireless, until one dark and stormy night a strange young man is washed up on their shore.

This is Andrea Marowski (Daniel Bruhl). He is handsome, sweet, and speaks hardly a word of English. But Janet Widdington (Maggie Smith) discovers he has some German, and unearths her ancient textbook. Soon she and her sister, Ursula (Dench), discover that Andrea is Polish, a violinist, and a gifted one at that. What they do not discover is how he happened to be in the sea on that stormy night, which is the very thing we want to know. There is no word of a shipwreck. Perhaps he is a magical creature, left over from *The Tempest*.

The sisters have lived in calm and contentment for many years. Janet is a widow; Ursula has never married, and probably never had sex, although from the way she regards Andrea she may be thinking it's never too late to start. Ursula becomes possessive of the handsome young man; Janet observes this, doesn't like it, and mostly but not entirely keeps her thoughts to herself.

Andrea is visited by good Dr. Mead (David Warner), who advises bed rest, although perhaps not as much as Andrea chooses to enjoy; it is pleasant, watching the sun stream in through the window and being served tea by the sisters' crusty maid, Dorcas (Miriam Margolyes), who was born to play Doll Tearsheet. Eventually, however, Andrea ventures outside and catches the eye of Olga Danilof (Natascha McElhone), a landscape painter; she is not a very good painter, but she is a beautiful young woman, speaks German, and is soon spending time with Andrea while Ursula goes into a quiet and tactful form of anguish. Of course, coincidentally, Olga happens to possess the key to Andrea's fate as a violinist.

There is a moment's suspense when Dr. Mead, who also fancies Olga, ventures the suggestion that Olga and Andrea, chattering away in German, might be spies observing coastal activities; in which case, apparently, he thinks an appropriate punishment would be for Andrea to go to prison and Olga to fall in love with the doctor. It is 1936, and Europe seems on the brink of war, although for the Widdington sisters that's not much of a concern. The local police chief drops by for a chat, is satisfied, and leaves. He is so polite that if they had been spies, I wonder if he would have wanted to spoil such a nice day by mentioning it.

Ladies in Lavender, directed by the actor Charles Dance, is perfectly sweet and civilized, and ends with one of those dependable scenes where—gasp!—look who's in the audience at the concert! It's a pleasure to watch Smith and Dench together; their acting is so natural it could be breathing. But Daniel Bruhl is tiresome as Andrea; he has no dark side, no anger, no fierceness, and although we eventually discover why he left Poland, we do not know if it was from passion or convenience. He is an ideal dinner guest; the kind of person you are happy enough to have at the table, but could not endure on a three-day train journey.

I am reminded of Lindsay Anderson's *The Whales of August* (1987), also about two elderly sisters in a house on a coast. That one starred Bette Davis and Lillian Gish, who engaged in subtle verbal gamesmanship, both as characters and as actors. It is probably true that we should not attend a movie about old ladies in a big old house expecting much in the way of great drama (although *Whatever Happened to Baby Jane?* has its moments), but *The Whales of August* had a fire that the relaxed *Ladies in Lavender* is entirely lacking.

In the category of movies about older women risking a last chance on love, you could hardly improve on *A Month by the Lake* (1995), with Vanessa Redgrave falling for, and being dropped by, Edward Fox. We want her to win her man, and the problem with *Ladies in Lavender* is that although Ursula can kid herself, we can't.

The Ladykillers ★ ★ ½
R, 104 m., 2004

Tom Hanks (Professor G. H. Dorr), Marlon Wayans (Gawain MacSam), J. K. Simmons (Garth Pancake), Tzi Ma (The General), Ryan Hurst (Lump Hudson), Irma P. Hall (Marva Munson). Directed by Joel Coen and Ethan Coen and produced by Ethan Coen, Joel Coen, Tom Jacobson, Barry Sonnenfeld, and Barry Josephson. Screenplay by Joel Coen and Ethan Coen, based on *The Ladykillers,* written by William Rose.

The genius of Alec Guinness was in his anonymity. He could play a character so ingratiating that he ingratiated himself right into invisibility, and that was the secret of his work in *The Ladykillers,* a droll 1955 British comedy that also starred Peter Sellers and Herbert Lom. Now comes a Coen brothers remake with Tom Hanks in the Guinness role, and although Hanks would be the right actor to play a low-key deceiver, the Coens have made his character so bizarre that we get distracted just by looking at him.

Hanks plays Goldthwait Higginson Dorr, who claims to be a professor of Latin and Greek, who dresses like Colonel Sanders, and who seems to be channeling Tennessee Williams, Edgar Allen Poe, and Vincent Price. As in the original, he rents a room from a sweet little old lady, and plans to use her home as a base for a criminal scheme. In this case, he and four associates will tunnel from her root cellar into the cash room of a nearby casino named the Bandit Queen. The professor explains to the little old lady that the five of them are a classical music ensemble who need a quiet place to practice; they play music on a boom box to cover the sounds of their tunneling.

The other crooks represent the extremes of available casting choices; all of them, like the professor, are over the top in a way rarely seen outside Looney Tunes. Gawain MacSam (Marlon Wayans) is a trash-talking hip-hop janitor at the casino; Garth Pancake (J. K. Simmons) is a mustachioed explosives expert who asphyxiates a dog in an unfortunate gas mask experiment; the General (Tzi Ma) is a chain-smoker who once apparently specialized in tunnels for the Viet Cong; and Lump (Ryan Hurst) is a dim-witted muscle man who will do the hard labor.

The little old lady is named Marva Munson, and she is played by Irma P. Hall in the one completely successful comic performance in the movie. Yes, she's a caricature, too: a church-going widow who doesn't allow smoking in the house, has regular conversations with the portrait of her dead husband, and is not shy about complaining to the sheriff. But her character is exaggerated from a recognizable human base, while the others are comic-strip oddities.

Even Marva is sometimes betrayed by the Coens, who give her speeches that betray themselves as too clever by half (protesting a neighbor's loud "hippity-hop" music, she complains that the songs use the n-word "2,000 years after Jesus! Thirty years after Martin Luther King! In the Age of Montel!" If she'd said "Oprah," it might have been her talking, but when she says "Montel" you can feel the Coens' elbow digging in your side. There's also a subplot involving Mrs. Munson's generous donations to Bob Jones University; she is apparently unaware of its antediluvian attitudes about race. There are too many moments where dialogue seems so unmatched to the characters that they seem to be victims of a drive-by ventriloquist.

Now let me say that although the movie never jells, its oddness keeps it from being boring. Tom Hanks provides such an eccentric performance that it's fun just to watch him behaving—to listen to speeches that coil through endless, florid ornamentation. That the purpose of a criminal in such a situation would be to become invisible—as Guinness, despite the bad teeth, tried to do in the 1955 film—escapes the Coens. But I am importing unwanted logic into a narrative that manifestly is uninterested in such fineries of specification, as the professor might declare. There are some big laughs in the movie, some of them involving body disposal and another one as Garth Pancake demonstrates the safe handling of explosives. When Mrs. Munson invites the church ladies over for tea and invites the nice gentlemen in the basement to play something, Hanks offers a poem by Poe as a consolation prize, and rises to a peak of mannered sublimity. As the church ladies gaze in speechless astonishment at his performance, I was reminded of a day in the 1960s I was in a working-class pub in a poor neighborhood of Sligo, in the west of Ireland. The TV set over the bar was tuned to *The Galloping Gourmet*. The regulars stared at him speechlessly, until finally one said: "Will you *look* at that fellow!" That's how they feel about Professor G. H. Dorr.

There's a lot of high-spirited gospel music in the movie, which brings the plot to a halt for a concert in Mrs. Munson's church. It's wonderful as music, but not really connected to the movie, unlike the music in the Coens' *O Brother, Where Art Thou?* For that matter, the four- and twelve-letter dialogue of the Wayans

character fits awkwardly into a story where no one else talks that way; his potty mouth also wins the film an otherwise completely unnecessary "R" rating.

What the movie finally lacks, I think, is modesty. The original *Ladykillers* was one of a group of small, inspired comedies made at the low-rent Ealing Studios near London, where Alec Guinness was the resident genius; his other titles from the period include *Kind Hearts and Coronets* (1949), *The Lavender Hill Mob* (1950), and *The Man in the White Suit* (1951). These were self-effacing films; much of their humor grew out of the contrast between nefarious schemes and low-key, almost apologetic behavior.

The Coens' *Ladykillers*, on the other hand, is always wildly signaling for us to notice it. Not content to be funny, it wants to be *funny!* Have you ever noticed that the more a comedian wears funny hats, the less funny he is? The old and new *Ladykillers* play like a contest between Buster Keaton and Soupy Sales.

Lana's Rain ★ ★ ★
R, 107 m., 2004

Oksana Orlenko (Lana), Nickolai Stoilov (Darko Lucev), Luoyong Wang (Julian), Stephanie Childers (Katrina), Stacey Slowid (Vermonica), David Darlow (General Donoffrio). Directed by Michael S. Ojeda and produced by Joel Goodman. Screenplay by Ojeda.

Lana's Rain tells the dark, hard-edged story of a brother and sister who escape from the war-torn Balkans, conceal themselves in a shipping container to travel to America, and try to survive on Chicago streets that have never seemed meaner. The picture is even bleaker than that: The brother is a war criminal who forces his sister into prostitution, and by the end of the film he's a low-life Scarface, with a stable of hookers, a big cigar, and a bottle and gun under his coat.

The story is seen through the eyes of the sister, Lana (Oksana Orlenko), who grew up apart from her brother and meets him again after many years on the eve of his escape from the Balkans. In a grisly prelude, the brother is having facial reconstruction to disguise himself, and is interrupted in the middle of the surgery;

he wears an eye patch through the movie, while his enemies and Interpol search for him.

Lana speaks no English, is naive, is dominated by her brother, and despises the life of prostitution. She is savagely beaten by one client. Darko (Nickolai Stoilov), her brother, keeps all her earnings, scornfully tossing her $10 for "spending money." She speaks so little English that she tries to learn the language from a Dr. Seuss book she finds in a Dumpster. Her only friend is an Asian-American sculptor named Julian (Luoyong Wang), who befriends her, likes her, offers her shelter, but cannot get her away from the insidious domination of her brother.

The film, written and directed by Michael S. Ojeda, shows a sure sense of *noir* style and a toughness that lasts right up to the very final scene, which feels contrived and tacked-on. It lives through the performance of Oksana Orlenko, who won the best actress award at Milan. On the basis of his work as the brother, Nickolai Stoilov has a future as a Bond villain. They are both never less than convincing, and Ojeda makes no effort to glamorize their lifestyle; even after Darko is running three or four call girls (advertising "Eastern European Beauties"), he lives in a shabby trailer in a neighborhood that looks more like Siberia than Chicago.

The movie has a lot of plot, including a revenge twist so ingenious I will not even hint of it. It also has too many endings; there is a time when it seems that Darko must certainly be dead, but with the resilience of a zombie he reappears. In a late confrontation where they are both drenched with gasoline, Lana's decision is drawn out for too long, and then the situation is settled with a shameless *deus ex machina*. And as for the nice Asian man, is it really that nice of him to make love to her in the night and reveal in the morning that he is committed to another woman? Well, given her need and desperation, maybe he did the right thing, but the subplot disappears just when we think it might amount to something interesting.

So *Lana's Rain* is not a perfect picture, but it has the flaws of ambition, not compromise. It doesn't soften the character of the brother, who is unremittingly evil from beginning to end, and it doesn't sentimentalize the sister's ordeal. Her stamina and endurance, during a harsh Chicago winter, give some hint of the harsh world she was raised in, and her struggle is all the more moving because it comes from courage, not cleverness. Even as I noted a glitch here and there in the plot, I was aware that the movie itself, and especially the character of Lana, had enlisted my sympathy.

La Petite Lili ★ ★ ★
NO MPAA RATING, 104 m., 2004

Nicole Garcia (Mado Marceaux), Bernard Giraudeau (Brice), Jean-Pierre Marielle (Simon Marceaux), Ludivine Sagnier (Lili), Robinson Stevenin (Julien Marceaux), Julie Dépardieu (Jeanne-Marie), Yves Jacques (Serge), Anne Le Ny (Leone), Marc Betton (Guy). Directed by Claude Miller and produced by Annie Miller. Screenplay by Claude Miller and Julien Boivent, based on Anton Chekhov's *The Seagull*.

There is nothing the equal of a summer cottage to assemble all the characters needed for a drama, and nobody else. There are spare bedrooms and secluded groves for adultery, and long tables on the shady lawn for boozy lunches at which truth is told. European films get enormous mileage out of the device; Hollywood is more likely to send the parents off with their kids to Wally World or the Johnson family reunion, which is why this adaptation of Chekhov's *The Seagull* would play strangely in a station wagon.

The play, you will recall, if you received a liberal education and didn't major in ways to make money, involves a family gathering that includes an aging diva, a famous writer, the diva's idealistic son, and a young actress. The son falls in love with the actress, who knows which side of her bread she wants buttered and goes after the writer, who is the lover of the diva. Minor characters have minor dalliances, and the point of the play is to show how all of these passions are transmuted into art.

Claude Miller, a French director of dry humor and great skill, has taken the Chekhov outline and updated it to present-day France, substituting the cinema for literature. His film stars the elegant Nicole Garcia as Mado Marceaux, a movie star acutely aware of her age and determined to retain possession of her lover, the successful director Brice (Bernard Giraudeau). Her son, Julien (Robinson Stevenin),

371

is one of those intolerable young men who guards the candle of integrity on the birthday cake of materialism. As the movie opens, Julien and Lili (Ludivine Sagnier), an ambitious young actress, are found making love, but Julien is like the young filmmaker in *Last Tango in Paris*, and sees his life as a movie and his lover as a character in need of direction.

Filling out the cast are old Uncle Simon (Jean-Pierre Marielle), who likes to nap in the sun and pose as a cynic, the handyman Guy (Marc Betton), his wife, Leone (Anne Le Ny), and their daughter, Jeanne-Marie (Julie Dépardieu), who is genuinely in love with Julien and believes he is a genius.

Whether he is or not becomes clear one day when Julien announces the world premiere of his new experimental film. All of the guests troop out to the barn for a viewing, especially the famous director Brice; Julien despises him, his work, and everything he stands for, but desires his praise and support. The film, which stars Lili, is awful. Everybody knows it, but finds ways to praise it (Gene Siskel's response in such a situation: "Thank you for making a film"). Lili doesn't find her future in Julien's avant-garde, and goes after Brice: "I could make you happy again." This is true only if it would give him joy to make her a star. Mado is crushed to lose to her younger rival. Jeanne-Marie stands by alertly to pick up Julien's pieces.

Flash forward five years and Julien is making a film on a set built to look like the location of their summer of passion. Some of the actors are playing themselves; others have been cast by famous look-alikes (the beloved Michel Piccoli among them). It is ironic that art has been transmuted into life, but more ironic that Julien has been transmuted into Brice, and now works on a sound stage with a full crew and a big budget. "Why did you make your movie for $24,000?" I heard an indie filmmaker asked at Sundance. "So I will never have to again."

The third act departs from Chekhov and is original with Miller; it not only makes a nicely ironic point, but, because he takes his time with it, allows for a meditation on the distance between art and life. We see that even the actors playing "themselves" are not playing the selves we have seen, but new selves invented by Julien. The character who best understands this, and actually forgives it, is the older director Brice.

And did Brice find happiness with young Lili? Almost on the very day he became her lover, he knew he would "fall into a well of loneliness." It has been said that the reason we establish relationships is to assure ourselves of a witness to our lives. Happy relationships have two witnesses, but Brice's has only one.

The Last Samurai ★ ★ ★ ½
R, 150 m., 2003

Tom Cruise (Nathan Algren), Timothy Spall (Simon Graham), Ken Watanabe (Katsumoto), Billy Connolly (Zebulon Gant), Tony Goldwyn (Colonel Bagley), Hiroyuki Sanada (Ujio), Koyuki (Taka), Shichinosuke Nakamura (Emperor). Directed by Edward Zwick and produced by Tom Cruise, Tom Engelman, Marshall Herskovitz, Scott Kroopf, Paula Wagner, and Zwick. Screenplay by John Logan, Herskovitz, and Zwick.

Edward Zwick's *The Last Samurai* is about two warriors whose cultures make them aliens, but whose values make them comrades. The battle scenes are stirring and elegantly mounted, but they are less about who wins than about what can be proven by dying. Beautifully designed, intelligently written, acted with conviction, it's an uncommonly thoughtful epic. Its power is compromised only by an ending that sheepishly backs away from what the film is really about.

Tom Cruise and Ken Watanabe costar, as a shabby Civil War veteran and a proud samurai warrior. Cruise plays Nathan Algren, a war hero who now drifts and drinks too much, with no purpose in life. He's hired by Americans who are supplying mercenaries to train an army for the Japanese emperor, who wants to move his country into the modern world and is faced with a samurai rebellion.

The role of the samurai leader Katsumoto (Watanabe) is complex; he is fighting against the emperor's men, but out of loyalty to the tradition the emperor represents; he would sacrifice his life in an instant, he says, if the emperor requested it. But Japan has been seized with a fever to shake off its medieval ways and copy the West, and the West sees money to be made in the transition: Representatives from the Remington arms company are filling big contracts for weapons, and the U.S. Embassy is a clearinghouse for lucrative trade arrangements.

Into this cauldron Algren descends as a cynic. He is told the samurai are "savages with bows and arrows," but sees that the American advisers have done a poor job of training the modernized Japanese army to fight them. Leading his untried troops into battle, he is captured and faces death—but is spared by a word from Katsumoto, who returns him as a prisoner to the village of his son.

It's at this point that *The Last Samurai* begins to reveal itself as more than an action picture. Katsumoto, who conveniently speaks English, explains he has kept Algren alive because he wants to know his enemy. Algren at first refuses to speak, but gradually, during a long, rainy winter of captivity, he begins to have philosophical conversations with the other man about the ethics of war and warriors. Some of these talks sound like Socratic exchanges:

Katsumoto: Do you believe a man can change his destiny?

Algren: I believe a man does what he can until his destiny is revealed.

For Algren, the traditional village life is a soothing tonic. Haunted by nightmares from his wartime experiences, he confesses, "Here I have known my first untroubled sleep in many years." He has been lodged in the house of Taka (Koyuki), the widow of a man he killed in battle, and although she complains bitterly to Katsumoto, she maintains a smiling facade in Algren's presence.

Algren: I killed her husband!

Katsumoto: It was a good death.

Katsumoto has pledged his life to defending the dying code of the samurai. Algren finds himself gradually shifting allegiances, away from the mercenaries and toward the samurai, but his shift is visceral, not ideological. He bonds with Katsumoto, respects him, wants to find respect in his eyes. The movie illustrates the universal military truth that men in battle are motivated not by their cause but by loyalty to their comrades.

The Last Samurai breaks with the convention that the Western hero is always superior to the local culture he immerses in. It has been compared to *Lawrence of Arabia* and *Dances with Wolves*, films in which Westerners learn to respect Arabs and Indians, but this film goes a step further, clearly believing that Katsumoto's traditional society is superior to the modernism being unloaded by the Americans. Katsumoto is the teacher and Algren is the student, and the film wonderfully re-creates the patterns and textures of the Japanese past; its production design, sets, and costumes are astonishing.

Watanabe is a deep, powerful presence; he has the potential to become the first world star from Japan since Toshiro Mifune. Cruise is already a star, and will be targeted by those predisposed to see him and not his character, but here I think his stardom works for the film, because he takes with him into battle both the cocksure pilot of *Top Gun* and the war-weary veteran of *Born on the Fourth of July*. The casting helps the film with its buried message, which is about the reeducation of a conventional American soldier.

The supporting cast is splendid: Koyuki quietly stirs as the widow who feels sexual attraction but suppresses it; Tony Goldwyn blusters and threatens as the hard American mercenary; Timothy Spall is the British translator who knows the words but not the music. Shichinosuke Nakamura plays the emperor as a tormented, shy man who admires Katsumoto's values even while agreeing with his advisers that the rebellion must be put down. "I am a living god—as long as I do what they say is right," he muses at one point, in words I somehow doubt any Japanese emperor would ever have employed.

The director is Edward Zwick, whose other war films *(Glory, Legends of the Fall, Courage Under Fire)* have also dealt with men whose personal loyalties have figured more importantly than political ideology. Here he gives Algren a speech attacking Custer, whose last stand was fresh in everyone's mind. ("He was a murderer who fell in love with his own legend, and his troops died for it.") Yes, but how would Algren describe this film's final battle scene, in which Katsumoto leads his men into what appears to be certain death? To be sure, his men share his values, but is there an element of seeking "a good death"? Is there a line between dying *for* what you believe in, and dying *because* of what you believe in?

That the film raises this question shows how thoughtful it is. If *The Last Samurai* had ended in a way that was consistent with its tone and direction, it would have been true to its real feelings. But the ending caves in to Hollywood requirements, and we feel the air going out of the picture. An art film can trust its audience to follow along to the necessary conclusion. A Hollywood ending assumes that the audience caves in at the end, turns dim-witted and sentimental, and must be fed its lollypop. *The Last Samurai* has greatness in it, but sidesteps the ending that would have given it real impact. If there's going to be an alternative ending on the DVD, I know what it would have to show—and so, I suspect, does Edward Zwick.

Note: Which character is the "last samurai"—Katsumoto or Algren? A case can be made for either answer, which suggests the nature of their relationship.

The Last Shot ★ ★ ★
R, 93 m., 2004

Matthew Broderick (Steven Schats), Alec Baldwin (Joe Devine), Toni Collette (Emily French), Calista Flockhart (Valerie Weston), Ray Liotta (Jack Devine), Tim Blake Nelson (Marshal Paris), James Rebhorn (Abe White), Tony Shalhoub (Tommy Sanz), Buck Henry (Lonnie Bosco). Directed by Jeff Nathanson and produced by Larry Brezner and David Hoberman. Screenplay by Nathanson, based on an article by Steve Fishman.

Like *Danny Deckchair, The Last Shot* is based on a real story that provides the inspiration for otherwise unbelievable events. Yes, the FBI really did once produce a phony movie as a sting operation. And yes, the filmmakers had no idea their producer was an undercover agent. Directors get screwed all the time by phony money men, but this was one time they couldn't go to the FBI.

The movie stars Matthew Broderick and Alec Baldwin as two men who desperately want to escape dead-end jobs. Broderick plays Steven Schats, an usher at Graumann's Chinese Theater, who, like almost everyone with even the most tenuous connection to the movie industry, has a screenplay he'd like to make into a movie. Baldwin plays Joe Devine, an FBI agent trapped in a low-level job in Rhode Island and hungry to move up. When he learns that mob-connected firms are muscling in on show-biz jobs in Providence, he has a brainstorm: He will set a trap by producing a movie that will tempt mobsters into incriminating themselves.

But first he needs a screenplay, probably from a would-be filmmaker so naive he could be deceived by Joe Devine's lack of credentials and, for that matter, his blissful ignorance of the movie business. Steven Schats is his pigeon. With the innocent enthusiasm that Broderick specializes in, the usher pitches a screenplay set in Arizona, about a tragic heroine who staggers out of the desert and into a series of murky flashbacks.

Devine green-lights *Arizona*, but has one stipulation: The movie has to be shot in Providence. Schats is thunderstruck: How can he shoot a location Western in Rhode Island? Devine says it's necessary for "production reasons," and talks about backdrops, special effects, and fake cacti. Schats needs a Hopi Indian cave for a sacred ceremony. Devine suggests a storage locker.

The Last Shot is not a well-oiled enterprise but more of a series of laughs separated by waits for more laughs. It has a kind of earnest, eager quality, and it's so screwy you feel affection for it; it creates completely gratuitous characters like the production executive played by an unbilled Joan Cusack, who barks into her intercom, "Bring me my back brace and my banjo!" There is no reason for the Cusack character except that she is relentlessly hilarious.

The screenplay, by the director Jeff Nathanson, has a nice line on funny free-standing dialogue. My favorite is probably, "Your dog is dead. She killed herself." I also like Tony Shaloub, as a gangster, saying: "I see you noticed my face. My wife set me on fire. Six months later, our marriage fell apart." And Devine boasting to Schats, "My wife did the hair on *Jaws*." She must have been very young at the time, but never mind. I also liked the moment when Schatz talks about "the business" and Devine thinks he means prostitution. A mistake anyone could make.

Toni Collette is funny as a ditzy would-be sex bomb who desperately needs the lead and desperately plays it, staggering out of the Rhode Island "desert" in full overacting mode. Calista Flockhart plays Valerie, Steven's flywheel girlfriend, who takes acting so seriously that she stabs herself in the leg to generate a Method "sense memory" of anguish. Familiar actors like Tim Blake Nelson, Buck Henry, and Ray Liotta work their supporting roles for everything they can get out of them.

I had the sense that one more trip through the word processor might have done the screenplay some good, but at the same time I enjoyed *The Last Shot* almost unreasonably, considering its rough edges. If a comedy makes you laugh you can forgive its imperfections. What is seductive about this one is the way Joe Devine begins to think of himself as a real movie producer, and gets caught up in the struggle to bring *Arizona* to the screen. What the movie gets right is the way even the most hopeless production can engender love and loyalty from its cast and crew, who talk themselves into believing it could be great. Nobody ever sets out to make a bad movie, and that's the lesson Joe Devine learns in spite of himself.

Latter Days ★ ★ ½
NO MPAA RATING, 108 m., 2004

Steve Sandvoss (Davis), Wes Ramsey (Christian), Rebekah Jordan (Julie), Amber Benson (Traci), Khary Payton (Andrew), Jacqueline Bisset (Lila), Joseph Gordon-Levitt (Ryder), Rob McElhenney (Harmon). Directed by C. Jay Cox and produced by Kirkland Tibbels and Jennifer Schafer. Screenplay by Cox.

A movie should present its characters with a problem and then watch them solve it, not without difficulty. So says an old and reliable screenplay formula. Countless movies have been made about a boy and a girl who have a problem (they haven't slept with each other) and after difficulties (family, war, economic, health, rival lover, stupid misunderstanding) they solve it, by sleeping with each other. Now we have a movie about two homosexuals that follows the same reliable convention.

Although much will be made of the fact that one of the characters in *Latter Days* is a Mormon missionary and the other is a gay poster boy, those are simply titillating details. Consider the subgenre of pornography in which nuns get involved in sex. We know they're not really nuns, but the costuming is supposed to add a little spice. By the same token, Davis (Steve Sandvoss) is a Mormon only because that makes his journey from hetero- to homosexual more fraught and daring. He could have been a Presbyterian or an atheist vegan and the underlying story would have been the same: A character who considers himself straight is seduced by an attractive gay man, and discovers he has been homosexual all along.

Since it is obvious to us from the opening shots that these two characters are destined for each other, the plot functions primarily to add melodrama to the inevitable. And there's change in both men. Christian (Wes Ramsey), who at the beginning is a shameless slut, bets a friend $50 he can seduce his new neighbor, but by the end of the film he truly loves him, and has been so transformed by this experience that he volunteers for an AIDS charity and in general is transformed into a nice guy. It's as if the Mormon missionary achieved his goal and converted him, in slightly different terms than he expected.

The $50 bet is a cliché as old as the movies, and of course it always results in the bettor *really* falling in love, while the quarry finds out about the bet and is crushed. One of the sly pleasures of *Latter Days* is the sight of this gay-themed movie recycling so many conventions from straight romantic cinema, as if it's time to catch up.

The film is made with a certain conviction, and the actors deliver more than their roles require; there are times when they seem about to veer off into true and accurate drama (as when Christian encounters a bitter dying man), but by the end, when Davis is back in Pocatello, Idaho, and his homophobic mother (Mary Kay Place) is sending him for shock treatment, we realize the movie could have been (a) a gay love story, or (b) an attack on the Mormon church, but is an awkward fit by trying to be (c) both at the same time.

I also question the character of one of Davis's fellow missionaries, who is outspokenly antigay in a particularly ugly way. Is this character modeled on life, or he is a version of the mustache-twirling villain? And then there's Christian's best friend, Julie (Rebekah Jordan), who of course is a hip and sympathetic African-American woman. You get to the point where you realize everyone in this movie has been ordered off the shelf from the Stock Characters Store, and none of them wandered in from real life.

Is there a way in which the movie works? Yes, it works by delivering on its formula. We sense immediately that Davis and Christian are destined to be lovers, and so we watch patiently as the screenplay fabricates obstacles to their destiny. We identify to some degree with them because—well, because we always tend to identify with likable characters in love stories. Maybe the fact that they're gay will help some homophobic audience members to understand homosexuality a little better, although whether they will attend the movie in the first place is a good question.

What I'm waiting for is a movie in which the characters are gay and that's a given, and they get on with a story involving their lives. Or maybe for a satire in which two heterosexuals move in next to each other and battle their inner natures until finally love tears down the barriers and they kiss, even though one is a boy and the other a girl. That would obviously be silly, and the day will come when a movie like this seems silly, too.

L'Auberge Espagnole ★ ★ ★
R, 122 m., 2003

Romain Duris (Xavier), Cécile De France (Isabelle), Judith Godrèche (Anne-Sophie), Audrey Tautou (Martine), Kelly Reilly (Wendy), Kevin Bishop (William), Federico D'Anna (Alessandro), Christian Pagh (Lars), Cristina Brondo (Soledad), Barnaby Metschurat (Tobias). Directed by Cédric Klapisch and produced by Bruno Levy. Screenplay by Klapisch.

Xavier, a French student worried about his career choices, is advised by a family friend that learning Spanish will be his ticket to success. He signs up for the Erasmus program of the European Community, which arranges student exchanges as a way for the young people of the New Europe to get to know one another by living and studying together for a year.

L'Auberge Espagnole is the story of Xavier's adventures during a year in Barcelona with, if I have this straight, fellow students from Spain, England, Belgium, Germany, Italy, and Denmark. An American wanders through, but makes no impression. Although all of their languages make cameo appearances, English is the common language of choice.

That makes the title all the more puzzling. I saw this movie for the first time at the 2002 Karlovy Vary Film Festival in the Czech Republic, where it won the audience award under the title *Europudding*. It opened in England as *Pot Luck*, in Spain as *Una Casa de Locos*, was announced for North America as *The Spanish Hotel*, and now arrives with the Spanish version of that title. This is not a good omen for the movie's message about the harmony of national cultures.

The movie has Xavier (Romain Duris) say good-bye for a year to his French girlfriend (Audrey Tautou, of *Amelie*) and fly to Spain on an odyssey which he narrates, not very helpfully (much dialogue along the lines of, "My story starts here . . . no, not here, but . . . "). In Barcelona he shares an apartment with six other students plus a revolving roster of lovers, most straight, one gay. Imagine the American students in *The Real Cancun* as if they were literate, cosmopolitan, and not substance abusers, and you've got it.

The subplots edge up to screwball comedy without ever quite reaching it, except in a sequence where a girl is in bed with the wrong boy and her current boyfriend arrives unexpectedly at the apartment. Writer-director Cédric Klapisch uses a three-way split screen to show the roommates racing to head off the boyfriend and provide an alibi, and what they come up with provides the movie's biggest laugh.

The romantic adventures of all of the students provide, not surprisingly, most of the movie's plot. I don't remember a whole lot of discussion about the euro as a currency. Unlike *The Real Cancun*, which was dripping with sex but was subtly homophobic, *L'Auberge Espagnole* is refreshingly frank about its lesbian, the Belgian girl named Isabelle (Cécile De France, who won the César Award as most promising newcomer). Although Xavier fancied himself an adequate lover when he arrived in Spain, he benefits greatly from Isabelle's expert lecture-demonstration about what really turns a woman on.

The movie is as light and frothy as a French comedy, which is what it is, a reminder that Cédric Klapisch also directed *When the Cat's Away* (1996), the lighthearted story of a woman who involves an entire neighborhood in the search for her cat. Klapisch likes a casual tone in which human eccentricity is folded into the story and taken for granted.

For Xavier, the year in the Erasmus program leads to a fundamental change in his career goals; he can't face a lifetime of French bureaucracy after the anarchy of his year of Europudding. Travel broadens the mind, they say, and certainly living for a year or so outside your native land helps you view it as part of the larger world. Depressing to contrast these young people with the cast of *The Real Cancun*, who hardly realize they're in Mexico.

Laurel Canyon ★ ★
R, 103 m., 2003

Frances McDormand (Jane), Christian Bale (Sam), Kate Beckinsale (Alex), Natascha McElhone (Sara), Alessandro Nivola (Ian). Directed by Lisa Cholodenko and produced by Susan A. Stover and Jeffrey Levy-Hinte. Screenplay by Cholodenko.

Frances McDormand's first film was *Blood Simple* (1984), but I really noticed her for the first time in *Mississippi Burning* (1988), standing in that doorway, talking to Gene Hackman, playing a battered redneck wife who had the courage to do the right thing. From that day to this I have been fascinated by whatever it is she does on the screen to create such sympathy with the audience.

Her Marge Gunderson in *Fargo* is one of the most likable characters in movie history. In almost all of her roles, McDormand embodies an immediate, present, physical, functioning, living, breathing person as well as any actor ever has, and she plays radically different roles as easily as she walks.

Laurel Canyon is not a successful movie—it's too stilted and preprogrammed to come alive—but in the center of it McDormand occupies a place for her character and makes that place into a brilliant movie of its own. There is nothing wrong with who she is and what she does, although all around her actors are cracking up in strangely written roles.

She plays Jane, a woman in her forties who has been a successful record producer for a long time—long enough to make enough money to own one house in the hills of Laurel Canyon and another one at the beach, which in terms of Los Angeles real estate prices means that when she goes to the Grammys a lot of people talk to her. A sexual free spirit from her early days, she is currently producing an album with a British rock singer named Ian (Alessandro Nivola), who is twenty years younger and her lover.

Jane has a son about Ian's age named Sam (Christian Bale), who is the product of an early and fleeting liaison. Sam is the opposite of his mother, fleeing hedonism for the rigors of Harvard Medical School, where he has found a fiancée named Alex (Kate Beckinsale). He studies psychiatry, she studies fruit flies, and true to their professions he will grow neurotic while she will buzz around seeing who lands on her.

Sam and Alex drive west; he'll do his residency, she'll continue her studies, and they'll live in the Laurel Canyon house while Jane moves to the beach. Alas, Laurel Canyon is occupied by Jane—and Ian and various members of the band—when they arrive because Jane has given the beach place to an ex-husband who needed a place to live.

Significant close-ups and furtive once-overs within the first few scenes make the rest of the movie fairly inevitable. Ian and Jane, whose relationship is so open you could drive a relationship through it, telepathically agree to include Alex in their embraces. Alex is intrigued by a freedom that she never experienced, shall we say, at Harvard Medical School, while Sam meanwhile meets the sensuous Sara (Natascha McElhone), a colleague at the psychiatric hospital, and soon they are in one of those situations where he gives her a ride home and they get to talking so much that he has to turn the engine off. (That act—turning the key in the ignition—is the often-overlooked first step in most adulteries.)

Sam and Alex are therefore on separate

trajectories, and *Laurel Canyon* makes that so clear with intercutting that we uneasily begin to sense the presence of the screenplay. The movie doesn't have the headlong inevitability of *High Art* (1998), by the same writer-director, Lisa Cholodenko. The earlier movie starred Radha Mitchell in a role similar to Alex, as a woman lured away from a safe relationship by the dark temptations of new friends. But *High Art* seemed to *happen,* and *Laurel Canyon* seems to unfold from an obligatory scenario.

Still, there is Frances McDormand, whose character happens and does not unfold, and who is effortlessly convincing as a sexually alluring woman of a certain age. In fact, she's a babe. Of the three principal female characters in the movie—played by McDormand, Beckinsale, and McElhone—it's McDormand whom many wise males (and females) would choose. She promises playful carnal amusement while the others threaten long, sad conversations about their needs.

How McDormand creates her characters I do not understand. This one is the opposite of the mother who worries about her rock-writer son in *Almost Famous.* She begins with a given—her physical presence—but even that seems to transmute through some actor's sorcery. In this movie she's a babe, a seductive, experienced woman who trained in the 1970s and is still a hippie at heart. Now go to the Internet Movie Database and look at the photo that goes with her entry. Who does she look like? A high school teacher chaperoning at the prom. How she does it is a mystery, but she does, reinventing herself, role after role. *Laurel Canyon* is not a success, but McDormand is ascendant.

Lawless Heart ★ ★ ★
R, 102 m., 2003

Bill Nighy (Dan), Tom Hollander (Nick), Douglas Henshall (Tim), Clementine Celarie (Corrine), Stuart Laing (David), Josephine Butler (Leah), Ellie Haddington (Judy), Sukie Smith (Charlie), Dominic Hall (Darren), David Coffey (Stuart). Directed by Tom Hunsinger and Neil Hunter and produced by Martin Pope. Screenplay by Hunsinger and Hunter.

Lawless Heart begins with a funeral, which, like all funerals, assembles people who may not often see one another but have personal connections—old, new, hidden, and potential. The dead man, named Stuart, ran a restaurant on the Isle of Man, off the British coast. To his funeral come Nick, who was his lover; Dan, who was his brother-in-law; and Tim, a childhood friend who has been long absent from the village.

The film opens with the reception after the funeral. We meet the characters and get to know them a little, we think, and we hear the kinds of profundities and resolutions that people utter when reminded of the possibility of their own deaths. The conversation is bright and quick, the people are likable, and at the end of the afternoon they go their various ways.

It's then that the film, written and directed by Tom Hunsinger and Neil Hunter, reveals its own hidden connections. It follows the three men, one after another, in sequences that take place at the same time but change their meaning depending on the point of view, so that the sight of a man crouching out of sight behind a car makes perfect sense, or no sense at all, depending on what you know about why he is doing it.

Nick (Tom Hollander) helped Stuart run the restaurant, and if Stuart had left a will, we learn, he would have left the business to his lover. But he left no will. Stuart's sister Judy therefore inherits the business, but discusses with her husband, Dan (Bill Nighy), the possibility of giving it to Nick anyway.

Nick, meanwhile, discovers that the long-lost friend Tim (Douglas Henshall) is broke and homeless, and lets him stay in the house he shared with Stuart. Tim moves in, drinks too much, and throws a party. The next morning Nick finds a girl named Charlie (Sukie Smith) in his bed, and she wants to know if they had sex. She had sex, all right, but not with the gay Nick—who throws out Tim but begins a friendship with Charlie that leads, to his own amazement, to them having sex after all. Judy discovers this heterosexual excursion by her brother's lover, and takes it as a reason (or an excuse) to keep the restaurant for herself.

Meanwhile, her husband, Dan, follows up on an intriguing conversation he had at the funeral with Corrine (Clementine Celarie), a

Frenchwoman who lives in the town, thinks he is single, and boldly invites him to dinner. Will he accept? The way that he handles himself on the crucial night is true, funny, and ultimately ironic.

These intrigues and others are all interconnected, as we gradually understand. *Lawless Heart* is an exercise in interlocking narratives, in which the same scene means first one thing and then another, the more we know about it. But it isn't simply an exercise; the characters are full-bodied and authentic, capable of surprising themselves, and their dialogue is written with a good ear for how smart people try to be truthful and secretive at the same time.

We discover, for example, that the reason Tim threw his apparently senseless party at Nick's was to create a place to which he could invite Leah (Josephine Butler), whom he met at the funeral. What Tim doesn't know is that his brother David had an unhappy affair with Leah. Tim is in love with Leah himself, or thinks he is, and the outcome of this liaison is one that none of the three could have anticipated.

My description of the plot no doubt makes it sound like a jigsaw puzzle, and yet it's surprising how clear all these relationships become when we're actually seeing and hearing the characters. They're so well drawn, so clear in their needs and fears, that we get drawn into the plot just as we might get drawn into the intrigues of a real village; the movie watches its characters like a nosy neighbor, changing its view as more information surfaces.

The purpose of the movie is perhaps to show us, in a quietly amusing way, that while we travel down our own lifelines, seeing everything from our own points of view, we hardly suspect the secrets of the lives we intersect with. We tend to think people exist when we are with them, but stay on hold the rest of the time. Our lives go forward—but so, *Lawless Heart* reminds us, do theirs.

Laws of Attraction ★ ★
PG-13, 90 m., 2004

Pierce Brosnan (Daniel Rafferty), Julianne Moore (Audrey Woods), Parker Posey (Serena), Michael Sheen (Thorne Jamison), Nora Dunn (Judge Abramovitz), Frances Fisher (Sara Miller). Directed by Peter Howitt and produced by Julie Durk, David T. Friendly, Beau St. Clair, and Marc Turtletaub. Screenplay by Aline Brosh McKenna and Robert Harling.

Opposites attract, it's true, but the problem with the two divorce lawyers in *Laws of Attraction* is that they're not opposites. They're perfectly well suited to each other, recognize that almost immediately, and tumble into bed at least half an hour, maybe an hour, before that's permitted by the movie's formula. Then they annoy us by trying to deny the attraction while the plot spins its wheels, pretending to be about something.

The two attractive people are Daniel Rafferty (Pierce Brosnan) and Audrey Woods (Julianne Moore). Neither one has ever lost a case. Both are, somewhat oddly, still single despite being awesomely attractive. Maybe it's because of all the divorces they see. Audrey blames it on being the plain daughter of a raving beauty (Frances Fisher), but, I don't know about you, I can't picture Julianne Moore as plain. As for Pierce Brosnan, anyone who thinks he needs to be replaced as James Bond is starkers.

As we all know, the formula for this kind of movie requires the two protagonists to hate each other at first sight. Only gradually do they discover they're in love. I recommend *Two Weeks Notice* (2002), with Sandra Bullock and Hugh Grant, as a superior example of the formula. But in *Laws of Attraction*, Brosnan is always more or less in love with Moore, usually more, and so the movie has to resort to wheezy devices to be about anything at all.

It gives him offices, for example, above a grocery in Chinatown. Why? Because Chinatown is a colorful location, although an undefeated divorce lawyer could afford uptown rents. I am reminded of *What a Girl Wants* (2003), in which Amanda Bynes and her mother, Kelly Preston, live in an apartment in Chinatown, again without a single Chinese person saying one word in the movie, simply because you get the colorful location for free.

One colorful location is not enough. Brosnan and Moore find themselves on opposite sides of a divorce case involving a rock star (Michael Sheen) and a dress designer (Parker Posey), who both want possession of a castle in Ireland, which of course requires Brosnan and Moore to jet to Ireland, visit the castle, attend a local fete, participate in Irish jigs, get drunk, and get married. Come to think of it, they were drunk when they went to bed for the first time too. Maybe Brosnan was drunk when he rented the apartment in Chinatown.

Now these two actors are perfectly lovable people, and so we are happy for them, and enjoy watching them and listening to them, but this is a movie, not an audition, and they really deserved more from the director, Peter Howitt, and cowriters Aline Brosh McKenna and Robert Harling, who between them come up with less than one serviceable screenplay.

One of the consequences of a reedy story like this is that you start looking in the corners. I remember that during *What Women Want* (2000), a much better movie starring Mel Gibson, I was gobsmacked by the office for his ad agency, which was the neatest office I had ever seen in a movie. In *Laws of Attraction,* I liked Brosnan's apartment, which is not in Chinatown and so we don't need to know where it is. It looks like a showroom for the Arts and Crafts Movement, with dark wood everywhere. It was a little shadowy, to be sure, but I wonder if even things like the sink and the sofa were made out of wood. Possibly even the sheets. This apartment looks so odd that one of the movie's most implausible moments comes when Moore sees it and says nothing about it. Oh, she was drunk.

Layer Cake ★ ★ ★ ½
R, 105 m., 2005

Daniel Craig (XXXX), Colm Meaney (Gene), Sienna Miller (Tammy), Michael Gambon (Eddie Temple), Kenneth Cranham (Jimmy Price), George Harris (Morty), Jamie Foreman (Duke). Directed by Matthew Vaughn and produced by Adam Bohling, David Reid, and Vaughn. Screenplay by J. J. Connolly, based on his novel.

Like Scorsese's *Casino* and *GoodFellas,* the British crime movie *Layer Cake* opens with a narration describing a criminal world made in heaven. Also like *Casino* and *GoodFellas,* it is about an inexorable decline toward the torments of hell. The voice explaining everything to us belongs to Daniel Craig, who plays the competent and conservative middleman in a well-run London cocaine operation. Nobody ever calls him by name during the movie, and

in the closing credits he's referred to as "XXXX," which may be one-upmanship on "XXX," or probably not.

Craig's credo, spelled out as if he's lecturing at a management seminar, involves knowing your suppliers, knowing your customers, paying your bills, and never getting too greedy. His front is real estate. His exit plan is retirement in the near future. All of that changes when he is summoned to a private club for a luncheon meeting with his immediate superior, Jimmy Price (Kenneth Cranham), a hard man with cold eyes and a menacing Cockney charm. Jimmy wants him to sort out an Ecstasy deal that went bad, and as a sort of twofer, also find the missing daughter of *his* boss, Eddie Temple (Michael Gambon), the kind of man whose soul has warts on its scars.

XXXX does not much like either assignment. They involve cleaning up the kinds of messes he has scrupulously avoided in his own dealings. What's the use of playing it safe if you work for people who want you to take their chances for them? The Ecstasy deal is especially dicey: One of Jimmy's cronies named Duke (Jamie Foreman) stole Ecstasy pills allegedly worth a million pounds. The Serbs he stole them from want them back. Jimmy's ideal scenario, never stated in so many words, would involve XXXX grabbing the pills for Jimmy while Duke is thrown to the Serbs.

XXXX has some hard men who work for him and might be able to get this job done. More complicated is the matter of the girl, especially when another girl named Tammy (Sienna Miller) enters the picture. There are key supporting roles for such actors as the indispensable Colm Meaney, who looks as if he should be found guilty and sent down for life just for the way he has of listening to you.

The movie was directed by Matthew Vaughn, who produced *Lock, Stock and Two Smoking Barrels* and *Snatch,* and this one works better than those films because it doesn't try so hard to be clever and tries harder to be menacing. It's difficult to take danger seriously when it's packaged in fancy camera work, although Guy Ritchie's *Lock, Stock* did have a carefree visual genius. *Layer Cake* is more in the Scorsese vein, in which a smart and ambitious young man has it all figured out, and then gradually loses control to old-fashioned hoods who don't have the patience for prudence when it's easier to just eliminate anyone who gets in their way. The problem is that every dead enemy tends to leave a more dangerous living enemy standing next in line.

There is a kind of scene that both American and British crime movies do very well, in which low-lifes enjoy high life. They've had success in their business of crime, but their preparation for life has not equipped them with interesting ways to stay amused. They almost always lack imagination about what constitutes fun, and dutifully spend their money on cars, cigars, women, champagne, and memberships in private clubs, none of which finally seem to be worth the trouble. We are reminded of the last days of Scarface, a young man who desperately needed something constructive to do with his spare time.

XXXX's dilemma is that he has the resources to enjoy himself, but works for people who speak a different language. He is really in the wrong line of work. He could steal more money with the kinds of high finance that distinguished Enron, and run a smaller risk of finding his head in a bucket of ice and his body elsewhere. As his life begins to heat up and events unfold more quickly than he can follow them, we're reminded of Ray Liotta in *GoodFellas*, whose life spun out of control.

Daniel Craig was said to be the front-runner for the next James Bond, until it began to be said that Pierce Brosnan might return for a farewell lap. My own money is on Clive Owen, but who would wish James Bond on anyone? Craig is fascinating here as a criminal who is very smart, and finds that is not an advantage because while you might be able to figure out what another smart person is about to do, dumbos like the men he works for are likely to do anything.

The League of Extraordinary Gentlemen ★

PG-13, 110 m., 2003

Sean Connery (Allan Quatermain), Shane West (Tom Sawyer), Stuart Townsend (Dorian Gray), Peta Wilson (Mina Harker), Jason Flemyng (Jekyll and Hyde), Naseeruddin Shah (Captain Nemo), Tony Curran (Rodney Skinner), Richard Roxburgh (M). Directed by Stephen Norrington and produced by Trevor Albert and Don Murphy. Screenplay by James Robinson, based on comic books by Alan Moore and Kevin O'Neill.

The League of Extraordinary Gentlemen assembles a splendid team of heroes to battle a plan for world domination, and then, just when it seems about to become a real corker of an adventure movie, plunges into incomprehensible action, idiotic dialogue, inexplicable motivations, causes without effects, effects without causes, and general lunacy. What a mess.

And yet it all starts so swimmingly. An emissary from Britain arrives at a private club in Kenya, circa 1899, to invite the legendary adventurer Allan Quatermain (Sean Connery) to assist Her Majesty's Government in averting a world war. Villains have used a tank to break into the Bank of England and have caused great destruction in Germany, and each country is blaming the other. Quatermain at first refuses to help, but becomes annoyed when armored men with automatic rifles invade the club and try to kill everybody. Quatermain and friends are able to dispatch them with some head butting, a few rights to the jaw, and a skewering on an animal horn, and then he goes to London to attend a meeting called by a spy master named—well, he's named M, of course.

Also assembled by M are such fabled figures as Captain Nemo (Naseeruddin Shah), who has retired from piracy; Mina Harker (Peta Wilson), who was involved in that messy Dracula business; Rodney Skinner (Tony Curran), who is the Invisible Man; Dorian Gray (Stuart Townsend), who, Quatermain observes, seems to be missing a picture; Tom Sawyer (Shane West), who works as an agent for the U.S. government; and Dr. Henry Jekyll (Jason Flemyng), whose alter ego is Mr. Hyde.

These team members have skills undreamed of by the authors who created them. We are not too surprised to discover that Mina Harker is an immortal vampire, since she had those puncture wounds in her throat the last time we saw her, but I wonder if Oscar Wilde knew that Dorian Gray was also immortal and cannot die (or be killed!) as long as he doesn't see his portrait; at one point, an enemy operative perforates him with bullets, and he comes up smiling. Robert Louis Stevenson's Mr. Hyde was about the same size as Dr. Jekyll, but here Hyde expands into a creature scarcely smaller than the Hulk and gets his pants from the same tailor, since they expand right along with him while his shirt is torn to shreds. Hyde looks uncannily like the WWF version of Fat Bastard.

Now listen carefully. M informs them that the leaders of Europe are going to meet in Venice, and that the mysterious villains will blow up the city to start a world war. The league must stop them. When is the meeting? In three days, M says. Impossible to get there in time, Quatermain says, apparently in ignorance of railroads. Nemo volunteers his submarine, the *Nautilus,* which is about ten stories high and as long as an aircraft carrier, and which we soon see cruising the canals of Venice.

It's hard enough for gondolas to negotiate the inner canals of Venice, let alone a sub the size of an ocean liner, but no problem; *The League of Extraordinary Gentlemen* either knows absolutely nothing about Venice, or (more likely) trusts that its audience does not. At one point, the towering *Nautilus* sails under the tiny Bridge of Sighs and only scrapes it a little. In no time at all there is an action scene involving Nemo's newfangled automobile, which races meaninglessly down streets that do not exist, because there are no streets in Venice and you can't go much more than a block before running into a bridge or a canal. Maybe the filmmakers did their research at the Venetian Hotel in Las Vegas, where Sean Connery arrived by gondola for the movie's premiere.

Bombs begin to explode Venice. It is Carnival time, and Piazza San Marco is jammed with merrymakers as the basilica explodes and topples into ruin. Later there is a scene of this same crowd engaged in lighthearted chatter, as if they have not noticed that half of Venice is missing. Dozens of other buildings sink into the lagoon, which does not prevent Quatermain from exalting, "Venice still stands!"

Now back to that speeding car. Its driver, Tom Sawyer, has been sent off on an urgent mission. When he finds something—an underwater bomb, I think, although that would be hard to spot from a speeding car—he's supposed to fire off a flare, after which I don't know what's supposed to happen. As the car hurtles down the nonexistent streets of Venice, enemy operatives stand shoulder-to-shoulder on the rooftops and fire at it with machine guns, leading us to hypothesize an enemy meeting at which the leader says, "Just in case they should arrive by submarine with a fast car, which hasn't been invented yet, I want thousands of men to line the rooftops and fire at it, without hitting anything, of course."

But never mind. The action now moves to the frozen lakes of Mongolia, where the enemy leader (whose identity I would not dream of revealing) has constructed a gigantic factory palace to manufacture robot soldiers, apparently an early model of the clones they were manufacturing in *Attack* of the same. This palace was presumably constructed recently at great expense (it's a bitch getting construction materials through those frozen lakes). And yet it includes vast, neglected, and forgotten rooms.

I don't really mind the movie's lack of believability. Well, I mind a little; to assume audiences will believe cars racing through Venice is as insulting as giving them a gondola chase down the White House lawn. What I do mind is that the movie plays like a big wind came along and blew away the script and they ran down the street after it and grabbed a few pages and shot those. Since Oscar Wilde contributed Dorian Gray to the movie, it may be appropriate to end with his dying words: "Either that wallpaper goes, or I do."

Le Cercle Rouge ★ ★ ★ ★
NO MPAA RATING, 140 m., 2003

Alain Delon (Corey), Gian Maria Volonté (Vogel), Yves Montand (Jansen), André Bourvil (Captain Mattei), François Périer (Santi), Paul Crauchet (The Fence), Pierre Collet (Prison Guard), André Ekyan (Rico). Directed by Jean-Pierre Melville and produced by Robert Dorfmann. Screenplay by Melville.

Gliding almost without speech down the dawn streets of a wet Paris winter, these men in trench coats and fedoras perform a ballet of crime, hoping to win and fearing to die. Some are cops and some are robbers. To smoke for them is as natural as breathing. They use guns, lies, clout, greed, and nerve with the skill of a magician who no longer even thinks about the cards. They share a code of honor that is not about what side of the law they are on, but about how a man must behave to win the respect of those few others who understand the code.

Jean-Pierre Melville watches them with the eye of a concerned god in his 1970 film *Le Cercle Rouge*. His movie involves an escaped prisoner, a diamond heist, a police manhunt, and mob vengeance, but it treats these elements as the magician treats his cards; the cards are insignificant, except as the medium through which he demonstrates his skills.

Melville is a director whose films are little known in America; he began before the French New Wave, died in 1973, worked in genres but had a stylistic elegance that kept his films from being marketed to the traditional genre audiences. His *Bob le Flambeur,* now available on a Criterion DVD, has been remade as *The Good Thief* and inspired elements of the two *Ocean's Eleven* films, but all they borrowed was the plot, and that was the least essential thing about it.

Melville grew up living and breathing movies, and his films show more experience of the screen than of life. No real crooks or cops are this attentive to the details of their style and behavior. Little wonder that his great 1967 film about a professional hit man is named *Le Samourai;* his characters, like the samurai, place greater importance on correct behavior than upon success. (Jim Jarmusch's *Ghost Dog* owes something to this value system.)

Le Cercle Rouge, or *The Red Circle* (restored for 2003 release by his admirer John Woo), refers to a saying of the Buddha that men who are destined to meet will eventually meet, no matter what. Melville made up this saying, but no matter; his characters operate according to theories of behavior, so that a government minister believes all men, without exception, are bad; and a crooked nightclub owner refuses to be a police informer because it is simply not in his nature to inform.

The movie stars two of the top French stars of the time, Alain Delon and Yves Montand, as well as Gian Maria Volonté, looking younger here than in the spaghetti Westerns, and with hair. But it is not a star vehicle—or, wait, it is a star vehicle, but the stars ride in it instead of the movie riding on them. All of the actors seem directed to be cool and dispassionate, to guard their feelings, to keep their words to them-

selves, to realize that among men of experience almost everything can go without saying.

As the film opens, we meet Corey (Delon) as he is released from prison. He has learned of a way to hold up one of the jewelry stores of Place Vendôme. Then we meet Vogel (Volonté), who is a handcuffed prisoner on a train, but he picks the locks of the cuffs, breaks a window, leaps from the moving train, and escapes from the veteran cop Mattei (André Bourvil).

Fate brings Vogel and Corey together. On the run in the countryside, Vogel hides in the trunk of Corey's car. Corey sees him do this, but we don't know he does. He drives into a muddy field, gets out of his car, stands away from it, and tells the man in the trunk he can get out. The man does, holding a gun that Corey must have known he would find in the trunk. They regard each other, face to face in the muddy field. Vogel wants a smoke. Corey throws him a pack and a lighter.

Notice how little they actually say before Corey says, "Paris is your best chance," and Vogel gets back in the trunk. And then notice the precision and economy of what happens next. Corey's car is being tailed by gunmen for a mob boss he relieved of a lot of money. It was probably due him, but still, that is no way to treat a mob boss. Corey pulls over. The gunsels tell him to walk toward the woods. He does. Then we hear Vogel tell them to drop their guns and raise their hands. Vogel picks up each man's gun with a handkerchief and uses it to shoot the other man—so the fingerprints will indicate they shot each other. Corey risked his life on the expectation that Vogel would know what to do and do it, and Corey was right.

There is one cool, understated scene after another. Note the way the police commissioner talks to the nightclub owner after he knows that the owner's son, picked up in an attempt to pressure the owner, has killed himself. Note what he says and what he doesn't say, and how he looks. And note, too, how Jansen, the Yves Montand character, comes into the plot, and think for a moment about why he doesn't want his share of the loot.

The heist itself is performed with the exactness we expect of a movie heist. We are a little startled to realize it is not the point of the film. In most heist movies, the screenplay cannot think beyond the heist, and is satisfied merely to deliver it. *Le Cercle Rouge* assumes that the crooks will be skillful at the heist because they are good workmen. The movie is not about their jobs but about their natures.

Melville fought for the French Resistance during the war. Manohla Dargis of the *Los Angeles Times*, in a review of uncanny and poetic perception, writes: "It may sound far-fetched, but I wonder if his obsessive return to the same themes didn't have something to do with a desire to restore France's own lost honor." The heroes of his films may win or lose, may be crooks or cops, but they are not rats.

Le Divorce ★ ★ ★
PG-13, 115 m., 2003

Kate Hudson (Isabel Walker), Naomi Watts (Roxeanne de Persand), Leslie Caron (Suzanne de Persand), Stockard Channing (Margeeve Walker), Glenn Close (Olivia Pace), Sam Waterston (Chester Walker), Bebe Neuwirth (Julia Manchevering), Matthew Modine (Tellman), Thierry Lhermitte (Edgar Cosset), Stephen Fry (Piers Janely), Melvil Poupaud (Charles-Henri de Persand). Directed by James Ivory and produced by Ismail Merchant and Michael Schiffer. Screenplay by Ruth Prawer Jhabvala and Ivory, based on the novel by Diane Johnson.

Le Divorce, which is about contrary French and American standards for marriage, adultery, divorce, and affairs, finds that the two nations are simply incompatible. While there are too many characters in too much story for the movie to really involve us, it's amusing as a series of sketches about how the French they are a funny race (or the Americans, take your choice). I am reminded of the British writer Peter Noble, who said everything he knew about France could be summed up in this story: "An English guy walks into a café in Cannes and asks if they have a men's room. The waiter replies: 'Monsieur! I have only two hands!'"

The movie stars Naomi Watts as Roxeanne, a pregnant American whose faithless French husband, Charles-Henri de Persand (Melvil Poupaud), has walked out on her because of his obsession with a married Russian woman named Magda. Roxeanne's sister Isabel (Kate Hudson) flies to Paris to support her sister, and soon promotes an affair for herself with Edgar (Thierry Lhermitte), the brother of Roxeanne's mother-in-law. Meanwhile, Magda's American husband (Matthew Modine) becomes a stalker, threatening Roxeanne. Doesn't he understand that it was her *husband* who stole away his wife?

Roxeanne's husband begs for a divorce. "She must understand," her husband patiently explains to Isabel, "that I have met the love of my life." He sees himself as the wronged party. Meanwhile, Edgar moves swiftly on his first lunch date with Isabel, explaining that the only question before them is whether she will become his mistress. What . . . ah . . . what exactly would that involve, Isabel asks, in a moment that reminds us that Kate Hudson is Goldie Hawn's daughter and has that same eyelid-batting trick of seeming naive and insinuating at the same time. Edgar explains that they would amuse each other: "I find you entertaining, and I hope you find me entertaining." Isabel says she wouldn't want their families to know. "Frankly," he says, "it would never occur to me to tell them."

The movie is based on a best-selling novel by Diane Johnson, and has been directed by James Ivory and produced by Ismail Merchant, working with their usual screenwriter, Ruth Prawer Jhabvala. The Merchant-Ivory firm are masters of movies about manners, and have fun with the rules by which Edgar conducts his affairs. A new conquest is immediately given a Kelly bag; that's a $6,000-and-up purse from Hermés, of the sort Grace Kelly always carried. Glenn Close, who plays an expatriate American writer in Paris, was a lover of Edgar's years ago, we learn, and observes that his affairs always begin with the bag and end with the gift of a scarf.

What is remarkable is that Suzanne de Persand (Leslie Caron), Edgar's sister, immediately finds out about the affair, and soon so does his wife. Caron makes a bracing analysis of the situation: It is bad enough that her son has behaved foolishly by allowing such a troublesome emotion as love to cause disrepair to his marriage, but for Isabel to fall for Edgar's tired routine is unforgivable, especially at a time like this. The Americans, she observes, have no idea how to conduct affairs, and do not realize they are intended to be temporary. When one ends, they get all serious and tragic. Even Edgar has his doubts, telling Isabel, "If you are keeping a diary, I hope your style will meet the expectations of the French public." And then, fearing the feckless American will not understand the Gallic sense of humor: "You're not, are you?"

The movie is so heavy on story that no character fully engages our sympathy—although some don't take long to make us dislike them. There's a subplot involving a painting that belongs to Isabel and Roxeanne's family, and which the faithless husband, incredibly, believes is half his. That leads to an amusing excursion into art values, with an expert from the Louvre pronouncing the painting inferior, and an expert from Christie's insisting it is by the master Georges de la Tour. The Christie's man is played by Stephen Fry, tall, cheery, and plummy, who explains why museums undervalue paintings and auction houses overvalue them. It's entertaining, but is it on topic?

I could have done without Matthew Modine's jealous husband, a dizzy basket case who generates a contrived and unnecessary scene atop the Eiffel Tower. But Stockard Channing is wonderful as the mother of the American girls. As sophisticated in her American way as the Leslie Caron character, she takes the wind out of French sails with her no-B.S. California style. I admire those who speak French whether or not they can, as when she orders in a restaurant: "Could I just get like a steak poivre and a salad vert, trés well?"

Le Divorce doesn't work on its intended level because we don't care enough about the interactions of the enormous cast. But it works in another way, as a sophisticated and knowledgeable portrait of values in collision. If you are familiar with France and have a love-hate affair with that most cryptic of nations, you are likely to enjoy the movie from moment to moment, whether or not it adds up for you.

Legally Blonde 2: Red, White and Blonde ★ ★
PG-13, 105 m., 2003

Reese Witherspoon (Elle Woods), Sally Field (Representative Victoria Rudd), Bob Newhart (Sidney Post), Luke Wilson (Emmett Richmond), Jennifer Coolidge (Paulette Bonafonte), Regina King (Grace Stoteraux), Jessica Cauffiel (Margot), Alanna Ubach (Serena McGuire), Bruce McGill (Stanford Marks). Directed by Charles Herman-Wurmfeld and produced by David Nicksay and Marc Platt. Screenplay by Kate Kondell.

Legally Blonde 2: Red, White and Blonde evokes a fairy-tale America in which a congresswoman's ditzy blonde junior staff member, pretty in pink, is asked to address a joint session of Congress and sways them with her appeal for animal rights. Not in this world. It might happen, though, in the world of the movie—but even then, her big speech is so truly idiotic she'd be laughed out of town. That the movie considers this speech a triumph shows how little it cares about its "ideas." The model for the movie is obviously *Mr. Smith Goes to Washington*, but in that one James Stewart's big speech was actually sort of about something.

The movie chronicles the continuing adventures of Elle Woods, the Reese Witherspoon character introduced in the winning *Legally Blonde* (2001). Elle, for whom pink is not a favorite color but a lifestyle choice, is like a walking, talking beauty and cosmetics magazine, whose obsession with superficial girly things causes people, understandably, to dismiss her at first sight. Ah, but beneath the Jackie Kennedy pillbox hat there lurks a first-class brain; Elle is a Harvard Law graduate who, as the sequel opens, has a job in a top legal firm.

It's impossible to determine if Elle knows what she's doing—if it's all a strategy—or whether she truly is *über*-ditzy. Always smiling, never discouraged, deaf to insults, blind to sneers, dressed in outfits that come from a fashion universe of their own, she sails through life like the good ship *Undefeatable*. How she stumbles upon the cause of animal rights is instructive. It begins with her search for the biological birth parent of Bruiser, her beloved Chihuahua. When she finds the mother captive in an animal testing laboratory ("We test makeup on animals so you don't have to"), she becomes an animal rights advocate, is fired from her law firm, and finds herself on the staff of Representative Victoria Rudd (Sally Field), who is sponsoring an animal-rights bill.

The movie's vision of Congress is hopelessly simplistic and idealistic. Characters have the same kinds of instant conversions that are standard on sitcoms, where the unenlightened oppose something, have a sudden epiphany, and then see the light. Consider the character of Stan, a self-described Southern conservative who discovers, along with Elle, that both their dogs are gay and have fallen in love with each other. This softens him up on the pending legislation because he loves his gay dog, you see.

The movie has its share of funny lines ("This is just like C-SPAN except it's not boring") and moments (congressional interns form a pom-pom squad), but the plot developments in Congresswoman Rudd's office are heavy-handed. Rudd's top aide (Regina King) is cold and antagonistic to Elle when the plot needs her to be and then turns on a dime. Rudd herself admits to dropping her bill in return for big campaign contributions. And Elle's top adviser is a hotel doorman (Bob Newhart) who knows how Washington works because of what he overhears. Uh-huh. Meanwhile, back home in Boston, Elle's fiancé (Luke Wilson) is incredibly understanding when his marriage is put on hold during Elle's legislative campaign. There could be a whole comedy just about being engaged or married to the creature in pink.

Ramping up for this review, I came across a curious column by Arianna Huffington, who attended a preview screening and wrote, "Sitting between my teenage daughters while watching Elle take on the U.S. Congress, I was struck by the palpable effect it had on them: They left the theater inspired, empowered, and talking about the things they wanted to change and the ways they might be able to change them." She quotes approvingly from Elle's big speech: "So speak up, America. Speak up for the home of the brave. Speak up for the land of the free gift with purchase. Speak up, America!"

Amazing, that the usually tough-minded Huffington fell for the movie. Amazing, too, that two teenage girls who have their own mother as a role model were inspired and empowered by the insipid Elle. I have a movie for them to see together: *Whale Rider*. Now there's a great movie about female empowerment, and the heroine doesn't even wear makeup.

America will no doubt speak up, alas, by spending millions of dollars on *Legally Blonde 2* in obedience to the movie's advertising blitz (buses in several cities have been painted entirely pink). And so the myth of a populist Congress will live on, entirely apart from the real world of lobbyists, logrolling, punishment to

the disloyal, and favors for friends. In the real world, Elle Woods would be chewed up faster than one of little Bruiser's Milk-Bones.

Lemony Snicket's A Series of Unfortunate Events ★ ★ ½
PG, 97 m., 2004

Jim Carrey (Count Olaf), Jude Law (Lemony Snicket), Emily Browning (Violet Baudelaire), Liam Aiken (Klaus Baudelaire), Kara and Shelby Hoffman (Sunny), Timothy Spall (Mr. Poe), Catherine O'Hara (Justice Strauss), Billy Connolly (Uncle Monty), Meryl Streep (Aunt Josephine). Directed by Brad Silberling and produced by Laurie MacDonald and Walter F. Parkes. Screenplay by Robert Gordon, based on the books by Daniel Handler.

The first time I picked up a Lemony Snicket adventure in a bookstore, I was intrigued by the message on the back cover: "I'm sorry to say that the book you are holding in your hands is extremely unpleasant . . ." It goes on to warn that "the three youngsters encounter a greedy and repulsive villain, itchy clothing, a disastrous fire, a plot to steal their fortune, and cold porridge for breakfast" and suggests "putting this book down at once."

As a marketing ploy, this is brilliant. It was all I could do to prevent myself from buying the book. And the film *Lemony Snicket's A Series of Unfortunate Events* opens on the same note, with Lemony Snicket himself (Jude Law) bent double over an old typewriter and typing out the dire story of the three Baudelaire children who suddenly and decisively become orphans. The family banker, Mr. Poe (Timothy Spall), breaks the news that a fire has destroyed their mansion and killed their parents.

The children seem to take this news rather well. I would say they take it too well, except that demonstrations of grief are not helpful in macabre comedies, where there is so much to grieve about that there would be no end to it. Perhaps tragedy is in the family tree; I assume they are descended from the French poet Charles Baudelaire, whose poems about sex and death "became a byword for unwholesomeness," according to Wikipedia.com. The only thing standing in the way of this theory is that Charles left no descendants.

The Baudelaire children are Violet (Emily Browning), Klaus (Liam Aiken), and the infant Sunny (Kara and Shelby Hoffman), who possesses only two teeth but such a firm bite that she can hang in midair from the edge of a table for minutes on end, an occupation she finds amusing. Violet is beautiful, Klaus is intense, and they are immediately beset with life-threatening difficulties.

Mr. Poe takes them to live with their "closest relative," a fourth cousin three times removed, or perhaps it's the other way around. This is Count Olaf (Jim Carrey), who lives in a Gothic mansion so creepy his interior decorator must have been Nosferatu. The count wants to kill the children and inherit the family fortune, and is not very subtle in his methods, parking his ancient Imperial on the train tracks with the children locked inside. As there are eleven novels so far in the series, they necessarily escape.

It's odd how the movie's gloom and doom are amusing at first, and then dampen down the humor. Although many Unfortunate Events do indeed occur in *Lemony Snicket*, they cannot be called exciting because everyone is rather depressed by them. There is no one in the movie to provide a reasonable reaction to anything; the adults are all demented, evil, or, in the case of Mr. Poe, stunningly lacking in perception, and the kids are plucky enough, but rather dazed by their misfortunes.

Jim Carrey is over the top as Count Olaf, but I suppose a character named Count Olaf is over the top by definition. The next relative to harbor the children is nice Uncle Monty (Billy Connolly), a herpetologist who shares his mansion with countless snakes, vipers, and other reptiles, and announces an immediate departure for Peru. Before the expedition can get under way, Count Olaf turns up again, this time in disguise as an Italian; although he prides himself on his acting and makeup skills, the kids take one look at him and announce that he is obviously Count Olaf. Uncle Monty, alas, is slow to take heed.

The children eventually arrive at yet another potential foster home, this one the residence of Aunt Josephine (Meryl Streep), whose Victorian mansion teeters on spindly supports that allow it to extend far above a rocky coast and stormy sea. Strange that her house is so precarious, since Josephine is literally afraid of everything, a condition I believe is called phobiaphobia.

The movie looks wonderful. Director Brad Silberling *(Moonlight Mile, City of Angels)* has assembled production designer Rick Heinrichs *(Sleepy Hollow)* and art directors John Dexter *(Planet of the Apes)* and Martin Whist, who have created wondrous and creepy spaces. The cinematography by Emmanuel Lubezki finds foreboding even in sunlight.

But there is a problem, and the problem is, everything seems to be an act. Nothing really seems to be at stake. The villains are teeth-gnashing hams, the hazards are more picturesque than frightening, and the children are unnaturally collected and capable. There is some kind of family secret, involving spyglasses, which will be resolved no doubt in later films; it's brought onstage and then not really dealt with.

I liked the film, but I'll tell you what. I think this one is a tune-up for the series, a trial run in which they figure out what works and what needs to be tweaked. The original *Spider-Man* was a disappointment, but the same team came back and made *Spider-Man 2* the best superhero movie ever made. The Lemony Snicket series has enormous potential, and I expect the next film will look just as good, and have the same wonderful kids, and be scarier and tell more of a real story, and discover that while gloom is an atmosphere, depression is a condition.

Levity ★ ½
R, 100 m., 2003

Billy Bob Thornton (Manuel Jordan), Morgan Freeman (Miles Evans), Holly Hunter (Adele Easley), Kirsten Dunst (Sofia Mellinger), Manuel Aranguiz (Señor Aguilar), Geoffrey Wigdor (Abner Easley), Luke Robertson (Young Abner Easley), Dorian Harewood (Mackie Whittaker). Directed by Ed Solomon and produced by Richard N. Gladstein, Adam Merims, and Solomon. Screenplay by Solomon.

Levity is an earnest but hopeless attempt to tell a parable about a man's search for redemption. By the end of his journey, we don't care if he finds redemption, if only he finds wakefulness.

He's a whiny slug who talks like a victim of over-medication. I was reminded of the Bob and Ray routine about the Slow Talkers of America.

That this unfortunate creature is played by Billy Bob Thornton is evidence, I think, that we have to look beyond the actors in placing blame. His costars are Morgan Freeman, Holly Hunter, and Kirsten Dunst. For a director to assemble such a cast and then maroon them in such a witless enterprise gives him more to redeem than his hero. The hero has merely killed a fictional character. Ed Solomon, who wrote and directed, has stolen two hours from the lives of everyone who sees the film, and weeks from the careers of these valuable actors.

The movie stars Thornton as Manuel Jordan, a man recently released from custody after serving twenty-two years of a sentence for murder. That his first name reminds us of Emmanuel and his surname echoes the Jordan River is not, I fear, an accident; he is a Christ figure, and Thornton has gotten into the spirit with long hair that looks copied from a bad holy card. The only twist is that instead of dying for our sins, the hero shot a young convenience store clerk—who died, I guess, for Manuel's sins.

Now Manuel returns to the same district where the killing took place. This is one of those movie neighborhoods where all the characters live close to one another and meet whenever necessary. Manual soon encounters Adele Easley (Holly Hunter), the sister of the boy he killed. They become friendly and the possibility of romance looms, although he hesitates to confess his crime. She has a teenage son (Geoffrey Wigdor), named Abner after her late brother.

In this district a preacher named Miles Evans (Freeman) runs a storefront youth center, portrayed so unconvincingly that we suspect Solomon has never seen a store, a front, a youth, or a center. In this room, which looks ever so much like a stage set, an ill-assorted assembly of disadvantaged youths are arrayed about the room in such studied "casual" attitudes that we are reminded of extras told to keep their places. Preacher Evans intermittently harangues them with apocalyptic rantings, which they attend patiently. Into the center walks Sofia Mellinger (Dunst), a lost girl who is tempted by drugs and

late-night raves, who wanders this neighborhood with curious impunity.

We know that sooner or later Manuel will have to inform Adele that he murdered her brother. But meanwhile the current Abner has fallen in with bad companions, and a silly grudge threatens to escalate into murder. This generates a scene of amazing coincidence, during which in a lonely alley late at night, all of the necessary characters coincidentally appear as they are needed, right on cue, for fraught action and dialogue that the actors must have studied for sad, painful hours, while keeping their thoughts to themselves.

Whether Manuel finds forgiveness, whether Sofia finds herself, whether Abner is saved, whether the preacher has a secret, whether Adele can forgive, whether Manuel finds a new mission in life, and whether the youths ever tire of sermons, I will leave to your speculation. All I can observe is that there is not a moment of authentic observation in the film; the director has assembled his characters out of stock melodrama. A bad Victorian novelist would find nothing to surprise him here, and a good one nothing to interest him. When this film premiered to thunderous silence at Sundance 2003, Solomon said he had been working on the screenplay for twenty years. Not long enough.

The Life Aquatic with Steve Zissou ★ ★ ½
R, 118 m., 2004

Bill Murray (Steve Zissou), Owen Wilson (Ned Plimpton), Cate Blanchett (Jane Winslett-Richardson), Anjelica Huston (Eleanor Zissou), Willem Dafoe (Klaus Daimler), Jeff Goldblum (Alistair Hennessey), Michael Gambon (Oseary Drakoulias), Noah Taylor (Vladimir Wolodarsky), Bud Cort (Bill Ubell). Directed by Wes Anderson and produced by Anderson, Barry Mendel, and Scott Rudin. Screenplay by Anderson and Noah Baumbach.

My rational mind informs me that this movie doesn't work. Yet I hear a subversive whisper: Since it does so many other things, does it have to work too? Can't it just *exist*? "Terminal whimsy," I called it on the TV show. Yes, but isn't that better than halfhearted whimsy, or no whimsy at all? Wes Anderson's *The Life Aquatic with Steve Zissou* is the *damnedest* film. I can't recommend it, but I would not for one second discourage you from seeing it.

To begin with, it has a passage of eerie beauty, in which the oceanographer Steve Zissou (Bill Murray) and his shipmates glide in a submarine past an undersea panorama of wondrous and delightful creatures. They are seeking the dreaded jaguar shark that ate Steve's beloved partner, and when they find it, well, they fall silent and just regard it, because it's kind of beautiful. This could have been a scene from *20,000 Leagues Under the Sea* if Captain Nemo had been a pothead.

Zissou is, we learn, the auteur of a series of increasingly uneventful undersea documentaries, in which the momentum is sliding down a graph that will intersect in the foreseeable future with a dead standstill. *The Life Aquatic* opens with the premiere of his latest work, which ends with the audience gazing up at the screen as if it is more interesting now that it is blank. Zissou himself seems to be in the later stages of entropy, and may become one of those Oliver Sacks people who just sit there on the stairs for decades, looking at you. His crew would seem slack-witted to SpongeBob.

On board the good ship Belafonte, Zissou has assembled his ex-wife, Eleanor (Anjelica Huston), her ex-husband, Alistair (Jeff Goldblum), the salty dog Klaus Daimler (Willem Dafoe), the plummy producer Oseary Drakoulias (Michael Gambon), and the financial guy Bill (Bud Cort, so that's what happened to him). Along the way they collect Ned Plimpton (Owen Wilson), who thinks he may be Steve's son, although my theory is he's just another one of George Plimpton's unfinished projects. Their mission is to find the deadly shark, exact revenge, and film the adventure. Covering the expedition is Jane Winslett-Richardson (Cate Blanchett), whose surname suggests she is the result of an affair involving the matriarchs of two great acting families and a designated male, perhaps Ned's birth father.

These characters involve themselves in great plot complications, which are facilitated by the design of the boat, which looks like a rust bucket on the outside but conceals innumerable luxuries, including a spa. There is also a "scientific laboratory" with equipment that looks as if it might have been bought at auction from a bankrupt high school in 1955. Anderson has built a wonderful set with a cutaway front wall so that we can look into all the rooms of the boat at once; it's the same idea Jerry Lewis used in *The Ladies' Man*.

Events on the boat are modulated at a volume somewhere between a sigh and a ghostly exhalation. Steve Zissou is very tired. I suggest for his epitaph: "Life for him was but a dreary play; he came, saw, dislik'd, and passed away." Ned makes an effort to get to know his father, a task made difficult because Steve may not be his father and is not knowable. Jane, Ned, and Steve form a romantic triangle, or perhaps it is just a triangle. A folksinger performs the works of David Bowie in Portuguese, and the ship is boarded by Filipino pirates.

So you see, it's that kind of movie. The colors are like the pastels produced by colored pencils, and kind of beautiful, like the shark. The action goes through the motions of slapstick at the velocity of dirge. Steve Zissou seems melancholy, as if simultaneously depressed that life is passing him by, and that it is taking so long to do it. Anjelica Huston seems privately amused, which is so much more intriguing than seeming publicly amused. Cate Blanchett proves she can do anything, even things she should not do. I forgot to mention that Steve's friend is played by Seymour Cassel, who I think I remember told me one night in Dan Tana's that he had always wanted to be eaten by a shark in a movie. ☞

The Life of David Gale no stars

R, 130 m., 2003

Kevin Spacey (Dr. David Gale), Kate Winslet (Elizabeth [Bitsey] Bloom), Laura Linney (Constance Harraway), Gabriel Mann (Zack), Matt Craven (Dusty), Rhona Mitra (Berlin), Leon Rippy (Braxton Belyeu). Directed by Alan Parker and produced by Nicolas Cage and Parker. Screenplay by Charles Randolph.

The Life of David Gale tells the story of a famous opponent of capital punishment, who, in what he must find an absurdly ironic development, finds himself on Death Row in Texas, charged with the murder of a woman who was also opposed to capital punishment. This is a plot, if ever there was one, to illustrate King Lear's complaint, "As flies to wanton boys, are we to the gods; They kill us for their sport." I am aware this is the second time in two weeks I have been compelled to quote Lear, but there are times when Eminem simply will not do.

David Gale is an understandably bitter man, played by Kevin Spacey, who protests his innocence to a reporter named Bitsey Bloom (Kate Winslet), whom he has summoned to Texas for that purpose. He claims to have been framed by right-wing supporters of capital punishment, because his death would provide such poetic irony in support of the noose, the gas, or the chair. Far from killing Constance Harraway (Laura Linney), he says, he had every reason not to, and he explains that to Bitsey in flashbacks that make up about half of the story.

Bitsey becomes convinced of David's innocence. She is joined in her investigation by the eager and sexy intern Zack (Gabriel Mann), and they become aware that they are being followed everywhere in a pickup truck by a gaunt-faced fellow in a cowboy hat, who is either a right-wing death penalty supporter who really killed the dead woman, or somebody else. If he is somebody else, then he is obviously following them around with the MacGuffin, in this case a videotape suggesting disturbing aspects of the death of Constance.

The man in the cowboy hat illustrates my recently renamed Principle of the Unassigned Character, formerly known less elegantly as the Law of Economy of Character Development. This principle teaches us that any prominent character who seems to be extraneous to the action will probably hold the key to it. The cowboy lives in one of those tumbledown shacks filled with flies and peanut butter, with old calendars on the walls. The yard has more bedsprings than the house has beds.

The acting in The Life of David Gale is splendidly done, but serves a meretricious cause. The direction is by the British director Alan Parker, who at one point had never made a movie I wholly disapproved of. Now has he ever. The secrets of the plot must remain unrevealed by me, so that you can be offended by them yourself, but let it be said this movie is about as corrupt, intellectually bankrupt, and morally dishonest as it could possibly be without David Gale actually hiring himself out as a joker at the court of Saddam Hussein.

I am sure the filmmakers believe their film is against the death penalty. I believe it supports it and hopes to discredit the opponents of the penalty as unprincipled fraudsters. What I do not understand is the final revelation on the videotape. Surely David Gale knows that Bitsey Bloom cannot keep it private without violating the ethics of journalism and sacrificing the biggest story of her career. So it serves no functional purpose except to give a cheap thrill to the audience slackjaws. It is shameful.

One of the things that annoys me is that the story is set in Texas and not just in any old state—a state like Arkansas, for example, where the 1996 documentary Paradise Lost: The Child Murders at Robin Hood Hills convincingly explains why three innocent kids are in prison because they wore black and listened to heavy metal, while the likely killer keeps pushing himself on-screen and wildly signaling his guilt. Nor is it set in my own state of Illinois, where Death Row was run so shabbily that Governor George Ryan finally threw up his hands and declared the whole system rotten.

No, the movie is set in Texas, which in a good year all by itself carries out half the executions in America. Death Row in Texas is like the Roach Motel: Roach checks in, doesn't check out. When George W. Bush was Texas governor, he claimed to carefully consider each and every execution, although a study of his office calendar shows he budgeted fifteen minutes per condemned man (we cannot guess how many of these minutes were devoted to pouring himself a cup of coffee before settling down to the job). Still, when you're killing someone every other week and there's an average of 400 more waiting their turn, you have to move right along.

Spacey and Parker are honorable men. Why did they go to Texas and make this silly movie? The last shot made me want to throw something at the screen—maybe Spacey and Parker.

You can make movies that support capital punishment (The Executioner's Song) or oppose it (Dead Man Walking) or are conflicted (In Cold Blood). But while Texas continues to warehouse condemned men with a system involving lawyers who are drunk, asleep, or absent; confessions that are beaten out of the helpless; and juries who overwhelmingly prefer to execute black defendants instead of white ones, you can't make this movie. Not in Texas.

Lilya 4-Ever ★ ★ ★
R, 109 m., 2003

Oksana Akinshina (Lilya), Artyom Bogucharsky (Volodya), Lyubov Agapova (Lilya's mother), Liliya Shinkaryova (Aunt Anna), Elina Benenson (Natasha), Pavel Ponomaryov (Andrei), Tomas Neumann (Witek). Directed by Lukas Moodysson and produced by Lars Jonsson. Screenplay by Moodysson.

Lilya 4-Ever provides a human face for a story that has become familiar in the newspapers. It follows a sixteen-year-old girl from the former Soviet Union as she is abandoned by her mother, places her faith in the wrong stranger, and is sold into prostitution. She is naive and innocent, and what looks like danger to us looks like deliverance to her. That there are countless such stories makes this one even more heartbreaking.

Lilya (Oksana Akinshina) lives in a barren urban wasteland of shabby high-rises and wind-swept vacant lots. Her best friend Volodya (Artyom Bogucharsky) plays basketball by throwing a tin can through a rusty hoop. Her mother announces that she is engaged to marry a Russian who now lives in the United States. Lilya is joyous, and brags to Volodya that she is going to America. But her mother has other plans, and explains Lilya must stay behind, to be "sent for" later.

The mother is heartless, but then this is a society crushed by poverty and despair. There must be better neighborhoods somewhere, but we do not see them and Lilya does not find them. Within a day of her mother's departure, she is ordered by an embittered aunt to clear out of her mother's apartment and move into the squalor of a tenement room. Here she hosts glue-sniffing parties for her friends, and Volodya comes to live after his father throws him out. Volodya is young—perhaps eleven or twelve—and although he talks hopefully about sex, he is a child and she treats him like a little brother.

Lilya's descent into prostitution does not surprise us. There is no money for food, no one cares for her, she is pretty, she is desperate, and when she finds her first client in a disco, the movie focuses closely on her blank, indifferent face, turned away from the panting man above her. Later there is a montage of clients, seen from her point of view (although she is not seen), and it says all that can be said about her disgust with them.

The money at least allows her to buy junk food and cigarettes, and give a basketball to Volodya, whose father is enraged by the gift. Then friendship seems to come in the form of a young man named Andrei (Pavel Ponomaryov), who does not want sex, offers her a ride home, takes her on a date (bumper cars, that reliable movie cliché), and says he works in Sweden and can get her a job there. We see through him, and even Volodya does, but she is blinded by the prospect he describes: "You'll make more money there in a week than a doctor here makes in a month." Perhaps, but not for herself.

The movie, written and directed by Lukas Moodysson, has the directness and clarity of a documentary, but allows itself touches of tenderness and grief. It is so sad to see this girl, even after weeks of prostitution, saying the Lord's Prayer in front of a framed drawing of a guardian angel. And there are two fantasy sequences toward the end that provide her with an escape, however illusory.

The movie should inspire outrage, but I read of thousands of women from Eastern Europe who are lured into virtual slavery. I hope some of their clients will attend this movie, even if for the wrong reasons, and see what they are responsible for.

Lipstick & Dynamite, Piss & Vinegar: The First Ladies of Wrestling ★ ★ ½
NO MPAA RATING, 83 m., 2005

Featuring Ella Waldek, Gladys "Killem" Gillem, Ida May Martinez, Johnnie "The Great" Mae Young, Lillian "The Fabulous Moolah" Ellison, Penny Banner, and Diamond Lil. A documentary directed by Ruth Leitman and produced by Anne Hubbell, James Jernigan, Leitman, and Debbie Nightingale.

Lipstick & Dynamite, Piss & Vinegar: The First Ladies of Wrestling tells us just enough about the early days of professional women wrestlers to suggest there must be a great deal more to tell. The documentary visits elderly women who, then and now, can best be described as tough broads, and listens as they describe the early days of women's wrestling. What they say is not as revealing as how they say it; as they talk we envision not a colorful chapter in showbiz history, but a hard-scrabble world in which they were mistreated, swindled, lied to, injured, sometimes raped or beaten—and tried, it must be said, to give as good as they got.

The documentary, by Ruth Leitman, does an extraordinary job of assembling the survivors from the early days of a disreputable sport, beginning with Gladys "Killem" Gillem, whose sideshow act began as a change of pace from the strippers. Footage from the late 1930s and 1940s includes a sideshow barker describing the unimaginable erotic pleasures to be found inside the All-Girl Revue. I remember such sideshows at the Champaign County Fair, where you worked your way past the Octopus and the Tilt-a-Whirl to the girlie tent, always at the bottom of the midway, where dancers in ratty spangled gowns paraded before we horny teenagers, and then the barker said, "All right, girls, back inside the tent!" We followed them in, slamming down the exact change; if a murder had taken place during the show, there would have been no witnesses, because there was absolutely no eye contact between the sinners.

But I digress. The appeal of women's wrestling, then and, I suspect, even now, had a lot to do with the possibility of a Janet Jackson moment. But the sideshow wrestlers gave way to a sport that toured the same venues as men's professional wrestling; sometimes the women were the curtain-raisers, although, as they tell it, the men were terrified that the women would become a bigger draw. We meet such legends of the sport as The Fabulous Moolah (Lillian Ellison), who was the biggest star of the sport and had the most longevity, surviving even into the heyday of the WWF and finding a new generation of fans.

Moolah, now in her eighties, still works as a wrestling promoter. We get a glimpse of her home life; she lives with The Great Mae Young and Diamond Lil, a dwarf wrestler, in a house-

hold that would give pause to John Waters. Although Moolah and Young are apparently a couple, the role of Diamond Lil becomes harder to define the more Moolah praises her skills as an invaluable maid of all work. Among the film's other unforgettable characters are Penny Banner, "the blond bombshell," and Ella Waldek, who sounds as if she has chain-smoked Camels from birth and later went into the detective business.

Men seem to have come into the lives of these women primarily as exploiters, rapists, and occasional transient husbands. The promoter Billy Wolfe, a key figure in the early days, is remembered without affection for taking half of what he said were their earnings, and sleeping with as many of them as he could. When the women describe their sexual experiences, their voices reflect more hardened realism than indignation. They were often abandoned when young, made their way on their own, paid their dues.

Magicians have a credo: "The trick is told when the trick is sold." They don't give away their secrets for free. Neither, I suspect, do women wrestlers. Glimpsed on every face in this movie, echoing in every voice, are hints of the things they've seen and the stories they could tell if they didn't have a lifelong aversion to leveling with the rubes. What we get is essentially the press-book version of their careers, which is harrowing enough; Ruth Leitman is said to be working on a fictional screenplay based on her material, and I have a suspicion it may be blood-curdling. At the end of the film, at the Gulf Coast Wrestlers' Reunion, there is not a lot of sentiment, and no visible tears. One woman after another seems to have attended in order to say, "I'm still here," as if being alive after what they've been through is a form of defiance.

Little Black Book ★ ★ ★
PG-13, 95 m., 2004

Brittany Murphy (Stacy Holt), Kathy Bates (Kippie Kann), Holly Hunter (Barb), Ron Livingston (Derek), Josie Maran (Lulu Fritz), Julianne Nicholson (Joyce), Rashida Jones (Dr. Rachel Keyes), Stephen Tobolowsky (Carl). Directed by Nick Hurran and produced by Elaine Goldsmith-Thomas, Deborah Schindler,

William Sherak, and Jason Shuman. Screenplay by Melissa Carter and Elisa Bell.

Well, in the first place, I think Brittany Murphy is a great deal more talented than some people do. I wouldn't compare her with Marilyn Monroe, who is incomparable, but she has a similar ability to draw our eyes to her segment of the screen, even when the action is ostensibly elsewhere. She does this not with sex appeal but with life force. See her in such completely various roles as Eminem's tough girlfriend in *8 Mile* and a rich girl's nanny in the underrated *Uptown Girls*; she has the quality of seeming immediately there on the screen, open to possibility, unrehearsed, unstudied, natural, appealing. She hasn't had the roles yet to prove it, but she is a born movie star.

In *Little Black Book*, Murphy has the necessary qualities to function as a sort of decoy. She lures us into the picture on false pretenses; she's cute and chirpy in the early scenes, we assume this is going to be a routine career-girl comedy, and we're surprised when it moves deeper into its subject until finally it's a satirical comedy about television that invades some of the same territory as *Network* or *Broadcast News*.

Murphy plays Stacy Holt, who worships above all living beings Diane Sawyer, and dreams not of becoming Diane Sawyer, but simply of becoming her assistant, to serve this great woman with the devotion she deserves. Stacy begins a little more humbly, in cable TV, and works her way up to the Kippie Kann show, a daytime talk show whose hostess, played by Kathy Bates, is a wannabe Jerry Springer/Jenny Jones. Stacy's mentor on the show is a producer named Barb (Holly Hunter), who could be a more experienced, more cynical version of the TV news producer Hunter played in *Broadcast News*.

Kippie Kann is on the brink of being canceled. Her ratings are tanking, and the show is shamelessly seeking sensationalism. Young Stacy suggests a show on "little black books"—in particular, the Palm Pilot, Treo, or Blackberry of the person you're dating, which may contain evidence that you're being cheated on. She is meanwhile dating the hunky Derek (Ron Livingston), a hockey scout who's maybe ten years older and has dated a lot of women.

Stacy meets some of them: a supermodel named Lulu Fritz (Josie Maran), a chef named Joyce (Julianne Nicholson), a gynecologist named Dr. Rachel Keyes (Rashida Jones). Abusing her position on the Kippie Kann show, Stacy calls them in for interviews. They think they're possible guests; she thinks they're possible rivals.

Where the movie goes with this is fairly hard to anticipate, although by the end we have been given a convincing demonstration of the amorality of a television show in search of better ratings. The long closing sequence is virtuoso, redefining what went before and requiring Murphy to become a more complex character than she gave any hint of in the opening scenes.

The movie, directed by Nick Hurran and written by Melissa Carter and Elisa Bell, is every bit as cynical as *Network*, but at the same time engenders a sweet onscreen romance, although not between the people we anticipate. Certain tricky scenes work well because of the presence of Julianne Nicholson, an actress of fresh charm and uninflected honesty who glowed in a movie named *Tully* that you should rent immediately. There is nothing false about her, which is very important.

As for Brittany Murphy, for me it goes back to the 2003 Independent Spirit Awards, held the day before the Oscars in a big tent on the beach at Santa Monica, California. Murphy was assigned to present one of the awards. Her task was to read the names of the five nominees, open an envelope, and reveal the name of the winner.

This she turned into an opportunity for screwball improvisational comedy, by pretending she could not follow this sequence, not even after the audience shouted instructions and the stage manager came out to whisper in her ear not once but twice. There were those in the audience who were dumbfounded by her stupidity. I was dumbfounded by her brilliance. I had a front-row seat, and was convinced her timing was too good, her double-takes too perfect, her pauses too wicked, to even possibly be authentic. She was taking a routine task and turning it into the opportunity to steal a scene and leave everybody in the tent chattering about her performance. You can't screw up that entertainingly by accident. You have to know exactly what you're doing.

The Longest Yard ★ ★ ★
PG-13, 113 m., 2005

Adam Sandler (Paul "Wrecking" Crewe), Chris Rock (Caretaker), Burt Reynolds (Coach Nate Scarborough), James Cromwell (Warden Hazen), Walter Williamson (Errol Dandridge), Michael Irvin (Deacon Moss), Nelly (Earl Megget), Edward Bunker (Skitchy Rivers). Directed by Peter Segal and produced by Jack Giarraputo. Screenplay by Sheldon Turner, based on the story by Albert S. Ruddy and the screenplay by Tracy Keenan Wynn.

Before I left for the Cannes Film Festival, I saw *The Longest Yard*, and I did an advance taping of an episode of *Ebert & Roeper* on which I gave a muted thumbs-up to Roeper's scornful thumbs-down. I kinda liked it, in its goofy way. There was a dogged ridiculousness to the film that amused me, especially in the way Adam Sandler was cast as a star quarterback. Once you accept Sandler as a quarterback, you've opened up the backfield to the entire membership of the Screen Actors Guild.

Now I have seen twenty-five films at Cannes, most of them attempts at greatness, and I sit here staring at the computer screen and realizing with dread that the time has come for me to write a review justifying that vertical thumb, which is already on video and will go out to millions of TV viewers seeking guidance in their moviegoing.

I do not say that I was wrong about the film. I said what I sincerely believed at the time. I believed it as one might believe in a good cu p of coffee; welcome while you are drinking it, even completely absorbing, but not much discussed three weeks later. Indeed, after my immersion in the films of Cannes, I can hardly bring myself to return to *The Longest Yard* at all, since it represents such a limited idea of what a movie can be and what movies are for.

Yet there are those whose entire lives as moviegoers are spent within the reassuring confines of such entertainments. In many cities and some states, there are few ways for them to get their eyes on movies that can feed their souls. They will have to be content with a movie in which Adam Sandler plays an alcoholic has-been football hero who gets drunk, drives dangerously, is thrown into jail, and becomes the pawn in a football game pitting a team of fellow prisoners against a team made up of prison guards. As I sit here, so help me God, I can't remember who got the idea for this game or why. I could look it up, but it's fascinating to watch myself trying to reconstruct a movie that was not intended to be remembered as long as it takes to get to the parking lot. This is how you learn. Through experience.

I recall that for some reason the big game is broadcast live on a sports network, maybe because the Sandler character was once a football hero and went down in flames over the drunk-driving scandal, and so there is a possibility of good ratings. His mentor is a former prisoner, played by Burt Reynolds, who starred in Robert Aldrich's original *The Longest Yard* (1974) and whose character this time is described in my notes as the Heisman Trophy winner of 1955. Assuming my notes are correct, he was about twenty-one when he won the trophy and now Reynolds is about seventy-one, although now that I have done the math I don't know where to go with it. Certainly he is older than Sandler and younger than God.

James Cromwell plays the warden. I have met him on industry occasions. He is a militant Screen Actors Guild spokesman and a fiercely intelligent man who takes roles like this for the same reason I review them, because we are professionals and this is what we do. He would rather be in better movies and I would rather review them, but we have both seen a lot worse than this. There is a sense in which attacking this movie is like kicking a dog for not being better at calculus.

You think you know where I am headed. I am going to admit that I was wrong. I am going to withdraw that upturned thumb even as its ghostly video image beams out across the nation. I will compare it to the shimmering authority of a hologram of Obi-Wan Kenobi, expressing wisdom that was true enough when the hologram was recorded, but may not be helpful by the time it is seen.

But no, I am not going to do that at all. When

the show was recorded I said what I believed, and for my sins I am appending three stars to the top of this review. I often practice a generic approach to film criticism, in which the starting point for a review is the question of what a movie sets out to achieve. *The Longest Yard* more or less achieves what most of the people attending it will expect. Most of its audiences will be satisfied enough when they leave the theater, although few will feel compelled to rent it on video to share with their friends. So, yes, it's a fair example of what it is.

I would, however, be filled with remorse if I did not urge you to consider the underlying melancholy of this review and seek out a movie you could have an interesting conversation about. After twelve days at Cannes, I was reminded that movies can enrich our lives, instead of just helping us get through them.

It may be that your local multiplex is not showing any films that have, or will, or would qualify for Cannes. There is a studied unwillingness among the major distributors to rise very frequently above the lowest common denominator, except during Oscar season. But there are actually some very worthy films in national release. If *Kontroll* is playing in your town, for example, that would be an idea. Or *Brothers,* or *Dominion: Prequel to the Exorcist,* or *Layer Cake,* or *Unleashed.* These are not great films, you understand, but they exist in a world that knows what greatness is, and they urge themselves toward it. If you can get to *Crash,* that is the movie you must see, and you should immediately drop any thought of seeing anything else instead.

Note: I attended a press conference of the Cannes jury. Its president, Emir Kusturica, said at one point that Cannes "kills uniformity." Its films are made one at a time. "To be global," he said, "to make a film that plays everywhere, you have to be slightly stupid." How do you like that; the bastard went and spoiled The Longest Yard *for me.*

Look at Me ★ ★ ★ ½
PG-13, 100 m., 2005

Marilou Berry (Lolita Cassard), Jean-Pierre Bacri (Etienne Cassard), Agnes Jaoui (Sylvia Miller), Laurent Grevill (Pierre Miller), Virginie Desarnauts (Karine Cassard), Keine Bouhiza (Sebastien), Gregoire Oestermann (Vincent), Serge Riaboukine (Felix), Michele Moretti (Edith). Directed by Agnes Jaoui and produced by Jean-Philippe Andraca and Christian Berard. Screenplay by Jean-Pierre Bacri and Jaoui.

Here is a difference, small but not insignificant, between Hollywood and French films. Consider the inevitable scene where the child is performing onstage, and the theater door opens, and there is the parent who has denied the child's talent, but now nods and smiles and sees that the child is truly gifted after all.

Now turn to *Look at Me,* the unforgiving new French film about a chubby classical singer and her egotistical father. She rehearses stubbornly and has a beautiful voice. He is a famous writer and a snob, absorbed in the appreciation of himself. She gives a recital in an old church in the country, and the audience admires her singing. Does the father arrive late, his eyes filled with tears as he acknowledges her gifts? No, the father arrives on time, but sneaks out to smoke and make cell calls.

People can be cruel out of ignorance or carelessness, but it takes a knack to be cruel as a strategy. Etienne Cassard (Jean-Pierre Bacri), the father, is a man full of himself. He has written great books, or at least people assure him they are great, and he is a publisher. People are wary of him and suck up to him.

Etienne has a gift for ignoring his twenty-year-old daughter, Lolita (Marilou Berry), perhaps because he doesn't think it helps his image to have her plumpness in view. He has a sleek, younger trophy wife named Karine (Virginie Desarnauts), who he is happy to display, but he ignores her, puts her down, ridicules her, gently corrects her, doesn't listen to her.

Given this situation, you'd think you could anticipate the drift of the film, but no: It doesn't pity its characters just because they are badly treated. Lolita, for example, is suspicious and defensive. She has felt unpopular for so long that she's developed a paranoia that prevents her from trusting others. No, not even Sebastien (Keine Bouhiza), the boy who cares for her, attends to her, would like her if she were not so sure no one could possibly like her.

There is also the matter of Lolita's music

teacher, Sylvia, played by Agnes Jaoui, who cowrote the movie with Bacri and directs it. Sylvia's teaching helps support her husband, Pierre (Laurent Grevill), a novelist who is stuck in obscurity. Does Sylvia's attitude toward Lolita change when she learns that the girl's father is a famous writer and publisher? A man who could help her Pierre? Lolita thinks it does, and is probably right. So Lolita uses her father as leverage with her teacher, and soon Etienne has seen to the publication of Pierre's book.

Now watch closely. Pierre's book is an enormous success. This (a) reflects well upon Etienne because he discovered Pierre and sponsored him, but (b) underlines the inconvenience that Etienne himself has published nothing much in recent years. Pierre meanwhile follows Etienne like a fawning dog, ignoring his wife because he's blinded by the famous people at Etienne's parties. Lolita observes all of this and detests it, and carefully nurtures her misery.

There are scenes in this movie of social cruelty beyond all compare. Etienne is capable of making his daughter think he is calling her attractive, and then correcting her: He was talking to the woman next to her. Whoever he's talking to on his cell phone is always more important than whoever he's talking to in person. At dinner, when the attention strays from him for long, Etienne's eyes narrow and his conversational knives are thrown.

This performance comes from an actor who was so vulnerable in the previous movie he made with Jaoui. That was *The Taste of Others* (2000), where he plays an unremarkable man who falls in love with an amateur actress and her circle in a local theater company. In that movie, he was essentially playing the Pierre character—the adoring dog. He goes from meekness to arrogance so convincingly he even seems to have a different face in the two films. Marilou Berry's performance is remarkable, too, in the defiant way she faces the world, and in the way she uses a miraculous voice that is not miracle enough for her.

The most sympathetic character is the one who would be the heavy in the Hollywood version: Karine, the young stepmother. She reaches out to Lolita even after being rejected. She wants to be the girl's friend. She puts up with the boorish behavior of her husband, and she tries to repair the wounds he causes to their friends. In some sense, the overbearing father and the resentful daughter have created each other; the stepmother is the innocent bystander. The thing about a movie like this is, the characters may be French, but they're more like people I know than they could ever be in the Hollywood remake.

Looney Tunes: Back in Action ★ ★ ★
PG, 91 m., 2003

Brendan Fraser (D. J. Drake/Himself), Jenna Elfman (Kate Houghton), Steve Martin (Mr. Chairman), Timothy Dalton (Damien Drake), Joan Cusack (Mother), Heather Locklear (Dusty Tails). With the voices of: Joe Alaskey: Bugs Bunny, Daffy Duck, Beaky Buzzard, Sylvester, Mama Bear; Jeff Glenn Bennett: Yosemite Sam, Foghorn Leghorn, Nasty Canasta; Billy West: Elmer Fudd, Peter Lorre; Eric Goldberg: Tweety Bird, Marvin the Martian, Speedy Gonzales. Directed by Joe Dante and produced by Paula Weinstein and Bernie Goldmann. Screenplay by Larry Doyle.

As *Looney Tunes: Back in Action* opens, Daffy Duck is in a heated salary dispute with Warner Bros. For years Bugs Bunny has been pulling down the big bucks, and now, as they prepare to costar in another movie, Daffy is fed up. He wants equal pay for equal work. But Kate (Jenna Elfman), the studio VP in charge of animated characters, won't budge. She cites demographic studies that indicate Daffy's fan base "is limited to angry fat guys in basements." Daffy throws a tantrum, and Kate orders a security guard (Brendan Fraser) to throw him off the lot.

I don't mind telling you my sympathies were entirely with Daffy in this scene. Let me tell you a personal story involving Daffy Duck, which also takes place on the Warner lot. I quote from an interview I did with Albert Brooks in 1991, when his movie *Defending Your Life* was about to be released.

As I was getting up to leave his office, Brooks said, "Look at these funny coffee mugs the studio sent over."

He had four or five of them on a shelf, cups shaped like the Warner cartoon heroes.

"Here," he said. "Have one. I want you to have one."

He pressed Elmer Fudd into my hands.

"No, that's okay," I said.

"Take one. What is this, a bribe? They're worth ten cents apiece. Twenty-five cents, tops."

"You know," I said, looking at the shelf, "I've never really been a fan of Elmer Fudd. My hero has always been Daffy Duck."

Brooks took the Daffy Duck mug from the shelf.

"Here, take it," he said. "I want you to have it. Really."

I could tell from the subtle intonation in his voice exactly what had happened. He had given me Elmer Fudd because he didn't like Elmer Fudd, either. He liked Daffy Duck. I had taken his favorite mug.

"No, you keep Daffy," I said. "I'll bet it's your favorite."

"Come on, come on," he said. "Take Daffy Duck. Take the one you want."

I tried to put Daffy back on the shelf. He pressed Daffy into my hands. I left with Daffy, but I would have bet a hundred bucks that the moment I was out of his office, Brooks had his secretary call Warner to see if they could send another Daffy Duck over.

And so now we are back in the present, and my eyes lift up from this review and regard the very same Daffy Duck coffee mug, which has pride of place in my office. And I reflect that while things always came easily for Bugs, Daffy had to fight every inch of the way. Bugs was insouciant. Daffy was outraged. Bugs was always a step ahead. Daffy was always a step behind.

In *Looney Tunes: Back in Action*, Daffy walks out of the meeting, and it doesn't take Kate and Bugs long to realize that without a foil the bunny is just spinning his paws. The security guard, whose name is D. J. Drake, and who is the twin brother of the egotistical Brendan Fraser, joins them in following Daffy to Vegas, where they get into trouble with the Acme megacorporation run by Steve Martin, discover Drake's dad is a secret agent (Timothy Dalton), and encounter the new Q (Joan Cusack) and a lot of amazing new inventions.

With the same kind of anarchic temporal and spatial logic that always inspired the Warner cartoons, the animals are soon in Paris and jumping into paintings in the Louvre. You

can imagine the characters in a painting by Dali, and maybe even in Serrault's pointillist style, but in Munch's *The Scream*? You have to see that for yourself. This segment is possibly a tribute to the late, beloved Chuck Jones, who liked to plunge his cartoon characters into high art.

A whole gallery of cartoon stars eventually gets involved, including Sylvester, Yosemite Sam, Foghorn Leghorn, Elmer Fudd, Tweety Bird, and Speedy Gonzales, who may be seen in some circles as politically incorrect, but seems quite correct to himself, thank you. How the action ends up in Earth orbit I will leave you to discover.

The director is Joe Dante, whose segment of *Twilight Zone* (1983) involved a traveler who unwisely entered a house where the reality was warped by a kid's obsession with cartoon characters. Again this time, he combines live action with animation, in a film not as inspired as *Who Framed Roger Rabbit* but in the same spirit. It's goofy fun. Or maybe we should make that daffy fun.

The Lord of the Rings: The Return of the King ★ ★ ★ ½
PG-13, 200 m., 2003

Elijah Wood (Frodo), Ian McKellen (Gandalf), Liv Tyler (Arwen), Viggo Mortensen (Aragorn), Sean Astin (Sam), Cate Blanchett (Galadriel), John Rhys Davies (Gimli), Bernard Hill (Theoden), Billy Boyd (Pippin), Dominic Monaghan (Merry), Orlando Bloom (Legolas), Hugo Weaving (Elrond), Miranda Otto (Eowyn), David Wenham (Faramir), Karl Urban (Eomer), John Noble (Denethor), Andy Serkis (Gollum/Smeagol). Directed by Peter Jackson and produced by Jackson, Barrie M. Osborne, and Fran Walsh. Screenplay by Walsh, Philippa Boyens, Jackson, and Steven Sinclair, based on the novel by J. R. R. Tolkien.

At last the full arc is visible, and the *Lord of the Rings* trilogy comes into final focus. I admire it more as a whole than in its parts. The second film was inconclusive, and lost its way in the midst of spectacle. But *The Return of the King* dispatches its characters to their destinies with a grand and eloquent confidence. This is the best of the three, redeems the earlier meandering, and certifies the *Ring* trilogy as a work of bold ambition at a time of cinematic timidity.

That it falls a little shy of greatness is perhaps inevitable. The story is just a little too silly to carry the emotional weight of a masterpiece. It is a melancholy fact that while the visionaries of a generation ago, like Francis Ford Coppola with *Apocalypse Now,* tried frankly to make films of great consequence, an equally ambitious director like Peter Jackson is aiming more for popular success. The epic fantasy has displaced real contemporary concerns, and audiences are much more interested in Middle Earth than in the world they inhabit.

Still, Jackson's achievement cannot be denied. *The Return of the King* is such a crowning achievement, such a visionary use of all the tools of special effects, such a pure spectacle, that it can be enjoyed even by those who have not seen the first two films. Yes, they will be adrift during the early passages of the film's 200 minutes, but to be adrift occasionally during this nine-hour saga comes with the territory; Tolkien's story is so sweeping and Jackson includes so much of it that only devoted students of the *Ring* can be sure they understand every character, relationship, and plot point.

The third film gathers all of the plot strands and guides them toward the great battle at Minas Tirith; it is "before these walls that the doom of our time will be decided." The city is a spectacular achievement by the special effects artisans, who show it as part fortress, part Emerald City, topping a mountain, with a buttress reaching out over the plain below where the battle will be joined. In a scene where Gandalf rides his horse across the drawbridge and up the ramped streets of the city, it's remarkable how seamlessly Jackson is able to integrate computer-generated shots with actual full-scale shots, so they all seem of a piece.

I complained that the second film, *The Two Towers,* seemed to shuffle the hobbits to the sidelines—as humans, wizards, elves, and orcs saw most of the action. The hobbits are back in a big way this time, as the heroic little Frodo (Elijah Wood) and his loyal friend Sam (Sean Astin) undertake a harrowing journey to return the Ring to Mount Doom—where, if he can cast it into the volcano's lava, Middle Earth will be saved and the power of the enemy extinguished. They are joined on their journey by the magnificently eerie, fish-fleshed, bug-eyed creature Smeagol, who is voiced and modeled by Andy Serkis in collaboration with CGI artists, and introduced this time around with a brilliant device to illustrate his dual nature: He talks to his reflection in a pool, and the reflection talks back. Smeagol loves Frodo but loves the Ring more, and indeed it is the Ring's strange power to enthrall its possessors (first seen through its effect on Bilbo Baggins in *The Fellowship of the Ring*) that makes it so tricky to dispose of.

Although the movie contains epic action sequences of awe-inspiring scope (including the massing of troops for the final battle), the two most inimitable special-effects creations are Smeagol, who seems as real as anyone else on the screen, and a monstrous spider named Shelob. This spider traps Frodo as he traverses a labyrinthine passage on his journey, defeats him, and wraps him in webbing to keep him fresh for supper. Sam is very nearly not there to save the day (Smeagol has been treacherous), but as he battles the spider we're reminded of all the other movie battles between men and giant insects, and we concede that, yes, this time they got it right.

The final battle is kind of magnificent. I found myself thinking of the visionaries of the silent era, like Fritz Lang *(Metropolis)* and F. W. Murnau *(Faust),* with their desire to depict fantastic events of unimaginable size and power, and with their own cheerful reliance on visual trickery. Had they been able to see this scene, they would have been exhilarated. We see men and even an army of the dead join battle against orcs, flying dragons, and vast lumbering elephantine creatures that serve as moving platforms for machines of war. As a flaming battering ram challenges the gates of the city, we feel the size and weight and convincing shudder of impacts that exist only in the imagination. Enormous bestial trolls pull back the springs for catapults to hurl boulders against the walls and towers of Minas Tirith, which fall in cascades of rubble (only to seem miraculously restored in time for a final celebration).

And there is even time for a smaller-scale personal tragedy; Denethor (John Noble), steward of the city, mourns the death of his older and favored son, and a younger son named Faramir (David Wenham), determined to gain his father's respect, rides out to certain death. The outcome is a tragic sequence in which the deranged Denethor attempts to cremate Faramir on a funeral pyre, even though he is not quite dead.

The series has never known what to do with its female characters. J. R. R. Tolkien was not much interested in them, certainly not at a psychological level, and although the half-elf Arwen (Liv Tyler) here makes a crucial decision to renounce her elven immortality in order to marry Aragorn (Viggo Mortensen), there is none of the weight or significance in her decision that we feel, for example, when an angel decides to become human in *Wings of Desire.*

There is little enough psychological depth anywhere in the films, actually, and they exist mostly as surface, gesture, archetype, and spectacle. They do that magnificently well, but one feels at the end that nothing actual and human has been at stake; cartoon characters in a fantasy world have been brought along about as far as it is possible for them to come, and while we applaud the achievement, the trilogy is more a work for adolescents (of all ages) than for those hungering for truthful emotion thoughtfully paid for. Of all the heroes and villains in the trilogy, and all the thousands or hundreds of thousands of deaths, I felt such emotion only twice, with the ends of Faramir and Smeagol. They did what they did because of their natures and their free will, which were explained to us and known to them. Well, yes, and I felt something for Frodo, who has matured and grown on his long journey, although as we last see him it is hard to be sure he will remember what he has learned. Life is so pleasant in Middle Earth, in peacetime.

Lords of Dogtown ★ ★
PG-13, 107 m., 2005

Emile Hirsch (Jay Adams), Victor Rasuk (Tony Alva), John Robinson (Stacy Peralta), Michael Angarano (Sid), Nikki Reed (Kathy Alva), Heath Ledger (Skip Engblom), Rebecca De Mornay (Philaine), Johnny Knoxville (Topper Burks). Directed by Catherine Hardwicke and produced by John Linson. Screenplay by Stacy Peralta.

In the summer of 1975, modern skateboarding was invented in the Santa Monica and Venice Beach areas of California. The young members of the Zephyr Team, sponsored by a permanently stoned surfboard store owner, revolutionized the sport, performing acrobatics and crazy stunts on skateboards that had until then been seen as fancy scooters. They became famous, they made a lot of money, they grew up, and one of them, Stacy Peralta, made a 2002 documentary about them named *Dogtown and Z-Boys.*

It was a good documentary. As I wrote at the time: "It answers a question I have long been curious about: How and why was the first skateboarder inspired to go aerial, to break contact with any surface and do acrobatics in midair? Consider that the pioneer was doing this for the very first time over a vertical drop of perhaps fifteen feet to a concrete surface. It's not the sort of thing you try out of idle curiosity."

Now we have *Lords of Dogtown,* a fiction film based on the very same material, and indeed, written by Peralta. Not only is there no need for this movie, but its weaknesses underline the strength of the doc. How and why Peralta found so much old footage of skateboarding in 1975 is a mystery, but he was able to give us a good sense of those kids at that time. Although Catherine Hardwicke, the director of *Lords of Dogtown,* has a good feeling for the period and does what she can with her actors, we've seen the originals, and these aren't the originals. Nobody in the fiction film pulls off stunts as spectacular as we see for real in the documentary.

The story line remains the same. The kids live in what was then one of the remaining beachfront slums, down the coast from the expensive Malibu area. The beach was ruled by surfers, but in the afternoon, when the waves died down, some of the surfers, or their younger brothers, fooled around on skateboards. One day, Skip Engblom, the shop owner, comes up with a key breakthrough, polyurethane wheels: "They grip." With the additional traction, the Z-Boys try skating the sides of the big open drainage canal that runs through the area. Then comes a brainstorm: Because of a drought, the area's swimming pools were drained. They started "borrowing" pools when the owners weren't home, to skate the curved sides.

Emile Hirsch stars as Jay Adams, Victor Rasuk is Tony Alva, and John Robinson, with long blond hair that gets him photographed a lot in the emerging skateboarding magazines, plays Stacy Peralta. They all seem like pale imitations of the originals, as indeed they must be. Heath Ledger plays Skip, their mentor, who sponsors the Zephyr Team, gives them their first priceless T-shirts, and eventually, stoned and drunk, ends up making surfboards in somebody else's back room. But he was the catalyst.

In the documentary, there was a Z-Girl along with the Z-Boys, but here all we get is Nikki Reed as Kathy, Tony's sister. We also meet Rebecca De Mornay, as Jay's mother, who, like all mothers in southern California films, looks like she oughta be in pictures. Both the surfing and skateboarding sequences are fun to watch, within reason, but after seeing *Dogtown and Z-Boys* and the haunting surfing documentary *Riding Giants* (2004), we know the real thing is more awesome. The best surfing scenes take place when surfers ride waves dangerously close to the Pacific Island Pier and the rocks at its base; the pier mysteriously burns down that summer. "They wanted it gone," Skip mourns.

Skateboarding is a sport combining grace, courage, and skill, and here we see it being born. What we do not quite understand is how long one can be a skateboarder before you feel like you've been there and done that. Stacy Peralta obviously feels great nostalgia for that period in his life, which was the foundation for fame and fortune, but at this point it is time for him to either (a) move on to films about something else, or (b) deal with the dark aftermath of those golden days.

There were a lot of drugs around; although we see Skip here as a survivor, he's more of a victim. And like the earlier movie, this one doesn't really deal with injuries or accidents. In a sport where you can free fall to concrete, were there deaths? Was anyone paralyzed? There's a touching scene here where the kids take a friend in a wheelchair into one of the empty swimming pools and let him ride the sides a little, but he's in the chair because of cancer, not skateboarding.

Lost in La Mancha ★ ★ ★
R, 93 m., 2003

Featuring Terry Gilliam, Phil Patterson, Toni Grisoni, Nicola Pecorini, René Cleitman, Bernard Bouix, Johnny Depp, and Jean Rochefort. Narrated by Jeff Bridges. A documentary directed by Keith Fulton and Louis Pepe and produced by Lucy Darwin. Screenplay by Fulton and Pepe.

Blow, winds, and crack your cheeks! rage! blow!
You cataracts and hurricanoes, spout
Till you have drench'd our steeples ...

History does not record whether these words of King Lear passed through Terry Gilliam's mind as his beloved film about Don Quixote turned to ashes. It is hard to believe they did not. *Lost in La Mancha*, which started life as one of those documentaries you get free on the DVD, ended as the record of swift and devastating disaster.

Gilliam, the director of such films as *Brazil, 12 Monkeys,* and *The Fisher King,* arrived in Spain in August 2000 to begin filming a project he had been preparing for ten years. *The Man Who Killed Don Quixote* would star Johnny Depp as a modern-day hero who is transported back in time, and finds himself acting as Sancho Panza to old Don Quixote, who tilts at windmills and remains the most bravely romantic figure in Western literature.

The film was budgeted at $32 million, making it the most expensive production ever financed only with European money, although, as Gilliam observes, that's "far below what a film like this would usually cost."

In the title role he had cast Jean Rochefort, the tall, angular French star of more than 100 films, including *The Tall Blond Man with One Black Shoe* and *The Hairdresser's Husband*. Rochefort arrives on the set looking suitably gaunt and romantic, and showing off the English he has learned during seven months of lessons.

The first day of the shoot begins ominously. Someone has forgotten to rehearse the extras who are yoked to Depp in a chain gang. F-16 fighter planes roar overhead, spoiling shot after shot. Gilliam's optimism remains unchecked, and we get a notion of the film from his sketches and storyboards and his conferences with members of the production team. There's an amusing episode when he casts three men as giants.

Day two involves a change of location and an adjustment in the shooting schedule. The actors have arrived late in Spain, but are on hand, and as Gilliam and his first assistant director, Philip Patterson, juggle the schedule, the location becomes too windy and dusty. And then all hell breaks loose.

Thunderheads form overhead and rain begins to fall. Then hail. Winds blow over sets, tents, props. A flash flood crashes down the mountain and turns the area into a muddy quagmire. The damned jets continue to fly. Gilliam and his team regroup and are able to cobble together a shot involving Don Quixote on his horse. But: "Did you see Jean Rochefort's face as he was riding on the horse? He was in pain."

So much pain, as it develops, that although the actor is an experienced horseman, he cannot mount the horse alone, and needs two men and an hour of struggle to get himself down from it. Rochefort flies off to Paris to see his doctors, and the company shuts down, except for a day when they go through some motions to impress a busload of doomed visiting investors.

Rochefort will be gone three days, a week, ten days, indefinitely. His problem is described as two herniated discs. Or perhaps prostate trouble. Like vultures, the insurance agents begin to gather, followed by the completion bond guarantors, who step in when a film goes over budget. There are discussions, not with the optimism of Don Quixote, about what constitutes an act of God.

Midway through the second week of the shooting schedule, with brutal swiftness, *The Man Who Killed Don Quixote* is shut down. Some films end with a whimper; this one banged into a stone wall. The camera often rests on Gilliam's face, as the enormity of the disaster sinks in. "The movie already exists in here," he says, tapping his head. "I have visualized it so many times." But that is the only place it will ever exist.

Many films play dice with nature. I once stood in a barren field outside Durango, Colorado, as workers placed thousands of melons on the ground because the melon crop had failed, and the movie was about a melon farmer. I watched on the Amazon as an expensive light and all of its rigging slowly leaned over and fell forever beneath the waters. Once in the Ukraine, I waited for days with 20,000 extras, all members of the Red Army, who were dressed as Napoleon's Old Guard—and who could not be filmed without a lens that was being held up in customs.

There are many sad sights in *Lost in La Mancha*. One comes when the producers try to evoke the oldest rule in the book: "Fire the first assistant director." Gilliam stands firm behind his longtime assistant Patterson. It is not his fault. Day by day, it becomes increasingly clear that the film will never be made. Finally comes the shot of props being loaded into cardboard shipping boxes and sealed with tape. Maybe they are destined for eBay.

Other men have tilted at Quixote's windmill. Orson Welles famously spent years trying to piece together a film of the material, even after some of his actors had died. Peter O'Toole starred in *Man of La Mancha* (1972), not a good movie. Of that production I wrote: "I've always thought there was a flaw in the logic of *Man of La Mancha*. What good does it do to dream the impossible dream when all you're doing anyway is killing time until the Inquisition chops your block off?"

Lost in Translation ★ ★ ★ ★
R, 105 m., 2003

Bill Murray (Bob Harris), Scarlett Johansson (Charlotte), Giovanni Ribisi (John), Anna Faris (Kelly). Directed by Sofia Coppola and produced by Coppola and Ross Katz. Screenplay by Coppola.

The Japanese phrase *mono no aware* is a bittersweet reference to the transience of life. It came to mind as I was watching *Lost in Translation*, which is sweet and sad at the same time it is sardonic and funny. Bill Murray and Scarlett Johansson play two lost souls rattling around a Tokyo hotel in the middle of the night, who fall into conversation about their marriages, their happiness, and the meaning of it all.

Such conversations can really be held only

with strangers. We all need to talk about metaphysics, but those who know us well want details and specifics; strangers allow us to operate more vaguely on a cosmic scale. When the talk occurs between two people who could plausibly have sex together, it gathers a special charge: You can only say, "I feel like I've known you for years" to someone you have not known for years. Funny, how your spouse doesn't understand the bittersweet transience of life as well as a stranger encountered in a hotel bar. Especially if drinking is involved.

Murray plays Bob Harris, an American movie star in Japan to make commercials for whiskey. "Do I need to worry about you, Bob?" his wife asks over the phone. "Only if you want to," he says. She sends him urgent faxes about fabric samples. Johansson plays Charlotte, whose husband, John, is a photographer on assignment in Tokyo. She visits a shrine and then calls a friend in America to say, "I didn't feel anything." Then she blurts out: "I don't know who I married."

She's in her early twenties; Bob's in his fifties. This is the classic setup for a May-November romance, since in the mathematics of celebrity intergenerational dating you can take five years off the man's age for every million dollars of income. But *Lost in Translation* is too smart and thoughtful to be the kind of movie where they go to bed and we're supposed to accept that as the answer. Sofia Coppola, who wrote and directed, doesn't let them off the hook that easily. They share something as personal as their feelings rather than something as generic as their genitals.

These are two wonderful performances. Bill Murray has never been better. He doesn't play "Bill Murray" or any other conventional idea of a movie star, but invents Bob Harris from the inside out, as a man both happy and sad with his life—stuck, but resigned to being stuck. Marriage is not easy for him, and his wife's voice over the phone is on autopilot. But he loves his children. They are miracles, he confesses to Charlotte. Not his children specifically, but—children.

He is very tired, he is doing the commercials for money and hates himself for it, he has a sense of humor and can be funny, but it's a bother. She has been married only a couple of years, but it's clear her husband thinks she's in the way. Filled with his own importance, flattered that a starlet knows his name, he leaves her behind in the hotel room because—how does it go?—he'll be working, and she won't have a good time if she comes along with him.

Ingmar Bergman's *Scenes from a Marriage* was about a couple who met years after their divorce and found themselves "in the middle of the night in a dark house somewhere in the world." That's how Bob and Charlotte seem to me. Most of the time nobody knows where they are, or cares, and their togetherness is all that keeps them both from being lost and alone. They go to karaoke bars and drug parties, pachinko parlors and, again and again, the hotel bar. They wander Tokyo, an alien metropolis to which they lack the key. They don't talk in the long, literate sentences of the characters in *Before Sunrise*, but in the weary understatements of those who don't have the answers.

Now from all I've said you wouldn't guess the movie is also a comedy, but it is. Basically, it's a comedy of manners—Japan's, and ours. Bob Harris goes everywhere surrounded by a cloud of white-gloved women who bow and thank him for—allowing himself to be thanked, I guess. Then there's the director of the whiskey commercial, whose movements for some reason reminded me of Cab Calloway performing *Minnie the Moocher*. And the hooker sent up to Bob's room, whose approach is melodramatic and archaic; she has obviously not studied the admirable Japanese achievements in porno. And the B-movie starlet (Anna Faris), intoxicated with her own wonderfulness.

In these scenes there are opportunities for Murray to turn up the heat under his comic persona. He doesn't. He always stays in character. He is always Bob Harris, who *could* be funny, who *could* be the life of the party, who *could* do impressions in the karaoke bar and play games with the director of the TV commercial, but doesn't—because being funny is what he does for a living, and right now he is too tired and sad to do it for free. Except . . . a little. That's where you see the fine-tuning of Murray's performance. In a subdued, fond way, he gives us wry, faint comic gestures, as if to show what he could do, if he wanted to.

Well, I loved this movie. I loved the way Coppola and her actors negotiated the hazards of romance and comedy, taking what little they

tory, and a sexy girl named Animala, whose role

needed and depending for the rest on the truth of the characters. I loved the way Bob and Charlotte didn't solve their problems, but felt a little better anyway. I loved the moment near the end when Bob runs after Charlotte and says something in her ear, and we're not allowed to hear it. We shouldn't be allowed to hear it. It's between them, and by this point in the movie they've become real enough to deserve their privacy. Maybe he gave her his phone number. Or said he loved her. Or said she was a good person. Or thanked her. Or whispered, "Had we but world enough, and time . . ." and left her to look up the rest of it.

The Lost Skeleton of Cadavra ★ ½
PG, 90 m., 2004

Larry Blamire (Dr. Paul Armstrong), Fay Masterson (Betty Armstrong), Jennifer Blaire (Animala), Brian Howe (Dr. Roger Fleming), Susan McConnell (Lattis), Andrew Parks (Krobar), Dan Conroy (Ranger Brad), Robert Deveau (The Farmer). Directed by Larry Blamire and produced by F. Miguel Valenti. Screenplay by Blamire.

"It is a curious attribute of camp that it can only be found, not made." So observes Dave Kehr, in his *New York Times* review of *The Lost Skeleton of Cadavra*. I did not read the rest of the review, because (1) I had to write my own, and (2), well, his first sentence says it all, doesn't it? True camp sincerely wants to be itself. In this category I include the works of Ed Wood and the infinitely more talented Russ Meyer. False camp keeps digging you in the ribs with a bony elbow. In this category falls *The Lost Skeleton of Cadavra*. Movies like the *Austin Powers* series are in a different category altogether, using the framework of satire for the purpose of comedy.

The Lost Skeleton of Cadavra, which is a loving tribute to the worst science fiction movies ever made, is about a three-way struggle for possession of the rare element atmosphereum. The contestants include an American scientist and his wife, a married (I think) couple from outer space, and a mad scientist and his sidekick, which is, of course, the lost skeleton of Cadavra. There is also a creature that seems to have been created by an explosion at a sofa fac-

tory, and a sexy girl named Animala, whose role is to appear in the movie and be a sexy girl. More about her later.

The photography, the dialogue, the acting, the script, the special effects, and especially the props (such as a space ship that looks like it would get a D in shop class) are all deliberately bad in the way that such films were bad when they were *really* being made. The locations remind me of the old *Captain Video* TV series, in which the same fake rocks were always being moved around to indicate we were in a new place on the alien planet. The writer and director, Larry Blamire, who also plays the saner of the scientists, has the look so well mastered that if the movie had only been made in total ignorance fifty years ago, it might be recalled today as a classic. A minor, perhaps even minuscule, classic.

A funny thing happened while I was watching it. I began to flash back to *Trog* (1970). This is an example of camp that was made, not found. That it was directed by the great cinematographer Freddie Francis I have absolutely no explanation for. That it starred Joan Crawford, in almost her final movie role, I think I understand. Even though she was already enshrined as a Hollywood goddess, she was totally unable to stop accepting roles, and took this one against all reason.

The plot of *Trog*, which I will abbreviate, involves a hairy monster. When it goes on a killing spree and is captured, Joan Crawford, an anthropologist, realizes it is a priceless scientific find: the Missing Link between ape and man. Then Trog kidnaps a small girl and crawls into a cave, and reader, although many years have passed since I saw the movie, I have never forgotten the sight of Joan Crawford in her designer pants suit and all the makeup crawling on her hands and knees into the cave and calling out, "Trog! Trog!" As if Trog knew the abbreviation of its scientific name.

But never mind; you see the point. *Trog* is perfect camp because Freddie Francis and Joan Crawford would never have allied themselves with a movie that was deliberately bad. (I am not so sure about Joe Cornelius, who played Trog.) It is bad all on its own. *The Lost Skeleton of Cadavra* has been made by people who are trying to be bad, which by definition reveals that they are playing beneath their ability. Poor

403

Ed Wood, on the other hand, always and sincerely made the very best film he possibly could. How rare is a director like Russ Meyer, whose work satirizes material that doesn't even exist except in his satire of it, and who is also very funny; no coincidence that the *Austin Powers* movies are always careful to quote him.

But what have I neglected to tell you about *The Lost Skeleton of Cadavra*? Reading my notes, I find that "there is enough atmosphereum in one teaspoon to go to the moon and back six times," which is not quite the statement it seems to be. Oh, and the sexy girl named Animala is described as: "part human, part four different forest animals, and she can dance! Oh, how she can dance! Like I've never seen a woman dance before!" A possible mate for Trog?

A Lot Like Love ★

PG-13, 95 m., 2005

Ashton Kutcher (Oliver), Amanda Peet (Emily), Kathryn Hahn (Michelle), Kal Penn (Jeeter), Ali Larter (Gina), Taryn Manning (Ellen), Gabriel Mann (Peter), Jeremy Sisto (Ben). Directed by Nigel Cole and produced by Armyan Bernstein and Kevin J. Messick. Screenplay by Colin Patrick Lynch.

A Lot Like Love is a romance between two of the dimmer bulbs of their generation. Judging by their dialogue, Oliver and Emily have never read a book or a newspaper, seen a movie, watched TV, had an idea, carried on an interesting conversation, or ever thought much about anything. The movie thinks they are cute and funny, which is embarrassing, like your uncle who won't stop with the golf jokes. This is not the fault of the stars, Ashton Kutcher and Amanda Peet, who are actors forced to walk around in Stupid Suits.

When I was at Boulder for a conference at the University of Colorado, I found myself walking across campus with a kid who confessed he was studying philosophy.

"What do you plan to do with it?" I asked.

He said he wasn't sure. All of his friends were on career tracks, but "I dunno. I just find this stuff interesting."

Yes! I said. Yes! Don't treat education as if it's only a trade school. Take some electives just because they're interesting. You have long years to get through, and you must guard against the possibility of becoming a bore to yourself.

A Lot Like Love, written by Colin Patrick Lynch and directed by Nigel Cole, is about two people who have arrived at adulthood unequipped for the struggle. The lives of Oliver and Emily are Idiot Plots, in which every misunderstanding could be solved by a single word they are vigilant never to utter. They Meet Cute, over and over again. They keep finding themselves alone because their lovers keep walking out on them. Well, no wonder. "I'm going," one of her lovers says, and goes. Any more of an explanation and she might have had to take notes.

He has an Internet start-up selling diapers over the Web. She's dumped by a rock musician in the opening scene, where she seems to be a tough Goth chick, but that's just the costume. Later Ollie gives her a camera and she becomes a photographer, and even has a gallery exhibit of her works, which look like photos taken on vacation with cell phone cameras and e-mailed to you by the children of friends.

The movie is ninety-five minutes long, and neither character says a single memorable thing. You've heard of being too clever by half? Ollie and Emily are not clever enough by three-quarters. During a dinner date they start spitting water at each other. Then she crawls under the table, not for what you're thinking, but so they can trade sides and spit in the opposite direction. Then it seems like she's choking on her food, but he refuses to give her the Heimlich maneuver, and even tells the waitress not to bother. So take a guess: Is she really choking, or not? If she's playing a trick, she's a doofus, and if she isn't, he's a doofus. They shouldn't be allowed to leave the house without a parent or adult guardian.

They continue to Meet Cute over many long years, which are spelled out in titles: "Three Years Later," "Six Months Later," and so on. I was reminded of the little blue thermometers telling you the software will finish downloading in nineteen hours. Their first Meet Cute is a doozy: On a flight to New York, she enlists him in the Mile-High Club before they even know each other's names. But that's

Strike One against him, she says, because she had to make the first move. Yeah, like a guy on an airplane should push into the rest room for sex with a woman he doesn't know. That's how you get to wear the little plastic cuffs.

Later they Meet Cute again, walk into a bar, drink four shots of Jack Daniels in one minute, and order a pitcher of beer. No, they're not alcoholics. This is just Movie Behavior; for example, at first she smokes and then she stops and then she starts again. That supplies her with a Personality Characteristic. Still later, they sing together, surprisingly badly. The movie is filled with a lot of other pop music. These songs tend toward plaintive dirges complaining, "My life can be described by this stupid song." At one point he flies to New York to pitch his dot-com diapers to some venture capitalists, and is so inarticulate and clueless he could be a character in this movie. To call the movie dead in the water is an insult to water.

Love Actually ★ ★ ★ ½
R, 129 m., 2003

Hugh Grant (Prime Minister), Liam Neeson (Daniel), Colin Firth (Jamie), Laura Linney (Sarah), Emma Thompson (Karen), Alan Rickman (Harry), Keira Knightley (Juliet), Martine McCutcheon (Natalie), Bill Nighy (Billy Mack), Rowan Atkinson (Rufus), Billy Bob Thornton (The U.S. President), Rodrigo Santoro (Karl), Thomas Sangster (Sam), Lucia Moniz (Aurelia). Directed by Richard Curtis and produced by Tim Bevan, Eric Fellner, and Duncan Kenworthy. Screenplay by Curtis.

Love Actually is a belly flop into the sea of romantic comedy. It contains about a dozen couples who are in love; that's an approximate figure because some of them fall out of love and others double up or change partners. There's also one hopeful soloist who believes that if he flies to Milwaukee and walks into a bar he'll find a friendly Wisconsin girl who thinks his British accent is so cute she'll want to sleep with him. This turns out to be true.

The movie is written and directed by Richard Curtis, the same man who wrote three landmarks in recent romantic comedy: *Four Weddings and a Funeral, Notting Hill,* and *Brid-*

get Jones's Diary. His screenplay for *Love Actually* is bursting with enough material for the next three. The movie's only flaw is also a virtue: It's jammed with characters, stories, warmth, and laughs, until at times Curtis seems to be working from a checklist of obligatory movie love situations and doesn't want to leave anything out. At 129 minutes it feels a little like a gourmet meal that turns into a hot dog–eating contest.

I could attempt to summarize the dozen (or so) love stories, but that way madness lies. Maybe I can back into the movie by observing the all-star gallery of dependable romantic comedy stars, led by Hugh Grant, and you know what? Little by little, a movie at a time, Hugh Grant has flowered into an absolutely splendid romantic comedian. He's getting to be one of those actors like Christopher Walken or William Macy who make you smile when you see them on the screen. He has that Cary Grantish ability to seem bemused by his own charm, and has so much self-confidence that he plays the British prime minister as if he took the role to be a good sport.

Emma Thompson plays his sister, with that wry way she has with normality, and Alan Rickman plays her potentially cheating husband with the air of a lawyer who hates to point out the escape clause he's just discovered. Laura Linney plays his assistant, who is shy to admit she loves her coworker Karl (Rodrigo Santoro), who is also shy to admit he loves her, and so you see how the stories go round and round.

Oh, and the prime minister walks into 10 Downing Street his first day on the job and Natalie the tea girl (Martine McCutcheon) brings him his tea and biscuits, and the nation's most prominent bachelor realizes with a sinking heart that he has fallen head over teapot in love. "Oh, no, that is *so* inconvenient," he says to himself, with the despair of a man who wants to be ruled by his head but knows that his netherlands have the votes.

Wandering past these lovable couples is the film's ancient mariner, a broken-down rock star named Billy Mack, who is played by Bill Nighy as if Keith Richards had never recorded anything but crap, and knew it. By the time he is fifty, George Orwell said, a man has the face he deserves, and Nighy looks as if he spent those years turning his face into a warning for

405

young people: look what can happen to you if you insist on being a naughty boy.

Billy Mack is involved in recording a cynical Christmas version of one of his old hits. The hit was crappy, the Christmas version is crap squared, and he is only too happy to admit it. Billy Mack is long past pretending to be nice just because he's on a talk show. At one point he describes his song with a versatile torrent of insults of which the only printable word is "turd." And on another show, when he's told he should spend Christmas with someone he loves, he replies, "When I was young I was greedy and foolish, and now I'm left with no one. Wrinkled and alone." That this is true merely adds to his charm, and Nighy steals the movie, especially in the surprising late scene where he confesses genuine affection for (we suspect) the first time in his life.

Look who else is in the movie. Billy Bob Thornton turns up as the president of the United States, combining the lechery of Clinton with the moral complacency of Bush. After the president makes a speech informing the British that America is better than they are, America is stronger than they are, America will do what is right and the Brits had better get used to it, Hugh Grant's PM steps up to the podium, and what he says is a little more pointed than he intended it to be because his heart is breaking: He has just glimpsed the president flirting with the delectable tea girl.

The movie has such inevitable situations as a school holiday concert, an office party, a family dinner, a teenage boy who has a crush on a girl who doesn't know he exists, and all sorts of accidental meetings, both fortunate and not. Richard Curtis always involves a little sadness in his comedies (like the funeral in *Four Weddings*), and there's genuine poignancy in the relationship of a recently widowed man (Liam Neeson) and his wife's young son by a former marriage (Thomas Sangster). Their conversations together have some of the same richness as *About a Boy.*

The movie has to hop around to keep all these stories alive, and there are a couple I could do without. I'm not sure we need the wordless romance between Colin Firth, as a British writer, and Lucia Moniz, as the Portuguese maid who works in his cottage in France. Let's face it: The scene where his manuscript blows into the lake and she jumps in after it isn't up to the standard of the rest of the movie.

I once had ballpoints printed up with the message, "No good movie is too long. No bad movie is short enough." *Love Actually* is too long. But don't let that stop you.

Love Don't Cost a Thing ★ ★ ★
PG-13, 100 m., 2003

Nick Cannon (Alvin Johnson), Christina Milian (Paris Morgan), Steve Harvey (Clarence Johnson), Al Thompson (Big Ted), Kal Penn (Kenneth Warman), Kenan Thompson (Walter Colley), Vanessa Bell Calloway (Vivian Johnson), Melissa Schuman (Zoe Parks). Directed by Troy Beyer and produced by Mark Burg, Reuben Cannon, Broderick Johnson, and Andrew A. Kosove. Screenplay by Michael Swerdlick and Beyer.

Love Don't Cost a Thing is a remake of *Can't Buy Me Love* (1987), a movie I despised, and yet this version is sweet and kind of touching, and I liked it. The difference, I think, is that the new one is lower on cynicism and higher on wisdom, and might actually contain some truth about the agonies of high school insecurity.

Both films have the same premise: A nerd in his senior year is getting good grades, but doesn't have a clue about dating. In desperation he bribes the most popular girl in school to date him long enough to change his image. She agrees. The 1987 movie painted its characters (played by Patrick Dempsey and Amanda Peterson) in fairly mercenary terms, but the characters in the remake are softened and made more likable.

Alvin Johnson (Nick Cannon) sees his chance when Paris Morgan (Christina Milian) turns up at the auto shop where he works, seeking emergency repairs to the front end of her mother's Cadillac SUV. The shop can't meet her deadline, but Alvin offers to help her out—in return for two weeks of dating. What she doesn't know is that he'll have to take the money he was saving for a science fair in order to pay for a replacement part.

Their high school is portrayed as a series of cruel no-go zones; an unpopular student would never venture into the corridor where the popular kids have their lockers, and so the first time

Alvin (with Paris) ventures into that forbidden territory, it's a giddy victory. And it goes to his head; intoxicated by his newfound popularity, which has indeed rubbed off from Paris, he drops his old buddies from science class and starts acting out like a demented Chris Rock.

The movie's buried message is that Alvin really is a nice guy, if only he could learn to trust himself. Paris begins to realize that, values their long talks, and at one crucial point really would like to be kissed by Alvin—but he can't see that, or admit it. At home, he mystifies his parents (Steve Harvey and Vanessa Bell Calloway) with an overnight transformation, complete with the new wardrobe Paris has dressed him in. His old friends come to visit, but are turned away, forlorn.

Alvin's act is all bravado; Paris is so high-powered she intimidates him. "Chicks like Paris don't date outside the NBA," one of Alvin's friends observes early in the film, and indeed her alleged boyfriend is in his first year in the pros. But when he disses her on ESPN by claiming that, romantically, he's a "free agent," Paris is wounded—and more available than Alvin realizes.

The movie, directed by the actress Troy Beyer and written by her and Michael Swerdlick, makes a low-key attempt to teach some lessons. Steve Harvey's acting may go over the top in a scene where he lectures his son on the theory and use of condoms, but it's useful information and more realistic than the blissful sexual ignorance of most high school movies. And Paris shares some wisdom, too, explaining, "Popularity is a job, Alvin."

Nick Cannon is in his second starring role (he was infectiously likable as the kid from Harlem who's recruited by a southern university in *Drumline*), and he shows again an easy screen presence; maybe he, too, goes a little over the top in showing Alvin in full egotistical explosion, but in this script it comes with the territory. Christina Milian has had a lot of smaller roles, but this is her first lead, and she fills it with confidence and charm; if she's the most popular girl in school, she convinces us she deserves the title and wasn't simply assigned it by the screenplay.

Movies like this are lightweight and forgettable; only this sequel reminded me of *Can't Buy Me Love*, which had otherwise faded from memory. But for its running time *Love Don't*

Cost a Thing does its job, and a little more. It has better values than the original, a little more poignancy, some sweetness. And Cannon and Milian have a natural appeal that liberates their characters, a little, from the limitations of the plot.

Love Liza ★ ★ ★
R, 90 m., 2003

Philip Seymour Hoffman (Wilson Joel), Kathy Bates (Mary Ann Bankhead), Jack Kehler (Denny), Sarah Koskoff (Maura Haas), Stephen Tobolowsky (Tom Bailey), Erika Alexander (Brenda). Directed by Todd Louiso and produced by Ruth Charny, Corky O'Hara, Chris Hanley, Jeffrey Roda, and Fernando Sulichin. Screenplay by Gordy Hoffman.

Diane Lane, who worked on Philip Seymour Hoffman's second movie, remembers that the cast almost tiptoed around him, he seemed so fragile. He's a bulky man, substantial, and yet in many of his roles he seems ready to deflate with a last exhausted sigh. It is a little startling to meet him in person and discover he is outgoing, confident, humorous. On the other hand, who knows him better than his brother Gordy, whose screenplay for *Love Liza* creates a Hoffman role teetering on the brink of implosion.

Hoffman plays Wilson Joel, a tech-head whose wife has recently committed suicide, although it takes us a while to figure that out. He presents a facade of conviviality in the office, sometimes punctuated by outbursts of laughter that go on too long, like choked grief. His home seems frozen in a state of mid-unpacking, and he sleeps on the floor. Eventually he stops going in to work altogether.

What he feels for his late wife is never usefully articulated. She left a letter for him, but he has not opened it; her mother, played by Kathy Bates, would like to know what it says, but what can she do to influence this man whose psyche is in meltdown? Wilson gives the sense of never having really grown up. One day he begins sniffing gasoline, a dangerous way to surround himself with a blurred world. He doesn't even have grown-up vices like drinks or drugs, but reverts to something he may have tried as a teenager.

The movie proceeds with a hypnotic relent-lessness that hesitates between horror and black comedy. Searching to explain all the gas he's buying, he blurts out that he needs it for his model airplanes (this would have been a teenager's alibi). A friendly coworker thinks maybe this is an opening to lure him back into life, and sends over a relative who is an enthu-siast of remote-controlled planes and boats. This sends Wilson careening into a series of cover-ups; he has to buy a model airplane, he finds himself attending remote control gather-ings in which he has not the slightest interest, and finally, after a series of events that Jim Car-rey could have performed in another kind of movie, he finds himself inexplicably swimming in a lake while angry little remote-controlled boats buzz like hornets around him.

Love Liza, directed by Todd Louiso, is not about a plot but about a condition. The con-dition is familiar to students of some of Hoffman's other characters, and comes to full flower in *Happiness* (1998), where he plays a man who lives in solitary confinement with his desperate and antisocial sexual fantasies. Sex hardly seems the issue with Wilson Joel, but he seems incapable of any kind of normal socializing, other than a kind of fake office ca-maraderie he might have copied from others. The mystery is not why Liza killed herself, but why she married him.

The purpose of a movie like this is to in-spire thoughts about human nature. Most movies do not contain real people; they con-tain puppets who conform to popular stereo-types and do entertaining things. In the recent and relatively respectable thriller *The Recruit*, for example, Colin Farrell doesn't play a three-dimensional human, nor is he required to. He is a place-holder for a role that has been played before and will be endlessly played again—the kid who chooses a mentor in a dangerous spy game. He is pleasant, sexy, wary, angry, baffled, ambitious, and relieved, all on cue, but these emotions do not proceed from his personality. They are generated by the requirements of the plot. Leaving the movie, we may have learned something about CIA spycraft (and a lot more about the manufacture of thrillers), but there is not one single thing we will have learned about being alive.

Al Pacino is the costar of that movie, defined and motivated as narrowly as Farrell is. In a new movie named *People I Know*, he plays a breathing, thinking human being, a New York press agent driven by drugs, drink, duty, and a persistent loyalty to his own political idealism. We learn something about life from that per-formance. Pacino teaches us, as he is always capable of doing in the right role.

Philip Seymour Hoffman is a teacher, too. You should see *Love Liza* in anticipation of his new movie, *Owning Mahowny*, which I saw at Sundance this year (*Love Liza* was at the 2002 festival, where it won the prize for best screen-play). The Mahowny character is at right an-gles to Wilson, but seems similarly blocked at an early stage of development. Observing how Mahowny, an addicted gambler, relates to his long-suffering fiancée (Minnie Driver), we can guess at the ordeal Wilson put Liza through. He's not cruel or angry or mean; he's simply not . . . there. His eyes seek other horizons.

In an age when depression and Prozac are not unknown, when the popularity of New Age goofiness reflects an urgent need for reas-surance, Hoffman may be playing characters much closer to the American norm than an action hero like Colin Farrell. We cannot all outsmart the CIA and win the girl, but many of us know what it feels like to be stuck in doubt and confusion, and cornered by our own evasions.

There is a kind of attentive concern that Hoffman brings to his characters, as if he has been giving them private lessons, and now it is time for their first public recital. Whether or not they are ready, it can be put off no longer, and so here they are, trembling and blinking, wondering why everyone else seems to know the music.

Love Me If You Dare ★ ★

R, 99 m., 2004

Guillaume Canet (Julien), Marion Cotillard (Sophie), Thibault Verhaeghe (Julien at Eight), Josephine Lebas-Joly (Sophie at Eight), Gerard Watkins (Julien's Father), Emmanuelle Gronvold (Julien's Mother), Laetizia Venezia (Christelle). Directed by Yann Samuell and produced by Christophe Rossignon. Screenplay by Jacky Cukier and Samuell.

Do I dislike this film, or only its characters? There can be good films about bad people. Remember Travis Bickle. For that matter, do I dislike it because the characters are bad, or simply because they make me feel uneasy? Perhaps they're simply insane, and trapped in their mutual obsession. Perhaps because the film makes me feel so crawly, it is actually good. Yet still I cannot like it.

Love Me If You Dare tells the story of Julien and Sophie, who meet in grade school and make a pact that binds them together for a lifetime. Their treaty revolves around a little tin box, a toy painted to look like a merry-go-round. When one hands the other the box, along with it comes a dare. The other *must* do what they've been dared to do. This begins as a childhood game and continues into adulthood, where it gathers dangerous and dark undertones.

The movie will appeal to lovers of *Amelie,* according to the ads. Not if they loved *Amelie* for its good cheer. This is *Amelie* through the looking-glass. Yes, it has some of the same visual invention and delight, and director Yann Samuell's camera swoops and circles and flies through windows and into dreams. Yes, there's a bright color palate. Yes, the movie riffs through techniques, including animated sequences. Yes, Marion Cotillard has sweetness and appeal as Sophie, and yes, she and Julien (Guillaume Canet) seem destined to spend their lives together. But like this?

When they meet, they're eight years old and Sophie is being picked on at school because she's a foreigner. Julien defends her. They become friends for life. Even their first childish dares are risky, as when Sophie dares Julien to release the parking brake on the school bus; as it rolls downhill, do they get a fix of excitement that hooks them for life? Before long Julien is in the principal's office, peeing his pants—not because he's scared, but because Sophie dared him to.

The dares get riskier and more embarrassing as they grow older. Julien dares Sophie to take an oral exam at university while wearing her panties and bra outside her clothes. Sophie dares Julien to say "no" at the altar on his wedding day. Of course he won't be marrying her; that would be too easy, because she'd be in on the joke.

For that matter, what *is* their relationship? Are they in love, or simply trapped in a hypnotic mutual fascination? There's a flashforward in the movie from a scene where Sophie sleeps over at Julien's house when they're eight, to the two of them as adults, still in the same position in bed. But have they had sex in the meantime? Does it matter? Their bond is deeper than sex and love; it's the bond of shared madness.

At one point in the movie, they dare each other to stay completely out of contact for ten years. Will they get their pact out of their system? Not at all. Every moment of those ten years, they're acutely aware of the passage of time and the fulfillment of their dare, and when they meet again at the end it's to escalate the dare to a new and disturbing level.

The movie's first shot tells us something we don't understand at the time. The last scene explains it, and is profoundly creepy. There is, I suppose, a tradition of lovers' pacts, but are they lovers, and what are they proving with the way they end their own pact? I know these are questions not intended for answers. I realize that the movie establishes a premise and follows it relentlessly. I understand that the playful camera strategies are supposed to take the edge off, and that scenes are played like comedy so that we won't grow completely depressed by the strange fate of Sophie and Julien.

But at the end, I didn't like them. In fact, reader, I loathed them. Did I loathe them as people, or as characters? Are their characters intended as real people, or as a fictional device? I'm not sure. What I do know is that the movie is strangely frustrating, because Julien and Sophie choose misery and obsession as a lifestyle, and push far beyond reason. Perhaps I should applaud the movie for its conviction? Perhaps the snakier it made me feel, the better it was? Perhaps, but I can't say so if I don't think so. I can say this: If despite everything my description has intrigued you, go ahead and take a chance. You won't be bored, he said with a little smile.

Love Object ★ ★
R, 88 m., 2004

Desmond Harrington (Kenneth), Melissa Sagemiller (Lisa), Rip Torn (Novak), Brad Henke

(Dotson), Udo Kier (Radley), John Cassini (Jason), Lyle Kanouse (Stan). Directed by Robert Parigi and produced by Kathleen Haase and Lawrence Levy. Screenplay by Parigi.

Robert Parigi's *Love Object* tells the story of a painfully shy writer of software manuals, a man inhibited to the point of paralysis, who discovers a Web site that sells realistic, life-size love dolls. Kenneth (Desmond Harrington) is already a user of porn, frequenting a cryptlike adult shop that looks like the horror chamber at Madame Tussaud's and seems to have the Elephant Man behind the cash register. Now he maxes out his line of credit to order Nikki, a custom-crafted mannequin made to his specifications: hair color, eyes, etc.

While this drama is unfolding in his private life, Kenneth is under pressure from his boss. That would be Mr. Novak (Rip Torn), who seems to have modeled his performance on Samuel Ramey as Mephistopheles. Gravel-voiced and goateed, he alternates threat and praise as he assigns Kenneth to produce a three-volume instruction manual in a month. To assist him, Novak supplies a temp who can do the typing. This is Lisa (Melissa Sagemiller), an attractive young blond.

Kenneth doesn't want help. He prefers to work alone. But then an eerie thing occurs; Lisa, as it happens, looks a little like the love doll, Nikki. Kenneth starts buying things for the doll: dresses, wigs, lipstick, fingernail polish. He rigs up a harness so he can dance with the doll. And meantime, Lisa makes no secret of her attraction to him, which is odd, since Kenneth is so odd he might as well have "Weirdo Freak" tattooed on his forehead.

The establishing scenes of *Love Object* are voyeuristic in a creepy way; there's a strange fascination in stories about sexual fetishes, and as Kenneth works to make Nikki look more like Lisa, and then to make Lisa look more like Nikki, the music by Nicholas Pike subtly reminds us of the *Vertigo* theme. The *Vertigo* connection seems deliberate: There's even a scene in a dress store, where Kenneth takes Lisa to buy the same dress he earlier bought for Nikki, and the sales clerk looks at him in that same complicit way the clerk regarded James Stewart in the Hitchcock film. Kenneth wants Lisa and Nikki to look alike, just as Stewart coached Kim Novak to resemble the woman of his dreams.

Both times there was a trap for the man: In Hitchcock, because Novak secretly really was the woman Stewart was obsessed by, and in Parigi, because Kenneth begins to confuse the woman and the doll. We can't be sure exactly what defines the level of his madness, but certainly he believes Nikki has the upper hand—she orders him around, calls him at work, handcuffs him in his sleep, and so on. Sooner or later Lisa is going to find out about this, and then . . .

Well, up to that point Parigi had me fairly well involved. I was reminded of Michael Powell's *Peeping Tom* (1960), about a voyeuristic photographer who kills with his camera, and *Kissed* (1996), the Canadian film about a woman's strangely sympathetic necrophilia. It wasn't as good as those films, but it had the same attention to the sad, inward obsession of the character. If Parigi had continued in the way he began, he might have produced a successful film.

But he lacks confidence in Kenneth and his inward life, and so the movie reaches with increasing desperation toward humor and grisly sadism, and the mood is broken. There is a workable subplot involving Kenneth's strange building manager (Udo Keir), who listens in amazement through the walls, but another neighbor, a Los Angeles detective named Dotson (Brad Henke), is a goofball who does everything wrong that he possibly can, just to wring cheap laughs out of a situation that by then is desperately unfunny.

And the film's violent conclusion is too gruesome to be earned by what has gone before. Instead of somehow finding a psychological climax for his hero's dilemma, as Hitchcock and Powell did, Parigi goes for horror film developments that he pushes far beyond any possible interest we have in seeing them. The movie turns cruel and ugly, and hasn't paid the dues to earn its last scenes. Parigi had me there for a while, but when he lost me, it was big time.

A Love Song for Bobby Long ★ ★ ★
R, 119 m., 2005

John Travolta (Bobby Long), Scarlett Johansson (Pursy Will), Gabriel Macht (Lawson Pines),

Deborah Kara Unger (Georgianna), Dane Rhodes (Cecil), David Jensen (Junior), Clayne Crawford (Lee), Sonny Shroyer (Earl). Directed by Shainee Gabel and produced by Gabel, David Lancaster, R. Paul Miller, and Bob Yari. Screenplay by Gabel, based on the novel *Off Magazine Street* by Ronald Everett Capps.

There is a lazy, seductive appeal to the lives of the two boozers in *A Love Song for Bobby Long.* The notion of moving to New Orleans and drinking yourself to death is the sort of escape plan only an alcoholic could come up with, involving the principle of surrender to the enemy. If you are a writer and a failed English professor like Bobby Long, you can even wrap yourself in the legend of other literary drunks. It's all wonderfully romantic, especially in the movies, where a little groaning in the morning replaces nausea, headaches, killer hangovers, and panic attacks. A realistic portrait of suicidal drinking would contain more terror and confusion, but never mind. *Leaving Las Vegas* did that, and this is a different movie.

Bobby Long is played by John Travolta like a living demonstration of one of those artist's conceptions of what Elvis would look like at seventy. White-haired, unshaven, probably smelly, he lives on Magazine Street in the Quarter with a former student named Lawson Pines (Gabriel Macht), who thinks he is a genius. Years ago, Bobby was a legend on campus, Lawson's charismatic mentor. Then something happened, which we are pretty sure we will find out about, and here he is without wife or family, living on the sofa surrounded by piles of books.

He and Lawson spend a lot of time quoting literature to each other. Ben Franklin, Charles Dickens, the usual twentieth century gods. This is entertaining all by itself, apart from the good it does for the characters. It reminded me of Alan Bennett's play, *The History Boys,* in which memorizing literary quotations is recommended as a means of fertilizing the mind. Bobby and Lawson are well fertilized, but too disorganized to plant anything; an unfinished novel and a would-be memoir languish in the shadows. In *Sideways,* when Miles (Paul Giamatti) says he can't commit suicide because he has a responsibility to his unpublished novel, his buddy Jack (Thomas Haden Church)

helpfully points out that the New Orleans legend John Kennedy Toole killed himself before *A Confederacy of Dunces* was published. So there is a precedent.

Bobby and Lawson seem prepared to keep on drinking and quoting and smoking forever, when a sudden change occurs in their lives. Their housemate, a jazz singer named Lorraine, has died. Now her daughter, Pursy (Scarlett Johansson), materializes, too late for the funeral. Pursy is a discontented and suspicious eighteen-year-old, who will soon prove to be the most mature member of the household. The boys tell Pursy her mother left her a third of the house, which is sort of true; actually, her mother left Pursy all of the house, but information like that could only confuse Pursy about the right of Bobby and Lawson to continue living there forever.

Pursy moves in, creating a form of family in which she is both the child and the adult, and Bobby and Lawson drift in between. At one point Lawson's halfway girlfriend Georgianna (Deborah Kara Unger) asks, "They know you're not going to school?" Pursy: "Yeah, it ranks right up there with being out of vodka and cigarettes."

The revelations in *A Love Song for Bobby Long* are not too hard to spot coming. There are only a few fictional developments that seem possible, and it turns out that they are. The movie is not about plot anyway, but about characters and a way of living. Pursy acts as a catalyst to create moments of truth and revelation, and those in turn help Bobby find a limited kind of peace with his past, and Lawson to find a tentative hope in his own possible future.

What can be said is that the three actors inhabit this material with ease and gratitude: It is good to act on a simmer sometimes, instead of at a fast boil. It's unusual to find an American movie that takes its time. It's remarkable to listen to dialogue that assumes the audience is well read. It is refreshing to hear literate conversation.

These are modest pleasures, but real enough. The movie tries for tragedy and reaches only pathos, but then Bobby lost his chance to be a tragic hero by living this long in the first place. Travolta has an innate likability quotient that works with characters like this;

411

you can sense why a student would follow him to New Orleans and join him in foggy melancholy. There doesn't have to be a scene explaining that. You can also sense how Pursy would change things, just by acting as a witness. Alcoholics get uncomfortable when they're surrounded by people with insights. They like to control the times and conditions of their performances, and don't want an audience to wander backstage. Just by seeing them, Pursy forces them to see themselves. Once they do that, something has to give.

Love the Hard Way ★ ★ ★
NO MPAA RATING, 104 m., 2003

Adrien Brody (Jack), Charlotte Ayanna (Claire), Jon Seda (Charlie), August Diehl (Jeff), Pam Grier (Linda Fox). Directed by Peter Sehr and produced by Wolfram Tichy. Screenplay by Marie Noelle and Sehr.

The Pianist was not only a fine movie but also served the purpose of bringing Adrien Brody into focus for moviegoers who might otherwise have missed this lean, smart, tricky actor. Odd, that his Oscar-winning role displayed him as passive and quiet, when Brody fits more comfortably into roles like Jack in *Love the Hard Way*—a street hustler and con artist, playing the angles, getting into danger "to feel the juice." He teams up with his partner, Charlie (Jon Seda), and a couple of young actresses to play a risky game of street theater: The actresses pretend to be hookers, and then Jack and Charlie, dressed as cops, bust them in hotel rooms—and can be bribed by the johns, of course, to drop the charges.

There is another side to Jack, in this movie made in 2001 but released now on the strength of *The Pianist*. He drops certain names in conversation—Pound, Kerouac, Melville—that lead us to suspect he is not your average street guy, and in the opening scene of the movie we glimpse his secret life. He rents a cubicle in a storage facility, and inside he jams a cramped office where he keeps a journal and works on a novel. He's not exactly a con artist only to get material, however; it's more like one of his personalities is criminal and the other personality is a shy intellectual watching to see what the first guy will do next.

One day he goes to the movies at a Lower Manhattan art theater (I guess this is the shy guy) and meets Claire (Charlotte Ayanna), a Columbia student. He uses the usual pickup lines, which should turn off your average college woman, but Claire is intrigued, and agrees to meet him again, and the better half of him falls in love with all of her.

This story, written by director Peter Sehr and Marie Noelle, is a little like David Mamet's *House of Games*, in which an academic woman falls for the dangerous appeal of a con man. The difference is Mamet's heroine took revenge on the guy who deceived her, and Claire, in a way, wants to be deceived and degraded. When she takes revenge, it is against herself.

One day a con goes wrong. Jack and Charlie are not arrested, but to stay in business they're going to need new bait. "Maybe we should give Claire a try," Charlie muses. "She's not built for it," Jack says, and indeed he tries his best to break up with her, maybe because he senses how dangerous he is to a woman like her.

But Claire will not be rejected, keeps coming back, wants to know the secret of Jack's other life, and eventually turns a trick—after which, in a pitiful and lonely scene, she sits alone with her sadness in a photo booth. Jack did not intend this, tries again to alienate her, and then is repaid in full for his deceptions when Claire drops out of school to become a hooker full-time, as if proving something.

This is the kind of psychological self-punishment we might expect in a French film, not in an American film where plot is usually more important than insight. But *Love the Hard Way* is curious about the twisted characters it has set into motion and follows them through several more twists and turns—perhaps a few more than necessary. The film approaches several possible endings as if flirting with them.

Charlotte Ayanna is very good as Claire—we realize, as the film goes on and the character deepens, how challenging the role really is. Brody brings a kind of slick complexity to his role; he's so conflicted about what he's doing and why that he may be the real target of all his own cons.

It is not unknown for authors to embrace the experiences they want to write about (of Jack's heroes, Melville went to sea, Kerouac went on the road, and Pound journeyed into madness), but we sense that Jack is on the edge of schizophrenia; his criminal persona scares him, despite all his bravado, and he wants to push Claire away to save her. The secret Jack, huddled in the container, writing in his journal, is an attempt to diagnose and understand himself.

Love the Hard Way is not perfect; a vice cop played by Pam Grier is oddly conceived and unlikely in action, and the movie doesn't seem to know how to end. But as character studies of Jack and Claire, it is daring and inventive and worthy of comparison with the films of a French master of criminal psychology like Jean-Pierre Melville. The success of *The Pianist* made Adrien Brody visible, probably won this film a theatrical release, and promises him many more intriguing roles. Surely Brody was born to play Bobby Fischer.

Lucía, Lucía ★ ★ ½
R, 113 m., 2003

Cecilia Roth (Lucía), Carlos Álvarez-Novoa (Félix), Kuno Becker (Adrián), Javier Díaz Dueñas (Inspector Garcia), Margarita Isabel (Lucía's Mom), Max Kerlow (Old Wehner), Mario Iván Martínez (Mr. Wehner), Jose Elias Moreno (Ramon), Héctor Ortega (The Cannibal). Directed by Antonio Serrano and produced by Matthias Ehrenberg, Christian Valdelievre, and Epigmenio Ibarrar. Screenplay by Serrano.

Perhaps because they have grown bored beyond all imagining with the formula plots in most crime stories, a lot of young directors play tricks with the facts. Audiences, who also know the basic plots by heart, think they're seeing another one and are willingly fooled. *Swimming Pool* is an example of the technique when it works; *Lucía, Lucía* illustrates the technique grown a little tiresome.

If the trickery is tiresome, the movie at least has life, especially in the lead performance by Cecilia Roth, from Pedro Almodóvar's *All About My Mother*. She plays a happily married woman who is stunned when her husband disappears at the Mexico City airport, just as they're leaving for a holiday in Brazil. The police seem incompetent to find him, but an elderly neighbor named Félix (Carlos Álvarez-Novoa) volunteers

to help, and so does a handsome kid named Adrián (Kuno Becker) whom they literally run into on the stairs.

There's a ransom call. The husband is being held by a revolutionary group. He tells his wife where she can find millions of pesos in a safe-deposit box. That is only the beginning of the story. And in a way, not even that, because Lucía, who narrates, reveals that she has made things up. She doesn't look like the woman we've been seeing. She doesn't live in the apartment we've been shown. And so on. Her inventions are the stuff of fiction (she writes children's books), but her husband's deceptions are part of a tangled web of political corruption and intrigue that unravels and unravels and unravels and unravels, until we want to get out the knitting needles.

The movie is within the recent tradition of colorful, fast-paced, Mexican films that play with narrative; remember *Amores Perros* and *Y Tu Mama También*. But director Antonio Serrano also wants to really tell a story, and to make a political statement with his depiction of a corrupt political system; in that it resembles *Herod's Law*. The date of the story is a little obscure, but since Félix fought in the Spanish civil war and says he is now seventy, it perhaps takes place in the 1970s or 1980s. That means the ruling party, not named, is the Institutional Revolutionary Party (PRI).

Serrano is a dues-paying member of the New Mexican Cinema, if that is what we should be calling it; his first film, *Sex, Shame and Tears*, was one of Mexico's biggest box-office winners. Fox Searchlight has prudently released this one as *Lucía, Lucía* instead of under its original title, "Daughter of the Cannibal," no doubt figuring that English-speaking audiences would not know the title referred to a political, not a dietetic, cannibal.

This Félix is quite a guy. A lifelong leftist whose résumé includes all the best Latin American revolutionary causes, he's still quick on his feet and fast to draw, if not to fire, a gun. He loves Lucía for her spirit. Adrián, on the other hand, lusts after her, although she protests she is too old for him; if the characters are the same age as the actors playing them, he is twenty-five and she is forty-seven—a young forty-seven, who begins to glow with excitement as the plot thickens and the risks begin to mount. Roth has a wonderful way of keeping the kid at arm's length with her don't-tempt-me smile.

There are some sweet interludes in the film, including one when the three partners take a long road trip through vast canyons to visit an old friend of Félix's. And a nice sequence the first time they try to deliver the ransom. But the ransom refuses to be delivered, and the millions of pesos hang around so long we grow impatient with them, and with the plot twists that revolve around them. The fancy stuff and foolery impedes the story and its emotions. The underlying story was strong enough that maybe a traditional narrative would have been best, after all. Heresy, but there you are.

Luther ★ ★
PG-13, 112 m., 2003

Joseph Fiennes (Martin Luther), Alfred Molina (Johann Tetzel), Jonathan Firth (Girolamo Aleandro), Claire Cox (Katharina von Bora), Peter Ustinov (Frederick), Bruno Ganz (Johann von Staupitz), Uwe Ochsenknecht (Pope Leo XII), Mathieu Carriere (Cardinal Cajetan), Marco Hofschneider (Ulrick). Directed by Eric Till and produced by Brigitte Rochow, Christian P. Stehr, and Alexander Thies. Screenplay by Bart Gavigan and Camille Thomasson, based on the play by John Osborne.

Martin Luther was the moral force of the Reformation, the priest who defied Rome, nailed his 95 theses to the castle door, and essentially founded the Protestant movement. He must have been quite a man. I doubt if he was much like the uncertain, tremulous figure in *Luther*, who confesses, "Most days, I'm so depressed I can't even get out of bed." It is unlikely audiences will attend this film for an objective historical portrait; its primary audience is probably among believers who seek inspiration. What they will find is the Ralph Nader of his time, a scold who has all his facts lined up to prove the Church is unsafe at any speed.

Who was Joseph Fiennes channeling when he chose this muddled tone? Obviously, he was reluctant to give a broad, inspirational performance of the kind you find in deliberately religious films. Jesus comes across in some Christian films as a Rotarian in a robe, a tall, blue-eyed athlete who showers every morning.

I remember defending *The Last Temptation of Christ* against a critic who complained that all of the characters were dirty. At a time when most people owned only one garment and walked everywhere in the desert heat, it's unlikely Jesus looked much like the Anglo hunks on the holy cards.

Martin Luther's world is likewise sanitized, converted into a picturesque movie setting where everyone is a type. The movie follows the movie hat rule: The more corrupt the character, the more absurd his hat. Of course Luther has the monk's shaven tonsure. He's one of those wise guys you find in every class who knows more than the teacher. When one hapless cleric is preaching "There is no salvation outside the church," Luther asks, "What of the Greek Christians?" and the professor is stumped.

The film follows the highlights of Luther's life, from his early days as a law student, through his conversion during a lightning storm, to his days as a bright young Augustinian monk who catches the eye of his admiring superior, Johann von Staupitz (Bruno Ganz). He is sent to Rome, where he's repelled by the open selling of indulgences (Alfred Molina plays a church retailer with slogans like Burma-Shave: "When a coin in the coffer rings, a soul from Purgatory springs"). He's also not inspired by the sight of the proud Pope Leo XII (Uwe Ochsenknecht) galloping off to the hunt, and when he returns to Germany it is with a troubled conscience that eventually leads to his revolt.

One thing the movie leaves obscure is the political climate that made it expedient for powerful German princes to support the rebel monk against their own emperor and the power of Rome. In scenes involving Frederick the Wise (Peter Ustinov), we see him using Luther as a way to define his own power, and we see bloody battles fought between Luther's supporters and forces loyal to the church. But Luther stands aside from these uprisings, is appalled by the violence, and, we suspect, if he had it all to do over again, would think twice.

That's the peculiar thing about Fiennes's performance: He never gives us the sense of a Martin Luther filled with zeal and conviction. Luther seems weak, neurotic, filled with self-doubt, unwilling to embrace the implications of his protest. When he leaves the priesthood and marries the nun Katharina von Bora (Claire Cox), where is the passion that should fill him? Their romance is treated like an obligatory stop on the biographical treadmill, and although I am sure Katharina told Martin many tender things, I doubt one of them was "We'll make joyous music together." This Martin Luther is simply not a joyous music kind of guy.

The most fun comes from the performance of grand old Sir Peter, who treasures his collection of sacred relics but sweeps them all aside after Luther casts doubt on their worth and authenticity (Luther has a funny speech pointing out that many saints left behind more body parts than they started out with). Ustinov here reminded me a little of his great Nero in *Quo Vadis*, collecting his tears in tiny crystal goblets—a big boy, playing with the toys of power.

Another major role is the papal adviser Giro-lamo Aleandro (Jonathan Firth), who correctly sees the threat posed by Luther and demands his excommunication and punishment, but for a political insider, misjudges the climate among the princes of Germany. The movie makes it clear to us, as it should to him, that for the power brokers in Germany, Luther's rebellion has as much secular as spiritual significance: He provides the moral rationale for a break they already desired to make.

I don't know what kind of movie I was expecting *Luther* to be, or what I wanted from it, but I suppose I anticipated that Luther himself would be an inspiring figure, filled with the power of his convictions. What we get is an apologetic outsider with low self-esteem, who reasons himself into a role he has little taste for.

M

The Machinist ★ ★ ★
R, 102 m., 2004

Christian Bale (Trevor Reznik), Jennifer Jason Leigh (Stevie), Aitana Sanchez-Gijon (Marie), John Sharian (Ivan), Michael Ironside (Miller). Directed by Brad Anderson and produced by Julio Fernandez. Screenplay by Scott Kosar.

"If you were any thinner," Stevie tells him, "you wouldn't exist." Trevor Reznik weighs 121 pounds and you wince when you look at him. He is a lonely man, disliked at work, up all night, returning needfully to two women who are kind to him: Stevie, a hooker, and Marie, the waitress at the all-night diner out at the airport. "I haven't slept in a year," he tells Marie.

Christian Bale lost more than sixty pounds to play this role, a fact I share not because you need to know how much weight he lost, but because you need to know that is indeed Christian Bale. He is so gaunt, his face so hollow, he looks nothing like the actor we're familiar with. There are moments when his appearance even distracts from his performance, because we worry about him. Certainly we believe that the character, Trevor, is at the end of his rope, and I was reminded of Anthony Perkins's work in Orson Welles's *The Trial*, another film about a man who finds himself trapped in the vise of the world's madness.

Trevor works as a machinist. There's a guy like him in every union shop, a guy who knows all the rules and works according to them and is a pain in the ass about them. His coworkers think he is strange; maybe he frightens them a little. His boss asks for a urine sample. One day he gets distracted and as a result one of his coworkers loses a hand. The victim, Miller (Michael Ironside), almost seems less upset about the accident than Trevor is. But then Trevor has no reserve, no padding; his nerve endings seem exposed to pain and disappointment.

Stevie (Jennifer Jason Leigh) is a consolation. They have sex, yes, but that's the least of it. She sees his need. Trevor is reading Dostoyevsky's *The Idiot* and perhaps there is a parallel between Stevie and Nastassia, Dostoyevsky's heroine, who is drawn to a self-destructive and dangerous man. Leigh has played a lot of prostitutes in her career, but each one is different because she defines them by how they are needed as well as by what they need.

Marie (Aitana Sanchez-Gijon) is the other side of the coin, a cheerful presence in the middle of the night. "You're lonely," she tells Trevor. "When you work graveyard shift as long as I have, you get to know the type." She wonders why he comes all the way out to the airport just for a cup of coffee and a slice of pie. She wouldn't mind dating him.

Then there is the matter of Ivan (John Sharian), the distracting and disturbing coworker who perhaps contributed to the accident. He lost some fingers in a drill press once, and the docs replaced them with his toes. "I can't shuffle cards like I used to," he says. Nor, apparently, can he punch in on the time clock: The guys at the shop claim he doesn't exist. Is Trevor imagining him? And what is the meaning of the Post-it notes that look like an incomplete version of a Hangman puzzle?

The Machinist has an ending that provides a satisfactory, or at least a believable, explanation for its mysteries and contradictions. But the movie is not about the plot, and while the conclusion explains Trevor's anguish, it doesn't account for it. The director Brad Anderson, working from a screenplay by Scott Kosar, wants to convey a state of mind, and he and Bale do that with disturbing effectiveness. The photography by Xavi Gimenez and Charlie Jiminez is cold slates, blues and grays, the palate of despair. We see Trevor's world so clearly through his eyes that only gradually does it occur to us that every life is seen through a filter.

We get up in the morning in possession of certain assumptions through which all of our experiences must filter. We cannot be rid of those assumptions, although an evolved person can at least try to take them into account. Most people never question their assumptions, and so reality exists for them as they think it does, whether it does or not. Some assumptions are necessary to make life bearable, such as the assumption that we will not die in the next ten minutes. Others may lead us, as they lead Trevor, into a bleak solitude. Near the end of the movie, we understand him when he simply says, "I just want to sleep."

Madagascar ★ ★ ½
PG, 80 m., 2005

With the voices of: Ben Stiller (Alex the Lion), Chris Rock (Marty the Zebra), David Schwimmer (Melman the Giraffe), Jada Pinkett Smith (Gloria the Hippo), Sacha Baron Cohen (Julian), Cedric the Entertainer (Maurice). Directed by Eric Darnell and Tom McGrath and produced by Teresa Cheng and Mireille Soria. Screenplay by Mark Burton and Billy Frolick.

One of the fundamental philosophical questions of our time is why Goofy is a person and Pluto is a dog. From their earliest days when Mickey Mouse was still in black and white, cartoons have created a divide between animals who are animals and animals who are human— or, if not human in the sense that Paris Hilton is human, then at least human in the sense that they speak, sing, have personalities, and are voiced by actors like Ben Stiller, Chris Rock, David Schwimmer, and Jada Pinkett Smith.

Now comes *Madagascar,* an inessential but passably amusing animated comedy that has something very tricky going on. What happens if the human side of a cartoon animal is only, as they say, a veneer of civilization? Consider Alex the Lion. In the Central Park Zoo, he's a star, singing "New York, New York" and looking forward to school field trips because he likes to show off for his audiences.

Alex (voice by Ben Stiller) lives the good life in the zoo, dining on prime steaks every day provided by his keepers. His friends include Marty the Zebra (Chris Rock), Melman the Giraffe (David Schwimmer) and Gloria the Hippo (Jada Pinkett Smith). If Alex likes it in the zoo, Marty has wanderlust. He wants to break out and live free. One night he escapes from the zoo, and his three friends catch up with him just as he's about to board a train for Connecticut, acting on bad advice from the giraffe, who has informed him that is where "the wild" can be found.

The animals are captured, crated up, and shipped off aboard a cargo ship to a wild animal refuge in Africa. On the way, a mutiny by rebellious penguins leads to them being swept off the deck and washed ashore in Madagascar. They're back in the wild, all right, but without survival training. The local population, primarily a colony of lemurs, is ruled by King Julian (Sacha Baron Cohen) and his right-paw man Maurice (Cedric the Entertainer).

Some of the locals think maybe the New Yorkers are obnoxious tourists, even though Alex stages his zoo act, much in the same sense captured prisoners of war entertain the commandant. Then the intriguing problem of the human/animal divide comes into play. Alex misses his daily stacks of sirloin and porterhouse. He is a meat-eater. He eats steak. "Which is you," Marty the Zebra is warned. At one point, driven wild by hunger, Alex even tries to take a bite out of Marty's butt.

This is the kind of chaos that always lingers under the surface of animal cartoons. How would Goofy feel if Pluto wanted to marry one of his daughters? There is a moment at which *Madagascar* seems poised on the brink of anarchy, as the law of the wild breaks down the detente of the zoo, and the animals revert to their underlying natures. Now that could have been interesting, although one imagines children being led weeping from the theater while Alex basks on a zebra-skin rug, employing a toothpick.

The movie is much too safe to follow its paradoxes to their logical conclusions, and that's probably just as well. The problem, though, is that once it gets the characters to the wild it doesn't figure out what to do with them there, and the plot seems to stall. *Madagascar* is funny, especially at the beginning, and good-looking in a retro cartoon way, but in a world where the stakes have been raised by *Finding Nemo, Shrek,* and *The Incredibles,* it's a throwback to a more conventional kind of animated entertainment. It'll be fun for the smaller kids, but there's not much crossover appeal for their parents.

Madame Sata ★ ★
NO MPAA RATING, 105 m., 2003

Lázaro Ramos (Madame Satã/João Francisco), Marcelia Cartaxo (Laurita), Flavio Bauraqui (Taboo), Felipe Marques (Renatinho), Emiliano

Queiroz (Amador), Renata Sorrah (Vítoria dos Anjos), Giovana Barbosa (Firmina), Ricardo Blat (José), Guilherme Piva (Alvaro). Directed by Karim Ainouz and produced by Marc Beauchamps, Isabel Diegues, Vincent Maraval, Mauricio Andrade Ramos, Donald Ranvaud, Juliette Renaud, and Walter Salles. Screenplay by Ainouz.

Madame Sata is a portrait of João Francisco dos Santos, a flamboyant, fiercely proud drag queen with a hair-trigger temper, who became a legend in the clubs and slums and prisons of Brazil. Born about 1900, dead in 1976, he spent nearly thirty of those years in prison, ten of them for murder. "There's something eating me up inside," he tells a friend. Performing his drag act provides a release, but requires a lifestyle that attracts trouble.

The character is never called Madame Sata during the film; we learn from the closing credits that he took the name, inspired by the De Mille film *Madame Satan,* later in life, when he began to win drag contests. The film opens not in victory but defeat: There is a long close-up of the hero, played by Lázaro Ramos, as his police record is read. It's quite a reading.

The movie has the same familiarity with the slums of Rio as the great film *City of God,* but provides less insight into the characters. João Francisco remains a puzzle to the end of the film, a person who fascinates us but doesn't share his secrets. The writer-director, Karim Ainouz, understands the milieu, and Ramos provides an electrifying, sometimes scary, performance, but it is always a performance, just as João is always, in a sense, onstage. Whatever is eating him up remains inside.

Homosexuality was an invitation to violence in the milieu of the film, but João is more than able to defend himself, and indeed makes a point of telling one of his attackers that being a queen makes him no less of a man. His domestic life is a parody of the nuclear family; he lives with a female prostitute named Laurita (Marcelia Cartaxo) and her child, not by him. They share a servant named Taboo (Flavio Bauraqui), who is more effeminate than his two employers put together. At home, João rules with the short temper and iron hand of the stereotypical dominant male, and is in many ways the most masculine character I've

seen in any recent movie—certainly more macho than, say, Ben Affleck in *Gigli.*

The story occupies the dives, cabarets, brothels, and jail cells of the Rio underworld, where João starts as a backstage assistant to an European singer; in an effective early scene, he mimics the onstage performance from his position just offstage, and when a friendly bartender gives him a gig, at first he simply imitates the European woman's act, while cranking up the voltage. He quickly becomes the object of curiosity and lust for the half-hidden but numerous gay population, and has a passionate, violent affair with a lover named Renatinho (Felippe Marques), who is a thief and sees no reason why being João's lover and stealing João's money should not be compatible.

If we never really understand João, there is another problem with the character, and that is: He isn't very nice. I refer not to his crimes, but to the way he treats those who care for him. He clouts the faithful Taboo, insults his admirers, is not imperious so much as just simply hostile. That would not be an objection if the film dealt with it, but the film seems as uneasy about João as we are. He serves as our guide to the world of 1930s sex and crime in Rio, but there comes a point when we want to leave the tour and continue on our own, because this man's demons are not only eating him, but devouring everyone around him.

Madison ★ ★ ★
PG, 94 m., 2005

James Caviezel (Jim McCormick), Jake Lloyd (Mike McCormick), Mary McCormack (Bonnie McCormick), Bruce Dern (Harry Volpi), Brent Briscoe (Tony Steinhart), Paul Dooley (Mayor Vaughn). Directed by William Bindley and produced by William Bindley and Martin Wiley. Screenplay by William Bindley and Scott Bindley.

What is it about Indiana that inspires movies about small-town dreamers who come from behind to win? William Bindley's *Madison,* the story of a town that races its own hydroplane on the Ohio River, joins *Breaking Away* (a bicycle race), *Hoosiers* (high school basketball), and *Rudy* (local boy is too small to play football for Notre Dame, but that doesn't stop him). All four stories are inspired by fact; maybe that has something to do with it. A story about Bobby Knight would of course have to be based on fiction.

As *Madison* opens in 1971, times are hard for the town, which was once the busiest port above New Orleans and one of the richest cities in the state. Factories are closing, people are moving to big cities to find work, and although Madison is the only town to enter its own boat in the Gold Cup, things look grim for this year's race.

The boat is *Miss Madison,* an unlimited hydroplane (I think that means anything goes with engines and speed). The Gold Cup has been held since 1950; local businessman Jim McCormick (James Caviezel) used to pilot the boat, but retired after an injury ten years earlier. Now he is suddenly needed again, by the town and the boat, and comes out of retirement to the pride of his son, Mike (Jake Lloyd), and the concern of his wife, Bonnie (Mary McCormack), who like so many movie wives frets that her spouse is either (a) going to get killed, or (b) not be home for dinner.

Miss Madison's engine has exploded during a time trial and the boat itself is seriously damaged. It looks as if the town will not have an entry in the very year it hosts the famous annual race, but then Mike and his crew go to work. They need a new engine and can't afford one, so under cover of darkness they slip off to a nearby town and steal the engine from an airplane displayed in the courthouse square. Without being a mechanic, I am fairly sure such an engine, if it were indeed still in the plane, would be filled with dead leaves and hornets' nests and would need more than a trip through Jiffy-Lube, but never mind: It purrs right along on race day.

For the town, meanwhile, the race is heaven-sent. It provides a boost for civic morale, keeps a few more citizens from moving away, attracts tourist dollars and television publicity, and gives everyone a chance to sit on the river banks in their lawn chairs with their picnic baskets. Much of this is made possible by Mayor Don Vaughn (Paul Dooley, who played the father in *Breaking Away*). He shifts some city funds, probably illegally, to find the money to back *Miss Madison.*

As sporting events go, hydroplane racing is pretty straightforward. The powerful boats race around a river course, making lots of waves and noise. Some of the boats have commercial sponsors, and one of the unique elements in *Madison* is negative product placement. One of the boats has "Budweiser" written all over it, and much is made about the rich and high-powered brewery team, but they're the bad guys and we want to see Bud lose to *Miss Madison.*

The cast is stalwart. Jim Caviezel, who made this movie in his pre-*Passion* days, is a salt-of-the-earth small-town dad who shares a secret with his son: a hidden cave that's "one of the special things about where we live." Mary McCormack, as wife and mother, is stuck with the obligatory speech, "You have a choice to make—me or the boat." But after she pays her dues with that tired line, she perks up and brings some sunshine into the movie. There is also sadness, which I will not reveal, except to say that driving one of these boats might be a good way to compete for the Darwin Award.

Who else? Oh: Bruce Dern. He's the expert mechanic who can turn around a stolen antique airplane engine in twenty-four hours. I saw him not long ago while revisiting *After Dark, My Sweet* (1993) and was happy to see him again. He has a way of chewing his dialogue as if he wants to savor it first before sharing it with us.

The Magdalene Sisters ★ ★ ★ ½
R, 119 m., 2003

Geraldine McEwan (Sister Bridget), Anne-Marie Duff (Margaret), Nora-Jane Noone (Bernadette), Dorothy Duffy (Rose/Patricia), Eileen Walsh (Crispina), Mary Murray (Una), Britta Smith (Katy), Frances Healy (Sister Jude), Eithne McGuinness (Sister Clementine). Directed by Peter Mullan and produced by Frances Higson. Screenplay by Mullan.

I was an unmarried girl
I'd just turned twenty-seven
When they sent me to the sisters
For the way men looked at me.
— Joni Mitchell, *The Magdalene Laundries*

Here is a movie about barbaric practices against women, who were locked up without trial and sentenced to forced, unpaid labor for such crimes as flirting with boys, becoming pregnant out of wedlock, or being raped. These inhuman punishments did not take place in Afghanistan under the Taliban, but in Ireland under the Sisters of Mercy. And they are not ancient history. The Magdalene Laundries flourished through the 1970s and processed some 30,000 victims; the last were closed in 1996.

The Magdalene Sisters is a harrowing look at institutional cruelty, perpetrated by the Catholic Church in Ireland and justified by a perverted hysteria about sex. "I've never been with any lads ever," one girl says, protesting her sentence, "and that's the god's honest truth." A nun replies: "But you'd like to, wouldn't you?" And because she might want to, because she flirted with boys outside the walls of her orphanage, she gets what could amount to a life sentence at slave labor.

This film has been attacked by the Catholic League, but its facts stand up; a series of *Irish Times* articles on the Internet talks of cash settlements totaling millions of pounds to women who were caught in the Magdalene net. What is inexplicable is that this practice could have existed in our own time, in a western European nation. The laundries were justified because they saved the souls of their inmates—but what about the souls of those who ran them?

Raised in the Catholic Church in America at about the same time, I had nothing but positive experiences. The Dominican sisters who taught us were dedicated, kind, and brilliant teachers, and when I see a film like this I wonder what went wrong in Ireland—or right at St. Mary's Grade School in Champaign-Urbana.

The Magdalene Sisters focuses on the true stories of three girls who fell into the net. As the film opens, we see Margaret (Anne-Marie Duff) lured aside by a relative at a family wedding and raped. When she tells a friend what has happened, the word quickly spreads, and within days it is she, not the rapist, who is punished. Her sentence, like most of the Magdalene sentences, is indefinite, and as she goes to breakfast on her first morning she passes a line of older women who have been held here all their lives.

Two others: Bernadette (Nora-Jane Noone) is the girl who flirted with boys outside her orphanage, and Rose (Dorothy Duffy) is pregnant out of wedlock. She bears her child because abortion would be a sin, only to have it taken

from her by the parish priest, who ships her off to a Magdalene institution.

Other inmates include Crispina (Eileen Walsh), whose crime is that she is mentally handicapped and might fall victim to men if not institutionalized. And there is an older prisoner who acts as a snitch to gain favor with the sisters. The nun in charge of this institution is a figure of pure evil named Sister Bridget (Geraldine McEwan), a sadist with a cruel streak of humor, who in one scene presides as new girls are forced to strip so their bodies and the size of their breasts can be compared. This is not fiction; the screenplay, by director Peter Mullan, is based on testimony by Magdalene inmates. Geraldine McEwan's powerful, scary performance evokes scarcely repressed sadomasochism.

The drama in *The Magdalene Sisters* is not equal to its anger. The film turns, as I suppose it must, into a story of escape attempts. A previously inexperienced girl finds herself making direct carnal offers to a young truck driver, if he will slip her a key to the gate. A priest who violates Crispina is paid back with poison ivy in his laundry. There is an escape attempt at the end that belongs more in an action film than in this protest against injustice.

But the closing credits remind us once again that the Magdalene Laundries existed and did their evil work in God's name. The church in Ireland has changed almost beyond recognition in recent years, and is now, like the American church, making amends for the behavior of some clergy. And the *Irish Times* articles report that some Protestant denominations had (and have) similar punishments for sexuality, real or suspected. The movie is not so much an attack on the Catholic Church as on the universal mind-set that allows transgressions beyond all decency, if they are justified by religious hysteria. Even today there are women walled up in solitary confinement in closed rooms in their own homes in the Middle East, punished for crimes no more serious, or trivial, than those of the Magdalene laundresses.

Malibu's Most Wanted ★ ★ ½
PG-13, 86 m., 2003

Jamie Kennedy (Brad Gluckman), Taye Diggs (Sean), Anthony Anderson (P. J.), Blair

Underwood (Tom Gibbons), Damien Dante Wayans (Tec), Regina Hall (Shondra), Ryan O'Neal (Bill Gluckman), Snoop Dogg (Ronnie Rizat), Bo Derek (Bess Gluckman). Directed by John Whitesell and produced by Fax Bahr, Mike Karz, and Adam Small. Screenplay by Bahr, Nick Swardson, Small, and Jamie Kennedy.

"This is my ghetto—the mall," Brad Gluckman explains at the beginning of *Malibu's Most Wanted*. He's the son of a millionaire who is running for governor of California under the slogan "California is my family," but the candidate has had little time for his own son, who has morphed into a gangsta rapper. Since he's rich and white and lives in Malibu, he's warned against "posing," but explains, "I ams who I say I ams."

Brad is played by Jamie Kennedy, star of the Fox show *JKX: The Jamie Kennedy Experiment*. The movie has a good satirical idea and does some nice things with it, but not enough. Flashes of inspiration illuminate stretches of routine sitcom material; it's the kind of movie where the audience laughs loudly and then falls silent for the next five minutes.

Brad's parents (Ryan O'Neal and Bo Derek) have not been around much to raise him; in a flashback to his childhood, they're seen communicating with him via satellite video from Tokyo and Paris. Although Brad has "never been east of Beverly Hills," he identifies with "his" homies in the inner city and talks about the hardships of his youth, for example when "the public be up on your private beach." He and his mall-rat friends like to pose as gangstas, but one ferocious and intimidating visit to a convenience store turns out to be about getting parking validation, and picking up some aromatherapy candles.

Brad's image is awkward for his father, especially when the kid unfurls a new political slogan on live TV: "Bill Gluckman is down with the bitches and hos." Gluckman's black campaign manager (Blair Underwood) advises a desperation move: Have the boy kidnapped by actors posing as gangstas and let them take him on a tour of the hood, so that he'll understand his own act is a fake.

Taye Diggs and Anthony Anderson play Sean and P. J., the two actors hired for the roles. They know exactly nothing about the hood. "I stud-ied at Julliard," Sean explains. "I was at the Pasadena Playhouse," says P. J. Still, the campaign manager's money talks, and they enlist the help of the only hood dweller they know, P. J.'s cousin Shondra (Regina Hall). Before long the kidnappers and their victim are kidnapped by real gangstas, led by Tec (Damien Dante Wayans), and there's a gun battle that's supposed to be funny because Brad thinks it's all an act and the bullets aren't real.

The movie has one comic insight: The gangsta lifestyle is not authentic to any place or race, but is a media-driven behavioral fantasy. Why should it be surprising that Eminem is the most successful rapper in America when most rap music is purchased by white suburban teenagers? Many of those who actually live in the ghetto have seen too much violence first-hand to be amused by gangsta rap.

Jamie Kennedy is a success on TV, where this same character, nicknamed B-Rad, originated. He's fresh and aggressive, a natural clown, and has a lot of funny lines, as when he's asked where he learned to handle an automatic rifle and he replies, "Grand Theft Auto 3." This inspires a detailed conversation with a real gangster about competing game platforms.

The elements here might have added up to a movie with real bite, but *Malibu's Most Wanted* plays it safe. It doesn't help that Eminem's *8 Mile* provided a recent and convincing treatment of what it might be like for a white rapper in the inner city. The subject is touchy, of course—race often is—but the solution might have been to push harder, not to fall back on reliable formulas.

Mambo Italiano ★ ★
R, 99 m., 2003

Luke Kirby (Angelo Barberini), Ginette Reno (Maria Barberini), Paul Sorvino (Gino Barberini), Claudia Ferri (Anna Barberini), Peter Miller (Nino Paventi), Sophie Lorain (Pina Lunetti), Mary Walsh (Lina Paventi), Tara Nicodemo (Aunt Yolanda). Directed by Émile Gaudreault and produced by Daniel Louis and Denise Robert. Screenplay by Gaudreault, based on a play by Steve Galluccio.

In *Mambo Italiano*, which we can refer to for convenience as *My Big Fat Gay Wedding*, the hero's Italian-Canadian parents grade sex for their son as follows: (1) No sex at all is best—just stay here at home with us; (2) if you must have sex, have it with a nice Italian girl; (3) if you get engaged to a non-Italian we'll kill you; but (4) if you become a homosexual we will first die of mortification and *then* kill you, and (5) no points for having gay sex with an Italian boy, because no Italian boy has ever been gay except for you, and you're not really gay anyway, you just haven't met the right girl, and look, here she is.

The movie takes place in a colorfully romanticized version of the Petite Italie neighborhood in Montreal, where the neighbors line up beside their garden allotments like the chorus members in an opera, and anyone is likely to break into song. Of their Italian accents, let it be said that none clash with Dean Martin's version of the title song. And, of course, there is one family member who pretends she knows nothing about homosexuality just so she can drop big clanging questions in the middle of tense family situations.

The movie stars Luke Kirby, looking here like a skinny John Belushi, as Angelo Barberini, teased since his childhood for being a sissy. Now he is grown and still living at home, which is fine with his parents, Maria (Ginette Reno) and Gino (Paul Sorvino). They nod approvingly at a neighbor's porch, where an elderly mother is still whacking her middle-aged son alongside the head. Angelo is growing increasingly desperate, and finally moves out, breaking the hearts of his parents, which are easily and frequently broken.

Love arrives unexpectedly. Nino Paventi (Peter Miller), one of the kids who picked on Angelo in school, has grown up to be a cop and a closeted gay man. They move in together, each one trying to keep his sexuality a secret, and then their families start churning, as families will, with matchmaking and awkward questions. Angelo has an ally in his sister Anna (Claudia Ferri), who is also quietly growing mad under the thumb of their parents. If they're told Angelo is gay, she says, "This is going to kill them." She pauses, and adds: "Tell them."

Meanwhile, there's a concerted push by Nino's parents to fix him up with an eligible woman, Pina Lunetti (Sophie Lorain). The plot unfolds in basic sitcom style, with surprise rev-

elations, sudden reversals, and very, very broad characterizations (Sorvino, an amateur opera singer, doesn't distinguish himself with underacting). There are laughs in the movie, and a lot of good feeling, but it seems more interested in its Italian stereotypes than its gay insights, and it must be said there is absolutely no feeling that Angelo and Nino are really lovers. I don't know anything about the personal sexuality of these actors, but let it be said that in this movie they're straight.

Note: For a better movie dealing with homosexuality and ethnic stereotypes, there's What's Cooking? *with its fraught yet hilarious scenes involving Kyra Sedgwick, her lover, Julianna Margulies, and her parents, Lainie Kazan and Maury Chaykin.*

A Man Apart ★ ★
R, 114 m., 2003

Vin Diesel (Sean Vetter), Larenz Tate (Demetrius Hicks), Timothy Olyphant (Hollywood Jack Slayton), Geno Silva ("Memo" Lucero), George Sharperson (Big Sexy), Jacqueline Obradors (Stacy Vetter), Mateo Santos (Juan Fernandez). Directed by F. Gary Gray and produced by Robert John Degus, Vincent Newman, Joey Nittolo, and Tucker Tooley. Screenplay by Christian Gudegast and Paul Scheuring.

A Man Apart sets chunks of nonsense floating down a river of action. The elements are all here—the growling macho dialogue, the gunplay, the drugs, the cops, the revenge—but what do they add up to? Some sequences make no sense at all, except as kinetic energy.

The movie stars Vin Diesel and Larenz Tate as drug cops named Vetter and Hicks. They're partners in the DEA, attempting to slam shut the Colombia-Mexico-California cocaine corridor. When they capture a cartel kingpin named Memo Lucero (Geno Silva), the cartel has its revenge by attacking Vetter's home and killing his beloved wife, Stacy (Jacqueline Obradors).

I have not given anything away by revealing her death; the movie's trailer shows her dying. Besides, she has to die. That's why she's in the movie. My colleague Richard Roeper has a new book named *Ten Sure Signs a Movie Character*

Is Doomed. One of the surest signs is when a wife or girlfriend appears in a cop-buddy action picture, in gentle scenes showing them dining by candlelight, backlit by the sunset on the beach, dancing in the dawn, etc. Action movies are not about dialogue or relationships, and women characters are a major dialogue and relationship hazard. The function of the woman is therefore inevitably to die, inspiring revenge. This time, as they say, it's personal.

Vin Diesel inhabits *A Man Apart* easily, and continues to establish himself as a big action star. Tate gets good mileage from the thankless sidekick role. Geno Silva, as the drug kingpin, gives us glimpses of a character who was probably more fully developed in the earlier drafts: There is very little of Memo, but what there is suggests much more.

The plot is routine. Cops capture kingpin. Kingpin is replaced by shadowy successor named El Diablo. Successor sends hit men to shoot at Vetter and wife. Vetter loses his cool during a drug bust when a guy disses dead wife. As a result, three cops are killed. The chief takes away Vetter's badge. Then the rogue ex-cop goes on a personal mission of revenge against El Diablo, with ex-partner obligingly helping. We have seen this plot before. But Vin Diesel has an undeniable screen charisma. And the movie is good-looking, thanks to cinematographer Jack N. Green, who gives scenes a texture the writing lacks. So everything is in place, and then we find ourselves confused about the basic purpose of whole sequences.

Example. Early in the movie, the DEA raids a club where Memo is partying. "You expect us to go into a building full of drunken cartel gunmen unarmed?" asks Vetter, who conceals a gun. So does everyone else, I guess, since the subsequent gun battle is loud and long and includes automatic weapons. While I was trying to find the logic of the "unarmed" comment, Memo flees from the club through an underground tunnel and emerges on the street to grab a getaway cab.

Okay. Later in the film, Vetter and Hicks return to the same club, enter through the getaway hatch, wade through waist-high water in the tunnels, emerge in the original room, and find a man sitting all by himself, who they think is El Diablo. "You think . . . I am El Diablo?" the man asks, all but cackling. As an action sequence unfolds and the guys retrace their steps through the flooded tunnel, etc., I'm asking what the purpose of this scene was. To provide mindless action, obviously. But was it also a strategy to use the same set twice, as an economy move?

The closing scene is even more illogical. I will give away no details except to say that, from the moment you see Vetter in the funny sun hat, smoking the cigarette and walking in the dusty village street, the entire scene depends on backward choreography: The omnipotent filmmakers know what is going to happen at the end of the scene and rewind it to the beginning. (Even so, the specific logistics of the payoff shot are muddled.)

Faithful readers will know I am often willing to forgive enormous gaps of logic in a movie that otherwise amuses me. But here the Vin Diesel character often seems involved in actions that are entirely without logical purpose. The movie's director is F. Gary Gray, whose *Set It Off* (1996) and *The Negotiator* (1998) were notable for strong characters and stories. This time the screenplay tries to paper over too many story elements that needed a lot more thought. This movie has been filmed and released, but it has not been finished.

The Manchurian Candidate ★ ★ ★
R, 130 m., 2004

Denzel Washington (Ben Marco), Meryl Streep (Eleanor Shaw), Liev Schreiber (Raymond Shaw), Jon Voight (Senator Thomas Jordan), Kimberly Elise (Rosie), Jeffrey Wright (Al Melvin), Ted Levine (Colonel Howard), Bruno Ganz (Richard Delp), Simon McBurney (Dr. Atticus Noyle), Vera Farmiga (Jocelyn Jordan), Robyn Hitchcock (Laurent Toker). Directed by Jonathan Demme and produced by Scott Rudin, Tina Sinatra, Ilona Herzberg, and Demme. Screenplay by Daniel Pyne and Dean Georgaris.

Corporations, not commies, are the sinister force behind Jonathan Demme's *The Manchurian Candidate,* in which poor Raymond Shaw is told by a liberal senator: "You are about to become the first privately owned and operated vice president of the United States." There's a level of cynicism here that is scarier than the Red Chinese villains in John Frankenheimer's 1962 classic. It's a stretch to imagine a Communist takeover of America, but the idea that corporations may be subverting the democratic process is plausible in the age of Enron.

Demme is not shy about suggesting parallels with current politics, and he borrows a neat bit of indirection from Frankenheimer: In the 1962 version, Communists posed as anti-Communists to drum up hysteria that could be used to subvert American freedoms. In the new version, right-wingers pose as liberals to win office while neutering the left. Meryl Streep plays Senator Eleanor Shaw, who has sold her soul to the Manchurian Global corporation. A stage mother from hell, she pushes her son, Raymond (Liev Schreiber), into the vice presidency; a timely assassination will make him president. Raymond has a chip implanted in his skull that will allow Manchurian to control him.

This plan is on track and will succeed unless two men can make sense of their nightmares. Ben Marco (Denzel Washington) and Al Melvin (Jeffrey Wright) both fought in the Kuwait War as members of a patrol that was saved by the heroism of Sergeant Shaw—whose Medal of Honor launched his political career. But did Shaw really save them? Marco and Melvin have fragmented nightmares of an alternate reality. Marco notes that all the patrol members use identical words to describe their experience. "I remember that it happened," Shaw confesses to Marco, "but I don't remember it happening."

Audiences of the earlier film will know that during the patrol's missing days, as Marco eventually concludes, "Somebody got into our minds with chain saws." The brainwashing is front-loaded in Demme's version; it's revealed fairly early, perhaps because he and his writers concluded there was no use being coy about a secret that most of the audience already knows. Instead, Demme wisely conceals other secrets, leading to a wickedly different ending just when you think you know everything that will happen.

Washington plays Marco as a man with the public face of a decorated officer and the private tortures of a haunted man. After he discovers a chip under the skin of his shoulder,

he desperately tries to get to Shaw to talk about their experience. At one point Marco actually leaps upon the vice presidential candidate, rips off his shirt, and tries to bite a chip out from under his skin. The Secret Service comes to the rescue, but Shaw declines to press charges, leaving us to wonder how the news organizations cover the remarkable spectacle of a decorated veteran biting a heroic candidate. Somehow, it should be a bigger story.

Schreiber, as Shaw, has the role played by Laurence Harvey in the original, and Washington follows Frank Sinatra. Meryl Streep has the assignment of playing the alarming and incestuous Mrs. Shaw, a role for which Angela Lansbury won an Oscar nomination, while essentially stealing the movie. Streep wisely goes for oblique humor rather than straight-ahead villainy, making the character different and yet just as loathsome. Gossips have whispered for months that her performance is modeled on Senator Hillary Clinton, but I dunno; Streep has mentioned Peggy Noonan, Condi Rice, and Dick Cheney.

Making parallels like that is risky. Demme's movie has all sorts of characters on the screen who tempt us to name their real-life counterparts, but he doesn't do simplistic one-to-one parallels; instead, he allows sly contemporary references to enter the film through many characters, as when one candidate calls for "compassionate vigilance." Another bold line, by Mrs. Shaw: "The assassin always dies, baby. It's necessary for the national healing."

Frank Rich writes in the *New York Times* that the movie is "more partisan" than *Fahrenheit 9/11*, but that requires a simpler and more translatable plot than the one I saw. Demme sticks his knife in everywhere, suggesting that the whole system and both parties have been compromised by the power of corporations. (For truly uninhibited parallelism in interpreting the movie, read Paul Krugman's *NYT* column "The Arabian Candidate."

Every time I watch the original *Manchurian Candidate*, I'm teased by the possibility that there may be another, deeper, level of conspiracy, one we're intended to sense without quite understanding. It involves the character of the woman named Rose or Rosie, whom Marco meets on a train; she was played in 1962 by Janet Leigh and this time by Kimberly Elise. These characters materialize out of nowhere, fall instantly in love with Marco, and say inexplicable things. To accept them as simply a romantic opportunity is too easy; why would a woman fall for a complete stranger who (in the Sinatra version) is shaking so badly he can't light his cigarette and (in the Washington version) biting vice-presidential candidates? She's up to something.

To compare Demme's version with Frankenheimer's is sort of irrelevant. That was then and this is now. Frank Sinatra and Denzel Washington are both complete and self-contained and cannot be meaningfully compared. What we can say is that Demme has taken a story we thought we knew and, while making its outlines mostly recognizable, rotated it into another dimension of conspiracy. Are corporations really a threat to America's security? The rotten ones are. When you consider that the phony California electric crisis, with its great cost in lives and fortune, was an act of corporate terrorism, he has a point.

Manic ★ ★
R, 100 m., 2003

Don Cheadle (David), Joseph Gordon-Levitt (Lyle), Michael Bacall (Chad), Zooey Deschanel (Tracey), Cody Lightning (Kenny), Elden Henson (Michael), Sara Rivas (Sara). Directed by Jordan Melamed and produced by Trudi Callon and Kirk Hassig. Screenplay by Michael Bacall and Blayne Weaver.

I haven't seen Manic before, but it feels like I have. The opening scenes place us in a familiar setting and more or less reveal what we can expect. In an institution for troubled teenagers, an encounter group is overseen by a therapist who tries his best to steer his clients toward healing. But the unruly young egos have wills of their own, and there will be crisis and tragedy before the eventual closure.

The plot is a serviceable device to introduce characters who need have no relationship to one another, and to guarantee conflict and drama. We are all indoctrinated in the wisdom of psychobabble, and know that by the end of

the film some of the characters will have learned to deal with the anger, others will have stopped playing old tapes, and with any luck at all there will even be a romance.

The screenplay by Michael Bacall and Blayne Weaver finds no new approaches to the material, but it does a skillful job of assembling the characters and watching them struggle for position within the group dynamic. Don Cheadle, who plays the counselor, has a thankless task, since the heroes and heroines will all eventually heal themselves, but Cheadle is a fine actor and finds calm and power in the way he tries to reason with them: "You don't think you chose the actions that caused you to be in this room with me?"

Joseph Gordon-Levitt, from Third Rock from the Sun, shows the dark side of his funny TV personality, as Lyle, a newcomer to the group, who was institutionalized for outbursts of angry violence in school, one leading to the serious injury of a classmate. His challenge now is to somehow learn to control his rage despite the provocations of the aggressive fellow inmate Michael (Elden Henson), who learns how to push his buttons. He shows promise as a serious actor.

With admirable economy, the screenplay provides Lyle not only with an antagonist, but also with a close friend, his Native American roommate, Kenny (Cody Lightning), and a romance (with Tracey, played by Zooey Deschanel). In stories of this sort, a minority group member who is the best friend of the hero has a disquieting way of dying when the movie requires a setback. Just as the romance must seem to have ended just before it finds a new beginning.

If the movie is not original, at least it's a showcase for the actors and writers. It does not speak as well, alas, for director Jordan Melamed and his cinematographer, Nick Hay. The movie was shot on video, which is an appropriate choice, giving the story an immediate, pseudo-documentary quality, but Melamed and Hay made an unfortunate decision to use the handheld style that specializes in gratuitous camera movement, just to remind us it's all happening right now. There are swish-pans from one character to another, an aggressive POV style, and so much camera movement that we're forced to the conclusion that it's a deliberate choice. A little subtle handheld movement creates a feeling of actuality; too much is an affectation.

There are moments of truth and close observation in *Manic*, and a scene where the Cheadle character does what we're always waiting for a long-suffering group leader to do, and completely loses it. Deschanel and Gordon-Levitt succeed in keeping their problems in the foreground of their romance, so those scenes don't simply descend into courtship. But at the end of *Manic* I'd seen nothing really new, and the camera style made me work hard to see it at all.

Manito ★ ★ ★ ½
NO MPAA RATING, 77 m., 2003

Franky G. (Junior Moreno), Leo Minaya (Manny Moreno), Manuel Cabral (Oscar Moreno), Julissa Lopez (Miriam), Jessica Morales (Marisol), Héctor González (Abuelo). Directed by Eric Eason and produced by Allen Bain and Jesse Scolaro. Screenplay by Eason.

Manito sees an everyday tragedy with sadness and tenderness, and doesn't force it into the shape of a plot. At the end, the screen goes dark in the same way a short story might end; there isn't one of those final acts where we learn the meaning of it all. Sometimes in life, bad things happen, and they just happen. There's nothing you could have done, and no way to fix them, and you are never going to get over the pain.

The movie, a heartfelt debut by writer-director Eric Eason, takes place in Washington Heights, a Latino neighborhood of New York City, where we meet the Moreno family. Junior (Franky G.) runs a plastering and painting crew, and his kid brother, Manny (Leo Minaya), is an honor student who is graduating today from high school, and headed to Syracuse on a scholarship.

In an unforced, natural way, we meet the characters. Junior spent time in prison, and is determined to stay straight. Manny, known as Manito, is not tough like his brother. Junior is a ladies' man; there's a well-observed scene with his wife, Miriam (Julissa Lopez), who won't even listen to his excuses when he sends her home without him. Manito is more shy, but gets up the nerve to ask Marisol (Jessica Morales), his classmate, to the graduation party in his honor.

This party is a big deal. The family is proud of Manito and his scholarship, and has rented a hall and hired a band—paid for by Junior, and also by Abuelo (Héctor González), who in a scene of sly comedy visits a local bordello and brings out his line of trashy lingerie. Humor pops up unexpectedly, as when Junior needs to hire day laborers and discovers that all of the prospects are wearing white shirts and ties. Why? A restaurant closed, and they lost their jobs.

There is a man on the fringes of the story, seen drinking alone, and that is Oscar (Manuel Cabral), the father. We learn later that he was responsible for Junior going to jail; he let his son take the rap for him. Now he wants to send one of those six-foot sub sandwiches to the party, but Junior furiously takes it right back.

Will this man, drinking heavily, do something violent to spoil the big day? It's a possibility. But the movie isn't about overplotted angst between family members. It's about how the city is a dangerous place to live, and has people in it who are not nice, and how it can break your heart and change your destiny in the blink of an eye. One thing leads to another and the result is tragedy. But *Manito* pushes further, to what happens then, and can never be fixed, and helps nothing, and leads to a place where all you can do is sob helplessly.

The film has been compared to *Mean Streets*, and has the same driving energy as the 1973 picture. But some of Scorsese's characters wanted to be criminals—you could see that again in *GoodFellas*. The Morales family has had all the crime it wants, thanks to the father, and wants only to pay the bills, have a party, and see Manito succeed.

Where do the actors come from, who can walk into their first picture and act with such effortless effect? Franky G. has had three roles since he finished *Manito*, in big pictures like *The Italian Job*, and we'll hear more of him. Leo Minaya and Jessica Morales have not worked before or since, but what freshness and truth they bring to their performances.

The film's flaw, not a crucial one, is in the handheld camera style. There are times when the camera is too close for comfort, too jerky, too involved. Just because you can hold a digital camera in your hand doesn't mean you have to; the danger is that a shot will not be about what is seen, but about the act of seeing it. *Manito* settles down a little after the opening scenes, too absorbed in its story to insist on its style.

Man on Fire ★ ★ ½
R, 146 m., 2004

Denzel Washington (Creasy), Dakota Fanning (Pita), Marc Anthony (Samuel), Radha Mitchell (Lisa), Christopher Walken (Rayburn), Giancarlo Giannini (Manzano), Rachel Ticotin (Mariana), Jesus Ochoa (Fuentes), Mickey Rourke (Jordan). Directed by Tony Scott and produced by Lucas Foster, Arnon Milchan, and Scott. Screenplay by Brian Helgeland, based on a novel by A. J. Quinnell.

Tony Scott's *Man on Fire* employs superb craftsmanship and a powerful Denzel Washington performance in an attempt to elevate genre material above its natural level, but it fails. The underlying story isn't worth the effort. At first we're seduced by the jagged photography and editing, which reminds us a little of *City of God* and *21 Grams.* We're absorbed by Washington's character, an alcoholic with a past he cannot forgive himself for. And we believe the relationship he slowly develops with the young Mexico City girl he's hired to protect. But then the strong opening levels out into a long series of action scenes, and the double-reverse ending works more like a gimmick than a resolution.

The screenplay is by Brian Helgeland, whose work on *Mystic River* dealt with revenge in deep, painful, personal terms. But this time, action formulas take over. The hero outshoots and outsmarts half the bad guys in Mexico City. He seems to be homeless, yet has frequent changes of wardrobe and weaponry, even producing a shoulder-mounted missile launcher when necessary. And as he plows his way through the labyrinth of those responsible for kidnapping the girl, the body count becomes a little ridiculous, and Washington's character, who seemed very human, begins uncomfortably to resemble an invulnerable superhero. Sure, he gets shot now and again, but can you walk around Mexico City as an accused cop-killer and outgun professional killers indefinitely? When it seems that everyone who could possibly be killed is dead and the movie must surely be over, there's another whole chapter. We count those still alive, and ask ourselves if the Law of Economy of Characters applies: That's the one that says a movie contains no unnecessary characters, and so the otherwise unexplained presence of a star in a seemingly insignificant role will be richly explained by the end.

All of this is true, and yet the movie has real qualities. Denzel Washington creates a believable, sympathetic character here—a character complex enough to deserve more than fancy action scenes. Even the last scene involving his character is a disappointment; there's a moment when one thing and one thing only should happen to him, and it doesn't, and the movie lets him, and us, down gently.

Washington plays Creasy, whose résumé includes antiterrorism. He's fallen on hard times, drinks too much, and travels to Mexico for a reunion with his old military buddy Rayburn (Christopher Walken). "Do you think God will forgive us for what we've done?" Creasy asks Rayburn. "No," says Rayburn. "Me either," says Creasy.

Rayburn has a job for him: acting as a bodyguard for Mexico City industrialist Samuel Ramos (Marc Anthony), his American wife, Lisa (Radha Mitchell), and their daughter, Pita (Dakota Fanning). At the job interview, Creasy is frank about himself: "I drink." Ramos is able to live with this information, but advises Creasy to tell nobody, especially Mrs. Ramos. As we think back over the film, this conversation will take on added importance.

Creasy keeps his distance on the job. Pita wants to be his friend; he explains he was hired as a bodyguard, not a friend. But eventually he bottoms out in his despair, begins to love the little girl, and becomes her swimming coach, Marine-style. These scenes have a real resonance. After she is kidnapped, the movie goes through the standard routine (police called in, telephones tapped, ransom drop arranged), but with additional local color, since off-duty Mexico City police were apparently involved in the snatch, and Creasy feels surrounded by vipers. Rayburn may be the only person he can trust.

At the Ramos home, Samuel negotiates with the kidnappers, gets advice from his family lawyer (Mickey Rourke), and consults with the head of the Anti-Kidnap Squad, who is a busy man if the movie is correct in its claim that someone is kidnapped in Mexico every ninety minutes. Creasy, meanwhile, depends on a plucky journalist named Mariana (Rachel Ticotin), and she depends on an ex-Interpol expert named Manzano (Giancarlo Giannini). As the net and the cast widen, we begin to wonder if anyone in Mexico City is not involved in the kidnapping in one way or another, or related to someone who was.

Man on Fire has a production too ambitious for the foundation supplied by the screenplay. It plays as if Scott knows the plot is threadbare and wants to patch it with an excess of style. He might have gotten away with that in a movie of more modest length, but *Man on Fire* clocks in at close to two and a half hours, and needs more depth to justify the length.

Too bad, because the performances deserve more. Denzel Washington projects the bleak despair he's revealed before, and his character arc involves us. Christopher Walken supplies another of his patented little speeches: "Creasy's art is death. He's about to paint his masterpiece." Dakota Fanning *(Uptown Girls)* is a pro at only ten years old, and creates a heart-winning character. Ticotin and Giannini supply what is needed, when it's needed. There are scenes that work with real conviction. The movie has the skill and the texture to approach greatness, but Scott and Helgeland are content with putting a high gloss on formula action.

The Man on the Train ★ ★ ★ ★
R, 90 m., 2003

Jean Rochefort (Manesquier), Johnny Hallyday (Milan), Charlie Nelson (Max), Pascal Parmentier (Sadko), Jean-François Stévenin (Luigi), Isabelle Petit-Jacques (Viviane). Directed by Patrice Leconte and produced by Philippe Carcassonne. Screenplay by Claude Klotz.

Two men meet late in life. One is a retired literature teacher. The other is a bank robber. Both are approaching a rendezvous with destiny. By chance, they spend some time together.

Each begins to wish he could have lived the other's life.

From this simple premise, Patrice Leconte has made one of his most elegant films. It proceeds as if completely by accident and yet foreordained, and the two men—who come from such different worlds—get along well because both have the instinctive reticence and tact of born gentlemen. When the robber asks the teacher if he can borrow a pair of slippers, we get a glimpse of the gulf that separates them: He wants them, not because he needs them, but because, well, he has never worn a pair of slippers.

The teacher is played by Jean Rochefort, seventy-three, tall, slender, courtly. It tells you all you need to know that he was once cast to play Don Quixote. The robber is played by Johnny Hallyday, fifty-nine, a French rock legend, who wears a fringed black leather jacket and travels with three handguns in his valise. This casting would have a divine incongruity for a French audience. In American terms, think of James Stewart and Johnny Cash.

Leconte is a director who makes very specific films, usually with an undertone of comedy, about characters who are one of a kind. His *The Hairdresser's Husband,* which also starred Rochefort, was about a man who loved to watch women cut hair. His *The Girl on the Bridge* was about a sideshow knife-thrower. His *The Widow of Saint Pierre* was about a nineteenth-century community on a French-Canadian fishing island that comes to love a man condemned to death. His *Ridicule* was about an eighteenth-century provincial who has an ecological scheme, and is told that the king favors those who can make him laugh. His *Monsieur Hire* was about a meek little man who spies on a woman, who sees him spying, and boldly challenges him to make his move.

These films have nothing in common except the humor of paradox, and Leconte's love for his characters. He allows them to talk with wit and irony. "Were you a good teacher?" the robber asks the teacher, who replies: "Not one pupil molested in thirty years on the job." "Not bad," the robber says dryly.

I have seen *The Man on the Train* twice, will see it again, cannot find a flaw. The man gets off the train in a drear November in a French provincial town, and falls into conversation with the teacher, who is quietly receptive. The teacher's elegant old house is unlocked ("I lost the key"). The village hotel is closed for the winter. "I know," the teacher says when the man returns. "I'll show you to your room."

Over a period of a few days, they talk, eat together, drink, smoke, gaze at the stars. There is no reason for them to be together, and so they simply accept that they are. There is a coincidence: At 10:00 A.M. on Saturday, the teacher is scheduled for a triple heart bypass, and the man from the train is scheduled to stick up a bank. The teacher offers the man money if he will abandon the plan, but the man cannot, because he has given his word to his confederates.

Early in the film, the teacher goes into the man's room, tries on his leather jacket, and imitates Wyatt Earp in the mirror. A little later, he gets a new haircut, telling the barber he wants a style "halfway between fresh out of jail, and world-class soccer player." One day when the teacher is away, one of his young tutorial pupils appears, and the robber says, "I'll be your teacher today," and leads him through a lesson on Balzac while successfully concealing that he has never read the novel, or perhaps much of anything else.

It is so rare to find a film that is about male friendship, uncomplicated by sex, romance, or any of the other engines that drive a plot. These men become friends, I think, because each recognizes the character of the other. Yes, the bank robber is a criminal, but not a bad man; the teacher tells him, quite sincerely, that he wishes he could help with the holdup. They talk about sex (the teacher points out the 200-year-old oil painting he masturbated before when he was young). They agree "women are not what they once were." The robber observes that, after a point, they're simply not worth the trouble. When the teacher's longtime friend Viviane (Isabelle Petit-Jacques) chatters away during dinner, the robber snaps, "He wants tenderness and sex, not news of your brat."

At the end of the film, the two men do exchange places, in a beautiful and mysterious way. Leconte brings his film to transcendent closure without relying on stale plot devices or the clanking of the plot. He resorts to a kind of poetry. After the film is over, you want to sigh with joy, that in this rude world such civilization is still possible.

The Manson Family ★ ★ ★
NO MPAA RATING, 95, m., 2004

Marcelo Games (Charlie), Marc Pitman (Tex), Leslie Orr (Patty), Maureen Allisse (Sadie), Amy Yates (Leslie), Jim Van Bebber (Bobbi). Directed by Jim Van Bebber and produced by Carl Daft, David Gregory, and Mike King. Screenplay by Van Bebber.

The Manson Family has scenes so foul and heartless they can hardly be believed. Killers stab victims again and again and again, relentlessly, with glee. A throat is cut on camera. A dog is sacrificed. Victims plead piteously for their lives.

The action is recorded in low-tech film and video footage, some of it scratched and faded to look archival. There are passages as amateurish as a home movie. Actors snarl at the camera as if they're doing screen tests for snuff films. Some images (like an opening shot of blood dripping onto white flowers) are groaningly ham-handed. Although Charles Manson is extolled in the film by members of his "family" as a messiah and seer, he says nothing of value and has the charisma of a wino after a night in a Dumpster.

All of this will lead you to conclude that *The Manson Family* is a wretched film, but I am not sure I would agree with you. It filled me with disgust and dismay, but I believe it was intended to, and in that sense was a success. It has an undeniable power and effect, but be sure you understand what you are getting yourself into. This is not a "horror" film or an "underground" film, but an act of transgression so extreme and uncompromised, and yet so amateurish and sloppy, that it exists in a category of one film, this film.

I'm tempted to say you should see it just because you will never see a film like this again, but then I wonder: What need is there to see a film like this at all? Its insight into the Manson Family is that they were usually drugged, had absorbed the half-assed hippie philosophy of the time, and fell into the hands of a persuasive, gravely damaged man who convinced them to gladly murder for him.

I do accept that those who did the actual killing were acting under the influence of Manson. What I cannot find in this film is the slightest clue as to how Manson obtained or exercised such power. He seems like the kind of deranged and smelly lunatic any reasonable person would get away from quickly and permanently. That such figures as Dennis Wilson of the Beach Boys even briefly gave him friendship and shelter makes a persuasive argument against drug abuse.

The Manson Family has been around in several unfinished forms for many years. Its director, Jim Van Bebber, began shooting it in 1988, ran out of funds on various occasions, showed rough cuts at underground venues, and finally found completion money to make this theatrical version. If there is not perfect continuity because the actors grew older during the shooting, you'll never notice it because the filming technique uses such fragmentation, jagged editing, and chronological anarchy that we're rarely sure anyway what shot belongs before or after another shot.

What we absorb from the experience, as if wringing it free from the miasma of its making, is that Manson gathered followers with the lure of drugs and sex orgies, that they lured others, that they found an old and confused man and turned his farm into a commune.

Charlie was addled by dreams that he would become a rock 'n' roll god and found portents, patterns, and messages in rock songs and, for all I know, in his tea leaves. In a way that is far from clear, his disappointment at his lack of progress led to Helter-Skelter, an operation during which innocent people, including the pregnant Sharon Tate, were murdered. His theory was that the Black Panthers would be framed and a race war would result in—what? Charlie taking over? This makes no sense, but did you expect it to?

What Van Bebber does accomplish is to make a film true to its subject. It doesn't bring reason, understanding, analysis, or empathy to Manson; it wants only to evoke him. It is not pro-Manson, simply convinced of the power he had over those people at that time. In a paradoxical way, it exhibits sympathy for his victims by showing their deaths in such horrifying detail. In its technical roughness, its raw blatant crudeness, it finds a style suitable to the material; to the degree that it was more smooth and technically accomplished, to that degree it would distance itself from its subject and purpose.

We come to the question of a star rating. Convention requires me to assign stars to every film. Do I give *The Manson Family* four stars because it does what it does so successfully and uncompromisingly, or do I give it zero stars, for the same reason? I will settle on three, because it is remarkable enough I do not want to dismiss it. That doesn't mean I think you should see it.

The Man Without a Past ★ ★ ★ ½
PG-13, 97 m., 2003

Markku Peltola (Man), Kati Outinen (Irma), Juhani Niemela (Nieminen), Kaija Pakarinen (Kaisa Nieminen), Sakari Kuosmanen (Anttila), Annikki Tahti (Flea Market Manageress), Anneli Sauli (Bar Owner), Elina Salo (Shipyard Clerk). Directed and produced by Aki Kaurismäki. Screenplay by Kaurismäki.

We sense that the parcel the man clutches contains everything he owns, or has managed to hang onto. He gets off the train as if it doesn't much matter what city it is. He settles down on a park bench, falls asleep, and is beaten by muggers to within an inch of his life. He flatlines in the hospital, then suddenly awakens and walks out onto the street with no idea who he is. He finds a community of people who live in shipping containers. There is a kind of landlord, who agrees to rent him one.

"If you don't pay up," the landlord says, "I'll send my savage dog to bite your nose off."

"It only gets in the way," the man says.

"You wouldn't be able to smoke in the shower," the landlord points out.

The dog regards all of this, curious and friendly. He never barks once during the entire film.

Aki Kaurismäki's *The Man Without a Past*, from Finland, was a 2003 Oscar nominee for best foreign film. It follows the adventures of its nameless hero in a series of episodes that are dry, deadpan, and either funny or sad, maybe both. The man has no job, no name, no memory, and yet his face reflects such a hard and sorrowful past that we suspect he has never been happier.

The man (Markku Peltola) gets to know his neighbors. A security guard and his wife help him settle in; their generosity is casual, not dramatic. He goes to the Salvation Army for help, work, anything, and meets an Army officer named Irma (Kati Outinen). I remember her from Kaurismäki's *Drifting Clouds* (1996), where she and her husband both lost their jobs and faced destitution with quiet resolve. She has a face, too; one of those faces that tells us there are sometimes small joys in the midst of the general devastation.

To describe the plot is sort of pointless, because it doesn't unfold so much as just plain happen. Without a name, a plan, or (despite the evidence of his callused hands) even an occupation, the man depends on luck and the kindness of strangers—and the love of the Salvation Army woman, who sees him as a soul only marginally more bereft than herself. The only thing keeping her going is rock 'n' roll.

Eventually, through a happy or perhaps unhappy chance, he is identified and journeys to meet the woman who says she was his wife. "You were my first love," she tells him. "That was beautifully said," he says. "Yes," she says. She tells him a little about the past he has forgotten: "You gambled. You lost all your LPs playing blackjack." The former wife is living with a man now, and the two men step outside because they think they probably ought to fight, but that turns out to be unnecessary.

Kaurismäki is an acquired taste—hard to acquire, because most of his films have never played here. You may have come across *Leningrad Cowboys Go America* (1989), about a group of Finnish rock 'n' rollers who hope to make the big time in this country. His characters tend to plant their feet and deliver their dialogue as if eternal truths are being spoken, and the camera tends to plant itself and regard them without a lot of fancy work. His characters don't smile much; they nod sadly a lot, they smoke and think and expect the worst.

And yet there is a joy in them, a deep humor that's all the richer because it springs from human nature and the absurdity of existence, instead of depending on one-liners and gags. If there is something funny about a container having a landlord with a savage watchdog, we

have to figure that out for ourselves, because the movie is not going to nudge us in the ribs and laugh for us.

At the end of *The Man Without a Past*, I felt a deep but indefinable contentment. I'd seen a comedy that found its humor in the paradoxes of existence, in the way that things may work out strangely, but they do work out. I felt a real affection for the man, and for the Salvation Army officer, and for the former wife who is not too happy to see her onetime husband again, and even for the poor sap who thinks he has to fight to preserve appearances.

Maria Full of Grace ★ ★ ★ ½
R, 101 m., 2004

Catalina Sandino Moreno (Maria), Yenny Paola Vega (Blanca), Giulied Lopez (Lucy), Jhon Alex Toro (Franklin), Patricia Rae (Carla), Orlando Tobon (Don Fernando). Directed by Joshua Marston and produced by Paul S. Mezey. Screenplay by Marston.

Long-stemmed roses must come from somewhere, but I never gave the matter much thought until I saw *Maria Full of Grace*, which opens with Maria working an assembly line in Colombia, preparing the roses for shipment overseas. I guess I thought the florist picked them early every morning, while mockingbirds trilled. Maria is young and pretty and filled with fire, and when she finds she's pregnant she isn't much impressed by the attitude of Juan, her loser boyfriend. She dumps her job and gets a ride to Bogotá with a man who tells her she could make some nice money as a mule—a courier flying to New York with dozens of little Baggies of cocaine in her stomach.

Maria (Catalina Sandino Moreno) is being exploited by the drug business, but she sees it as an opportunity. Her best friend, Blanca (Yenny Paola Vega), comes along, and they get tips from Lucy (Giulied Lopez), who has been a mule before—it's a way to visit her sister in New York.

At Kennedy Airport, the customs officials weren't born yesterday and consider the girls obvious suspects, but Maria can't be X-rayed because she's pregnant. The girls slip through and make contact with two witless drug work-

431

ers whose job is to guard them while the drug packets emerge. But Lucy is feeling ill. A packet has broken in her stomach, and soon she's dead of an overdose. Her body is crudely disposed of by the two workers; her death is nothing more than a cost of doing business.

Maria is a victim of economic pressures, but she doesn't think like a victim. She has spunk and intelligence and can think on her feet. The movie wisely avoids the usual clichés about the drug cartel and instead shows us a fairly shabby importing operation, run by people more slack-jawed than evil. Here is a drug movie with no machine guns and no chases. It focuses on its human story, and in Catalina Sandino Moreno finds a bright-eyed, charismatic actress who engages our sympathy.

The story of the making of the movie is remarkable. It was filmed on an indie budget by Joshua Marston, a first-time American director in his thirties, who found Moreno at an audition, cast mostly unknowns, and used real people in some roles—notably Orlando Tobon, who in life as in the film operates out of a Queens storefront, acting as middleman and counselor to Colombian immigrants in need.

The movie has the freshness and urgency of life actually happening. There's little feeling that a plot is grinding away; instead, Maria takes this world as she finds it and uses common sense to try to survive. She makes one crucial decision that a lesser movie would have overlooked; she goes to find the sister that Lucy came to visit.

I learn from Ella Taylor's article in the *LA Weekly* that one of Marston's favorite directors is Ken Loach, the British poet of working people. Like Loach, Marston has made a film that understands and accepts poverty without feeling the need to romanticize or exaggerate it. Also like Loach, he shows us how evil things happen because of economic systems, not because villains gnash their teeth and hog the screen. Hollywood simplifies the world for moviegoers by pretending evil is generated by individuals, not institutions; kill the bad guy, and the problem is solved.

Maria Full of Grace is an extraordinary experience for many reasons, including, oddly, its willingness to be ordinary. We see everyday life here, plausible motives, convincing deci-

sions, and characters who live at ground level. The movie's suspense is heightened by being generated entirely at the speed of life, by emerging out of what we feel probably would really happen. Consider the way the two drug middlemen are seen as depraved and cruel, but also as completely banal, as bored by their job as Maria was with the roses. Most drug movies are about glamorous stars surrounded by special effects. Meanwhile, in a world almost below the radar, the Marias and Lucys hopefully board their flights with stomachs full of death.

Masculine, Feminine ★ ★ ★
NO MPAA RATING, 103 m., 2005

Jean-Pierre Leaud (Paul), Chantal Goya (Madeleine), Marlene Jobert (Elisabeth), Michel Debord (Robert), Catherine-Isabelle Duport (Catherine-Isabelle). Directed by Jean-Luc Godard and produced by Anatole Dauman. Screenplay by Godard, based on *La Femme de Paul* and *Le Signe* by Guy de Maupassant.

"We went seeking greatness in movies, and were most often disappointed. We waited for a movie like the one we wanted to make, and secretly wanted to live."

That's the line I remember best from Godard's *Masculine, Feminine,* and not the more famous "We are the children of Marx and Coca-Cola." When we found a movie like the one we secretly wanted to live, we did not even seek greatness; greatness could take care of itself. The joke at the center of *Masculine, Feminine* (1966) is that its young French characters were fascinated by America, and its young American audiences were fascinated by them. When the movie came out, we all focused on "Marx and Coca-Cola," but now I see that the operative word is "children."

I was barely older than the characters when I wrote my review of the film. I affected a certain detachment ("the French New Wave is coming full circle and recording what has happened to those influenced by it"). I didn't own up to what I really liked about the movie: the way its young hero moves casually through a world of cafés and bistros and the bedrooms of beautiful young girls, including a pop star who is maddeningly indifferent to him.

I wanted to be Paul, the character played by Jean-Pierre Leaud, or at least be Leaud, and appear in movies by Truffaut and Godard, or at least live in Paris and walk down the same streets. All of the rest—the radical politics, the sex talk, the antiwar graffiti Paul sprayed on the car of the American ambassador—was simply his performance art. By acting in that way, he could meet girls like the pop singer Madeleine (Chantal Goya) and her sexy roommates. If you didn't have the money to live in the world of a girl like that, it was a useful strategy to convince her of the purity of your poverty.

I call them "girls" deliberately, and Leaud's character is a boy. Pauline Kael, who loved the film, was even more heartless in her description, calling them "this new breed between teenagers and people." She is alert to the way they boldly discuss birth control, but don't in fact have the pill or know much about sex. Yes, the French are said to be great sophisticates, but the birth control method promised to Madeleine by Paul is one with many a slip 'twixt the method and the control.

The movie has been restored in a new 35mm print. You can appreciate Godard's vigorous early visual style; long before the Dogma movement, he shoots with natural sound and light, he inserts his characters into real times and places, and he practices his own form of withdrawal by separating the movie into fifteen chapters, each one with a title. There is an extended sequence where Leaud's character "interviews" a beauty contest winner, and the entire conversation is completely understood by both of them to be a pick-up attempt.

In a buried sense, everything Leaud does in the film is single-mindedly designed to get him into bed with girls who are not very interested (or interesting). He says he is a Communist. He supports the workers. He paints slogans. He makes radical political comments. He is at the barricades in the sense that barricades are found in the streets, and when he hangs out in cafés the streets are right outside. In the movie's first shot, we see him trying to flip a cigarette into his mouth in one smooth movement, Belmondo-style, as in Godard's first film, *Breathless*. He never gets it right.

From the way he smokes we suspect that smoking is not the point: Smoking like Belmondo is the point.

The movie was inspired by two short stories by Guy de Maupassant. I have just read one of them, *The Signal*, which is about a married woman who observes a prostitute attracting men with the most subtle of signs. The woman is fascinated, practices in the mirror, discovers she is better than the prostitute at attracting men, and then finds one at her door and doesn't know what to do about him. If you search for this story in *Masculine, Feminine*, you will not find it, despite some talk of prostitution. Then you realize that the signal has been changed but the device is still there: Leaud's character went to the movies, saw Belmondo attracting women, and is trying to master the same art. Like the heroine of de Maupassant's story, he seems caught off guard when he makes a catch.

The actress Chantal Goya was interviewed about her experience on the movie. She remembers the first day: "Jean-Pierre Leaud, whom I didn't know from Adam, or Eve, came over to me and, looking me straight in the eye, asked me point blank, 'Will you marry me?' I told him, 'We'll see later. I'm in a hurry. Bye.' I went home at noon." I'll have to see the film again to be sure, but I have the strangest feeling that moment is in the movie. The appeal of *Masculine, Feminine* may be that it's not a movie like the one they wanted to make and secretly wanted to live, but the movie they did make, and were living.

Masked and Anonymous ½★
PG-13, 107 m., 2003

Jeff Bridges (Tom Friend), Penelope Cruz (Pagan Lace), Bob Dylan (Jack Fate), John Goodman (Uncle Sweetheart), Jessica Lange (Nina Veronica), Luke Wilson (Bob Cupid). Directed by Larry Charles and produced by Nigel Sinclair and Jeff Rosen. Screenplay by Rene Fontaine and Sergei Petrov.

Bob Dylan idolatry is one of the enduring secular religions of our day. Those who worship him are inexhaustible in their fervor, and every enigmatic syllable of the great poet is cherished and analyzed as if somehow he conceals profound truths in his lyrics, and if we could only decrypt them, they would be the solution to— I dunno, maybe everything.

In *Masked and Anonymous,* where he plays a legendary troubadour named (I fear) Jack Fate, a religious fanatic played by Penelope Cruz says: "I love his songs because they are not precise—they are completely open to interpretation." She makes this statement to characters dressed as Gandhi and the pope, but lacks the courtesy to add, "But hey, guys, what do *you* think?"

I have always felt it ungenerous to have the answer but wrap it in enigmas. When Woody Guthrie, the great man's inspiration, sings a song, you know what it is about. Perhaps Dylan's genius was to take simple ideas and make them impenetrable. Since he cannot really sing, there is the assumption that he cannot be performing to entertain us, and that therefore, there must be a deeper purpose. The instructive documentary *The Ballad of Ramblin' Jack* suggests that it was Ramblin' Jack Elliott who was the true follower of Woody, and that after he introduced Dylan to Guthrie he was dropped from the picture as Dylan studiously repackaged the Guthrie genius in 1960s trappings.

That Dylan still exerts a mystical appeal there can be no doubt. When *Masked and Anonymous* premiered at Sundance 2003, there was a standing ovation when Dylan entered the room. People continued to stand during the film, in order to leave, and the auditorium was half-empty when the closing credits played to thoughtful silence. One of the more poignant moments in Sundance history then followed, as director Larry Charles stood on the stage with various cast members, asking for questions and then asking, "Aren't there any questions?"

The movie's cast is a tribute to Dylan's charisma. Here are the credits which, after Dylan, proceed alphabetically: Bob Dylan, Jeff Bridges, Penelope Cruz, John Goodman, Jessica Lange, Luke Wilson. Also Angela Bassett, Steven Bauer, Paul Michael Chan, Bruce Dern, Ed Harris, Val Kilmer, Cheech Marin, Chris Penn, Giovanni Ribisi, Mickey Rourke, Richard Sarafian, Christian Slater, Fred Ward, Robert Wisdom. In a film where salaries must have been laughable, these people must have thought it would be cool to be in a Dylan movie. Some of them exude the aw-shucks gratitude of a visiting singer beckoned onstage at the Grand Ole Opry. Ironically, the credits do not name the one performer in the movie whose performance actually was applauded; that was a young black girl named Tinashe Kachingwe, who sang "The Times They Are a-Changin' " with such sweetness and conviction that she was like a master class.

The plot involves a nation in the throes of postrevolutionary chaos. This is "a ravaged Latin American country" *(Variety)* or perhaps "a sideways allegory about an alternative America" *(Salon).* It was filmed in run-down areas of Los Angeles, nudge, nudge. A venal rock promoter named Uncle Sweetheart (John Goodman) and his brassy partner Nina Veronica (Jessica Lange) decide to spring Jack Fate from prison to give a benefit concert to raise funds for poverty relief (maybe) and Uncle and Nina (certainly). That provides the pretense for Dylan to sing several songs, although the one I liked best, "Dixie," seemed a strange choice for a concert in a republic that, wherever it is, looks in little sympathy with the land of cotton.

The enormous cast wanders bewildered through shapeless scenes. Some seem to be improvising, and Goodman and Jeff Bridges (as a rock journalist) at least have high energy and make a game try. Others look like people who were asked to choose their clothing earlier in the day at the costume department; the happenings of the 1960s come to mind.

Dylan occupies this scenario wearing a couple of costumes borrowed from the Tinhorn Dictator rack. Alarmingly thin, he sprawls in chairs in postures that a merciful cinematographer would have talked him out of. While all about him are acting their heads off, he never speaks more than one sentence at a time, and his remarks uncannily evoke the language and philosophy of Chinese fortune cookies.

Masked and Anonymous is a vanity production beyond all reason. I am not sure, however, that the vanity is Dylan's. I don't have any idea what to think about him. He has so long since disappeared into his persona that there is little received sense of the person there. The vanity belongs perhaps to those who flattered their own by working with him, by assuming (in the face of all they had learned during hard days of honest labor on a multitude of pictures) that his genius would somehow redeem a screenplay that could never have seemed other than what it was—incoherent, raving, juvenile meanderings. If I had been asked to serve as consultant on this picture, my advice would have amounted to three words: more Tinashe Kachingwe.

Master and Commander: The Far Side of the World ★ ★ ★ ★
PG-13, 139 m., 2003

Russell Crowe (Captain Jack Aubrey), Paul Bettany (Dr. Stephen Maturin), Billy Boyd (Barrett Bonden), James D'Arcy (Lieutenant Thom Pullings), Lee Ingleby (Hollom), George Innes (Joe Plaice), Mark Lewis Jones (Mr. Hogg) Chris Larkin (Marine Captain Howard), Richard McCabe (Mr. Higgins), Robert Pugh (Mr. Allen), David Threlfall (Killick), Max Pirkis (Lord Blakeney), Edward Woodall (2nd Lieutenant William Mowett), Ian Mercer (Mr. Hollar), Max Benitz (Peter Calamy). Directed by Peter Weir and produced by Samuel Goldwyn Jr., Duncan Henderson, John Bard Manulis, and Weir. Screenplay by Weir and John Collee, based on the novels by Patrick O'Brian.

Peter Weir's *Master and Commander* is an exuberant sea adventure told with uncommon intelligence; we're reminded of well-crafted classics before the soulless age of computerized action. Based on the beloved novels of Patrick O'Brian, it re-creates the world of the British Navy circa 1805 with such detail and intensity that the sea battles become stages for personality and character. They're not simply swashbuckling—although they're that, too, with brutal and intimate violence.

The film centers on the spirits of two men, Captain Jack Aubrey and ship's surgeon Stephen Maturin. Readers of O'Brian's twenty novels know them as friends and opposites—Aubrey, the realist, the man of action; Maturin, more intellectual and pensive. Each shares some of the other's qualities, and their lifelong debate represents two sides of human nature. There's a moment in *Master and Commander* when Maturin's hopes of collecting rare biological specimens are dashed by Aubrey's determination to chase a French warship, and the tension between them at that moment defines their differences.

Aubrey, captain of HMS *Surprise*, is played by Russell Crowe as a strong but fair leader of men, a brilliant strategist who is also a student, but not a coddler, of his men. He doesn't go by the books; his ability to think outside the envelope saves the *Surprise* at one crucial moment and wins a battle at another. Maturin is played by Paul Bettany, whom you may recall as Crowe's imaginary roommate in *A Beautiful Mind*. He's so cool under pressure that he performs open-skull surgery on the deck of the *Surprise* (plugging the hole with a coin), and directs the removal of a bullet from his own chest by looking in a mirror. But his passion is biology, and he is onboard primarily because the navy will take him to places where there are beetles and birds unknown to science.

The story takes place almost entirely onboard the *Surprise*, a smaller vessel outgunned by its quarry, the French warship *Acheron*. Using an actual ship at sea and sets in the vast tank in Baja California where scenes from *Titanic* were shot, Weir creates a place so palpable we think we could find our own way around. It is a very small ship for such a large ocean, living conditions are grim, some of the men have been shanghaied on board, and one of the junior officers is thirteen years old. For risking their lives, the men are rewarded with an extra tot of grog, and feel well paid. There are scenes at sea, including the rounding of Cape Horn, which are as good or better than any sea journey ever filmed, and the battle scenes are harrowing in their closeness and ferocity; the object is to get close enough in the face of withering cannon fire to board the enemy vessel and hack its crew to death.

There are only two major battle scenes in the movie (unless you count the storms of the Cape as a battle with nature). This is not a movie that depends on body counts for its impact, but on the nature of life on board such a ship. Maturin and Aubrey sometimes relax by playing classical duets, the captain on violin, the doctor on cello, and this is not an affectation but a reflection of their well-rounded backgrounds; their arguments are as likely to involve philosophy as strategy. The reason O'Brian's readers are so faithful (I am one) is because this friendship

435

provides him with a way to voice and consider the unnatural life of a man at sea: By talking with each other, the two men talk to us about the contest between man's need to dominate and his desire to reflect.

There is time to get to know several members of the crew. Chief among them is young Lord Blakeney (Max Pirkis), the teenager who is actually put in command of the deck during one battle. Boys this young were often at sea, learning in action (Aubrey was not much older when he served under Nelson), and both older men try to shape him in their images. With Maturin he shares a passion for biology, and begins a journal filled with sketches of birds and beetles they encounter. Under Aubrey he learns to lead men, to think clearly in battle. Both men reveal their characters in teaching the boy, and that is how we best grow to know them.

There is a sense here of the long months at sea between the dangers, of loneliness and privation on "this little wooden world." One subplot involves an officer who comes to be considered bad luck—a Jonah—by the men. Another involves the accidental shooting of the surgeon. There is a visit to the far Galapagos, where Darwin would glimpse the underlying engines of life on earth. These passages are punctuation between the battles, which depend more on strategy than firepower—as they must, if the *Surprise* is to stand against the dangerous French ship. Aubrey's charge is to prevent the French from controlling the waters off Brazil, and although the two-ship contest in *Master and Commander* is much scaled down from the fleets at battle in O'Brian's original novel, *The Far Side of the World*, that simply brings the skills of individual men more into focus.

Master and Commander is grand and glorious, and touching in its attention to its characters. Like the work of David Lean, it achieves the epic without losing sight of the human, and to see it is to be reminded of the way great action movies can rouse and exhilarate us, can affirm life instead of simply dramatizing its destruction.

Matchstick Men ★ ★ ★ ★
PG-13, 120 m., 2003

Nicolas Cage (Roy), Sam Rockwell (Frank Mercer), Alison Lohman (Angela), Bruce McGill (Frechette), Bruce Altman (Dr. Klein). Directed by Ridley Scott and produced by Sean Bailey, Ted Griffin, Jack Rapke, Scott, and Steve Starkey. Screenplay by Nicholas Griffin and Ted Griffin, based on the book by Eric Garcia.

Ridley Scott's *Matchstick Men* tells three stories, each one intriguing enough to supply a movie. It is: (1) the story of a crisis in the life of a man crippled by neurotic obsessions; (2) the story of two con men who happen onto a big score; and (3) the story of a man who meets the teenage daughter he never knew he had, and finds himself trying to care for her. The hero of all three stories is Roy (Nicolas Cage), who suffers from obsessive-compulsive disorder, agoraphobia, panic attacks, you name it. His con-man partner is Frank (Sam Rockwell). His daughter is Angela (Alison Lohman), and Roy is so fearful that when he decides to contact her, he persuades his shrink to make the phone call.

I wish that you had seen the movie so we could discuss what a sublime job it does of doing full justice to all three of these stories, which add up to more, or perhaps less, than the sum of their parts. The screenplay for *Matchstick Men* is an achievement of Oscar caliber— so absorbing that whenever it cuts away from "the plot," there is another, better plot to cut to. Brothers Ted and Nicholas Griffin adapted it from the novel by Eric Garcia. Cage bought the movie rights before it was published, and no wonder, because the character of Roy is one of the great roles of recent years; he's a nut case, a clever crook, and a father who learns to love, all in one. Cage effortlessly plays these three sides to his character, which by their nature would seem to be in conflict.

As the movie opens, Roy and Frank are playing a sophisticated form of the Pigeon Drop, in which victims are convinced they have a tax refund coming, and are then visited by Frank and Roy themselves, posing as federal agents who want cooperation in catching the tax frauds. Elegant. Frank keeps wondering when Roy will be ready to pull a really big job, but it's all Roy can do to get out of bed in the morning.

An open door can cause a panic attack. He goes into spasms of compulsive behavior, and only the pills prescribed by Dr. Klein (Bruce Altman) seem to hold him together at all. When he spills his pills down the drain and

Klein's office is closed, Cage has a scene in a pharmacy that is the equal of his opening moments in *Leaving Las Vegas* as an illustration of a man desperately trying to get what he needs before he implodes.

Enter the mark: Frechette (Bruce McGill), a man who might want to turn a profit laundering large sums of British money that Roy and Frank happen to have on hand. The way they bait this trap, spring it, and then move Frechette up to a really large sum has the fascination of any good con. The secret, Roy explains, is that he doesn't take people's money: "They give it to me." The victims always think it's their own idea. And since they're breaking the law, who can they complain to?

Meanwhile, Dr. Klein learns more about Roy's early, unhappy marriage, which produced a daughter after Roy left. Would it help to meet this girl, who would now be about fifteen? It might. After Klein makes the first advance, Roy approaches Angela after school, his tics and jerks and twitches all in demo mode. Angela comes for a "trial weekend," stays for a while, and eventually becomes a steadying influence for her father. At first Roy is reluctant to tell her about himself, but when he finally does admit he's not very proud of what he does, that's the first moment in the movie when he seems calm and even relaxed.

Nicolas Cage is accused of showboating, but I prefer to think he swings for the fences. Sometimes he strikes out *(Gone in 60 Seconds)*, but more often he connects (he took enormous risks in *Leaving Las Vegas, Bringing Out the Dead,* and *Adaptation*). He has a kind of raging zeal that possesses his characters; what in another actor would be overacting is, with Cage, a kind of fearsome intensity.

Rockwell, Lohman, McGill, and Altman are all perfectly cast, which is essential, since they must convince us without the movie making any effort to insist. Lohman in particular is effective; I learn to my astonishment that she's twenty-four, but here she plays a fifteen-year-old with all the tentative love and sudden vulnerability that the role requires when your dad is a whacko confidence man.

Because this is a movie about con men and a con game, there are elements I must not reveal. But let's talk about the very last scene—the one that begins "One Year Later." This is a scene that could have gone terribly wrong, spoiled by being too obvious, sentimental, angry, or tricky. Ridley Scott and his players know just how to handle it; they depend on who these characters really are. If you consider what the characters have gone through and mean to one another, then this scene has a kind of transcendence to it. It doesn't trash the story or add one more twist just for fun, but looks with dispassionate honesty at what, after all, people must believe who do this sort of thing for a living.

The Matrix Reloaded ★ ★ ★ ½
R, 138 m., 2003

Keanu Reeves (Neo), Laurence Fishburne (Morpheus), Carrie-Anne Moss (Trinity), Hugo Weaving (Agent Smith), Jada Pinkett Smith (Niobe), Gloria Foster (Oracle), Monica Bellucci (Persephone), Collin Chou (Seraph), Nona Gaye (Zee), Randall Duk Kim (Keymaker), Harry Lennix (Commander Lock), Harold Perrineau (Link), Neil and Adrian Rayment (Twins), Lambert Wilson (Merovingian), Helmut Bakaltis (Architect). Directed by Andy Wachowski and Larry Wachowski and produced by Joel Silver. Screenplay by Wachowski and Wachowski.

Commander Lock: "Not everyone believes what you believe."

Morpheus: "My beliefs do not require that they do."

Characters are always talking like this in *The Matrix Reloaded,* which plays like a collaboration involving a geek, a comic book, and the smartest kid in Philosophy 101. Morpheus in particular unreels extended speeches that remind me of Laurence Olivier's remarks when he won his honorary Oscar—the speech that had Jon Voight going "God!" on TV, but in print turned out to be quasi-Shakespearean doublespeak. The speeches provide, not meaning, but the effect of meaning: It sure sounds like those guys are saying some profound things.

That will not prevent fanboys from analyzing the philosophy of *The Matrix Reloaded* in endless Web postings. Part of the fun is becoming an expert in the deep meaning of shallow pop mythology; there is something refreshingly ironic about becoming an authority on the transient extrusions of mass culture, and Morpheus (Laurence Fishburne) now joins Obi Wan Kenobi as the Plato of our age.

I say this not in disapproval, but in amusement. *The Matrix* (1999), written and directed by the brothers Andy and Larry Wachowski, inspired so much inflamed pseudophilosophy that it's all *The Matrix Reloaded* can do to stay ahead of its followers. It is an immensely skillful sci-fi adventure, combining the usual elements: heroes and villains, special effects and stunts, chases and explosions, romance and oratory. It develops its world with more detail than the first movie was able to afford, gives us our first glimpse of the underground human city of Zion, burrows closer to the heart of the secret of the Matrix, and promotes its hero, Neo, from confused draftee to a Christ figure in training.

As this film opens, we learn that the Machines need human bodies, millions and millions of them, for their ability to generate electricity. In an astonishing sequence, we see countless bodies locked in pods around central cores that extend out of sight above and below. The Matrix is the virtual reality that provides the minds of these sleepers with the illusion that they are active and productive. Questions arise, such as, is there no more efficient way to generate power? And, why give the humans dreams when they would generate just as much energy if comatose? And, why create such a complex virtual world for each and every one of them when they could all be given the same illusion and be none the wiser? Why is each dreamer himself or herself occupying the same body in virtual reality as the one asleep in the pod?

But never mind. We are grateful that 250,000 humans have escaped from the grid of the Matrix and gathered to build Zion, which is "near the Earth's core—where there is more heat." And as the movie opens we are alarmed to learn that the Machines are drilling toward Zion so quickly that they will arrive in thirty-six hours. We may also wonder if Zion and its free citizens really exist, or if the humans only think so, but that leads to a logical loop ending in madness.

Neo (Keanu Reeves) has been required to fly, to master martial arts, and to learn that his faith and belief can make things happen. His fights all take place within virtual reality spaces, while he reclines in a chair and is linked to the cyberworld, but he can really be killed, because if the mind thinks it is dead, "the body is controlled by the mind." All of the fight sequences, therefore, are logically contests not between physical bodies, but between videogame players, and the Neo in the big fight scenes is actually his avatar.

The visionary Morpheus, inspired by the prophecies of the Oracle, instructs Neo—who gained the confidence to leap great distances, to fly, and in *Reloaded* destroys dozens of clones of Agent Smith (Hugo Weaving) in martial combat. That fight scene is made with the wonders of digital effects and the choreography of the Hong Kong action director Yuen Wo Ping, who also did the fights in *Crouching Tiger, Hidden Dragon*. It provides one of the three great set pieces in the movie.

The second comes when Morpheus returns to Zion and addresses the assembled multitude—an audience that looks like a mosh pit crossed with the underground slaves in *Metropolis*. After his speech, the citizens dance in a percussion-driven frenzy, which is intercut with Neo and Trinity (Carrie-Anne Moss) having sex. I think their real bodies are having the sex, although you can never be sure.

The third sensational sequence is a chase involving cars, motorcycles, and trailer trucks, with gloriously choreographed moves including leaps into the air as a truck continues to move underneath. That this scene logically takes place in cyberspace does not diminish its thrilling fourteen-minute fun ride, although we might wonder—when deadly enemies meet in one of these virtual spaces, who programmed it? (I am sure I will get untold thousands of e-mails explaining it all to me.)

I became aware, during the film, that a majority of the major characters were played by African Americans. Neo and Trinity are white, and so is Agent Smith, but consider Morpheus; his superior, Commander Lock (Harry Lennix); the beautiful and deadly Niobe (Jada Pinkett Smith), who once loved Morpheus and now is with Lock, although she explains enigmatically that some things never change; the programmer Link (Harold Perrineau); Link's wife, Zee (Nona Gaye), who has the obligatory scene where she complains he's away from home too much; and the Oracle (the late Gloria Foster, very portentous). From what we can see of the extras, the population of Zion is largely black.

It has become commonplace for science fiction epics to feature one or two African-American stars, but we've come a long way since Billy Dee Williams in *Return of the Jedi*. The Wachowski brothers use so many African Americans, I suspect, not for their box-office appeal, because the Matrix is the star of the movie, and not because they are good actors (which they are), but because to the white teenagers who are the primary audience for this movie, African Americans embody a cool, a cachet, an authenticity. Morpheus is the power center of the movie, and Neo's role is essentially to study under him and absorb his mojo.

The film ends with "To Be Concluded," a reminder that the third film in the trilogy arrives on November 5, 2003. Toward the end there are scenes involving characters who seem pregnant with possibilities for part three. One is the Architect (Helmut Bakaltis), who says he designed the Matrix, and revises everything Neo thinks he knows about it. Is the Architect a human, or an avatar of the Machines? The thing is, you can never know for sure. He seems to hint that when you strip away one level of false virtual reality, you find another level beneath. Maybe everything so far is several levels up?

Stephen Hawking's *A Brief History of Time* tells the story of a cosmologist whose speech is interrupted by a little old lady who informs him that the universe rests on the back of a turtle. "Ah, yes, madame," the scientist replies, "but what does the turtle rest on?" The old lady shoots back: "You can't trick me, young man. It's nothing but turtles, turtles, turtles, all the way down."

The Matrix Revolutions ★ ★ ★
R, 130 m., 2003

Keanu Reeves (Neo), Laurence Fishburne (Morpheus), Carrie-Anne Moss (Trinity), Hugo Weaving (Agent Smith), Jada Pinkett Smith (Niobe), Mary Alice (The Oracle). Directed by Andy Wachowski and Larry Wachowski and produced by Grant Hill and Joel Silver.

Screenplay by Andy Wachowski and Larry Wachowski.

My admiration for *The Matrix Revolutions* is limited only by the awkward fact that I don't much give a damn what happens to any of the characters. If I cared more about Neo, Morpheus, Niobe, and the others, there'd be more fire in my heart. But my regard is more for the technical triumph of the movie, less for the emotions it evokes. Neo is no more intended to have deep psychological realism than Indiana Jones, but the thing is, I *liked* Indy and hoped he got out in one piece—while my concern about Neo has been jerked around by so many layers of whether he's real or not, and whether he's really doing what he seems to be doing, that finally I measure my concern for him not in affection but more like the score in a video game.

Consider, too, the apocalyptic battle scene of the movie, as the vast, mechanical, all-too-symbolic screw of the Machines penetrates the dome of Zion and unleashes the Sentinels, nasty whiplashing octopi. The humans fight back by climbing into fearsome robotic fighting machines, so their muscles control more powerful muscles made of steel and cybernetics. Each of their surrogate arms ends in a mighty machine gun that sprays limitless streams of ammo at the enemy. All well done in a technical way (the computer-generated special effects are awesome), but I'm thinking: (a) The Machines use machines, so shouldn't the humans be fighting back in a more human manner? And then (b) but it's silly of me to think in this way, because neither the humans nor Machines are really there, and what we're seeing are avatars in a computer program. Who wins the battle wins the world, but the world is not what we see; what we see is a projection of the cyber-reality of the Matrix.

Or is it? See, that's where I get confused. Do humans have a separate physical reality and did they really construct Zion, that city buried deep within the Earth, and is it really there, made of molecules and elements? Because if they do and if they did, then why don't the Machines just nuke them? Why all the slithering mechanical octopi? And why, in a society that is unimaginably advanced over our own, do they still use machine guns anyway? So it would seem that the battle is a virtual battle, not a real one, and that impression is reinforced by the way the laws of physics seem to be on hold; as Niobe and Morpheus race to the rescue in their speeding ship, for example, it bounces off the walls and sheds so many vital parts that if it were a real ship it would have crashed.

I am sure my information is flawed. No doubt I will get countless e-mails demonstrating my ignorance in tiresome detail. But the thing is: A movie should not depend on the answers to questions like this for its effect. The first *Matrix* was the best because it really did toy with the conflict between illusion and reality—between the world we think we inhabit and its underlying nature. The problem of *The Matrix Reloaded* and *The Matrix Revolutions* is that they are action pictures that are forced to exist in a world that undercuts the reality of the action.

There is, to be sure, the movie's underlying philosophy, but this grows more underwhelming as the series continues. When Neo finally sits down with the Oracle (Mary Alice) and demands the 411, what he gets is about what you'd pay fifty bucks for from a storefront Tarot reader. When the dust has settled and we all look back on the trilogy from a hype-free zone, we'll realize that the first movie inspired its fans to imagine that astonishing philosophical revelations would be made, and the series hasn't been able to live up to those anticipations. Maybe that would have been impossible. No matter how luridly the barker describes the wonders inside his tent, it's always just another sideshow.

Still, in a basic and undeniable sense, this is a good movie, and fans who have earned their credit hours with the first two will want to see this one and graduate. To the degree that I was able to put aside my questions, forget logic, disregard continuity problems, and immerse myself in the moment, *The Matrix Revolutions* is a terrific action achievement. Andy and Larry Wachowski have concluded their trilogy with all barrels blazing. Their final apocalypse in the bowels of the Earth plays like *Metropolis* on steroids. There are sights here to stir the sense of wonder, and a marriage between live action and special effects that is about as good as these things get in the movies. It's a rich irony that the story is about humans occupying a world

generated by computers, and the movie consists of actors occupying a world also created by computers. Neo may or may not exist in a universe created by computers, but Keanu Reeves certainly does.

Note: The Matrix Reloaded was notable for the number of key characters who were black; this time, what we notice is how many strong women there are. Two women operate a bazooka team, Niobe flies the ship, the women have muscles, they kick ass, and this isn't your grandmother's Second Sex anymore.

May ★ ★ ★★
R, 95 m., 2003

Angela Bettis (May Canady), Jeremy Sisto (Adam Stubbs), Anna Faris (Polly), James Duval (Blank), Nichole Hiltz (Ambrosia), Kevin Gage (Papa), Merle Kennedy (Mama), Chandler Hect (Young May). Directed by Lucky McKee and produced by Marius Balchunas and Scott Sturgeon. Screenplay by McKee.

May is a horror film and something more and deeper, something disturbing and oddly moving. It begins as the story of a strange young woman, it goes for laughs and gets them, it functions as a black comedy, but then it glides past the comedy and slides slowly down into a portrait of madness and sadness. The title performance by Angela Bettis is crucial to the film's success. She plays a twisted character who might easily go over the top into parody, and makes her believable, sympathetic, and terrifying.

The movie will inevitably be compared with *Carrie*, not least because Bettis starred in the 2002 TV version of that story. Like *Carrie*, it is about a woman who has been wounded by society and finds a deadly revenge. But *May* is not a supernatural film. It follows the traditional outlines of a horror or slasher film, up to a point—and then it fearlessly follows its character into full madness. We expect some kind of a U-turn or cop-out, but no; the writer and director, Lucky McKee, never turns back from his story's implacable logic. This is his solo directing debut, and it's kind of amazing. You get the feeling he's the real thing.

Bettis plays May Canady, who as a girl had a "lazy eye" that made her an outcast at school.

After a brief prologue, we meet her in her twenties, as an assistant in a veterinary clinic. She is shy, quirky, askew, but in a curiously sexy way, so that when she meets the good-looking Adam Stubbs (Jeremy Sisto), he is intrigued. "I'm weird," she tells him. "I like weird," he says. "I like weird a lot."

Uh-huh. His idea of weird is attending the revival of a Dario Argento horror film. He shows May his own student film, which begins with a young couple kissing and caressing and then moves on inexorably into mutual cannibalism. May likes it. She snuggles closer to him on the sofa. Afterward, she gives him her review: "I don't think that she could have gotten his whole finger in one bite, though. That part was kind of far-fetched."

Bettis makes May peculiar but fully human. There are scenes here of such close observation, of such control of body language, voice, and behavior, evoking such ferocity and obsession, that we are reminded of Lady Macbeth. It is as hard to be excellent in a horror film as in Shakespeare. Harder, maybe, because the audience isn't expecting it. Sisto's performance as Adam is carefully calibrated to show an intelligent guy who is intrigued, up to a point, and then smart enough to prudently back away. He's not one of those horror movie dumbos who makes stupid mistakes. Notice the look in his eye after he asks her to describe some of the weird stuff that goes on at the animal hospital, and she does, more graphically than he requires.

May's colleague at the clinic is Polly (Anna Faris), a lesbian, always open to new experiences. One day when May cuts herself with a scalpel, Polly is fascinated. Then May unexpectedly cuts her. Polly recoils, screams, considers, and says, "I kind of liked it. Do me again." Like Adam, she is erotically stirred by May's oddness—up to a point. There is an erotic sequence involving May and Polly, not explicit but very evocative, and it's not just a "sex scene," but a way to show that for Polly sex is entertainment and for May it is of fundamental importance.

McKee uses various fetishes in an understated way. May is not a smoker, but she treasures a pack of cigarettes that Adam gave her, and the precious cigarettes are measured out one by one as accomplices to her actions. She has a doll from childhood that gazes from its glass cabinet; in a lesser movie, it would come alive, but in this one it does all the necessary living within May's mind. When May volunteers to work with blind kids, we fear some kind of exploitation, but the scenes are handled to engender suspense, not disrespect.

The movie subtly darkens its tone until, when the horrifying ending arrives, we can see how we got there. There is a final shot that would get laughs in another kind of film, but *May* earns the right to it, and it works, and we understand it.

There are so many bad horror movies. A good one is incredibly hard to make. It has to feel a fundamental sympathy for its monster, as movies as different as *Frankenstein, Carrie,* and *The Silence of the Lambs* did. It has to see that they suffer, too. The crimes of too many horror monsters seem to be for their own entertainment, or ours. In the best horror movies, the crimes are inescapable, and the monsters are driven toward them by the merciless urgency of their natures.

Mayor of the Sunset Strip ★ ★ ★
R, 94 m., 2004

As themselves: Rodney Bingenheimer, David Bowie, Deborah Harry, Courtney Love, Cher, Nancy Sinatra, Mick Jagger. A documentary directed by George Hickenlooper and produced by Chris Carter, Greg Little, and Tommy Perna. Screenplay by Hickenlooper.

Mayor of the Sunset Strip tells the story of Rodney Bingenheimer, a man who loved music and musicians so much that he willed himself from obscurity into a position of power as the most influential hit-maker on the most important rock radio station in Los Angeles, and then faded from view as his moment passed. Now he is like a ghost, haunting the scenes of his former triumphs, clinging to a last gig from midnight to 3 A.M. every Sunday night on the station he once ruled. "They're afraid to fire him," another employee speculates, "because he's the soul of KROQ."

The Rodney Bingenheimer of today seems always to be smiling through a deep sadness. He is a small man who still has the youthful cuteness that must have won him friends in his early days. His hair is still combed in the same tousled, mid-1970s, rock star style, and his T-shirts are the real thing, not retro. He lives now in an inexpensive apartment jammed with records, tapes, discs, and countless autographed photos of his friends the stars. And, yes, they are still his friends; they have not forgotten him, and David Bowie, Cher, Deborah Harry, Courtney Love, Nancy Sinatra, and Mick Jagger all appear in this film and seem genuinely fond of Rodney.

Well they might. He introduced some of them—Bowie in particular—to American radio. He was known for finding new music and playing it first: the Ramones, the Sex Pistols, the Clash, Nirvana. Stations all over the country stole their playlists from Rodney. "Sonny and Cher were kinda like my mom and my dad," he says wistfully at one point. He ran a little club for a while, featuring British glam rock, and the stars remember with a grin that it was so small the "VIP Area" consisted simply of a velvet rope separating a few chairs from the dance floor.

The story of how Bingenheimer entered into this world is apparently true, unlikely as it sounds. As a kid, he was obsessed with stars, devoured the fan magazines, collected autographs. One day when he was a teenager, his mother dropped him off in front of Connie Stevens's house and told him he was on his own. He didn't see his mother for another five or six years. Connie wasn't home.

He migrated to Sunset Strip, but instead of dying there or disappearing into drugs or crime, he simply ingratiated himself. People liked him. He hustled himself into a job as a gofer for Davy Jones of the Monkees (they looked a little alike), and then became a backstage caterer; a survivor of a Doors tour remembers a Toronto concert where Rodney had enormous platters of fresh shrimp backstage. But the Beatles were backstage visitors, and Rodney gave them the shrimp, so there were only a few left for the Doors, who had paid for them. Challenged by the Doors, Rodney shrugged and said, "Well, they're the Beatles."

Wherever Bingenheimer went in the music and club scene, his face was his passport. Robert Plant says, "Rodney got more girls than I did." We hear a little of his radio show from the old days, and what comes across is not a vibrating personality or a great radio voice—it's kind of tentative, really—but an almost painful sincerity. He loves the music he plays, and he introduces it to you like a lover he thinks is right for you.

The road downhill was gradual, apparently. We get glimpses of Rodney today, repairing his mom's old Nova with a pair of pliers, shuffling forlornly through souvenirs of his glory days. He seems very even, calm, sad but resigned, except for one moment the documentary camera is not supposed to witness, when he finds that another deejay, a person he sponsored and gave breaks to, is starting a show of new music—stealing Rodney's gig. He explodes in anger. We're glad he does. He has a lot to feel angry about.

The film was directed by George Hickenlooper, who made the classic doc *Hearts of Darkness* (1991) about the nightmare of Francis Ford Coppola's *Apocalypse Now,* and the wonderful fiction film *The Man from Elysian Fields* (2001). Why did he make this film (apart from the possibility that someone named Hickenlooper might feel an affinity for someone named Bingenheimer)? Hickenlooper has been around fame from an early age. He was twenty-six when he released the doc about the Coppola meltdown. He cast Mick Jagger and James Coburn in *Elysian Fields.* He was aware of Rodney Bingenheimer when the name opened doors. His film evokes what the Japanese call "mono no aware," which refers to the impermanence of life and the bittersweet transience of things. There is a little Rodney Bingenheimer in everyone, but you know what? Most people aren't as lucky as Rodney.

Mean Creek ★ ★ ★
R, 89 m., 2004

Rory Culkin (Sam), Ryan Kelley (Clyde), Scott Mechlowicz (Marty), Trevor Morgan (Rocky), Josh Peck (George), Carly Schroeder (Millie). Directed by Jacob Aaron Estes and produced by Susan Johnson, Rick Rosenthal, and Hagai Shaham. Screenplay by Estes.

Mean Creek opens with a schoolyard bully picking on a smaller kid, develops into a story of revenge, and then deepens into the surprisingly complex story of young teenagers trying to do the right thing. It could have been simpleminded and predictable, but it becomes a rare film about moral choices, about the difficulty of standing up against pressure from your crowd.

Sam (Rory Culkin) is small for his age, bright, articulate. He has become the favorite target of George (Josh Peck), a chubby, spoiled kid whose aggression, we eventually learn, masks a deep loneliness. Certainly George is obnoxious on the surface; I was reminded of specific bullies who operated in the schools of my youth, bullies who never seem to attend our class reunions, although if they did I would cross the room to avoid them. Childhood wounds are not forgiven.

Sam gets pounded by George in a schoolyard fight one day, and that angers his older brother, Rocky (Trevor Morgan). Rocky is a teenager whose triumphs are behind him: He got points for smoking and drinking before anyone else did, was probably sexually active at an early age, was macho and good-looking, was popular within a narrow range, and is now facing his working years without the skills or education to prevail. He's a type familiar from Richard Linklater's *Dazed and Confused,* the recent high school graduate still hanging out with younger kids because those his own age have moved on.

Sam runs with a crowd of close friends, including Marty (Scott Mechlowicz), Clyde (Ryan Kelley), and Millie (Carly Schroeder), who will become his girlfriend when they figure out their half-formed feelings. Marty has problems including a father's suicide and an older brother who picks on him, and of course, the bully George knows how to push his buttons.

George is smart and observant, able to hurt with his words as well as his fists, and it's only in a scene where he's alone at home that we see how desperately he depends on his video toys and the neat stuff in his room as compensation for a deep loneliness. His problem is his big mouth, his habit of using words to wound even when they put him in danger. His out-of-control rant at a crucial moment is a very bad idea.

The other kids hang out as a crowd, and, pushed by Rocky and Marty, decide to pull a practical joke on George. "We need to hurt him without really hurting him," Sam says. They devise a fake birthday party as a way of luring George along on a boat trip, and it is during that trip that their practical joke begins to seem like a bad idea.

Jacob Aaron Estes, who wrote and directed *Mean Creek,* shows in this first film a depth of empathy for his characters, and for the ways the strong-willed ones control the others. It's extraordinary, the small words and events he uses to demonstrate the discovery by the more sensitive kids—Sam and especially Millie—that George isn't a monster after all. They begin to feel sorry for him, and talk quietly among themselves about calling off the practical joke. But Rocky and Marty, who personally have nothing against George, want to go ahead; they're using a crude interpretation of justice to mask their own needs.

The final act of the film is extraordinary. How unusual it is to see kids this age in the movies seriously debating moral rights and wrongs and considering the consequences of their actions. *Mean Creek* makes us realize how many films, not just those about teenagers but particularly the one-dimensional revenge-driven adult dramas, think the defeat of the villain solves everything. Such films have a simplistic, playground morality: The bully is bad, we will destroy him, and our problems will be over. They don't pause to consider the effects of revenge—not on the bully, but on themselves.

Mean Creek joins a small group of films, including *The River's Edge* and *Bully,* that deal accurately and painfully with the consequences of peer-driven behavior. Kids who would not possibly act by themselves form groups that cannot stop themselves. This movie would be an invaluable tool for moral education in schools, for discussions of situational ethics and refusing to go along with the crowd.

But the MPAA in its wisdom has recommended it not be seen by those who would find it most useful and challenging; it has the R rating. At Cannes, where the movie was selected for the Director's Fortnight, Jacob Aaron Estes ruefully said the rating was "because of a scene where the f-word is used about 1,000 times." Let it be said that the f-word has been heard and undoubtedly used by everyone the MPAA is shielding from it, and that the dialogue in that scene and throughout *Mean Creek* is accurate in the way it hears these kids talking.

It is especially accurate, in fact, in showing how the f-word lends power to half-formed and wrong ideas, coloring them with a dangerous aura. Kids who are familiar with the f-word but uncertain about the f-act are likely to feel challenged and insecure when they hear it, suspecting that those who use it must have access to hidden knowledge. All forbidden words work that way, which is how rap music gets some of its power; people who obsessively use that kind of language are covering up for their inability to articulate or even know what they really mean. The kids in *Mean Creek* learn such lessons in a hard and painful way, and will be forever touched by them.

Me and You and Everyone We Know ★ ★ ★ ★
R, 95 m., 2005

John Hawkes (Richard), Miranda July (Christine), Miles Thompson (Peter), Brandon Ratcliff (Robby), Carlie Westerman (Sylvie), Hector Elias (Michael), Brad Henke (Andrew), Natasha Slayton (Heather), Najarra Townsend (Rebecca), Tracy Wright (Nancy). Directed by Miranda July and produced by Gina Kwon. Screenplay by July.

Miranda July's *Me and You and Everyone We Know* is a film that with quiet confidence creates a fragile magic. It's a comedy about falling in love when, for you, love requires someone who speaks your rare emotional language. Yours is a language of whimsy and daring, of playful mind games and bold challenges. Hardly anybody speaks that language, the movie suggests—only me and you and everyone we know, because otherwise we wouldn't bother knowing them.

As a description of a movie, I suppose that sounds maddening. An example. A young woman walks into a department store, and in the shoe department she sees a young man who fascinates her. His hand is bandaged. She approaches him and essentially offers the gift of herself. He is not interested; he's going through a divorce and is afraid of losing his children. She asks him how he hurt his hand. "I was trying to save my life," he says. We've already seen how it happened: He covered his hand with lighter fluid and set it on fire to delight his two sons. He didn't think lighter fluid really burns you when you do that. He was wrong. He was thinking of rubbing alcohol.

Now imagine these two characters, named Christine (Miranda July) and Richard (John Hawkes), as they walk down the street. She suggests that the block they are walking down is their lives. And so now they are halfway down the street and halfway through their lives, and before long they will be at the end. It is impossible to suggest how poetic this scene is; when it's over, you think, that was a perfect scene, and no other scene can ever be like it.

Richard and Christine are at the center of the film, but through Richard's sons we meet other characters. His seven-year-old is named Robby, and is played by Brandon Ratcliff, who read my review from Sundance and wrote me a polite and helpful letter in which he assured me he's as smart as an eleven-year-old. In the movie, he visits an online sex chat room even though he knows nothing about sex. He knows enough about computers to sound like he does, however, by cutting and pasting words, and using open-ended questions. Asked what turns him on, he writes "poop," not because it does, but possibly because it is the only word he can spell that he thinks has something to do with the subject.

His fourteen-year-old brother, Peter (Miles Thompson), is being persecuted by two girls in his class named Heather (Natasha Slayton) and Rebecca (Najarra Townsend). They are intensely interested in oral sex, but unsure about its theory and technique. They decide to practice on Peter. I know this sounds perverse and explicit, and yet the fact is, these scenes play with an innocence and tact that is beyond all explaining. They are about what an embarrassment and curiosity sex is when you're old enough to know it exists but too young to know how it's done and what it's for. They are much intrigued by a neighbor who is a dirty old man in theory but not in practice.

Other characters have other plans for perfect lifetimes. Young Peter, once he shakes off the relentless Heather and Rebecca, is fascinated by Sylvie (Carlie Westerman), a ten-year-old neighbor who does comparison shopping to get the best price on kitchen appliances. Peter catches her ironing some towels. They are going straight into her hope chest, she explains. She is preparing her own dowry. Her future husband, when she grows up and finds him, had better be ready to be good and married.

There is also an art curator (Tracy Wright) who has a strange way of evaluating art, as if she's afraid it may violate rules she's afraid she doesn't know. She has a sexual hunger that proves particularly hard to deal with. She is, however, able to project her longings into the uncomprehending world; the strategy she uses, and the result it brings, is a scene of such inevitability and perfection that we laugh at least partly out of admiration.

Miranda July is a performance artist; this is her first feature film (it won the Special Jury Prize at Sundance, and at Cannes won the Camera d'Or as best first film, and the Critics' Week grand prize). Performance art sometimes deals with the peculiarities of how we express ourselves, with how odd and wonderful it is to be alive. So does this film. As Richard slowly emerges from sadness and understands that Christine values him, and he must value her, for reasons only the two of them will ever understand, the movie holds its breath, waiting to see if their delicate connection will hold.

Me and You and Everyone We Know is a balancing act, as July ventures into areas that are risky and transgressive, but uses a freshness that disarms them, a directness that accepts human nature and likes to watch it at work. The MPAA gave it an R rating "for disturbing sexual content involving children," but the one thing it isn't is disturbing. When the movie was over at Sundance, I let out my breath and looked across the aisle at another critic. I wanted to see if she felt how I did. "What did you think?" she said. "I think it's the best film at the festival," I said. "Me too," she said.

Mean Girls ★ ★ ★
PG-13, 93 m., 2004

Lindsay Lohan (Cady Heron), Rachel McAdams (Regina George), Lizzy Caplan (Janis), Daniel Franzese (Damian), Jonathan Bennett (Aaron), Lacey Chabert (Gretchen), Tina Fey (Ms. Norbury),Tim Meadows (Mr. Duvall), Amanda Seyfried (Karen). Directed by Mark S. Waters and produced by Lorne Michaels. Screenplay by Tina Fey, based on the book *Queen Bees and Wannabes* by Rosalind Wiseman.

In a wasteland of dumb movies about teenagers, *Mean Girls* is a smart and funny one. It even contains some wisdom, although I hesitate to mention that, lest I scare off its target audience. The TV ads, which show Lindsay Lohan landing ass over teakettle in a garbage can, are probably right on the money; since that scene is nothing at all like the rest of the movie, was it filmed specifically to use in the commercials?

Lindsay Lohan stars as Cady Heron, a high school junior who was home-schooled in Africa while her parents worked there as anthropologists. She is therefore the smartest girl in school when her dad is hired by Northwestern and she enrolls in Evanston Township High School—which, like all American high schools in the movies, is physically located in Toronto. What she's not smart about are the ways cliques work in high school, and how you're categorized and stereotyped by who you hang with and how you dress.

Cady makes two friends right away: Janis (Lizzy Caplan), a semi-Goth whose own anthropology includes an analysis of who sits where in the cafeteria, and why; and Damian (Daniel Franzese), Janis's best friend, described as "too gay to function." They clue her in: The three most popular girls in the junior class are the Plastics, so-called because they bear an uncanny resemblance to Barbie. They're led by Regina George (Rachel McAdams), a skilled manipulator whose mother's boob job has defined her values in life. Her sidekicks are Gretchen (Lacey Chabert) and Karen (Amanda Seyfried).

Janis and Damian warn Cady against the girls from hell. But when Regina invites Cady to join their table, Janis urges her to: She can be a spy and get inside information for their campaign to destroy Regina. And she can recommend an obscure brand of Swedish "diet bar" actually used by athletes to gain weight, so that slim Regina with her flawless complexion can find out how it feels to be chubby and spotty.

Mean Girls dissects high school society with a lot of observant detail that seems surprisingly well informed. The screenplay by *Saturday Night Live*'s Tina Fey is both a comic and a sociological achievement, and no wonder; it's inspired not by a novel but by a nonfiction book by Rosalind Wiseman. Its full title more or less summarizes the movie: *Queen Bees and Wannabes: Helping Your Daughter Survive Cliques, Gossip, Boyfriends, and Other Realities of Adolescence.* The mothers in the movie are not much help, however, and Fey's screenplay wisely uses comedy as a learning tool.

Fey also plays a math teacher named Ms. Norbury, who is more plausible and likable than most high school teachers in the movies, and also kind of lovable, especially in the vicinity of the school principal, Mr. Duvall (Tim Meadows, a former *SNL* star). Although many of producer Lorne Michaels's movies with *SNL* cast members have been broad, dumb, and obvious, this one has a light and infectious touch, and it's a revelation to see how Meadows gets real laughs not with big gestures but with small ones: Notice particularly his body language and tone of voice during the new prom queen's speech.

The movie was directed by Mark S. Waters, who also made *Freaky Friday* (2003), a superior remake, and emerged from Sundance 1997 with *The House of Yes*, an uneven but intriguing dark comedy with Parker Posey convinced she was Jackie Onassis. Here he avoids amazing numbers of clichés that most teenage comedies cannot do without. When Cady throws a party while her parents are out of town, for example, a lot of uninvited guests do crash, yes, but amazingly they do *not* trash the house. Although Principal Duvall lectures the student body about a pushing-and-shoving spree, he does *not* cancel the prom ("We've already hired the deejay"). When Cady gets a crush on Aaron (Jonathan Bennett), who sits in front of her in math class, she deals with it in a reasonable way that does *not* involve heartbreak. When there are misunderstandings, they're understandable, and *not* awkward contrivances manufactured for the convenience of the plot.

In the middle of all this, Lindsay Lohan, who was seventeen when the movie was filmed, provides a center by being centered. She has a quiet self-confidence that prevents her from getting shrill and hyper like so many teenage stars; we believe her when she says that because of her years in Africa, "I had never lived in a world where adults didn't trust me." She never allows the character to tilt into caricature, and for that matter, even the Plastics seem real, within their definitions of themselves, and not like the witch-harridans of some teenage movies.

Will teenage audiences walk out of *Mean Girls* determined to break with the culture of cliques, gossip, and rules for popularity? Not a chance. That's built into high school, I think. But they may find it interesting that the geeks are more fun than the queen bees, that teachers have feelings, and that you'll be happier as yourself than as anybody else. I guess the message is, you have to live every day as if you might suddenly be hit by a school bus.

The Medallion ★ ★ ★

PG-13, 90 m., 2003

Jackie Chan (Eddie Yang), Lee Evans (Arthur Watson), Claire Forlani (Nicole), Christy Chung (Charlotte Watson), Julian Sands (Snakehead), John Rhys-Davies (Hammerstock-Smythe), Anthony Wong Chau-Sang (Lester). Directed by Gordon Chan and produced by Alfred Cheung. Screenplay by Bey Logan and Chan.

The child who was born in the fourth month of the Year of the Snake and is destined to meld the two halves of the sacred medallion is always surrounded by candles. Well, of course he is. He sits in the lotus position and gazes into infinity and there are hundreds, maybe thousands of candles surrounding him, and I am left with questions:

1. Who obtains the candles? Is there a wholesale source?

2. Is the child's meditation disturbed when it takes hours to light all of those candles, with some burning down before others have even been lighted? Do the candle-lighters work in shifts?

3. What kind of a kid can sit still for that long? When we went on vacation with our grandsons, Taylor and Emil, we made the mistake of buying them pedometers, and they clocked 4,000 steps before they even got out of bed.

These questions are of course utterly beside the point, but to ask them is one of the pleasures with a movie like *The Medallion*. I realize I am not stern enough with such movies, permitting myself to be entertained when I should be appalled, but just when I am trying to adjust my frown, in walks John Rhys-Davies and introduces himself as "Commander Hammerstock-Smythe," and there I go again.

The movie stars Jackie Chan, who has never to my knowledge been described as handsome, and who pokes fun at his own nose in this movie. His command of the English language should more properly be called a duel, and most of his movies are sensationally derivative of most of his other movies. Yet he is so likeable that if you let him, he'll grow on you. And every once in a while he'll pull something like the stunt in this movie, where he approaches a locked gate and gracefully climbs right up the wall next to it and jumps over it—and then, in that endearing touch he often uses after a feat like that, he shakes his head and grins as if to suggest even he can't believe how good he is.

The plot of *The Medallion* involves the two halves of an ancient medallion, which the above-mentioned child can join, after which it can grant eternal life, but first you have to die. There are some other complications, so study the instructions before attempting this at home. The evil Snakehead (Julian Sands) wants to get his hands on the child and the medallion, and Jackie Chan is a Hong Kong cop who tries to prevent him. His allies include an Interpol operative named Arthur Watson (Lee Evans), and another Interpol cop named Nicole (Claire Forlani), who used to have something going with Jackie, as we can tell because she slaps him a lot and then smiles at him.

The plot we will sidestep. The effects we can talk about. Jackie Chan does a lot of his own stunts, and then there's a sensational climactic scene in which Chan and Snakehead have a duel in midair, which I think is fairly pointless since by then they are both immortal—or sort of immortal, which is the loophole. Earlier, there's a nice scene where Jackie is locked into a shipping container with the boy (but without the candles) and then the container is dumped into the ocean, which would seem to be the wrong strategy if you want to grab the kid. How or if they get out of that, I'm not telling.

The Medallion is what it is, disposable entertainment, redeemed by silliness, exaggeration,

and Jackie Chan's skill and charm. I would not want to see it twice, but I liked seeing it once. If you are the kind of person who doubts you will ever see a Jackie Chan movie, this is not the one to start with. If you are an admirer of Chan, you will find this a big step above *The Tuxedo* but not up to *Shanghai Knights*.

Meet the Fockers ★ ★

PG-13, 116 m., 2004

Robert De Niro (Jack Byrnes), Ben Stiller (Greg Focker), Dustin Hoffman (Bernie Focker), Barbara Streisand (Roz Focker), Blythe Danner (Dina Byrnes), Teri Polo (Pam Byrnes), Owen Wilson (Kevin Rawley), Spencer and Bradley Pickren (Little Jack), Alanna Ubach (Isabel). Directed by Jay Roach and produced by Jane Rosenthal, Robert De Niro, and Roach. Screenplay by Jim Herzfeld and John Hamburg.

As a categorical rule, I avoid statements beginning, "If you loved/liked (name of movie), you'll love/like (name of another movie)." So let me put it this way. If you went to *Meet the Parents* (2000), you will probably find yourself going to *Meet the Fockers*, because having met one set of crazy parents, you are curious about the other set. Also, you may be the kind of person who finds it entertaining to mention that you are on your way to meet the Fockers. When the MPAA objected to the title, by the way, the filmmakers produced several real people who said they were Fockers, and proud of it.

The movie opens with Greg Focker (Ben Stiller) and Pam Byrnes (Teri Polo) still in the embrace of their interminable courtship. In the original film, Pam took Greg home to meet her parents, Jack and Dina (Robert De Niro and Blythe Danner), and you will recall that Greg was a threat to Jack's beloved cat, human ashes made an inappropriate appearance, a septic tank overflowed, and Jack the ex-CIA man gave Greg a lie-detector test.

Now it is time to drive down to Focker Isle in Florida, where live Father and Mom Focker (Dustin Hoffman and Barbra Streisand). Roz is a successful sex therapist, author of books such as *Meet Your Orgasm!* Bernie was a lawyer until he took paternity leave to raise Greg and never went back to work. The Fockers only had the one child, Jack Byrnes discovers. And with a memory so long that I hope audiences can also recall the funniest moment in the first movie, he accuses Greg: "I thought you had a sister. You said you milked your sister's cat."

Hoffman and Streisand are such positive thinkers, so quick to hug and approve and embrace (and meet their orgasms) that it's amazing they produced such an uptight child as Greg. The household is so open-minded, there's a breeze. Consider, for example, Roz Focker's collection of erotic wood carvings of small ethnic people sporting enormous phalli. Jack scowls at such displays, and doesn't want to take his shirt off when Roz offers him a massage. The massage scene, sad to say, doesn't really pay off. Its only point is that Roz works him over so thoroughly that he's stiff and sore afterward. There must have been some comic way, I think, for Jack to meet his orgasm, or at least give it a friendly wave.

There is a tradition at dinners in these families that something unappetizing makes its appearance at the table, but Greg's childhood souvenir is so *very* unappetizing that, I dunno, I cringed instead of laughing. To the cat of the first movie we now add the Fockers' sex-mad dog, which, like a curious number of dogs, has a pants-leg fetish, proving Darwin was right because dogs have existed so much longer than pants. The cat is not only toilet-trained but knows how to flush, leading to another septic joke. And Jack calls on his old CIA buddies to investigate suspicions he has involving his future son-in-law and the family's former maid, the buxom Isabel (Alanna Ubach).

The movie is pleasant enough, but never quite reaches critical mass as a comedy. The director, Jay Roach, who made *Meet the Parents* and the Austin Powers movies, has some funny stuff, including Father Focker's proud display of all of his son's trophies ("I didn't know they made ninth-place ribbons," Jack muses). There's some wordplay involving the Byrnes family Circle of Trust and who is in it, who is outside it, and whose circle it is. Streisand and Hoffman create characters who are, under the circumstances, not only likable but actually sort of believable. And yet, even if you loved *Meet the Parents,* you will only sorta, kinda like *Meet the Fockers.*

Note: There's a cute baby in the movie, Jack Jr., played by twins Spencer and Bradley Pickren. The kid is too young to talk, but Jack Sr. has already started him on sign language. I learn that the Pickren twins actually can sign, and that long before they can speak, babies can learn and use signs.

Melinda and Melinda ★ ★ ★ ½
PG-13, 99 m., 2005

Radha Mitchell (Melinda), Chloe Sevigny (Laurel), Jonny Lee Miller (Lee), Will Ferrell (Hobie), Amanda Peet (Susan), Chiwetel Ejiofor (Ellis), Wallace Shawn (Sy), Larry Pine (Max). Directed by Woody Allen and produced by Letty Aronson. Screenplay by Allen.

Woody Allen's *Melinda and Melinda* begins with friends having dinner in a Chinese restaurant. One of the friends is played by Wallace Shawn, who (Allen's audiences will know) has had a famous restaurant meal or two. Shawn is a playwright, debating another playwright (Larry Pine) about whether the world is essentially tragic or comic. They devise two versions of a story, which changes in detail and tone according to whether it is comedy or tragedy, and the film cuts between those possibilities.

The exercise involves two couples, both disrupted by the unexpected entrance of a character named Melinda (played by Radha Mitchell). For Susan the independent filmmaker (Amanda Peet) and her husband, Hobie (Will Ferrell), an out-of-work actor, she is the downstairs neighbor. For the rich woman Laurel (Chloe Sevigny) and her husband, Lee (Jonny Lee Miller), an alcoholic actor, she is Laurel's old college friend.

In both cases, Melinda is the catalyst for adultery, which does not play out the same way in the two stories. Indeed, almost all the characters except Melinda are different in the two stories because you would cast a comedy differently than a tragedy. Unexpected characters like Ellis Moonsong (Chiwetel Ejiofor), a composer, turn up to supply the third point in two romantic triangles at once.

From time to time, Allen reminds us that all of these characters are being imagined by people at dinner, and all of their feelings are being created out of thin air. The film's last shot, a bold masterstroke, leaves this perfectly clear, and strands us looking at the closing credits, which as always are played over some good traditional jazz. Why won't Woody choose one of these stories or the other? Why won't he either cheer or sadden us? When he abandoned comedy for neo-Bergman exercises like *Interiors*, at least they were Bergmanesque all the way through, with no excursions into romantic comedy. Why can't he make up his mind?

But you see, he has. Allen has made up his mind to pull the rug out from under us as we stand at the cocktail party of life, chattering about how we got there, when we plan to leave, and how we'll get back home. He has shown that the rug, the party, and all of the guests are shadows flickering on the walls. *Melinda and Melinda* is a movie about the symbiosis of the filmmaker and the audience, who are required to conspire in the creation of an imaginary world. He shows us how he does it and how we do it. In its complexity and wit, this is one of his best films.

That creates a particular challenge for the actors, who are expected to act as if they are in either a comedy or a tragedy and do not know about the other half of the movie. Radha Mitchell, who is the crossover character, rises to the challenge and is impudent in the comedy and touching in the tragedy; she must have had to compartmentalize her emotions, but then that's what actors do.

The two stories are a little sketchy because neither one is required to have a beginning, middle, and end—to deliver in traditional terms. They're works in progress. That may sound frustrating, but it's sort of exciting, as if Allen is allowing us to read his early drafts. Perhaps in Woody Allen's mind a dinner party is held nightly at which his optimistic and pessimistic selves argue about his next project. *Melinda and Melinda* may be a dramatization of his creative process.

Before the movie opened, A. O. Scott wrote a provocative article in the *New York Times*, concluding: "Instead of making the movies we expect him to, (Allen) stubbornly makes the movies he wants to make, gathering his A-list casts for minor exercises in whimsy and bile that tend not to be appreciated when they arrive in theaters. How could they be? Mr. Allen

will never again be his younger self, and his audience, as long as we refuse to acknowledge that fact, will never grow up, guaranteeing our further disappointment. Maybe what we have on our hands is a dead shark."

That's a reference to *Annie Hall*, which won the Oscar and was the high point of America's relationship with Woody Allen ("A relationship is like a shark. It has to constantly move forward or it dies"). With Scott's words I have some sympathy. Woody Allen made members of my generation laugh when we were young, and now he doesn't make us feel young anymore. Scott argues that by refusing to repeat himself, Allen has left himself open to the charge of repeating himself: There he goes again, doing something different. I cannot escape the suspicion that if Woody had never made a previous film, if each new one was Woody's Sundance debut, it would get a better reception. His reputation is not a dead shark but an albatross, which, with admirable economy, Allen has arranged for the critics to carry around their own necks.

Melinda fails the standards of most audiences because it doesn't deliver a direct emotional charge. It doesn't leave us happy or sad for the characters, or even knowing which characters we were supposed to care about. That, however, is not Allen's failure, but his purpose. More than any other film that comes to mind, *Melinda and Melinda* says, clearly and without compromise, that movies are only movies. They're made up of thin air, the characters are not real, they could turn out however the director wants them to. We get all worked up about what Frankie does in *Million Dollar Baby*, and would get just as worked up if he did the opposite, both times talking about Frankie as if he were real and had actually done something. At the end of *Melinda and Melinda*, we realize that neither Melinda nor Melinda is real, but Woody Allen certainly is. ☞

The Merchant of Venice ★ ★ ★ ½
R, 138 m., 2005

Al Pacino (Shylock), Jeremy Irons (Antonio), Joseph Fiennes (Bassanio), Lynn Collins (Portia), Zuleikha Robinson (Jessica), Kris Marshall (Gratiano), Charlie Cox (Lorenzo). Directed by

Michael Radford and produced by Cary Brokaw, Michael Cowan, Barry Navidi, and Jason Piette. Screenplay by Radford, based on the play by William Shakespeare.

Thinking to read *The Merchant of Venice* one more time, I took down the volume of Shakespeare's tragedies, only to be reminded that this dark and troubling play is classified with his comedies. Its two natures come from different spheres; sunny scenes of romance alternate with sadness, desperation, and guile. When Jessica, Shylock's daughter, steals his fortune and leaves his home to marry Lorenzo, it's as if she's escaping from one half of the play to the other.

Michael Radford's new production is, incredibly, the first theatrical film of the play in the sound era. There were several silent versions, and it has been done for television, but among the most important titles in Shakespeare's canon this is the play that has been sidestepped by not only Hollywood but every film industry in the world. The reason is plain to see: Shylock, the moneylender who demands repayment with a pound of flesh, is an anti-Semitic caricature; filmmakers turn away and chose more palatable plays.

Yet Shylock is an intense, passionate character in a great play, and Radford's film does him justice. Although Shylock embodies anti-Semitic stereotypes widely held in Shakespeare's time, he is not a one-dimensional creature like Marlowe's *The Jew of Malta,* but embodies, like all of Shakespeare's great creations, a humanity that transcends the sport of his making. Radford's Shylock, played with a rasping intensity by Al Pacino, is not softened or apologized for—that would deny the reality of the play—but he is *seen* as a man not without his reasons.

The film opens by visualizing an event referred to only in dialogue in the original: We see the merchant Antonio (Jeremy Irons) spit at Shylock on the Rialto bridge, as part of a demonstration against the Jews who are both needed and hated in Venice—needed, because without moneylenders the city's economy cannot function, and hated, because Christians must therefore do business with the same people they have long executed a blood libel against.

That Antonio spits at Shylock, asks him for a loan of 3,000 ducats, and boldly tells him he would spit at him again is, in modern terms, asking for it. That Shylock loans him the money against the guarantee of a pound of flesh is not simply a cruelty, but has a certain reason; Shakespeare's dialogue makes it clear that Shylock proudly declines to accept any monetary interest from Antonio and has every reason to think Antonio can repay the loan, which means that Shylock will have borrowed the money at cost to himself and loaned it to Antonio for free.

That Antonio comes within a whisper of losing his flesh and his life is, after all, the result of a bargain he quickly agreed to, because he also thought he would escape without paying interest. Shakespeare's great courtroom scene, in which the Doge must decide between the claims of Shylock and the life of Antonio, is undercut by the farce of the cross-dressing Portia's last-second appeal; on the merits of the case, Shylock should win.

But I have written as if you know who Shylock and Antonio and Portia are, and you may not; *The Merchant of Venice* is studiously avoided in those courses that seek to introduce Shakespeare to students, who can tell you all about Romeo and Juliet. One of the strengths of the film is its clarity. A written prologue informs us of the conditions of Jewish life in Venice in 1586; Jews were forced to live in a confined area that gave the word "ghetto" to the world, were forbidden to move through the city after dark (although they seem to do a lot of that in the film), and were tolerated because Christians were forbidden to lend money at interest, and somebody had to.

The plot is driven from the comic side by the desire of Bassanio (Joseph Fiennes) to wed the fair Portia (Lynn Collins). She has been left by her father's will in the position of a game show prize; her suitors are shown chests of gold, silver, and lead, and made to choose one; inside the lucky chest is the token of their prize. Elementary gamesmanship cries out "Lead! Choose the lead!" but one royal hopeful after another goes for the glitter, and the impoverished Bassanio still has a chance.

He will need money to finance his courtship, and turns to his friend Antonio. The play famously opens with Antonio's melancholy ("I know not why I am so sad"), but the casting of Jeremy Irons makes that opening speech unnecessary; he is an actor to whom sadness comes without effort, and a dark gloom envelops him throughout the play. The reason for this is implied by Shakespeare and made clear by Radford: Antonio is in love with Bassanio, and in effect is being asked for a loan to finance his own romantic disappointment. Whether he and Bassanio were actually lovers is a good question. How genuinely Bassanio can love Portia the lottery prize is another. That these two questions exist in the same place is a demonstration of the way in which Shakespeare boldly juxtaposes inner torment and screwball comedy.

Shylock is a cruel caricature, but isn't he also one of the first Jews allowed to speak for himself in gentile European literature, to argue his case, to reveal his humanity? It's possible that Shakespeare never actually met a Jew (to be a Catholic was a hanging offense in his England), but then he never visited Venice, either—or France, Denmark, or the seacoast of Bohemia. His Shylock begins as a lift from literary sources, like so many of his characters, and is transformed by his genius into a man of feelings and deep wounds. There is a kind of mad incongruity in the play's intersecting stories, one ending in sunshine, marriage, and happiness, the other in Shylock's loss of everything—daughter, fortune, home, and respect. And Shylock's great speech, beginning "Hath not a Jew eyes?" is a cry against anti-Semitism that rings down through the centuries. It is wrong to say that *The Merchant of Venice* is not "really" anti-Semitic—of course it is—but its venom is undercut by Shakespeare's inability to objectify any of his important characters. He always sees the man inside.

Pacino is a fascinating actor. As he has grown older he has grown more fierce. He is charged sometimes with overacting, but never with bad acting; he follows the emotions of his characters fearlessly, not protecting himself, and here he lays bare Shylock's lacerated soul. He has a way of attacking and caressing Shakespeare's language at the same time. He

loves it. It allows him reach and depth. His performance here is incandescent.

Of the others, Irons finds the perfect note for the treacherous role of Antonio; making his love for Bassanio obvious is the way to make his behavior explicable, and so Antonio for once is poignant, instead of merely a mope. The young people, Bassanio and Portia, resolutely inhabit their comedy, unaware of the suffering their romance is causing for others. Only Jessica (Zuleikha Robinson) still seems inexplicable; how can she do what she does to her father, Shylock, with such vacuous contentment?

The film is wonderful to look at, saturated in Renaissance colors and shadows, filmed in Venice, which is the only location that is also a set. It has greatness in moments, and is denied greatness overall only because it is such a peculiar construction; watching it is like channel-surfing between a teen romance and a dark abysm of loss and grief. Shylock and Antonio, if they were not made strangers by hatred, would make good companions for long, sad conversations punctuated by wounded silences.

Metallica: Some Kind of Monster ★ ★ ★
NO MPAA RATING, 120 m., 2004

A documentary directed and produced by Joe Berlinger and Bruce Sinofsky.

Metallica: Some Kind of Monster doesn't require you to know anything about the band Metallica or heavy metal music, but it supplies a lot of information about various kinds of monsters. Some of them have been around since childhood, some live in the bottle, and others are generated by the act of making millions as a rock god. When the film opens, the band has been around some twenty years and its surviving members, now middle-aged, are exhausted, neurotic, and on each other's nerves. Their bass player, Jason Newsted, has quit the band, citing "the physical damage I've done to myself playing the music live."

In 2001, Metallica goes into an improvised studio in San Francisco's Presidio to create a new album from scratch. They're starting with "no riffs, no songs, no titles, nothing."

For reasons that must have seemed excellent at the time, they invite two documentary filmmakers to film them in this process. Joe Berlinger and Bruce Sinofsky have made some of the best docs of recent years, including *Paradise Lost: The Child Murders at Robin Hood Hills* (1996), which follows the trial and conviction of three heavy metal fans who almost certainly had nothing to do with the grisly murders they're charged with (in a 2000 sequel, *Paradise Lost 2: Revelations,* the likely murderer does all he can to draw suspicion to himself).

Sinofsky and Berlinger possibly thought this assignment would be more routine, even music-driven. In fact, there is little music in *Metallica* and a great deal of talking, as the three band members (lead singer James Hetfield, drummer Lars Ulrich, and guitarist Kirk Hammett) recruit their producer, Bob Rock, to play bass. There is another recruit: a therapist named Phil Towle. The relationship between Hetfield and Ulrich has become poisonous, and Towle's assignment is to bring peace and healing—or at least the ability to function.

The band members exhibit a certain courage in allowing their sessions to be filmed warts and all, as tempers flare, hurtful words are exchanged, and Towle's skills as a therapist make us wonder if his scenes were deleted from *This Is Spinal Tap.* That he is being paid $40,000 a month makes him feel like keeping his job, until finally Hetfield and Ulrich find they agree on something at last, getting rid of him.

The progress of the album is interrupted when Hetfield unexpectedly signs into rehab. For weeks and months the others have no idea how long he'll be gone; he returns in a year, sober and solemnly following instructions from the rehab center. He can work only four hours a day, for example. This drives Ulrich up the wall: How can you make an album without sleepless nights? He charges Hetfield with being "self-regarding," which was probably more true before he went into rehab; now, in his free time, we see him attending his daughter's ballet class and otherwise trying to learn how to be a husband and father.

There are hints in the film that a little rehab would not be amiss for Ulrich. He gets a visit from his long-haired hippie Danish father, who still treats him like a kid taking music lessons, and at one point suggests deleting a song from the album because "It just doesn't sound right." Hammett meanwhile keeps a low profile, like the child in a dysfunctional marriage who has learned how to stay below the radar.

The band eventually finishes the album *(St. Anger).* The movie opens with the press junket promoting it, at which they repeat conventional sound bites that the movie shows bear little correspondence with reality. If *Metallica: Some Kind of Monster* has a message, it's that it's great being a rock god up to a point, but most rock gods play the role long after it's much fun. Some people sing and tour forever (Willie Nelson, the Stones, McCartney). What Dr. Phil should probably advise Metallica is to call it a day. Why work with people you can't stand, doing work you're sick of, and that may be killing you? Lots of people have jobs like that, but Metallica has a choice.

A Mighty Wind ★ ★ ½
PG-13, 92 m., 2003

Christopher Guest (Alan Barrows), Michael McKean (Jerry Palter), Fred Willard (Mike LaFontaine), Catherine O'Hara (Mickey), Eugene Levy (Mitch), Bob Balaban (Jonathan Steinbloom), Parker Posey (Sissy Knox), Ed Begley Jr. (Lars), Harry Shearer (Mark Shubb), David Blasucci (Tony Pollono), Laura Harris (Miss Klapper), Michael Hitchcock (Lawrence Turpin), Jane Lynch (Laurie Bohner). Directed by Christopher Guest and produced by Karen Murphy. Screenplay by Guest and Eugene Levy.

If your idea of the ultimate circle of hell is singing along with Burl Ives on "I Know an Old Lady Who Swallowed a Fly"—if even as a child you refused to go "hee haw, hee haw"—then *A Mighty Wind* will awaken old memories. Christopher Guest's new mockumentary is about a reunion of three groups from the 1960s folk boom, and in the film's final concert the audience is indeed required to imitate chickens and horses.

The premise: The beloved folk promoter Irving Steinbloom has passed away, and his son Jonathan (Bob Balaban) wants to stage a concert in his honor at Town Hall, legendary site of so many folk performances. He assembles the relentlessly upbeat New Main Street Singers, the Folksmen (Christopher Guest, Harry Shearer, Michael McKean) and—the stars of the show—the long-estranged Mitch and Mickey (Eugene Levy and Catherine O'Hara).

These acts are all uncannily close to types we vaguely remember from *Hootenanny* and other shows, if we are over forty, and *A Mighty Wind* does for aging folkies what Rob Reiner's *This Is Spinal Tap* did for aging heavy-metal fans. If you ever actually spent money on an album by the Brothers Four, you may feel you vaguely remember some of the songs.

Guest follows the general outlines of the real (and wonderful) documentary *The Weavers: Wasn't That a Time!*, joining his characters in their current lives and then leading them through apprehensions and rehearsals to their big concert. The Folksmen are the most analytical about their comeback ("It wasn't retro then, but it's retro now"), the New Main Street Singers the most inanely cheerful (most of the members weren't born when the original group was formed), and Mitch and Mickey the most fraught with painful old memories and (in Mitch's case) new emotional traumas.

Mitch and Mickey dominate the film, providing a dramatic story that takes on a life of its own. Mitch is played by Levy as a deeply neurotic man who doubts he can still sing or even remember lyrics, and who still has a broken heart because a famous onstage kiss with Mickey did not lead to lasting offstage romance. When he disappears from backstage shortly before show time, we may be reminded of Ringo's solo walk in *A Hard Day's Night*.

Guest surrounds his talent with the usual clueless types he likes to skewer in his films. Fred Willard, hilarious as the color commentator in *Best in Show*, is back playing a promoter and onetime TV star who was famous for five minutes for the catchphrase "Wha' happened?" He laughs at his own jokes to demonstrate to his silent listeners that they are funny. Ed Begley Jr. plays an obtuse public television executive named Lars, whose speech is punctuated by an impenetrable thicket of Yiddish. Bob Balaban, as the dutiful son and impresario, frets over every detail of

the performance, and is the singularly ill-at-ease emcee.

A lot of the movie consists of music, much of it written by Guest and other collaborators in the cast, and that is an enjoyment and a problem. The songs actually do capture the quality of the lesser groups of the time. They are performed in uncanny imitations of early TV musical staging. The movie demolishes any number of novelty songs with the Folksmen's version of "Eat at Joe's," based on a faulty neon sign that reads, "E . . . A . . . O."

But there comes a point when the movie becomes . . . well, performances and not comedy. The final act of the movie mostly takes place during the televised concert, and almost against its will takes on the dynamic of a real concert and not a satirical one.

There is another difficulty: Christopher Guest is rather fond of his characters. He didn't hate his targets in *Best in Show* or *Spinal Tap*, but he skewered them mercilessly, while the key characters in *A Mighty Wind*, especially Levy and O'Hara, take on a certain weight of complexity and realism that edges away from comedy and toward sincere soap opera.

There were many times when I laughed during *A Mighty Wind* (not least at lines like, "the kind of infectious that it's good to spread around"). But the edge is missing from Guest's usual style. Maybe it's because his targets are, after all, so harmless. The deluded *Spinal Tap* and the ferocious dog owners in *Best in Show* want to succeed and prevail. The singers in *A Mighty Wind* are grateful to be remembered, and as we watch them, we cut them the kind of slack we often do for aging comeback acts. Hey, the Beach Boys may be old, fat, and neurotic, but we don't want to spoil the fun by taking their T-Bird away.

Million Dollar Baby ★ ★ ★ ★
PG-13, 132 m., 2004

Clint Eastwood (Frankie Dunn), Hilary Swank (Maggie Fitzgerald), Morgan Freeman (Scrap), Jay Baruchel (Danger), Mike Colter (Big Willie Little), Lucia Rijker (Billie [The Blue Bear]), Brian F. O'Byrne (Father Horvak), Margo Martindale (Earline Firzgerald). Directed by Clint Eastwood and produced by Tom Rosenberg, Paul Haggis, Albert S. Ruddy, and Eastwood. Screenplay by

Haggis, based on stories from *Rope Burns,* by F. X. Toole.

Clint Eastwood's *Million Dollar Baby* is a masterpiece, pure and simple, deep and true. It tells the story of an aging fight trainer and a hillbilly girl who thinks she can be a boxer. It is narrated by a former boxer who is the trainer's best friend. But it's not a boxing movie. It is a movie about a boxer. What else it is, all it is, how deep it goes, what emotional power it contains, I cannot suggest in this review, because I will not spoil the experience of following this story into the deepest secrets of life and death. This is the best film of the year.

Eastwood plays the trainer, Frankie, who runs a seedy gym in Los Angeles and reads poetry on the side. Hilary Swank plays Maggie, from southwest Missouri, who has been waitressing since she was thirteen and sees boxing as the one way she can escape waitressing for the rest of her life. Otherwise, she says, "I might as well go back home and buy a used trailer, and get a deep fryer and some Oreos." Morgan Freeman is Scrap, whom Frankie managed into a title bout. Now he lives in a room at the gym and is Frankie's partner in conversations that have coiled down through the decades. When Frankie refuses to train a "girly," it's Scrap who convinces him to give Maggie a chance: "She grew up knowing one thing. She was trash."

These three characters are seen with a clarity and truth that is rare in the movies. Eastwood, who doesn't carry a spare ounce on his lean body, doesn't have any padding in his movie, either: Even as the film approaches the deep emotion of its final scenes, he doesn't go for easy sentiment, but regards these people, level-eyed, as they do what they have to do.

Some directors lose focus as they grow older. Others gain it, learning how to tell a story that contains everything it needs and absolutely nothing else. *Million Dollar Baby* is Eastwood's twenty-fifth film as a director, and his best. Yes, *Mystic River* is a great film, but this one finds the simplicity and directness of classical storytelling; it is the kind of movie where you sit very quietly in the theater and are drawn deeply into lives that you care very much about.

Morgan Freeman is the narrator, just as he was in *The Shawshank Redemption,* which this film resembles in the way the Freeman character describes a man who became his lifelong study. The voice is flat and factual: You never hear Scrap going for an effect or putting a spin on his words. He just wants to tell us what happened. He talks about how the girl walked into the gym, how she wouldn't leave, how Frankie finally agreed to train her, and what happened then. But Scrap is not merely an observer; the film gives him a life of his own when the others are offscreen. It is about all three of these people.

Hilary Swank is astonishing as Maggie. Every note is true. She reduces Maggie to a fierce intensity. Consider the scene where she and Scrap sit at a lunch counter, and Scrap tells the story of how he lost the sight in one eye, how Frankie blames himself for not throwing in the towel. It is an important scene for Freeman, but what I want you to observe is how Hilary Swank has Maggie do absolutely nothing but listen. No "reactions," no little nods, no body language except perfect stillness, deep attention, and an unwavering gaze.

There's another scene, at night driving in a car, after Frankie and Maggie have visited Maggie's family. The visit didn't go well. Maggie's mother is played by Margo Martindale as an ignorant and selfish monster. "I got nobody but you, Frankie," Maggie says. This is true, but do not make the mistake of thinking there is a romance between them. It's different and deeper than that. She tells Frankie a story involving her father, whom she loved, and an old dog she loved too.

Look at the way the cinematographer, Tom Stern, uses the light in this scene. Instead of using the usual "dashboard lights" that mysteriously seem to illuminate the whole front seat, watch how he has their faces slide in and out of shadow, how sometimes we can't see them at all, only hear them. Watch how the rhythm of this lighting matches the tone and pacing of the words, as if the visuals are caressing the conversation.

It is a dark picture overall. A lot of shadows, many scenes at night, characters who seem to be receding into their private fates. It is also a "boxing movie" in the sense that it follows

Maggie's career, and there are several fight scenes. She wins right from the beginning, but that's not the point; *Million Dollar Baby* is about a woman who is determined to make something of herself, and a man who doesn't want to do anything for this woman, and will finally do everything.

The screenplay is by Paul Haggis, who has worked mostly on TV but with this work will earn an Oscar nomination. Other nominations, and possibly Oscars, will go to Swank, Eastwood, Freeman, the picture, and many of the technicians—and possibly the original score composed by Eastwood, which always does what it required and never distracts. *[Indeed, the film won four Oscars.]*

Haggis adapted the story from *Rope Burns: Stories from the Corner*, a 2000 book by Jerry Boyd, a seventy-year-old fight manager who wrote it as "F. X. Toole." The dialogue is poetic but never fancy. "How much she weigh?" Maggie asks Frankie about the daughter he hasn't seen in years. "Trouble in my family comes by the pound." And when Frankie sees Scrap's feet on the desk: "Where are your shoes?" Scrap: "I'm airing out my feet." The foot conversation continues for almost a minute, showing the film's freedom from plot-driven dialogue, its patience in evoking character.

Eastwood is attentive to supporting characters, who make the surrounding world seem more real. The most unexpected is a Catholic priest who is seen, simply, as a good man; the movies all seem to put a negative spin on the clergy these days. Frankie goes to Mass every morning and says his prayers every night, and Father Horvak (Brian F. O'Byrne) observes that anyone who attends daily Mass for twenty-three years tends to be carrying a lot of guilt. Frankie turns to him for advice at a crucial point, and the priest doesn't respond with church orthodoxy but with a wise insight: "If you do this thing, you'll be lost, somewhere so deep you will never find yourself." Listen, too, when Haggis has Maggie use the word "frozen," which is what an uneducated backroads girl might say, but is also the single perfect word that expresses what a thousand could not.

Movies are so often made of effects and sensation these days. This one is made out of three people and how their actions grow out of who they are and why. Nothing else. But isn't that everything? ☞

Millions ★ ★ ★ ★
PG, 97 m., 2005

James Nesbitt (Ronnie Cunningham), Daisy Donovan (Dorothy), Lewis McGibbon (Anthony Cunningham), Alex Etel (Damian Cunningham), Christopher Fulford (The Man). Directed by Danny Boyle and produced by Graham Broadbent, Andrew Hauptman, and Damian Jones. Screenplay by Frank Cottrell Boyce.

"It isn't the money's fault it got stolen."

That is the reasoning of Anthony Cunningham, who at nine is more of a realist than his seven-year-old brother, Damian. Therefore, it isn't their fault that a bag containing 265,000 British pounds bounced off a train and into Damian's playhouse and is currently stuffed under their bed.

Danny Boyle's *Millions*, a family film of limitless imagination and surprising joy, follows the two brothers as they deal with their windfall. They begin by giving some of it away, taking homeless men to Pizza Hut. Damian wants to continue their charity work, but Anthony leans toward investing in property. They have a deadline: In one week the U.K. will say goodbye to the pound and switch over to the euro; maybe, thinks Anthony, currency speculation would be the way to go.

Here is a film that exists in that enchanted realm where everything goes right—not for the characters, for the filmmakers. They take an enormous risk with a film of sophistication and whimsy, about children, money, criminals, and saints. Damian collects the saints— "like baseball cards," says Richard Roeper. He knows all their statistics. He can see them clear as day, and have conversations with them. His favorite is St. Francis of Assisi, but he knows them all: When a group of Africans materializes wearing halos, Damian is ecstatic: "The Ugandan martyrs of 1881!"

The boys' mother has died, and Damian asks his saints if they have encountered a Saint Maureen. No luck, but then heaven is limitless. Their dad, Ronnie (James Nesbitt), has recently moved them into a newly built suburb outside Liverpool, where the kids at school are hostile at first. Anthony finds it cost-efficient to bribe them with money and neat stuff. Damian, under advice from St. Francis, wants to continue giving money to the poor. Anthony warns him urgently that throwing around too much money will draw attention to them, but Damian drops 10,000 pounds into a charity collection basket. When the boys find out the money was stolen, Damian thinks maybe they should give it back, which is when Anthony comes up with the excellent reasoning I began with.

Perhaps by focusing on the money and the saints I have missed the real story of *Millions*, which involves the lives of the boys, their father, and the woman (Daisy Donovan) who works at the charity that finds the fortune in its basket. The boys are dealing with the death of their mother, and the money is a distraction. Their father is even lonelier; maybe too lonely to ever marry again, maybe too distracted to protect his boys against the bad guy (Christopher Fulford), who dreamed up the perfect train robbery and is now skulking about the neighborhood looking for his missing bag of loot.

By now you may have glanced back to the top of the review to see if I really said *Millions* was directed by Danny Boyle, who made *Shallow Grave*, *Trainspotting*, and the zombie movie *28 Days Later*. Yes, *the* Danny Boyle. And the original screenplay and novel are by Frank Cottrell Boyce, who wrote *Hilary and Jackie* and *24 Hour Party People*. What are these two doing making a sunny film about kids?

I don't require an answer for that, because their delight in the film is so manifest. But they are serious filmmakers who do not know how to talk down to an audience, and although *Millions* uses special effects and materializing saints, it's a film about real ideas, real issues, and real kids. It's not sanitized, brainless eye candy. Like all great family films, it plays equally well for adults—maybe better, since we know how unusual it is.

One of its secrets is casting. In Alex Etel and Lewis McGibbon the film has found two of the most appealing child actors I've ever seen. Alex is like the young Macaulay Culkin *(Home Alone)* except that he has no idea he is cute, and like the young Haley Joel Osment *(The Sixth Sense)* in that he finds it perfectly reasonable to speak with dead people. There is no overt cuteness, no

affected lovability, not a false note in their performances, and the movie allows them to be very smart, as in Anthony's theory about turning the pounds into dollars and buying back into euros after the new currency falls from its opening-day bounce.

Of course, that involves the difficulty of two boys ages seven and nine trying to convert 265,000 pounds into anything. They can't just walk into a bank with a note from their dad. The movie handles this and other problems with droll ingenuity, while also portraying a new suburban community in the making. An opening shot by Boyle, maybe a sly dig at Lars von Trier's *Dogville*, shows the boys visiting the site of their new neighborhood when it consists only of chalk outlines on the ground. After the new homeowners move in, a helpful policeman cheerfully advises a community meeting that they should expect to be burgled, and he tells them which forms to ask for at the police station.

Boyce, a screenwriter who often works with Michael Winterbottom, is so unpredictable and original in his work that he could be called the British Charlie Kaufman, if they were not both completely distinctive. He got the inspiration for *Millions*, he says, from an interview in which Martin Scorsese said he was reading the lives of the saints.

The idea of characters getting a sudden cash windfall is not new, indeed has been a movie staple for a century. What's original about the movie is the way it uses the money as a device for the young brothers to find out more about how the world really works, and what is really important to them. The closing sequence is a bit of a stretcher, I will be the first to admit, but why not go for broke? One of the tests of sainthood is the performance of a miracle, and since Damian is clearly on the road to sainthood, that is permitted him. For that matter, Boyce and Boyle have performed a miracle with their movie. This is one of the best films of the year.

Mindhunters ★ ★ ½
R, 106 m., 2005

Val Kilmer (Jake Harris), Christian Slater (J. D. Reston), LL Cool J (Gabe Jensen), Jonny Lee Miller (Lucas Harper), Kathryn Morris (Sara Moore), Clifton Collins Jr. (Vince Sherman), Will

Kemp (Rafe Perry), Patricia Velasquez (Nicole Willis), Eion Bailey (Bobby Whitman). Directed by Renny Harlin and produced by Cary Brokaw, Akiva Goldsman, Robert F. Newmyer, Jeffrey Silver, and Rebecca Spikings. Screenplay by Wayne Kramer and Kevin Brodbin.

One of Those Among Us Is a Killer, and We Cannot Leave This (a) Isolated Country Estate, (b) Besieged Police Station, (c) Antarctic Research Outpost, (d) Haunted House, (e) Space Station, (f) Rogue Planet, or (g) Summer Camp Until We Find Out Who It Is—or Until We All Die. It is a most ancient and dependable formula, invariably surprising us with the identity of the killer, because the evidence is carefully rigged to point first to one suspect and then another, until they persuasively clear their names by getting murdered.

In *Mindhunters,* a thriller directed by Renny Harlin, the suspects and/or victims are assembled on an isolated island that has been rigged up by the FBI as a training facility. It looks like a real town, but is equipped with video cameras and hidden technology so supervisors can see how well trainees handle real-life problems, not that getting your head shattered into supercooled fragments is a challenge they'll be facing every day on the job.

The formula was used early and well by Agatha Christie, whose influence on *Mindhunters* has been cited by such authorities as the *Hollywood Reporter* and *Film Threat.* In the London play *The Mousetrap,* which is now in the second century of its run, she assembled a group of characters in a snowbound country house; one of them died, and the others tried to solve the murder during long conversations in the sitting room involving much malt whiskey, considerable tobacco, unwise "looks around the house," and the revelation that some of the people are not really strangers to one another. It was possibly this play that gave us the phrase, "Where were you when the lights went out?"

To the Agatha Christie formula, *Mindhunters* adds another literary inspiration: George Orwell's *Decline of the English Murder,* a brilliant essay in which he celebrated the golden age of British poisoning and other ingenious methods of disposal. The victims were usually married to their killer, who tended to be a meek accountant who had

fallen into a trap set by a floozy: "In the last analysis," Orwell writes, "he (commits) murder because this seems to him less disgraceful, and less damaging to his career, than being detected in adultery."

But by 1946, when Orwell was writing, British standards had fallen off fearfully, and in the famous case of the Cleft Chin Murder, "The background was not domesticity, but the anonymous life of the dance-halls and the false values of the American film." So there we go again, vulgar Americans with our wicked influence on the Brits, who in murder as elsewhere maintained elegant traditions until we spoiled the game by just having people kill each other.

Orwell might have been cheered by *Mindhunters,* although Christie would have wanted a more ingenious solution. They both might have thought that the killer in the movie goes to a dubious deal of difficulty to create elaborate murder situations that depend on perfect timing, skillful mechanics, a deep knowledge of the characters, and a single-minded focus on providing the movie with Gotcha! scenes. Does the killer in any one of these movies ever have a moment of weariness and depression? ("What the hell, instead of rigging the liquid nitrogen and rewiring the town, I think I'll just shoot somebody.")

Not in *Mindhunters.* The people who arrive on the island are there for an exercise in the profiling of a mass killer. Can they construct a psychological profile to narrow the search to the likely suspects? Val Kilmer plays their instructor, as the kind of expert you suspect has studied *The Dummy's Guide to Profiling.* The others include LL Cool J as Gabe Jensen, a Philadelphia cop who is along as an observer; the brainy Sara Moore (Kathryn Morris); the sexy Nicole Willis (Patricia Velasquez); Vince Sherman (Clifton Collins Jr.), who uses a wheelchair; J. D. Reston (Christian Slater), a cocky showboat, and so on.

They all have a single character trait, announced with such frequency that apparently, when they packed for the island, they were allowed to bring along only one. There is the character who likes to smoke. The character who will not go anywhere without a gun. Perhaps not amazingly, each victim dies because of the weakness revealed by his trait. The ingenuity of their deaths is impressive. Murder traps are rigged all over the island; you may think they are unbelievably complicated, but I say they're nothing a rogue agent couldn't accomplish if he were assisted by an army of key grips, carpenters, best boys, electricians, set designers, art directors, special effects wizards, makeup experts, and half a dozen honey wagons.

Is the film worth seeing? Well, yes and no. Yes, because it is exactly what it is, and no, for the same reason. What always amuses me in Closed World Murders is how the survivors keep right on talking, scheming, suspecting, and accusing: They persist while bodies are piling up like cordwood. At some point, even if you were FBI material, wouldn't you run around screaming and looking for a boat so you could row the hell off that island?

The mystery, when it is solved, is both arbitrary and explained at great length. The killer gives a speech justifying his actions, which is scant comfort for those already dead. As a courtesy, why not post a notice at the beginning: "The author of a series of murders that will begin this evening would like his victims to know in advance that he has good reasons, which follow." Of course, expert profilers might be able to read the note and figure out his identity, although not, I suspect, in this case.

I will leave you with only one clue. In *House of Wax*, the movie theater is playing *Whatever Happened to Baby Jane?* In this movie, the theater marquee advertises *The Third Man*. No, the male characters are not numbered in order, so you can't figure it out that way, nor is the killer necessarily a woman. So think real hard. What else do you know about *The Third Man*? If you have never seen *The Third Man*, I urge you to rent it immediately, as a preparation (or substitute) for *Mindhunters*.

Miracle ★ ★ ★
PG, 135 m., 2004

Kurt Russell (Herb Brooks), Patricia Clarkson (Patti Brooks), Noah Emmerich (Craig Patrick), Michael Mantenuto (Jack O'Callahan), Eddie Cahill (Jim Craig), Patrick O'Brien Dempsey (Mike Eruzione), Nathan West (Rob McClanahan). Directed by Gavin O'Connor and produced by Mark Ciardi and Gordon Gray. Screenplay by Eric Guggenheim.

Miracle is a sports movie that's more about the coach than about the team, and that's a miracle too. At a time when movies are shamelessly aimed at the young male demographic, here's a film with a whole team of hockey players in their teens and early twenties, and the screenplay hardly bothers to tell one from another. Instead, the focus is on Herb Brooks (Kurt Russell), a veteran hockey coach from Minnesota who is assigned the thankless task of assembling a team to represent America in the 1980 Winter Olympics. The United States hasn't won since 1960, and the professionals on the Soviet team—not to mention the Swedes, the Finns, and the Canadians—rule the sport.

This is a Kurt Russell you might not recognize. He's beefed up into a jowly, steady middle-aged man who still wears his square high school haircut. Patricia Clarkson, playing his wife, has the thankless role of playing yet another movie spouse whose only function in life is to complain that his job is taking too much time away from his family. This role, complete with the obligatory shots of the wife appearing in his study door as the husband burns the midnight oil, is so standard, so ritualistic, so boring, that I propose all future movies about workaholics just make them bachelors, to spare us the dead air. At the very least, she could occasionally ask her husband if he thinks he looks good in those plaid sport coats and slacks.

Herb Brooks was a real man (he died just after the film was finished), and the movie presents him in all his complexity. It's fascinated by the quirks of his personality and style; we can see he's a good coach, but, like his players, we're not always sure if we like him. That's what's good about the film: the way it frankly focuses on what a coach does, and how, and why. Brooks knows hockey and disappointment: He was cut from the 1960 American hockey team only a week before the first game, and so in this film, when he has to cut one more player at the last moment, we know how he feels—and he knows how the player feels.

Brooks's strategy is to weave an air of mystery about himself. He assigns his assistant coach, Craig Patrick (Noah Emmerich), to become a friend to the players—because Brooks deliberately does not become a friend, stays aloof, wants to be a little feared and a little resented. At one point, after chewing out his team in the locker room, he stalks out and, passing Patrick, says in a quiet aside, "That oughta wake 'em up."

After Brooks is selected for the job, his first task is to select his team. He immediately breaks with tradition. Amateur sports are overrun with adults who are essentially groupies, loving to get close to a team, treasuring their blazers with the badges on the breast pockets. These guys think they will join Brooks in choosing the American finalists after a week of tryouts, but Brooks announces his final cut on the first day of practice; he already knows who he wants, and doesn't require any advice. He's looking for kids who are hungry and passionate and *need* to win.

Most of the time, the team is seen as a unit. We begin to recognize their faces, but not much is done to develop them as individuals. The exception is the goaltender, Jim Craig (Eddie Cahill). He refuses to take a psychological exam that Brooks hands out, and Brooks tells him that, by not taking it, "you just took it." Later, when Craig seems to falter, he benches him, and says, "I'm looking for the guy who refused to take the test."

We know all the clichés of the modern sports movie, but *Miracle* sidesteps a lot of them. Eric Guggenheim's screenplay, directed by Gavin O'Connor, is not about how some of the players have little quirks that they cure, or about their girl, or about villains that have to be overcome. It's about practicing hard and winning games. It doesn't even bother to demonize the opponents. When the team finally faces the Soviets, they're depicted as—well, simply as the other team. Their coach has a dark, forbidding manner and doesn't smile much, but he's not a Machiavellian schemer; and the Soviets don't play any dirtier than most teams do in hockey.

Oddly enough, the movie this one reminds me of is Robert Altman's *The Company*, about the Joffrey Ballet. Altman was fascinated by the leadership style of the company's artistic director, and how he deliberately uses strategy and underlings to create an aura of mysterious authority. And he dealt dispassionately with injuries, which are a fact of life and end a career in a second. *Miracle* has a similar orientation.

In keeping with its analytical style, the movie doesn't use a lot of trick photography in the hockey games. Unlike the fancy shots in a movie like *The Mighty Ducks*, this one films the hockey matches more or less the way they might look in a good documentary, or a superior TV broadcast. We're in the middle of the confusion on the ice, feeling the energy rather than focusing on plot points.

That leaves Kurt Russell and his character Herb Brooks as the center and reason for the film. Although playing a hockey coach might seem like a slap shot for an actor, Russell does real acting here. He has thought about Brooks and internalized him; the real Brooks was available as a consultant to the film. And Russell and O'Connor create a study of a personality, of a man who is leading young men through a process that led him to disappointment twenty years earlier. He has ideas about hockey and ideas about coaching, and like the Zen master Phil Jackson, begins with philosophy, not strategy. The film doesn't even end with the outcome of the Big Game. It ends by focusing on the coach, after it is all over.

Miss Congeniality 2: Armed and Fabulous ★ ½
PG-13, 115 m., 2005

Sandra Bullock (Gracie Hart), Regina King (Sam Fuller), William Shatner (Stan Fields), Heather Burns (Cheryl), Ernie Hudson (McDonald), Diedrich Bader (Joel), Enrique Murciano (Jeff Foreman), Treat Williams (Collins). Directed by John Pasquin and produced by Sandra Bullock and Marc Lawrence. Screenplay by Lawrence.

Having made the unnecessary *Miss Congeniality*, Sandra Bullock now returns with the doubly unnecessary *Miss Congeniality 2: Armed and Fabulous.* Perhaps it is not entirely unnecessary in the eyes of the producers, since the first film had a worldwide gross of $212 million, not counting home video, but it's unnecessary in the sense that there is no good reason to go and actually see it.

That despite the presence of Sandra Bullock, who remains a most agreeable actress and brings what charm she can to a character who never seems plausible enough to be funny. Does a character in a comedy need to be plausible? I think it helps. It is not enough for a character to "act funny." A lot of humor comes from tension between who the character is and what the character does, or is made to do. Since Miss Congeniality is never other than a ditz, that she acts like one is not hilarious.

You will recall that Gracie Hart (Bullock) is an FBI agent who in the first film impersonated a beauty pageant contestant in order to infiltrate—but enough about that plot, since all you need to know is that the publicity from the pageant has made her so famous that *MC2* opens with a bank robber recognizing her and aborting an FBI sting. Gracie is obviously too famous to function as an ordinary agent, so the FBI director makes her a public relations creature—the new "face of the bureau."

Since the Michael Caine character in the first film successfully groomed her into a beauty pageant finalist, you'd think Gracie had learned something about seemly behavior, but no, she's still a klutz. The bureau supplies her with Joel (Diedrich Bader), a Queer Guy for the Straight Agent, who gives her tips on deportment (no snorting as a form of laughter), manners (chew with your mouth closed), and fashion (dress like a Barbie doll). She is also assigned a new partner: Sam Fuller (Regina King), a tough agent with anger management issues, who likes to throw people around and is allegedly Gracie's bodyguard, assuming she doesn't kill her.

As Gracie is rolled out as the FBI's new face, there's a funny TV chat scene with Regis Philbin (Regis: "You don't look like J. Edgar Hoover." Gracie: "Really? Because this is his dress"). Then comes an emergency: Miss United States (Heather Burns), Gracie's buddy from the beauty pageant, is kidnapped in Las Vegas, along with the pageant manager (William Shatner).

Gracie and Sam fly to Vegas and humiliate the bureau by tackling the real Dolly Parton under the impression she is an imposter. Then they find themselves doing Tina Turner impersonations in a drag club. They also reenact the usual clichés of two partners who hate each other until they learn to love each other. And they impersonate Nancy Drew in their investigation, which leads to the thrilling rescue of Miss United States from the least likely place in the world where any kidnapper would think of hiding her.

Now a word about the name of Regina King's character, Sam Fuller. This is, of course, the same name as the famous movie director Sam Fuller *(The Big Red One, Shock Corridor, The Naked Kiss)*. Fuller (1912–1997) was an icon among other directors, who gave him countless cameo roles in their movies just because his presence was like a blessing; he appeared in films by Amos Gitai, Aki Kaurismaki, his brother Mika Kaurismaki, Larry Cohen, Claude Chabrol, Steven Spielberg, Alexandre Rockwell (twice), Wim Wenders (three times), and Jean-Luc Godard, the first to use him, in *Pierrot le Fou*, where he stood against a wall, puffed a cigar, and told the camera, "film is like a battleground."

It may seem that I have strayed from the topic, but be honest: You are happier to learn these factoids about Sam Fuller than to find out which Las Vegas landmark the kidnappers use to imprison Miss United States and William Shatner. The only hint I will provide is that they almost drown, and Sandra Bullock almost drowns, too, as she did most famously in *Speed 2*, a movie about a runaway ocean liner. I traditionally end my reviews of the *Miss Congeniality* movies by noting that I was the only critic in the world who liked *Speed 2*, and I see no reason to abandon that tradition, especially since if there is a *Miss Congeniality 3* and it doesn't have Sam Fuller in it, I may be at a loss for words.

The Missing ★ ★
R, 135 m., 2003

Tommy Lee Jones (Samuel Jones), Cate Blanchett (Maggie Gilkeson), Evan Rachel Wood (Lily), Jenna Boyd (Dot Gilkeson), Aaron Eckhart (Brake Baldwin), Eric Schweig (Chidin). Directed by Ron Howard and produced by Brian Grazer and Daniel Ostroff. Screenplay by Ken Kaufman, based on the novel by Thomas Eidson.

New York magazine ran a cover story years ago calling John Ford's *The Searchers* the most influential movie in American history. Movies like *Taxi Driver, Hard Core,* and *Paris, Texas* consider the theme of an abducted girl and the father or husband or cab driver who tries to rescue her from sexual despoliation at the hands of people he despises. The beat goes on with Ron Howard's *The Missing*, a clunky Western that tries so hard to be politically correct that although young women are kidnapped by Indians to be sold into prostitution in Mexico, they are never molested by their captors.

In the tradition of Robert De Niro *(Taxi Driver)*, George C. Scott *(Hard Core)*, and Harry Dean Stanton *(Paris, Texas)*, the movie has Tommy Lee Jones as a craggy loner who turns up when needed for the rescue. But in its update of the story, *The Missing* supplies a strong woman as the heroine. This is Maggie Gilkeson (Cate Blanchett), as a frontier rancher who lives with two daughters and has a hired man (Aaron Eckhart) who provides sex but isn't allowed to spend the night because she doesn't want to give anyone the wrong idea. She has some doctoring skills, and as the film opens is pulling an old woman's tooth—her last one, ho, ho.

Jones plays Maggie's father, Samuel, who abandoned the family years ago and has been living with Indians, learning their customs and sharing their firewater. He turns up desperate, but she sends him away. Then her daughter Lily (Evan Rachel Wood) is captured by Indians, and she needs his expertise in the ways of the Indian; she asks him to join her in the search. Also coming along is her younger daughter, Dot (Jenna Boyd).

So okay. An old drunk, a woman, and a kid are chasing a resourceful band of Indians and half-breeds, led by a psychic male witch named Chidin (Eric Schweig). What are their chances? Excellent, I'd say, although of course there will have to be several close calls, assorted escapes and recaptures, and gunfights so prolonged that our attention drifts.

Sorry, but I couldn't believe any part of this movie. It's such a preposterous setup that I was always aware of the plot chugging away, and the logistics of the chase defy all common sense. The underlying assumption (that an old white coot and his daughter can out-Injun the Injuns) would be offensive if it did not border on the comedic, and why else, really, did they bring the ten-year-old along except to provide a young girl who'd be handy for scenes in which she is in danger?

When you see good actors in a story like this, you suspect they know how bad it is, but work to keep their self-respect. Tommy Lee Jones has

sad eyes in the film, and underplays his role to avoid its obvious opportunities for parody; Cate Blanchett is strong and determined, and the only flaw in her performance is that it's in the wrong movie.

At 135 minutes, *The Missing* is way too long. This is basically a B Western jumped up out of its category. As a lean little oater, this story could have held down half of a double bill back when Westerns were popular, but these days audiences need a reason to see a Western. Kevin Costner gives them one in *Open Range*, but Ron Howard, who often makes wonderful movies, has taken a day off.

Mona Lisa Smile ★ ★ ★
PG-13, 117 m., 2003

Julia Roberts (Katherine Watson), Kirsten Dunst (Betty Warren), Julia Stiles (Joan Brandwyn), Maggie Gyllenhaal (Giselle Levy), Ginnifer Goodwin (Constance Baker), Dominic West (Bill Dunbar), Juliet Stevenson (Amanda Armstrong), John Slattery (Paul Moore), Marcia Gay Harden (Nancy Abbey), Marian Seldes (Jocelyn Carr). Directed by Mike Newell and produced by Elaine Goldsmith-Thomas, Paul Schiff, and Deborah Schindler. Screenplay by Lawrence Konner and Mark Rosenthal.

I find it hard to believe that Wellesley College was as reactionary in the autumn of 1953 as *Mona Lisa Smile* says it was—but then I wasn't there. Neither were the screenwriters, who reportedly based their screenplay on Hillary Clinton's experience at Wellesley in the early 1960s. The film shows a school that teaches, above all, that a woman's duty is to stand by her man, and if Clinton learned that, she also learned a good deal more. No doubt she had a teacher as inspiring as Katherine Watson (Julia Roberts), who trades in the bohemian freedom of Berkeley for a crack at Wellesley's future corporate wives.

This is the kind of school that actually offers classes in deportment, grooming, and table-setting, and the teacher of those classes, Nancy Abbey (Marcia Gay Harden), takes them so seriously that we begin to understand the system that produced Cathy Whitaker, Julianne Moore's showpiece wife in *Far from Heaven*. Watson finds her students scornful of her California background (every student makes it a point to be able to identify every slide of every painting in her first lecture), but she counterattacks with a blast of modern art, and there is a scene where she takes them to watch the uncrating of a new work by Jackson Pollock.

Of course, the board of trustees is suspicious of Katherine Watson, modern art, and everything else that is potentially "subversive," and resistance among the undergraduates is led by Betty (Kirsten Dunst), whose mother is a trustee, whose plans include marrying an upward-bound but morally shifty Harvard man, and whose editorials in the school paper suggest Watson is leading her girls in the direction of communism and, worse, promiscuity. (A school nurse who gives advice on contraception has to leave her job.)

We are pretty sure what the story parabola of *Mona Lisa Smile* will be (the inspiring teacher will overcome adversity to enlighten and guide), but the movie is more observant and thoughtful than we expect. It doesn't just grind out the formula, but seems more like the record of an actual school year than about the needs of the plot. In the delicate dance of audience identification, we get to be both the teacher and her students—to imagine ourselves as a free spirit in a closed system, and as a student whose life is forever changed by her. But, you're wondering, how can I identify with a thirtyish teacher and her twentyish female students? Don't you find yourself identifying with just about anybody on the screen, if the movie is really working? Katherine Watson is smart and brave and stands by her beliefs, and so of course she reminds us of ourselves.

Julia Roberts is above all an actress with a winning way; we like her, feel protective toward her, want her to prevail. In *Mona Lisa Smile* she is the conduit for the plot, which flows through her character. The major supporting roles are played by luminaries of the first post-Julia generation, including not only Dunst, but Julia Stiles as Joan Brandwyn, a girl smart enough to be accepted by Yale Law but perhaps not smart enough to choose it over marriage; Maggie Gyllenhaal as Giselle Levy, who is sexually advanced and has even, it is said, slept with the studly young Italian professor; and Ginnifer Goodwin as Constance Baker, who is too concerned about her looks.

"A few years from now," the Wellesley students are solemnly informed, "your sole responsibility will be taking care of your husband and children." This is not a priority Watson can agree to. She tells the competent but conservative school president (Marian Seldes), "I thought I was headed to a place that would turn out tomorrow's leaders—not their wives." Unlike the typical heroes of movies about inspiring teachers, however, she doesn't think the answer lies in exuberance, freedom, and letting it all hang out, but in actually studying and doing the work, and she despairs when competent students throw away their futures (as she sees it) for marriage to men who have already started to cheat before their wedding days.

Watson herself has a fairly lively love life, with a boyfriend in California (John Slattery) and now a warmth for the above-mentioned studly Italian teacher (Dominic West), although it is probably not true, as a student rumor has it, that she had to come east because of a torrid affair with William Holden. The movie is not really about her romances at all, but about her function as a teacher and her determination to install feminism on the campus before that noun was widely in use. The movie, directed by Mike Newell, may be a little too aware of its sexual politics and might have been more absorbing if Katherine and her students were fighting their way together out of the chains of gender slavery. But the characters involve us, we sympathize with their dreams and despair of their matrimonial tunnel vision, and at the end we are relieved that we listened to Miss Watson and became the wonderful people that we are today.

Mondays in the Sun ★ ★ ½
R, 115 m., 2003

Javier Bardem (Carlos "Santa" Santamaria), Luis Tosar (José Suarez), José Ángel Egido (Paulino "Lino" Ribas Casado), Nieve de Medina (Ana), Enrique Villén (Reina), Celso Bugallo (Amador), Joaquin Climent (Rico), Laura Domínguez (Ángela). Directed by Fernando León de Aranoa and produced by Elías Querejeta and Jaume Roures. Screenplay by de Aranoa and Ignacio del Moral.

Mondays in the Sun chronicles the lives of men who were shipbuilders in Spain until the yards closed, and now measure out their lives in drinking and despair. One still goes to apply for jobs, but is too old, and considers hair dye to make himself look younger. Others buy lottery tickets, hoping for good luck, and benefit from the free cheese samples at the supermarket. They all feel unmanned by the inability to support themselves and their families, and free time is like a swamp they have to wade through every day.

The film stars Javier Bardem, whose range as an actor is demonstrated here by the way he seems to have aged, put on weight, lost his athletic poise, and become a bar stool jockey. He plays "Santa," the unelected leader of a small group of friends who meet most days in a bar opened by Rico (Joaquin Climent) when he was laid off at the shipyards. Among the regulars: Amador (Celso Bugallo), who has developed into a pitiful alcoholic and won't go home even when he has clearly had too much to drink; Reina (Enrique Villén), who found a job as a security guard and whose employment is like a silent rebuke to them all; and José (Luis Tosar), whose wife, Ana (Nieve de Medina), has a job at the cannery and drowns herself in deodorants to get rid of the fishy smell.

In one of the movie's most sharply focused scenes, José and Ana go to the bank to apply for a loan, and the questions of the loan officer, on top of José's bitterness that his wife works and he does not, lead to an angry outburst. But outburst or no, there was no way they were going to get the loan. All of these characters are at a dead end.

There are moments of sad insight, as when they take Amador home to his apartment and find it an emptied-out mess; the wife he keeps talking about has abandoned him. And when Santa meets a friendly woman named Ángela (Laura Domínguez), there's no way he feels able to pursue a relationship because he has nothing to offer her, not even self-esteem. Better to stay in Rico's bar and drink, and go through a pretend flirtation with Rico's teenage daughter.

You can see here fairly clearly the way in which a neighborhood bar can become a surrogate family for men with nowhere to go, nothing to do, and a tendency to drink too much. The bartender is the authority figure, and day after day, week after week, his customers appear in his court for their daily sentence. Sometimes Santa and a friend sit outside in the sun, talking aimlessly about nothing much, because even with the tabs that Rico runs for them they lack the funds to be as drunk as they would like.

The movie, directed by Fernando León de Aranoa, was the most honored film in Spain in 2002, chosen by the Spanish as their Oscar contender over Pedro Almodóvar's *Talk to Her*. Bardem won the Goya, Spain's Oscar, as best actor, and the picture picked up four other Goyas, including one for best film. It is intensely involving at the outset, but it faces an insoluble problem: The story, like the characters, has no place to go. If they get jobs or win the lottery, the movie would be dishonest, and if they do not, then day will follow day with increasing gloom. For the viewer, it seems as if *Mondays in the Sun* is simply repeating the same dilemma over and over. For its characters, of course, it feels that way, too.

Mondovino ★ ★ ★
PG-13, 135 m., 2005

Featuring Michael Broadbent, Hubert de Montille, Aime Guibert, Jonathan Nossiter, Robert Parker, Michel Rolland, and Neal Rosenthal. A documentary directed by Jonathan Nossiter and produced by Emmanuel Giraud and Nossiter. Screenplay by Nossiter.

Mondovino applies to the world of wine the same dreary verdict that has already been returned about the worlds of movies, books, fashion, politics, and indeed modern life: Individuality is being crushed, marketing is the new imperialism, people will like what they are told to like, and sales are the only measurement of good. Briefly (although his movie is not brief), the wine lover Jonathan Nossiter argues that modern tastes in wine are being policed by an unholy alliance involving the most powerful wine producer, the most ubiquitous wine adviser, and the most influential wine critic. Together, they are enforcing a bland, mass-produced taste on a world of wine drinkers who fancy themselves connoisseurs, but basically like what they are told to like.

This does not surprise me, since I have long suspected that "oenophile" is a polite word for a trainee alcoholic who has money and knows how to pronounce the names of several wines that have worked for him in the past. I thought *Sideways* was particularly observant as it watched Miles, the oenophile played by Paul Giamatti, advance during the course of a day from elaborate sniffing, chewing, and tasting rituals to pouring the bucket of slops over his head. I treasure the Mike Royko column in which he advised the insecure on how to deal with a snotty sommelier: He will present you with the cork. Salt it lightly and eat it. This will clear your palate.

There are people who know good wine from bad, and some of them are in this movie, although you will have to take their word for it, all the time remembering that every wine drinker thinks he knows good wine from bad, even at the level where Paisano is judged superior to Mogen David, as indeed some believe. *Mondovino* says distinctive wines are being punished because they do not taste familiar; the unique local taste of great wines is being leveled by "microoxygenization," a mysterious process that is recommended by the wine consultant Michel Rolland, which produces wines that are approved by the wine critic Robert Parker, and therefore becomes the standard for mass producers like Robert Mondavi. As Mondavi and other giants march through Europe buying up ancient vineyards, Rolland and Parker are right behind him to standardize the product.

Rolland is described in the movie as "always laughing; you have to like him." Indeed, the man seems bubbling over with private humor as he speeds in his chauffeured car from one vineyard to another, dispensing valued advice one step ahead of the serious, even self-effacing Parker, whose opinion can make or break a vineyard. That Parker is so powerful is proof that countless wine drinkers do not have taste of their own, because by definition there can be no such thing as a wine that everyone values equally; a great wine should be a wine that you think is great, and if you think it's great because Parker does, then you don't know what you like and simply require a prelubrication benediction.

This much I know from common sense. How many of the rest of Nossiter's charges are true, I cannot know, but he is persuasive. He is fluent in the language of every country he vis-

its, talks with the powerful vintners and the little local growers, visits veteran retailers, and consults with a wine expert from Christie's who wonders "to what extent individuality has flown out the window," and concludes it has taken wing to a very great extent indeed.

Much is made of "terroir," a French word meaning "soil" but also meaning a region, a specific place, a magical quality that a particular area imparts to the grapes it produces. Every great wine should be specifically from its own time and place, in theory, but in practice that would mean that some wines were great and most wines were not, and that's no way to run a global industry. The new goal, Nossiter believes, is to produce pretty good wine and train consumers to consider it great because they're told it is and can find the real thing only with some difficulty. Nossiter thinks some French vineyards are holding out, but that the Italians have more or less caved in to Mondavism.

He makes this argument in a film that is too long and needlessly mannered. There is no particular reason for a restless hand-held camera in a documentary about wine. If we are watching a documentary about cockfighting or the flight of the bumble bee, we can see the logic of a jumpy camera, but vineyards don't move around much and are easy to keep in frame. I am more permissive about Nossiter's other camera strategy, which is to interrupt a shot whenever a dog comes into view, in order to focus on the dog. This I understand. Whenever a dog appears at a social occasion, I immediately interrupt my conversation to greet the dog, and often find myself turning back to its owner with regret.

Despite its visual restlessness and its dogs, *Mondovino* is a fascinating film, not because Nossiter turns red-faced with indignation, but because he allows his argument to make itself. There comes a point when we learn all we are likely to learn about modern wine, and the movie continues cheerfully for another 30 or 40 minutes, just because Nossiter is having so much fun. Although modern wines may have lost their magic, traveling from one vineyard to another has not, and just when we think Nossiter is about to wrap it up, off he goes to Argentina. It was certainly only by an effort of will that he prevented himself from visiting our excellent Michigan vineyards. They have some magnificent dogs.

Monsieur Ibrahim ★ ★ ★
R, 95 m., 2004

Omar Sharif (Monsieur Ibrahim), Pierre Boulanger (Momo), Gilbert Melki (Momo's Father), Isabelle Renauld (Momo's Mother), Lola Naynmark (Myriam), Anne Suarez (Sylvie), Mata Gabin (Fatou), Celine Samie (Eva), Isabelle Adjani (Brigitte Bardot). Directed by François Dupeyron and produced by Michele Petin and Laurent Petin, based on the book and play by Eric-Emmanuel Schmitt.

On the rue Bleue in a working-class Jewish neighborhood in Paris, people know each other and each other's business, and live and let live. That includes the streetwalkers who are a source of fascination to young Momo, who studies them from the window of his flat before preparing supper for his father. Momo's mother is dead, an older brother has left the scene, and his father is distant and cold with the young teenager. But his life is not lonely; there is Monsieur Ibrahim, who runs the shop across the street. And there is Sylvie, who provides Momo with his sexual initiation after the lad breaks open his piggy bank.

Although Brigitte Bardot (played by Isabelle Adjani) pays a visit to the street one day to shoot a scene in a movie, there was another movie character I almost expected to see wandering past: Antoine Doinel, the hero of *The 400 Blows* and four other films by François Truffaut. Not only are both films set within about five years of each other (circa 1958 and 1963), but they share a similar theme: the lonely, smart kid who is left alone by distant parents and seeks inspiration in the streets.

Antoine found it at the movies and in the words of his hero, Balzac. Momo (Pierre Boulanger), whose life is sunnier and his luck better, finds it from Monsieur Ibrahim (Omar Sharif). Although Ibrahim is Turkish, his store is known in Parisian argot as "the Arab's store," because only Arabs will keep their stores open at night and on weekends. Ibrahim establishes himself like a wise old sage behind his counter, knows everyone who comes in, and everything they do, so of course he knows that Momo is a shoplifter. This he does not mind so much: "Better you should steal here, than somewhere you could get into real trouble."

The old man sees that the young one needs a friend and guidance, and he provides both, often quoting from his beloved Koran. He knows things about Momo's family that Momo does not know, and is discreet about Momo's friendship with the hookers. What Ibrahim dreams about is to return someday to the villages and mountains of his native land, to the bazaars and dervishes and the familiar smells of the food he grew up with. What Momo desires is a break with a home life that is barren and crushes his spirit.

The movie was directed by François Dupeyron, based on a book and play by Eric-Emmanuel Schmitt. Its best scenes come as the characters are established and get to know one another. Omar Sharif at seventy-one still has the fire in his eyes that we remember from *Lawrence of Arabia,* and is still a handsome presence, but he settles comfortably into Monsieur Ibrahim's shabby life, and doesn't bore us with his philosophy. And young Boulanger, like Jean-Pierre Leaud all those years ago, has a quick, open face that lets us read his heart.

The last third of the film is more like a fantasy. Momo and Ibrahim both want to escape. Ibrahim buys a fancy red sports car (like the one Bardot was driving), and they drive off to Turkey. What happens there, you will have to discover on your own, but while *The 400 Blows* ended on a note of bleak realism, *Monsieur Ibrahim* settles for melodrama and sentiment. Well, why not? Momo is not as star-crossed as Antoine Doniel, and Ibrahim achieves a destiny he accepts.

But isn't it sort of sad that a movie has to be set forty years ago for us to accept an elderly storekeeper buying a sports car and driving away with a teenager, without ever for an instant suspecting the purity of his motives? The innocence that Antoine and Momo lose in their stories is nothing compared to the world teenagers live in today.

Monster ★ ★ ★ ★
R, 109 m., 2004

Charlize Theron (Aileen Wuornos), Christina Ricci (Selby Wall), Bruce Dern (Thomas), Scott

Wilson (Horton Rohrback), Lee Tergesen (Vincent Corey), Pruitt Taylor Vince (Gene), Annie Corley (Donna Tentler), Marco St. John (Evan). Directed by Patty Jenkins and produced by Mark Damon, Donald Kushner, Clark Peterson, Charlize Theron, and Brad Wyman. Screenplay by Jenkins.

What Charlize Theron achieves in Patty Jenkins's *Monster* isn't a performance but an embodiment. With courage, art, and charity, she empathizes with Aileen Wuornos, a damaged woman who committed seven murders. She does not excuse the murders. She simply asks that we witness the woman's final desperate attempt to be a better person than her fate intended.

Wuornos received a lot of publicity during her arrest, trial, conviction, and 2002 execution for the Florida murders of seven men who picked her up as a prostitute (although one wanted to help her, not use her). The headlines, true as always to our compulsion to treat everything as a sporting event or an entry for the *Guinness Book*, called her "America's first female serial killer." Her image on the news and in documentaries presented a large, beaten-down woman who did seem to be monstrous. Evidence against her was given by Selby Wall (Christina Ricci), an eighteen-year-old who became the older woman's naive lesbian lover and inspired Aileen's dream of earning enough money to set them up in a "normal" lifestyle. Robbing her clients led to murder, and each new murder seemed necessary to cover the tracks leading from the previous one.

I confess that I walked into the screening not knowing who the star was, and that I did not recognize Charlize Theron until I read her name in the closing credits. Not many others will have that surprise; she won the Academy Award for Best Actress. I didn't recognize her— but more to the point, I hardly tried, because the performance is so focused and intense that it becomes a fact of life. Observe the way Theron controls her eyes in the film; there is not a flicker of inattention, as she urgently communicates what she is feeling and thinking. There's the uncanny sensation that Theron has forgotten the camera and the script and is directly channeling her ideas about Aileen

Wuornos. She has made herself the instrument of this character.

I have already learned more than I wanted to about the techniques of disguise used by makeup artist Toni G. to transform an attractive twenty-eight-year-old into an ungainly street prostitute, snapping her cigarette butt into the shadows before stepping forward to talk with a faceless man who has found her in the shadows of a barren Florida highway. Watching the film, I had no sense of makeup technique; I was simply watching one of the most real people I had ever seen on the screen. Jenkins, the writer-director, has made the best film of the year. Movies like this are perfect when they get made, before they're ground down by analysis. There is a certain tone in the voices of some critics that I detest—that superior way of explaining technique in order to destroy it. They imply that because they can explain how Theron did it, she didn't do it. But she does it.

The movie opens with Wuornos informing God that she is down to her last $5, and that if God doesn't guide her to spend it wisely she will end her life. She walks into what happens to be a lesbian bar and meets the eighteen-year-old Selby, who has been sent to live with Florida relatives and be "cured" of lesbianism. Aileen is adamant that she's had no lesbian experience, and indeed her sordid life as a bottom-rung sex worker has left her with no taste for sex at all. Selby's own sexuality functions essentially as a way to shock her parents and gratify her need to be desired. There is a stunning scene when the two women connect with raw sexual energy, but soon enough sex is unimportant compared to daydreaming, watching television, and enacting their private soap opera in cheap roadside motels.

Aileen is the protector and provider, proudly bringing home the bacon—and the keys to cars that Selby doesn't ask too many questions about. Does she know that Aileen has started to murder her clients? She does and doesn't. Aileen's murder spree becomes big news long before Selby focuses on it. The crimes themselves are triggered by Aileen's loathing for prostitution—by a lifetime's hatred for the way men have treated her since she was a child. She has only one male friend, a shattered Vietnam veteran and fellow drunk (Bruce Dern). Although she kills for the first time in self-defense, she is also lashing out against her past. Her experience of love with Selby brings revulsion uncoiling from her memories; men treat her in a cruel way and pay for their sins and those of all who went before them. The most heartbreaking scene is the death of a good man (Scott Wilson) who actually wants to help her, but has arrived so late in her life that the only way he can help is to be eliminated as a witness.

Aileen's body language is frightening and fascinating. She doesn't know how to occupy her body. Watch Theron as she goes through a repertory of little arm straightenings and body adjustments and head tosses and hair touchings, as she nervously tries to shake out her nervousness and look at ease. Observe her smoking technique; she handles her cigarettes with the self-conscious bravado of a thirteen-year-old trying to impress a kid. And note that there is only one moment in the movie where she seems relaxed and at peace with herself; you will know the scene, and it will explain itself. This is one of the greatest performances in the history of the cinema.

Christina Ricci finds the correct note for Selby Wall—so correct some critics have mistaken it for bad acting, when in fact it is sublime acting in its portrayal of a bad actor. She plays Selby as clueless, dim, in over her head, picking up cues from moment to moment, cobbling her behavior out of notions borrowed from bad movies, old songs, and barroom romances. Selby must have walked into a gay bar for the first time only a few weeks ago, and studied desperately to figure out how to present herself. Selby and Aileen are often trying to improvise the next line they think the other wants to hear.

We are told to hate the sin but not the sinner, and as I watched *Monster* I began to see it as an exercise in the theological virtue of charity. It refuses to objectify Wuornos and her crimes and refuses to exploit her story in the cynical manner of true crime sensationalism—insisting instead on seeing her as one of God's creatures worthy of our attention. She has been so cruelly twisted by life that she seems incapable of goodness, and yet when she feels love for the first time she is inspired to try to be a better person.

She is unequipped for this struggle, and lacks the gifts of intelligence and common sense. She is devoid of conventional moral standards. She is impulsive, reckless, angry, and violent, and she devastates her victims, their families, and herself. There are no excuses for what she does, but there are reasons, and the purpose of the movie is to make them visible. If life had given her anything at all to work with, we would feel no sympathy. But life has beaten her beyond redemption.

Monster-in-Law ★
PG-13, 100 m., 2005

Jennifer Lopez (Charlie Cantilini), Jane Fonda (Viola Fields), Michael Vartan (Kevin Fields), Wanda Sykes (Ruby), Adam Scott (Remy), Annie Parisse (Morgan), Monet Mazur (Fiona), Will Arnett (Kit). Directed by Robert Luketic and produced by Paula Weinstein, Chris Bender, and J. C. Spink. Screenplay by Anya Kochoff and Richard La Gravenese.

Faithful readers will know I'm an admirer of Jennifer Lopez, and older readers will recall my admiration for Jane Fonda, whom I first met on the set of *Barbarella* (1968), so it has been all uphill ever since. Watching *Monster-in-Law*, I tried to transfer into Fan Mode, enjoying their presence while ignoring the movie. I did not succeed. My reveries were interrupted by bulletins from my conscious mind, which hated the movie.

I hated it above all because it wasted an opportunity. You do not keep Jane Fonda offscreen for fifteen years only to bring her back as a specimen of rabid Momism. You write a role for her. It makes sense. It fits her. You like her in it. It gives her a relationship with Jennifer Lopez that could plausibly exist in our time and space. It gives her a son who has not wandered over after the *E.R.* auditions. And it doesn't supply a supporting character who undercuts every scene she's in by being more on-topic than any of the leads.

No, you don't get rid of the supporting character, whose name is Ruby and who is played by Wanda Sykes. What you do is lift the whole plot up on rollers, and use heavy equipment to relocate it in Ruby's universe, which is a lot more promising than the rabbit hole this movie falls into. *Monster-in-Law* fails the Gene Siskel Test: "Is this film more

467

interesting than a documentary of the same actors having lunch?"

The movie opens by establishing Charlotte "Charlie" Cantilini (Lopez) as an awfully nice person. She walks dogs, she works as a temp, she likes to cook, she's friendly and loyal, she roughs it on Venice Beach in an apartment that can't cost more than $2,950 a month, she has a gay neighbor who's her best bud. I enjoyed these scenes, right up until the Meet Cute with Young Dr. Kevin Fields (Michael Vartan), a surgeon who falls in love with her. She can't believe a guy like that would really like a girl like her, which is unlikely, since anyone who looks like Jennifer Lopez and walks dogs on the boardwalk has already been hit on by every dot.com entrepreneur and boy band dropout in Santa Monica, and Donald Trump and Charlie Sheen.

Dr. Kevin's mother, Viola, played by Fonda, is not so much a clone of Barbara Walters as a rubbing. You get the outlines, but there's a lot of missing detail. In a flashback, we see that she was a famous television personality, fired under circumstances no one associated with this movie could possibly have thought were realistic—and then allowed to telecast one more program, when in fact security guards would be helping her carry cardboard boxes out to her car. Her last show goes badly when she attempts to kill her guest.

When we meet her, she's "fresh off the funny farm," guzzling booze, taking pills, and getting wake-up calls from Ruby, who is played by Sykes as if she thinks the movie needs an adult chaperone. Viola is seen as a possessive, egotistical, imperious monster who is, and I quote, "on the verge of a psychotic break." The far verge, I would say. When she learns that Dr. Kevin is engaged to marry Charlie, she begins a campaign to sabotage their romance, moaning, "My son the brilliant surgeon is going to marry a temp."

The movie's most peculiar scenes involve Charlie being steadfastly and heroically nice while Viola hurls rudeness and abuse at her. There is a sequence where Viola throws a "reception" for her prospective daughter-in-law and invites the most famous people in the world, so the little temp will be humiliated; Charlie is so serene in her self-confidence that even though she's dressed more for volleyball than diplomacy, she keeps her composure.

All during her monster act, we don't for a second believe Fonda's character because if she really were such a monster, she would fire Ruby, who insults her with a zeal approaching joy. Anyone who keeps Ruby on the payroll has her feet on the ground. Another problem is that Dr. Kevin is a world-class wimp, who actually proposes marriage to Charlie while his mother is standing right there. No doubt Dr. Phil will provide counsel in their wedding bed.

Eventually we realize that Fonda's character consists entirely of a scene waiting to happen: The scene where her heart melts, she realizes Charlie is terrific and she accepts her. Everything else Viola does is an exercise in postponing that moment. The longer we wait, the more we wonder why (a) Charlie doesn't belt her, and (b) Charlie doesn't jump Dr. Kevin—actually, I meant to write "dump," but either will do. By the time the happy ending arrives, it's too late, because by then we don't want Charlie to marry Dr. Kevin. We want her to go back to walking the dogs. She was happier, we were happier, the dogs were happier.

Monty Python's Life of Brian ★ ★ ★
R, 94 m., 2004

Multiple roles by Monty Python's Flying Circus: Graham Chapman, John Cleese, Terry Gilliam, Eric Idle, Terry Jones, and Michael Palin. Directed by Terry Jones and produced by John Goldstone. Screenplay by the Monty Python Troupe.

Monty Python's Life of Brian has been re-released, I suspect, because of the enormous box office of *The Passion of the Christ*. This is a classic bait-and-switch, because Brian, of course, is not Christ, but was born in the next stable. In cinema as in life, poor Brian never did the big numbers. When the film was released in 1979 it was attacked as blasphemous by many religious groups. Consulting my original review, I find I quoted Stanley Kauffmann in the *New Republic*, who speculated that Jesus might have enjoyed it; he had a sense of humor, proven by his occasional puns. That opens up another line of controversy: Are puns funny? Certainly *Monty Python's Life of Brian* is funny, in that peculiar British way where jokes are told sideways, with the obvious point and then the delayed zinger.

The tragedy of Brian (Graham Chapman) is that he has everything it takes be a success, except divinity. Not that he has any desire to found a religion. He attracts followers who convince themselves he is the savior, is the object of cult veneration, and unsuccessfully tries to convince his (small) multitudes that he is not who they think he is. No, that's the other guy. His followers seize upon the smallest hints and misunderstood fragments of his speech to create an orthodoxy they claim to have received from him.

We see the real Jesus twice, once in the next manger (unlike Brian, he has a halo) and again when he delivers the Sermon on the Mount. Most biblical movies show the sermon from a point of view close to Jesus, or looking over his shoulder. *Life of Brian* has the cheap seats, way in the back at the bottom of the mount, where it's hard to hear: "What did he say? Blessed are the cheesemakers?"

Unlike Brian, Monty Python's Flying Circus gang had a distinguished family line. It was in direct descent from the *The Goon Show* on BBC radio (Spike Milligan, Peter Sellers) and the satirical revue *Beyond the Fringe* (Peter Cook, Dudley Moore, Jonathan Miller, Alan Bennett), which was inspired by Second City. Cook and Moore also had a TV show named "Not Only . . . But Also," which along with Second City more or less invented *Saturday Night Live.* Then came the Pythons, who adapted best to movies *(Monty Python and the Holy Grail, Monty Python's The Meaning of Life).*

The success of *Life of Brian* is based first of all on Brian's desperation at being a redeemer without portfolio. He's like one of those guys you meet in a bar who explains how he would have been Elvis if Elvis hadn't been so much better at it. Brian is, in fact, not a religious leader at all but the member of an underground political organization seeking to overthrow Pontius Pilate and kick the Romans out of the Holy Land. There are uncomfortable parallels with the real-life situation in the Middle East, and a jab at the second-class status of women in the scene where men stone a blasphemer. The joke is that the "men" are women pretending to be men, because as women they never get to have fun attending stonings and suchlike. Monty Python rotates the joke into another dimension, since all of the women in the movie are men in drag (some of them risking discovery, you would think, by wearing beards).

The movie benefits by looking vaguely historically accurate (it used the sets built by Lord Lew Grade for Franco Zeffirelli's *Jesus of Nazareth*). It incorporates familiar figures such as Pontius Pilate (Michael Palin), but observes that he speaks with a lisp (his centurions helplessly crack up behind his back). At crucial moments it breaks into song, and there is a particular irony, considering how it is used in the movie, that "The Bright Side of Life" has taken on a long life in exactly the opposite context.

If the film has a message, and it may, it's that much of what passes in religion for truth is the result of centuries of opinion and speculation. Its version of the Brian legend is like a comic parallel to the theories of Christian history in *The Da Vinci Code*—itself a ripe target for Pythonizing. The difficulty with a literal interpretation of the Bible is that it is a translation of a translation of a translation of documents that were chosen by the early church from among a much larger cache of potential manuscripts. "You've all got to think for yourselves!" Brian exhorts his followers, who obediently repeat after him: "We've all got to think for ourselves!"

Moolaade ★ ★ ★ ★

NO MPAA RATING, 124 m., 2004

Fatoumata Coulibaly (Colle Ardo Gallo Sy), Maimouna Helene Diarra (Hadjatou), Salimata Traore (Amasatou), Dominique T. Zeida (Mercenaire), Mah Compaore (Doyenne des Exciseuses), Aminata Dao (Alima Ba). Directed and produced by Ousmane Sembene. Screenplay by Sembene.

Sometimes I seek the right words and I despair. What can I write that will inspire you to see *Moolaade*? This was, for me, the best film at Cannes 2004, a story vibrating with urgency and life. It makes a powerful statement and at the same time contains humor, charm, and astonishing visual beauty.

But even my words of praise may be the wrong ones, sending the message that this is an important film, and therefore hard work. Moviegoers who will cheerfully line up for trash are cautious, even wary, about attending a film they fear might be great. And if I told you the subject of the film is female circumcision—would I lose you? And if I placed the story in an African village, have you already decided to see *National Treasure* instead?

All I can tell you is, *Moolaade* is a film that will stay in my memory and inform my ideas long after other films have vaporized. It takes place in a village in Senegal, where ancient customs exist side-by-side with battery-powered radios, cars, and trucks, and a young man returning from Paris. Traditional family compounds surround a mosque; they are made in ancient patterns from sun-baked mud and have the architectural beauty of everything that is made on the spot by the people who will use it, using the materials at hand. The colors of this world are the colors of sand, earth, sky, and trees, setting off the joyous colors of the costumes.

It is the time for several of the young women in the village to be "purified." This involves removing parts of their genitals so they will have no feeling during sex. The practice is common throughout Africa to this day, especially in Muslim areas, although Islam in fact condemns it. Many girls die after the operation, and during the course of this movie two will throw themselves down a well. But men, who in their wisdom assume control over women's bodies, insist on purification. And because men will marry no woman who has not been cut, the older women insist on it too; they have daughters who must find husbands.

Colle (Fatoumata Coulibaly), the second of four wives of a powerful man, has refused to let her daughter be cut. Now six girls flee from a purification ritual, and four of them seek refuge with her. Colle agrees to help them, and invokes "moolaade," a word meaning "protection." She ties a strand of bright yarn across the entrance to her compound, and it is understood by everyone that as long as the girls stay inside the compound, they are safe, and no one can step inside to capture them.

These details are established not in the mood of a dreary ethnographic docudrama, but with great energy and life. The writer and director is Ousmane Sembene, sometimes called the father of African cinema, who at eighty-one can look back on a life during which he has made nine other films, founded a newspaper, written a novel, and become, in the opinion of his distributor, the art film pioneer Dan Talbot, the greatest living director. Sembene's stories are not the tales of isolated characters; they always exist within a society that observes and comments, and sometimes gets involved. Indeed, his first film, *Black Girl* (1966), is the tragedy of a young African woman who is taken away from this familiarity and made to feel a stranger in Paris.

The village in *Moolaade* has an interesting division of powers. All authority allegedly resides with the council of men, but all decisions seem to be made by the women, who in their own way make up their minds and achieve what they desire. Men insist on purification, but it is really women who enforce it—not just the fearsome women who actually conduct the ceremony, but ordinary women who have undergone it and see no reason why their daughters should be spared.

Colle has seen many girls sicken and die, and does not want to risk her daughter. She knows, as indeed most of those in the village know, that purification is dangerous and unnecessary and has been condemned even by their own government. But if a man will not marry an unpurified daughter, what is a mother to do? This is particularly relevant for Colle, whose own daughter, Amasatou (Salimata Traore), is engaged to be married to a young man who will someday rule their tribe, and who is a successful businessman in Paris. Yes, he is modern, is educated, is cosmopolitan, but in returning to his village for a bride, of course he desires one who has been cut.

Local characters stand out in high relief. There is Mercenaire (Dominique T. Zeida), a peddler whose van arrives at the village from time to time with pots, pans, potions, and dry goods, and who brings news from the wider world. There's spontaneous fun in the way the women bargain and flirt with him. And there is the *doyenne des exciseuses* (Mah Compaore), whose livelihood depends on her purification rituals, and who rules a fierce band of assistants who could play the witches in *Macbeth*.

Much of the humor in the film comes from the ineffectual debates of the council of men, who deplore Colle's action but have been checkmated by the invocation of moolaade. One ancient tradition is thwarted by another. Colle's husband, who has been away, returns to the village and insists that she hand over the girls, but she flatly refuses, and in a scene of drama and rich humor, the husband's first wife backs up the second wife's position and supports her.

All of this nonsense is caused by too much outside influence, the men decide. All of the radios in the village are collected and thrown onto a big pile near the mosque—where, in an image that lingers through the last scenes of the film, some of them continue to play, so that the heap seems filled with disembodied voices. Colle stands strong. Then the young man from Paris arrives, and the whole village holds its breath, poised between the past and the future.

The Mother ★ ★ ★ ½

R, 112 m., 2004

Anne Reid (May), Peter Vaughan (Toots), Cathryn Bradshaw (Paula), Steven Mackintosh (Bobby), Daniel Craig (Darren), Oliver Ford Davies (Bruce), Anna Wilson-Jones (Helen). Directed by Roger Michell and produced by Kevin Loader. Screenplay by Hanif Kureishi.

The Mother peers so fearlessly into the dark needs of human nature that you almost wish it would look away. It's very disturbing. It begins as one of those conventional family dramas with a little love, a little sadness, and a few easy truths, but it's anything but conventional. By the end we've seen lives that aren't working and probably can't be fixed, and we've seen sex used so many different ways it seems more a weapon than a comfort.

The film opens in the reassuring environs of British domesticity. A long-married couple travel into London to visit their children. May (Anne Reid) still has her health and the remains of her beauty, but Toots (Peter Vaughan) seems always out of breath. They arrive at the expensive new home of their son, Bobby (Steven

Mackintosh), go for dinner at the flat of their daughter, Paula (Cathryn Bradshaw), and then Toots dies of a heart attack.

It's clear that Bobby and Paula do not much love their mother, although Paula goes through the motions; Bobby is always darting away for urgent conversations on his cell phone. May understands this, and yet when she returns home she finds she simply cannot stay there: "I'll be like all the other old girls around here, and then I'll go into a home. I'd rather kill myself." She returns to London, is greeted coolly by Bobby and his wife, but finds a role with Paula, who needs a baby-sitter.

At Bobby's expensive house, work is under way: His best friend, Darren (Daniel Craig), is building a new solarium. One night May hears Paula having sex in her living room, peers into the room, and discovers that Darren is Paula's lover. This discovery causes something to shift within May, who becomes friendly with Darren, brings him breakfast and lunch on a tray, and asks him, "Would you come to the spare room with me?"

She is in her sixties; he is in his thirties (and married, with an autistic child). She is a sweet-faced matron; he is bearded and muscular. I was reminded of Fassbinder's *Ali: Fear Eats the Soul* (1974), with its tall Moroccan immigrant and its doughy German widow, and indeed Anne Reid looks a little like Brigitte Mira, Fassbinder's star. But Fassbinder's couple had nothing in common but need; May and Darren find that they talk easily, laugh at the same things, are comfortable together. We follow them to lunch along the Thames and to the churchyard where Hogarth is buried; they are probably the only two people in the story who know who Hogarth was.

We think we know where the film stands: It will be about love transcending age. Not at all. That reassuring subject would leave Paula out of the picture, and she desperately pursues Darren and expects him to leave his wife. As sex gives May an inner glow and inspires her to improve her hair and wardrobe, desperation eats away at Paula until she looks almost as old as her mother, and more haggard and needy. She drinks, which doesn't help. After she and her brother guess the truth about May and Darren, Paula pushes to the center of the story with cold, unforgiving fury.

The Mother was written by Hanif Kureishi, whose screenplays include *My Beautiful Laundrette* and *My Son the Fanatic*. It has been directed by Roger Michell, who, hard to believe, is also the director of the comedy *Notting Hill*. Kureishi is relentless in peeling away the defenses of his characters, exposing their naked needs and fears. Familiar with the conventions of fiction, we expect to like someone in this movie. In the middle stretch we like May and Darren, even while we're aware of something not right in their relationship (it isn't the age gap, it's something trickier). But by the end there is nobody to like; we're faced with the possibility that to truly know someone is to wish you knew them less.

There is courage everywhere you look in *The Mother*. In Anne Reid, who follows May with unflinching honesty into the truth of her life. In Cathryn Bradshaw, whose Paula has never felt loved or valued by anyone. In Daniel Craig, who seems to understand why Darren wants to have sex with May, and helps us understand it, and then, when we think we do, shows us we don't. By the end, *The Mother* has told us all we need to know about the characters, except how to feel about them. It shows how people play a role and grow comfortable with it, and how that role is confused with the real person inside. And then it shows the person inside, frightened and pitiful and fighting for survival. I have a lot of questions about what happens in this movie. I am intended to.

The Motorcycle Diaries ★ ★ ½
R, 128 m., 2004

Gael Garcia Bernal (Ernesto "Che" Guevara), Rodrigo de la Serna (Alberto Granados), Mia Maestro (Chichina Ferreyra), Mercedes Moran (Celia de la Serna), Jorge Chiarella (Dr. Bresciani). Directed by Walter Salles and produced by Michael Nozik, Edgard Tenenbaum, and Karen Tenkhoff. Screenplay by Jose Rivera, based on books by Che Guevara and Alberto Granado.

The Motorcycle Diaries tells the story of an 8,000-mile trip by motorcycle, raft, truck, and foot from Argentina to Peru, undertaken in 1952 by Ernesto Guevara de la Serna and his friend Alberto Granados. If Ernesto had not later become "Che" Guevara and inspired countless T-shirts, there would be no reason to tell this story, which is interesting in the manner of a travelogue but simplistic as a study of Che's political conversion. It belongs to the dead-end literary genre in which youthful adventures are described, and then ". . . that young man grew up to be (Benjamin Franklin, Einstein, Rod Stewart, etc.)."

Che Guevera makes a convenient folk hero for those who have not looked very closely into his actual philosophy, which was repressive and authoritarian. He said he loved the people but he did not love their freedom of speech, their freedom to dissent, or their civil liberties. Cuba has turned out more or less as he would have wanted it to.

But all of that is far in the future as Ernesto (Gael Garcia Bernal) and Alberto (Rodrigo de la Serna) mount their battered old 1939 motorcycle and roar off for a trip around a continent they'll be seeing for the first time. Guevara is a medical student with one year still to go, and Alberto is a biochemist. Neither has ever been out of Argentina. From the alarming number of times their motorcycle turns over, skids out from under them, careens into a ditch, or (in one case) broadsides a cow, it would appear neither has ever been on a motorcycle, either.

First stop, the farm of Ernesto's girlfriend, whose rich father disapproves of him. Chichina (Mia Maestro) herself loves him, up to a point: "Do you expect me to wait for you? Don't take forever." Shy around girls and not much of a dancer, Ernesto is unable to say whether he does or not.

The film, directed by Walter Salles (*Central Station*), follows them past transcendent scenery; we see forests, plains, high chaparral, deserts, lakes, rivers, mountains, spectacular vistas. And along the way the two travelers depend on the kindness of strangers; they're basically broke, and while Ernesto believes in being honest with people, Alberto gets better results by conning them.

They do meet some good new friends. A doctor in Lima, for example, who gets them an invitation to stay at a leper colony. The staff at the colony, and the lepers. A farmer and his wife, whom they meet on the road, and who were forced off their land by evil capitalists.

Day laborers and their sadistic foreman. A garage owner's lonely wife. To get to the leper colony, they take a steamer down a vast lake. Guevera stands in the stern and looks down at a shabby smaller boat that the steamer is towing: This is the boat carrying the poor people, who have no decks, deck chairs, dining rooms, orchestras, and staterooms, but must hang their hammocks where they can.

By the end of the journey, Ernesto has undergone a conversion. "I think of things in different ways," he tells his friend. "Something has changed in me." The final titles say he would go on to join Castro in the Cuban Revolution, and then fight for his cause in the Congo and Bolivia, where he died. His legend lives on, celebrated largely, I am afraid, by people on the left who have sentimentalized him without looking too closely at his beliefs and methods. He is an awfully nice man in the movie, especially as played by the sweet and engaging Gael Garcia Bernal (from *Y Tu Mama Tambien*). Pity how he turned out.

The movie is receiving devoutly favorable reviews. They are mostly a matter of Political Correctness, I think; it is uncool to be against Che Guevera. But seen simply as a film, *The Motorcycle Diaries* is attenuated and tedious. We understand that Ernesto and Alberto are friends, but that's about all we find out about them; they develop none of the complexities of other on-the-road couples, like Thelma and Louise, Bonnie and Clyde, or Huck and Jim. There isn't much chemistry. For two radical intellectuals with exciting futures ahead of them, they have limited conversational ability, and everything they say is generated by the plot, the conventions of the situation, or standard pieties and impieties. Nothing is startling or poetic.

Part of the problem may be that the movie takes place before Ernesto became Che and Alberto became a doctor who opened a medical school and clinic in Cuba (where he still lives). They are still two young students, middle-class, even naive, and although their journey changes them, it ends before the changes take hold.

Salles uses an interesting device to suggest how their experiences might have been burned into their consciousness so that lessons could be learned. He has poor workers, farmers, miners, peasants, beggars pose for the camera, not in still photos, but standing as still as they can, and he uses black-and-white for these tableaux, so that we understand they represent memory. It's an effective technique, and we are meant to draw the conclusion that the adult Che would help these people, although it is a good possibility he did more harm to them.

As a child I faithfully read all of the titles in a book series named *Childhoods of Famous Americans*. George Washington chopped down a cherry tree, Benjamin Franklin got a job at a print shop, Luther Burbank looked at a potato and got thoughtful. The books always ended without really dealing with the adults those children became. But, yes, in retrospect, we can see how crucial the cherry tree, print shop, potato, and Che's motorcycle were, because Those Young Men Grew Up, etc. It's a convenient formula, because it saves you the trouble of dealing with who they became.

Note: To be fair, I must report that a Spanish-speaking friend tells me the spoken dialogue is much richer than the subtitles indicate.

Mr. and Mrs. Smith ★ ★ ★
PG-13, 119 m., 2005

Brad Pitt (John Smith), Angelina Jolie (Jane Smith), Adam Brody (Benjamin), Kerry Washington (Jasmine), Vince Vaughn (Eddie). Directed by Doug Liman and produced by Lucas Foster, Akiva Goldsman, Eric McLeod, Arnon Milchan, and Partrick Wachsberger. Screenplay by Simon Kinberg.

There is a kind of movie that consists of watching two people together on the screen. The plot is immaterial. What matters is the "chemistry," a term that once referred to a science, but now refers to the heat we sense, or think we sense, between two movie stars. Brad Pitt and Angelina Jolie have it, or I think they have it, in *Mr. and Mrs. Smith,* and because they do, the movie works. If they did not, there'd be nothing to work with.

The screenplay is a device to revive their marriage by placing them in mortal danger, while at the same time providing an excuse for elaborate gunfights and chase scenes. I learn from *Variety* that it was written by Simon Kinberg as his master's thesis at Columbia. If he had been studying chemistry instead of the cinema, he might have blown up the lab, but it wouldn't have been boring.

Pitt and Jolie play John and Jane Smith, almost certainly not their real names, who met in Bogota "five or six" years ago, got married, and settled down to a comfortable suburban lifestyle while not revealing to each other that they are both skilled assassins. John keeps his guns and money in a pit beneath the tool shed. Jane keeps her knives and other weapons in trays that slide out from under the oven.

As the movie opens, they're in marriage counseling; the spark has gone out of their relationship. On a typical day, they set off separately to their jobs: He to kill three or four guys, she to pose as a dominatrix while snapping a guy's neck. Can you imagine Rock Hudson and Doris Day in this story? Gable and Lombard and Hepburn and Tracy have also been invoked, but given the violence in their lives, the casting I recommend is The Rock and Vin Diesel. In the opening scene, they could fight over who has to play Mrs. Smith.

Sorry. Lost my train of thought. Anyway, John and Jane individually receive instructions to travel to a remote desert location in the Southwest and take out a mysterious target. They travel there separately, only to discover that their targets are themselves. It's one of those situations where they could tell each other, but then they'd have to kill each other. "If you two stay together, you're dead," says Eddie (Vince Vaughn), another tough guy, who lives at home with his mother because it's convenient and she cooks good and on and on.

The question becomes: Do John and Jane kill each other like the professionals they are, or do they team up to save their lives? The solution to this dilemma requires them to have a fight that reminded me of the showdown between Uma Thurman and Daryl Hannah in *Kill Bill 2*. After physical violence that should theoretically have broken every bone in both their beautiful bodies, they get so excited that, yes, they have sex, which in their case seems to involve both the martial and marital arts.

There is a chase scene. The movie was directed by Doug Liman (*The Bourne Identity*), who is good at chase scenes, and here he gets a laugh by having Jolie drive a van while being pursued by three muscle cars. Liman is able to find a lot of possibilities in the fact that it's one of those vans with two sliding doors in the rear.

The movie pauses from time to time for more sessions with the marriage counselor, during which it appears that professional killing is good for their relationship. After we get our money's worth of action, their problems are resolved, more or less. Although many lives have been lost, the marriage is saved.

None of this matters at all. What makes the movie work is that Pitt and Jolie have fun together on the screen, and they're able to find a rhythm that allows them to be understated and amused even during the most alarming developments. There are many ways that John and Jane Smith could have been played awkwardly, or out of sync, but the actors understand the material and hold themselves at just the right distance from it; we understand this is not really an action picture, but a movie star romance in which the action picture serves as a location.

I've noticed a new trend in the questions I'm asked by strangers. For years it was, "Seen any good movies lately?" Now I am asked for my insights into Brad and Angelina, Tom and Katie, and other couples created by celebrity gossip. I reply that I know nothing about their private lives except what I read in the supermarket tabloids, which also know nothing about their private lives. I can see this comes as a disappointment. So I think I'll start speculating about threesomes enlisting The Rock, Vin Diesel, and Vince Vaughn, selected at random. This may be an idea for the sequel.

Mr. 3000 ★ ★ ★
PG-13, 104 m., 2004

Bernie Mac (Stan Ross), Angela Bassett (Mo Simmons), Brian J. White (T-Rex Pennebaker), Michael Rispoli (Boca), Chris Noth (General Manager Shembri), Paul Sorvino (Coach Gus Panas). Directed by Charles Stone III and produced by Gary Barber, Roger Birnbaum, and Maggie Wilde. Screenplay by Eric Champnella, Keith Mitchell, and Howard Gould.

Baseball heroes are not necessarily the nicest guys on earth, but do moviegoers want to know that? Two movies about flawed legends, Ty Cobb and Babe Ruth, bombed at the box office. Now here is *Mr. 3000,* starring Bernie Mac as a player so disliked that even the team's mascot disses him. This time, however, the movie is a comedy, not a dirge, and Bernie Mac gives a funny and kind of touching performance as a man who attains greatness once and then has to do it again.

Mac plays Stan Ross, a legend in more ways than one with the Milwaukee Brewers, where he retired after getting 3,000 hits. In fact, he retired immediately after hit No. 3,000, leaving his team in the middle of the season to devote himself to his car dealership and TV commercials. Even his best friend doesn't sound sincere when he speaks on Stan Ross Day. Maybe there's still some bad feeling because Stan climbed into the stands to get the ball he hit for No. 3,000, and grabbed it out of the hands of a little kid.

Time passes. Stan basks in the afterglow of his 3,000 hits. He is considered for the Baseball Hall of Fame, and then a statistician discovers a crucial error: Because of a discontinued game, some of his hits were counted twice, and he in fact only has 2,997 hits. Too bad he didn't finish out that season.

That's all setup. The fun is in the payoff, as Stan comes out of retirement at forty-seven to try to get three more hits. He's past his prime and even past his decline, but his comeback makes a good story and ticket sales zoom. But the kids on the team hardly know who he is, and his attitude wears badly when he's batting 0 for 27. You may be in trouble if you're starring every night in Jay Leno monologues.

The thing about Stan, though, is that he knows baseball. He thinks his team is loafing, and he's right. He calls them a Little League team. He notices things, like an opposing pitcher's "tell" before he throws a curve. He starts passing out advice and criticism in the dugout. There's room for that, because the team's manager (Paul Sorvino) sits with sphinxlike detachment at the end of the bench, never uttering a single word.

The Bernie Ross story is a big one for ESPN, which assigns ace reporter Mo Simmons (Angela Bassett). She's an old girlfriend of Stan's, maybe the only woman he ever loved, although love for Stan does not come easily. She puts the pieces in place for what becomes the redemption of Mr. 3000, as he struggles to attain his crucial hits, but somehow at the same time becomes a nicer and even a wiser guy.

Bernie Mac is a meat-and-potatoes kind of actor, at least in the roles he's given to play. In his characters, what you see is what you get: a no-BS straight talker with unlimited self-confidence. He's a good choice to play Stan Ross because we believe him when he says what he thinks, and we especially believe him when he says what he shouldn't be thinking. Stan's romantic relationship with Mo Simmons is obviously based on a lot of history, and Angela Bassett plays what could have been a routine role with a convincing emotional spirit; she'll cover the story, but Mr. 3000 has not earned an entry in her record book.

Almost all sports movies end with the big play, the big point, the big pass, the big putt, whatever. I guess they have to. There's not much point in showing the *next* play, point, etc. And, of course, the big moment has to come in the last moment of the last game of the season, after countless setbacks, in a sudden death situation. *Mr. 3000* follows this formula up to a point, and then, to my surprise, it finds a variation. Don't assume I'm hinting that Stan Ross doesn't get hit No. 3000, or, for that matter, that he does. It's more a case of allowing the implacable logic of baseball strategy to take over.

The Mudge Boy ★ ★ ★
R, 94 m., 2004

Emile Hirsch (Duncan Mudge), Tom Guiry (Perry Foley), Richard Jenkins (Edgar Mudge), Pablo Schreiber (Brent), Zachary Knighton (Travis), Ryan Donowho (Scotty), Meredith Handerhan (Tonya), Beckie King (April). Directed by Michael Burke and produced by Beth Alexander, Alison Benson, and Randy Ostrow. Screenplay by Burke.

The Mudge Boy tells the story of a strange and quiet mama's boy whose mother dies in the film's first scene, leaving him defenseless in the hard world of men—men like his stern and distant father, and the beer-swilling local kids who haunt the back roads in their red pickup truck.

They're in basic training for a lifetime of alcoholism and wife-beating.

Duncan Mudge (Emile Hirsch) doesn't fit into this rural world. He is so direct we think at first he might be retarded; but no, he's simply clueless about how to relate to the louts who circle him. The great love of his life is a chicken, named Chicken, who follows him around and rides in the basket of his bicycle. Chicken is called "she" by just about everybody, but looks like a rooster to me; this may be a reference to the sexual uncertainty that uncoils during the film.

Duncan, who is fifteen or sixteen, has no friends as the story opens, but makes one: Perry (Tom Guiry), a neighbor, who is friendlier to him than the other local boys. One day at the swimming hole Duncan reaches out to feel the muscles in Perry's arm, and Perry recoils as if stung. But the touch sets something into motion between them. We think at first it may be Duncan's discovery that he is gay, but we're getting ahead of the plot, and Duncan may not be gay at all. Perry, the macho tough kid with the swagger, is another story.

Watching the movie, I wondered if *The Mudge Boy* is supposed to take place in the real world, and decided it is not quite. Duncan and his father, Edgar (Richard Jenkins), live not in a farmhouse but in a Farmhouse, an archetypal place filled not with furniture but with props—a dresser, a chair, a couch, a kitchen table. The district seems less like working farmland than like offstage in a psychological problem play. The local boys arrive in their pickup like messengers of fate, and Duncan passively allows himself to be swept up in their ignorance. He buys his way in by paying for their beer; when they come by looking for him, Edgar stares at them long and hard, suspecting their motives.

Edgar is not a cruel father. He is simply unable to talk with his son, except for a few rigid rules no doubt handed down by his own father. After he catches Duncan in an embarrassing situation, his response is to make him dig a hole, wide and deep, to learn what work is like. "You can't even get into trouble like a normal boy," he complains.

Some scenes work with cruel precision. Others seem uncertain—like the scene in church, with Duncan singing "The Old Rugged Cross" way off-key. The movie doesn't seem to know the point of this scene. Certainly it understands Perry, the neighbor boy, whose behavior toward Duncan is directly related to the fact that his father beats him. Duncan has at least been freed by his upbringing to be the person that he is; Perry is trapped in a maze of macho acting-out and baffled by his own behavior.

The film was written and directed by Michael Burke, who seems to be tapping deep, fearful feelings. The movie wants to be dark and truthful, but the spell is sometimes broken by scenes that edge too close to silly, such as the chicken cemetery, and others that seem just plain weird: Did you know you can "becalm" a chicken by putting its head in your mouth? Dr. Johnson said it was a brave man who ate the first oyster, but that was nothing compared to the discovery of chicken becalming.

At the end there is a scene of sudden emotional truth that explains nothing but feels like it does. Duncan will go out into life and probably find a way, in a big city, to be himself. We should seek Perry's future adventures on the shelves of true crime books. *The Mudge Boy* is odd and intense, very well acted, and impossible to dismiss. I think the key is to understand that Duncan is not the one with the problems, but the kind of person who, by being completely and mysteriously on his own wavelength, causes the uncertain people around him to insist loudly and with growing unease on how certain they are of themselves.

My Architect: A Son's Journey ★ ★ ★ ½
NO MPAA RATING, 116 m., 2004

A documentary directed by Nathaniel Kahn and produced by Susan Rose Behr and Kahn. Screenplay by Kahn.

What a sad film this, and how filled with the mystery of human life. When Nathaniel Kahn read the obituary of his father, the great American architect Louis I. Kahn, he expected, somehow, to see his own name listed among the survivors. But in death as in life his father kept his secrets. Louis Kahn had an "official" family including his wife, Esther, and daughter Sue Ann. He had two other secret families: With fellow architect Anne Tyng he had a daughter,

Alexandra, and with his colleague Harriet Pattison he had Nathaniel.

That Kahn was a great architect is clear from the loving photography of his work by his son. His masterpiece, the capitol of Bangladesh in Dhaka, is a building that invites the spirit to soar. His other works included the Kimball Art Museum in Fort Worth, the Yale Art Gallery, the Salk Institute in California, and, most surprising, a "music boat" he designed almost like a vessel from a cartoon. The boat sails into a harbor, folds up into a proscenium stage, and presents a concert for the listeners on shore.

Against these achievements the movie sets a lifetime of struggle, secrecy, stubbornness, deception, and frequent failure. He was "short, scarred, and ugly, and had a funny voice," a colleague states flatly. His face badly burned by a fire when he was an infant, Louis moved with his family from Estonia to Philadelphia when he was six. Called "Scarface" in school, he buried himself in his studies, won a college scholarship, had grand ideas about architecture, but was supported for twenty years by his first wife and didn't open his own office until he was almost fifty.

He would die at seventy-three, and only in the last ten years of his life did he achieve the stature for which he is remembered. But what a death. Returning from Bangladesh—a hard journey for a man his age—he collapsed and died in a rest room of Penn Station, and his body went unclaimed for two days because he had scratched out his address on his passport, and the police did not recognize his name. To this day, Nathaniel's mother remains convinced he blotted out the address because he planned to make good on a promise to come and live with them. Nathaniel is not so sure.

The movie begins as the story of a son searching for his father, and ends as the story of the father searching for himself. Kahn would visit Nathaniel and Harriet unexpectedly, always leaving before morning. He told the boy stories about his life, drew him a book of funny boats (at the time he was designing the music ship), but "left no physical evidence he had ever been in our home—not even a bow tie hanging in the closet."

Nathaniel interviews both his mother and Anne; Esther, who died in 1996, is seen in an old video. He talks to many of his father's col-leagues, from contemporaries like Philip Johnson and I. M. Pei to Frank Gehry, who once worked in Kahn's shop. Their memories mix affection and respect with exasperation. He was a difficult man. When his plan to redesign downtown Philadelphia was rejected, there was a hint that anti-Semitism might have been involved, but when Nathaniel tracks down Ed Bacon, the czar in charge of the project, he gets a sharp verdict: "Totally irresponsible. Totally impractical." Kahn wanted Philadelphians to park their cars in a ring around the city and walk to work, a utopian idea not likely to win tax dollars.

There are moments of sudden poignance. A colleague remembers that Kahn always spent Christmas with them, and Nathaniel repeats "Christmas?" and we realize he never spent a Christmas with his father. And Robert Boudreau, the man who commissioned the music ship, realizes he is talking to Louis's son, and tears well in his eyes. "I saw you when you were six years old," he says. "At the wake." Kahn's wife had sent orders for Anne and Harriet to stay away from the funeral, but they came anyway, and were ignored.

A portrait emerges of Louis I. Kahn as a man constantly in motion, an elusive target who lived more at his office than in any home, who worked his employees beyond the endurance of some of them, who would appear for two or three days and then fly off in search of a commission or to supervise a job. It was his great disappointment that his plans for a synagogue in Jerusalem were never taken up; ironic, that his greatest work was built by a Muslim country.

When he died, Nathaniel says, his father was $500,000 in debt. He narrates a catalog of projects that were canceled or never commissioned. At the end of the film, meeting with his two half-sisters, he wonders if they are a family, and they decide they are because they choose to be—not because of who their father was. That was the only choice Louis left them.

My Life Without Me ★ ★ ½

R, 106 m., 2003

Sarah Polley (Ann), Amanda Plummer (Laurie), Scott Speedman (Don), Leonor Watling (Neighbor Ann), Deborah Harry (Ann's Mother), Mark Ruffalo (Lee), Alfred Molina

(Ann's Father), Julian Richings (Dr. Thompson). Directed by Isabel Coixet and produced by Esther Garcia and Gordon McLennan. Screenplay by Coixet.

It's not probable that I will die before attending Sofia Coppola's Lifetime Achievement Award, but I can't deny that death has been on my mind these days. Having surgery for cancer concentrates the mind wonderfully. I have some notions of what I would do if I had little time to live, and things I would not do. I would not, for example, do any of the things that are done by Ann, the heroine of *My Life Without Me*, who would be a cruel egocentric if she weren't so obviously just a fictional pawn.

I would let everyone know what was what. I would expect them to be open with me. I would try to remember the dying woman in Ingmar Bergman's *Cries and Whispers*, who writes in her journal: "This is happiness. I cannot wish for anything better. I feel profoundly grateful to my life, which gives me so much." I would remember my dying Aunt Marjorie, who told me with total contentment, "I've enjoyed my life, Rog, and you know this day comes for all of us sooner or later." And I would start reading a long novel. We both knew Margie had maybe a month to live. She was a great reader. I asked her what she was reading. "I've just started Tom Clancy's new novel," she said, and her smile finished the sentence.

The heroine of *My Life Without Me*, on the other hand, engineers her death as a soap opera that would be mushy if it were about her, but is shameless because it is by her. Told she has inoperable ovarian cancer, she keeps it a secret from everyone in her life, lies to cover up her growing weakness, and on good days works through a checklist of "Ten Things to Do Before I Die." Number eleven should maybe be, rent the video of *Things to Do in Denver When You're Dead*.

One of the items on her list is, "Find out what it would be like to make love with another man." She was married at seventeen, to the only boy she ever slept with, and now she is twenty-three and lives with Don and their daughters in a house trailer in her mother's backyard. They have the happiest marriage I have ever seen in the movies, maybe because strict plot economy allows no time to provide them with problems.

Nevertheless when she meets a guy named Lee at the Laundromat, she allows them to drift into a relationship that quickly leads to love.

I don't understand her need to do this. I understand that a twenty-three-year-old woman might be curious about sleeping with a second man, but would she act on mere curiosity if she loved her husband, they were happy, and had great sex? Okay, maybe, although I think she'd be wrong. But to do it when she's dying is so unfair to the other guy, who doesn't understand part of her appeal is the urgent, bittersweet quality that dying has given her. And it's not enough for her to have sex. She wants to make someone fall in love with her. It's not enough to spring a mournful surprise on one man who loves her. She wants two heartbreaks. Maybe she stops at only two because of time pressure. At her funeral they should play, "Don't Cry for Me, Argentina."

Her egocentric decision puts enormous pressure on the kind doctor who gives her the bad news and is forbidden to treat her. And on her kids, who know something is very wrong, because kids always do, and who have to believe her lies about being tired. And on her husband, her mother, her best friend at work, and even the woman (also named Ann) who has moved in next door. After testing her baby-sitting skills, she has chosen this Ann as Don's next wife, and arranges a dinner they don't realize is their first date. It's bad enough for a second wife to feel like she's sharing her husband with the ghost of his first wife, but how does it feel during sex when the ghost is cheering, "You go, girl!"

Now of course all of this is handled with exquisite taste. Actors do not often get roles this challenging, and they find honesty in the moments even while the movie as a whole grows into a manipulation. Ann is played by Sarah Polley, from *The Sweet Hereafter*, and she accepts the character's decisions and invests them, wrong as they are, with simplicity and glowing conviction. Lee, the second lover, is played by Mark Ruffalo, who amazes me in one movie after another with the intensity of his presence and his gentle response to other actors. Scott Speedman is Ann's husband, Deborah Harry is her mother, Alfred Molina is her father, currently in prison; Amanda Plummer is the best friend, and Leonor Watling is the other Ann, who tells a story about dying Siamese twins that starts out sad and then becomes increasingly inconceivable.

And an actor named Julian Richings is Dr. Thompson, the man who tells her she has ovarian cancer. He sits next to her in a row of chairs while telling her this, and admits he has never been able to look a patient in the eye when telling them they're about to die. This character, and this scene, point to a better way the movie could have gone. The doctor has the empathy for other humans that Ann lacks. What he does may be professionally questionable, but it comes from his heart.

That the performances are so good, that they find truth in scenes to which we have fundamental objections, makes this a tricky movie to review. I think the screenplay, written by director Isabel Coixet, is shameless in its weepy sentiment. But there is truth here, too, and a convincing portrait of working-class lives. These people don't stagger under some kind of grim proletarian burden, but are smart and resourceful, and I suspect Ann—had she lived—might have someday turned into a pretty good writer.

On the other hand, there are several scenes of Ann making tape recordings intended to be played by her daughters on their birthdays until they're eighteen. If I were one of those daughters and had grown old enough to have a vote on the matter, I would burn the goddamn tapes and weep and pound the pillow and ask my dead mother why she was so wrapped up in her stupid, selfish fantasies that she never gave me the chance to say good-bye.

My Sister Maria ★ ★ ★ ½
NO MPAA RATING, 90 m., 2004

With Maria and Maximilian Schell and members of their family. A documentary directed by Maximilian Schell and produced by Dieter Pochlatko. Screenplay by Schell and Gero von Boehm.

My Sister Maria is brave, heartless, and exceedingly strange, a quasi-documentary in which the actor Maximilian Schell mercilessly violates the privacy of his older sister, Maria. It is filmed mostly on the Schells' family farm in Austria, where Maria, a famous star from the 1940s through the 1960s, lives in decline and seclusion. Like a modern Norma Desmond

from *Sunset Boulevard,* she is surrounded by television sets, all playing videos of her old movies. "It all comes back, and I'm inside the scene," she says. "I was happy then."

She is not senile, precisely, or at least Maximilian refuses her the escape of that diagnosis. She has simply arrived at a decision: Having given her life to entertaining others, she has arrived at a time when the others must care for her. A psychiatrist explains to Max that his sister's mental "center for discipline" has been destroyed—something that sounds more like a punishment in a horror film than an actual condition.

For Maximilian, his sister's condition is explicable, and her recovery clear: She has given up and wants to spend all day in bed, and if she will only get up and walk, each day a little farther, her heart will pump blood to her brain and she will—what? Recover? That this regimen is forced upon Maria in the middle of an Alpine winter leads to scenes bordering on black comedy, as the pathetic old woman is sent out into the snow to laboriously walk a slippery path. More than once, she slips and falls. That a body double is obviously being used relieves us of concern that she will break a hip, but provides us with unsettling questions about the movie: How much of it is real, and how much devised, staged, or contrived? Once after the double falls, there is a close-up of Maria's face on the ground. Is she willingly acting here? Was the scene contrived? You rarely know exactly what the screenplay means with a documentary, and certainly not this time.

The film opens with paparazzi forcing themselves into Maria's home to grab photos of the old woman, which appear the next day in a paper. What are we to make of this? Did Maximilian use secret cameras to record this transgression? Unlikely, since we see the paparazzi approaching the wrong house, talking with a housekeeper and moving on to the right house; and then we see them inside. So the paparazzi were actors, apparently, directed by Maximilian for the film. And when Maria is shown the newspaper, her dialogue is right on target: "I used to be on Page One. Now I'm on Page Three." We can accept that the film restaged a paparazzi invasion that may really have happened, but how much indignation can we feel when Maximilian himself shows his sister at length, her beauty ravaged by time?

There is another strangeness in the scenes when Maximilian, his Russian-born wife, Natasha, and their children talk with Maria. To me, at least, Maria seems of essentially sound mind. Max asks her about their family, about her husbands, about her career, about romance, and her answers are lucid, concise, and sometimes even witty. What we want to hear, and never do, is how she feels about this use of herself, her history, and her present life.

Max must love his sister, and yet he resents her, too, especially in the way she has spent herself into bankruptcy. He asks on the sound track why others should be asked to sacrifice their financial status to support her. Max is finally forced to auction his art, and there are scenes perhaps a little boastful, where we're shown what famous artists he has collected ("This is Rothko's last painting"), and what enormous bids they inspire.

The film is intercut with scenes from Maria's long career. She was a star in Europe and Hollywood, was the first actress on the cover of *Time*, acted opposite everyone from Gary Cooper and Yul Brynner to Oskar Werner, had a radiant smile and a quick, healthful beauty, and then, gradually, faded away into age, as we all must.

I agree that a documentary that simply reviewed her career would be routine and pointless. I know Maximilian is a filmmaker obsessed with the subject of the loss of fame and beauty, because he demonstrated that so memorably in his 1984 documentary about Marlene Dietrich. But Dietrich resolutely (perhaps wisely) refused to appear on screen. Was Maria given a choice? Because we don't know if she's as sane as she seems or as crazy as the movie claims, we can't decide. If she is indeed demented, then the movie is not fair to her, and might even be interpreted as a form of revenge for the demands she has made on Maximilian's time, patience, and financial resources.

There is, however, another possibility: That the film, in some bold and original way, is a conscious collaboration between brother and sister to devise a work about the loss of fame and youth—a work that is all the more powerful because it seems to be factual, and seems

to violate Maria's right to privacy. That this film may be substantially fictional, devised in its "documentary" form as an artistic tactic, is a fascinating possibility.

I was always, in any event, fascinated by the experience of watching it, and of trying to decide exactly what I was watching. If we accept the film on its own terms, then it takes, I think, immoral liberties with a woman powerless to protect herself. Yet Maria Schell in this film does not seem unaware, and retains enough authority that those around her do her bidding (even bringing her another TV set on a sled, through a blizzard). So I am unsure what to think.

Whatever the underlying reality, the film is now a fact, and if damage has been done, it is too late to undo it. To watch *My Sister Maria* requires us to decide what we think a film is, what we think a documentary should do, how far we think art justifies its cost in human feelings. Those who think *Fahrenheit 9/11* blurs the line between fact and interpretation have no idea how mysterious and challenging that line can become. The fundamental drama of *My Sister Maria* takes place within our own minds, as we struggle with the enigma of viewing it.

Mysterious Skin ★ ★ ★ ½
NO MPAA RATING, 99 m., 2005

Joseph Gordon-Levitt (Neil McCormick), Brady Corbet (Brian Lackey), Michelle Trachtenberg (Wendy Peterson), Jeffrey Licon (Eric Peterson), Bill Sage (Coach Heider), Mary Lynn Rajskub (Avalyn Friesen), Elisabeth Shue (Ellen McCormick), George Webster (Young Brian), Chase Ellison (Young Neil). Directed by Gregg Araki and produced by Araki, Jeffrey Levy-Hinte, and Mary Jane Skalski. Screenplay by Araki, based on a novel by Scott Heim.

"The summer I was eight years old," a character says at the beginning of *Mysterious Skin*, "five hours disappeared from my life." He remembers being at a Little League game, and then the next thing he remembers is being found hiding in his basement at home, with blood from a nosebleed all over his shirt. What happened during those five hours? And why does he continue to have blackouts, nosebleeds, and nightmares for the next ten years?

This character's name is Brian, and he is played as a child by George Webster, wearing glasses too large for his face. As a teenager, played by Brady Corbet, he has grown into the glasses, but remains a shy and inward boy. He sees a TV show about a girl named Avalyn in a nearby Kansas town who believes she was abducted by aliens. He meets her, solemnly regards the scar on her leg where a "tracking device" was implanted, and when he talks about his nosebleeds she nods knowingly: "The old nose trick, so the scar can't be seen."

Although Brian's narration opens *Mysterious Skin,* he isn't the film's central character. That would be Neil, played by Chase Ellison as an eight-year-old and by Joseph Gordon-Levitt as a young man. He remembers Little League very well. He idolized his coach (Bill Sage), went home with him, was seduced with video games and sexually molested. The molestation continued that whole summer, as Neil identified with the coach as a father figure, valued his importance in the coach's life, and developed a compulsion to please older men. That leads him in adolescence to become a prostitute, not so much for the money as because he has been programmed that way.

Mysterious Skin, written and directed by Gregg Araki and based on a novel by Scott Heim, is at once the most harrowing and, strangely, the most touching film I have seen about child abuse. It is unflinching in its tough realism; although there is no graphic sex on the screen, what is suggested, and the violence sometimes surrounding it, is painful and unsentimental. There is little sense that Neil enjoys sex, or that he is "gay" in the way, for example, that his friend Eric is—Eric, who likes flamboyant hairstyles and black lipstick but never seems to have sex. Then there's Neil's soul mate, Wendy (Michelle Trachtenberg). "If I hadn't been queer, we would have gotten married and had kids and all of that," Neil tells us. She accepts Neil's nature, warns him of its risks, and at one point objectively observes, "Where normal people have a heart, Neil McCormick has a bottomless black hole."

The film's scenes set in childhood are filled with the kinds of mysteries childhood contains, including Neil's feelings about the endless string of boyfriends brought home by his mother (Elisabeth Shue), and Brian's conviction that a UFO hovered one night over his house. In their later teen years, the two boys have no contact. Neil turns tricks at the public park, while Brian hangs out at the library and keeps a notebook of his nightmares about aliens. His friendship with Avalyn (Mary Lynn Rajskub) is based on memories of balloon-headed aliens performing weird sex probes, until Avalyn tries a weird probe of her own, which Brian is completely unable to deal with.

Neil's experiences are sad and harsh, and sometimes comic, as when he has sex while stoned, and simultaneously provides the public address commentary on a local baseball game. He follows Wendy to New York, and in the early 1990s learns some things about AIDS that cause him to leave hustling for a while and test opportunities in the fast food industry. His encounter with a dying AIDS victim is sad and tender ("This is going to be the safest encounter you've ever had. If you could just rub my back. I really need to be touched"). And then there is a brutal encounter that sends him fleeing home to Kansas on Christmas Eve, and to a crucial encounter with Brian, who thinks maybe since they were on the same Little League team, Neil might remember something helpful. He does.

Mysterious Skin begins in the confusion of childhood experiences too big to be processed, and then watches with care and attention as its characters grow in the direction that childhood pointed them. It is not a message picture, doesn't push its agenda, is about discovery, not accusation. Above all it shows how young people interpret experiences in the terms they have available to them, so that for Neil the memory of the coach remains a treasured one, until he digs more deeply into what really happened, and for Brian the possibility of alien abduction seems so obvious as to be beyond debate. The film begins with their separate myths about what happened to them when they were eight, and then leads them to a moment when their realities join. How that happens, and what is revealed, is astonishing in its truthfulness.

There is accomplished acting in this film, and there needs to be. This is not an easy story. Joseph Gordon-Levitt evokes a kind of detached realism that holds him apart from the sordid details of his life, while Brady Corbet's character seems frozen in uncertain childhood, afraid to grow up. Both are lucky to have friends of tact and kindness: Michelle Trachtenberg's Wendy knows there is something deeply wounded about Neil, but accepts it and worries about him. And Jeffrey Licon, as Eric, becomes Brian's closest friend without ever seeming to require a sexual component; he watches, he is curious about human nature, he cares.

Mysterious Skin is a complex and challenging emotional experience. It's not simplistic. It hates child abuse, but it doesn't stop with hate; it follows the lives of its characters as they grow through the aftermath. The movie clearly believes Neil was born gay; his encounter with the coach didn't "make" him gay, but was a powerful influence that aimed his sexuality in a dangerous direction. Brian on the other hand was unable to process what happened to him, has internalized great doubts and terrors, and may grow up neither gay nor straight, but forever peering out of those great big glasses at a world he will never quite bring into focus.

Mystic River ★ ★ ★ ★
R, 137 m., 2003

Sean Penn (Jimmy Markum), Tim Robbins (Dave Boyle), Kevin Bacon (Sean Devine), Laurence Fishburne (Whitey Powers), Marcia Gay Harden (Celeste Boyle), Laura Linney (Annabeth Markum), Thomas Guiry (Brendan), Emmy Rossum (Katie). Directed by Clint Eastwood and produced by Eastwood, Judie Hoyt, and Robert Lorenz. Screenplay by Brian Helgeland, based on the novel by Dennis Lehane.

Clint Eastwood's *Mystic River* is a dark, ominous brooding about a crime in the present that is emotionally linked to a crime in the past. It involves three boyhood friends in an Irish neighborhood of Boston, who were forever marked when one of them was captured by a child molester; as adults, their lives have settled into uneasy routines that are interrupted by the latest tragedy. Written by Brian Helgeland, based on the novel by Dennis Lehane, the movie uses a group of gifted actors who are able to find true human emotion in a story that could have been a whodunit, but looks too deeply and evokes too much honest pain.

The film centers on the three friends: Jimmy (Sean Penn), an ex-con who now runs the corner store; Dave (Tim Robbins), a handyman; and Sean (Kevin Bacon), a homicide detective. All are married; Jimmy to a second wife, Annabeth (Laura Linney), who helps him raise his oldest daughter and two of their own; Dave to Celeste (Marcia Gay Harden), who has given him a son; Sean to an absent, pregnant wife who calls him from time to time but never says anything. The other major character is Whitey (Laurence Fishburne), Sean's police partner.

Jimmy keeps a jealous eye on his nineteen-year-old daughter, Katie (Emmy Rossum), who works with him at the store. She's in love with Brendan (Thomas Guiry), a boy Jimmy angrily disapproves of. Theirs is a sweet puppy love; they plan to run away together, but before that can happen Katie is found brutally beaten and dead. Sean and Whitey are assigned to the case. Brendan is obviously one of the suspects, but so is Dave, who came home late the night of the murder, covered with blood and talking to his wife in anguish about a mugger he fought and may have killed.

Although elements in *Mystic River* play according to the form of a police procedural, the movie is about more than the simple question of guilt. It is about pain spiraling down through the decades, about unspoken secrets and unvoiced suspicions. And it is very much about the private loyalties of husbands and wives. Jimmy says that he will kill the person who killed his daughter, and we have no reason to doubt him, especially after he hires neighborhood thugs to make their own investigation. Laura Linney, as his wife, has a scene where she responds to his need for vengeance, and it is not unreasonable to compare her character to Lady Macbeth. Marcia Gay Harden, as Celeste, Dave's wife, slowly begins to doubt her husband's story about the mugger, and shares her doubts. We see one wife fiercely loyal, and another who suspects she has been shut out from some deep recess of her husband's soul.

Although the story eventually arrives at a solution, it is not about the solution. It is about the journey, and it provides each of the actors with scenes that test their limits. Both Penn and Robbins create urgent and breathtaking suspense as they are cross-examined by the police. There is tension between Whitey, who thinks Dave is obviously guilty, and Sean, who is reluctant to suspect a childhood friend. There are such deep pools of hatred and blood lust circling the funeral that we expect an explosion at any moment, and yet the characters are all inward, smoldering.

And always that day in the past lingers in their memories. The three boys were writing their names in wet concrete when two men in a car drove up, flashed a badge, and took one of the boys away with them. Flashbacks show that he was abused for days. Compounding his suffering was the uneasiness the other two boys always felt about him; maybe they didn't entirely understand what happened to him, but in some sense they no longer felt the same about their violated friend—whose name, half-finished, remains in the old concrete like a life interrupted in midstream.

This is Clint Eastwood's twenty-fourth film as a director, and one of the few titles where he doesn't also act. He shows here a deep rapport with the characters and the actors, who are allowed lancing moments of truth. Always an understated actor himself, he finds in his three actors pools of privacy and reserve. Robbins broods inside his own miseries and watches vampire movies on TV to find metaphors for the way he feels. Bacon hurts all the time, we feel, because of the absence of his wife. Penn is a violent man who prepares to act violently but has not, we see, found much release that way in the past.

To see strong acting like this is exhilarating. In a time of flashy directors who slice and dice their films in a dizzy editing rhythm, it is important to remember that films can look and listen and attentively sympathize with their characters. Directors grow great by subtracting, not adding, and Eastwood does nothing for show, everything for effect.

My Summer of Love ★ ★ ★
R, 85 m., 2005

Natalie Press (Mona), Emily Blunt (Tamsin), Paddy Considine (Phil), Dean Andrews (Ricky), Paul Antony-Barger (Tamsin's Father), Lynette Edwards (Tamsin's Mother), Kathryn Sumner (Sadie). Directed by Pawel Pawlikovsky and produced by Chris Collins and Tanya Seghatchian. Screenplay by Pawlikovksy and Michael Wynne, based on the novel by Helen Cross.

Her brother has gone bonkers. He's pouring all the booze down the drain and announcing he's turning the pub into a worship center for Jesus people. Mona and Phil inherited the pub from their parents, and live upstairs; Phil (Paddy Considine) has come to Jesus belatedly, after a spell in prison. Mona (Natalie Press) gets on her moped, which has no engine but nevertheless functions as a symbol of escape, and wheels it into the country outside their small Yorkshire town. That's the day she meets Tamsin.

The title of *My Summer of Love* gives away two games at once: that she will fall in love, and that autumn will come. Mona is a tousled blonde, sixteen years old, dressed in whatever came to hand when she got up in the morning, bored by her town, her brother, and her life. Her boyfriend has just broken up with her in a particularly brutal way. Tamsin (Emily Blunt) is a rich girl, about the same age, sleek and brunette, on horseback the first time Mona sees her. She's spending the summer at her family's country house. "You're invited," she tells Mona. "I'm always here."

Tamsin's mother is absent. Her father is present but seems absent. The first time Mona visits, Tamsin shows her the room of her dead sister: "It's been kept as a shrine." The sister died, Tamsin says, of anorexia. The country girl and the city girl become friends almost by default; there seems to be no one else in the town they would want to talk to—certainly not the members of Phil's worship group.

That their summer leads to love is not quite the same thing as that it leads to a lesbian relationship. It's more like a teenage crush, composed in equal parts of hormones and boredom. But Tamsin and Mona promise to love each other forever, and as they swim in forest pools and ride around the countryside, they form their own secret society.

Phil, in the meantime, is engaged in the construction of a giant cross, made of iron and wood, which he wants to place on the top of a hill overlooking the town. Mona passes through the pub on her way upstairs, avoiding the prayer groups; left unexplained is how the brother and sister are supporting themselves. For Phil, religion seems less a matter of spiritual conviction than emotional hunger; he has been bad, now is good, and requires forgiveness and affirmation. Nothing wrong with that, unless he begins to impose his new lifestyle on Mona.

The movie is sweet and languid when the girls are together, edgier when Mona is around Phil. The question of Tamsin's father is complicated by the presence of his "personal assistant." The big summer house is empty and lonely, lacking a mother and haunted by the ghost of the dead sister. Pawel Pawlikovsky, the director and cowriter (with Michael Wynne), wisely allows the time to seem to flow, instead of pushing it. That's why, when Phil visits Tamsin's house looking for Mona, how Tamsin behaves and what happens is such a cruel surprise. She is, we realize, a convincing actress. When more revelations come in a closing scene, they are not exactly a surprise, not exactly a tragedy, not exactly very nice. We begin to sense the buried irony in the title.

Emily Blunt is well cast as Tamsin, a rich girl, product of the best schools, who cultivates decadence as her way of standing apart from what's expected of her. Natalie Press as Mona, on the other hand, is straight from the shoulder: She's without illusions about life, has given up on her brother, looks forward to marriage and family as a dreary prospect. Without quite saying so, she knows she'll never find a husband in her Yorkshire valley who is up to her speed. Will she, after this summer, identify as a lesbian? Doubtful. The summer stands by itself.

I'm not sure if the movie has a point. I'm not sure it needs one. I learn from *Variety* that the screenplay is inspired by a novel by Helen Cross that also involves a miner's strike and some murders. All of that is missing here, and what's left is a lazy summer of sweaty, uncertain romance; this isn't a coming-of-age movie so much as a movie about being of an age. At the end, when Tamsin tries to explain herself to Mona, we understand how completely different these two teenage girls are; how one deals in irony and deception, and with the other, what you see is what you get, whether you want it or not.

N

Napoleon Dynamite ★ ½
PG, 86 m., 2004

Jon Heder (Napoleon Dynamite), Jon Gries (Uncle Rico), Aaron Ruell (Kip Dynamite), Efren Ramirez (Pedro), Tina Majorino (Deb), Diedrich Bader (Rex), Haylie Duff (Summer). Directed by Jared Hess and produced by Jeremy Coon, Sean Covel, and Chris Wyatt. Screenplay by Jared Hess and Jerusha Hess.

There is a kind of studied stupidity that sometimes passes as humor, and Jared Hess's *Napoleon Dynamite* pushes it as far as it can go. Its hero is the kind of nerd other nerds avoid, and the movie is about his steady progress toward complete social unacceptability. Even his victory toward the end, if it is a victory, comes at the cost of clowning before his fellow students.

We can laugh at comedies like this for two reasons: because we feel superior to the characters, or because we pity or like them. I do not much like laughing down at people, which is why the comedies of Adam Sandler make me squirmy (most people, I know, laugh because they like him). In the case of Napoleon Dynamite (Jon Heder), I certainly don't like him, but then, the movie makes no attempt to make him likable. Truth is, it doesn't even try to be a comedy. It tells his story and we are supposed to laugh because we find humor the movie pretends it doesn't know about.

Napoleon is tall, ungainly, depressed, and happy to be left alone. He has red hair that must take hours in front of the mirror to look so bad. He wants us to know he is lonely by choice. He lives outside of town with his brother, Kip (Aaron Ruell), whose waking life is spent online in chat rooms, and with his grandmother, who is laid up fairly early in a dune buggy accident.

It could be funny to have a granny on a dune buggy; I smile at least at the title of the Troma film *Rabid Grannies*. But in this film the accident is essentially an aside, an excuse to explain the arrival on the farm of Napoleon's Uncle Rico (Jon Gries), a man for whom time has stood still ever since the 1982 high school sports season, when things, he still believes, should have turned out differently. Rico is a door-to-door salesman for an herbal breast enlargement potion, a product that exists only for the purpose of demonstrating Rico's cluelessness. In an age when even the Fuller Brush Man would be greeted with a shotgun (does anyone even remember him?), Rico's product exists in the twilight zone.

Life at high school is daily misery for Napoleon, who is picked on cruelly and routinely. He finally makes a single friend, Pedro (Efren Ramirez), the school's only Latino, and manages his campaign for class president. He has a crush on a girl named Deb (Tina Majorino), but his strategy is so inept that it has the indirect result of Deb going to the prom with Pedro. His entire prom experience consists of cutting in.

Watching *Napoleon Dynamite*, I was reminded of *Welcome to the Dollhouse*, Todd Solondz's brilliant 1996 film, starring Heather Matarazzo as an unpopular high school girl. But that film was informed by anger and passion, and the character fought back. Napoleon seems to passively invite ridicule, and his attempts to succeed have a studied indifference, as if he is mocking his own efforts. I'm told the movie was greeted at Sundance with lots of laughter, but then, Sundance audiences are concerned to be cool, and to sit through this film in depressed silence would not be cool, however urgently it might be appropriate.

Narc ★ ★ ★
R, 105 m., 2003

Ray Liotta (Lieutenant Henry Oak), Jason Patric (Sergeant Nick Tellis), Chi McBride (Captain Cheevers), Busta Rhymes (Beery), Anne Openshaw (Kathryn Calvess), Richard Chevolleau (Steeds), John Ortiz (Ruiz), Thomas Patrice (Marcotte), Alan Van Sprang (Michael Calvess). Directed by Joe Carnahan and produced by Diane Nabatoff, Julius Nasso, Ray Liotta, and Michelle Grace. Screenplay by Carnahan.

Joe Carnahan's *Narc* is a cold, hard film about Detroit narcotics detectives. Ray Liotta and Jason Patric star, as a veteran whose partner has been killed, and a younger cop assigned to join him in the investigation. If many cop-partner movies have an undertone of humor, even a splash of *The Odd Couple*, this one is hard-bitten and grim: The team consists of Bad Cop and Bad Cop. The twist is that both of them are good at their work; their problem is taking the job too personally.

The film opens with a virtuoso handheld chase scene, as Nick Tellis (Patric) pursues a suspect through backyards and over fences until the chase ends in a shooting—and it's not the perp who is hit, but a pregnant woman. Tellis is put on suspension and cools off at home with his wife and a baby he loves. It's clear this is a man with big problems involving anger and overcompensation; is there such a thing as being too dedicated as a cop?

More than a year later, his captain (Chi McBride) calls in Tellis and makes him an offer: He can be reinstated on the force if he becomes the partner of Henry Oak (Liotta). Oak's former partner, a cop named Calvess, has been murdered. The captain thinks Tellis's contacts with drug dealers and other lowlifes, plus his unique brand of dedication, are needed to track down the cop killer. He warns Tellis that Oak is a good cop but sometimes unstable, and there are quick subjective cuts to the older man beating a prisoner.

Tellis and Oak do not fit the usual pattern of cop partners in the movies. Either of them could be the lead. Neither one is supporting. As cops, they think independently and are self-starters, and cooperation doesn't come easily. Tellis is startled, too, at Oak's methods, which are quick and practical and amoral, and produce results, but are not always legal.

The movie's writer and director, Joe Carnahan, brings a rough, aggressive energy to the picture. His first film, *Blood, Guts, Bullets & Octane* (1998), was all style, but here he creates believable characters. His screenplay stays within the broad outlines of the cop-buddy formula, but brings fresh energy to the obligatory elements. It is no surprise, for example, that Tellis's wife doesn't want him back out on the streets, and that there's tension between his home life and his job. This is an ancient action cliché: A man's gotta do what a man's gotta do. But the details of the domestic scenes ring true.

In terms of its urban wasteland, the movie descends to a new level of grittiness. These streets aren't mean, they're cruel, and to work them is like being the garbageman in hell. Liotta's character stalks them as a man on a mission, driven by private agendas we only begin to suspect. The Patric character is stunned to see the other man not only violating protocol, but apparently trying to shut him out of the investigation, as if this business can only be settled privately between him and his demons.

Both Liotta and Patric have played similar roles. Patric starred in *Rush* (1992), in a brilliant performance as an undercover narcotics cop who, along with his rookie partner (Jennifer Jason Leigh), gets hooked on drugs himself. Liotta has appeared in countless crime pictures, both as a cop and most memorably in *GoodFellas* (1990) as a cocaine-addled criminal. Here they bring a kind of rawness to the table. Liotta, heavier, wearing a beard, leaves behind his days as a handsome leading man and begins edging into interesting Brian Cox territory. Patric, ten years after *Rush*, looks less like he's playing a cop and more like he might be one.

The investigation itself must remain undescribed here. But its ending is a neat and ironic exercise in poetic justice. Pay attention during one of the very last shots, and tell me if you think the tape recorder was on or off. In a way, it makes a difference. In another way, it doesn't.

National Treasure ★ ★
PG, 100 m., 2004

Nicolas Cage (Benjamin Franklin Gates), Harvey Keitel (Agent Sadusky), Jon Voight (Patrick Henry Gates), Diane Kruger (Dr. Abigail Chase), Sean Bean (Ian Howe), Justin Bartha (Riley Poole), Christopher Plummer (John Adams Gates). Directed by Jon Turteltaub and produced by Jerry Bruckheimer and Turteltaub. Screenplay by Jim Kouf, Cormac Wibberley, and Marianne Wibberley.

Here is a movie about a fabled ancient treasure from the Middle East, protected through the ages by the Knights Templar and the Masons, and hidden for centuries until a modern investigator follows a series of baffling clues that lead him first to a priceless work in a national gallery, and then to a hiding place beneath an ancient church.

If you are one of the millions, like me, who plowed through *The Da Vinci Code,* you can be forgiven for thinking they've made it into a movie. And in a way, they have, but the movie is titled *National Treasure.* This new Jerry Bruckheimer production is so similar in so many ways to the plot of the Dan Brown bestseller that either (a) the filmmakers are the only citizens of the entertainment industry who have never heard of *The Da Vinci Code,* no, not even while countless people on the set must have been reading the book, or (b) they have ripped it off. My attorneys advise me that (a) is the prudent answer.

That I have read the book is not a cause for celebration. It is inelegant, pedestrian writing in service of a plot that sets up cliff-hangers like clockwork, resolves them with improbable escapes, and leads us breathlessly to a disappointing anticlimax. I should read a potboiler like *The Da Vinci Code* every once in a while, just to remind myself that life is too short to read books like *The Da Vinci Code.*

The Da Vinci movie will be directed by Ron Howard, who should study this one for clues about what to avoid. The central weakness of the story is the absurdity of the clues, which are so difficult that no sane forefather could have conceivably believed that anyone could actually follow them. That the movie's hero, named Benjamin Franklin Gates and played by Nicolas Cage, is able to intuitively sense the occult meanings of ancient riddles and puzzles is less a tribute to his intelligence than to the screenplay supplying him with half a dozen bonus A-ha! Moments. An A-Ha! Moment, you will recall, is that moment at which a movie character suddenly understands something which, if he did not understand it, would bring the entire enterprise to a halt.

Benjamin Franklin Gates is named, of course, after the famous software millionaire. His family of historians has been scorned for generations because of its belief that a vast treasure was brought back from the Crusades by the Knights Templar and has been hidden by the Masons—in this case, Masons who were the Founding Fathers of America. Benjamin's father, Patrick Henry Gates (played by Jon Voight and named after O. Henry), scoffs at the family legend, but his grandfather, John

Adams Gates (played by Christopher Plummer and named after the inventor of the toilet), gives Benjamin a clue handed down through the generations from Charles Carroll, the last surviving signer of the Declaration of Independence.

This clue, which involves the word "Charlotte," seems baffling until Benjamin has an A-Ha! and leads an expedition north of the Arctic Circle in search of a nineteenth-century sailing ship that, he calculates, must have frozen in the ice and then been shifted miles inland by the gradual movement of the floes. To say the expedition finds the ship without much trouble is putting it mildly; Benjamin digs about a foot down into the permafrost, and then bends over and wipes clean a brass nameplate that helpfully says "Charlotte."

Clues on the ship lead him to believe the map to the treasure may be written in invisible ink on the back of the Declaration of Independence—a safe place for it, because such a document would be guarded down through the ages. Of course, there is the problem of convincing the National Archives to allow you to remove the Declaration from its vacuum-sealed vault and molest it with lemon juice and a hair dryer. Luckily the national archivist, Dr. Abigail Chase (Diane Kruger), named after her scenes in the movie, is convinced by Benjamin, and together they team up to steal the Declaration before the villain (Sean Bean) can steal it first.

After many chases and close calls and quick thinking and fast footwork and hanging from swinging doors and leaping chasms, etc., the heroes find themselves in a collapsing mine shaft beneath a church tomb—a shaft that must have been created secretly, although it seems roughly the size of Boston's Big Dig. Whether they're on a wild goose chase or find the fortune of the ages, I will leave for you to discover. I understand why it is necessary in *The Da Vinci Code* to conceal information associated with the Holy Grail, but I am less convinced in *National Treasure* that the treasure had to be hidden because it was so vast that if all that wealth came suddenly into the world it would, I dunno, capsize the economy or cause the brains of accountants to explode.

Nicolas Cage, one of my favorite actors, is

ideal for this caper because he has the ability to seem uncontrollably enthusiastic about almost anything. Harvey Keitel, who plays FBI agent Sadusky, falls back on his ability to seem grim about almost anything. Jon Voight calls on his skill at seeming sincere at the drop of a pin. Diane Kruger has a foreign accent even though she is the national archivist, so that our eyes can mist at the thought that in the land of opportunity, even a person with a foreign accent can become the national archivist. *National Treasure* is so silly that the Monty Python version could use the same screenplay, line for line.   ☞

Never Die Alone ★ ★ ★ ½
R, 90 m., 2004

DMX (King David), David Arquette (Paul), Michael Ealy (Mike), Clifton Powell (Moon), Reagan Gomez-Preston (Juanita), Aisha Tyler (Nancy), Jennifer Sky (Janet), Keesha Sharp (Edna). Directed by Ernest Dickerson and produced by Earl Simmons and Alessandro Camon. Screenplay by James Gibson, based on a novel by Donald Goines.

Ernest Dickerson's *Never Die Alone* is a doom-laden morality tale centered on a character who not only refers to *Scarface*'s Tony Montana but is more evil, more vicious, more self-pitying, and more cold-blooded. This is a man named King David, played by DMX as a midlevel drug dealer whose favorite trick is to hook a girl on cocaine and then switch her to heroin without telling her, so that she'll be completely dependent on him. If that is vile, he has a little "test" for them that is monstrous.

The movie begins with King David dead and in his coffin. I am not giving anything away; it's the first shot. Dead he may be, but he narrates the story of his own life from beyond the grave, like Tupac Shakur in *Tupac: Resurrection*. He has kept a diary on cassette tapes, and they come into the possession of an earnest white writer named Paul (David Arquette). Paul has a poster of Hemingway on the wall of his shabby rented room, and engages in the risky business of hanging out around tough types in Harlem drug bars. He's doing research, he thinks, or looking for trouble, we think.

The movie's plot is not nearly as linear and simple as I've made it sound so far. It loops back and forth through ten years of time, in flashbacks and memories, and there are several other major players. As it opens, King David has returned from Los Angeles to New York in order to "make amends" by repaying a debt to a higher-level drug kingpin named Moon (Clifton Powell), and Moon has sent his relatively untested lieutenant Mike (Michael Ealy) and another man to collect the cash payment. When that turns violent against Moon's specific instructions, it sets in motion a chain of events with beginnings that coil back through time, including the connection King David does not know he has with Mike.

Never Die Alone, written by James Gibson and based on a novel by the legendary ex-con writer Donald Goines, is not a routine story of drugs and violence, but an ambitious, introspective movie in which a heartless man tells his story without apology. The evil that he did lives after him, but there is no good to inter with his bones. What he cannot quite figure out at the end is how this white kid came into his life, and is driving him to the hospital, and seems to know his story.

There's action in the movie, but brief and brutal; this is not an action picture but a drama that deserves comparison with *Scarface* and *New Jack City*. The many characters are all drawn with care and dimension, especially the three women who have the misfortune to enter David's life; they're played by Reagan Gomez-Preston, Jennifer Sky, and Keesha Sharp. Each is onscreen relatively briefly; each makes a strong impression.

DMX is hard and cold as King David, and never more frightening than when he seems so charming to the women he encounters. It's a fearless performance, made more effective because we begin the movie by sort of liking him—so that we're being set up just like his victims. Michael Ealy, as Mike, has the difficult assignment of going through most of the movie being motivated by events we don't yet know about, so that we have to change our idea of him as the story develops. David Arquette is more the pawn of the plot than its mover, and his character functions mostly as a witness and facilitator; that's scary, because most of the time he has no idea how much danger he's in. After he inherits King David's

Stutz pimpmobile, he essentially turns himself into a shooting gallery target.

The director Dickerson, who began as Spike Lee's NYU classmate and cinematographer, has done strong work before, starting with his debut film *Juice* (1992) and including the overlooked *Our America* (2002), based on the true story of two Chicago ghetto teenagers who were given a tape recorder by NPR and made an award-winning documentary. *Never Die Alone* is his best work, with the complexity of serious fiction and the nerve to start dark and stay dark, to follow the logic of its story right down to its inevitable end.

New York Minute ★ ½
PG, 91 m., 2004

Mary-Kate Olsen (Roxy Ryan), Ashley Olsen (Jane Ryan), Eugene Levy (Lomax), Andy Richter (Bennie Bang), Jared Padalecki (Trey), Riley Smith (Jim Wessler), Andrea Martin (Senator). Directed by Dennie Gordon and produced by Denise Di Novi, Mary-Kate Olsen, Ashley Olsen, and Robert Thorne. Screenplay by Emily Fox, Adam Cooper, and Bill Collage.

They say baseball is popular because everyone thinks they can play it. Similar reasoning may explain the popularity of the Olsen twins: Teenage girls love them because they believe they could *be* them. What, after all, do Mary-Kate and Ashley do in *New York Minute* that could not be done by any reasonably presentable female adolescent? Their careers are founded not on what they do, but on the vicarious identification of their fans, who enjoy seeing two girls making millions for doing what just about anybody could do.

The movie offers the spectacle of two cheerful and attractive seventeen-year-olds who have the maturity of silly thirteen-year-olds and romp through a day's adventures in Manhattan, a city that in this movie is populated entirely by hyperactive character actors. Nothing that happens to them has any relationship with anything else that happens to them, except for the unifying principle that it all happens to *them*. That explains how they happen to be (1) chased by a recreational vehicle through heavy traffic, (2) wading through the sewers of New York, (3) getting a beauty makeover in a Harlem salon, (4) in possession of a kidnapped dog, (5) pursued by music pirates, (6) in danger in Chinatown, and (7) . . . oh, never mind.

Given the inescapable fact that they are twins, the movie of course gives them completely opposite looks and personalities, and then leads us inexorably to the moment when one will have to impersonate the other. Mary-Kate Olsen plays Roxy Ryan, the sloppy girl who skips school and dreams of getting her demo tape backstage at a "punk rock" video shoot. Ashley Olsen plays Jane Ryan, a Goody Two-shoes who will win a four-year scholarship to Oxford University if she gives the winning speech in a competition at Columbia. Perhaps in England she will discover that the university is in the town of Oxford, and so can correct friends who plan to visit her in London. (I am sure the screenwriters knew the university was in Oxford, but were concerned that audience members might confuse "going to" Oxford and "being in" Oxford, and played it safe, since London is the only city in England many members of the audience will have heard of, if indeed they have.)

But I'm being mean, and this movie is harmless, and as eager as a homeless puppy to make friends. In fact, it has a puppy. It also has a truant officer, played by Eugene Levy in a performance that will be valuable to film historians, since it demonstrates what Eugene Levy's irreducible essence is when he plays a character who is given absolutely nothing funny to say or do. His performance suggests that he stayed at home and phoned in his mannerisms. More inexplicable is Andy Richter's work as a limousine driver with sinister connections to music piracy rackets. He is given an accent, from where I could not guess, although I could guess why: At a story conference, the filmmakers looked in despair at his pointless character and said, "What the hell, maybe we should give him an accent."

Because the movie all takes place during one day and Roxy is being chased by a truant officer, it compares itself to *Ferris Bueller's Day Off*. It might as reasonably compare itself to *The Third Man* because they wade through sewers. *New York Minute* is a textbook example of a film created as a "vehicle," but without any ideas about where the vehicle should go. The Olsen twins are not children any longer, yet not quite poised to become adults, and so they're given the props and costumes of seventeen-year-olds, but carefully shielded from the reality. That any seventeen-year-old girl in America could take seriously the rock band that Roxy worships is beyond contemplation. It doesn't even look like a band to itself.

The events involving the big speaking competition are so labored that occasionally the twins seem to be looking back over their shoulders for the plot to catch up. Of course, there is a moment when all the characters and plot strands meet on the stage of the speech contest, with the other competitors looking on in bafflement, and of course (spoiler warning, ho, ho), Jane wins the scholarship. In fact (major spoiler warning), she does so without giving the speech, because the man who donates the scholarship reads her notes, which were dropped on the stage, and *knows* it would have been the winning speech had she only been able to deliver it. Unlikely as it seems that Jane could win in such a way, this scenario certainly sidesteps the difficulty of having her deliver a speech that would sound as if she could win.

Nicholas Nickleby ★ ★ ★ ½
PG, 132 m., 2003

Charlie Hunnam (Nicholas Nickleby), Hugh Mitchell (Young Nicholas), Jamie Bell (Smike), Nathan Lane (Vincent Crummles), Barry Humphries (Mrs. Crummles), Christopher Plummer (Ralph Nickleby), Tom Courtenay (Newman Noggs), Jim Broadbent (Wackford Squeers), Edward Fox (Sir Mulberry Hawk), Timothy Spall (Charles Cheeryble), Gerald Horan (Ned Cheeryble), Juliet Stevenson (Mrs. Squeers), Romola Garai (Kate Nickleby), Anne Hathaway (Madeline Bray), Stella Gonet (Mrs. Nickleby), Alan Cumming (Mr. Folair). Directed by Douglas McGrath and produced by Simon Channing-Williams, John Hart, and Jeff Sharp. Screenplay by McGrath, based on the novel by Charles Dickens.

Nicholas Nickleby was the third novel by Charles Dickens, following *The Pickwick Papers* and *Oliver Twist* and sharing with them a riot of colorful characters. One of them, the sadistic boarding school proprietor Wackford Squeers, was a portrait taken so much from life that it resulted in laws being passed to reform the private education industry. The novel followed a familiar Dickens pattern—a young man sets out in the world to win fortune and love despite a rogue's gallery of villains. It contained characters improbably good or despicable, and with admirable economy tied together several of the key characters in a web of melodramatic coincidences. It is not placed in the first rank of Dickens's art, but I would place it near the top for sheer readability.

The new film version by Douglas McGrath, who made *Emma* (1996), is much more reasonable than the 1980 nine-hour stage version of the Royal Shakespeare Company, which I have on laser disk and really mean to get to one of these days. The movie is jolly and exciting and brimming with life, and wonderfully well acted. McGrath has done some serious pruning, but the result does not seem too diluted; there is room for expansive consideration of such essential characters as Nicholas's vindictive Uncle Ralph (Christopher Plummer), secretly undermined by his dipsomaniac and disloyal servant Newman Noggs (Tom Courtenay). The movie gives full screen time to Wackford Squeers (Jim Broadbent, looking curiously Churchillian) and his wife (Juliet Stevenson)—and hints that psychosexual pathology inspired their mistreatment of students. Their most pathetic target, Smike (Jamie Bell, who played *Billy Elliott*), is seen as less of a caricature and more of a real victim.

To balance the scales are two of the happiest comic couples Dickens ever created: the touring theatricals Vincent and Mrs. Crummles (Nathan Lane and Barry Humphries), and the brothers Cheeryble (Timothy Spall and Gerald Horan). The Crummles rescue Nicholas (Charlie Hunnam) after his escape from the Squeers's school, turn him into an actor, and even find talent in the hapless Smike. Their touring company is a loving exaggeration of companies Dickens must have worked with, and is rich with such inspirations as their aging and expanding daughter the Child Phenomenon. Barry Humphries uses his alter ego, Dame Edna Everage, to play Mrs. Crummles, and if you look closely you will notice Humphries as a man, playing opposite the formidable Dame.

The Cheerybles are the lawyer brothers who agree on everything, especially that Nicholas must be hired in their firm, all of his problems solved, and his romantic future secured through a liaison with Madeline Bray (Anne Hathaway), whose tyrannical father has long ruled her life. It is particularly good to see Timothy Spall nodding and smiling as brother Charles, after seeing him so depressed in role after role.

Nicholas himself is more of a placeholder than a full-blooded character: the handsome, feckless, and earnest young man who leads us through the story as he encounters one unforgettable character after another. The most striking member of the Nickleby family is, of course, Uncle Ralph, played by Plummer in a performance so cold-blooded it actually reminded me of his stage Iago. Ralph lives only for the accumulation of money. His opinion of the poor is that poverty is their own fault, and they deserve as a result to be put to work to enrich him (in this he reflects some of the latest tax reforms). Nicholas he more or less sells to Squeers, and he lodges Mrs. Nickleby (Stella Gonet) and her daughter Kate (Romola Garai) in a hovel while Kate is put to work doing piecework. Kate is a beauty, however, and so Ralph's larger scheme is to marry her off to the vile Sir Mulberry Hawk (Edward Fox), in return for various considerations involving their business interests.

The actors assembled for *Nicholas Nickleby* are not only well cast, but well typecast. Each one by physical appearance alone replaces a page or more of Dickens's descriptions, allowing McGrath to move smoothly and swiftly through the story without laborious introductions: They are obviously who they are. The result is a movie that feels like a complete account of Dickens's novel, even though the Royal Shakespeare found an additional seven hours of inspiration.

The physical production is convincing without being too charming or too realistic. The clothes of some of the characters remind us that in those days their wardrobes would have consisted only of what they wore. The countryside is picturesque but falls short of greeting cards (except for the Nicklebys' cottage at the end). The story takes place at about the same time as Scorsese's *Gangs of New York,* but London is heavier on alehouses, lighter on blood in the gutters. The movie makes Dickens's world look more pleasant to inhabit than it probably was, but then so did his novels.

What animates the story is Dickens's outrage, and his good heart. *The Pickwick Papers* was essentially a series of sketches of comic characters, but in *Oliver Twist* and *Nicholas Nickleby* we find him using fiction like journalism, to denounce those who would feed on the poor and exploit the helpless. One senses that in Dickens's time there were more Uncle Ralphs than Cheerybles, but that perhaps he helped to improve the ratio.

Nobody Knows ★ ★ ★ ½
PG-13, 141 m., 2005

Yuya Yagira (Akira), Ayu Kitaura (Kyoko), Hiei Kimura (Shigeru), Momoko Shimizu (Yuki), Hanae Kan (Saki), You (Keiko). Directed and produced by Hirokazu Kore-eda. Screenplay by Kore-eda.

As *Nobody Knows* opens, we watch a mother and two kids moving into a new apartment. They wrestle some heavy suitcases up the stairs. When the movers have left, they open the suitcases and release two younger children, who are a secret from the landlord. "Remember the new rules," the mother says. "No going outside. Not even on the veranda—except for Kyoko, to do the laundry."

Kyoko is the second oldest, about ten. The oldest, a boy named Akira, is about twelve. He regards his mother with guarded eyes. So do we. There is something too happy about her, as she acts like one of the kids. It is not the forced happiness of a person trying to keep up a brave front, or the artificial happiness of someone who is high, but the crazy happiness of a person who is using laughter to mask the reality of her behavior. It fools the little kids, Shigeru and Yuki, who are perhaps seven and four.

The mother, named Keiko, played by a pop star named You, leaves Akira some money and goes away. She returns very late at night, still cheerful, as if it is the most natural thing in the world to leave her children alone, let them prepare their own dinners, and save some for her. "She stinks of booze," Akira says quietly to Kyoko.

Keiko confides in Akira that she has met a

new guy, who seems "sincere" and might marry her. "Again?" he says. He is very quiet around her. She goes away again, for a much longer time, until the money she left runs out, and then she returns with gifts, including a backpack for Kyoko—ironic, since Kyoko is forbidden to leave the building. Keiko gives Akira more money, leaves again, and days and weeks pass; when Kyoko asks if she will return, Akira says she will not.

This story, written and filmed by Hirokazu Kore-eda, is based on a true story from Tokyo, where four children were abandoned by their mother and lived in an apartment for months, unmissed and undetected. He tells the story not as a melodrama about kids in danger, but as a record of long, lonely days, of the younger children playing their games and watching TV, of Akira going out into the city to buy food and find money. He gets some from a man in a pachinko parlor, who tells him not to ask again: "You know, Yuki isn't my kid." All four of the children have different fathers. Now they have no mother, but they have each other. Akira could contact the authorities, but "that happened before," he tells a friend, "and it was a real mess."

Akira is played by Yuya Yagira, who filmed the role over eighteen months, during which he grew a little and his voice broke. It is not just a cute kid performance, but real acting, because Kore-eda doesn't give him dialogue and actions to make his thoughts clear, but prefers to observe him observing, coping, and deciding. Yagira won the best actor award at Cannes.

What is most poignant is the sight of these kids wasting their lives. Kyoko asks her mother if she can go to school, but her mother laughs and says she will be happier at home. Akira was in school at one point, and studies his books at night, until finally his only subject is arithmetic—figuring how much longer their money will last. There's a wistful shot of him looking at kids in a schoolyard, and one idyllic moment when he is asked to join a baseball game, and given a shirt and cap to wear.

He meets a girl his age named Saki (Hanae Kan), who prefers the streets to her home. They are too young for sex, but too old to be children. She picks up a guy, goes into a bar with him, comes out, and gives Akira some money.

He tries to push it away, but she says, "All I did was sing karaoke with him." This time.

Kore-eda is the most gifted of the young Japanese directors. His *Maborosi* (1995), about a widow who remarries and takes her child to live in a small village, and *After Life* (1998), about a waiting room in heaven, are masterful. Here he is more matter-of-fact, more realistic, in suggesting the slow progress of time, the cold winter followed by the hot summer days, the desperation growing behind Akira's cautious expression. The fact that he doesn't crank up the energy with manufactured emergencies makes the impending danger more dramatic: This cannot go on, and it is going to end badly.

But don't the adults in the building, or anywhere else, know what is happening in the apartment? Hard to say. The landlady comes at one point to collect the rent, but then seems to let the subject drop. The gas, lights, and water are turned off, but that doesn't ring an alarm bell. Yuki's possible father knows Keiko has been away, but doesn't follow up to see if she's returned; perhaps he'd rather not know.

There are moments in Yuya Yagira's performance that will break your heart. One comes when he takes a few precious coins to a pay telephone to call a number where he might find his mother, or news of her. He's put on hold, and drops in one coin after another until they are all gone and he is disconnected, and bends his head forward against the telephone.

Kore-eda creates a sense of intimacy within the apartment. He shoots close to the kids (there's no room to get farther away), and underlines their claustrophobic imprisonment. They like each other, they have some toys, they get more or less enough to eat, usually less. One day Akira even takes their shoes out of a closet and lets them put them on, and takes them outside for a walk in the great, free, wide-open world that is so indifferent to them.

Noel ★ ★
PG, 96 m., 2004

Penelope Cruz (Nina), Susan Sarandon (Rose), Paul Walker (Mike), Alan Arkin (Artie), Robin Williams (Charlie), Marcus Thomas (Jules), Chazz Palminteri (Arizona), Erika Rosenbaum

(Merry). Directed by Chazz Palminteri and produced by Al Corley, Eugene Musso, Bart Rosenblatt, and Howard Rosenman. Screenplay by David Hubbard.

Noel tells the usual story of sad strangers who seek happiness on Christmas Eve, with the variation that most of the characters are stark staring mad. Christmas is a holiday fraught with hazards anyway, and these people are clearly not up to it. Thanksgiving is the most angst-free holiday, with no presents to buy, no cards to send, and mountains of turkey. But the genre of Thanksgiving movies is dominated by miserable, destructive family reunions; only the wonderful *What's Cooking?* gives the holiday a break.

If Thanksgiving in the movies is about lethal families, Christmas movies tend to be about loners who most keenly feel their aloneness as they engage in that quintessential activity of the Lonely Person, watching a Yule log on TV. The thing is, we're obsessed with the conviction that we're *supposed* to feel happy at Christmastime.

In Chazz Palminteri's film, the most miserable character is probably Rose (Susan Sarandon), a divorced, middle-aged book editor whose mother has disappeared into Alzheimer's. At one point she stands on the banks of a river, looking longingly at the icy water, but she's talked back from the edge by Charlie (Robin Williams), whom she met in her mother's nursing home, where he was sitting in the corner in the dark in a room with an unmoving body on the bed—a body that Rose, in her desperation, one night told, "I love you!"

Well, she needs somebody to love. "You need sex. Good sex," advises her secretary, who seems to speak from experience. Rose gets fixed up with the office stud, but at the point of decision she finds that it's all just too sad and sordid. Meanwhile, we meet Nina (Penelope Cruz), who is engaged to a cop named Mike (Paul Walker), who is consumed by such anger and jealousy that she threatens to postpone their wedding.

Mike has his own problems: Artie (Alan Arkin), a waiter in a restaurant, follows him around with lovesick eyes, not because he is gay, but because it only took him one look at

Mike to realize he is the reincarnation of his dead wife. He could see it in the eyes. Even people who believe in reincarnation would probably not want to meet Artie.

Oh, and then there's the sad case of Jules (Marcus Thomas), who has had only one happy Christmas in his entire life, and that was when he was in a hospital emergency room and they had a Christmas party. Early in the film, he wanders into his local ER and asks what time the party starts, but is informed, alas, that he will require an emergency. This leads to easily the movie's most peculiar scene, in which Jules approaches a sinister man who seems to live on the stage of an abandoned theater, and says to him: "Glenn said that you break hands."

All of these plot developments are further complicated by the movie's intersecting plotlines and time lines; this is one of those stories where the characters always seem to be crossing paths. Some of the characters, like Susan Sarandon's Rose, are convincing and poignant; others, like Arkin's lovesick waiter, are creepy, and the guy who gets his hand broken should have tried the party at the Salvation Army, where they have great hot chocolate and sometimes you get a slice of pumpkin pie.

Only a cynic could dislike this movie, which may be why I disliked it. I can be sentimental under the right circumstances, but the movie is such a calculating tearjerker that it played like a challenge to me. There's a point at which the plot crosses an invisible line, becoming so preposterous that it's no longer moving and is just plain weird. If it's this much trouble to be happy on Christmas, then maybe Rose should consider doing what Susan Sontag does every year, which is to fly to Venice all by herself, walk around alone in the fog and the mist, cross lonely bridges over dark canals, and let the chill seep into her bones, and then curl up in bed in an empty hotel with a good book. It's kind of a judo technique: You use loneliness as a weapon against itself.

No Good Deed ★ ★ ★
R, 103 m., 2003

Samuel L. Jackson (Jack Friar), Milla Jovovich (Erin), Stellan Skarsgård (Tyrone), Doug

Hutchison (Hoop), Joss Ackland (Mr. Quarre), Grace Zabriskie (Mrs. Quarre), Jonathan Higgins (David Brewster). Directed by Bob Rafelson and produced by Barry Berg, David Braun, Peter Hoffman, Herb Nanas, Sam Perlmutter, Andre Rouleau, and Maxime Remillard. Screenplay by Christopher Canaan and Steve Barancik, based on *The House on Turk Street* by Dashiell Hammett.

Bob Rafelson's two best movies are *Five Easy Pieces* and *The Postman Always Rings Twice*, and *No Good Deed* is like a mingling of their themes. From *Postman* comes hard-boiled American crime fiction, and from *Five Easy Pieces* and its musical family comes the cop played by Samuel L. Jackson, a diabetic who plays the cello. He is, in fact, looking forward to a week at a "fantasy camp" where he can play with Yo-Yo Ma when fate intervenes.

Jackson's character, Jack Friar, is asked by a friend to help find her runaway daughter. He's a cop assigned to grand theft auto and usually finds runaway cars, but he postpones his vacation to ask around in the last neighborhood where the girl was seen, and that leads him to help out Mrs. Quarre, a sweet little old lady who has fallen on her steps with bags of groceries. Once inside her house, he discovers the little old lady is not sweet, and that her criminal partners think the cop is looking for them. So they tie him to a chair, where he will spend most of the movie.

The story is based on *The House on Turk Street*, a 1924 short story by Dashiell Hammett, whose work also inspired *The Maltese Falcon* and *The Thin Man*. The *noir* origins are evident in Jackson's resigned, laconic hero, and in the character of Erin (Milla Jovovich), with a blond Veronica Lake haircut, who guards Jack, talks to him, and eventually joins in a scene that improbably combines sex and the art of cello playing.

Jack Friar, who was only trying to do a good deed, has walked into the final stages of a bank robbery. A gang led by the precise Tyrone (Stellan Skarsgård) and including the violent hothead Hoop (Doug Hutchison) is about to commit a multimillion-dollar computer fraud with the help of an inside man named David (Jonathan Higgins), a bank official who thinks Erin is in love with him.

More than one man shares that misapprehension, including Hoop, who thinks he and Erin will do away with Tyrone and skip with the money. And Tyrone, who trusts Erin to stay with him. To be sure, she left him once before, but "this is how Tyrone says you shouldn't have left," Erin says, showing Jack Friar a foot with four toes.

As Erin and Jack wait in the house for the bank robbery to take place, the old couple are at an airport. Mr. Quarre (Joss Ackland) is a feisty old fart who has a pipe collection and memories of flying a lot of missions in Korea, and has been signed up to fly the robbers to the Bahamas. Mrs. Quarre (Grace Zabriskie, who was the angry hitchhiker in *Five Easy Pieces*) is along for the ride; as they wait in the rain for their passengers to turn up, they make love in the plane, which is more than any of Erin's men can claim.

The long delay gives Jack and Erin an opportunity to share secrets. Turns out Tyrone brought Erin over from Russia, where she was a piano prodigy, which she proves with a solo. Then she releases Jack long enough for a surprisingly erotic cello duet, involving only one cello, that eludes the question: Why doesn't Jack overpower her and escape? Later, tied up again, he tries to burn through his cords by holding his feet over a flame on the kitchen range; it's surprising how painful and effective that scene is.

In a story based on double-crosses, the possibility emerges that Jack and Erin could make a deal on their own. But can Erin be trusted by anyone? The movie's ending strikes an unsentimental note that remembers the cynicism of classic *film noir*. And its look is *noir*, too; cinematographer Juan Ruiz Anchia seems inspired by the paintings of Jack Vettriano with his shadowy interiors glowing with reds, golds, and oranges.

The movie doesn't rank with Rafelson's best work, which also includes the crime melodrama *Blood and Wine* (1996), with Jack Nicholson and Jennifer Lopez. But it's an absorbing, atmospheric *noir* with nice little touches, including Skarsgård's speech patterns, the jolly greed of the Quarres, and the way that the cop and the blond relate to each other on three levels: as prisoner and captor, as man and woman, and as musicians.

Northfork ★ ★ ★ ★
PG-13, 103 m., 2003

Peter Coyote (Eddie), Anthony Edwards (Happy), Duel Farnes (Irwin), Daryl Hannah (Flower Hercules), Nick Nolte (Father Harlan), Mark Polish (Willis O'Brien), James Woods (Walter O'Brien), Claire Forlani (Mrs. Hadfield), Robin Sachs (Cup of Tea), Ben Foster (Cod), Clark Gregg (Mr. Hadfield). Directed by Michael Polish and produced and written by Mark Polish and Michael Polish.

There has never been a movie quite like *Northfork*, but if you wanted to put it on a list, you would also include *Days of Heaven* and *Wings of Desire*. It has the desolate open spaces of the first, the angels of the second, and the feeling in both of deep sadness and pity. The movie is visionary and elegiac, more a fable than a story, and frame by frame it looks like a portfolio of spaces so wide, so open, that men must wonder if they have a role beneath such indifferent skies.

The film is set in Montana in 1955, as the town of Northfork prepares to be submerged forever beneath the waters of a dam. Three two-man evacuation teams travel the countryside in their fat black sedans, persuading the lingering residents to leave. The team members have a motivation: They've all been promised waterfront property on the lake to come. Most of the residents have already pulled out, but one stubborn citizen opens fire on the evacuators, and another plans to ride out the flood waters in his ark, which does not have two of everything but does have two wives, a detail Noah overlooked.

Other lingerers include Irwin (Duel Farnes), a pale young orphan who has been turned back in by his adoptive parents (Claire Forlani and Clark Gregg) on the grounds that he is defective. "You gave us a sick child, Father," they tell Father Harlan, the parish priest (Nick Nolte). "He can't stand the journey." The priest cares for the child himself, although the lonely little kid is able to conjure up company by imagining four angels who come to console him. Or are they imaginary? They are real for little Irwin, and that should be real enough for us.

The town evokes the empty, lonely feeling you get when you make a last tour of a home you have just moved out of. There is a scene where the six evacuators line up at the counter in a diner to order soup. "Bowl or cup?" asks the waitress, and as they consider this choice with grave poker faces, we get the feeling that only by thinking very hard about soup can they avoid exploding in a frenzy of madness. One of Father Harlan's final church services is conducted after the back wall has already been removed from his church, and the landscape behind him looks desolate.

This is the third film by the Polish twins. Michael directs, Mark acts, and Mark and Michael coproduce and cowrite. Their first was the eerie, disquieting *Twin Falls Idaho*, about Siamese twins who deal with the fact that one of them is dying. The next was *Jackpot*, about a man who tours karaoke contests, looking for his big break. Now *Northfork*, which in its visual strategy presents Montana not as a scenic tourist wonderland, but as a burial ground of foolish human dreams. Indeed, one of the subplots involves the need to dig up the bodies in the local cemetery, lest the coffins bob to the surface of the new lake; Walter O'Brien (James Woods), one of the evacuators, tells his son Willis O'Brien (Mark Polish) that if they don't move the coffin of the late Mrs. O'Brien, "When this small town becomes the biggest lake this side of the Mississippi, your mother will be the catch of the day."

Funny? Yes, and so is the soup scene in the diner, but you don't laugh out loud a lot in this film because you fear the noise might echo under its limitless leaden sky. This is like a black-and-white film made in color. In some shots, only the pale skin tones contain any color at all. In talking with the Polish brothers after the film premiered at Sundance 2003, I learned that they limited all the costumes, props, and sets to shades of gray, and the cinematographer, M. David Mullen, has drained color from his film so that there is a bleakness here that gets into your bones.

Against this cold is the pale warmth of the angels, who are evoked by Irwin. To console himself for being abandoned by his adoptive parents, he believes that he is a lost angel, fallen to Earth and abducted by humans who amputated his wings. Indeed, he has scars on his shoulder blades. The angels include Flower Hercules (Daryl Hannah), who seems neither man nor woman; Cod (Ben Foster), a cowboy who never speaks; Happy (Anthony Edwards), who is almost blind, but perhaps can see something through the bizarre glasses he wears, with their multiple lenses; and Cup of Tea (Robin Sachs), who talks enough to make up for Happy.

Of these the most moving is Flower Hercules, who seems to feel Irwin's loneliness and pain as her/his own. Daryl Hannah evokes a quality of care for the helpless that makes her a tender guardian angel. Since the evacuators have a stock of angel's wings, which they sometimes offer as inducements to reluctant homeowners, the thought persists that angels are meant to be real in the film, just as they are in *Wings of Desire*, and only those who cannot believe think Irwin has dreamed them up.

Northfork is not an entertaining film so much as an entrancing one. There were people at Sundance, racing from one indie hipness to another, who found it too slow. But the pace is well chosen for the tone, and the tone evokes the fable, and the fable is about the death of a town and of mankind's brief purchase on this barren plat of land, and it is unseemly to hurry a requiem. The film suggests that of the thousands who obeyed the call, "Go West, young man!" some simply disappeared into the wilderness and were buried, as Northfork is about to be buried, beneath the emptiness of it all.

The Notebook ★ ★ ★ ½
PG-13, 120 m., 2004

Rachel McAdams (Young Allie Nelson), Ryan Gosling (Young Noah Calhoun), Gena Rowlands (Allie Nelson), James Garner (Noah Calhoun), Joan Allen (Allie's Mother), Heather Wahlquist (Sara Tuffington), Nancy De Mayo (Mary Allen Calhoun), Sylvia Jefferies (Rosemary). Directed by Nick Cassavetes and produced by Lynn Harris and Mark Johnson. Screenplay by Jeremy Leven and Jan Sardi, based on the novel by Nicholas Sparks.

The Notebook cuts between the same couple at two seasons in their lives. We see them in the urgency of young romance, and then we see them as old people, she disappearing into the shadows of Alzheimer's, he steadfast in his love. It is his custom every day to read to her from a notebook that tells the story of how they met and fell in love and faced obstacles to their happiness. Sometimes, he says, if only for a few minutes, the clouds part and she is able to remember who he is and who the story is about.

We all wish Alzheimer's could permit such moments. For a time, in the earlier stages of the disease, it does. But when the curtain comes down, there is never another act and the play is over. *The Notebook* is a sentimental fantasy, but such fantasies are not harmful; we tell ourselves stories every day, to make life more bearable. The reason we cried during *Terms of Endearment* was not because the young mother was dying, but because she was given the opportunity for a dignified and lucid parting with her children. In life it is more likely to be pain, drugs, regret, and despair.

The lovers are named Allie Nelson and Noah Calhoun, known as Duke. As old people they're played by Gena Rowlands and James Garner; as young people, by Rachel McAdams and Ryan Gosling. The performances are suited to the material, respecting the passion at the beginning and the sentiment at the end, but not pushing too hard; there is even a time when young Noah tells Allie, "I don't see how it's gonna work," and means it, and a time when Allie gets engaged to another man.

She's a rich kid, summering at the family's mansion in North Carolina. He's a local kid who works at the sawmill but is smart and poetic. Her parents are snobs. His father (Sam Shepard) is centered and supportive. Noah loves her the moment he sees her, and actually hangs by his hands from a bar on a Ferris wheel until she agrees to go out with him. Her parents are direct: "He's trash. He's not for you." One day her mother (Joan Allen) shows her a local working man who looks hard-used by life, and tells Allie that twenty-five years ago she was in love with him. Allie thinks her parents do not love one another, but her mother insists they do; still, Joan Allen is such a precise actress that she is able to introduce the quietest note of regret into the scene.

The movie is based on a novel by Nicholas Sparks, whose books inspired *Message in a Bottle* (1999), unloved by me, and *A Walk to Remember* (2002), which was so sweet and positive it persuaded me (as did Mandy Moore as its star). Now here is a story that could have been a tearjerker, but—no, wait, it *is* a tearjerker, it's just that it's a good one. The director is Nick Cassavetes, son of Gena Rowlands and John Cassavetes, and perhaps his instinctive feeling for his mother helped him find the way past soap opera in the direction of truth.

Ryan Gosling has already been identified as one of the best actors of his generation, although usually in more hard-edged material. Rachel McAdams, who just a few months ago was the bitchy high school queen in *Mean Girls,* here shows such beauty and clarity that we realize once again how actors are blessed by good material. As for Gena Rowlands and James Garner: They are completely at ease in their roles, never striving for effect, never wanting us to be sure we get the message. Garner is an actor so confident and sure that he makes the difficult look easy, and loses credit for his skill. Consider how simply and sincerely he tells their children: "Look, guys, that's my sweetheart in there." Rowlands, best known for highstrung, even manic characters, especially in films by Cassavetes, here finds a quiet vulnerability that is luminous.

The photography by Robert Fraisse is striking in its rich, saturated effects, from sea birds at sunset to a dilapidated mansion by candlelight to the texture of southern summer streets. It makes the story seem more idealized; certainly the retirement home at the end seems more of heaven than of earth. And the old mansion is underlined, too, first in its decay and then in its rebirth; Young Noah is convinced that if he makes good on his promise to rebuild it for Allie, she will come to live in it with him, and paint in the studio he has made for her. ("Noah had gone a little mad," the notebook says.) That she is engaged to marry another shakes him but doesn't discourage him.

We have recently read much about Alzheimer's because of the death of Ronald Reagan. His daughter Patti Davis reported that just before he died, the former president opened his eyes and gazed steadily into those of Nancy, and there was no doubt that he recognized her. Well, it's nice to think so. Nice to believe the window can open once more before closing forever.

Nowhere in Africa ★ ★ ★ ★
NO MPAA RATING, 140 m., 2003

Juliane Köhler (Jettel Redlich), Merab Ninidze (Walter Redlich), Lea Kurka (Younger Regina), Karoline Eckertz (Teenage Regina), Sidede Onyulo (Owuor [Cook]), Matthias Habich (Süsskind). Directed by Caroline Link and produced by Peter Herrmann. Screenplay by Link, based on the novel by Stefanie Zweig.

It is so rare to find a film where you become quickly, simply absorbed in the story. You want to know what happens next. Caroline Link's *Nowhere in Africa* is a film like that, telling the story of a German Jewish family that escapes from the Nazis by going to live and work on a farm in rural Kenya. It's a hardscrabble farm in a dry region, and the father, who used to be a lawyer, is paid a pittance to be the manager. At first his wife hates it. Their daughter, who is five when she arrives, takes to Africa with an immediate and instinctive love.

We see the mother and daughter, Jettel and Regina Redlich (Juliane Köhler and Lea Kurka), in their comfortable world in Frankfurt. The mother likes clothes, luxury, elegance. Her husband, Walter (Merab Ninidze), reading the ominous signs of the rise of Nazism, has gone ahead to East Africa, and now writes asking them to join him—"and please bring a refrigerator, which we will really need, and not our china or anything like that." What Jettel brings is a ballroom gown, which will be spectacularly unnecessary.

The marriage is a troubled one. Jettel thinks herself in a godforsaken place, and Walter, who works hard but is not a natural farmer, has little sympathy with her. Their sex life fades: "You only let me under your shirt when I'm a lawyer," he tells her once when his advance is turned away. But little Regina loves every moment of every day. She makes friends with the African children her age, with that uncomplicated acceptance that children have, and seems to learn their language overnight. She picks up their lore and stories, and is at home in the bush.

Jettel, meanwhile, has a rocky start with Owuor (Sidede Onyulo), the farm cook. He is a tall, proud, competent man from the regional tribe, the Masai, who soon loves Regina like his own daughter. Jettel makes the mistake of treating him like a servant when he sees himself as a professional. He never compromises local custom regarding cooks. Asked to help dig a well, he explains, "I'm a cook. Cooks don't dig in the ground." And for that matter, "Men don't carry water."

They are outsiders here in three ways: as white people, as Germans, and as Jews. The first presents the least difficulty, because the tribal people on the land are friendly and helpful. Their status as Germans creates an ironic situation when war is declared and they are rounded up by the British colonial authorities as enemy aliens; this is absurd, since they are refugees from the enemy, but before the mistake can be corrected they are transported to Nairobi and interred—ironically, in a luxury hotel that has been pressed into service. As high tea is served to them, a British officer asks the hotel manager if the prisoners need to be treated so well. "These are our standards, and we are not willing to compromise," the manager replies proudly.

To the Africans, they are not Jews, Germans, or aliens, but simply white farmers; the rise of anticolonialism is still in the future in this district. Regina, so young when she left Europe, therefore hasn't tasted anti-Semitism until her parents send her into town to a boarding school. Now a pretty teenager (played by Karoline Eckertz), she is surprised to hear the headmaster say, "The Jews will stand outside the classroom as we recite the Lord's Prayer."

As time passes and the beauty and complexity of the land become clear to Jettel, she begins slowly to feel more at home. Her husband is vindicated in moving his family to Africa; letters arrive with sad news of family members deported to death camps. But he always considers Africa a temporary haven, and his attention is focused on a return to Europe. Each member of the Redlich family has a separate arc: The mother grows to like Africa as the father likes it less, and their daughter loves it always.

The story is told through the eyes of the daughter (Eckertz is the narrator); Caroline Link's screenplay is based on a best-selling German novel by Stefanie Zweig, who treats such matters as Jettel's brief affair with a British officer as they might have been perceived, and interpreted, by the daughter. Link's style permits the narrative to flow as it might in memory, and although there are dramatic high points (such as a fire and a plague of locusts), they are not interruptions but part of the rhythm of African life, and are joined by the sacrifice of a lamb (for rain) and an all-night ritual ceremony that the young girl will never forget.

Link's film, which won five German Oscars, including best film, won the 2003 Academy Award as best foreign film, and comes after another extraordinary film, her 1997 *Beyond Silence*, which was an Oscar nominee. That one was also about the daughter of a troubled marriage; the heroine was the hearing child of a deaf couple. I respond strongly to her interest in good stories and vivid, well-defined characters; this film is less message than memory, depending on the strength of the material to make all of the points. We feel as if we have lived it.

O

Oasis ★ ★ ★
NO MPAA RATING, 133 m., 2004

Sol Kyung-gu (Hong Jong-du), Moon So-ri (Han Gong-ju), Ahn Nae-sang (Hong Jong-il), Ryoo Seung-wan (Hong Jong-sae), Chu Kwi-jung (Jong-sae's Wife), Son Byung-ho (Han Sang-shik), Yun Ga-hyun (Sang-shik's Wife). Directed by Lee Chang-dong and produced by Cho Min-cheul, Jeon Jay, and Myeong Gye-nam. Screenplay by Chang-dong.

Oasis is a love story involving two young people abandoned by families unwilling to give them the love and attention they require. We in the audience may be equally unwilling to give them love and attention, and that's why the film works so powerfully. Its heroine is a woman rendered almost powerless by cerebral palsy. Its hero is a man so obnoxious and clueless that while he's in prison his family moves and leaves no forwarding address. They meet when he rapes her.

The new South Korean cinema is transgressive and disturbing, open to forms of behavior that are almost never seen in the films of the West. It can be about urgent, undisciplined, perverse needs; it can have the graphic detail of pornography yet show no hint of an erotic purpose; it can accept extreme characters and make no attempt to soften them or make them likable. There's something stunning and even inspiring in its indifference to popular taste. *Oasis* depends on scenes that could not be contemplated within the Western commercial cinema; it is unconventional to the point of aggression.

The movie opens with Hong Jong-du (Sol Kyung-gu), newly released from prison, seeking out his younger brother. He needs help because, in his passive-aggressive way, he has ordered food in a restaurant without being able to afford it (no, they don't want to accept his shoes as payment).

Jong-du is one of those people the rest of us instinctively avoid. He looks at people strangely, asks inappropriate questions, assumes an unwanted intimacy, violates their space, doesn't know the rules of social interaction, and in general inspires his targets to make a perfunctory and inane response and get away as quickly as possible. He may be retarded, but the movie doesn't make that judgment; perhaps he is intelligent enough, but socially dysfunctional.

Jong-du has just served time for a hit-and-run episode. He has no money and no job prospects, and his family would be happy to never see him again. One day he buys a fruit basket and goes to visit the family of the man he killed with his drunk driving. It is impossible to say why he thinks this gesture would be appropriate, and his manner is so odd that the dead man's son and his wife are understandably enraged.

But it is through this visit that Jong-du learns of the existence of the dead man's daughter, Han Gong-ju (Moon So-ri). Severely disabled, she remains in what was the family apartment; her brother and sister-in-law have moved out and have as little to do with her as possible. We gather she is cared for by a combination of sketchy social services and the kindness of neighbors.

Jong-du returns to the apartment when Gong-ju is alone, rapes her, and leaves. He is amazed when, a few days later, he receives a message from her. He goes to see her, and they begin a romance that seems to meet their particular needs. For Jong-du, who senses other people trying to shrink from him, Gong-ju has the admirable quality of not being able to avoid him—or even, without immeasurable effort, arguing with him. For Gong-ju, her new friend is a prize who provides sex, companionship, and a way to get out of the house. Their needs and motives come together, for example, when Jong-du takes his new friend to dinner with his family; we (and they) are completely unable to read his motive. Is he being kind to her, standing up for what he believes in, or merely hoping to piss them off?

There are fantasy scenes when Gong-ju seems miraculously restored, and can move with grace and speak with eloquence. I am not sure if these moments are poetic, or somehow cruel. I am reminded of a better film involving a similar character: Rolf de Heer's *Dance Me to My Song* (1998), which starred and was written by the late Heather Rose, herself a victim of cerebral palsy. For her there was no possibility of fantasy scenes in which she danced about the screen, and her limitations became the movie's greatest strength.

Still, *Oasis* is a brave film in the way it shows two people who find any relationship almost impossible, and yet find a way to make theirs work. The problems with the film come because it overstays its welcome. There's a scene in which Gong-ju's family misinterprets something they witness, and their reaction leads to dire consequences that could surely have been avoided by a simple explanation. This is an Idiot Plot situation, in which the plot continues only because everyone acts stupidly. The closing scenes dissipate what has been accomplished, and seem not only unnecessary but harmful.

In the matter of romance between the disabled and the able-bodied, sentiment is usually the great weakness. A magnificent film like *Dance Me to My Song* was denied an American release because *The Theory of Flight* (1998, with Kenneth Branagh and Helena Bonham Carter) offered a more commercial, palatable treatment of a similar subject. Heather Rose's film was frank and graphic. *Oasis* falls somewhere in between, with the twist that the able-bodied character is more incapable of dealing with everyday life than the CP victim.

Ocean's Twelve ★ ★ ★
PG-13, 125 m., 2004

George Clooney (Danny Ocean), Brad Pitt (Rusty Ryan), Matt Damon (Linus Caldwell), Catherine Zeta-Jones (Isabel Lahiri), Andy Garcia (Terry Benedict), Don Cheadle (Basher Tarr), Bernie Mac (Frank Catton), Julia Roberts (Tess Ocean), Elliott Gould (Reuben Tishkoff), Vincent Cassel (Francois Toulour). Directed by Steven Soderbergh and produced by Jerry Weintraub. Screenplay by George Nolfi.

Just as most caper movies end with the thieves comfortably basking in retirement, so most sequels to caper movies begin with the thieves forced to go back to work and pull one more job. *Ocean's Twelve* does not disappoint. Tess Ocean (Julia Roberts) is chatting on the phone with her husband, Danny (George Clooney), when she looks out the window and says, "Oh, no." Terry Benedict (Andy Garcia) is ringing the door bell.

You will recall that in *Ocean's Eleven* Benedict was the owner of the Bellagio, a casino in Las Vegas from which the eleven stole—well, let's see, with interest, it works out to about $19 million apiece. Benedict is accompanied on his visit by evil-looking twins and has an off-putting practice of poking people with a putter, the better to suggest dire consequences if his money is not returned. Yes, the insurance company has already paid off, but he envisions double indemnity.

With some movies, you begin to notice implausibilities. With others, you begin to admire them. For example, since Terry Benedict eventually pays a personal call on each and every one of the original eleven, why don't Danny and Tess simply telephone the other nine and warn them Benedict is coming? The reason you don't want to ask that question is because it would prevent the movie from introducing all the crooks and showing us what they're doing now.

One of the problems with a movie like this is directing traffic: How do you establish eleven characters (not counting Benedict, police inspector Catherine Zeta-Jones, rival thief Vincent Cassel, etc.) and keep them alive? You have a roll call every once in a while, is what you do, or you have them thrown in jail so the camera can pan across their faces and remind us who they are. Occasionally you have a scene for no other reason than to get an actor's face on the screen for five seconds, so he will not be misplaced. Elliott Gould puffs on his cigar three different times for this very reason.

The movie takes inventory of its characters with the same droll wit it does everything else. The *original* original *Ocean's Eleven*, made in 1960 by the Rat Pack, was a send-up of 1950s caper movies (it was inspired by Jean-Pierre Melville's French classic *Bob le Flambeur*). The *new* original *Ocean's Eleven* (2001) was a successful attempt by Soderbergh to doodle with the formula, much as a pianist might pick out a tune just well enough to show he could play it if he wanted to. Now, with *Ocean's Twelve*, Soderberg and his scenarist, George Nolfi, are doing a jazz riff. This isn't a caper movie at all; it's an improvisation on caper themes. If at times it seems like a caper, well, as the fellow said when he got up from the piano, it might not be Beethoven, but it has a lot of the same notes.

What Soderbergh is working with here is the charm of his actors, particularly Clooney, Roberts, Brad Pitt, and Zeta-Jones, who have the key roles, and the puppy-dog earnestness of Matt Damon, who wakes up Pitt on a transatlantic flight to tell him he thinks he's ready to play "a more central role." Damon's character is named Linus, a good choice of role model, since he is sincere and intense, and everyone else in the movie seems inspired by Snoopy.

When one character is excoriated as agoraphobic (what a wonderful phrase that is, "excoriated as agoraphobic"; don't you think it's almost musical?), Linus earnestly argues, "I don't think we have to be the kind of organization that labels people." There is a scene of mad invention in which Clooney and Pitt take him along for a meeting with Robbie Coltrane, an underworld contact, and their entire conversation is nonsense—an exchange of elegantly meaningless paradoxes. Linus doesn't understand a word, which is reasonable, but what he doesn't realize is that they don't either.

Their scheme has to do with stealing enough stuff to pay Benedict the $19 million apiece that they owe him. They doubt they can raise this much money in the three weeks until their deadline, especially since it appears that another thief, the Night Fox, is in business against them, and is either more skilled than they are or a supernatural being. As they contemplate the security surrounding one of their targets, Pitt flatly states: "In the physical universe we live in, it cannot be done." But the Night Fox can do it.

Occasionally their plans take the long way around. Consider a man in Amsterdam who has sealed himself and his treasures inside a house guarded with multiple alarm systems, and never leaves home. Surveillance indicates there is a control pad on an inner wall that might be manipulated to bypass the alarms. How to reach it? Their plan involves getting *underneath* the house, which is beside a canal and rests on underwater pylons, and using hy-

draulic lifts to raise the house one inch, so that a difficult shot with an arrow becomes possible. Uh-huh. With overhead like that, when do they reach their break-even point?

Rather than describe some of their other targets, such as a priceless jeweled egg, I will observe that all of the targets are MacGuffins, that it matters not what they go after but how they do it, and what they say in the process. The movie is all about behavior, dialogue, star power, and wiseass in-jokes. I really sort of liked it.

Example of the cleverness: There are two cameos in the movie that, for once, contribute something more than allowing us to say, "Hey! There's (name of star)!" The genius is that one of the stars is really there, and the other star is not really there, although she is there in the person of the character who seems to be her. This will all become clear when you see the movie. What I liked is that the one cameo role is used to expose the other cameo role. When you get to the point of interlocking cameos, you have ascended to a level of invention that is its own reward.

Off the Map ★ ★ ★ ½
PG-13, 108 m., 2005

Joan Allen (Arlene Groden), Valentina de Angelis (Bo Groden), Sam Elliott (Charley Groden), J. K. Simmons (George), Jim True-Frost (William Gibbs), Amy Brenneman (Adult Bo). Directed by Campbell Scott and produced by Scott and George Van Buskirk. Screenplay by Joan Ackermann.

Somewhere in the back of nowhere, in an adobe house with no lights or running water, a family lives in what could be called freedom or could be called poverty. We're not sure if they got there because they were 1960s hippies making a lifestyle experiment, or were simply deposited there by indifference to conventional life. They grow vegetables and plunder the city dump and get $320 a month in veteran's benefits, but they are not in need and are apparently content with their lot.

Now there is a problem. "That was the summer of my father's depression," the narrator tells us. She is Bo Groden, played in the movie by Valentina de Angelis at about age twelve, and heard on the sound track as an adult (Amy Brenneman). "I'm a damn crying machine," says her dad, Charley (Sam Elliott). He sits at the kitchen table, staring at nothing, and his wife and daughter have learned to live their lives around him.

His wife is Arlene, played by Joan Allen in a performance of astonishing complexity. Here is a woman whose life includes acceptance of what she cannot change, sufficiency within her own skin, and such simple pleasures as gardening in the nude. She is a good wife and a good mother, but not obviously; it takes us the whole movie to fully appreciate how profoundly she observes her husband and daughter, and provides what they need in ways that are below their radar.

Charley has a friend named George (J. K. Simmons), who sort of idolizes him. Sometimes they fish, sometimes they talk. Arlene wants George to impersonate Charley, visit a psychiatrist, and get some antidepressants. George would rather fish. One day a stranger arrives at their home, which is far from any road. He carries a briefcase, says he is from the IRS, and is there to audit them, since the Groden family has reported an annual income of less than $5,000 for several years.

This man is William Gibbs (Jim True-Frost). He is stung by a bee, takes to the sofa, confesses his dissatisfaction with tax-collecting and, what with one thing and another, never leaves. Eventually he lives in an old school bus on the property. He falls in love with Arlene, in a nondemonstrative way, and is good company for Charley. "Ever been depressed?" Charley asks him. "I've never not been," William says.

These characters in this setting could become caricatures or grotesques. But the director, Campbell Scott, and the writer, Joan Ackermann, refuse to underline them or draw arrows pointing to their absurdities. They accept them. Their movie is freed from a story that must hurry things along; life unfolds from day to day. Will Charley recover from his depression? Will William leave? Will Bo, who is being home-schooled, get to go to a real school? The movie suggests no urgency to get these questions answered.

Instead, in a stealthy and touching way, it shows how people can work on one another.

Charley may be depressed because of a chemical imbalance, or he may be stuck because his life offers him no opening for heroism. Arlene keeps herself entertained by surprising herself with her oddities; she handles financial emergencies by observing with detachment that sooner or later they will probably have to deal with them. Bo keeps busy writing letters to food corporations, complaining about insect parts found in their products, and composing personal questions for the "Ask Beth" newspaper column. William Gibbs starts to paint, and completes a watercolor, three feet high by forty-one long, showing the earth meeting the sky.

It is not clear if William has joined them to heal, to escape, or to die. But his presence in the family, which is accepted without comment, budges the emotional ground under Charley just enough so that he slides toward the edge of his depression. Perhaps it is William's undemonstrative love for Arlene, never acted on, that reawakens Charley's desire for this magnificent beast, his wife.

Campbell Scott is an actor, and as a director he is able to trust his actors entirely. If they are doing their jobs, we will watch, no matter if the story centers on a man sitting at a table and everyone else essentially waiting for him to get up. The life force bubbling inside young Bo, suggested by Valentina de Angelis in a performance of unstudied grace, lets us know things will change, if only because she continues to push at life. *Off the Map* is visually beautiful, as a portrait of lives in the middle of emptiness, but it's not about the New Mexico scenery. It's about feelings that shift among people who are good enough, curious enough, or just maybe tired enough to let that happen.

Variety, the show-biz bible, always assesses a movie's commercial prospects in its reviews. Its chief critic, the dependable Todd McCarthy, loves this film, but does his duty to the biz by noting: "Pic's unmelodramatic nature and unmomentous subject matter will make this a tough sell even on the review-driven specialized circuit." True, and by now you have sensed whether you would like it or not. If you think you would not, be patient, for sooner or later you will find yourself compelled to get up from the table.

Oldboy ★ ★ ★ ★
R, 120 m., 2005

Min-sik Choi (Dae-su Oh), Ji-tae Yoo (Woo-jin Lee), Hye-jung Gang (Mido). Directed by Chan-wook Park and produced by Dong-joo Kim. Screenplay by Jo-yun Hwang, Joon-hyung Lim, and Park.

A man gets violently drunk and is chained to the wall in a police station. His friend comes and bails him out. While the friend is making a telephone call, the man disappears from an empty city street in the middle of the night. The man regains consciousness in what looks like a shabby hotel room. A bed, a desk, a TV, a bathroom cubicle. There is a steel door with a slot near the floor for his food tray. Occasionally a little tune plays, the room fills with gas, and when he regains consciousness the room has been cleaned, his clothes have been changed, and he has received a haircut.

This routine continues for fifteen years. He is never told who has imprisoned him, or why. He watches TV until it becomes his world. He fills one journal after another with his writings. He pounds the wall until his fists grow bloody, and then hardened. He screams. He learns from TV that his blood and finger-prints were found at the scene of his wife's murder. That his daughter has been adopted in Sweden. That if he were to escape, he would be a wanted man.

Oldboy, by the Korean director Chan-wook Park, watches him objectively, asking no sympathy, standing outside his plight. When, later, he does talk with the man who has imprisoned him, the man says: "I'm sort of a scholar, and what I study is you."

In its sexuality and violence, this is the kind of movie that can no longer easily be made in the United States; the standards of a puritanical minority, imposed on broadcasting and threatened even for cable, make studios unwilling to produce films that might face uncertain distribution. But content does not make a movie good or bad—it is merely what it is about. *Oldboy* is a powerful film not because of what it depicts, but because of the depths of the human heart it strips bare.

The man, named Dae-su Oh (Min-sik Choi), is a wretch when we first meet him, a drunk who has missed his little daughter's birthday and now sits forlornly in the police station, ridiculously wearing the angel's wings he bought her as a present. He is not a bad man, but alcohol has rendered him useless.

When he suddenly finds himself freed from his bizarre captivity fifteen years later, he is a different person, focused on revenge, ridiculously responsive to kindness. Wandering into a restaurant, he meets a young woman who, he knows from the TV, is Korea's "Chef of the Year." This is Mido (Hye-jung Gang). Sensing that he has suffered, feeling an instinctive sympathy, she takes him home with her, hears his story, cares for him, comes to love him. Meanwhile he sets out on a methodical search to find the secret of his captivity. He was fed pot stickers day after day, until their taste was burned into his memory, and he travels the city's restaurants until he finds the one that supplied his meals. That is the key to tracking down his captors.

It is also, really, the beginning of the movie, the point at which it stops being a mystery and becomes a tragedy in the classical sense. I will not reveal the several secrets that lie ahead for Dae-su, except to say that they come not as shabby plot devices, but as one turn after another of the screws of mental and physical anguish and poetic justice. I can mention a virtuoso sequence in which Dae-su fights with several of his former jailers, his rage so great that he is scarcely slowed by the knife sticking in his back. This is a man consumed by the need for revenge, who eventually discovers he was imprisoned by another man whose need was no less consuming, and infinitely more diabolical.

I am not an expert on the Korean cinema, which is considered in critical circles as one of the most creative in the world (*Oldboy* won the Grand Jury Prize at Cannes 2004). I can say that of the Korean films I've seen, only one (*The YMCA Baseball Team*) did not contain extraordinary sadomasochism. *Oldboy* contains a tooth-pulling scene that makes Laurence Olivier's Nazi dentist in *Marathon Man* look like a healer. And there is a scene during which an octopus is definitely harmed during the making of the movie.

These scenes do not play for shock value, but are part of the whole. Dae-su has been locked up for fifteen years without once seeing another living person. For him the close presence of anyone is like a blow to all of his senses. When he says in a restaurant, "I want to eat something that is alive," we understand (a) that living seafood is indeed consumed as a delicacy in Asia, and (b) he wants to eat the life, not the food, because he has been buried in death for fifteen years.

Why would Mido, young, pretty, and talented, take this wretched man into her life? Perhaps because he is so manifestly helpless. Perhaps because she believes his story, and even the reason why he cannot reclaim his real name or identity. Perhaps because in fifteen years he has been transformed into a man she senses is strong and good, when he was once weak and despicable. From his point of view, love is joined with salvation, acceptance, forgiveness, and the possibility of redemption.

All of this is in place during the several scenes of revelation that follow, providing a context and giving them a deeper meaning. Yes, the ending is improbable in its complexity, but it is not impossible, and it is not unmotivated. *Oldboy* ventures to emotional extremes, but not without reason. We are so accustomed to "thrillers" that exist only as machines for creating diversion that it's a shock to find a movie in which the action, however violent, makes a statement and has a purpose.

Old School ★
R, 90 m., 2003

Luke Wilson (Mitch), Will Ferrell (Frank), Vince Vaughn (Beanie), Ellen Pompeo (Nicole), Juliette Lewis (Heidi), Jeremy Piven (Gordon), Craig Kilborn (Mark), Leah Remini (Lara). Directed by Todd Phillips and produced by Daniel Goldberg, Joe Medjuck, and Phillips. Screenplay by Phillips and Scot Armstrong.

Luke Wilson, Will Ferrell, and Vince Vaughn clock in at an average age of thirty-four, which is a little old to be a frat boy. It is not their age but their longevity, however, that I question. In *Old School,* where they occupy a series of off-campus party houses, they follow lifestyles more appropriate for the college students in *Flatliners.* Anyone stuck in the jugular by an animal-disabling tranquilizer dart who then rolls into a swimming pool is not likely to have to face the kinds of questions about retirement confronting the hero of *About Schmidt.*

There is a type of older student who never seems to leave the campus. Some are actually graduate students, some are "finishing their thesis," others are gaining job experience (i.e., are bartenders or drug dealers). I graduated from Illinois, returned ten years later, and found my old friend Mike still at his usual table in the Illini Union, drinking the bottomless cup of coffee and working the crossword puzzle.

Wilson, Ferrell, and Vaughn do not play this type of student. They are not really students at all, in fact. Wilson plays a businessman who returns home early to discover that his fiancée (Juliette Lewis) is hosting an orgy. Ferrell is engaged to be married, and Vaughn is married. They stumble into founding their own fraternity after discovering by accident that you can get a lot of action if you throw nude wrestling matches in K-Y jelly.

Old School wants to be *National Lampoon's Animal House,* but then, don't they all. It assumes that the modern college campus is a hotbed, or is it a sinkhole, of moral squalor, exhibitionism, promiscuity, kinky sex, and rampant rampantness. Perhaps it is.

I have also heard, on the other hand, that the politically correct modern male undergraduate, terrified of sexual harassment charges, must have a notarized statement in hand giving him permission to even think about getting to first base, and a judge's order authorizing him to advance to second. (All women in movies set on such campuses are issued at birth a blanket license to kick groins.)

Unsure of myself, I avoid altogether the question of *Old School*'s veracity, and move on to its humor, which is easier to master because there is so little of it. This is not a funny movie, although it has a few good scenes and some nice work by Will Ferrell as an apparently compulsive nudist.

It follows the same old story about a bunch of fun-loving guys who only want to throw orgies and meet chicks, and a young fogey dean (Jeremy Piven) who wants to spoil their fun. One of the cute co-eds is played by Ellen Pompeo, who was so absolutely wonderful in *Moonlight Mile.* She should not be discouraged by this sophomore effort. Even Meryl Streep had to make a second movie after *Julia*. Oh, and I just found the title right here: *The Deer Hunter*.

The movie has been slapped together by director Todd Phillips, who careens from scene to scene without it occurring to him that humor benefits from characterization, context, and continuity. Otherwise, all you have is a lot of people acting goofy. The movie was screened before an "invited audience" in a Chicago theater, where two small groups of audience members laughed loudly at almost everything, and just about everybody else waited politely until it was over and they could leave. Critics are sometimes required to see comedies at such screenings because we can appreciate them better when we see them with a general audience, and to be sure, I learn a lot that way.

Once Upon a Time in Mexico ★ ★ ★
R, 101 m., 2003

Antonio Banderas (El Mariachi), Salma Hayek (Carolina), Johnny Depp (CIA Agent Sands), Rubén Blades (Jorge), Eva Mendes (Special Agent Ajedrez), Willem Dafoe (Barillo), Mickey Rourke (Billy), Cheech Marin (Belini). Directed by Robert Rodriguez and produced by Elizabeth Avellan, Carlos Gallardo, and Rodriguez. Screenplay by Rodriguez.

After Robert Rodriguez made his $7,000 first film, *El Mariachi* (1992), and his $3 million *Desperado* (1995), Quentin Tarantino told him they were the Mexican equivalents of Sergio Leone's first two spaghetti Westerns. After the low-budget *A Fistful of Dollars* and *For a Few Dollars More*, Leone moved up to bigger budgets for *The Good, the Bad and the Ugly* and *Once Upon a Time in the West*—and therefore, Tarantino told his friend, Rodriguez should now make *Once Upon a Time in Mexico*. And so he has, for $30 million—still a relatively modest budget, as action movies go.

Like Leone's movie, the Rodriguez epic is more interested in the moment, in great shots, in surprises and ironic reversals and close-ups of sweaty faces, than in a coherent story. Both movies feed on the music of heroism and lament. Both paint their stories in bold, bright colors. Both go for sensational kills; if Clint Eastwood kills three men with one bullet,

Salma Hayek kills four men with four knives, all thrown at once.

In my review of *Desperado*, I praised Rodriguez for his technical skill and creative energy, but said he hadn't learned to structure a story so we cared about what happened. That's still true in *Once Upon a Time in Mexico*, but you know what? I didn't mind. I understood the general outlines of the story, I liked the bold strokes he uses to create the characters, and I was amused by the camera work, which includes a lot of shots that are about themselves.

The actors in a movie like this have to arrive on the screen self-contained; there are flashbacks to their earlier lives, but they explain what happened to them, not who they are. With Antonio Banderas, Salma Hayek, and Johnny Depp as his leads, and a supporting cast including Rubén Blades, Eva Mendes, Willem Dafoe, and Mickey Rourke, Rodriguez has great faces, bodies, eyes, hair, sneers, snarls, and personalities to work with. Banderas is as impassive as Eastwood, Hayek steams with passion, and Johnny Depp steams with something—maybe fermenting memories of *Pirates of the Caribbean*.

The plot is at least technically a sequel to the first two movies, once again with El Mariachi as a troubadour with a sideline in killing (early in the movie, he cocks his guitar). I didn't remember the particulars of the first two films well enough to follow this continuation in detail, but so what? Essentially, El Mariachi (Banderas) is in self-imposed exile after the deaths of Carolina (Hayek) and their daughter. Depp, who is a CIA agent of sorts, tracks him down with the help of a talkative bartender (Cheech Marin). He wants El Mariachi to stop a plot against the president by the drug kingpin Barillo (Dafoe). Mickey Rourke's role is to carry a little dog in his arms, look sinister, and seem capable of more colorful dialogue than the screenplay provides for him. It's time for him to be rehabilitated in a lead.

There are lots of fancy shots in the movie, but nothing quite equals a sensational sequence in which Banderas and Hayek, chained together, escape from a high-rise apartment and somehow rappel to the ground with one hanging on while the other swings down to the next level. Neat.

Rodriguez is the one-man band of contemporary filmmakers, making his movies not quite by himself, but almost. His credits here say he "chopped, shot and scored" the movie, as well as writing and directing it, and he personally operated the new Sony 24-fps digital hi-def camera. As a skeptic about digital feature photography and a supporter of light through celluloid, I have to admit that this movie looks great. Maybe the camera has been improved, maybe the Boeing digital projectors are a step up from the underpowered Texas Instruments machines, but the picture is bright, crisp, and detailed. Maybe it was a little too sharp-edged, since there is something to be said for the tactile softness of celluloid, but it was impressive, and an enormous improvement over what I've seen before, including Rodriguez's own *Spy Kids 2*. (*Spy Kids 3-D* doesn't count because of the murkiness inherent in 3-D.)

What bubbles beneath all of Rodriguez's work is an impatient joy in the act of filmmaking. He started with hundreds of home movies when he was a kid, made *Desperado* for peanuts and somehow got a studio to buy it, and is still only thirty-five.

He talks about how easy digital filmmaking makes it for him and the actors—no fussing over lights, no worrying about film costs, lots of freedom to try things different ways. *Once Upon a Time in Mexico* sometimes feels as if he's winging it, but you have to admit he has an instinctive, exuberant feel for moving images. I am not sure a thoughtful and coherent story can be made using his methods, but maybe that's not what he's interested in doing.

Once Upon a Time in the Midlands ★ ★ ★

R, 104 m., 2003

Robert Carlyle (Jimmy), Rhys Ifans (Dek), Shirley Henderson (Shirley), Kathy Burke (Carol), Ricky Tomlinson (Charlie), Finn Atkins (Marlene). Directed by Shane Meadows and produced by Andrea Calderwood. Screenplay by Paul Fraser and Meadows.

Once Upon a Time in the Midlands has a score that sounds familiar, with its echoing hoof beats, harmonicas, and far-off whistles. It evokes the atmosphere of a Sergio Leone Western, sneaking up under the movie's human

comedy and adding a smile. The film is set not in the West (or Spain), but in Nottingham, in the British Midlands, where its lovable working-class characters get involved in a story of love, loss, revenge, clowns, and country-and-western music.

The movie opens on the British version of the Jerry Springer show, with the love-struck Dek (Rhys Ifans) proposing marriage to his longtime live-in lover, Shirley (Shirley Henderson). To his dismay, she turns him down. Watching the show is her former husband, Jimmy (Robert Carlyle), who, as it happens, has a reason to visit their little town—he's lying low after a botched stickup. His reappearance confronts Shirley with a classic Western decision, between the respectable shopkeeper and the gunslinger from out of town.

Dek and Shirley live with Marlene (Finn Atkins), her daughter by Jimmy, which gives the snaky ex-husband an excuse to reenter their lives. He wants to reconnect with his daughter. Uh-huh. And for a time he's able to kindle once again in Shirley the excitement she once felt around this dangerous and unpredictable man. Down at his business, the Clutch Hutch, Dek fantasies about a showdown with Jimmy, but all it leads up to is a classic Western gunfight pose with Dek holding not a revolver but a power drill.

Shirley and Dek are part of an extended family including two best friends left over from her marriage. Carol (Kathy Burke), Jimmy's foster sister, is a loud, confident woman who thinks nothing of leaping across the room to topple a man from his La-Z-Boy; her husband, Charlie (Ricky Tomlinson), is a country-and-western singer, or so he says. They provide a running commentary as Shirley tentatively decides to let Jimmy back into her life.

Dek, a gentle soul who is devastated by being turned down on national TV, is now prepared almost to surrender, since Shirley obviously doesn't love him. But her daughter Marlene does, and in her mind Dek has always been her father. That leads to scenes of surprising tenderness, in a movie that has enormous affection for all of its characters—except for Jimmy.

There's a slapstick sequence in the film: the botched robbery, which involves clowns and a Morris Mini, and it would almost break the spell except that we can just about believe these characters are goofy enough to pull off something like that (maybe they saw it in a movie?). And there's always the undertone of danger with Jimmy, who can be charming and then turn mean in an instant.

Rhys Ifans is the key player. You may remember him as Hugh Grant's Welsh roommate in *Notting Hill*, the one with such a fascination for his bodily functions. He can play peculiar, but here he plays normal, even low-key, as a guy who doubts himself so much that, if Shirley says she won't marry him, she must be right.

The movie doesn't really press its parallels with Sergio Leone; maybe the title and the music are simply supposed to suggest that even in Nottingham there can be showdowns between good and evil, and a loser can learn to stand up like a man. Some of the photography by Brian Tufano also quietly echoes the Leone look, including a lovely night exterior of the outside of a bingo parlor, outlined against the evening sky.

Note: Will American audiences have trouble with the accents? I ask because people at the screening asked me. I think it's a matter of listening to the music instead of the words. You may be a little put off at the beginning, especially by Carlyle, but it's funny how as the characters develop and the story gets interesting, somehow we hear all the words and stop thinking about the accents.

Ong-Bak: The Thai Warrior ★ ★ ★
R, 107 m., 2005

Tony Jaa (Ting), Petchthai Wongkamlao (George), Pumwaree Yodkamol (Muay Lek), Rungrawee Borrijindakul (Ngek), Chetwut Wacharakun (Peng), Sukhaaw Phongwilai (Khom Tuan). Directed by Prachya Pinkaew and produced by Pinkaew and Sukanya Vongsthapat. Screenplay by Suphachai Sithiamphan.

"No stunt doubles.
"No computer graphics.
"No strings attached."

These nine words represent the most astonishing element of *Ong-Bak: The Thai Warrior*, the first Thai film to break through in the martial arts market. Having seen documentaries showing how stunt men are "flown" from wires that are eliminated in postproduction, having seen entire action sequences made on computers, I sat through the movie impressed at how real the action sequences seemed. Then I went to the Web site and discovered that they *were* real.

Yes, they do a lot with camera angles and editing tricks. With the right lens and angle and slow-motion you can make it look like an actor is defying gravity, when in fact he is simply making a big jump from a trampoline. But some of the shots cannot easily be faked.

In *Red Trousers* (2004), a documentary about Hong Kong stuntmen, we find that they perform a lot of falls simply by—falling. *Ong-Bak* opens with a tree-climbing contest in which the competitors try to capture a red flag at the top of a tree, while kicking and shoving their opponents off the limbs. Say all you want about wide-angle lenses that exaggerate distance, but we see the tree in an undistorted shot that establishes its height, and these guys are falling a long way and they are landing hard.

The movie stars Tony Jaa, a young actor who is already an accomplished stuntman and expert in Muay Thai boxing, a sentence I have typed just as if I had the slightest idea what Muay Thai boxing is. Thank you, Web site. Jaa, who plays the hero, Ting, is an acrobat and stuntman in the league of Jackie Chan or Buster Keaton, and there's an early chase through city streets where he does things just for the hell of it, like jumping through a large coil of barbed wire, jumping over two intersecting bicycles, and sliding under a moving truck.

This chase, and the tree-climbing scene, set the pace for the movie. It is 107 minutes long, and approximately seven minutes are devoted to the plot, which involves the theft of an ancient Buddhist statue from the hero's village. He has been trained by Buddhist monks and will not fight for reasons of vengeance, money, or personal gain, but he agrees to go to Bangkok and retrieve the sacred statue, and for a monk with a vow of pacifism he certainly relaxes his rule against fighting. One bloody sequence has him taking on three opponents in an illegal boxing club where enormous sums are wagered by Khom Tuan (Sukhaaw Phongwilai), the local crime lord.

I arrived at the movie prepared to take notes on my beloved Levenger Pocket Briefcase, which I lost at Sundance and then miraculously had restored to me. But I found when the movie was over that I had written down its title, and nothing else. That's because there's really nothing to be done with this movie except watch it. My notes, had I taken them, would have read something like this:

"Falls from tall tree.

"Chase through streets.

"Runs on tops of heads of people.

"Runs across the tops of market stalls, cars, and buses.

"Barbed wire!

"Fruit Cart Scene!!! Persimmons everywhere!

"Illegal boxing club. Breakaway chairs and tables pounded over heads.

"Chase scene with three-wheeled scooter-taxis, dozens of them.

"Ting catches fire, attacks opponents with blazing legs."

And so on, and on. The movie is based on the assumption, common to almost all martial arts movies, that the world of the hero has been choreographed and cast to supply him with one prop, location, and set of opponents after another. Ting needs a couple dozen three-wheelers for a chase scene? They materialize, and all other forms of transportation disappear. He fights twenty opponents at once? Good, but no one is ever able to whack him from behind; they obediently attack him one at a time, and are smashed into defeat.

The plot includes a pretty girl (Pumwaree Yodkamol), who I think is the girlfriend of George (Petchthai Wongkamlao), a friend of Ting's from the village who has become corrupted by Bangkok and betrays him. I was paying pretty close attention, I think, but I can't remember for sure if Ting and the girl ever get anything going, maybe because any romance at all would drag the action to a halt for gooey dialogue. I think they look at each other like they'll get together after the movie.

Did I enjoy *Ong-Bak*? As brainless but skillful action choreography, yes. And I would have enjoyed it even more if I'd known going in that the stunts were being performed in the old-fashioned, precomputer way. *Ong-Bak* even uses that old Bruce Lee strategy of re-peating shots of each stunt from two or three angles, which wreaks havoc with the theory that time flows ceaselessly from the past into the future, but sure does give us a good look when he clears the barbed wire.

On_Line ★ ★

R, 97 m., 2003

Josh Hamilton (John Roth), Harold Perrineau (Moe Curley), Isabel Gillies (Moira Ingalls), John Fleck (Al Fleming), Vanessa Ferlito (Jordan Nash), Eric Millegan (Ed Simone), Liz Owens (Angel). Directed by Jed Weintrob and produced by Tanya Selvaratnam and Adam Brightman. Screenplay by Andrew Osborne and Weintrob.

I refuse to sign up for instant messaging for the same reason I won't carry a cell phone: Don't call me, I'll call you. The characters in Jed Weintrob's *On_Line* are on call more or less all the time, living their barren lives in cyberspace, where the members of a suicide Webcam chat are bored, waiting around for someone to overdose. The film's redeeming feature is that it knows how sad these people are and finds the correct solution to their problems: They meet in the flesh.

The movie stars Josh Hamilton and Harold Perrineau as John and Moe, roommates who run an on-line sex site named InterconX. It's a little like the real-life iFriends.com; on screens that display simultaneous cybercams, its members flirt, chat, engage in virtual sex, and charge for interaction. So mesmerized is John by this process that he follows, on another screen, a twenty-four-hour live cam where Angel (Liz Owens) lives her life in public view.

This can get to be a way of life. I have a friend who became so obsessed with one woman's Webcam that he kept its window constantly open on his desktop, no doubt getting up in the night to check that she was sleeping well. This is the geek equivalent of looking in on the kids. And at Sundance 1999 I saw *Home Page*, a documentary about a pioneering on-line blogger (as they were not called then) named Justin Hall, whose life seemed to be lived just so he could report on it.

That would also describe John, who keeps his own on-line journal in which he sighs about the emptiness of his existence and the futility of it all, and whose sex life at one point is reduced to masturbating not into his own sock, which would be pathetic enough, but into his roommate's.

The movie charts its lives through a split-screen technique that resembles the Web pages where the characters hang out. Digital video is combined with screen shots in a way that is intriguing and sometimes beautiful; the way the movie chops up the screen to follow simultaneous events is a little like Ang Lee's technique in *Hulk,* and the visuals use filters, textures, and colored lighting to create an effect not unlike some of the weirder pages of the early *Wired* magazine. Even when my interest in the characters flagged, I liked looking at the movie; credit to cinematographer Toshiaki Ozawa and visual effects supervisor Christian D. Bruun.

The film's relationships suggest that although you might find a soul mate on-line, you might be better off sticking with your roommate's sock. John, for example, falls for Jordan (Vanessa Ferlito), one of the women who pays him to rent space on InterconX. When he dates her in real life, he discovers she is frighteningly real and maybe more than he can handle; we hear his thoughts while he watches her dance at a nightclub, and suspect he would be happier going home and experiencing the date on-line.

Another couple consists of an older gay man in New York (John Fleck) who develops a friendship with a teenager (Eric Millegan) who fears he is the only adolescent homosexual in Ohio. When the kid gets off the bus in New York City, I was not ready to cheer this as a victory over the loneliness of cyberspace, because I believe that teenage boys in Ohio, whatever their sexual identity, cannot solve their problems by meeting strange older men in New York. The movie is more optimistic here than I am.

The movie's weakness is in its strength. It does a good job of portraying the day-to-day life of these on-line obsessives, but we realize eventually that they are more interesting *because* they are on-line. Their problems and personalities would not necessarily be movie material if it weren't for the cyberspace overlay. When it comes to those who try to live in cyberspace, I am reminded of Dr. Johnson's comment about a dog standing on its hind legs: "It is not done well, but you are surprised to find it done at all."

Open Hearts ★ ★ ★
R, 114 m., 2003

Sonja Richter (Cecilie), Mads Mikkelsen (Niels), Paprika Steen (Marie), Nikolaj Lie Kaas (Joachim), Stine Bjerregaard (Stine), Birthe Neumann (Hanne), Niels Olsen (Finn), Ulf Pilgaard (Thomsen), Ronnie Hiort (Gustav). Directed by Susanne Bier and produced by Jonas Frederiksen and Vibeke Windelov. Screenplay by Anders Thomas Jensen.

A life can be forever changed in an instant. Joachim proposes marriage to Cecilie, they are in love, they kiss, he steps heedlessly out of the car, he is struck by another car, and is paralyzed from the neck down. All of that happens at the outset in *Open Hearts,* which is about how this instant echoes in the lives of others.

Most movies about such injuries are sentimental, like *The Other Side of the Mountain.* What I have learned from disabled friends who have had such devastating events in their lives is that sentimentality is for greeting cards. They face a new reality, and they have to be hard and brave, and sometimes they use dark humor as a relief or shield. I will never forget the puckish humor of Heather Rose, the star and author of *Dance Me to My Song,* who could control only one finger of one hand, and used it to tap out a computer message to a college audience that had just seen her film: "Let's go get pissed."

What is unusual about *Open Hearts* is how forthright it is about the reaction of Joachim (Nikolaj Lie Kaas) to his injury. We have seen him as an athlete, a rock climber, an extrovert, a man in love. But when Cecilie (Sonja Richter) is at his bedside, after he hears that he will never walk again, he turns away from her pledges of love and tells her to get lost. He is angry and doesn't even want to look at her.

This is not unreasonable. He is furious at the instant of fate that has taken his youth and his movement from him. Furious that he cannot do the things he loves. And he recoils from her love because . . . because . . . well, because it hurts him too much, and because he wants to release her from their engagement, spare her a lifetime with him on these new terms.

His anger is a stage that he has to go through. Eventually will come the other stages we hear about, involving negotiation, acceptance, and so on. Kübler-Ross's five stages for the dying get reversed for the gravely handicapped: They awaken feeling they are dead, and have to track back into accepting and embracing life.

Open Hearts is not simply about Joachim and Cecilie, however. It is about a matrix of lives affected by the accident. We meet Marie (Paprika Steen), who was driving the car that struck Joachim. While the accident was not precisely her fault, she was distracted at the time and believes she might have been able to avoid it. Her husband, Niels (Mads Mikkelsen) is by coincidence the doctor on duty in the emergency ward where Joachim is taken. He's the one who has to break the news to Cecilie.

In the weeks and months that follow, Joachim continues to be hostile to Cecilie. He issues orders that she is not to be allowed in his room. He is also startlingly hostile to a nurse, who can take it, and does, creating an intriguing dynamic. Cecilie, who has no one to confide in, begins to share her feelings with Niels, the doctor. His wife knows and approves, but does not know that Niels is falling helplessly, obsessively, in love with the younger woman.

The movie is fascinated by the nature of his love. This is not a romance, not adultery, not an affair, not any of the things that can be explained with a word. It is helpless intoxicating infatuation, so powerful he is ready to consider leaving his long and happy marriage with Marie, which has given him three children he loves.

Now it is up to us. What do we think? Two men have decided to abandon women who love them. Cecilie is in the middle—pushed away by one, loved by another. Joachim and Marie are the outsiders—he by choice, she by—well, you could call this an accident, too, a blow of fate when she does not expect it. Marie's way of dealing with Neils's new love is seen with clarity and intelligence by Susanne Bier, the director. She doesn't respond on cue with screaming and accusations, like soap opera wives, but tries to size up the new reality and see what can be saved or salvaged.

As for Joachim—well, I feel he's a rat. He should not leave his wife and children to move in with the sort-of fiancée of his patient. As Pascal once said (and Woody Allen once quoted), "The heart has its reasons of which reason knows nothing." At the end, it's all a mess. Love causes such pain and regret. Can Neils be strong and reject his love for Cecilie? Can he be as strong as Joachim? Why do we want Neils to abandon his love and Joachim to reassert his? And what is so amazingly unique about Cecilie, anyway? She is sweet and pretty but not in any way extraordinary, yet has taken possession of both these men.

It must be noted that *Open Hearts* is a Dogma film, subscribing to the Danish manifesto calling for a simpler, more direct, and less artful approach to filmmaking. This was the twenty-eighth film to receive the Dogma certificate, but I am weary of sifting each Dogma production through the same dogmatic sieve, and will simply note that it is filmed directly, intimately, without heightened effects or facile emotion-boosters. It is intensely curious about these people, sees them clearly, has no answers. I wish there were a manifesto that forgot about the stylistic stuff and simply required that.

Open Range ★ ★ ★ ½
R, 135 m., 2003

Kevin Costner (Charley Waite), Robert Duvall (Boss Spearman), Annette Bening (Sue Barlow), Abraham Benrubi (Mose), Michael Gambon (Denton Baxter), Michael Jeter (Percy), Diego Luna (Button). Directed by Kevin Costner and produced by Costner, Jake Eberts, and David Valdes. Screenplay by Craig Storper, based on the novel by Lauran Paine.

One of the many ways in which the Western has become old-fashioned is that the characters have values and act on them. Modern action movies have replaced values with team loyalty; the characters do what they do because they want to win and they want the other side to lose. The underlying text of most classic Westerns is from the Bible: "What does it profit a man if he gains the whole world, but loses his soul?" The underlying text of most modern action movies is from Vince Lombardi: "Winning isn't everything; it's the only thing."

Kevin Costner's *Open Range*, an imperfect but deeply involving and beautifully made new Western, works primarily because it expresses the personal values of a cowboy named Boss (Robert Duvall) and his employee of ten years,

Charley (Costner). Boss does not believe in unnecessary violence, and is willing to put his own life at risk rather than kill someone just to be on the safe side. Charley was an expert killer during the Civil War, and has spent ten years under Boss trying to tame that side of his character. Boss is not only his friend but also his mentor and, in a sense, his spiritual leader. Charley doesn't merely work with him, but follows him as a sort of disciple.

Boss grazes his cattle on the open range. His group includes Charley, the younger man Mose (Abraham Benrubi), big and bearded, and the kid Button (Diego Luna), who would sometimes rather play with the dog than do his work. They halt outside a town, Mose is sent in on an errand, and when he doesn't return the two men ride in after him and find him in jail. The town is run by a rancher named Baxter (Michael Gambon), whose dislike of free grazers is violent, and whose payroll includes a gang of hired thugs.

When the two men free Mose and return to camp, they find the kid in bad shape. He needs to see a doctor. That means returning to the town, and they all know that to return to Baxter's domain is to risk death. "This may mean killing," Boss says. "I got no problem with that," says Charley. The subtext of the movie is that while Boss's way is best, when actual evil is encountered, Charley's way is required.

At the doctor's house, the men meet not only the doc but a woman named Sue (Annette Bening), whom they first take for his wife and later discover is his sister. Sue's and Charley's eyes meet, setting up a strong attraction that continues through the movie. She sees that he is a good man despite his rough ways and cowboy grunge. For him, this is perhaps the first good woman he has known. The movie wisely doesn't push them into a quick kiss, but underlines their awareness and reinforces it with some quiet conversations, shy and painfully sincere on Charley's part.

I can see what Costner is getting at here, and I admire his reticence, his unwillingness to push the romance beyond where it wants to go, and yet somehow the romance itself seems like an awkward fit in this story. Only a few days are involved, violence and illness overshadow everything, and it's clear that this visit will end in a gunfight. The romance, sweet and well acted as it is, seems imposed on the essential story.

The town is thoroughly cowed by Baxter. But the townspeople behave differently than they do in many Westerns, where gunfights are treated as a spectator sport. People in a settlement this size know everything that's going to happen, and as the showdown approaches, they get out of town, climbing the hill to the safety of the church. Afterward, they gather again to study and deal with the dead bodies; Costner says he saw that detail over and over in old photographs, although in many Westerns bodies seem to disappear after they serve their purpose as targets.

Most gunfights consist of the two sides blazing away at each other until the good guys win. The gunfight in *Open Range*, which is the high point of the movie, is different. Charley has been under fire, has killed, knows how men respond to the terror of being shot at. Although he and Boss (and their few confederates, including an ornery coot played by Michael Jeter) are outnumbered, Charley thinks they have a chance. In the movie's most intriguing speech, he outlines for Boss how Baxter's men are likely to react: who will freeze, who will run, who will shoot first.

All of the elements involving Boss and his men and the showdown with Baxter are achieved with the skill of a classic Western. But again at the end, the relationship between Charley and Sue seems a little forced. They have two scenes of leave-taking when one would do, possibly because their romance even at this point seems undefined and incomplete. We suspect they will meet again, although that doesn't belong in this story; for the purposes of *Open Range*, their time together is either too much or too little, and their bittersweet parting seems unsatisfying.

That is not to fault Bening's and Costner's acting in their scenes together, which is as convincing as the material permits—maybe more so. There is a lovely scene where she serves them tea, and Costner's fingers are too big to fit through the handle on his teacup. But to bring a woman into this story at all seems like a stretch, even though I can see she's supposed to underline Costner's uncertainty about his two sides, the killer side and the Boss-following side. It is Boss, after all, who sends Charley back for a proper farewell: "She's entitled to more than just your backside, walking away." What Charley tells her is to the point: "Men are gonna get killed here today, Sue, and I'm gonna kill them."

As for Duvall, here is an actor. He embodies Boss's values rather than having to explain them. His pauses are as fascinating as his actions. Consider the scene where he buys chocolates and cigars for himself and Charley: "Best smoke these while we got the chance." He is the center of the story, the man for whom values are important, and whose response to this violent situation is based on what he believes is right, not what he believes will work. "Cows is one thing," he says, "but one man telling another man where he can go in this country is something else." His character elevates *Open Range* from a good cowboy story into the archetypal region where the best Westerns exist.

Open Water ★ ★ ★ ½

R, 79 m., 2004

Blanchard Ryan (Susan), Daniel Travis (Daniel), Saul Stein (Seth), Estelle Lau (Estelle), Michael E. Willimson (Davis), Jon Charles (Junior), Christina Zenarro (Linda). Directed by Chris Kentis and produced by Laura Lau. Screenplay by Kentis.

Rarely, but sometimes, a movie can have an actual physical effect on you. It gets under your defenses and sidesteps the "it's only a movie" reflex and creates a visceral feeling that might as well be real. *Open Water* had that effect on me. So did *Touching the Void,* the mountain-climbing movie. After both movies were over, I felt the need to go outside and walk in the sunshine and try to cheer myself up.

That's not to say *Open Water* is a thriller that churned my emotions. It's a quiet film, really, in which less and less happens as a large, implacable reality begins to form. The ending is so low-key we almost miss it. It tells the story of a couple who go scuba diving and surface to discover that a curious thing has happened: The boat has left without them. The horizon is empty in all directions. They feel very alone.

Touching the Void affected me because I'm not fond of heights and cannot imagine hang-ing from a mountainside. *Open Water* reached me in a different way. I'm not afraid of water and don't spend much time thinking about sharks, but the prospect of being lost, of being forgotten about, awakens emotions from deep in childhood. To be left behind stirs such anger and hopelessness.

When night follows day, when thirst becomes unbearable, when jellyfish sting, when sharks make themselves known, when the boat *still* does not come back for them, their situation becomes a vast, dark, cosmic joke. It is one thing to be in danger of losing your life. It is another thing to have hours and hours to think about it, and to discuss how casually the Caribbean vacation was settled on, instead of a ski holiday. The angriest line in the whole movie may be: "We paid to do this." They went to a good deal of trouble and expense in order to be abandoned at sea.

The movie stars Blanchard Ryan and Daniel Travis as Susan and Daniel. They come from a world of SUVs and cell phones and busy work schedules, and now their lives have been reduced to the fact that they are floating in the ocean. With their scuba outfits, they can float for a long time. Much longer, indeed, than will be of any interest to them.

The sea is calm. The water is cold but not cold enough to kill them. The opening scenes explain, with implacable logic, the series of events that leads to two scuba divers being counted twice, so that the boat returns to port with eighteen divers, although it left with twenty. If this seems like inexcusable carelessness, well, we can kind of understand how it happened. And the movie is based on a true story of two divers left behind.

The movie, written, directed, and edited by Chris Kentis, tells its story with a direct simplicity that is more harrowing than any fancy stuff could possibly be. The movie was filmed with digital video cameras, but of course it was; what would a 35mm camera be doing out there? And they are out there; the actors were in deep water, I learn, with real sharks.

For most of an hour we are essentially watching Susan and Daniel float, and talk, and think. Their dialogue is believable: no poetry, no philosophy, no histrionics, just the way people talk when they know each other well and are trying to kid themselves that things are not as bad as they seem. How could they be *forgotten*? How could the crew not notice their gear on board, or their missing air tanks? Surely the boat will return. Certainly there will be a search.

They try to remember information from the Discovery Channel. Daniel knows it is fatal to drink seawater. (You can drink urine, but that's tricky when you're floating in a scuba suit.) Those are certainly shark fins cutting the surface of the sea. Most sharks won't bother you, but the word "most" is not anywhere near inclusive enough to reassure them. There is even a period when Susan discusses whether this might have all been Daniel's fault: He spent too much time on the bottom looking at that damned eel.

"Fault" is as meaningless as any other concept. Nothing they think or believe has any relevance to the reality they are in. Their opinions are not solicited. Their past is irrelevant. Their success, dreams, fears, loves, plans, and friends are all separated from them now by this new thing that has become their lives. To be still alive, but removed from everything they know about how and why to live, is peculiar: Their senses continue to record their existence, but nothing they can do has the slightest utility.

So you see I was not afraid as I watched the movie. I was not afraid of sharks, or drowning, or dehydration. I didn't feel any of the *Jaws* emotions. But when it began to grow dark, when a thunderstorm growled on the far horizon, a great emptiness settled down upon me. The movie is about what a slender thread supports our conviction that our lives have importance and make sense. We need that conviction in order to live at all, and when it is irreversibly taken away from us, what a terrible fate to be left alive to know it.

Osama ★ ★ ★ ½
PG-13, 82 m., 2004

Marina Golbahari (Osama), Arif Herati (Espandi), Zubaida Sahar (Mother), Khwaja Nader (Mullah), Hamida Refah (Grandmother). Directed by Siddiq Barmak and produced by Barmak, Julia Fraser, Julie LeBrocquy, and Makoto Ueda. Screenplay by Barmak.

The movies are a little more than a century old. Imagine if we could see films from previous centuries—records of slavery, the Great Fire of London, the Black Plague. *Osama* is like a film from some long-ago age. Although it takes place in Afghanistan, it documents practices so cruel that it is hard to believe such ideas have currency in the modern world. What it shows is that, under the iron hand of the Taliban, the excuse of "respect" for women is used to condemn them to a lifetime of inhuman physical and psychic torture. No society that loves and respects women could treat them in this way.

The heroine of the film, Osama (Marina Golbahari), is a preadolescent in a household without a man. Under the rules of the Taliban, women are not to leave the house without a male escort or take jobs, so Osama, her mother, and grandmother are condemned to cower inside and starve, unless friends or relatives bring food. They do not. Finally the grandmother suggests that Osama cut her hair and venture out to find work, pretending to be a boy.

This story is told against a larger context of institutional sadism against women. An opening scene shows women in blue burkhas holding a demonstration—they want the right to take jobs—and being attacked by soldiers who begin with water cannons and eventually start shooting at them. Obviously, Osama is risking her life to venture out into this world, and soon she's in trouble: She is snatched away from her job and sent to a school to indoctrinate young men in the ways of the Taliban.

Then it is only a matter of time until her real sex is discovered. The punishment handed down by a judge is revealing: This child becomes one of the many wives of a dirty old man, a mullah who keeps his young women as prisoners. At that, Osama gets off lightly; another woman in the film is buried up to her neck and stoned for . . . well, for behaving like a normal person in a civilized society.

The movie touches some of the same notes as *Baran* (2001), an Iranian movie about an unspoken love affair between a young Iranian worker and an Afghan immigrant who is a girl disguised as a boy. The film is not as tragic as *Osama*, in part because Iran is a country where enlightened and humanistic attitudes are fighting it out side-by-side with the old, hard ways.

But in both cases Western audiences realize that to be a woman in such a society is to risk becoming a form of slave.

What is remarkable is the bravery with which filmmakers are telling this story in film after film. Consider Tahmineh Milani's *Two Women* (1999), which briefly landed her in jail under threat of death. Or Jafar Panahi's harrowing *The Circle* (2000), showing women without men trying to survive in present-day Tehran, where they cannot legally work or pause anywhere or be anywhere except inside and out of sight. The real weapons of mass destruction are . . . men.

Who will go to see *Osama*? I don't know. There is after all that new Adam Sandler movie, and it's a charmer. And *The Lost Skeleton of Cadavra* is opening, for fans of campy trash. I'm not putting them down. People work hard for their money, and if they want to be entertained, that's their right. But brave, dissenting Islamic filmmakers are risking their lives to tell the story of the persecution of women, and it is a story worth knowing, and mourning. In this country Janet Jackson bares a breast and causes a silly scandal. The Taliban would have stoned her to death. If you put these things into context, the Jackson case begins to look like an affirmation of Western civilization.

Oscar Short Subject Nominees ★ ★ ★

NO MPAA RATING, 120 m., 2005

The 2005 short subject Oscar nominees. Animated: *Birthday Boy,* directed by Sejong Park; *Ryan,* directed by Chris Landreth; and *Gopher Broke* directed by Jeff Fowler. Live action: *Two Cars, One Night,* directed by Taika Waititi and Ainsley Gardiner; *7:35 in the Morning,* directed by Nacho Vigalondo; *Wasp,* directed by Andrea Arnold; and *Little Terrorist,* directed by Ashvin Kumar.

Seven of 2005's Oscar-nominated short subjects and the 2004 Oscar-winning student animated film have been gathered into a two-hour package going into release around the country. Every year readers ask me where and how they can see the shorts nominated for Oscars, and every year until now I've had to reply that, well, they can't. The distribution of short subjects is a notoriously difficult challenge, but a package like this, timed for release at Oscar time, is the perfect solution.

Only one of the animated films and none of the live-action shorts are by American directors. The finalists come from Australia, Canada, New Zealand, Spain, India, and Britain. (The student Oscar winner saves the day; it's from filmmakers at the New York University film school.)

Also a trend: One of the animated nominees and three of the four live-action films are about children who are neglected or in danger.

And the nominees are:

Live Action Short Subjects
—*Wasp,* from the United Kingdom, directed by Andrea Arnold, is a heartbreaking and angering twenty-three-minute drama about a single mother and her four children, one a baby. She fears having the children taken away from her, and with good reason: During a long day and night, she chats up a former boyfriend, claims she is only baby-sitting the children, takes them home, and finds only white sugar from a bag to feed them. Then she brings them along to the pub where she's meeting the boyfriend, parking them outside and rushing out to give them potato chips and a Coke, "to share around." Hour follows hour as she plays pool and is sweet-talked by her date, while the kids wait outside, sad and hungry. The film is notable above all for not underlining its points, but simply making them: This woman should not be a mother, and these children should not have these lives. The movie won the 2005 Oscar.

—*7:35 in the Morning,* from Spain, directed by Nacho Vigalondo, is an odd and haunting eight-minute film that begins with a woman entering a café and sitting down with coffee and a pastry. She notices two musicians standing by the back wall. "What's with that?" she asks the owner, who does not answer. The customers all seem stiff, frightened, uncertain. A man appears and begins to sing a song about the woman, her coffee and pastry, and his thoughts about her. The customers and employees have already been rehearsed, and sing parts of the song from lyrics cupped in their hands. Then there is a scene where, frightened and awkward, they dance. The reason for their behavior eventually becomes clear, and terrifying.

—*Little Terrorist*, from India, directed by Ashvin Kumar, takes place along the border between India and Pakistan. A young boy crawls beneath a barbed-wire fence and enters a minefield in order to retrieve a cricket ball. Guards, who cannot see how young he is, fire warning shots and he runs in fear—to the other side of the field. Now he is in another country. A village schoolmaster and his wife give him shelter and a quick alibi during a house-to-house search, but now he must get back home. In fifteen minutes, the film builds genuine and poignant drama.

—*Two Cars, One Night*, from New Zealand, directed by Taika Waititi and Ainsley Gardiner, begins with two cars parked in the lot of a hotel with a bar and restaurant. There are two boys, one nine, one younger, in one car, and a twelve-year-old girl in the other. The adults who brought them are in the bar for the evening. The kids make faces and then they make friends, sharing without even mentioning it the loneliness of sitting in the cars at night and waiting for who knows how long.

Animated Short Subjects

—*Ryan*, from Canada, the 2005 Oscar winner by Chris Landreth, is an animated fourteen-minute documentary that cuts deeply into the truth of a human life. The subject is Ryan Larkin, who circa 1970 made animated films considered among the best and most influential in Canadian history, and then went astray into drug addiction and alcoholism. The film takes place largely in a vast room filled with long, empty tables, where Landreth talks with Larkin about his life; there are cutaways to important figures from his past.

The animation technique is dramatic, striking, and wholly original. Apparently beginning with live-action footage, Landreth converts the figures into grotesque cutaways of skull and sinew, eyes and hair, partial faces surrounded by emptiness or marred by bright visual scars representing angst. The effect is hard to describe, impossible to forget; the animation takes the documentary content to another emotional level.

—*Birthday Boy*, from Australia, by Sejong Park, is set in Korea in 1951 and shows a young boy all alone in a deserted wartime village. He plays, he wanders, he talks to himself, he sees tanks passing on rail cars, he sees planes flying overhead, he misses his mother. Like *Grave of the Fireflies*, it shows war providing a landscape in which childhood is exposed and vulnerable.

—*Gopher Broke*, from the USA, directed by Jeff Fowler, is in the tradition of Hollywood animated cartoons; it follows a gopher who digs a hole in a dirt road so that produce trucks will bounce fruit and vegetables into the road. All fine, except for the squirrels, crows, and other varmints who are faster than the gopher. Then there is a problem with a cow.

—*Rex Steele: Nazi Smasher*, is the bonus film, winner of the 2004 student animation Oscar. Directed by Alexander Woo, it's Indiana Jones crossed with Sky Captain, as a superhero enters a Nazi citadel atop a South American volcano and faces dire peril. High-spirited and kinetic.

Not included in the program, presumably because their makers chose not to participate, are the animated shorts *Guard Dog*, by Bill Plympton, and *Lorenzo*, by Mike Gabriel and Baker Bloodworth of Disney, and the live-action short *Everything in This Country Must*, by Gary McKendry.

The Other Side of the Bed ★ ★
R, 114 m., 2003

Ernesto Alterio (Javier), Paz Vega (Sonia), Guillermo Toledo (Pedro), Natalia Verbeke (Paula), Alberto San Juan (Rafa), María Esteve (Pilar), Ramón Barea (Sagaz), Nathalie Poza (Lucia). Directed by Emilio Martínez Lázaro and produced by Tomás Cimadevilla and José Antonio Sáinz de Vicuña. Screenplay by David Serrano.

Nobody quite makes it to the other side of the bed in the Spanish musical comedy *The Other Side of the Bed*, but that's not for lack of talking about it. Although they don't come right out and say so, I gather that this side of the bed is for heterosexuals, and that side is for homosexuals, and the movie is about a lot of people who are cheating on their partners while speculating that a lot of other people are gay.

515

I would like to tell you who all of these people are, but my space and your time are limited, and there are so many lovers and couples and would-be lovers and would-be couples that I was reminded of that limerick that ends,

> They argued all night
> As to who had the right
> To do what, and with which, and to
>   whom.

I'll give you just a sample. As the film opens, Pedro (Guillermo Toledo) is told by his girlfriend Paula (Natalia Verbeke) that she is in love with another and must end their relationship. Meanwhile, we discover that Paula is having a secret affair with Pedro's best friend, Javier (Ernesto Alterio), who has promised to break up with his girlfriend Sonia (Paz Vega), but lacks the nerve, possibly because he still loves her. When the men and two other friends get together to discuss their romantic miseries, one of them, of course, is keeping a big secret—and another, a macho taxi driver named Rafa (Alberto San Juan), delivers his women-hating theories and speculates that they are all lesbians at heart.

There is a lesbian in the movie, Lucia (Nathalie Poza), and she has the thankless task of standing there while other characters reveal their astonishing ignorance of lesbianism, sexuality, and indeed the nature of life on the planet that we occupy. For people who do nothing about it, these characters spend an inordinate amount of time discussing homosexuality; in this case, where there's smoke, there's smoke. Their knowledge extends to the theory that "we are all bisexual," and we keep expecting the theory to be tested in the laboratory on the other side of the bed, but this is a discussion, like what you would do if you won the lottery, that remains hypothetical and can be extended indefinitely.

The movie is a musical, which is kind of fun, with the characters expanding into song now and again. Like the heroes of a Bollywood musical from India, they seem able to materialize large numbers of backup dancers at a moment's notice. The choreography depends heavily on architecture and furniture, as the characters dance on motel balconies, lunchroom tables, etc.

All of the actors are extremely likable. And it's refreshing that the movie has a grown-up European attitude toward nudity, so that we're spared the Omniscient Bed Sheet, which always knows exactly where to fall in order to conceal a nipple. In its bright colors and zest, *The Other Side of the Bed* looks a little like an Almodóvar film—but Almodóvar knows a lot more about sexuality and, what's more important, he cares about his characters and allows them to be complicated and convincing.

Everyone in *The Other Side of the Bed*, alas, has the depth of a character in a TV commercial: They're all surface, clothes, hair, and attitude, and the men have the obligatory three-day beards. You realize after a while that it's just as well they're all so extraordinarily stupid about sex and human nature, because if they knew more, they would be wretchedly depressed about themselves.

Out of Time ★ ★ ★
PG-13, 114 m., 2003

Denzel Washington (Matt Lee Whitlock), Sanaa Lathan (Anne Merai Harrison), Dean Cain (Chris Harrison), Eva Mendes (Alex Diaz-Whitlock), John Billingsley (Chae), Alex Carter (Dr. Cabbot). Directed by Carl Franklin and produced by Jesse Beaton and Neal H. Mortiz. Screenplay by David Collard.

Denzel Washington, who played a hateful bad guy in *Training Day,* is a more sympathetic slickster in *Out of Time,* where he cheats on his wife and steals money, but has his reasons: His wife has already left him and is filing for divorce, he's cheating with his first love from high school, she's married to a wife-beater, and he steals the money to help her afford cancer therapy. So we sympathize with him as he digs himself into a hole. Any reasonable observer would consider him guilty of murder, theft, and arson—and one such observer is his estranged wife, who is also the detective assigned to the case.

Washington plays Matt Lee Whitlock, the sheriff of Banyan Key, Florida, a sleepy backwater where nothing much goes wrong. He is still on good terms with Alex (Eva Mendes), but their marriage has wound down and they're preparing for a split. That gives him time for a torrid affair with Anne Harrison (Sanaa Lathan), whose husband, Chris (Dean Cain), is a violent and jealous man. Matt narrowly avoids being caught by the husband, and that's the first of many narrow escapes in a plot that cheerfully piles on the contrivances.

Anne reveals to Matt that she's dying from lung and liver cancer. Chris has purchased a $1 million life insurance policy; she changes the beneficiary to Matt, who steals $500,000 in impounded drug loot from his office safe so that she can go to Europe for alternative therapy. The theory is that he can replace the money with the insurance payout, but alas, Anne and Chris both die in a suspicious fire, and the feds suddenly decide they need the drug money immediately. Matt seems guilty any way you look at it—his name on the insurance policy even provides a motive—and to make things worse, a neighbor saw him lurking around the house shortly before it burned down.

There are more details, many more, which I will suppress because they provide the central entertainments of the movie (what I've described is the setup, before Matt's troubles really get sticky). The movie is in the spirit of those overplotted 1940s crime movies where the hero's dilemma is so baffling that it seems impossible for him to escape; the screenplay by David Collard is inspired in part by *The Big Clock* (1948). All circumstantial evidence points to Matt; Hitchcock described this dilemma as "the innocent man wrongly accused," but the catch is, Matt isn't entirely innocent. He did steal the money, for starters.

Director Carl Franklin (*One False Move*), who also worked with Washington on *Devil in a Blue Dress* (1995), is frankly trying to manipulate the audience beyond the edge of plausibility. The early scenes seem to follow more or less possibly, but by the time Matt is hanging from a hotel balcony, or concealing incriminating telephone records, we care more about the plot than the characters; suspension of disbelief, always necessary in a thriller, is required here in wholesale quantities. But in a movie like *Out of Time* I'm not looking for realism; I'm looking for a sense of style brought to genre material.

Washington is one of the most likable of actors, which is essential to this character, preventing us from concluding that he's getting what he deserves. Eva Mendes makes the ex-wife, Alex, into a curiously forgiving character,

who feels little rancor for the straying Matt and apparently still likes him; maybe there would have been more suspense if she were furious with him. Sanaa Lathan has a tricky role as Anne—trickier the deeper we go into the plot—and is plausible at many different speeds, and Dean Cain is convincingly vile as the violent husband. John Billingsley is Chae, the local medical examiner, who is Matt's sidekick and supplies low-key, goofy support in some tight situations.

Another one of the movie's stars is its Florida location. It was photographed in and around Miami, Boca Grande, and Cortez, and reminds us how many Hollywood crime movies depend on the familiar streets of Los Angeles (or Toronto). Banyan Key seems like a real place, sleepy and laid-back, where everybody knows one another and high school romances could still smolder. As the net of evidence tightens around the sheriff, it seems more threatening because there are few places for him to hide, and few players who don't know him.

Overnight ★ ★ ★
R, 82 m., 2004

Featuring Troy Duffy, Willem Dafoe, Billy Connolly, and Jeffrey Baxter. A documentary directed by Tony Montana and Mark Brian Smith and produced by Montana.

Overnight tells a riches-to-rags story, like Project Greenlight played in reverse. Greenlight, you will recall, is the Miramax contest to choose and produce one screenplay every year by a hopeful first-time filmmaker. In *Overnight*, the director starts out with a contract and money from Miramax, and works his way back to no contract, no film, and no money. Call it Project Red Light.

The documentary tells the Hollywood story of a nine-day wonder named Troy Duffy. He was a bartender at a sports bar named J. Sloan's on Melrose, and had written a screenplay named *The Boondock Saints*. He, his brothers, and some friends had a rock band. In Los Angeles, every bartender under the age of seventy has a screenplay and is in a rock band, and they all want Harvey Weinstein of Miramax to read their script. After all, Harvey made Matt Damon and Ben Affleck stars by producing their screenplay of *Good Will Hunting*.

Troy Duffy hits the trifecta. Not only does Harvey buy his screenplay, but he signs Duffy to direct it, *and* the band gets a recording contract, *and* he agrees to buy the bar; they'll own it together. To celebrate his good fortune, Duffy asked two friends, Tony Montana and Mark Brian Smith, to make a documentary of his rise. It turned out to be about his fall.

I'd give anything to see footage of the early meetings between Weinstein and Duffy. What magic did the bartender have to so bedazzle Harvey? By the opening scenes of *Overnight*, Duffy has sold a $300,000 script, has been given a $15 million budget, has signed with the William Morris Agency, and brags, "I get drunk at night, wake up the next morning hungover, go into those meetings in my overalls, and they're all wearing suits." Being Hollywood agents, they are probably also more familiar with the danger signals of alcoholism than Duffy is.

One of the subtexts of the movie involves how people look at Troy Duffy. He is very full of himself. At one point he actually says that Harvey Weinstein would like to be him. He keeps all of the money, tells the guys in the band they will get paid later, later tells them they don't deserve a dime, and still later tells them, "You do deserve it, but you're not gonna get it."

He is deeply satisfied with himself: "We got a deep cesspool of creativity here," he says, and boasts, "This is the first time in history they've signed a band sight unseen." Also, he might have reflected, sound unheard. As he's acting out his ego trip, the camera shows the others in the room looking at him with what can only be described as extremely fed-up expressions. His family, we sense during one scene, has been listening to this blowhard for a lifetime, and although they are happy to share his success, they're sort of waiting to see how he screws up.

So are we. The movie is pieced together out of uneven footage, and the idea of a documentary seems to have occurred in the midst of filming; at one point, a Morris agent walks into the room, looks at the lens, and says, "Oh, you got a better camera!" There are unfortunately no scenes between Duffy and Weinstein; the initial infatuation happens before the film starts, and then Weinstein pulls out of the deal by putting *The Boondock Saints* into dreaded "turnaround." The recording contract is also canceled.

Eventually a Hollywood producer named Elie Samada, who has been behind some good films but is a controversial character, picks up *The Boondock Saints* for much less than the Miramax price, and Duffy is elated again. Having dissed Keanu Reeves, Ethan Hawke, and Jon Bon Jovi ("I didn't even know he was an actor"), he hires the excellent Willem Dafoe; we see one scene being filmed, in which characters a lot like Duffy and his friends get drunk and go berserk. The finished movie is taken to the Cannes marketplace, where not one single offer is made to purchase it. *Saints* eventually plays for one week in five theaters. The sound track album sells less than 600 copies. Then a car jumps the curb and hits Duffy, who "flees his apartment and arms himself."

Ah, but there's a happy ending! *The Boondock Saints* becomes a cult favorite on DVD, and Duffy is currently directing *Boondock II: All Saint's Day*. Unfortunately, the Morris agency neglected to secure for him any portion of the DVD profits.

Owning Mahowny ★ ★ ★ ★
R, 107 m, 2003

Philip Seymour Hoffman (Dan Mahowny), Minnie Driver (Belinda), John Hurt (Victor Foss), Maury Chaykin (Frank Perlin), Sonja Smits (Dana Selkirk), Ian Tracey (Ben Lock), Roger Dunn (Bill Gooden). Directed by Richard Kwietniowski and produced by Andras Hamori and Seaton McLean. Screenplay by Maurice Chauvet, based on a book by Gary Ross.

Owning Mahowny is about a man seized helplessly with tunnel vision, in the kind of tunnel that has no light at either end. He is a gambler. Cut off temporarily by his bookie, he asks incredulously, "What am I supposed to do? Go out to the track and *watch*?" Given the means to gamble, he gambles—thoughtless of the consequences, heedless of the risks, caught in the vise of a power greater than himself. Like all addictive gamblers he seeks the sensation of losing more money than he can afford. To win a great deal before losing it all back again creates a kind of fascination: Such gamblers need to confirm over and over that they cannot win.

The film is based on the true story of a Toronto bank vice president who began by stealing exactly as much as he needed to clear his debts at the track ($10,300) and ended by taking his bank for $10.2 million. So intent is he on this process that he rarely raises his voice, or his eyes, from the task at hand. Philip Seymour Hoffman, that fearless poet of implosion, plays the role with a fierce integrity, never sending out signals for our sympathy because he knows that Mahowny is oblivious to our presence. Like an artist, an athlete, or a mystic, Mahowny is alone within the practice of his discipline.

There have been many good movies about gambling, but never one that so single-mindedly shows the gambler at his task. Mahowny has just been rewarded at work with a promotion and a raise. He drives a clunker even the parking lot attendants kid him about. His suits amuse his clients. He is engaged to Belinda (Minnie Driver), a teller who is the very embodiment of a woman who might be really pretty if she took off those glasses and did something about her hair.

He is so absorbed in gambling that even his bookie (Maury Chaykin) tries to cut him off, to save himself the trouble of making threats to collect on the money Mahowny owes him. "I can't do business like this," the bookie complains, and at another point, when Mahowny is so rushed he only has time to bet $1,000 on all the home teams in the National League and all the away teams in the American, the bookie finds this a breach of ethics: He is in business to separate the gambler from his money, yes, but his self-respect requires the gambler to make reasonable bets.

When Mahowny moves up a step by stealing larger sums and flying to Atlantic City to lose them, he encounters a more ruthless and amusing professional. John Hurt plays the manager of the casino like a snake fascinated by the way a mouse hurries forward to be eaten. Hurt has seen obsessive gamblers come and go and is familiar with all the manifestations of their sickness, but this Mahowny brings a kind of grandeur to his losing.

The newcomer is quickly singled out as a high roller, comped with a luxury suite, offered French cuisine and tickets to the Pointer Sisters, but all he wants to do is gamble ("and maybe . . . some ribs, no sauce, and a Coke?"). Hurt sends a hooker to Mahowny's room, and a flunky reports back: "The only woman he's interested in is Lady Luck." Certainly Mahowny forgets his fiancée on a regular basis, standing her up, disappearing for weekends, even taking her to Vegas and then forgetting that she is upstairs waiting in their suite. (The fiancée is a classic enabler, excusing his lapses, but Vegas is too much for her; she tries to explain to him that when she saw the size of the suite she assumed they had come to Vegas to get married: "That's what normal people do in Vegas.")

It is impossible to like Mahowny, but easy to identify with him, if we have ever had obsessions of our own. Like all addicts of anything, he does what he does because he does it. "He needs to win in order to get more money to lose," one of the casino professionals observes.

Of course he will eventually be caught. He knows it, we know it, but being caught is beside the point. The point is to gamble as long as he can before he is caught. Mahowny refers at one point to having had a lot of luck, and he is referring not to winning, but to being able to finance a great deal of gambling at a level so high that, asked by a psychiatrist to rate the excitement on a scale of zero to one hundred, he unhesitatingly answers, "One hundred." And his greatest excitement in life outside of gambling? "Twenty."

Philip Seymour Hoffman's performance is a masterpiece of discipline and precision. He spends a lot of time adjusting his glasses or resting his fingers on his temples, as if to enhance his tunnel vision. He never meets the eye of the camera, or anyone else. Even when a casino security guard is firmly leading his fiancée away from his table, he hardly looks up to notice that she is there, or to say a word in her defense. He is . . . gambling. The movie has none of the false manipulation of most gambling movies, in which the actors signal their highs and lows. Hoffman understands that for this gambler, it is not winning or losing, but all process.

The movie, written by Maurice Chauvet, has been directed by Richard Kwietniowski, whose only other feature was *Love and Death on Long Island* (1998). That one also starred John Hurt, playing a reclusive British literary intellectual who becomes as obsessed as Mahowny, but with an erotic fixation. So unworldly he does not own a television and never goes to the movies, the Hurt character takes refuge from the rain in a cinema, finds himself watching a teenage comedy starring Jason Priestley, and becomes so fascinated by this young man that he keeps a scrapbook like a starstruck teenager and eventually travels to Long Island just in the hopes of meeting him. We get the impression that the Hurt character has been unaware of his homosexuality and indeed even his sexuality before being thunderstruck by this sudden fixation. In both films, Kwietniowski understands that conscious choice has little to do with his characters, that risk and humiliation are immaterial, that once they are locked in on the subjects of their obsessions, they have no choice but to hurry ahead to their dooms.

P

The Pacifer ★ ★
PG, 90 m., 2005

Vin Diesel (Shane Wolfe), Lauren Graham (Claire Fletcher), Faith Ford (Julie Plummer), Carol Kane (Helga), Brad Garrett (Vice Principal Murney), Brittany Snow (Zoe Plummer), Max Thieriot (Seth Plummer), Morgan York (Lulu Plummer). Directed by Adam Shankman and produced by Gary Barber, Roger Birnbaum, and Jonathan Glickman. Screenplay by Thomas Lennon and Ben Garant.

In *The Pacifier*, Vin Diesel follows in the footsteps of those Arnold Schwarzenegger comedies where the muscular hero becomes a girly-man. Diesel doesn't go to the lengths of Schwarzenegger in *Junior*, where Arnold was actually pregnant, but he does become a baby-sitter, going where no Navy SEAL has gone before.

Diesel plays Shane Wolfe, hard-edged commando ("We are SEALs—and this is what we do"). In the pretitle sequence, he and three other scuba-diving SEALs shoot down a helicopter, wipe out four gunmen on jet skis, bomb a boat, and rescue Plummer, an American scientist kidnapped by Serbians. They want "Ghost," the scientist's foolproof encryption key. That the scientist uses the names of his children as the password for his locked briefcase suggests that the Serbians could have saved themselves a lot of trouble by just finding the geek who hacked Paris Hilton's cell phone and aiming him at Plummer's hard drive.

Anyway. One thing leads to another, and soon Wolfe has a new assignment, which is to baby-sit and protect Plummer's five children while his wife and a navy intelligence officer go to Geneva to open his safety deposit box. They're supposed to be gone only a couple of days, but one week follows another as they unsuccessfully try to, yes, guess the password.

From time to time the movie cuts to a Swiss bank, where two executives wait patiently while the wife and the navy guy try one word after another. That two Swiss bank officials are willing to sit in a room day after day and listen to people guessing a password is yet one more example of why the Swiss banking system has such an exemplary reputation.

That leaves Wolfe in charge of an unhappy teenage boy, a boyfriend-crazy teenage girl, and three noisy moppets. Because he is not good at names, he tags them the Red Team, and calls them "Red One," "Red Two," and so on. They do not much take to this, and make his life a living hell.

This premise is promising, but somehow the movie never really takes off. We know that Diesel will begin as gravel-voiced and growly, and that he'll soften up and get to love the kids. We know that in two weeks all of the kids' personal problems will be solved, their behavior will improve, and they'll start cleaning up around the house. We're not much surprised when the Plummer nanny, a curious creature created by Carol Kane with an impenetrable accent, stalks out. Using the Law of Economy of Characters, we know that any neighbors who seem unnecessary yet are given dialogue will be more than merely neighbors.

There's one subplot that seems to offer more opportunities for comedy than it does. Seth (Max Thieriot), the older Plummer boy, wants to be an actor, despite the kidding he gets at high school. He's appearing in a production of *The Sound of Music*, where, unfortunately, he keeps dropping members of the Trapp family. The play's director, who seems to have been imported from *Waiting for Guffman*, walks off the job, and Shane Wolfe takes over the direction. Uh-huh. And he has a tender heart-to-heart with the kid about following his dream and being an actor if that's what will make him happy.

Meanwhile, Wolfe is also supposed to be guarding the kids against, I dunno, more Serbian kidnappers, maybe, although North Koreans also come into the mix. He has an uncanny ability to follow events on supermarket security monitors, which are not usually positioned where customers can see them, and so protects the Plummer girls when their firefly Girls cookie stand is attacked by rival scouts. He is also challenged to a wrestling match with a coach who is more than strange (Brad Garrett), and deals with an anal-retentive school principal by showing that Navy SEALs have better split-second timing than clock-watching bureaucrats.

All very nice, sometimes we smile, but nothing compelling. The director is Adam Shankman, whose previous film, *Bringing Down the House,* starred Queen Latifah as a convict who moves in on Steve Martin's middle-class life. Shankman begins with situations that should work, but he doesn't quite boost them over the top into laugh-out-loud. Maybe he's counting too much on the funny casting. Casting is funny only when the cast is given something funny to do, a truth that should be engraved above the portals of every film school.

Palindromes ★ ★ ★ ½

NO MPAA RATING, 100 m., 2005

Ellen Barkin (Joyce Victor), Stephen Adly Guirgis (Joe/Earl/Bob), Jennifer Jason Leigh (Aviva), Emani Sledge (Aviva), Will Denton (Aviva), Hannah Freiman (Aviva), Shayna Levine (Aviva), Valerie Shusterov (Aviva), Sharon Wilkins (Aviva), Rachel Corr (Aviva/Henrietta), Richard Masur (Steve Victor), Debra Monk (Mama Sunshine), Matthew Faber (Mark Wiener), Robert Agri/John Gemberling (Judah), Stephen Singer (Dr. Fleischer), Alexander Brickel (Peter Paul), Walter Bobbie (Bo Sunshine), Richard Riehle (Dr. Dan). Directed by Todd Solondz and produced by Mike S. Ryan and Derrick Tseng. Screenplay by Solondz.

Todd Solondz's *Palindromes* is a brave and challenging film for which there may not be much of an audience. That is not a fault of the film, which does not want to be liked and only casually hopes to be understood. What it wants is to provoke. You do not emerge untouched from a Solondz film. You may hate it, but you have seen it, and in a strange way it has seen you.

Palindromes contains characters in favor of abortion and characters opposed to it, and finds fault with all of them. The film has no heroes without flaws and no villains without virtues, and that is true no matter who you think the heroes and villains are. To ambiguity it adds perplexity by providing us with a central character named Aviva, a girl of about thirteen played by eight different actresses, two of them adults, one a boy, one a six-year-old girl. She is not always called Aviva.

The point, I think, is to begin with the fact of a girl becoming pregnant at a too-early age and then show us how that situation might play out in different kinds of families with different kinds of girls.

The method by which Aviva becomes pregnant is illegal in all cases, since she is underage, but there is a vast difference between a scenario in which Aviva persuades a reluctant young son of a family friend to experiment with sex, and another where she runs away from home and meets a truck driver.

Perhaps Solondz is suggesting that our response to Aviva's pregnancy depends on the circumstances. He doesn't take an obvious position on anything in the movie, but simply presents it and leaves us to sort it out. We probably can't. *Palindromes* is like life: We know what we consider to be good and bad, but we can't always be sure how to apply our beliefs in the messy real world.

Consider an early scene in the film where one of the Avivas gets pregnant and wants to have the child. Her mother (Ellen Barkin) argues that this will destroy her life; an abortion will allow her to continue her education and grow up to be a normal adolescent, rather than being a mother at thirteen. The mother goes on to make a long list of possible birth defects that might occur in an underage pregnancy.

Later in the film, we meet the "Sunshine Family," a household full of adopted children with birth defects: one with Down's syndrome, one born without arms, and so on. It occurs to us that these are the hypothetical children Barkin did not want her daughter to bear. The children are happy and seem pleased to be alive. Yes, but does Solondz consider the adoptive parents of the Sunshine Family to be good and moral people? Not precisely, not after we find Father Sunshine conspiring to bring about a murder.

The plot circles relentlessly, setting up moral situations and then pulling the moral ground out from under them. The movie is almost reckless in the way it refuses to provide us with a place to stand. It is all made of paradoxes. Pregnancy is pregnancy, rape is rape, abortion is abortion, murder is murder, and yet in the world of *Palindromes* the facts and categories shift under the pressure of human motives—some good, some bad, some misguided, some well-intentioned but disastrous.

We look for a clue in the movie's title. A "palindrome" is a word which is spelled the same way forward and backward: Aviva, for example, or madam or racecar. Is Solondz saying that it doesn't matter which side of the issue we enter from, it's all the same and we'll wind up where we started?

While following the news during the Terri Schiavo case, I was struck by how absolutely sure of their opinions everyone was, on both sides. Could the reporters have found a few people willing to say that after giving the matter a lot of thought, they'd decided it was a tragedy no matter which way you looked at it? Solondz is perhaps arguing for moral relativism, for the idea that what is good in a situation is defined by the situation itself, not by absolute abstractions imposed from outside.

Todd Solondz has made a career out of challenging us to figure out what side of any issue he's on. You can't walk out of one of his movies *(Welcome to the Dollhouse, Happiness, Storytelling)* and make a list of the characters you like and the ones you don't. There's something to be said for and against everybody. Most movies, like most people, are so certain, and we like movies we can agree with. He makes movies where, like a member of the debate team, you sometimes feel as if you're defending a position just because that's the side you were assigned.

If the movie is a moral labyrinth, it is paradoxically straightforward and powerful in the moment; each individual story has an authenticity and impact of its own. Consider the pathos brought to Aviva by the actress Sharon Wilkins, who is a plus-size adult black woman playing a little girl, and who creates perhaps the most convincing little girl of them all. Or Jennifer Jason Leigh, three times as old as Aviva but barely seeming her age. These individual segments are so effective that at the end of each one we know how we feel, and why. It's just that the next segment invalidates our conclusions.

I look at a movie like this, and I consider what courage it took to make it. Solondz from the beginning has made a career out of refusing to cater to broad, safe tastes. He shows us transgressive or evil characters, invites us to identify with their pathos, then shows us that despite our sympathy, they're rotten anyway. You walk out of one of his films feeling like you've just failed a class in ethics, and wondering if in this baffling world anyone ever passes.

Paper Clips ★ ★ ★
G, 82 m., 2005

Linda Hooper (Herself), Sandra Roberts (Herself), Dagmar Schroeder-Hildebrand (Herself), Peter Schroeder (Himself), David Smith (Himself). A documentary directed by Elliot Berlin and Joe Fab and produced by Fab, Robert M. Johnson, and Ari Daniel Pinchot. Screenplay by Fab.

In 1998, three middle-school teachers in Whitwell, Tennessee (population 1,500), came up with a project for the eighth-grade class: Learn about intolerance by studying the Holocaust. The students read *The Diary of Anne Frank* and did Internet research, discovering that during World War II, the Norwegians wore paper clips in their lapels as a silent gesture of solidarity and sympathy with Hitler's victims.

A student, no one seems to remember which one, said it was impossible to imagine 6 million of anything, let alone Jews who died in the Holocaust. That led somehow to the notion of gathering 6 million paper clips in one place at one time, as a tribute to the victims. The project started slowly, with a clip here and a clip there, and 50,000 from one donor, and then *The Washington Post* and Tom Brokaw got on the story and by the time Whitwell's third group of eighth-graders were running the project, they had 29 million paper clips.

That could be a story like the one about the kid who was dying and wanted to collect business cards, and got millions and millions as his desperate parents announced he had recovered and no longer wanted more cards. But the Whitwell story goes to another level, a touching one, as the students make new friends through their project. Two of them are Peter and Dagmar Schroeder, White House correspondents from Germany, who visit the town and write about it. Many more were Holocaust survivors, who as a group visited Whitwell for a potluck dinner at the Methodist church, classes at the school, and a community reception.

And then there was the train car. The Schroeders found one of the actual rail cars used to transport Jews to the death camps, and arranged for it to be shipped to Whitwell. Local carpenters repaired the leaky roof and rotting floor, and the car was placed outside the high school as a Holocaust memorial. Inside were 11 million paper clips, representing 6 million Jews and 5 million gypsies, homosexuals, Jehovah's Witnesses, and others who were murdered by the Nazis. Also a suitcase that German children had filled with notes to Anne Frank.

Paper Clips, which tells this story, is not a sophisticated or very challenging film, nor should it be. It is straightforward, heartfelt, and genuine. It plays more like a local news report, and we get the sense that the documentary, like the paper clip project, grows directly out of the good intentions of the people involved. Whitwell at the time had no Jews, five African-Americans, and one Hispanic, we learn; there weren't even any Catholics. By the time the project was completed, the horizons of the population had widened considerably.

David Smith, one of the teachers involved, says he knows he is stereotyped as a southerner, and admits that he stereotypes northerners. In changing their perceptions about minorities, the students of Whitwell also changed perceptions others may have held about them. That America has been divided by pundits into blue states and red states does not mean there are not good-hearted people living everywhere; in a time of divisiveness, there is something innocently naive about the paper clip project, which transforms a silly mountain of paper clips into a small town's touching gesture.

Party Monster ★ ★ ★
NO MPAA RATING, 98 m., 2003

Macaulay Culkin (Michael Alig), Seth Green (James St. James), Chloë Sevigny (Gitsie), Natasha Lyonne (Brooke), Justin Hagan (Freeze), Wilson Cruz (Angel Melendez), Wilmer Valderrama (Disc Jockey Keoki), Dylan McDermott (Peter Gatien). Directed by Fenton Bailey and Randy Barbato and produced by Bailey and Barbato, Jon Marcus, Bradford Simpson, and Christine Vachon. Screenplay by Bailey and Barbato, based on the book *Disco Bloodbath* by James St. James.

Party Monster is based on a book named *Disco Bloodbath,* and there's a tug-of-war in both titles between fun and horror. Horror wins. Michael Alig, the movie's subject, looks innocent with his baby face and cute little outfits, but he is a creature of birdbrained vanity. After the drugs take over he becomes not merely dangerous but deadly, and we are reminded of George Carlin's answer when he was asked how cocaine makes you feel: "It makes you feel like having some more cocaine."

Alig is played by Macaulay Culkin, in his first movie since *Richie Rich* (1994), and it is a fearless performance as a person so shallow, narcissistic, and amoral that eventually even his friends simply stare at him in disbelief. Alig, who is now thirty-seven and serving a prison sentence for manslaughter, was a Manhattan media creature of the early 1990s, promoting parties whose primary purpose was to draw attention to their promoter. At the Limelight and other venues, including a fast-food store and the back of a trailer truck, he assembled androgynous crowds of substance abusers who desperately had fun.

Alig came to New York from South Bend, Indiana, where, needless to say, he did not fit in. Perhaps his whole identity was formed by the need to build a wall against childhood bullying, and it is possible to feel some sympathy, not for the man he became, but for the boy who had to become that man. In New York, broke but blissfully drunk on himself, he convinces club owner Peter Gatien (Dylan McDermott) to let him throw parties at the famous Limelight nightclub, and sets himself up as the next Andy

Warhol. The difference (apart from the fact that Warhol was an important artist) is that Warhol defined the notion of fifteen minutes of fame, and Alig only illustrated it.

Alig has a way of instantly annexing a court of admirers. His first conquest is James St. James (Seth Green), also a party organizer, who becomes the "best friend" of a person with no gift for friendship, and who watches in dismay as Michael embraces self-destruction. Then there's Keoki (Wilmer Valderrama)—"you'll be my boyfriend." And Angel Melendez (Wilson Cruz)—"I'll make you a drug dealer." Various other moths fly into his flame, including Gitsie (Chloë Sevigny) and Brooke (Natasha Lyonne), and the grown-up and straight club owner Gatien is sometimes amazed at himself for putting up with this creature.

Michael Alig is gay as a default. Obviously he cannot be straight and be the person he is, so gay is what's left, but the movie gives the sense that sexuality is of little importance to him. Perhaps sex involves an intimacy he was uninterested in. Of course, after a certain point in his drug spiral it would have become impossible. He wanted to use not the bodies of his friends but their appearances and identities; he selects his circle as if furnishing a room.

James St. James (who wrote the book) is the relatively sane observer of the madness, a person screwed up in more conventional ways. His drugs and lifestyle are a problem, but at least there is a human being there, who attempts to reason with Michael and warn him, and who sees the train wreck coming. Fatal not to Michael but to Angel, who is killed in an agonizing way with hammer blows and injections of Drano. Yes, Alig was drugged out of his mind at the time, but if you can think of Drano while in a chemical stupor, that indicates the evil extends pretty far down your brain stem.

Culkin plays Alig as clueless to the end, living so firmly in his fantasy world that nothing can penetrate his chirpy persona. Whether this is accurate—whether indeed any of the facts in the film are accurate—is not for me to say, but it works. Seth Green is more dimensional and reachable as James, but it is Culkin's oblivious facade that makes him scary; any attempt to bring "humanity" to this character would miss the point.

That said, I am not sure what the movie accomplishes, except to portray an extreme and impenetrable personality type. The film was written and directed by Fenton Bailey and Randy Barbato, who made a 1999 documentary about Michael Alig and then decided on this fictional docudrama. Unlike such real-life crime movies as *In Cold Blood*, they find no insights into the humanity of their subject, but that may be because Alig was a cipher known only to himself (if that). The movie lacks insight and leaves us feeling sad and empty—sad for ourselves, not Alig—and maybe it had to be that way.

Passionada ★ ★ ★
PG-13, 108 m., 2003

Jason Isaacs (Charles Beck), Sofia Milos (Celia Amonte), Emmy Rossum (Vicky Amonte), Theresa Russell (Lois Vargas), Seymour Cassel (Daniel Vargas), Lupe Ontiveros (Angelica Amonte), Chris Tardio (Gianni Martinez). Directed by Dan Ireland and produced by David Bakalar. Screenplay by Jim Jermanok and Steve Jermanok.

Passionada assembles the elements for a soap opera, and turns them into a bubble bath. The movie is populated with lovable rogues, cuddly coots, passionate widows, and beloved ghosts, and is about a romance between a professional gambler and a torch singer in mourning, but somehow all of these elements fall into place; we feel surprising affection for these people from New Bedford, Massachusetts.

The movie has been directed by Dan Ireland, from a first screenplay by the brothers Jim and Steve Jermanok, whose freelance writing credits sound like homework for this story. Steve wrote the book *New England Seacoast Adventures*, and here the brothers create an emotional adventure for a down-and-out gambler and a Portuguese-American widow who sings of lost love and vows she will never marry again.

The widow is named Celia Amonte, and is played by Sofia Milos, from the TV show *CSI: Miami*. Dark of hair, eyes, and mood, she raises her teenage daughter, Vicky (Emmy Rossum), lives beneath her mother-in-law, Angelica (Lupe Ontiveros), and remains faithful to the memory of her first love, a fisherman who died at sea.

Into her life stumbles Charles Beck, played by Jason Isaacs, who plays the villain Lucius Malfoy in the *Harry Potter* films. Here he's not a villain but a luckless card-counter who has been barred from most of the casinos in North America, and has drifted into New Bedford to find support from his old gambling buddy Daniel (Seymour Cassel) and his younger wife, Lois (Theresa Russell), who is so besotted with him that she carries a cocktail kit in her purse in case he requires a martini in a restaurant without a liquor license.

Once all of these pieces are in place, we can guess what the movie will do with them, and we will be correct. It is important that Charles stop lying about himself, that Celia move on with her life, and that Vicky, Lois, and Daniel be an amusing chorus to egg them on. Yet the movie is able to surprise us with how it arrives at a happy ending, as when Lupe Ontiveros delivers a line that we did not expect from the mother-in-law, and fills it with emotion while remaining absolutely matter-of-fact. And there is a nice twist when Vicky, Celia's daughter, proposes a deal to Charles: "Teach me to card-count, and I'll get you a date with my mom."

Sofia Milos successfully plays a character who should be all but unplayable; she sings sad love songs night after night in a local club, while never permitting love for herself. (Her singing voice is supplied by the Portuguese singer Misia.) In the economy of love stories, a widow is a wife in waiting, but the movie doesn't hurry to end her wait. Charles has too many secrets, too much baggage, too many lies to move confidently in her direction—and, besides, he likes her, and then loves her, and that will require a basic readjustment in the way he's been living his life. Isaacs's character has a way of lightly sidestepping difficult issues, in conversation and life, and it is absorbing to see him gradually realize that a moment of truth is at hand.

Strictly speaking, there is no real need for the characters of Daniel and Lois, and that has been true of many of the characters Seymour Cassel has played; he comes on to swell a progress, start a scene or two, and then the central characters march on without him. But Cassel is indispensable for bringing a relaxed, gentle humanity into a story. He provides a context and a reference for Charles; if he thinks the gambler is okay, then we can trust him with Celia. Theresa Russell is a surprising choice for the loving younger wife, until we reflect that she has long been married to the director Nicolas Roeg, twenty-nine years her senior.

Dan Ireland's first feature, *The Whole Wide World* (1996), was also about a romance between a serious young woman (Renée Zellweger) and an elusive eccentric (Vincent D'Onofrio, as the pulp fiction writer Robert E. Howard). There comes a moment when Howard is challenged to open up about elements of his life he would rather keep secret, and Charles Beck has a moment like that in *Passionada*—handled well, and without quite the payoff we expect.

The movie makes evocative use of its locations in New Bedford, the whaling port where Ishmael set sail in *Moby-Dick*. "In summer time," wrote Melville, "the town is sweet to see; full of fine maples—long avenues of green and gold." Melville did not anticipate the nearby casinos run by Indian tribes where Charles plies his trade, but the trees are still sweet to see all the same.

The Passion of the Christ ★ ★ ★
R, 126 m., 2004

James Caviezel (Jesus, the Christ), Maia Morgenstern (Mary), Monica Bellucci (Mary Magdalene), Mattia Sbragia (Caiphas), Hristo Shopov (Pontius Pilate), Claudia Gerini (Pilate's Wife), Luca Lionello (Judas). Directed by Mel Gibson and produced by Bruce Davey, Gibson, and Stephen McEveety. Screenplay by Gibson and Benedict Fitzgerald.

If ever there was a film with the correct title, that film is Mel Gibson's *The Passion of the Christ*. Although the word *passion* has become mixed up with romance, its Latin origins refer to suffering and pain; later Christian theology broadened that to include Christ's love for mankind, which made him willing to suffer and die for us. The movie is 126 minutes long, and I would guess that at least 100 of those minutes, maybe more, are concerned specifically and graphically with the details of the torture and death of Jesus. This is the most violent film I have ever seen.

I prefer to evaluate a film on the basis of what it intends to do, not on what I think it should have done. It is clear that Mel Gibson wanted to make graphic and inescapable the price that Jesus paid (as Christians believe) when he died for our sins. Anyone raised as a Catholic will be familiar with the stops along the way; the screenplay is inspired not so much by the Gospels as by the fourteen Stations of the Cross. As an altar boy, serving during the Stations on Friday nights in Lent, I was encouraged to meditate on Christ's suffering, and I remember the chants as the priest led the way from one station to another:

At the Cross, her station keeping . . .
Stood the mournful Mother weeping . . .
Close to Jesus to the last.

For us altar boys, this was not necessarily a deep spiritual experience. Christ suffered, Christ died, Christ rose again, we were redeemed, and let's hope we can get home in time to watch the Illinois basketball game on TV. What Gibson has provided for me, for the first time in my life, is a visceral idea of what the Passion consisted of. That his film is superficial in terms of the surrounding message—that we get only a few passing references to the teachings of Jesus—is, I suppose, not the point. This is not a sermon or a homily, but a visualization of the central event in the Christian religion. Take it or leave it.

David Anson, a critic I respect, finds in *Newsweek* that Gibson has gone too far. ". . . (T)he relentless gore is self-defeating," he writes. "Instead of being moved by Christ's suffering, or awed by his sacrifice, I felt abused by a filmmaker intent on punishing an audience, for who knows what sins." This is a completely valid response to the film, and I quote Anson because I suspect he speaks for many audience members, who will enter the theater in a devout or spiritual mood and emerge deeply disturbed. You must be prepared for whippings, flayings, beatings, the crunch of bones, the agony of screams, the cruelty of the sadistic centurions, the rivulets of blood that crisscross every inch of Jesus' body. Some will leave before the end.

This is not a Passion like any other ever filmed. Perhaps that is the best reason for it. I grew up on those pious Hollywood biblical epics of the 1950s, which looked like holy cards brought to life. I remember my grin when *Time* magazine noted that Jeffrey Hunter, starring as Christ in *King of Kings* (1961), had shaved his armpits. (Not Hunter's fault; the film's crucifixion scene had to be reshot because preview audiences objected to Jesus' hairy chest.) If it does nothing else, Gibson's film will break the tradition of turning Jesus and his disciples into neat, clean, well-barbered middle-class businessmen. They were poor men in a poor land. I debated Scorsese's *The Last Temptation of Christ* with Michael Medved before an audience from a Christian college, and was told by an audience member that the characters were filthy and needed haircuts.

The Middle East in biblical times was a Jewish community occupied against its will by the Roman Empire, and the message of Jesus was equally threatening to both sides—to the Romans, because he was a revolutionary, and to the establishment of Jewish priests because he preached a new covenant and threatened the status quo. In the movie's scenes showing Jesus being condemned to death, the two main players are Pontius Pilate, the Roman governor, and Caiphas, the Jewish high priest. Both men want to keep the lid on, and while neither is especially eager to see Jesus crucified, they live in a harsh time when such a man is dangerous.

Pilate is seen going through his well-known doubts before finally washing his hands of the matter and turning Jesus over to the priests, but Caiphas, who also had doubts, is not seen as sympathetically. The critic Steven D. Greydanus, in a useful analysis of the film, writes: "The film omits the canonical line from John's gospel in which Caiphas argues that it is better for one man to die for the people that the nation be saved. Had Gibson retained this line, perhaps giving Caiphas a measure of the inner conflict he gave to Pilate, it could have underscored the similarities between Caiphas and Pilate and helped defuse the issue of anti-Semitism."

This scene and others might justifiably be cited by anyone concerned that the movie contains anti-Semitism. My own feeling is that Gibson's film is not anti-Semitic, but reflects a range of behavior on the part of its Jewish characters, on balance favorably. The Jews who seem to desire Jesus' death are in the priesthood, and have political as well as theological reasons for acting; like today's Catholic bishops who were slow to condemn abusive priests, Protestant TV preachers who confuse religion with politics, or Muslim clerics who are silent on terrorism, they have an investment in their positions and authority. The other Jews seen in the film are viewed positively; Simon helps Jesus to carry the cross, Veronica brings a cloth to wipe his face, Jews in the crowd cry out against his torture.

A reasonable person, I believe, will reflect that in this story set in a Jewish land, there are many characters with many motives, some good, some not, each one representing himself, none representing his religion. The story involves a Jew who tried no less than to replace the established religion and set himself up as the Messiah. He was understandably greeted with a jaundiced eye by the Jewish establishment while at the same time finding his support, his disciples, and the founders of his church entirely among his fellow Jews. The libel that the Jews "killed Christ" involves a willful misreading of testament and teaching: Jesus was made man and came to Earth *in order* to suffer and die in reparation for our sins. No race, no religion, no man, no priest, no governor, no executioner killed Jesus; he died by God's will to fulfill his purpose, and with our sins we *all* killed him. That some Christian churches have historically been guilty of the sin of anti-Semitism is undeniable, but in committing it they violated their own beliefs.

This discussion will seem beside the point for readers who want to know about the movie, not the theology. But *The Passion of the Christ*, more than any other film I can recall, depends upon theological considerations. Gibson has not made a movie that anyone would call "commercial," and if it grosses millions, that will not be because anyone was entertained. It is a personal message movie of the most radical kind, attempting to re-create events of personal urgency to Gibson. The filmmaker has put his artistry and fortune at the service of his conviction and belief, and that doesn't happen often.

Is the film "good" or "great"? I imagine each person's reaction (visceral, theological, artistic) will differ. I was moved by the depth of feeling, by the skill of the actors and technicians, by their desire to see this project through, no matter what. To discuss individual performances, such as James Caviezel's heroic depiction of the ordeal, is almost beside the point. This isn't a movie about performances, although it has powerful ones; or about technique, although it is awesome; or about cinematography (although Caleb Deschanel paints with an artist's eye); or music (although John Debney supports the content without distracting from it). It is a film about an idea. An idea that it is necessary to fully comprehend the Passion if Christianity is to make any sense. Gibson has communicated his idea with a single-minded urgency. Many will disagree. Some will agree, but be horrified by the graphic treatment. I myself am no longer religious in the sense that a long-ago altar boy thought he should be; but I can respond to the power of belief whether I agree or not, and when I find it in a film I must respect it.

Note: I said the film is the most violent I have ever seen. It will probably be the most violent you have ever seen. This is not a criticism but an observation; the film is unsuitable for younger viewers, but works powerfully for those who can endure it. The MPAA's "R" rating is definitive proof that the organization either will never give the NC-17 rating for violence alone, or was intimidated by the subject matter. If it had been anyone other than Jesus up on that cross, I have a feeling that NC-17 would have been automatic. ☞

Paycheck ★ ★
PG-13, 119 m., 2003

Ben Affleck (Michael Jennings), Uma Thurman (Rachel Porter), Aaron Eckhart (Rethrick), Paul Giamatti (Shorty), Joe Morton (Agent Dodge), Emily Holmes (Betsy), Colm Feore (Mr. Wolf), Joe Morton (Agent Dodge), Michael C. Hall (Agent Klein). Directed by John Woo and produced by Terence Chang, John Davis, Michael Hackett, and Woo. Screenplay by Dean Georgaris, based on the short story by Philip K. Dick.

Paycheck begins with a thought-provoking idea from Philip K. Dick, exploits it for its action and plot potential, but never really develops it. By the end, the film seems to have lost enthusiasm for itself, and should be scored with "Is

That All There Is?" It's like an assembly of off-the-shelf parts from techno-thrillers: the vast laboratory, the cold-blooded billionaire industrialist, the hero in a situation he doesn't understand, the professional security men who line up to get bumped off by the amateur computer nerd. Because the director is John Woo, we expect a chase and a martial arts sequence, and we get them, but they're strangely detached; they feel like exercises, not exuberances.

Ben Affleck and Uma Thurman establish a strong presence as the leads, having some fun (and shedding a few tears) over the fact that they've been deeply in love but he can't remember it. That's in the nature of Affleck's job. He plays Michael Jennings, a brilliant engineer who hires himself out to reverse-engineer new computer breakthroughs. He starts with impenetrable code or uncrackable chips, takes them apart, sees what makes them work, and reassembles them as elegant little rip-offs that sidestep copyright infringement. Because big bucks are involved in what he does, and because corporations wouldn't want a guy like this blabbing on TechTV, they write a sneaky clause into his contract: After he completes a job, his memory is wiped clean, and he's left with a gap of several weeks and a big paycheck.

For a writer with Dick's pulp origins, Michael is an ideal character type—sort of a cyber version of Johnny Dollar, the man with the action-packed expense account. Give him his salary and he's happy to walk away from the job (although we get a brief glimpse of a check that wouldn't be much of a payday for a program that essentially does the same thing as Al Pacino's software in *Simone*—creates a 3-D digital actress who looks and sounds like the real thing).

Next assignment. Michael is hired by Rethrick (Aaron Eckhart), head of the ominous Allcom. This assignment will take a little longer—three years of his life, as he tries to crack an invention that can see into the future. Yes, Rethrick wants to steal a lens so powerful that it follows the curvature of space and time right back to where it started and then some. Theory is, if you can predict the future, your stock price will go up. Yes, and you can win the lottery, too—although once the fundamental principles of stock markets and lotteries have

been capsized, what do you do for an encore? See if you're going to enjoy lunch?

At a party at Rethrick's house, Michael exchanges small talk with the beautiful biologist Rachel (Uma Thurman), demonstrating once again that we should never, ever worry about the cleverness of our small talk because in the movies it can be gormless and banal and yet be repeated as a motif for an entire film. After Michael suggests that they "go somewhere else" and talk, she turns him down, and then she says, "You don't believe in second chances, do you?" Not a line to rank with "I want you to hold [the chicken salad] between your knees," but it will be repeated with variations, tears, irony, fondness, and urgency, to prove that the movie has not had its own memory erased.

The ingenious element in the plot is that when Michael's three years are up and he's free again, he discovers he has signed away millions of dollars and is left only with a manila envelope containing nineteen objects. These are apparently objects that the prewipe Michael knew he would need postwipe; he has to figure out what to use them for, and when. (Clue: He's being chased by killers at a bus station, and whoa!—He has a bus pass!) There's an echo here of *The Bourne Identity* (2002), starring Affleck's buddy Matt Damon as an amnesiac who takes possession of a Swiss safe-deposit box containing clues to several identities, perhaps including his own.

Okay, so the idea is for Michael and Rachel to stop Allcom before it can destroy the world. Destruction is likely, it's explained, because if world leaders could foresee that their enemies planned to use weapons of mass destruction, they would launch a preemptive strike to respond to the attack before it takes place. Those wacky sci-fi guys! Their way to derail this scenario, of course, involves a long motorcycle chase sequence and a martial arts battle.

Although Woo is famous for his mastery of action scenes, the motorcycle chase is played by the numbers; there hardly seems to be risk or danger involved, and the computer nerd and his biologist girlfriend don't seem particularly amazed when lots of men in black cars try to shoot them dead. Later, when Rachel does some hand-to-hand combat, we're reminded how much more convincing Thurman was in

Kill Bill—although there's a scene involving a mechanical hand that shows some wit and gets a chuckle.

There was a basic level at which I enjoyed the movie, just for the scope of the production and the way Affleck doggedly puzzled his way through that manila envelope. But at the end we get the sense that Woo is operating with a clipboard and a checklist, making sure everyone is killed in the right order. There's simply not enough urgency involved. And the attempts of the Allcom security staff to deal with the various locks and alarms in their top-secret lab had me thinking of *Dumb and Dumber*. There are countless fascinating possibilities involved in Philip K. Dick's story, and I'm kind of sad that the one ranking highest in the minds of the filmmakers was the opportunity to have chase scenes and blow stuff up real good.

The Perfect Man ★

PG, 96 m., 2005

Hilary Duff (Holly Hamilton), Heather Locklear (Jean Hamilton), Chris Noth (Ben Cooper), Mike O'Malley (Lenny Horton), Ben Feldman (Adam Forrest), Aria Wallace (Zoe Hamilton), Vanessa Lengies (Amy). Directed by Mark Rosman and produced by Susan Duff, Marc E. Platt, and Dawn Wolfrom. Screenplay by Gina Wendkos.

Is there no one to step forward and simply say that Heather Locklear's character in *The Perfect Man* is mad? I will volunteer. Locklear plays Jean Hamilton, a woman whose obsessive search for the "perfect man" inspires sudden and impulsive moves from one end of the country to another, always with her teenage daughter, Holly (Hilary Duff), and Holly's seven-year-old sister, Zoe (Aria Wallace). Apparently, there can only be one Perfect Man candidate per state.

As the movie opens, Holly is preparing to attend a prom in Wichita when her mother announces, "It's moving time!" Her latest boyfriend has broken up with her, so they all have to pile into the car and head for New York, where Mom providentially has a job lined up at a bakery—a job that pays well enough for them to move into an apartment that would rent for, oh, $4,000 a month.

Holly keeps an online blog named GirlOnTheMove.com, where she chronicles her mom's craziness for all the world. "Post me on Match.com," her mom tells Holly after they arrive in New York, but Holly thinks maybe it might be fun to see if her mom just—you know, *meets* someone. Jean's way of meeting someone is certainly direct: She attends a PTA meeting at Holly's new school, and suggests special PTA meetings for single parents and teachers. In desperation, Holly creates an imaginary online friend for her mom, who says all the things a woman wants to hear.

How does Holly know this is true? Because she's made a new friend at school (she's always making new friends, because she's always moving to new schools). This friend, named Amy (Vanessa Lengies) has an Uncle Ben (Chris Noth) who runs a bistro and is a bottomless well of information about what women want to hear, and what a Perfect Man consists of. Holly names the imaginary friend Ben, sends her mom Uncle Ben's photo, and recycles what he tells her into the e-mail. Example of his wisdom: "When a woman gets an orchid, she feels like she's floating on a cloud of infinite possibility." If I met a woman who felt like she was floating on a cloud of infinite possibility after receiving an orchid, I would be afraid to give her anything else until she'd had a good physical.

The Perfect Man takes its idiotic plot and uses it as the excuse for scenes of awesome stupidity. For example, when Jean walks into Uncle Ben's restaurant and there is a danger they might meet, Holly sets off the sprinkler system. And when Holly thinks Ben is marrying another woman, she interrupts the wedding—while even we know, because of the tortured camera angles that strive not to reveal this, that Ben is only the best man.

Meanwhile, Jean has another prospect, a baker named Lenny (Mike O'Malley), who is a real nice guy but kind of homely, and invites her to a concert by a Styx tribute band. This involves driving to the concert in Lenny's pride and joy, a 1980 Pontiac Trans-Am two-door hardtop; Jean has to take off her shoes before entering the sacred precincts of this car. My personal opinion is that Lenny would be less boring after six months than the cloud of infinite possibilities guy.

The Perfect Man crawls hand over bloody hand up the stony face of this plot, while we in the audience do not laugh because it is not nice to laugh at those less fortunate than ourselves, and the people in this movie are less fortunate than the people in just about any other movie I can think of, simply because they are in it.

The Perfect Score ★ ★
PG-13, 93 m., 2004

Scarlett Johansson (Francesca), Erika Christensen (Anna), Chris Evans (Kyle), Darius Miles (Desmond), Leonardo Nam (Roy), Bryan Greenberg (Matty), Fulvio Cecere (Francesca's Father), Kyle Labine (Dave), Bill Mackenzie (Bernie). Directed by Brian Robbins and produced by Roger Birnbaum, Jonathan Glickman, Robbins, and Michael Tollin. Screenplay by Mark Schwahn, Marc Hyman, and Jon Zack.

The dialogue in *The Perfect Score* mentions *The Breakfast Club*, which is nice (how come the characters in movies never seem to know there are movies—except the ones they attend but never watch?). And there are similarities between the two films, not least in the way that Scarlett Johansson, with her red lips and brunette haircut, resembles Molly Ringwald. There is also a certain seriousness linking the two films, although this one tilts toward a caper comedy.

The film takes place in Princeton, New Jersey, which in addition to being Albert Einstein's place of last employment is also home to the Princeton Testing Center, home of the SAT exam. The SATs, we learn, were once known as the Scholastic Aptitude Test, but since this name presumably reeked of common sense, it was dropped, and now "SAT" simply stands for—SAT. "Ess Ay Tee," the Website explains, making it easy for us.

We meet Kyle (Chris Evans), who for as long as he can remember has wanted to be an architect. That for him translates into being admitted to Cornell, but for Cornell, alas, he will need to score a 1,430 on his SAT, and his first score is

down close to triple digits. He can take the test again, but he doubts he can improve his score.

"Kyle," says one of his buddies, "this is your dream, man. If they want to put a number on that, then the hell with them." Yeah. So Kyle and his posse decide to break into the Princeton Testing Center, steal the answers to the test, and realize their dream. And that they set out to do, in a film that sketches various motives for a half-dozen characters. You may be able to find parallels between these characters and those in *The Breakfast Club*. On the other hand, you may decide life is too short.

I wasn't thinking about *The Breakfast Club* anyway, while I watched the film. I was thinking about *Better Luck Tomorrow*, the 2002 film by Justin Lin about a group of Asian-American high school students in Orange County, who started by selling exam answers and ended up involved in drugs and murder, all without getting caught. In the original ending of the film when it played at Sundance, the central character considers turning himself in to the police, but "I couldn't let one mistake get in the way of everything I'd worked for. I know the difference between right and wrong, but I guess in the end I really wanted to go to a good college."

Lin reshot some of the film, including that ending, but I've always thought it was a good one. It shows an ability to separate achievement from morality, and places so much value on success that it finally justifies any action. Lin's young heroes, I wrote in my article about the best films of the year, have positioned themselves to take over from the fallen leaders of Enron.

I thought about the film because *The Perfect Score* considers similar material without the bite and anger and savage determination. It's too palatable. It maintains a tone of light seriousness, and it depends on the caper for too much of its entertainment value. *Better Luck Tomorrow* also has a plot that involves crime, but the difference is, *The Perfect Score* is about the intended crime and depends on it, while in *Better Luck Tomorrow* we see a process by which the behavior of the characters leads them where they never thought to go.

There is a kind of franchising of movies going on right now, in which the big studio product is like fast food: bad for you, but available on every corner. Good and challenging movies are limited to release in big cities and in a handful of independently booked cinemas. Whole states and sections of the country never see the best new films on big screens, and they're not always easy to find on video.

And that's a shame. What does it say when a dozen of the titles nominated for major Academy Awards this year did not play in a majority of the markets? Have I drifted from the movie under review? I'm not drifting, I'm swimming.

Peter Pan ★ ★ ★ ½
PG, 105 m., 2003

Jason Isaacs (Captain Hook/Mr. Darling), Olivia Williams (Mrs. Darling), Lynn Redgrave (Aunt Millicent), Jeremy Sumpter (Peter Pan), Rachel Hurd-Wood (Wendy Darling), Harry Newell (John Darling), Freddie Popplewell (Michael Darling), Richard Briers (Smee), Ludivine Sagnier (Tinker Bell). Directed by P. J. Hogan and produced by Lucy Fisher, Patrick McCormick, and Douglas Wick. Screenplay by Michael Goldenberg and Hogan, based on the book by J. M. Barrie.

I'm not sure how to describe this *Peter Pan* to you. It's so different from what I expected. I walked in anticipating a sweet kiddie fantasy, and was surprised to find a film that takes its story very seriously indeed, thank you, and even allows a glimpse of underlying sadness. To be Peter Pan is fun for a day or a year, but can it be fun forever? Peter is trapped in Groundhog Day, repeating the same adventures, forever faced with the tiresome Captain Hook, always shackled to Tinker Bell, who means well but would get on your nerves if you took a three-day bus trip with her.

"Peter," asks Wendy, "what are your real feelings?" Those are precisely what Peter is unable to share. This expensive production, shot in Australia and unveiling a young unknown as the beautiful Wendy, is aware of the latent sexuality between the two characters, and Peter is a little scared of that. They are at precisely the age when it is time to share their first real kiss—and they do so, astonishing the other characters

(they've never seen that before—not in the cartoon, not on the stage—never!).

The movie has been directed by P. J. Hogan, best known for Julia Roberts comedies *(My Best Friend's Wedding)*. Here he stays closer to the J. M. Barrie book, which is about to celebrate its centenary, and also closer to the book's buried themes, which are side-stepped by most versions of *Peter Pan*. When a muscular and bare-chested gamin appears on the windowsill of the prettiest twelve-and-a-half-year-old in London and asks her to fly away from home and family to join him with the Lost Boys in Neverland, he is exactly the kind of strange man her mother should have warned her about. When the other major player in Neverland is the one-armed Captain Hook, who takes an uncomfortably acute interest in both Peter and Wendy, there's enough inspiration here to have Freud gnawing on his cigar.

It's not that the movie is overtly sexual; it's just that the sensuality is *there*, and the other versions have pretended it was not. The live action contributes to the new focus; Peter Pan is played by Jeremy Sumpter, who was so effective in Bill Paxton's *Frailty*, and Wendy Darling is Rachel Hurd-Wood, who was selected at an open casting call and is delightful in her first role. They're attractive young people in roles that in the past have been played by such as Robin Williams and Mary Martin, and there is chemistry on the screen.

The special effects, of course, are endless, but there is a method to their excess. The movie's not simply a riot of pretty pictures, but begins with a Neverland that seems overgrown and pungent—more like Louisiana than Middle Earth. There is a vast, gloomy castle and all manner of paths into the darkness, but then scenes will turn as delicate as *A Midsummer Night's Dream*. At a point when lesser films would be giving us swashbuckling by the numbers, Peter and Wendy dance in midair, emulating the fairy ballet.

As the film narrows into its crucial themes, we realize there are two: Wendy's desire to free Peter Pan from eternal boyhood, and Hook's envy of the affection they have for each other. It is no accident that the poison made of droplets from Hook's red eye is composed of envy, malice, and disappointment.

Captain Hook and John Darling are both played by Jason Isaacs, in a dual role made traditional by decades of holiday pantomimes; each character is short on qualities the other has in abundance. Hook is all gnash and bluster, while John Darling is so shy he can hardly talk to himself in the mirror. Mrs. Darling (Olivia Williams), mother of Wendy and her two younger brothers, seems awfully composed during her long nights by the open window, waiting for her children to return, but maybe she has seen the earlier versions.

Wendy finds a role for herself in Neverland. It's touching, the way the Lost Boys so desperately want to be found, and crowd around Wendy, asking her to be their mother. (What does a mother do? "Tell us a story!" Later, when the Lost Boys join Wendy and her brothers, John and Michael, back home in their bedroom, they ask Mrs. Darling to be their mother—and she agrees, although when Smee arrives late and is motherless, the new character of Aunt Millicent (Lynn Redgrave) steps in joyfully.

It was Aunt Millicent who really started all the trouble, by observing that Wendy was not a girl anymore and offering to take her into hand and make her a woman. This offer is vaguely alarming to Wendy, and what Peter offers her is the chance to drift in her preadolescent dream forever. What she offers him is a chance to grow up. "To grow up is such a barbarous business," Hook observes. "Think of the inconvenience—and the pimples!" But to never grow up is unspeakably sad, and this is the first *Peter Pan* where Peter's final flight seems not like a victory but an escape.

The Phantom of the Opera ★ ★ ★
PG-13, 143 m., 2004

Gerard Butler (The Phantom), Emmy Rossum (Christine), Patrick Wilson (Raoul), Miranda Richardson (Madame Giry), Minnie Driver (Carlotta), Ciaran Hinds (Firmin), Simon Callow (Andre), Victor McGuire (Piangi). Directed by Joel Schumacher and produced by Andrew Lloyd Webber. Screenplay by Webber, based on the novel by Gaston Leroux.

The question at this point is whether *The Phantom of the Opera* is even intended to be frightening. It has become such a product of modern popular art that its original inspiration, "the loathsome gargoyle who lives in hell but dreams of heaven," has come dangerously close to becoming an institution, like Dracula, who was also scary a long, long time ago.

Lon Chaney's Phantom in the 1925 production had a hideously damaged face, his mouth a lipless rictus, his eyes off-center in gouged-out sockets. When Christine tore off his mask, she was horrified, and so was the audience. In the Andrew Lloyd Webber version, now filmed by Joel Schumacher, the mask is more like a fashion accessory, and the Phantom's "good" profile is so chiseled and handsome that the effect is not an object of horror but a kinky babe magnet.

There was something unwholesome and pathetic about the 1925 Phantom, who scuttled like a rat in the undercellars of the Paris Opera and nourished a hopeless love for Christine. The modern Phantom is more like a perverse Batman with a really neat cave. The character of Raoul, Christine's nominal lover, has always been a fatuous twerp, but at least in the 1925 version Christine is attracted to the Phantom only until she removes his mask. In this version, any red-blooded woman would choose the Phantom over Raoul, even knowing what she knows now.

But what I am essentially disliking is not the film but the underlying material. I do not think Andrew Lloyd Webber wrote a very good musical. The story is thin beer for the time it takes to tell it, and the music is maddeningly repetitive. When the chandelier comes crashing down, it's not a shock, it's a historical reenactment. You do remember the tunes as you leave the theater, but you don't walk out humming them; you wonder if you'll be able to get them out of your mind. Every time I see Webber's *Phantom*, the bit about the "darkness of the music of the night" bounces between my ears, as if, like Howard Hughes, I am condemned to repeat the words until I go mad. (I have the same difficulty with "Waltzing Matilda.") Lyrics such as

Let your mind start a journey through a strange new world,
leave all thoughts of the world you knew before,
let your soul take you where you long to be,
only then can you belong to me.

wouldn't get past Simon Cowell, let alone Rodgers and Hammerstein.

Yet Joel Schumacher has bravely taken aboard this dreck and made of it a movie I am pleased to have seen. To have seen, that is, as opposed to have heard. I concede that Emmy Rossum, who is only eighteen and sings her own songs and carries the show, is a phenomenal talent, and I wish her all the best—starting with better material. What an Eliza Dolittle she might make. But the songs are dirges or show-lounge retreads, the dialogue laboriously makes its archaic points, and meanwhile the movie looks simply sensational. Schumacher knows more about making a movie than the material deserves, and he simply goes off on his own, bringing greatness to his department and leaving the material to fend for itself.

I attended a rehearsal of the Lyric Opera's new production of *A Wedding* and talked with its cowriter and director, Robert Altman. "I don't know $#!+ about the music," he told me. "I don't even know if they're singing on key. That's not my job. I focus on how it moves, how it looks, and how it plays." One wonders if Schumacher felt the same way—not that it would be polite to ask him.

He has a sure sense for the macabre, going back to his 1987 teenage vampire movie *The Lost Boys* and certainly including his *Flatliners* (1990), about the medical students who induce technical death and then resuscitate themselves to report on what death was like—whether they saw the white tunnel, and so on. His *Batman Forever* was the best of the Batman movies, not least because of its sets, and here, working with production designer Anthony Pratt *(Excalibur)*, art director John Fenner *(Raiders of the Lost Ark)*, set decorator Celia Bobak (Branagh's *Henry V* and *Hamlet*), and costume designer Alexandra Byrne *(Eliz-*

abeth), he creates a film so visually resonant you want to float in it.

I love the look of the film. I admire the cellars and dungeons and the Styx-like sewer with its funereal gondola, and the sensational Masked Ball, and I was impressed by the rooftop scenes, with Paris as a backdrop in the snow. The scarlet of the Phantom's cape acts like a bloodstain against the monochrome cityscape and Christina's pale skin, and she rises to an occasion her rival lovers have not earned. She responds to more genuine tragedy than the film provides for her, she has feelings her character must generate from within, she is so emotionally tortured and romantically torn that both Raoul and the Phantom should ask themselves if there is another man.

I know there are fans of the Phantom. For a decade in London, you couldn't go past Her Majesty's Theater without seeing them with their backpacks, camped out against the north wall, waiting all night in hopes of a standby ticket. People have seen it ten, twenty, a hundred times—have never done anything else in their lives but see it. They will embrace the movie, and I congratulate them, because they have waited too long to be disappointed.

Some still feel Michael Crawford should have been given the role he made famous on stage; certainly Gerald Butler's work doesn't argue against their belief. But Butler is younger and more conventionally handsome than Crawford, in a *GQ* kind of way, and Lloyd Webber's production has long since forgotten that the Phantom is supposed to be ugly and aging and, given the conditions in those cellars, probably congested, arthritic, and neurasthenic.

This has been, I realize, a nutty review. I am recommending a movie I do not seem to like very much. But part of the pleasure of moviegoing is pure spectacle—of just sitting there and looking at great stuff and knowing it looks terrific. There wasn't much Joel Schumacher could have done with the story or the music he was handed, but in the areas over which he held sway, he has triumphed. This is such a fabulous production that by recasting two of the three leads and adding some better songs it could have been, well, great.

Phone Booth ★ ★ ★
R, 81 m., 2003

Colin Farrell (Stu Shepard), Forest Whitaker (Captain Ramey), Katie Holmes (Pamela McFadden), Radha Mitchell (Kelly Shepard), Kiefer Sutherland (The Caller [voice]). Directed by Joel Schumacher and produced by Gil Netter and David Zucker. Screenplay by Larry Cohen.

Phone Booth is a religious fable, a showbiz fable, or both. It involves a fast-talking, two-timing Broadway press agent who is using the last phone booth in Manhattan (at 53d and Eighth) when he's pinned down by a sniper. The shooter seems to represent either God, demanding a confession of sins, or the filmmakers, having their revenge on publicists.

The man in the crosshairs is Stu Shepard (Colin Farrell), who we've already seen striding the streets, lying into his cell phone, berating his hapless gofer. Why does he now use a pay phone instead of his cellular? Because he's calling his mistress Pamela (Katie Holmes) and doesn't want the call to turn up on the monthly bill scrutinized by his wife, Kelly (Radha Mitchell).

The phone in the booth rings, and Stu follows the universal human practice of answering it. The voice is harsh, sardonic, sounds like it belongs to a man intelligent and twisted, and with a sense of humor. For the next hour or so, in a movie that is only eighty-one minutes long, Stu will be trying to keep the man on the other end from pulling the trigger. The Voice (for so we may call him) seems to know a lot about Stu—personal secrets, but also things anyone could see, like the way he rudely treated a pizza delivery man. He seems to think Stu is a reprehensible man who deserves to die—and may, unless Stu can talk or think his way out of this situation.

The movie is essentially a morality play, and it's not a surprise to learn that Larry Cohen, the writer, came up with the idea twenty years ago—when there were still phone booths and morality plays. If the movie had been conceived more recently, Stu would have been the hero for the way he lies and cheats. The movie is an instructive contrast to *People I Know*, which played at Sundance 2003 and stars Al Pacino as a press agent who doggedly tries to do the right thing despite all of his (many) sins.

The director, Joel Schumacher, discovered Colin Farrell in the tense, quirky basic training drama *Tigerland* (2000). Farrell played a recruit who was too smart and too verbal to be a good trainee, and stirred up trouble in a fraught situation. Now comes a similar character, further twisted by civilian life. The movie is Farrell's to win or lose, since he's on-screen most of the time, and he shows energy and intensity.

As the crisis builds in tension, he forms a rapport with Captain Ramey (Forest Whitaker), a cop experienced at hostage situations, who at first believes Stu might be the perp and not the victim. The two actors have to communicate nonverbally to keep the sniper from realizing what's happening, and the movie shows them figuring that out.

The movie was premiered at Toronto 2002, scheduled for immediate release, and then yanked when the Beltway Sniper went into action. Then it opened during the Iraqi war. Hard to pick a safe opening date these days. Schumacher is the director of many blockbuster titles, like two of the *Batman* movies, but he sometimes leaves the big budgets behind (he shot *Phone Booth* on one set in ten days).

For the voice of his sniper, he calls on Kiefer Sutherland, who also starred in Schumacher's *The Lost Boys* (1987), *Flatliners* (1990), and *A Time to Kill* (1996) and here takes the mostly (but not quite entirely) invisible role as a very useful favor to Schumacher—because if the voice doesn't work, neither does the movie. It does. I especially like the way the caller taunts Stu: "Do you see the tourists with their video cameras, hoping the cops will shoot so they can sell the tape?"

Pieces of April ★ ★ ★
PG-13, 81 m., 2003

Katie Holmes (April Burns), Patricia Clarkson (Joy Burns), Oliver Platt (Jim Burns), Derek Luke (Bobby), Alison Pill (Beth Burns), Alice Drummond (Grandma Dottie), John Gallagher Jr. (Timmy Burns), Sean Hayes (Wayne). Directed by Peter Hedges and produced by Alexia Alexanian, John S. Lyons, and Gary Winick. Screenplay by Hedges.

Thanksgiving is not a conventional religious or political holiday but consists simply of families gathering to love one another and express gratitude. That's the tricky part. There are no theologies to fall back on. It has inspired a uniquely North American group of films. Most of the families in them are troubled, but there is usually a reconciliation, comforting to everyone except the turkey.

The best Thanksgiving film is Woody Allen's *Hannah and Her Sisters,* and the most entertaining are *Planes, Trains and Automobiles* and *What's Cooking?* The most depressing is *The Ice Storm,* and the best single line is by Lou Jacobi in *Avalon:* "You cut the turkey without me?" The spirit of the genre is summed up in *Home for the Holidays* when two family members are fighting on the lawn while the father hoses them down. Seeing the neighbors gawking across the street, the father snarls, "Go back to your own goddamn holidays!"

Peter Hedges's *Pieces of April* ends prematurely and has a side plot that's a distraction and a cheat, but it contains much good humor and works anyway. It consists of two and a half parallel stories. Story one: The Burns family is driving from the suburbs to New York to have Thanksgiving dinner with a troublesome daughter. Story two: The daughter, who has never cooked a Thanksgiving dinner before, is trying to cope despite a broken oven. Story two and a half: Her boyfriend disappears on a mission that is unnecessary, distracting, and misleading.

Katie Holmes plays April Burns, the tattooed daughter who has been the family's despair. Derek Luke is her boyfriend, a sweet guy whose subplot hints he's up to no good, but that's just a cheap tease. Driving into the city are Jim Burns (Oliver Platt), wife Joy (Patricia Clarkson), daughter Beth (Alison Pill), son Timmy (John Gallagher Jr.), and Grandma Dottie (Alice Drummond), who is in that stage of movie-induced Alzheimer's that allows her to provide perfectly timed zingers when necessary.

The movie belongs to April and her mother. Joy is dying of breast cancer and this may be her final Thanksgiving, but she uses her mortality as a springboard for brave humor; at one point, she asks for silence to reflect on an approaching crisis. "We all have to give a lot of thought . . ."

she says, and they wait for a declaration about her impending death, "to how we are going to hide the food we don't eat."

In April's apartment, all is chaos. She's gone through a punk/Goth rebellion, but a yearning for family ritual runs deep, and her new boyfriend has helped her believe that she has a home she can invite her family to. The turkey is the problem. April's oven is broken, and that sends her on a quest through her building for someone with an oven she can borrow. Most of the neighbors are suspicious or hostile, but there's a Chinese family that illustrates the same message as *What's Cooking?:* Thanksgiving is a reminder that all Americans, even Native Americans, are immigrants to this continent.

There's lots of humor in the car with the dysfunctional Burnses. Beth is outraged that they're visiting her sister; April was the apple of the family eye before she went wrong, and Beth feels threatened that she seems about to go right again. Young Timmy is a pothead whose supply of grass provides comfort to his dying mom, who after a few inhales likes the rapper on the radio. Jim, the dad, tries to put down rebellion and see the bright side: "This new guy, Bobby, sounds very promising. Apparently he reminds her of me." A measure of the family's goofiness comes when they stop to conduct a burial service for an animal they've run over. Their eulogy: "We're sorry we didn't know you. We hope it was quick."

The wild card is Bobby, the boyfriend, and here Hedges, the writer-director, halfheartedly tries to do something that doesn't work and is a little offensive. Bobby is middle-class, kind, soft-spoken, and a good influence on April, but the screenplay sends him out of the apartment on an obscure mission and hints that it may involve something illegal or dangerous; his behavior and deliberately misleading dialogue plays on clichés about young black men.

And consider the scene where he first encounters April's family. He's bleeding and looks dangerous and they think they're under attack. Bobby's behavior indicates an undigested idea of who the character is and how it would be funny to portray him. It's not mean-spirited so much as half-assed; Hedges has a confused idea that it would be funny to play on negative associations about young black men, to make it a joke when we find out how nice Bobby is. Not funny.

The movie ends rather abruptly, as if it ran out of money. Maybe it did; it was shot on digital for $200,000 in three weeks (and looks remarkably good given those constraints). The closing montage of photographs looks uncannily like a way to represent a scene Hedges didn't have time to shoot (the eighty-one-minute running time is another hint). Despite its flaws, *Pieces of April* has a lot of joy and quirkiness; it's well intentioned in its screwy way, with flashes of human insight, and actors who can take a moment and make it glow. You forgive the lapses. You have the feeling that Hedges sees the same stuff that bothers you and it makes him squirm, too; a movie made this close to the line has no room for second thoughts.

Hedges is a novelist who wrote the screen adaptation for his own wonderful *What's Eating Gilbert Grape* in 1993, and adapted Nick Hornby's *About a Boy* (2002) for the screen, winning an Oscar nomination in the process. He has a feeling for his characters and tries to find humor in true observation. *Pieces of April* was a success at Sundance 2003, where Patricia Clarkson was honored for her acting. The movie is an enjoyable calling card that will set the stage, I suspect, for a new Hedges movie made with more resources and under less time pressure, and that is a movie I am looking forward to seeing.

Pirates of the Caribbean:
The Curse of the Black Pearl ★ ★ ★
PG-13, 134 m., 2003

Johnny Depp (Captain Jack Sparrow), Geoffrey Rush (Captain Barbossa), Orlando Bloom (Will Turner), Keira Knightley (Elizabeth Swann), Jack Davenport (Commodore Norrington), Jonathan Pryce (Governor Weatherby Swann). Directed by Gore Verbinski and produced by Jerry Bruckheimer. Screenplay by Ted Elliott and Terry Rossio.

There's a nice little 90-minute B movie trapped inside the 134 minutes of *Pirates of the Caribbean: The Curse of the Black Pearl,* a movie that charms the audience and then outstays its welcome. Although the ending leaves open the possibility of a sequel, the movie feels like it already includes the sequel; maybe that explains the double-barreled title. It's a good thing that Geoffrey Rush and Johnny Depp are on hand to jack up the acting department. Their characters, two world-class goofballs, keep us interested even during entirely pointless swordfights.

Pointless? See if you can follow me here. Captain Jack Sparrow (Depp) has a deep hatred for Captain Barbossa (Rush), who led a mutiny aboard Sparrow's pirate ship, the *Black Pearl,* and left Captain Jack stranded on a deserted island. Barbossa and his crew then ran afoul of an ancient curse that turned them into the Undead. By day they look like normal if dissolute humans, but by the light of the moon they're revealed as skeletal cadavers.

Now here's the important part: Because they're already dead, they cannot be killed. Excuse me for supplying logic where it is manifestly not wanted, but doesn't that mean there's no point in fighting them? There's a violent battle at one point between the *Black Pearl* crew and sailors of the Royal Navy, and unless I am mistaken the sailors would all eventually have to be dead, because the skeletons could just keep on fighting forever until they won. Yes?

The only reason I bring this up is that the battle scenes actually feel as if they go on forever. It's fun at first to see a pirate swordfight, but eventually it gets to the point where the sword clashing, yardarm swinging, and timber shivering get repetitious. I also lost count of how many times Jack Sparrow is the helpless captive of both the British and the pirates, and escapes from the chains/brig/noose/island.

And yet the movie made me grin at times and savor the daffy plot and enjoy the way Depp and Rush fearlessly provide performances that seem nourished by deep wells of nuttiness. Depp in particular seems to be channeling a drunken drag queen, with his eyeliner and the way he minces ashore and slurs his dialogue ever so insouciantly. Don't mistake me: This is not a criticism, but admiration for his work. It can be said that his performance is original in its every atom. There has never been a pirate, or for that matter a human being, like this in any other movie. There's some talk about how he got too much sun while he was stranded on that island, but his behavior shows a lifetime of rehearsal. He is a peacock in full display.

Consider how boring it would have been if Depp had played the role straight, as an Errol Flynn or Douglas Fairbanks (Sr. or Jr.) might have. To take this material seriously would make it unbearable. Captain Sparrow's behavior is so rococo that other members of the cast actually comment on it. And yet because it is consistent and because you can never catch Depp making fun of the character, it rises to a kind of cockamamy sincerity.

Geoffrey Rush is relatively subdued—but only by contrast. His Barbossa, whose teeth alone would intimidate a congregation of dentists, brings gnashing to an art form. Only the film's PG-13 rating prevents him from doing unthinkable things to the heroine, Elizabeth Swann (Keira Knightley), whose blood, it is thought, can free the captain and his crew from the curse of the *Black Pearl*. Elizabeth is the daughter of the governor (Jonathan Pryce) of Port Royal, a British base in the Caribbean, and seems destined to marry Commodore Norrington (Jack Davenport), a fate that we intuit would lead to a lifetime of conversations about his constipation.

She truly loves the handsome young swordsmith Will Turner (Orlando Bloom), whom she met when they were both children, after spotting him adrift on a raft with a golden pirate medallion around his neck, which turns out to hold the key to the curse. Jack Sparrow takes a fatherly interest in young Turner, especially when he discovers who his father was . . . and that is quite enough of the plot.

Orlando Bloom is well cast in a severely limited role, as the heroic straight arrow. He has the classic profile of a silent film star. Keira Knightley you will recall as the best friend of the heroine in *Bend It Like Beckham*, where she had a sparkle altogether lacking here. Truth be told, she doesn't generate enough fire to explain why these swashbucklers would risk their lives for her, and in close-up seems composed when she should smolder. Parminder K. Nagra, the star of *Beckham*, might have been a more spirited choice here.

The movie is based on the theme park ride at Disney World, which I have taken many times. It is also inspired (as the ride no doubt was) by the rich tradition of pirate movies and excels in such departments as buried treasure, pirates' caves, pet parrots, and walking the plank, although there is a shortage of eye patches and hooks. The author Dave Eggers has opened a pirates' store, complete with planks measured and made to order, and the movie plays like his daydreams.

Polar Express ★ ★ ★ ★
G, 100 m., 2004

Body movement performers: Tom Hanks (Hero Boy/Father/Conductor/Hobo/Scrooge/Santa), Michael Jeter (Smokey/Steamer), Nona Gaye (Hero Girl), Peter Scolari (Lonely Boy), Eddie Deezen (Know-It-All), Charles Fleischer (Elf General), Steven Tyler (Elf Lieutenant/Elf Singer), Leslie Zemeckis (Sister Sarah/Mother). Voice performers if different than above: Daryl Sabara (Hero Boy), Andre Sogliuzzo (Smokey/Steamer), Jimmy Bennett (Lonely Boy), Isabella Peregrina (Sister Sarah). Directed by Robert Zemeckis and produced by Gary Goetzman, Steve Starkey, William Teitler, and Zemeckis. Screenplay by Zemeckis and William Broyles Jr., based on the book by Chris Van Allsburg.

The Polar Express has the quality of a lot of lasting children's entertainment: It's a little creepy. Not creepy in an unpleasant way, but in that sneaky, teasing way that lets you know eerie things could happen. There's a deeper, shivery tone, instead of the mindless jolliness of the usual Christmas movie. This one creates a world of its own, like *The Wizard of Oz* or *Willy Wonka*, in which the wise child does not feel too complacent.

Those who know the Chris Van Allsburg book will feel right at home from the opening moments, which quote from the story: *On Christmas Eve, many years ago, I lay quietly in my bed* . . . The young hero, who is never given a name, is listening for the sound of sleigh bells ringing. He is at just the age when the existence of Santa Claus is up for discussion.

The look of the film is extraordinary, a cross between live action and Van Allsburg's artwork. Robert Zemeckis, the same director whose *Who Framed Roger Rabbit* juxtaposed live action with animation, this time merges them, using a process called "performance capture," in which human actors perform the movements that are translated into lifelike animation. The characters in *Polar Express* don't look real, but they don't look unreal, either; they have a kind of simplified and underlined reality that makes them visually magnetic. Many of the body and voice performances are by Tom Hanks, who is the executive producer and worked with Zemeckis on *Forrest Gump* (1994) — another film that combined levels of reality and special effects.

The story: As Hero Boy lies awake in bed, there is a rumble in the street and a passenger train lumbers into view. The boy runs outside in his bathrobe and slippers, and the conductor advises him to get onboard. Having refused to visit a department store Santa, having let his little sister put out Santa's milk and cookies, Hero Boy is growing alarmingly agnostic on the Santa question, and the *Polar Express* apparently shuttles such kids to the North Pole, where seeing is believing.

Already on board is Hero Girl, a solemn and gentle African-American, who becomes the boy's friend, and also befriends Lonely Boy, who lives on the wrong side of the tracks and always seems sad. Another character, Know-It-All, is one of those kids who can't supply an answer without sounding obnoxious about it. These four are the main characters, in addition to the conductor, a hobo who lives on top of the train, Santa, and countless elves.

There's an interesting disconnect between the movie's action and its story. The action is typical thrill-ride stuff, with the *Polar Express* careening down a "179-degree grade" and racing through tunnels with a half-inch of clearance, while Hero Boy and the Hobo ski the top of the train to find safety before the tunnel. At the North Pole, there's another dizzying ride when the kids spin down a corkscrewing toy chute.

Those scenes are skillful, but expected. Not expected is a dazzling level of creativity in certain other scenes. Hero Girl's lost ticket, for example, flutters through the air with as much freedom as the famous floating feather at the start of *Forrest Gump*. When hot chocolate is served on the train, dancing waiters materialize with an acrobatic song-and-dance. And

the North Pole looks like a turn-of-the-century German factory town, filled with elves who not only look mass-produced but may have been, since they mostly have exactly the same features (this is not a cost-cutting device, but an artistic decision).

Santa, in this version, is a good and decent man, matter-of-fact and serious: a professional man, doing his job. The elves are like the crowd at a political rally. A sequence involving a bag full of toys is seen from a high angle that dramatizes Santa's operation, but doesn't romanticize it; this is not Jolly St. Nick, but Claus Inc. There is indeed something a little scary about all those elves with their intense, angular faces and their mob mentality.

That's the magic of *The Polar Express:* It doesn't let us off the hook with the usual reassuring Santa and Christmas clichés. When a helicopter lifts the bag of toys over the town square, of course it knocks a star off the top of the Christmas tree, and of course an elf is almost skewered far below. When Santa's helpers hitch up the reindeer, they look not like tame cartoon characters, but like skittish purebreds. And as for Lonely Boy, although he does make the trip and get his present, and is fiercely protective of it, at the end of the movie we suspect his troubles are not over, and that loneliness may be his condition.

There are so many jobs and so many credits on this movie that I don't know who to praise, but there are sequences here that are really very special. Some are quiet little moments, like a reflection in a hubcap. Some are visual masterstrokes, like a POV that looks straight up through a printed page, with the letters floating between us and the reader. Some are story concepts, like the train car filled with old and dead toys being taken back to the Pole for recycling. Some are elements of mystery, like the character of the hobo, who is helpful and even saves Hero Boy's life but is in a world of his own up there on top of the train and doesn't become anybody's buddy (when he disappears, his hand always lingers a little longer than his body).

The Polar Express is a movie for more than one season; it will become a perennial, shared by the generations. It has a haunting magical quality because it has imagined its world freshly and played true to it, sidestepping all the tiresome Christmas clichés that children have inflicted on them this time of year. The conductor tells Hero Boy he thinks he really should get on the train, and I have the same advice for you.

Note: I've seen the movie twice, once in the IMAX 3-D process that will be available in larger markets. New oversized 3-D glasses, big enough to fit over your own glasses, light enough so you can forget them, made this the best 3-D viewing experience I've ever had. If there's a choice, try the IMAX version. Or go twice. This is a movie that doesn't wear out. ☞

Poolhall Junkies ★ ★ ★
R, 94 m., 2003

Gregory "Mars" Callahan (Johnny Doyle), Chazz Palminteri (Joe), Rick Schroder (Brad), Rod Steiger (Nick), Michael Rosenbaum (Danny Doyle), Alison Eastwood (Tara), Christopher Walken (Mike). Directed by Gregory "Mars" Callahan and produced by Karen Beninati, Vincent Newman, and Tucker Tooley. Screenplay by Chris Corso and Callahan.

One of the things I like best about *Poolhall Junkies* is its lack of grim desperation. Its characters know that pool is a game, and do not lead lives in which every moment is a head-butt with fate. Yes, there are fights, weapons are drawn, and old scores are settled, but the hero's most important bet is made to help his girl get a job she wants, the two archrivals are clearly destined to become friends, and Christopher Walken gets to deliver one of his famous monologues. He starts out, "Have you ever watched one of those animal channels?" and we are grinning already.

This is a young man's film, humming with the fun of making it. It was directed and cowritten by Gregory "Mars" Callahan, who also plays the leading role, Johnny Doyle, who was so good when he was a kid that "the cue was part of his arm and the balls had eyes." He never wanted to grow up to be a pool hustler. He wanted to join the pro tour. He's a good player, but he's not one of those nuts whose eyeballs spin like pinwheels when he's lining up a shot.

Johnny was more or less abandoned by his parents, and adopted by Joe (Chazz Palminteri), a manager of young pool talent. Joe likes taking his cut from the kid's earnings, and Johnny grows up before he discovers that Joe destroyed his invitation to join the pros. That leads to a scene in which Joe breaks the kid's hand, but not his thumb, and then seeks more revenge by taking a new protégé named Brad (Rick Schroder) under his management. Joe also involves Johnny's kid brother Danny (Michael Rosenbaum) in big trouble.

Johnny has a girlfriend named Tara (Alison Eastwood), who's in law school and doesn't approve of pool hustling, so Johnny gets a job as a construction carpenter, but the nails do not have eyes. Johnny and Tara are invited to a party at the home of a rich lawyer, where they meet her uncle Mike (Walken), one of the few actors in movie history who always draws a quiet rustle of pleasure from the audience the first time he appears on the screen.

And so on. The plot you are already generally familiar with. There will be high-stakes games of pool with lives and fortunes, etc., hanging in the balance. That goes with the territory. *Poolhall Junkies* is a pleasure not because it rivets us with unbearable poolhall suspense, but because it finds a voluptuous enjoyment in the act of moviemaking. You get the sense that "Mars" Callahan, whom I have never met, woke during the night to hug himself that he was getting to make this movie.

Poolhall Junkies has big moments of inspiration, like the Walken speech and a couple of other monologues. It has movie-fan moments, as when Rod Steiger, as the manager of a poolhall, gets to stick out his lower jaw and lay it on the line (this was Steiger's final role). It has Callahan as a serious kid with chiseled dark Irish features, who is cool like McQueen was cool—no big thing, just born that way.

And then it has, well, this corny stuff that Callahan kept in the screenplay because he's no doubt the kind of guy who doesn't like to walk into a bar without a joke to tell. There's a lawyer joke ("What do you call it when you have 10,000 lawyers buried up to their necks in the sand?"). And the oldest trick bet in the book ("I'll bet you I can tell you where you got your shoes"). And a barroom hustle recycled directly out of

Steve Buscemi's *Trees Lounge* ("I'll bet I can drink both of these pints faster than you can drink both of those shots"). I mean, come on.

These little hustles set up bigger ones that are also the oldest gags in the book, but the movie delivers on them and has fun while it's doing it. Callahan plays the character of Johnny Doyle not to convince you he's the meanest mother in the city, but simply to demonstrate that it would not be wise to bet large sums of money against him in the game of pool. There is an innocence at work here that reminds me of young Sylvester Stallone, who gave Rocky Balboa pet turtles named Cuff and Link.

Is this a great movie? Not at all. Is it more or less consistently entertaining? Yes. Do Walken and Palminteri do things casually that most actors could not do at all? Yes. Did I feel afterward as if I had been dragged through the blood and grime of the mean streets? No, but I felt like I had a good time at the movies.

Postmen in the Mountains ★ ★ ★
NO MPAA RATING, 90 m., 2004

Teng Rujun (Father), Liu Ye (Son), Gong Yehong (Grandmother), Chen Hao (Dong Girl). Directed by Huo Jianqi and produced by Kang Jianmin and Han Sanping. Screenplay by Si Wu, based on a short story by Peng Jianming.

The father prepares the postbag the night before, arranging the mail in the order it will be needed, and wrapping everything carefully against the possibility of bad weather. This will be the last time he packs the bag, and the first time the route will be carried by his son—who is inheriting his job.

The next morning unfolds awkwardly. The boy's mother is worried: Will he find the way? Will he be safe? The father (Teng Rujun) is unhappy to end the job that has defined his life. But his son (Liu Ye) will be accompanied by the family dog, who has always walked along with the father and knows the path. It is a long route, 112 kilometers through a mountainous rural region of China, and the trip will take three days. The son shoulders the bag and sets off, and then there is a problem: The dog will not come along. It looks uncertainly at the father. It runs between them. It is not right that

the son and the bag are leaving, and the father is staying behind.

This is the excuse the father is looking for to walk the route one last time and show his son the way. The two men and the dog set off together in Huo Jianqi's *Postmen in the Mountains*, a film so simple and straightforward that its buried emotions catch us a little by surprise.

The trek represents the longest time father and son have ever spent together; the boy was raised by his mother while his father was away, first for long periods, then for three days at a time. They've never even had much of a talk. Now the son observes that his father, who seemed so distant, has many friendships and relationships along the way—that he plays an important role as a conduit to the outside world, a bringer of good news and bad, a traveler in gossip, a counselor, adviser, and friend.

The villages and isolated dwellings are located in a region that must have been chosen for its astonishing beauty. Here are no factories, freeways, or fast food to mar the view, and the architecture has the beauty that often results when poverty and necessity dictate the function, and centuries evolve the form. The dog seems proud to show these things to his new young master.

There are several vignettes, as the postman brings personal news between villages, and in one case continues a long-running deception he has practiced on a blind woman. Her son in the city sends money, but does not write; the postman invents a letter to go with every delivery, "reading" to her out of his imagination. Now that will become part of the son's job.

They receive food and shelter along the way. One night they build a campfire under the stars. They don't share deep, philosophical truths, but simple facts about the job, which gradually become the father's explanation to his son about the life he has led, about his satisfactions and regrets. It is too bad he was never at home very much—but now his son will find out for himself that carrying the mail is an important job and must be taken seriously.

And that's about it. The movie consists of the journey, the conversations, the scenery, the little human stories. No big drama. No emergencies. Just carrying the mail, which over the years has supplied the threads to bind together all of these lives. When the son sets out alone on his next journey, the dog cheerfully goes along.

how the girl's parents in both movies seem to have been assembled from the same kit.

Primer ★ ★ ★ ½
PG-13, 78 m., 2004

Shane Carruth (Aaron), David Sullivan (Abe), Casey Gooden (Robert), Anand Upadhyaya (Phillip), Carrie Crawford (Kara). Directed and produced by Shane Carruth. Screenplay by Carruth.

Shane Carruth's *Primer* opens with four tech-heads addressing envelopes to possible investors; they seek venture capital for a machine they're building in the garage. They're not entirely sure what the machine does, although it certainly does something. Their dialogue is halfway between shop talk and one of those articles in *Wired* magazine that you never finish. We don't understand most of what they're saying, and neither, perhaps, do they, but we get the drift. Challenging us to listen closely, to half-understand what they half-understand, is one of the ways the film sucks us in.

They steal a catalytic converter for its platinum, and plunder a refrigerator for its xenon. Their budget is so small, they could cash the checks on the bus. Aaron and Abe, agreeing that whatever they've invented, they're the ones who invented it, subtly eliminate the other two from the enterprise. They then regard something that looks like an insulated shipping container with wires and dials and coils and stuff. This is odd: It secretes protein. More protein than it has time to secrete. Measuring the protein's rate of growth, they determine that one minute in the garage is equal to 1,347 minutes in the machine.

Is time in the machine different from time outside the machine? Apparently. But that would make it some kind of time machine, wouldn't it? Hard to believe. Aaron (Shane Carruth) and Abe (David Sullivan) ponder the machine and look at their results, and Aaron concludes it is "the most important thing any living being has ever witnessed." But what is it?

There's a fascination in the way they talk with each other, quickly, softly, excitedly. It's better, actually, that we don't understand everything they say, because that makes us feel more like eavesdroppers and less like the passive audience for predigested dialogue. We can see where they're heading, especially after . . . well, I don't want to give away some of the plot, and I may not understand the rest, but it would appear that they can travel through time. They learn this by seeing their doubles before they have even tried time travel—proof that later they will travel back to now. Meanwhile (is that the word?) a larger model of the machine is/was assembled in a storage locker by them/their doubles.

Should they personally experiment with time travel? Yes, manifestly, because they already have. "I can think of no way in which this thing would be considered even remotely close to safe," one of them says. But they try it out, journeying into the recent past and buying some mutual funds they know will rise in value.

It seems to work. The side effect, however, is that occasionally there are two of them: the Abe or Aaron who originally lived through the time, and the one who has gone back to the time and is living through it simultaneously. One is a double. Which one? There is a shot where they watch "themselves" from a distance, and we assume those they're watching are themselves living in ordinary time, and they are themselves having traveled back to observe them. But which Abe or Aaron is the real one? If they met, how would they speak? If two sets of the same atoms exist in the same universe at the same time, where did the additional atoms come from? It can make you hungry, thinking about questions like that. "I haven't eaten since later this afternoon," one complains.

Primer is a puzzle film that will leave you wondering about paradoxes, loopholes, loose ends, events without explanation, chronologies that don't seem to fit. Abe and Aaron wonder, too, and what seems at first like a perfectly straightforward method for using the machine turns out to be alarmingly complicated; various generations of themselves and their actions prove impossible to keep straight. Carruth handles the problems in an admirably understated way; when one of the characters begins to bleed a little from an ear, what does that mean? Will he be injured in a past he has not yet visited? In that case, is he the double? What happened to the being who arrived at this moment the old-fashioned way, before having traveled back?

The movie delights me with its cocky confidence that the audience can keep up. *Primer* is a film for nerds, geeks, brainiacs, academic decathlon winners, programmers, philosophers, and the kinds of people who have made it this far into the review. It will surely be hated by those who "go to the movies to be entertained," and embraced and debated by others, who will find it entertains the parts the others do not reach. It is maddening, fascinating, and completely successful.

Note: Carruth wrote, directed, and edited the movie, composed the score, and starred in it. The budget was reportedly around $7,000, but that was enough: The movie never looks cheap, because every shot looks as it must look. In a New York Times *interview, Carruth said he filmed largely in his own garage, and at times he was no more sure what he was creating than his characters were.* Primer *won the award for best drama at Sundance 2004.*

The Prince & Me ★ ★ ½
PG, 111 m., 2004

Julia Stiles (Paige Morgan), Luke Mably (Prince Edvard), Ben Miller (Soren), James Fox (King Haraald), Miranda Richardson (Queen Rosalind), Eliza Bennett (Princess Anabella), Alberta Watson (Amy Morgan), John Bourgeouis (Ben Morgan). Directed by Martha Coolidge and produced by Mark Amin. Screenplay by Jack Amiel, Michael Begler, and Katherine Fugate.

The Prince & Me recycles a story so old that it must satisfy some basic yearning in the human psyche—or at least that portion of the psyche installed in teenage girls. It is, as you have probably guessed, about a romance between a prince and a commoner—in this case, between the future king of Denmark and a Wisconsin farm girl. He enrolls in a Wisconsin university, they fall into hate and then into love, but when she follows him back to Denmark she has to ask herself if she really wants to be the future queen.

If the story felt more than usually familiar, maybe it's because I saw *Win a Date with Tad Hamilton!* In that version, a small-town girl won a date with a big Hollywood star, flew to Los Angeles, and in her simplicity and sincerity inspired the star to fall in love. But was she really cut out to be a movie star's wife? In both cases, the movies start by establishing the men as targets of paparazzi because of their steamy romantic lives; in both cases, the men are won over by the freshness of a woman unlike any they have ever dated.

The Prince & Me is an efficient, sweet, sometimes charming PG-rated version of the story, ideal for girls of a certain age but perhaps not for everybody else. It stars Julia Stiles as Paige Morgan, a serious, focused student of biochemistry, who was raised on an organic dairy farm and is famous as "the last unengaged girl in town." Stiles is gifted at conveying intelligence, which is a mixed blessing here; any smarter, and she'd realize she was in a movie.

Luke Mably plays Prince Edvard of Denmark, a.k.a. "Eddie," who flies to Wisconsin to escape the paparazzi and also because he saw a video in which Wisconsin college girls flash their boobs for the camera, and he assumes this is typical behavior in Wisconsin. This is such a stupid motivation for the prince's trip that it throws the character a little out of balance; it takes him several scenes in Wisconsin to reestablish himself as a person of normal intelligence.

Eddie arrives incognito with his valet Soren (Ben Miller) in tow, but because his parents have cut off his allowance he's short on funds and has to take a job in the campus cafeteria where Paige works. They clash almost at once, and find a temporary truce when she can help him with chemistry and he can help her with Shakespeare (he knows a lot about princes of Denmark). This stretch of the film is fun because it's based on tension; not so much fun is the formulaic part where she discovers his true identity, is angry at the deception, he returns to his father's sickbed, she follows him to Denmark, he proposes marriage, and so forth.

The movie does struggle to make something interesting of the royal family. The king (Edward Fox) and queen (Miranda Richardson) are played by fine actors who bring dimension and conviction to their roles; they are not simply marching through clichés. The queen's initial disapproval of Paige and her gradual acceptance are well handled. But the plot jerks Paige and Eddie back and forth romantically so many times we lose patience with it; we know, because the story is so familiar, that she must accept his proposal, then have second thoughts, then . . . well, you know.

As pure escapism, there are some sublime moments. I like the one where the queen takes Paige into the royal vault to show her the crown jewels, and ask her to pick out something to wear to the coronation ball. As Paige's eyes sweep the glittering shelves, there is a certain intake of breath among some of the women in the audience, and I was reminded of a similar moment in *The Greek Tycoon* when Aristotle Onassis outlines their marriage contract to Jackie Kennedy, and adds, "plus a million dollars a month walking-around money."

So there's good stuff here, and the stars are likable, but the director, Martha Coolidge, throws so many logical roadblocks in our path that we keep getting distracted from the story. When Paige arrives unannounced in Denmark and stands in the crowd at a royal parade, Eddie sees her and sweeps her up on his horse as the Danes shout, "Paige! It's Paige!" That's because they know her from photos the paparazzi took in Wisconsin. Okay, but how about later, when Eddie is giving his first speech as king, and Paige walks through the middle of the crowd and *no one* notices her, just because at that point the plot doesn't want them to? Despite the fact that she's now infinitely more famous in Denmark as the girl who accepted Eddie's proposal and then rejected it?

Quibble, quibble. The movie's target audience won't care. Others will. *The Prince & Me* has the materials to be a heartwarming mass-market love story, but it doesn't assemble them convincingly. *Win a Date with Tad Hamilton!* is less obviously blessed, but works better. Strange,

The Princess Diaries 2: Royal Engagement ★ ½

G, 120 m., 2004

Julie Andrews (Clarisse Renaldi), Anne Hathaway (Mia Thermopolis), Hector Elizondo (Joe), Heather Matarazzo (Lilly Moscovitz), Chris Pine (Sir Nicholas). Kathleen Marshall (Charlotte), John Rhys-Davies (Viscount Mabrey), Callum Blue (Andrew Jacoby). Directed by Garry Marshall and produced by Debra Martin Chase, Whitney Houston, and Mario Iscovich. Screenplay by Shonda Rhimes.

The Princess Diaries 2: Royal Engagement offers the prudent critic with a choice. He can say what he really thinks about the movie, or he can play it safe by writing that it's sure to be loved by lots of young girls. But I avoid saying that anything is sure to be loved by anybody.

In this case, I am not a young girl, nor have I ever been, and so how would I know if one would like it? Of course, that's exactly the objection I get in e-mails from young readers, who complain that no one like me can possibly like a movie like this. They are correct. I have spent a long time, starting at birth and continuing until this very moment, evolving into the kind of person who could not possibly like a movie like this, and I like to think the effort was not in vain.

So to girls who think they might like this movie, I say: Enjoy! Movies are for fun, among other things, and if you love *The Princess Diaries 2*, then I am happy for you, because I value the movies too much to want anyone to have a bad time at one.

But to Garry Marshall, the often-talented director of the original *Princess Diaries* as well as this sequel, I say: Did you deliberately assemble this movie from off-the-shelf parts, or did it just happen that way? The film is like an homage to the clichés and obligatory stereotypes of its genre. For someone like Marshall, it must have been like playing the scales.

The beautiful Anne Hathaway, still only twenty-two, stars as Princess Mia. You will remember that she was a typical American teenager whose mother raised her in a converted San Francisco firehouse, where she could slide down the pole every morning. Then a visit from Queen Clarisse of Genovia (Julie Andrews) revealed that she was, in fact, the queen's granddaughter and next in line to the throne.

In *Part 2*, she is the beloved Princess Mia of Genovia, a kingdom the size of a movie set, which is apparently located somewhere in Europe and populated by citizens who speak American English, except for a few snaky types with British accents. This kingdom has two peculiarities: (1) The shops and homes all seem to be three-quarter-scale models of the sorts of structures an American Girl doll would occupy; and (2) a great many of the extras get a few extra frames, in order to look uncannily as if they might be personal friends of the director. So many prosperous men in their sixties, so well barbered, groomed, and dressed, so southern California in their very bearing, are unlikely to be visiting Genovia for any other reason, since the kingdom doesn't seem to have a golf course.

There's no need for me to spoil the plot; as I was saying about *The Village*, it spoils itself. If I were to describe the characters, you could instantly tell me what happens in the movie. Let's try that, as an experiment.

There is Princess Mia, who is given a deadline of one month to either marry or forfeit her rights to the throne. The evil Viscount Mabrey (John Rhys-Davies) wants to disqualify her because his nephew, Sir Nicholas (Chris Pine), is next in line to the throne. Desperate for a husband, and learning that Queen Clarisse was perfectly happy in an arranged marriage, Mia decides to marry for the love of her country.

A suitable bachelor is discovered: nice Andrew Jacoby, duke of Kensington (Callum Blue). Mia accepts his proposal, despite, as she writes in her diary on the Web site, "He's everything a girl should want in a husband-to-be. It's . . . just that . . . something . . . you know." Meanwhile, of course, she hates the handsome young Sir Nicholas, who hangs around a lot and annoys her. Dear Diary: "Just look at him . . . all sneaky and smug and . . . and . . . cute."

Okay now, given those clues, see if you can figure out who she ends up with. And for that matter, consider Joseph (Hector Elizondo), the chief of palace security. He has been in love with the widow Clarisse for years, and she knows it, and is pleased. That provides us with a romance without closure that has persisted ever since the first movie, and if there is anything nature abhors more than a vacuum, it is a loving couple kept asunder when they should be sundering.

Director Marshall puts his cast and plot through their paces with the speed and delib-

eration of Minnesota Fats clearing the table. He even provides a fountain for two characters to stand beside, so they can illustrate Gene Siskel's maxim that nobody in a comedy ever comes within ten yards of water without falling in.

Yes, it's nice to see Julie Andrews looking great and performing a song, although the line "Give the queen a shout-out, and she'll sing" is one I doubt will ever be heard in Buckingham Palace. It is also rather original that at her slumber party, Mia and her friends don't get wasted at a private club, but engage in the jolly indoor sport of mattress surfing. ☞

P.S. ★ ★ ★
R, 97 m., 2004

Laura Linney (Louise Harrington), Topher Grace (F. Scott Feinstadt), Gabriel Byrne (Peter Harrington), Paul Rudd (Sammy), Marcia Gay Harden (Missy Goldberg), Lois Smith (Louise's Mother), Jennifer Carta (Sarah), Ross A. McIntyre (Jimmy). Directed by Dylan Kidd and produced by Anne Chaisson, John Hart, Robert Kessel, and Jeff Sharp. Screenplay by Kidd, based on the novel by Helen Schulman.

P.S. is the second movie in 2004 to use reincarnation as the excuse for transgressive sex. The earlier film was *Birth*, in which a woman in her mid-thirties becomes convinced that her dead husband has been reincarnated as a ten-year-old boy. Now comes *P.S.*, in which a woman in her late thirties is struck by the uncanny resemblance, in name and appearance, between a twenty-year-old student and the boy she loved when she was that age. The age gap makes both relationships problematic; *P.S.* involves sex, while *Birth* prudently sidesteps it.

Both films are fascinating because they require us to see the younger character through two sets of eyes—our own, which witness an attractive woman drawn to a younger male, and the women's, which see a lost love in a new container. *Birth* considers the possibility that actual reincarnation is involved, while *P.S.* is willing to consider the possibility of an amazing coincidence. In *Birth*, it is the little boy who insists he is the dead husband, and tries to prove it; in *P.S.*, the woman is struck by the uncanny similarity between a student and the young man she once loved, and tries to prove it—to him, and to a friend her own age who once loved him too. That both her dead boyfriend and the young student are named F. Scott Feinstadt seems too good to be true. Even, indeed, if only one were named F. Scott Feinstadt, it would be a reach.

Watching these movies, we are fascinated by the disconnect between romance and reality. If the ten-year-old boy in *Birth* really is the dead husband, what then? The older woman (Nicole Kidman) actually suggests at one point that they wait until he comes of age, and then, well, what? It might have been wiser for her to say: "It's been ten years since you died. Life goes on. You should grow up and find a girl your age. Look at it this way: You're the first person in history who gets his wish to be ten again, knowing what you know now."

As for *P.S.* and the new F. Scott (Topher Grace), there's little doubt in the mind of Louise Harrington (Laura Linney) about what she should do, which is to take him home in the middle of the afternoon so they can have safe sex immediately. That she is a Columbia University admissions officer and he is a student applying for admission creates an ethical conflict, but should ethics stand in the way of earth-shaking metaphysical lust? We would all agree that ethics certainly should not, although of course if a thirty-nine-year-old male admissions officer were to sleep with a twenty-year-old female applicant, castration would be too good for the fiend.

These logical considerations are not much discussed in *P.S.*, although one of the best things about *Birth* is that the woman's family think she's crazy and her mother threatens to call the cops. In *P.S.*, reincarnation is not insisted on, and while Louise sleeps with F. Scott because she wants to relive her treasured memories of first love, F. Scott sleeps with Louise because he can. Both genders are programmed by eons of Darwinian genetic strategy, and so we believe them, and because Linney and Grace are sexy and play well together, the age gap is not a barrier so much as additional seasoning.

In *Birth*, it must be admitted, the ten-year-old doesn't bring much to the party. He stands there like a little scold, insisting on his identity and completely failing to see the humor in his predicament. F. Scott, on the other hand, is a wiseass who treats Louise with an informality bordering on rudeness; she likes this, because it reminds her of the other F. Scott, and because it means she is being treated more like an equal than like an older authority figure. Louise has been saving up for a long time for the opportunity to get medieval on some guy. Like the fortyish Kim Basinger character in *Door in the Floor,* who has a wild fling with a sixteen-year-old boy (who resembles her dead son, of course), she brings great appetites to the task.

Louise comes supplied with an ex-husband, a brother, and a best friend who complicate matters. The ex-husband, inevitably named Peter (Gabriel Byrne), has decided he is a sex addict, and is twelve-stepping his way to restraint at just that moment when Louise casts it to the winds. Her brother Sammy (Paul Rudd) is a recovering addict with a fund of handy mantras. Her friend Missy Goldberg (Marcia Gay Harden) flies in from the coast to get a good look at F. Scott, and invites him to her hotel suite to get a better look. There is some question whether it was Louise or Missy who loved the original F. Scott first, or last, or best.

The plot mechanisms of these movies are at the service of justifying scenes that would otherwise be impossible, improbable, or criminal. The achievement of *Birth* is to take an entirely unacceptable situation (older woman, child) and make it dramatically possible by inhabiting the young body, so it would seem, with an older man. *P.S.* uses the stunning power of the boy's uncanny resemblance to the lost love, and *Door in the Floor* uses the grief of the mourning mother, who is reminded of her dead son by this teenage boy, although that doesn't exactly explain why she sleeps with him.

Watching these movies negotiate the hazards of their plots is part of the fun. Watching good actresses at the top of their form is another. Because these are not European films like Louis Malle's *Murmur of the Heart* or Agnes Varda's *Kung Fu Master,* they depend on plot more than emotion to motivate their forbidden behavior, but they seem to be taking chances even when they aren't really, and besides, stories like this are gold mines of terrific reaction shots.

The Punisher ★ ★
R, 124 m., 2004

Thomas Jane (Frank Castle [Punisher]), John Travolta (Howard Saint), Will Patton (Quentin Glass), Laura Harring (Livia Saint), Rebecca Romijn-Stamos (Joan), Samantha Mathis (Maria Castle), John Pinette (Mr. Bumpo), Ben Foster (Spacker Dave), Marcus Johns (Will Castle), Roy Scheider (Mr. Castle). Directed by Jonathan Hensleigh and produced by Avi Arad and Gale Anne Hurd. Screenplay by Michael France and Hensleigh, based on the comic book by Gerry Conway, Garth Ennis, Johnny Romita, and Michael Tolkin.

The Punisher is a long, dark slog through grim revenge. Unlike most movies based on comic book heroes, it doesn't contain the glimmer of a smile, and its hero is a depressed alcoholic—as well he might be, since his entire family, including wife, child, father, and even distant cousins have been massacred before his eyes. As he seeks vengeance, he makes the Charles Bronson character in *Death Wish* look relatively cheerful and well adjusted.

I wonder if the filmmakers understand quite how downbeat and dark their movie is? It opens with an FBI sting that leads to the death of a mobster's son. The operation, we learn, was the last assignment before retirement for agent Frank Castle (Thomas Jane). The criminal, a wealthy, high-profile money launderer named Mr. Saint (John Travolta), orders Castle's death, and then his wife, Livia (Laura Harring), adds, "His family. His whole family."

This sets up a sequence from which the movie hardly recovers. Castle has a romantic walk on the beach with his wife, Maria (Samantha Mathis), a hug with his child, and sentimental moments as his father (Roy Scheider) speaks at a family reunion. Then Saint's gunmen mow down the entire family in a series of gruesome vignettes, not neglecting to linger on the death of wife and child after their pitiful attempt to flee.

Castle kills a few of the attackers, but is cornered on a pier, shot repeatedly, doused with gasoline, blown up, and lands in the water. This establishes a pattern for the movie: No one is killed only once. (Later in the film, a target is shot, chained to the back of a car and dragged into a car lot where all of the cars explode.) Miraculously, Castle survives and is nursed back to health by one of those useful clichés, the black loner who lives by himself on an island and possesses the wisdom of the ages.

The rest of the movie involves his recovery, his preparations, and his methodical revenge against Mr. Saint and all of his people. Several colorful supporting characters are introduced, especially the three oddballs who live in the shabby rooming house Castle occupies. They are Joan (Rebecca Romijn-Stamos), a sexy but frightened woman with an abusive boyfriend; Mr. Bumpo (John Pinette), a tubby sissy, and Spacker Dave (Ben Foster), who is pierced in ways you don't even want to think about. We have all been indoctrinated in the notion that "we are family!" and these three attempt to include Castle in their circle despite his need to isolate, drink, kill, and brood. There is something a little odd when he's invited over for ice cream and cake.

The movie is relentless in its violence. There is a scene where Spacker Dave is tortured by having his piercings removed with pliers; the scene breaks the fabric of the film and moves into a different and macabre arena. *The Punisher* opened on the same weekend as another movie about a gruesome massacre and an elaborate revenge, *Kill Bill: Vol. 2*, but they are as different as night and day; *Kill Bill* vibrates with humor, irony, over-the-top exaggeration, and the joy of filmmaking. *The Punisher* is so grim and cheerless you wonder if even its hero gets any satisfaction from his accomplishments.

That said, I have to note that the film, directed by Jonathan Hensleigh, is consistently well acted, and has some scenes of real power. That the Punisher is a drear and charmless character does not mean that Thomas Jane doesn't play him well: He goes all the way with the film's dark vision, and is effective in the action scenes. John Travolta, as Mr. Saint, finds a truth you would not think was available in melodrama of this sort; his grief over his son and possessive jealousy over his wife are compelling.

The film doesn't simply set up Saint as a bad guy and a target, but devotes attention to the character, and develops an intriguing relationship between Saint and his right-hand man Quentin Glass (the always effective Will Patton). The Punisher is able to use Saint's jealousy to drive a wedge between the two men, but here's the strange thing: What happens between Saint and Glass is convincing, but what the Punisher does to sabotage their relationship is baffling and ludicrous, involving false fire hydrants and the improbable detail that Saint would allow his wife to go to the movies alone after he knows the Punisher is alive and at war.

Right down the line, the performances are strong. Even the three misfits in the run-down rooming house are given the dimension and screen time to become interesting. The screenplay, by Michael France and Jonathan Hensleigh, based on the Marvel comic, doesn't simply foreground the Punisher and make everyone else into one-dimensional cartoons. There's so much that's well done here that you sense a good movie slipping away. That movie would either be lighter than this one or commit to its seriousness, like *Scarface*. This one loses control of its mood and doesn't know what level of credibility it exists on. At the end, we feel battered down and depressed, emotions we probably don't seek from comic book heroes.

Q

The Quiet American ★ ★ ★ ★
R, 118 m., 2003

Michael Caine (Thomas Fowler), Brendan Fraser (Alden Pyle), Do Thi Hai Yen (Phuong), Rade Serbedzija (Inspector Vigot), Tzi Ma (Hinh), Robert Stanton (Joe Tunney), Holmes Osborne (Bill Granger), Quang Hai (The General), Ferdinand Hoang (Mr. Muoi). Directed by Phillip Noyce and produced by Staffan Ahrenberg and William Horberg. Screenplay by Christopher Hampton and Robert Schenkkan, based on the novel by Graham Greene.

The Englishman is sad and lonely. He suffers from the indignity of growing too old for romance while not yet free of yearning. He is in love for one last time. He doesn't even fully understand it is love until he is about to lose it. He is a newspaper correspondent in Saigon, and she is a dance-hall girl thirty or forty years younger. She loves him because he pays her to. This arrangement suits them both. He tells himself he is "helping" her. Well, he is, and she is helping him.

His name is Fowler, and he is played by Michael Caine in a performance that seems to descend perfectly formed. There is no artifice in it, no unneeded energy, no tricks, no effort. It is there. Her name is Phuong (Do Thi Hai Yen), and like all beautiful women who reveal little of their true feelings, she makes it possible for him to project his own upon her. He loves her for what he can tell himself about her.

Between them steps Alden Pyle (Brendan Fraser), the quiet young American who has come to Vietnam, he believes, to save it. Eventually he also believes he will save Phuong. Young men, like old ones, find it easy to believe hired love is real, and so believe a girl like Phuong would prefer a young man to an old one, when all youth represents is more work.

Graham Greene's novel *The Quiet American* (1955) told the story of this triangle against the background of America's adventure in Vietnam in the early 1950s—when, he shows us, the CIA used pleasant, presentable agents like Pyle to pose as "aid workers" while arranging terrorist acts that would justify our intervention there.

The novel inspired a 1958 Hollywood version in which the director Joseph Mankiewicz turned the story on its head, making Fowler the bad guy and Pyle the hero. Did the CIA have a hand in funding this film? Stranger things have happened: The animated version of *Animal Farm* (1954) was paid for by a CIA front, and twisted Orwell's fable about totalitarianism both East and West into a simplistic anti-Communist cartoon.

Now comes another version of *The Quiet American,* this one directed by the Australian Phillip Noyce and truer to the Greene novel. It is a film with a political point of view, but often its characters lose sight of that in their fascination with each other and with the girl. A question every viewer will have to answer at the end is whether a final death is the result of moral conviction or romantic compulsion.

The film is narrated by Caine's character in that conversational voice weary with wisdom; we are reminded of the tired cynicism of the opening narration in the great film of Greene's *The Third Man.* Pyle has "a face with no history, no problems," Fowler tells us; his own face is a map of both. "I'm just a reporter," he says. "I offer no point of view, I take no action, I don't get involved." Indeed, he has scarcely filed a story in the past year for his paper, the *Times* of London; he is too absorbed in Phuong and opium.

The irony is that Pyle, whom he actually likes at first, jars him into action and involvement. What he finally cannot abide is the younger man's cheerful certainty that he is absolutely right: "Saving the country and saving a woman would be the same thing to a man like that."

As luck would have it, *The Quiet American* was planned for release in the autumn of 2001. It was shelved after 9/11, when Miramax president Harvey Weinstein decided, no doubt correctly, that the national mood was not ripe for a film pointing out that the United States is guilty of terrorist acts of its own. Caine appealed to Weinstein, who a year later allowed the film to be shown at the Toronto Film Festival, where it was well received by the public and critics.

It would be unfortunate if people went to

the movie, or stayed away, because of its political beliefs. There is no longer much controversy about the CIA's hand in stirring the Vietnam pot, and the movie is not an exposé but another of Greene's stories about a worn-down, morally exhausted man clinging to shreds of hope in a world whose cynicism has long since rendered him obsolete. Both men "love" Phuong, but for Pyle she is less crucial. Fowler, on the other hand, admits: "I know I'm not essential to Phuong, but if I were to lose her, for me that would be the beginning of death." What Phuong herself thinks is not the point with either man, since they are both convinced she wants them.

Fraser, who often stars as a walking cartoon (*Dudley Do-Right, George of the Jungle*), has shown in other pictures, like *Gods and Monsters,* that he is a gifted actor, and here he finds just the right balance between confidence and blindness: What he does is evil, but he is convinced it is good, and has a simple, sunny view that maddens an old hand like Fowler. The two characters work well together because there is an undercurrent of commonalty: They are both floating in the last currents of colonialism, in which life in Saigon can be very good, unless you get killed.

Phillip Noyce made two great pictures close together, this one and *Rabbit-Proof Fence.* He feels anger as he tells this story, but he conceals it, because the story as it stands is enough. Some viewers will not even intercept the political message. It was that way with Greene: The politics were in the very weave of the cloth, not worth talking about. Here, in a rare Western feature shot in Vietnam, with real locations and sets that look well-worn enough to be real, with wonderful performances, he suggests a worldview more mature and knowing than the simplistic pieties that provide the public face of foreign policy.

R

Racing Stripes ★ ★
PG, 101 m., 2005

Bruce Greenwood (Nolan Walsh), Hayden Panettiere (Channing Walsh), M. Emmet Walsh (Woodzie), Wendie Malick (Clara Dalrymple). And the voices of: Frankie Muniz (Stripes), Mandy Moore (Sandy), Michael Clarke Duncan (Clydesdale), Jeff Foxworthy (Reggie), Joshua Jackson (Trenton's Pride), Joe Pantoliano (Goose), Michael Rosenbaum (Ruffshodd), Steve Harvey (Buzz), David Spade (Scuzz), Snoop Dogg (Lightning), Fred Dalton Thompson (Sir Trenton), Dustin Hoffman (Tucker), Whoopi Goldberg (Franny). Directed by Frederik Du Chau and produced by Broderick Johnson, Andrew A. Kosove, Edward McDonnell, and Lloyd Phillips. Screenplay by David Schmidt.

Racing Stripes is a compromise between *National Velvet* and *Babe,* leading to the inescapable question: Why not see them instead of this? It tells the story of the young girl who has faith in a disregarded animal and rides it to victory in a derby, and it has the barnyard full of cute talking animals. There are kids who will like it, but then there are kids who are so happy to be at the movies that they like everything. Adults are going to find it a little heavy on barnyard humor.

The story: On a night journey, a circus truck breaks down, and when the caravan resumes its journey, a basket has been forgotten by the side of the road. It contains a baby zebra. Horse trainer Nolan Walsh (Bruce Greenwood) and his daughter, Channing (Hayden Panettiere), find the orphan. Nolan wants to trace its owners, but Channing, of course, falls in love with it and wants it for a pet. It wouldn't seem that hard to find the owners of a baby zebra in Kentucky, but Nolan agrees, and the baby is named Stripes.

The Walsh farm occupies high ground above a race track, which absorbs much of the attention of the farm's animals. Walsh himself was a trainer, we learn, until he fell into depression after his wife died in a riding accident. He has forbidden Channing to follow her lifelong dream of being a jockey, but are we all agreed it's only a matter of time until she rides Stripes to victory in the local derby?

The animals in the movie are all real animals, except for the animated flies (voices by Steve Harvey and David Spade). Computer effects are used, however, to synch their mouths with the dialogue—an effect that's a little creepy. Cartoon animals have a full range of facial expressions, but when real animals are given CGI lip movements there often seems to be a disconnect between the lips and the face.

The Walsh farm is that anachronism in these days of agribusiness, a diversified barnyard filled with examples of every farm animal that might show promise as a character. They're voiced by actors who are quickly identifiable (Dustin Hoffman as a short-tempered Shetland, Joe Pantoliano as a goose who seems to be hiding out from the mob, Whoopi Goldberg as a goat, and Mandy Moore as a mare who falls in love with Stripes, although the movie wisely avoids the question of what would happen should they decide to begin a family). Stripes is voiced by Frankie Muniz of *Agent Cody Banks* and the wonderful *My Dog Skip* (an infinitely better movie about a friendship between a kid and his pet).

The racetrack is run by a Cruella DeVille type named Clara Dalrymple (Wendie Malick), reminding us of how reliable Dalrymple is as a movie name for upper-crust snobs. Her own horse, Trenton's Pride (voiced by Joshua Jackson), is favored to win the derby, and she doesn't see any point in letting a zebra enter the race. In a way, she has logic on her side. It's a horse race. There aren't any gazelles or ostriches, either.

I will get the usual feedback from readers who took their children to see *Racing Stripes* and report that the whole family loved the movie. For them, I am happy. It is a desperate thing to be at a movie with children who are having a bad time. But when you think of the *Babe* pictures, and indeed, even an animated cartoon like *Home on the Range,* you realize *Stripes* is on autopilot with all of the usual elements: a heroine missing one parent, an animal missing both, an underdog (or underzebra), cute animals, the big race. This is the

kind of movie you might grab at the video store, but it's not worth the trip to the theater.
☞

Radio ★ ★ ★
PG, 109 m., 2003

Cuba Gooding Jr. (James "Radio" Kennedy), Ed Harris (Coach Harold Jones), Alfre Woodard (Principal Daniels), Debra Winger (Linda Jones), S. Epatha Merkerson (Maggie), Riley Smith (Johnny Clay), Sarah Drew (Mary Helen Jones), Chris Mulkey (Frank Clay). Directed by Michael Tollin and produced by Brian Robbins and Tollin. Screenplay by Mike Rich and Gary Smith.

I don't know the slightest thing about the true story that inspired *Radio,* and I don't really want to, because the movie has convinced me that it's pretty close to real life. I believe that because (1) the closing credits include footage of the real Radio Kennedy and Coach Jones, and (2) because the movie isn't hyped up with the usual contrivances. Here is a film about football that doesn't even depend for its climax on the Big Game.

There are scenes that in another movie might have seemed contrived—the way the local boosters's club gathers after every game in the downtown barbershop, for example, to get the coach's report and grill him. Isn't this the sort of thing that happens only in movie small towns? Just like there's always a diner filled with regulars who apparently sit there twenty-four hours a day waiting to act as the local Greek chorus?

Maybe, but by the end of *Radio* I was half-convinced that if I were to visit Anderson, South Carolina, on the night of a high school game, I could walk downtown and see the boosters right there through the barbershop window.

The movie is based on a *Sports Illustrated* story about the way a series of Anderson teams and coaches have adopted James "Radio" Kennedy, a mentally disabled local man, as a team mascot and cheerleader. He is much beloved, and we sense that his good heart and cheer needed only the right opportunity to give him this mission in life. The movie focuses in fictional form on Radio's first season with the team, and about the bond that forms between the youngish man (Cuba Gooding Jr.) and lean, no-nonsense Coach Harold Jones (Ed Harris).

Radio, when first seen, goes on his harmless daily rounds through the town, pushing a shopping cart filled with treasures and listening to a beloved portable radio. One day a few football players lock him in an equipment shed and throw footballs at it, frightening him, and after Jones rescues Radio he becomes committed to a project—an obsession, really—to involve Radio with the team.

Jones's wife, Linda (Debra Winger), of course has the obligatory scenes complaining that his mind is always on his work. His daughter, Mary Helen Jones (Sarah Drew), of course has the obligatory scenes in which she stays out too late and gives other signs of needing more of her father's attention. But here's an unexpected thing: Not much is made in the obligatory way of these subplots, because Jones is a nice guy and his family understands him and the daughter sort of solves her own problems.

There are villains of a sort. Johnny Clay (Riley Smith) is the star player who instinctively picks on Radio, maybe because his dad, Frank (Chris Mulkey), is also a bully (does it go without saying that Frank is the town banker, and a big cheese in the booster club?). Frank thinks Radio is a "distraction" to the team, but Radio is so beloved and Coach Jones such a big-hearted man that even the villains seem to be going through the motions just to be good sports and lend the film some drama.

Radio is such a sweet expression of the better side of human nature, indeed, that it's surprising to find it in theaters and not on one of the more innocuous cable channels. In Gooding and Harris it has top-line talent, and a screenplay by Mike Rich (who wrote *Finding Forrester*) and Gary Smith (who wrote the *SI* story). Director Michael Tollin (*Summer Catch,* unreviewed by me) tells his story as simply and directly as he can, with no fancy stuff, and what we get is just what we're promised: a story about a town that adopts a disadvantaged young man for its benefit and his own. Radio teaches the town, Jones says, by treating everyone the way we should all treat one another; the young man is incapable of meanness, spite, or dishonesty.

The role is tricky for an actor; Gooding wants to make Radio lovable without being grotesquely cute, and mostly he succeeds, although Gooding is by instinct an expansive actor (the kind of man you imagine underlines his signature), and maybe a calmer actor like Ice Cube would have been a good choice. It was enough for Gooding to make me like Radio; in a few scenes I think he wanted me to pet him. Ed Harris is well cast in a role like Coach Jones, because he brings along confident, masculine authority without even having to think about it. The other actors are pretty much pro forma; Alfre Woodard plays the sensible high school principal, S. Epatha Merkerson is convincing as Radio's loving mom, and Debra Winger is strong in a small role that makes me want to see her in a larger one.

Now if the movie's story sounds too good to be true, that's probably how you'll find it. There is no cynicism in *Radio*, no angle or edge. It's about what it's about, with an open, warm, and fond nature. Every once in a while human nature expresses itself in a way we can feel good about, and this is one of those times. For families, for those who find most movies too cynical, for those who want to feel good in a warm and uncomplicated way, *Radio* is a treasure. Others may find it too slow or sunny or innocent. You know who you are.

Raise Your Voice ★
PG, 103 m., 2004

Hilary Duff (Terri Fletcher), Rita Wilson (Frances Fletcher), David Keith (Simon Fletcher), Jason Ritter (Paul Fletcher), Oliver James (Jay), Rebecca De Mornay (Aunt Nina), John Corbett (Mr. Torvald), Lauren C. Mayhew (Robin), Dana Davis (Denise). Directed by Sean McNamara and produced by David Brookwell, A. J. Dix, McNamara, Anthony Rhulen, Sara Risher, and William Shively. Screenplay by Sam Schreiber.

Hilary Duff has a great smile, and she proves it by smiling pretty much all the way through *Raise Your Voice*, except when there's a death in the family, or her roommate Denise says something mean to her, or she sees her kind-of boyfriend Jay kissing Robin after he said he'd broken up with her, or when her dad says she can't go to music camp. The rest of the time she smiles and smiles, and I love gazing upon her smile, although a still photo would achieve the same effect and be a time-saver.

She smiles in *Raise Your Voice*, a carefully constructed movie that doesn't make her a contemporary teenager so much as surround her with them. She plays Terri Fletcher, a young music student, who after a personal tragedy wants to begin again by attending a three-week camp for gifted young musicians in Los Angeles. Her dad (David Keith) is against it: Terrible things can happen to a young woman in Los Angeles. Her mother (Rita Wilson) conspires with her artistic Aunt Nina (Rebecca De Mornay) to sneak her off to the camp while Dad thinks she's visiting Nina in Palm Desert. Aunt Nina is one of those artists who does alarming things up on stepladders with an acetylene torch.

All the kids are snobs at the camp, primarily so they can soften later. (If they soften right away, there goes the plot.) Terri's new roommate is Denise (Dana Davis), who plans to work hard for a scholarship, and resents Terri as a distraction. Sizing up Terri's wardrobe and her smile, Denise tells her: "You're like some kind of retro Brady Buncher." I hate it when a movie contains its own review. For that matter, earlier in the movie her brother tells her she's a "Stepford daughter," but he encourages her to go to the camp, direly predicting: "If you don't, you're going to end up doing *Cats* at the Y when you're forty."

Terri meets a nice kid named Jay (Oliver James), who has a British accent and is very encouraging and warm, and brings her out of herself and encourages her to sing with joy, and writes a song with her and says he doesn't date the bitchy Robin (Lauren C. Mayhew) anymore because she was "last summer." There is also an inspiring music teacher (John Corbett), who wants to find the best in her, and doesn't have to look very deep.

All of this plays out against the backdrop of Terri's deception of her dad, who is convinced she's in Palm Desert because Terri and Aunt Nina phone him on a conference call. Dad only wants the best for her, of course, but when he finds out about the deception, he declares, "I want her home, right now!"

Does that mean (a) she comes home, right now, or (b) her mom and Aunt Nina work on Dad, and, wouldn't you know, the auditorium door opens and Dad walks in just in time for his daughter to see him from the stage halfway through her big solo. The answer of course is

553

(b), right down to the obligatory moment when the disapproving parent in the audience nods at the gifted child onstage and does the heartfelt little nod that means, "You were right, honey." But her dad was right about one thing. Something terrible did happen to her in Los Angeles. She made this movie.

Raising Helen ★ ★

PG-13, 119 m., 2004

Kate Hudson (Helen Harris), John Corbett (Pastor Dan), Joan Cusack (Jenny), Hector Elizondo (Mickey Massey), Helen Mirren (Dominique), Hayden Panettiere (Audrey), Spencer Breslin (Henry), Abigail Breslin (Sarah), Sakina Jaffrey (Nilma Prasad), Felicity Huffman (Lindsay). Directed by Garry Marshall and produced by Ashok Amritraj and David Hoberman. Screenplay by Jack Amiel and Michael Begler.

Raising Helen is a perfectly pleasant comedy in which nice people do good things despite challenges that are difficult but not excessive. As a pilot for a TV sitcom it would probably be picked up, but it's not compelling enough to involve a trip to the movies. From beginning to end, we've been there, seen that.

Kate Hudson, who stars, seems to be following in the footsteps of her mother, Goldie Hawn; both have genuine talent, but choose too often to bury themselves in commercial formulas. Hudson plays Helen Harris, a high-powered Manhattan career woman who works as the personal assistant to the head (Helen Mirren) of a famous modeling agency. She works hard, is on call 24-7, and even when she parties she's talent-scouting. She has a sister named Jenny (Joan Cusack) who lives in the suburbs and raises her children as a disciplined time-and-motion study. Jenny's house, Helen observes, looks like a showroom at Pottery Barn.

Tragedy strikes. Their sister Lindsay (Felicity Huffman) and her husband are killed in an accident, and in her will Lindsay leaves custody of her small son and daughter not to Jenny the perfect homemaker, but to Helen the fast-track girl. How can this be? Helen and Jenny are both appalled, but Helen takes on the task of raising

little Henry and Sarah, played by real-life siblings Spencer and Abigail Breslin.

If Helen has any notions that she can be a mom and keep her agency job, she's disabused by Mirren, who expects total dedication. Soon Helen has lost her job, moved her little family to a lower-middle-class neighborhood in Queens, and enrolled the kids in a nearby Lutheran school run by Pastor Dan (John Corbett), who is single and therefore preordained to fall in love with Helen, although not before many plot-laden details have been worked through. She gets a job in a car dealership run by the unfailingly dynamic Hector Elizondo.

The movie, directed by Garry Marshall (*Pretty Woman*), is not unaware of the lifestyle differences between single Manhattan career women and receptionists in Queens. Not even after Helen unloads an eyesore green Lincoln and is promoted to sales does she have the money, or the skills, to make things work—even though she learns fast. But she's let off fairly easily. The movie exists in the kind of economy where one working-class paycheck can just about support a family, and where city kids go to the wholesome parochial school down the street. Times are harder now, but the movie doesn't know it—can't afford to, if its sunny disposition is to prevail.

Most of Helen's lessons in survival come not from her sister, a forbiddingly humorless caricature, but from her across-the-hall Indian neighbor Nilma Prasad (Sakina Jaffrey), who, just like all neighbors in sitcoms, is willing to drop her own life at a moment's notice to play a supporting role in the heroine's; she channels Ethel Mertz.

The romance between Helen and Pastor Dan progresses with agonizing slowness, complicated by Helen's belief that Lutheran ministers cannot marry (her attempts to fake Lutheranism to get her kids into the school are amusing, but could have been subtler). Finally, Pastor Dan breaks the ice: "I'm a sexy man of God, and I know it." Then there are the scenes where the kids resent this man who seems about to replace their father, and the obligatory group visit to the zoo, scored with the obligatory use of Simon and Garfunkel's "At the Zoo."

Garry Marshall is a smart director with more of a comic edge than this movie allows him. I wonder if at any point he considered darkening the material even a little, and making Hudson's character a shade more desperate and less Lucy-like. There's nothing at risk in *Raising Helen*. We're not even surprised the kids go to Helen and not her sister, because the sister is written in a way that makes her impossible as a parental candidate.

Pastor Dan is the conveniently available, nearby eligible male, but somehow we doubt there are many ordained Lutheran bachelors in Queens; why not rotate the plot toward more complexity? Surely that nice Mrs. Prasad across the hall has a brother who is a widower with two children of his own? To obtain comedy, you don't give Helen problems and then supply a man who solves them; you supply a man who brings in additional problems. I can imagine this premise being passed through the imagination of a director like Gurinder Chadha *(Bend It Like Beckham, What's Cooking?)* and emerging fresh and exciting. *Raising Helen* is tame and timid from beginning to end, and relentlessly conventional. Because Helen takes no real risks, because she lives surrounded by the safeguards of formula fiction, the movie is fated from its first shot to be obedient to convention.

Raising Victor Vargas ★ ★ ★ ½
R, 88 m., 2003

Victor Rasuk (Victor Vargas), Judy Marte (Judy Ramirez), Melonie Diaz (Melonie), Altagracia Guzman (Grandma), Silvestre Rasuk (Nino Vargas), Krystal Rodriguez (Vicki Vargas), Kevin Rivera (Harold), Wilfree Vasquez (Carlos). Directed by Peter Sollett and produced by Sollett, Scott Macaulay, Robin O'Hara, and Alain de la Mata. Screenplay by Sollett.

Raising Victor Vargas tells the heartwarming story of first love that finds a balance between lust and idealism. Acted by fresh-faced newcomers who never step wrong, it sidesteps the clichés of teenage coming-of-age movies and expands into truth and human comedy. It's the kind of movie you know you can trust, and you give yourself over to affection for these characters who are so lovingly observed.

We meet the Vargas family, who live on the Lower East Side of New York. Grandma (Altagracia Guzman) came from the Dominican Republic. She is raising her three grandchildren: Victor (Victor Rasuk), Nino (Silvestre Rasuk), and Vicki (Krystal Rodriguez). Victor, who is about sixteen, fancies himself a ladies' man but is not as experienced as he seems. Nino looks up to him. Vicki, who is plump and seems to live on the sofa, is fed up with both boys—and Grandma lives in fear of the hazards that surround them.

In another movie those hazards might involve gangs, drugs, and guns. Not in *Raising Victor Vargas*, which eliminates the usual urban dangers and shows us a home where the values may be old-fashioned but have produced three basically good kids. It's refreshing to find a movie where a Latino family in a poor neighborhood is not portrayed with the usual tired conventions about poverty and crime, but is based on love and strong values. It's only natural that Nino reveals himself as a moderately talented pianist.

If Victor thinks constantly about dating and sex, what boy his age doesn't? As the film opens, he is interrupted during the conquest of Fat Donna, who lives upstairs. It would appear, however, that the interruption came just in time to qualify him still as a virgin. Fat Donna is apparently a neighborhood legend, and although he swears her to secrecy the gossip quickly spreads and his sister cheerfully informs him, "You'll always be known as Fat Donna's boy."

This causes him no small agony, because at the swimming pool he sees the girl of his dreams: Judy Ramirez (Judy Marte), who seems beautiful and elegant and forever inaccessible. The movie's romantic plot involves a complicated scheme in which he convinces Judy's younger brother to arrange an introduction in return for Victor's influence in helping the younger brother meet his sister, Vicki. Meanwhile, Victor's friend Harold falls for Judy's friend Melonie (Melonie Diaz), who seems to be a classic type—the plain girl who is the popular girl's best friend. But then, in a movie tradition that I continue to love, Melonie takes off her glasses and lets down her hair.

The movie is not simply about these three

inexperienced and uncertain pairs of lovers. If it were, it would be a typical teenage comedy. It is much deeper and more knowing than that, especially in the way it shows Grandma waging a losing battle to maintain her idea of the family's innocence. Although Victor is a good boy, Grandma imagines his life as a hotbed of sin, and the city as the devil's workshop. When Victor invites Judy to dinner it is a disaster because Grandma has not even suspected their friendship.

There is a delicate progress in the relationship of the two young lovers. Judy for a long time plays hard to get; she's determined to resist the relentless male lust all around her, and demands respect and attention from the boy who will win her heart. Victor is not strong in these qualities, but in a subtle and moving way he begins to learn about them, and the tentative progress of their love is a tender delight.

It is also touching that while Victor, Nino, and Vicki are exasperated by their grandmother's old world ways, they love her and need her. And the film is careful not to make Grandma into a caricature: What she does, she does from love, and when there is a crisis involving a social worker, which threatens the family, Victor finds a silent and tactful way to end it. The screenplay finds reconciliation in a touching story Grandma tells about her childhood.

I was in a discussion the other day about whether a movie can be erotic. Sexual, yes, and explicit, yes—but truly erotic? To achieve that, a film must abandon the details of sexual congress and focus instead on the personalities of its characters. When Victor and Judy finally kiss in this movie, it is a moment more real and joyous than miles of "sex scenes," because by then we know who they are, how they have traveled together to this moment, and what it means to them.

Raising Victor Vargas was written and directed by Peter Sollett. It grew from an award-winning short subject he made with the same actors, who are not experienced professionals but are fresh and true in a way that suggests they're the real thing, and will have fruitful careers.

Note: Like so many movies dealing intelligently with teenage sexuality, Raising Victor Vargas *has been rated R by the MPAA, which awards the PG-13 to comedies celebrating cheap vulgarity, but penalizes sincere expressions of true experience and real-life values.*

Rana's Wedding ★ ★ ★
NO MPAA RATING, 90 m., 2004

Clara Khoury (Rana), Khalifa Natour (Khalil), Ismael Dabbag (Ramzy), Walid Abed Elsalam (Marriage Official), Zuher Fahoum (Father), Bushra Karaman (Grandmother). Directed by Hany Abu-Assad and produced by Bero Beyer and George Ibrahim. Screenplay by Ihab Lamey and Liana Badr.

Rana's father is going to the airport at 4 P.M., and she can either get married or leave the country with him. He supplies her with a list of eligible bachelors who have asked for her hand in marriage. But she is in love with Khalil. Can she find him, ask him to marry her, find a registrar, get her hair done, gather the relatives, and get married—all before 4 o'clock?

This could be the description of a Hollywood romantic comedy. And indeed it is a romantic comedy of sorts, as romance and comedy survive in the midst of the conflict between Palestinians and Israelis. The movie takes place on both sides of the armed border separating Jerusalem and the Palestinian settlement of Ramallah, and although the comedy occupies the foreground, the background is dominated by checkpoints and armed soldiers, street funerals and little boys throwing rocks, bulldozers tearing down buildings and a general state of siege.

Rana (Clara Khoury) is a Palestinian who is seventeen; her lover, Khalil (Khalifa Natour), a theater director, seems to be around forty. Although her father has grave doubts about their marriage, they cite Islamic law that allows them to wed if they inform the father in the presence of a registrar. Her problem is to find her lover, find the registrar, find her father, and get them all together in the same place at the same time. This involves several trips back and forth through armed roadblocks that quietly make the point that Palestinians spend all day every day facing hostility and suspicion.

What's interesting is that the movie, made by the Netherlands-based Palestinian filmmaker Hany Abu-Assad, makes little overt point of its political content; the politics are the air that the characters breathe, but the story is about their short-term romantic goals. And those are made more complicated because Rana is not a simple woman. She changes her mind, she gets jealous, she risks missing the deadline in order to get her hair done, she sometimes seems older, sometimes like a child.

The premise is a little hard to accept: Has her father actually sent her a note on the morning when he is to leave the country, setting the 4 P.M. deadline? She seems very independent; is there any way she can stay behind? Could she have considered marriage days or weeks earlier, or has all of this come about at the last moment? And what, exactly, is her father's reasoning? Although we see him briefly, we have no real ideas about who he is and how he thinks.

It is also rather startling that Khalil is prepared to get married at a moment's notice. Rana finally tracks him down on the stage of a theater in the Palestinian sector, where he's asleep with some of his cast; the roadblocks make that easier than going home. She awakens him with the news that they are to get married this very day, and he takes it fairly well, I'd say. Enlisting a friend with a yellow VW beetle, he sets off with Rana on a mission to find the registrar (who is not at home, of course) and meet the deadline.

We have to accept this unlikely plot, I suppose, because there it is—a device to add suspense. More suspense comes because Rana sometimes seems in no hurry. But the strength of the movie comes in its observation of details, as when Rana sees small boys throwing rocks at a barricade, and Israeli soldiers firing back; this scene, and other border scenes, look like real life captured by the film, although I have no way of knowing if that's true. There's also a scene where Rana and Khalil stop for a quiet talk, and notice a security camera pointed at them, and when Rana forgets the plastic carryall with her possessions in it, and runs back to find she's too late: the police, thinking it might contain a bomb, have just blown it up with a remote-controlled cannon.

There are, of course, two sides to such an experience; if Palestinians use hidden explosives and suicide bombers, then the Israelis of course must try to prevent them. But the movie doesn't preach; it simply observes. This is how daily life is. The movie is passable as a story but fascinating as a document. It gives a more complete visual picture of the borders, the Palestinian settlements, and the streets of Jerusalem than we ever see on the news, and we understand that the Palestinians are not all suicide bombers living in tents, as the news sometimes seems to imply, but in many cases middle-class people like Rana and her circle, sharing the same abilities and aspirations as their neighbors. I think the point is to show how their conditions of life are like a water torture, breaking them down a drop at a time, reminding them that having lived in this place for a long time, they are nevertheless homeless.

Rare Birds ★ ★ ★
R, 104 m., 2003

William Hurt (Dave), Andy Jones (Phonse), Molly Parker (Alice). Directed by Sturla Gunnarsson and produced by Paul Pope and Janet York. Screenplay by Edward Riche, based on his novel.

People who live at the edge of the sea sometimes have a restless look in their eyes, as if they have gone as far as they can go, and it is not far enough. Consider Dave Purcell (William Hurt), who has opened a fine dining restaurant named The Auk on a rocky seaside outcrop of Newfoundland, far from large numbers of fine diners. He is a quiet, moody perfectionist, his food is splendid, his business is lousy, and he is going broke. There is also the matter of his addiction to drugs and alcohol, which he is struggling to overcome.

Dave's best friend is Phonse (Andy Jones), an optimistic codger who comes up with a scheme to help business: They'll report the sighting of a rare duck, the area will be swamped with bird-watchers, and even birders have to eat, no? This fraud works so well that Dave can no longer run The Auk as a one-man show, and hires a waitress. This is Alice (Molly Parker), and soon the two are in love. (There was once a Mrs. Purcell, whose love for Dave did not extend to joining him on the rocky Newfoundland outcrop, etc.)

Sturla Gunnarsson's *Rare Birds,* adapted by Edward Riche from his novel, is a sweetheart of a film, whimsical and touching. It positions itself somewhere between a slice of life and a screwball comedy. Hurt plays Dave tenderly, as an inward and unsocial man who apparently enjoys running his restaurant in complete privacy. His life is complicated enormously not only by the rush of business and the arrival of Alice, but also by Phonse's discovery of a large amount of cocaine floating in the bay. Can this be resold? Can Dave stay away from it?

There are, we should note, men skulking about who are obviously not bird fanciers. Dave might not notice them. Phonse does. He is obsessed with the possibilities of marketing a "recreational submarine," and thinks maybe they're industrial spies. Of course, they could also be narcs. This plot gets a little overheated by the end of the film; I could have done with less action and more whimsy, but Hurt stays true to his character and the film weaves a goofy spell.

The film was made in 2001 by Gunnarsson, whose previous work was the wonderful *Such a Long Journey,* inspired by the novel by Rohinton Mistry. *Rare Birds* was scheduled for its world premiere at the Toronto Film Festival on September 11, 2001. That premiere never happened, the public did not see the film, and its fate was forever changed; a few critics were able to attend a makeup screening in a little twenty-seat theater. It's now in limited theatrical release, and also available on tape and DVD. Best to see it in a theater; The Auk may be in an unlikely location, but it has a magnificent view.

Ray ★ ★ ★ ★
PG-13, 152 m., 2004

Jamie Foxx (Ray Charles), Kerry Washington (Della Bea Robinson), Clifton Powell (Jeff Brown), Harry Lennix (Joe Adams), Terrence Dashon Howard (Gossie McKee), Larenz Tate (Quincy Jones), Richard Schiff (Jerry Wexler), Aunjanue Ellis (Mary Ann Fisher), Bokeem Woodbine (Fathead Newman), Sharon Warren (Aretha Robinson), Curtis Armstrong (Ahmet Ertegun), Regina King (Margie Hendricks), Warwick Davis (Oberon). Directed by Taylor Hackford and produced by Howard Baldwin, Stuart Benjamin, and Hackford. Screenplay by James L. White.

Ray Charles became blind at age seven, two years after witnessing the drowning death of his little brother. In a memory that haunted his life, he stood nailed to the spot while the little boy drowned absurdly in a bath basin. Why didn't Ray act to save him? For the same reason all five-year-olds do dumb and strange things: Because they are newly in possession of the skills of life, and can be paralyzed by emotional overload. No one seeing the scene in *Ray,* Taylor Hackford's considerable new musical biography, would think to blame the boy, but he never forgives himself.

If he had already been blind, he could not have blamed himself for the death, and would not have carried the lifelong guilt that, the movie argues, contributed to his drug addiction. Would he also then have not been driven to become the consummate artist that he was? Who can say? For that matter, what role did blindness play in his genius? Did it make him so alive to sound that he became a better musician? Certainly he was so attuned to the world around him that he never used a cane or a dog; for Charles, blindness was more of an attribute than a handicap.

Jamie Foxx suggests the complexities of Ray Charles in a great, exuberant performance. He doesn't do the singing—that's all Ray Charles on the sound track—but what would be the point? Ray Charles was deeply involved in the project for years, until his death in June 2004, and the film had access to his recordings, so of course it should use them, because nobody else could sing like Ray Charles.

What Foxx gets just right is the physical Ray Charles, and what an extrovert he was. Not for Ray the hesitant blind man of cliché, feeling his way, afraid of the wrong step. In the movie and in life, he was adamantly present in body as well as spirit, filling a room, physically dominant, interlaced with other people. Yes, he was eccentric in his mannerisms, especially at the keyboard; I can imagine a performance in which Ray Charles would come across like a manic clown. But Foxx correctly interprets his body language as a kind of choreography, in which he was conducting his music with himself, instead of with a baton. Foxx so accurately reflects my own images and memories of Charles that I abandoned thoughts of how much "like" Charles he was, and just accepted him as Charles, and got on with the story.

The movie places Charles at the center of key movements in postwar music. After an early career in which he seemed to aspire to sound like Nat "King" Cole, he loosened up, found himself, and discovered a fusion between the gospel music of his childhood and the rhythm and blues of his teen years and his first professional gigs. The result was, essentially, the invention of soul music, in early songs like "I Got a Woman."

The movie shows him finding that sound in Seattle, his improbable destination after he leaves his native Georgia. Before and later, it returns for key scenes involving his mother, Aretha (Sharon Warren), who taught him not to be intimidated by his blindness, to dream big, to demand the best for himself. She had no education and little money, but insisted on the school for the blind, which set him on his way. He heads for Seattle after hearing about the club scene, but why there and not in New York, Kansas City, Chicago, or New Orleans? Certainly his meeting with the Seattle teenager Quincy Jones was one of the crucial events in his life (as was his friendship with the dwarf emcee Oberon, played by Warwick Davis, who turns him on to pot).

The movie follows Charles from his birth in 1930 until 1966, when he finally defeats his heroin addiction and his story grows happier but also perhaps less dramatic. By then he had helped invent soul, had moved into the mainstream with full orchestration, had moved out of the mainstream into the heresy of country music (then anathema to a black musician), and had, in 1961, by refusing to play a segregated concert in Georgia, driven a nail in the corpse of Jim Crow in the entertainment industry.

In an industry that exploits many performers, he took canny charge of his career, cold-bloodedly leaving his longtime supporters at Atlantic Records to sign with ABC Paramount and gain control of his catalog. (It's worth noting that the white Atlantic owners Ahmet Ertegun and Jerry Wexler are portrayed positively, in a genre that usually shows music execs as bloodsuckers.) Charles also fathered more children than the movie can tell you about, with more women than the movie has time for, and yet found the lifelong love and support of his wife, Della Bea Robinson (Kerry Washington).

The film is two and a half hours long—not too long for the richness of this story—but to cover the years between 1966 and his death in 2004 would have required more haste and superficial summary than Hackford and his writer, James L. White, are willing to settle for. When we leave him, Ray is safely on course for his glory years, although there is a brief scene set in 1979 where he receives an official apology from his home state of Georgia over the concert incident, and "Georgia on My Mind" is named as the state song.

Charles's addictions were to drugs and women. He beat only drugs, but Ray is perceptive and not unsympathetic in dealing with his roving ways. Of the women we meet, the most important is his wife, Della Bea, played by Washington as a paragon of insight, acceptance, and with a certain resignation; when one of his lovers dies, she asks him, "What about her baby?" "You knew?" says Charles. She knew everything.

His two key affairs are with Mary Ann Fisher (Aunjanue Ellis), a blues singer, and Margie Hendricks (Regina King), a member of his backup group, the Raelettes. Who knows what the reality was, but in the film we get the sense that Charles was honest, after his fashion, about his womanizing, and his women understood him, forgave him, accepted him, and were essential to him. Not that he was easy to get along with during the heroin years, and not that they were saints, but that, all in all, whatever it was, it worked. "On the road," says Margie, in a line that says more than it seems to, "I'm Mrs. Ray Charles."

The movie would be worth seeing simply for the sound of the music and the sight of Jamie Foxx performing it. That it looks deeper and gives us a sense of the man himself is what makes it special. Yes, there are moments when an incident in Ray's life instantly inspires a song (I doubt "What'd I Say?" translated quite so instantly from life to music). But Taylor Hackford brings quick sympathy to Charles as a performer and a man, and we remember that he directed Hail! Hail! Rock 'n' Roll, a great documentary about Chuck Berry, a performer whose onstage and offstage moves more than braced Hackford for this film. Ray Charles was quite a man; this movie not only knows it, but understands it.

The Reckoning ★ ★ ★
R, 112 m., 2004

Willem Dafoe (Martin), Paul Bettany (Nicholas), Gina McKee (Sarah), Brian Cox (Tobias), Ewen Bremner (Damian), Vincent Cassel (Lord de Guise), Simon McBurney (Stephen), Elvira Minguez (Martha). Directed by Paul McGuigan and produced by Caroline Wood. Screenplay by Mark Mills, based on the novel *Morality Play* by Barry Unsworth.

In England circa 1380, a troupe of traveling actors makes its way across the medieval landscape, where to go twenty miles from home was to enter a world of strangers. In London at about the same time, Geoffrey Chaucer was writing about another group on the road—pilgrims on their way to Canterbury. His Knight, learning from the journey, declared:

This world is but a thoroughfare full of woe,
And we be pilgrims, passing to and fro.
Death is an end to every worldly sore.

The actors arrive at much the same conclusion in *The Reckoning*, when they arrive at a village where a murder trial is under way. A mute woman (Elvira Minguez) has been charged with the death of a local boy, and been sentenced to death as a witch. The actors by their nature are more worldly and sophisticated than the village folk, and after questioning the woman through sign language, they begin to doubt her guilt.

It is at first no affair of theirs, however, and they unload their props and costumes from a lumbering covered wagon and stage the wheezer they've been touring with: a morality tale about Adam and Eve. That this is probably the first play ever seen by the locals does not give it the virtue of novelty; it is ever so much more entertaining to hang witches than to attend allegory. In desperation, the players decide to devise a play based on the murder case, and the more they discover, the more they doubt the woman's guilt. The village in fact is a hotbed of sin and suspicion, and only a con-

spiracy of fear has kept the lid on. The actors are stirring the pot.

Ah, but there's a twist. One of the troupe, Nicholas (Paul Bettany, the surgeon in *Master and Commander*), is not an actor at all, but a priest who was discovered at the wrong kind of devotions with a wife from his congregation—not the Wife of Bath, alas, or he might have gotten away with it. Fleeing for his life, he is taken on by the troupe, whose leader, Martin (Willem Dafoe), agrees to shelter him. Martin's sister Sarah (Gina McKee) is intrigued by Nicholas's aura of sensual guilt, but the veteran actor Tobias (Brian Cox) thinks they have enough mouths to feed without a freeloader. These tensions all play a role when the troupe begins to suspect a village scandal, and Lord Robert de Guise (Vincent Cassel) orders them to leave.

The Reckoning has been directed, perhaps incredibly, by Paul McGuigan, the Scots filmmaker whose previous work (*Gangster No. 1*) did not seem to point him in this direction. And yet the previous movie shows the same taste for dissecting the evil beneath the skin. Basing his film on the novel *Morality Play* by Barry Unsworth and a screenplay by Mark Mills, McGuigan shows a world in which characters project a rigid self-confidence which, when cracked, reveals venom.

The medieval world of the film has been convincingly re-created (it was photographed in Spain), and the ambience and plot suggest connections with three other medieval mystery films: *The Name of the Rose*, about a murder at a monastery, *The Return of Martin Guerre*, about a man who may be Martin or may have murdered him, and Bergman's *The Virgin Spring*, about a girl murdered by itinerant farmworkers. In those years, superstition and ignorance were the key elements in any criminal investigation.

The Reckoning has just a little too much of the whodunit and the thriller and not enough of the temper of its clash between cultures, but it works, maybe because the simplicity of the underlying plot is masked by the oddness of the characters. Willem Dafoe is invaluable in an enterprise like this, always seeming to speak from hard experience, giving mercy because he has needed it. Bettany plays the priest as a man left rudderless by his loss of status, and Cox plays the kind of malcontent who, on a modern movie location, would be angry about the quality of the catering. Given the vast scale of a quasi-medieval epic like *The Lord of the Rings*, it is refreshing to enter the rude poverty of the real Middle Ages, where both the peasant and his lord lived with death and disease all around, and trusted sorcery and superstition to see them through.

The Recruit ★ ★ ½
PG-13, 105 m., 2003

Al Pacino (Walter Burke), Colin Farrell (James Clayton), Bridget Moynahan (Layla Moore), Gabriel Macht (Zack). Directed by Roger Donaldson and produced by Roger Birnbaum, Jeff Apple, and Gary Barber. Screenplay by Roger Towne, Kurt Wimmer, and Mitch Glazer.

The Recruit reveals that the training process of the Central Intelligence Agency is like a fraternity initiation, but more dangerous. At one point would-be agents are given a time limit to walk into a singles bar and report back to the parking lot with a partner willing to have sex with them. Uh-huh. As for the Company's years of embarrassments and enemy spies within the ranks? "We reveal our failures but not our successes," the senior instructor tells the new recruits. Quick, can you think of any event in recent world history that bears the stamp of a CIA success?

The senior instructor is Walter Burke, played by Al Pacino in a performance that is just plain fun to watch, gruff, blunt, with a weathered charm. He recruits an MIT whiz kid named James Clayton (Colin Farrell), who turns down a big offer from Dell Computers because he wants to know more about the fate of his late father, a CIA agent. Or maybe because he uses a Macintosh.

Clayton is taken to The Farm, a rustic hideaway somewhere in Ontario, doubling for Virginia, where during the entrance exam he locks eyes with the lovely and fragrant Layla (Bridget Moynahan). He also meets Zack (Gabriel Macht), a former Miami cop who speaks English, Spanish, and Farsi.

The training process involves a series of Bondian sequences in which the agents learn such skills as blowing up cars: (a) Throw bomb under car; (b) detonate. They are also taught about biodegradable listening devices, weapons usage, and how to shadow someone. And they are told of an agency superweapon that (I think I heard this right) can plug into an electric socket and disable every digital device connected to the grid. Agents: Be sure Mr. Coffee has completed his brewing cycle before employing weapon.

The early scenes in the film are entertaining, yes, because Pacino works his character for all its grizzled charm, and Colin Farrell is not only enormously likable but fascinates us with his permanent four-day beard. His chemistry with Layla is real enough, but come on: When he walks into that bar to pick up someone, doesn't it occur to him that it is hardly a coincidence that Layla is already there? Mata Hari would make mincemeat of this guy, but the girl shows promise; as Marlene Dietrich usefully observed, "It took more than one man to change my name to Shanghai Lily."

Still, it's intriguing to see these young trainees learning their job, and to hear Pacino's observations, which are epigrammatic ("I don't have answers. Only secrets"), hardboiled ("They show you your medal. You don't even get to take it home"), complacent ("Our cause is just"), and helpful ("Nothing is what it seems. Trust no one"). Pacino's character wisely sticks to political generalities so that the film can play in foreign markets; the closest it comes to current events is in the mention of Farsi, which is the language of Iran, although, as Michael Caine likes to say, not many people know that.

The first two acts of the film are fun because they're all setup and buildup, and because the romance between James and Layla is no more cornball and contrived than it absolutely has to be. The third act is a mess. It saddles Pacino with the thankless role of the Talking Killer (not that he necessarily kills). That's the guy who has to stand there and explain the complexities of the plot when any real CIA veteran would just blow the other guy away. By the time Pacino wraps things up, we're realizing that the mantras "Nothing is what it seems" and "Trust no one," if taken seriously, reveal the entire plot. There is, however, a neat little misunderstanding at the end that earns a chuckle.

The movie was directed by Roger Donaldson, who does political thrillers about as well as anyone; his *Thirteen Days* (2001), about the Cuban missile crisis, and *No Way Out* (1987), about a scandal in the Department of Defense, were gripping and intelligent, and *The Recruit* is so well directed and acted that only a churl such as myself would question its sanity. It's the kind of movie you can sit back and enjoy, as long as you don't make the mistake of thinking too much.

Red Betsy ★ ★ ★
PG, 98 m., 2003

Alison Elliott (Winifred Rounds), Leo Burmester (Emmet Rounds), Lois Smith (Helen Rounds), Chad Lowe (Orin Sanders), William Wise (Grandpa Charles), Isa Thomas (Grandma K), Brent Crawford (Dale Rounds), Courtney Jines (Jane Rounds). Directed by Chris Boebel and produced by James Calabrese. Screenplay by Boebel, based on a short story by Charles Boebel.

Red Betsy takes place in a corner of rural Wisconsin, and it contains more truth about World War II than *Pearl Harbor* even dreamed of. There are no battle scenes in this movie, no special effects—not even any airplanes, except for one powered with a Model A engine from a junkyard. The movie sees World War II and the following years through the eyes of those who went away and those who stayed at home, and it tells one small true story that represents the incalculable effect of the war.

The movie opens in 1941, on a farm near Delafield, Wisconsin, where a small group has gathered to watch nervously as a little red airplane prepares to take off from a flat field. "Don't worry, Mom; it's guaranteed to fly," says Dale Rounds (Brent Crawford), not very reassuringly, and his plane does fly; he circles overhead in the *Red Betsy*, in what will be the most glorious moment of his short life.

Dale is engaged to Winifred (Alison Elliott). They plan to go to school in Madison in the fall, but he hasn't quite gotten around to breaking the news to his parents, Emmet and Helen (Leo Burmester and Lois Smith). Emmet is crusty and old-fashioned, and expects the young couple to move into the Little House on the property and work the farm until he dies, then they can move into the Big

House and Dale can take over. Helen says she'll break the news to her husband. She's had a lot of practice at telling him things he doesn't want to hear. He accepts the plans—not cheerfully, but he accepts them.

(Spoiler warning.) The happiness of the wedding day is brief. Helen dies suddenly and leaves Emmet alone and feeling abandoned. Pearl Harbor is attacked, and Dale can't wait to sign up. Winifred agrees uneasily to move into the Little House, "just for a year," look after Emmet, and wait for Dale to return. Within a few months a telegram arrives with the news that Dale has been killed in action in the Pacific; another piece of news is that Winifred is pregnant.

All of that is prologue to the real subject of the movie, which involves those whose lives were changed by the war, and how they coped. Emmet doesn't need much looking after. He runs the farm as always, and has nothing but scorn for the tree-trimmers of the Rural Electrification Authority, who plan to bring electricity to the district. By 1949, Winifred is teaching in the local school, and she and her daughter, Jane, are still living in the Little House.

There were countless stories like this. Born in downstate Illinois seven months after Pearl Harbor, I grew up hearing about fiancés and sons killed in the war, and saw their pictures—so young and serious in uniform—on the living-room mantel. My aunt never married after her boyfriend died aboard the USS *Indianapolis*. People carried on with their lives and coped, and *Red Betsy* is about that—how the years pass, how Winifred changes and adapts to a life she never imagined, how Jane grows up, how Emmet wages his lonely war against everything that has changed the serenity and predictability that ruled his life for so long.

The movie isn't too sentimental. It is told in the direct terms that we use to relate family stories; they're sad, but we've told them many times and they no longer make us cry. The director is Chris Boebel, a graduate of the NYU film school, and he wrote the screenplay with his father, Charles, an English teacher. It's based on one of the father's short stories. The family comes from rural Wisconsin stock, and Chris's grandmother still lives on a farm. This is not the country postcard of Hollywood fantasies, but just a working farm in a district where there are few enough people that every personality seems backlighted.

Their faces are important in the movie. Although all the leads are professional actors (Lois Smith is the Oscar-nominated Steppenwolf Theatre Company legend, Burmester was in *Gangs of New York*, Elliott is a veteran, and Chad Lowe plays an REA official), they're unaffected and understated; they've observed how midwestern farm people are embarrassed by making displays of themselves. I don't know if the extras in the wedding scene are locals, and I don't need to know, because I can see that they are. I like the way Alison Elliott, as Winifred, really does stand out in the crowd, with her red lipstick, her stylish 1940s dresses, her cigarettes sneaked with a girlfriend on the screened-in porch. I can look at Winifred and look at Emmet and know precisely how and why they will never really understand each other.

And yet the years bring accommodations, and the new becomes routine, and if people want to do the right thing, sooner or later they work their way around to it. That's what *Red Betsy* is about. How long has it been since you saw a movie about that?

Red Trousers: The Life of the Hong Kong Stuntmen ★ ★

R, 93 m., 2004

Robin Shou (Himself), Beatrice Chia (Silver), Keith Cooke (Kermuran), Hakim Alston (Eyemarder), Ridley Tsui (Himself), Craig Reid (Jia Fei). A documentary directed and produced by Robin Shou. Screenplay by Shou.

There's no room for the concept of workman's compensation in the world of the Hong Kong stuntman. Although certain stunts involve an 80 percent chance of a trip to the hospital, that's all in a day's work, and the stuntman who complains risks losing face with his employers—and his fellow stuntmen.

So we learn in *Red Trousers: The Life of the Hong Kong Stuntmen*, a rambling and frustrating documentary that nevertheless contains a lot of information about the men and women who make the Hong Kong action film possible. Not for them the air bags and safety precautions of Hollywood stuntmen. Quite often, we're stunned to learn, their stunts are done ex-

actly as they seem: A fall from a third-floor window, for example, involves a stuntman falling from a third-floor window.

There is a sequence in the film where a stuntman is asked to fall off a railing, slide down a slanting surface to a roof, and bounce off the roof to the floor below. It is rehearsed with pads on the floor. When the shot is ready, the director tells his stuntman, "No pads. Concrete floor." And when the stuntman lands on the concrete incorrectly the first time, he insists on doing the stunt again: "I came off the roof at the wrong angle. This time I will get it right."

Are stuntmen ever killed? No doubt they are, but you will not hear about it in this doc, directed by the onetime stuntman and current actor and director Robin Shou *(Mortal Kombat)*. We do learn of a stuntman who was gravely injured when his wire snapped and he fell from a great height to land on jagged rocks. We see the shot as the wire snaps, and then the cameras keep rolling, Jackie Chan–style, as the crew race over to the man, who is screaming in pain. There's a call for pads to put him on, and then he's carried off on the shoulders of five or six crew members. We realized with astonishment that there is no medical team standing by, no ambulance, no provision at all should the stunt go wrong.

Later, visiting the injured stuntman in his village, we learn that he needed many operations over a period of two years on a shattered leg, but thank goodness his facial cuts didn't leave scars. He was paid $25 a day for two days of work, he observes. What about compensation? No mention. Good thing they have socialized medicine.

Wires are, of course, often used in stunts, to make the characters appear to defy gravity, but it would be wrong to assume they make stunts any easier. We see stunts where the wires are used to slam a stuntman against a wall, or spin him into a fall. The wires do not break the impact or slow the fall.

We hear a lot about how carefully Hollywood stuntmen prepare their "gags," but consider a scene in this movie where a stuntman jumps off a highway overpass, lands on top of a moving truck, and then rolls off the truck onto the top of a van before falling to the highway. How was the stunt done? Just as it looks. "My call was for 5:30 and the stunt was finished by 5:45," the stuntman reports cheerfully. Good thing the truck and the van were in the right places, or he might have been run over, or have fallen from the overpass to the pavement.

There are a lot of interviews with stuntmen in the movie, who repeat over and over how they love their work, how excited they are to be in the movies, how of course they're frightened but it's a matter of pride to do a stunt once you have agreed to it—if word gets around that they've balked, the jobs might dry up. They take pride in the fact that Hong Kong stuntmen are allowed to make physical contact with the stars, while in Hollywood, the stars must never be touched.

All of this has a fascination, and yet *Red Trousers* is a jumbled and unsatisfying documentary. It jumps from one subject to another, it provides little historical context, it shows a lot of stunts being prepared and executed but refuses to ask the obvious questions in our minds: Are there no laws to protect injured stuntmen? Are they forced to sign releases? How many are killed or crippled? Why not use more safety measures?

Instead, Shou devotes way too much screen time to scenes from *Lost Time* (2001), a short action film he directed. Yes, we see stunts in preparation and then see them used in the movie, but sometimes he just lets the movie run, as if we want to see it. He explains that the term "red trousers" originated with the uniforms of students at the Beijing Opera School, which produced many of the early stuntmen, and shows us students of the opera school today; they begin as children, their lives controlled from morning to night, just as depicted in Kaige Chen's great Chinese film *Farewell, My Concubine* (1993). He interviews some of the students, who are still children, and as they affirm their ambitions and vow their dedication, we glimpse a little of where the stuntman code comes from. But if the wire breaks some day, they may, during the fall, find themselves asking basic questions about their working conditions.

Resident Evil: Apocalypse ½ ★
R, 93 m., 2004

Milla Jovovich (Alice), Sienna Guillory (Jill Valentine), Oded Fehr (Carlos Olivera), Thomas Kretschmann (Major Cain), Jared Harris (Dr. Charles Ashford), Sandrine Holt (Terri Morales). Directed by Alexander Witt and produced by Paul W. S. Anderson, Jeremy Bolt, and Don Carmody. Screenplay by Anderson.

I'm trying to remember what the city was called in the original *Resident Evil* (2002). I don't think it was called anything, but in *Resident Evil: Apocalypse*, it's called Raccoon City, just like in the original video game. Call it what you will, it has the Toronto skyline. Toronto played Chicago in *Chicago* and now it plays Raccoon City. Some you win, some you lose.

The movie is an utterly meaningless waste of time. There was no reason to produce it except to make money, and there is no reason to see it except to spend money. It is a dead zone, a film without interest, wit, imagination, or even entertaining violence and special effects.

The original film involved the Umbrella Corp. and its underground research laboratory called The Hive. The experimental T-virus escaped, and to contain it, The Hive was flooded and locked. But its occupants survived as zombies and lurched about infecting others with their bites. Zombies can appear in interesting movies, as George Romero proved in *Dawn of the Dead* and Danny Boyle in *28 Days Later*. But zombies themselves are not interesting because all they do is stagger and moan. As I observed in my review of the first film, "they walk with the lurching shuffle of a drunk trying to skate through urped Slushies to the men's room."

Now time has passed and the Umbrella Corp. has decided to reopen The Hive. Well, wouldn't you know that the T-virus escapes *again*, and creates even more zombies? Most of the population of Raccoon City is infected, but can be easily contained because there is only one bridge out of town. The story involves three sexy women (Milla Jovovich, Sienna Guillory, and Sandrine Holt), the first a former Umbrella Corp. scientist, the second a renegade cop, the third a TV reporter. Picking up some guys along the way, they battle the zombies and try to rescue a little girl so her dad can pull some strings and get them out of the quarantined city before it is nuked.

We pause here for logistical discussions. In a scene where several characters are fighting zombies inside a church, the renegade scientist comes to the rescue by crashing her motorcycle through a stained-glass window and landing in the middle of the fight. This inspires the question: How did she know what was on the other side of the window? Was she crashing through the stained glass on spec?

My next logistical puzzlement involves killing the zombies. They die when you shoot them. Fine, except Umbrella Corp. has developed some mutants who wear bulletproof armor. Zillions of rounds of ammo bounce off this armor, but here's a funny thing: The mutants do not wear helmets, so we can see their ugly faces. So why not just shoot them in the head? Am I missing something here?

What I was missing were more of the mutants from the first picture, where they were little monsters with nine-foot tongues. They have a walk-on (or maybe a lick-on) in the sequel, but it's no big deal. *Resident Evil: Apocalypse* could have used them, but then this is a movie that could have used anything. The violence is all video-game target practice, the zombies are a bore, we never understand how Umbrella hopes to make money with a virus that kills everyone, and the characters are spectacularly shallow. Parents: If you encounter teenagers who say they liked this movie, do not let them date your children.

Respiro ★ ★ ★
PG-13, 90 m., 2003

Valeria Golino (Grazia), Vincenzo Amato (Pietro), Francesco Casisa (Pasquale), Veronica D'Agostino (Marinella), Filippo Pucillo (Filippo). Directed by Emanuele Crialese and produced by Dominic Process. Screenplay by Crialese.

That there is something not right about Grazia, all the village agrees. "Bring her shot!" her husband calls out at fraught moments, and the children and neighbors hold her down while he jabs her with a needle filled with—what? It calms her down, anyway. There is said to be a doctor in Milan who could help her, but when the entire village unites in favor of the Milan trip, Grazia runs away and is thought to be dead in the sea.

The village is angry at her because Grazia opened the doors of an old stone building and released dozens of stray dogs to run about the streets. Whether they were rabid or just homeless is not clear, and why they were being held instead of put down is not explained, but the men of the village are resourceful, and take to their rooftops with rifles to shoot all the dogs. Then it becomes clear that Grazia must go to Milan: "This can't go on."

The village is on the Italian island of Lampedusa, not far from Tunisia. Whether *Respiro* paints an accurate portrait of its society, I cannot say. Fishing and canning are the local industries, everybody lives in everybody else's pockets, and the harsh sun beats down on a landscape of rock and beach, sea and sky, and sand-colored homes surrounded by children and Vespas.

In this world Grazia (Valeria Golino) is a legend. Young-looking to be the mother of three children, one a teenager, she is married to Pietro (Vincenzo Amato), a handsome fisherman who loves her, but is understandably disturbed when his boat passes a beach where Grazia is swimming nude with their children. More accurately, she is nude, and her son Pasquale (Francesco Casisa) wants her to put her clothes back on and come home with him.

Pasquale tries to protect his mother. She has what we in the audience diagnose as manic depression, although the movie never declares itself. Mostly she's in the manic phase, too happy, too uncontrolled, burning with a fierce delight that wears out everyone else. Rather than go to Milan, she runs away, and Pasquale helps her hide in a cave he knows, and brings her food while the village searches for her and Pietro grows bereft.

But the story of Grazia is only one of the pleasures of *Respiro*, which won the grand prize in the Critics' Week program at Cannes 2002. The movie, written and directed by the New York University graduate Emanuele Crialese, has a feeling for the rhythms of life on the island, and especially for the way the boys—Grazia's two sons and others—run wild as boys will. We see them trapping birds and cooking them for a treat, depantsing each other, forming tribes constantly at war, and swimming out to returning fishing boats hoping to be thrown a few fish they can trade in the marketplace for chances at winning a train set in the lottery.

When the boys actually win the train set, their bearded and sun-bronzed fishermen fathers behave as all fathers do everywhere, and set up the train "for the kids" because they want to play with it themselves. In the middle of this enterprise, Grazia lures Pietro away for a "nap." It's clear they are still passionately in love. Sex indeed is not far from the surface in this family, and the teenage daughter, Marinella (Veronica D'Agostino), flirts with the new policeman in town, who seems a good deal less sure of his moves than she is.

That's why it's all the more sad when Grazia disappears and Pasquale helps in her deception. Pietro mourns on the beach while Grazia is not far away, living in the cave. How could she do such a heartless thing? Well, because she really does need the man in Milan, although the movie sidesteps that inescapable reality with an ending both poetic and unlikely.

Respiro is a cheerful, life-affirming film, strong in its energy, about vivid characters. It uses mental illness as an entertainment, not a disease. As I watched it, I wondered—do such people really live on Lampedusa, and is this film an accurate reflection of their lives? I have no idea. I tend to doubt it. But perhaps it doesn't matter, since they exist for the ninety minutes of this film, and engage us with their theatricality. Grazia needs help, but her island will not be such a lively place to live if she gets it.

The Return ★ ★ ★

NO MPAA RATING, 106 m., 2004

Vladimir Garin (Andrey), Ivan Dobronravov (Ivan), Konstantin Lavronenko (Father), Natalia Vdovina (Mother). Directed by Andrey Zvyagintsev and produced by Dmitry Lesnevsky. Screenplay by Vladimir Moiseenko and Alexander Novototsky.

Here is the latest and most disturbing of three films about children and their ominous fathers. Bill Paxton's *Frailty* was about two brothers who are fearful about their father's conviction that an angel of God has assigned him to kill the Satan-possessed among us. *I'm Not Scared*, by Gabriele Salvatores of Italy, was about a small boy who stumbles upon a chained kidnap victim and gradually realizes his father is the kidnapper. Now we have *The Return*, from Russia, which is all the more frightening because two young brothers never do fully understand their father's alarming behavior. It is a Kafkaesque story, in which ominous things follow each other with a certain internal logic, but make no sense at all.

As the movie opens, Andrey (Vladimir Garin) and his younger brother Ivan (Ivan Dobronravov) return home one day to hear their mother whisper, "Quiet! Dad's sleeping." This is a father they have not seen for years, if ever, and the movie gives us no explanation for his absence. Almost immediately he proposes a fishing trip, and the boys are less than overjoyed at this prospect of leaving home with a man who is essentially a stranger.

The father (Konstantin Lavronenko) drives them to a lakeside. He attempts to impose stern discipline in the car, but this seems less the result of cruelty than because of his awkwardness around young boys. Indeed, the movie's refusal to declare the father a villain adds to the ambiguity; eventually he creates a disturbing situation, but does he act by design, compulsion, or impulse? And what are his motives?

Whatever they are, it's clear that catching fish is not one of them. There is an ominous scene under a lowering sky and scattered rain, as he and the boys row a small boat to an island far away in the middle of the lake. On the island, the boys explore, and there is a tower that tests their fear of heights. They spy on their father, and see him retrieve a small buried trunk. What's in it? We think perhaps he is a paroled convict, returning for his loot. Or a man who has learned of buried treasure. Or . . .

Doesn't matter. The box, which has caused so much trouble, is lost to history by the end of the film, along with the reason why the father thought he needed to bring his two sons along. Was he acting from some kind of stunted impulse to make up time with his boys? Was he subjecting them to an experience he had undergone? Are they safe with him?

The Return, directed by Andrey Zvyagintsev and cowritten by Vladimir Moiseenko and Alexander Novototsky, does not conceal information from the audience, which would be a technique of manipulation—but from the young boys, which is a technique of drama. The movie is not about the father's purpose but the boys' confusion and alarm. Like the other two films I mentioned, it eventually arrives at the point where the boys must decide whether or not to act, and here the interior dynamic of their own relationship is more important than how they feel about their father.

Zvyagintsev films on chilly, overcast days, on an island that in this season is not a vacation spot. His cinematographer, Mikhail Kritchman, denatures the color film stock to deny us cheer. We do not like this island, or trust this father, or like the looks of the boat—which for a long time is left untethered on the beach, so that there's a constant underthought that it might float away. What finally happens is not anything we could have anticipated, except to observe that something like that seemed to be hanging in the damp, cold air.

Note: An additional sadness creeps into the film if we know that Vladimir Garin, the older of the two boys, drowned not long after the film was completed, in a situation not unlike one in the film.

The Revolution Will Not Be Televised
★ ★ ★ ½
NO MPAA RATING, 74 m., 2003

Featuring Hugo Chavez, Pedro Carmona, Jesse Helms, Colin Powell, and George Tenet. A documentary directed by Kim Bartley and Donnacha O'Briain and produced by David Power.

Was the United States a shadowy presence in the background of the aborted coup in Venezuela in 2002? The democratically elected government of Hugo Chavez was briefly overthrown by a cabal of rich businessmen and army officers, shortly after their representatives had been welcomed in the White House. Oh, the United States denied any involvement in the episode; there's Colin Powell on TV, forthrightly professing innocence. But earlier we heard ominous rumblings from Jesse Helms, Ari Fleischer, and George Tenet, agreeing that Chavez was no friend of the United States, and after the coup there was no expression of dismay from Wash-ington, no announcement that we would work to restore the elected government.

Why was Chavez not our friend? It all comes down to oil, as it so often does these days. Venezuela is the fourth-largest oil-producing nation in the world, and much of its oil comes to the United States. Its price has been guaranteed by the cooperation of the nation's ruling class. Chavez was elected primarily by the poor. He asked a simple question: Since the oil wells have always been nationalized and the oil belongs to the state, why do the profits flow directly to the richest, whitest 20 percent of the population, while being denied to the poorer, darker 80 percent? His plan was to distribute the profits equally among all Venezuelans.

This was, you may agree, a fair and obvious solution. But not to the 20 percent, of course. And not to other interested parties, including our friends the Saudis, whose people get poorer as the sheiks get richer. Charging Chavez with being a Communist who wanted to bring Castroism to Venezuela, the rich and powerful staged a coup on April 12, 2002. Chavez was put under arrest and held on an island, and the millionaire businessman Pedro Carmona was sworn in as president. This was in violation of the constitution, but he blandly assured TV audiences he was in power because "of a mandate better than any referendum." There was no disagreement from Washington.

Incredibly, the coup failed. Hundreds of thousands of Chavez supporters surrounded the presidential palace, and the loyal presidential guard put the interlopers under arrest. Although the state-run Channel 8 was taken off the air and the private channels told lies and showed falsified news footage, Venezuelans learned from CNN and other cable channels that Chavez had not resigned and a coup had taken place; they demanded his return, and a few days later he arrived by helicopter at the presidential palace and resumed office.

These events are recounted in *The Revolution Will Not Be Televised,* a remarkable documentary by two Irish filmmakers. It is remarkable because the filmmakers, Kim Bartley and Donnacha O'Briain, had access to virtually everything that happened within the palace during the entire episode. They happened to be in

567

Caracas to make a doc about Chavez, they had access to his cabinet meetings, they were inside the palace under siege, they faced a tense deadline after which it would be bombed, they stayed after Chavez gave himself up to prevent the bombing, and they filmed the new government. There are astonishing shots, such as the one where Chavez's men, now back in power, go down to the basement to confront coup leaders who have been taken prisoner. Why no one on either side thought to question the presence of the TV crew is a mystery, but they got an inside look at the coup—before, during, and after—that is unique in film history.

Film can be made to lie. Consider footage shown on the private TV channels to justify the coup. Learning that the right wing was sponsoring a protest march against Chavez, his supporters also marched on the palace. Scuffles broke out, and then concealed snipers began to fire on the Chavez crowd. Some in the crowd fired back. Although the dead and wounded were Chavez supporters, the private TV showed footage of them firing, and said they were firing at the anti-Chavez protest march. Bartley and O'Briain use footage of the same moment, from another angle, to show that there is no protest march in view, and that the fire is aimed at snipers above the parade route. That this deception was deliberate is confirmed by a producer for the private TV channels, who resigned in protest and explains how the footage was falsified. (Private TV did have one interesting slip; in a talk show the morning after the coup, one of its elated leaders talks frankly about the plan to disrupt the Chavez march and overthrow the government, while others on the program look like they'd like to throttle him.)

If private TV lied to the nation in support of the coup, the doc itself is clearly biased in favor of Chavez—most clearly so in depicting his opponents. When the right-wing leaders are introduced, it's in slo-mo, with ominous music and funeral drums. He may have articulate opponents in Venezuela, but the only ones we see are inane society people who warn each other, "Watch your servants!" Does everyone on the right in Venezuela dress like (a) an undertaker, (b) a military officer, or (c) a disco guest circa 1990?

Interestingly, there was relative civility on both sides. Chavez and his cabinet were arrested, but not harmed. After Chavez regained power, he said there would be no "witch hunt" of those who opposed him; although Carmona fled to Miami, several of the coup's military leaders (stripped of rank) remained in Venezuela and still continue as members of the opposition. This shows remarkable confidence on the part of Chavez, and a commitment to the democratic process.

It is, of course, impossible to prove that the coup was sponsored by the CIA or any other U.S. agency. But what was the White House thinking when it welcomed two antigovernment leaders who soon after were instrumental in the coup? Not long ago, reviewing another film, I wrote about the CIA-sponsored overthrow of Chile's democratically elected president, Salvador Allende. I got a lot of e-mail telling me the CIA had nothing to do with it. For anyone who believes that, I have a bridge I'd like to sell them.

Note: The last words in George Orwell's notebook were: "At age 50, every man has the face he deserves." Although it is outrageously unfair and indefensibly subjective of me, I cannot prevent myself from observing that Chavez and his cabinet have open, friendly faces, quick to smile, and that the faces of his opponents are closed, shifty, hardened.

Rick ★ ★ ★
R, 100 m., 2004

Bill Pullman (Rick), Aaron Sanford (Duke), Agnes Bruckner (Eve), Dylan Baker (Buck), Sandra Oh (Michelle). Directed by Curtiss Clayton and produced by Ruth Charny, Jim Czarnecki, and Sofia Sondervan. Screenplay by Daniel Handler.

Rick is a vicious SOB and a bully. He ridicules those weaker than he is, and rolls on the floor to please his boss. In other words, he's in middle management. Bill Pullman brings the character to full bloom in *Rick,* a movie that paints a corporate world of lust, hypocrisy, racism, and cruelty. No mention is made of the product or service produced by the corporation where Rick works, perhaps because the product is beside the point: This corporate culture works to produce itself.

The movie goes beyond dark comedy into dank comedy. Rick and his boss, Duke (Aaron Sanford), are creatures without redeeming merit, and Rick's old buddy Buck (Dylan Baker) is a killer for hire. His daughter is a regular in an X-rated chat room. Perhaps it is not astonishing that the screenplay is by Daniel Handler, who writes the Lemony Snicket books, the first of which warns its young readers: "These books are among the most miserable in the world."

With Lemony Snicket he's kidding, I think. With *Rick*, we have misanthropy run riot. I don't know if it works, but it's not boring, and there is a kind of terrible thrill in seeing an essentially nice guy like Bill Pullman play a character who is hateful beyond all measure. The story line is lifted from Verdi's *Rigoletto*, but if you could not sit down right now and compose 200 words summarizing the plot of that opera, it matters little; the movie has a life of its own.

The tone is set in a remarkable early scene in which Rick (Pullman) bounds into the office of Duke, who is half his age, and debases himself in a paroxysm of male bonding behavior. They curse, they drink, they smoke cigars, they pound each other to show what great guys they are, and Rick at one point actually crawls on the floor and seems likely to hump Duke's leg. They go out for a drink in a curious club supplied with video monitors so the customers can spy on each other, and then Duke excuses himself to go back to the office, where he can't wait to log on as BIGBOSS in that X-rated Web chat room.

Earlier in the film, a young woman named Michelle (Sandra Oh) came to Rick's office to be interviewed for a job. He made her go out, come in, go out, and wait and then come in again, and then systematically and cruelly humiliated and insulted her, deliberately confusing her Asian origins. In the club, wouldn't you know she's his waitress. Rick starts in on her again. She takes a little more than she should, and then, in a magnificent scene, she retaliates: "You're an evil person and you can't get away with it. I curse you. Your evil will come right back at you." This curse resonates through the

film, reaching that deep part of Rick's ego where even he is disgusted by himself.

Rick has a daughter named Eve (Agnes Bruckner, so good as the student who deals with a molesting teacher in *Blue Car*). She's a regular in the chat room, logging on as VIXXXEN, and she and BIGBOSS have worked up to the point where a meeting might be in order. Meanwhile, Duke sees Rick with the pretty Eve on his arm, and concludes that Eve is Rick's wife, not his daughter. As his wife, she's fair game, Duke concludes; but then, as his daughter she probably would be too.

Enter Buck the alleged college chum. "I've started my own company," Buck tells Rick, and hands him his card:

Buck—My Own Company

What Buck does is eliminate your competitors at work, clearing the way for your own advancement. He does this by killing them, which he justifies as the price of getting ahead in business. In *Rigoletto* as in Shakespeare, much depends on improbably mistaken identities, and so we're not in much suspense about whether the wrong person will get killed, or be seduced, or whatever.

There is no one in this movie to like. It has a heroine, the young woman Michelle, but she's around only long enough to stand up for herself, put a curse on Rick, and get the hell out of there. The remaining characters are hateful, except for Eve the daughter, who is blameless apart from her practice of inflaming the fantasies of anonymous men with her chat room scenarios.

Movies like this are kind of a test for a viewer. If you require that you "like" a movie, then *Rick* is not for you, because there is nothing likable about it. It's rotten to the core and right down to the end. But if you find that such extremes can be fascinating, then the movie may cheer you, not because it is happy, but because it goes for broke.

Note: The director is Curtiss Clayton, who has edited many of Gus Van Sant's movies. He was scheduled to be the editor of Vincent Gallo's The Brown Bunny, *but walked off the job on the first day of postproduction when* Rick *was green-lighted. I don't know what passed between them, but Gallo told me he "freaked out" when Clayton bailed; is it possible that Gallo's propensity for putting hexes on people was the inspiration for Michelle's great scene?*

Riding Giants ★ ★ ★ ½
PG-13, 105 m., 2004

A documentary directed by Stacy Peralta and produced by Peralta, Agi Orsi, and Jane Kachmer. Screenplay by Peralta and Sam George.

For fifteen years, Jeff Clark surfed alone. He paddled through forty-five minutes of wave and chop to reach Maverick's, "a veritable graveyard of jagged rocks" in the Pacific off San Francisco. There he found the most challenging surfing he had ever seen or heard about. For all those years other surfers didn't join him; the area was too remote, and they were focused on southern California and Hawaii.

Well, you wonder, how dangerous could the "graveyard" be if Clark survived it solo for fifteen years? Then word of Maverick's gets around, and legendary surfers from Hawaii's North Shore come to visit. One of the sport's champions, Mark Foo, is killed after wiping out on a medium wave. One theory is that the tether to his board got caught on rocks and he drowned. Another surfer thinks he felt or sensed somebody under the water who shouldn't have been there. Exactly one year later, during a memorial to Foo, another surfer is drowned.

The documentary *Riding Giants* shows surfers gathered to discuss and mourn the lost men. It does not show Jeff Clark during those previous fifteen years because, of course, he was alone. And what a species of aloneness it was, to plunge into the cold ocean and swim out forty-five minutes for a few seconds of exhilaration at the risk of your life. Clark and his kind live at the intersection of courage, madness, skill, and obsession.

Consider Laird Hamilton, the current golden boy of the sport, who has cashed in with endorsement contracts, modeling assignments, and magazine covers. But no, I am not comparing him unfavorably to Clark, because Hamilton is also a superb athlete and a driven man. Hanging around as a kid with Hawaii's big wave riders of the 1960s, he intro-

duced his divorced mom to one of them, who became his stepfather and tutor; Laird grew up to become surfing's first superstar.

What Hamilton has done is go farther from land than any rider had thought to go, seeking "remote offshore reefs capable of producing unimaginable waves." At first this involved paddling two hours and then waiting up to two hours for a wave. Then Hamilton invents "towing surfing," in which a jet ski tows him out to the far reefs and slings him onto waves moving so fast it is impossible to access them any other way.

The jet ski driver's other job is to pick up Hamilton again after the ride, or be prepared to rescue him. The thriller *Open Water* shows a couple lost at sea after being left behind on a scuba-diving tour. For Hamilton, being lost at sea is a possibility several times a day. *Riding Giants* was directed by Stacy Peralta, whose *Dogtown and Z-Boys* (2002) documented the invention and culture of southern California skateboarding. In both films his archival work is the key; he seems to have access to limitless historical footage, sometimes in home movie form; we see Hamilton at the dawn of towing surfing, when at first it was scorned and then embraced by the sport's champions.

In August 2000, Hamilton goes to Tahiti in search of a legendary wave so big it is "a freak of hydroponics." He finds it and rides it, and we see him precariously balanced on its terrifying immensity in what the movie calls "the most significant ride in surfing history." Other surfers, providing voice-over commentary, say the wave's characteristics were so different from ordinary waves that Hamilton had to improvise new techniques, some of them violating years of surfing theory and instinct, right there on the wave.

What a long time it seems since that summer of 1967, when I sat in a Chicago beer garden with the suntanned and cheerful Bruce Brown. He'd just made a documentary named *Endless Summer,* and was touring the country with it, at the moment when surfing was exploding (there were 5,000 surfers in 1959, 2 million today). For Brown, surfing was a lark. With a $50,000 budget, he followed two surfers on an odyssey that led to Senegal, Ghana, South Africa, Australia, New Zealand, Tahiti, and Hawaii. They were searching for the "perfect wave" and found it off Durban, South Africa: "A four-foot curl that gave rides of fifteen minutes and came in so steadily it looked like it was made by a machine."

A four-foot curl? Hamilton and his contemporaries challenge waves of sixty or seventy feet. *Endless Summer* charts a world of beaches and babes, brews and Beach Boys songs, and surfers who live to "get stoked." In *Riding Giants* the sport is more like an endless winter—solitary and dangerous. Even as Brown was making *Endless Summer,* modern surfing was being invented by pioneers like Greg Noll of Hawaii, who ventured fifteen miles up the coast from Honolulu to Waimea Bay. It was thought to be unsurfable; a surfer asks himself, "Can the human body survive the wipeout?" It could. The discovery of the North Shore of Oahu, the movie says, "was surfing's equivalent of Columbus discovering the New World."

More vintage footage. The "storm of the century" descends upon Hawaii, and Noll, known as "The Bull," determines to surf it. His chances of surviving are rated at 50/50 by the movie, at zero by any reasonable person watching it. He survived. It was "the biggest wave ever ridden"—until, perhaps, a monster that Hamilton found off Tahiti, too big to be measured.

After Bruce Brown finds his Perfect Wave in *Endless Summer,* he marvels: "The odds against a wave like this are twenty million–to-one!" The odds that Laird Hamilton could get stoked on a four-foot curl are higher than that. Before seeing *Riding Giants,* my ideas about surfing were formed by the Gidget movies, *Endless Summer,* the Beach Boys, Elvis, and lots of TV commercials. "Surfin' Safari" was actually running through my head on the way into the screening.

Riding Giants is about altogether another reality. The overarching fact about these surfers is the degree of their obsession. They live to ride, and grow depressed when there are no waves. They haunt the edge of the sea like the mariners Melville describes on the first pages of *Moby-Dick.* They seek the rush of those moments when they balance on top of a wave's fury and feel themselves in precarious harmony with the ungovernable force of the ocean. They are cold and tired, battered by

waves, thrown against rocks, visited by sharks, held under so long they believe they are drowning—and over and over, year after year, they go back into the sea to do it again.

The Ring Two ★ ★ ½
PG-13, 111 m., 2005

Naomi Watts (Rachel Keller), David Dorfman (Aidan Keller), Simon Baker (Max Rourke), Sissy Spacek (Evelyn), Elizabeth Perkins (Dr. Emma Temple), Gary Cole (Martin Savide). Directed by Hideo Nakata and produced by Laurie MacDonald, Walter F. Parkes, and Mark Sourian. Screenplay by Ehren Kruger, based on the novel *Ringu* by Koji Suzuki.

I am not sure I entirely understand the deer. In *The Ring Two,* Rachel and her young son, Aidan, visit a farmer's market. Aidan wanders off and observes some deer that emerge from a nearby forest and stare at him. He stares back. Later, as mother and son are driving down a little-traveled road, a deer appears in front of their car. "Keep moving," Aidan says urgently, but his mother hesitates, and soon the car is under attack by a dozen stags, their antlers crashing through the windows. She speeds away and hits another stag, doing considerable damage to the car's front end.

This is in a movie that also involves a mysterious video that brings death to whoever watches it, unless they pass it on to someone else within a week. The video is connected to the death of a young girl named Samara who had a cruel childhood. Samara's ghost is trying to possess Aidan's body. Because she died at the bottom of a well, much water is produced wherever her ghost manifests itself. Usually the water is on the floor, but sometimes it flows up to the ceiling.

Rachel visits the old farm where the girl was mistreated and died. In the basement, she finds antlers. A whole lot of antlers. So maybe the deer sense Samara's ghost's presence in Aidan and are attacking the car in revenge? But Samara was presumably not the deer hunter, being far too occupied as a cruelly mistreated little girl at the time. So is it that the deer are psychic, but not very bright?

One does not know but, oddly, one does not care. The charm of *The Ring Two,* while limited, is real enough; it is based on the film's ability to make absolutely no sense, while nevertheless generating a convincing feeling of tension a good deal of the time. It is like an exercise in cinema mechanics: Images, music, photography, and mood conspire to create a sense of danger, even though at any given moment we cannot possibly explain the rules under which that danger might manifest itself.

We do get some information. Samara, for example, can hear everything Rachel (Naomi Watts) and Aidan (David Dorfman) say to each other, except when Aidan is asleep. So Rachel talks to him a lot while he's asleep, with dubious utility. They also appear in each other's dreams, where they either (a) find a loophole by talking to each other while they're asleep, or (b) are only dreaming.

Meanwhile, the video gimmick, which supported *The Ring* (2002), is retired and the action centers on Samara's assaults on Aidan's body and Rachel's attempts to defend him. At one point this involves almost drowning him in a bathtub, which is the second time (after *Constantine*) that being almost drowned in a bathtub is employed as a weapon against supernatural forces.

The movie has been directed by Hideo Nakata, who directed the two famous Japanese horror films *Ringu* (1998) and *Ringu 2* (1999), although *The Ring Two* is not a remake of *Ringu 2*. It is a new departure, as Rachel, a newspaper reporter, leaves Seattle and gets a job on the paper in the pretty but rainy coastal town of Astoria, Oregon. Here perhaps the tape and its associated menace will not follow them.

Naomi Watts and David Dorfman are always convincing, sometimes very effective, in their roles; in the scene where she's going down into the basement, we keep repeating, "It's only a basement," but I was surprised that the ancient cinematic techniques still worked for me. In all such scenes it is essential for the camera to back into the basement while focused on the heroine, so that we cannot see what she sees, and therefore, through curious movie logic, neither can she.

The scenes involving Aidan's health are also well handled, as his body temperature goes up and down like an applause meter, reflecting the current state of Samara's success in taking

over his body. If he becomes entirely a ghost, does he go down to room temperature? Elizabeth Perkins plays a psychiatrist who thinks Aidan may have been abused, and there is a creepy cameo by Sissy Spacek, wearing scary old lady makeup, as Samara's birth mother. Aidan always calls his mother "Rachel," by the way, and when he starts calling her "Mommy" this is not a good sign.

When I say the film defies explanation, that doesn't mean it discourages it. Websites exist for no other reason than to do the work of the screenwriters by figuring out what it all means. At the end, for example, when Rachel rolls the heavy stone across the top of the well, does that mean Samara is out of business? Rachel seems to think so, but wasn't the stone *always* on top of the well?

Rivers and Tides: Andy Goldsworthy Working with Time ★ ★ ★ ½

NO MPAA RATING, 90 m., 2003

A documentary about Scottish environmental artist Andy Goldsworthy. Directed by Thomas Riedelsheimer and produced by Annedore von Donop. Screenplay by Riedelsheimer.

Have you ever watched—no, better, have you ever *been* a young child intent on building something out of the materials at hand in the woods, or by a stream, or at the beach? Have you seen the happiness of an adult joining kids and slowly slipping out of adulthood and into the absorbing process of this . . . and now . . . and over here . . . and build this up . . . and it should go like this?

The artist Andy Goldsworthy lives in that world of making things. They have no names; they are Things. He brings order to leaves or twigs or icicles and then surrenders them to the process of nature. He will kneel for hours by the oceanside, creating a cairn of stones that balances precariously, the weight on the top holding the sides in place, and then the tide will come in and wash away the sand beneath, and the cairn will collapse, as it must, as it should.

"The very thing that brought the thing to be is the thing that will cause its death," Goldsworthy explains, as his elegant, spiraled constructions once again become random piles of stones on the beach. As with Andy's stones, so with our lives.

Rivers and Tides: Andy Goldsworthy Working with Time is a documentary that opened in San Francisco in mid-2002 and just kept running, moving from one theater to another, finding its audience not so much through word of mouth as through hand-on-elbow, as friends steered friends into the theater, telling them that this was a movie they had to see. I started getting E-mail about it months ago. Had I seen it? I hadn't even heard of it.

It is a film about a man wholly absorbed in the moment. He wanders woods and riverbanks, finding materials and playing with them, fitting them together, piling them up, weaving them, creating beautiful arrangements that he photographs before they return to chaos. He knows that you can warm the end of an icicle just enough to make it start to melt, and then hold it against another icicle, and it will stick. With that knowledge, he makes an ice sculpture, and then it melts in the sun and is over.

Some of his constructions are of magical beauty, as if left behind by beings who disappeared before the dawn. He finds a way to arrange twigs in a kind of web. He makes a spiral of rocks that fans out from a small base and then closes in again, a weight on top holding it together. This is not easy, and he gives us pointers: "Top control can be the death of a work."

Often Andy will be . . . almost there . . . right on the edge . . . holding his breath as one last piece goes into place . . . and then the whole construction will collapse, and he will look deflated, defeated for a moment ("Damn!"), and then start again: "When I build something I often take it to the very edge of its collapse, and that's a very beautiful balance."

His art needs no explanation. We go into modern art galleries and find work we cannot comprehend as art. We see Damien Hirst's sheep, cut down the middle and embedded in plastic, and we cannot understand how it won the Turner Prize (forgetting that no one thought Turner was making art, either). We suppose that concepts and statements are involved.

But with Andy Goldsworthy, not one word of explanation is necessary because every single one of us has made something like his art. We have piled stones or made architectural constructions out of sand, or played Pick-Up Stix, and we know *exactly* what he is trying to do—and why. Yes, why, because his art takes him into that zone where time drops away and we forget our left-brain concerns and are utterly absorbed by whether this . . . could go like this . . . without the whole thing falling apart.

The documentary, directed, photographed, and edited by Thomas Riedelsheimer, a German filmmaker, goes home with Goldsworthy to Penpont, Scotland, where we see him spending some time with his wife and kids. It follows him to a museum in the south of France, and to an old stone wall in Canada that he wants to rebuild in his own way. It visits with him old stone markers high in mountains, built by early travelers to mark the path.

And it offers extraordinary beauty. We watch as he smashes stones to release their content, and uses that bright red dye to make spectacular patterns in the currents and whirlpools of streams. We see a long rope of linked leaves, bright green, uncoil as it floats downstream. Before, we saw only the surface of the water, but now the movement of the leaves reveals its current and structure. What a happy man. Watching this movie is like daydreaming.

Rize ★ ★ ★

PG-13, 85 m., 2005

Featuring Tommy the Clown, Lil Tommy, Larry, Swoop, El Nino, Dragon, Lil C, Tight Eyez, Baby Tight Eyez, Daisy, Big X, Miss Prissy, La Nina, and Quinesha. A documentary directed by David LaChapelle and produced by Marc Hawker, Ellen Jacobson-Clarke, and LaChapelle. Screenplay by LaChapelle.

"The footage in this movie has not been speeded up in any way."

We need to be told that, right at the beginning of *Rize*, because krumping, the dance style shown in the movie, looks like life in fast-forward. You haven't heard of krumping? Neither had I. And I didn't know that dressing up like a clown has become an alternative to joining a street gang in the South Central and Watts areas of Los Angeles. When this movie was made, there were more than 50 clown groups; now there are said to be more than 100.

Rize is the rare documentary that plays as breaking news. Krumping and clowning have become so big in L.A. that the fifth annual krumping competition, known as Battle Zone, was held in the Great Western Forum. Yet until this movie was made by *Vanity Fair* photographer David LaChapelle, it was a phenomenon that existed below the radar of the media. It's an alternative to the hip-hop style that is growing a little old; because recording labels and cable TV have so much invested in hip-hop, however, they have been slow to embrace it. Or maybe they just couldn't believe their eyes.

The clowns in these groups are real clowns. Bozo should get royalties. They have rainbow wigs and putty noses and weirdly made-up faces and wildly colored costumes, and they would have floppy shoes except then they couldn't dance. The dance they do, krumping, sometimes looks like a fistfight in fast motion, sometimes borrows moves from strippers, sometimes looks like speeded-up martial arts, sometimes is beyond description.

Borrowing a page from poetry jams, krumpers face off one-on-one and try to out-krump one another, and the final showdown in Battle Zone V is between the two main factions of the movement, the krumps and the clowns. (Just to spell out the difference: While clowns krump, not all krumps are clowns. Krumping was invented by Lil C, Tight Eyez, and Dragon after they left Tommy to start their own school. So now you know.)

This world is the invention, we learn, of Tommy the Clown (Tom Johnson), who as a young man was into drugs and gangs. "Living like that," he says, "you either wind up shot dead or in jail. I was lucky. I wound up in jail." When he was released and unsure what direction his life would take, he was asked to play a clown at a friend's birthday party. He liked the way people responded to him as a clown; they regarded him as if he had dropped out of ordinary categories and lived in a separate world.

Tommy the Clown became "a ghetto celebrity," he tells us, and we see footage of Tommy making unannounced appearances at shopping malls, movie theater lines, and street corners. He takes his first disciple, Lil Tommy

("When my mom was in jail, he took me in"), and soon he's running a clown academy. A key moment comes when the clowns evoke a new kind of dancing; a clown named Larry is a key innovator. Soon there are groups of krump-dancing clowns all over the streets of neighborhoods that were once afire (the film opens with footage from the Watts and Rodney King rioting).

In these neighborhoods to wear the wrong gang colors in the wrong place at the wrong time is to risk being shot dead. But a clown wears every possible color at once, and in a way becomes disqualified. "The gangs sort of leave us alone," one of the clowns says, and there is a sense that joining a clown group may be a way to survive outside the gang culture. It is also a very weird lifestyle.

We see clowns devising elaborate facial makeup, owing more to Batman villains than to Bozo. We witness artistic rivalries between various styles of clowning and dancing. And there are suggestions that not everyone loves clowns; while Tommy is running the face-off at the Forum, his home is trashed. Late in the film, one of the most lovable characters is shot dead by drive-by killers, firing at random. Guns don't kill people; people with guns kill people.

Still, *Rize* on the whole brings good news, of a radical social innovation that simultaneously sidesteps street gangs and bypasses hip-hop. Krumping should turn up any day now on BET and MTV, if it hasn't already; whether the dancers will be dressed as clowns is less likely. There is something a little eerie about clowns, and to see dozens of them at once perhaps inspires even gang members to go elsewhere.

The most remarkable thing about *Rize* is that it is real. I remember hearing vaguely at Sundance about an earlier short subject that LaChapelle made about this phenomenon; was it on the level or a mockumentary? If *Rize* were a fake doc, it would look about the same as it does now, and would be easier to absorb, since the idea of gangs of clowns sounds like a put-on. But it isn't.

Robots ★ ★ ★ ½
PG, 91 m., 2005

With the voices of: Ewan McGregor (Rodney Copperbottom), Halle Berry (Cappy), Greg

Kinnear (Phineas T. Ratchet), Mel Brooks (Big Weld), Amanda Bynes (Piper Pinwheeler), Drew Carey (Crank Casey), Jim Broadbent (Madame Gasket), Jennifer Coolidge (Aunt Fanny), Robin Williams (Fender), Stanley Tucci (Herb Copperbottom). Directed by Chris Wedge and Carlos Saldanha and produced by Jerry Davis, John C. Donkin, and William Joyce. Screenplay by David Lindsay-Abaire, Lowell Ganz, and Babaloo Mandel.

The thing that struck me first of all about *Robots* was its pictorial beauty. I doubt that was the intention of the animators, who've made a slapstick comedy set in a futurist city that seems fresh off the cover of a 1942 issue of *Thrilling Wonder Stories*. Towers and skyways and strange architectural constructions look like an Erector set's erotic dreams, and the ideal skyscraper is a space needle ringed by metallic doughnuts.

This world is inhabited by robots who are human in every respect except that they are not human in any respect, if you follow me. They even have babies. As the movie opens, Herb Copperbottom and his wife are unwrapping their new little boy, who has arrived in a shipping crate, some assembly required. This being a PG-rated movie aimed at the whole family, the robots even have the ability to fart, which is a crucial entertainment requirement of younger children.

But look at the design and artistic execution. Each robot is a unique creation, made of nuts and bolts, but also expressing an individual personality, and moving in a way that seems physical and mechanical at the same time. And consider the color palate, which seems to have been borrowed from Fiestaware, which was inspired by the cheap table settings that used to be given away as prizes at Saturday matinees and is now collected by those who inexplicably find it beautiful, such as myself. Even the shapes of some of the robots resemble the plump art deco lines of a Fiestaware teapot or water pitcher.

Like *Finding Nemo*, this is a movie that is a joy to behold entirely apart from what it is about. It looks happy, and more to the point, it looks harmonious. One of the reasons this entirely impossible world works is because it looks like it belongs together, as if it evolved organically.

Of course, organics are the last concern of young Rodney Copperbottom (voice by Ewan McGregor), who is born in Rivet City but dreams of a journey to Robot City, where he hopes that a mysterious tycoon named Big Weld will be amazed by his inventions. Rodney's father (Stanley Tucci) is a dishwasher (the appliance is built right into his midsection), and Rodney has invented a tiny helicopter robot that can whiz around the kitchen, stacking plates and silverware. What is served on the plates I will leave to your imagination.

Encouraged by his father to follow his dream, Rodney takes the train to Robot City. This train apparently uses the same technology as the *Polar Express;* it's pulled by a traditional steam locomotive, which casually takes off and chugs through the air. In Robot City, almost the first robotperson Rodney meets is Fender (Robin Williams), a tourist tout who snaps pictures, sells postcards, and introduces Rodney to the city's public transportation system.

Their trip across town is when we realize how joyously the filmmakers have imagined this world. Chris Wedge and Carlos Saldanha, who worked together on *Ice Age* (2002), create a Rube Goldberg series of ramps, pulleys, catapults, spring-loaded propulsion devices, spiraling chutes, and dizzying mechanical slingshots that hurtle Fender and poor Rodney on a stomach-churning ride, or would if they had stomachs.

Robots has a plot that centers on the availability of spare parts, and uses a lot of them itself, borrowed from other movies. There's a little of *The Wizard of Oz* in the character of Big Weld (Mel Brooks), who does a TV program extolling the virtues and perfection of his vast corporation, but does not seem findable when Rodney visits Big Weld headquarters. Nor are Big Weld's executives interested in Rodney's inventions.

The company is being run day-to-day by Phineas T. Ratchet (Greg Kinnear), who is uninterested in improving the product because a perfect product would be bad for sales. "Upgrades! That's how we make the dough!" he explains, sounding like a consumer electronics executive.

Phineas is dominated by his mother, Madame Gasket, played by Jim Broadbent. Yes, Jim Broadbent, but reflect that in a robot society the genders are elements of design, not function. If you have a screwdriver and swappable attachments, you can come out of the closet as whatever you feel like. Madame Gasket's master plan is to create a shortage of spare parts, so that robots will have to be replaced, instead of being indefinitely repaired like a 1959 Chevy in Havana.

Rodney now meets a sexpot, or would that be an oilpot, named Cappy (Halle Berry), who serves as his guide to some of the secrets of Robot City. She looks great, but of course in a robot society everybody has had some work done. She becomes his sidekick in an invasion of Big Weld headquarters, which leads to a confrontation with the Weld himself.

I have observed before that giant corporations have replaced Nazis as dependable movie villains. Phineas T. Ratchett, who plans an inside takeover of Big Weld's empire, is obviously a student of the theories of conspicuous consumption and planned obsolescence. Such truths of human marketing would presumably have no place in the logical world of robots, but perhaps somewhere in the dim prehistory of Robot City there were human programmers, who added a few lines of code to make the robots endearingly greedy, selfish, and wasteful.

Darwinian processes seem irrelevant in robot society since, as nearly as I can tell, every robot is a unique example of intelligent design, including Aunt Fanny (Jennifer Coolidge), whose enormous derriere would no doubt confer an evolutionary advantage not immediately apparent, if robots reproduced according to the laws of DNA instead of the whims of manufacturers and repairmen. Imagine going to the garage after a breakdown and asking, "How long will it be before I can get myself back?"

Rock School ★ ★ ★
R, 93 m. 2005

With Paul Green, C. J. Tywoniak, Will O'Connor, Madi Diaz Svalgard, Tucker Collins, Asa Collins, Napoleon Murphy Brock, Eric Svalgard, Andrea Collins, Chris Lampson, Monique Del Rosario, Brandon King, Lisa Rubens, Lisa Green, and Jimmy Carl Black. A documentary directed by Don Argott and produced by Argott and Sheena M. Joyce.

Paul Green is a great teacher. We have this on the authority of Paul Green. He wanted to be a great rock musician, and when that didn't pan out, he picked something he could be great at, and now, he admits, he is great at it. He is the founder and apparently the entire faculty at the Paul Green School of Rock, a Philadelphia after-school program that takes kids ages nine to seventeen and trains them to be rock musicians. Maybe he would like to start even sooner; at one point he asks his infant son, "Can you say 'Jethro Tull'?"

The school is crammed into a narrow brick building where every classroom seems jammed with kids who do not measure up to Green's standards. He warns them, berates them, shouts at them, waves his arms, issues dire predictions, and somehow gets them to play music. Some of them are pretty good. There is a guitar player named C. J. Tywoniak, who stands about five feet tall and can play better than most of the guitarists you see on *Saturday Night Live*. And a singer named Madi Diaz Svalgard, who comes out of a Quaker background and knows people involved in a group named Quaker Gangsta.

"The whole thing in education now is that you don't compare children," Green says. "Well, I do." It's difficult to figure out what the kids are thinking as they stare at him during his tirades, but he has a certain level of self-mockery that takes the edge off. Green is not an angry jerk so much as a guy playing an angry jerk because he loves rock music and wants these kids to play it well. He is not Mr. Nice Guy, like the Jack Black character in *School of Rock*.

But what does he mean by rock music? "I wanted life as a rock star in 1972," he said. "I'd never want to be a rock star now." His god is Frank Zappa, and he leads the kids through difficult Zappa songs like *Inca Roads*, preparing them for the annual Zappanale Festival in Germany. "We gotta be the best band there," he says, and during his preshow pep talks he sounds uncannily like a coach in a high school sports movie. In Germany they get a chance to play with two Zappa veterans, Napoleon Murphy Brock and Jimmy Carl Black, and Murphy Brock gets down on his knees and bows to young C. J., and is about half-serious.

One of the most intriguing students in the school is Will O'Connor, who provides a description of his rocky beginnings: His was a difficult birth, his head was too large, he had to wear a neck brace for three years, he was misdiagnosed as mentally challenged, he was suicidal, etc., and then he discovered the School of Rock, and while he has not emerged as much of a musician, he no longer thinks of suicide and can even kid about it. Paul Green establishes the school's "Will O'-Connor Award for Student Most Likely to Kill Himself," which sounds one way when it's an in-joke in the school corridors and another way when it's quoted in the *Philadelphia Inquirer.* One thing becomes clear when O'-Connor is on the screen: Far from being "slow," he talks like the smartest person in the movie. The School of Rock is made for difficult cases like his.

There are scenes showing Lisa, Paul's wife, and his home life, which looks conventional. There are interviews with a few parents, who seem pleased with what their children are learning at school. One even styles her kid's hair in a spiky punk style, but draws the line at stenciling pentagrams on his face. Scenes of nine-year-olds rehearsing to sing in a menacing fashion are illuminating, revealing the nine-year-olds inside many rock singers.

Green uses the f-word incessantly, along with all the other words he can think of, and anyone in the conventional educational system would be horrified, I suspect, by moments in this film. What is important is that he doesn't talk down to the students, and he is deadly serious about wanting them to work hard, practice more, and become good musicians. He rants and raves, but at least he doesn't condescend. "By the time I'm thirty," his student Will O'Connor says, evaluating his musical progress, "I think I could be decent. If I live that long."

All very well, but how good a teacher is Paul Green, really? There are no scenes in the movie showing him actually teaching his students to play a guitar. Not a single musical note is discussed. No voice lessons. There are

times when the point of the school doesn't seem to be making students into rock stars, but rewriting Green's own lost childhood. There are other times when the students regard him blankly, waiting for his wacky behavior to be over so that they can get back to playing. We see no friendships between the students. Not much school spirit; they're playing for Green's glory, not their own. Green's approach certainly opens up opportunities for his students, and is a refreshing change from the lockstep public school approach, which punishes individualism. But sooner or later, a kid like C. J. Tywoniak is going to have to move on—to Julliard, maybe.

Rory O'Shea Was Here ★ ★ ★
R, 104 m., 2005

James McAvoy (Rory O'Shea), Steven Robertson (Michael Connolly), Romola Garai (Siobhan), Gerard McSorley (Fergus Connolly), Tom Hickey (Con O'Shea), Brenda Fricker (Eileen). Directed by Damien O'Donnell and produced by James Flynn and Juanita Wilson. Screenplay by Jeffrey Caine.

Don't you want to get drunk, get arrested, get laid?

—Rory to Michael

When Rory O'Shea arrives at the Carrigmore Home for the Disabled, Michael Connolly's life is on hold. Michael's cerebral palsy makes his speech difficult to decipher, except by Rory, who understands every word. Rory himself is exuberantly verbal, but muscular dystrophy has left him with control over two fingers of one hand, and that's it.

Are you still even reading this review? "Marketing challenges don't come much tougher," says *Variety,* the showbiz bible. So I should shift gears and say that *Rory O'Shea Was Here* is funny and moving, and more entertaining than some of the movies you are considering—more than *Son of the Mask* or *Constantine,* that's for sure.

In fact, trying to keep you from tuning out because of the subject matter, I've just gone back and added the quote at the top of this review. That's said by Rory to Michael in his attempt to blast him out of his silent corner at

577

the care home, and get him out in the world—where, Rory is convinced, they both belong.

Rory wears his hair in a weird arrangement of spikes. I didn't notice his shoes, but they were probably Doc Martens. Yes, muscular dystrophy has thrown him a curve, but he's still at the plate and swinging. In no time at all he has Michael following him into a pub, where he tries to pick up girls and at one point seems prepared to start a fight, which with anybody else would be a bad sign but for Rory may actually represent growth.

Rory wants to get out of the institutional world and into independent living. A well-meaning board of supervisors doesn't think he's ready for that yet, not with his disabilities combined with his recklessness. Michael is perfectly prepared to spend forever in the home, until Rory blasts him loose and uses him as his ticket to freedom. He convinces Michael to apply for independent living, and after Michael's application is approved by the board, Rory adds sweetly that of course Michael will need an interpreter.

They'll also need a care giver, and they interview the usual assortment of hopeless cases. There should be a *Little Glossary* entry about the obligatory scene where a job interview or an audition inevitably involves several weirdly unacceptable candidates, before the perfect choice steps forth.

In this case, they meet Siobhan (Romola Garai) in a supermarket, and convince her that life with them will have to be more exciting than stacking toilet tissues. It is more or less inevitable that they'll both get a crush on Siobhan, made more poignant because Rory will have to interpret whatever Michael wants to say to her. How this works out is not predictable, and is the occasion for some of the film's best written and acted scenes.

James McAvoy plays Rory as a would-be Dublin punk turned into the R. P. McMurphy of the care home. It's a performance combining joy and determination as if they feed off each other. Steven Robertson has more limited opportunities with his character, but let it be said that by the end of the film we can sort of understand what Michael is saying, and we always know what he means. Sometimes, on the other hand, amusingly, a word or two of Rory's Dublin accent slips past undetected.

Both actors are able-bodied in real life. I could not watch the movie without being powerfully reminded of an Australian film that never got theatrical distribution in the United States, Rolf de Heer's *Dance Me to My Song*. It was the first film in my first Overlooked Film Festival, and on stage we greeted Heather Rose, who, like Rory, could control only a finger or two. Yet she wrote the film and starred in it, as a woman with two goals in life, which Rory would have approved of: (1) get revenge on the minder who is mistreating her and stealing from her, and (2) meet a bloke and get laid. Heather Rose was a great and funny woman, who died last year. After the Q&A session, she typed out on her voice synthesizer, in the true Aussie spirit, "Now let's all go out and get pissed."

You can rent *Dance Me to My Song*, and you may want to, after seeing *Rory O'Shea Was Here*. There has been much talk involving the messages about disability sent by two major recent movies. Here is a movie that sends the message that if you want to be a punk and you're in a wheelchair, you can be a punk in a wheelchair. If you're in a chair and want to play rugby, you can, as a documentary named *Murderball* makes perfectly clear. Some are more disabled than others; Rory will not be able to play wheelchair rugby, but he'd make a hell of a coach.

Rugrats Go Wild! ★ ★
PG, 81 m., 2003

With the voices of: Michael Bell (Drew Pickles/Chaz Finster), Jodi Carlisle (Marianne Thornberry), Nancy Cartwright (Chuckie Finster), Lacey Chabert (Eliza Thornberry), Melanie Chartoff (Didi Pickles), Cheryl Chase (Angelica C. Pickles), Tim Curry (Sir Nigel Thornberry), Elizabeth Daily (Tommy Pickles), Danielle Harris (Debbie Thornberry), Bruce Willis (Spike). Directed by John Eng and Norton Virgien and produced by Gabor Csupo and Arlene Klasky. Screenplay by Kate Boutilier.

The Rugrats meet the Thornberrys in *Rugrats Go Wild!* a merger of the two popular Nickelodeon franchises that confirms our suspicion that Angelica Pickles can shout down anybody, even Debbie Thornberry. The movie has so much shouting, indeed so much noise in general, that I pity parents who will have to listen to it again and again and again after the DVD comes home and goes into an endless loop. The most persuasive argument for the animation of Hayao Miyazaki is that it's sometimes quiet and peaceful.

In the movie, the Pickles family goes on a cruise—not on the magnificent ocean liner that's pulling out just as they arrive at the dock, but on a leaky gutbucket that soon runs into big trouble, as the movie sails into *Perfect Storm* territory with a wall of water that towers above them.

Marooned by the storm on a deserted island, they discover it isn't deserted when they stumble upon Debbie Thornberry sunning herself beside the family's luxury camper. Yes, the Wild Thornberrys are on the island to film a documentary, and Sir Nigel and family more or less rescue the Pickles family, not without many adventures. One intriguing development: Spike, the Pickles's dog, talks for the first time, thanks to the ability of little Eliza Thornberry to speak with animals. (Spike's voice is by Bruce Willis.)

I sat watching the movie and was at a loss for an entry point. Certainly this is not a film an adult would want to attend without a child; unlike *Finding Nemo*, for example, it doesn't play on two levels, but just on one: shrill, nonstop action. That doesn't mean it lacks humor and charm, just that it pitches itself on the level of the Nickelodeon show instead of trying to move it beyond the target audience.

That's what I think, anyway, but as an adult, am I qualified to judge this film? Not long ago I (and 80 percent of the other critics in America) disliked Eddie Murphy's *Daddy Day Care*, only to be reprimanded by Al Neuharth, founder of *USA Today*, who wrote a column saying we critics were out of touch because he went with his children, aged five to twelve, and they liked it.

I offered Mr. Neuharth a list of a dozen other films his kids would probably like infinitely more, and which would also perhaps challenge and enlighten them, instead of simply bludgeoning them with sitcom slapstick. But on the off chance he was right, I took my grandsons, Emil, aged nine, and Taylor, age five, along with me to *Rugrats Go Wild!* and afterward asked them to rate it on a scale of one to ten.

They both put it at five. "Not as much fun as the TV show," said Emil. "Angelica didn't get to do as much funny stuff." What did they think about the Pickles family meeting the Thornberrys? They were unmoved, not to say indifferent.

My own feeling is that the film is one more assault on the notion that young American audiences might be expected to enjoy films with at least some subtlety and depth and pacing and occasional quietness. The filmmakers apparently believe their audience suffers from ADD, and so they supply breakneck action and screaming sound volumes at all times. That younger viewers may have developed ADD from a diet of this manic behavior on television is probably a fruitful field for study.

Note: The movie is presented in "Odorama." At most screenings, including the one I attended, audience members are given scratch-and-sniff cards with six scents, keyed to numbers that flash on the screen. We can smell strawberries, peanuts, tuna fish, etc. Scratching and sniffing, I determined that the root beer smells terrific, but the peanut butter has no discernible smell at all. The kids around me seemed pretty underwhelmed by this relic from the golden age of exploitation, which was last used by John Waters with his Polyester (1981).

Runaway Jury ★ ★ ★
PG-13, 127 m., 2003

John Cusack (Nicholas Easter), Gene Hackman (Rankin Fitch), Dustin Hoffman (Wendell Rohr), Rachel Weisz (Marlee), Bruce Davison (Durwood Cable), Bruce McGill (Judge Harkin), Jeremy Piven (Lawrence Greer), Nick Searcy (Doyle), Cliff Curtis (Frank Herrera). Directed by Gary Fleder and produced by Fleder, Christopher Mankiewicz, and Arnon Milchan. Screenplay by Brian Koppelman, David Levien, Rick Cleveland, and Matthew Chapman, based on the novel by John Grisham.

Although the jury selection process is intended to weed out bias among prospective jurors, it's an open secret that both sides look for bias—in their own favor, of course. There's an argument that juries would be more fairly selected by a random process, and *Runaway Jury* plays like the poster child for that theory. The new John

Grisham thriller is about a jury consultant who tries to guarantee a friendly panel, and a juror who does a little freelance jury consulting on his own.

The case involves a widow who is suing a gun manufacturer because her husband was killed in an office massacre involving an easily obtained weapon. The widow has hired the traditional, decent Wendell Rohr (Dustin Hoffman) to represent her, and the gun manufacturer is defended by a lawyer named Durwood Cable (Bruce Davison), who is the instrument of the evil, brilliant jury consultant Rankin Fitch (Gene Hackman).

Fitch has been hired by the reptilian head of the gun company to find a jury stacked in the company's favor. The most interesting sequence in the movie, a virtuoso montage of image, dialogue, and music by the director Gary Fleder, shows him doing just that. Fitch stands in front of an array of computer and television monitors, apparently able to summon at will the secrets of all the prospective jurors. I was reminded a little of Tom Cruise manipulating those floating digital images in *Minority Report*. Spying on dozens of jury pool members is probably not legal, especially when blackmailable information is obtained, but apart from that—wouldn't it cost millions, and could it be done in such a short time?

Such quibbles disappear in the excitement of the chase, as Fitch presides over his screens like an orchestra conductor, offering pithy comments on possible jurors and their faults. "I hate Baptists as much as I hate Democrats," he says. I don't know who that means he likes (atheist Republicans?), but Hackman can sell a line like that and make us believe Fitch can see into jurors' souls.

There is, however, one juror who gets on the panel despite Fitch's grave misgivings. This is Nicholas Easter (John Cusack), a feckless young man who seems to come from nowhere and appears to be trying to get off the jury (he feeds the judge a rambling explanation about the video game contest he's involved in). Easter's evasions inspire the judge (Bruce McGill) to lecture him on doing his duty, and puts indirect pressure on both sides to accept him.

(Spoiler warning.) Easter, as it turns out, is involved in a freelance arrangement with his woman friend Marlee (Rachel Weisz) to sell the jury to the highest bidder. He'll work on the inside, she'll handle the negotiations, and the highest bidder gets the verdict. This is an ingenious plot device, saving the movie from being a simple confrontation between good and evil and adding a wild card, forcing both sides to choose their own morality. Will the decent Wendell Rohr pay in order to win the verdict he believes his client deserves? Will the devious Durwood Cable add this expense to the massive Fitch operation? Can Easter sway a jury that Fitch thinks he has hand-picked for acquittal? These questions are so absorbing that we neglect to ask ourselves how Easter could be so sure of being called up for jury duty in the first place. If I missed the explanation, it must have been a doozy.

The movie hums along with a kind of sublime craftsmanship, fueled by the consistent performances of Hackman and Hoffman (in their first film together), the remarkable ease of John Cusack (the most relaxed and natural of actors since Robert Mitchum), and the juicy typecasting in the supporting roles. Several jury members are given back stories (there's a marine veteran, played by Cliff Curtis, who thinks the case is nonsense), and a little jury rebellion that leads to their defiant reciting of the Pledge of Allegiance in the courtroom. McGill, as the judge, treats them like an unruly grade-school class.

The movie's ending is underwhelming. There's a whole lot of explaining going on, as we discover everyone's hidden motives long after they've ceased to be relevant. And there's not enough behind-the-scenes stuff in the jury room showing Easter at work (what we see is a study in applied psychology). The jury room itself looks curiously like the one in *12 Angry Men*, reminding us of a movie where the jury really did decide a case. Here the jury is getting the case decided for it. "There are some things," say the movie's ads, "that are too important to be left to juries."

The Rundown ★ ★ ★ ½
PG-13, 104 m., 2003

Dwayne Johnson [The Rock](Beck), Seann William Scott (Travis), Rosario Dawson (Mariana), Christopher Walken (Hatcher), Stephen Bishop (Quarterback), Ewen Bremner

(Declan), Jeff Chase (Kambui), Jon Gries (Harvey), William Lucking (Billy Walker). Directed by Peter Berg and produced by Marc Abraham, Karen Glasser, and Kevin Misher. Screenplay by R. J. Stewart and James Vanderbilt.

Early in *The Rundown,* The Rock is entering a nightclub to confront some tough guys, and he passes Arnold Schwarzenegger on the way out. "Have a good time," Arnold says. It's like he's passing the torch. Whether The Rock will rival Schwarzenegger's long run as an action hero is hard to say—but on the basis of *The Rundown,* he has a good chance. I liked him in his first starring role, *The Scorpion King* (2002), but only up to a point: "On the basis of this movie," I wrote, "he can definitely star in movies like this." That's also true on the basis of *The Rundown*—but it's a much better movie, and he has more to do.

He plays a man named Beck, a "retrieval expert" who in the early scene is trying to retrieve a bad debt from an NFL quarterback. He does, beating up the entire defensive line in the process. Then his boss sends him on another mission—to bring back his son, who is somewhere in the Amazon. The moment I heard "Amazon" I perked up, because I'm getting tired of action movies shot entirely within Los Angeles County. Hawaii doubles for South America in the movie, and does a great job of it, apparently aided at times by computer effects; and the jungle locations give the film a texture and beauty that underlines the outsized characters.

Beck's mission takes him to a town named El Dorado, run by the evil Hatcher (Christopher Walken, whose first appearance, as usual, cheers up the audience). Beck's quarry is Travis Walker, a feckless fortune hunter played by Seann William Scott, who, yes, is the same Seann William Scott who plays Stiffler in the *American Pie* series. Here he has the same cocky in-your-face personality, has added a beard, and is once again a natural comic actor.

So is The Rock, within the limits set by his character (there is some kind of a sliding scale in action pictures in which the star can be funny up to a point, but the second banana can go beyond that point). I liked, for example, Beck's call to his boss before beating up half the

NFL team: He doesn't want to pound on them because "They may have a chance to repeat."

Just about the first person Beck meets in El Dorado is the bartender Mariana, played by Rosario Dawson, who later sees a lot of action and is convincing in it, reminding me a little of Linda Hamilton in *The Terminator.* "Have more beautiful lips ever been photographed?" I asked in my review of her performance in *Chelsea Walls.* On the basis of her performance here, I suggest that the answer is no.

Walken's character runs El Dorado as the kind of company town where all your wages go right back into the pocket of the boss (you have to rent your shovel by the day). Dawson's character doesn't like this, but I will not reveal more. Scott's character wants to find and steal a priceless Indian relic that will free the Indians in some unspecified way, but not if he sells it on eBay first. The Rock's character gets in the middle.

It goes without saying that Beck and Travis have to get lost in the jungle at some point, but how to arrange this? The film is admirably direct: Beck causes a Jeep to crash, and he and Travis roll down a hillside that is about nine miles long. I was reminded of the similar scene in *Romancing the Stone,* and indeed the two movies have a similar comic spirit. Once in the jungle they have all sorts of harrowing adventures, and I enjoyed it that real things were happening, that we were not simply looking at shoot-outs and chases, but at intriguing and daring enterprise.

So determined is the film to avoid shootouts on autopilot that Beck makes it a point not to use firearms. "Guns take me to a place I don't want to go," he says. When the chips are down and the going is very heavy, however, he reconsiders. There's a lurid, overheated montage showing close-ups of guns and ammo and close-ups of The Rock's eyes, and the pressure to pick up a gun builds and builds until it's like the drunk in *The Lost Weekend* contemplating falling off the wagon.

Christopher Walken has a specialty these days: He walks on-screen and delivers a febrile monologue that seems to come from some steamy bog in his brain. In *Poolhall Junkies,* he had a riff about the law of the wild. In *Gigli* he wondered if aliens had kidnapped the judge's brother. Here he tells a torturous parable about the Tooth Fairy, which the locals have a lot of trouble understanding. He also has a hat that reminds me of the hat rule: Hero wears normal hat, sidekick wears funny hat, villain wears ugly hat.

The movie was directed by Peter Berg, the actor, whose first directorial job was *Very Bad Things* (1998), a movie I thought was a very bad thing. Since I am quoting my old reviews today, let it be noted that I wrote in my review of that one: "Berg shows that he can direct a good movie, even if he hasn't." Now he has.

Russian Ark ★ ★ ★ ★
NO MPAA RATING, 96 m., 2002

Sergey Dontsov (The Marquis), Mariya Kuznetsova (Catherine the Great), Leonid Mozgovoy (The Spy), Mikhail Piotrovsky (Himself), David Giorgobiani (Orbeli), Aleksandr Chaban (Boris Piotrovsky), Lev Yeliseyev (Himself), Oleg Khmelnitsky (Himself), Maksim Sergeyev (Peter the Great). Directed by Aleksandr Sokurov and produced by Andrey Deryabin, Jens Meuer, and Karsten Stöter. Screenplay by Anatoly Nikiforov, Boris Khaimsky, Svetlana Proskurina, and Sokurov.

Every review of *Russian Ark* begins by discussing its method. The movie consists of one unbroken shot lasting the entire length of the film, as a camera glides through the Hermitage, the repository of Russian art and history in St. Petersburg. The cinematographer, Tilman Buttner, using a Steadicam and high-definition digital technology, joined with some 2,000 actors in a high-wire act in which every mark and cue had to be hit without fail; there were two broken takes before the third time was the charm.

The subject of the film, which is written, directed, and (in a sense) hosted by Aleksandr Sokurov, is no less than three centuries of Russian history. The camera doesn't merely take us on a guided tour of the art on the walls and in the corridors, but witnesses many visitors who came to the Hermitage over the years. Apart from anything else, this is one of the best-sustained *ideas* I have ever seen on the screen. Sokurov reportedly rehearsed his all-important camera move again and again with the cinematographer, the actors, and the invis-

ible sound and lighting technicians, knowing that the Hermitage would be given to him for only one precious day.

After a dark screen and the words "I open my eyes and I see nothing," the camera's eye opens upon the Hermitage and we meet the Marquis (Sergey Dontsov), a French nobleman who will wander through the art and the history as we follow him. The voice we heard, which belongs to the never-seen Sokurov, becomes a foil for the Marquis, who keeps up a running commentary. What we see is the grand sweep of Russian history in the years before the Revolution, and a glimpse of the grim times afterward.

It matters little, I think, if we recognize all of the people we meet on this journey; such figures as Catherine II and Peter the Great are identified (Catherine, like many another museum visitor, is searching for the loo), but some of the real people who play themselves, like Mikhail Piotrovsky, the current director of the Hermitage, work primarily as types. We overhear whispered conversations, see state functions, listen as representatives of the Shah apologize to Nicholas I for the killing of Russian diplomats, even see little flirtations.

And then, in a breathtaking opening-up, the camera enters a grand hall and witnesses a formal state ball. Hundreds of dancers, elaborately costumed and bejeweled, dance to the music of a symphony orchestra, and then the camera somehow seems to float through the air to the orchestra's stage and moves among the musicians. An invisible ramp must have been put into place below the camera frame for Buttner and his Steadicam to smoothly climb.

The film is a glorious experience to witness, not least because, knowing the technique and understanding how much depends on every moment, we almost hold our breath. How tragic if an actor had blown a cue or Buttner had stumbled five minutes from the end! The long, long single shot reminds me of a scene in *Nostalgia*, the 1982 film by Russia's Andrei Tarkovsky, in which a man obsessively tries to cross and recross a littered and empty pool while holding a candle that he does not want to go out: The point is not the action itself, but its duration and continuity.

It will be enough for most viewers, as it was for me, to simply view *Russian Ark* as an original and beautiful idea. But Stanley Kauffmann raises an inarguable objection in his *New Republic* review, when he asks, "What is there intrinsically in the film that would grip us if it had been made—even excellently made—in the usual edited manner?" If it were not one unbroken take, if we were not continuously mindful of its 96 minutes—what then? "We sample a lot of scenes," he writes, "that in themselves have no cumulation, no self-contained point. . . . Everything we see or hear engages us only as part of a directorial tour de force."

This observation is true, and deserves an answer, and I think my reply would be that *Russian Ark,* as it stands, is enough. I found myself in a reverie of thoughts and images, and some-times, as my mind drifted to the barbarity of Stalin and the tragic destiny of Russia, the scenes of dancing became poignant and ironic. It is not simply what Sokurov shows about Russian history, but what he does not show—doesn't need to show, because it shadows all our thoughts of that country. Kauffmann is right that if the film had been composed in the ordinary way out of separate shots, we would question its purpose. But it is not, and the effect of the unbroken flow of images (experimented with in the past by directors like Hitchcock and Max Ophuls) is uncanny. If cinema is sometimes dreamlike, then every edit is an awakening. *Russian Ark* spins a daydream made of centuries.

S

The Saddest Music in the World
★ ★ ★ ½
NO MPAA RATING, 99 m., 2004

Mark McKinney (Chester Kent), Isabella Rossellini (Lady Port-Huntly), Maria de Medeiros (Narcissa), David Fox (Fyodor), Ross McMillan (Roderick/Gavrillo). Directed by Guy Maddin and produced by Niv Fichman, Daniel Iron, and Jody Shapiro. Screenplay by Maddin and George Toles, based on an original screenplay by Kazuo Ishiguro.

So many movies travel the same weary roads. So few imagine entirely original worlds. Guy Maddin's *The Saddest Music in the World* exists in a time and place we have never seen before, although it claims to be set in Winnipeg in 1933. The city, we learn, has been chosen by the *London Times,* for the fourth year in a row, as "the world capital of sorrow." Here Lady Port-Huntly (Isabella Rossellini) has summoned entries for a contest which will award $25,000 "in depression-era dollars" to the performer of the saddest music.

This plot suggests, no doubt, some kind of camp musical, a sub–Monty Python comedy. What Maddin makes of it is a comedy, yes, but also an eerie fantasy that suggests a silent film like *Metropolis* crossed with a musical starring Nelson Eddy and Jeannette McDonald, and then left to marinate for long forgotten years in an enchanted vault. The Canadian filmmaker has devised a style that evokes old films from an alternate time line; *The Saddest Music* is not silent and not entirely in black and white, but it looks like a long-lost classic from decades ago, grainy and sometimes faded; he shoots on 8mm film and video, and blows it up to look like a memory from cinema's distant past.

The effect is strange and delightful; somehow the style lends quasi-credibility to a story that is entirely preposterous. Because we have to focus a little more intently, we're drawn into the film, surrounded by it. There is the sensation of a new world being created around us. The screenplay is by the novelist Kazuo Ishig-

uro, who wrote the very different *Remains of the Day.* Here he creates, for Maddin's visual style, a fable that's *Canadian Idol* crossed with troubled dreams.

Lady Port-Huntly owns a brewery, and hopes the contest will promote sales of her beer. Played by Rossellini in a blond wig that seems borrowed from a Viennese fairy tale, she is a woman who has lost her legs and propels herself on a little wheeled cart until being supplied with fine new glass legs, filled with her own beer.

To her contest come competitors like the American Chester Kent (Mark McKinney of *The Kids in the Hall*), looking uncannily like a snake-oil salesman, and his lover, Narcissa (Maria de Medeiros), who consults fortune-tellers on the advice of a telepathic tapeworm in her bowels. If you remember de Medeiros and her lovable little accent from *Pulp Fiction* (she was the lover of Bruce Willis's boxer), you will be able to imagine how enchantingly she sings "The Song Is You."

Kent's brother Roderick (Ross McMillan) is the contestant from Serbia. Their father, Fyodor (David Fox), enters for Canada, singing the dirge "Red Maple Leaves." One night while drunk, he caused a car crash and attempted to save his lover by amputating her crushed leg— but, alas, cut off the wrong leg, and is finally seen surrounded by legs. And that lover, dear reader, was Lady Port-Huntly.

Competitors are matched off two by two. "Red Maple Leaves" goes up against a pygmy funeral dirge. Bagpipers from Scotland compete, as does a hockey team that tries to lift the gloom by singing "I Hear Music." The winner of each round gets to slide down a chute into a vat filled with beer. As Lady Port-Huntly chooses the winners, an unruly audience cheers. Suspense is heightened with the arrival of a cellist whose identity is concealed by a long black veil.

You have never seen a film like this before, unless you have seen other films by Guy Maddin, such as *Dracula: Pages from a Virgin's Diary* (2002), or *Archangel* (1990). Although his

Tales from the Gimli Hospital was made in 1988, his films lived on the fringes, and I first became aware of him only in 2000, when he was one of the filmmakers commissioned to make a short for the Toronto Film Festival. His *The Heart of the World,* now available on DVD with *Archangel* and *Twilight of the Ice Nymphs* (1997), was a triumph, selected by some critics as the best film in the festival. It, too, seemed to be preserved from some alternate universe of old films.

The more films you have seen, the more you may love *The Saddest Music in the World.* It plays like satirical nostalgia for a past that never existed. The actors bring that kind of earnestness to it that seems peculiar to supercharged melodrama. You can never catch them grinning, although great is the joy of Lady Port-Huntly when she poses with her sexy new beer-filled glass legs. Nor can you catch Maddin condescending to his characters; he takes them as seriously as he possibly can, considering that they occupy a mad, strange, gloomy, absurd comedy. To see this film, to enter the world of Guy Maddin, is to understand how a film can be created entirely by its style, and how its style can create a world that never existed before, and lure us, at first bemused and then astonished, into it.

Safe Conduct ★ ★ ★ ★
NO MPAA RATING, 170 m., 2003

Jacques Gamblin (Jean Devaivre), Denis Podalydès (Jean Aurenche), Charlotte Kady (Suzanne Raymond), Marie Desgranges (Simone Devaivre), Ged Marlon (Jean-Paul Le Chanois), Philippe Morier-Genoud (Maurice Tourneur), Laurent Schilling (Charles Spaak), Maria Pitarresi (Reine Sorignal). Directed by Bertrand Tavernier and produced by Frédéric Bourboulon and Alain Sarde. Screenplay by Jean Cosmos and Tavernier, based on the book by Jean Devaivre.

More than 200 films were made in France during the Nazi Occupation, most of them routine, a few of them good, but none of them, Bertrand Tavernier observes, anti-Semitic. This despite the fact that anti-Semitism was not unknown in the French films of the 1930s. Tav-

ernier's *Safe Conduct* tells the story of that curious period in French film history through two central characters, a director and a writer, who made their own accommodations while working under the enemy.

The leading German-controlled production company, Continental, often censored scenes it objected to, but its mission was to foster the illusion of life as usual during the Occupation; it would help French morale, according to this theory, if French audiences could see new French films, and such stars as Michel Simon and Danielle Darrieux continued to work.

Tavernier considers the period through the lives of two participants, the assistant director Jean Devaivre (Jacques Gamblin) and the writer Jean Aurenche (Denis Podalydès). The film opens with a flurry of activity at the hotel where Aurenche is expecting a visit from an actress; the proprietor sends champagne to the room, although it is cold and the actress would rather have tea. Aurenche is a compulsive womanizer who does what he can in a passive-aggressive way to avoid working for the Germans while not actually landing in jail. Devaivre works enthusiastically for Continental as a cover for his activities in the French Resistance.

Other figures, some well known to lovers of French cinema, wander through: We see Simon so angry at the visit of a Nazi "snoop" that he cannot remember his lines, and Charles Spaak (who wrote *The Grand Illusion* in 1937) thrown into a jail cell, but then, when his screenwriting skills are needed, negotiating for better food, wine, and cigarettes in order to keep working while behind bars.

Like Francois Truffaut's *The Last Metro* (1980), the movie questions the purpose of artistic activity during wartime. But Truffaut's film was more melodramatic, confined to a single theater company and its strategies and deceptions, while Tavernier is more concerned with the entire period of history.

The facts of the time seem constantly available just beneath the veneer of fiction, and sometimes burst through, as in a remarkable aside about Jacques Dubuis, Devaivre's brother-in-law; after he was arrested as a Resistance member, the film tells us, Devaivre's wife never saw her brother again—except once, decades later, as an extra in a French film of the period. We see the moment in a film clip, as the long-dead man collects tickets at a theater. There was debate within the film community about collaborating with the Nazis, and some, like Devaivre, risked contempt for their cooperative attitude because they could not reveal their secret work for the Resistance. Tavernier shows him involved in a remarkable adventure, one of those wartime stories so unlikely they can only be true. Sent home from the set with a bad cold, he stops by the office and happens upon the key to the office of a German intelligence official who works in the same building. He steals some papers, and soon, to his amazement, finds himself flying to England on a clandestine flight to give the papers and his explanation to British officials. They fly him back; a train schedule will not get him to Paris in time, and so he rides his bicycle all the way, still coughing and sneezing, to get back to work. Everyone thinks he has spent the weekend in bed.

You would imagine a film like this would be greeted with rapture in France, but no. The leading French film magazine, *Cahiers du Cinema,* has long scorned the filmmakers of this older generation as makers of mere "quality," and interprets Tavernier's work as an attack on the New Wave generation that replaced them. This is astonishingly wrongheaded, since Tavernier (who worked as a publicist for such New Wavers as Godard and Chabrol) is interested in his characters not in terms of the cinema they produced but because of the conditions they survived, and the decisions they made.

Writing in the *New Republic,* Stanley Kauffmann observes: "Those who now think that these film people should have stopped work in order to impede the German state must also consider whether doctors and plumbers and teachers should also have stopped work for the same reason." Well, some would say yes. But that could lead to death, a choice it is easier to urge upon others than to make ourselves.

What Tavernier does here is celebrate filmmakers who did the best they could under the circumstances. Tavernier knew many of these characters; Aurenche and Pierre Bost, a famous screenwriting team, wrote his first film, *The Clockmaker of St. Paul,* and Aurenche worked on several others. In the film's closing moments, we hear Tavernier's own voice in narration, saying that at the end of his life, Aurenche told him he would not have done anything differently.

The Safety of Objects ★ ★
R, 121 m., 2003

Glenn Close (Esther Gold), Dermot Mulroney (Jim Train), Jessica Campbell (Julie Gold), Patricia Clarkson (Annette Jennings), Joshua Jackson (Paul Gold), Moira Kelly (Susan Train), Robert Klein (Howard Gold), Timothy Olyphant (Randy), Alex House (Jake Train), Mary Kay Place (Helen). Directed by Rose Troche and produced by Dorothy Berwin and Christine Vachon. Screenplay by Troche, based on stories by A. M. Homes.

Side by side on a shady suburban street, in houses like temples to domestic gods, three families marinate in misery. They know one another, but what they don't realize is how their lives are secretly entangled. We're intended to pity them, although their troubles are so densely plotted they skirt the edge of irony; this is a literate soap opera in which beautiful people have expensive problems and we wouldn't mind letting them inherit some undistinguished problems of our own.

To be sure, one of the characters has a problem we don't envy. That would be Paul Gold (Joshua Jackson), a bright and handsome teenager who has been in a coma since an accident. Before that he'd been having an affair with the woman next door, Annette Jennings (Patricia Clarkson), so there were consolations in his brief conscious existence.

Now his mother, Esther (Glenn Close), watches over him, reads to him, talks to him, trusts he will return to consciousness. His father, Howard (Robert Klein), doesn't participate in this process, having written off his heir as a bad investment, but listen to how Esther talks to Howard: "You never even put your eyes on him. How do you think that makes him feel?" The dialogue gets a laugh from the heartless audience, but is it intended as funny, thoughtless, ironic, tender, or what? The movie doesn't give us much help in answering that question.

In a different kind of movie, we would be deeply touched by the mother's bedside vigil. In a *very* different kind of movie, like Pedro Almodóvar's *Talk to Her,* which is about two men at the bedsides of the two comatose women they love, we would key in to the weird-sad tone that somehow rises above irony into a kind of sincere, melodramatic excess. But here—well, we know the Glenn Close character is sincere, but we can't tell what the film thinks about her, and we suspect it may be feeling a little more superior to her than it has a right to.

Written and directed by Rose Troche, based on stories by A. M. Homes, *The Safety of Objects* hammers more nails into the undead corpse of the suburban dream. Movies about the Dread Suburbs are so frightening that we wonder why everyone doesn't flee them, like the crowds in the foreground of Japanese monster movies.

The Safety of Objects travels its emotional wastelands in a bittersweet, elegiac mood. We meet a lawyer named Jim Train (Dermot Mulroney), who is passed over for partnership at his law firm, walks out in a rage, and lacks the nerve to tell his wife, Susan (Moira Kelly). Neither one of them knows their young child, Jake (Alex House), is conducting an affair—yes, an actual courtship—with a Barbie doll.

Next door is Helen (Mary Kay Place), who, if she is really going to spend the rest of her life picking up stray men for quick sex, should develop more of a flair. She comes across as desperate, although there's a nice scene where she calls the bluff of a jerk who succeeds in picking her up—and is left with the task of explaining why, if he really expected to bring someone home, his house is such a pigpen.

Let's see who else lives on the street. Annette, the Clarkson character, makes an unmistakable pitch to a handyman, who gets the message, rejects it, but politely thanks her for the offer. Annette is pathetic about men: She forgives her ex-husband anything, even when he skips his alimony payments, and lets a child get away with calling her a loser because she can't afford summer camp.

What comes across is that all of these people are desperately unhappy, are finding no human consolation or contact at home, are fleeing to the arms of strangers, dolls, or the comatose, and place their trust, if the title is to be believed, in the safety of objects. I don't think that means objects will protect them. I think it means they can't hurt them.

Strewn here somewhere are the elements of an effective version of this story—an *Ice Storm* or *American Beauty,* even a *My New Gun.* But Troche's tone is so relentlessly, depressingly monotonous that the characters seem trapped in a narrow emotional range. They live out their miserable lives in one lachrymose sequence after another, and for us there is no relief. *The Safety of Objects* is like a hike through the swamp of despond, with ennui sticking to our shoes.

Sahara ★ ★ ★
PG-13, 127 m., 2005

Matthew McConaughey (Dirk Pitt), Steve Zahn (Al Giordino), Penelope Cruz (Eva Rojas), Lambert Wilson (Massarde), Glynn Turman (Dr. Hopper), Delroy Lindo (Carl), William H. Macy (Admiral Sandecker), Rainn Wilson (Rudi), Lennie James (General Kazim). Directed by Breck Eisner and produced by Stephanie Austin, Howard Baldwin, Karen Elise Baldwin, and Mace Neufeld. Screenplay by Thomas Dean Donnelly, Joshua Oppenheimer, John C. Richards, and James V. Hart, based on the novel by Clive Cussler.

Clive Cussler, who wrote the novel that inspired *Sahara,* is said to have rejected untold drafts of the screenplay, and sued Paramount over this one. One wonders not so much what Cussler would have left out as what else could have gone in. *Sahara* obviously contains everything that could possibly be included in such a screenplay, and more. It's like a fire sale at the action movie discount outlet.

Do not assume I mean to be negative. I treasure the movie's preposterous plot. It's so completely over the top, it can see reality only in its rearview mirror. What can you say about a movie based on the premise that a Confederate ironclad ship from the Civil War is buried beneath the sands of the Sahara, having ventured there 150 years ago when the region was, obviously, damper than it is now?

Matthew McConaughey plays Dirk Pitt, the movie's hero, who is searching for the legendary ship. Dirk Pitt. Dirk Pitt. Or Pitt, Dirk. Makes Brad Pitt sound like William Pitt. Dirk has a thing about long-lost ships; readers may recall that he was also the hero of *Raise the Titanic* (1980), a movie so expensive that its producer,

Lord Lew Grade, observed, "It would have been cheaper to lower the ocean."

Dirk has a sidekick named Al Giordino, played by Steve Zahn in the time-honored Movie Sidekick mode. Was it Walter Huston who explained that movie heroes need sidekicks "because somebody has to do the dance." You know, the dance where the sidekick throws his hat down on the ground and stomps on it in joy or anger? You can't have your hero losing his cool like that.

The two men arrive in Africa to find that a dangerous plague is spreading. The plague is being battled by the beautiful Eva Rojas (Penelope Cruz), and it turns out that Dirk and Eva share mutual interests, since if the plague spreads down rivers and "interacts with salt water," there is a danger that "all ocean life will be destroyed." Actually, I am not sure why that is only a mutual interest; it's more of a universal interest, you would think, although General Kazim (Lennie James), the African dictator, and an evil French zillionaire (Lambert Wilson) don't seem much disturbed. That's because they're getting rich in a way I will not reveal, although there is something grimly amusing about converting pollutants into other pollutants.

The movie, directed by Breck Eisner, son of Michael, is essentially a laundry line for absurd but entertaining action sequences. Dirk, Eva, and Al have an amazing series of close calls in the desert, while Admiral Sandecker (ret.) (William H. Macy) keeps in touch with them by radio and remains steadfast in his course, whatever it is. There are chases involving planes, trains, automobiles, helicopters, dune buggies, wind-propelled airplane carcasses, and camels. The heroes somewhat improbably conceal themselves inside a tank car on a train going toward a secret desert plant (improbably, since the car going in that direction should have been full), and then find themselves one of those James Bondian vantage points inside the plant, from where they can observe uniformed clones carrying out obscure tasks.

There is a race against time before everything explodes, of course, and some bizarre science involving directing the sun's rays, and then what do you suppose turns up? If you slapped yourself up alongside the head and

shouted out, "The long-lost Civil War ironclad?" you could not be more correct. Gee, I wonder if its cannons will still fire after this length of time?

I enjoyed this movie on its own dumb level, which must mean (I am forced to conclude) in my own dumb way. I perceive that I have supplied mostly a description of what happens in the film, filtered through my own skewed amusement. Does that make this a real review?

Funny you should ask. As it happens, I happened to be glancing at Gore Vidal's article about the critic Edmund Wilson in a 1993 issue of the *New York Review of Books*. There Vidal writes: "Great critics do not explicate a text; they describe it and then report on what they have described, if the description itself is not the criticism." In this case, I think the description itself is the criticism. Yes, I'm almost sure of it.

Saints and Soldiers ★ ★ ★
PG-13, 90 m., 2004

Corbin Allred (Nathan "Deacon" Greer), Lawrence Bagby (Shirl Kendrick), Kirby Heyborne (Oberon Winley), Peter Asle Holden (Gordon Gunderson), Alexander Niver (Steven Gould), Lincoln Hoppe (Heinrich), Ruby Chase O'Neil (Sophie), Melinda Renee (Catherine), Ethan Vincent (Rudy). Directed by Ryan Little and produced by Adam Abel and Little. Screenplay by Geoffrey Panos and Matt Whitaker.

Just as it stands, *Saints and Soldiers* could have been made in 1948. That is not a bad thing. It has the strengths and the clean lines of a traditional war movie, without high-tech special effects to pump up the noise level. I saw it when the new restoration of Sam Fuller's *The Big Red One* (1980), made by a director who was an infantryman throughout World War II, and was struck by how the two films had similar tone: The No. 1 job of a foot soldier is to keep from getting killed. Doing his duty is a close second.

The film is inspired by actual events. We're told of a massacre of American soldiers at Malmedy, in Belgium, six months after the Normandy invasion; Nazis opened fire on

U.S. prisoners and most were killed, but four were able to lose themselves in the surrounding forest. The movie is about their attempt to walk back to the American lines through snow and bitter cold; along the way, they're joined by a British paratrooper who has intelligence about a major Nazi offensive, and they decide they have to get that to the Allies in time to do some good.

These five soldiers are ordinary people; well, the Americans are, although the Brit seems odd to them, and they don't always appreciate his sense of humor. They are tired and hungry all the time, and guard cigarettes like a precious hoard. Unlike the characters in modern war movies, they don't use four-letter words, and we don't miss them. I don't know if that's accurate or not. Certainly in the 1940s that language was much rarer that it is now, but Norman Mailer uses the f-word all through *The Naked and the Dead*, spelling it "fugg" to get it past the censors.

The movie's hero is quiet and troubled rather than gung-ho. That would be Corporal Nathan Greer (Corbin Allred), nicknamed "Deacon" because he treasures his Bible and was once a missionary in Berlin. That's where he learned the German that saves them. We assume he's a Mormon, but aren't actually told so. His little group is led by Sergeant Gordon Gunderson (Peter Holden), who shields him from criticism after he freezes at a crucial moment; he's the best sharpshooter in the group, but can he actually kill someone? Steven Gould (Alexander Niver), the medic, is the obligatory soldier from Brooklyn who is required in all World War II movies, and Shirl Kendrick (Lawrence Bagby) is the equally obligatory farm boy from the South. The British pilot, Oberon Winley (Kirby Heyborne), may have seen one David Niven movie too many.

The story follows them as they trek through the forest and try to stay alive. There are some close calls as German troops comb the area, but also a friendly Belgian housewife (who will remind film lovers of the farm wife in *Grand Illusion*), and maybe a little too coincidentally, a German soldier who was friendly with Deacon during his missionary days in Berlin.

The director, Ryan Little, used the mountains of Utah for Belgium, and a firm hand to insist on character and story in a movie that doesn't have a lot of money for extras and effects; many of the Germans are played by military hobbyists who stage battle reenactments, and they also lent Little some of their equipment. *Saints and Soldiers* isn't a great film, but what it does, it does well.

Saved! ★ ★ ★ ½
PG-13, 92 m., 2004

Jena Malone (Mary), Mandy Moore (Hilary Faye), Macaulay Culkin (Roland), Patrick Fugit (Patrick), Martin Donovan (Pastor Skip), Mary-Louise Parker (Lillian), Eva Amurri (Cassandra), Chad Faust (Dean). Directed by Brian Dannelly and produced by Michael Stipe, Sandy Stern, Michael Ohoven, and William Vince. Screenplay by Dannelly and Michael Urban.

Saved! is a satire aimed at narrow-minded Christians, using as its weapon the values of a more tolerant brand of Christianity. It is also a high school comedy, starring names from the top shelf of teenage movie stars: Mandy Moore *(The Princess Diaries)*, Jena Malone *(Donnie Darko)*, Patrick Fugit *(Almost Famous)*, and Macaulay Culkin, who is twenty-three but looks younger than anyone else in the cast. That Hollywood would dare to make a comedy poking fun at the excesses of Jesus people is, I think, an encouraging sign; we have not been entirely intimidated by the religious right.

The film follows the traditional pattern of many other teenage comedies. There's a clique ruled by the snobbiest and most popular girl in school, and an opposition made up of outcasts, nonconformists, and rebels. We saw this formula in *Mean Girls*. What's different this time is that the teen queen, Hilary Faye, is the loudest Jesus praiser at American Eagle Christian High School, and is played by Mandy Moore, having a little fun with her own good-girl image.

Her opposition is a checklist of kids who do not meet with Hilary Faye's approval. That would include Dean (Chad Faust), who thinks he may be gay; Cassandra (Eva Amurri), the only Jew in school and an outspoken rebel, and Roland (Culkin), Hilary Faye's brother, who is in a wheelchair but rejects all forms of sympathy and horrifies his sister by becoming Cassandra's boyfriend. There's also Patrick (Fugit), member of a Christian skateboarding team and the son of Pastor Skip (Martin Donovan), the school's principal. Patrick is thoughtful and introspective, and isn't sure he agrees with his father's complacent morality.

The heroine is Mary (Jena Malone), whose mother, Lillian (Mary-Louise Parker), has recently been named the town's No. 1 Christian Interior Decorator. Mary's boyfriend is Dean (Chad Faust, an interesting name in this context). One day they're playing a game that involves shouting out secrets to each other while underwater in the swimming pool, and Dean bubbles: "I think I'm gay!" Mary is shocked, bangs her head, thinks she sees Jesus (he's actually the pool maintenance guy), and realizes it is her mission to save Dean. That would involve having sex with him, she reasons, since only such a drastic act could bring him over to the hetero side. She believes that under the circumstances, Jesus will restore her virginity.

Jesus does not, alas, intervene, and Mary soon finds herself staring at the implacable blue line on her home pregnancy kit. Afraid to tell her mother, she visits Planned Parenthood, and is spotted by Cassandra and Roland.

> Cassandra: There's only one reason
> Christian girls come downtown to the
> Planned Parenthood!
> Roland: She's planting a pipe bomb?

You see what I mean. The first half of this movie is astonishing in the sharp-edged way it satirizes the knee-jerk values of Hilary Faye and her born-again friends. Another target is widower Pastor Skip, who is attracted to Mary's widowed mother, Lillian; she likes him, too, but they flirt in such a cautious way we wonder if they even realize what they're doing. A big complication: Skip is married, and his estranged wife is doing missionary work in Africa, making his feelings a torment.

At the time Mary sacrifices her virginity to conquer Dean's homosexuality, she's a member of Hilary Faye's singing trio, the Christian Jewels, and a high-ranking celebrity among the school's Jesus boosters. But the worldly Cassandra spots her pregnancy before anyone else does, and soon the unwed mother-to-be is hanging out with the gay, the Jew, and the kid in the wheelchair. They're like a hall of fame of outsiders.

Dean's sexuality is discovered by his parents, and he's shipped off to Mercy House, which specializes in drug detox and "degayification." Once again the screenplay, by director Brian Dannelly and Michael Urban, is pointed: "Mercy House doesn't really exist for the people that go there, but for the people who send them," says Patrick, who is having his own rebellion against Pastor Skip, and casts his lot with the rebels.

Now if the film were all pitched on this one note, it would be tiresome and unfair. But having surprised us with its outspoken first act, it gets religion of its own sort in the second and third acts, arguing not against fundamentalism but against intolerance; it argues that Jesus would have embraced the cast-outs and the misfits, and might have leaned toward situational ethics instead of rigid morality. Doesn't Mary, after all, think she's doing the right thing when she sleeps with Dean? (What Dean thinks remains an enigma.)

Saved! is an important film as well as an entertaining one. At a time when the FCC is enforcing a censorious morality on a nation where 8.5 million listeners a day are manifestly not offended by Howard Stern, here is a movie with a political message: Jesus counseled more acceptance and tolerance than some of his followers think. By the end of the movie, mainstream Christian values have not been overthrown, but demonstrated and embraced. Those who think Christianity is just a matter of enforcing their rule book have been, well, enlightened. And that all of this takes place in a sassy and smart teenage comedy is, well, a miracle. Oh, and *mirabile dictu*, some of the actors are allowed to have pimples.

Saw ★ ★
R, 100 m., 2004

Leigh Whannell (Adam), Cary Elwes (Dr. Lawrence Gordon), Danny Glover (Detective David Tapp), Ken Leung (Detective Steven Sing), Dina Meyer (Kerry), Mike Butters (Paul), Paul Gutrecht (Mark), Michael Emerson (Zep Hindle), Benito Martinez (Brett). Directed by James Wan and produced by Mark Burg, Gregg

Hoffman, and Oren Koules. Screenplay by
Leigh Whannell.

Saw is an efficiently made thriller, cheerfully gruesome, and finally not quite worth the ordeal it puts us through. It's a fictional machine to pair sadistic horrors with merciless choices, and so the question becomes: Do we care enough about the characters to share what they have to endure? I didn't.

Two films, *Touching the Void* and *Open Water*, involved characters who experienced almost unimaginable ordeals of pain and despair, and I was with them every step of the way—not least because I understood how they found themselves in their terrifying situations, and how they hoped to escape.

Saw, by contrast, depends on an improbably devious and ingenious villain who creates complications for the convenience of the screenplay. Named "The Jigsaw Killer," he joins that sturdy band of movie serial killers with time on their hands to devise elegant puzzles for their victims and the police. Sometimes that works, as in *The Silence of the Lambs,* and sometimes we simply feel toyed with. That said, *Saw* is well made and acted, and does what it does about as well as it could be expected to. Horror fans may forgive its contrivances.

The movie opens in a locked public toilet. A clock on the wall says it is 2 o'clock. Two men are chained by leg irons to opposite walls. In the center of the floor is a corpse in a pool of blood. Near the corpse are a revolver, a tape recorder, and a saw. The men are Adam (played by Leigh Whannell, who wrote the screenplay) and Dr. Lawrence Gordon (Cary Elwes). The corpse remains a mystery for a long time, but the tape recording is helpful: It informs both men that Dr. Gordon has to kill Adam by 6 o'clock, or his wife and daughter will be murdered.

A parallel story involves the efforts of two detectives to track down the Jigsaw Killer, who has posed such deadly ultimatums to earlier victims. (One involves a machine bolted to the victim's head, with a mechanism inserted into the mouth that is timed to rip the jaws apart after the deadline. I hate it when that happens.) The detectives are David Tapp (Danny Glover) and Steven Sing (Ken Leung), and

they're racing, as you might expect, against time.

Who is the Jigsaw Killer, and why has he gone to such diabolical lengths to devise such cruel predicaments? Well might you ask. The answer, of course, is that he is a plot device lowered into the movie with a toolbox filled with horrors, dangers, and unspeakable choices. He exists not because he has his reasons or motivations (although some are assigned to him, sort of as a courtesy, at the end). He exists because he tirelessly goes to great trouble and expense to fabricate a situation that the movie can exploit for 100 minutes. And he is almost certainly not who he seems to be, because of the screenwriting workshop principle that a false crisis and a false dawn must come before the real crisis and the real dawn.

Elwes and Whannell, chained by their ankles in the locked room, not only have to act their socks off but perhaps even their feet. Actors like roles like this, I suppose, because they can vibrate at peak intensity for minutes on end, screaming and weeping and issuing threats and pleas, and pretty much running through the gamut of emotions by knocking over all of the hurdles. You hope at the end of the movie they have a hot shower, a change of clothes, and a chicken dinner waiting for them.

As for the (possible) Jigsaw Killer, he of course is glimpsed imperfectly in some kind of a techno-torture lair, doing obscure things to control or observe the events he has so painstakingly fabricated. We see another version of the killer, also annoying: Jigsaw (or someone) disguises himself as a grotesque clownlike doll on a tricycle. Uh-huh. Whenever a movie shows me obscure, partial, oblique, fragmented shots of a murderous mastermind, or gives him a mask, I ask myself—why? Since the camera is right there in the lair, why not just show us his face? The answer, of course, is that he is deliberately obscured because he's being saved up for the big revelatory climax at the end.

A movie that conceals the identity of a killer is of a lower order, in general, than one that actually deals with him as a character. To get to know someone is infinitely more pleasing than to meet some guy behind a hockey mask, or in a puppet suit, or whatever. There is always the moment when the killer is unmasked and spews out his bitterness and hate and vindictive triumph over his would-be victims. I find it a wonder this obligatory scene has survived so long, since it is so unsatisfying. How about just once, at the crucial moment, the killer gets squished under a ton of canned soup and we never do find out who he was?

Scary Movie 3 ★ ½
PG-13, 90 m., 2003

Anna Faris (Cindy Campbell), Charlie Sheen (Tom Logan), Regina Hall (Brenda Meeks), Denise Richards (Annie Logan), Jeremy Piven (Ross Giggins), Queen Latifah (Shaniqua), Eddie Griffin (Orpheus), Anthony Anderson (Mahalik), Simon Rex (George). Directed by David Zucker and produced by Robert K. Weiss and Zucker. Screenplay by Brian Lynch, Craig Mazin, Pat Proft, Kevin Smith, and Zucker.

Scary Movie 3 understands the concept of a spoof but not the concept of a satire. It clicks off several popular movies *(Signs, The Sixth Sense, The Matrix, 8 Mile, The Ring)* and recycles scenes from them through a spoofalator, but it's feeding off these movies, not skewering them. The average issue of *Mad* magazine contains significantly smarter movie satire, because Mad goes for the vulnerable elements, and *Scary Movie 3* just wants to quote and kid.

Consider the material about *8 Mile*. Eminem is talented and I liked his movie, but he provides a target that *Scary Movie 3* misses by a mile. The Eminem clone is played by Simon Rex, whose material essentially consists of repeating what Eminem did in the original movie, at a lower level. He throws up in the john (on somebody else, ho, ho), he duels onstage with a black rapper, he preempts criticism by attacking himself as white, he pulls up the hood on his sweatshirt and it's shaped like a Ku Klux Klan hood, and so on. This is parody, not satire, and no points against Eminem are scored.

Same with the crop circles from *Signs*, where farmer Tom Logan (Charlie Sheen) finds a big crop circle with an arrow pointing to his house and the legend ATTACK HERE. That's level one. Why not something about the way the movie extended silence as far as it could go? His part-

ing scene with his wife (Denise Richards), who is being kept alive by the truck that has her pinned to a tree, is agonizingly labored.

The Ring material is barely different from *The Ring* itself; pop in the cassette, answer the phone, be doomed to die. *The Sixth Sense* stuff is funnier, as a psychic little kid walks through the movie relentlessly predicting everyone's secrets. Funny, but it doesn't build. Then there's an unpleasant scene at the home of news reader Cindy Campbell (Anna Faris), involving a salivating priest who arrives to be a baby-sitter for her young son (ho, ho).

The movie is filled with famous and semi-famous faces, although only two of them work for their laughs and get them. That would be in the pre–opening credits, where Jenny McCarthy and Pamela Anderson take the dumb blond shtick about as far as it can possibly go, while their push-up bras do the same thing in another department.

Other cameos: Queen Latifah, Eddie Griffin, William Forsythe, Peter Boyle, Macy Gray, George Carlin, Ja Rule, Master P, and Leslie Nielsen, the Olivier of spoofs, playing the president. But to what avail? The movie has been directed by David Zucker, who with his brother Jerry and Jim Abrahams more or less invented the genre with the brilliant *Airplane!* (1980). Maybe the problem isn't with him. Maybe the problem is that the genre is over and done with and dead. *Scream* seemed to point in a new and funnier direction—the smart satire—but *Scary Movie 3* points right back again. It's like it has its own crop circle, with its own arrow pointing right at itself.

School of Rock ★ ★ ★ ½
PG-13, 108 m., 2003

Jack Black (Dewey Finn), Joan Cusack (Rosalie Mullins), Mike White (Ned Schneebly), Sarah Silverman (Patty), Joey Gaydos (Zack), Miranda Cosgrove (Summer), Maryam Hassan (Tomika), Kevin Clark (Kevin), Rebecca Brown (Katie), Robert Tsai (Lawrence),Brian Falduto (Billy). Directed by Richard Linklater and produced by Scott Rudin. Screenplay by Mike White.

Jack Black is a living, breathing, sweating advertisement for the transformative power of rock and roll in *School of Rock*, the first kid movie that parents will like more than their children. He plays Dewey Finn, failed rocker, just kicked out of the band he founded. Rock is his life. When he fakes his way into a job as a substitute fifth-grade teacher, he ignores the lesson plans and turns the class into a rock band; when the kids ask about tests, he promises them that rock "will test your head, and your mind, and your brain, too."

Now that's a cute premise, and you probably think you can guess more or less what the movie will be like. But you would be way wrong, because *School of Rock* is as serious as it can be about its comic subject, and never condescends to its characters or its audience. The kids aren't turned into cloying little clones, but remain stubborn, uncertain, insecure, and kidlike. And Dewey Finn doesn't start as a disreputable character and then turn gooey. Jack Black remains true to his irascible character all the way through; he makes Dewey's personality not a plot gimmick, but a way of life.

If quirky, independent, grown-up outsider filmmakers set out to make a family movie, this is the kind of movie they would make. And they did. The director is Richard Linklater *(Dazed and Confused, Before Sunrise)*, the indie genius of Austin, Texas, who made *Waking Life* in his garage and revolutionized animation by showing that a commercial film could be made at home with a digital camera and a Macintosh. The writer and costar is Mike White, who since 2000 has also written *Chuck and Buck, Orange County* (which costarred Black as a rebel couch potato), and the brilliant *The Good Girl*, with Jennifer Aniston as a married discount clerk who falls in love with the cute checkout kid.

White's movies lovingly celebrate the comic peculiarities of everyday people, and his Dewey Finn is a goofy original—a slugabed who complains, when his roommate (White) asks for the rent, "I've been mooching off of you for years!" He truly believes that rock, especially classic rock, will heal you and make you whole. His gods include Led Zeppelin, The Ramones, and The Who. His own career reaches a nadir when he ends a solo by jumping ecstatically off the stage and the indifferent audience lets him fall to the floor.

He needs money. A school calls for his roommate, he fakes his identity, and later that day is facing a suspicious group of ten-year-olds and confiding, "I've got a terrible hangover." It's an expensive private school, their parents pay $15,000 a year in tuition, and Summer (Miranda Cosgrove), the smarty-pants in the front row, asks, "Are you gonna teach us anything, or are we just gonna sit here?"

The class files out for band practice, Dewey listens to their anemic performance of classical chestnuts, and has a brainstorm: He'll convert them into a rock group and enter them in a local radio station's Battle of the Bands.

The movie takes music seriously. Dewey assigns instruments to the talented students, including keyboardist Lawrence (Robert Tsai), lead guitarist Zack (Joey Gaydos), drummer Kevin (Kevin Clark), and backup singer Tomika (Maryam Hassan), who is shy because of her weight. "You have an issue with *weight?*" Dewey asks. "You know who else has a weight issue? *Me!* But I get up there on the stage and start to sing, and people *worship* me!"

There's a job for everyone. Billy (Brian Falduto) wants to be the band's designer, and produces glitter rock costumes that convince Dewey the school uniforms don't look so bad. Busybody Summer is made the band's manager. Three girls are assigned to be groupies, and when they complain that groupies are sluts, Dewey defines them as more like cheerleaders.

Of course there is a school principal. She is Rosalie Mullins (Joan Cusack), and, miraculously, she isn't the standard old prune that movies like this usually supply, but a good soul who loves her school and has been rumored to be capable, after a few beers, of getting up on the table and doing a Stevie Nicks imitation. The big payoff is the Battle of the Bands, and inevitably all of the angry parents are in the front row, but the movie stays true, if not to its school, at least to rock and roll, and you have a goofy smile most of the time.

I saw a family film named *Good Boy!* that was astonishingly stupid, and treated its audience as if it had a tragically slow learning curve and was immune to boredom. Here is a movie that proves you can make a family film that's alive and well acted and smart and perceptive and funny—and that rocks.

Note: I have absolutely no clue why the movie is rated PG-13. There's "rude humor and some drug references," the MPAA says. There's not a kid alive who would be anything but delighted by this film. It belongs on the MPAA's List of Shame with Whale Rider *and* Bend It Like Beckham, *two other PG-13 films perfect for the family.*

Schultze Gets the Blues ★ ★ ★ ½

PG, 114 m., 2005

Horst Krause (Schultze), Harald Warmbrunn (Jurgen), Karl Fred Muller (Manfred), Ursula Schucht (Jurgen's Wife), Hannelore Schubert (Manfred's Wife), Wolfgang Boos (Gatekeeper), Leo Fischer (Head of Music Club), Loni Frank (Schultze's Mother). Directed by Michael Schorr and produced by Jens Korner. Screenplay by Schorr.

Do they have salt mines in Germany? Or is Schultze's job simply a symbol of a lifetime of thankless toil? Day after day he ventures down into the salt mine until, with a shock, he and three friends are forced to retire. There is a little party at the beer hall, his coworkers singing a lugubrious song of farewell, and Schultze is a retired man. Not married, he passes his days in the sad enjoyment of unwanted freedom. Sometimes he contemplates his retirement present, a lamp made from large block of crystallized salt with a bulb inside. If it ever falls into other hands, will its new owners think to lick it?

Schultze (Horst Krause) is a bulky, stolid, unlovely man who wipes the dust from his garden gnomes, spends as much time as possible napping on his sofa, visits his mother in a nursing home, plays the accordion at a polka club, and plays chess at a club where the level of play is not too high; one should not reach retirement age as a chess player still arguing over applications of the "touch-move" rule. He gets around town on his bicycle, dealing with the delays caused by a rail crossing guard who is distracted by the study of alchemy.

One night Schultze's world changes forever. On the radio he hears zydeco music from Louisiana. I was reminded of *Genghis Blues*, the 1999 film where a blind musician in San Francisco, Paul Pena, hears Tuva throat-singing over the radio, teaches it to himself, and travels to the Republic of Tuva for the annual competition. Schultze becomes a man possessed. He takes up his accordion, begins to pump through a tired song he has played a thousand times, and then gradually increases the tempo and turns up the heat until he is playing, well, zydeco polka.

That is not an impossible musical genre. David Golia, a friend of mine from San Francisco, leads a polka band that explores what he sees as the underlying connection between polka, rock, and Mexican and Brazilian music. It's not all about beer barrels.

Schultze now becomes a man obsessed. His lonely life is filled with fantasies of far-off bayous. He gets a cookbook and prepares jambalaya on his kitchen stove. His polka club listens to his zydeco arrangements and votes to send him to a German music festival in the town's sister city in Texas—not so much to honor him, we suspect, as to get him out of town.

Schultze is not much of a traveler, and speaks perhaps a dozen words of English. Unlike the travelers in many movies, he doesn't magically learn many more. The Texas festival does not nurture his inner man, and he does what any sensible person in Schultze's position would do, which is to purchase a boat and set off across the Gulf and into the waterways of Louisiana.

What may not be clear in my description is that *Schultze Gets the Blues* is not entirely, or even mostly, a comedy, even though it has passages of droll, deadpan humor. It is essentially the record of a man who sets himself into motion and is amazed by the results. I was reminded of Aki Kaurismaki's *The Man without a Past* (2002), the story of a man whose amnesia frees him to begin an altogether different life. The film has also been compared with *About Schmidt* (2002), although Schmidt was a madcap compared to Schultze.

Schultze is not an object of fun, but a focus of loneliness and need, a man who discovers too late that he made no plans for his free time and is deeply bored by his life. His American journey is not travel but exploration—not of a new land, but of his own possibilities. He suddenly realizes that he, Schultze, can move from one continent to another, can medicate his blues with Louisiana hot sauce, and play music that sends his accordion on crazy trills of joy.

He does not, during his journey, meet a soul mate, fall in love, become discovered on

American Idol, or do anything else than live his new life. He meets people easily because he is so manifestly friendly and harmless, but finds it hard to form relationships because of his handful of words. No matter. We suspect it was the same for him even in Germany, and now he wanders where every single thing he sees is new to his eyes.

The writer and director, Michael Schorr, is making his first film, but has the confidence and simplicity of someone who has been making films forever. Unlike many first-timers, he isn't trying to see how much of his genius one film can contain. He begins, I think, not with burning ambition, but with a simple love and concern for Schultze. He creates the character, watches him asleep on the sofa, and then follows a few steps behind as Schultze backs away from the dead-end of retirement. He begins his journey with a single step, as we know all journeys must begin, and arrives at last on a boat in the Gulf of Mexico, where not all journeys end, and where Schultze must be as surprised as his director to find himself.

Scooby-Doo 2: Monsters Unleashed ★ ★
PG, 93 m., 2004

Freddie Prinze Jr. (Fred), Sarah Michelle Gellar (Daphne), Matthew Lillard (Shaggy), Linda Cardellini (Velma), Seth Green (Patrick), Peter Boyle (Old Man Wickles), Tim Blake Nelson (Jacobo), Alicia Silverstone (Heather). Directed by Raja Gosnell and produced by Charles Roven and Richard Suckle. Screenplay by James Gunn.

The Internet was invented so that you can find someone else's review of Scooby-Doo. *Start surfing.*

Those were the closing words of my 2002 review of the original *Scooby-Doo,* a review that began with refreshing honesty: "I am not the person to review this movie." I was, I reported, "unable to generate the slightest interest in the plot, and I laughed not a single time, although I smiled more than once at the animated Scooby-Doo himself, an island of amusement in a wasteland of fecklessness."

Whoa, but I was in a bad mood that day. I gave the movie a one-star rating. Now I am faced with *Scooby-Doo 2.* There is a subtitle: *Monsters Unleashed.* As the story commences, our heroes in Mystery Inc. are attending the opening night of a museum exhibiting souvenirs from all of the cases they have solved. The event turns into a disaster when one of the monster costumes turns out to be inhabited and terrorizes the charity crowd.

Now I don't want you to think I walked into 2 with a chip on my shoulder because of the 2002 film. I had completely forgotten the earlier film, and so was able to approach the sequel with a clean slate. I viewed it as the second movie on a day that began with a screening of *Taking Lives,* with Angelina Jolie absorbing vibes from the graves of serial killer victims. The third movie was Bresson's 1966 masterpiece *Au Hasard Balthazar,* which could have been called *The Passion of the Donkey.* So you see, we have to shift gears quickly on the film crit beat.

What I felt as I watched *Scooby-Doo* was not the intense dislike I had for the first film, but a kind of benign indifference. There was a lot of eye candy on the screen, the colors were bright, the action was relentless, Matthew Lillard really is a very gifted actor, and the animated Scooby-Doo is so jolly I even liked him in the first movie. This film is no doubt ideally constructed for its target audience of ten-year-olds and those who keenly miss being ten-year-olds.

Once again, to quote myself, I am not the person to review this movie, because the values I bring to it are irrelevant to those who will want to see it. This is a silly machine to whirl goofy antics before the eyes of easily distracted audiences, and it is made with undeniable skill. Watching it is a little like watching synchronized swimming: One is amazed at the technique and discipline lavished on an enterprise that exists only to be itself.

But a little more about the movie. The original cast is back, led by Lillard as Scooby-Doo's friend Shaggy, and containing Freddie Prinze Jr., Sarah Michelle Gellar, and Linda Cardellini. Alicia Silverstone plays a trash-TV reporter who is determined to debunk the myth of Mystery Inc. The always reliable Peter Boyle is mean Old Man Wickles, who, if he is not involved in skullduggery, is in the movie under false pretenses.

Seth Green is funny as the museum curator. And there are a lot of cartoon monsters.

Is this better or worse than the original? I have no idea. I'll give it two stars because I didn't feel anything like the dislike I reported after the first film, but no more than two, because while the film is clever it's not really trying all that hard. I think the future of the republic may depend on young audiences seeing more movies like *Whale Rider* and fewer movies like *Scooby-Doo 2*, but then that's just me.

The Scoundrel's Wife ★ ★ ½
R, 99 m., 2003

Tatum O'Neal (Camille Picou), Julian Sands (Dr. Lenz), Tim Curry (Father Antoine), Lacey Chabert (Florida Picou), Eion Bailey (Ensign Jack Burwell), Patrick McCollough (Blue Picou). Directed by Glen Pitre and produced by Peggy Rajski and Jerry Daigle. Screenplay by Michelle Benoit and Pitre.

The Scoundrel's Wife takes place in the small but real bayou fishing village of Cut Off, Louisiana, during World War II. German submarines have been sighted offshore, and the Coast Guard suspects local shrimp boat operators of trading with the enemy. If the premise seems far-fetched, the movie's closing titles remind us that some 600 vessels were attacked by U-boats in American coastal waters, and the movie's plot is inspired by stories heard in childhood by the director, Glen Pitre, who lives in Cut Off to this day.

Pitre is a legendary American regional director, a shrimper's son who graduated from Harvard and went back home to Louisiana to make movies. His early films were shot in the Cajun dialect, starred local people, and played in local movie houses where they quickly made back their investment. I met him at Cannes and again at the Montreal festival—French enclaves where he was being saluted as arguably the world's only Cajun-language filmmaker.

He broke into the mainstream with *Belizaire the Cajun* (1986), starring Armand Assante as a Cajun who defends his people's homes against marauding bands of Anglo rabble-rousers. Found guilty of murder, he stands on a scaffold between two (symbolic?) thieves and tries to talk his way free. He's sort of a bayou version of

Gandhi, restraining his anger, able to see the comic side of his predicament, possessed of physical strength and quiet charm.

Now Pitre is back with *The Scoundrel's Wife*, again filmed near home, with local extras joining such stars as Tatum O'Neal, Julian Sands, Tim Curry, Lacey Chabert, and Eion Bailey (of *Band of Brothers*). The film is frankly melodramatic and the climax is hard to believe, but the movie has such a fresh sense of place and such a keen love for its people that it has genuine qualities despite its narrative shortcomings.

O'Neal stars, in her first role since *Basquiat* (1996), as Camille Picou, the widow of a shrimp boat captain who was making ends meet by smuggling in Chinese aliens. He may have been guilty of the murder of some of them, and Camille may have been an accomplice—at least that's what the local people think. She's raising her two teenagers, her son, Blue (Patrick McCollough), and daughter, Florida (Chabert), when World War II begins, and the Coast Guard entrusts a local boy, the untested young ensign Jack Burwell (Bailey), to monitor fishing activities and keep an eye out for spies.

Are there spies in Cut Off? There are certainly suspicious characters. One of them is the German refugee Dr. Lenz (Julian Sands), said to be Jewish, who has settled in as the only local doctor. Another, oddly enough, is the local priest, Father Antoine (Tim Curry), who is charmingly drunk much of the time but also spends ominous evenings in the cemetery, using an iron cross as an antenna for his shortwave radio.

Whether the priest is a spy (and whether the doctor is all he says he is) will not be discussed here. There are two possible romances in the film, one between the widow Picou and the German, the other between the ensign and young Florida. There is also much malicious gossip, all adding up to a scene in the doctor's front yard when a lynch crowd turns up and seems remarkably easy to convince of first one story and then another.

Objectively, *The Scoundrel's Wife* has problems, and there will not be a person in the audience convinced of what happens in the last scene. But I just fired off a note to a campus film critic who was being urged to write more objectively, and asked him, what is a review if not subjective? So let me confess my subjectivity.

I like the bayou flavor of this film, and the

fact that it grows from a local story that has been retailed, no doubt, over hundreds of bowls of gumbo. I like the quiet dignity O'Neal brings to her guilt-ridden widow, and I like Curry's willingness to make his priest a true eccentric, instead of trying to hunker down into some bayou method performance. I like the soft, humid beauty of Uta Briesewitz's photography. And if the ending does not convince, well, a lot of family legends do not bear close scrutiny. The movie is finally just a little too ungainly, too jumbled at the end, for me to recommend, but it has heart, and I feel a lot of affection for it.

The Sea ★ ★

NO MPAA RATING, 109 m., 2003

Gunnar Eyjolfsson (Thordur), Hilmir Snaer Gudnason (Agust), Helene De Fougerolles (Francoise), Kristbjorg Kjeld (Kristin), Sven Nordin (Morten), Gudrun S. Gisladottir (Ragnheidur), Sigurdur Skulason (Haraldur), Elva Osk Olafsdottir (Aslaug), Nina Dogg Filippusdottir (Maria), Herdis Thorvaldsdottir (Kata). Directed by Baltasar Kormakur and produced by Kormakur and Jean-Francois Fonlupt. Screenplay by Kormakur and Olafur Haukur Simonarson, based on a play by Simonarson.

How to spot a film inspired by *King Lear*: An old fart summons home three children amid hints of dividing the kingdom. Once we've spotted this early telltale clue, there can't be many surprises. Each child will fail to do or say what is expected, and the odds are good the O.F. will eventually be wandering in some kind of a wilderness. I've seen the story set in Japan and a farm in Iowa, and now here is *The Sea*, which begins with the Lear figure thundering against changes in the Icelandic fishing industry.

The patriarch is Thordur (Gunnar Eyjolfsson), who owns a fish processing factory in a fading Icelandic fishing village, and refuses to change his ways. His fish are still cleaned by hand, by local women in spotless uniforms, and he rails against the mechanized factory ships that process and ice the fish at sea. He is also loyal to the aging operators of the port's small fishing boats, which are no longer economic.

Still, there is money to be made, or salvaged,

from the family business, especially if Thordur sells out to his hated rival and there is a redistribution of local fishing quotas. That is what, in various ways, his desperately neurotic and unhappy family hopes will happen.

We meet the three children, Agust (Hilmir Snaer Gudnason), Haralder (Sigurdur Skulason), and the daughter, Ragnheidur (Gudrun S. Gisladottir). Each is unhappy in a different way. Agust has been living in Paris with his pregnant girlfriend, Maria (Nina Dogg Filippusdottir), squandering his business-school tuition on *la vie bohème*. Haraldur has to endure his harpy of a wife, Aslaug (Elva Osk Olafsdottir), a drunk who runs a sexy lingerie shop. And Ragnheidur, who as the youngest daughter might be suspected of Cordelia tendencies, is a would-be filmmaker in an unhappy marriage.

Ah, but there are more characters. Thordur's wife, Kristin (Kristbjorg Kjeld), is the sister of his first wife, who died in a way that still inspires festering bitterness. And we meet Thordur's old mother, who specializes in spitting out the painful truth at the wrong moment; and various former mistresses, colorful cops, crotchety fishermen, and disloyal business associates.

The characters in Baltasar Kormakur's film are thoroughly wretched, but lack the stature of tragic heroes and are mainly sniveling little rats. They hate their father and each other. The father is clearly wrong about the fishing business, and probably knows it, but hangs onto his old ways out of sheer bloody-mindedness, or to make his family miserable. Since there seems to be no joy in the little village except the kinds that can be purchased with money, it seems ill-mannered of old Thordur to refuse to cash in, and merely sensible of Agust to relocate to Paris.

The Sea is overcrowded and overwritten, with too many shrill denunciations and dramatic surprises; we don't like the characters and, worse, they don't interest us. Surprisingly, the film was nominated by Iceland for this year's Best Foreign Film Oscar. I am surprised because in July 2002 at the Karlovy Vary film festival, I saw a much better film about Icelandic families named *The Seagull's Laughter*, a human comedy about a teenage girl whose life is changed by the return home of a sexy local woman, a bit of a legend who has lived abroad for years. It has the grace and humanity that the lumbering *The Sea* is lacking.

597

Seabiscuit ★ ★ ★ ½
PG-13, 140 m., 2003

Tobey Maguire (Red Pollard), Jeff Bridges (Charles Howard), Chris Cooper (Tom Smith), Gary Stevens (George Woolf), Elizabeth Banks (Marcela Howard), William H. Macy (Tick Tock McGlaughlin), Eddie Jones (Samuel Riddle). Directed by Gary Ross and produced by Kathleen Kennedy, Frank Marshall, Ross, and Jane Sindell. Screenplay by Ross, based on the book by Laura Hillenbrand.

Seabiscuit was a small horse with a lazy side. Sleeping and eating were his favorite occupations early in life, and he wasn't particularly well behaved. That was before he met three men who would shape him into the best-loved sports legend of the 1930s: the owner Charles Howard, who had a knack for spotting potential in outcasts, the trainer Tom Smith, who was called a screwball for thinking he could heal horses other trainers would have shot, and the jockey Red Pollard, who started out as an exercise boy and stable cleaner because in the depression he would settle for anything.

Seabiscuit, based on the best-seller by Laura Hillenbrand, tells the stories of these three men and the horse against the backdrop of the times. The depression had brought America to its knees. The nation needed something to believe in. And in the somewhat simplified calculus of the movie, both Seabiscuit and Roosevelt's New Deal, more or less in that order, were a shot in the American arm. If an underdog like Seabiscuit could win against larger and more famous horses with distinguished pedigrees, then maybe there was a chance for anyone.

The story has the classic structure of a sports movie, with a setback right before the big race at the end, but, like Seabiscuit, it's a slow starter. There is a leisurely introduction to the times and the three men before the horse makes its appearance, and we see once again the classic battle between the automobile and the horse. Charles Howard (Jeff Bridges) begins as a bicycle salesman, is asked to repair a Stanley Steamer, takes it apart and makes some improvements, and before long is a millionaire who buys a farm and turns the stables into a garage.

After a family tragedy, however, he changes directions and becomes a horse owner and breeder. And there are sequences showing how he encounters Pollard (Tobey Maguire) and Smith (Chris Cooper). Soon he has everything in place except a horse, and Smith has unaccountable faith in Seabiscuit. It has to do with the horse's heart.

The movie doesn't make the mistake of treating the horse like a human. It is a horse all the time, a horse with the ability to run very fast and an inability to lose, when guided by Smith's strategy and Pollard's firm love. The movie's races are thrilling because they must be thrilling; there's no way for the movie to miss on those, but writer-director Gary Ross and his cinematographer, John Schwartzman, get amazingly close to the action; it's hard for us to figure out where the camera is, since we seem to be suspended at times between two desperately striving horses and their jockeys.

The movie gives me a much better sense of how difficult and dangerous it is to ride one of those grand animals in a race. The jockeys are sometimes friends, sometimes mortal enemies, and they often shout at one another during races. Sometimes this works, sometimes it is a little improbable, as when Red says "goodbye" to a friend as Seabiscuit shifts into winning gear.

As horses compete, so do owners. After Seabiscuit has conquered all of the champion horses of the West, Charles Howard begins a strategy to force a match race between his horse and War Admiral, the eastern champion and Triple Crown winner owned by Samuel Riddle (Eddie Jones). He goes on a whistle-stop campaign across the country (this seems to anticipate Truman's 1948 campaign) and builds up such an overwhelming groundswell of public sentiment that Riddle caves in and agrees—on his terms, of course, which makes the race all the more dramatic. The radio broadcast of that historic race was heard, we are told, by the largest audience in history. Businesses closed for the afternoon so their employees could tune in.

If *Seabiscuit* has a weakness, it's the movie's curious indifference to betting. Horses race and bettors bet, and the relationship between the two is as old as time, except in this movie, where the Seabiscuit team seems involved in pure sport and might even be shocked! shocked! to learn that there is gambling at the track. Since a subplot about betting would no doubt be a complicated distraction, perhaps this is not such a loss.

I liked the movie a whole lot without quite loving it, maybe because although I can easily feel love for dogs, I have never bonded much with horses. I was happy for Seabiscuit without being right there with him every step of the way. The character I liked the best was Tom Smith, and once again Chris Cooper shows himself as one of the most uncannily effective actors in the movies. Here he seems old, pale, and a little worn out. In *Adaptation,* he was a sunburned swamp rat. In John Sayles's *Lone Star* he was a ruggedly handsome Texas sheriff. How does he make these transformations? Here, with a few sure movements and a couple of quiet words, he convinces us that what he doesn't know about horses isn't worth knowing.

Tobey Maguire and Jeff Bridges are wonderful, too, in the way they evoke their characters; Maguire as a jockey who commits his whole heart and soul, Bridges as a man who grows wiser and better as he ages. And then there is William H. Macy as Tick Tock McGlaughlin, a manic radio announcer who throws in corny sound effects and tortured alliterations as he issues breathless bulletins from the track. If Tick Tock McGlaughlin did not exist in real life, I don't want to know it.

Seabiscuit will satisfy those who have read the book, and I imagine it will satisfy those like myself, who have not. I have recently edged into the genre of racing journalism, via *My Turf* by William A. Nack, the great writer for *Sports Illustrated.* I was at a reading where he made audience members cry with his description of the death of Secretariat, and I saw people crying after *Seabiscuit,* too. More evidence for my theory that people more readily cry at movies not because of sadness, but because of goodness and courage.

The Seagull's Laughter ★ ★ ★ ½
NO MPAA RATING, 102 m., 2004

Margrét Vilhjálmsdóttir (Freya), Ugla Egilsdóttir (Agga), Heino Ferch (Björn Theódór), Hilmir Snær Guðnason (Magnús), Kristbjörg Kjeld (Grandma), Edda Bjorg Eyjólfsdóttir (Dodo), Guðlaug Ólafsdóttir (Ninna), Eyvindur Erlendsson (Granddad). Directed by Ágúst Guðmundsson and produced by Kristin Atladóttir. Screenplay by Guðmundsson, based on the novel by Kristin Marja Baldursdóttir.

The most beautiful woman in the Icelandic village of Hafnarfjordur ran off to New York with an American serviceman, or so it is said, and now returns to her hometown without her husband but with seven trunks of sexy dresses. Is she a widow, as she claims, or did she never marry the serviceman, or did he come to a bad end? Freya is the kind of woman who inspires such speculation, especially in the inflamed imagination of her eleven-year-old cousin Agga, who adores and hates her, sometimes at the same time.

The Seagull's Laughter, an uncommonly engaging comedy with ripe, tragic undertones, begins with the fact that everybody in town lives in everybody else's pockets. There are few secrets. Certainly Freya (Margret Vilhjálmsdóttir) is a sex bomb in search of a husband, and there are only two eligible men in the village: an engineer who lives with his mother and is engaged to the mayor's daughter, and a young policeman. The engineer has the better job and house, and so the mayor's daughter must go.

All of this is seen through the eyes of Agga, played by Ugla Egilsdóttir with such spirit and deviousness that when I was on the jury at the Karlovy Vary festival in 2002, we gave her the best actress award. She is on the trembling edge of adolescence, and her ambiguous feelings about sexuality cause her to worship the older woman while at the same time trying to frame her with arson, murder, and other crimes, during regular visits to the young cop. He dismisses her breathless eyewitness reports as the fantasies of an overwrought would-be Nancy Drew, but the movie suggests some of her reports—especially involving the mysterious fire that kills the wife-beating husband of Freya's best friend—may contain bits of truth.

Freya has essentially returned from America with no prospects at all. She takes a job in the chemist's shop, and finds popularity with the local drunks by selling them rubbing alcohol. She has moved into her grandfather's house, displacing the resentful Agga from her bed, and joins a matriarchy. The grandfather is almost always away at sea, and his house is ruled by his wife, Agga's grandmother, who also provides a home for her daughters, Dodo and Ninna, and her pipe-smoking sister-in-law, Kidda. Death is a fact in this home; Kidda's husband has died, and so have young Agga's parents. (When the police arrive at the door and ask to speak with her mother, she calmly tells them, "That will be difficult. She's dead.") The women are supportive of Freya and delighted by all of her dresses; they hold a spontaneous dress-up parade, and end by admiringly measuring her waist, bustline, and long hair.

Freya captures the eye of the engineer, Björn Theódór (Heino Ferch), at a village dance, spirits him away, and doesn't return, Agga breathlessly tattles to the policeman, until 5 A.M. ("Five thirteen," he corrects her). Freya tells Agga how they spent the night, leaving out the detail of their lovemaking, but speaking of the softness of long summer nights, the look of the sea, and the stroll they took on the path through the . . . well, through the fish-drying racks.

The racks come up later, after winter sets in and Freya begins to take long, despairing walks in the snow. She hates Iceland, she cries out: the cold and the snow and the seagulls laughing at her, and the smell of fish. But home is where, when you have to go there, they have to take you in.

The understory involves Agga's gradual transition into womanhood. Watching Freya, sometimes spying on her, she gets insights into the adult world and translates them into bulletins for the young cop. She plays both sides of the street, at one point forging a letter to keep Freya and the engineer in contact. And she learns hard lessons when Freya's best friend is mistreated by her husband and threatens suicide, and Freya calms her in an extraordinary scene by getting on her hands and knees, letting down her long hair, creeping to the friend, and calming her with its smell. This seems to refer to a childhood memory, and has an unexpected emotional impact.

The movie balances between dark and light, between warmth and cold, like an Icelandic year. It's scored with Glenn Miller and other swing bands from the war era, and opens and closes with the 1950s hit "Sh-boom." The message I think is that tragedy is temporary and the dance of life goes on. Soon it will be Agga's turn to choose a partner.

The Sea Inside ★ ★ ★
PG-13, 125 m., 2004

Javier Bardem (Ramon Sampedro), Belen Rueda (Julia), Lola Duenas (Rosa), Clara Segura (Gene), Mabel Rivera (Manuela), Celso Bugallo (Jose), Tamar Novas (Javi), Joan Dalmau (Joaquin), Francesc Garrido (Marc). Directed and produced by Alejandro Amenabar. Screenplay by Amenabar and Mateo Gil.

When you can't escape and you depend on others, you learn to cry by smiling.

So says Ramon Sampedro, who has been in the same bed in the same room for twenty-six years, not counting trips to the hospital. He was paralyzed from the neck down in a diving accident as a young man. He has his music, his radio and television, his visitors, his window view. He can control a computer, and write using a pen he holds in his mouth. He is cared for by his family, who love him and welcome the money they get from the government for his support. As *The Sea Inside* opens, Ramon demands the right to die.

"A life in this condition has no dignity," he says. He is tired of his bed, his limitations, and his life. He argues his point with great conviction, aided above all by his smile. Ramon is played by Javier Bardem, that Spanish actor of charm and gentle masculine force, and the smile lights up his face in a way that isn't forced or false, but sunny and with love. People truly care for him—his brother and sister-in-law, his nephew, the lawyer from a right-to-die organization, and Rosa, the woman from town who works as a disc jockey and peddles her bike out one day to meet him. Those who love me, he lets them all know, will help me to die.

The Sea Inside is based on the true story of a quadriplegic from Galicia, Spain, who in 1998 did succeed in dying, after planning his death in such an ingenious way that even if all the details were discovered no one could be legally charged with the crime. What we see in *The Sea Inside* is fiction, based on the final months. His lawyer, Julia (Belen Rueda), is herself suffering from a degenerative disease, and he feels that will make her more sympathetic to his cause. They fall in love with each other. The local woman Rosa certainly loves him. His family loves him and doesn't complain about the burden; his brother, in fact, is adamantly opposed to euthanasia. Ramon waits in his bed, smiles, is charming, and figures out how this thing can be made to happen.

Bardem and Alejandro Amenabar, the film's director, are adamant that they do not believe everyone in Ramon's position should die. This is simply the story of one man. Yes, and on those terms I accept it, and was moved by the humanity and logic of the character. But it happens I know a few things about paraplegia, which I hope you will allow me to share.

At the University of Illinois, my alma mater, there are more students in wheelchairs than at any other university in the country (the campus is completely lacking in hills, a great convenience), and they were in all my classes; when I was editor of the student paper, our photo editor was in a chair. The most outspoken student radical on campus could walk only with an exoskeleton of braces and crutches—it would have been easier in a chair, but not for him. Among other paraplegics I have known, a lifelong friend recently retired as a sportscaster, a young woman was largely responsible for getting the Americans with Disabilities Act passed, and I once joined a dozen wheelchair athletes on a teaching tour of southern Africa. A high school classmate was paralyzed in his senior year; a few years ago I got news of his romance and marriage. Some of these people have had children, and have raised them competently, lovingly, and well. I remember the remarkable Heather Rose, whose condition limited her to the use of one finger, which she used to tap on a voice synthesizer. She wrote and starred in *Dance Me to My Song*, and flew from Australia to attend my first Overlooked Film Festival. Only recently I got an e-mail from a fellow film critic I have been in communication with for years; discussing this movie, he revealed to me that he is a quadriplegic.

These people are all functioning usefully, and it is clear they have happy and productive days, no doubt interrupted sometimes by pain, doubt, and despair. To be sure, most of them are not quads. But whatever their reality, they deal with it. Ramon, on the other hand, refuses to be fitted with a breath-controlled wheelchair because he finds it a parody of the freedom he once had.

What would I do in the same situation as the man in Spain? I am reminded of something written by another Spaniard, the director Luis Buñuel. What made him angriest about dying, he said, was that he would be unable to read tomorrow's newspaper. I believe I would want to live as long as I could, assuming I had my sanity and some way to communicate. If I were trapped inside my mind, like the hero of Dalton Trumbo's *Johnny Got His Gun*, that would be another matter—although consider the life of Helen Keller.

In *The Sea Inside*, Ramon Sampedro has considered all these notions, and is not persuaded. He does not care to live any longer. Julia, the woman from the right-to-die agency, supports him, and so do "backers" from around the country. Rosa, the local girl, desperately wants him to live. A quadriplegic priest visits to talk Ramon out of his decision, and there is a macabre scene in which messages are carried up and down stairs between the two men. Julia's own health becomes an issue.

What finally happens to Ramon Sampedro I will not say. The movie invites us to decide if we are pleased or not. I agree with Ramon that, in the last analysis, the decision should be his to make: To be or not to be. But if a man is of sound mind and not in pain, how in the world can he decide he no longer wants to read tomorrow's newspaper? ☞

The Sea Is Watching ★ ★ ½
R, 119 m., 2003

Misa Shimizu (Kikuno), Nagiko Tono (O-Shin), Masatoshi Nagase (Ryosuke), Hidetaka Yoshioka (Fusanosuke), Eiji Okuda (Ginji), Renji Ishibashi (Zenbei), Miho Tsumiki (Okichi), Michiko Kawai (Osono). Directed by Kei Kumai and produced by Naoto Sarukawa. Screenplay by Akira Kurosawa, based on the novel by Shugoro Yamamoto.

Prostitutes are a great convenience in stories, allowing the author to dispense with courtship and begin immediately with sex and intrigue. Little wonder, then, that the Japanese master Akira Kurosawa, who rarely focused on women in his movies and said he did not much understand them, would use a brothel as the setting for his screenplay *The Sea Is Watching*. Based on a novel by Shugoro Yamamoto, left unfilmed when Kurosawa died in 1998, it has been directed by Kei Kumai as a film that seems more melodramatic and sentimental than Kurosawa's norm. Perhaps when you do not really understand someone, in fiction or in life, you are a little nicer to them.

The movie is set in the Edo period, circa 1850, in a village that would later become Tokyo. Into a brothel one night stumbles a callow young samurai named Fusanosuke (Hidetaka Yoshioka), who has disgraced himself by getting drunk, killing a man, and losing his sword. A prudent prostitute would show him the door, but O-Shin (Nagiko Tono) feels tender and protective, and besides, as her fellow prostitutes never tire of telling her, she's a sucker for a hard-luck story. She disguises the samurai to protect him from the dead man's friends, and after he is banished from his father's house he returns to O-Shin again and again for long, heartfelt conversations—and no sex.

O-Shin's best friend in the house is Kikuno (Misa Shimizu), who is protective of the girl and worried about her tendency to mix business with pleasure. It appears, though, that O-Shin might achieve what few prostitutes could in Japan's feudal society, and make a marriage with a nice man. The other girls in the house begin to service her clients so that she can cleanse herself, in a sense, by a period of celibacy.

There are other men whom O-Shin also feels tenderness for. One of them is Ginji (Eiji Okuda), an elderly businessman who wants O-Shin to come and live with him, and whose offer is probably more sincere and practical than the romantic delusions she harbors about Fusanosuke.

The movie does a good job of evoking daily life in the brothel, which meets not only the sexual needs of its clients but also, and perhaps more urgently, their need for a place to escape from the rigors of the caste system and find sympathetic conversation. We also see something of the district, which is separated from the main town by the river, and is understood by everyone to be a haven of vice. When O-Shin discovers rather cruelly what a shallow and feckless creature Fusanosuke really is, there is yet a third client who touches her heart, and

he could be real trouble. This is Ryosuke (Masatoshi Nagase).

We are always aware of the nearby presence of the sea—today's Tokyo Bay. And when a great, cleansing, violent typhoon roars in and the district is evacuated, Kikuno refuses to leave because she has been entrusted with the house keys by the madam; O-Shin stays with her out of loyalty and a general indifference to life. As they sit on the roof beam of the house, surrounded by floodwaters, they find out at last if anyone cares enough to come and rescue them.

It must not be a coincidence that Kurosawa named his heroine O-Shin, creating an English pun on "ocean." But the connection between O-Shin and the rising sea is murky to me, unless perhaps they share an underlying sympathy so that the sea comes, in a sense, to her rescue. The movie is slow and unabashedly melodramatic. Without looking at the credits I would never have identified it as Kurosawa's work, but it has a sweetness and a directness that's appealing. It might never have been made without Kurosawa's name attached to it, and that is true as well of the master's own last film, *Madadayo* (1993), a touching elegy about an old professor honored by his students. But Kurosawa was a great artist, and so even his lesser work is interesting—just as we would love to find one last lost play, however minor, by his hero Shakespeare.

Secondhand Lions ★ ★ ★
PG, 107 m., 2003

Michael Caine (Garth), Robert Duvall (Hub), Haley Joel Osment (Walter), Kyra Sedgwick (Mae), Emmanuelle Vaugier (Princess Jasmine). Directed by Tim McCanlies and produced by David Kirschner, Scott Ross, and Corey Sienega. Screenplay by McCanlies.

Secondhand Lions is about the uncles every boy should have, and the summer every boy should spend. No uncles or summers like this ever existed, but isn't it nice to think that Uncle Garth and Uncle Hub are waiting there on their Texas ranch, shooting at fish and salesmen, and waiting for their twelve-year-old nephew to be dumped on them?

They are two completely inexplicable and unlikely characters, and we doubt we can believe anything we learn about them, but in the hands of those sainted actors Robert Duvall and Michael Caine they glow with a kind of inner conviction even while their stories challenge even the kid's credulity. Maybe Hub really was a foreign legionnaire and led thousands of men into battle and won and lost a dozen fortunes, and maybe he really was in love with a desert princess named Jasmine, and then again maybe he's just been sitting there on the porch with Garth making up tall tales for gullible nephews.

The nephew's name is Walter, and he is played by Haley Joel Osment, the child actor from *The Sixth Sense* and *A.I.: Artificial Intelligence,* now on the edge of adolescence but still with that clear-eyed directness that cuts right to the heart of a scene. Some actors have trouble standing up to that kind of unadorned presence, but Caine and Duvall are not ordinary, and they look the kid straight in the eye and tell him exactly what he needs to know.

Walter is dumped with the uncles after his mother, Mae (Kyra Sedgwick), decides to attend court reporting school and ends up engaged to a guy in Vegas. Things like that are always happening to her. Walter's first impression of Garth and Hub is a fearful one; they seem carved from a block of American Gothic, and sit in their high-backed chairs on the porch like men who are prepared to wait for death no matter how long it takes. The summer will, however, not be boring, Walter understands, when the uncles start firing shotguns at unwanted visitors.

They have a lot of traffic on the farm because word has it they've got millions stashed away somewhere. Maybe they used to work with Al Capone (one local rumor), or maybe they kept one of those dozen fortunes Hub won, or maybe there aren't any millions at all. Hub and Garth go through life like a double act, feeding each other straight lines as they plant a garden that is unexpectedly heavy on corn, or order a used circus lion to be delivered to the farm. (A giraffe also shows up, but the movie loses track of him.)

The plot, such as it is, is hardly necessary. Yes, Mae turns up with the fiancé from Vegas, and yes, he wants to get his hands on the money, but of course Hub can handle him. Even on the day he collapses and then checks himself out of the hospital, we see him punch out four louts in a local saloon, and then give them the special speech he always gives to young men. It has to do with being able to believe in something even if it's not true, because the believing part is what's important.

The movie, written and directed by Tim Mc-Canlies, is a gentle and sweet whimsy, attentive to the love between the two brothers, respectful of the boy's growth and curiosity. There are flashbacks to the story of Princess Jasmine and her jealous lover, and it appears that Hub as a swordsman would have shamed Zorro. True? Who cares, as long as you believe it is.

Watching the movie, I was reminded of *Unstrung Heroes* (1995), the Diane Keaton film about a young boy who goes to live with his uncles, who are world-class eccentrics. That movie was based on a memoir by Franz Lidz; Tim McCanlies, who wrote and directed *Secondhand Lions,* seems to have made it up, although his friend Harry Knowles thinks maybe it's inspired by the childhood of Bill Watterson, the creator of *Calvin & Hobbes.* Certainly young Walter grows up to become a cartoonist whose characters include a couple of goofy but heroic uncles and a used lion. To have the kind of childhood you can use as inspiration for a comic strip should be the goal of every kid.

The Secret Lives of Dentists ★ ★ ★
R, 104 m., 2003

Campbell Scott (David Hurst), Hope Davis (Dana Hurst), Denis Leary (Slater), Robin Tunney (Laura). Directed by Alan Rudolph and produced by Campbell Scott and George Van Buskirk. Screenplay by Craig Lucas, based on the novel *The Age of Grief* by Jane Smiley.

They met in dental school, where he was awed by her brilliance, and now they share a practice and a family. Their three daughters are a handful, especially the little one, who is going through a phase of preferring daddy to mommy, but slaps daddy whenever she gets the chance. They are happy, apparently, but something strange is going on under the surface of this marriage, and one day David accidentally glimpses his wife sharing a tender and loving moment with another man.

What should he do then? Alan Rudolph's *The Secret Lives of Dentists* is about a quiet, inward man. David (Campbell Scott) is a good father and certainly loves his wife, but when Dana (Hope Davis) tries to talk to him he seems to be asleep. She says she wishes they were closer: "You scare me a little." And yet what about her affair? For the time being, David determines to say nothing and do nothing, and hope that, whatever it is, it plays itself out and Dana comes back to him—to them.

David has the kind of patient a dentist must dread: a cocky wiseass named Slater (Denis Leary) who masks his fear with hostility, hates dentists, is keeping an appointment made by his ex-wife. David fills a cavity, only to be confronted at the community opera by Slater, who holds up a filling that dropped out and informs the audience that David is a lousy dentist. This is on the same night he saw his wife with the strange man. Not a good night.

The story advances through a mixture of everyday realism and fantasy. We get a deep, real, convincing portrait of a family going through a period of crisis (the family doctor insists on diagnosing all of the children's illnesses as emotional reactions to tension between the parents). We see meals served, fights stopped, love expressed, weekends planned. At the same time, Slater begins to turn up in David's mind as an imaginary guest, and we see him, too—standing in the kitchen, offering free advice in the dining room, even sliding out from under the bed.

Slater hates his ex-wife and thinks women have it coming to them. He advises David to cut and run. David tries to explain himself: He won't confront Dana about her affair because he doesn't want to have to do something about it. Perhaps he is afraid that, if forced, she will chose her lover instead of her husband.

Whether she chooses, and whether he acts, you will have to discover for yourself. What you will find is a film with an uncanny feeling for the rhythms of daily life, acted by Scott and Davis with attention to those small inflections of speech that can turn words into weapons. There is also a lot of physical acting; the youngest child, in particular, has a great need to be held and touched and hauled around in her parents' arms. And then there are the five days of the flu, as first one and then another family member develops a fever and starts throwing up. Scott is wonderful here in the way he shows

his character caring for the family while coming apart inside.

I suppose the Slater character is essential to Rudolph's idea of the movie, which is based on the novel *The Age of Grief* by Jane Smiley. To introduce Slater's imaginary presence is a risk, and a reach, and I suppose it deserves credit, especially since Leary plays the character about as well as he can probably be played. But I wanted less, in a way. I wanted to lose the whole fantasy overlay and stay with the movie's strength, which is to show the everyday life of a family in crisis. There are real feelings here, which go deep and are truly felt, and the whole Slater apparatus is only a distraction. *The Secret Lives of Dentists* tries hard to be a good film, but if it had relaxed a little, it might have been great.

Secret Things ★ ★ ★

NO MPAA RATING, 115 m., 2004

Coralie Revel (Natalie), Sabrina Seyvecou (Sandrine), Roger Mirmont (Delacroix), Fabrice Deville (Christophe), Blandine Bury (Charlotte), Olivier Soler (Cadene), Viviane Theophildes (Mme. Mercier). Directed by Jean-Claude Brisseau and produced by Brisseau and Jean-Francois Geneix. Screenplay by Brisseau.

Secret Things is a rare item these days: an erotic film made well enough to keep us interested. It's about beautiful people, has a lot of nudity, and the sex is as explicit as possible this side of porno. If you enjoyed *Emmanuelle,* you will think this is better. And, like Bertolucci's more considerable film *The Dreamers,* it will remind you of the days when movies dealt as cheerfully with sex as they do today with action. Of course, it is French.

What is amazing is how seriously the French take it. I learn from *Film Journal International* that *Secret Things* was named Film of the Year by *Cahiers du Cinema,* the magazine that brought Godard, Truffaut, Chabrol, and Rohmer into the world, and became the bible of the auteur theory. But then *Cahiers* has long been famous for jolting us out of our complacency by advocating the outrageous.

The movie is an erotic thriller that opens with a woman alone on a sofa, doing what such women do on such sofas in such movies. The camera slowly draws back to reveal the location: a strip club. We hear the voice of the narrator, Sandrine (Sabrina Seyvecou), who is a bartender in the club and new to this world; she needed the job. When she seems reluctant to have sex with the customers, the performer, named Natalie (Coralie Revel), tells her that is her right, and they are both fired.

Sandrine cannot go to her flat because she is behind on the rent. Natalie invites her to spend the night with her. You see how these situations develop in erotic fiction. They have a tête-à-tête, and vice versa. We hear frank, revealing, and well-written dialogue about their sexual feelings. Natalie is a realist about sex, she says. When it comes to pleasure, she is more interested in herself than in her partners, who are nonparticipants in the erotic theater of her mind. What turns her on is being watched by strangers, and although Sandrine is shocked at first, in no time at all they are doing things in a Metro station that would get you arrested if you were not in a movie.

"Let's climb the social ladder," Natalie suggests to Sandrine. They target a small but wealthy company whose cofounder is about to die. His son, a notorious rake and pervert, will inherit. Sandrine gets a job as a secretary and is provocative in just such a way as to attract the attention of the other cofounder, Delacroix (Roger Mirmont). Soon she is his private secretary, and almost immediately his lover; her boldness in seducing him shows a nerve that is almost more interesting than her technique. She has him so completely in her power, she feels sorry for the poor guy.

Sandrine arranges for Natalie to be hired by the company, and soon they have both fallen into the orbit of Christophe (Fabrice Deville), the son and heir. This is a disturbed man. As a child, he watched his mother die and sat for days beside her body. As an adult, he has been such a cruel lover that not one but two women committed suicide by setting themselves afire in front of him. He has a sister, Charlotte (Blandine Bury), and feels about her as such men do in such movies.

If the film is erotic on the surface, its undercurrent is as hard and cynical as *In the Company of Men*. The difference is that, this time, women are planning the cruel jokes and deceptions—or they would like to think they are. The writer and director, Jean-Claude Brisseau, devises an ingenious plot that involves corporate intrigue and blackmail, double-crossing and sabotage, and sex as the key element in the control of the country.

And all the time, Sandrine's narration adds another element. She is detached, observant, and a little sad in her comments on the action; unlike an American narrator, who would try to be steamy, she talks to us like one adult to another, commenting on what she really felt, who she felt sorry for, what she regretted having to do, and who she trusted but shouldn't have. The ending, which resolves all the plotting and intrigue with clockwork precision, is ironic not like a Hitchcock film, but like a French homage to Hitchcock; Truffaut's *The Bride Wore Black*, perhaps.

The film is well made, well acted, cleverly written, photographed by Wilfrid Sempe as if he's a conspirer with the sexual schemers. There's an especially effective scene where Natalie stands behind an open door and drives poor Delacroix frantic as coworkers pass by right outside. The movie understands that even powerful men can be rendered all but helpless by women with sufficient nerve. *Secret Things* is not the film of the year, or even of the fortnight, but it is a splendid erotic film with a plot so cynical that we're always kept a little off balance.

Secret Window ★ ★ ★
PG-13, 106 m., 2004

Johnny Depp (Mort Rainey), John Turturro (John Shooter), Maria Bello (Amy Rainey), Timothy Hutton (Ted), Charles S. Dutton (Ken Karsch), Len Cariou (Sheriff). Directed by David Koepp and produced by Gavin Polone. Screenplay by Koepp, based on a Stephen King novella.

The first shot after the credits of *Secret Window* is an elaborate one. It begins with a view across a lake to a rustic cabin. Then the camera moves smoothly in to the shore and across the grounds and in through a window of the cabin, and it regards various rooms before closing in on a large mirror that reflects a man asleep on a couch.

The framing narrows until we no longer see the sides of the mirror, only the image. And then we realize we aren't looking at a reflection, but are in fact now in the real room. Not possible logically, but this through-the-looking-glass shot, along with a wide-brimmed black hat and some Pall Mall cigarettes, are the only slight ripples in the smooth surface of the movie's realism.

The movie stars Johnny Depp in another of those performances where he brings a musing eccentricity to an otherwise straightforward role. He plays Mort Rainey, a best-selling novelist of crime stories; like the hero of *Misery,* he reminds us that the original story is by Stephen King. The computer on his desk in the loft contains one paragraph of a new story, until he deletes it. He spends a lot of time sleeping, and has possibly been wearing the same ratty bathrobe for months. His hair seems to have been combed with an eggbeater, but of course with Johnny Depp you never know if that's the character or the actor.

A man appears at his door. He is tall and forbidding, speaks with a Mississippi accent, wears the wide-brimmed black hat, and says, "You stole my story." This is John Shooter (John Turturro), a writer who leaves behind a manuscript that is, indeed, almost word for word the same as Rainey's story *Secret Window.* The plot deals with a man who has been betrayed by his wife, murders her, and buries her in her beloved garden—where, after a time, she will be forgotten, "perhaps even by me." Rainey knows he did not steal the story, but Shooter is an angry and violent man who stalks the author and causes bad things to happen: a screwdriver through the heart of his beloved dog, for example. Shooter says he wrote his story in 1997, and Rainey has his comeback: He wrote his in 1994, and thinks he has an old issue of *Ellery Queen's Mystery Magazine* to prove it.

But that leads him back into the world of his estranged wife, Amy (Maria Bello), who is living with her new lover (Timothy Hutton). She has the big house in town, and that's why Rainey is living in sloth and despond in the lake cottage. To tell more would be wrong, except to note Rainey's decision to hire an ex-cop (Charles S. Dutton) as a bodyguard, and to complain to the local sheriff (Len Cariou), an arthritic whose hobby is knitting.

Rainey appears to be the classic Hitchcock hero, an innocent man wrongly accused. He has been cheated on by his wife, and now this nut from nowhere is threatening his life because of a story he did not steal. The situation is magnified nicely by the location at the isolated cottage, which leaves many opportunities for disturbing sounds, strange omens, broken lightbulbs, threatening letters, and Shooter himself, who appears at disconcerting moments and seems to be stalking Rainey wherever he goes.

All of this could add up to a straight-faced thriller about things that go boo in the night, but Johnny Depp and director David Koepp (who wrote *Panic Room* and directed *Stir of Echoes*) have too much style to let that happen. Like many men who have lived alone for a long time, Rainey carries on a running conversation with himself—dour, ironic, sometimes amused. He talks to the dog until the dog is killed. Aroused from a nap, he stumbles through a confused investigation, asks himself, "Now, where was I?" and returns to the same position on the couch.

Even his friends are entertaining. When he talks with the ex-cop, they use a chess clock, banging their button when the other guy starts talking. Maybe this has something to do with billing arrangements, or maybe they're just competitive. Probably the latter, since bodyguards are always on duty.

The story is more entertaining as it rolls along than it is when it gets to the finish line. But at least King uses his imagination right up to the end, and spares us the obligatory violent showdown that a lesser storyteller would have settled for. A lot of people were outraged that he was honored at the National Book Awards, as if a popular writer could not be taken seriously. But after finding that his book *On Writing* had more useful and observant things to say about the craft than any book since Strunk and White's *The Elements of Style,* I have gotten over my own snobbery.

King has, after all, been responsible for the movies *The Shawshank Redemption, The Green Mile, The Dead Zone, Misery, Apt Pupil, Christine, Hearts in Atlantis, Stand by Me,* and *Carrie. Secret Window* is somewhere in the middle of that range storywise, and toward the top in Depp's performance. And we must not be ungrateful for *Silver Bullet,* which I awarded three stars because it was "either the worst movie ever made from a Stephen King story, or the funniest," and you know what side of that I'm gonna come down on.

Seed of Chucky ★ ★
R, 86 m., 2004

Herself (Jennifer Tilly), Himself (Redman), Hannah Spearritt (Joan), John Waters (Pete Peters), Billy Boyd (Voice of Glen/Glenda Doll), Brad Dourif (Voice of Chucky Doll), Jennifer Tilly (Voice of Tiffany Doll). Directed by Don Mancini and produced by David Kirschner and Corey Sienega. Screenplay by Mancini.

Midway through *Seed of Chucky*, Jennifer Tilly complains: "I'm an Oscar nominee, and now I'm f---ing a puppet!" Yeah, and I'm a Pulitzer winner, and I was being f---ed by a puppet movie. Because Focus Features declined to preview its new movie for the press, and indeed went so far as to station a guard at the Thursday night sneak preview in case I could not contain my eagerness to attend, I went on Saturday morning. I'm not complaining. They had those poppable Snickers bits.

Seed of Chucky is actually two movies, one wretched, the other funny. The funny one involves the Jennifer Tilly scenes. She plays "herself" in the movie—a horror film star making *Chucky Goes Psycho* and little realizing that both the Chucky doll and its wife, the Jennifer doll, have been brought back to life by the Glen or Glenda doll, their child.

Tilly, who seems to supply most of her own dialogue and is certainly a good sport if she didn't, is portrayed as a has-been actress who hopes to make a comeback by starring as the Virgin Mary in a film being prepared by the rap artist Redman. After an audition, Redman tells her he's going with his first choice for the role, Julia Roberts. But he tells Tilly he loved that movie with her and the other girl. "'Bound'?" she says. "Yeah, everyone loves that one." He asks if, uh, she is still, uh, friends with the other girl. "Gina Gershon? Me and Gina are *very* close friends. Gee, maybe the three of us could hang out." Then she shamelessly suggests that Redman come over to her place so they can get better acquainted.

"You're prostituting yourself to play the Virgin Mary!" her best friend tells her. "You'll go to hell!"

"Hell," says Tilly, "would be ending up on *Celebrity Fear Factor* in a worm-eating contest with Anna Nicole Smith."

Tilly has lots of good one-liners ("They're executing Martha Stewart this morning") and argues convincingly that if she had played Erin Brockovich instead of Julia Roberts, she wouldn't have had to wear a push-up bra. She is completely unaware that Chucky and Tiffany have come to life, until she finds the prop man's head and thinks it's a prop until it starts to drip.

The Chucky side of the movie tells the story of how Chucky and Tiffany's child sees them on television, realizes he's not alone in the world, and escapes from a British ventriloquist to fly to L.A. and bring his parents back to life with an ancient incantation. They're delighted to find they have offspring, but get into a fight over whether the kid is a boy or a girl. Full frontal doll nudity solves nothing. Chuck likes Glen as a name; Tiffany likes Glenda. Ed Wood, director of *Glen or Glenda* (1953) would be proud (and another cult filmmaker, John Waters, turns up here long enough to have his face eaten away).

Chucky's master plan is to impregnate Jennifer Tilly so Glen/Glenda can have a brother/sister. This involves the first doll masturbation scene that, offhand, I can remember in the movies, as Chucky produces a sperm sample (as a visual aid, he rejects skin magazines and chooses *Fangoria*). A turkey baster makes its inevitable appearance.

If you're thinking of *Seed of Chucky* as a horror movie, you can forget about it. It's not scary. If you do not by now find Chucky and the other killer dolls tiresome, I do (this is their fifth movie). If you like the way Jennifer Tilly has fun with her image (and, in what can only be called selfless generosity, with Gina Gershon's image), *Seed of Chucky* is a movie to be seen on television. Free television.

Note: The print at the Webster Place theater in Chicago looked dim, murky, and washed-out. I complained to the management, suggesting that perhaps the projector bulb was set too low. There was no improvement. The movie's trailers on the Web have bright and vivid colors. The movie I saw was drab, as if filmed through a dirty window. So were the other trailers they showed.

Seeing Other People ★ ★ ½
R, 90 m., 2004

Jay Mohr (Ed), Julianne Nicholson (Alice), Lauren Graham (Claire), Bryan Cranston (Peter), Josh Charles (Lou), Andy Richter (Carl), Matthew Davis (Donald), Jill Ritchie (Sandy), Helen Slater (Penelope). Directed by Wallace Wolodarsky and produced by Gavin Polone. Screenplay by Maya Forbes and Wolodarsky.

Alice and Ed are happy. They've been happy for five years. They're engaged to be married. But then Alice begins to mope. She wonders if she's been unfairly shortchanged in the sexual experience sweepstakes, since before Ed she slept with only three guys, and two of them don't count, one because he was not a guy. So she makes a modest proposal: They should both fool around a little before they get married. That will jump-start their own fairly tame sex life, and reconcile her to a lifetime of faithfulness.

Seeing Other People takes her suggestion and runs with it through several sexual encounters, arriving at the conclusion that the biggest danger of meaningless sex is that it can become meaningful. It isn't a successful movie, but is sometimes a very interesting one, and there is real charm and comic agility by the two leads, Julianne Nicholson and Jay Mohr. There is also finally a role for which Andy Richter seems ideally cast.

The movie has to overcome one problem: We like Ed and Alice. Their friends like them. They seem intended for each other. They aren't sitcom types, but solid, loyal, comfortable, smart people; Alice reminds me a little of Nicholson's great performance in *Tully* (2000) as a veterinarian who knows who she wants to marry and captures him with infinite subtlety and tenderness.

Here she suggests the rules. They will be completely honest with each other. They will be honest with their partners. They will somehow know when to stop. Alice takes the first leap: "I made out with someone," she tells Ed. "Made out?" "Yeah, like . . . made out." As she describes her experience, they grow excited, and have, they tell friends the next day, the best sex they've had—ever. It'll be downhill from there, as Alice meets a contractor named Donald (Matthew Davis) and Ed meets a waitress named Sandy (Jill Ritchie). Neither Sandy nor

Donald see themselves as one-night stands, and are not content to play walk-through roles in the sexual adventures of an engaged couple.

Other characters include Alice's sister (Lauren Graham) and brother-in-law (Bryan Cranston), and Ed's two best friends, played by Josh Charles as a sexual cynic, and Andy Richter as a sincere, salt-of-the-earth guy who just absolutely knows no good can come of this experiment.

Seeing Other People is not so much about sex as about its consequences, and although we see some heaving blankets, what the characters mostly bare are their souls. I liked it best in the tentative early stages, when Ed and Alice were unsure about their decision, not very brave about acting on it, and fascinated by talking about it. Then the movie starts working out various permutations of possible couples, and we get a traffic jam. I don't want to give away all the secrets, but Alice gets into bed with one person she should not, would not, and probably could not get into bed with—not if she's the person she seems to be.

There's a quiet joke in the fact that Alice wants to fool around and Ed is reluctant to go along. And there's a nice irony when Alice decides to call off the experiment just when Sandy has promised Ed a three-way with her college roommate. Ed perseveres, only to learn what many have discovered before him, that three-way sex tends to resemble a three-car race where one car is always in the pits.

This is not a boring movie, and the dialogue has a nice edge to it. It was written by a married couple, Maya Forbes and Wallace Wolodarsky, and directed by Wolodarsky; his credits include *The Simpsons* and hers include *The Larry Sanders Show*. I liked the way they had Alice and Ed actually discuss their experiment, instead of simply presenting it as a comic setup. But I don't know if the filmmakers ever decided how serious the movie should be, and so fairly harrowing moments of truth alternate with slapstick (man escapes through bedroom window as wife enters through door, etc.). And there are so many different pairings to keep track of that the movie loses focus and becomes a juggling act. Too bad, because in their best scenes together Nicholson and Mohr achieve a kind of intimacy and immediate truth that is hard to find, and a shame to waste.

September 11 ★ ★ ★
NO MPAA RATING, 135 m., 2003

Segments directed by Alejandro Gonzalez Inarritu, Ken Loach, Mira Nair, Amos Gitai, Youssef Chahine, Danis Tanovic, Samira Makhmalbaf, Claude Lelouch, Shohei Imamura, Sean Penn, and Idrissa Ouedraogo, and produced by Alain Brigand.

The recent release of the audio recordings of calls from the doomed World Trade Center adds an eerie timeliness to *September 11*, a film in which eleven directors from around the world contribute eleven segments of eleven minutes each. Voices and sounds without pictures force us to internalize a catastrophe almost impossible to visualize.

That's illustrated in the best of the segments, an overpowering film by Alejandro Gonzalez Inarritu of Mexico, best known for *Amores Perros*. He keeps his screen entirely black for most of the eleven minutes, occasionally interrupting it with flashes of bodies falling from the burning World Trade Center. We realize after a while that the muffled thuds on the sound track are the bodies landing.

The sound track begins and ends with a collage of excited voices, and during the eleven minutes we also hear snatches of newscasts and part of a cell phone call from a passenger on one of the hijacked airplanes ("We have a little problem on the plane, and I wanted to say I love you . . ."). Toward the end, there is the sound of fearsome hammering, and we realize with a chill that this is the sound of the floors collapsing, one on top of another, growing louder. It must have been recorded from a radio inside the building; it is the last thing the terrified people inside the towers heard. This film is so strong because it allows us to use our imaginations. It generates almost unbearable empathy.

Another of the best films is by Ken Loach of Great Britain, who films a Chilean writing a letter to Americans in which he offers his sympathy. Then he recalls that on another Tuesday, September 11—this one in 1973—the democratically elected government of Chile was overthrown by a CIA-funded military coup, President Salvador Allende was murdered, and the right-wing dictator Augusto Pinochet

was installed as the U.S. puppet to rule over a reign of torture and terror. I wrote in my notes: "Do unto others as you would have them do unto you."

The third powerful film is by Mira Nair of India, who tells the true story of a Pakistani mother in New York whose son got on the subway to go to medical school and never returned. She was questioned by the FBI, her son was named as a suspected terrorist, and only six months later was his body found in the rubble, where, as a trained medic, he had gone to help. His hero's coffin was draped in the American flag.

One of the most sympathetic films comes from Iran. Samira Makhmalbaf's film shows a teacher trying to explain to her students—Afghan refugees in Iran—what has happened in New York. The kids get into a discussion about God, and whether he would kill some people to make others; "God isn't crazy," one child finally decides. None of the children can imagine a tall building, so the teacher takes them to stand beneath a smokestack, and the smoke from the top makes an eerie mirror of the catastrophe.

Other films miss the mark. Amos Gitai of Israel shows a TV news reporter broadcasting live from the scene of a suicide bombing when she is taken off the air because of the news from New York. This situation could have generated an interesting film, but the reporter is depicted as so self-centered and goofy that the piece derails. A film by Egypt's Youssef Chahine also has an interesting premise—a director is visited by the ghost of a U.S. Marine who was killed in the Beirut bombing—but the piece is unfocused, half-realized.

The only note of humor comes in a charming film by Idrissa Ouedraogo, from Burkina Faso in Africa, where five poor boys believe they have spotted Osama bin Laden in their town, and plot to capture him and win the $25 million reward. They are not entirely off the track; the actor hired to play Bin Laden could be his double.

Other films are from Bosnia's Danis Tanovic, who shows women continuing to march with the names of their dead despite the deaths in New York; Japan's Shohei Imamura, who shows a man who survived the atomic bombing but has become convinced he is a snake; Sean Penn

609

of the United States, who stars Ernest Borgnine as an old man who rejoices when his dead wife's flowers bloom, not realizing they get sunlight because the towers have fallen; and France's Claude Lelouch, with a sentimental piece about a deaf woman who does not realize what has happened until her boyfriend returns alive, covered with dust.

Emerging from *September 11*, shaken particularly by Inarritu's use of sound with a mostly black screen, I could not help wondering: Would it have killed one of these eleven directors to make a clear-cut attack on the terrorists themselves? 9/11 was a savage and heartless crime, and after the symbolism and the history and the imagery and the analysis, that is a point that must be made.

Sex Is Comedy ★ ★ ½
NO MPAA RATING, 92 m., 2004

Anne Parillaud (Jeanne), Gregoire Colin (Actor), Roxane Mesquida (Actress), Ashley Wanninger (Leo), Dominique Colladant (Willy), Bart Binnema (Cinematographer), Yves Osmu (Sound Man). Directed by Catherine Breillat and produced by Jean-Francois Lepetit. Screenplay by Breillat.

Sex Is Comedy watches a French director as she attempts to film two sex scenes. She doesn't have an easy time of it. Her actor and actress hate each other, and she and the actor are having an affair. She begins with a summer beach scene that is being filmed on a cold day out of season. Her crew is bundled up warmly but her actors shiver in their swimsuits while she urges them to seem more sincere and passionate. Their hearts are clearly not in their work. When an actor's body is there but not his soul, she believes, "that is moral ugliness." Perhaps so, but as Woody Allen observed: "Sex without love is an empty experience, but, as empty experiences go, it's one of the best."

This is the new film by Catherine Breillat, the French woman who often takes sex—its mystery, its romance, its plumbing—as her subject. When her *Anatomy of Hell* opened, it showed a woman who pays a man to watch her, simply watch her, as she reveals her innermost physical and emotional secrets. Now here is another film about watching, this time

curious about the director's personal and professional needs for sex, and how they differ.

The director, named Jeanne and played by Anne Parillaud *(La Femme Nikita)*, is pretty clearly supposed to be Breillat herself. The film within the film seems inspired by her *Fat Girl* (2002), a brave and shocking movie about two sisters, one fifteen and pretty, one twelve and pudgy, and the younger one's desire to follow her sister prematurely into the world of sexuality. The sex scenes in *Sex Is Comedy* are similar to scenes in *Fat Girl*, and indeed the actress is Roxane Mesquida, who played the older sister in that film.

Breillat is making a film, then, about herself making an earlier film. Like other films about filmmaking, ranging from Truffaut's *Day for Night* to Tim Burton's *Ed Wood*, it sees the director and the stars existing in a fever of their own, while the assistant director holds things together and the crew looks on dubiously. "It's always the same with her male leads," the sound man observes. "She picks them for their looks, then grows disillusioned."

Known as the Actor (Gregoire Colin) and the Actress (Mesquida), the two stars indeed seem to hate each other, although Jeanne suspects, probably correctly, that they're exaggerating their feelings as a way of dodging the scene. It is cold on the beach, soon it will rain, their lips are blue, it is a ridiculous situation, and the director seems to doubt her own wisdom. The second sex scene is at least in bed, but here, too, authentic feeling seems to be lacking, and finally the director climbs into bed with her leading man to rehearse, while the crew stands by—"for twenty-six minutes," observes the assistant director, whose job is to keep the production on schedule.

The bed scene is further complicated by the use of a large artificial phallus, which doubles (perhaps literally) for the Actor's own. The Actor walks around the set with the device bobbling out of his dressing gown, something Breillat thinks is funnier than it is; she should study the glow-in-the-dark condom scene from Blake Edwards's *Skin Deep* (1989).

The Actress is having difficulty "expressing herself" in the scene, which means that she doesn't seem to be faking an orgasm truthfully enough, and Jeanne shoots take after take as everyone's frustration grows. Finally there is a breakthrough, as the Actress experiences what may be hysteria but at least plays as sex, and Jeanne, obviously moved, hugs her afterward. It is not so much the Actress who must be aroused, apparently, as the director. This is a theory I heard more than once from Russ Meyer, with whom Breillat might have enjoyed shoptalk.

Sex Is Comedy is not really a comedy and not really about sex. It's about the way a director works with actors and uses them in a godlike way to create a new reality; first directors remake the world the way they see it, and then they guide us into seeing it that way too. It is often said that the movies allow us to empathize with the characters, but aren't we empathizing even more with the directors, since they're the ones who take over our eyes, ears, minds, and imaginations? A great director, by this definition, would be one who most successfully involves us in voyeurism.

Movie sex scenes are famously faked—except in porn and, on several occasions, in films by Breillat (who showed real sex in *Romance* and the *Anatomy of Hell*, where she used porn stars as actors or, sometimes, as body doubles). Her films are not pornography, however, because they do not share the purpose of pornography, which is to arouse. She is fascinated by our fascination with sex, and her movies demystify and deconstruct it. That is an interesting purpose, but *Sex Is Comedy* is not sure what it's really about, or how to get there; the director is seen as flighty and impulsive, the situations seem like setups, and we never know what the Actor and Actress are really thinking—or if thinking has anything to do with it.

Shall We Dance? ★ ★ ★
PG-13, 106 m., 2004

Richard Gere (John Clark), Jennifer Lopez (Paulina), Susan Sarandon (Beverly), Stanley Tucci (Link), Bobby Cannavale (Chic), Lisa Ann Walter (Bobbie), Anita Gillette (Miss Mitzi), Omar Benson Miller (Vern). Directed by Peter Chelsom and produced by Simon Fields. Screenplay by Masayuki Suo and Audrey Wells.

Richard Gere plays John Clark, not an unhappy man, in *Shall We Dance?* He loves his wife and daughter, he enjoys his job as a Chicago lawyer, and when his wife (Susan Sarandon) gets that funny look in her eye and asks him if everything is okay, he says sure, of course, everything is fine. But there is something missing.

One night as he is returning home on the L train, he notices a woman standing alone in the window of Miss Mitzi's Dance Studio. There is something intriguing about her solitude, her pensive attitude, and, let it be said, her figure. A few days later, he gets off the train, walks into the studio, and signs up for classes in ballroom dancing.

Is he interested in dancing? No. Is he interested in the woman, named Paulina and played by Jennifer Lopez? Yes. Is she interested in him? No: "I prefer not to socialize with students." What does he think of the others, including the giant-size Vern (Omar Benson Miller), the homophobic Chic (Bobby Cannavale), the would-be bombshell Bobbie (Lisa Ann Walter), the manic dynamo Link (Stanley Tucci), and of course dear Miss Mitzi (Anita Gillette)? Let us say these are not the kinds of people he usually associates with.

But Paulina exudes a true fascination, especially when she personally dances the rumba with him. In talking about dance, she allows herself a freedom and sensuality she denies herself in life. Listen to her: "The rumba is the vertical expression of a horizontal wish. You have to hold her like the skin on her thigh is your reason for living. Let her go like your heart's being ripped from your chest. Throw her back like you're going to have your way with her right here on the dance floor. And then finish, like she's ruined you for life."

And then ask her if it was as good for her as it was for you. *Shall We Dance?* is a reasonably close remake of *Dansu Wo Shimasho Ka*, a 1996 Japanese film that set box-office records at home and won audiences around the world. If you've seen it, you know precisely what happens in the Hollywood version, but the movie is a star vehicle; the plot isn't the point, Gere and Lopez are. When they dance together, it's a reminder that when dancing became rare from the movies, so did a lot of grace and sexiness.

This is not a cutting-edge movie. The characters are broad, what happens is predictable, and of course everything ends up in a big ballroom dancing competition, and (are you ready for this?) at the crucial moment we get the obligatory scene where the loved one arrives in the audience, sees what is happening, and understands all. I'm averaging two versions of that scene a month; think of *Raise Your Voice.*

Conventional as it may be, *Shall We Dance?* offers genuine delights. The fact that Paulina is uninterested in romance with John comes as sort of a relief, freeing the story to be about something other than the inexorable collision of their genitals. It can be about how John feels about his life, about why it might be useful for a middle-aged lawyer to jump the rails and take up ballroom dance. And about the gallery of supporting characters, who get enough screen time to become engaging.

Stanley Tucci, for example, has fun with Link, who is John Clark's mild-mannered colleague in a Loop law firm. On the dance floor, wearing a flamboyant hairpiece, he becomes a wild man. His dream: "I want to dance before the world in my own name." He fears he would lose his job if he did that, but when John joins the class, he gains courage. He's one of the reasons John stays at Miss Mitzi's even after it becomes clear that Paulina is not available. "Ballroom is all or nothing," Link tells him.

There's one area where the American remake is less than convincing. In the Japanese version, we believe that a faithful wife might remain at home evening after evening while her salaryman husband returned long after work. That's part of the Japanese office culture. That an American wife would put up with it is more problematical. The Clark household, including their teenagers, is not very realistic, but then it exists only as the staging area for the last big scene. I enjoyed the Japanese version so much I invited it to my Overlooked Film Festival a few years ago; it's available on DVD, but this remake offers pleasures of its own.

Shanghai Knights ★ ★ ★
PG-13, 107 m., 2003

Jackie Chan (Chon Wang), Owen Wilson (Roy O'Bannon), Aaron Johnson (Charlie), Thomas Fisher (Artie Doyle), Aidan Gillen (Rathbone), Fann Wong (Chon Lin), Donnie Yen (Wu Chow), Oliver Cotton (Jack the Ripper). Directed by David Dobkin and produced by Roger Birnbaum, Gary Barber, and Jonathan Glickman. Screenplay by Alfred Gough and Miles Millar.

Shanghai Knights has a nice mix of calculation and relaxed goofiness, and in Jackie Chan and Owen Wilson it once again teams up two playful actors who manifestly enjoy playing their ridiculous roles. The world of the action comedy is fraught with failure, still more so the period-Western-kung-fu comedy, but here is a movie, like its predecessor *Shanghai Noon* (2000), that bounds from one gag to another like an eager puppy.

The movie opens with the obligatory action prologue required in the Screenwriter's Code: The Great Seal of China is stolen by sinister intruders, and its guardian killed. The guardian, of course, is the father of Chon Wang (Jackie Chan), who, as we join him after the titles, is sheriff of Carson City, Nevada, and busy ticking off the names of the bad guys he has apprehended. Hearing of the tragedy from his beautiful sister, Chon Lin (Fann Wong), Wang hurries to New York to join up with his old comrade in arms Roy O'Bannon (Owen Wilson).

The movie's plot is entirely arbitrary. Nothing has to happen in Nevada, New York, or its ultimate location, London, although I suppose the setup does need to be in China. Every new scene simply establishes the setting for comedy, martial arts, or both. Because the comedy is fun in a broad, genial way, and because Jackie Chan and his costars (including Fann Wong) are martial arts adepts, and because the director, David Dobkin, keeps the picture filled with energy and goodwill, the movie is just the sort of mindless entertainment we're ready for after all of December's distinguished and significant Oscar finalists.

The plot moves to London because, I think, that's where the Great Seal and the evil plotters are, and even more because it needs fresh locations to distinguish the movie from its predecessor. The filmmakers click off locations like Sheriff Chan checking off the bad guys: the House of Lords, Buckingham Palace (fun with the poker-faced guards), Whitechapel and an encounter with Jack the Ripper, Big Ben (homage to Harold Lloyd), Madame Tussaud's. Charlie Chaplin and Arthur Conan Doyle make surprise appearances, surprises I will not spoil.

For Jackie Chan, *Shanghai Knights* is a comeback after the dismal *The Tuxedo* (2002), a movie that made the incalculable error of depriving him of his martial arts skills and making him the captive of a cybernetic suit. Chan's character flip-flopped across the screen in computer-generated action, which is exactly what we don't want in a Jackie Chan movie. The whole point is that he does his own stunts and the audience knows it.

They know it, among other reasons, because over the closing credits there are always outtakes in which Jackie and his costars miss cues, fall wrong, get banged and bounced on assorted body parts, and break up laughing. The outtakes are particularly good this time, even though I cannot help suspecting (unfairly, maybe) that some of them are just as staged as the rest of the movie.

Shaolin Soccer ★ ★ ★
PG-13, 87 m., 2004

Stephen Chow (Sing), Vicki Zhao (Mui), Man Tat Ng (Golden Leg Fung), Patrick Tse (Hung), Yut Fei Wong (Iron Head). Directed by Stephen Chow and produced by Kwok-fai Yeung. Screenplay by Chow and Kan-Cheung Tsang.

Shaolin Soccer is like a poster boy for my theory of the star rating system. Every month or so, I get an anguished letter from a reader wanting to know how I could possibly have been so ignorant as to award three stars to, say, *Hidalgo* while dismissing, say, *Dogville* with two stars. This disparity between my approval of kitsch and my rejection of angst reveals me, of course, as a superficial moron who will do anything to suck up to my readers.

What these correspondents do not grasp is that to suck up to *my* demanding readers, I would do better to praise *Dogville*. It takes more nerve to praise pop entertainment; it's easy and safe to deliver pious praise of turgid deep thinking. It's true, I loved *Anaconda* and did not think *The United States of Leland* worked, but does that mean I drool at the key-

board and prefer man-eating snakes to suburban despair?

Not at all. What it means is that the star rating system is relative, not absolute. When you ask a friend if *Hellboy* is any good, you're not asking if it's any good compared to *Mystic River*, you're asking if it's any good compared to *The Punisher*. And my answer would be, on a scale of one to four, if *Superman* (1978) is four, then *Hellboy* is three and *The Punisher* is two. In the same way, if *American Beauty* gets four stars, then *Leland* clocks in at about two.

And that is why *Shaolin Soccer*, a goofy Hong Kong action comedy, gets three stars. It is piffle, yes, but superior piffle. If you are even considering going to see a movie where the players zoom fifty feet into the air and rotate freely in violation of everything Newton held sacred, then you do not want to know if I thought it was as good as *Lost in Translation*.

Shaolin Soccer has become a legend. It's the top-grossing action comedy in Hong Kong history, and was a big hit at Toronto 2002 (although, for some reason, I didn't see it; I must have been sidetracked by *Bowling for Columbine*). Miramax bought it, and shelved it for two years, apparently so Harvey Weinstein could cut it by thirty minutes, get rid of the English dubbing, restore the subtitles, and open it one week after his own *Kill Bill: Vol. 2*. To put this movie up against Tarantino is like sending Simon Cowell against William H. Rehnquist, but Simon has his fans.

The movie has been directed and cowritten by Stephen Chow, who stars as Sing, a martial arts master turned street cleaner, who uses his skills in everyday life and is in love with Mui (Vicki Zhao), who sells buns from her little street stand and combs her hair forward to conceal a complexion that resembles pizza with sausage and mushrooms. It is a foregone conclusion that by the end of this film Mui will be a startling beauty. Less predictable is that Sing recruits seven soccer players from his former monastery to form a soccer team.

His inspiration to do this is Fung (Man Tat Ng), known as the Golden Leg because he was, years ago, a great soccer hero until his leg was broken by Hung (Patrick Tse). Hung now rules the soccer world as owner of Team Evil (yes, Team Evil), while Fung drags his leg like the Hunchback of Notre Dame. It is another foregone conclusion that Team Evil will meet the Shaolin soccer team formed by Fung and Sing in a thrilling match played before what looks like a vast crowd that has been borrowed from a computer game.

The game doesn't follow any known rules of soccer, except that there is a ball and a goal. As the players swoop high into the air and do acrobatics before kicking the ball, I was reminded more of Quidditch. There is also the matter of ball velocity. The players can kick the ball so hard that it actually catches fire as it rockets through the air, or digs a groove in the ground as it plows toward the goal.

Since the game is impossible and it is obvious Team Evil will lose, there's not much suspense, but there is a lot of loony comedy, a musical number, and the redemption of the Poor Spotted Little Bun Girl. As soccer comedies go, then, I say three stars. It's nowhere near as good as *Bend It Like Beckham* (2002), of course, but *Beckham* is in a different genre, the coming-of-age female-empowerment film. It's important to keep these things straight.

The Shape of Things ★ ★ ★ ½
R, 96 m., 2003

Paul Rudd (Adam), Rachel Weisz (Evelyn), Gretchen Mol (Jenny), Fred Weller (Phillip). Directed by Neil LaBute and produced by LaBute, Gail Mutrux, Philip Steuer, and Rachel Weisz. Screenplay by LaBute.

The world of Neil LaBute is a battleground of carnage between the sexes. Men and women distrust one another, scheme to humiliate one another, are inspired to fearsome depths of cruelty. Their warfare takes place in the affluent habitats of the white upper-middle class—restaurants, bookstores, coffee shops, corporate offices, campuses, museums, and apartments of tasteful sterility. Although one of his gender wars films was shot in Fort Wayne, Indiana, and the other two in southern California, there is no way to tell that from the information on the screen. All of his characters seem to live in clean, well-lighted, interchangeable places.

The Shape of Things is the third of these films. First came *In the Company of Men* (1997) and *Your Friends and Neighbors* (1998). Then there were two mainstream films, *Nurse Betty* (2000) and *Possession* (2002). Now we are back in the world of chamber dramas involving a handful of intimately linked characters. The first film was driven by a man of ferocious misanthropy. The second involved characters whose everyday selfishness and dishonesty were upstaged by a character of astonishing cruelty. In *The Shape of Things*, while the two couples have their share of character defects, they seem generally within the norm, until we fully understand what has happened.

In a museum, we see Evelyn (Rachel Weisz) step over a velvet rope to take Polaroids of a male nude statue—or, more specifically, of a fig leaf added at a later date. The museum guard, named Adam (Paul Rudd), asks her to step outside the rope, but eventually steps inside it himself, to plead with her not to cause trouble just before his shift ends. He's a student, working part-time.

They begin to see each other. She's a graduate student, working on a project that she describes, as she describes a great many things, as a "thingy." Eventually we meet an engaged couple, Jenny (Gretchen Mol) and Phillip (Fred Weller), who are friends of Adam's. Over a period of months, they notice changes in him. He loses weight. Gets a haircut. Rids himself of a nerdy corduroy jacket that, we learn, Phillip has been urging him to throw away since freshman year. He even has a nose job, which he tries to explain as an accidental injury.

What, or who, is responsible for these changes? Can it be Evelyn, who is now Adam's girlfriend? Adam denies it, although it is not unknown for a woman to make over the new man in her life, and even Jenny observes that most men have traits that stand between them and perfection—traits women are quick to observe and quite willing to change.

The movie unfolds as a series of literate conversations between various combinations of these four articulate people. Their basic subject is one another. They are observant about mannerisms, habits, values, and changes, and feel licensed to make suggestions. There is even a little low-key sexual cheating, involving kissing, and low-key emotional assaults, involving telling about the kissing.

And then . . . but I will not say one more word because the rest of the movie is for you to discover. Let it simply be said that there are no free passes in LaBute's class in gender studies.

The Shape of Things builds a sense of quiet dread under what seems to be an ordinary surface. Characters talk in a normal way, and we suspect that their blandness disguises buried motives. Often they are quite happy to criticize each other, and none of them takes criticism well. These characters are perhaps in training to become the narcissistic, self-absorbed monsters in *Your Friends and Neighbors.*

LaBute has that rarest of attributes, a distinctive voice. You know one of his scenes at once. His dialogue is the dialogue overheard in trendy midscale restaurants, with the words peeled back to suggest the venom beneath. He also has a distinctive view of life, in which men and women are natural enemies—and beyond that, every person is an island surrounded by enemies. This seems like a bleak and extreme view, and yet what happens in his films often feels like the logical extension of what happens to us or around us every day. It is the surface normality of the characters and their world that is scary.

LaBute has been compared to David Mamet, and no doubt there was an influence, seen in the devious plots and the precisely heard, evocative language. But Mamet is much more interested in plotting itself, in con games and deceptions, while in LaBute there is the feeling that some kind of deeper human tragedy is being enacted; his characters deceive and wound one another not for gain or pleasure, but because that is their nature.

Actors have a thankless task in a film like this. All four players are well cast in roles that ask them to avoid "acting" and simply exist on a realistic, everyday level. Like the actors in a Bresson film, they're used for what they intrinsically represent, rather than for what they can achieve through their art. They are like those all around us, and like us, except that LaBute is suspicious of their hidden motives. One person plays a cruel trick in *The Shape of Things,* but we get the uneasy sense that, in LaBute's world, any one of the four could have been that person.

Shark Tale ★ ★

PG, 100 m., 2004

With the voices of: Will Smith (Oscar), Robert De Niro (Don Lino), Renee Zellweger (Angie), Jack Black (Lenny), Angelina Jolie (Lola), Martin Scorsese (Sykes), Katie Couric (Katie Current), Doug E. Doug (Bernie), Ziggy Marley (Ernie), Michael Imperioli (Frankie). Directed by Bibo Bergeron, Vicky Jenson, and Rob Letterman and produced by Bill Damaschke, Janet Healy, and Allison Lyon Segan. Screenplay by Letterman, Damian Shannon, Mark Swift, and Michael J. Wilson.

Casablanca was only twenty-five years old when I started as a movie critic, but I thought of it as an old movie. *The Godfather,* which supplies most of the inspiration for *Shark Tale,* is thirty-two years old, and *Jaws,* its other inspiration, is twenty-nine years old. Time slips into the future, and movies still fresh in our hearts are considered by younger audiences to be ancient classics.

Since the target audience for *Shark Tale* is presumably kids and younger teenagers, how many of them have seen the R-rated *Godfather* and will get all the inside jokes? Not a few, I suppose, and some of its characters and dialogue have passed into common knowledge. But it's strange that a kid-oriented film would be based on a parody of a 1972 gangster movie for adults. Strange, too, that the movie's values also seem to come from *The Godfather,* a study in situational ethics that preferred good gangsters with old-fashioned values (the Corleone family) to bad gangsters who sold drugs. Sure, it would be better for your kids to grow up to be more like Don Vito than Scarface, but what a choice.

The movie is the latest production of DreamWorks Animation, codirected by Vicky Jenson *(Shrek),* Bibo Bergeron *(The Road to El Dorado),* and Rob Letterman. It takes place on an underwater reef where sharks are the local gangsters, and run things from their headquarters on the hulk of the *Titanic.* Coral formations, undersea debris, and vegetation combine to create an aquatic Times Square, and, as in *Shrek 2,* real retailers have their "toon" equivalents.

The movie doesn't follow the plot of *The Godfather* so much as recycle its characters, and the *Jaws* inspiration gets an early smile when the famous theme music, scary for people, is as inspiring to sharks as the national anthem. The story's hero is Oscar (voice by Will

Smith), who works down at the Whale Wash. It's a mob front, run by Sykes (voice by Martin Scorsese), a puffer fish who has extraordinary eyebrows, for a fish. Oscar is deep in debt to Sykes, who assigns a couple of Rastafarian enforcers (Ziggy Marley and Doug E. Doug) to take Oscar on a trip and teach him a lesson he'll never forget.

The mob is ruled by Don Lino (voice by Robert De Niro, channeling Marlon Brando), who is a ruthless, but by his own standards, fair shark. His two sons are Frankie (Michael Imperioli), who has grown up to be a shark any dad can be proud of, and Lenny (Jack Black), who has disgraced the family by becoming a vegetarian. Lenny could found a reef chapter of PETA (Predators for the Ethical Treatment of Animals) on the basis of his activist intervention one night at dinner, when he sets a shrimp cocktail free.

Don Lino is fed up with Lenny, and orders Frankie to take the lad on a swimabout and teach him the life lessons of sharkhood. As luck would have it, they cross paths with Oscar and the enforcers, and when a falling ship's anchor kills Frankie, Oscar gets the credit. Since the reef lives in terror of the sharks, this makes him a local hero and creates romantic suspense: Will he remain faithful to his longtime girlfriend, Angie (Renée Zellweger), or be seduced by the charms of the local "finne fatale," Lola (Angelina Jolie)? Reporting on all of this is the local anchorwoman, Katie Current, voiced by Katie Couric.

The problem with this story is that the movie pays too much attention to it, as if we really cared. Most successful animation has a basic level that even small children can easily identify. Little Nemo wanted to escape from the fish tank and return to his father in the ocean. Every kid understood that. But how much will they care in *Shark Tale* that Oscar wants to clear his debt with the loan sharks and become rich and famous? Will they follow the romantic struggle involving the Zellweger and Jolie characters?

The movie lacks a port of entry for young viewers in a character they can identify with. All of the major characters are adults with adult problems like debt, romance, and running (or swimming) away from the mob. In dealing with their concerns, the characters do way too much talking, maybe because the filmmakers were so thrilled to have great voice-over talent.

In earlier days the voice-over dubbers for cartoons were anonymous, unless they were named Mel Blanc. Now they "star" in the movie, so that the posters for *Shark Tale* list De Niro, Smith, Zellweger, and Jolie in big type at the top, as if we were really going to see them in the movie. To be sure, the fish look a little like their voice talents; I wonder if salaries go up when the voices for animation agree to have their faces and mannerisms borrowed.

There are a lot of funny moments in *Shark Tale*, free-standing gags, clever lines, neat twists, but the movie never comes together into a convincing enterprise. It's so in love with its origins in gangster movies, and has so much fun with the voices of its famous actors, that it never really defines and sells the characters in a way the audience cares about. There's a point when you wish the filmmakers would drop the in-jokes and the subtle Hollywood references and just get on with it. The movie is likely to appeal to movie buffs more than to typical family audiences.

Shattered Glass ★ ★ ★ ½
PG-13, 99 m., 2003

Hayden Christensen (Stephen Glass), Peter Sarsgaard (Chuck Lane), Chloë Sevigny (Caitlin Avey), Melanie Lynskey (Amy Brand), Steve Zahn (Adam Penenberg), Hank Azaria (Michael Kelly), Rosario Dawson (Andie Fox), Luke Kirby (Rob Gruen). Directed by Billy Ray and produced by Craig Baumgarten, Marc Butan, Tove Christensen, Gaye Hirsch, and Adam Merims. Screenplay by Ray, based on the article by Buzz Bissinger.

"Are you mad at me?" Stephen Glass asks. He's like a puppy who's made a mess on the carpet but knows he's cute and all of the kids are crazy about him. The kids in this case are his fellow staffers at the *New Republic*, and the mess consists of twenty-seven steaming piles of fabricated falsehoods that he deposited on its pages.

You may remember some of Glass's stories. I know I did. I loved his piece about the young hacker who terrified corporations with raids on their computers, and then sold them his expertise to shoot down other hackers. This guy was so successful he had his own agent. Then there was the gathering of Young Republicans at a Washington hotel, partying all night like drunken fraternity boys. And the convention of the political novelties industry, with display tables of racist, homophobic, and anti-Clinton T-shirts, bumper stickers, and books.

Terrific stories. Problem is, Stephen Glass (Hayden Christensen) made them all up. Without realizing it, The *NR* had started publishing fiction. Magazines employ fact-checkers to backstop their writers, and they're a noble crowd, but sometimes they check the trees and not the forest; it doesn't occur to them that a piece might be a total fraud.

The first puncture of Stephen Glass's balloon came from Adam Penenberg (Steve Zahn), who as a writer for the Web-based Forbes Digital Tool was several steps down the ladder from the *New Republic*'s superstar. But when he tries to follow up on that rich hacker with his own agent, he can't find him—or his agent, or the company that hired him, or his Website, or anything. When he calls the *NR*, his query lands on the desk of Charles Lane (Peter Sarsgaard), the magazine's new editor. Lane has enough to worry about: He has recently replaced the beloved Michael Kelly, he lacks Kelly's charisma, and the staffers instinctively side with Glass against the cool, distant Lane.

When you hear about a case like this, or the similar fraud committed against the *New York Times* by Jayson Blair, you wonder how a world-class publication gets itself conned by some kid. Maybe the key word is "kid." Maybe the hotshot newcomers generate an attractive aura around themselves so that editors would rather jump on the bandwagon than seem like old fogeys.

Shattered Glass, written and directed by Billy Ray and based on a *Vanity Fair* article by Buzz Bissinger, relates the rise and fall of the young charmer in terms of the office culture at the *New Republic*, which is written by and for smart people and, crucially, doesn't use photographs. ("Photos would have saved us," one staffer notes, "because there wouldn't have been any." There were, however, photos with Jayson Blair's stories—it's just that the photographer could never seem to find him at the scene of the story.)

The movie is smart about journalism be-cause it is smart about offices; the typical news-room is open space filled with desks, and jour-nalists are actors on this stage; to see a good writer on deadline with a big story is to watch not simply work, but performance.

Stephen Glass was a better actor than most, playing the role of a whiz kid with bashful nar-cissism. There is a fascinating and agonizing se-quence during which Lane tries to pin down the slippery details of a Glass story, and Glass tries to wriggle free. Phone numbers go miss-ing, files are left at home, phone calls aren't an-swered, and as it becomes obvious to Lane that the story will not hold water, a kind of dread begins to grow.

We like Glass, too, and we can see he's trapped; he channels those nightmares we all have about flunking the big exam. There are a couple of times when Lane seems to have him nailed down and he squirms free with a des-perate but brilliant improvisation, and we're reminded of Frank Abagnale Jr., the hero of *Catch Me If You Can,* who found an addictive joy in getting praise he did not deserve.

Glass's fellow workers admire him because (a) he's turning in work they would have died to have written, and (b) he doesn't rub it in. Two of his most admiring colleagues, Caitlin Avey (Chloë Sevigny) and Amy Brand (Melanie Lynskey), feel protective toward him; like sisters, they worry that he works too hard, pushes him-self, doesn't take credit, doesn't know how good he is. A more typical newsroom colleague is Andie Fox, played by Rosario Dawson over at Forbes Digital Tool; she senses that Penenberg (Zahn) is onto a really big story, wants a piece of it, and keeps trying to elbow in.

Because *Shattered Glass* is cast so well, with actors who seem to instinctively embody their parts, it's worth another look at some of Billy Ray's choices. Hayden Christensen, who makes Glass's career believable by being utterly plausi-ble himself, played young Anakin Skywalker in *Star Wars: Attack of the Clones.* Steve Zahn often plays clueless losers, and Rosario Dawson specializes in sex and action roles; not here. Chloë Sevigny is a versatile actress, but you might not have thought of her as a *New Repub-lic* staffer until you see her here, and she's pitch-perfect. Peter Sarsgaard has the balancing act as a new editor who happens to be right but is under enormous pressure to be wrong.

Shattered Glass deserves comparison with *All the President's Men* among movies about journalism, but it's about a type known in many professions: The guy who seems to be pursuing the office agenda when actually he's pursuing his own. Filled with a vision of his own success, charming and persuasive, smart, able to create whole worlds from fictions that work as well as facts, he has an answer for everything until someone finally thinks to ask the fundamental question: Is it all a fraud, right down to the bone?

In recent years we have seen vast corporations built on lies and political decisions based more on wishes than facts. The engineers of those deceptions have all been enormously likable, of course. They need to be. We are saved, from time to time, not so much by the rectitude of the Charles Lanes as by the dogged curiosity of the Adam Penenbergs.

Shaun of the Dead ★ ★ ★
R, 99 m., 2004

Simon Pegg (Shaun), Kate Ashfield (Liz), Nick Frost (Ed), Lucy Davis (Dianne), Dylan Moran (David), Bill Nighy (Phil), Penelope Wilton (Barbara). Directed by Edgar Wright and produced by Nira Park. Screenplay by Simon Pegg and Wright.

As movie characters, zombies are boring by definition: All they can do is shuffle, moan, catch up with much faster people, and chew on their arms. *Shaun of the Dead* shares my sentiments so exactly that during the opening scenes of the movie its hero walks among the undead and doesn't even notice them. He's too hungover and worried that his girlfriend will leave him.

The movie is a new British comedy about clueless layabouts whose lives center on the pub; for them, the zombies represent not a threat to civilization as we know it, but an interference with valuable drinking time. When it becomes clear that London is crawling (or shuffling) with zombies, best buddies Shaun (Simon Pegg) and Ed (Nick Frost) lead a small band of survivors to the obvious stronghold: the Winchester, their local.

The irony is that Shaun's girlfriend, Liz (Kate Ashfield), has been issuing ultimatums, asking Shaun to choose between her and the pub. She lives with Di (Lucy Davis) and David (Dylan Moran), who think that in a showdown Shaun would choose the pub over his girl; when Shaun urges them to barricade themselves inside the Winchester, David is not encouraging: "Do you think his master plan is going to amount to anything more than sitting and eating peanuts in the dark?" This is not really fair, since Shaun is at least armed: He uses his cricket bat to wham zombies on the head. A cricket bat is to British movies as a baseball bat is to American movies: the weapon of choice for clueless heroes going downstairs to investigate a noise that was inevitably made by somebody packing a lot more than a bat.

Liz, Shaun, and Ed the best friend have a relationship not unlike the characters played by Jennifer Aniston, John C. Reilly, and Tim Blake Nelson in *The Good Girl* (2002). Liz is smart and ambitious and wants to get ahead in the world, but Shaun is happy with his entry-level job in retail and his leisure hours spent with Ed, watching the telly and drinking beer—at the pub, preferably, or at home in a pinch. When Liz complains that Ed is always around, Shaun says, "He doesn't have too many friends," which is often an argument for not becoming one.

Shaun of the Dead, written by Simon Pegg and Edgar Wright and directed by Wright, is a send-up of zombie movies, but in an unexpected way: Instead of focusing on the undead and trying to get the laughs there, it treats the living characters as sitcom regulars whose conflicts and arguments keep getting interrupted by annoying flesh-eaters. In the first two or three scenes, as he crawls out of bed and plods down the street wrapped in the misery of his hangover, Shaun doesn't even notice the zombies. Sure, they're on the TV news, but who watches the news? For Shaun and Ed, the news functions primarily as reassurance that the set will be operating when the football match begins.

The supporting characters include Shaun's stepfather, Phil (Bill Nighy), and mother, Barbara (Penelope Wilton). Nighy is that elongated character actor who looks as if he may have invaded Rhys Ifans's gene pool. He has a quality that generates instinctive sympathy, as in *Love Actually* (2002), where he played the broken-down rock star still hoping patiently in middle age for a comeback. Here there's something endearing about his response when he is bitten by a zombie. It has been clearly established that such bites always lead to death and then rebirth as a zombie. Once bitten, your doom is sealed. But listen to Phil reassure them, "I ran it under the tap."

Shaun of the Dead has its pleasures, which are mild but real. I like the way the slacker characters maintain their slothful gormlessness in the face of urgent danger, and I like the way the British bourgeois values of Shaun's mum and dad assert themselves even in the face of catastrophe. There is also that stubborn British courage in times of trouble. "We never closed," bragged the big neon sign outside the Windmill strip club in Soho, which stayed open every night during the Blitz. In this movie, the Winchester pub exhibits the same spirit.

Good thing the movie is about more than zombies. I am by now more or less exhausted by the cinematic possibilities of killing them. I've seen thousands of zombies die, and they're awfully easy to kill, unless you get a critical mass that piles on all at once. George Romeo, who invented the modern genre with *Night of the Living Dead* and *Dawn of the Dead,* was essentially devising video-game targets before there were video games: They pop up, one after another, and you shoot them, or bang them on the head with a cricket bat. It's more fun sitting in the dark eating peanuts.

She Hate Me ★ ★ ★
R, 138 m., 2004

Anthony Mackie (Jack Armstrong), Kerry Washington (Fatima Goodrich), Ellen Barkin (Margo Chadwick), Monica Bellucci (Simona Bonasera), Jim Brown (Geronimo Armstrong), Chiwetel Ejiofor (Frank Wills), Brian Dennehy (Bill Church), Woody Harrelson (Leland Powell), John Turturro (Angelo Bonasera). Directed by Spike Lee and produced by Preston L. Holmes, Lee, and Fernando Sulichin. Screenplay by Michael Genet and Lee.

Spike Lee's *She Hate Me* will get some terrible reviews. Scorched-earth reviews. Its logic, style, presumption, and sexual politics will be ridiculed. The Tomatometer will be down around 20. Many of the things you read in those reviews may be true from a conventional point of view. Most of the critics will be on safe ground. I will seem to be wrong. Seeming to be wrong about this movie is one of the most interesting things I've done recently. I've learned from it.

After seeing the movie once, I would have complained that *She Hate Me* contains enough for five movies, but has no idea which of those movies it wants to be. Movie One: the story of a corporate whistle-blower (Anthony Mackie) and an indictment of the corporate culture. Movie Two: The hero inexplicably becomes a stud who is hired to impregnate lesbians at $10,000 a pop. Movie Three: He impregnates a Mafia daughter (Monica Bellucci), and John Turturro turns up as her father to do a Marlon Brando imitation. Movie Four: a free-standing sidebar about Frank Wills (Chiwetel Ejiofor), the Watergate security guard who brought down the Nixon administration, and reaped nothing but personal unhappiness. Movie Five: how a black man steps up to the plate and accepts responsibility for raising his kids, by bonding with his lesbian ex-girlfriend (Kerry Washington) and her lover, who have both borne one of his children.

What do these stories have to do with one another? How can we be expected to believe that not one but eighteen lesbians would pay a man to make them pregnant? And that he could perform with six women in the same night and bring every one of them to a loud and even thrashing climax? That his sperm count would go the distance? That seventeen of them would get pregnant after one encounter? That none of them would be alarmed at being sixth or eighteenth in a row of unprotected sex? And that when the movie shows its hero ready to "be there" for his children, it ignores the question of whether a lesbian couple would need or desire his presence, however noble his intentions?

Oh, I could go on and on. But read some of the other reviews for that. The standard review of this movie is unanswerable, unless you look beneath the surface.

I went to see the movie a second time, because

my first response, while immediate and obvious, left me feeling unsatisfied. I knew I could plow into the movie and spare not a single frame, using implacable logic and withering sarcasm. But some seed of subversion in the film made that feel too easy. Whatever its faults, the movie had engaged and fascinated me in its various parts, even if it seemed to have no whole.

Spike Lee is a filmmaker on a short list with directors like Herzog, Sayles, Jarmusch, Altman, Paul Thomas Anderson, Todd Solondz, and the new kid, David Gordon Green. He dances to his own music. He no doubt knows all the objections that can be raised against his film. He knows that structurally it's all over the map. He knows the lesbian story line is logically and emotionally absurd. He knows Frank Wills came in from left field. He knows he begins with a conventional drama about rotten corporations, and then jumps ship. He knows all of that. He teaches film at Harvard, for chrissakes. *So why did he make this movie, this way?*

I could call him up and ask him, but maybe the point is to look at this film, ask myself that question, and avoid the easy answer, which is that he made a preposterous movie because he didn't know any better. He knows better. He could have delivered a safe, politically correct, well-made film without even breathing hard.

But this is the work of a man who wants to dare us to deal with it. Who is confronting generic expectations, conventional wisdom, and political correctness. Whose film may be an attack on the sins it seems to commit. Who is impatient with the tired, rote role of the heroic African-American corporate whistle-blower (he could phone that one in). Who confronts the pious liberal horror about such concepts as the inexhaustible black stud and lesbians who respond on cue to sex with a man—and instead of skewering them, which would be the easy thing to do, flaunts them.

His movie seems to celebrate those forbidden ideas. Why does he do this? Perhaps because to attack those concepts would be simplistic, platitudinous, and predictable. But to work without the safety net, to deliberately be offensive, to refuse to satisfy our generic expectations, to dangle the conventional for-mula in front of us and then yank it away, to explode the structure of the movie, to allow it to contain anger and sarcasm, impatience, and wild, imprudent excess, to find room for both unapologetic melodramatic romance *and* satire—well, that's audacious. To go where this film goes and still have the nerve to end the way he does (with a reconciliation worthy of soap opera, and the black hero making a noble speech at a congressional hearing) is a form of daring beyond all reason.

My guess is that Lee is attacking African-American male and gay/lesbian stereotypes not by conventionally preaching against them, but by boldly dramatizing them. The inspiration for *She Hate Me* may be his *Bamboozled* (2000), an attack on black stereotypes that was one of his least successful films. Having failed with a frontal assault, he returns to the battle using indirection. By getting mad at the movie, we arrive at the conclusions he intends. In a sense, he is sacrificing himself to get his message across.

Either that, or I have completely misread *She Hate Me*, but I couldn't write the obvious review. I couldn't convince myself I believed it. This film is alive and confrontational and aggressively in our face, and the man who made it has abandoned all caution even to the point of refusing to signal his intentions, to put in a wink to let us see he knows what he's doing.

It is exciting to watch this movie. It is never boring. Lee is like a juggler who starts out with balls and gradually adds baseball bats, top hats, and chainsaws. It's not an intellectual experience, but an emotional one. Spike Lee is like a jazz soloist who cuts loose, leaving behind the song and the group, walking offstage and out of the club, and keeps on improvising right down the street, looking for someone who can keep up with him. True, the movie is not altogether successful. It's so jagged, so passionate in its ambition, it raises more questions than it answers. But isn't that better than the way most films answer more questions than they raise? *She Hate Me* invites anger and analysis about the stereotypes it appears to celebrate; a film that attacked those stereotypes would inspire yawns. Think what you want on a "politically correct" level, but concede that *She Hate Me* is audacious and recklessly risky. ☞

Shrek 2 ★ ★ ★
PG, 105 m., 2004

With the voices of: Mike Myers (Shrek), Eddie Murphy (Donkey), Cameron Diaz (Princess Fiona), John Cleese (King Harold), Julie Andrews (Queen Lillian), Jennifer Saunders (Fairy Godmother), Antonio Banderas (Puss-in-Boots), Rupert Everett (Prince Charming), Larry King (The Ugly Stepsister). An animated film directed by Andrew Adamson, Kelly Asbury, and Conrad Vernon and produced by David Lipman, Aron Warner, and John H. Williams. Screenplay by J. David Stem, Joe Stillman, and David N. Weiss, based on the characters by William Steig.

Shrek 2 is bright, lively, and entertaining, but it's no *Shrek*. Maybe it's too much to expect lightning to strike twice. *Shrek* was so original in its animation and such an outpouring of creative imagination that it blindsided us; *Shrek 2* is wonderful in its own way, but more earthbound. It's more fun to see Shrek battle a dragon than to watch him meeting his new in-laws.

Shrek (voiced again by Mike Myers) actually seems teetering on the brink of middle-class respectability in the sequel. There's nothing like a good woman to tame an ogre. His outsider status as the loner in the swamp has changed dramatically through his romance with Princess Fiona (Cameron Diaz), although his table manners could stand improvement when he has dinner with her parents, King Harold (John Cleese) and Queen Lillian (Julie Andrews).

In the first film, as you may remember, Fiona's curse was that she had been taken captive by a dragon, but could be freed if the dragon was slain and she was kissed by the hero who did the deed. Ideally, that would be Prince Charming (Rupert Everett), but in *Shrek 2*, when he finally arrives in the neighborhood he discovers to his intense disappointment that the ogre has already dispatched the dragon and wed the princess—and that Shrek's kiss dramatically transformed Fiona. No longer petite, she is tall and broad and green, and an ogre.

A summons comes from the Kingdom of Far Far Away: Her parents want to meet her new husband. This involves a very long journey by Shrek, Fiona, and Donkey (Eddie Murphy), who insists on coming along. Donkey is the comic high point of the movie, with Murphy's nonstop riffs and inability to guess when he is not welcome. "The trick isn't that he talks," Shrek observed in the first movie. "The trick is to get him to shut up." The kingdom is indeed far, far away, which gives Donkey endless opportunities to ask, "Are we there yet?"

Their arrival at the castle of Fiona's parents provides big laughs; Harold and Lillian are shocked to find that their daughter has not only married an ogre, but also become one. A basket of doves is released to celebrate their arrival, and one of them is so astonished it flies bang into the castle wall, and drops dead at Harold's feet. Eventually the plot leads us into the environs of the Fairy Godmother (Jennifer Saunders), a sinister figure who operates a vast factory manufacturing potions and hexes. Is it possible that her Happily Ever After potion could transform ogres into humans? Not if she can help it; she wants to get rid of Shrek and marry Fiona to Prince Charming, according to her original plan.

The screenplay, by J. David Stem, Joe Stillman, and David N. Weiss, has the same fun *Shrek* did in playing against our expectations. Who would anticipate a fight between the ogre and his bride, with Shrek marching out of the house? What about the arrivals ceremony at the matrimonial ball, with all of the kingdom's celebrities walking down a red carpet while an unmistakable clone of Joan Rivers does the commentary? And there's real sweetness when Shrek and Fiona start smooching.

The movie has several songs, none of which I found very memorable, although of course I am the same person who said the Simon and Garfunkel songs in *The Graduate* were "instantly forgettable." The first song, "Accidentally in Love," explains how Shrek and Fiona fell for each other. It's cut like a music video, which is okay, but I think it comes too early in the film, before we really feel at home with the narrative.

A few minor characters from the first film, like the Gingerbread Man and the Three

Blind Mice, return for the sequel, and there's a new major character: Puss-in-Boots, a cat who seems to have been raised on Charles Boyer movies, and is voiced by Antonio Banderas. Donkey and Puss build an enormous mutual resentment, because each one thinks he's the star.

Sequels have their work cut out for them. Some people think *Godfather, Part II* is better than *The Godfather,* but the first film loomed so tall in my mind that I gave "Part II" only three stars. In the same way, perhaps I would have liked *Shrek 2* more if the first film had never existed. But I'll never know. Still, *Shrek 2* is a jolly story, and Shrek himself seems durable enough to inspire *Shrek 3* with no trouble at all. Maybe it will be *Shrek Meets Cheaper by the Dozen.*

Sideways ★ ★ ★

R, 124 m., 2004

Paul Giamatti (Miles Raymond), Thomas Haden Church (Jack Lopate), Virginia Madsen (Maya), Sandra Oh (Stephanie). Directed by Alexander Payne and produced by Michael London. Screenplay by Payne and Jim Taylor, based on the novel by Rex Pickett.

"There was a tasting last night," Miles Raymond explains, on one of those alcoholic mornings that begin in the afternoon and strain eagerly toward the first drink. That's why he's a little shaky. He's not an alcoholic, you understand; he's an oenophile, which means he can continue to pronounce French wines long after most people would be unconscious. We realize he doesn't set the bar too high when he praises one vintage as "quaffable." No wonder his unpublished novel is titled *The Day After Yesterday;* for anyone who drinks a lot, that's what today always feels like.

Miles is the hero of Alexander Payne's *Sideways,* which is as lovable a movie as *Fargo,* although in a completely different way. He's an English teacher in middle school whose marriage has failed, whose novel seems in the process of failing, whose mother apparently understands that when he visits her, it is because he loves her, and also because he needs to steal some of her money. Miles is not perfect, but the way Paul Giamatti plays him, we

forgive him his trespasses, because he trespasses most of all against himself.

Miles's friend Jack is getting married in a week. They would seem to have little in common. Jack is a big, blond, jovial man at the peak of fleshy middle-aged handsomeness, and Miles looks like—well, if you know who Harvey Pekar is, that's who Giamatti played in his previous movie. But Jack and Miles have been friends since they were college roommates, and their friendship endures because together they add up to a relatively complete person.

Miles, as the best man, wants to take Jack on a week-long bachelor party in the California wine country, which makes perfect sense, because whatever an alcoholic says he is planning, at the basic level he is planning his drinking. Jack's addiction is to women. "My best man gift to you," he tells Miles, "will be to get you laid." Miles is so manifestly not layable that for him this would be less like a gift than an exercise program.

Jack (Thomas Haden Church) is a not very successful actor; he tells people they may have heard his voice-over work in TV commercials, but it turns out he's the guy who rattles off the warnings about side effects and interest rates in the last five seconds. The two men set off for wine country, and what happens during the next seven days adds up to the best human comedy of the year—comedy, because it is funny, and human, because it is surprisingly moving.

Of course they meet two women. Maya (Virginia Madsen) is a waitress at a restaurant where Miles has often stopped in the past, to yearn but not touch. She's getting her graduate degree in horticulture, and is beautiful, in a kind way; you wonder why she would be attracted to Miles until you find out she was once married to a philosophy professor at Santa Barbara, which can send a woman down-market in search of relief. The next day they meet Stephanie (Sandra Oh), a pour girl at a winery tasting room, and when it appears that the two women know each other, Jack seals the deal with a double date, swearing Miles to silence about the approaching marriage.

Miles has much to be silent about. He has been in various forms of depression for years, and no wonder, since alcohol is a depressant.

He is still in love with his former wife, and mourns the bliss that could have been his, if he had not tasted his way out of the marriage. Although his days include learned discourses about vintages, they end with him drunk, and he has a way of telephoning the poor women late at night. "Did you drink and dial?" Jack asks him.

The movie was written by Payne and Jim Taylor, from the novel by Rex Pickett. One of its lovely qualities is that all four characters are necessary. The women are not plot conveniences, but elements in a complex romantic and even therapeutic process. Miles loves Maya and has for years, but cannot bring himself to make a move because romance requires precision and tact late at night, not Miles's peak time of day. Jack lusts after Stephanie, and casually, even cruelly, fakes love for her even as he cheats on his fiancée.

What happens between them all is the stuff of the movie, and must not be revealed here, except to observe that Giamatti and Madsen have a scene that involves some of the gentlest and most heartbreaking dialogue I've heard in a long time. They're talking about wine. He describes for her the qualities of the Pinot Noir grape that most attract him, and as he mentions its thin skin, its vulnerability, its dislike for being too hot or cold, too wet or dry, she realizes he is describing himself, and that is when she falls in love with him. Women can actually love us for ourselves, bless their hearts, even when we can't love ourselves. She waits until he is finished, and then responds with words so simple and true they will win her an Oscar nomination, if there is justice in the world. *[They did.]*

Terrible misunderstandings (and even worse understandings) take place, tragedy grows confused with slapstick, and why Miles finds himself creeping through the house of a fat waitress and her alarming husband would be completely implausible if we had not seen it coming every step of the way. Happiness is distributed where needed and withheld where deserved, and at the end of the movie we feel like seeing it again.

Alexander Payne has made four wonderful movies: *Citizen Ruth, Election,* the Jack Nicholson tragicomedy *About Schmidt,* and now this. He finds plots that service his char-acters, instead of limiting them. The characters are played not by the first actors you would think of casting, but by actors who will prevent you from ever being able to imagine anyone else in their roles.   ☞

Silver City ★ ★ ★ ½
R, 129 m., 2004

Chris Cooper (Dickie Pilager), Danny Huston (Danny O'Brien), Maria Bello (Nora Allardyce). Thora Birch (Karen Cross), Richard Dreyfuss (Chuck Raven), Miguel Ferrer (Cliff Castleton), Daryl Hannah (Madeleine Pilager), Kris Kristofferson (Wes Benteen), Mary Kay Place (Grace Seymour), Michael Murphy (Senator Judd Pilager), Billy Zane (Chandler Tyson). Directed by John Sayles and produced by Maggie Renzi. Screenplay by Sayles.

John Sayles's *Silver City* can be read as social satire aimed at George W. Bush—certainly the film's hero mirrors the Bush quasi-speaking style—but it takes wider aim on the entire political landscape we inhabit. Liberals and conservatives, the alternative press and establishment dailies, environmentalists, and despoilers are all mixed up in a plot where it seems appropriate that the hero is a private detective. Even the good guys are compromised.

Sayles, like Robert Altman, is a master at the tricky art of assembling large casts and keeping all the characters alive. Here, as in his *City of Hope* (1991), he shows how lives can be unexpectedly connected, how hidden agendas can slip in under the radar, how information can travel and wound or kill.

The movie centers on the campaign of Dickie Pilager (Chris Cooper), who is running for governor of Colorado with the backing of his father (Michael Murphy), the state's senior senator. Dickie is the creature of industrial interests who want to roll back pollution controls and penalties, but as the movie opens he's dressed like an L.L. Bean model as he stands in front of a lake and repeats, or tries to repeat, platitudes about the environment. Cooper deliberately makes him sound as much like George II as possible.

The younger Pilager may be clueless, but he's not powerless. His campaign is being managed by a Karl Rove type named Chuck Raven

623

(Richard Dreyfuss), who tells him what to say and how to say it. There's not always time to explain why to say it. Surrounding the campaign, at various degrees of separation, other characters develop interlocking subplots.

The most important involves the discovery of a dead body in a lake, and the attempts of private eye Danny O'Brien (Danny Huston) to investigate the case. O'Brien is in the tradition of Elliott Gould in Altman's *The Long Goodbye*; he's an untidy, shambling, seemingly distracted, superficially charming loser who often seems to be talking beside the point, instead of on it.

Maria Bello plays Nora Allardyce, a local journalist who used to be involved with Danny. She sniffs a connection between the body and politics. Once she was a fearless reporter for a fearless newspaper, but a conglomerate swallowed up the paper and taught it fear, and now she is an outsider. She's currently engaged to a lobbyist (Billy Zane), who knows where all the bodies are buried and swells with his pleasure in this knowledge. Other important characters include Kris Kristofferson as a millionaire mine owner and polluter, who is funding Pilager's campaign and is one of those gravel-voiced cynics who delight in shocking people with their disdain for conventional wisdom.

The best of the supporting characters is Madeleine Pilager, Dickie's renegade sister, played by Daryl Hannah with audacious boldness. She likes to shock, she likes to upset people, she detests Dickie, and she provides an unexpected connection between the private eye and the campaign manager. Those connections beneath the surface, between people whose lives in theory should not cross, is the organizing principle of Sayles's screenplay; one of the reasons his film is more sad than indignant is that it recognizes how people may be ideologically opposed and yet share unworthy common interests.

Sayles's wisdom of linking a murder mystery to a political satire seems questionable at first, until we see how Sayles uses it, and why. One of his strengths as a writer-director is his willingness to allow uncertainties into his plots. A Sayles movie is not a well-oiled machine rolling inexorably toward its conclusion, but a series of dashes in various directions, as if the plot is trying to find a way to escape a preordained conclusion. There's a dialogue scene near the end of *Silver City* that's a brilliant demonstration of the way he can deflate idealism with weary reality. Without revealing too much about it, I can say that it involves acknowledging that not all problems have a solution, not all wrongs are righted, and sometimes you find an answer and realize it doesn't really answer anything. To solve a small puzzle is not encouraging in a world created to generate larger puzzles.

It's a good question whether movies like this have any real political influence. Certainly Sayles is a lifelong liberal, and so is his cinematographer, the great Haskell Wexler. (So are Murphy and Dreyfuss, for that matter.) They create a character who is obviously intended to be George W. Bush. How do we know that? Because Dickie Pilager speaks in short, simplistic sound bites, uses platitudes to conceal his real objectives, and has verbal vertigo. Now, then: Am I attacking the president with that previous sentence, or only describing him? Perhaps to describe George W.'s speaking style in that way is not particularly damaging, because America is familiar with the way he talks, and about half of us are comfortable with it.

That's why *Silver City* may not change any votes. There is nothing in the movie's portrait of Pilager/Bush that has not already been absorbed and discounted by the electorate. Everybody knows that Bush expresses noble thoughts about the environment while his administration labors to license more pollution and less conservation. We know Bush's sponsors include the giant energy companies, and that Enron and Ken Lay were his major contributors before Lay's fall from grace. So when Dickie Pilager is revealed as the creature of antienvironment conglomerates, it comes as old news.

The movie's strength, then, is not in its outrage, but in its cynicism and resignation. There is something honest and a little brave about the way Sayles refuses to provide closure at the end of his movie. Virtue is not rewarded, crime is not punished, morality lies outside the rules of the game, and because the system is rotten no one who plays in it can be entirely untouched. Some characters are better than others, some are not positively bad, but their options are limited and their will is fading. Thackeray described *Vanity Fair* as "a novel without a hero." Sayles has made this film in the same spirit—so much so, that I'm reminded of the title of another Victorian novel, *The Way We Live Now.*

Sinbad: Legend of the Seven Seas ★ ★ ★ ½
PG, 85 m., 2003

With the voices of: Brad Pitt (Sinbad), Catherine Zeta-Jones (Marina), Joseph Fiennes (Proteus), Michelle Pfeiffer (Eris), Dennis Haysbert (Kale). Directed by Patrick Gilmore and Tim Johnson and produced by Jeffrey Katzenberg and Mireille Soria. Screenplay by John Logan.

Sinbad: Legend of the Seven Seas plays like a fire sale in three departments of the genre store: Vaguely Ancient Greek, Hollywood Swashbuckler, and Modern Romance. That it works is because of the high-energy animation, some genuinely beautiful visual concepts, and a story that's a little more sensuous than we expect in animation.

Sinbad, whose voice is by Brad Pitt, is a sailor and pirate whose name and legend have been stretched to accommodate an astonishing range of movie adventures. This time we learn he was a resident of Syracuse, a commoner friend of Prince Proteus (Joseph Fiennes), and left town after his first look at Proteus's intended, Marina (Catherine Zeta-Jones). "I was jealous for the first time," he remembers.

Sinbad runs away and finds a career commanding a pirate vessel with his first mate, a stalwart giant named Kale (Dennis Haysbert). They have indeed sailed the seven seas, all right, if we're to believe his talk of retirement in Fiji. Considering how far Fiji was from Greece in the centuries before the Suez Canal, we rather doubt he has really been there, but no matter: Maybe he's been talking to Realtors.

As the film opens, Sinbad's pirate ship attacks a ship commanded by Proteus, who is in possession of the *Book of Peace,* a sacred volume of incalculable value to the future of Syracuse. This attempted theft goes ahead despite the fact

that the two men are old friends and happy to see each other; a pirate is never off duty. Sinbad's scheme is interrupted by Eris (Michelle Pfeiffer), the goddess of chaos, who likes to mix things up and creates a gigantic sea monster to threaten both ships. The battle with the seemingly indestructible monster is one of several astonishing sequences in the film; the others involve sailing off the edge of the world; Tartarus, the realm of the dead, which awaits them over the edge; and a winter vastness presided over by an awesome snowbird. These scenes are animated so fluidly and envision strange sights so colorfully that there is real exhilaration.

The story, directed by Patrick Gilmore and Tim Johnson and written by John Logan, involves the shape shifting, deceptions, switches, and parental ultimatums much beloved by legend. It also exploits the tendency throughout Greek legend for the gods to interfere in the affairs of man. As flies to wanton boys are, Sinbad is to Eris. Although Sinbad did not actually steal the *Book of Peace,* the meddlesome Eris impersonates him and he seems to steal it, and Sinbad is taken prisoner and condemned to die by King Dymas, father of Proteus. Sinbad protests his innocence; Proteus believes him and offers himself as hostage to free Sinbad to sail off in search of the book. There's a ten-day deadline.

Here's where the sensuous stuff ramps up. Marina, who says she has always wanted to go away to sea, stows away on Sinbad's ship, and that comes in handy when all of the sailors on board are bewitched by seductive Sirens. A female immune to their charms, Marina takes the helm, saves the ship, and furthers the inevitable process by which she falls in love with Sinbad, who, as the character with his name in the title, of course must get the girl.

The scene where the ship sails off the edge of the world to the land of Tartarus involves physics of a nature that Archimedes, a famous native son of Syracuse, would probably not have approved, but what wondrous visuals, and what a haunting realm they discover, filled with the hulls of wrecked ships and the bones of doomed sailors. *Sinbad* is rich with ideas and images, and it exploits the resources of mythology to create such creatures as the snowbird, who at one point locks Syracuse in a grip of ice.

Syracuse itself, for that matter, is a magically

625

seen place, a city of towering turrets atop a mountain range. When Sinbad returns, it is to deal with the crucial question of whether Marina will return to her betrothed or stay with him. This is handled with great tact in a conversation in which both men agree that her basic motivation is to sail away and see the world, although she also, I suspect, has a burning desire to see the bunk in Sinbad's cabin.

Sinbad: Legend of the Seven Seas is another worthy entry in the recent renaissance of animation, and in the summer that also gave us *Finding Nemo*, it's a reminder that animation is the most liberating of movie genres, freed of gravity, plausibility, and even the matters of lighting and focus. There is no way that Syracuse could exist outside animation, and as we watch it, we are sailing over the edge of the human imagination.

Since Otar Left ★ ★ ★

NO MPAA RATING, 102 m., 2004

Esther Gorintin (Eka [Grandmother]), Nino Khomassouridze (Marina [Daughter]), Dinara Droukarova (Ada [Granddaughter]), Temour Kalandadze (Tenguiz), Roussoudan Bolkvadze (Roussiko), Sacha Sarichvili (Alexo), Dputa Skhirtladze (Niko). Directed by Julie Bertuccelli and produced by Yael Fogiel. Screenplay by Bertuccelli, Bernard Renucci, and Roger Bohbot.

Since Otar Left tells a story of conventional melodrama and makes it extraordinary because of the acting. The characters are so deeply known, so intensely observed, so immediately alive to us, that the story primarily becomes the occasion for us to meet them. Nothing at the plot level engaged me much, not even the ending, which is supposed to be so touching. But I was touched deeply, again and again, simply by watching these people live their lives.

Three women live in a book-lined flat in Tbilisi, the capital of the one-time Soviet republic of Georgia. Eka is the grandmother, very old, very determined (she is played by Esther Gorintin, who was eighty-five when she began her acting career five years ago). Marina (Nino Khomassouridze) is her daughter, around fifty, a woman of quick peremptory dismissals and sudden rushes of feeling. Ada (Dinara Droukarova), late twenties, is Marina's daughter, a student of literature, bored with her life.

We gather that Eka was French, moved to Georgia with her Soviet husband, was a committed Communist. She still thinks Stalin was a great man. Marina says he was a murderer. Ada looks incredulous that they are still having this argument. The cramped quarters are made into an arena when Eka turns up her television, and both Marina and Ada crank up their CD players.

But look at the way these actresses move. Every step, every gesture, suggests long familiarity with these lives. A visit to the post office observes the body language of people long buried in their jobs. The way that Marina discards her fork as the three women have tea says everything about her impatience. The women use verbal and physical shorthand to illuminate what goes without saying. Eka is always certain of herself. Marina is never satisfied ("I wish I loved you," she says to her patient man friend). Ada is fed up and trapped.

The crowded flat is dominated by the person who isn't there—Otar, Eka's son, who has moved to Paris to look for work. He telephones, but the lines fail. He sends money, but the postal service is uncertain. Things worked better in Stalin's day, Eka is certain. When news comes that Otar has been killed in an accident, Marina decides they will not tell old Eka, to spare her. This leads to a deception, the details of which are familiar from similar films.

What is not familiar, what becomes increasingly fascinating, is the direct and relentless way Eka marches toward the truth. She determines to go to Paris to visit her son, takes along the other two, finds them missing from their hotel room, and mutters "Those two are leading me on."

What is clear is that this old woman has a life and will of her own. There is a wonderful scene while she is still at home in Georgia. She leaves the house alone, looks up some information in the library, buys two cigarettes, and smokes them while riding on a Ferris wheel. With a lesser actor or character, this would be a day out for a lovable granny. With Esther Gorintin playing Eka, it is the day of a woman who thinks she has it coming to her.

What happens, and how, need not concern us. What I remember is the way Julie Bertuccelli, the director and cowriter, sees right into the beings of her characters. Consider two scenes in which the old woman gets a foot massage. In one, her granddaughter absently massages her foot while reading aloud from Proust. In the other, her daughter, usually so wounded and stern, giggles helplessly while tickling her feet, and old Eka laughs and squirms like a child. After seeing this movie, you watch another one with less gifted actors, and the characters seem to have met each other for the first time on the set, earlier that day.

Sin City ★ ★ ★ ★
R, 126 m., 2005

Bruce Willis (Hartigan), Jessica Alba (Nancy), Rosario Dawson (Gail), Benicio Del Toro (Jackie Boy), Clive Owen (Dwight), Mickey Rourke (Marv), Brittany Murphy (Shellie), Nick Stahl (Yellow Bastard), Alexis Bledel (Becky), Devon Aoki (Miho), Jaime King (Goldie), Frank Miller (Priest), Powers Boothe (Senator Roark), Michael Clarke Duncan (Manute), Carla Gugino (Lucille). Directed by Robert Rodriguez, Frank Miller, and Quentin Tarantino and produced by Elizabeth Avellan, Miller, and Rodriguez. Screenplay by Rodriguez and Miller.

If *film noir* was not a genre but a hard man on mean streets with a lost lovely in his heart and a gat in his gut, his nightmares would look like *Sin City.* The new movie by Robert Rodriguez and Frank Miller plays like a convention at the movie museum in Quentin Tarantino's subconscious. A-list action stars rub shoulders with snaky villains and sexy wenches in a city where the streets are always wet, the cars are ragtops, and everybody smokes. It's a black-and-white world, except for blood that is red, eyes that are green, hair that is blond, and the Yellow Bastard.

This isn't an adaptation of a comic book; it's like a comic book brought to life and pumped with steroids. It contains characters who occupy stories, but to describe the characters and summarize the stories would be like replacing the weather with a weather map.

The movie is not about narrative but about style. It internalizes the harsh world of the Frank Miller *Sin City* comic books and processes it through computer effects,

grotesque makeup, lurid costumes, and dialogue that chops at the language of *noir.* The actors are mined for the archetypes they contain; Bruce Willis, Mickey Rourke, Jessica Alba, Rosario Dawson, Benicio Del Toro, Clive Owen, and the others are rotated into a hyperdimension. We get not so much their presence as their essence; the movie is not about what the characters say or what they do, but about who they are in our wildest dreams.

On the movie's Website there's a slide show juxtaposing the original drawings of Frank Miller with the actors playing the characters, and then with the actors transported by effects into the visual world of graphic novels. Some of the stills from the film look so much like frames of the comic book as to make no difference. And there's a narration that plays like the captions at the top of the frame, setting the stage and expressing a stark, existential world view.

Rodriguez has been aiming toward *Sin City* for years. I remember him leaping out of his chair and bouncing around a hotel room, pantomiming himself filming *Spy Kids 2* with a digital camera and editing it on a computer. The future! he told me. This is the future! You don't wait six hours for a scene to be lighted. You want a light over here, you grab a light and put it over here. You want a nuclear submarine, you make one out of thin air and put your characters into it.

I held back, wondering if perhaps the spy kids would have been better served if the films had not been such a manic demonstration of his method. But never mind; the first two *Spy Kids* were exuberant fun (*Spy Kids 3-D* sucked, in great part because of the 3-D). Then came his *Once Upon a Time in Mexico* (2003), and I wrote it was "more interested in the moment, in great shots, in surprises and ironic reversals and close-ups of sweaty faces, than in a coherent story." Yes, but it worked.

And now Rodriguez has found narrative discipline in the last place you might expect, by choosing to follow the Miller comic books almost literally. A graphic artist has no time or room for drifting. Every frame contributes, and the story marches from page to page in vivid action snapshots. *Sin City* could easily have looked as good as it does and still been a mess, if it were not for the energy of

Miller's storytelling, which is not the standard chronological account of events, but more like a tabloid murder illuminated by flashbulbs.

The movie is based on three of the *Sin City* stories, each more or less self-contained. That's wise, because at this velocity a two-hour, one-story narrative would begin to pant before it got to the finish line. One story involves Bruce Willis as a battered old cop at war with a pedophile (Nick Stahl). One has Mickey Rourke waking up next to a dead hooker (Jaime King). One has a good guy (Clive Owen) and a wacko cop (Benicio Del Toro) disturbing the delicate balance of power negotiated between the police and the leader of the city's hookers (Rosario Dawson), who despite her profession moonlights as Owen's lover. Underneath everything is a deeper layer of corruption, involving a senator (Powers Boothe), whose son is not only the pedophile but also the Yellow Bastard.

We know the Bastard is yellow because the movie paints him yellow, just as the comic book did; it was a masterstroke for Miller to find a compromise between the cost of full-color reproduction and the economy of two-color pages; red, green, and blue also make their way into the frames. Actually, I can't even assume Miller went the two-color route for purposes of economy, because it's an effective artistic decision.

There are other vivid characters in the movie, which does not have leads so much as actors who dominate the foreground and then move on. In a movie that uses nudity as if the 1970s had survived, Rosario Dawson's stripper is a fierce dominatrix, Carla Gugino shows more skin than she could in Maxim, and Devon Aoki employs a flying guillotine that was borrowed no doubt from a circa-1970 Hong Kong exploiter.

Rodriguez codirected, photographed, and edited the movie, collaborated on the music and screenplay, and is coproducer. Frank Miller and Quentin Tarantino are credited as codirectors, Miller because his comic books essentially act as storyboards, which Rodriguez follows with ferocity, Tarantino because he directed one brief scene on a day when Rodriquez was determined to wean him away from celluloid and lure him over to the

dark side of digital. (It's the scene in the car with Clive Owen and Del Toro, who has a pistol stuck in his head.) Tarantino also contributed something to the culture of the film, which follows his influential *Pulp Fiction* in its recycling of pop archetypes and its circular story structure. The language of the film, both dialogue and narration, owes much to the hard-boiled pulp novelists of the 1950s.

Which brings us, finally, to the question of the movie's period. Skylines suggest the movie is set today. The cars range from the late 1930s to the 1950s. The costumes are from the trench coat and g-string era. I don't think *Sin City* really has a period, because it doesn't really tell a story set in time and space. It's a visualization of the pulp *noir* imagination, uncompromising and extreme. Yes, and brilliant. ☞

The Singing Detective ★ ★ ★
R, 109 m., 2003

Robert Downey Jr. (Dan Dark), Robin Wright Penn (Nicola/Nina/Blond), Mel Gibson (Dr. Gibbon), Jeremy Northam (Mark Binney), Katie Holmes (Nurse Mills), Adrien Brody (First Hood), Jon Polito (Second Hood), Carla Gugino (Betty Dark/Hooker), Saul Rubinek (Skin Specialist), Alfre Woodard (Chief of Staff). Directed by Keith Gordon and produced by Bruce Davey, Mel Gibson, and Steven Haft. Screenplay by Dennis Potter.

He calls himself "a human pizza." His skin looks like sausage and mushrooms with extra tomato sauce and an occasional eruption of cheese. He is in excruciating pain but surprisingly articulate about it, considering that his lips are so chapped they can hardly move. During a painful treatment, he announces, "I'm gonna go back to my bed. It's vivid and exciting there."

It certainly is. To escape from his agony, he evokes daydreams from a pulp novel he once wrote, luridly populated by *noir* characters who look just like people in his own life—his mother, his nurse, himself. He varies this sometimes by visualizing song-and-dance numbers done in the style of 1950s musicals. In the middle of a difficult medical procedure, the hospital staff or his visitors are likely to break into choreographed versions of '50s hits like "Walking in the Rain," "Doggie in the Window," or "At the Hop."

Keith Gordon's *The Singing Detective* involves the world of Dan Dark (Robert Downey Jr.), once a writer, now living in a world so encompassed by pain that it has become the single fact of his life. The movie is based on an eight-hour BBC series that ran in 1986; both were written by Dennis Potter, whose own psoriasis was nearly unbearable. We know the story was autobiographical, but now it seems to be based on two lives: Potter's and Downey's. What horrors Downey has endured during his struggle with addiction we can easily imagine. Dan Dark's sardonic view of the world and his insulting, sarcastic manner of speech is a defense mechanism familiar to anyone who has known a user.

The film played at Sundance 2003, where the buzz decided it didn't work. I am as guilty as anyone of employing the concept of a film "working," but in this case I wonder how anyone *thought* it would work. It can't be the eight-hour series because it's two hours long. It can't misrepresent Potter's vision because it is his vision; this was the last big project he worked on before he died, and he wanted to see a feature-length movie version of what in some ways was his life story. Of course the medical details don't "work" with the pulp detective story, nor do the musical numbers "work" anywhere, but wouldn't it take a facile compromise to make them fit smoothly together? Here is a character in agony, who deliberately breaks the reality of his world to escape to a more bearable one.

It might be more useful to ask, who would want to see this movie, and why? When I saw it at Sundance, my attention was divided because I was trying to process the meaning of the jagged structure. Seeing it again, knowing what to expect, I found it a more moving experience. I knew, for example, that the *film noir* sequences were not simply pulp escapism, but represented Dan Dark's lurid resentments against people he hated, such as his mother (Carla Gugino) and his cheating wife (Robin Wright Penn).

The movie does not propose to be a comedy, a musical, a *film noir* story, or a medical account. It proposes to be a subjective view of suffering and the ways this character tries to cope with it. Understand that, and the pieces

fall into place. Hospitals have a chart with numbers from 1 to 8 and ask you to "rate" the level of your pain. For Dan Dark such a chart is a ghastly joke.

The Singing Detective is a movie about a man who has been failed by science and drugs, and turns in desperation to his mind, seeking temporary insanity as a release. His sharp intelligence is an asset. He knows the 1950s songs are trash, and that's the point; you don't throw songs you love onto the bonfire. Eventually, slowly, he begins to get better. Perhaps his skin condition was partly psychosomatic after all. Or perhaps he simply healed himself, mind over matter. Norman Cousins wrote a book about how he cured himself by laughter. Dennis Potter and his surrogate Robert Downey Jr. seem to be trying anger and resentment as a cure. If it works, don't fix it.

The Sisterhood of the Traveling Pants ★ ★ ★
PG, 119 m., 2005

Amber Tamblyn (Tibby), Alexis Bledel (Lena), America Ferrera (Carmen), Blake Lively (Bridget), Jenna Boyd (Bailey), Bradley Whitford (Al), Nancy Travis (Lydia Rodman), Rachel Ticotin (Carmen's Mother). Directed by Ken Kwapis and produced by Debra Martin Chase, Denise Di Novi, Broderick Johnson, and Andrew A. Kosove. Screenplay by Delia Ephron and Elizabeth Chandler, based on the novel by Ann Brashares.

Four teenage girls in a clothing store, trying on things, kidding around, giggling. Girls of four different sizes and shapes. What makes them all want to try on the same pair of pre-owned jeans? And why are the jeans a perfect fit all four times? It's the summer before the girls begin their senior year in high school, and all four have big summer plans. Because the jeans magically fit them all, and perhaps because they all saw *Divine Secrets of the Ya-Ya Sisterhood,* they come up with a plan: Each girl will wear the jeans for a week and then FedEx them to the next on the list.

Along with the solemn vow to forward the jeans on schedule comes a list of rules that must not be violated, of which the most crucial is that the girls must never let anyone else remove the jeans from their bodies. There is, however, a loophole: They can take them off themselves. Here we have a premise that could easily inspire a teenage comedy of comprehensive badness, but *The Sisterhood of the Traveling Pants* is always sweet and sometimes surprisingly touching, as the jeans accompany each girl on a key step of her journey to adulthood.

The movie, like *Mystic Pizza* (1988), assembles a group of talented young actresses who have already done good work separately and now participate in a kind of showcase. America Ferrera (whose *Real Women Have Curves* remains one of the best recent coming-of-age films) plays Carmen, who lives with her Puerto Rican mother and is thrilled to be spending the summer with her absentee non–Puerto Rican father. Alexis Bledel, who struck entirely different notes in *Sin City,* is Lena, off to visit her grandparents and other relatives on a Greek island. Blake Lively plays Bridget, who attends a soccer camp in Mexico and falls in love with one of the hunky young counselors. And Amber Tamblyn (of *Joan of Arcadia*) is Tibby, the one with the sardonic angle on life, who wants to be a filmmaker and takes a low-paying job for the summer at a suburban megastore where she plans to shoot a video documentary about life and work.

The stories of the four girls comes, I learn, from a novel by Ann Brashares, who has written two more in the series. The usefulness of her four-story structure is that none of the stories overstays its welcome, and the four girls aren't trapped in the same dumb suburban teenage romantic plot. They live, and they learn.

Carmen has idealized her father, Al (Bradley Whitford), even though he dumped her mother (Rachel Ticotin) years earlier. She values her Puerto Rican roots and discovers, with a shock, that her dad is planning marriage with a WASP named Lydia (Nancy Travis), who comes equipped with children and a suburban home that her father seems to desire as much as his new bride. Is he ashamed of his golden-skinned daughter whose jeans show off a healthy and rounded but technically overweight body?

Tibby has perhaps been watching IFC too much, and possibly envisions herself at Sundance as she heads off to the Wal-Mart clone with her video camera. She gets a young assistant named Bailey (Jenna Boyd), who is a good soul, open and warmhearted, and with a secret that Tibby discovers one day when Bailey passes out right there on the floor of a store corridor. Tibby's tendency was to look at everything through a lens, objectively; Bailey removes the lens cap on her heart.

In Greece, Lena finds her family living a salt-of-the-earth existence in what are surely outtakes from a tourism commercial. If there really is an island this sun-drenched, with a village this filled with white stucco and deep shade, populated by people who are this jolly and loving and throw a feast on a moment's notice, then I don't know why I'm not there instead of here. Lena's Greek relatives are, however, extremely protective of her chastity, which may exist primarily in their dreams, and she gets a crush on a local teen god.

Meanwhile, in Mexico, Bridget and the counselor know they are violating unbreakable rules by even spending private time together, but Bridget sets her sights on the guy and stages a campaign of attraction and seduction that is more or less irresistible.

The role played by the jeans in all of these stories is, it must be said, more as a witness than as a participant, sometimes from a vantage point draped over a chair near to a bed. But no, the PG-rated movie isn't overloaded with sex, and its values are in the right place. The message for its primary audience of teenage girls is that to some degree they choose their own destinies and write their own stories, and while boys may be an unexplored country, they are not necessarily a hostile one. As for fathers who would like to become Anglo by marriage, and daughters who fiercely resent them, perhaps after all he is still her father and she is still his daughter, and there is hope.

Because the *Ya-Ya Sisterhood* was such a disappointment, I expected even less from what looked, going in, like a teenage retread. But in a world where one pair of jeans fits all, miracles can happen. This *Sisterhood* is real pleasure, a big-hearted movie where a group of gifted actresses find opportunities most younger movie stars can only dream about.

Sky Captain and the World of Tomorrow ★ ★ ★ ★
PG, 107 m., 2004

Jude Law (Joe "Sky Captain" Sullivan), Gwyneth Paltrow (Polly Perkins), Angelina Jolie (Captain Franky Cook), Giovanni Ribisi (Dex Dearborn), Michael Gambon (Editor Morris Paley), Ling Bai (Mysterious Woman). Directed by Kerry Conran and produced by Jon Avnet, Sadie Frost, Jude Law, and Marsha Oglesby. Screenplay by Conran.

Sky Captain and the World of Tomorrow is even more fun than it sounds like. In its heedless energy and joy, it reminded me of how I felt the first time I saw *Raiders of the Lost Ark*. It's like a film that escaped from the imagination directly onto the screen, without having to pass through reality along the way.

Before I got into serious science fiction, I went through a period when my fantasies were fed by a now-forgotten series of books about Tom Corbett, Space Cadet. There was a gee-whiz vigor to those adventures, a naive faith in science and pluck, evoking a world in which evil existed primarily as an opportunity for Tom to have fun vanquishing it. *Sky Captain* has that kind of innocence.

Jude Law and Gwyneth Paltrow star, as Joe "Sky Captain" Sullivan, a free-lance buccaneer for truth and justice, and Polly Perkins, a scoop-crazy newspaperwoman who hitches a ride in his airplane. Manhattan has come under attack from giant mechanical men who lumber through the skies like flying wrestlers, and stomp down the city streets sending civilians scurrying. This is obviously a case for Sky Captain, who must be the richest man on Earth, judging by his secret hideaway and what seems to be his private air force and science lab.

The robots have been sent by the mysterious Dr. Totenkopf, a World War I–vintage German scientist who has nurtured his plans for world domination ever since. He has kidnapped many leading scientists, and now his metal men will enforce his rule, unless Joe and Polly can stop him. Also on the side of the good guys are Franky (Angelina Jolie), a sexy pilot with her own agenda, and Dex Dearborn (Giovanni Ribisi), Sky Captain's head of research and development.

To summarize the plot would spoil the fun, and be pointless anyway, since the plot exists essentially to inspire silly grins. What needs to be described is the look and technique of the film. *Sky Captain* is filmed halfway between full color and sepiatone, so that it has the richness of color and yet the distance and nostalgic quality of an old photograph. Its production design and art direction remind me of covers for ancient pulp magazines like *Thrilling Wonder Stories.*

Much will be written about the technique, about how the first-time director, Kerry Conran, labored for years to bring forth on his Macintosh a six-minute film illustrating his vision for *Sky Captain.* This film caught the attention of the director Jon Avnet, who agreed to produce Conran's film and presented the idea to Paltrow and Law.

The actors did almost all of their scenes in front of a blue screen, which was then replaced with images generated on computers. The monsters, the city, and most of the sets and props never really existed except as digital files. This permitted a film of enormous scope to be made with a reasonable budget, but it also freed Conran and his collaborators to show whatever they wanted to, because one digital fantasy costs about as much as another.

The film is not good because it was filmed in this way, however; it's just plain good. The importance of the technique is that it allows the movie to show idealized versions of sci-fi fantasies that are impossible in the real world and often unconvincing as more conventional special effects. It removes the layers of impossibility between the inspiration and the audience.

Paltrow and Law do a good job of creating the kind of camaraderie that flourished between the genders in the 1930s and 1940s, in films like *The Lady Eve,* with Henry Fonda and Barbara Stanwyck, or *His Girl Friday,* with Cary Grant and Rosalind Russell. The women in this tradition are tomboys (Katharine Hepburn is the prototype), and although romance is not unknown to them, they're often running too fast to kiss anyone. We gather that Polly and Joe had a romance a few years ago that ended badly (Franky may have had a role in that), but now their chemistry renews itself as they fly off to Nepal in search of Dr. Totenkopf's lair.

The evil doctor is played by Laurence Olivier, who died in 1989, and who is seen here through old shots recycled into a new character. A posthumous performance makes a certain sense, given the nature of Dr. Totenkopf. There's something ghoulish about using a dead actor's likeness without his knowledge, and in the past I've deplored such desecrations as the Fred Astaire dust-buster ads, but surely every actor on his deathbed, entering the great unknown, hopes he has not given his last performance.

Sky Captain will probably not inspire the universal affection of a film like *Indiana Jones,* in part because Steven Spielberg is a better director than Kerry Conran, in part because many of *Sky Captain*'s best qualities are more cinematic than dramatic; I responded to the texture and surfaces and very feel of the images, and felt some of the same quickening I remember from the cover of a new Tom Corbett book. If the Space Cadet ever graduated, he probably grew up to be Sky Captain. ☞

Sleepover ★

PG, 90 m., 2004

Alexa Vega (Julie), Mika Boorem (Hannah), Scout Taylor-Compton (Farrah), Kallie Flynn Childress (Yancy), Sam Huntington (Ren), Jane Lynch (Gabby), Jeff Garlin (Jay), Sara Paxton (Staci). Directed by Joe Nussbaum and produced by Bob Cooper and Charles Weinstock. Screenplay by Elisa Bell.

I take it as a rule of nature that all American high schools are ruled by a pack of snobs, led by a supremely confident young woman who is blond, superficial, catty, and ripe for public humiliation. This character is followed everywhere by two friends who worship her, and are a little bit shorter. Those schools also contain a group of friends who are not popular and do not think of themselves as pretty, although they are smarter, funnier, and altogether more likable than the catty-pack.

In the classic form of this formula, the reigning blond dates a hunk whom the mousy outcast has a crush on, and everything gets cleared up at the prom when the hunk realizes

the mouse is the real beauty, while the evil nature of the popular girl is exposed in a sensationally embarrassing way.

Sleepover, a lame and labored comedy, doesn't recycle this plot (the blond gets dumped by her boyfriend) but works more as a series of riffs on the underlying themes. It moves the age group down a few years, so that the girls are all just entering high school. And it lowers the stakes—instead of competing for the football captain, the rivals enter into a struggle over desirable seating in the school's outdoor lunchroom. Winners get the "popular" table, losers have to sit by the Dumpster. That a school would locate a lunch area next to the garbage doesn't say much for its hygiene standards, but never mind.

Julie is the girl we're supposed to like. She's played by Alexa Vega, from *Spy Kids.* Staci (Sara Paxton) is the girl we're supposed to hate. Julie's posse includes Hannah (Mika Boorem), a good friend who is moving to Canada for no better reason, as far as I can tell, than to provide an attribute for a character with no other talking points; and Farrah (the wonderfully named Scout Taylor-Compton), who functions basically as an element useful to the cinematographer in composing groups of characters.

Julie decides to have a sleepover, and at the last minute invites poor Yancy (the also wonderfully named Kallie Flynn Childress), who is plump and self-conscious about her weight. Julie's invitation is so condescending it's a form of insult, something that doesn't seem to occur to the grateful Yancy. Julie's mom, the wonderfully named Gabby (Jane Lynch), lays down rules for the sleepover, all of which will be violated by the end of the evening without anything being noticed by her dad, Jay (Jeff Garlin), reinforcing the rule that the parents in teenage comedies would remain oblivious if their children moved the Ringling Bros. and Barnum and Bailey Circus into their bedrooms.

Staci, the popular one, visits the slumber party to suggest a scavenger hunt, with the winner to get the desirable lunch table. So it's up to the girls to sneak out of the house and snatch all the trophies, including, of course, the boxer shorts of the high school hunk. There is a tradition in which movie teenagers almost always have bedrooms with windows opening onto roofs, porches, trellises, etc., which function perfectly as escape routes when necessary, but collapse instantly (a) when used by an unpopular character or (b) when the risk of discovery and betrayal needs to be fabricated.

What happens during the scavenger hunt I will leave to you to discover, if you are so unwise as to attend this movie instead of *Mean Girls*. One of the movie's strangest scenes has Julie, who is about fourteen, sneaking into a bar because the scavenger hunt requires her to get a photo of herself being treated to a drink by a grown-up. This scene is outrageous even if she orders a Shirley Temple, but is even weirder because the guy she chooses is a teacher from her junior high, who must live in a wonderland of his own since he obviously has no idea of the professional hazards involved in buying a drink in public for one of his barely pubescent students, and then posing for a photo so she will have proof.

I don't require all high school (or junior high) comedies to involve smart, imaginative, articulate future leaders. But I am grateful when the movie at least devises something interesting for them to do or expresses empathy with their real natures. The characters in *Sleepover* are shadows of shadows, diluted from countless better, even marginally better, movies. There was no reason to make this movie, and no reason to see it.

A Slipping-Down Life ★ ★ ★
R, 111 m., 2004

Lili Taylor (Evie Decker), Guy Pearce (Drumstrings Casey), John Hawkes (David Elliot), Sara Rue (Violet), Irma P. Hall (Clotelia), Tom Bower (Mr. Decker), Shawnee Smith (Faye-Jean), Veronica Cartwright (Mrs. Casey). Directed by Toni Kalem and produced by Richard Raddon. Screenplay by Kalem, based on the novel by Anne Tyler.

I first became aware of Lili Taylor in *Mystic Pizza* (1988), a star-making film that also introduced Julia Roberts. She plays the girl who walks away from the altar because her husband-to-be doesn't believe in sex before marriage and she doesn't think it's worth mar-

rying him just to get him into bed. That kind of almost-logical circular reasoning is common in her characters; you can see it in other Taylor masterpieces, like *Dogfight* (1991), *Household Saints* (1993), *Girls Town* (1996), her great work in *I Shot Andy Warhol* the same year, and in *Casa de los Babys* (2003).

I don't suppose Taylor was born to play Evie Decker, the heroine of *A Slipping-Down Life*, but I can't imagine any other actress getting away with this role. She has a kind of solemnity she can bring to goofy characters, elevating them to holy (and usually lovable) fools. Here she plays a young woman from a small town who is lonely and isolated and lives with her father, who loves her but spends his evenings talking to ham radio operators in Moscow. She needs for something to happen to her.

Something does. She hears a rock singer on the radio one night. His off-balance ad lib philosophizing turns off the disc jockey, but sends her out to a local bar to see him in person. He becomes to her a demigod, a source of light and wisdom, but she is too inept to attract his attention. So she goes into the rest room and uses a piece of a broken bottle to carve his name into her forehead.

His name is Drumstrings Casey. She just carves the "Casey." "Why didn't you use my first name?" he asks her. "I didn't have room on my forehead," she says. "They call me Drum," he says. "I wish I'd known that," she says. There is another problem: She carved the name backward, because that way it looked right in the mirror. But at least when she looks at herself in the mirror it looks okay to her.

Drumstrings is played by Guy Pearce, of *Memento* and *L.A. Confidential*. He fits easily into the role of a third-rate, small-town rock god. When his agent finds out what Evie did, he talks Drumstrings into coming to the hospital to get his picture taken with her, and the publicity leads to an offer to have her appear at his concerts, to drum up business. This works well enough that he gets a gig in a nearby town, and doesn't invite her along, which breaks her heart. But somehow without that crazy girl in the audience, Drumstrings has an off night, and realizes he needs her.

The movie, written by the director Toni Kalem and based on a novel by Anne Tyler, performs a delicate maneuver as it slips along. The film opens with Evie totally powerless and miserable, and with Drumstrings holding all the cards. But her self-mutilation empowers her, and it provides a way for her to hold Drum's attention long enough for him to begin to like her. What she doesn't understand at first is that he's holding cards as bad as her own.

The film is like a tightrope walk across possible disasters. It could so easily go wrong. The plot itself is not enough to save it; indeed, this plot in the wrong hands could be impossible. But Kalem, an actress herself, understands how mood and nuance shape film stories; it's not what it's about, but how it's about it. Lili Taylor never overplays, never asks us to believe anything that isn't right there for us to see and hear. She changes by almost invisible steps into a woman who knows what she wants in a man and in marriage, and is able to communicate that to Drumstrings in a way he can, eventually, imperfectly, understand.

The supporting performances are like sturdy supports when the movie needs them. Tom Bower plays Evie's father as a man who has receded into his own loneliness. Irma P. Hall plays their maid, who is the de facto head of the household. John Hawkes is Drumstring's manager, who understands managing and publicity only remotely, but with great enthusiasm. Drum's mother (Veronica Cartwright) does not consider it a plus that this woman has carved her son's name into her forehead. Backward.

The movie is not a great dramatic statement, but you know that from the modesty of the title. It is about movement in emotional waters that had long been still. Taylor makes it work because she quietly suggests that when Evie's life has stalled, something drastic was needed to shock her back into action, and the carving worked as well as anything. Besides, when she combs her bangs down, you can hardly see it.

Something's Gotta Give ★ ★ ★ ½
PG-13, 124 m., 2003

Jack Nicholson (Harry Sanborn), Diane Keaton (Erica Barry), Amanda Peet (Marin Barry), Keanu Reeves (Julian Mercer), Frances McDormand (Zoe), Jon Favreau (Leo). Directed by Nancy Meyers and produced by Bruce A. Block and Meyers. Screenplay by Meyers.

"Some say I'm an expert on the younger woman—since I've been dating them for forty years."

Who's talking here? Jack Nicholson, or the character he plays in *Something's Gotta Give*? Maybe it doesn't make any difference. After playing an older man entirely unlike himself in *About Schmidt*, Nicholson here quite frankly and cheerfully plays a version of the public Jack, the guy who always seems to be grinning like he got away with something. This has inspired scoldings from the filmcrit police ("This is Jack playing 'Jack,'" says *Variety*), but who would you rather have playing him? Nicholson's quasi-autobiographical role is one of the pleasures of the film.

Nicholson's character, named Harry Sanborn, is a rich music executive who is currently dating the nubile young Marin Barry (Amanda Peet). She takes him for a weekend to her mother's home in the Hamptons—where, horrors, he is found raiding the refrigerator in the middle of the night by her mother, Erica (Diane Keaton), and Aunt Zoe (Frances McDormand). Erica is a famous playwright, too worldly to object to her grown daughter's taste in men, and the four spend the weekend together. We learn that Harry and Marin have not yet actually had sex, and alas, as they circle for a landing Harry is seized with chest pains and rushed to the hospital.

Only in the Hamptons would the doctor be handsome Julian Mercer (Keanu Reeves), who is instantly smitten by the sexy older woman. He prescribes bed rest for Harry, who takes refuge in Erica's guest room as the others return to the city. And that's the setup for a witty sitcom, written and directed by Nancy Meyers, who in movies like *Baby Boom* and *What Women Want* has dealt skillfully with the sexual adventures of characters whose ages fall between those who remember where they were when John Kennedy was shot, and when John Lennon was shot. It is more or less foreordained that Harry and Erica will fall in love, despite his taste for younger women. The twist is that Dr. Mercer also falls in love with Erica, supplying her with two possible lovers at a time in her life when she thought she'd gone into sexual retirement.

How, why, and whether Harry and Julian do or don't become Erica's lovers is entirely a matter of sitcom accounting, and need not concern us. What's intriguing about the movie is what they say in between. Meyers gives them more and smarter dialogue than we expect in a romantic comedy, because if Erica and Harry are ever to have sex, they're going to have to talk themselves into it. She has strong opinions about this man whose lifestyle is so notorious he made the cover of *New York* magazine as "The Escape Artist." And Harry, shocked by his sudden brush with mortality, finds that for the first time in his life he needs someone he can actually talk with in the middle of the night.

The movie is true enough to its characters that at one point, when Harry and Erica both find themselves crying at the same time, we find ourselves surprisingly moved by this recognition of their humanity. And when Harry goes back to his old ways, as we know he must, we're moved again, this time by how lonely he feels, and how sad it is when he plays his old tapes. Harry and Erica are convincing characters, at least in the world of romantic comedy.

It's Dr. Mercer who seems like nothing more than a walking plot complication. We don't believe or understand his relationship with Erica, and it must be said that a young man who would propose to a woman twenty-five years his senior, fly to Paris with her, plan marriage, and yet immediately surrender her to his rival without a struggle (out of good manners and breeding, it would seem) has desires that are all too easily contained. There is sexual mystery surrounding the whole situation. Harry doesn't know (for sure) whether Erica and young Dr. Mercer have had sex, which perhaps makes the situation easier for him; in the Hamptons, a virgin is anyone who hasn't slept with anyone you know since you met them.

A movie like this depends crucially on its stars. To complain that Nicholson is playing "himself"—or that Keaton is also playing a character very much like her public persona—is missing the point. Part of the appeal depends on the movie's teasing confusion of reality and fiction. Harry defends himself by telling Erica, "I have never lied to you. I have always told you

some version of the truth," and we smile at the backward morality in that statement; we wonder if Nicholson himself contributed that line to the screenplay. We are meant to wonder.

The film's nudity observes the usual double standard; we get three opportunities for a leisurely study of Nicholson's butt, but the nude shot of Diane Keaton is so brief it falls only a frame this side of subliminal. Their faces are more interesting, anyway. "At fifty," Orwell tells us, "every man has the face he deserves." I don't know what Harry and Erica did to deserve theirs, but they didn't skip any payments. They bring so much experience, knowledge, and humor to their characters that the film works in ways the screenplay might not have even hoped for.

Note: The paintings in the Hamptons house are by Jack Vettriano, and the drawings are by Paul Cox. I have not reason for telling you that, but I couldn't stop myself.

The Son ★ ★ ★ ★
NO MPAA RATING, 103 m., 2003

Olivier Gourmet (Olivier), Morgan Marinne (Francis), Isabella Soupart (Magali), Remy Renaud (Philippo), Nassim Hassaini (Omar), Kevin Leroy (Raoul), Felicien Pitsaer (Steve). Directed by Jean-Pierre Dardenne and Luc Dardenne and produced by the Dardennes and Denis Freyd. Screenplay by the Dardennes.

The Son is complete, self-contained, and final. All the critic can bring to it is his admiration. It needs no insight or explanation. It sees everything and explains all. It is as assured and flawless a telling of sadness and joy as I have ever seen.

I agree with Stanley Kauffmann, in the *New Republic*, that a second viewing only underlines the film's greatness, but I would not want to have missed my first viewing, so I will write carefully. The directors, Jean-Pierre Dardenne and Luc Dardenne, do not make the slightest effort to mislead or deceive us. Nor do they make any effort to explain. They simply (not so simply) show, and we lean forward, hushed, reading the faces, watching the actions, intent on sharing the feelings of the characters.

Let me describe a very early sequence in

enough detail for you to appreciate how the Dardenne brothers work. Olivier (Olivier Gourmet), a Belgian carpenter, supervises a shop where teenage boys work. He corrects a boy using a power saw. We wonder, because we have been beaten down by formula films, if someone is going to lose a finger or a hand. No. The plank is going to be cut correctly.

A woman comes into the shop and asks Olivier if he can take another apprentice. No, he has too many already. He suggests the welding shop. The moment the woman and the young applicant leave, Olivier slips from the shop and, astonishingly, scurries after them like a feral animal and spies on them through a door opening and the angle of a corridor. A little later, strong and agile, he leaps up onto a metal cabinet to steal a look through a high window.

Then he tells the woman he will take the boy after all. She says the boy is in the shower room. The handheld camera, which follows Olivier everywhere, usually in close medium shot, follows him as he looks around a corner (we intuit it is a corner; two walls form an apparent join). Is he watching the boy take a shower? Is Olivier gay? No. We have seen too many movies. He is simply looking at the boy asleep, fully clothed, on the floor of the shower room. After a long, absorbed look he wakes up the boy and tells him he has a job.

Now you must absolutely stop reading and go see the film. Walk out of the house today, tonight, and see it, if you are open to simplicity, depth, maturity, silence, in a film that sounds in the echo chambers of the heart. *The Son* is a great film. If you find you cannot respond to it, that is the degree to which you have room to grow. I am not being arrogant; I grew during this film. It taught me things about the cinema I did not know.

What did I learn? How this movie is only possible because of the way it was made, and would have been impossible with traditional narrative styles. Like rigorous documentarians, the Dardenne brothers follow Olivier, learning everything they know about him by watching him. They do not point, underline, or send signals by music. There are no reaction shots because the entire movie is their reaction shot. The brothers make the consciousness of the Olivier character into the auteur of the film.

. . . So now you have seen the film. If you

were spellbound, moved by its terror and love, struck that the visual style is the only possible one for this story, then let us agree that rarely has a film told us less and told us all, both at the once.

Olivier trains wards of the Belgian state—gives them a craft after they are released from a juvenile home. Francis (Morgan Marinne) was in such a home from his eleventh to sixteenth years. Olivier asks him what his crime was. He stole a car radio.

"And got five years?"

"There was a death."

"What kind of a death?"

There was a child in the car, whom Francis did not see. The child began to cry and would not let go of Francis, who was frightened and "grabbed him by the throat."

"Strangled him," Olivier corrects.

"I didn't mean to," Francis says.

"Do you regret what you did?"

"Obviously."

"Why obviously?"

"Five years locked up. That's worth regretting."

You have seen the film and know what Olivier knows about this death. You have seen it and know the man and boy are at a remote lumberyard on a Sunday. You have seen it and know how *hard* the noises are in the movie, the heavy planks banging down one upon another. How it hurts even to hear them. The film does not use these sounds or the towers of lumber to create suspense or anything else. It simply respects the nature of lumber, as Olivier does and is teaching Francis to do. You expect, because you have been trained by formula films, an accident or an act of violence. What you could not expect is the breathtaking spiritual beauty of the ending of the film, which is nevertheless no less banal than everything that has gone before.

Olivier Gourmet won the award for best actor at Cannes 2002. He plays an ordinary man behaving at all times in an ordinary way. Here is the key: *Ordinary for him.* The word for his behavior—not his performance, his behavior—is "exemplary." We use the word to mean "praiseworthy." Its first meaning is "fit for imitation."

Everything that Olivier does is exemplary. Walk like this. Hold yourself just so. Measure exactly. Do not use the steel hammer when the wooden mallet is required. Center the nail. Smooth first with the file, then with the sandpaper. Balance the plank and lean into the ladder. Pay for your own apple turnover. Hold a woman who needs to be calmed. Praise a woman who has found she is pregnant. Find out the truth before you tell the truth. Do not use words to discuss what cannot be explained. Be willing to say, "I don't know." Be willing to have a son and teach him a trade. Be willing to be a father.

A recent movie got a laugh by saying there is a rule in *The Godfather* to cover every situation. There can never be that many rules. *The Son* is about a man who needs no rules because he respects his trade and knows his tools. His trade is life. His tools are his loss and his hope.

Son of the Mask ★ ½
PG, 86 m., 2005

Jamie Kennedy (Tim Avery), Alan Cumming (Loki), Liam Falconer and Ryan Falconer (Alvey Avery), Bob Hoskins (Odin), Traylor Howard (Tonya Avery), Ben Stein (Dr. Arthur Neuman), Bear (Otis the Dog). Directed by Lawrence Guterman and produced by Erica Huggins and Scott Kroopf. Screenplay by Lance Khazei.

One of the foundations of comedy is a character who must do what he doesn't want to do because of the logic of the situation. As Auden pointed out about limericks, they're funny not because they end with a dirty word, but because they have no choice but to end with the dirty word—by that point, it's the only word that rhymes and makes sense. Lucille Ball made a career out of finding herself in embarrassing situations and doing the next logical thing, however ridiculous.

Which brings us to *Son of the Mask* and its violations of this theory. The movie's premise is that if you wear a magical ancient mask, it will cause you to behave in strange ways. Good enough, and in Jim Carrey's original *The Mask* (1994), the premise worked. Carrey's elastic face was stretched into a caricature, he gained incredible powers, he exhausted himself with manic energy. But there were rules. There was a baseline of sanity from which the mania proceeded. *Son of the Mask* lacks a baseline. It is all mania, all the time; the behavior in the movie is not inappropriate, shocking, out of character, impolite, or anything else except behavior.

Both *Mask* movies are inspired by the zany world of classic cartoons. The hero of *Son of the Mask*, Tim Avery (Jamie Kennedy), is no doubt named after Tex Avery, the legendary Warner Bros. animator, although it is *One Froggy Evening* (1955), by the equally legendary Chuck Jones, that plays a role in the film. Their films all obeyed the Laws of Cartoon Thermodynamics, as established by the distinguished theoreticians Trevor Paquette and Lieutenant Justin D. Baldwin. (Examples: Law III: "Any body passing through solid matter will leave a perforation conforming to its perimeter"; Law IX: "Everything falls faster than an anvil.")

These laws, while seemingly arbitrary, are consistent in all cartoons. We know that Wile E. Coyote can chase the Road Runner off a cliff and keep going until he looks down; only then will he fall. And that the Road Runner can pass through a tunnel entrance in a rock wall, but Wile E. Coyote will smash into the wall. We instinctively understand Law VIII ("Any violent rearrangement of feline matter is impermanent"). Even cartoons know that if you don't have rules, you're playing tennis without a net.

The premise in *Son of the Mask* is that an ancient mask, found in the earlier movie, has gone missing again. It washes up on the banks of a little stream, and is fetched by Otis the Dog (Bear), who brings it home to the Avery household, where we find Tim (Kennedy) and his wife, Tonya (Traylor Howard). Tim puts on the Mask, and is transformed into a whiz-kid at his advertising agency, able to create brilliant campaigns in a single bound. He also, perhaps unwisely, wears it to bed and engenders an infant son, Alvey, who is born with cartoonlike abilities and discovers them by watching the frog cartoon on TV.

Tim won an instant promotion to the big account, but without the Mask he is a disappointment. And the Mask cannot be found, because Otis has dragged it away and hidden it somewhere—although not before Otis snuffles at it until it attaches itself to his face, after which he is transformed into a cartoon dog and careens wildly around the yard and the sky, to his alarm.

A word about baby Alvey (played by the twins Liam and Ryan Falconer). I have never much liked movie babies who do not act like babies. I think they're scary. The first *Look Who's Talking* movie was cute, but the sequels were nasty, especially when the dog started talking. About *Baby's Day Out* (1994), in which Baby Bink set Joe Mantegna's crotch on fire, the less said the better.

I especially do not like Baby Alvey, who behaves not according to the rules for babies, but more like a shape-shifting creature in a Japanese anime. There may be a way this could be made funny, but *Son of the Mask* doesn't find it.

Meanwhile, powerful forces seek the Mask. The god Odin (Bob Hoskins) is furious with his son Loki (Alan Cumming) for having lost the Mask, and sends him down to Earth (or maybe these gods already live on Earth, I dunno) to get it back again. Loki, who is the god of mischief, has a spiky punk hairstyle that seems inspired by the jester's cap and bells, without the bells. He picks up the scent and causes no end of trouble for the Averys, although of course the dog isn't talking.

But my description makes the movie sound more sensible than it is. What we basically have here is a license for the filmmakers to do whatever they want to do with the special effects, while the plot, like Wile E. Coyote, keeps running into the wall.

Spanglish ★ ★ ★
PG-13, 128 m., 2004

Adam Sandler (John Clasky), Tea Leoni (Deborah Clasky), Paz Vega (Flor), Cloris Leachman (Evelyn), Shelbie Bruce (Cristina), Sarah Steele (Bernice Clasky). Directed by James L. Brooks and produced by Brooks, Julie Ansell, and Richard Sakai. Screenplay by Brooks.

James L. Brooks' *Spanglish* tells the story of a Mexican woman and her daughter who travel all the way to Los Angeles to bring sanity to a crazy Anglo family. When I mention that the father of the family is played by Adam Sandler and is not its craziest member, you will see she has her work cut out for her. And yet the movie is not quite the sitcom the setup seems to suggest; there are some character quirks that make it intriguing.

Consider Deborah Clasky, the mother of the Los Angeles family. She is played by Tea Leoni like an explosion at the multiple personalities factory. She is kind, enlightened, and politically correct. She is also hysterical, manic, and a drama queen whose daily life is besieged by one crisis after another. I am not sure this character has any connection to a possible human being, but as a phenomenon it's kind of amazing; Deborah doesn't just go over the top, she waves good-bye as she disappears into cuckooland. Somehow Leoni is able to play Deborah without frothing at the mouth, and indeed makes her kind of lovable.

One who loves her is her husband, John (Adam Sandler), although he treacherously observes, "I'm running out of excuses for the woman of the house." John is a chef—in fact, according to the *New York Times,* the finest chef in America. You would therefore expect him to be a perfectionist tyrant with anger management problems, but in fact he's basically just that sweet Sandler boy, and at one point he is asked, "Could you stop being so stark raving calm?"

Deborah's mother, Evelyn (Cloris Leachman), is a practicing alcoholic whose rehearsals start at noon. She's a former jazz singer, now relegated to resident Golden Girl, sending in zingers from the sidelines. Her drinking pays off in the last act, however, when she sobers up (no one notices) and gives her daughter urgent advice.

Into this household come Flor (Paz Vega) and her daughter, Cristina (Shelbie Bruce), who is about the same middle-school age as the Claskys' daughter, Bernice (Sarah Steele). Flor and Cristina have lived in the barrio for six years, and now venture into Anglo-land because Flor needs a better job. The story is narrated by the seventeen-year-old Cristina as an affectionate memory of her mother, who learned English the better to treat this needful family with enormous doses of common sense.

Now that we have all the characters on stage, what is their story about? Is it about Flor, whose daughter narrates the story, or about the Claskys' marriage, or about the way the two daughters, both smart, both sane, are the go-to members of their families? I'm not sure there's a clear story line; it's more as if all these people meet, mix, behave, and almost lose their happiness (if happiness it is) before all is restored and the movie can end.

Along the way there are some wonderful scenes. My favorite involves a sequence where Flor decides she must finally explain to the Claskys exactly what she thinks, and why. At this point she still speaks no English, and so Cristina acts as her interpreter. As mother and daughter, Paz Vega and Shelbie Bruce play the scene with virtuoso comic timing, the mother waving her arms and the girl waving her same arms exactly the same way a second later, as they stalk around the room, Cristina acting as translator, shadow, and mime.

There's also ironic dialogue in a sequence involving the *Times* review of John's restaurant, which to John is a catastrophe. Restaurants are ruined by four-star reviews, he explains: A line of @$$#o!>s immediately forms out in front. Please, lord, he prays, just give me three and a quarter stars. The restaurant isn't really crucial to the story, however; it's more like a way for John to get out of the house.

Oh, and Tea Leoni has the first onscreen orgasm that can seriously be compared with Meg Ryan's show-stopper in *When Harry Met Sally.* After Ryan's, you'll recall, another woman in the restaurant said, "I'll have what she's having." After Leoni's, you just want to dial 911.

When it comes to the experiences of a Latino maid in an Anglo household, nothing is likely to improve on the adventures of Zaide Silvia Gutierrez in *El Norte* (1983), where the space-age automatic washer-dryer proved so baffling that the young maid just spread the washing out on the lawn to dry in the sun. But *Spanglish* isn't really about being a maid; it's more about being a life force, as Paz Vega heals this family with a sunny disposition and an anchor of normality.

There are a couple of excursions toward adultery in the film, one offscreen, the other not quite realized, but they, too, exist not to cause trouble, but to provide trouble that can be cured. The movie is all about solutions, and the problems are more like test questions. At the end, I felt there hadn't been much at risk,

but I got to see some worthy characters stumbling toward improvement.

Spartan ★ ★ ★ ★
R, 106 m., 2004

Val Kilmer (Robert Scott), Derek Luke (Curtis), William H. Macy (Stoddard), Ed O'Neill (Burch), Tia Texada (Jackie Black), Kristen Bell (Laura Newton). Directed by David Mamet and produced by Art Linson, David Bergstein, Elie Samaha, and Moshe Diamant. Screenplay by Mamet.

Spartan opens without any credits except its title, but I quickly knew it was written by David Mamet because nobody else hears and writes dialogue the way he does. That the film tells a labyrinthine story of betrayal and deception, a con within a con, also stakes out Mamet territory. But the scope of the picture is larger than Mamet's usual canvas: This is a thriller on a global scale, involving the Secret Service, the FBI, the CIA, the White House, a secret Special Ops unit, and Middle Eastern kidnappers. Such a scale could lend itself to one of those big, clunky action machines based on 700-page best-sellers that put salesmen to sleep on airplanes. But no. Not with Mamet, who treats his action plot as a framework for a sly, deceptive exercise in the gradual approximation of the truth.

Before I get to the plot, let me linger on the dialogue. Most thrillers have simpleminded characters who communicate to each other in primary plot points ("Cover me." "It goes off in ten minutes." "Who are you working for?") *Spartan* begins by assuming that all of its characters know who they are and what they're doing, and do not need to explain this to us in thriller-talk. They communicate in elliptical shorthand, in shoptalk, in tradecraft, in oblique references, in shared memories; we can't always believe what they say, and we don't always know that. We get involved in their characters and we even sense their rivalries while the outline of the plot is still murky. How murky we don't even dream.

Val Kilmer, in his best performance since *Tombstone,* plays a Special Ops officer named Scott, who as the movie opens is doing a field exercise with two trainees: Curtis (Derek Luke) and Jackie Black (Tia Texada). He's called off that assignment after the daughter of the president is kidnapped. The Secret Service was supposed to be guarding her, but . . . what went wrong is one of the movie's secrets. Ed O'Neill plays an agent in charge of the search for the daughter, William H. Macy is a political operative from the White House, and it turns out that the daughter, Laura Newton (Kristen Bell), was taken for reasons that are not obvious, by kidnappers you would not guess, who may or may not know she is the president's daughter. Kilmer's assignment: go anywhere and get her back by any means necessary. Curtis and Jackie want to get involved, too, but Kilmer doesn't want them, which may not be the final word on the subject.

And that is quite enough of the plot. It leaves me enjoying the way Mamet, from his earliest plays to his great films like *House of Games, Wag the Dog, Homicide,* and *The Spanish Prisoner,* works like a magician who uses words instead of cards. The patter is always fascinating, and at right angles to the action. He's like a magician who gets you all involved in his story about the king, the queen, and the jack, while the whole point is that there's a rabbit in your pocket. Some screenwriters study Robert McKee. Mamet studies magic and confidence games. In his plots, the left hand makes a distracting movement, but you're too smart for that, and you quick look over at the right hand to spot the trick, while meantime the left hand does the business while still seeming to flap around like a decoy.

The particular pleasure of *Spartan* is to watch the characters gradually define themselves and the plot gradually emerge like your face in a steamy mirror. You see the outlines, and then your nose, and then you see that somebody is standing behind you, and then you see it's you, so who is the guy in the mirror? Work with me here. I'm trying to describe how the movie operates without revealing what it does.

William H. Macy, who has been with Mamet since his earliest theater days, is an ideal choice for this kind of work. He always seems like the ordinary guy who is hanging on for retirement. He's got that open, willing face, and the flat, helpful voice with sometimes the little complaint in it, and in *Spartan* he starts out with what looks like a walk-on role (we're thinking

David found a part for his old pal) and ends up walking away with it. Val Kilmer, a versatile actor who can be good at almost anything (who else has played Batman and John Holmes?), here plays lean and hard, Sam Jackson style. His character is enormously resourceful with his craft, but becomes extremely puzzled about what he can do safely, and who he can trust. Derek Luke, a rising star with a quiet earnestness that is just right here, disappears for a long stretch and then finds out something remarkable, and Tia Texada, in the Rosario Dawson role, succeeds against all odds in actually playing a woman soldier instead of a sexy actress playing a woman soldier.

I like the safe rooms with the charts on the walls, and I like the casual way that spycraft is explained by being used, and the way Mamet keeps pulling the curtain aside to reveal a new stage with a new story. I suppose the last scene in the film will remind some of our friend the *deus ex machina,* but after reflection I have decided that, in that place, at that time, what happens is about as likely to happen as anything else, maybe likelier.

Spellbound ★ ★ ★
G, 95 m., 2003

The Spellers: Harry Altman, Angela Arenivar, Ted Brigham, April DeGideo, Neil Kadakia, Nupur Lala, Emily Stagg, Ashley White. A documentary directed by Jeffrey Blitz and produced by Blitz and Sean Welch.

It is useful to be a good speller, up to a point. After that point, you're just showing off. The eight contestants in *Spellbound,* who have come from all over the country to compete in the 1999 National Spelling Bee, are never likely to need words such as "opsimath" in their daily rounds, although "logorrhea" might come in handy. As we watch them drilling with flash cards and work sheets, we hope they will win, but we're not sure what good it will do them.

And yet for some of them, winning the bee will make a substantial difference in their lives— not because they can spell so well, but because the prizes include college scholarships. Take Angela Arenivar, for example. She makes it all the way to the finals in Washington, D.C., from the Texas farm where her father works as a laborer. He originally entered the country illegally, still speaks no English, and is proud beyond all words of his smart daughter.

We cheer for her in the finals, but then we cheer for all of these kids, because it is so easy to remember the pain of getting something wrong in front of the whole class. None of these teenagers is good only at spelling. Jeffrey Blitz takes his documentary into their homes and schools, looks at their families and ambitions, and shows us that they're all smart in a lot of other ways—including the way that makes them a little lonely at times.

Consider Harry Altman. He is a real kid, but has so many eccentricities that he'd be comic relief in a teenage comedy. His laugh would make you turn around in a crowded room. He screws his face up into so many shapes while trying to spell a word that it's a wonder the letters can find their way to the surface. High school cannot be easy for Harry, but he will have his revenge at the twentieth class reunion, by which time he will no doubt be a millionaire or a Nobel winner, and still with that unlikely laugh.

To be smart is to be an outsider in high school. To be seen as smart is even worse (many kids learn to conceal their intelligence). There is a kind of rough populism among adolescents that penalizes those who try harder or are more gifted. In talking with high school kids, I find that many of them go to good or serious movies by themselves, and choose vulgarity and violence when going with their friends. To be a kid and read good books and attend good movies sets you aside. Thank God you have the books and the movies for company—and now the Internet, where bright teenagers find each other.

In *Spellbound,* which was one of this year's Oscar nominees, Blitz begins with portraits of his eight finalists and then follows them to Washington, where they compete on ESPN in the bee, which was founded years ago by Scripps-Howard newspapers. The ritual is time-honored. The word is pronounced and repeated. It may be used in a sentence. Then the contestant has to repeat it, spell it, and say it again.

We've never heard most of the words (cabotinage?). General spelling rules are useful only up to a point, and then memory is the only resource. Some of these kids study up to eight hours a day, memorizing words they may never hear, write, or use. Even when they think they know a word, it's useful to pause and be sure, because once you get to the end of a word you can't go back and start again. You don't win because of your overall score, but because you have been perfect longer than anyone else; the entire bee is a sudden-death overtime.

Oddly enough, it's not tragic when a kid loses. Some of them shrug or grin, and a couple seem happy to be delivered from the pressure and the burden. One girl is devastated when she misspells a word, but we know it's because she knew it, and knew she knew it, and still got it wrong. They're all winners, in a way, and had to place first in their state or regional contests to get to Washington. When the finalist Nupur Lala, whose parents came from India, returns home to Florida, she's a local hero, and a restaurant hails her on the sign out in front: "Congradulations, Nupur!"

Spider ★ ★ ★
R, 98 m., 2003

Ralph Fiennes (Dennis "Spider" Cleg), Miranda Richardson (Yvonne/Mrs. Cleg), Gabriel Byrne (Bill Cleg), Lynn Redgrave (Mrs. Wilkinson), John Neville (Terrence), Bradley Hall (Young Spider), Gary Reineke (Freddy), Philip Craig (John). Directed by David Cronenberg and produced by Catherine Bailey, Cronenberg, and Samuel Hadida. Screenplay by Patrick McGrath, based on his novel.

He looked like a man cut away from the stake, when the fire has overrunningly wasted all the limbs without consuming them....

So Ahab is described in *Moby-Dick.* The description matches Dennis Cleg, the subject (I hesitate to say "hero") of David Cronenberg's *Spider.* Played by Ralph Fiennes, he is a man eaten away by a lifetime of inner torment; there is not one ounce on his frame that is not needed to support his suffering. Fiennes, so jolly as J. Lo's boyfriend in *Maid in Manhattan,* looks here like a refugee from the slums of hell.

We see him as the last man off a train to London, muttering to himself, picking up stray bits from the sidewalk, staring out through blank, uncomprehending eyes. He finds a boardinghouse in a cheerless district, and is shown to a barren room by the gruff landlady (Lynn Redgrave). In the lounge he meets an old man who explains kindly that the house has a "curious character, but one grows used to it after a few years."

This is a halfway house, we learn, and Spider has just been released from a mental institution. In the morning the landlady bursts into his room without knocking—just like a mother, we think, and indeed later he will confuse her with his stepmother. For that matter, his mother, his stepmother, and an alternate version of the landlady are all played by the same actress (Miranda Richardson); we are meant to understand that her looming presence fills every part of his mind that is reserved for women.

The movie is based on an early novel by Patrick McGrath. It enters into the subjective mind of Spider Cleg so completely that it's impossible to be sure what is real and what is not. We see everything through Spider's eyes, and he is not a reliable witness. He hardly seems aware of the present, so traumatized is he by the past. Whether they are trustworthy or not, his childhood memories are the landscape in which he wanders.

In flashbacks, we meet his father, Bill Cleg (Gabriel Byrne) and mother (Richardson). Then we see his father making a rendezvous in a garden shed with Yvonne (also Richardson), a tramp from the pub. The mother discovers them there, is murdered with a spade, and buried right then and there in the garden, with the little boy witnessing everything. Yvonne moves in, and at one point tells young Dennis, "Yes, it's true he murdered your mother. Try and think of me as your mother now."

Why are the two characters played by the same actress? Is this an artistic decision, or a clue to Spider's mental state? We cannot tell for sure, because there is almost nothing in his life that Spider knows for sure. He is adrift in fear. Fiennes plays the character as a man who wants to take back every step, reconsider every word, question every decision. There is a younger version of the character, Spider as a boy, played by Bradley Hall. He is solemn and wide-eyed, is beaten with a belt at one point, has a child-

hood that functions as an open wound. We understand that this boy is the most important inhabitant of the older Spider's gaunt and wasted body.

The movie is well-made and -acted, but it lacks dimension because it essentially has only one character, and he lacks dimension. We watch him and perhaps care for him, but we cannot identify with him, because he is no longer capable of change and decision. He has long since stopped trying to tell apart his layers of memory, nightmare, experience, and fantasy.

He is alone and adrift. He wanders through memories, lost and sad, and we wander after him, knowing, somehow, that Spider is not going to get better—and that if he does, that would simply mean the loss of his paranoid fantasies, which would leave him with nothing. Sometimes people hold onto illnesses because they are defined by them, given distinction, made real. There seems to be no sense in which Spider could engage the world on terms that would make him any happier.

There are three considerable artists at work here: Cronenberg, Fiennes, and Richardson. They are at the service of a novelist who often writes of grotesque and melancholy characters; he is Britain's modern master of the gothic. His Spider Cleg lives in a closed system, like one of those sealed glass globes where little plants and tiny marine organisms trade their energy back and forth indefinitely. In Spider's globe he feeds on his pain and it feeds on him. We feel that this exchange will go on and on, whether we watch or not. The details of the film and of the performances are meticulously realized; there is a reward in seeing artists working so well. But the story has no entry or exit, and is cold, sad, and hopeless. Afterward, I felt more admiration than gratitude.

Spider-Man 2 ★ ★ ★ ★
PG-13, 125 m., 2004

Tobey Maguire (Peter Parker/Spider-Man), Kirsten Dunst (Mary Jane Watson), Alfred Molina (Dr. Otto Octavius/Doc Ock), James Franco (Harry Osborn), Rosemary Harris (Aunt May), J. K. Simmons (J. Jonah Jameson). Directed by Sam Raimi and produced by Avi

Arad and Laura Ziskin. Screenplay by Alvin Sargent, Michael Chabon, Miles Millar, and Alfred Gough, based on the comic book by Stan Lee and Steve Ditko.

Now this is what a superhero movie should be. *Spider-Man 2* believes in its story in the same way serious comic readers believe, when the adventures on the page express their own dreams and wishes. It's not camp and it's not nostalgia, it's not wall-to-wall special effects and it's not pickled in angst. It's simply and poignantly a realization that being Spider-Man is a burden that Peter Parker is not entirely willing to bear. The movie demonstrates what's wrong with a lot of other superhero epics: They focus on the superpowers and short-change the humans behind them (has anyone ever been more boring than Clark Kent or Bruce Wayne?).

Spider-Man 2 is the best superhero movie since the modern genre was launched with *Superman* (1978). It succeeds by being true to the insight that allowed Marvel Comics to upturn decades of comic book tradition: Readers could identify more completely with heroes like themselves than with remote, god-like paragons. Peter Parker was an insecure high school student, in grade trouble, inarticulate in love, unready to assume the responsibilities that came with his unexpected superpowers. It wasn't that Spider-Man could swing from skyscrapers that won over his readers; it was that he fretted about personal problems in the thought balloons above his Spidey face mask.

Parker (Tobey Maguire) is in college now, studying physics at Columbia, more helplessly in love than ever with Mary Jane Watson (Kirsten Dunst). He's on the edge of a breakdown: He's lost his job as a pizza deliveryman, Aunt May faces foreclosure on her mortgage, he's missing classes, the colors run together when he washes his Spider-Man suit at the Laundromat, and after his web-spinning ability inexplicably seems to fade, he throws away his beloved uniform in despair. When a bum tries to sell the discarded Spidey suit to Jonah Jameson, editor of the *Daily Bugle,* Jameson offers him $50. The bum says he could do better on eBay. Has it come to this?

I was disappointed by the original *Spider-Man* (2002), and surprised to find this film working from the first frame. Sam Raimi, the director of both pictures, this time seems to know exactly what he should do, and never steps wrong in a film that effortlessly combines special effects and a human story, keeping its parallel plots alive and moving. One of the keys to the movie's success must be the contribution of novelist Michael Chabon to the screenplay; Chabon understands in his bones what comic books are, and why. His inspired 2000 novel, *The Amazing Adventures of Kavalier and Clay,* chronicles the birth of a 1940s comic book superhero and the young men who created him; Chabon worked on the screen story that fed into Alvin Sargent's screenplay. *See entry in the Answer Man section.*

The seasons in a superhero's life are charted by the villains he faces (it is the same with James Bond). *Spider-Man 2* gives Spider-Man an enemy with a good nature that is overcome by evil. Peter Parker admires the famous Dr. Otto Octavius (Alfred Molina), whose laboratory on the banks of the East River houses an experiment that will either prove that fusion can work as a cheap source of energy, or vaporize Manhattan. To handle the dangerous materials of his experiments, Octavius devises four powerful tentacles that are fused to his spine and have cyber-intelligence of their own; a chip at the top of his spine prevents them from overriding his orders, but when the chip is destroyed the gentle scientist is transformed into Doc Ock, a fearsome fusion of man and machine, who can climb skyscraper walls by driving his tentacles through concrete and bricks. We hear him coming, hammering his way toward us like the drums of hell.

Peter Parker meanwhile has vowed that he cannot allow himself to love Mary Jane because her life would be in danger from Spider-Man's enemies. She has finally given up on Peter, who is always standing her up; she announces her engagement to no less than an astronaut. Peter has heart-to-hearts with her and with Aunt May (Rosemary Harris), who is given full screen time and not reduced to an obligatory cameo. And he has to deal with his friend Harry Osborn (James Franco), who likes Peter but hates Spider-Man, blaming him for the death of his father (a.k.a. the Green Goblin, although much is unknown to the son).

There are special effects, and then there are special effects. In the first movie I thought Spider-Man seemed to move with all the realism of a character in a cartoon. This time, as he swings from one skyscraper to another, he has more weight and dimension, and Raimi is able to seamlessly match the CGI and the human actors. The f/x triumph in the film is the work on Doc Ock's four robotic tentacles, which move with an uncanny life, reacting and responding, doing double-takes, becoming characters of their own.

Watching Raimi and his writers cut between the story threads, I savored classical workmanship: The film gives full weight to all of its elements, keeps them alive, is constructed with such skill that we care all the way through; in a lesser movie from this genre, we usually perk up for the action scenes but wade grimly through the dialogue. Here both stay alive, and the dialogue is more about emotion, love, and values, less about long-winded explanations of the inexplicable (it's kind of neat that Spider-Man never does find out why his web-throwing ability sometimes fails him).

Tobey Maguire almost didn't sign for the sequel, complaining of back pain; Jake Gyllenhaal, another gifted actor, was reportedly in the wings. But if Maguire hadn't returned (along with Spidey's throwaway line about his aching back), we would never have known how good he could be in this role. Kirsten Dunst is valuable, too, bringing depth and heart to a girlfriend role that in lesser movies would be conventional. When she kisses her astronaut boyfriend upside-down, it's one of those perfect moments that rewards fans of the whole saga; we don't need to be told she's remembering her only kiss from Spider-Man.

There are moviegoers who make it a point of missing superhero movies, and I can't blame them, although I confess to a weakness for the genre. I liked both of *The Crow* movies, and *Daredevil*, *The Hulk*, and *X2*, but not enough to recommend them to friends who don't like or understand comic books. *Spider-Man 2* is in another category: It's a real movie, full-blooded and smart, with qualities even for those who have no idea who Stan Lee is. It's a superhero movie for people who don't go to superhero movies, and for those who do, it's the one they've been yearning for. ☞

The SpongeBob SquarePants Movie ★ ★ ★
PG, 90 m., 2004

With the voices of: Tom Kenny (SpongeBob SquarePants), Bill Fagerbakke (Patrick Star), Mr. Lawrence (Plankton), Clancy Brown (Eugene H. Krabs), Jeffrey Tambor (King Neptune), Alec Baldwin (Dennis), Rodger Bumpass (Squidward Tentacles). Directed by Sherm Cohen and Stephen Hillenburg and produced by Derek Drymon, Albie Hecht, Hillenburg, Julia Pistor, and Gina Shay. Screenplay by Hillenburg, Drymon, Tim Hill, Kent Osborne, Aaron Springer, and Paul Tibbett.

Q: Why does a lobster make the ideal pet?
A: It doesn't bark, and it knows the secrets of the deep.

I've been telling that joke for years, to people who regard me in silence and mystification. If it made you smile even a little, you are a candidate for *The SpongeBob SquarePants Movie.* This is the "Good Burger" of animation, plopping us down inside a fast-food war being fought by sponges, starfish, crabs, tiny plankton, and mighty King Neptune.

SpongeBob (voice by Tom Kenny) has a ready-made legion of fans, who follow his adventures every Saturday morning on Nickelodeon. I even know parents who like the show, which is fast-paced and goofy and involves SpongeBob's determination to amount to something in this world. In the movie, he dreams of becoming manager of Krusty Krab II, the new outlet being opened by Eugene H. Krabs (Clancy Brown), the most successful businesscrab in the ocean-floor community of Bikini Bottom. SpongeBob may only be a kid, but he's smart and learns fast, and reminded me of Ed, the hero of the live-action Nickelodeon series *Good Burger* ("Welcome to Good Burger, home of the Good Burger! Can I take your order *please?*").

SpongeBob, like all sponges I suppose, has a thing about cleanliness, and to watch him take a shower is inspiring. First he eats a cake of soap. Then he plunges a hose into the top of his head and fills up with water, exuding soap bubbles from every pore, or would that be orifice, or crevice? Then he pulls on his SquarePants and hurries off for what he expects to be a richly deserved promotion.

Alas, the job goes to Squidward Tentacles (Rodger Bumpass), who has no rapport with the customers but does have seniority. A kid can't handle the responsibility, Eugene Krabs tells SpongeBob. This is a bitter verdict, but meanwhile, intrigue is brewing in Bikini Bottom. Plankton, who runs the spectacularly unsuccessful rival food stand named Chum Bucket, plans to steal Eugene's famous recipe for Krabby Patties. As part of this plot, Plankton (Mr. Lawrence) has King Neptune's crown stolen and frames Eugene Krabs with the crime, so it's up to SpongeBob and his starfish friend Patrick (Bill Fagerbakke) to venture to the forbidden no-go zone of Shell City (which is no doubt near Shell Beach, and you remember Shell Beach). There they hope to recapture the crown, restore it to King Neptune (Jeffrey Tambor), save Mr. Krabs from execution, and get SpongeBob the promotion.

All of this happens in jolly animation with bright colors and is ever so much more entertaining than you are probably imagining. No doubt right now you're asking yourself why you have read this far in the review, given your near-certainty that you will not be going anywhere near a SpongeBob SquarePants movie, unless you are the parent or adult guardian of a SpongeBob SquarePants fan, in which case your fate is sealed. Assuming that few members of SpongeBob's primary audience are reading this (or can read), all I can tell you is, the movie is likely to be more fun than you expect.

The opening, for example, is inexplicable, unexpected, and very funny, as a boatload of pirates crowd into the front of a movie theater to see SpongeBob. These are real flesh-and-blood pirates, not animated ones, and part of the scene's charm comes because it is completely gratuitous. So, for that matter, is the appearance of another flesh-and-blood actor in the movie, David Hasselhoff, who gives SpongeBob and Patrick a high-speed lift back to Bikini Bottom and then propels them to the deeps by placing them between his pectoral muscles and flexing and popping. This is not quite as disgusting as it sounds, but it comes close.

I confess I'm not exactly sure if the residents of Bikini Bottom are cannibals; what, exactly, is in Eugene H. Krabs's Krabby Patties if not ... krabs? Does the Chum Bucket sell chum? No doubt faithful viewers of the show will know. I am reminded of the scene in *Shark Tale* when Lenny, the vegetarian shark, becomes an activist and frees a shrimp cocktail.

One of the stranger scenes in *SBSP* comes when SpongeBob and Patrick get wasted at Goofy Goober's nightclub, where ice cream performs the same function as booze. This leads to the ice-cream version of a pie fight, and terrible hangovers the next morning; no wonder, as anyone who has ever used a sponge on ice cream can testify.

Spun ★ ★ ★
R, 101 m., 2003

Jason Schwartzman (Ross), Mickey Rourke (Cook), Brittany Murphy (Nikki), John Leguizamo (Spider Mike), Mena Suvari (Cookie), Patrick Fugit (Frisbee), Peter Stormare (Cop No. 1), Alexis Arquette (Cop No. 2), Chloe Hunter (April). Directed by Jonas Akerlund and produced by Chris Hanley, Fernando Sulichin, Timothy Wayne Peternel, and Danny Vinik. Screenplay by Will De Los Santos and Creighton Vero.

Spun is a movie about going around and around and around on speed. Sometimes it can be exhausting to have a good time. The characters live within the orbit of Cook, who converts enormous quantities of nonprescription pills into drugs, and Spider Mike, who sells these and other drugs to people who usually can't pay him, leading to a lot of scenarios in which bodily harm is threatened in language learned from TV.

Because Cook is played with the studied weirdness of Mickey Rourke and Spider Mike with the tireless extroversion of John Leguizamo, *Spun* has an effortless wickedness. Rourke in particular has arrived at that point where he doesn't have to play heavy because he is heavy.

Leguizamo has the effect of trying to talk himself into and out of trouble simultaneously.

Their world includes characters played by Jason Schwartzman (from *Rushmore*), Mena Suvari (from *American Beauty*), Patrick Fugit (from *Almost Famous*), and Brittany Murphy (from *8 Mile* and *Just Married*). Uncanny, in a way, how they all bring along some of the aura of their famous earlier characters, as if this were a doc about Hollywood youth gone wrong.

Brittany Murphy made quite an impact at the Independent Spirit Awards by being unable to master the concept of reading the five nominees *before* opening the envelope, despite two helpful visits from the stage manager and lots of suggestions from the audience, but with Murphy, you always kind of wonder if she doesn't know exactly what she's doing.

Here she plays Nikki, Cook's girlfriend, which is the kind of situation you end up in when you need a lot of drugs for not a lot of money. She depends on Ross (Schwartzman) to chauffeur her everywhere in his desperately ill Volvo, sometimes taking him off on long missions through the city. These journeys have a queasy undertone since we know (although Ross sometimes forgets) that he has left his own current stripper girlfriend handcuffed to a bed. April (Chloe Hunter), the handcuffed girlfriend, is all the more furious because she realizes Ross is not sadistic but merely confused and absent-minded.

The movie plays like a dark screwball comedy in which people run in and out of doors, get involved with mistaken identities, and desperately try to keep all their plates in the air. The film's charm, which is admittedly an acquired and elusive taste, comes from the fact that *Spun* does not romanticize its characters, does not enlarge or dramatize them, but seems to shake its head incredulously as these screwups persist in ruinous and insane behavior.

Leguizamo is fearless when it comes to depictions of sexual conduct. You may recall him as the transvestite Miss Chi-Chi Rodriguez in *To Wong Foo, Thanks for Everything! Julie Newmar* (1995), or more probably as the energetic Toulouse-Lautrec in *Moulin Rouge,* and he toured in his stage show *John Leguizamo's Sexaholixs.* In *Spun* he demonstrates that although black socks have often played important roles in erotic films, there are still frontiers to be ex-

plored. What I have always enjoyed about him is the joy and abandon with which he approaches the right kind of role, as if it is play, not work. Here his energy inspires the others, causing even Patrick Fugit's slothful Frisbee to stir.

The movie is like the low-rent, road show version of those serious drug movies where everybody is macho and deadly. The characters in *Narc* would crush these characters under their thumbs. *Spun* does have two drug cops, played by Peter Stormare and Alexis Arquette, but they work for some kind of TV reality show, are followed by cameras, and are also strung out on speed.

The director, Jonas Akerlund, comes from Sweden via commercials and music videos, and has obviously studied *Requiem for a Dream* carefully, since he uses the same kind of speeded-up visual disconnections to suggest life on meth. His feel for his characters survives his technique, however, and it's interesting how this story and these people seem to have been living before the movie began and will continue after it is over; instead of a plot, we drop in on their lives. When Cook starts the mother of all kitchen fires, for example, he walks toward the camera (obligatory fireball behind him), already looking for a new motel room.

Stage Beauty ★ ★ ★
R, 110 m., 2004

Billy Crudup (Ned Kynaston), Claire Danes (Maria), Rupert Everett (King Charles II), Tom Wilkinson (Thomas Betterton), Ben Chaplin (Duke of Buckingham), Hugh Bonneville (Samuel Pepys), Richard Griffiths (Sir Charles Sedley), Edward Fox (Sir Edward Hyde), Zoe Tapper (Nell Gwynn). Directed by Richard Eyre and produced by Robert De Niro, Hardy Justice, and Jane Rosenthal. Screenplay by Jeffrey Hatcher, based on his play *Compleat Female Stage Beauty.*

Stage Beauty opens in a London weary of Puritan dreariness. The monarchy has been restored, and Charles II is a fun-loving king whose mistress, Nell Gwynn, whispers mischief in his ear. They take a lively interest in the theater. Women are not allowed to perform on the stage, so all the women's roles are played by men—chief among them Ned Kynaston (Billy Crudup), whom Samuel Pepys described in his diary as the most beautiful woman on the London stage.

Ned is most comfortable playing a woman both onstage and off. But is he gay? The question doesn't precisely occur in that form, since in those days gender lines were not rigidly enforced, and heterosexuals sometimes indulged their genitals in a U-turn. Certainly Ned has inspired the love of Maria (Claire Danes), his dresser, who envies his art while she lusts for his body. We see her backstage during one of Ned's rehearsals, mouthing every line and mimicking every gesture; she could play Desdemona herself, and indeed she does one night, in an illicit secret theater, even borrowing Ned's costumes.

Word of her performance reaches the throne, and Charles (Rupert Everett) is intrigued; a courtier tells him the French have long allowed women on the stage. His adviser Sir Edward Hyde (Edward Fox) observes, "Whenever one is about to do something truly horrible, we always say the French have been doing it for years." But Charles, nudged by Nell, decrees that henceforth women shall be played by women. This puts Ned Kynaston out of work, and turns Maria into an overnight star. "A woman playing a woman?" Ned sniffs. "What's the trick of that?"

The film, written by Jeffrey Hatcher and based on his play *Compleat Female Stage Beauty,* is really about two things at once: the craft of acting and the bafflement of love. It must be said that Ned is not a very convincing woman onstage (although he is pretty enough); he plays a woman as a man would play a woman, lacking the natural ease of a woman born to the role. Curiously, when Maria takes over his roles, she also copies his gestures, playing a woman as a woman might play a man playing a woman. Only gradually does she relax into herself. "I've always hated your Desdemona," she confesses to Ned. "You never fight; you only die."

Like *Shakespeare in Love,* which is set half a century earlier and also centers on men playing women (and on a woman playing a man, and a woman playing a man playing a woman), *Stage Beauty* explores the boundaries between reality and performance. The difference is the Gwyneth Paltrow character in

Shakespeare knows she is a woman in real life, while Ned Kynaston (based on a real actor) knows he is a woman on the stage but is not so sure about life.

It is a cruel blow when he finds fame and employment taken from him in an instant and awarded to Maria. Yet Maria still has feelings for Ned, and rescues him from a bawdy music hall to spirit him off to the country—where their lovemaking has the urgency of a first driving lesson. Like the couple in the limerick, they:

Argue all night
As to who has the right
To do what, and with which, and to whom.

Claire Danes is as fresh as running water in this role, exhibiting the clarity and directness that has become her strength; her characters tend to know who they are and why. That makes her a good contrast to Crudup, playing a character who is adrift between jobs and genders. Life for him is confusing, as men like the duke of Buckingham (Ben Chaplin) court him as a woman, forgiving him the inconvenience that he is not one, while saucy women delight in rummaging through his netherlands on a treasure hunt.

The movie lacks the effortless charm of *Shakespeare in Love,* and its canvas is somewhat less alive with background characters and details. But it has a poignancy that *Shakespeare* lacks, because it is about a real dilemma and two people who are trying to solve it; must Ned and Maria betray their real natures in order to find love, or accept them?

The London of the time is fragrantly evoked, as horses attend to their needs regardless of whose carriage they are drawing, and bathing seems a novelty. I wonder if the court of Charles II was quite as Monty Pythonesque as the movie has it, and if Nell Gwynn was quite such a bold wench, but the details involving life in the theater feel real, especially in scenes about the fragility of an actor's ego. Poor Ned. "She's a star," the theater owner Thomas Betterton (Tom Wilkinson) tells Ned about Maria. "She did what she did first; you did what you did last."

Note: Our best record of this period, of course, is Pepys's diary (if you do not have six months to read it all, try the audiobook abridgement by

Kenneth Branagh, or look at the daily entries at www.pepysdiary.com). Pepys was a high official in the navy, with access to the court, and is the source for some of what we know about Ned Kynaston. We often see him at the edge of the screen, busily scribbling (in fact, he wrote at home in code). "Mr. Pepys," he is asked at one point, "who do you write down all those little notes for?"

Stander ★ ★ ½

R, 111 m., 2004

Thomas Jane (Andre Stander), Dexter Fletcher (Lee McCall), David Patrick O'Hara (Allan Heyl), Deborah Kara Unger (Bekkie Stander), Ashley Taylor (Deventer). Directed by Bronwen Hughes and produced by Martin Katz, Chris Roland, and Julia Verdin. Screenplay by Bima Stagg.

Stander begins with white South African police firing on black demonstrators during an infamous massacre at Soweto. Andre Stander, a police captain, has ordered his men to stand fast, but after a sniper in a helicopter starts firing, the tragedy begins. Stander kills a man and fires three more times. He is appalled by what he has done. When some of his men ask, "Think we'll get paid double-time on this?" he attacks them.

Stander, played by Thomas Jane, is in conflict with himself and his society. He hates his job, which he does so well he is about to be promoted. "A white man could get away with anything while the police are out watching the blacks," he observes. To prove it, he holds up a bank. He gets away with it.

The real Andre Stander was eventually to rob twenty-seven banks on his way to becoming a South African folk legend. He was bold to the point of recklessness, at one point returning as a police officer to the bank he had just robbed. He asks a teller for a description. "He looked just like you," the teller says. The cops get a good laugh out of that. On another occasion, he robs the bank next door to the special task force set up to catch him. On a third, when a bank manager brags he missed his other safe, he goes back to empty it.

He gathers a gang of two partners, whom he met in prison after being convicted of some of his earlier robberies. After their escape, they roam South Africa robbing banks almost on impulse. Yes, they use disguises, but disguises that look like disguises—and besides, everybody knows anyway that it's the Stander gang. Various girlfriends cause conflicts and problems, and Stander has a problematic relationship with his furious wife, Bekkie (Deborah Unger).

In court, the real Stander made the statement, "I'm tried for robbing banks—but I have killed unarmed people." So were his robberies a protest against apartheid and the cruel laws of white South Africa? In this movie, not precisely. He steals from the rich and gives to himself. The robberies seem to continue because the first one fed some kind of a need. It was self-destructive and thrilling at the same time; there may be a key in the opening scene, where he is drunk and driving recklessly, and is stopped by cops who apologize when they realize who he is. Does he need to flaunt his lawlessness as a way of dealing with his conflicts as a police officer? It's not so much that he wants to get caught, as that he wants a cop to get caught.

Stander, directed by Bronwen Hughes and written by Bima Stagg, is as conflicted as its hero. Does it see Stander as an antihero or a case study? There's a long middle passage devoted mostly to bank robberies that seems almost perfunctory. We miss the timing, irony, and drama of the robberies in *Bonnie and Clyde*, where comedy was punctuated by violence, but don't get that tension here. The style is more deadpan, as if to demystify Stander: He was famous as a turncoat cop who performed dozens of daring daylight robberies, but he was not a criminal mastermind, and at times seemed almost childish.

The movie has few intimate insights into Andre Stander; it knows him as the reader of a newspaper might know him. It uses apartheid as a backdrop, but an uninformed moviegoer would not learn much about the South Africa of those days from this movie. The ending, which takes place in Fort Lauderdale during spring break, is ironic, yes, but all too conveniently existential; in a way it lets Stander off the hook.

There is one extraordinary scene. In his personal version of the Truth and Reconciliation process, Stander walks boldly into Soweto to visit the family of the man he killed. His audacity protects him, up to a point: A white man walking alone down those angry streets must have a good reason to think he can get away with it. When he finds the family, he identifies himself as the policeman who killed their son, and says he has come to apologize. Then he is beaten almost to death by young men from the crowd that has gathered. Well, of course he is, as he must have known he would be.

This scene involves elements that, properly presented and understood, might have provided insights into Stander and his culture, but it is played as a stand-alone event, an enigmatic choice by Stander that doesn't seem to connect with what comes later. We are not sure if his motive is to rid himself of guilt, to seek forgiveness, or simply to invite death in a form of suicide.

Stander's long run of brazen bank robberies would have made him a legend in any nation, but in South Africa there was the additional crucial factor that he was not only white, but had been a respected police official. His court statement, contrasting robbery with the killing of unarmed civilians, must have had wide circulation. What did black South Africans think of him? The movie gives us no real idea. The blacks provide backdrop and context, their deaths motivate the plot, but none of them emerge as individuals and their opinion of Stander is not solicited.

Starsky & Hutch ★ ★ ★
PG-13, 97 m., 2004

Ben Stiller (Dave Starsky), Owen Wilson (Ken Hutchinson), Snoop Dogg (Huggy Bear), Vince Vaughn (Reese Feldman), Juliette Lewis (Kitty), Fred Williamson (Captain Doby). Directed by Todd Phillips and produced by William Blinn, Stuart Cornfeld, Akiva Goldsman, Tony Ludwig, and Alan Riche. Screenplay by John O'Brien, Phillips, Scot Armstrong, and Stevie Long.

As Hollywood works its way through retreads of TV series from the 1960s and 1970s, I find I can approach each project with a certain purity, since I never saw any of the original shows. Never saw a single Starsky and Hutch. Not one

episode of *I Spy*. No *Mod Squad*. No *Charlie's Angels*. What was I doing instead, apart from seeing thousands of movies? Avoiding episodic television like a communicable disease, and improving myself with the great literature of the ages. Plus partying.

So here is *Starsky & Hutch*, adding the ampersand for a generation too impatient for "and." It's a surprisingly funny movie, the best of the 1970s recycling jobs, with one laugh ("Are you okay, little pony?") almost as funny as the moment in *Dumb and Dumber* when the kid figured out his parakeet's head was Scotch-taped on.

Ben Stiller and Owen Wilson star, in their sixth movie together. They use the same comic contrasts that worked for Hope and Crosby and Martin and Lewis: one is hyper and the other is sleepy-eyed and cool. In a genial spoof of the cop buddy genre, they're both misfits on the Bay City police force. Starsky (Stiller) is the kind of cop who would ask another cop if he had a license for his firearm. Hutch (Wilson) has done nothing useful at all for months, aside from enriching himself illegally by stealing from dead bodies. Their captain (Fred Williamson) thinks they deserve each other, and makes them partners in a scene where Hutch immediately insults Starsky's perm.

The bad guy is Reese Feldman (Vince Vaughn), coils of cigarette smoke constantly rising in front of his face. He's a big-time cocaine dealer who has invented, or discovered, a form of cocaine that has no taste or smell and can fool police dogs. He's also a vicious boss who kills an underling in the opening scene and pushes him off his yacht. Discovery of the floater gives Starsky and Hutch their first big case, although they almost blow it, since Hutch's first suggestion is to push it back out to sea and hope it floats to the next precinct.

Although the plot survives sporadically, the movie is mostly about the rapport between Stiller and Wilson, who carry on a running disagreement about style while agreeing on most other issues, such as the importance of partying with sexy cheerleaders as part of their investigation. Carmen Electra and Amy Smart are the cheerleaders, improbably attracted to the guys, and there's a very funny scene where Wilson croons a minor David Soul hit from the

1970s while a psychedelically fueled cartoon bird chirps on his shoulder.

The movie doesn't make the mistake of relying entirely on its stars. Apart from Vaughn and the cheerleaders, the supporting cast benefits mightily from Juliette Lewis, as Vaughn's mistress, and Snoop Dogg as Huggy Bear, a combo pimp/superfly/police informer whose outfits are like retro cubed. Will Ferrell turns up in a weird cameo as a jailhouse source whose sexual curiosity falls far outside anything either Starsky and Hutch had ever imagined ("arch your back and look back at me over your shoulder, like a dragon").

Another character is Starsky's beloved bright-red, supercharged Ford Gran Torino, which he drives like a madman while obsessing about the smallest scratch. The closing stunt involves something we've been waiting to happen in car stunt scenes for a very long time.

The film's director is Todd Phillips, of *Road Trip* and *Old School*. I was not a big fan of either movie, but they both contained real laughs, and now in *Starsky & Hutch* he reaches critical mass. Will the movie inspire me to watch reruns of the original series? No. I want to quit while I'm ahead.

Star Wars: Episode III — Revenge of the Sith ★ ★ ★ ½
PG-13, 140 m., 2005

Ewan McGregor (Obi-Wan Kenobi), Hayden Christensen (Anakin Skywalker), Natalie Portman (Padme Amidala), Ian McDiarmid (Chancellor Palpatine), Samuel L. Jackson (Mace Windu), Jimmy Smits (Senator Bail Organa), Christopher Lee (Count Dooku), Frank Oz (voice) (Yoda), Anthony Daniels (C-3PO), Kenny Baker (R2-D2). Directed by George Lucas and produced by Rick McCallum. Screenplay by Lucas.

George Lucas comes full circle in more ways than one in *Star Wars: Episode III—Revenge of the Sith*, which is the sixth and allegedly, but not necessarily, the last of the *Star Wars* movies. After *Episode II* got so bogged down in politics that it played like the Republic covered by C-Span, *Episode III* is a return to the classic space opera style that launched the series. Because the story leads up to where the

original *Star Wars* began, we get to use the immemorial movie phrase, "This is where we came in."

That Anakin Skywalker abandoned the Jedi and went over to the dark side is known to all students of *Star Wars*. That his twins, Luke Skywalker and Princess Leia, would redeem the family name is also known. What we discover in *Episode III* is how and why Anakin lost his way—how a pleasant and brave young man was transformed into a dark, cloaked figure with a fearsome black metal face. As Yoda sadly puts it in his inimitable word-order: "The boy who dreamed, gone he is, consumed by Darth Vader." Unexplained is how several inches grew he in the process.

As *Episode III* opens, Anakin Skywalker (Hayden Christensen) and his friend Obi-Wan Kenobi (Ewan McGregor) are piloting fighter crafts, staging a daring two-man raid to rescue Chancellor Palpatine (Ian McDiarmid). He has been captured by the rebel General Grievous (whose voice, by Matthew Woods, sounds curiously wheezy considering the general seems to use replacement parts). In the spirit of all the *Star Wars* movies, this rescue sequence flies in the face of logic, since the two pilots are able to board Grievous's command ship and proceed without much trouble to the ship's observation tower, where the chancellor is being held. There is a close call in an elevator shaft, but where are the guards and the security systems? And why, for that matter, does a deep space cruiser need an observation tower when every porthole opens onto the universe? But never mind.

Back within the sphere of the Jedi Council, Anakin finds that despite his heroism he will not yet be named a Jedi Master. The council distrusts Palpatine and wants Anakin to spy on him; Palpatine wants Anakin to spy on the council. Who to choose? McDiarmid has the most complex role in the movie as he plays on Anakin's wounded ego. Anakin is tempted to go over to what is not yet clearly the dark side; in a movie not distinguished for its dialogue, Palpatine is insidiously snaky in his persuasiveness.

The way Anakin approaches his choice, however, has a certain poignancy. Anakin has a rendezvous with Padme (Natalie Portman); they were secretly married in the previous film, and now she reveals she is pregnant. His reaction is that of a nice kid in a teenage comedy, trying to seem pleased while wondering how this will affect the other neat stuff he gets to do. To say that George Lucas cannot write a love scene is an understatement; greeting cards have expressed more passion.

The dialogue throughout the movie is once again its weakest point: The characters talk in what sounds like Basic English, without color, wit, or verbal delight, as if they were channeling Berlitz. The exceptions are Palpatine and, of course, Yoda, whose speech (voiced by Frank Oz) reminds me of Wolcott Gibbs's famous line about the early style of *Time* magazine: "Backward ran sentences until reeled the mind."

In many cases the actors are being filmed in front of blue screens, with effects to be added later, and sometimes their readings are so flat they don't seem to believe they're really in the middle of amazing events. How can you stand in front of exploding star fleets and sound as if you're talking on a cell phone at Starbucks? "He's worried about you," Anakin is told at one point. "You've been under a lot of stress." Sometimes the emphasis in sentences is misplaced. During the elevator adventure in the opening rescue, we hear, "Did I miss *something*?" when it should be, "Did I *miss* something?"

The dialogue is not the point, however; Lucas's characters engage in sturdy oratorical pronunciamentos and then leap into adventure. *Episode III* has more action per square minute, I'd guess, than any of the previous five movies, and it is spectacular. The special effects are more sophisticated than in the earlier movies, of course, but not necessarily more effective. The dogfight between fighters in the original *Star Wars* and the dogfight that opens this one differ in their complexity (many more ships this time, more planes of action, complex background) but not in their excitement. And although Lucas has his characters attend a futuristic opera that looks like a cross between Cirque du Soleil and an ultrasound scan of an unborn baby, if you regard the opera hall simply as a place, it's not as engaging as the saloon on Tatooine in the first movie.

The lesson, I think, is that special effects should be judged not by their complexity but by the degree that they stimulate the imagination, and *Episode III* is distinguished not by

how well the effects are done, but by how amazingly they are imagined. A climactic duel on a blazing volcanic planet is as impressive, in its line, as anything in *The Lord of the Rings*. And Yoda, who began life as a Muppet but is now completely animated (like about 70 percent of the rest of what we see), was to begin with and still is the most lifelike of the *Star Wars* characters.

A word, however, about the duels fought with lightsabers. When they flashed into life with a mighty whizzing "thunk" in the first "Star Wars" and whooshed through their deadly parabolas, that was exciting. But the thrill is gone. The duelists are so well matched that saber fights go on forever before anyone is wounded, and I am still not sure how the sabers seem able to shield their bearers from incoming ammo. When it comes to great movie swordfights, Liam Neeson and Tim Roth took home the gold medal in *Rob Roy* (1995), and the lightsaber battles in *Episode III* are more like isometrics.

These are all, however, more observations than criticisms. George Lucas has achieved what few artists do, and created and populated a world of his own. His *Star Wars* movies are among the most influential, both technically and commercially, ever made. And they are fun. If he got bogged down in solemnity and theory in *Episode II: Attack of the Clones*, the Force is in a jollier mood this time, and *Revenge of the Sith* is a great entertainment.

Note: I said this is not necessarily the last of the Star Wars movies. Although Lucas has absolutely said he is finished with the series, it is inconceivable to me that 20th Century-Fox will willingly abandon the franchise, especially as Lucas has hinted that parts VII, VIII, and IX exist at least in his mind. There will be enormous pressure for them to be made, if not by him, then by his deputies. ☞

The Statement ★ ★
R, 120 m., 2004

Michael Caine (Pierre Brossard), Tilda Swinton (Anne-Marie Livi), Jeremy Northam (Colonel Roux), Charlotte Rampling (Nicole), Noam Jenkins (Michael Levy), Matt Craven (David Manenbaum), Alan Bates (Armand Bertier). Directed by Norman Jewison and produced by

651

Jewison and Robert Lantos. Screenplay by Ronald Harwood, based on a novel by Brian Moore.

Michael Caine is such a lovely actor. In a movie like *The Statement*, where he is more or less adrift among competing themes, it's a pleasure to watch him craft a character we can care about even when the story keeps throwing him curves. He has such patience with a moment, such an ability to express weariness or fear without seeming to try. Here he plays a weak man baffled by life and by his own motives, and he arouses so much sympathy that even though he's supposed to be the villain, the movie ends up with substitute villains who are shadowy and ill-explained.

Caine plays Pierre Brossard, a Frenchman who was involved in the execution of Jews during World War II. Wanted as a war criminal, he has been living in hiding ever since, in a series of Roman Catholic monasteries and other safe houses. It's explained that he is a member of an ultrasecret Catholic society that protects its own, and that presents one of the movie's many hurdles: Although the story is based on fact, the movie never convinced me of its truth.

The screenplay, by Ronald Harwood *(The Pianist)*, based on a novel by Brian Moore, is inspired by the real-life Paul Touvier, who executed Jewish hostages and then was protected for many years by an informal network of right-wing Catholics. Would a series of abbots and cardinals place the church at risk for this insignificant man for years after the war has ended? Yes, apparently, some did; but a movie must seem to be based on its own facts, not those in research consulted by the screenwriters. The situation on screen is not made to seem real.

Caine himself is virtually made to play two different characters. Early in the film we see him cool and merciless as he perceives that he is being followed, and calmly kills the man who wants to kill him. Later, we see him weak, pathetic, and confused. Perhaps he contains both men, but the movie seems to write the character first one way and then the other, showing not contrasts but simply contradictions.

Scene after scene works on its own terms. The director, Norman Jewison, has skill and conscience and obviously feels for the material,

even if he hasn't found the way to tell it. There is a confrontation, for example, between Brossard and his estranged wife (Charlotte Rampling), which for edge and emotional danger could come from Le Carré or Graham Greene, but in *The Statement* it works on its own terms but doesn't fit into the whole, giving us one more facet of a personality that doesn't seem to fit together in any sensible way.

Presumably the moral thrust of the movie is against elements within the Church that supported anti-Semitism and continued to protect war criminals after the war. That there were such elements, and that the real Touvier was such a criminal, is beyond doubt. But then why does the movie supply a murky third element—a conspiracy to murder Brossard and pin the death on Zionists? The film fails to explain who these conspirators are, or to make clear exactly what they hope to achieve. We are not even quite sure which side they are on: Do they want to attack anti-Semites, or protect the Church, or support Israel, or what? I don't require that a movie have a message, but in a message movie it is helpful to know what the message is.

Stateside ★ ★
R, 96 m., 2004

Rachel Leigh Cook (Dori Lawrence), Jonathan Tucker (Mark Deloach), Agnes Bruckner (Sue Dubois), Joe Mantegna (Mr. Deloach), Carrie Fisher (Mrs. Dubois), Diane Venora (Mrs. Hengen), Ed Begley Jr. (Father Concoff), Val Kilmer (SDI Skeer). Directed by Reverge Anselmo and produced by Robert Greenhut and Bonnie Wells-Hlinomaz.

Stateside tells the story of a rich kid who joins the marines to stay out of jail, and then finds himself in love with a famous actress and rock singer who is being treated for schizophrenia. Stated as plainly as that, the plot could have been imported from a soap opera, but the writer-director, Reverge Anselmo, assures us it is "based on a true story." Perhaps. Certainly he rotates it away from sensationalism, making it the story of an irresponsible kid who is transformed by boot camp and then becomes obsessed with what he sees as his duty to the actress.

The kid is named Mark (Jonathan Tucker). He goes to an upscale Catholic high school, drinks too much one night, and is driving a car that broadsides the car of the headmaster, Father Concoff (Ed Begley Jr.). The priest is paralyzed from the waist down, but doesn't sue (he explains why, but so enigmatically it doesn't work). Mark's millionaire father (Joe Mantegna) pulls strings to have the charges dropped in exchange for Mark enlisting in the marines.

Mark goes to Parris Island for basic training, under the command of a drill instructor named Skeer (Val Kilmer). Skeer doesn't like the rich kid and makes it hard on him; the kid puts his head down and charges through, emerging at the end of the ordeal as what Skeer, if not all of the rest of us, would consider a success.

Home on leave before more training, he visits his girlfriend. That would be Sue (Agnes Bruckner), who lost her front teeth in the crash, but lost her freedom after her mother (Carrie Fisher) found some sexually explicit letters she wrote. The letters are obviously evidence of madness, so she's institutionalized, in the Connecticut version of *The Magdalene Sisters*. When Mark visits her, he meets her roommate, Dori (Rachel Leigh Cook), and they fall in love.

All of this sounds simpler than the movie makes it. The opening scenes are disjointed and confusing, and it doesn't help that the characters sometimes seem to be speaking in poetic code. We meet Dori early in the film, before Mark does, when she has a breakdown onstage and walks away from her band. But the movie doesn't make it clear who she is or what has happened, and we piece it together only later.

Famous as she is, she is also troubled, and Mark's steadfast loyalty and level gaze win her heart. She wouldn't ordinarily date a man from boot camp, even a rich one, but Mark's letters tell her he will stand by her, and she believes him. So do we, after he manages to balance the marines with trips home, springing her at various times from mental institutions and hospitals. These moments of freedom are heady for her, and she enjoys getting out from under her medication too. But her therapist (Diane Venora) solemnly explains to Mark that he is bad for Dori, that she needs her medication, that she can be a danger to herself. One conversation between them is especially well handled. The point of the movie, I think, is that the

marines make Mark into a man, but he takes his newfound self-confidence and discipline and uses it to commit to a lost cause. He doggedly persists in his devotion to Dori because he loves her, yes, but also because her helplessness makes him feel needed, and her illness is a test of his resolve.

Perhaps the movie is based on more of the true story than was absolutely necessary. Toward the end of the film, Mark is part of the marine landing in Lebanon, and returns home gravely wounded. This happens too late in the film for the consequences to be explored, especially in terms of his relationship with Dori. *Stateside* might have been wiser to bring the Mark-Dori story to some kind of a bittersweet conclusion without opening a new chapter that it doesn't ever really close.

The performances are strong, although undermined a little by Anselmo's peculiar style of dialogue, which sometimes sounds more like experimental poetry or song lyrics than like speech. It is also hard to know how to read Dori; we believe the therapist who says she is very ill, but her illness is one of those movie conveniences in which she is somehow usually able to do or say what the screenplay requires. There's also the enigma of Mark's father, played by Mantegna as a remote, angry man who carts an oxygen bottle around with him. We sense there's more Anselmo wants to say about the character than he has time for. *Stateside* plays like urgent ideas for a movie that Anselmo needed to make, but they're still in note form.

The Station Agent ★ ★ ★ ½
R, 88 m., 2003

Peter Dinklage (Finbar McBride), Patricia Clarkson (Olivia Harris), Bobby Cannavale (Joe Oramas), Michelle Williams (Emily), Raven Goodwin (Cleo), Paul Benjamin (Henry Styles). Directed by Thomas McCarthy and produced by Robert May, Mary Jane Skalski, and Kathryn Tucker. Screenplay by McCarthy.

"It's really funny how people see me and treat me, since I'm really just a simple, boring person."

So says Finbar McBride, the hero of *The Station Agent*. Nothing in life interests him more than trains. Model trains, real trains, books about trains. He likes trains. Finbar is a dwarf, and nothing about him interests other people more than his height. It's as if he's always walking in as the next topic of conversation. His response is to live in solitude. This works splendidly as a defense mechanism, but leaves him deeply lonely, not that he'd ever admit it.

Finbar is a character of particular distinction, played by Peter Dinklage as a man who is defiantly himself. Rarely have I seen a movie character more *present* in every scene. He is the immovable object, resisting approaches by strangers, and at first no one can get through his defenses except for a little African-American girl who looks straight at him and is not intimidated and will not be dismissed.

As the movie opens, Finbar is working in a model train store owned by apparently his only friend in the world, Henry Styles (Paul Benjamin). Henry drops dead, and Finbar inherits from him an abandoned train station near a town with the unlikely but real name of Newfoundland, New Jersey. Nothing prevents Finbar from moving immediately to New Jersey and living in the station, and so he does, exciting enormous curiosity from Joe Oramas (Bobby Cannavale), who runs a roadside coffee wagon on a road where hardly anyone ever seems to stop for coffee. Joe has unlimited time on his hands, is lonely in a gregarious rather than a reclusive way, and forces himself into Finbar's life with relentless cheerfulness. Cannavale is such an eruption of energy that the two quieter characters almost have to shield themselves from him. There's humor in Finbar's persistent attempts to slam the door on a man who totally lacks the ability to be rejected.

There is a third lonely soul in Newfoundland. She is Olivia Harris (Patricia Clarkson), who is going through a divorce and is in mourning for the death of her child. Olivia is a very bad driver. As Finbar walks to the convenience store one morning, she nearly hits him with her car. At the store, he has to endure posing for a snapshot taken by the clerk. Walking back home, he's nearly hit by her a second time, and takes a tumble into the ditch.

That would be a slapstick scene in another kind of movie, but writer-director Thomas McCarthy is aiming a bit more deeply. Yes, this is a comedy, but it's also sad, and finally it's simply a story about trying to figure out what you

love to do and then trying to figure out how to do it. Joe has that part mastered, since the coffee wagon represents a lifestyle so perfect that the only way to improve it would be if, say, a dwarf moved into the train station. Finbar thinks he has life mastered—he thinks all he wants to do is sit in his train station and think about trains—but perhaps there are possibilities of friendship and sex that he has not considered.

Finbar is a handsome man, which does not escape the attention of a local librarian named Emily (Michelle Williams). But she wants him not for his mind, or his trains, but for his body, and he is not interested in satisfying that kind of curiosity. Olivia is a more complex case, since perhaps she sees in the little man her lost child, or perhaps that is only the avenue into what she really sees. It is a great relief in any event that *The Station Agent* is not one of those movies in which the problem is that the characters have not slept with each other and the solution is that they do. It's more about the enormous unrealized fears and angers that throb beneath the surfaces of their lives; Finbar and Olivia could explode in one way or another at any moment, and the hyperactive Joe is capable of anything.

The movie's island of sanity is Cleo (Raven Goodwin), whom you may remember as the young adopted girl in *Lovely and Amazing*. Goodwin, like Dinklage, has a particular and unshakable presence on the screen, and I hope the movies do not misplace her, as they do so many child actors. As she regards Finbar and asks him if he is a midget ("No. A dwarf"), we realize that Finbar hates such questions, but is happy to answer hers, because he understands that Cleo is simply gathering information.

There was a documentary on cable about little people, describing their lives in their own words, and its subtext seemed to be: "Yes, I'm short. Get over it." I remember my face burning with shame early one morning when I was six years old and went with my father to where the circus was setting up. I gawked through a flap in the dining tent at the circus giant, and he scowled and said, "Can't you find anything else to stare at?" and I learned something that I never had to be taught again.

The Station Agent makes it clear that too many people make it all the way to adulthood without manners enough to look at a little person without making a comment. It isn't necessarily a rude comment—it's that any comment at all is rude. In a way, the whole movie builds up to a scene in a bar. A scene that makes it clear why Finbar does not enjoy going to bars. The bar contains a fair number of people so witless and cruel that they must point and laugh, as if Finbar has somehow chosen his height in order to invite their moronic behavior. Finally he climbs up on a table and shouts, "Here I am! Take a look!" And that is the moment you realize there is no good reason why Peter Dinklage could not play Braveheart.

Steamboy ★ ★
PG-13, 106-126 m., 2005

With the voices of: Anna Paquin (Ray Steam), Alfred Molina (Eddie Steam), Patrick Stewart (Lloyd Steam). Directed by Katsuhiro Otomo and produced by Shinji Komori and Hideyuki Tomioka. Screenplay by Sadayuki Murai and Katsuhiro Otomo.

Steamboy is a noisy, eventful, and unsuccessful venture into Victorian-era science fiction, animated by a modern Japanese master. It's like H. G. Wells and Jules Verne meet *Akira*. The story follows three generations of a British family involved in a technological breakthrough involving steam, which the movie considers the nineteenth-century equivalent of nuclear power. There may be possibilities here, but they're lost in the extraordinary boredom of a long third act devoted almost entirely to loud, pointless, and repetitive action.

The movie opens in 1866 with the collection of water from an ice cave; its extraordinary purity is necessary for experiments by the Steam family, which is perfecting the storage of power through steam under high pressures. Young Ray Steam (voice by Anna Paquin) is the boy hero, whose father, Eddie (Alfred Molina), and grandfather, Lloyd Steam (Patrick Stewart), are rivals in the development of the technology. One day Ray gets a package in the mail from his grandfather, its delivery followed immediately by ominous men dressed in alarming dark Victorian fashions that proclaim, "I am a sinister villain."

The box contains a steam ball, which we learn contains steam under extraordinary pressure. The ball, invented by Lloyd, is either a revolutionary power source or an infernal device that could explode at any moment, take your choice. Ray tries to escape on a peculiar invention that seems to combine the most uncomfortable experiences of riding a unicycle and being trapped in a washing machine, but is captured and taken to the headquarters of the O'Hara Foundation, which wants to control the invention and use it to power new machines of war. It goes without saying, or does it, that the O'Hara family daughter is named Scarlett.

The movie is the result of ten years of labor by Katsuhiro Otomo, whose *Akira* (1988) was the first example of Japanese anime to break through to world theatrical markets. That one created a futuristic Tokyo where a military dictatorship cannot control rampaging motorcycle gangs. The animation was state of the art, the vision was bleak, the tone was a radical departure for American audiences raised to equate animation with cute animals and fairy tales.

Otomo also wrote *Rojin Z* (1991), about a computerized machine that contains elderly patients within an exoskeleton/bed that transports, diagnoses, treats, massages, and entertains its occupants; once installed in the new Z-100 model, owners are expected never to leave, whether or not they want to.

The movie has intriguing ideas about human lives ruled by machines, which is why the technology in *Steamboy* seems promising. Otomo has reportedly been working on the film for ten years, drawing countless animation cels by hand and also using computer resources; why, with all the effort he put into the film's construction, did he neglect to go anywhere interesting with the plot?

We have hope at first, just because Otomo creates Manchester and London at the dawn of the industrial era, when steam power offered limitless possibilities and the internal combustion engine was still impractical. His machines and the interior of the O'Hara Foundation look like the ancestors of pulp sci-fi magazine covers, but without the bright colors. For reasons that don't pay off, Otomo's visuals tend toward the pale and drab. Maybe he's going for period atmosphere. I wondered at first if the movie was being projected on video, but no, Otomo wants it to look washed-out.

His plot holds promise: The evil O'Hara Foundation wants to hijack the Great Exhibition, for which Prince Albert built the Crystal Palace to showcase Britain's leadership of the industrial revolution. But the Great Exhibition was held in 1851, and if the movie is set in 1866, is the chronology off? There may have been an explanation that eluded me, this not being a question that riveted my attention at the time.

The O'Hara people want to jettison the notion of progress for peace, and use the exhibition to promote its expensive new engines of war, hoping every country will buy some, go to war, and need to buy more. At this point, when the movie could potentially get its teeth into something, Otomo goes nuts with brainless action sequences in which one retro-futuristic device after another does battle, explodes, dives, surfaces, floats, opens fire, flies, attacks, defends, and so on.

Some of his ideas are promising, including a zeppelin fitted with iron claws that can lift a speeding train car from the tracks. A fearsome strategy indeed, although it would be awkward for the dirigible if the train ever went through a tunnel or under a bridge, or raced past big hard buildings close to the tracks. Other ideas are just collisions of hardware, punctuated by frantic expostulations.

It is a theory of mine that action does not equal interest. Objects endlessly in motion are as repetitive as objects forever at rest. Context is everything. Why are they moving, who wants them to move, what is at risk, what will be gained? By the end of *Steamboy* I was convinced the answers to all of these questions were: Otomo has abandoned the story and, in despair, is filling the screen with wonderfully executed but pointless and repetitive kinetic energy. Action doodles.

Note: The movie is available in a 106-minute English-dubbed version and a 126-minute Japanese version with English subtitles.

The Stepford Wives ★ ★ ★
PG-13, 93 m., 2004

Nicole Kidman (Joanna Eberhart), Matthew Broderick (Walter Kresby), Bette Midler

(Bobbie Markowitz), Jon Lovitz (Dave Markowitz), Roger Bart (Roger Bannister), David Marshall Grant (Jerry Harmon), Faith Hill (Sarah Sunderson), Glenn Close (Claire Wellington), Christopher Walken (Mike Wellington). Directed by Frank Oz and produced by Donald De Line, Gabriel Grunfeld, Scott Rudin, and Edgar J. Scherick. Screenplay by Paul Rudnick, based on the book by Ira Levin.

The Stepford Wives depends for some of its effect on a plot secret that you already know, if you've been paying attention at any time since the original film version was released in 1975. If you don't know it, stay away from the trailer, which gives it away. It's an enticing premise, an opening for wicked feminist satire, but the 1975 movie tilted toward horror instead of comedy. Now here's a version that tilts the other way, and I like it a little better.

The experience is like a new production of a well-known play. The original suspense has evaporated, and you focus on the adaptation and acting. Here you can also focus on the new screenplay by Paul Rudnick, which is rich with zingers. Rudnick, having committed one of the worst screenplays of modern times (*Isn't She Great*, the Jacqueline Susann story), redeems himself with barbed one-liners; when one of the community planners says he used to work for AOL, Joanna asks, "Is that why the women are so slow?"

Nicole Kidman stars, as Joanna Eberhart, a high-powered TV executive who is fired after the victim of one of her reality shows goes on a shooting rampage. Her husband, Walter (Matthew Broderick), resigns from the same network, where he worked under her, and moves with his wife and two children to the gated community of Stepford, Connecticut.

It's weird there. The women all seem to be sexy clones of Betty Crocker. Glenn Close is Claire Wellington, the real-estate agent, greeter, and community cheerleader, and she gives Joanna the creeps (she's "flight attendant friendly"). Nobody in Stepford seems to work; they're so rich they don't need to, and the men hang out at the Men's Association while the women attend Claire's exercise sessions. In Stepford, the women dress up and wear heels even for aerobics (no sweaty gym shorts), and

Claire leads them in pantomimes of domestic chores ("Let's all be washing machines!").

Walter loves it in Stepford. Joanna hates it. She bonds with Bobbie Markowitz (Bette Midler), author of a best-selling memoir about her mother, *I Love You, But Please Die*. Her house is a pigpen. Every other house in Stepford is spotlessly clean, even though there seem to be no domestic servants; the wives cheerfully do the housework themselves. They also improve themselves by attending Claire's book club. A nice example of Rudnick's wit: When Joanna shares that she has finished volume two of Robert Caro's biography of Lyndon Johnson, Claire takes a beat, smiles bravely, and suggests they read *Christmas Keepsakes* and discuss celebrating Jesus' birthday with yarn.

Christopher Walken is Claire's husband and seems to be running Stepford; it's the kind of creepy role that has Walken written all over it, and he stars in a Stepford promotional film that showcases another one of his unctuous explanations of the bizarre. A new touch this time: Stepford has a gay couple, and Roger (Roger Bart), the "wife," is flamboyant to begin with, until overnight, strangely, he becomes a serious-minded congressional candidate.

What's going on here? You probably know, but I can't tell you. When Ira Levin's original novel was published in 1972, feminism was newer, and his premise satirized the male desire for tame, sexy wives who did what they were told and never complained. Rudnick and director Frank Oz don't do anything radical with the original premise (although they add some post-1972 touches like the Stepford-style ATM machine), but they choose comedy over horror, and it's a wise decision. Kidman plays a character not a million miles away from her husband-killer in *To Die For*, even though this time she's the victim. Bette Midler is defiantly subversive as the town misfit. And Walken is . . . Walken.

The movie is surprisingly short, at 93 minutes including end titles (the 1975 film was 115 minutes long). Maybe it needs to be short. The secret is obvious fairly early (a woman goes berserk and when Walter says she was probably just sick, Joanna says, "Walter, she was sparking!"). It could probably work as a springboard for heavy-duty social satire, but that's not what audiences expect from this material, and Rudnick pushes about as far as he can without tearing the envelope. Some movies are based on short stories, some on novels. *The Stepford Wives* is little more than an anecdote, and like all good storytellers, Oz and Rudnick don't meander on their way to the punch line.

Stevie ★ ★ ★ ½

NO MPAA RATING, 140 m., 2003

A documentary directed by Steve James and produced by James, Adam Singer, and Gordon Quinn.

Stevie is a brave and painful film, the story of a man who goes looking for the youngster he met ten years earlier through the Big Brother program. He finds that the news about him is not good, and will get worse. This is a story involving a family so dysfunctional it seems almost to exist for the purpose of wounding and warping this child, Stephen Fielding. As he was wounded, so he has wounded others. That's often the way it goes. They say that child abusers were almost always abused as children. Stevie could be Exhibit A.

The movie is by Steve James, who directed the great documentary *Hoop Dreams* (1994). For years people asked him, "Whatever happened to those kids?"—to the two young basketball players he followed from eighth grade to adulthood. James must often have wondered about the kid nobody ever asked about, Stevie. While he was a student at Southern Illinois University, Steve was a Big Brother to Stevie, but he lost touch in 1985 after graduating. Ten years later, he went back downstate to the little town of Pomona, ten or fifteen miles down the road from Carbondale, to seek out Stevie.

That must have taken some courage, and even on his first return James must have suspected that this story would not have a happy ending. But it has so much truth, as it shows an unhappy childhood reaching out through the years and smacking down its adult survivor.

Here are a few facts, for orientation. Stevie Fielding was not wanted. He was born out of wedlock, does not know who his father is, was raised by a mother who didn't want him, was beaten by her. When she did marry, she turned him over to her new husband's mother to raise. He also made a circuit of foster homes and juvenile centers, where he was raped and beaten regularly.

When we meet Stevie again he is twenty-three and not doing well. His tattoos and Harley T-shirt express a bravado he does not possess, and he makes a poor impression with haystack hair, oversized thick glasses, and bad teeth. The most important person in his life is his girlfriend, Tonya Gregory, who on first impression seems slow, but who on longer acquaintance reveals herself to be smart about Stevie, and loyal to him. His stepsister Brenda is also a support, a surrogate mother who seems the best-adjusted member of his family, perhaps because, as her husband tells us, "They didn't beat her."

Stevie freely expresses hatred for his mother, Bernice ("Someday I am going to kill her"), and she is one of the villains of the piece, but having stopped drinking, she feels remorse and even blames herself, to a degree, for Stevie's problems—especially the latest one. Between 1995, when Steve James first revisits Stevie, and 1997, when production proper started on this documentary, Stevie was charged with molesting an eight-year-old girl.

Stevie says he is innocent. Even Tonya thinks he is guilty. We do not forgive him this crime because of his tragic childhood, but it helps us understand it—even predict it, or something like it. And as he goes through the court system, Tonya stands by him, Brenda helps him as much as she can, and Bernice, his mother, seems slowly to change for the better—to move in the direction she might have taken if it had not been for her own troubles.

There is no sentimentality in *Stevie*, no escape, no release. "The film does not come to a satisfying ending," writes the critic David Poland. He wanted more of a "lift," and so, I suppose, did I—and Steve James. But although *Hoop Dreams* ended in a way that a novelist could not have improved upon, *Stevie* seems destined to end the way it does, and is the more courageous and powerful for it. A satisfying ending would have been a lie. Most of us are blessed with happy families. Around us are others, nursing deep hurts and guilts and secrets—punished as children for the crime of being unable to fight back.

To watch *Stevie* is to wonder if anything could have been done to change the course of

this history. Steve James's Big-Brothering was well intentioned, and his wife, a social worker, believes in help from outside. But this extended family seems to form a matrix of pain and abuse that goes around and around in each generation, and mercilessly down through time to the next. To be born into the family is to have a good chance of being doomed, and Brenda's survival is partly because she got out fast, married young, and kept her distance.

Philip Larkin could have been thinking of this family in his most famous poem, whose opening line cannot be quoted here, but which ends:

Man hands on misery to man.
It deepens like a coastal shelf.
Get out as early as you can,
And don't have any kids yourself.

Search the Web using the first two lines, and you will find a poem that Stevie Fielding might agree with.

The Stoneraft ★ ★ ★

NO MPAA RATING, 117 m., 2003

Ana Padrão (Joana), Gabino Diego (Jose), Icíar Bollain (Maria), Diogo Infante (Joaquim), Federico Luppi (Pedro). Directed and produced by George Sluizer. Screenplay by Yvette Biro and Sluizer, based on the novel by José Saramago.

Certain unexpected shots send an uneasy shudder through the audience. In *Close Encounters* there was the pickup truck waiting at the train crossing when two headlights appeared in the rear window and then, inexplicably, began to rise vertically. In George Sluizer's new film *The Stoneraft*, a dog trots doggily through a country field, and then for no reason leaps across a patch of ground, and continues on his doggy way. A second later, a crack opens up in the ground right where he jumped. How did the dog know?

The film is a low-key disaster picture, made about characters who are inward, thoughtful, talkative. It's about the Iberian Peninsula breaking loose from Europe and sending Spain and Portugal very quickly out into the Atlantic toward a collision with the Azores.

Like all disaster movies, it follows the

larger story through several smaller ones. There are five of them, drawn together finally by the dog. Jose (Gabino Diego) discovers that he is being followed everywhere by a flock of birds. Joana (Ana Padrão) uses a stick to idly trace a line in the earth, and finds she cannot erase the line. Joaquim (Diogo Infante) picks up a heavy stone and heaves it into the sea, only to watch amazed as it skips over the waves like a pebble. Maria (Icíar Bollain) starts to unravel a knitted blue sock that has gone wrong, and discovers that her task is never done: "No matter how long I work, there is still more wool." An older man named Pedro (Federico Luppi) can feel the earth trembling even if no one else can.

These people end up in an increasingly crowded Citroën 2CV, driving toward the collision coast as crowds flee in the opposite direction. Eventually the car breaks down and they switch to a horse cart. Some villages are being looted by mobs; in others, people dance in the streets, for tomorrow they may die.

Television covers the fallout. Britain reasserts its claim to Gibraltar. Americans arrive to try to close the widening rift with cables and earth-moving machinery. Governments resign. No one has an explanation, although many believe the film's five heroes may have had something to do with it.

Sluizer is the same director who made *The Vanishing* (1993), one of the best thrillers ever made, about a man whose wife disappears at a highway rest stop. He later remade it in a Hollywood version that vulgarized his own material. This time, he has reversed the process, taking the tacky American disaster movie and translating it into a quieter and more elegant European version.

It's amusing how few special effects he gets away with. Two entire nations break off from Europe and set sail, and he covers it with a trench in the ground, a flock of birds, a ball of blue wool, and a trained dog. The effect is uncanny and haunting, and I was reminded a little of *On the Beach* (1959), in which the nuclear destruction of the Northern Hemisphere is observed from Australia via low-tech shortwave broadcasts and hearsay reports.

The movie is meant partly as satire; after years of reports about nations breaking away from the EUC, here are two that literally do.

There's some social observation: Why does the public assume the man followed by birds represents the cause, not the solution? Much of the story is told at the pace of a leisurely day in the country, as the five characters and the dog muse about the curious turn of events. Is it possible that the small actions of these people could have set into motion the partitioning of subcontinents? After all, doesn't chaos theory teach us that the beating of a butterfly's wings in Asia could theoretically begin a chain of events leading to a hurricane in . . . the Azores, wasn't it?

Stone Reader ★ ★ ★ ½
PG-13, 128 m., 2003

With Carl Brandt, Frank Conroy, Bruce Dobler, Robert C. S. Downs, Robert Ellis, Leslie Fiedler, Ed Gorman, Robert Gottlieb, Dan Guenther, John Kashiwabara, Mark Moskowitz, Dow Mossman, William Cotter Murray, John Seelye. Directed by Mark Moskowitz and produced by Moskowitz and Robert M. Goodman. Screenplay by Moskowitz.

In 1972, a man reads a review of a new novel named *The Stones of Summer* in the *New York Times*. The reviewer believes it is one of the most extraordinary novels of its generation—a masterpiece. The man buys the novel, can't get into it, puts it on the shelf, moves it around with his books for years, and finally reads it. He thinks it's a masterpiece too. He goes on the Internet to find out what else the author, Dow Mossman, has written. Mossman has written nothing—has disappeared, it would appear, from the face of the Earth.

Stone Reader is the story of the reader's quest for that missing writer. Mark Moskowitz, whose day job is directing political commercials, embarks on a quixotic quest for Dow Mossman, finds him after much difficulty, and discovers why he has been silent for thirty years, and what he has been up to. It will occur to any attentive viewer of the film that Moskowitz could have found Mossman more quickly and easily than he does—that at times he is stretching out the search for its own sake—but then the movie is not really about Mossman anyway. It is about a reader who goes in search of other readers, and it is a love poem to reading.

It is the kind of movie that makes you want to leave the theater and go directly to a bookstore. Maybe to buy *The Stones of Summer*, which got a new edition in autumn 2003, but also to buy—well, it reawakened my interest in Joseph Heller's *Something Happened,* which has been lost in the shadow of his *Catch-22,* and it observes correctly that Kerouac's *On the Road* is a better novel than a lot of people think it is, and it reminded me of Frederick Exley's *A Fan's Notes,* which has been described as the kind of book that, when you meet someone at a party who has also read it, forces you to seek out a quiet corner to talk urgently about it, with much laughter and shaking of heads.

Moskowitz, who narrates the movie and appears in much more of it than Dow Mossman, is a Woody Allenish character who makes the filming into the subject of the film. At one point, he phones his mother for advice on what he should ask Mossman. (At another, he asks her what sort of kid he was at eighteen, when he first bought the novel, and she remembers: "You had a beard, and you used to like to wear only the linings of coats.") When he encounters a fresh interview subject, he is likely to produce a box jammed with books and stack them up between them, reciting the titles like a litany of touchstones. I do not travel around with boxes of books, but get me in conversation with another reader, and I'll recite titles, too. Have you ever read *Quincunx? The Raj Quartet? A Fine Balance?* Ever heard of that most despairing of all travel books, *The Saddest Pleasure,* by Moritz Thomsen? Does anybody hold up better than Joseph Conrad and Willa Cather? Know any Yeats by heart? Surely P. G. Wodehouse is as great at what he does as Shakespeare was at what he did.

Shakespeare, as it turns out, has been one of Dow Mossman's companions during his missing years. Without telling you very much about where he is now or why he didn't write another novel or what his work has been since 1972, I can nevertheless evoke his presence as a person you would very much like to talk books with. He turns out not to be a tragic recluse, a sad alcoholic, or a depressive, but a man filled with words and good cheer. When he came to my Overlooked Film Festival, where the film played in April, he and the French director

Bertrand Tavernier seemed always to be in a corner together, trading enthusiasm about books.

Mark Twain is one of his heroes, and he can cite the chapter of Twain's autobiography that you must read. He is awestruck by Casanova's memoirs. He hated *Shakespeare in Love* because of those scenes where Shakespeare crumpled up a page of foolscap in frustration and threw it away: Paper was too expensive to throw away in those days, Mossman observes, and he is convinced Shakespeare created his plays in his mind while walking around London, and then taught them to his players. Since many of the plays show evidence of being based on actors' prompt copies and scholars can sometimes identify the actor-source who may have been more familiar with some scenes than others, he may be right.

Doesn't matter. What matters is listening to him talk about books with Moskowitz. In the scene where Moskowitz first encounters him, they are soon talking about Shakespeare, not Mossman. Here, we feel, is a man who should appear regularly on National Public Radio, just talking about books he loves.

Before he finds Mossman, Moskowitz interviews several men of letters (no women). Some of them, he hopes, might remember *The Stones of Summer*—such as Robert Gottlieb, the famous editor, or John Kashiwabara, who designed the book cover, or Frank Conroy, who was Mossman's adviser at the University of Iowa. John Seelye, who wrote the original review for the *New York Times,* remembers the book. The late Leslie Fiedler, a towering literary critic, has never heard of it — but Moskowitz interviews him anyway, about the phenomenon of one-book novelists. (Some writers who write many books, like Kerouac, Salinger, Malcolm Lowry, and James T. Farrell, are nevertheless really one-book novelists, they decide.)

Stone Reader is a meandering documentary, frustrating when Moskowitz has Mossman in his sights and *still* delays bagging him while talking to other sources. But at the end, we forgive his procrastination (and remember, with Laurence Sterne and *Tristam Shandy,* that procrastination can be an art if it is done delightfully). Moskowitz has made a wonderful film about readers and reading, writers and writing. Now somebody needs to go to Cedar Rapids and make a whole documentary about Dow Mossman. Call it *The Stone Writer.*

The Story of the Weeping Camel ★ ★ ★
PG, 90 m., 2004

Janchiv Ayurzana (Janchiv [Great Grandfather]), Chimed Ohin (Chimed [Great Grandmother]), Amgaabazar Gonson (Amgaa [Grandfather]), Zeveljamz Nyam (Zevel [Grandmother]), Ikhbayar Amgaabazar (Ikchee [Father]), Odgerel Ayusch (Odgoo [Mother]), Enkhbulgan Ikhbayar (Dude [Older Brother]), Uuganbaatar Ikhbayar (Ugna [Younger Brother]), Guntbaatar Ikhbayar (Guntee [Baby Brother]), Ingen Temee (Mother Camel), Botok (Baby Camel). Directed by Byambasuren Davaa and Luigi Falorni and produced by Tobias Siebert. Screenplay by Davaa and Falorni.

On the edges of the Gobi Desert live to this day nomadic herders who travel with their animals and exist within an ancient economy that requires no money. *The Story of the Weeping Camel,* which despite its title is a joyous movie, tells the story of one of those families, and of their camel, which gives birth to a rare white calf and refuses to nurse it. It is a terrible thing to hear the cry of a baby camel rejected by its mother.

The movie has been made in the same way that Robert Flaherty made such documentaries as *Nanook of the North, Man of Aran,* and *Louisiana Story.* It uses real people in real places, and essentially has them play themselves in a story inspired by their lives. That makes it a "narrative documentary," according to the filmmakers. A great many documentaries are closer to this model than their makers will admit; even *cinema verité* must pick and choose from the available footage and reflect a point of view.

We meet four generations of the same family. Do not think of them as primitive; it takes great wisdom to survive in their manner. I learn from the press materials that the older brother, Dude (Enkhbulgan Ikhbayar), went away to boarding school but then returned to his family because he enjoyed the way of life. Certainly these people live close to the land and to their animals, and their yurts are masterpieces of construction—sturdy, portable homes that can be carried on the back of a camel, but are sturdy enough to withstand winter storms.

It is spring when the movie begins, and a mother camel (Ingen Temee) has just given painful birth to her white calf (Botok). It is only reasonable to supply the names of these animals, since they are so much a part of their nomad families. Does the mother refuse her milk because the calf looks strange to her, or because of her birth agony? No matter; unless the calf is fed, it will die, and the family needs it.

When bottle-feeding fails, Dude and his younger brother Ugna (Uuganbaatar Ikhbayar) travel by camel some fifty kilometers to the nearest town to bring back a musician who will play a traditional song to the camel and perhaps persuade it to relent. While in the village, they watch television and brush against other artifacts of modern life with curiosity, but without need.

The musician accompanies them to the village. He plays the traditional song. Legend has it that if a camel finally agrees to nurse her young, this will cause her to weep. There are also a few damp eyes among members of the family. All of this is told in a narrative that is not a cute true-life animal tale, but an observant and respectful record of the daily rhythms and patterns of these lives. We sense the dynamics among the generations, how age is valued and youth is cherished, how the lives of these people make sense to them in a way that ours never will, because they know why they do what they do, and what will come of it. The causes and effects of their survival are visible, and they are responsible.

The filmmakers are Byambasuren Davaa and Luigi Falorni. They cowrote and directed; he photographed. They met at the Munich Film School, where she told him that her grandparents had been herders. Their film was shot on location in about a month, and has an authenticity in its very bones. In a commercial movie, sentiment would rule, and we would feel sorry for the cute baby camel. Well, yes, we feel sorry for the calf in *The Story of the Weeping Camel,* but we also understand that the camel represents wealth and survival for its owners, and in what they do, they're thinking, as they should, more about themselves than about the camel.

I believe this film would be fascinating for

smart children, maybe the same ones who liked *Whale Rider,* because so much of it is told through the eyes of the younger brother. Although the desert society is alien to everything we know, in another way it is instantly understandable, because we know about parents and grandparents, about working to put food on the table, about the need of babies to nurse. Here is a film that is about life itself, and about those few humans who still engage it at first hand.

Note: Two other splendid documentaries cover similar ground. Taiga *(1995), the remarkable eight-hour documentary by Ulrike Ottinger, lives and travels with nomads for a year, and witnesses their private lives and religious ceremonies.* Genghis Blues *is the wonderful 1999 documentary about a blind San Francisco blues singer who hears Tuvan throat singing on the radio, teaches himself that difficult art, and journeys to Tuva, which is between Mongolia and Siberia, to enter a throat-singing contest.*

Strayed ★ ★ ★
NO MPAA RATING, 95 m., 2004

Emmanuelle Béart (Odile), Gaspard Ulliel (Yvan), Grégoire Leprince-Ringuet (Philippe), Clémence Meyer (Cathy), Jean Fornerod (Georges), Samuel Labarthe (Robert). Directed by André Téchiné and produced by Jean-Pierre Ramsay-Levi. Screenplay by Gilles Taurand and Téchiné, based on the novel *The Boy with Gray Eyes* by Gilles Perrault.

Who is this Yvan, this boy with the shaved head who has crawled out of the mud to lead them to safety? And why should she trust him? Odile (Emmanuelle Béart) is a bourgeois Parisian woman with two children and no way to protect them, and Yvan (Gaspard Ulliel) has a toughness that is reassuring and at the same time menacing. She really has no choice but to follow him into the forest, after Nazi planes have strafed and bombed the column of refugees streaming south from Paris.

It is 1940, and all of the certainties of Odile's life have evaporated. She is a pretty widow in her late thirties, a teacher, who fled Paris and joined the flight from the Germans with her thirteen-year-old son, Philippe, and her daughter, Cathy, who is seven. Her children trust her, but she doesn't trust herself, because her experience and values are irrelevant in this sudden war. "It's every man for himself," someone shouts on the road, not originally but cogently, as bullets kill some and spare others.

Yvan is tough and sure of himself, and her instincts as a teacher tell her he is dangerous. The teenager Philippe is frightened but more realistic; he believes they need this strange young man. Yvan has a sweet side, and seems to want to help them; there is perhaps even the suggestion that he needs this family to replace one he lost, and he needs this chance to be helpful and competent. Or perhaps the fact that Philippe secretly bribed him with his father's watch convinced him to stay; we never know for sure what he's thinking.

Strayed begins and ends with facts of war, but it is really a film about the nature of male and female, about middle-class values and those who cannot afford them, about how helpless we can be when the net of society is broken. The French director André Téchiné, no sentimentalist, creates a separate world for his four characters, and the war goes on elsewhere.

Separated from the other refugees, they walk through a forest of such beauty that war seems impossible, and they sleep under the stars. The next day, they come upon a country home, comfortable, isolated, and tempting. The owners have fled. Yvan believes they should break in and stay there for a while; the roads are mobbed, there is no sure safety in the south, and no one will look for them here. Odile argues that the house is private property. Her bourgeois instincts are so strong that she would sleep with her children in the woods, or try to rejoin the exodus, rather than break in. For Yvan, there is no choice: They must survive.

We realize that the war is very new to her, that she clings to the certainties of her ordered life and must learn that the rules have changed. They break in, of course. There is a wine cellar, many bedrooms, some food. Yvan hunts for game. Odile establishes a domestic routine. They could almost be on holiday, the children vibrating with the sense of adventure, Odile putting good French food on the table, and Yvan . . . Yvan . . . enjoying it too, but on guard, and always aware of their danger. Their danger and, we sense, his own.

When you put a beautiful woman and a forceful young man in an isolated situation where they must live closely together, sexual tension coils under the surface. At first it is not obvious, because Odile's bourgeois certainties make it impossible that she could sleep with a rough working-class stranger twenty years younger. And there are the children, although Philippe admires Yvan: Here is an older brother, or perhaps a father figure, who can protect them when his own father has failed.

There are certain mysteries, which I will not reveal, involving secrets Odile keeps from Yvan and those he keeps from her, and certain questions about how long they should stay in the house—questions that seem to depend, in Yvan's mind, on more than the simple matter of survival. There are things Philippe observes and keeps to himself. And always there is the knowledge between Odile and Yvan that they could sleep together, that the nature of their relationship is shifting, that the war has changed the rules and that Yvan has become necessary to her family.

We sense the story will not end here, and we know this temporary family cannot live in this house forever, with time suspended. We are not sure how near a town might be, and Odile wonders why the telephone doesn't work. Someone will find them, and what will happen then? Those questions occur to us as they occur to the characters, adding an urgency, an unreality, as the days pass comfortably. Téchiné, a master of buried power struggles, increases the level of uncertainty and apprehension until we know something must happen, and then something does, and the essential natures of Yvan and Odile, and their way their society formed them, becomes clear.

Stuck on You ★ ★ ★
PG-13, 118 m., 2003

Matt Damon (Bob), Greg Kinnear (Walt), Cher (Herself), Eva Mendes (April), Seymour Cassel (Morty), Wen Yann Shih (May), Ray "Rocket" Valliere (Rocket), Jay Leno (Himself), Jack Nicholson (Himself), Meryl Streep (Herself), Griffin Dunne (Himself). Directed by Bobby Farrelly and Peter Farrelly and produced by Bobby Farrelly, Peter Farrelly, Bradley Thomas, and Charles B. Wessler. Screenplay by Bobby Farrelly and Peter Farrelly.

Bob and Walter are joined at the hip, and they like it that way. Their life has become a double act, and they're so efficient behind the counter of their diner in Martha's Vineyard that customers get a free burger if they have to wait more than three minutes. There are, of course, difficulties involved with being conjoined twins, but they're amiable souls and have learned to accommodate each other. Bob (Matt Damon) would happily stay on the island for a lifetime, but Walt (Greg Kinnear) is restless and has ambitions; he wants to be an actor. This has already led to an annual crisis involving the local amateur production; as Walt acts, Bob battles stage fright.

Stuck on You is the new movie by the Farrelly brothers, who have earlier dealt with schizophrenics *(Me, Myself and Irene)*, fat people *(Shallow Hal)*, a one-handed bowler *(Kingpin)*, stupidity *(Dumb and Dumber)*, and hair gel *(There's Something About Mary)*. Their next film, *The Ringer*, will be about an imposter who tries to crash the Special Olympics. The subjects of their comedies are defiantly non-P.C., but their hearts are in the right place, and it's refreshing to see a movie that doesn't dissolve with embarrassment in the face of handicaps.

Walter and Bob are a case study of how to live happily while bonded for life to another person. An operation to separate them would be risky, because their shared liver is mostly on Bob's side, and Walt's chances of survival would only be 50-50. Thus, when Walt determines that he must go to Hollywood to try his fortunes as an actor, Bob is a good sport and sadly says good-bye to the gang at the burger bar.

Up until now they have done everything together, including sports; being conjoined is an advantage in baseball, where the twins stand on the mound, one staring down the hitter while the other catches a runner off base. But in Hollywood life changes, because Walt has an immediate stroke of good luck in his career, while Bob is reduced, literally, to a bystander.

Walt's break comes through a lucky meeting with Cher, who is auditioning for a new TV series she hates and wants to get out of. She thinks maybe a conjoined twin would be the ideal costar to sink the ratings. Some of the movie's funniest scenes involve Walt acting with Cher while Bob stands behind scenery or is removed by special effects—but when the press discovers that Cher's costar is a still-joined twin, the ratings go through the roof.

Meanwhile, romance beckons. Bob has been flirting with an online Los Angeles pen pal for three years, but when he meets May (Wen Yann Shih), he's too shy to reveal his condition; keeping the secret involves contortions, evasions, and misunderstandings, mostly based on the fact that Walt always seems to be right there at Bob's side. Walt, meanwhile, strikes up a friendship with a poolside babe at their motel. She's April (Eva Mendes), a dumb brunette who interprets everything in southern California terms; seeing the bridge of flesh that joins the brothers at the hip, she casually asks them, "So—where'd you get this done?" Mendes adds this role of broad comedy to her dramatic work as Denzel Washington's wife in Out of Time and an action role in 2 Fast 2 Furious, showing herself at home across a range of genres.

The movie's showbiz milieu is much helped by the appearance of famous stars in cameo roles. Jack Nicholson turns up briefly, Jay Leno interviews both twins at once, Cher pokes fun at her own image, Griffin Dunne is the self-important director of her TV show, and Meryl Streep is the very definition of a good sport in a surprise appearance late in the film.

Many of the characters are challenged minorities in one way or another, including Morty (Seymour Cassel), who lives in a retirement home, uses a scooter to get around, but still chain smokes cigars and considers himself a full-service agent. There's a scene where the brothers reduce his fee by pointing out he will, after all, be representing only one of them.

The movie is funny, but also kindhearted. Much screen time is given to Rocket (Ray "Rocket" Valliere), a waiter in the burger joint. He's a mentally challenged friend of the Farrellys, who makes it clear here why they like him. Their approach to handicaps is open and natural, and refreshing compared to the anguished, guilt-laden treatment usually given to handicapped characters in movies. The fact that Walt hopes to be a movie star is less amazing, really, than that the Farrellys had the nerve to make a comedy about it.

Super Size Me ★ ★ ★

NO MPAA RATING, 96 m., 2004

A documentary directed by Morgan Spurlock and produced by Spurlock. With Dr. Daryl Isaacs, Ronald McDonald, and Dr. Lisa Ganjhu.

Of course it is possible to eat responsibly at McDonald's, as spokesmen for the chain never tire of reminding us. Fast food is simply one element of a balanced nutritional plan. Of course, it's the *unbalanced element* unless you order the fish filet sandwich with no mayonnaise and one of those little salads with the lo-cal dressing; then you'll be fine, except for the refined white flour in the bun and the high intake of sodium. Eating responsibly at McDonald's is like going to a strip club for the iced tea.

I say this having eaten irresponsibly at McDonald's since I was in grade school, and one of the very first McDonald's outlets in the nation opened in Urbana, Illinois. Hamburgers were fifteeen cents; fries were a dime. Make it two burgers and we considered that a meal. Today it is possible to ingest thousands of calories at McDonald's and zoom dangerously over your daily recommended limits of fat, sugar, and salt. I know because Morgan Spurlock proves it in *Super Size Me.*

This is the documentary that caused a sensation at Sundance 2004 and allegedly inspired McDonald's to discontinue its "supersize" promotions as a preemptive measure. In it, Spurlock vows to eat three meals a day at McDonald's for one month. He is examined by three doctors at the beginning of the month and found to be in good health. They check him again regularly during the filming, as his weight balloons thirty pounds, his blood pressure skyrockets, his cholesterol goes up sixty-five points, he has symptoms of toxic shock to his liver, his skin begins to look unhealthy, his energy drops, he has chest pains, and his girlfriend complains about their sex life. At one point his doctors advise him to abandon McDonald's before he does permanent damage. The doctors say they have seen similar side effects from binge drinkers, but never dreamed you could get that way just by eating fast food.

It's amazing, what you find on the menu at McDonald's. Let's say you start the day with a sausage and egg McMuffin. You'll get ten grams of saturated fat—50 percent of your daily recommendation, not to mention 39 percent of your daily sodium intake. Add a Big Mac and medium fries for lunch, and you're up to 123 percent of your daily saturated fat recommendation and 96 percent of your sodium. For dinner, choose a quarter-pounder with cheese, add another medium order of fries, and you're at 206 percent of daily saturated fat and 160 percent of sodium. At some point add a strawberry shake to take you to 247 percent of saturated fat and 166 percent of sodium. And remember that most nutritionists recommend less fat and salt than the government guidelines.

There is a revisionist interpretation of the film, in which Spurlock is identified as a self-promoter who, on behalf of his film, ate more than any reasonable person could consume in a month at McDonald's. That is both true and not true. He does have a policy that whenever he's asked if he wants to "supersize it," he must reply "yes." But what he orders for any given meal is not uncommon, and we have all known (or been) customers who ordered the same items. That anyone would do it three times a day is unlikely. Occasionally you might want to go upscale at someplace like Outback, where the Bloomin' Onion Rings all by themselves provide more than a day's worth of fat and sodium, and 1,600 calories. Of course, they're supposed to be shared. For best results, share them with everyone else in the restaurant.

We bear responsibility for our own actions, so . . . is it possible to go to McDonald's and order a healthy meal? A Chicago nutritionist told a *Sun-Times* reporter that of course Spurlock put on weight, because he was eating 5,000 calories a day. She suggested a McDonald's three-meal menu that would not be fattening, but as I studied it, I wondered: How many customers consider a small hamburger, small fries and a diet Coke as their dinner? When was the last time you even *ordered* a small hamburger (that's not a quarter-pounder) at McDonald's? Don't all raise your hands at once.

Oh, I agree with the nutritionist that her recommended three meals would not add weight; her daily caloric intake totaled 1,460 calories, which is a little low for a child under four, according to the USDA. But even her menu would include fifty-four grams of fat (fifteen saturated), or about one-third of calories (for best heart health, fat should be down around 20 percent). And her diet included an astonishing 3,385 megagrams of sodium (daily recommendation: 1,600 megagrams to 2,400 megagrams). My conclusion: Even the nutritionist's bare-bones 1,460-calorie McDonald's menu is dangerous to your health.

I approached *Super Size Me* in a very particular frame of mind because in December 2002, after years of fooling around, I began seriously following the Pritikin program of nutrition and exercise, and I have lost about eighty-six pounds. Full disclosure: Fifteen of those pounds were probably lost as a side effect of surgery and radiation; the others can be accounted for by Pritikin menus and exercise (the 10,000 Step-a-Day Program plus weights two or three times a week). So of course that makes me a true believer.

You didn't ask, but what I truly believe is that unless you can find an eating program you can stay on for the rest of your life, dieting is a waste of time. The pounds come back. Instead of extreme high-protein or low-carb diets with all their health risks, why not exercise more, avoid refined foods, and eat a balanced diet of fruits and veggies, whole grains, fish, and a little meat, beans, soy products, low-fat dairy, low fat, low salt? Of course, I agree with McDonald's that a visit to Mickey D's can be part of a responsible nutritional approach. That's why I've dined there twice in the last seventeen months.

Suspect Zero ★ ★
R, 99 m., 2004

Aaron Eckhart (Thomas Mackelway), Carrie-Anne Moss (Fran Kulok), Ben Kingsley (Benjamin O'Ryan). Directed by E. Elias Merhige and produced by Gaye Hirsch and Paula Wagner. Screenplay by Zak Penn and Billy Ray.

We should be grateful, I suppose, when the serial killers in movies pause in their carnage long enough to concoct elaborate webs of clues, hints, and tantalizing challenges for their pursuers. Lives may be saved because of the time it takes them to plant enigmatic clues, send cryptic faxes, and pose for extreme close-ups in which they look like some guy in a photo booth trying to look tortured.

The serial killer or killers in *Suspect Zero* have obviously spent a lot of time watching old thrillers. They have learned in particular that it is important to zero in on one particular lawman, show that they're familiar with his secrets, and then challenge him to stop them before they kill or fax again.

In *Suspect Zero*, the fated target is FBI agent Thomas Mackelway (Aaron Eckhart), who got in some kind of trouble in Texas and has been demoted to New Mexico. He chews handfuls of aspirin to ease his pain, as Travis Bickle did in *Taxi Driver*, this is a behavior limited almost entirely to the movies, where the characters are too masochistic to wash them down with water.

Never mind. Mackelway investigates a murder involving a man whose car is found precisely on the state line between Arizona and New Mexico. "The killer must have used a global positioning system," Mackelway deduces. Why? To take the crime out of the jurisdiction of state authorities and make it the business of the FBI. And not just the FBI, but Mackelway personally, as a series of taunting faxes makes clear.

The faxes come from someone with inside knowledge about a serial killer. The problem with this killer is that he has no modus operandi, no pattern, no telltale habits, and strikes entirely at random, which makes him difficult to find. Does the writer of the faxes know the killer, or is he the killer? Or is there a third, more occult, explanation? As we ponder these possibilities, what looks like the world's longest and blackest semitrailer truck cruises inappropriately down city streets near playgrounds, and we wonder: Assuming the truck is not in the movie by accident, could it be connected to the killings, and, if so, wouldn't the presence of such a gargantuan truck be the very M.O. the killer allegedly lacks?

Mackelway has been joined in New Mexico by agent Fran Kulok (Carrie-Anne Moss). They share some unsuccessful romantic history. He has issues. Maybe they both do. But they have to work together, and so inevitably they will come to a new knowledge of each other in order to provide the fax writer with additional insights, and the ending with additional chills.

Ben Kingsley meanwhile looks like he should be chewing aspirin too. He plays a man named Benjamin O'Ryan who is often seen in such extreme close-ups that if pores could talk, the movie would be over. Is he the killer? The Law of Economy of Characters would seem to suggest that he must be, since the movie contains no other eligible candidate. But perhaps there is another, more bizarre and involved explanation, and the killer is either hidden in plain view among the major characters or is never seen at all until the climax. I am not spoiling any secrets, but simply applying logic to a plot that offers zero sum as well as zero suspects.

The director, E. Elias Merhige, made the splendid *Shadow of the Vampire* (2001), a macabre thriller about the filming of F. W. Murnau's silent classic *Nosferatu* (1922). Murnau, played by John Malkovich, has a dreadful secret he was keeping from his cast: Max Schreck (Willem Dafoe), who is playing the vampire, is so good in the role because he is in fact a vampire, and has been promised the blood of the leading lady, which even in an industry famous for its catering is one star perk too many. (Midway through production, Schreck dines on the cinematographer and when Murnau is furious at him, wonders to himself if they really need the writer.)

Merhige is a gifted director with a good visual sense and a way of creating tension where it should not exist. But *Suspect Zero* is too devised and elaborate to really engage us. There's a point at which its enigmatic flashes of incomprehensible action grow annoying, and a point at which we realize that there's no use paying close attention, because we won't be able to figure out the film's secrets until they're explained to us. All of the clues and faxes and close-ups and flashbacks are revealed as devices that are in the movie not because they add up to anything, but because they surround a fairly simple story with gratuitous stylistic mystery.

One final thought. Imagine the underlying material rewritten so that it was all seen and told from the point of view of the Ben Kingsley character. Wouldn't it be more interesting that way? His dilemma is much more dramatic than the elaborate charade concocted for the FBI. In a movie where one character knows everything and the others know nothing, it seems unkind to stick the audience with the dummies.

S.W.A.T. ★ ★ ★
PG-13, 111 m., 2003

Samuel L. Jackson (Hondo Harrelson), Colin Farrell (Jim Street), Brian Gamble (Jeremy Renner), Michelle Rodriguez (Chris Sanchez), James Todd Smith [LL Cool J] (David "Deke" Kay), Olivier Martinez (Alex). Directed by Clark Johnson and produced by Dan Halsted, Chris Lee, and Neal H. Moritz. Screenplay by David Ayer and David McKenna.

Half an hour into watching *S.W.A.T.*, I realized the movie offered pleasures that action movies hardly ever allow themselves anymore:

1. The characters had dialogue and occupied a real plot, which involved their motivations and personalities.

2. The action scenes were more or less believable. The cops didn't do anything that real cops might not really almost be able to do, if they had very, very good training.

I started taking notes along these lines, and here are a few of my jottings:

"When a cop shoots at a robber in a hostage situation, the hostage is wounded."

"The chief punishes two hotshots with demotions instead of pulling their badges and guns and kicking them off the force."

"When the bad guy steals a cop car, we expect a chase, but he backs up and crashes it within a block."

"When the chase leads down to the Los Angeles subway system, the cops approach a stopped train, board it, and look for their quarry. Astonishingly, there is not a fight scene atop a speeding train."

"In a S.W.A.T. team training scene, the trainees are running toward a target while shooting, and somebody asks, 'No rolls?' The veteran cop in charge replies: 'They only roll in John Woo movies—not in real life.'"

That's the point with *S.W.A.T.* This isn't a John Woo movie, or *Bad Boys 2*, or any of the other countless movies with wall-to-wall action and cardboard characters. It isn't exactly real life, either, and I have to admit some of the stunts and action scenes are a shade unlikely, but the movie's ambition is essentially to be the

same kind of police movie they used to make before special effects upstaged human beings.

The result is one of the best cop thrillers since *Training Day*. Samuel L. Jackson and Colin Farrell costar, playing the time-honored roles of veteran officer and young hothead. Michelle Rodriguez and James Todd Smith (a.k.a. LL Cool J), both effective actors, give depth to the S.W.A.T. team. And Olivier Martinez, who played Diane Lane's lover in *Unfaithful*, is the smirking playboy arms dealer who offers a $100 million reward to anyone who springs him from custody.

The plot begins with a hostage situation gone wrong. A S.W.A.T. team member (Brian Gamble) disobeys orders, enters a bank, and wounds a hostage. He and his partner, Jim Street (Farrell), are offered demotions. Street accepts; his partner leaves the force. But Street, a talented officer and a great shot, is spotted by the legendary veteran Hondo Harrelson (Samuel L. Jackson) and chosen for his hand-picked elite S.W.A.T. team.

One of the pleasures of the movie is the training sequence, where Jackson leads his team through physical and mental maneuvers. Many recent action movies have no training scenes because, frankly, you can't train to do their impossible stunts—you need an animator to do them for you.

A routine traffic bust leads to the unexpected arrest of Alex (Olivier Martinez), an internationally wanted fugitive. Alex offers the $100 million reward on television, the cops assume there will be a lot of escape masterminds hoping to collect the reward, and it's up to Hondo and his team to safely escort the prisoner to a federal penitentiary.

That it does not go smoothly goes without saying. I'm not arguing that the last forty-five minutes of the movie are, strictly speaking, likely or even plausible, but nothing violates the laws of physics and you can kind of see how stuff like that might sort of happen, if you get my drift.

S.W.A.T. is a well-made police thriller, nothing more. No Academy Awards. But in a time when so many action pictures are mindless assaults on the eyes, ears, and intelligence, it works as superior craftsmanship. The director, Clark Johnson, is a veteran of TV, both as an actor and director, and supplies a well-made film that trusts its story and actors. What a pleasure, after movies that merely wanted to make my head explode.

Sweet Sixteen ★ ★ ★ ½

R, 106 m., 2003

Martin Compston (Liam), Annmarie Fulton (Chantelle), William Ruane (Pinball), Michelle Abercromby (Suzanne), Michelle Coulter (Jean), Gary McCormack (Stan), Tommy McKee (Rab), Calum McAllees (Calum). Directed by Ken Loach and produced by Rebecca O'Brien. Screenplay by Paul Laverty.

Sweet Sixteen is set in Scotland and acted in a local accent so tricky it needs to be subtitled. Yet it could take place in any American city, in this time of heartless cuts in social services and the abandonment of the poor. I saw the movie at about the same time our lawmakers attacked the pitiful $400 child tax credit, while transferring billions from the working class to the richest 1 percent. Such shameless greed makes me angry, and a movie like *Sweet Sixteen* provides a social context for my feelings, showing a decent kid with no job prospects and no opportunities, in a world where only crime offers a paying occupation.

Yes, you say, but this movie is set in Scotland, not America. True, and the only lesson I can learn from that is that in both countries too many young people correctly understand that society has essentially written them off.

The director of *Sweet Sixteen*, Ken Loach, is political to the soles of his shoes, and his films are often about the difficulties of finding dignity as a working person. His *Bread and Roses* (2000) starred the future Oscar winner Adrien Brody as a union activist in Los Angeles, working to organize a group of nonunion office cleaners and service employees. In *Sweet Sixteen*, there are no jobs, thus no wages.

The movie's hero is a fifteen-year-old named Liam (Martin Compston) who has already been enlisted into crime by his grandfather and his mother's boyfriend. We see the three men during a visit to his mother in prison, where Liam is to smuggle drugs to her with a kiss. He refuses: "You took the rap once for that bastard." But the mother is the emotional and

physical captive of her boyfriend, and goes along with his rules and brutality.

The boy is beaten by the two older men, as punishment, and his precious telescope is smashed. He runs away, finds refuge with his seventeen-year-old sister, Chantelle (Annmarie Fulton), and begins to dream of supporting his mother when she is released from prison. He finds a house trailer on sale for 6,000 pounds, and begins raising money to buy it.

Liam and his best friend, Pinball (William Ruane), have up until now raised money by selling stolen cigarettes, but now he moves up a step, stealing a drug stash from the grandfather and the boyfriend and selling it himself. Eventually he comes to the attention of a local crime lord, who offers him employment—but with conditions, he finds out too late, that are merciless.

Some will recall Loach's great film *Kes* (1969), about a poor English boy who finds joy in training a pet kestrel—a season of self-realization, before a lifetime as a miner down in the pits. *Sweet Sixteen* has a similar character; Liam is sweet, means well, does the best he can given the values he has been raised with. He never quite understands how completely he is a captive of a system that has no role for him.

Yes, he could break out somehow—but we can see that so much more easily than he can. His ambition is more narrow. He dreams of establishing a home where he can live with his mother, his sister, and his sister's child. But the boyfriend can't permit that; it would underline his own powerlessness. And the mother can't make the break with the man she has learned to be submissive to.

The movie's performances have a simplicity and accuracy that are always convincing. Martin Compston, who plays Liam, is a local seventeen-year-old discovered in auditions at his school. He has never acted before, but is effortlessly natural. Michelle Coulter, who plays his mother, is a drug rehab counselor who has also never acted before, and Annmarie Fulton, who plays the sister Chantelle, has studied acting but never appeared in a film.

By using these inexperienced actors (as he often does in his films), Loach gets a spontaneous freshness; scenes feel new because the actors have never done anything like them before, and there are no barriers of style and technique between us and the characters. At the end of *Sweet Sixteen,* we see no hope in the story, but there is hope in the film itself, because to look at the conditions of Liam's life is to ask why, in a rich country, his choices must be so limited. The first crime in his criminal career was the one committed against him by his society. He just followed the example.

Note: The flywheels at the MPAA still follow their unvarying policy of awarding the PG-13 rating to vulgarity and empty-headed violence (2 Fast 2 Furious), while punishing with the R any film like this, which might actually have a useful message for younger viewers.

Swimming Pool ★ ★ ★
R, 102 m., 2003

Charlotte Rampling (Sarah Morton), Ludivine Sagnier (Julie), Charles Dance (John Bosload), Marc Fayolle (Marcel, the Keeper), Jean-Marie Lamour (Franck, the Bartender), Mireille Mossé (Marcel's Daughter). Directed by François Ozon and produced by Olivier Delbosc and Marc Missonnier. Screenplay by Emmanuéle Bernheim and Ozon.

"She threw me a look I caught in my hip pocket," Robert Mitchum's private eye says of Charlotte Rampling's femme fatale in *Farewell, My Lovely* (1975). You don't know what that means, but you know exactly what it means. Rampling has always had the aura of a woman who knows things you would like to do that you haven't even thought of. She played boldly sexual roles early in her career, as in *The Night Porter* (1974), and now, in *Swimming Pool,* a sensuous and deceptive new thriller, she becomes fascinated by a young female predator.

Rampling plays Sarah Morton, a British crime writer whose novels seem to exist somewhere between those of P. D. James and Ruth Rendell. Now she is tired and uncertain, and her publisher offers her a holiday at his French villa. She goes gratefully to the house, shops in the nearby village, and finds she can write again. She is alone except for a taciturn caretaker, who goes into the village at night to live with his daughter, a dwarf who seems older than he is.

Then an unexpected visitor turns up: Julie (Ludivine Sagnier), the daughter her publisher didn't think to tell her about. Sarah is annoyed. Her privacy has been violated. Her privacy and her sense of decorum. Julie is gravid with self-confidence in her emerging sexuality, appears topless at the villa's swimming pool, brings home men to sleep with—men who have nothing in common except Julie's willingness to accommodate them. Sarah is surprised, intrigued, disapproving, curious. She looks down from high windows, spying on the girl who seems so indifferent to her opinion. Eventually she even steals glimpses of the girl's diary.

There is a waiter in the town named Franck (Jean-Marie Lamour), whom Sarah has chatted with and who is perhaps not unaware of her enduring sexuality. But he becomes one of Julie's conquests, too—maybe because Julie senses the older woman's interest in him.

At this point the film takes a turn toward violence, guilt, panic, deception, and concealment, and I will not take the turn with it, because a film like this must be allowed to have its way with you. Let us say that François Ozon, the director and cowriter (with Emmanuéle Bernheim), understands as Hitchcock did the small steps by which a wrong decision grows in its wrongness into a terrifying paranoid nightmare. And how there is nothing more disturbing than trying to conceal a crime that cries out to be revealed.

There is one moment late in the film that displays Rampling's cool audacity more than any other. The caretaker is about to investigate something that is best not investigated. What she does to startle and distract him I will not hint at, but what a startling moment, and what boldness from Rampling!

Ozon is a director who specializes in films where the absent is more disturbing than the present. Rampling starred in his *Under the Sand* (2000), a film about a husband who apparently drowns and a wife who simply refuses to accept that possibility. He also made the terrifying fifty-seven-minute film *See the Sea* (1997), in which the mother of an infant befriends a young woman hitchhiker and begins to feel that it was a dangerous mistake.

Swimming Pool is more of a conventional thriller than those two—or if it is unconventional, that is a development that doesn't affect the telling of most of the story. After it is over you will want to go back and think things through again, and I can help you by suggesting there is one, and only one, interpretation that resolves all of the difficulties, but if I told you, you would have to kill me.

Sylvia ★ ★ ★
R, 110 m., 2003

Gwyneth Paltrow (Sylvia Plath), Daniel Craig (Ted Hughes), Blythe Danner (Aurelia Plath), Lucy Davenport (Doreen), Michael Gambon (Professor Thomas), Jared Harris (Al Alvarez), Eliza Wade (Frieda Hughes), Amira Casar (Assia Wevill). Directed by Christine Jeffs and produced by Alison Owen. Screenplay by John Brownlow.

> Fame will come. Fame especially for you.
> Fame cannot be avoided. And when it
>   comes
> You will have paid for it with your
>   happiness,
> Your husband and your life.

So (perhaps) the spirit of the Ouija board whispered to Sylvia Plath, one evening when she and Ted Hughes were spelling out their futures and she suddenly refused to continue. Hughes uses the speculation to close his poem "Ouija" in *Birthday Letters*, the book of poetry he wrote about his relationship with Plath. It was started after her suicide in 1963 and published after his death in 1998. It broke his silence about Sylvia, which persisted during years when the Plath industry all but condemned him of murder.

But if there was ever a woman who seemed headed for suicide with or without this husband or any other, that woman must have been Plath, and there is a scene in *Sylvia* where her mother warns Hughes of that, not quite in so many words. "The woman is perfected," Plath wrote in a poem named "Edge." "Her dead body wears the smile of accomplishment." Of course, it is foolhardy to snatch words from a poem and apply them to a life as if they make a neat fit, but "Edge" was her last poem, written on February 5, 1963, and six days later she left

out bread and milk for her children, sealed their room to protect them, and put her head in the gas oven.

Christine Jeffs's *Sylvia* is the story of the short life of Plath (1932–1963), an American who came as a student to Cambridge, met the young poet Ted Hughes at a party, was kissed by him before the evening had ended, and famously bit his cheek, drawing blood. It was not merely love at first sight, but passion, and the passion continued as they moved back to Massachusetts, where she was from, and where he taught. Then back to England, and to a lonely cottage in the country, and to the birth of their children, and to her (correct) suspicion that he was having an affair, and to their separation, and to February 11, 1963. He was famous before she was, but the posthumous publication of *Ariel*, her final book of poems, brought greater fame to her. In the simplistic accounting that governs such matters, her death was blamed on his adultery, and in the thirty-five years left to him he lived with that blame.

Hughes became Britain's poet laureate. He married the woman he was having the affair with (she died a suicide, too). He burned one of Plath's journals—he didn't want the children to see it, he said—and was blamed for covering up an indictment of himself. He edited her poetry. He saw her novel *The Bell Jar* to press, and kept his silence. *Birthday Letters* is all he had to write about her. When you read the book you can feel his love, frustration, guilt, anger, sense of futility. When you read her poetry, you experience the clear, immediate voice of a great poet more fascinated by death than life. "Somebody's done for," she wrote in the last line of "Death & Co." (November 14, 1962), and although that line follows bitter lines that are presumably about Hughes, there is no sense that he's done for. It's her.

A movie about their lives was probably inevitable. It will be bracketed with *Iris*, the 2001 film about the British novelist Iris Murdoch, who died of Alzheimer's. I deplored the way that that movie made so much of Iris the wild young thing and Iris the tragic Alzheimer's victim, and left out the middle Iris who was a great novelist—whose work made her life worth filming in the first place. I am not so bothered by the way *Sylvia* focuses on the poet's neurosis, because her life and her work were so entwined. She wrote:

> Dying
> is an art, like everything else.
> I do it exceptionally well.

The film stars Gwyneth Paltrow as Sylvia and Daniel Craig as Ted. They are well cast, not merely because they look something like the originals but because they sound like people who live with words and value them; there's a scene where they hurl quotations at each other, and it sounds like they know what they're doing. Paltrow's great feat is to underplay her character's death wish. There was madness in Sylvia Plath, but of a sad, interior sort, and one of the film's accomplishments is to show in a subtle way how it was so difficult for Hughes to live with her. The movie doesn't pump up the volume. Yes, she does extreme things, like burning his papers and wrecking his office, but he does extreme things, too. Adultery is an extreme thing. In this consider the scene where Hughes meets Mrs. Plath for the first time. Played by Blythe Danner (Paltrow's mother), Aurelia tells her daughter's lover that Sylvia had tried to kill herself and was a person who was capable of getting it right one of these times.

It is difficult to portray a writer's life. *Sylvia* handles that by incorporating a good deal of actual poetry into the movie, read by or to the characters, or in voice-over. It also captures the time of their lives; they were young in the 1950s, and that was another world. England gloomed through postwar poverty, there were shortages of everything, red wine and candles made you a bohemian, poets were still considered ex-tremely important, and Freud was being ported wholesale into literature; poets took their neuroses as their subjects. Literary criticism was taken seriously because it was written in English that could be understood and had not yet imploded into academic puzzle-making. To be good in that time was to be very good, and Plath and Hughes were both first-rate.

There are two questions the movie dodges. We don't know the precise nature of Hughes's cheating, and we don't understand how Plath felt about the children she was leaving behind—why she thought it was acceptable to leave them. The second question has no answer. The answer to the first is supplied by Hughes's critics, who accuse him of womanizing, but the film dilutes that with the suggestion that he simply could not stay in the same house any longer with Sylvia.

Imagine a hypothetical moviegoer who has not heard of Plath or Hughes or read any of their poetry. That would include almost everyone at the multiplex. Is there anything in *Sylvia* for them? Yes, in a way: a glimpse of literary lives at a time when they were more central than they are now, a touching performance by Paltrow, and a portrait of a depressive. But for those who have read the poets and are curious about their lives, *Sylvia* provides illustrations for the biographies we carry in our minds. We see the milieu, the striving, the poverty, the passion, and we hear the poetry, and in the way Paltrow's performance allows Sylvia to grow subtly distant from her daily life, we sense the approach of the end. There is not even the feeling that we are intruding, because the poems of these two poets violated their privacy in a manner both thorough and brutal.

T

The Take ★ ★ ★
NO MPAA RATING, 87 m., 2005

A documentary directed by Avi Lewis and produced by Lewis and Naomi Klein. Screenplay by Klein.

As one documentary after another attacks the International Monetary Fund and its pillaging of the Third World, I wish I knew the first thing about global economics. If these films are as correct as they are persuasive, international monetary policy is essentially a scheme to bankrupt smaller nations and cast their populations into poverty, while multinational corporations loot their assets and whisk the money away to safe havens and the pockets of rich corporations and their friends. But that cannot be, can it? Surely the IMF's disastrous record is the result of bad luck, not legalized theft?

I am still haunted by *Life and Debt* (2001), a documentary explaining how tax-free zones were established on, but not of, Jamaican soil. Behind their barbed-wire fences, Jamaican law did not apply, workers could not organize or strike, there were no benefits, wages were minimal, and factories exported cheap goods without any benefit to the Jamaican economy other than subsistence wages.

Meanwhile, Jamaican agriculture was destroyed by IMF requirements that Jamaica import surplus U.S. agricultural products, which were subsidized by U.S. price supports and dumped in Jamaica for less than local (or American) farmers could produce them for. That destroyed the local dairy, onion, and potato industries. Jamaican bananas, which suffered from the inconvenience of not being grown by Chiquita, were barred from all markets except England. Didn't seem cricket, especially since Jamaican onions were so tasty.

Now here is *The Take*, a Canadian documentary by Avi Lewis and Naomi Klein, shot in Argentina, where a prosperous middle-class economy was destroyed during ten years of IMF policies, as enforced by President Carlos Menem (1989–1999). Factories were closed, their assets were liquidated, and money fled the country, sometimes literally by the truckload. After most of it was gone,

Menem closed the banks, causing panic. Today more than half of all Argentineans live in poverty, unemployment is epidemic, and the crime rate is scary.

In the face of this disaster, workers at several closed factories attempted to occupy the factories, reopen them, and operate them. Their argument: The factories were subsidized in the first place by public money, so if the owners didn't want to operate them, the workers deserved a chance. The owners saw this differently, calling the occupations theft. Committees of workers monitored the factories to prevent owners from selling off machinery and other assets in defiance of the courts. And many of the factories not only reopened, but were able to turn a profit while producing comparable or superior goods at lower prices.

A success story? Yes, according to the Movement of Recovered Companies. No, according to the owners and the courts. But after Menem wins his way into a run-off election he suddenly drops out of the race, a moderate candidate becomes president, the courts decide in favor of the occupying workers, and the movement gains legitimacy. The film focuses on an auto parts plant and ceramics and garment factories that are running efficiently under worker management.

Is this sort of thing a threat to capitalism, or a revival of it? The factories are doing what they did before—manufacturing goods and employing workers—but they are doing it for the benefit of workers and consumers, instead of as an exercise to send profits flowing to top management. This is classic capitalism, as opposed to the management pocket-lining system, which is essentially loot for the bosses and bread and beans for everybody else. Sounds refreshing to anyone who has followed the recent tales of corporate greed in North America. Is it legal? Well, if the factories are closed, haven't the owners abandoned their moral right to them? Especially if the factories were built with public subsidies in the first place?

I wearily anticipate countless e-mails advising me I am a hopelessly idealistic dreamer, and explaining how when the rich get richer, everybody benefits. I will forward the most inspiring of these messages to minimum-wage workers at Wal-Mart, so they will understand why labor unions would be bad for them, while working unpaid overtime is good for the economy. All I know is that the ladies at the garment factory are turning out good-looking clothes, demand is up for Zanon ceramics, and the auto parts factory is working with a worker-controlled tractor factory to make some good-looking machines. I think we can all agree that's better than just sitting around.

Taking Lives ★ ★ ★
R, 103 m., 2004

Angelina Jolie (Illeana Scott), Ethan Hawke (James Costa), Kiefer Sutherland (Martin Asher), Olivier Martinez (Paquette), Tcheky Karyo (Leclair), Gena Rowlands (Mrs. Asher). Directed by D. J. Caruso and produced by Mark Canton and Bernie Goldmann. Screenplay by Jon Bokenkamp, based on the novel by Michael Pye.

Taking Lives is another one of those serial killer thrillers where the madman is not content with murder but must also devise an ingenious and diabolical pattern so that it can be intuited by an investigator who visits the crime scene and picks up his vibes. The vibe jockey this time is FBI agent Illeana Scott (Angelina Jolie), and the first time the other cops see her, she's on her back in the open grave of one of the victims, feeling the pain or sensing the hate or just possibly freaking out the cops so they won't take her for granted.

Although she's American, she's in Canada because her special skills have been called in by the Montreal police. Before you find it odd that the Canadian cops lack a single law enforcement person with her expertise, reflect on this: They don't even know they're not in Montreal. At almost the very moment we hear "Montreal" on the sound track, there is a beautiful shot of the Chateau Frontenac in Quebec City. This is a little like Chicago cops not noticing they are standing beneath Mount Rushmore.

But I quibble. *Taking Lives* is actually an effective thriller, on its modest but stylish level. Agent Scott quickly figures out that there's a

pattern behind the killings—each victim is a few years older than the previous one, and the killer steals his identity, so he must be a person so unhappy to be himself that he has to step into a series of other lives. A moment's reflection might have informed him that his victims, were they not dead, would be keeping up with him chronologically, but maybe, you know what, he's insane.

There's a big break in the case when an artist and gallery owner named James Costa (Ethan Hawke) surprises the killer at work, and is able to supply a high-quality sketch of a suspect. Another development: Mrs. Asher (Gena Rowlands), mother of one of the supposed victims, says the dead body is not her son. Then, not long after, she sees her son quite alive on a ferry. "He's a dangerous man," she tells the cops. He was one of twins, but let's not go there.

The cops include Olivier Martinez and Tcheky Karyo, one of whom resents Scott, while the other respects her. Her methods include devising elaborate time lines of the victims and their photographs, but her greatest gift is to notice little clues. When she spots a draft beneath a bookcase, for example, Nancy Drew is the only other sleuth who would have guessed that behind the case is a hidden door to a secret room.

The movie gets a lot more complicated than I have indicated, and I will not even refer to the last act except to observe that it recycles a detail from *Fatal Attraction* in an ingenious and merciful way. The ending is, in fact, preposterous, depending as thrillers so often do on elaborate plans that depend on the killer hitting all his marks and the cops picking up on all his cues.

For that matter (I will speak cautiously), why is there a person under that bed? To kill Scott, I suppose, but when they struggle, why oh why does she not recognize him? To sacrifice this scene would have meant losing the clue of the draft under the bookcase, but with a little more imagination the hidden room could have been played for creepy chills and occult clues, and we could have lost the big *Carrie* moment. Another excellent question: How can a driver crash a speeding car and be sure who will live and who will die?

This keeps reading like a negative review. I've got to get a grip on myself. See, I *like* movies that make me ask goofy questions like this, as long as they absorb and entertain me, and have actors who can go the distance. Angelina Jolie, like Daryl Hannah, is one of those beauties you somehow never see playing a domesticated housewife. She's more of a freestanding object of wonder, a force of intrigue. Ethan Hawke has the ability to be in a thriller and yet actually seem like a real gallery owner; the art on the walls during his gallery opening looks like a group show from Mrs. Gradgrind's third-grade class, but that's contemporary art for you. And all I can say about Kiefer Sutherland, apart from praise for his good work in the past, is that he seems to have graduated from prime suspect to the parallel category of obvious suspect.

The movie was directed by D. J. Caruso, whose *The Salton Sea* (2002) included the most unforgettably weird villain in recent memory; you remember Vincent D'Onofrio's Pooh-Bear and his little plastic nose. In *Taking Lives,* he understands that a certain genre of thriller depends more upon style and tone than upon plot; it doesn't matter if you believe it walking out, as long as you were intrigued while it was happening.

Taking Sides ★ ★ ★

NO MPAA RATING, 105 m., 2003

Harvey Keitel (Major Steve Arnold), Stellan Skarsgård (Wilhelm Furtwängler), Moritz Bleibtreu (Lieutenant David Wills), Birgit Minichmayr (Emmi Straube), Oleg Tabakov (Oberst Dymshitz), Ulrich Tukur (Helmut Rode), Hanns Zischler (Rudolf Werner), August Zirner (Captain Ed Martin). Directed by István Szabó and produced by Yves Pasquier. Screenplay by Ronald Harwood, based on his play.

The death of Leni Riefenstahl was a reminder of the "de-Nazification" process in which Allied tribunals investigated possible Nazi collaborators. The subjects were not blatant war criminals like those tried at Nuremberg, yet neither were they innocent bystanders. They were German civilians of power or influence whose contribution to the war now had to be evaluated.

Some said they didn't agree with the Nazis and never joined the party, but merely continued in their civilian jobs and tried to remain outside politics. Such a man was Wilhelm Furtwängler, the conductor of the Berlin Philharmonic, who was known as "Hitler's favorite conductor," just as Riefenstahl was his favorite filmmaker. *Taking Sides* is the record of Furtwängler's postwar interrogation at the hands of Steve Arnold, a U.S. Army major who in civilian life had been an insurance investigator, and who approaches the great man as if Furtwängler's restaurant had just burned down and he smelled of kerosene.

Many German artists, Jewish and not, fled their country with the rise of Hitler. Furtwängler's contemporary and rival Otto Klemperer left in 1933 and took over the podium at the Los Angeles Philharmonic. But Furtwängler (Stellan Skarsgård) remained behind, and tells Arnold (Harvey Keitel) he did it out of loyalty to his music, his orchestra, and his nation. Art for him was above politics, he said, and he never joined the Nazi Party or gave the Nazi salute. Ah, says Arnold, but you played at Hitler's birthday party. Furtwängler splits hairs: He played at an event the night before.

To remain in Germany and not be a loyal Nazi was "to walk a tightrope between exile and the gallows," he says. The impression he wants to give is that he never liked Hitler, never liked the Nazis, was loyal to the decent traditions of Germany's past. Yes, but if the Nazis had won—would he have then tried to slip out to some safe haven? That is the great question with Riefenstahl too; we can't help suspecting their postwar dislike for the Nazis was greatly amplified by their defeat.

Taking Sides, based on a play by Ronald Harwood *(The Dresser),* has been directed by the distinguished Hungarian István Szabó, whose great *Mephisto* (1981) tells the story of an actor whose career is promoted by the Nazis he loathes; he plays the roles of his dreams but loses his soul. Szabó himself remained in Hungary during the Soviet occupation, true to his country, loyal to his art, working with the Soviets but hating them, so this material must resonate with him. *Mephisto* was at one level clearly about Soviets, not Nazis, and was about Szabó's own situation. In *Mephisto,* as the title signals, the hero sold his soul to evil. But Furtwängler is a more complicated case, and one of the problems of the film is that it doesn't clearly take sides. Another is that Furtwängler is presented as a man of pride and character, and the American comes across as a vulgar little toady who wants to impress his superiors by bagging the great man: "I'm not after small fish," he brags. "I'm after Moby-Dick." He calls the conductor a "bandleader," and says, "Musicians, morticians, they're all the same."

Major Arnold treats Furtwängler with deliberate contempt, making him wait for hours when he arrives on time for appointments and playing childish games involving the chair he sits in. Sharing his office are an aide and a secretary: Lieutenant David Wills (Moritz Bleibtreu), a German Jew in the American army, and Emmi Straube (Birgit Minichmayr), whose father was one of the Nazi officers killed in a belated uprising against Hitler. Both grew up thinking of Furtwängler as a great man, both are shocked by the contempt with which Arnold treats him, and Emmi finally announces she is leaving: "I've been questioned by the Gestapo—just like that."

Furtwängler's case is a murky one. Yes, he made anti-Semitic comments. But he also helped many Jewish musicians escape to Switzerland and the West. Yes, his recording of Beethoven's *Ninth* was played on German radio after Hitler's death. But of course it was. Yes, he was naive to think that art and politics could be kept separate. But you know how those longhairs are. The de-Nazification courts eventually cleared him, but he remained under a cloud and never toured in America.

The movie is both interesting and unsatisfying. The Keitel performance is over the top, inviting us to side with Furtwängler simply because his interrogator is so vile. There are maddening lapses, as when Furtwängler's rescue of Jewish musicians is mentioned but never really made clear. But Skarsgård's performance is poignant; it has a kind of exhausted passivity, suggesting a man who once stood astride the world and now counts himself lucky to be insulted by the likes of Major Arnold. Furtwängler chose the wrong side, and tried to have it both ways, living at arm's length with the Nazis. Klemperer left not necessarily because he was Furtwängler's moral superior, but because as a Jew it was a matter of survival. Furtwängler, ambitious, vain like many conductors, perhaps under the illusion that Hitler would win, stayed and held his nose.

At the end of a movie that never clearly chooses sides, Szabó finds the perfect image to close with. It's from an old newsreel of the real Furtwängler, conducting the philharmonic for an audience of Nazi officers. After the concert is over, an officer approaches the podium and shakes his hand. And then Furtwängler quietly takes a handkerchief out of his pocket and wipes off his hand. Szabó shows the gesture a second time, in close-up. And there you have it. Better not to shake hands with the devil in the first place.

Tarnation ★ ★ ★
NO MPAA RATING, 88 m., 2004

With Jonathan Caouette, Renee LeBlanc, Adolph and Rosemary Davis, and David Sanin Paz. A documentary directed by Jonathan Caouette and produced by Caouette and Stephen Miller. Screenplay by Caouette.

The child is father of the man.

—Wordsworth

Renee LeBlanc was a beautiful little girl; she was a professional model before she was twelve. Then Renee was injured in a fall from the family garage, and descended into depression. Her parents agreed to shock therapy; in two years she had more than 200 treatments, which her son blames for her mental illness, and for the pain that coiled through her family.

Tarnation is the record of that pain, and a journal about the way her son, Jonathan Caouette, dealt with it—first as a kid, now as the director of this film, made in his early thirties. It is a remarkable film, immediate, urgent, angry, poetic, and stubbornly hopeful. It has been constructed from the materials of a lifetime: old home movies, answering-machine tapes, letters and telegrams, photographs, clippings, new video footage, recent interviews, and printed titles that summarize and explain Jonathan's life. "These fragments I shored against my ruins," T. S. Eliot wrote in *The Waste Land,* and Caouette does the same thing.

His film tells the story of a boy growing up gay in Houston and trying to deal with a schizophrenic mother. He had a horrible childhood. By the time he was six, his father

675

had left the scene, he had been abused in foster homes, and he traveled with his mother to Chicago, where he witnessed her being raped. Eventually they both lived in Houston with her parents, Adolph and Rosemary Davis, who had problems of their own.

Caouette dealt with these experiences by stepping outside himself and playing roles. He got a video camera, and began to dress up and film himself playing characters whose problems were not unlike his own. In a sense, that's when he began making *Tarnation*; we see him at eleven, dressed as a woman, performing an extraordinary monologue of madness and obsession.

He was lucky to survive adolescence. Drugs came into his life, he tried suicide, he fled from home. His homosexuality seems to have been a help, not a hindrance; new gay friends provided a community that accepted this troubled teenager. He was diagnosed with "depersonalization disorder," characterized by a tendency to see himself from the outside, like another person. This may have been more of a strategy than a disorder, giving him a way to objectify his experiences and shape them into a story that made sense. In *Tarnation* he refers to himself in the third person. The many printed titles that summarize the story are also a distancing device; if he had spoken the narration, it would have felt first-person and personal, but the written titles stand back from his life and observe it.

The *Up* series of documentaries began with several children at the age of seven. It revisits them every seven years (most recently, in *42 Up*). The series makes it clear that the child is indeed the father of the man; every one of its subjects is already, at seven, a version of the adult he or she would become. *Tarnation* is like Caouette's version of that process, in which the young boy, play-acting, dressing up, dramatizing the trauma in his life, is able to deal with it. Eventually, in New York, he finds a stable relationship with David Sanin Paz, and they provide a home for Renee, whose troubles are still not over.

The method of the film is crucial to its success. *Tarnation* is famous for having been made for $218 on a Macintosh, and edited with the free iMovie software that came with the computer. Of course, hundreds of thousands

were later spent to clear music rights, improve the sound track, and make a theatrical print (which was invited to play at Cannes). Caouette's use of iMovie is virtuoso, with overlapping wipes, dissolves, saturation, split screens, multiple panes, graphics, and complex montages. There is a danger with such programs that filmmakers will use every bell and whistle just because it is available, but *Tarnation* uses its jagged style without abusing it.

Caouette's technique would be irrelevant if his film did not deliver so directly on an emotional level. We get an immediate, visceral sense of the unhappiness of Renee and young Jonathan. We see the beautiful young girl fade into a tortured adult. We see Jonathan not only raising himself, but essentially inventing himself. I asked him once if he had decided he didn't like the character life had assigned for him to play, and simply created a different character, and became that character. "I think that's about what happened," he said.

Looking at *Tarnation*, I wonder if the movie represents a new kind of documentary that is coming into being. Although home movies have been used in docs for decades, they were almost always, by definition, brief and inane. The advent of the video camera has meant that lives are recorded in greater length and depth than ever before; a film like *Capturing the Friedmans* (2003), with its harrowing portrait of sexual abuse and its behind-the-scenes footage of a family discussing its legal options, would have been impossible before the introduction of consumer video cameras. Jonathan Caouette not only experienced his life, but recorded his experience, and his footage of himself as a child says what he needs to say more eloquently than any actor could portray it or any writer could describe it.

The film leaves some mysteries. Caouette visits his grandfather and asks hard questions, but gets elusive answers; we sense that the truth is lost in the murkiness of memory and denial. The 200 shock treatments destroyed his mother's personality, Caouette believes, and they could have destroyed him by proxy, but in *Tarnation* we see him survive. His is a life in which style literally prevailed over substance; he defeated the realities that would have destroyed him by becoming someone they could not destroy.

Taxi ★
PG-13, 97 m.,2004

Queen Latifah (Belle), Jimmy Fallon (Washburn), Henry Simmons (Jesse), Jennifer Esposito (Lieutenant Marta Robbins), Gisele Bundchen (Vanessa), Ann-Margret (Washburn's Mom). Directed by Tim Story and produced by Luc Besson. Screenplay by Ben Garant, Thomas Lennon, and Jim Kouf.

The taming of Queen Latifah continues in the dismal *Taxi*, as Queen, a force of nature in the right roles, is condemned to occupy a lame-brained action comedy. In a film that is wall-to-wall with idiocy, the most tiresome delusion is that car chases are funny. Movie audiences are bored to the point of sullen exhaustion by car chases, especially those without motivation, and most especially those obviously created with a computer.

As the movie opens, Latifah plays a bicycle messenger who races through Macy's, rattles down the steps of the subway, zips through a train to the opposite platform, goes up a ramp, bounces off the back of a moving truck, lands on the sidewalk, jumps off a bridge onto the top of another truck, and so on. This is, of course, not possible to do, and the sequence ends with that ancient cliché in which the rider whips off a helmet and—why, it's Queen Latifah!

It's her last day on the job. She has finally qualified for her taxi license, and before long we see the customized Yellow Cab she's been working on for three years. In addition to the titanium supercharger given by her fellow bike messengers as a farewell present (uh, huh), the car has more gimmicks than a James Bond special; a custom job like this couldn't be touched at under $500,000, which of course all bike messengers keep under the bed. Her dream, she says, is to be a NASCAR driver. In her Yellow Cab?

Then we meet a cop named Washburn (Jimmy Fallon), who is spectacularly incompetent, blows drug busts, causes traffic accidents, and has not his badge, but his driver's license confiscated by his chief, Lieutenant Marta Robbins (Jennifer Esposito), who used to be his squeeze, but no more. When he hears about a bank robbery, he commandeers Queen Latifah's cab, and soon she is racing at speeds well over 100 mph down Manhattan streets in pursuit of the robbers, who are, I kid you not, four supermodels who speak Portuguese. Luckily, Queen Latifah speaks Portuguese, too, because, I dunno, she used to be the delivery girl for a Portuguese take-out joint.

Oh, this is a bad movie. Why, oh why, was the lovely Ann-Margret taken out of retirement to play Fallon's mother, an alcoholic with a blender full of margaritas? Who among the writers (Ben Garant, Thomas Lennon, and Jim Kouf) thought it would be funny to give Latifah and the cop laughing gas, so they could talk funny? What's with Latifah's fiancé, Jesse (Henry Simmons), who looks like a *GQ* cover boy and spends long hours in fancy restaurants waiting for Queen Latifah, who is late because she is chasing robbers, etc.? Is there supposed to be subtle chemistry between Latifah and the cop? It's so subtle, we can't tell. (He's afraid to drive because he had a trauma during a driving lesson, so she coaches him to sing while he's driving, and he turns into a stunt driver and a pretty fair singer. Uh, huh.)

All these questions pale before the endless, tedious chase scenes, in which cars do things that cars cannot do, so that we lose all interest. If we were cartoons, our eyes would turn into X-marks. What is the *point* of showing a car doing 150 miles an hour through midtown Manhattan? Why is it funny that the cop causes a massive pile-up, with the cars in back leapfrogging onto the top of the pile? The stunt must have cost a couple of hundred thousand dollars; half a dozen indie films could have been made for that money. One of them could have starred Queen Latifah.

Latifah has been in movies since 1991, but first flowered in F. Gary Gray's *Set It Off* (1996), about four black working women who rob a bank. She was wonderful in *Living Out Loud* (1998), as a torch singer who has an unexpectedly touching conversation with a lovelorn elevator operator (Danny DeVito). She walked away with her scenes in *Chicago*.

Why was it thought, by Latifah or anyone, that she needed to make a movie as obviously without ambition, imagination, or purpose as *Taxi*? Doesn't she know that at this point in her career she should be looking for some lean and hungry Sundance type to put her in a zero-budget masterpiece that could win her the Oscar? True, it could turn out to be a flop. But better to flop while trying to do something good than flop in something that could not be good, was never going to be good, and only gets worse as it plows along.

Team America: World Police ★
R, 98 m., 2004

With the voices of Trey Parker, Matt Stone, Kristen Miller, Daran Norris, and Phil Hendrie. Directed by Trey Parker and produced by Scott Rudin, Matt Stone, Parker, and Pam Brady. Screenplay by Stone, Parker, and Brady.

What're you rebelling against, Johnny? Whaddya got?
    —Marlon Brando in *The Wild One*

If this dialogue is not inscribed over the doors of Trey Parker and Matt Stone, it should be. Their *Team America: World Police* is an equal opportunity offender, and waves of unease will flow over first one segment of their audience, and then another. Like a cocky teenager who's had a couple of drinks before the party, they don't have a plan for who they want to offend, only an intention to be as offensive as possible.

Their strategy extends even to their decision to use puppets for all of their characters, a choice that will not be universally applauded. Their characters, one-third life-size, are clearly artificial, and yet there's something going on around the mouths and lips that looks halfway real, as if they were inhabited by the big faces with moving mouths from Conan O'Brien. There are times when the characters risk falling into the Uncanny Valley, that rift used by robot designers to describe robots that alarm us by looking too humanoid.

The plot seems like a collision at the screenplay factory between several half-baked world-in-crisis movies. Team America, a group not unlike the Thunderbirds, bases its rockets, jets, and helicopters inside Mount Rushmore, which is hollow, and race off to battle terrorism wherever it is suspected. In the opening sequence, they swoop down on Paris and fire on caricatures of Middle East desperadoes, missing most of them but managing to destroy the Eiffel Tower, the Arch of Triumph, and the Louvre.

Regrouping, the team's leader, Spottswoode (voice by Daran Norris), recruits a Broadway actor named Gary to go undercover for them. When first seen, Gary (voice by Parker) is starring in the musical *Lease*, and singing "Everyone Has AIDS." Ho, ho. Spottswoode tells Gary: "You're an actor with a double major in theater and world languages! Hell, you're the perfect weapon!" There's a big laugh when Gary is told that, if captured, he may want to kill himself, and is supplied with a suicide device I will not reveal.

Spottswoode's plan: Terrorists are known to be planning to meet at "a bar in Cairo." The Team America helicopter will land in Cairo, and four uniformed team members will escort Gary, his face crudely altered to look "Middle Eastern," to the bar, where he will go inside and ask whazzup. As a satire on our inability to infiltrate other cultures, this will do, I suppose. It leads to an ill-advised adventure where in the name of fighting terrorism, Team America destroys the pyramids and the Sphinx. But it turns out the real threat comes from North Korea and its leader, Kim Jong Il (voice also by Parker), who plans to unleash "9/11 times 2,356."

Opposing Team America is the Film Actors Guild, or F.A.G., ho, ho, with puppets representing Alec Baldwin, Tim Robbins, Matt Damon, Susan Sarandon, and Sean Penn (who has written an angry letter about the movie to Parker and Stone about their comments, in *Rolling Stone*, that there is "no shame in not voting"). No real point is made about the actors' activism; they exist in the movie essentially to be ridiculed for existing at all, I guess. Hans Blix, the UN chief weapons inspector, also turns up, and has a fruitless encounter with the North Korean dictator. Some of the scenes are set to music, including such tunes as "Pearl Harbor Sucked and I Miss You" and "America, F***, Yeah!"

If I were asked to extract a political position from the movie, I'd be baffled. It is neither for nor against the war on terrorism, just dedicated to ridiculing those who wage it and those who oppose it. The White House gets a free pass, since the movie seems to think Team America makes its own policies without political direction.

I wasn't offended by the movie's content so much as by its nihilism. At a time when the world is in crisis, the response of Parker, Stone, and company is to sneer at both sides—indeed, at anyone who takes the current world situation seriously. They may be right that some of us are puppets, but they're wrong that all of us are fools, and dead wrong that it doesn't matter.

Tears of the Sun ★ ★ ★
R, 121 m., 2003

Bruce Willis (A. K. Waters), Monica Bellucci (Dr. Lena Hendricks), Cole Hauser (Red Atkins), Tom Skerritt (Bill Rhodes), Eamonn Walker (Zee Pettigrew), Nick Chinlund (Slo Slowenski), Fionnula Flanagan (Nurse Grace), Johnny Messner (Kelly Lake). Directed by Antoine Fuqua and produced by Ian Bryce, Mike Lobell, Arnold Rifkin, and Bruce Willis. Screenplay by Patrick Cirillo and Alex Lasker.

Tears of the Sun is a film constructed out of rain, cinematography, and the face of Bruce Willis. These materials are sufficient to build a film almost as good as if there had been a better screenplay. In a case like this, the editor often deserves the credit for concealing what is not there with the power of what remains.

The movie tells the story of a Navy Seals unit that is dropped into a Nigerian civil war zone to airlift four U.S. nationals to safety. They all work at the same mission hospital. The priest and two nuns refuse to leave. The doctor, widow of an American, is also hostile at first ("Get those guns out of my operating room!"), but then she agrees to be saved if she can also bring her patients. She cannot. There is no room on the helicopters for them, and finally Waters (Bruce Willis) wrestles her aboard.

But then he surprises himself. As the chopper circles back over the scene, they see areas already set afire by arriving rebel troops. He cannot quite meet the eyes of the woman, Dr. Lena Hendricks (Monica Bellucci). "Let's turn it around," Willis says. They land, gather about twenty patients who are well enough to walk, and call for the helicopters to return.

But he has disobeyed direct orders, his superior will not risk the choppers, and they will all have to walk through the jungle to Cameroon to be rescued. Later, when it is clear Willis's decision has placed his men and mission in jeopardy, one of his men asks, "Why'd you turn it around?" He replies: "When I figure that out, I'll let you know." And later: "It's been so long since I've done a good thing—the right thing."

There are some actors who couldn't say that dialogue without risking laughter from the audience. Willis is not one of them. His face smeared with camouflage and glistening with rain, his features as shadowed as Marlon Brando's in *Apocalypse Now,* he seems like a dark, violent spirit sent to rescue them from one hell only to lead them into another. If we could fully understand how he does what he does, we would know a great deal about why some actors can carry a role that would destroy others. Casting directors must spend a lot of time thinking about this.

The story is very simple, really. Willis and his men must lead the doctor and her patients through the jungle to safety. Rebel troops pursue them. It's a question of who can walk faster or hide better; that's why it's annoying that Dr. Hendricks is constantly telling Waters, "My people have to rest!" Presumably (a) her African patients from this district have some experience at walking long distances through the jungle, and (b) she knows they are being chased by certain death, and can do the math.

Until it descends into mindless routine action in the climactic scenes, *Tears of the Sun* is essentially an impressionistic nightmare, directed by Antoine Fuqua, the director who emerged with the Denzel Washington cop picture *Training Day.* His cinematographers, Mauro Fiore and Keith Solomon, create a visual world of black-green saturated wetness, often at night, in which characters swim in and out of view as the face of Willis remains their implacable focal point. There are few words; Willis scarcely has 100 in the first hour. It's all about the conflict between a trained professional soldier and his feelings. There is a subtext of attraction between the soldier and the woman doctor (who goes through the entire film without thinking to button the top of her blouse), but it is wisely left as a subtext.

This film, in this way, from beginning to end,

679

might have really amounted to something. I intuit "input" from producers, studio executives, story consultants, and the like, who found it their duty to dumb it down by cobbling together a conventional action climax. The last half-hour of *Tears of the Sun*, with its routine gun battles, explosions, and machine-gun bursts, is made from off-the-shelf elements. If we can see this sort of close combat done well in a film that is really about it, like Mel Gibson's *We Were Soldiers*, why do we have to see it done merely competently, in a movie that is not really about it?

Where the screenplay originally intended to go, I cannot say, but it's my guess that at an earlier stage it was more thoughtful and sad, more accepting of the hopelessness of the situation in Africa, where "civil war" has become the polite term for genocide. The movie knows a lot about Africa, lets us see that, then has to pretend it doesn't.

Willis, for example, has a scene in the movie where, as a woman approaches a river, he emerges suddenly from beneath the water to grab her, silence her, and tell her he will not hurt her. This scene is laughable, but effective. Laughable, because (a) hiding under the water and breathing through a reed, how can the character know the woman will approach the river at precisely that point? and (b) since he will have to spend the entire mission in the same clothes, is it wise to soak all of his gear when staying dry is an alternative?

Yet his face, so fearsome in camouflage, provides him with a sensational entrance and the movie with a sharp shudder of surprise. There is a way in which movies like *Tears of the Sun* can be enjoyed for their very texture. For the few words Willis uses, and the way he uses them. For the intelligence of the woman doctor, whose agenda is not the same as his. For the camaraderie of the Navy Seals unit, which follows its leader even when he follows his conscience instead of orders. For the way the editor, Conrad Buff, creates a minimalist mood in setup scenes of terse understatement; he doesn't hurry, he doesn't linger. If only the filmmakers had been allowed to follow the movie where it wanted to go—into some existential heart of darkness, I suspect—instead of detouring into the suburbs of safe Hollywood convention.

Tell Them Who You Are ★ ★ ★ ½
R, 95 m., 2005

With Mark Wexler, Haskell Wexler, Peter Bart, Verna Bloom, Billy Crystal, Michael Douglas, Conrad L. Hall, Julia Roberts, Jane Fonda, Sidney Poitier, John Sayles, Albert Maysles, Tom Hayden, Studs Terkel, Norman Jewison, Dennis Hopper, Milos Forman, and Paul Newman. Directed and produced by Mark Wexler. Screenplay by Robert DeMaio and Wexler.

I have known Haskell Wexler for thirty-six years. When Haskell had a rough cut of *Medium Cool*, his docudrama shot at the 1968 Democratic Convention, he asked me to see it after Paramount got cold feet about distribution. Like many people since then, I thought it was a powerful and courageous film. Haskell and I became friends over the years. I remember swimming in Jamaica with Haskell and his wife, the actress Rita Taggart. I remember going through *Blaze* a frame at a time with Haskell at the Hawaii Film Festival, and taking apart *Casablanca* with him on Dusty Cohl's Floating Film Festival.

So he is a friend. He is also a great cinematographer. And he is an activist for progressive causes, a sometime director of features and documentaries, and the subject of a new documentary named *Tell Them Who You Are*. The documentary is by his son, Mark, who tells his father very clearly: "I'm not a fan. I'm a son." Mark made a previous doc, *Me and My Matchmaker*, which I found fascinating; he meets a matchmaker, thinks it would be interesting to watch her at work, asks her to find him a wife, and gets involved in a process neither he nor the matchmaker could possibly have anticipated.

Mark's new doc is frankly intended, we learn, as an attempt to get to know his father better. The child of Haskell's second marriage, he has an almost Oedipal rivalry that has, among other things, led him to politics that are the opposite of his father's. Haskell, now in his eighties, agreed to participate with misgivings, and is not very happy with the results.

Two of Haskell's longtime friends, the director John Sayles and producer Maggie Renzi, told me Mark has "issues" with his father and the film doesn't reflect Haskell's big-hearted kindness. Then again, they share Haskell's left-wing beliefs. Mark, perhaps not coincidentally, does not. "Haskell gets up every morning and he rants against what's happening in the world," says Haskell's fellow documentarian Pam Yates, with admiration. In the film, he takes Mark along to a peace rally in San Francisco, where he seems to know everybody.

All fathers and sons have issues. If *Tell Them Who You Are* had been a sunny doc about how great the old man was, it wouldn't be worth seeing—and wouldn't be the kind of film Haskell himself makes. What Mark does, better perhaps than either he or his father realizes, is to capture some aspects of a lifelong rivalry that involves love but not much contentment.

Mark remembers his father advising him, "Tell them you're Haskell Wexler's son," which would have done him some good in Hollywood, but Mark has been trying for years to be defined as *not* simply Haskell's son, and this film about his father is paradoxically part of that struggle. This generational thing has been going on for a while with the Wexlers; as a young man, Haskell organized a strike against his own father's factory. And, although he came from a well-to-do family, we learn that Haskell volunteered for the Merchant Marines in World War II and survived a torpedoed ship. This is a man who has been there.

"I don't think there's a movie that I've been on that I wasn't sure I could direct it better," Haskell says in the film. We learn of a few films he was fired from when the directors felt he was making that all too clear; one of them was *One Flew Over the Cuckoo's Nest,* and we get the memories of director Milos Forman ("He was sharing his frustrations with the actors") and producer Michael Douglas ("He reminds me of my own father: critical and judging").

There were also films he walked away from on matters of principle. After one, he told me the director was lazy and didn't treat people with respect. Haskell isn't an obedient hired hand, but a strong-willed artist who gets the admiration of strong directors like John Sayles (*Limbo, The Secret of Roan Inish*), Norman Jewison (*In the Heat of the Night*), Mike Nichols (*Who's Afraid of Virginia Woolf*), and

Hal Ashby (*Bound for Glory*). He won Oscars for his work on *Virginia Woolf* and *Bound for Glory,* and was nominated three other times.

On the other hand, Francis Ford Coppola replaced him on *The Conversation* (after Haskell had finished the legendary opening sequence). Haskell's version: He was working too quickly for Coppola, who wasn't prepared. Coppola's version: unstated. And Haskell believes he shot more than half of Terrence Malick's *Days of Heaven,* which Nestor Almendros won an Oscar for.

After the lights went up at the Toronto Film Festival premiere of the doc, there was Norman Jewison sitting across the aisle and observing, "He could be a son of a bitch." The way he said it, it sounded affectionate.

What Haskell is sure of is that he knows more about making documentaries than Mark does. He tells Mark he should have employed a sound man for some scenes shot at a party, and he turns out to be right. The two men get into a heated argument when Mark tries to set up a shot with his father standing in front of a sunset, and Haskell thinks his son is valuing form over content; forget the sunset, he says, because "I desperately want to say something." On the other hand, he criticizes Mark for having him "say everything" instead of using the technique of telling through showing.

Mark provides a good overview of his father's career: the Academy Awards, the great films, the legendary reputation. He talks to some who love him and some who don't. We learn of Haskell's business partnership and close friendship with Conrad L. Hall, another great cinematographer; Mark sometimes felt closer to Conrad than to his own father, and strangely enough, Conrad's son, also a great cinematographer, felt closer to Haskell.

Then there is the issue of Mark's mother, Marian, Wexler's wife for thirty years, now a victim of Alzheimer's. I've known Haskell only with his third wife, Rita, and I see a couple glowing with love. Mark resents his father for leaving his mother. But then we see probably the film's strongest scene, and it involves Haskell visiting Marian in a nursing home. Marian doesn't recognize him, but Haskell speaks softly to her: "We've got secrets, you, me. We've got secrets. We know things about each other that nobody else in the world knows." There are tears in his eyes.

Certainly only a family member could have had access to such a scene. Possibly Haskell did not expect it to be in the documentary. But it reflects well on him, and on Mark for including it. There is this: Haskell agreed to be in the film, to some degree in order to help his son. And although Mark shows the tension between himself and his father, he also shows a willingness to look beyond the surface of his resentments. Jane Fonda says of them: "Intimacy was not their gift." They are still working at it. This is a film about a relationship in progress.

Ten ★ ★

NO MPAA RATING, 94 m., 2003

Mania Akbari (The Woman), Amin Maher (Her Son), Roya Arabshahi (Passenger), Katayoun Taleidzadeh (Passenger), Mandana Sharbaf (Passenger), Amene Moradi (Passenger). Directed by Abbas Kiarostami and produced by Kiarostami and Marin Karmitz. Screenplay by Kiarostami.

I am unable to grasp the greatness of Abbas Kiarostami. His critical reputation is unmatched: His *Taste of Cherry* (1997) won the Palme d'Or at Cannes, and *The Wind Will Carry Us* (1999) won the Golden Lion at Venice. And yet his films, for example his latest work *Ten,* are meant not so much to be watched as to be written about; his reviews make his points better than he does.

Any review must begin with simple description. *Ten* consists of ten scenes set in the front seat of a car. The driver is always the same. Her passengers include her son, her sister, a friend, an old woman, and a prostitute. The film is shot in digital video, using two cameras, one focused on the driver, the other on the passenger. The cameras are fixed. The film has been described as both fiction and documentary, and is both: What we see is really happening, but some of it has been planned, and Amin, for example, does not seem to be the driver's son.

Kiarostami's method, I learn from Geoff Andrew's review in *Sight & Sound,* was to audition real people, choose his actors, talk at length with them about their characters and dialogue, and then send them out in the car without him, to play their characters (or perhaps themselves) as they drove the streets and the cameras watched. Beginning with twenty-three hours of footage, he ended with this ninety-four-minute film.

Now you might agree that is a provocative and original way to make a movie. Then I might tell you that *Taste of Cherry* was also set entirely in the front seat of a car—only in that film Kiarostami held the camera and sat alternatively in the seat of the driver and the passenger. And that *The Wind Will Carry Us* was about a man driving around trying to find a place where his cell phone would work. You might observe that his method has become more daring, but you would still be left with movies about people driving and talking.

Ah, but what do we learn about them, and about modern Iran? Andrew, who thinks this is Kiarostami's best film, observes the woman complaining about Iran's "stupid laws" that forbid divorce unless she charges her husband with abuse or drug addiction. He observes that the movie shows prostitution exists in Iran, even though it is illegal. The old woman argues that the driver should try prayer, and she does, showing the nation's religious undercurrent. The friend removes her scarf to show that she has shaved her head, and this is transgressive because women are not allowed to bare their heads in public. And little Amin, the son, seems like a repressive Iranian male in training, having internalized the license of a male-dominant society to criticize and mock his mother.

All very well. But to praise the film for this is like praising a child for coloring between the lines. Where is the reach, the desire to communicate, the passion? If you want to see the themes in *Ten* explored with power and frankness in films of real power, you would turn away from Kiarostami's arid formalism and look instead at a film like Tahmineh Milani's *Two Women* (1998) or Jafar Panahi's *The Circle* (2001), which have the power to deeply move audiences, instead of a willingness to alienate or bore them.

Anyone could make a movie like *Ten.* Two digital cameras, a car, and your actors, and off you go. Of course, much would depend on the actors, what they said, and who they were playing (the little actor playing Amin is awesomely self-confident and articulate on the screen, and effortlessly obnoxious). But if this approach were used for a film shot in Europe or America, would it be accepted as an entry at Cannes?

I argue that it would not. Part of Kiarostami's appeal is that he is Iranian, a country whose films it is somewhat daring to praise. Partly, too, he has a lot of critics invested in his cause, and they do the heavy lifting. The fatal flaw in his approach is that no ordinary moviegoer, whether Iranian or American, can be expected to relate to his films. They exist for film festivals, film critics, and film classes.

The shame is that more accessible Iranian directors are being neglected in the overpraise of Kiarostami. Brian Bennett, who runs the Bangkok Film Festival, told me of attending a Tehran Film Festival with a fair number of Western critics and festival directors. "The moment a film seemed to be about characters or plot," he said, "they all got up and raced out of the room. They had it fixed in their minds that the Iranian cinema consisted of minimalist exercises in style, and didn't want to see narrative films." Since storytelling is how most films work and always have, it is a shame that Iranian stories are being shut out of Western screenings because of a cabal of dilettantes.

The Terminal ★ ★ ★ ½
PG-13, 121 m., 2004

Tom Hanks (Viktor Navorski), Catherine Zeta-Jones (Amelia Warren), Stanley Tucci (Frank Dixon), Chi McBride (Joe Mulroy), Diego Luna (Enrique Cruz), Barry Shabaka Henley (Ray Thurman), Kumar Pallana (Gupta Rajan), Zoe Saldana (Dolores Torres). Directed by Steven Spielberg and produced by Laurie MacDonald, Walter F. Parkes, and Spielberg. Screenplay by Sacha Gervasi and Jeff Nathanson.

Steven Spielberg and Tom Hanks have made, in *The Terminal*, a sweet and delicate comedy, a film to make you hold your breath, it is so precisely devised. It has big laughs, but it never seems to make an effort for them; it knows exactly, minutely, and in every detail who its hero is, and remains absolutely consistent to what he believes and how he behaves.

The hero is named Viktor Navorski. He has arrived in a vast American airport just as his nation, Krakozia, has fallen in a coup. Therefore his passport and visa are worthless, his country no longer exists, and he cannot go forward or go back. Dixon, the customs official, tells him he is free to remain in the International Arrivals Lounge, but forbidden to step foot on American soil.

This premise could have yielded a film of contrivance and labored invention. Spielberg, his actors, and writers (Sacha Gervasi and Jeff Nathanson) weave it into a human comedy that is gentle and true, that creates sympathy for all of its characters, that finds a tone that will carry them through, that made me unreasonably happy.

There is a humanity in its humor that reminds you of sequences in Chaplin or Keaton where comedy and sadness find a fragile balance. It has another inspiration, the work of the French actor-filmmaker Jacques Tati. Spielberg gives Hanks the time and space to develop elaborate situations like those Tati was always getting himself into, situations where the lives of those around him became baffling because of Tati's own profound simplicity.

In *The Terminal*, Viktor Navorski's unintended victim is Dixon, the customs and immigrations official, played by Stanley Tucci with an intriguing balance between rigidity and curiosity. He goes by the rules, but he has no great love of the rules. Sometimes the rules are cruel, but he takes no joy in the cruelty. As Navorski lingers day after day in the arrivals lounge, Dixon's impatience grows. "He's found out about the quarters," he says one day, staring grimly at a surveillance monitor. Navorski is returning luggage carts to the racks to collect the refund, and spending his profits on food.

Navorski is a man unlike any Dixon has ever encountered—a man who is exactly who he seems to be and claims to be. He has no guile, no hidden motives, no suspicion of others. He trusts. The immigration service, and indeed the American legal system, has no way of dealing with him because Viktor does not do, or fail to do, any of the things the system is set up to prevent him from doing, or not doing. He has slipped through a perfect logical loophole. *The Terminal* is like a sunny Kafka story, in which it is the citizen who persecutes the bureaucracy.

Dixon wants Navorski out of the terminal because, well, he can't live there forever, but he shows every indication of being prepared to. "Why doesn't he escape?" Dixon asks his underlings, as Navorski stands next to an open door that Dixon has deliberately left unguarded. Dixon's plan is to pass Navorski on to another jurisdiction: "You catch a small fish and unhook him very carefully. You place him back in the water, so that someone else can have the pleasure of catching him."

Dixon could arrest Navorski unfairly, but refuses to: "He has to break the law." Navorski, who speaks little English but is learning every day, refuses to break the law. He won't even lie when Dixon offers him political asylum. "Are you afraid of returning to your country?" "Not afraid," he says simply. "But aren't you afraid of *something?*" "I am afraid for . . . ghosts," says Navorski. The terminal is filled with other characters Navorski gets to know, such as Amelia the flight attendant (Catherine Zeta-Jones), who is having an affair with a married man and finds she can open her heart to this strange, simple man. And Gupta the janitor (Kumar Pallana), who leaves the floor wet and watches as passengers ignore the little yellow warning pyramids and slip and fall. "This is the only fun I have," he says. And a food services employee (Diego Luna), who is in love with an INS official (Zoe Saldana) and uses Navorski as his go-between.

These friends and others have secret social lives in the terminal, feasting on airline food, playing poker. Navorski becomes their hero when he intervenes in a heart-rending case. A Russian man has medicine he needs to take to his dying father, but Dixon says it must stay in the United States. The man goes berserk, a hostage situation threatens, but Navorski defuses the situation and finds a solution that would have pleased Solomon.

Tom Hanks does something here that many actors have tried to do and failed. He plays his entire role with an accent of varying degrees of impenetrability, and it never seems like a comic turn or a gimmick, and he never seems to be doing it to get a laugh. He gets laughs, but his acting and the writing are so good they seem to evolve naturally. That is very hard to do. He did the same thing in *Forrest Gump,* and Navorski is another character that audiences will, yes, actually love. The screenplay also sidesteps various hazards that a lesser effort would have

fallen to, such as a phony crisis or some kind of big action climax. *The Terminal* doesn't have a plot; it *tells a story.* We want to know what will happen next, and we care.

Most of this movie was shot on a set, a vast construction by production designer Alex McDowell. We're accustomed these days to whole cities and planets made of computerized effects. Here the terminal with all of its levels, with its escalators and retail shops and food courts and security lines and passenger gates actually exists. The camera of the great Janusz Kaminski can go anywhere it wants, can track and crane and pivot, and everything is real. Not one viewer in one hundred will guess this is not a real airline terminal.

Spielberg and Hanks like to work together *(Saving Private Ryan, Catch Me If You Can),* and here they trust each other with tricky material. It is crucial, perhaps, that they're so successful as to be unassailable, which allows them to relax and take their time on a production that was burning dollars every second. Others might have heard the clock ticking and rushed or pushed, or turned up the heat by making the Dixon character into more of a villain and less of a character study. Their film has all the time in the world. Just like Viktor Navorski. He isn't going anywhere.

Terminator 3: Rise of the Machines ★ ★ ½

R, 109 m., 2003

Arnold Schwarzenegger (Terminator), Kristanna Loken (T-X), Nick Stahl (John Connor), Claire Danes (Kate Brewster), David Andrews (Robert Brewster), Mark Famiglietti (Scott Petersen). Directed by Jonathan Mostow and produced by Mario F. Kassar and Andrew G. Vajna. Screenplay by John Brancato and Michael Ferris.

In the dawning days of science fiction, there was a chasm between the concept-oriented authors and those who churned out space opera. John W. Campbell Jr.'s *Astounding Science Fiction,* later renamed *Analog* to make the point clear, was the home of the brainy stuff. Bug-eyed monsters chased heroines in aluminum brassieres on the covers of *Amazing, Imagination,* and *Thrilling Wonder Stories.*

The first two Terminator movies, especially the second, belonged to Campbell's tradition of sci-fi ideas. They played elegantly with the paradoxes of time travel, in films where the action scenes were necessary to the convoluted plot. There was actual poignancy in the dilemma of John Connor, responsible for a world that did not even yet exist. The robot Terminator, reprogrammed by Connor, provided an opportunity to exploit Isaac Asimov's Three Laws of Robotics.

But that was an age ago, in 1991. *T2* was there at the birth of computer-generated special effects, and achieved remarkable visuals, especially in the plastic nature of the Terminator played by Robert Patrick, who was made of an infinitely changeable substance that could reconstitute itself from droplets. Now we are in the latter days of CGI, when the process is used not to augment action scenes but essentially to create them. And every week brings a new blockbuster and its $50 million–plus gross, so that audiences don't so much eagerly anticipate the latest extravaganza as walk in with a show-me attitude.

Terminator 3: Rise of the Machines is made in the spirit of these slick new action thrillers and abandons its own tradition to provide wall-to-wall action in what is essentially one long chase and fight punctuated by comic, campy, or simplistic dialogue. This is not your older brother's *Terminator*. It's in the tradition of *Thrilling Wonder Stories; T2* descended from Campbell's *Analog*. The time-based paradoxes are used arbitrarily and sometimes confusingly and lead to an enormous question at the end: How, if that is what happens, are the computer-based machines of the near future created?

Perhaps because the plot is thinner and more superficial, the characters don't have the same impact, either. Nick Stahl plays John Connor, savior of mankind, in the role created by the edgier, more troubled Edward Furlong. Stahl seems more like a hero than a victim of fate, and although he tells us at the outset he lives "off the grid" and feels "the weight of the future bearing down on me," he seems more like an all-purpose action figure than a man who really (like Furlong) feels trapped by an impenetrable destiny.

Early in the film he meets a veterinarian named Kate Brewster (Claire Danes), and after they find they're on the same hit list from the killers of the future, they team up to fight back and save the planet. They are pursued by a new-model Terminator named T-X, sometimes called the Terminatrix, and played by the icy-eyed Kristanna Loken. I know these characters are supposed to be blank-faced and impassive, but somehow Robert Patrick's evil Terminator was ominous and threatening, and Loken's model is more like the mannequin who keeps on coming; significantly, she first appears in the present after materializing in a Beverly Hills shop window. The movie doesn't lavish on her the astonishing shape-shifting qualities of her predecessor.

To protect John and Kate, Terminator T-101 arrives from the future, played by Arnold Schwarzenegger, who has embodied this series from the very first. The strange thing is, this is not the same Terminator he played in *T2*. "Don't you remember me?" asks Connor. But "hasta la vista, baby" doesn't ring a bell. T-101 does, however, inexplicably remember some old Schwarzenegger movies and at one point intones, "She'll be back."

The movie has several highly evolved action set pieces, as we expect, and there's a running gag involving the cumbersome vehicles that are used. The Terminatrix commandeers a huge self-powered construction crane to mow down rows of cars and buildings, a fire truck is used at another point, and after Kate, John, and the Terminator find a cache of weapons in the coffin of John's mother, a hearse is put into play—at one point, in a development that is becoming a cliché, getting its top sheared off as it races under a truck trailer, so that it becomes a convertible hearse. (Why do movies love convertibles? Because you can see the characters.)

Kate's father is a high-up muckety-muck whose job is a cover for top-secret security work, and that becomes important when the three heroes discover that a nuclear holocaust will begin at 6:18 P.M. Can they get to the nation's underground weapons control facility in time to disarm the war? The chase leads to a genuinely creative development when a particle accelerator is used to create a magnetic field so powerful it immobilizes the Terminatrix.

The ending of the film must remain for you

to discover, but I will say it seems perfunctory—more like a plot development than a denouement in the history of humanity. The movie cares so exclusively about its handful of characters that what happens to them is of supreme importance, and the planet is merely a backdrop.

Is *Terminator 3* a skillful piece of work? Indeed. Will it entertain the Friday-night action crowd? You bet. Does it tease and intrigue us like the earlier films did? Not really. Among recent sci-fi pictures, *Hulk* is in the tradition of science fiction that concerns ideas and personalities, and *Terminator 3* is dumbed down for the multiplex hordes.

The Texas Chainsaw Massacre no stars
R, 98 m., 2003

Jessica Biel (Erin), Jonathan Tucker (Morgan), Eric Balfour (Kemper), Andrew Bryniarski (Leatherface), Erica Leerhsen (Pepper), Mike Vogel (Andy), R. Lee Ermey (Sheriff Hoyt), Terrence Evans (Old Monty). Directed by Marcus Nispel and produced by Michael Bay and Mike Fleiss. Screenplay by Scott Kosar, based on the screenplay by Kim Henkel and Tobe Hooper.

The new version of *The Texas Chainsaw Massacre* is a contemptible film: vile, ugly, and brutal. There is not a shred of a reason to see it. Those who defend it will have to dance through mental hoops of their own devising, defining its meanness and despair as "style" or "vision" or "a commentary on our world." It is not a commentary on anything except the marriage of slick technology with the materials of a geek show.

The movie is a remake of, or was inspired by, the 1974 horror film by Tobe Hooper. That film at least had the raw power of its originality. It proceeded from Hooper's fascination with the story and his need to tell it. This new version, made by a man who has previously directed music videos, proceeds from nothing more than a desire to feed on the corpse of a once-living film. There is no worthy or defensible purpose in sight here: The filmmakers want to cause disgust and hopelessness in the audience. Ugly emotions are easier to evoke and often more commercial than those that contribute to the ongoing lives of the beholders.

The movie begins with grainy "newsreel" footage of a 1974 massacre (the same one as in the original film; there are some changes, but this is not a sequel). Then we plunge directly into the formula of a Dead Teenager Movie, which begins with living teenagers and kills them one by one. The formula can produce movies that are good, bad, funny, depressing, whatever. This movie, strewn with blood, bones, rats, fetishes, and severed limbs, photographed in murky darkness, scored with screams, wants to be a test: Can you sit through it? There were times when I intensely wanted to walk out of the theater and into the fresh air and look at the sky and buy an apple and sigh for our civilization, but I stuck it out. The ending, which is cynical and truncated, confirmed my suspicion that the movie was made by and for those with no attention span.

The movie doesn't tell a story in any useful sense, but is simply a series of gruesome events that finally are over. It probably helps to have seen the original film in order to understand what's going on, since there's so little exposition. Only from the earlier film do we have a vague idea of who the people are in this godforsaken house, and what their relationship is to one another. The movie is eager to start the gore and unwilling to pause for exposition.

I like good horror movies. They can exorcise our demons. *The Texas Chainsaw Massacre* doesn't want to exorcise anything. It wants to tramp crap through our imaginations and wipe its feet on our dreams. I think of filmgoers on a date, seeing this movie and then—what? I guess they'll have to laugh at it, irony being a fashionable response to the experience of being had.

Certainly they will not be frightened by it. It recycles the same old tired thriller tools that have been worn out in countless better movies. There is the scary noise that is only a cat. The device of loud sudden noises to underline the movements of half-seen shadows. The van that won't start. The truck that won't start. The car that won't start. The character who turns around and sees the slasher standing right behind her. One critic writes, "Best of all, there was not a single case of 'She's only doing that [falling, going into a scary space, not picking up the gun] because she's in a thriller.'" Huh?

Thirteen

Nobody does anything in this movie for any other reason. There is no reality here. It's all a thriller.

There is a controversy involving Quentin Tarantino's *Kill Bill: Volume 1*, which some people feel is "too violent." I gave it four stars, found it kind of brilliant, felt it was an exhilarating exercise in nonstop action direction. The material was redeemed, justified, illustrated, and explained by the style. It was a meditation on the martial arts genre, done with intelligence and wit. *The Texas Chainsaw Massacre* is a meditation on the geek-show movie. Tarantino's film is made with grace and joy. This movie is made with venom and cynicism. I doubt that anybody involved in it will be surprised or disappointed if audience members vomit or flee. Do yourself a favor. There are a lot of good movies playing right now that can make you feel a little happier, smarter, sexier, funnier, more excited—or more scared, if that's what you want. This is not one of them. Don't let it kill ninety-eight minutes of your life.

Thirteen ★ ★ ★ ½
R, 100 m., 2003

Evan Rachel Wood (Tracy), Nikki Reed (Evie), Holly Hunter (Melanie), Jeremy Sisto (Brady), Brady Corbet (Mason), Deborah Kara Unger (Brooke), Kip Pardue (Luke). Directed by Catherine Hardwicke and produced by Jeffrey Levy-Hinte and Michael London. Screenplay by Hardwicke and Nikki Reed.

"The two worst years of a woman's life," writes Nell Minow, "are the year she is thirteen and the year her daughter is." There are exceptions to the rule; I once attended a thirteenth birthday party at which daughter and mother both seemed to be just fine, thanks, but it is hard to imagine a worse year than the one endured by the characters in *Thirteen*. This is the frightening story of how a nice girl falls under the influence of a wild girl and barely escapes big, big, big trouble, by which I mean drugs, crime, unwanted pregnancies, and other hazards, which some teenagers seem inexplicably eager to experience.

That the horrors in this movie are worse than those found in the lives of most thirteen-year-olds, I believe and hope. It is painful enough to endure them at any age, let alone in a young and vulnerable season when life should be wondrous. But I believe such things really happen to some young teenagers, because at Sundance, I met Nikki Reed, who cowrote the screenplay when she was thirteen, and was fourteen when she played Evie, the movie's trouble maker. In real life Reed was the good girl; here, as a wild and seductive bad influence, she's so persuasive and convincing I'm prepared to believe the movie is a truthful version of real experiences.

Evie is the most popular girl in the seventh grade because of her bold personality, her clothes and accessories (mostly stolen), and her air of knowing more about sex than a thirteen-year-old should. The school's value system is suggested by the fact that some of the students are working on a "project" about J-Lo. One of Evie's admirers is Tracy (Evan Rachel Wood), a good student who hangs around with a couple of unpopular girls and wants to trade up. Evie is cruel to her ("Call me," she says, and gives her the wrong number). But when Tracy steals a purse and hands over the money, Evie takes her on a shopping spree and soon the girls are such close friends that Evie has, essentially, moved into Tracy's room.

Tracy lives with her divorced mother, Melanie, played by Holly Hunter in a performance where the character vibrates with the intensity of her life. Melanie lives in a sprawling house she can't afford, inherited from a marriage with a husband who is behind on his child support; she runs a beauty salon in her kitchen, and her house seems to be a drop zone for friends, acquaintances, their children, and their needs ("A $2 tip," she complains after one mob leaves, "and they ate half the lasagna").

Melanie is a recovering alcoholic, hanging onto AA for dear life, and with a boyfriend named Brady (Jeremy Sisto) who is in the program, too, although Melanie has painful memories from when he wasn't. Melanie is sober, but it would be fair to say her life is still unmanageable, and although she loves Tracy and protects her with a fierce mother's love, she's clueless about what's going on behind that bedroom door.

Evie's history is often described but somehow never very clear. She lives with someone named Brooke (Deborah Unger), who is not quite her mother, not quite her guardian, allegedly her cousin, more like her spaced-out roommate. Evie tells stories of violence and sexual abuse when she was young, and while we have no trouble believing such things could have happened, it's impossible to be sure when she's telling the truth.

Although Evie is trouble enough on her own, she reaches critical mass after she moves in with Tracy. Perhaps only a thirteen-year-old like Nikki Reed could have found the exact note in dialogue where the mother tries to get answers and information and is rejected and ignored like an unsolicited telephone call. You might doubt that a girl could conceal from her mother the fact that she has had her tongue and navel pierced, but this movie convinced me of that, and a lot more.

There are moments when you want to cringe at the danger these girls are in. They slip through the bedroom window and hang out on Hollywood Boulevard, they experiment sexually with kids older and tougher than they are, they all but rape "Luke the lifeguard boy" (Kip Pardue), a neighbor who accuses them, accurately, of being jailbait. They want to fly close to danger without getting hurt, and we wait for them to learn how hard and cruel the world can be.

When I met Reed at Sundance she was with the film's director, Catherine Hardwicke, who told one of those "only in southern California" stories: Hardwicke was dating Reed's father, Reed was having problems, Hardwicke suggested she keep a journal, she wrote a screenplay instead, Hardwicke collaborated on a final draft and became the director. Of Reed it can only be said that, like Diane Lane at a similar age, she has the gifts to do almost anything. Although this is Hardwicke's directing debut, she has many important credits as a production designer (*Tombstone, Three Kings, Vanilla Sky*), and the movie is smoothly professional, especially in the way it choreographs the comings and goings in Holly Hunter's chaotic household. Hunter gave a famous performance in *Broadcast News* (1987) as a hyperactive news producer who was forever trying to keep all her plates spinning. Her problems here are similar. We know exactly how she feels as she trips on a loose kitchen tile and starts tearing up "the goddamn $1.50-a-square-foot floor."

Who is this movie for? Not for most thirteen-year-olds, that's for sure. The R rating is richly deserved, no matter how much of a lark the poster promises. Maybe the film is simply for those who admire fine, focused acting and writing; *Thirteen* sets a technical problem that seems insoluble, and meets it brilliantly, finding convincing performances from its teenage stars, showing a parent who is clueless but not uncaring, and a world outside that bedroom window that has big bad wolves, and worse.

Note: Watching Thirteen, *I remembered another movie with the same title. David D. Williams's* Thirteen *(1997) tells the story of a thirteen-year-old African-American girl named Nina, who runs away from home and causes much concern for her mother, neighbors, and the police before turning up again. The movie is set in a more innocent place, a small Virginia town, and has a heroine who has not grown up too fast but is still partly a child, as she should be. The film, which I showed at my Overlooked Film Festival, is apparently not available on video; it would be a comfort after this one.*

13 Going on 30 ★ ★
PG-13, 97 m., 2004

Jennifer Garner (Jenna Rink), Mark Ruffalo (Matt Flamhaff), Judy Greer (Lucy Wyman), Andy Serkis (Richard Kneeland), Kathy Baker (Beverly Rink), Phil Reeves (Wayne Rink), Christa B. Allen (Young Jenna Rink). Directed by Gary Winick and produced by Susan Arnold, Gina Matthews, and Donna Roth. Screenplay by Cathy Yuspa, Josh Goldsmith, and Niels Mueller.

Jennifer Garner is indeed a charmer, but she's the victim of a charmless treatment in *13 Going on 30*, another one of those body-switch movies (think *Big, Vice Versa, Freaky Friday*, etc.) in which a child magically occupies an adult body. The director, Gary Winick, came out of Sundance with *Tadpole* (2003), a movie in which a sixteen-year-old boy was seduced by a forty-year-old woman, and some of us wondered how well that plot would have worked with a sixteen-year-old girl and a forty-year-old man. Now Winick finds out, by supplying a thirteen-year-old girl with a thirty-year-old body and a boyfriend who's a professional hockey star. Their big makeout scene goes wrong when she thinks he's "gross," and we fade to black, mercifully, before we find out what happens then. Can you be guilty of statutory rape caused by magical body-switching?

The movie introduces us to Jenna Rink when she's a teenager (played by Christa B. Allen), who allows the most popular girls in school to push her around because she wants to be just like them. (There's a much superior version of this angle in *Mean Girls*.) She throws a party in her rec room and the girls play a nasty trick on her, which inspires her to be cruel to her only true friend, Matt, a chubby kid who lives next door and adores her.

Then she's sprinkled with magic dust (I think we have to let the movie get away with this), and discovers that she is thirty, lives in New York, is an editor of a magazine named *Poise,* and looks like Jennifer Garner. Her snotty high school classmate Lucy (Judy Greer) now works with her on the magazine, and they're friends, sort of, although the movie teaches us that career women will betray each other to get ahead.

In the best examples of this genre, there are funny scenes in which adult actors get to act as if they're inhabited by kids. Tom Hanks did this about as well as it can be done in *Big,* and I also liked Judge Reinhold in *Vice Versa,* and of course Jamie Lee Curtis in the 2003 version of *Freaky Friday.* Strangely, *13 Going on 30* doesn't linger on scenes like that, maybe because Jenna is established in a high-powered Manhattan world where she has to learn fast. The result is that most of the movie isn't really about a thirteen-year-old in an adult body, but about a power struggle at the magazine, and Jenna's attempts to renew her friendship with Matt (now played by Mark Ruffalo).

He's not cooperative. Apparently her missing seventeen years all actually occurred; it's just that she can't remember them. And after the disastrous party in the rec room, she never talked to Matt again, so why should he believe she's any different now? She's desperate, because she has no real friends, but Matt is engaged to be married, and what happens to the time line to solve that dilemma would make *Eternal Sunshine of the Spotless Mind* look as linear as a Doris Day romance.

Logical quibbles are, of course, irrelevant with a movie like this. You buy the magic because it comes with the territory. What I couldn't buy was the world of the magazine office, and the awkward scenes in which high-powered professionals don't seem to notice that they're dealing with a thirteen-year-old mind. Jenna's bright idea to redesign the magazine is so spectacularly bad that it's accepted, I suppose, only because the screenwriters stood over the actors with whips and drove them to it.

The writers, by the way, are Cathy Yuspa, Josh Goldsmith, and Niels Mueller. Yuspa and Goldsmith wrote the vastly superior office comedy *What Women Want* (2000), in which Mel Gibson was able to read the minds of the women in his office. This time there are no minds worth reading. Although we understand why Jenna is attracted to the adult Matt (who has undergone a transition from pudgy to handsome), the movie never really deals with (1) whether he fully comes to grips with the fact that this is the *same* girl he knew at thirteen, and (2) how or why or whether or when a thirteen-year-old can successfully fall in love with a thirty-year-old man, with everything that would entail (in life, anyway, if not in this movie). There are so many emotional and sexual puzzles to tap-dance around, this should have been a musical.

This Girl's Life ★ ★ ★
R, 101 m., 2004

Juliette Marquis (Moon), James Woods (Pops), Kip Pardue (Kip), Tomas Arana (Aronson), Michael Rapaport (Terry), Rosario Dawson (Martine), Isaiah Washington (Shane), Ioan Gruffudd (Daniel), Cheyenne Silver (Cheyenne). Directed by Ash and produced by Ash, Chris Hanley, and David Hillary. Screenplay by Ash.

This Girl's Life is an imperfect movie with so many moments of truth that you forgive its stumbles. You also note that it's probably of historical value, because it centers on the first performance of an actress who is going to be a big star. Juliette Marquis, Ukrainian-born, Chicago-raised, is a great beauty, yes, but beauty is not hard to find in the movies. What she has is courage and an uncanny screen presence. She spends a lot of the movie talking directly to the audience, and she looks at the camera clear-eyed and calmly confident, and we feel she is ... *there.*

She plays a porn star named Moon, about twenty-three years old, who works for a Website that trains cameras on her house twenty-four hours a day. Whatever happens there, subscribers see. A lot happens (although she seems to be away from home for most of the movie). Moon went into porn with her eyes open, eagerly. She likes sex, and likes bold and risky situations, and she's articulate about her motives and feelings. There's a scene where she talks straight to the camera while ... well, while otherwise engaged, and her focus never wavers.

She's a porn star, but *This Girl's Life* isn't a porn movie. We get a lot of R-rated nudity and dialogue, but the story isn't about sex; it's about the complications of Moon's life. She's worried about her father, Pops (James Woods), who has Parkinson's. She cares for him, races home when he needs her, worries about him. She's frightened by an AIDS scare in the industry. She is also conflicted about a guy, a blind date named Kip (Kip Pardue), who didn't know she is a porn star and doesn't know if he's all right with that.

The movie surrounds her with friends, including the real porn star Cheyenne Silver, playing herself. They get together for a birthday party for Pops, which I think he enjoys, although Woods is good at showing a man disappearing into the sadness of his disease. A few days later, one of her friends confides that her boyfriend has proposed. Before the friend says yes, she wants Moon to do her a favor: test him out. See if she can seduce him. If she can, the would-be bride will know he's not the faithful type.

All of this sounds like the material of a trashy sex comedy, but *This Girl's Life* plays it thoughtfully and doesn't avoid real issues. Intrigued by her power in the original situation, Moon takes out an ad for a "Sexual Investigation Agency." She'll test your husband or boyfriend for faithfulness. This turns out to be a very bad idea, as she finds out when a car dealer (Michael Rapaport) flunks the test, finds out his wife hired her, shows her his son's photo, and says if she tells the wife, he'll lose his family. Does she want to be responsible for that?

The cards are stacked in her favor in her "investigations," since Moon is sexy and sub-

tle, and it would take a good and true man to resist her. She finds, indeed, that the more she exercises her sexual power, the less sure she is of herself; her early certainty shades into doubt and discontent. Should she renew her contract with Aronson (Tomas Arana), the porn king? He's played as a well-spoken, not uncharming businessman who is realistic about his business, not sleazy, and can be persuasive. But Moon's trip to an AIDS clinic is the sort of experience that makes you think.

This Girl's Life has a ragged construction and an ending that's patched together. I'm not sure I understood exactly why Moon's love for sex translated into employment in porn. And James Woods's performance, good as it is, is almost too strong for a supporting role in a movie that is, after all, not about him.

The film was made by a British writer-director named Ash, whose earlier films *Bang* (1995) and *Pups* (1999) showed real talent. The first starred Darling Narita as a woman who is abused by a cop, ties him up, steals his uniform and motorcycle, and learns a great deal about Los Angeles by impersonating a police officer. (Ash plugged her into real situations with people who didn't know they were in a movie.) *Pups* was about a couple of middle-school kids who find a gun and decide to stick up a bank. In those films and in *This Girl's Life,* Ash likes to place his characters in risky situations where a lot depends on their being able to act their way to safety.

Hollywood talks about good early roles as "calling cards." With this movie, Juliette Marquis proves she has the right stuff. She has completed two more films (one starring Steven Seagal, not necessarily a good sign), and after the casting directors see *This Girl's Life* I have a feeling she won't be looking for work.

Thunderbirds ★ ½
PG, 94 m., 2004

Bill Paxton (Jeff Tracy), Anthony Edwards (Brains), Sophia Myles (Lady Penelope), Ben Kingsley (The Hood), Brady Corbet (Alan Tracy), Soren Fulton (Fermat), Vanessa Anne Hudgens (Tin-Tin), Ron Cook (Parker), Philip Winchester (Scott Tracy), Lex Shrapnel (John Tracy), Dominic Colenso (Virgil Tracy), Ben Torgersen

(Gordon Tracy). Directed by Jonathan Frakes and produced by Tim Bevan, Eric Fellner, and Mark Huffam. Screenplay by William Osborne and Michael McCullers.

I run into Bill Paxton and Ben Kingsley occasionally, and have found them to be nice people. As actors they are in the first rank. It's easy to talk to them, and so the next time I run into one of them I think I'll just go ahead and ask what in the h-e-double-hockey-sticks they were *thinking* when they signed up for *Thunderbirds*. My bet is that Paxton will grin sheepishly and Kingsley will twinkle knowingly, and they'll both say the movie looked like fun, and gently steer the conversation toward other titles. *A Simple Plan,* say, or *House of Sand and Fog.*

This is a movie made for an audience that does not exist, at least in the land of North American multiplexes: fans of a British TV puppet show that ran from 1964 to 1966. "While its failure to secure a U.S. network sale caused the show to be canceled after thirty-two episodes," writes David Rooney in *Variety,* "the 'Supermarionation' series still endures in reruns and on DVD for funky sci-fi geeks and pop culture nostalgists." I quote Rooney because I had never heard of the series and, let's face it, never have you. Still, I doubt that "funky" describes the subset of geeks and nostalgists who like it. The word "kooky" comes to mind, as in "kooky yo-yos."

Thunderbirds is to *Spy Kids* as Austin Powers is to James Bond. It recycles the formula in a campy 1960s send-up that is supposed to be funny. But how many members of the preteen audience for this PG movie are knowledgeable about the 1960s Formica and polyester look? How many care? If the film resembles anything in their universe, it may be the Jetsons.

A solemn narrator sets the scene. The Thunderbirds, we learn, are in real life the Tracy family. Dad is Jeff Tracy (Paxton), a billionaire who has built his "secret" headquarters on a South Pacific island, where his secret is safe because no one would notice spaceships taking off. His kids are named after astronauts: Scott, John, Virgil, and Gordon, and the youngest, Alan (Brady Corbet), who is the hero and thinks he is old enough to be trusted with the keys to the family rocket. His best friend, Fermat (Soren Fulton), is named after

the theorem, but I am not sure if their best friend, Tin-Tin (Vanessa Anne Hudgens), is named after the French comic book hero or after another Tin-Tin. It's a common name.

The plot: The Hood (Kingsley) is a villain who (recite in unison) seeks world domination. His plan is to rob the Bank of London. The Thunderbirds are distracted when a Hood scheme endangers their permanently orbiting space station (did I mention Dad was a billionaire?), and when Dad and the older kids rocket off to save it, the coast is clear—unless plucky young Alan, Fermat, and Tin-Tin can pilot another rocket vehicle to London in time to foil them. In this they are helped by Lady Penelope (Sophia Myles) and her chauffeur (Ron Cook).

As the Tracys rocket off to rescue the space station, I was reminded of the Bob and Ray radio serial where an astronaut, stranded in orbit, is reassured that "our scientists are working to get you down with a giant magnet." Meanwhile, his mother makes sandwiches, which are rocketed up to orbit. ("Nuts!" he says. "She forgot the mayonnaise!")

Among the big *Thunderbirds* f/x scenes are one where the kids use their rocket ship to rescue a monorail train that has fallen into the Thames. This and everything else the Thunderbirds do seems to be covered on TV, but try to control yourself from wondering where the TV cameras can possibly be, and how they got there.

Paxton was in *Spy Kids 2* and at least knows this territory. Let it be said that he and Kingsley protect themselves, Paxton by playing a true-blue 1960s hero who doesn't know his lines are funny, and Sir Ben by trying his best to play no one at all while willing himself invisible. A movie like this is harmless, I suppose, except for the celluloid that was killed in the process of its manufacture, but as an entertainment it will send the kids tip-toeing through the multiplex to sneak into *Spider-Man 2.*

Till Human Voices Wake Us ★ ½
R, 101 m., 2003

Guy Pearce (Sam Franks), Helena Bonham Carter (Ruby), Lindley Joyner (Young Sam Franks), Brooke Harman (Silvy Lewis). Directed by Michael Petroni and produced by Thomas Augsberger, Matthias Emcke, Shana Levine, Dean Murphy, Nigel Odell, and David Redman. Screenplay by Petroni.

Till Human Voices Wake Us could have been a poem by Edgar Allen Poe, a short story by Stephen King, or a *Twilight Zone* episode by Rod Serling. Poe would have liked the part where the heroine drifts on her back down the river under the starry skies. King would have the hero gasping when he finds only his coat in the boat. And Serling would have informed us, "A man named T. S. Eliot once hinted that you can drown in your sleep and not have the nightmare until you wake up in the morning."

None of these artists would have, however, made this movie. That is because film makes it literal, and the story is too slight to bear up under the weight. *The Twilight Zone* could have done it as video, because it would have represented 20 minutes of running time (instead of 101), and been photographed in that stylized 1950s black-and-white television purity where the exterior shot of every residential street seemed to leave room for a mushroom cloud.

The movie tells a story that kept its key hidden for a long time in the Australian version, which began with two young people in a rural district and only switched over, much later, to a story about two adults (Guy Pearce and Helena Bonham Carter). At least in Australia you thought for half an hour or so that the whole story was about the teenagers (Lindley Joyner and Brooke Harman). In the version shown in the rest of the world, the two stories are intercut, which of course gives away the game, since Young Sam Franks grows up to be Sam Franks, and therefore, according to the Principle of the Unassigned Character, the mysterious girl he meets on the train must therefore be . . .

I am not giving anything away. This is the first movie I have seen where the plot device is revealed by the *fact* of the first flashback. Young Sam has journeyed on into adulthood with a heavy burden of guilt, which he hints at in a lecture he gives on psychology. Freud will be of no help to him, however. Maybe Jung would have some ideas, or Dionne Warwick.

The title comes from *The Love Song of J. Alfred Prufrock,* by T. S. Eliot, which is the favorite poem of—well, I was about to say both

women. It looks to me like Silvy, the young woman, is reading from the first edition, which would have been possible in Australia in those days. So is the older woman, named Ruby, at a time when the book was worth about $35,000. A book like that, you take the paperback when you go swimming.

But I am being way too cynical about a film that after all only wants to be sad and bittersweet, redemptive and healing. It doesn't really matter what your literal interpretation is for what happens in that adult summer, since there is a sense in which it doesn't really happen anyway, and the result would be the same no matter what the explanation.

There must still be a kind of moony young adolescent girl for which this film would be enormously appealing, if television has not already exterminated the domestic example of that species. The last surviving example in the wild was run over last week by a snowmobile in Yellowstone.

Timeline ★ ★
PG-13, 116 m., 2003

Paul Walker (Chris), Frances O'Connor (Kate), Gerard Butler (Andre Marek), Billy Connolly (Edward Johnston), Neal McDonough (Gorgdon), Ethan Embry (David Stern), Anna Friel (Lady Claire), David Thewlis (Robert Doniger). Directed by Richard Donner and produced by Donner, Lauren Shuler Donner, and Jim Van Wyck. Screenplay by Jeff Maguire and George Nolfi, based on the novel by Michael Crichton.

Timeline is inspired by a Michael Crichton story that's not so much about travel between the past and the present as about travel between two movie genres. After opening on an archeological dig (evoking memories of *Indiana Jones, The Exorcist* and *The Omen*), it's a corporate thriller crossed with a medieval swashbuckler. The corporation has discovered a way to beam objects from one place to another, and has big plans: It wants to put Federal Express out of business. Alas, its teleportation machine intersects with a wormhole, and inadvertently sends a group of scientists back into 14th-century France.

So far I don't have a problem. I'll accept any

premise that gets me into a good movie. But why can the screenwriters Jeff Maguire and George Nolfi think of nothing more interesting for their heroes to do than immerse themselves in a medieval swashbuckler? Why travel six hundred years into the past just so you can play "I Capture the Castle"? The movie follows the modern formula in which story is secondary to action, and the plot is essentially a frame for action scenes. I understand this is not the case with the Crichton novel, unread by me.

The movie has been directed by Richard Donner, who has given me some splendid times at the movies. His *Superman* remains one of the great superhero epics, his *Lethal Weapon* made my best ten list and *Lethal Weapon 2* was almost as good, and he made a lighthearted version of *Maverick* with Mel Gibson that brought cheer to the Western genre. But here I think he got off on the wrong foot, with a story whose parts don't fit.

Donner and his wife, the producer Lauren Shuler Donner, attended the Chicago press screening of *Timeline* and made some comments. When filmmakers do that, I kind of want to duck behind the seat in front of me. I'd rather see the movie cold. They told of their long odyssey to get the movie made, the corporate struggles that almost sank it, the difficult locations, their determination in spite of everything. Because of those travails, I wish the movie had been a triumph, but it's not.

Donner made it a special point that the movie doesn't contain nearly as many special effects as we might assume. When besieging armies hurl fireballs into a castle, for example, those are real fireballs—not the computer-generated version, as in *Gladiator*. Twenty years ago a filmmaker might have boasted that he had used computers for his effects. Now he gets points for using the traditional methods. The problem is, unless the shots involved are so bad they call attention to themselves (and these are certainly not), it's not whether we're watching real fireballs or fake fireballs but whether we care about the fireballs.

I didn't. I felt too much of the movie consisted of groups of characters I didn't care about, running down passageways and fighting off enemies and trying to get back to the present before the window of time slams shut (there's even a big clock ticking off the seconds). Just once I'd like to see a time-travel movie inspired by true curiosity about the past, instead of by a desire to use it as a setting for action scenes.

Together ★ ★ ★ ½
PG, 116 m., 2003

Tang Yun (Liu Xiaochun), Liu Peiqi (Liu Cheng), Chen Hong (Lili), Wang Zhiwen (Professor Jiang), Chen Kaige (Professor Yu Shifeng), Zhang Qing (Yu Lin). Directed by Chen Kaige and produced by Chen Hong, Kaige, Li Bolun, Yan Xiaoming, and Yang Buting. Screenplay by Kaige and Xue Xiao Lu.

Here is a movie not embarrassed by strong, basic emotions like love and ambition. It has the courage to face them head-on, instead of edging up to them through irony, or disarming them with sitcom comedy. Chen Kaige's *Together* is a movie with the nerve to end with melodramatic sentiment—and get away with it, because it means it. Lots of damp eyes in the audience.

The movie tells the story of Liu Xiaochun (Tang Yun), a thirteen-year-old violin prodigy who lives in a provincial town with his father, Liu Cheng (Liu Peiqi). His father is a cook who decides Xiaochun must advance his studies in Beijing—and so he takes them both there, with his meager savings hidden in his red peasant's hat. Because he is so naive, so direct, so obviously exactly who he is, and because his son really is talented, the uncultured father is able to convince a violin teacher named Jiang (Wang Zhiwen) to take the boy as a student.

Jiang is almost a recluse, a once-talented pianist whose heart was broken by a girl, and who has retreated to a shabby apartment with his cats and his dirty laundry. As he tutors the boy, the boy tutors him, lecturing him on his hygiene and self-pity. The two become close friends, but one day Xiaochun's father decides it is time for him to move up to a better teacher—the famous Yu Shifeng, played by director Chen Kaige himself. Jiang is a realist and agrees with this change, and the leave-taking between the two friends is handled in a touching, unexpected way.

The big city is exciting for young Xiaochun, who meets a woman in her twenties named Lili, played by Chen Hong, who in real life is the director's wife. She tips him for carrying her bag, hires him to play at a party, takes him shopping, and befriends him. She is also involved in a complex and traumatic episode when the boy sells his precious violin (all that is left from his mother, he is told) to buy her a coat.

The young violinist's goal is to be chosen by Professor Yu for an important international contest. A girl named Yu Lin (Zhang Qing), another of Yu's students, is his rival, and both the professor and the girl tell him secrets that force him to reevaluate his world and values. Torn between recognition and his love for his father, he finds a solution in the last scene that is physically impossible (unless the symphony orchestra is playing very, very loudly) but is the perfect outcome for the story—an emotional high point that's dramatic and heartwarming.

The movie is also a story about the old and new China, set in old and new Beijing. Professor Jiang lives in a crowded quarter of dwellings that lean cozily on each other, its streets filled with bicycles and gossip. People know each other. Professor Yu lives in a sterile modern building with Western furnishings. When he suggests that Xiaochun leave his father and live with him, he is essentially asking him to leave an older, more human China, and enter a modern world of ambition, success, and media marketing.

Lili, the pretty neighbor, is caught between those two worlds. She is clearly a good person, yet not above using her beauty to support herself. In this PG-rated movie, however, it's a little hard to figure out exactly what her profession is. I did some Web research and discovered she is "a goodhearted neighbor [who] offers some of the film's most tender moments" (U.S. Conference of Catholic Bishops), "a gold-digging glamour-puss" *(Village Voice)*, or "the proverbial hooker with the heart of gold" *(New York Post)*. Morality is in the eye of the beholder.

For Chen Kaige, *Together* is a comeback after the extravagant *Temptress Moon* (1996) and *The Emperor and the Assassin* (1999). His earlier credits include *Yellow Earth,* a touching story of a soldier collecting rural folk songs, and the masterful *Farewell My Concubine,* about two members of the Peking Opera who survive through a time of political tumult.

Together is powerful in an old-fashioned, big-studio kind of way; Hollywood once had the knack of making audience-pleasers like this, before it got too clever for its own good. Strange, but moviegoers who avoid "art films" and are simply in the mood for a good, entertaining movie would be better off with this Chinese film than with most of the multiplex specials.

Tokyo Godfathers ★ ★ ★
PG-13, 90 m., 2004

With the voices of: Toru Emori (Gin), Yoshiaki Umegaki (Hana), and Aya Okamoto (Miyuki). Directed by Satoshi Kon and produced by Masao Maruyama. Screenplay by Kon and Keiko Nobumotu.

In Japan, animation is not seen as the exclusive realm of children's and family films, but is often used for adult, science fiction, and action stories, where it allows a kind of freedom impossible in real life. Some Hollywood films strain so desperately against the constraints of the possible that you wish they'd just caved in and gone with animation (*Torque* is an example).

Now here is *Tokyo Godfathers,* an animated film both harrowing and heartwarming, about a story that will never, ever, be remade by Disney. It's about three homeless people—an alcoholic, a drag queen, and a girl of about eleven—who find an abandoned baby in the trash on a cold Christmas Eve, and try for a few days to give it a home. The title makes a nod to John Ford's *3 Godfathers* (1948), where three desperados (led by John Wayne) rescue a baby from its dying mother on Christmas Eve and try to raise it, at one point substituting axle grease for baby oil.

The three urban drifters live in a Tokyo of ice and snow, where they have fashioned a temporary shelter of cardboard and plywood, and outfitted it with all the comforts of home, like a portable stove. Here they've formed a family of sorts, but each has a story to tell, and during the movie they all tell them.

Gin, the alcoholic, claims to have been a bicycle racer who abandoned his family after losing everything by gambling. Hana, the transvestite, has felt like an outsider since birth. Miyuki, the little girl, ran away from home after a fight with her father. The others tell her she should return, but she's afraid to. And then the cries of the infant alert them, and their rescue of the little girl is a catalyst that inspires each of them to find what's good and resilient within themselves.

The movie was cowritten and directed by Satoshi Kon, whose *Perfect Blue* and *Millennium Actress* have been among the best-received and most popular anime titles. Unlike Hayao Miyazaki *(Spirited Away, My Neighbor Totoro)*, his style doesn't approach full-motion animation, but uses the simplified approach of a lot of anime, with simple backgrounds and characters who move and talk in a stylized way that doesn't approach realism. If you see this style for thirty seconds you're likely to think it's constrained, but in a feature film it grows on you and you accept it, and your imagination makes it expand into an acceptable version of the world.

The movie's story is melodrama crossed with pathos, sometimes startling hard-boiled action, and enormous coincidence. The streets of Tokyo seem empty and grim as the three godparents protect the child and eventually begin a search for its true parents. And the story involving those parents is more complicated than we imagine. There are scenes in an abandoned house, in an alley of homeless dwellings, in a drugstore, that seem forlorn and hopeless, and then other scenes of surprising warmth, leading up to a sensational ending and a quite remarkable development in which two lives are saved in a way possible only in animation.

Tokyo Godfathers is not appropriate for younger viewers, and I know there are older ones who don't fancy themselves sitting through feature-length adult animation from Japan. But there's a world there to be discovered. And sometimes, as with this film and the great *Grave of the Fireflies,* the themes are so harrowing that only animation makes them possible. I don't think I'd want to see a movie in which a real baby had the adventures this one has.

Torque ★ ★ ½
PG-13, 81 m., 2004

Martin Henderson (Cary Ford), Ice Cube (Trey Wallace), Monet Mazur (Shane), Jay Hernandez (Dalton), Christina Milian (Nina), Jaime Pressly (China), Matt Schulze (Henry). Directed by Joseph Kahn and produced by Brad Luff and Neal H. Moritz. Screenplay by Matt Johnson.

Long ago, at the dawn of motorcycle pictures, a critic who had been working for only four months encountered a film named *Hells Angels on Wheels* (1967). It was about a war between motorcycle gangs, and its cast included an actor named Jack Nicholson, whom the critic did not even name, although he found room to mention Adam Roarke, John Garwood, and Sabrina Scharf. The critic, observing that "sometimes good stuff creeps into exploitation pictures just because nobody cares enough to keep it out," made the following points:

— "The characters are authentically surly, irresponsible, mean, coarse, and human."

— Sabrina Scharf "makes you wonder how she keeps her makeup on while raising hell with the angels."

— The "accomplished camera work" includes "one shot where the camera moves in and out of focus through a field of green grass and then steals slowly across one of the big, brutal cycles. The contrast has an impact equal to David Lean's similar shots in *Doctor Zhivago* (remember the frosty window fading into the field of flowers?)."

— "The film is better than it might have been, and better than it had to be. Take it on its own terms and you might find it interesting."

Reader, that young critic was me. The film's director was Richard Rush, who went on to make *The Stunt Man.* The young cinematographer was "Leslie Kovacs," who, under his true Hungarian name of László, went on to shoot *Five Easy Pieces* with Jack Nicholson, and fifty other films, including some of the best photographed of his time.

Today I went to see *Torque,* also a motorcycle picture. Whether it contains a future Nicholson is hard to say, because the dialogue is all plot-driven and as sparse as possible. But the characters are surly, irresponsible, mean, and coarse, if not human; the actresses keep their makeup on; and the look of the picture is certainly accomplished. I use the word "look" because the cinematographer has been joined by squadrons of special-effects and animation artists, platoons of stunt men, and covens of postproduction wizards.

I enjoyed the two pictures about the same. I'd rate them both two and a half stars, meaning this as faint praise, but praise nevertheless. As genre exercises they are skillful, quick, and entertaining. There is a difference, though. *Hells Angels on Wheels* was frankly intended as an exploitation picture by everyone involved, who all hoped to move up to the A-list and make better films (all except for the producer, Joe Solomon, whom we will get to in a moment). *Torque,* I fear, considers itself to be a real movie—top of the world, man! Although it's been kept on the shelf for nearly a year by Warner Bros., reportedly to avoid competing with *2 Fast 2 Furious* and *Biker Boyz,* that is a marketing judgment, not an aesthetic opinion. I suspect no one at Warners has an aesthetic opinion about *Torque.*

I spent some time with Joe Solomon once, to profile him for *Esquire.* I liked him immensely. He wasn't too big to involve himself personally in the smallest details of a production, as when he demonstrated how ice cubes could be used as a perkiness enhancer. He was never happier than when producing motorcycle pictures, and his credits included *Angels from Hell; Run, Angel, Run; Wild Wheels;* and *Nam's Angels.*

What has happened between 1967 and 2004 is that Hollywood genres have undergone a fundamental flip-flop. Low-budget pictures are now serious and ambitious and play at Sundance. Big-budget exploitation work, on which every possible technical refinement is lavished, are now flashy and dispensable and open in 3,000 multiplexes. Little did Joe Solomon suspect that he was making the major studio pictures of the future.

Now as for *Torque.* The director is Joseph Kahn, who started by directing music videos and moved to this project, I learn, after long months of frustration trying to get *Crow 4* off the ground. The first three minutes convince us we are looking at a commercial before the feature begins. Then we realize the whole movie will look like this. It's flashy, skillful work—as much CGI as real, but that's the name of the game.

The plot is about a biker (Martin Henderson) who has returned to Los Angeles from exile in Thailand. The leader of a rival gang (Ice Cube) thinks he killed his brother, and wants revenge. The two gangs clash in a series of elaborate stunt and effects sequences, including a duel between two sexy women. A Hummer is tossed into the air and spun like a top before crushing a sports car. One motorcycle chase

takes place on top of a train, and then inside the train; we would care more if it were not on approximately the same level of reality as a *Road Runner* chase. One of the bikes is "built around a Rolls-Royce jet engine." It goes so fast it makes parking meters explode. The final fight sequence is so extravagantly choreographed that the props work together like a speeded-up version of a Buster Keaton sequence.

The film is better than it might have been, and better than it had to be. Take it on its own terms and you might find it interesting. Or did I say that already? One hopes that the filmmakers understand that *Torque* must be seen as the first step on their artistic journey, not its destination.

Touching the Void ★ ★ ★ ★
NO MPAA RATING, 106 m., 2004

Brendan Mackey (Simpson), Nicholas Aaron (Yates), Joe Simpson (Himself), Simon Yates (Himself). Directed by Kevin Macdonald and produced by John Smithson. Screenplay by Joe Simpson, based on his book.

For someone who fervently believes he will never climb a mountain, I spend an unreasonable amount of time thinking about mountain climbing. In my dreams my rope has come loose and I am falling, falling, and all the way down I am screaming: "Stupid! You're so stupid! You climbed all the way up there just so you could fall back down!"

Now there is a movie more frightening than my nightmares. *Touching the Void* is the most harrowing movie about mountain climbing I have seen, or can imagine. I've read reviews from critics who were only moderately stirred by the film (my friend Dave Kehr certainly kept his composure), and I must conclude that their dreams are not haunted as mine are.

I didn't take a single note during this film. I simply sat there before the screen, enthralled, fascinated, and terrified. Not for me the discussions about the utility of the "pseudo-documentary format," or questions about how the camera happened to be waiting at the bottom of the crevice when Simpson fell in. *Touching the Void* was, for me, more of a horror film than any actual horror film could ever be.

The movie is about Joe Simpson and Simon

Yates, two Brits in their mid-twenties who determined to scale the forbidding west face of a mountain named Siula Grande, in the Peruvian Andes. They were fit and in good training, and bold enough to try the "one push" method of climbing, in which they carried all their gear with them instead of establishing caches along the route. They limited their supplies to reduce weight, and planned to go up and down quickly.

It didn't work out that way. Snowstorms slowed and blinded them. The ascent was doable, but on the way down the storms disoriented them and the drifts concealed the hazard of hidden crevices and falls. Roped together, they worked with one man always anchored, and so Yates was able to hold the rope when Simpson had a sudden fall. But it was disastrous: He broke his leg, driving the calf bone up through the knee socket. Both of them knew that a broken leg on a two-man climb, with rescue impossible, was a death sentence, and indeed Simpson tells us he was rather surprised that Yates decided to stay with him and try to get him down.

We know that Simpson survived, because the movie shows the real-life Simpson and Yates, filmed against plain backgrounds, looking straight on into the camera, remembering their adventure in their own words. We also see the ordeal reenacted by two actors (Brendan Mackey as Simpson, Nicholas Aaron as Yates), and experienced climbers are used as stunt doubles. The movie was shot on location in Peru and also in the Alps, and the climbing sequences are always completely convincing; the use of actors in those scenes is not a distraction because their faces are so bearded, frostbitten, and snow-caked that we can hardly recognize them.

Yates and Simpson had a 300-foot rope. Yates's plan was to lower Simpson 300 feet and wait for a tug on the rope. That meant Simpson had dug in and anchored himself and it was safe for Yates to climb down and repeat the process. A good method in theory, but then, after dark, in a snowstorm, Yates lowered Simpson over a precipice and left him hanging in midair over a drop of unknowable distance. Since they were out of earshot in the blizzard all Yates could know was that the rope was tight and not moving, and his feet were slipping out of the holes he had dug to brace them.

After an hour or so he realized they were at an impasse. Simpson was apparently hanging helplessly in midair, Yates was slipping, and unless he cut the rope they would both surely die. So he cut the rope.

Simpson says he would have done the same thing under the circumstances, and we believe him. What we can hardly believe is what happens next, and what makes the film into an incredible story of human endurance.

If you plan to see the film—it will not disappoint you—you might want to save the rest of the review until later.

Simpson, incredibly, falls into a crevice but is slowed and saved by several snow bridges he crashes through before he lands on an ice ledge with a drop on either side. So there he is, in total darkness and bitter cold, his fuel gone so that he cannot melt snow, his lamp battery running low, and no food. He is hungry, dehydrated, and in cruel pain from the bones grinding together in his leg (two aspirins didn't help much).

It is clear Simpson cannot climb back up out of the crevice. So he eventually gambles everything on a strategy that seems madness itself, but was his only option other than waiting for death: He uses the rope to lower himself down into the unknown depths below. If the distance is more than 300 feet, well, then, he will literally be at the end of his rope.

But there is a floor far below, and in the morning he sees light and is able, incredibly, to crawl out to the mountainside. And that is only the beginning of his ordeal. He must somehow get down the mountain and cross a plain strewn with rocks and boulders; he cannot walk but must try to hop or crawl despite the pain in his leg. That he did it is manifest, since he survived to write a book and appear in the movie. How he did it provides an experience that at times had me closing my eyes against his agony.

This film is an unforgettable experience, directed by Kevin Macdonald (who made *One Day in September,* the Oscar-winner about the 1972 Olympiad) with a kind of brutal directness and simplicity that never tries to add suspense or drama (none is needed!), but simply tells the story, as we look on in disbelief. We learn at the end that after two years of surgeries Simpson's leg was repaired, and that (but you anticipated this, didn't you?) he went back to climbing again. Learning this, I was reminded of Boss Gettys's line about Citizen Kane: "He's going to need more than one lesson." I hope to God the rest of his speech does not apply to Simpson: ". . . and he's going to get more than one lesson."

The Tracker ★ ★ ★ ½
NO MPAA RATING, 90 m., 2004

David Gulpilil (The Tracker), Gary Sweet (The Fanatic), Damon Gameau (The Follower), Grant Page (The Veteran), Noel Wilton (The Fugitive). Directed by Rolf de Heer and produced by Bridget Ikin, Julie Ryan, and de Heer. Screenplay by de Heer.

The Tracker is one of those rare films that deserve to be called haunting. It tells the sort of story we might find in an action Western, but transforms it into a fable or parable. Four men set out into the Australian wilderness to track down an accused killer, and during the course of their journey true justice cries out to be done. The men never use their names, but the credits identify them as The Fanatic, a merciless officer; The Follower, a greenhorn new to the territory; The Veteran, an older man of few words; and The Tracker, an Aboriginal who will lead them to their quarry, also an Aboriginal.

The live action is intercut with paintings of events in the story, and the sound track includes songs about what happens. We assume the story is based on fact that became legend, and that the songs commemorate it; several critics have said the paintings are "probably Aboriginal" and done at the time (1922). Not so. The story is an original by the director, Rolf de Heer; the paintings were done on location by Peter Coad; and the songs were written by the director and Graham Tardif. They have created their own legend from their own facts, but it feels no less real; it is a distillation from Australia's shameful history with the Aboriginals, and contains echoes of the hunt for escaped Aboriginal children in *Rabbit-Proof Fence.*

De Heer used a small crew and shot in the wilderness, camping out every night, and we see the film's events not as heightened action but as a long, slow trek across a vast landscape. It seems to be unpopulated, but no; on the first

night, when the kid gets out his ukulele and starts to sing, the officer quiets him so they can hear anyone approaching. "You won't hear them," the older man says. "They're there," says the tracker.

They are there, everywhere, invisible, as spears materialize out of emptiness and pick off their horses and then one of the men. Once they come upon the camp of a small Aboriginal family group. These people are peaceful, the tracker tells the officer, but some of them are wearing discarded army uniforms, and so the officer kills them all. The greenhorn is shaken and distraught: "They were innocent." The tracker, who says what the officer likes to hear, tells him, "The only innocent black is a dead black."

This tracker is more complex than he seems. He plays a loyal army employee, but his eyes suggest other dimensions. And when one of the men is killed, how extraordinary that he recites a Catholic burial rite in Latin. He must have passed through a missionary school on his way to this day in the Outback, and is not the savage (however noble) imagined by the racist officer. At the same time, he knows his job, and when the greenhorn charges that he isn't really tracking but is only following his nose, the officer (who also knows his job) tells the tracker, "Show him," and he does—pointing out a small dislodged stone with the earth still damp where it has rested.

The tracker is played by David Gulpilil, whose career started in 1971 when he played the young Aboriginal boy who guides the lost white girl in *Walkabout.* He also played a tracker in *Rabbit-Proof Fence.* Here he has a disarming smile and an understated enthusiasm that seems genuine—to the officer, at least— while we sense a different agenda shifting beneath the surface. While it is clear that some kind of confrontation is coming, it would be unfair for me to suggest what happens.

The officer, played by Gary Sweet, is unbending and filled with certitude. There is not a doubt in his mind that he is justified in shooting innocent people, and he even claims to expect a medal. The greenhorn (Damon Gameau) is the moral weathervane; the mission at first seems justifiable, and then he wonders. The old-timer (Grant Page) is the taciturn type every society knows; he has accommodated himself to this way of doing business, but stands apart from it. Notice how while the massacre is under way, he sits on a log and smokes, and we guess something of his detachment from the way the smoke emerges as a very thin, steady stream.

The performances are all the more powerful for being in a minor key. De Heer seems determined to tell his story without calculated emotional boosts. "The brutal scenes," he told an Australian interviewer, "were basically shifted from the film itself to the paintings to make the viewer look at the death scenes and macabre scenes differently—to distance the audience." And when the officer is shouting at the family group, the volume of his dialogue is toned down and a song plays as counterpoint; here is a film about memory, sadness, tragedy, and distance, not a film that dramatizes what it laments. Truffaut said it was impossible to make an antiwar film because the action always argued for itself; de Heer may have found the answer.

The Triplets of Belleville ★ ★ ★ ½
PG-13, 91 m., 2003

With the voices of Jean-Claude Donda, Michel Robin, Monica Viegas, M. Beatrice Bonifassi, and Charles Prevost Linton. An animated film directed by Sylvain Chomet and produced by Didier Brunner and Paul Cadieux. Screenplay by Chomet.

The Triplets of Belleville will have you walking out of the theater with a goofy damn grin on your face, wondering what just happened to you. To call it weird would be a cowardly evasion. It is creepy, eccentric, eerie, flaky, freaky, funky, grotesque, inscrutable, kinky, kooky, magical, oddball, spooky, uncanny, uncouth, and unearthly. Especially uncouth. What I did was, I typed the word "weird" and when that wholly failed to evoke the feelings the film stirred in me, I turned to the thesaurus and it suggested the above substitutes—and none of them do the trick, either.

There is not even a way I can tell you what the film is "like," because I can't think of another film "like" it. Maybe the British cartoonists Ronald Searle and Gerald Scarfe suggest the visual style. Sylvain Chomet, the writer and director, has created an animated feature of appalling originality and scary charm. It's one of those movies where you keep banging your fist against your head to stop yourself from using the word "meets," as in Monsieur Hulot meets Tim Burton, or the Marquis de Sade meets Lance Armstrong.

Most animated features have an almost grotesque desire to be loved. This one doesn't seem to care. It creates a world of selfishness, cruelty, corruption, and futility—but it's not serious about this world and it doesn't want to attack it or improve upon it. It simply wants to sweep us up in its dark comic vision.

The movie opens in France, where a small boy and his dog live in the top floor of a narrow, crooked house. The Metro roars past on schedule, and his dog races upstairs on schedule to bark at it, and the boy's grandmother gives the boy a trike and eventually a bike, and soon he is the foremost bicycle racer in the world. Meanwhile, the Metro has been replaced by an elevated highway that shoulders the house to one side, so that it leans crookedly and the stairs are dangerous for the dog to climb.

The grandmother is a ferocious trainer. A little whistle seems welded to her jaw, and she toots relentlessly as the boy pedals. Then he is kidnapped by thugs who want to use him for a private gambling operation, and the key to his rescue may be the Triplets of Belleville, who were music hall stars in the era of Josephine Baker, so how old would that make them now?

The action leaves Paris for New York, maybe, although it is more likely Montreal, where Chomet lives. Doesn't matter so much, since there has never been a city like this. Jazz joints from the 1930s exist with *noir* hideouts and bizarre tortures. After a certain point it isn't the surprises that surprise us—it's the surprises about the surprises. We take it in stride, for example, when the Triplets go fishing for frogs with dynamite. What amazes us is that one of the exploded frogs survives, and crawls desperately from a scalding pot in its bid for freedom.

I am completely failing to do justice to this film. Now you think it is about frog torture. I will get letters from PETA. What happens to the frogs is nothing compared to what happens to the grandson, who is subjected to Rube Goldberg exercise machines, and at one point has his kneecaps vacuumed.

The movie's drawing style is haunting in a comic way. The energy of the story is inexorable. There is a concert that involves tuning bicycle wheels. Luis Buñuel wrote that when he and Salvador Dali were about to premiere their surrealist film *Un Chien Andalou,* he loaded his pockets with stones to throw at the audience in case it attacked. How can I best describe *The Triplets of Belleville* other than to suggest that Buñuel might have wanted to stone it? Some of my faithful readers went to see *Songs from the Second Floor* on my recommendation. *Triplets* comes from a similar mind-set, but is told in a manic fever, and is animated. Imagine Felix the Cat with firecrackers tied to his tail, in a story involving the French nephew and aunt of *The Reservoir Dogs,* and a score by Spike Jones. No, the other Spike Jones.

Troy ★ ★

R, 162 m., 2004

Brad Pitt (Achilles), Eric Bana (Hector), Orlando Bloom (Paris), Diane Kruger (Helen), Brian Cox (Agamemnon), Sean Bean (Odysseus), Brendan Gleeson (Menelaus), Peter O'Toole (Priam), Garrett Hedlund (Patroclus). Directed by Wolfgang Petersen and produced by Petersen, Diana Rathbun, and Colin Wilson. Screenplay by David Benioff, based on the poem "The Iliad" by Homer.

Troy is based on the poem by Homer, according to the credits. Homer's estate should sue. The movie sidesteps the existence of the Greek gods, turns its heroes into action movie clichés, and demonstrates that we're getting tired of computer-generated armies. Better a couple of hundred sweaty warriors than two masses of 50,000 men marching toward each other across a sea of special effects.

The movie recounts the legend of the Trojan War, as the fortress city is attacked by a Greek army led by Menelaus of Sparta and Agamemnon of Mycenae. The war has become necessary because of the lust of the young Trojan prince Paris (Orlando Bloom), who during a peace mission to Sparta seduces its queen, Helen (Diane Kruger). This understandably annoys her husband, Menelaus (Brendan Gleeson), not to mention Paris's brother Hector (Eric Bana), who points out, quite correctly, that when you visit a king on a peace mission it is counterproductive to leave with his wife.

What the movie doesn't explain is why Helen would leave with Paris after an acquaintanceship of a few nights. Is it because her loins throb with passion for a hero? No, because she tells him: "I don't want a hero. I want a man I can grow old with." Not in Greek myth, you don't. If you believe Helen of Troy could actually tell Paris anything remotely like that, you will probably also agree that the second night he slipped into her boudoir, she told him, "Last night was a mistake."

The seduction of Helen is the curtain-raiser for the main story, which involves vast Greek armies laying siege to the impenetrable city. Chief among their leaders is Achilles, said to be the greatest warrior of all time, but played by Brad Pitt as if he doesn't believe it. If Achilles was anything, he was a man who believed his own press releases. Heroes are not introspective in Greek drama, they do not have second thoughts, and they are not conflicted.

Achilles is all of these things. He mopes on the flanks of the Greek army with his own independent band of fighters, carrying out a separate diplomatic policy, kind of like Ollie North. He thinks Agamemnon is a poor leader with bad strategy, and doesn't really get worked up until his beloved cousin Patroclus (Garrett Hedlund) is killed in battle. Patroclus, who looks a little like Achilles, wears his helmet and armor to fool the enemy, and until the helmet is removed everyone thinks Achilles has been slain. So dramatic is that development that the movie shows perhaps 100,000 men in hand-to-hand combat, and then completely forgets them in order to focus on the Patroclus battle scene, with everybody standing around like during a fight on the playground.

Brad Pitt is a good actor and a handsome man, and he worked out for six months to get buff for the role, but Achilles is not a character he inhabits comfortably. Say what you will about Charlton Heston and Victor Mature, but one good way to carry off a sword-and-sandal epic is to be filmed by a camera down around your knees, while you intone quasi-formal prose in a heroic baritone. Pitt is modern, nuanced, introspective; he brings complexity to a role where it is not required.

By treating Achilles and the other characters as if they were human, instead of the larger-than-life creations of Greek myth, director Wolfgang Petersen miscalculates. What happens in Greek myth cannot happen between psychologically plausible characters. That's the whole point of myth. Great films like Michael Cacoyannis's *Elektra*, about the murder of Agamemnon after the Trojan War, know that and use a stark dramatic approach that is deliberately stylized. Of course, *Elektra* wouldn't work for a multiplex audience, but then maybe it shouldn't.

The best scene in the movie has Peter O'Toole creating an island of drama and emotion in the middle of all that plodding dialogue. He plays old King Priam of Troy, who at night ventures outside his walls and into the enemy camp, surprising Achilles in his tent. Achilles has defeated Priam's son Hector in hand-to-hand combat before the walls of Troy, and dragged his body back to camp behind his chariot. Now Priam asks that the body be returned for proper preparation and burial. This scene is given the time and attention it needs to build its mood, and we believe it when Achilles tells Priam, "You're a far better king than the one who leads this army." O'Toole's presence is a reminder of *Lawrence of Arabia*, which proved that patience with dialogue and character is more important than action in making war movies work.

As for the Greek cities themselves, a cliché from the old Hollywood epics has remained intact. This is the convention that whenever a battle of great drama takes place, all the important characters have box seats for it. When Achilles battles Hector before the walls of Troy, for example, Priam and his family have a sort of viewing stand right at the front of the palace, and we get the usual crowd reaction shots, some of them awkward close-ups of actresses told to look grieved.

In a way, *Troy* resembles *The Alamo*. Both are about fortresses under siege. Both are defeated because of faulty night watchmen. The Mexicans sneak up on the Alamo undetected, and absolutely nobody is awake to see the Greeks climbing out of the Trojan Horse. One difference between the two movies is that Billy Bob Thornton and the other *Alamo* actors are given evocative dialogue and deliver it well, while *Troy* provides dialogue that probably cannot be

delivered well because it would sound even sillier that way.

Tupac: Resurrection ★ ★ ★ ½
R, 90 m., 2003

Narrator . . . Tupac Shakur. Directed by Lauren Lazin and produced by Preston Holmes, Karolyn Ali, and Lazin.

"I didn't have a record until I had a record."

So says Tupac Shakur, the gangsta rap artist who was shot down in his youth on a Las Vegas street. And, yes, it is Tupac Shakur saying it. He narrates his own story about an American life that started badly, got a lot better, and then a whole lot worse. Because he was articulate and introspective, questioned his own behavior and had a philosophical streak, and because he left behind so many hours of interviews, the makers of *Tupac: Resurrection* are able to use his voice and only his voice to tell the story of his life from his birth to beyond the grave.

Shakur was a talented child who attended the Philadelphia High School for the Performing Arts and in another world might have made another kind of music. But he came up at the defining moment of rap and embraced gangsta imagery, which became his reality. He advocated some kind of half-baked philosophy named Thug Life, which was supposed to be a code to end the anarchy of inner-city street gangs. But like the rap artist Biggie Smalls, whose murder has been linked with Shakur's in the legend of the East-West rap war, and like Sean (Puffy) Combs, who has also been associated with violence, he was not a ghetto warrior but a rich, talented performer who pretended to be a lot tougher than he was.

Tupac: Resurrection, directed by Lauren Lazin, is essentially the autobiography of a young man who suddenly has to learn how to handle fame, money, and power, and whose impulses to do the right thing are clouded by the usual problems of too much, too soon. "I was immature," he observes at one point, and later, "I tried to get humble again." He attacked Spike Lee and Eddie Murphy for no good reason. He fought with the Hughes brothers, who were trying to direct him in a movie. He was accused of rape. He did time behind bars. He was involved in gunplay. He was making millions of dollars and did not fully realize what a target that made him in a new branch of the music industry where murder was a marketing strategy.

The most important person in his life was clearly his mother, Afeni Shakur, a Black Panther who was in jail when she was pregnant with Tupac, and who later fought and won a battle with drugs; her politics and feminism helped form him, and he talks about how comfortable he is with women, how he understands them, how he was the only male in the family. In the last months of his life, his relationship with his mother is the most positive input he has—and he knows it.

He's egotistical about his success, as he makes millions for Death Row Records and its notorious proprietor, Suge Knight. One movie that ought be viewed in connection with this one is Nick Broomfield's *Biggie and Tupac* (2002), which says Knight had both rappers murdered and even fingers the hit men (off-duty Los Angeles cops on Suge's payroll). The LAPD, not surprisingly, has a different theory, but Broomfield's movie is instructive for its portrait of Suge Knight, who actually was and is the kind of hard character Shakur and Smalls posed as.

Tupac: Resurrection is about rap music, the forces that created it, and the world it then created. Shakur talks about the experiences and politics that went into his own music, in a way that casts more light on rap than anything else I've come across in a movie. Although rap is not music in the sense that you come out humming the melody, it's as genuine an American idiom as jazz or the blues, and it is primarily a medium of words, of ideology; a marriage of turntables, poetry slams, autobiography, and righteous anger.

I remember seeing Vondie Curtis-Hall's *Gridlock'd* at Sundance 1996, soon after Tupac was murdered in Vegas. I'd admired Shakur's acting in *Poetic Justice* and *Juice*, and now here, opposite the great Tim Roth, he was distinctive and memorable in what was essentially a two-character study. Consider the scene where his character, desperate to get into detox, tries to persuade Roth's character to stab him in the side, and the two get into a hopeless discussion about which side the liver is on.

In the long run Shakur might have become

more important as an actor than as a singer (as Ice Cube has). As you listen to his uncanny narration of *Tupac: Resurrection*, which is stitched together from interviews, you realize you're not listening to the usual self-important vacancies from celebrity Q&As, but to spoken prose of a high order, in which analysis, memory, and poetry come together seamlessly in sentences and paragraphs that sound as if they were written. Let's assume you are a person who never intends to see a doc about rap music, but might have it in you to see one. This is the one.

Turtles Can Fly ★ ★ ★ ★
NO MPAA RATING, 95 m., 2005

Soran Ebrahim (Satellite), Avaz Latif (Agrin), Hirsh Feyssal (Henkov). Directed by Bahman Ghobadi and produced by Ghobadi. Screenplay by Ghobadi.

I wish everyone who has an opinion on the war in Iraq could see *Turtles Can Fly*. That would mean everyone in the White House and in Congress, and the newspaper writers, and the TV pundits, and the radio talkers, and you—especially you, because you are reading this and they are not.

You assume the movie is a liberal attack on George W. Bush's policies. Not at all. The action takes place just before the American invasion begins, and the characters in it look forward to the invasion and the fall of Saddam Hussein. Nor does the movie later betray an opinion one way or the other about the war. It is about the actual lives of refugees, who lack the luxury of opinions because they are pre-occupied with staying alive in a world that has no place for them.

The movie takes place in a Kurdish refugee camp somewhere on the border between Turkey and Iraq. That means, in theory, it takes place in "Kurdistan," a homeland that exists in the minds of the Kurds even though every other government in the area insists the Kurds are stateless. The characters in the movie are children and teenagers, all of them orphans; there are adults in the camp, but the kids run their own lives—especially a bright wheeler-dealer named Satellite (Soran Ebrahim), who organizes work gangs of other children.

What is their work? They disarm land mines, so they can be resold to arms dealers in the nearby town. The land mines are called "American," but this is a reflection of their value and not a criticism of the United States; they were planted in the area by Saddam Hussein, in one of his skirmishes with Kurds and Turks. (Well, technically, they were supplied to Saddam by the United States.) Early in the film, we see a character named Henkov (Hirsh Feyssal), known to everyone as The Boy With No Arms, who gently disarms a mine by removing the firing pin with his lips.

Satellite pays special attention to a girl named Agrin (Avaz Latif), who is Henkov's sister. They have a little brother named Risa, who is carried about with his arms wrapped around the neck of his armless brother. We *think* he is their brother, that is, until we discover he is Agrin's child, born after she was raped by Iraqi soldiers while still almost a child herself. The armless boy loves Risa; his sister hates him, because of her memories.

Is this world beginning to take shape in your mind? The refugees live in tents and huts. They raise money by scavenging. Satellite is the most resourceful person in the camp, making announcements, calling meetings, assigning work, and traveling ceremonially on a bicycle festooned with ribbons and glittering medallions. He is always talking, shouting, hectoring, at the top of his voice: He is too busy to reflect on the misery of his life.

The village is desperate for information about the coming American invasion. There is a scene of human comedy in which every household has a member up on a hill with a makeshift TV antenna; those below shout instructions: "To the left! A little to the right!" But no signal is received. Satellite announces that he will go to town and barter for a satellite dish. There is a sensation when he returns with one. The elders gather as he tries to bring in a signal. The sexy music video channels are prohibited, but the elders wait patiently as Satellite cycles through the sin until he finds CNN, and they can listen for English words they understand. They hate Saddam and eagerly await the Americans.

But what will the Americans do for them?

The plight of the Kurdish people is that no one seems to want to do much for them. Even though a Kurd has recently been elected to high office in Iraq, we get the sense he was a compromise candidate—chosen precisely because his people are powerless. For years the Kurds have struggled against Turkey, Iraq, and other nations in the region, to define the borders of a homeland the other states refuse to acknowledge.

From time to time the aims of the Kurds come into step with the aims of others. When they were fighting Saddam, the first Bush administration supported them. When they were fighting our ally Turkey, we opposed them. The *New York Times Magazine* ran a cover story about Ibrahim Parlak, who for ten years peacefully ran a Kurdish restaurant in Harbert, Michigan, only to be arrested in 2004 by the federal government, which hoped to deport him for Kurdish nationalist activities that at one point we approved. Because I supported Ibrahim's case, I could read headlines on right-wing sites such as, "Roger Ebert Gives Thumbs Up to Terrorism."

I hope Debbie Schlussel, who wrote that column, sees *Turtles Can Fly*. The movie does not agree with her politics, or mine. It simply provides faces for people we think of as abstractions. It was written and directed by Bahman Ghobadi, whose *A Time for Drunken Horses* (2000) was also about Kurds struggling to survive between the lines. Satellite has no politics. Neither does The Boy With No Arms, or his sister, or her child born of rape; they have been trapped outside of history.

I was on a panel at the University of Colorado where an audience member criticized movies for reducing the enormity of the Holocaust to smaller stories. But there is no way to tell a story big enough to contain all of the victims of the Holocaust, or all of the lives affected for good and ill in the Middle East. Our minds cannot process that many stories. What we can understand is The Boy With No Arms, making a living by disarming land mines like the one that blew away his arms. And Satellite, who tells the man in the city he will trade him fifteen radios and some cash for a satellite dish. Where did Satellite get fifteen radios? Why? You need some radios?

28 Days Later ★ ★ ★
R, 108 m., 2003

Cillian Murphy (Jim), Naomie Harris (Selena), Christopher Eccleston (Major Henry West), Megan Burns (Hannah), Brendan Gleeson (Frank), Noah Huntley (Mark). Directed by Danny Boyle and produced by Andrew MacDonald. Screenplay by Alex Garland.

Activists set lab animals free from their cages—only to learn, too late, that they're infected with a "rage" virus that turns them into frothing, savage killers. The virus quickly spreads to human beings, and when a man named Jim (Cillian Murphy) awakens in an empty hospital and walks outside, he finds a deserted London. In a series of astonishing shots, he wanders Piccadilly Circus and crosses Westminster Bridge with not another person in sight, learning from old wind-blown newspapers of a virus that turned humanity against itself.

So opens *28 Days Later*, which begins as a great science fiction film and continues as an intriguing study of human nature. The ending is disappointing—an action shoot-out, with characters chasing each other through the headquarters of a rogue army unit—but for most of the way, it's a great ride. I suppose movies like this have to end with the good and evil characters in a final struggle. The audience wouldn't stand for everybody being dead at the end, even though that's the story's logical outcome.

Director Danny Boyle (*Trainspotting*) shoots on video to give his film an immediate, documentary feel, and also no doubt to make it affordable; a more expensive film would have had more standard action heroes and less time to develop the quirky characters. Spend enough money on this story, and it would have the depth of *Armageddon*. Alex Garland's screenplay develops characters who seem to have a reality apart from their role in the plot—whose personalities help decide what they do and why.

Jim is the everyman, a bicycle messenger whose nearly fatal traffic accident probably saves his life. Wandering London, shouting (unwisely) for anyone else, he eventually encounters Selena (Naomie Harris) and Mark (Noah Huntley), who have avoided infection and explain the situation. (Mark: "Okay, Jim, I've got some bad news.") Selena, a tough-minded black woman who is a realist, says the virus had spread to France and America before the news broadcasts ended; if someone is infected, she explains, you have twenty seconds to kill them before they turn into a berserk, devouring zombie.

That twenty-second limit serves three valuable story purposes: (a) It has us counting "twelve . . . eleven . . . ten" in our minds at one crucial moment; (b) it eliminates the standard story device where a character can keep his infection secret; and (c) it requires the quick elimination of characters we like, dramatizing the merciless nature of the plague.

Darwinians will observe that a virus that acts within twenty seconds will not be an efficient survivor; the host population will soon be dead—and along with it, the virus. I think the movie's answer to this objection is that the "rage" virus did not evolve in the usual way, but was created through genetic manipulation in the Cambridge laboratory where the story begins.

Not that we are thinking much about evolution during the movie's engrossing central passages. Selena becomes the dominant member of the group, the toughest and least sentimental, enforcing a hard-boiled survivalist line. Good-hearted Jim would probably have died if he hadn't met her. Eventually they encounter two other survivors: a big, genial man named Frank (Brendan Gleeson) and his teenage daughter, Hannah (Megan Burns). They're barricaded in a high-rise apartment, and use their hand-cranked radio to pick up a radio broadcast from an army unit near Manchester. Should they trust the broadcast and travel to what is described as a safe zone?

The broadcast reminded me of that forlorn radio signal from the Northern Hemisphere that was picked up in post-bomb Australia in *On the Beach*. After some discussion the group decides to take the risk, and they use Frank's taxi to drive to Manchester. This involves an extremely improbable sequence in which the taxi seems able to climb over gridlocked cars in a tunnel, and another scene in which a wave of countless rats flees from zombies.

Those surviving zombies raise the question: How long can you live once you have the virus? Since London seems empty at the beginning, presumably the zombies we see were survivors until fairly recently. Another question: Since they run in packs, why don't they attack each other? That one, the movie doesn't have an answer for.

The Manchester roadblock, which is indeed maintained by an uninfected army unit, sets up the third act, which doesn't live up to the promise of the first two. The officer in charge, Major Henry West (Christopher Eccleston), invites them to join his men at one of those creepy movie dinners where the hosts are so genial that the guests get suspicious. And then . . . see for yourself.

Naomie Harris, a newcomer, is convincing as Selena, the rock at the center of the storm. We come to realize she was not born tough, but has made the necessary adjustments to the situation. In a lesser movie there would be a love scene between Selena and Jim, but here the movie finds the right tone in a moment where she pecks him on the cheek and he blushes. There is also a touching scene where she offers Valium to young Hannah. They are facing a cruel situation. "To kill myself?" Hannah asks. "No. So you won't care as much."

The conclusion is pretty standard. I can understand why Boyle avoided having everyone dead at the end, but I wish he'd had the nerve that John Sayles showed in *Limbo* with his open ending. My imagination is just diabolical enough that when that jet fighter appears toward the end, I wish it had appeared, circled back—and opened fire. But then I'm never satisfied. *28 Days Later* is a tough, smart, ingenious movie that leads its characters into situations where everything depends on their (and our) understanding of human nature.

21 Grams ★ ★ ★
R, 125 m., 2003

Sean Penn (Paul Rivers), Benicio Del Toro (Jack Jordan), Naomi Watts (Cristina Peck), Charlotte Gainsbourg (Mary Rivers), Melissa Leo (Marianne Jordan), Clea DuVall (Claudia), Danny Huston (Michael). Directed by Alejandro Gonzalez Inarritu and produced by Inarritu, Ted Hope, and Robert Salerno. Screenplay by Guillermo Arriaga.

---

21 Grams knows all about its story but only lets us discover it a little at a time. Well, every movie

does that, but usually they tell their stories in chronological order, so we have the illusion that we're watching as the events happen to the characters. In this film everything has already happened, and it's as if God, or the director, is shuffling the deck after the game is over. Here is the question we have to answer: Is this approach better than telling the same story from beginning to end?

The film is by Alejandro Gonzalez Inarritu, the almost unreasonably talented Mexican filmmaker whose *Amores Perros* (2000) was an enormous success. That film intercut three simultaneous stories, all centering on a traffic accident. *21 Grams* has three stories and a traffic accident, but the stories move back and forth in time, so that sometimes we know more than the characters, sometimes they know more than we do.

While the film is a virtuoso accomplishment of construction and editing, the technique has its limitations. Even though modern physics teaches that time does not move from the past through the present into the future, entertaining that delusion is how we make sense of our perceptions. And it is invaluable for actors, who build their characters emotionally as events take place. By fracturing his chronology, Inarritu isolates key moments in the lives of his characters, so that they have to stand alone. There is a point at which this stops being a strategy and starts being a stunt.

21 Grams tells such a tormenting story, however, that it just about survives its style. It would have been more powerful in chronological order, and even as a puzzle it has a deep effect. Remembering it, we dismiss the structure and recall the events as they happened to the characters, and are moved by its three sad stories of characters faced with the implacable finality of life.

Because the entire movie depends on withholding information and revealing unexpected connections, it is fair enough to describe the characters but would be wrong to even hint at some of their relationships. Sean Penn, Benicio Del Toro, and Naomi Watts play the key figures, and their spouses are crucial in ways that perhaps should not be described. Penn is Paul, a professor of mathematics (even that fact is withheld for a long time, and comes as a jolt because he does not seem much like one). He is dying of a heart condition, needs a transplant, and is badged by his wife (Charlotte Gainsbourg) to donate sperm so that she can have his baby—after his death, she does not quite say.

Benicio Del Toro is Jack, a former convict who now rules his family with firm fundamentalist principles. He is using Jesus as a way of staying off drugs and alcohol; his wife (Melissa Leo) is grateful for his recovery but dubious about his cure.

The third story centers on Cristina (Naomi Watts), first seen at a Narcotics Anonymous meeting; she has a husband (Danny Huston) and two daughters, and her life seems to be getting healthier and more stable until an event takes place that eventually links all of the characters in a situation that falls halfway between tragedy and fraught melodrama.

As you watch this film you are absorbed and involved, sometimes deeply moved; acting does not get much better than the work done here by Penn, Del Toro, and Watts, and their individual moments have astonishing impact. But in the closing passages, as the shape of the underlying structure becomes clear, a vague dissatisfaction sets in. You wonder if Inarritu took you the long way around, running up mileage on his storyteller's taxi meter. Imagining how heartbreaking the conclusion would have been if we had arrived at it in the ordinary way by starting at the beginning, I felt as if an unnecessary screen of technique had been placed between the story and the audience.

Yet I do not want to give the wrong impression: This is an accomplished and effective film, despite my reservations. It grips us, moves us, astonishes us. Some of the revelations do benefit by coming as surprises. But artists often grow by learning what to leave out (the great example is Ozu). I have a feeling that Inarritu's fractured technique, which was so impressive in his first film and is not so satisfactory in this one, may inspire impatience a third time around. He is so good that it's time for him to get out of his own way.

The Twilight Samurai ★ ★ ★ ★

NO MPAA RATING, 129 m., 2004

Hiroyuki Sanada (Seibei Iguchi), Rie Miyazawa (Tomoe Iinuma), Nenji Kobayashi (Choubei Hisasaka), Min Tanaka (Zenemon Yogo), Ren Osugi (Toyotarou Kouda), Mitsuru Fukikoshi (Michinojo Iinuma), Miki Ito (Kayana Iguchi), Erina Hashiguchi (Ito Iguchi). Directed by Yoji Yamada and produced by Hiroshi Fukazawa, Shigehiro Nakagawa, and Ichiro Yamamoto. Screenplay by Yamada Asama and Yoshitaka Asama, based on novels by Shuuhei Fujisawa.

One who is a samurai must before all things keep in mind, by day, and by night, the fact that he has to die. That is his chief business.
—Code of Bushido

The Twilight Samurai is set in Japan during the period of the Meiji Restoration, circa 1868—the same period as Kurosawa's great *Seven Samurai* and Edward Zwick's elegant *The Last Samurai*. The three films deal in different ways with a time when samurai still tried to live by the Code of Bushido, even as they faced poverty or unemployment in a changing society. *The Last Samurai* is about samurai opposing the emperor's moves to modernize Japan; ironically, we learn that the hero of *The Twilight Samurai* fought and died in that rebellion—after the story of this movie is over.

His name is Seibei (Hiroyuki Sanada), and he lives under the rule of his clan in northeast Japan, where he spends his days not in battle but as an accountant, keeping track of dried fish and other foods in storage. Seeing him bending wearily over a pile of papers, declining an invitation by his fellow workers to go out drinking, we're reminded of the hero of Kurosawa's film *Ikiru*. Seibei hurries home because he has a senile mother and two young daughters to support, and is in debt after the death of his wife.

His story is told by director Yoji Yamada in muted tones and colors, beautifully re-creating a feudal village that still retains its architecture, its customs, its ancient values, even as the economy is making its way of life obsolete. What kind of a samurai has to pawn his sword and make do with a bamboo replacement? The film is narrated by Seibei's oldest daughter (Erina Hashiguchi), who is young in the film but an old lady on the sound track, remembering her father with love.

After working all day in the office, Seibei hurries home to grow crops to feed his family and earn extra cash. His coworkers gossip that his kimono is torn, and that he smells. One day the lord of the clan comes to inspect the food stores, notices Seibei's aroma, and reprimands him. This brings such disgrace on the family that Seibei's stern uncle reminds him, "Only a generation ago, hara-kiri would have been called for." His uncle advises him to remarry to get another worker into the home to prepare meals and do laundry. It happens that his childhood sweetheart, Tomoe (Rie Miyazawa), has just divorced her wife-beating husband, and begins to help around the house. The girls love her, but Seibei is shy and tired and cannot imagine remarrying.

The clan comes to him with an assignment: He is to kill the unruly Yogo (Min Tanaka), a samurai who has been employed by the clan for only four years, after a long, destitute time of wandering the countryside. Yogo, considered crazy, has declined the clan's suggestion that he kill himself. That seems sane enough to me, but the clan must uphold its standards even as its time is passing, and so the reluctant Seibei is bribed and blackmailed into taking on the assignment.

The closing third of the film is magnificent in the way it gathers all we have learned about Seibei and uses it to bring depth to what could have been a routine action sequence, but is much more. We see Tomoe shyly preparing him for battle ("Allow me to comb your hair"), and after a crucial conversation, he leaves her and goes to Yogo's home, where the body of an earlier emissary lies in the courtyard, covered by a swarm of flies.

I will not, of course, tell you what happens inside the house, or what happens between Seibei and Tomoe. What I can refer to is the extraordinary conversation between Seibei and Yogo, while their swords remain undrawn. "I know, you're all keyed up," Yogo says. "But I'm going to run." He has no desire to fight. He recounts his weary history as a samurai in poverty, or in bondage to a clan: "I was an errand boy, too." At one extraordinary moment he takes the ashes of his dead daughter and crunches a piece of bone between his teeth. Yogo's motive for having this conversation may not be as clear as it seems; it is up to you to decide.

Director Yoji Yamada, now seventy-three, has made at least sixty-six films, according to IMDB.com. *The Twilight Samurai*, the first to be widely released in this country, was Japan's Oscar nominee this year. He has been nominated six times since he was sixty as Japan's best director, and won once. Yet no less than forty-eight of his films were B-pictures, involving the beloved character Tora-san, popular in Japan from 1970 until the death in 1996 of Kiyoshi Atsumi, who played him. Tora-san is little known outside Japan, but for a class on Japanese cinema, I obtained one of his movies from Shochiku Studios and we watched it. Apparently they are all much the same: Tora-san, a meek, self-effacing comic figure (a little Chaplin, a little Jerry Lewis, a little Red Skelton), is a salesman who stumbles into a domestic crisis, makes it worse, and then makes it better.

One can only imagine what it would be like to direct that formula forty-eight times. Perhaps Yamada felt a little like Seibei, as he remained loyal to the studio and this character year after year. Perhaps when Seibei finds, at the end of *The Twilight Samurai*, that he may be poor and stuck in a rut but he still has greatness in him—well, perhaps that's how Yamada felt when he entered the home stretch. There is a kind of perfection in laboring humbly all your life only to show, as the end approaches, that you had greatness all along. I am half-convinced that as Seibei's daughter remembers her father's life, she is also describing Yamada's. I could probably find out if that is true, but I don't want to know. I like it better as a possibility.

Note: The Twilight Samurai *swept the 2003 Japanese Academy Awards, winning twelve categories, including best picture, director, screenplay, actor, actress, supporting actor, and cinematography.*

Twisted ★ ½
R, 96 m., 2004

Ashley Judd (Jessica Shepard), Samuel L. Jackson (John Mills), Andy Garcia (Mike Delmarco), David Strathairn (Dr. Melvin Frank), Russell Wong (Lieutenant Tong), Camryn Manheim (Lisa), Mark Pellegrino (Jimmy Schmidt). Directed by Philip Kaufman and produced by Barry Baeres, Linne Radmin, Arnold Kopelson, and Anne Kopelson. Screenplay by Sarah Thorp and Kaufman.

Phil Kaufman's *Twisted* walks like a thriller and talks like a thriller, but squawks like a turkey.

And yet the elements are in place for a film that works—until things start becoming clear and mysteries start being solved and we start shaking our heads, if we are well mannered, or guffawing, if we are not.

Let me begin at the ending. The other day I employed the useful term *deus ex machina* in a review, and received several messages from readers who are not proficient in Latin. I have also received several messages from Latin scholars who helpfully translated obscure dialogue in *The Passion of the Christ* for me, and, as my Urbana High School Latin teacher Mrs. Link used to remind me, *"In medio tutissimus ibis."*

But back to *deus ex machina*. This is a phrase you will want to study and master, not merely to amaze friends during long bus journeys but because it so perfectly describes what otherwise might take you thousands of words. Imagine a play on a stage. The hero is in a fix. The dragon is breathing fire, the hero's sword is broken, his leg is broken, his spirit is broken, and the playwright's imagination is broken. Suddenly there is the offstage noise of the grinding of gears, and invisible machinery lowers a god onto the stage, who slays the dragon, heals the hero, and fires the playwright. He is the "god from the machine."

Now travel with me to San Francisco. Ashley Judd plays Jessica Shepard, a new homicide detective who has a habit of picking up guys in bars and having rough sex with them. She drinks a lot. Maybe that goes without saying. Soon after getting her new job, she and her partner, Mike Delmarco (Andy Garcia), are assigned to a floater in the bay. She recognizes the dead man, who has been savagely beaten. It's someone she has slept with.

She reveals this information, but is kept on the case by the police commissioner (Samuel L. Jackson), who raised her as his own daughter after her own father went berserk and killed a slew of people, including her mother. The commissioner trusts her. Then another body turns up, also with the killer's brand (a cigarette burn). She slept with this guy, too. She's seeing the department shrink (David Strathairn), who understandably suggests she has to share this information with her partner. Then a third dead guy turns up. She slept with him, too. Wasn't it Oscar Wilde who said, "To kill one

lover may be regarded as a misfortune. To kill three seems like carelessness"?

Detective Sheperd has a pattern. She goes home at night, drinks way too much red wine, and blacks out. The next day, her cell rings and she's summoned to the next corpse. Wasn't it Ann Landers who said that killing people in a blackout was one of the twenty danger signals of alcoholism? To be sure, Delmarco helpfully suggests at one point that she should drink less. Maybe only enough to maim?

So anyway, on a dark and isolated pier in San Francisco, three of the characters come together. I won't reveal who they are, although if one of them isn't Ashley Judd it wouldn't be much of an ending. Certain death seems about to ensue, and then with an offstage grinding noise . . . but I don't want to give away the ending. Find out for yourself.

And ask yourself this question: Assuming the premise of the first amazing development, how did the San Francisco police department know exactly which dark and isolated pier these three people were on, and how did they arrive in sixty seconds (by car, truck, motorcycle, and helicopter), and how come the cops who arrived were precisely the same cops who have already been established as characters in the story? And isn't it convenient that, fast as they arrived, they considerately left time for the Talking Killer scene, in which all is explained when all the Killer has to do is blow everyone away and beat it?

The movie does at least draw a moral: *Nemo repente fuit turpissimus.*

2 Fast 2 Furious ★ ★ ★
PG-13, 100 m., 2003

Paul Walker (Brian O'Connor), Tyrese (Roman Pearce), Eva Mendes (Monica Fuentes), Cole Hauser (Carter Verone), Chris "Ludacris" Bridges (Tej), James Remar (Agent Markham), Devon Aoki (Suki). Directed by John Singleton and produced by Neal H. Moritz. Screenplay by Michael Brandt and Derek Haas.

John Singleton's *2 Fast 2 Furious* tells a story so shamelessly preposterous all we can do is shake our heads in disbelief. Consider that the big climax involves a Miami drug lord who hires two street racers to pick up bags full of money in

Miami and deliver them in the Keys, and adds, "You make it, I'll personally hand you one hundred G's at the finish line." Hell, for ten G's I'd rent a van at the Aventura Mall and deliver the goods myself.

But this is not an ordinary delivery. The drivers are expected to drive at speeds ranging from one hundred mph to jet-assisted takeoff velocities, which of course might attract the attention of the police, so the drug lord has to arrange a fifteen-minute "window" with a corrupt cop, whom he persuades by encouraging a rat to eat its way into his intestines. Does it strike you that this man is going to a lot of extra trouble?

Despite the persuasive rat, the cops do chase the speed racers, but the racers have anticipated this, and drive their cars into a vast garage, after which dozens or hundreds of other supercharged vehicles emerge from the garage, confusing the cops with a high-speed traffic jam. Oh, and some guys in monster trucks crush a lot of squad cars first. It is my instinct that the owners of monster trucks and street machines treat them with tender loving care, and don't casually volunteer to help out a couple of guys (one they've never seen before) by crashing their vehicles into police cars. You can get arrested for that.

Does it sound like I'm complaining? I'm not complaining. I'm grinning. 2 Fast 2 Furious is a video game crossed with a buddy movie, a bad cop–good cop movie, a Miami drug lord movie, a chase movie, and a comedy. It doesn't have a brain in its head, but it's made with skill and style and, boy, is it fast and furious.

How much like a video game is it? The two drivers are named Brian O'Connor (Paul Walker) and Roman Pearce (Tyrese). As they race down city streets at one-fifth the speed of sound, they talk to each other. They can't hear each other, but that doesn't matter, because what they say is exactly the kind of stuff that avatars say in video games. I took some notes:

"Let's see what this thing can do!"

"Watch this, bro!"

"Let's see if you still got it, Brian!"

"How you like them apples!?"

Walker returns from the original *The Fast and the Furious* (2001), which established Vin Diesel as a star. Rather than appear in this movie, about cops infiltrating his car gang to bust the drug cartel, Diesel decided instead to make *A Man Apart*, playing a cop fighting the drug cartel. Oddly enough, *F&F2* is the better movie.

Walker's costar is Tyrese, a.k.a. Tyrese Gibson, who was so good in Singleton's *Baby Boy* (2001) and is the engine that drives 2 Fast 2 Furious with energy and charisma. He's like an angrier Vin Diesel. Walker, who gets top billing in both movies, is pleasant but not compelling, sort of a Don Johnson lite.

Other key roles are by Cole Hauser as Carter Verone, the drug lord, whose Colombian parents didn't name him after Jimmy because he's too old for that, but possibly after Mother Maybelle; and Eva Mendes, as Monica Fuentes, the sexy undercover cop who has been on Verone's payroll for nine months and is either sleeping with him or is a sensational conversationalist.

O'Connor and Pearce are teamed up to work undercover as drivers for Verone, and promised that their records will be cleaned up if the mission succeeds. First they have to win their jobs. Verone assembles several teams of drivers and tells them he left a package in his red Ferrari at an auto pound twenty miles away. First team back with the package "gets the opportunity to work with me."

That sets off a high-speed race down Route 95 during which one car is crushed under the wheels of a truck, several more crash, and various racers and, presumably, civilians are killed. O'Connor and Pearce return with the package. As they're driving back, they don't even seem to pass the scene of the incredible carnage they caused in the opposite lanes; just as well, because at 120 mph you don't want to hit a gapers' block.

All of the chases involve the apparently inexhaustible supply of squad cars in South Florida. There's also a traffic jam in the sky, involving police and news helicopters. At one point a copter broadcaster hears a loud noise, looks up, and says, "What was that?" but we never find out what it was, perhaps because the movie is just too fast and too furious to slow down for a helicopter crash.

Two Brothers ★ ★ ½
PG, 109 m., 2004

Guy Pearce (Aidan McRory), Jean-Claude Dreyfus (Eugene Normandin), Philippine Leroy-

Beaulieu (Mathilde Normandin), Freddie
Highmore (Raoul), Oanh Nguyen (His
Excellency), Moussa Maaskri (Saladin), Vincent
Scarito (Zerbino), Maï Anh Le (Naï-Rea).
Directed by Jean-Jacques Annaud and
produced by Annaud and Jake Eberts.
Screenplay by Alain Godard and Annaud.

The brothers in *Two Brothers* are tiger cubs
when we meet them, prowling the ruins of temples in the jungles of French Indochina, circa
1920. With their mother and father, Kumal and
Sangha live an idyllic life, romping and wrestling
and living on air, apparently, since no prey ever
seems to be killed. The movie never really fesses
up that tigers kill for their dinner; that would
undercut its sentimentality. The result is a reassuring fairy tale that will fascinate children and
has moments of natural beauty for their parents, but makes the tigers approximately as realistic as the animals in *The Lion King*.

The movie is astonishing in its photography
of the two tigers, played by an assortment of
trained beasts, augmented by CGI. It is less
wondrous in its human story, involving such
walking stereotypes as the great British hunter,
the excitable French administrator, the misunderstood Indochinese prince, and the little
French boy who makes friends with Sangha
and sleeps with him when Sangha is at an age to
be plenty old enough for his own bed, preferably behind bars.

Two Brothers was directed and cowritten by
Jean-Jacques Annaud, whose international hit
The Bear (1989) did not sentimentalize its bear
cub but treated it with the respect due to an animal that earns its living under the law of the
wild. In that one, the speech of the hunter (Jack
Wallace) was presented not so much as language as simply the sounds that human animals make. In *Two Brothers*, the cubs may not
understand English, but they get the drift. In
both films, Annaud achieves almost miraculous moments, the result no doubt of a combination of training, patience, and special effects.
We're usually convinced we are looking at real
tiger cubs doing what they really want to do,
even when it goes against their nature. Occasionally there will be a scene that stretches it, as
when Kumal, who was trained in a circus to
jump through a ring of fire, apparently uses
telepathy to convince Sangha he can do it too.

The first half-hour or so involves only the
cubs, and these scenes play like a scripted documentary. The beauty of the tigers and the exotic nature of the locations are so seductive we
almost forget the movie has human stars and
will therefore interrupt with a plot. But it does.

The villain, who becomes the hero, is Aidan
McRory (Guy Pearce), introduced as an ivory
hunter but then, after the bottom drops out of
the ivory market, a tomb raider. When one of
his assistants finds an ancient statue in the forest and regrets it's too heavy to bring back to
Europe, McRory coldly tells him, "cut off its
head." McRory is the one who kills the cubs' father and captures Kumal, selling him to a circus
run by the harsh trainer Zerbino (Vincent
Scarito).

Sangha is also captured, and adopted by
young Raoul (Freddie Highmore), son of the
French colonial administrator (Jean-Claude
Dreyfus). He eventually ends up in the
menagerie of a spoiled prince (Oanh Nguyen);
Sangha is no longer safe as Raoul's playmate, the
kid is told, "now that he has tasted blood." Apparently until that fatal taste, Sangha was a vegetarian. The prince decrees that the two tigers
fight to the death in an amphitheater, but of
course, being brothers, they ... well, do more or
less exactly what we expect them to do.

The story is broad melodrama that treats
Sangha and Kumal as if they were almost
human in their motivations and emotions.
Such comforting sentiment is a luxury wild animals cannot afford. Still, along with the beauty
of the animals and the photography, there are
moments of genuine tension, as when McRory
faces the tigers up close. That McRory does not
make his own contribution to their taste for
blood is because of the tiger's uncanny ability
to peer deeply into the eyes of the human actors
and learn there what they must do for the
benefit of the movie's plot.

There is a lot in *Two Brothers* I admire. Families will not go wrong in attending this film.
Some kids will think it's one of the best movies
they've seen. My objections are of a sort that
won't occur, I realize, to many of the viewers.
But I remember *The Bear* and its brave refusal
to supply its bear cub with human emotions
and motivations. W. G. Sebald writes that animals and humans view one another "through a
breach of incomprehension." That is pro-

foundly true, and helpful to keep in mind when making friends with the bears at Yellowstone, or reassuring tigers that we feel their pain.

Tycoon: A New Russian ★ ★ ½
NO MPAA RATING, 128 m., 2003

Vladimir Mashkov (Platon ["Plato"]), Andrei Krasko (Chmakov), Maria Mironova (Maria), Vladimir Golovin (Ahmet), Vladimir Goussav (Lomov), Alexandre Baluev (Koretski). Directed by Pavel Lounguine and produced by Catherine Dussart and Vladimir Grigoriev. Screenplay by Alexandre Borodianski, Lounguine, and Youli Doubov, adapted from the novel by Doubov.

Tycoon is subtitled *A New Russian*, and indeed its hero is a Russian unlike those we usually see in the movies: Plato Makovski is a killer capitalist, a onetime mathematics professor who seizes on the fall of Marxism as his opportunity to play capitalist tricks in a naive new economy. The character is based on the real-life billionaire Boris Berezovsky, who is even rumored to have financed it. Like *The Godfather*, it shows him as a crook with certain standards, surrounded by rats with none.

The movie is handicapped by a jittery editing style that prevents us from getting involved in the flow of the narrative, but it provides visuals for all those headlines about the Russian Mafia, go-go capitalists, and Moscow as Dodge City. It also suggests a series of recent Russian governments shot through with corruption and bribery, which may help explain why this was the most successful Russian film in history at the box office.

Makovski is played by Vladimir Mashkov, who in some lights looks handsome and in others feral. He has a charm based on brilliance. Most of his inner circle, like himself, came up through universities, since academia offered an alternative to bureaucracy and the army in the precollapse days. There are scenes where he dazzles the others with his audacious schemes, explaining how he will sell cars at a loss to make a profit, or pay off three debts with a nonexistent payment that circles through the debts back to the place where it does not exist.

If you don't understand that, neither do some of his admiring colleagues, but it must work, since Plato ends up fabulously wealthy.

He operates not by stealth, like old-model crooks, but in the modern style of audacious publicity. Like the con men at Enron, he presents his crimes as a thriving capitalist success story, and he has access to the highest levels of the Kremlin, just as Enron had in the White House. His empire is centered in a towering Moscow high-rise with the company name in giant letters on the roof.

All of this apparently comes to an end, however, in the assassination that opens the movie. His armored Mercedes is blown apart by an antitank missile; soon after it appears he will have to face criminal charges. ("I am a politician," he tells a TV interviewer, "and jail is part of the game.") The movie then flashes back over the past fifteen years to tell his story, using titles like "Three days before Plato's death" or "Five years before Plato's death" before each scene. These titles are of no help, because the structure makes it impossible for us to get a clear idea of chronology, and so the scenes have to be viewed as free-standing episodes involving recurring characters.

Among those characters is one of particular interest, a bulbous politician from Siberia named Lomov (Vladimir Goussav), whom Plato grooms to be the new premiere—only to be double-crossed. It's haunting, the way in which Lomov is created from nothing, grows popular through bald-faced lies, is forgiven his stupidity by an electorate tired of details, and is obedient to the interests of his billionaire backers. Lomov even becomes deluded that he has accomplished all of this on his own, and there is a strange confrontation in which he and Plato have entirely different ideas of their relationship. Plato has many other friends, including Koretski (Alexandre Baluev), a powerful minister who fights corruption mercilessly until his bribers mention the correct figure.

Another intriguing character is Chmakov (Andrei Krasko), a prosecuting judge from the provinces, brought in to investigate Plato's assassination. Although Plato and his confederates controlled an empire of bewildering size and complexity, this dogged and weary man is supposed to find the truth all by himself, and plods about in drizzly weather, looking uncannily like Mickey Spillane.

Chmakov drinks a lot, but then so does almost everyone in the movie. There isn't a major character who isn't an alcoholic, with the exception of Maria (Maria Mironova), Plato's sometime, arm's-length girlfriend. Watching this movie makes it easier to understand why the average Russian male doesn't live to be fifty: The wonder is that they live so long.

One particularly amusing character is Ahmet (Vladimir Golovin), a very old man who is brought in to deal with a gang of thugs who want 50 percent of Plato's auto dealings. He arranges a meeting for the next day. The ancient man, unprotected by bodyguards, greets the thugs in a grungy industrial area while seated behind a table with linen and crystal. He savors some caviar, informs them Plato is under his protection, and awes them into submission. It is not clear at the time whether Ahmet really is a legendary godfather or simply a bold con man. Certainly the thugs have no way of knowing.

Berezovsky, the real-life Plato, has been in trouble in recent years, including an arrest in the United Kingdom. Extradition is pending. At the end of his career Plato is lonely, isolated, and tired, and that is supposed to be the moral of the story. Yes, but since all of us face the possibility of loneliness, isolation, and exhaustion, perhaps it is better to face that fate as a billionaire.

U

Uncle Nino ★ ★
PG, 102 m., 2005

Joe Mantegna (Robert Micelli), Anne Archer (Marie Micelli), Pierrino Mascarino (Uncle Nino), Trevor Morgan (Bobby Micelli), Gina Mantegna (Gina Micelli). Directed by Robert Shallcross and produced by David James. Screenplay by Shallcross.

The loudest danger signal for Uncle Nino, after he arrives from Italy to visit his dead brother's family, is that the wine comes from a cardboard box with a spigot. There are other problems. The nephew and his wife are both working too hard, the kids are on the edge of rebellion, and the household has no dog. Obviously, a family in crisis; obviously, Uncle Nino is the solution. He will return them all to their old-world roots, and reawaken their sense of family.

And so he does, in *Uncle Nino*, a family movie that some will find wholesome and heartwarming and others will find cornball and tiresome. You know who you are. I know who I am. This is not my kind of movie, and I found myself feeling mighty restless by the end, or even halfway through, or even near the beginning, but objectively I know there are people who will embrace this movie, and my duty as a critic is to tell them about it.

The film goes into national release with an interesting marketing story behind it. Independently financed and made in Chicago, it was rejected by major distributors and festivals. It opened in one theater in Grand Rapids, Michigan, played fifty-five weeks, grossed $170,000, and has ecstatic user comments on the Internet Movie Database. It also has an IMDb "user rating" of 9.1, which is 0.1 higher than *The Godfather*. This rating is interesting because 79.4 percent of everyone voting for it gave it a perfect "10" rating, and because the breakdown of voters into males, females, age groups, U.S. and non–U.S. reveals that the approval rating in each and every group is uncannily close to 9 (every female under eighteen scored it 10, and the hardest to please were males thirty to thirty-four, at 7.4). Does

this suggest to you that someone has been force-feeding the database?

Never mind. Let's regard the movie. It stars Joe Mantegna and Anne Archer as Robert and Marie Micelli, a Glenview, Illinois, couple who have moved into an expensive new home and are working hard to keep up. Their son, Bobby (Trevor Morgan), is a fourteen-year-old who belongs to a band that can't find a place to practice, and their twelve-year-old daughter, Gina (Gina Mantegna), spends a lot of time at her best friend's house because nobody is home at her house. She wants a dog, but Robert doesn't want the mess and bother.

Enter Uncle Nino (Pierrino Mascarino), one of those lovable movie ethnic types who speaks no English except for each and every word he requires in a specific situation. He is making a belated visit to America to visit the grave of his late brother. A quick study, he perceives that the Micelli family needs more quality time, more music, wine in bottles, and a dog. In attempting to remedy these needs, he blunders into various episodes of mistaken intentions, mistaken identities, and mistaken mistakes. He is simultaneously saintly and comic, and filled with a wisdom at which American suburbanites can only shake their heads with envy.

The film ends with the high school battle of the bands. Does Bobby's band get enough rehearsal time to qualify? What role do Uncle Nino and his violin play? Is there a scene in which the busy dad is able to tear himself away from the office in order to sit in the audience and make significant eye contact with his son, indicating that a lifelong bond has been forged, and that he'll be a better father in the future?

As it happens, Joe Mantegna has appeared in a much better movie about an older Italian man with deep innocence in his heart. That would be David Mamet's wonderful *Things Change* (1988), starring Don Ameche as an old shoeshine man who is mistaken as a Mafia don because of his way of looking mysterious and issuing truisms that sound like profundities. *Uncle Nino* made me wish I was seeing that movie again.

I am quite aware, however, that *Uncle Nino*

will appeal to those who seek sunny, predictable, positive family entertainment and do not demand that it also be challenging or have any depth. The success in Grand Rapids was because of word-of-mouth, as people told each other about the film, and if it is allowed to find an audience in its national release, that will probably happen again. It's that kind of movie, for better or worse.

Under the Tuscan Sun ★ ★ ★
PG-13, 102 m., 2003

Diane Lane (Frances Mayes), Raoul Bova (Marcello), Sandra Oh (Patti), Vincent Riotta (Mr. Martini), Lindsay Duncan (Katherine), Giulia Steigerwalt (Chiara), Dan Bucatinsky (Rodney), Valentine Pelka (Jerzy), Ralph Palka (The German Man), Kristoffer Ryan Winters (David). Directed by Audrey Wells and produced by Tom Sternberg and Wells, based on the book *Under the Tuscan Sun: At Home in Italy* by Frances Mayes.

Under the Tuscan Sun is an alluring example of yuppie porn, seducing audiences with a shapely little villa in Italy. While once Katharine Hepburn journeyed to Venice, met Rosanna Brazzi, and jumped into the Grand Canal, now Diane Lane journeys to Tuscany and jumps into real estate. She does find romance, to be sure, but it's not what she's looking for and, besides, a villa pleasures her all day long.

Lane plays Frances Mayes, a San Francisco author who discovers her husband is cheating on her. She gets out of the marriage, and a friend (Sandra Oh) gives her a ticket to Italy on a gay tour—"so nobody will hit on you," she explains. The next thing she knows, Frances is getting off the tour bus and making an offer on a charming little villa that needs a lot of work. The contessa who owns it will not sell to anybody; she demands a sign from God, but when Frances is bombed by a pigeon, that's good enough for the contessa.

The movie is escapist in the time-honored Hollywood way, inviting us to share the heroine's joy as she moves in, meets the neighbors, and hires illegal workers from Poland to rehab the place. Diane Lane's assignment in many scenes is simply to be delighted. Although she wants to be alone, that would give her no one to talk to, and so the movie surrounds her with colorful and eccentric locals, including Katherine (Lindsay Duncan), who wears big hats and got a lot of good advice from Fellini, and Mr. Martini (Vincent Riotta), a friendly real estate agent who has a crush on her. There is also a jolly family next door with an aged grandmother who is heartbroken after being dumped by an e-mail lover from Ecuador.

The movie is inspired by *Under the Tuscan Sun: At Home in Italy,* a best-seller by Frances Mayes, unread by me. I gather that Mayes in real life did not have the divorce, etc., and I suspect she also did not experience certain events that are obligatory in movies of this sort, including the accidentally collapsing ceiling and the violent thunderstorm. As lightning flashed, windows banged open, rain poured in, and the heavens vented their fury, it occurred to me what convenient storytelling devices thunderstorms are: They allow heroines to get wet, run from room to room in desperation, be surrounded by drama, and wake up the next morning to a perfect day—all for free, without the slightest need to establish why the storm started or stopped. Any screenwriter seeking an exciting transition between two plot points is safe with a thunderstorm, which doesn't require dialogue or change anything, but gives the audience the impression something is happening.

So, yes, the movie is basically paint-by-numbers. The first time Frances sees the villa, it looks not so much run-down, but more like a crew of prop men had worked for a week to supply crooked shutters, peeling paint, and overgrown gardens. By the end, when it looks like a photo from *Conde Nast Traveler,* it looks as if the same prop men have been working with Martha Stewart. But that's the whole point: We don't want a realistic movie about illegal Polish workmen rehabbing a yuppie's new house (although such a movie exists: Jerzy Skolimowski's *Moonlighting,* from 1982). We want a fantasy in which after the colorful setbacks, the house emerges magically from its cocoon, and so does the heroine.

What redeems the film is its successful escapism and Diane Lane's performance. They are closely linked. Consider first Diane Lane. Some people are fortunate to have faces that can be decoded as a sign of good character. This has nothing to do with "beauty" and more to do with ineffables like smiles and eyes. Diane Lane involves us, implicates us. We don't stand outside her performance, and neither does she. We sign on for the ride, and when clichés happen (like the thunderstorm), in a way we're watching Diane Lane surviving the scene rather than her character surviving the storm. The dynamic is the same. She persuades us that she deserves to be happy. When her character has sex for the first time in a long time, the movie is shy about showing the sex but bold about showing her reaction, as she comes home, bounces up and down on her bed, pumps her fist in the air, and shouts, "Yes! Yes! I still got it!" More movie characters feel like that than ever admit it.

Of the supporting cast, I can say that Vincent Riotta can occasionally be seen winking from behind the ethic stereotypes, that Sandra Oh has that wonderful air of no-nonsense friendship, but that Frances's whirlwind lover Marcello (Raoul Bova) needn't have been so obviously ripped from the bodice of a romance novel.

That leaves Katherine (Lindsay Duncan), who dresses like the flamboyant mistress played by Sandra Milo in Fellini's 8½, turns up everywhere the plot requires her, shares memories of Fellini which, if they are true, would make her seventyish, and is inexplicable and therefore intriguing. There is absolutely no reason for this character to be in the movie, and really no explanation for who she is and what she wants. We keep waiting for the plot to give her something to do, but she exists firmly at the level of comic relief and ambiguous sexual implication. She's better than a thunderstorm, and I would not do without her.

Undertow ★ ★ ★ ★
R, 107 m., 2004

Jamie Bell (Chris Munn), Devon Alan (Tim Munn), Josh Lucas (Deel Munn), Dermot Mulroney (John Munn), Kristen Stewart (Lila), Shiri Appleby (Violet). Directed by David Gordon Green and produced by Terrence Malick, Lisa Muskat, and Edward R. Pressman. Screenplay by Joe Conway and Green.

The two boys live in a rural area of Georgia with their father. The older, Chris, is quietly building a reputation as a troublemaker; the younger, Tim, is an odd kid who eats mud and paint and explains he is "organizing my books by the way they smell." Their father, John, mourns his dead wife and keeps his boys so isolated that on his birthday Chris complains, "We can't even have friends. What kind of a birthday party is it with just the three of us?"

A fourth arrives. This is Deel, John's brother, fresh out of prison and harboring resentment. "I knew your mom first—she was my girl," he tells Chris. Deel and John's father had a hoard of Mexican gold coins with a legend attached to them: They belonged to the ferryman on the river Styx. Deel believes he should have inherited half of the coins, and believes John has them hidden somewhere around the place.

If this sounds as much like a Brothers Grimm tale as a plot, that is the intention of David Gordon Green, the gifted director of Undertow. Still only twenty-nine, he has made three films of considerable power, and has achieved what few directors ever do: After watching one of his films for a scene or two, you know who directed it. His style has been categorized as "southern Gothic," but that's too narrow. I sense a poetic merging of realism and surrealism; every detail is founded on fact and accurate observation, but the effect appeals to our instinct for the mythological. This fusion is apparent when his characters say something that (a) sounds exactly as if it's the sort of thing they would say, but (b) is like nothing anyone has ever said before. I'm thinking of lines like, "He thinks about infinity. The doctor says his brain's not ready for it." Or, "Can I carve my name in your face?"

Undertow, like Green's George Washington (2001) and All the Real Girls (2003), takes place in a South where the countryside coexists with a decaying industrial landscape. We see not the thriving parts of cities, but the desolate places they have forgotten. His central characters are usually adolescents, vibrating with sexual feelings but unsure how to express them, and with a core of decency they are not much aware of.

In writing Undertow, Green said at the Toronto Film Festival, he had in mind stories by the Grimms, Mark Twain, and Robert Louis Stevenson, and also Capote's In Cold Blood. He wears these sources lightly. While much is made about the family legends surrounding the gold coins, they inspire not superstition but greed and function in the story just as any treasure would. Although we see two generations in which there is a troubled brother and a strange brother, the parallels are not underlined.

Instead, we see largely through the eyes of Chris (Jamie Bell, from *Billy Elliot* and *Nicholas Nickleby*). He figures in the startling opening sequence, where he tries to get the attention of a girl he likes, is chased away, and lands on a board with a nail in it. The audience recoils in shock. But now watch how he *continues* to hobble along with the board still attached to his foot. This is technically funny, but in a very painful way, and who but Green would think of the moment when an arresting cop gives Chris his board back?

Chris is in rebellion against the isolated life created for them by their father (Dermot Mulroney). So is Tim (Devon Alan), but in an internal way, expressed by the peculiar things he eats and the chronic stomach pain that results. When their Uncle Deel (Josh Lucas) appears one day, he is at first a welcome change, with his laid-back permissiveness. John asks Deel to watch the kids during the day while he's at work, but Deel is not very good at this, and points his nephews toward more trouble than he saves them from.

The bad feeling over the gold coins comes to a head in an instant of violence, and the boys run away from home, entering a world that evokes *The Night of the Hunter* (1955). In both films, two siblings flee from a violent man through a haunted and dreamy southern landscape. The people they meet during their flight all look and sound real enough, but also have the qualities of strangers encountered in fantasies: the kindly black couple who lets them work for food, and the secret community of other kids, living in a junkyard. If these passages add up to a chase scene, Green directs not for thrills but for deeper, more ominous feelings, and the music by Philip Glass doesn't heighten, as it would during a conventional chase scene, but deepens, as if the chase is descending into ominous dreads.

Green has a visual style that is beautiful without being pretty. We never catch him photographing anything for its scenic or decorative effect. Instead, his landscapes have the kind of underlined ambiguity you'd find in the work of a serious painter; these are not trees and swamps and rivers, but Trees and Swamps and Rivers—it's here that the parallel with *The Night of the Hunter* is most visible.

Undertow is the closest Green has come to a conventional narrative, although at times you can sense him pulling away from narrative requirements to stay a little longer in a moment that fascinates him. He is not a director of plots so much as a director of tones, emotions, and moments of truth, and there's a sense of gathering fate even in the lighter scenes. His films remind me of *Days of Heaven,* by Terrence Malick (one of this film's producers), in the way they are told as memories, as if all of this happened and is over with and cannot be changed; you watch a Green film not to see what will happen, but to see what did happen.

Films like *Undertow* leave some audiences unsettled because they do not proceed predictably according to the rules. But they are immediately available to our emotions, and we fall into a kind of waking trance, as if being told a story at an age when we half-believed everything we heard. It takes us a while to get back to our baseline; Green takes us to that place where we keep feelings that we treasure, but are a little afraid of.

Underworld ★ ★

R, 121 m., 2003

Kate Beckinsale (Selene), Scott Speedman (Michael), Shane Brolly (Kraven), Michael Sheen (Lucian), Bill Nighy (Viktor), Erwin Leder (Singe), Sophia Myles (Erika). Directed by Len Wiseman and produced by Gary Lucchesi, Tom Rosenberg, and Richard S. Wright. Screenplay by Danny McBride.

Umberto Eco, the distinguished writer from Italy, offered a definition of pornography that has stood the test of time. A porno movie, he said, is a movie where you become acutely aware that the characters are spending too much time getting in and out of cars and walking in and out of doors. Eco's wisdom came to mind when Todd McCarthy, writing in *Variety,* observed of *Underworld* that "there may be more openings and closings of doors in this picture than in the entire oeuvre of Ernst Lubitsch." That is not the sort of detail that should occur to you while you're watching a movie about a war between werewolves and vampires.

But *Underworld* is all surfaces, all costumes and sets and special effects, and so you might as well look at the doors as anything else. This is a movie so paltry in its characters and shallow in its story that the war seems to exist primarily to provide graphic visuals. Two of those visuals are Kate Beckinsale, who plays Selene, a vampire with (apparently) an unlimited line of credit at North Beach Leather, and Scott Speedman as Michael, a young intern who is human, at least until he is bitten by a werewolf—and maybe even after, since although you become a vampire after one bites you, I am uncertain about the rules regarding werewolves.

Hold on, I just Googled it. A werewolf bite does indeed turn you into a werewolf, according to a Website about the computer game Castlevania, which helpfully goes on to answer the very question I was going to ask next: "What would be the result if a werewolf bites a vampire? It is called a were-pire or wolf zombie . . ." The reason intern Michael is bitten by the werewolf Lucian, I think, is because the werewolves want to create a new hybrid race and gang up on the vampires.

All of this is an emotional drain on Selene, who finds herself in love with a werewolf at the same time that her vampire kingdom is in grave danger. Exactly why she falls in love with Michael, or whether love bites are allowed in their foreplay, is not very clear, probably because romance and sex inevitably involve dialogue, and dialogue really slows things down. This is not a movie that lingers for conversation; its first words, "You're acting like a pack of rabid dogs," occur after fifteen minutes of nonstop and senseless action in a fight scene involving characters we have not been introduced to.

Selene is being challenged for leader of the vampires by Kraven (Shane Brolly), who, as you might have guessed from his name, is a villain, just as you can guess from his name that Viktor (Bill Nighy) is not. Viktor, in fact, is deep in a sleep of centuries when he's awakened prematurely by Selene, who needs his advice to deal with the werewolf/human/Kraven situation. The gradual transformation in appearance of the reawakened Viktor is an intriguing special-effects exercise; he begins as a terminal case of psoriasis and ends as merely cheerfully cadaverous.

Underworld is the directing debut of Len Wiseman, an art director *(Stargate, Independence Day)* who can stage great-looking situations but has few ideas about characters and plots. It's so impossible to care about the characters in the movie that I didn't care if the vampires or werewolves won. I might not have cared in a better movie, either, but I might have been willing to pretend.

The United States of Leland ★ ★
R, 108 m., 2004

Don Cheadle (Pearl Madison), Ryan Gosling (Leland P. Fitzgerald), Chris Klein (Allen Harris), Jena Malone (Becky Pollard), Lena Olin (Marybeth Fitzgerald), Kevin Spacey (Albert T. Fitzgerald), Martin Donovan (Harry Pollard), Ann Magnuson (Karen Pollard), Michelle Williams (Julie Pollard), Kerry Washington (Ayesha). Directed by Matthew Ryan Hoge and produced by Bernie Morris, Jonah Smith, Kevin Spacey, and Palmer West. Screenplay by Hoge.

Early in *The United States of Leland*, a teenager named Leland stabs an autistic boy twenty times, is arrested for the murder, and explains why he committed it: "Because of the sadness." The movie will cycle through many characters and much fraught dialogue to explain this statement, but it never seems sure what it thinks about Leland's action. I believe it is as cruel and senseless as the killings in *Elephant*, but while that film was chillingly objective, this one seems to be on everybody's side. It's a moral muddle.

Leland P. Fitzgerald (Ryan Gosling) is the alienated child of a distant mother (Lena Olin) and an absent father who is a famous novelist (Kevin Spacey). Much is made of his father's decision to send his son on a trip every year—to Paris, to Venice—but not to meet him there. Leland has recently broken up with Becky (Jena Malone), the drug-addicted sister of the murdered boy, but that doesn't seem to be the reason for his action.

We meet the victim's other sister, Julie (Michelle Williams), and her boyfriend, Allen (Chris Klein). They're also in a rocky time in their romance, but we can't be sure that's what prompts Allen to the action he takes in the film. The dead boy's parents are Harry and Karen Pollard (Martin Donovan and Ann Magnuson), and while they are bereft, they express themselves in ways borrowed from docudramas.

There are two perfectly crafted performances in the movie, by Spacey as Albert Fitzgerald, the novelist who flies in from Europe, and by Don Cheadle as Pearl Madison, a high school teacher in the juvenile detention facility where Leland is held. Pearl, who perhaps sees a book in the murder, encourages Leland to open up about his feelings, and much of the movie is narrated by Leland from writings in his journal.

Some of the scenes in the movie, written and directed by Matthew Ryan Hoge, are so perfectly conceived that they show up the rest. When the novelist and the teacher meet in a hotel bar, it's an opportunity for Spacey to exercise his gift for understated irony ("There are no private spaces in my son's heart reserved for me"), and for Cheadle to show a man conflicted between his real concern for Leland and his personal awe at meeting the great writer. Ryan Gosling, a gifted actor, does everything that can be done with Leland, but the character comes from a writer's conceits, not from life.

The movie circles through characters and subplots on its way to its final revelations, and some of the subplots are blatantly unnecessary. Why, for example, must Cheadle's character have an affair with a coworker (Kerry Washington) and then try to explain it to his apparently estranged girlfriend? What does this have to do with anything? Why, really, does Spacey's character fly in if he is only going to sit in a hotel bar and exude literate bitterness? Perhaps to show that his emotional distance from his son helped lead to the murder? But no, because Leland's problem is not alienation, but an excess of empathy.

Lost in all of this is the fate of the murdered boy. The character and his autism are used as plot points, and there is little concern about his fate except as it helps set the story into motion and provide the inspiration for Leland's action. Subplots involving his sisters, their problems, their romances, and their boyfriends are made more confusing because the movie makes it

difficult for us to be sure who they are; for a long time we're not sure they're sisters. That's not subtle writing, but needless confusion.

The reason for Leland's action, when we understand it, has a clarity and simplicity that would be at home in a short story. The problem is that the movie follows such a tortured path in arriving at it that, at the end, his motive is not so much a moment of insight as a plot point. And there is another murder in the movie that had me leaving the theater completely uncertain about how I was intended to feel about it. Is it that the first murder, however tragically mistaken, was at least committed with loftier motives than the second? Or what?

Unleashed ★ ★ ★
R, 103 m., 2005

Jet Li (Danny), Morgan Freeman (Sam), Bob Hoskins (Bart), Kerry Condon (Victoria). Directed by Louis Leterrier and produced by Luc Besson, Steven Chaseman, and Jet Li. Screenplay by Besson.

The story is familiar. The dog has been raised from infancy as a killer, obedient to its master. When it wears its collar it is passive. When the collar is removed and an order is given, it turns into a savage murder machine. Then a confusing thing happens. The dog experiences kindness for the first time in its life. Does this mean its master is wrong and must be disobeyed?

Luc Besson has produced or written some of the most intriguing movies of the last twenty years (*La Femme Nikita, The Fifth Element, Kiss of the Dragon, Ong-Bak*). He takes this classic animal story and makes a simple but inspired change: He turns the dog into a human being. Jet Li stars in *Unleashed* as Danny, a lethal martial arts warrior who has been raised in captivity since childhood and is used by Bart, a Glasgow gangster, as a fearsome weapon. Danny lives in a cage under the floor of Bart's headquarters, travels quietly in the gangster's car, and, when his collar is removed, explodes into violent fury and leaves rooms filled with his victims.

This is a story that could have made a laughable movie. That it works is because of the performances of Jet Li and Bob Hoskins, who plays his master. "Danny the dog" is fearful of his owner, passive in captivity, and obedient in action, because he has been trained that way for his whole life. Bart the gangster is another one of those feral characters Hoskins specializes in, a man who bares his teeth and seems prepared to dine on the throats of his enemies. Hoskins, who can be the most genial of men, has a dimension of pitiless cruelty that he revealed in his first starring role, *The Long Good Friday* (1980).

But *Unleashed* would be too simple if it were only about Bart and Danny. Besson's screenplay now adds the character of Sam, a blind piano tuner played by Morgan Freeman. Sam lives in a gentle world of musicians and pianos and his beloved stepdaughter, Victoria (Kerry Condon). Danny falls into their lives by accident, after running away from Bart, as a dog is likely to do when it becomes fed up with its master.

In Danny's early memories, a piano figures somehow. A drawing of a piano triggers some of those old shadows, and when he hears piano music with Sam and Victoria, and when they give him his first simple music lessons, a great cloud lifts from his mind and he knows joy for the first time. He also begins to recall his mother, who was a pianist, and remembers fragments of the events that led to him becoming Danny the dog.

The film is ingenious in its construction. It has all the martial arts action any Jet Li fan could possibly desire, choreographed by Yeun Woo-ping, who is the Gerald Arpino of kung fu and creates improbable but delightful ballets of chops and socks, leaps and twists, and kicks and improvisations. Everything happens in a denatured sepia tone that is not black and white nor quite color, but a palate drained of cheer and pressing down like a foggy day.

Because Hoskins is so good at focusing the ferocity of Bart, he distracts us from the impossible elements in the trained-killer plot. Because Morgan Freeman brings an unforced plausibility to every character he plays, we simply accept the piano tuner instead of noticing how implausibly he enters the story. Freeman handles the role in the only way that will work, by playing a piano tuner as a piano tuner, instead of as a plot device in a martial arts movie. His stepdaughter, Victoria, is invaluable because, as Ann Coulter was explaining when she was so rudely shouted down the other day, women are a civilizing influence on men, who will get up to mischief in each other's company; Victoria's gentleness stirs Danny's humanity more than it inflames his lust.

So many action movies are made on autopilot that I am grateful when one works outside the box. Luc Besson, as producer and writer, almost always brings an unexpected human element to his action stories. *Unleashed* ends with a confrontation between Bart and Danny in which Bart reveals the truly twisted depth of his attachment to the "dog." They say dogs and their owners eventually start to resemble each other, but in this case an actual transference seems to be going on.

The Untold Story of Emmett Louis Till ★ ★ ★
NO MPAA RATING, 70 m., 2005

A documentary directed and produced by Keith Beauchamp. Screenplay by Beauchamp.

There is no statute of limitations on murder. Fifty years after the death of Emmett Till, the U.S. Justice Department reopened the case of the fourteen-year-old black boy from Chicago who went to visit his grandfather in Mississippi and was kidnapped, tortured, and killed because he whistled at a white woman.

The case electrified the nation in 1955, not least because Emmett's indomitable mother, Mamie, enlisted Chicago officials in her fight to gain possession of the boy's body, which authorities in Money, Mississippi, wanted to bury as quickly and quietly as possible. In a heartbreaking sequence in *The Untold Story of Emmett Louis Till*, she recalls saying: "I told the funeral director, 'If you can't open the box, I can. I want to see what's in that box.'"

What she found was the already decomposing body of her son, which had spent three days in a bayou of the Tallahatchie River, a heavy cotton gin fan tied to his neck with barbed wire. The mother is deliberate as she describes what she saw. She always thought her son's teeth were "the prettiest thing I ever saw." All but two were knocked out. One eyeball was hanging on his chin. An ear was missing. She saw daylight through the bullet hole in his head. His skull had been chopped almost in two, the face separated from the back of the head.

What Mamie Till did then made history. She insisted that the casket remain open at the Chicago funeral. Thousands filed past the remains. A photograph in Jet magazine made such an impression that, fifty years later, 60 Minutes reporter Ed Bradley remembers seeing it; he discusses it on his program with Keith Beauchamp, director of this film, a much younger man who saw the photo and became obsessed with the case.

It was Beauchamp's nine years of investigation, summarized in the film, that was primarily responsible for Justice reopening the case. In the original trial, two white men, Roy Bryant and J. W. Milam, were charged with the crime. An all-white jury took only an hour to acquit them, later explaining they would have returned sooner, but took a "soda pop break" to make it look better. Only two months later, immune because of laws against double jeopardy, the two men sold their story to Look magazine for $4,000 and confessed to the crime.

Both are now dead. But Beauchamp's investigation indicates fourteen people were involved in one way or another in the murder, including five black employees of the white men, as well as the woman Till whistled at. Five of them are still alive.

The film inevitably invites comparison with 4 Little Girls (1997), Spike Lee's powerful documentary about the 1963 Birmingham church bombing, which includes the long-delayed conviction of Robert ("Dynamite Bob") Chambliss, one of the bombers. Lee is the better filmmaker, with better source materials to work with, and his film is more passionate.

Beauchamp's film, on the other hand, has an earnest solemnity that is appropriate to the material. He has a lot of old black-and-white TV and newsreel footage, including shots of the accused men before, during, and after their trial. He interviews Emmett's young cousins who were in the house on the night the white men took him away. He recounts the courage of Emmett's uncle, who in the courtroom fearlessly pointed out the men who had taken Emmett, when such an act was a death sentence in Mississippi.

It is startling, the way the local sheriff casually tells TV reporters, "We didn't have any problems until our niggers went up north and talked to the NAACP and came back down here and caused trouble." And the way reporter Dan Wakefield recalls, "Everybody in the town knew they did it," even before they confessed in Look magazine. The defense attorneys informed the jury their forefathers would "roll over in their graves" if they voted to convict. But the case would not go away, and has not gone away. Mamie Till died in January 2003, just a little too soon to learn that the case was reopened.

Up and Down ★ ★ ★
R, 108 m., 2005

Petr Forman (Martin Horecky), Emilia Vasaryova (Vera), Jiri Machacek (Frantisek Fikes), Natasa Burger (Miluska), Jan Triska (Otakar), Ingrid Timkova (Hana), Kristyna Liska-Bokova (Lenka), Jaroslav Dusek (Colonel). Directed by Jan Hrebejk and produced by Milan Kuchynka and Ondrej Trojan. Screenplay by Hrebejk and Petr Jarchovsky.

In the middle of the night on a back road of the Czech Republic, two truck drivers unload a group of illegal immigrants from India. Then they drive away, unaware that they still have a passenger—a baby, left behind in the confusion. Should they try to return the infant to its mother? No, because they don't know how to find her without risking arrest. Should they dump the baby by the roadside? One thinks that would be a good idea, but the other doesn't, and they end up selling the baby to the owners of a shady pawnshop.

This opening sets up one of the story lines in Up and Down, a Czech film about working-class and middle-class characters, former and present wives, infant and grown children, current and retired soccer fans, professors and hooligans, criminals and the police. Director Jan Hrebejk and his cowriter, Petr Jarchovsky, are interested not so much in making a statement about their society as seeing it reflected in specific lives; in this, their film resembles the early work of the Czech director Milos

Forman *(The Fireman's Ball)*, whose son Petr plays one of the film's leads.

The first couple we meet after the pawnshop are the Fikeses, Miluska and Frantisek (Natasa Burger and Jiri Machacek). They're not very bright, but not bad people. He's a night watchman, sensitive about his cleft palate, grateful to his wife for having dinner with him even though "I eat ugly." He's a member of a soccer team's fanatic group of supporters, who meet to watch the games on TV, get drunk, sing, chant slogans, and go through the emotional yo-yo of victory and defeat.

Miluska desperately wants a baby. She can't conceive. They can't adopt because Frantisek has a police record (he blames the soccer club for leading him into hooliganism). After almost stealing a baby in its carriage, she's afraid: "I'll do something and they'll arrest me." The baby at the pawn shop is a godsend. They buy it, bring it home, and love it. When Frantisek's booster club buddy makes racist remarks about the baby's dark skin, Frantisek boots him out, resigns from the club, and joins his wife in loving the baby.

Then we meet another family, the Horeckas. Martin (Petr Forman) has spent the last twenty years in Australia—a useful explanation for his English-accented Czech, no doubt. He returns home to visit his father, Otakar (Jan Triska), and mother, Vera (Emilia Vasaryova), who have divorced. He is also confronted with the fact that his former girlfriend, Hana (Ingrid Timkova), is now living with his father, and they have an eighteen-year-old daughter, Lenka (Kristana Bokova). No doubt the romance between Otakar and Hana was one of the reasons Martin left for Australia.

Czech movies seem to have some of their finest moments around the dining table, and a Horecky family dinner is funny, sad, and harrowing all at once. So is the uncertain relationship between Martin and his half-sister, Lenka. We learn that Vera is an alcoholic with the kinds of resentments, including racist ones, that drunks often use to deflect anger and attention away from themselves.

These two stories do not so much interact as reflect on each other with notions about families, parents, children, and class. For me, the most affecting character was Franta, the watchman, who is tattooed, muscular, and ferocious, yet so gentle with his wife and baby. He has been under the thumb of the "Colonel" (Jaroslav Dusek), a leader of the booster club, but for a brief moment breaks free into happiness and a content family life. The story of his history with the club is the story of the ups and downs of his life, and his final scene in the movie is heartbreaking in the way it shows the club becoming a substitute family.

There is, of course, the question of the baby's real parents. Can they go to the police without revealing their status as illegal immigrants? Another of the movie's ups and downs is about the way we're simultaneously required to sympathize with the baby's birth mother while witnessing how the baby transforms the marriage of Miluska and Frantisek.

Jan Hrebejk was also the director of *Divided We Fall* (2000), a film about a couple in Prague whose Jewish employers are victims of the Nazis. When the son of the employers appears at their door, they give him shelter in a hidden space within their house. Meanwhile, a local Nazi makes it clear he is attracted to the wife of the couple providing the shelter. He also begins to suspect their secret. What should happen next? Should the wife have sex with the Nazi to protect the man they are hiding?

Such moral puzzles are at the heart of Hrebejk's work, and he has no easy answers. *Up and Down* also lacks any formulas or solutions, and is content to show us its complicated characters, their tangled lives, and the way that our need to love and be loved can lead us in opposite directions.

The Upside of Anger ★ ★ ★ ★
R, 118 m., 2005

Joan Allen (Terry Wolfmeyer), Kevin Costner (Denny Davies), Erika Christensen, Andy Wolfmeyer), Evan Rachel Wood ("Popeye" Wolfmeyer), Keri Russell (Emily Wolfmeyer), Alicia Witt (Hadley Wolfmeyer), Mike Binder ("Shep" Goodman). Directed by Mike Binder and produced by Jack Binder, Alex Gartner, and Sammy Lee. Screenplay by Binder.

Joan Allen and Kevin Costner achieve something in *The Upside of Anger* that may have been harder than costarring in *Macbeth*. They create two imperfect, alcoholic, resentful ordi-

721

nary people, neighbors in the suburbs, with enough money to support themselves in the discontent to which they have become accustomed. I liked these characters precisely because they were not designed to be likable—or, more precisely, because they were likable in spite of being exasperating, unorganized, self-destructive, and impervious to good advice. That would be true of most of my friends. They say the same about me.

Allen plays Terry Wolfmeyer, suburban wife and mother of four daughters ("One of them hates me and the other three are working on it"). Her husband has walked out of the marriage, and all signs point to his having fled the country to begin a new life in Sweden with his secretary. "He's a vile, selfish pig," Terry says, "but I'm not gonna trash him to you girls." The girls, of college and high school age, dress expensively, are well groomed, prepare the family meals, and run the household, while their mother emcees with a vodka and tonic; her material is smart and bitter, although she sees the humor in the situation, and in herself.

Costner plays her neighbor, Denny Davies, once a star pitcher for the Detroit Tigers, now a sports-talk host who is bored by sports and talk. He spends his leisure time at the lonely but lucrative task of autographing hundreds of baseballs to sell online and at fan conventions. When Terry's husband disappears, Denny materializes as a friend in need. In need of a drinking partner, mostly. Neither one is a sensational *Barfly/Lost Weekend* kind of alcoholic, but more like the curators of a constant state of swizzledom. They are always a little drunk. Sometimes a little less little, sometimes a little more little.

Allen and Costner are so good at making these characters recognizable that we may not realize how hard that is to do. For Allen, the role comes in a season of triumph; she is also wonderful in Campbell Scott's *Off the Map*, and wait until you see her in Sally Potter's *Yes*. Costner reminds us that he is best when he dials down; he is drawn to epic roles, but here he's as comforting as your boozy best pal.

In *The Upside of Anger*, written and directed by Mike Binder, they occupy a comedy buried in angst. The camaraderie between Terry and Denny is like the wounded affection of two people with hangovers and plenty of time to drink them away. The four daughters have sized up the situation and are getting on with their lives in their own ways, mostly competently. Hadley (Alicia Witt) is a cool, centered college student; Andy (Erika Christensen) reacts as second children often do, by deciding she will not be Hadley and indeed will accept an offer to be an intern on Denny's radio show—an offer extended enthusiastically by Shep (Binder), the fortyish producer, who is a shameless letch. Emily (Keri Russell) is at war with her mother; she wants to be a dancer, and her mother says there's no money or future in it. Popeye (Evan Rachel Wood) is the youngest, but maturing way too rapidly, like Wood's character in *13*.

Terry deals imperfectly with events in the lives of her daughters, such as Hadley's impending marriage and Andy becoming Shep's girlfriend. Although Terry is wealthy, stylish, and sexy—a thoroughbred temporarily out of training—she has a rebel streak maybe left over from her teens in the late 1970s. At a lunch party to meet Hadley's prospective in-laws, she tells Denny, "I was like a public service ad against drinking."

It is inevitable that Denny and Terry will become lovers. The girls like him. He is lonely, and Terry's house feels more like home than his own, where the living room is furnished primarily with boxes of baseballs. It is also true, given the current state of the drunk driving laws, that alcoholics are wise to choose lovers within walking distance. So the movie proceeds with wit, intelligence, and a certain horrifying fascination. Sometimes Terry picks up the phone to call the creep in Sweden, but decides not to give him the satisfaction.

And then comes an unexpected development. Because *The Upside of Anger* opened a week earlier in New York than in Chicago, I am aware of the despair about this development from A. O. Scott in the *New York Times* (the ending "is an utter catastrophe") and Joe Morgenstern in the *Wall Street Journal* (the ending is "a cheat").

They are mistaken. Life can contain catastrophe, and life can cheat. The ending is the making of the movie, its transcendence, its way of casting everything in a new and ironic light, causing us to reevaluate what went before, and to regard the future with horror and pity. Without the ending, *The Upside of Anger* is a wonderfully made comedy of domestic manners. With it, the movie becomes larger and deeper. When life plays a joke on you, it can have a really rotten sense of humor.

Uptown Girls ★ ★ ★
PG-13, 93 m., 2003

Brittany Murphy (Molly Gunn), Dakota Fanning (Ray Schleine), Heather Locklear (Roma Schleine), Jesse Spencer (Neal), Marley Shelton (Ingrid), Donald Faison (Huey). Directed by Boaz Yakin and produced by Allison Jacobs, John Penotti, and Fisher Stevens. Screenplay by Julia Dahl, Mo Ogrodnik, and Lisa Davidowitz, based on the story by Jacobs.

The theory is that Brittany Murphy is trying to channel Marilyn Monroe, but as I watched *Uptown Girls* another name came to mind: Lucille Ball. She has a kind of divine ineptitude that moves beyond Marilyn's helplessness into Lucy's dizzy lovability. She is like a magnet for whoops! moments.

I remember her as a presenter at the 2003 Independent Spirit Awards, where her assignment was to read the names of five nominees, open an envelope, and read the winner. This she was unable to do, despite two visits by a stage manager who whispered helpful suggestions into her ear. She kept trying to read every nominee as the winner, and when she finally arrived triumphantly at the real winner, she inspired no confidence that she had it right.

Some thought she was completely clueless, or worse. I studied her timing and speculated that she knew exactly what she was doing, and that while it took no skill at all to get it right, it took a certain genius to get it so perfectly wrong. She succeeded in capturing the attention of every person in that distracted and chattering crowd, and I recalled Lucy shows where everyone in a restaurant would suddenly be looking at her.

Uptown Girls gives Murphy an opportunity to channel Lucy at feature length. She plays an improbable character in an impossible story, but of course she does. She is Molly Gunn, whose father was a rock star until both parents were killed in a plane crash, leaving her with a collection of guitars and a trust fund adminis-

tered by someone named Bob. As the story opens, Bob has disappeared with all of her money and she is forced to work for the first time in her life. This does not come easy to a girl whose only skills are as a consumer.

She gets a job as the nanny of an eight-year-old girl named Ray (Dakota Fanning), who seems so old and wise that when she tells Molly, "Act your age," we see what she means. Ray is a dubious little adult in a child's body, and although her family is rich she has never enjoyed any of the usual rich kid pleasures.

"You've never been to Disneyland?" asks Molly.

"Alert the media," says Ray.

Molly still makes some effort to preserve her pre-Ray, prepoverty lifestyle, and this includes an infatuation with a young singer named Neal (Jesse Spencer), who keeps his distance. He is only 274 days sober, he tells her, and has been advised to stay celibate for his first year. This turns out to be less than the truth, in a plot twist involving Ray's worldly mother Roma (Heather Locklear, yes, Heather Locklear as the mother, and how time flies).

Ray is a hypochrondiac who travels with her own soap and monitors her medications and whose basic inability is to act like a kid. Molly has never grown up. Although this scenario is as contrived as most such movie plots, there is a way in which it works because Ray does seem prematurely old and Molly does seem eternally childlike; in the case of Dakota Fanning I think we are looking at good acting, and in Brittany Murphy's case I think we are seeing something essential in her nature. Even in *8 Mile,* where she played Eminem's girlfriend in a landscape of urban grunge, there was a part of her that was identical with Molly's crush on Neal the singer.

I dismiss all cavils about the movie's logic and plausibility as beside the point. This is not a movie about plot but about personalities. Molly Gunn is a comic original, vulnerable and helpless, well-meaning and inept, innocent and guileless—or, more accurately, a person of touchingly naive guile. Murphy's performance has a kind of ineffable, mischievous innocence about it.

I also enjoyed the movie's emotional complexity. *Uptown Girls* could have been a simpleminded, relentlessly cheerful formula picture. There is an underlying formula there, of course, with all problems resolved at the end, but Ray is anything but another cookie-cutter little movie girl, and Molly's problems at times are really daunting. The surprise she gets about Neal's behavior is not the sort of thing that usually happens in this genre. The director is Boaz Yakin, who made the searing movie *Fresh* in 1994. That one, too, was about a young kid with a lot of adult wisdom and an underlying sad-ness. *Uptown Girls,* on a completely different wavelength, suggests some of the same under-tones. The screenplay, by Julia Dahl, Mo Ogrod-nik, and Lisa Davidowitz, based on a story by the producer, Allison Jacobs, takes what we might expect from this material and rotates it into a slightly darker dimension, where Brittany Murphy's Lucy act is not merely ditzy, but even a little brave.

V

Valentin ★ ★ ★
PG-13, 86 m., 2004

Rodrigo Noya (Valentin), Julieta Cardinali (Leticia), Carmen Maura (His Grandmother), Alejandro Agresti (His Father), Mex Urtizberea (Rufo). Directed by Alejandro Agresti and produced by Laurens Geels, Thierry Forte, and Julio Fernandez. Screenplay by Agresti.

Valentin is a nine-year-old boy who is solemn and observant, and peers out at the world through enormous glasses that correct his wandering eye. He lives with his grandmother in Buenos Aires in the late 1960s. His mother is not on the scene. His father appears from time to time with a girlfriend, usually a new one. Valentin spends a lot of time "building stuff for astronauts" and observing the adults in his life with analytical zeal.

He narrates his own story, but here's an interesting touch: The voice belongs to the young actor (Rodrigo Noya), but the sensibility is that of an adult remembering his childhood. There is an interesting explanation. The movie was written and directed by Alejandro Agresti, who tells us it is his own life story. Interesting that he plays the father who causes this little boy so much grief.

Valentin's grandmother (Carmen Maura) is not a lovable movie granny. She does what is necessary for the boy, is miserly with her affections, is trying to stage-manage her son into a second marriage. One day his father comes home with a girlfriend Valentin likes. This is Leticia (Julieta Cardinali), and she likes Valentin too. They get along famously, until one day he makes the mistake of telling her disturbing things about his father. She makes the mistake of repeating them to his father. As a result, Leticia breaks up with his father, and his father is angry with Valentin.

The movie sets its story against an Argentina carefully remembered by Agresti. Buenos Aires looks and sounds cosmopolitan and embracing, and there is a leisurely feeling to the streets and cafés, especially one in which Valentin observes a man sitting and reading and smoking, day after day. This is Rufo (Mex Urtizberea), a musician, who gives Valentin some piano lessons and becomes his confidant. "Rufo gave me the feeling I was older and more useful," he explains.

Valentin feels that since the adult world handles its affairs badly, he must sometimes take things into his own hands. When he decides his grandmother is ill, he convinces a doctor to visit her. Later, he gives the doctor a painting as a present. Outside events penetrate unevenly into his mind; he is up-to-date on the astronauts, but not so sure what it means when Che Guevara is killed. In church, people walk out of a sermon about Che; at home, anti-Semitism is prevalent, even though Valentin's mother was Jewish (we begin to suspect why she may have left the family).

I am not always sure what I mean when I praise a child actor, especially one as young as Rodrigo Noya. Certainly, casting has a lot to do with his appeal; he looks the part and exudes a touching solemnity. But there is more. There's something about this kid, and the way he talks and listens and watches people, that is very convincing. Perhaps it helped that he was directed by a man who was once Valentin himself. The film is warm and intriguing, and he is the engine that pulls us through it. We care about what happens to him; high praise.

By the end of the film, Valentin feels, with some reason, that he has been set adrift by the adult world. But he is smart and resourceful, and he has a simple but effective working knowledge of human nature. What he does and how he does it, and who he does it for I will leave for you to discover, since the movie's closing scenes are filled with a sublime serendipity. Let me just say he earns his name.

Van Helsing ★ ★ ★
PG-13, 131 m., 2004

Hugh Jackman (Gabriel Van Helsing), Kate Beckinsale (Anna Valerious), Richard Roxburgh (Count Dracula), Shuler Hensley (Frankenstein's Monster), David Wenham (Carl), Will Kemp (Velkan Valerious), Kevin J. O'Connor (Igor), Samuel West (Dr. Frankenstein), Robbie Coltrane (Mr. Hyde). Directed by Stephen

Sommers and produced by Bob Ducsay and Sommers. Screenplay by Sommers.

The zombies were having fun,
The party had just begun,
The guests included Wolf Man,
Dracula and his son.
　　　— "Monster Mash" by Bobby Pickett

Strange that a movie so eager to entertain would forget to play *Monster Mash* over the end credits. There have been countless movies uniting two monsters (*Frankenstein Meets the Wolf Man, King Kong vs. Godzilla*, etc.), but *Van Helsing* convenes Frankenstein, his Monster, Count Dracula, the Wolf Man, Igor, Van Helsing the vampire hunter, assorted other werewolves, werebats and vampires, and even Mr. Hyde, who as a bonus seems to think he is the Hunchback of Notre Dame.

The movie is like a greatest hits compilation; it's assembled like Frankenstein's Monster, from spare parts stitched together and brought to life with electricity, plus lots of computer-generated images. The plot depends on Dracula's desperate need to discover the secret of Frankenstein's Monster because he can use it to bring his countless offspring to life. Because Dracula (Richard Roxburgh) and his vampire brides are all dead, they cannot give birth, of course, to live children. That they give birth at all is somewhat remarkable, although perhaps the process is unorthodox, since his dead offspring hang from a subterranean ceiling wrapped in cocoons that made me think, for some reason, of bagworms, which I spent many a summer hand-picking off the evergreens under the enthusiastic direction of my father.

Van Helsing (Hugh Jackman, Wolverine in the X-Men movies) is sometimes portrayed as young, sometimes old in the Dracula movies. Here he's a professional monster-killer with a *Phantom of the Opera* hat, who picks up a dedicated friar named Carl (David Wenham) as his sidekick. His first assignment is to track down Mr. Hyde (Robbie Coltrane), who now lives in Notre Dame cathedral and ventures out for murder. That job doesn't end as planned, so Van Helsing moves on to the Vatican City to get new instructions and be supplied with high-tech weapons by the ecclesiastical equivalent of James Bond's Q.

Next stop: Transylvania, where the movie opened with a virtuoso black-and-white sequence showing a local mob waving pitchforks and torches and hounding Frankenstein's Monster into a windmill that is set ablaze. We know, having seen the old movies, that the Monster will survive, but the mob has worked itself into such a frenzy that when Van Helsing and Carl arrive in the village, they are almost forked and burnt just on general principles. What saves them is an attack by three flying vampiresses, who like to scoop up their victims and fly off to savor their blood; Van Helsing fights them using a device that fires arrows like a machine gun.

And that leads to his meeting the beautiful Anna Valerious (Kate Beckinsale), who with her brother, Velkan (Will Kemp), represents the last of nine generations of a family that will never find eternal rest until it vanquishes Dracula. (Conveniently, if you kill Dracula, all the vampires he created will also die.) Anna is at first suspicious of Van Helsing, but soon they are partners in vengeance, and the rest of the plot (there is a whole lot of it) I will leave you to discover for yourselves.

The director, Stephen Sommers, began his career sedately, directing a very nice *Adventures of Huckleberry Finn* (1993) and the entertaining *Jungle Book* (1994). Then Victor Frankenstein must have strapped him to the gurney and turned on the juice, because he made a U-turn into thrillers, with *Deep Rising* (1998), where a giant squid attacks a cruise ship, and *The Mummy* (1999) and *The Mummy Returns* (2001, introducing The Rock as the Scorpion King). Now comes *Van Helsing*, which employs the ultimate resources of CGI to create a world that is violent and hectic, bizarre and entertaining, and sometimes very beautiful.

CGI can get a little boring when it allows characters to fall hundreds of feet and somehow survive, or when they swoop at the ends of ropes as well as Spiderman, but without Spidey's superpowers. But it can also be used to create a visual feast, and here the cinematography by Allen Daviau (*E.T.*) and the production design by Allen Cameron join with Sommers's imagination for spectacular sights. The best is a masked ball in Budapest, which is part real (the musicians balancing on balls, the waiters circling on unicycles) and part fabricated in the computer. Whatever. It's a remarkable scene, and will reward study on the DVD. So will the extraordinary coach chase.

I also liked the movie's re-creation of Victor Frankenstein's laboratory, which has been a favorite of production designers, art directors, and set decorators since time immemorial (Mel Brooks's *Young Frankenstein* recycled the actual sets built for James Whale's *The Bride of Frankenstein*). Here Frankenstein lives in a towering Gothic castle just down the road from Dracula, and the mechanism lifts the Monster to unimaginable heights to expose him to lightning bolts. There are also plentiful crypts, stygian passages, etc., and a library in which a painting revolves, perhaps in tribute to Mel Brooks's revolving bookcase.

The screenplay by Sommers has humor, but restrains itself; the best touches are the quiet ones, as when the friar objects to accompanying Van Helsing ("But I'm not a field man") and when the Monster somewhat unexpectedly recites the 23rd Psalm. At the outset, we may fear Sommers is simply going for f/x overkill, but by the end he has somehow succeeded in assembling all his monsters and plot threads into a high-voltage climax. *Van Helsing* is silly, and spectacular, and fun.

Vanity Fair ★ ★ ★ ★
PG-13, 137 m., 2004

Reese Witherspoon (Becky Sharp), Eileen Atkins (Matilde Crawley), Jim Broadbent (Mr. Osborne), Gabriel Byrne (Marquess of Steyne), Romola Garai (Amelia Sedley), Bob Hoskins (Sir Pitt Crawley), Rhys Ifans (William Dobbin), Geraldine McEwan (Lady Southdown), James Purefoy (Rawdon Crawley), Jonathan Rhys-Meyers (George Osborne), Tony Maudsley (Joseph Sedley). Directed by Mira Nair and produced by Janette Day, Lydia Dean Pilcher, and Donna Gigliotti. Screenplay by Matthew Faulk, Julian Fellowes, and Mark Skeet, based on the novel by William Makepeace Thackeray.

I had thought her a mere social climber. I see now she's a mountaineer.

So says one of her fascinated observers as Becky Sharp transforms herself from the impoverished orphan of an alcoholic painter into an adornment of the middle, if not the upper, reaches of the British aristocracy. *Vanity Fair* makes her a little more likable than she was in the 1828 novel—but then, I always liked Becky anyway, because she so admirably tried to obey her cynical strategies and yet so helplessly allowed herself to be misled by her heart.

Reese Witherspoon reflects both of those qualities effortlessly in this new film by Mira Nair, and no wonder, for isn't there a little of Elle Woods, her character in *Legally Blonde*, at work here? Becky, to be sure, never goes through a phase when anyone thinks her stupid, but she does use her sexuality to advantage, plays men at their own game, and scores about as well as possible given the uneven nineteenth-century playing field.

When William Makepeace Thackeray wrote his funny and quietly savage novel, there were few career prospects for an educated young woman who did not fancy prostitution. She could become a governess, a teacher, a servant, a religious, or a wife. The only male profession open to her was writing, which she could practice without the permission or license of men; that accounts for such as Jane Austen, the Brontës, George Eliot, Mrs. Gaskell, and others who, as Virginia Woolf imagined them, wrote their masterpieces in a corner of the parlor while after-dinner chatter surrounded them.

Becky Sharp could probably have written a great novel, and certainly inspired one; Thackeray sees her dilemma and her behavior without sentiment, in a novel that must have surprised its first readers with its realism. We meet Becky just as she's leaving finishing school, where the French she learned from her Parisian mother won her a berth as a boarder and tutor. She made one good friend there: Amelia Sedley (Romola Garai), and now proposes to visit the Sedley family for a few days on her way to her first job, as a governess for the down-at-heels Sir Pitt Crawley (Bob Hoskins).

But working as a governess is not Becky's life goal. She wants to marry well, and since she has neither fortune nor title it would be best if her husband brought both of those attributes into the marriage. Does this make her an evil woman? Not at all; romantic love is a modern and untrustworthy motive for marriage, and in England and India (where both Thackeray and Mira Nair were born), marriage strategies have always involved family connections and financial possibilities.

Amelia likes Becky (she is the only one at school who did, Thackeray observes), and thinks it would be nice if Becky married her brother Joseph (Tony Maudsley). Amelia's own fiancé, Captain George Osborne (Jonathan Rhys-Meyers), discourages this plan, convincing the weak-willed Joseph that Becky is little better than a beggar with vague family irregularities, and would not adorn the Sedley household.

So Becky goes to Crawley Hall, where she mistakes the unshaven Sir Pitt for a servant. Servants, money, and provisions seem in short supply in the Crawley family, but Becky makes one important conquest; Sir Pitt's rich maiden sister, Matilde (played with magnificent, biting wit by Eileen Atkins), admires her pluck and becomes her friend and protector—up to a point. That point is reached when Becky secretly marries her nephew Rawdon Crawley (James Purefoy). As a second son, Rawdon will not inherit the title or house, and as a gambler can't live within his allowance, so this marriage gives Becky a liaison with a good family but not the benefits.

Some of the film's best moments come when characters administer verbal flayings to one another. Matilde is unforgiving when she is crossed. But the most astonishing dialogue comes from a character named Lord Steyne (Gabriel Byrne), whom Becky meets for the first time when she's a young girl in her father's studio. Steyne fancies a portrait of Becky's mother; her father prices it at three guineas, but Becky insists on ten, putting on a good show of sentimental attachment to her departed parent. Now, many years later, Steyne crosses Becky's path again. She reminds him of their first meeting. It occurs to him that having purchased a portrait of the parent, he might purchase the original of the daughter. This sets up a dinner-table scene in the Steyne household at which the lord verbally destroys every member of his family, not sparing the rich mulatto heiress from the Caribbean who married his son for

his title even though "the whole world knows he's an idiot."

The peculiar quality of *Vanity Fair*, which sets it aside from the Austen adaptations like *Sense and Sensibility* and *Pride and Prejudice*, is that it's not about very nice people. That makes them much more interesting. There are some decent blokes in the story, but on the fringes: William Dobbin (Rhys Ifans), for example, who persists in loving Amelia even though she falls for George, a thoroughgoing bounder. Joseph is a good sort, too.

And for that matter, how evil is Lord Steyne, really? He and Becky meet again after her husband, Rawdon, has lost everything at the gambling tables and the bailiff is literally moving their furniture out of the house. Steyne pays off their debts. This would not have been considered by anybody as an act of selfless charity. Of course, he expects Becky to show her gratitude, although oddly enough she shows it more frankly in the 1848 novel than in the 2004 movie; its PG-13 rating no doubt inspired Nair and her writers to suggest to their tender young audiences that Becky can be friendly and grateful without, as the saying goes, Steyne having sex with that young woman. In the real world, the furniture would have been back on the sidewalk.

Is the India-born Mira Nair a strange choice to adapt what some think is the best English novel of the nineteenth century? Not at all. She has an instinctive feel for the comic possibilities of marital alliances, as she showed in her wonderful *Monsoon Wedding* (2001). And she brings to the movie an awareness of the role India played in the English imagination; in the nineteenth century, hardly a well-born family lacked relatives serving or living in India, and wasn't it Orwell who said the two nations deserved each other, because they shared the same love of eccentricity?

Vera Drake ★ ★ ★

R, 125 m., 2004

Imelda Staunton (Vera Drake), Phil Davis (Stan Drake), Peter Wight (Inspector Webster), Adrian Scarborough (Frank), Heather Craney (Joyce), Daniel Mays (Sid Drake), Alex Kelly (Ethel Drake), Sally Hawkins (Susan), Eddie

Marsan (Reg), Ruth Sheen (Lily). Directed by Mike Leigh and produced by Simon Channing Williams and Alain Sarde. Screenplay by Leigh.

Vera Drake is a melodious plum pudding of a woman who is always humming or singing to herself. She is happy because she is useful, and likes to be useful. She works as a cleaning woman in a rich family's house, where she burnishes the bronze as if it were her own, and then returns home to a crowded flat to cook, clean, and mend for her husband, son, and daughter, and cheer them up when they seem out of sorts. She makes daily calls on invalids to plump up their pillows and make them a nice cup of tea, and once or twice a week she performs an abortion.

London in the 1950s. Wartime rationing is still in effect. A pair of nylons is bartered for eight packs of Players. Vera (Imelda Staunton) buys sugar on the black market from Lily (Ruth Sheen), who also slips her the names and addresses of women in need of "help." Lily is as hard and cynical as Vera is kind and trusting. Vera would never think of accepting money for "helping out" young girls when "they got no one to turn to," but Lily charges two pounds and two shillings, which she doesn't tell Vera about.

In a film of pitch-perfect, seemingly effortless performances, Imelda Staunton is the key player, and her success at creating Vera Drake allows the story to fall into place and belong there. We must believe she's naive to be taken advantage of by Lily, but we do believe it. We must believe she has a simple, pragmatic morality to justify abortions, which were a crime in England until 1967, but we do believe it.

Some of the women who come to her have piteous stories; they were raped, they are still almost children, they will kill themselves if their parents find out, or in one case there are seven mouths to feed and the mother lacks the will to carry on. But Vera is not a social worker who provides counseling; she is simply being helpful by doing something she believes she can do safely. Her age-old method involves lye soap, disinfectant, and, of course, lots of hot water, and another abortionist describes her method as "safe as houses."

The movie has been written and directed by Mike Leigh, the most interesting director now at work in England, whose *Topsy-Turvy, High Hopes, All or Nothing,* and *Naked* join this film in being partly "devised" by the actors themselves. His method is to gather a cast for weeks or months of improvisation in which they create and explore their characters. I don't think the technique has ever worked better than here; the family life in those cramped little rooms is so palpably real that as the others wait around the dining table while Vera speaks to a policeman behind the kitchen door, I felt as if I were waiting there with them. It's not that we "identify" so much as that the film quietly and firmly includes us.

The movie is not about abortion so much as about families. The Drakes are close and loving. Vera's husband, Stan (Phil Davis), who works with his brother in an auto repair shop, considers his wife a treasure. Their son, Sid (Daniel Mays), works as a tailor, has a line of patter, is popular in pubs, but lives at home because of the postwar housing crisis. Their daughter, Ethel (Alex Kelly), is painfully shy, and there is a sweet, tactful subplot in which Vera invites a lonely, tongue-tied bachelor named Reg (Eddie Marsan) over for tea, and essentially arranges a marriage.

Vera Drake tells a parallel story about a rich girl named Susan (Sally Hawkins), the daughter of the family Vera cleans for. Susan is raped by her boyfriend, becomes pregnant, and goes to a psychiatrist who can refer her to a private clinic for a legal abortion. Like everyone in the movie, Susan is excruciatingly shy about discussing sex, and ignorant. "Did he force himself upon you?" the psychiatrist asks, and Susan is not sure how to answer. Leigh's point is that those with £100 could legally obtain an abortion in England in 1950, and those with £2 had to depend on Vera Drake, or on women not nearly as nice as Vera Drake.

Vera's world falls apart when the police become involved in an abortion that almost leads to death, and the tightly knit little family changes when the police knock on the door. Inspector Webster (Peter Wight) is a considerable man, large, imposing, and not without sympathy. He believes in the law and enforces the law, but he quickly understands that Vera was not working for profit, and is not ungentle with her. In a courtroom scene, on the other hand, it is clear that the law makes no room for nuance or circumstance.

Some of the film's best scenes involve the family sitting around the table, shell-shocked (after Vera whispers into her husband's ear, telling him what he had never suspected). There are moments when Leigh uses his technique of allowing a reticent character to stir into conviction. At Vera's final Christmas dinner, Reg, now engaged to Ethel, makes what for him is a long speech: "This is the best Christmas I've had in a long time. Thank you very much, Vera. Smashing!" He knows telling Vera she has prepared a perfect meal means more to her than any speech about rights and wrongs, although later he blurts out: "It's all right if you're rich, but if you can't feed 'em you can't love 'em."

Vera Drake is not so much pro- or antiabortion as it is opposed to laws that do little to eliminate abortion but much to make it dangerous for poor p5ople. No matter what the law says, then or now, in England or America, if you can afford a plane ticket and the medical bill you will always be able to obtain a competent abortion, so laws essentially make it illegal to be poor and seek an abortion.

Even in saying that, I am bringing more ideology into *Vera Drake* than it probably requires. The strength of Leigh's film is that it is not a message picture, but a deep and true portrait of these lives. Vera is kind and innocent, but Lily, who procures the abortions, is hard, dishonest, and heartless. The movie shows the law as unyielding, but puts a human face on the police. And the enduring strength of the film is the way it shows the Drake family rising to the occasion with loyalty and love.

Veronica Guerin ★ ★ ★

R, 98 m., 2003

Cate Blanchett (Veronica Guerin), Gerard McSorley (John Gilligan), Ciaran Hinds (John Traynor), Brenda Fricker (Bernie Guerin), Don Wycherley (Chris Mulligan), Barry Barnes (Graham Turley), Simon O'Driscoll (Cathal Turley), Emmet Bergin (Aengus Fanning), Gerry O'Brien (Martin Cahill). Directed by Joel Schumacher and produced by Jerry Bruckheimer. Screenplay by Carol Doyle and Mary Agnes Donoghue.

Veronica Guerin may or may not have been a great journalist, but she was certainly a brave and foolish one. Disturbed by the sight of gangs selling drugs to children and teenagers in the Dublin of the 1990s, she began a high-profile, even reckless campaign to expose them. Was she surprised when her campaign ended with her own murder? She must have been, or she would have gone about it differently. That she struck a great blow against the Irish drug traffic is without doubt, but perhaps she could have done so and still survived to raise her son.

Cate Blanchett plays Guerin in a way that fascinated me for reasons the movie probably did not intend. I have a sneaky suspicion that director Joel Schumacher and his writers (Carol Doyle and Mary Agnes Donoghue) think of this as a story of courage and determination, but what I came away with was a story of bone-headed egocentrism. There are moments when Guerin seems so wrapped up in her growing legend and giddy with the flush of the hunt that she barely notices her patient husband, who seems quite gentle, under the circumstances, and his suggestions that she consider the danger she's in and think of their child.

Daily journalism in Britain and Ireland is miles more aggressive than in North America, no doubt because there is a truly competitive press. All of Dublin's papers are national, there are additional titles on Sundays, and, not incidentally, the Irish are great readers. It is unthinkable that an Irish politician would boast that he never reads the papers. Guerin was a well-known writer for the *Sunday Independent*—"a rag," she says at one point, unfairly. Her good looks and unbuttoned personality were popular. Sunday journalists go for the home run, and she hit hers in 1994 when young addicts told her of the gangs that used them as retailers in the housing projects.

Appalled, she tries to backtrack from the poor street sellers to the rich men who presumably lurk at a safe remove. The movie knows more than she does about the gangs, and intercuts her investigation with horrifying violence used by the gangs to maintain discipline. You may remember John Boorman's *The General* (1998), starring Brendan Gleeson as Martin Cahill, a criminal Robin Hood of sorts (he stole from the rich and gave to himself). In that film, he nails a suspected stool pigeon to a snooker table; in *Veronica Guerin,* the same character, now played by Gerry O'Brien, is nailing someone to the floor. He should have been called The Carpenter.

Cahill eventually got into trouble by interfering with the IRA's drug trade, but that hot potato goes unreported by Guerin, in part because she has an inside source feeding her information about the Dublin mob. This is a very nervous midlevel crook named John Traynor (Ciaran Hinds) who has a bit of a crush on her, actually worries about her safety, and couples his information with warnings that she is in very real danger. Traynor tries to play a double game and ends by outsmarting himself without helping her.

Cate Blanchett dominates the material with a headstrong, extroverted performance. Her Veronica Guerin is heady with excitement, and it doesn't hurt that enormous billboards promote the investigation by the *Independent*'s star journalist. Her editors look alternately grateful and alarmed when she breezes in with another scoop, and we get the feeling she considers her press card to be a guarantee of immunity—or at least, a bulletproof vest. We know Veronica is going to die because that happens in the first five minutes of the movie. All the rest is flashback, showing how she arrived at the day of her death. We cringe at the flamboyant risks she takes—as when she actually walks into the house of an Irish Mafia kingpin and asks him why he sells drugs to children. The film develops an undertone of horror; it's like watching fate unfold.

A lot of critics in England disliked it, which is valid enough, but some of them seemed to confuse Guerin's journalism and Blanchett's performance. The film ends with the obligatory public funeral, grateful proles lining the streets while type crawls up the screen telling how much Guerin's antidrug crusade accomplished. These are standard prompts for us to get a little weepy at the heroism of this brave martyr, but actually I think Blanchett and Schumacher have found the right note for their story. Their Veronica Guerin dies, essentially, because the excitement of a great story robs her of all common sense. Oh, certainly, she felt outrage and anger, and so should she have, but it was so much fun to skewer these hard, evil men. And then they did what everyone has

been telling her for weeks they would do, and she was dead.

A Very Long Engagement ★ ★ ★ ½
R, 134 m., 2004

Audrey Tautou (Mathilde), Gaspard Ulliel (Manech), Jean-Pierre Becker (Lieutenant Esperanza), Jodie Foster (Elodie Gordes), Albert Dupontel (Celestin Poux), Clovis Cornillac (Benoit Notre-Dame), Marion Cotillard (Tina Lombardi), Ticky Holgado (Germain Pire). Directed by Jean-Pierre Jeunet and produced by Francis Boespflug. Screenplay by Jeunet and Guillaume Laurant, based on the novel by Sebastien Japrisot.

In the horror of trench warfare during World War I, with French and Germans dug in across from each other during endless muddy, cold, wet, bloody months, not a few put their rifles into their mouths and sent themselves on permanent leave. Others, more optimistic, wounded themselves to get a pass to a field hospital, but if this treachery was suspected the sentence was death. *A Very Long Engagement* opens by introducing us to five French soldiers convicted of wounding themselves; one is innocent, but all are condemned, and it is a form of cruelty, perhaps, that instead of being lined up and shot they are sent out into No-Man's-Land and certain death.

The movie is seen largely through the eyes of Mathilde (Audrey Tautou), an orphan with a polio limp, who senses in her soul that her man is not dead. He is Manech (Gaspard Ulliel), son of a lighthouse tender, a boy so openfaced and fresh he is known to all as Cornflower. After the war, Mathilde comes upon a letter that seems to hint that not all five died on the battlefield, and she begins the long task of tracking down eyewitnesses and survivors to find the Manech she is sure is still alive and needs her help.

This story is told in a film so visually delightful that only the horrors of war keep it from floating up on clouds of joy. Having not connected with his earlier films *Delicatessen* and *The City of Lost Children,* I was enchanted, as everyone was, by Jean-Pierre Jeunet's first film with Audrey Tautou, *Amelie.* Now he brings everything together—his joyously poetic style, the lovable Tautou, a good story worth the telling—into a film that is a series of pleasures stumbling over one another in their haste to delight us. I will have to go back again to those early films; maybe I am learning the language.

That is not too say *A Very Long Engagement* is mindless jollity. From *Goodbye to All That* by Robert Graves and from a hundred films like *All Quiet on the Western Front, Paths of Glory,* and *King and Country,* we have an idea of the trench warfare that makes World War I seem like the worst kind of hell politicians and generals ever devised for their men. To be assigned to the front was essentially a sentence of death, but not quick death, more often death after a long season of cold, hunger, illness, shell shock, and the sheer horror of what you had to look at and think about. Jeunet depicts this reality as well as I have ever seen it shown on the screen, beginning with his opening shot of a severed arm hanging, Christ-like, from a shattered cross.

Against these fragments he buttresses his fancies, his camera swooping like a glad bird over Paris and the countryside, his narrator telling us of Mathilde and her quest. These moments have some of the charm of the early scenes in Truffaut's *Jules and Jim*, before the same war destroyed their happiness. Mathilde enlists a dogged old bird of a private detective (Ticky Holgado, who you may remember from the cover of Amelie's talking book). He plods about quizzing possible witnesses with the raised eyebrows of an Inspector Maigret, and gradually a scenario seems to form in which Manech is not necessarily dead.

As a counterpoint to Mathilde's hopeful search, Jeunet supplies another search among the same human remains, this one carried out by a prostitute named Tina (Marion Cotillard), who figures out who was responsible for the death of her lover. Her means of revenge are so unspeakably ingenious that Edgar Allan Poe would twitch in envy.

The barbarity of war and the implacable logic of revenge are softened by the voluptuous beauty of Jeunet's visuals and the magic of his storytelling. Here is a director who loves—adores!—telling stories, so that we sense his voluptuous pleasure in his own tales. He must work in a kind of holy trance, falling to his knees at night to give thanks that modern special effects have made his visions possible. Some directors abuse effects. He flies on their wings.

Whether Mathilde finds Manech is a question I should not answer, but reader, what do you think is the likelihood that an angel-faced girl with polio could spend an entire movie searching for her true love and not find him? Audiences would rip up their seats. The point is not whether she finds him, but how. Can Jeunet devise their reunion in a way that is not an anticlimax after such a glorious search? What can they do, Mathilde and Manech, and what can they say? Reader, the film's closing moments are so sad and happy that we know, yes, it has to end on just that perfect note, held and held and held.

View from the Top ★ ★ ★
PG-13, 87 m., 2003

Gwyneth Paltrow (Donna), Mark Ruffalo (Ted), Christina Applegate (Christine), Mike Myers (John Whitney), Candice Bergen (Sally), Kelly Preston (Sherry), Rob Lowe (Copilot Steve). Directed by Bruno Barreto and produced by Matthew Baer, Bobby Cohen, and Brad Grey. Screenplay by Eric Wald.

View from the Top stars Gwyneth Paltrow in a sweet and sort of innocent story about a small-town girl who knows life holds more for her, and how a job as a flight attendant becomes her escape route. Along the way she meets friends who help her and friends who double-cross her, a guy who dumps her, and a guy she dumps. And she finds love. What more do you want from a movie?

I confess I expected something else. Flight attendants have been asking me for weeks about this movie, which they are in a lather to see. It may be closer to their real lives than they expect. I anticipated an updated version of *Coffee, Tea or Me?* but what I got instead was *Donna the Flight Attendant.* The movie reminded me of career books I read in the seventh grade with titles like *Bob Durham, Boy Radio Announcer.* It's a little more sophisticated, of course, but it has the same good heart, and a teenager thinking of a career in the air might really enjoy it.

So did I, in an uncomplicated way. Paltrow

is lovable in the right roles, and here she's joined by two others who are sunny on the screen: Candice Bergen, as the best-selling author/flight attendant who becomes her mentor, and Mark Ruffalo (from *You Can Count on Me*) as the law student who wants to marry her. The movie knows a secret; most careers do not involve clawing your way to the top, but depend on the kindness of the strangers you meet along the way, who help you just because they feel like it.

We meet Donna (Paltrow) as the daughter of a much-married former exotic dancer from Silver Springs, Nevada. She seems doomed to a life working at the mall until she sees a TV interview with the best-selling Bergen, whose book inspires Donna to train as a flight attendant. Her first stop is a puddle jumper named Sierra Airlines, which flies mostly to and from Fresno, but then she enrolls in training at Royalty Airlines, where the instructor (Mike Myers) is bitter because his crossed eye kept him from flying. Myers finds a delicate balance between lampoon and poignancy—and that's some balance.

Ruffalo plays the sometime law student who comes into her life in Nevada and then again in Cleveland, where she's assigned not to Royalty's transatlantic routes but to the discount Royalty Express. Her first flight is comic (she runs down the aisle screaming, "We're gonna crash!") and then we follow her through intrigues and romantic episodes that lead to a lonely Christmas in Paris when she decides life *still* has to offer more than this.

The movie, directed by Bruno Barreto and written by Eric Wald, is surprising for what it doesn't contain: no scenes involving mile-high clubs, lecherous businessmen, or randy pilots, but the sincere story of a woman who finds her career is almost but not quite enough. Adult audiences may be underwhelmed. Not younger teenage girls, who will be completely fascinated.

The Village ★
PG-13, 130 m., 2004

Joaquin Phoenix (Lucius Hunt), Bryce Dallas Howard (Ivy Walker), Adrien Brody (Noah Percy), William Hurt (Edward Walker), Sigourney Weaver (Alice Hunt), Brendan Gleeson (August Nicholson). Directed by M. Night Shyamalan and produced by Sam Mercer, Scott Rudin, and Shyamalan. Screenplay by Shyamalan.

The Village is a colossal miscalculation, a movie based on a premise that cannot support it, a premise so transparent it would be laughable were the movie not so deadly solemn. It's a flimsy excuse for a plot, with characters who move below the one-dimensional and enter Flatland. M. Night Shyamalan, the writer-director, has been successful in evoking horror from minimalist stories, as in *Signs,* which if you think about it rationally is absurd—but you get too involved to think rationally. He is a considerable director who evokes stories out of moods, but this time, alas, he took the day off.

Critics were enjoined after the screening to avoid revealing the plot secrets. That is not because we would spoil the movie for you. It's because if you knew them you wouldn't want to go. The whole enterprise is a shaggy dog story, and in a way it is all secrets. I can hardly discuss it at all without being maddeningly vague.

Let us say that it takes place in an unspecified time and place, surrounded by a forest the characters never enter. The clothing of the characters and the absence of cars and telephones and suchlike suggests either the 1890s or an Amish community. Everyone speaks as if they had studied *Friendly Persuasion.* The chief civic virtues are probity and circumspection. Here is a village that desperately needs an East Village.

The story opens with a funeral attended by all the villagers, followed by a big outdoor meal at long tables groaning with corn on the cob and all the other fixin's. Everyone in the village does everything together, apparently, although it is never very clear what most of their jobs are. Some farming and baking goes on.

The movie is so somber, it's afraid to raise its voice in its own presence. That makes it dreary even during scenes of shameless melodrama. We meet the patriarch Edward Walker (William Hurt), who is so judicious in all things he sounds like a minister addressing the Rotary Club. His daughter Ivy (Bryce Dallas Howard) is blind but spunky. The stalwart young man, Lucius Hunt (Joaquin Phoenix), petitions the elders to let him take a look into the forest. His widowed mother, Alice (Sigourney Weaver), has feelings for Edward Walker. The village idiot (Adrien Brody), gambols about, and gamboling is not a word I use lightly. There is a good man and true (Brendan Gleeson). And a bridegroom who is afraid his shirt will get wrinkled.

Surrounding the village is the forest. In the forest live vile, hostile creatures who dress in red and have claws of twigs. They are known as Those We Do Not Speak Of (except when we want to end a designation with a preposition). We see Those We Do Not Speak Of only in brief glimpses, like the water-fixated aliens in *Signs*. They look better than the *Signs* aliens, who looked like large extras in long underwear, while Those We Do Not, etc., look like their costumes were designed at summer camp.

Watchtowers guard the periphery of the village, and flares burn through the night. But not to fear: Those We Do, etc., have arrived at a truce. They stay in the forest and the villagers stay in the village. Lucius wants to go into the forest, and petitions the elders, who frown at this desire. Ivy would like to marry Lucius, and tells him so, but he is so reflective and funereal it will take him another movie to get worked up enough to deal with her. Still, they love each other. The village idiot also has a thing for Ivy, and sometimes they gambol together.

Something terrible happens to somebody. I dare not reveal what, and to which, and by whom. Edward Walker decides reluctantly to send someone to "the towns" to bring back medicine for whoever was injured. And off goes his daughter Ivy, a blind girl walking through the forest inhabited by Those Who, etc. She wears her yellow riding hood, and it takes us a superhuman effort to keep from thinking about Grandmother's House.

Solemn violin dirges permeate the sound track. It is autumn, overcast and chilly. Girls find a red flower and bury it. Everyone speaks in the passive voice. The vitality has been drained from the characters; these are the Stepford Pilgrims. The elders have meetings from which the young are excluded. Someone finds something under the floorboards. Wouldn't you just know it would be there, exactly where it was needed, in order

for someone to do something he couldn't do without it.

Eventually the secret of Those, etc., is revealed. To call it an anticlimax would be an insult not only to climaxes but to prefixes. It's a crummy secret, about one step up the ladder of narrative originality from It Was All a Dream. It's so witless, in fact, that when we do discover the secret, we want to rewind the film so we don't know the secret anymore. And then keep on rewinding, and rewinding, until we're back at the beginning, and can get up from our seats and walk backward out of the theater and go down the up escalator and watch the money spring from the cash register into our pockets. ☞

Virgin ★ ★ ★
NO MPAA RATING, 113 m., 2005

Robin Wright Penn (Mrs. Reynolds), Elisabeth Moss (Jessie Reynolds), Daphne Rubin-Vega (Frances), Socorro Santiago (Lorna), Peter Gerety (Mr. Reynolds), Stephanie Gatchet (Katie Reynolds), Charles Socarides (Shane). Directed by Deborah Kampmeier and produced by Raye Dowell and Sarah Schenck. Screenplay by Kampmeier.

Jessie Reynolds is not the kind of girl who gets nice things written under her picture in the high school yearbook. She's probably never going to graduate, for one thing. When we see her for the first time in *Virgin*, she's trying to talk a stranger into buying some booze for her, and when he does, he gets a kiss.

Jessie is not bad, precisely. It would be more fair to say she is lost, and a little dim. She clearly feels left behind, even left out, by her family. Her sister, Katie (Stephanie Gatchet), is pretty, popular, and a track star who dedicates her victories to Jesus. Her parents (Robin Wright Penn and Peter Gerety) are fundamentalists, strict and unforgiving. Jessie doesn't measure up and doesn't even seem to be trying.

There is, however, someone she would like to impress: Shane (Charles Socarides), a boy at school. She wanders off from a dance with him, is drunk, is given a date-rape pill, is raped, and wakes up with no memory of the event. When she discovers she is pregnant, there is only one possible explanation in her mind: There has been an immaculate conception, and she will give birth to the baby Jesus.

Jessie is played by Elisabeth Moss, from *West Wing*, as a girl both endearing and maddening. Her near-bliss seems a little heavily laid on, under the circumstances, but director Deborah Kampmeier has ways of suggesting it's the real thing. Whether or not there is a God has nothing to do with whether or not we believe he is speaking to us, and although in this case there's every reason to believe God has not impregnated Jessie, there's every reason for Jessie to think so. Among other things, it certainly trumps the religiosity of her parents and sister.

Fundamentalists almost always appear in American movies for the purpose of being closed-minded, rigid, and sanctimonious. Anyone with any religion at all, for that matter, tends to be suspect (the priest in *Million Dollar Baby* is the first good priest I can remember in a film in a long time). Movies can't seem to deal with faith as a positive element in an admirable life, and the only religions taken seriously by Hollywood are the kinds promoted in stores that also sell incense and Tarot decks. So it's refreshing to see the Robin Wright Penn character allowed to unbend in *Virgin*, to become less rigid and more of an empathetic mother, who intuitively senses that although Jessie may be deluded, she is sincere.

There has, of course, been a great wrong committed here, but it would be cruel for Jessie to learn of that fact. How sad to believe you are bearing the Christ child and then be told, no, you got drunk and were raped. Better, perhaps, to let Jessie bear the child and find out gradually that, like all children, it displays divinity primarily in the eyes of its mother.

But Kampmeier is up to something a little more ambitious here. She uses visual strategies to suggest that Jessie, in the grip of her conviction, enters a state that is just as spiritual as if its cause were not so sad. The performance by Moss invests Jessie with a kind of zealous hope that is touching: Here is a slutty loser touched by the divine and transformed. What has happened to her is more real than the miracles hailed on Sundays by results-oriented preachers. The more you consider the theological undertones of *Virgin*, the more radical it becomes. Must you be the mother of God to experience the benefits of thinking that you are? Can those from a conventional religious background deal with your ecstasy?

There is a wonderful novel named *The Annunciation of Francesca Dunn* by Janis Hallowell, a friend of mine, that tells of a waitress in Boulder, Colorado, whom a homeless man becomes convinced is the Virgin Mary. The novel explores a little more poetically and explicitly than *Virgin* the experience of being blindsided by an unsolicited spiritual epiphany.

Both works are fascinating because in mainstream society, there are only two positions on such matters: either you believe, or you do not (and therefore, either you are saved, or you don't care). Is it not possible that faith is its own reward, apart from any need for it to be connected with reality? I am unreasonably stimulated by works that leave me theologically stranded like that. They're much more interesting than works that, one way or the other, think they know.

Theological footnote: Every once in a while my Catholic grade school education sounds a dogma alarm. Jessie is not a Catholic, which perhaps explains why she thinks the term "immaculate conception" refers to the birth of Jesus, when in fact it refers to the birth of Mary.

W

Walking Tall ★ ★
PG-13, 85 m., 2004

The Rock (Chris Vaughn), Neal McDonough (Jay Hamilton Jr.), Johnny Knoxville (Ray Templeton), John Beasley (Chris Vaughn Sr.), Barbara Tarbuck (Connie Vaughn), Kristen Wilson (Michelle), Khleo Thomas (Pete), Ashley Scott (Deni), Michael Bowen (Sheriff Watkins). Directed by Kevin Bray and produced by Ashok Amritraj, Jim Burke, Lucas Foster, and David Hoberman. Screenplay by David Klass, Channing Gibson, Brian Koppelman, and David Levien.

I didn't see the original *Walking Tall*. I was "out of town at the time," I explained in my review of *Walking Tall, Part 2*. Sounds reasonable. But I suspect the earlier film was tilted more toward populism and less toward superhero violence than the new *Walking Tall*, which is "dedicated to the memory of Buford Pusser," but turns the story into a cartoon of retribution and revenge.

The Rock stars as a war hero named Chris Vaughn who returns to his southern hometown and finds that the mill has closed, a casino has opened, and kids are addicted to drugs. His character is named Chris Vaughn and not Buford Pusser, possibly because The Rock, having gone to a great deal of trouble to adopt a name both simple and authoritative, could not envision himself being called "Buford" or "Sheriff Pusser" for any amount of money.

He finds that an old high school nemesis named Jay Hamilton Jr. (Neal McDonough) has closed the mill, opened the casino, and manufactures the drugs. We know Jay is the villain because he has that close-cropped, curly, peroxided hair that works like a name tag that says, "Hi! I'm the Villain!" Outraged by the corruption that has descended upon his town, The Rock picks up the famous Buford Pusser Model Oak Club, smashes up the casino, defends himself in court, and makes such an impassioned speech that he has soon been elected sheriff. I love those movie trials in which cases are settled not according to guilt and innocence and the law, but according to who is *really* right and *deserves* to go free.

Sheriff Vaughn hires an old high school pal named Ray Templeton to be his deputy. The role is played by Johnny Knoxville, famous for *Jackass*, who is, in fact, completely convincing and probably has a legitimate movie career ahead of him and doesn't have to stuff his underpants with dead chickens and hang upside down over alligator ponds anymore.

The scenes establishing all of these events are handled efficiently and have a certain interest, but then the movie, alas, goes on autopilot with a series of improbable fight scenes that are so heavy on stunts and special effects that we might as well be watching a cartoon. This is an action movie, pure and simple, and one can only wonder what the late Buford Pusser would have made of it. Maybe he would have advised Sheriff Vaughn that times have changed and he should forget the oak club and get himself an AK-47.

The Rock comes out of the movie more or less intact, careerwise. I've felt from the beginning that he had the makings of a movie star, and I still think so; he has a kind of inner quiet that allows him to inhabit preposterous scenes without being overwhelmed by them. His acting style is flat and uninflected, authoritative without pushing it; he's a little like John Wayne that way. Also like Wayne, he's a big, physically intimidating man who is able to suggest a certain gentleness; he's not inflamed, not looking for a fight, not shoving people around, but simply trying to right wrongs. I seriously doubt that he could play a convincing villain. Not even with a name tag.

War of the Worlds ★ ★
PG-13, 118 m., 2005

Tom Cruise (Ray Ferrier), Dakota Fanning (Rachel), Miranda Otto (Mary Ann), Tim Robbins (Harlan Ogilvy), Justin Chatwin (Robbie). Directed by Steven Spielberg and produced by Kathleen Kennedy and Colin Wilson. Screenplay by Josh Friedman and David Koepp, based on the novel by H. G. Wells.

War of the Worlds is a big, clunky movie containing some sensational sights but lacking the zest and joyous energy we expect from Steven Spielberg. It proceeds with the lead-footed deliberation of its 1950s predecessors to give us an alien invasion that is malevolent, destructive, and, from the alien point of view, pointless. They've "been planning this for a million years" and have gone to a lot of trouble to invade Earth for no apparent reason and with a seriously flawed strategy. What happened to the sense of wonder Spielberg celebrated in *Close Encounters of the Third Kind,* and the dazzling imagination of *Minority Report?*

The movie adopts the prudent formula of viewing a catastrophe through the eyes of a few foreground characters. When you compare it with a movie like *The Day After Tomorrow,* which depicted the global consequences of cosmic events, it lacks dimension: Martians have journeyed millions of miles to attack a crane operator and his neighbors (and if they're not Martians, they journeyed a lot farther).

The hero, Ray Ferrier (Tom Cruise), does the sort of running and hiding and desperate defending of his children that goes with the territory, and at one point even dives into what looks like certain death to rescue his daughter. There's a survivalist named Ogilvy (Tim Robbins) who has quick insights into surviving: "The ones that didn't flatline are the ones who kept their eyes open." And there are the usual crowds of terrified citizens looking up at ominous threats looming above them. But despite the movie's $135 million budget, it seems curiously rudimentary in its action.

The problem may be with the alien invasion itself. It is not very interesting. We learn that countless years ago, invaders presumably but not necessarily from Mars buried huge machines all over Earth. Now they activate them with lightning bolts, each one containing an alien (in what form, it is hard to say). With the aliens at the controls, these machines crash up out of the earth, stand on three towering but spindly legs, and begin to zap the planet with death rays. Later, their tentacles suck our blood and fill steel baskets with our writhing bodies.

To what purpose? Why zap what you later want to harvest? Why harvest humans? And, for that matter, why balance these towering machines on ill-designed supports? If evolution has taught us anything, it is that limbs of living things, from men to dinosaurs to spiders to centipedes, tend to come in numbers divisible by two. Three legs are inherently not

stable, as Ray demonstrates when he damages one leg of a giant tripod, and it falls helplessly to earth.

The tripods are indeed faithful to the original illustrations for H.G. Wells's novel *The War of the Worlds,* and to the machines described in the historic 1938 Orson Welles radio broadcast and the popular 1953 movie. But the book and radio program depended on our imaginations to make them believable, and the movie came at a time of lower expectations in special effects. You look at Spielberg's machines and you don't get much worked up, because you're seeing not alien menace but clumsy retro design. Perhaps it would have been a good idea to set the movie in 1898, at the time of Wells's novel, when the tripods represented a state-of-the-art alien invasion.

There are some wonderful f/x moments, but they mostly don't involve the pods. A scene where Ray wanders through the remains of an airplane crash is somber and impressive, and there is an unforgettable image of a train, every coach on fire, roaring through a station. Such scenes seem to come from a different kind of reality than the tripods.

Does it make the aliens scarier that their motives are never spelled out? I don't expect them to issue a press release announcing their plans for world domination, but I wish their presence reflected some kind of intelligent purpose. The alien ship in *Close Encounters* visited for no other reason, apparently, than to demonstrate that life existed elsewhere, could visit us, and was intriguingly unlike us while still sharing such universal qualities as the perception of tone.

Those aliens wanted to say hello. The alien machines in *War of the Worlds* seem designed for heavy lifting in an industry that needs to modernize its equipment and techniques. (The actual living alien being we finally glimpse is an anticlimax, a batlike bug-eyed monster, confirming the wisdom of Kubrick and Clarke in deliberately showing no aliens in *2001.*)

The human characters are disappointingly one-dimensional. Tom Cruise's character is given a smidgeon of humanity (he's an immature, divorced hotshot who has custody of the kids for the weekend), and then he wanders out with his neighbors to witness strange portents in the sky, and the movie becomes a story about grabbing and running and ducking and hiding and trying to fight back. There are scenes in which poor Dakota Fanning, as his daughter, has to be lost or menaced, and then scenes in which she is found or saved, all with much desperate shouting. A scene where an alien tentacle explores a ruined basement where they're hiding is a mirror of a better scene in *Jurassic Park* where characters hide from a curious raptor.

The thing is, we never believe the tripods and their invasion are *practical*. How did these vast metal machines lie undetected for so long beneath the streets of a city honeycombed with subway tunnels, sewers, water and power lines, and foundations? And why didn't a civilization with the physical science to build and deploy the tripods a million years ago not do a little more research about conditions on the planet before sending its invasion force? It's a war of the worlds, all right—but at a molecular, not a planetary, level.

All of this is just a way of leading up to the gut reaction I had all through the film: I do not like the tripods. I do not like the way they look, the way they are employed, the way they attack, the way they are vulnerable, or the reasons they are here. A planet that harbors intelligent and subtle ideas for science fiction movies is invaded in this film by an ungainly Erector set.

The Weather Underground ★ ★ ★ ½
NO MPAA RATING, 92 m., 2003

Featuring Billy Ayers, Kathleen Cleaver, Bernardine Dohrn, Brian Flanagan, David Gilbert, Todd Gitlin, Naomi Jaffe, Mark Rudd, Don Strickland, and Laura Whitehorn. Narrated by Lili Taylor. A documentary directed by Sam Green and Bill Siegel and produced by Green, Carrie Lozano, Siegel, and Marc Smolowitz.

I still have my membership card in Students for a Democratic Society, signed by Tom Hayden, who handed it to me at a National Student Congress in 1963 and tucked the $1 membership fee in the pocket of his flannel shirt. SDS in those days was still the student department of the League for Industrial Democracy, an old-line left-labor group headed by Norman Thomas, whose statement on the back of the card made it clear the organization was nonviolent and anti-Communist. Within a few years, SDS would be captured by a far-left faction that became the Weather Underground, the most violent protest group in modern American history.

The new documentary *The Weather Underground* chronicles those early days of idealism, and their transition into a period when American society seemed for an instant on the point of revolution. The Weathermen orchestrated a string of bombings, initiated the Days of Rage in Chicago, and were in a vanguard of a more widespread antiwar movement that saw National Guard troops on the campuses, the Pentagon under siege by protesters, including hippies who vowed to levitate it, and the infamous Chicago 7 trial. Whether the protest movement hastened the end of the Vietnam War is hard to say, but it is likely that Lyndon Johnson's decision not to run for reelection was influenced by the climate it helped to create.

One crucial moment documented in this film is when SDS, with 100,000 members an important force among American young people, was essentially hijacked at its 1969 national convention in Chicago by the more radical Weather faction. "Institutional piracy," Todd Gitlin called it; one of the founders of SDS and later the author of a landmark book about the student left, he watched in dismay as the Weather faction advocated the violent overthrow of the U.S. government. Their program of terrorist bombings, he said, "was essentially mass murder." When an innocent person was killed in one of its early bombings, the group, however, decided that was "a terrible error," and took care that nobody was injured in a long series of later bombings, including one at the U.S. Capitol building. But a Greenwich Village townhouse used by the Weathermen as a bomb factory was destroyed in an accidental explosion that killed three bomb makers.

The Weatherman tactics were "Custeristic," Black Panther leader Fred Hampton sardonically observed at the time. When the Weathermen called for Days of Rage in Chicago in 1969, he said they were "taking people into a situation where they can be massacred." He was right, but he was himself soon massacred, in a still-controversial shooting that Chicago law enforcement officials described as a shoot-out, but which physical evidence indicated was an assassination. (After the *Tribune* cited "bullet holes" proving Hampton had fired back, a *Sun-Times* team ran photographs revealing the holes to be nailheads.)

The documentarians, Sam Green and Bill Siegel, are too young to remember this period personally—and, indeed, many viewers of the film may discover for the first time how ferociously the war at home was fought. The film interviews surviving players in the drama, including Bernardine Dohrn, her husband Bill Ayers, Naomi Jaffe, Mark Rudd, David Gilbert, Brian Flanagan, and Gitlin. Dohrn, today the head of a program for juvenile justice at Northwestern University, still burns with the fire of her early idealism, as do Ayers and Jaffe, and you can hear in the voice of Gilbert (serving a life sentence for his involvement in a fatal robbery of a Brinks truck), the pain he felt because his country was committing what he considered murder in Vietnam.

Ironically, many charges against the Weathermen had to be dropped because the FBI had violated the law with its "Cointelpro," a secret agency to discredit the left. After the war ended and the Weatherman movement faded away, Dohrn and Ayers lived in hiding for several years with their children—an existence some say inspired the 1988 movie *Running on Empty*. Eventually they turned themselves in, and today are leading productive, unrepentant lives. I see Dohrn at the Conference on World Affairs at the University of Colorado, where she is as angry about the unnecessary criminalization of poor (often nonwhite) American young people as she was then about the war. She has, you must observe, the courage of her convictions.

The Wedding Date ★ ★ ½
PG-13, 90 m., 2005

Debra Messing (Kat Ellis), Dermot Mulroney (Nick Mercer), Amy Adams (Amy), Jack Davenport (Edward Fletcher-Wooten), Jeremy Sheffield (Jeffrey), Peter Egan (Victor Ellis), Holland Taylor (Bunny Ellis). Directed by Clare Kilner and produced by Jessica Bendinger, Paul Brooks, Michelle Chydzik, and Nathalie Marciano. Screenplay by Dana Fox.

The Wedding Date presents the curious case of two appealing performances surviving a bombardment of schlock. I have so many questions about the movie's premise that it seems, in memory, almost entirely composed of moments when I was shaking my head in disbelief. The character played by Dermot Mulroney is a romance novel fantasy, and yet that doesn't prevent him from also being subtle and intriguing. The character played by Debra Messing not only finds Mulroney through an article in the *Sunday New York Times Magazine,* but seems to have found herself there, too, in the spring fashion issue. But she is nevertheless lovable and touching.

The premise: Kat Ellis (Messing) is a British woman living in New York, who must fly back to London for her sister's wedding. The problem: The groom's best man, Jeff, is Kat's former fiancé, who dumped her. The solution: She hires a male escort named Nick (Mulroney) to go along with her and play the role of her fiancé, so that Jeff will be jealous and she won't look pathetic and single. Nick gets $6,000 plus his airfare on Virgin Upper Class, which is also what he offers: Sex would be extra.

The movie develops the usual assortment of impossible relatives and fun wedding activities; some scenes look like they're posed for snapshots in the *Tatler,* a British society magazine devoted to pretending to like twits. The story expertly compacts *Four Weddings and a Funeral, Pretty Woman,* and *My Best Friend's Wedding* into *One Wedding, an Ex-Best Friend, and a Pretty Man,* with Mulroney (who played the best friend in the original) as the escort with a heart of gold.

Yes, and yet the movie isn't giddy with silliness. There's a melancholy undertow. Mulroney seems to have taken a close look at his character and realized that the less Nick says, the better. His personal thoughts are a closely guarded secret, and he makes a point of separating his role as an escort from his feelings as a man. When there comes, as inevitably there must, a moment when his feelings win out, the movie signals this not with clunky dialogue but with the most romantic use of an anchovy I can recall.

Messing, from TV's *Will & Grace,* makes Kat a character who is dealing with two confusing situations at once. She doesn't know how she feels about hiring an escort, and she doesn't know how she feels about Jeff (Jeremy

Sheffield). Does she want Jeff back, or does she just want to make him miserable? Subplots grind away to create last-minute problems for her sister, Amy (Amy Adams), and her fiancé, the forthrightly named Edward Fletcher-Wooten (Jack Davenport). Nick the escort is so handsome, so mysteriously knowledgeable, so at home in every situation, and so wise that Kat forgets everything a grown-up girl like her should know about prostitution, role-playing, and the dangers of STDs, and relates to him as if she were the heroine on the cover of a novel by Jennifer Blake.

"Every woman has the exact love life she wants," Nick believes, according to the *Times* magazine article. It is his job to figure out what that is, and create the illusion that he is supplying it. "It's not about the sex," he says, "it's about what people need." And what does Kat need? Nick says he heard something in her voice on the phone. "Desperation?" she asks. "I think it was hope," he says. Down, boy!

Part of the movie's appeal comes from the way the Nick character negotiates the absurdities of the plot as if he stands outside it. A lesser performance, or one not as skillfully written (by Dana Fox) would have pitched him headlong into the fray. By withdrawing, so to speak, he creates a great curiosity about himself, and the other characters see in him what they need to see. As for Messing, she has an appeal similar to Nia Vardalos's in *My Big Fat Greek Wedding*. We want her to be happy. Whether that happiness will come at the hands of Nick is an excellent question, made simpler by the certainty that Jeff would only make her miserable. The answer to this and other questions, every single one of them, is supplied by one of those romantic comedy endings where false crisis and false hope and real crisis and real hope alternate like a clockwork mechanism. Everyone appears and disappears exactly on cue, driving around in sports cars with the top down and running around in shoes meant only for walking down the aisle.

As for Nick, what makes him happy? Is it also true that every man has the exact love life he wants? Does he want his? When he watches *Five Easy Pieces* and Jack Nicholson says, "I faked a little Chopin, and you faked a big re-sponse," does he see himself as the pianist, or the piano?

We Don't Live Here Anymore ★ ★
R, 101 m., 2004

Mark Ruffalo (Jack Linden), Laura Dern (Terry Linden), Peter Krause (Hank Evans), Naomi Watts (Edith Evans), Sam Charles (Sean Linden), Haili Page (Natasha Linden), Jennifer Bishop (Sharon Evans). Directed by John Curran and produced by Jonas Goodman, Harvey Kahn, and Naomi Watts. Screenplay by Larry Gross, based on stories by Andre Dubus.

Jack and Edith, who are married to other people, are seized with the need to have sex right then and there, in the middle of the night, in Edith's living room. But what about her husband, Hank? If he wakes up, she says, "he'll go to the bathroom first; we'll hear him." That kind of domestic detail compounds the betrayal, taking advantage of her husband's humanity at just that moment when the last thing they should be doing is listening for poor Hank to flush the toilet.

We Don't Live Here Anymore is set in the shabby moral surroundings of two couples who know each other too well, and themselves not well enough. Jack Linden (Mark Ruffalo) and Hank Evans (Peter Krause) are professors on a small campus in Oregon; Jack is married to Terry (Laura Dern) and Hank to Edith (Naomi Watts). One night at a party Jack finds that the beer supply has run low and says he'll go get some more. Edith says she'll go along for the ride. Later that night Terry asks her husband if it isn't time for him to stop going off with Edith on their phony little missions and leaving her behind with Hank.

Jack plays innocent, but fairly early in the film it's clear that both couples (and eventually their children) have a pretty good idea of what's going on. *We Don't Live Here Anymore* isn't about shocking discoveries and revelations, but about four people who move with varying degrees of eagerness toward, and then away from, the kinds of sexual cheating they may have read about in the pages of John Cheever, Philip Roth, or John Updike—whose characters are too sophisticated to be surprised by adultery, but not very good at it.

The movie, directed by John Curran and written by Larry Gross, is based on two stories by Andre Dubus. As with *In the Bedroom* (2001), also based on the work of Dubus, it listens carefully to what couples say in the privacy of their own long knowledge of themselves. What we hear this time is that Jack thinks Terry drinks too much, and Terry agrees. But Jack isn't cheating with Edith because his wife is a drunk; he's cheating because he wants too, because he and Edith have fallen into a season of lust. Hank, meanwhile, is not particularly alarmed by his cheating wife, because he's a serial cheater himself. His philosophy, explained to Jack: Sure, you should love your wife and kids, but it's okay to fool around sometimes "just because it feels good."

For Jack and Edith, it feels really good that first time, on the blanket in the woods near the bike trail. It feels so good that Jack has flashbacks to it every time he's near the place where it happened—while taking his kids on a bike ride, for example. The movie presents those flashbacks with an odd undertone, as if they're bothering him. Is that because he regrets what he did, or regrets he isn't doing it again right now? Hard to say.

As for his wife, Terry, she tells Jack that she and Hank have had sex, and Jack's response is not the emotional reaction of a wounded man, but the intellectual combativeness of an English professor who wants details of their conversations because he thinks somehow he can win this battle on a logical level. Hank, for that matter, also seems to prefer the theory to the practice of sex, although he confesses to Jack that he cried after breaking up with his last mistress.

These people are such whiners. They mope and complain and recycle their petty little marital grudges, and we yearn for—well, not for more passion, which doesn't come with the territory in stories of academic adultery, but more edge, cruelty, psychological wounding, slashing sarcasm, sadistic button-pushing. Consider George and Martha, virtuosos of verbal spousal abuse in *Who's Afraid of Virginia Woolf?* Or Neil LaBute's coldly evil characters in *Your Friends and Neighbors* (1998). Or the sardonic battle of wits between David Strathairn and Saul Rubinek (and their wives,

Bonnie Bedelia and Caroleen Feeney) in *Bad Manners* (1997).

Jack and Terry and Hank and Edith are halfhearted in their cheating. Yes, the sex is great between Jack and Edith when they're on the blanket in the woods, or downstairs listening for Hank to pee, but didn't Woody Allen observe that the worst sex he'd had wasn't that bad? That three children are involved, and all three sense what's happening, acts like an undertow, demonstrating to the adults that they don't really want to face the consequences of their actions.

What must be said is that the actors are better than the material. There are four specific people here, each one closely observed and carefully realized. Ruffalo's Jack, driven by his lust, finds his needs fascinating to himself; Naomi Watts's Edith finds them fascinating to her. Terry and Hank seem almost forced into their halfhearted affair, and Laura Dern and Peter Krause are precise in the way they show dutiful excitement in each other's presence, while Dern vibrates with anger and passion in her arguments with her husband.

The film's problem is that it's too desultory. Maybe the point of the Dubus stories was to show perfunctory transgressions between characters not sufficiently motivated to accept the consequences. They approach adultery the way they might approach a treadmill, jumping on, punching the speed and incline buttons, working up a sweat, coming back down to level, slowing to a walk, and then deciding the goddamn thing isn't worth the trouble.

Welcome to Mooseport ★ ★ ★
PG-13, 110 m., 2004

Gene Hackman (Monroe Cole), Ray Romano (Handy Harrison), Marcia Gay Harden (Grace Sutherland), Maura Tierney (Sally Mannis), Christine Baranski (Charlotte Cole), Fred Savage (Bullard), Rip Torn (Bert Langdon). Directed by Donald Petrie and produced by Marc Frydman, Basil Iwanyk, and Tom Schulman. Screenplay by Tom Schulman.

I knew a very good poker player who always lost money at bachelor parties. He'd turn a profit in Vegas, but down in the basement with the beer and the cigar smoke he invariably got cleaned out. The reason, he explained, was that the jerks he was playing against didn't know how to play poker. They bet on every hand. They raised when they should have folded. You couldn't tell when they were bluffing because they knew so little they were always bluffing.

Gene Hackman plays a character like that in *Welcome to Mooseport*. The movie isn't about poker but the principle is the same. He is a former president of the United States who has moved to a colorful Maine hamlet and suddenly finds himself running for mayor. His problem is, he knows way too much about politics to run for mayor of Mooseport. And way too little about Mooseport.

Hackman is one of the most engaging actors on the face of the earth. He's especially good at bluster. "The Eagle has landed," he declares, arriving in town. His name is Monroe "The Eagle" Cole, and don't forget the nickname. His opponent in the race is Handy Harrison (Ray Romano), a plumber who owns the local hardware store. "Let me get this straight," says The Eagle. "I'm running for mayor against the man who is repairing my toilet?"

There are romantic complications. Handy has been dating local beauty Sally Mannis (Maura Tierney) for seven years, without ever having gotten up the nerve to pop the question. As the movie opens, his face lights up with joy as he races over to tell her he's come into some money, and so the time is finally right to ... buy that pickup. When The Eagle asks her out to dinner, she accepts.

Of course, he has no idea Handy and Sally have been dating. For that matter, the only reason he's in Mooseport at all is that his bitchy ex-wife, Charlotte (Christine Baranski), got the big house in the divorce settlement. Now time hangs heavily on his hands, he's surrounded by a support staff with nothing to do, and a mayoral race has them all exercising their over-trained skills. The only sane voice in his entourage belongs to Grace Sutherland (Marcia Gay Harden), who may be hoping that someday The Eagle will land on her.

Rip Torn plays the Karl Rove role. What a pleasure Torn is. Like Christopher Walken and Steve Buscemi, he makes us smile just by appearing on the screen. His Machiavellian approach to Mooseport is all wrong, however, because the town is so guileless and good-hearted that schemes are invisible to them. We question that such a naive and innocent town could exist in America, and are almost relieved to find that the movie was shot in Canada. Has it seemed to you lately that Canada is the last remaining repository of the world Norman Rockwell used to paint?

There is a genre of movies about outsiders who arrive in small towns and are buffaloed by the guileless locals. Consider David Mamet's *State and Main* (2000) or *Win a Date with Tad Hamilton!*. There's always a romance with a local, always a visiting sophisticate who rediscovers traditional values, always a civic booster in a bow tie, always a microphone that deafens everyone with a shriek whenever it's turned on, always an embarrassing public display of dirty laundry, and almost always a Greek chorus of regulars at the local diner/tavern/launderette who pass judgment on events.

Whether the movie works or not depends on the charm of the actors. Gene Hackman could charm the chrome off a trailer hitch. Ray Romano is more of the earnest, aw-shucks, sincere, well-meaning kind of guy whose charm is inner and only peeks out occasionally. They work well together here, and Maura Tierney does a heroic job of playing a character who doesn't know how the story will end, when everybody else in the cast and in the audience has an excellent idea.

Whale Rider ★ ★ ★
PG-13, 105 m., 2003

Keisha Castle-Hughes (Pai), Rawiri Paratene (Koro), Vicky Haughton (Flowers), Cliff Curtis (Porourangi), Grant Roa (Rawiri), Mana Taumaunu (Hemi), Rachel House (Shilo), Taungaroa Emile (Dog). Directed by Niki Caro and produced by John Barnett, Frank Hubner, and Tim Sanders. Screenplay by Caro, based on the novel by Witi Ihimaera.

Whale Rider arrives in theaters already proven as one of the great audience-grabbers of recent years. It won the audience awards as the most popular film at both the Toronto and Sundance film festivals, played to standing ovations, left audiences in tears. I recite these facts right at the top of this review because I fear you might make a hasty judgment that you don't want to see a movie about a twelve-year-old Maori girl who dreams of becoming the chief of her people. Sounds too ethnic, uplifting, and feminist, right?

The genius of the movie is the way it sidesteps all of the obvious clichés of the underlying story and makes itself fresh, observant, tough, and genuinely moving. There is a vast difference between movies for twelve-year-old girls, and movies about twelve-year-old girls, and *Whale Rider* proves it.

The movie, which takes place in the present day in New Zealand, begins with the birth of twins. The boy and the mother die. The girl, Pai (Keisha Castle-Hughes), survives. Her father, Porourangi (Cliff Curtis), an artist, leaves New Zealand, and the little girl is raised and much loved by her grandparents, Koro and Nanny Flowers.

Koro is the chief of these people. Porourangi would be next in line, but has no interest in returning home. Pai believes that she could serve as the chief, but her grandfather, despite his love, fiercely opposes this idea. He causes Pai much hurt by doubting her, questioning her achievements, insisting in the face of everything she achieves that she is only a girl.

The movie, written and directed by Niki Caro, inspired by a novel by Witi Ihimaera, describes these events within the rhythms of daily life. This is not a simplistic fable, but the story of real people living in modern times. There are moments when Pai is lost in discouragement and despair, and when her father comes for a visit she almost leaves with him. But, no, her people need her—whether or not her grandfather realizes it.

Pai is played by Keisha Castle-Hughes, a newcomer of whom it can only be said: This is a movie star. She glows. She stands up to her grandfather in painful scenes, she finds dignity, and yet the next second she's running around the village like the kid she is. The other roles are also strongly cast, especially Rawiri Paratene and Vicky Haughton as the grandparents.

One day Koro summons all of the young teenage boys of the village to a series of compulsory lessons on how to be a Maori, and the leader of Maoris. There's an amusing sequence where they practice looking ferocious to scare their enemies. Pai, of course, is banned from these classes, but eavesdrops,

and enlists a wayward uncle to reveal some of the secrets of the males.

And then—well, the movie doesn't end as we expect. It doesn't march obediently to standard plot requirements, but develops an unexpected crisis, and an unexpected solution. There is a scene set at a school ceremony, where Pai has composed a work in honor of her people, and asked her grandfather to attend. Despite his anger, he will come, won't he? The movie seems headed for the ancient cliché of the auditorium door that opens at the last moment to reveal the person whom the child onstage desperately hopes to see—but no, that's not what happens.

It isn't that Koro comes or that he doesn't come, but that something else altogether happens. Something on a larger and more significant scale, that brings together all of the themes of the film into a magnificent final sequence. It's not just an uplifting ending, but a transcendent one, inspired and inspiring, and we realize how special this movie really is. So many films by and about teenagers are mired in vulgarity and stupidity; this one, like its heroine, dares to dream.

What a Girl Wants ★ ★
PG, 104 m., 2003

Amanda Bynes (Daphne Reynolds), Colin Firth (Henry Dashwood), Kelly Preston (Libby Reynolds), Eileen Atkins (Lady Jocelyn), Anna Chancellor (Glynnis), Jonathan Pryce (Alastair Payne), Oliver James (Ian Wallace), Christina Cole (Clarissa). Directed by Dennie Gordon and produced by Denise Di Novi, Bill Gerber, and Hunt Lowry. Screenplay by Jenny Bicks and Elizabeth Chandler, based on the screenplay by William Douglas Home.

Amanda Bynes, the star of *The Amanda Show*, is well known to fans of the Nickelodeon channel, who are so numerous that she is to 'tweeners as Jack Nicholson is to the Academy. She was sort of wonderful in *Big Fat Liar*, a comedy about kids whose screenplay is stolen by a Hollywood professional, and now here she is in *What a Girl Wants*, a comedy whose screenplay was stolen from *The Princess Diaries*.

But I am unfair. What goes around comes around, and to assume this is a retread of *The*

Princess Diaries is to overlook its own pedigree. It's based on the 1956 play and 1958 screenplay, *The Reluctant Debutante,* by William Douglas Home—who, by the way, was the brother of Sir Alec Douglas Home, briefly the British prime minister in the 1960s.

The point, I suppose, is that few movies are truly original, and certainly not *What a Girl Wants* or *The Princess Diaries.* Both are recycled from ancient fairy tales in which a humble child discovers a royal parent and is elevated from pauperdom to princehood, to coin a phrase.

I would not be surprised to learn that Jenny Bicks and Elizabeth Chandler, who adapted Home's screenplay, did homework of their own—because a key plot point in the movie mirrors Sir Alec's own decision, in 1963, to renounce his seat in the House of Lords in order to run for a seat in the Commons. He won, became prime minister after Macmillan, and quickly lost the next election to Harold Wilson.

Do you need to know this? Perhaps not, but then do you need to know the plot of *What a Girl Wants*? The movie is clearly intended for girls between the ages of nine and fifteen, and for the more civilized of their brothers, and isn't of much use to anyone else.

Bynes stars as Daphne Reynolds, who has been raised by her mother, Libby (Kelly Preston), in an apartment above a restaurant in Chinatown, for the excellent reason that we can therefore see shots of Daphne in Chinatown. As nearly as I can recall, no Chinese characters have speaking lines, although one helps to blow out the candles on her birthday cake.

Daphne is the love child of Sir Henry Dashwood (Colin Firth), a handsome British politician who has decided to renounce his seat in the House of Lords in order to run for the Commons (the movie dismisses such minutiae as that Tony Blair has already booted most of the lords out onto the street). Sir Henry had a Meet Cute with Libby in Morocco fifteen years ago, and they were married by a Bedouin prince, but never had a "real marriage" (a Bedouin prince not ranking as high in this system as a justice of the peace). Then Sir Henry's evil adviser (Jonathan Pryce) plotted to drive them apart, and she fled to Chinatown, believing Sir Henry did not love her and nobly saving

him the embarrassment of a pregnant American commoner.

So great is the wealth of the Dashwoods that their country estate, surrounded by a vast expanse of green lawns and many a tree, is smack dab in the middle of London, so central that Daphne can hop off a bus bound for Trafalgar Square and press her pert little nose against its cold iron gates. The Dashwoods, in short, live on real estate worth more than Rhode Island.

Daphne jumps the wall at Dashwood House in order to meet her father, her lovable but eccentric grandmother (Eileen Atkins), her father's competitive fiancée (Anna Chancellor), her father's future stepdaughter (Christina Cole), and her father's adviser (Pryce), who frowns on the notion of introducing a love child on the eve of the election. Now that you know all that, you can easily jot down the rest of the plot for yourself.

There are moments of wit, as when the eccentric grandmother recoils from the American teenager ("No hugs, dear. I'm British. We only show affection to dogs and horses"). And an odd scene where Daphne is locked in a bedroom, released just as Queen Elizabeth II is arriving at a party, and flees in tears—causing her father to choose between chasing her and greeting the queen. My analysis of this scene: (1) He should choose to greet the queen, or nineteen generations of breeding have been for nothing, and (2) Daphne won't get far before being returned, dead or alive, by the Scotland Yard security detail that accompanies the queen when she visits private homes.

I found it a little unlikely, by the way, that the guests at the party were all looking at Daphne and not the queen. Paul Theroux wrote of being at a dinner party for the queen and agonizing over what he should say when she entered the room. Suddenly seeing her famous profile, all he could think of was: "That reminds me! I need to buy postage stamps."

So is this movie worth seeing? Well, everybody in it is either sweet or cute, or eccentric and hateful, and the movie asks the timeless question: Can a little girl from America find love and happiness as the daughter of a wealthy and titled English lord? If you are a fan of Amanda Bynes, you will probably enjoy finding out the answer for yourself. If not, not.

What the #$*! Do We Know? ★ ★ ½

NO MPAA RATING, 108 m., 2004

Marlee Matlin (Amanda), Elaine Hendrix (Jennifer), John Ross Bowie (Elliot). And appearances by David Albert, Joe Dispenza, Amit Goswami, John Hagelin, Stuart Hameroff, Dr. Miceal Ledwith, Daniel Monti, Andrew B. Newberg, Candace Pert, Ramtha, Jeffrey Satinover, William Tiller, and Fred Alan Wolf. Directed by Mark Vicente, Betsy Chasse, and William Arntz, and produced by Arntz and Chasse. Screenplay by Arntz, Chasse, and Mathew Hoffman.

Why does anything exist? How do I know it exists? What do I mean when I say "I"? It's convenient to pin everything on God, but if there is a God, he provided us with brains and curiosity and put us in what seems to be a physical universe, and so we cannot be blamed for trying to figure things out. Newton seemed to have it about right, but it's been downhill ever since. And with the introduction of quantum physics, even unusually intelligent people like you and me have to admit we are baffled.

What the #$! Do We Know?* is a movie that attempts to explain quantum physics in terms anyone can understand. It succeeds, up to a point. I understood every single term. Only the explanation eluded me. Physicists, philosophers, astronomers, biologists, and neurologists describe their strange new world, in which matter (a) cannot be said to exist for sure, although (b) it can find itself in two places at the same time. Time need not flow in one direction, and our perception of reality may be a mental fabrication.

Among the experts on the screen, only one seemed to make perfect sense to me. This was a pretty, plumpish blond woman with clear blue eyes, who looked the camera straight in the eye, seemed wise and sane, and said that although the questions might be physical, the answers were likely to be metaphysical. Since we can't by definition understand life and the world, we might as well choose a useful way of pretending to.

Sounded good to me, especially compared to the cheerful evasions, paradoxes, and conundrums of the other experts. Only after the movie was over did I learn from my wife, who is informed on such matters, that the sane woman who made perfect sense was in fact Ramtha—or, more precisely, Ramtha as channeled by the psychic JZ Knight, who would seem to be quite distinctive enough without leaving the periods out of her name. And who is Ramtha? From Cathleen Falsani, the religion writer of the *Chicago Sun-Times,* I learn that Ramtha is a 35,000-year-old mystical sage from the lost continent of Atlantis. Well, weirder authorities have surfaced. Or maybe not.

What the Bleep Do We Know, as it is referred to for convenience, is not a conventional documentary about quantum physics. It's more like a collision in the editing room between talking heads, an impenetrable human parable and a hallucinogenic animated cartoon. The parts have so little connection and fit together so strangely that the movie seems to be channel surfing. This is not a bad thing, but wondrously curious. There are three directors, and I wonder if they made the movie like one of those party games where you write the first sentence of a story and pass it along, and someone else writes the second sentence and then folds the paper so the third person can't see the first sentence, and so on.

We meet many wise men and women from august institutions, who sit in front of bookshelves and landscapes and describe the paradoxes and inexplicabilities of quantum physics. They seem to agree that quantum physics accurately describes the universe, but they don't seem sure about the universe it describes. Perhaps the universe is going into and out of existence at every moment, or switching dimensions, or is a construct of our minds, or is mostly made of nothing. Perhaps we cannot observe it but only observe ourselves as we think we're observing it.

The experts do not know the answers to these questions, and admit it. They have quixotic little smiles as they explain why it is that there are no answers. What makes them experts? I guess it's because they have been able to formulate the questions, and intuit the ways in which they are prevented from being answered. Gene Siskel ended every interview by asking his subjects, "What do you know for sure?" These people know for sure that they can't know for sure. At some point in the movie I would have enjoyed, as a change of pace, a professor of French who explains he cannot speak the language, that perhaps nobody can, and cautions us that France may not exist.

Intercut with their intellectual flailing (which is charming, intelligent, articulate, and by definition baffled), we get the story of a young woman named Amanda (Marlee Matlin). She is a photographer who has many questions about her life. Many of these are the usual questions we all have, like what does my life mean, and why do I look like this in the mirror? She unhappily attends a wedding party at which people think they are dancing and having a good time, but may in fact be bouncing randomly through space and time without a clue. Well, most parties are like that, but what we don't suspect is that the subatomic particles in our bodies may be partying in exactly the same way.

To visualize this idea, the filmmakers use brightly colored animated blobs to represent emotions, tendencies, memes, engrams, delusions, behavior patterns, senses, and various forms of matter or energy, all wandering around the universe trying to get a drink or maybe meet someone. As we see how random everything is, how much chance is involved, and what the odds are of anything happening or not happening, we ask ourselves, "What the #$*! Do We Know?" And we conclude that we don't know s#!t.

That's where Ramtha comes in. Cathleen Falsani, who must have been taking notes while I was staring gobsmacked at the screen, quotes the 35,000-year-old Atlantean: "That we simply are has allowed this reality we call real, from the power of intangibility, to pull, out of inertness, action . . . and mold it into a form we call matter." Like I said, Ramtha makes perfect sense. That I simply am a film critic has allowed this reality we call *What the #$*! Do We Know?*, however intangible, to be molded into a form I call a movie review. Isn't life great? ☞

When Will I Be Loved ★ ★ ★ ★
R, 81 m., 2004

Neve Campbell (Vera), Fred Weller (Ford), Dominic Chianese (Count Tommaso), Karen Allen (Alexandra), Barry Primus (Victor), Mike Tyson (Himself). Directed by James Toback and produced by Ron Rotholz. Screenplay by Toback.

When Will I Be Loved is like a jazz solo that touches familiar themes on its way to a triumphant and unexpected conclusion. Neve Campbell plays the soloist, a rich girl who likes to walk on the wild side, is open to the opportunities of the moment, and improvises a devious and spontaneous revenge when her boyfriend betrays her. Here is a movie that doesn't start out to be about a con, but ends up that way.

Campbell's performance is carnal, verbally facile, physically uninhibited, and charged with intelligence. Not many actresses could have played this character, and fewer still could give us the sense she's making it up as she goes along. She plays Vera, daughter of wealth, girlfriend of a persuasive street hustler named Ford (Fred Weller). Ford is smart, quick, cynical, and believes in making his own opportunities. He's engaged in trying to scam Count Tommaso (Dominic Chianese), an Italian millionaire who turns out to be interested in only one thing Ford might have to offer: his girlfriend.

The count suggests an introduction. Ford mentions money. Money is not a problem. The count is a man of the world, cultivated, with taste but without scruples. He would never make the mistake of implying that cash will be exchanged for sex. He uses the soothing language of money as a gift or tribute or simply a gesture, as if Vera deserves his money because she is so splendid a person.

Ford pitches the idea to Vera, after a scene in which they have enthusiastic sex; Vera has earlier had spontaneous sex with a girlfriend, and is a thoroughly sensual creature. We begin to understand why she is attracted to Ford, why she even likes him, why she's entertained by the audacity of his pitch to the world. But Ford is poor and needs money, and pushes too hard in the wrong way.

Vera agrees to meet with the count, as much for her own amusement as anything. She quickly ups the talking price from $100,000 to $1 million—both sums negligible to the count. She discovers that Ford, as the middle man, was going to cheat her on her share. She is dealing with a man who wants to sell her and another who wants to buy her, and neither one understands two things: (1) She is offended by being bought and sold, and (2) she doesn't need the money.

Toback began as a writer *(The Gambler)* before going on to write and direct such films as *Fingers* and *Black and White,* and to write *Bugsy* for Warren Beatty. In his work and in his life, he likes risk, likes gambling, likes women, and once tried to pick up so many in a short span of time that the late *Spy* magazine ran a four-page foldout chart of whom he hit on, what he told them, and how he scored. There's a little of Ford in his character, but also a little of Vera and the count, especially in his delight in verbal negotiation.

The centerpiece of the film is an extended scene between Vera and the count, as they discuss the amount of money and what it is being paid for. Vera is very specific about the money, and the count is politely vague about exactly what he expects for it, until Vera makes it clear that the count is likely to be pleased with the outcome. It is possible that Vera might have gone through with the deal, not for $1 million but for the danger, excitement, and audacity of negotiating for the $1 million and then delivering; the count is not young, but he is trim, elegant, sophisticated, and probably good company—at dinner, you know, and the opera, and at what he means when he mentions dinner and the opera.

Now I can tell you no more of the plot, except to say that it involves Vera's evolving response to a situation that develops in ways no one could have foreseen. I've seen countless movies in which people were conned or double-crossed or trapped by a con within a con (*Criminal* is an example). They all have to clear one hurdle: How could the characters predict so accurately who would do what, right on schedule, to make the pieces fall into place?

What is fascinating and ingenious about *When Will I Be Loved* is that nothing need be anticipated, not even the possibility of a con. In scenes of flawless timing, logic, and execution, Vera improvises in a fluid situation and perhaps even surprises herself at where she ends up. The third act of this movie is spellbinding in the way Vera distributes justice and revenge, and adapts to the unexpected and

creates, spontaneously and in the moment, a checkmate.

Toback's structure backs into his perfect ending. There's an early scene where he plays a professor who is interviewing Vera for a job as his assistant, and then the two of them begin to speak openly about what is "really" going on; that's the curtain-raiser for the later high-stakes negotiation. There is a scene with Mike Tyson (so effective in *Black and White*) that plays like comic relief, until you think about it in the context of the movie. There's the lesbian scene, which seems gratuitous at the time but later seems necessary to establish Vera's carnal curiosity and Ford's ignorance of her complexity.

And the verbal sparring between Vera and the count is an exercise in the precise and stylish use of language to communicate exact meanings while using inexact euphemisms. Dominic Chianese and Neve Campbell are like virtuoso soloists with conversation as their instrument; the way they test and challenge each other is underlined by their obvious joy in performance. Both characters seem pleased to find another person who can engage them on their level of emotional negotiation.

The song "When Will I Be Loved" is about someone who complains, "I've been cheated—been mistreated." In the movie, the cheater and the mistreater have no idea who they're dealing with.

White Chicks ★ ½
PG-13, 100 m., 2004

Marlon Wayans (Marcus Copeland), Shawn Wayans (Kevin Copeland), Anne Dudek (Tiffany Wilson), Maitland Ward (Brittany Wilson), Brittany Daniel (Megan Vandergeld), Jaime King (Heather Vandergeld), Rochelle Aytes (Denise), Lochlyn Munro (Agent Harper), Frankie Faison (FBI Chief), Terry Crews (Latrell). Directed by Keenen Ivory Wayans and produced by Keenen Ivory Wayans, Shawn Wayans, and Marlon Wayans. Screenplay by Keenen Ivory Wayans.

Various combinations of the Wayans family have produced a lot of cutting-edge comedy, but *White Chicks* uses the broad side of the knife. Here is a film so dreary and conventional that it took an act of the will to keep me in the theater. Who was it made for? Who will it play to? Is there really still a market for fart jokes?

Marlon and Shawn Wayans play Marcus and Kevin Copeland, brothers who are FBI agents. Fired after a sting goes wrong, they're given a second chance. Their assignment: Protect Tiffany and Brittany Wilson (Anne Dudek and Maitland Ward), high-society bimbos who seem to be the target of a kidnapping scheme. The girls get tiny cuts in a car crash and are too vain to attend a big society bash in the Hamptons. Marcus and Kevin have the answer: They'll disguise themselves as the Wilsons and attend the party in drag.

Uh-huh. They call in experts who supply them with latex face masks, which fool everybody in the Hamptons but looked to me uncannily like the big faces with the talking lips on Conan O'Brien. There is also the problem that they're about six inches taller than the Wilsons. I guess they're supposed to be, I dunno, Paris and Nicky Hilton, but at least the Hiltons look like clones of humans, not exhibits in a third-rate wax museum.

The gag is not so much that black men are playing white women as that men learn to understand women by stepping into their shoes and dishing with their girlfriends. Womanhood in this version involves not empowerment and liberation, but shopping, trading makeup and perfume tips, and checking out the cute guys at the party. "Tiffany" and "Brittany" pick up a posse of three friendly white girls, inherit the Wilsons' jealous enemies, and engage in the most unconvincing dance contest ever filmed, which they win with a break-dancing exhibition.

Meanwhile, a pro athlete named Latrell (Terry Crews) is the top bidder at a charity auction for Marcus, who represents his ideal: "A white chick with a black woman's ass!" This leads to all sorts of desperately unfunny situations in which Marcus tries to keep his secret while Latrell goes into heat. Also meanwhile, a labyrinthine plot unfolds about who is really behind the kidnapping, and why.

The fact that *White Chicks* actually devotes expository time to the kidnap plot shows how lame-brained it is, because no one in the audience can conceivably care in any way about its details. Audiences who see the TV commercials and attend *White Chicks* will want sharp, transgressive humor, which they will not find, instead of a wheezy story about off-the-shelf bad guys, which drags on and on in one complicated permutation after another.

Are there any insights about the races here? No. Are there any insights into the gender gap? No. As men or women, black or white, the Wayans brothers play exactly the same person: an interchangeable cog in a sitcom.

Because they look so odd in makeup, the effect is quease-inducing. They fall victims, indeed, to the Uncanny Valley Effect. This phenomenon, named in 1978 by the Japanese robot expert Masahiro Mori, refers to the ways in which humans relate emotionally with robots. Up to a certain point, he found, our feelings grow more positive the more the robots resemble humans. But beyond a certain stage of reality, it works the other way: The closer they get to humans, the more we notice the differences and are repelled by them. In the same way, the not-quite convincing faces of the two white chicks provide a distraction every moment they're on the screen. We're staring at them, not liking them, and paying no attention to the plot. Not that attention would help.

The Whole Ten Yards ★
PG-13, 99 m., 2004

Bruce Willis (Jimmy "The Tulip" Tudeski), Matthew Perry (Nicholas "Oz" Oseransky), Amanda Peet (Jill St. Claire), Kevin Pollak (Lazlo Gogolak), Natasha Henstridge (Cynthia Oseransky). Directed by Howard Deutch and produced by Allan Kaufman, Arnold Rifkin, Elie Samaha, and David Willis. Screenplay by George Gallo.

A fog of gloom lowers over *The Whole Ten Yards*, as actors who know they're in a turkey try their best to prevail. We sense a certain desperation as dialogue mechanically grinds through unplayable scenes, and the characters arrive at moments that the movie thinks are funny but they suspect are not. This is one of those movies you look at quizzically: What did they think they were doing?

The movie is an unnecessary sequel to *The Whole Nine Yards* (2000), a movie in which many of the same actors sent completely different messages. "A subtle but unmistakable aura of jolliness sneaks from the screen," I wrote in my review of the earlier movie. "We suspect that the actors are barely suppressing giggles. This is the kind of standard material everyone could do in lockstep, but you sense inner smiles, and you suspect the actors are enjoying themselves."

The problem, I suspect, is that *The Whole Nine Yards* did everything that needed to be done with the characters, and did it well. Now the characters are back again, blinking in the footlights, embarrassed by their curtain call. The movie has the hollow, aimless aura of a beach resort in winter: The geography is the same, but the weather has turned ugly.

You will recall that the earlier film starred Bruce Willis as Jimmy "The Tulip" Tudeski, a professional hit man who has moved in next door to a Montreal dentist named Oz (Matthew Perry). The dentist's receptionist was Jill (Amanda Peet), a woman whose greatest ambition in life was to become a hit woman. Jimmy was in hiding from a Chicago gangster named Janni Gogolak (Kevin Pollak), who wanted him whacked.

In *The Whole Ten Yards*, Jimmy the Tulip and Jill are married and hiding out in Mexico, where Jill finds employment as a hit woman while Jimmy masquerades as a house-husband. That puts Willis in an apron and a head cloth during the early scenes, as if such a disguise would do anything other than call attention to him. Oz, meanwhile, has moved to Los Angeles and is married to Cynthia (Natasha Henstridge), who used to be married to the Tulip. (His first wife, played in the earlier movie by Rosanna Arquette with a hilarious French-Canadian accent, might have been useful here.)

Janni Gogolak was made dead by Oz and the Tulip in the first picture, but now his father, the crime boss Laszlo Gogolak, has been released from prison, and uses all of his power to find revenge against the two men; that fuels most of the plot, such as it is. Lazlo Gogolak is played by Kevin Pollak in one of the most singularly bad performances I have ever seen in a movie. It doesn't fail by omission, it fails by calling attention to its awfulness. His accent, his voice, his clothes, his clownish makeup, all conspire to create a character who brings the movie to a halt every time he appears on the screen. We stare in amazement, and I repeat: What did they think they were doing?

The movie's plot is without sense or purpose. It generates some action scenes that are supposed to be comic, but are not, for the inescapable reason that we have not the slightest interest in the characters and therefore even less interest in their actions. The movie is instructive in the way it demonstrates how a film can succeed or fail not only because of the mechanics of its screenplay, but because of the spirit of its making.

The Whole Nine Yards was not a particularly inspired project, but it was made with spirit and good cheer, and you felt the actors almost visibly expanding on the screen; Amanda Peet in particular seemed possessed. Here we see the actors all but contracting, as if to make themselves smaller targets for the camera. That there will never be a movie named *The Whole Eleven Yards* looks like a safe bet.

Wicker Park ★ ★ ★
PG-13, 113 m., 2004

Josh Hartnett (Matthew), Rose Byrne (Alex), Diane Kruger (Lisa), Matthew Lillard (Luke), Jessica Pare (Rebecca). Directed by Paul McGuigan and produced by Andre Lamal, Gary Lucchesi, Tom Rosenberg, and Marcus Viscidi. Screenplay by Brandon Boyce and Gilles Mimouni.

Strangely enough, I saw *Wicker Park* on the same day I saw another film, *What the #$*! Do We Know?* The what-the-bleep film was about quantum physics, and included a dozen experts testifying that we don't know s#!t. I have never understood quantum physics, so it was a relief to discover that no one else does, either. That set my mind at ease regarding *Wicker Park*. By substituting "Wicker Park" for "quantum physics," I was able to experience the movie in the same way that I experience the universe, by treating it as if it exists even if it doesn't.

The plot, for example, hums along as if it's really there, like matter, when in fact it's mostly a vacuum, like the insides of atoms. The chronology isn't confusing because scientists believe it's only an illusion that time originates in the past and moves through the present on its way to the future. It might move in any direction, like it does in this movie.

I especially appreciated *What the #$*!'s* claim that we cannot see something we do not understand. When Columbus arrived in the New World, the movie says, the Indians standing on the beach could not see his ships, because they had no concept of ships. But a wise old shaman noticed that the waves were flowing differently, and by standing on the beach for a long time, he was finally able to see the ships, and point them out to his friends.

In exactly the same way, I could not see the plot of this movie, because I had no concept of what it was. But by looking and listening carefully, I was at last able to perceive that it was a love quadrangle taking place in three Chicago apartments, which, for convenience, I thought of as the *Nina,* the *Pinta,* and the *Santa Maria.*

Am I a slow study? I think I'm ahead of the curve. The reviewer for the BBC Web site reports that the movie takes place in New York. It is set in Chicago and was filmed in Chicago and Montreal. Quantum physics, of course, explains how the characters, like subatomic particles, can be in Chicago and Montreal at the same time.

Faithful readers will notice that I have said almost nothing about the movie. That is because the movie consists entirely of plot twists and turns that cannot even be described without being revealed. Let me say, as vaguely as possible, that it involves a romance between Matthew (Josh Hartnett) and Lisa (Diane Kruger) that is the Real Thing, but comes to a sudden end because of a tragic lack of communication and a mutual misunderstanding. Although the characters spend half the movie on the phone, neither one succeeds in making the single call that would clear everything up; it's one of those plots where incredible coincidences happen right on cue, but common-sense events are impossible.

Two years pass. Matthew is engaged to Rebecca (Jessica Pare). He is supposed to fly to China to seal a deal for her father's firm, but in a restaurant he thinks he sees Lisa. This leads him on a trail involving mysterious addresses, hotel room keys, and notes that are, or are not, received by those they are intended for. Since he originally met Lisa by following her like a stalker, and since he searches for her now by acting the same way, past and present mingle delightfully, and we're not always sure if he's following the Lisa he wants to meet or the Lisa he's lost.

Then there are Alex (Rose Byrne) and Luke (Matthew Lillard). They start dating each other. Luke is Matthew's best friend, but Alex doesn't know that. Alex becomes Lisa's friend, but Lisa doesn't know . . . oh, never mind. And I won't even mention the true object of Alex's erotomania.

The strange thing is, I liked all of this while it was happening. The movie is a remake of *L'Appartement,* a 1996 French film I did not see—which is just as well, because the American film *Criminal* is a remake of *Nine Queens,* a 2000 Argentinean film I did see, so that I knew everything that was going to happen. Even if I had seen *L'Appartement,* I might not have known everything that was going to happen in *Wicker Park,* however, because I don't think anyone does, including the director, Paul McGuigan, and the writers, Brandon Boyce and Gilles Mimouni.

Once we understand the principle (if not the details) of the plot, *Wicker Park* works because the actors invest their scenes with what is, under the circumstances, astonishing emotional realism. There's a scene between Josh Hartnett and Rose Byrne during which so much is said, and left unsaid, that we feel real sympathy for both characters. There's an emotional craziness to the way the Hartnett character misses his plane to China and starts skulking around Chicago/Montreal like a sleuth. There's an open innocence to the way Matthew Lillard's character fails to realize he is about to become an innocent bystander. And Diane Kruger, whose Lisa is subjected to logical whiplash by the plot, always seems to know when it is and how she should feel. Now that's acting.

Wilbur Wants to Kill Himself ★ ★ ★ ½
R, 111 m., 2004

Jamie Sives (Wilbur), Adrian Rawlins (Harbour), Shirley Henderson (Alice), Lisa McKinlay (Mary), Mads Mikkelsen (Horst), Julia Davis (Moira). Directed by Lone Scherfig and produced by

Sisse Graum Olsen. Screenplay by Scherfig and Anders Thomas Jensen.

It strikes a note of optimism, I suppose, that *Wilbur Wants to Kill Himself* is not titled *Wilbur Kills Himself.* Wilbur certainly tries desperately enough, with pills, gas, hanging, and teetering on the edge of a great fall. But he never quite succeeds. He is saved more than once by his brother, Harbour, and on another occasion by Alice, who interrupts his hanging attempt. By this point we begin to suspect that *Wilbur Wants to Kill Himself* is not about suicide at all, that Wilbur is destined for better things, and that despite its title this is a warm human comedy.

The movie takes place in Glasgow, that chill city where many views are dominated by the Necropolis, the Gothic cemetery on a hillside overlooking the town. Such a view must be a daily inspiration for Wilbur (Jamie Sives). He is, from time to time, a patient at a local psychiatric clinic, where the therapists seem to have limited their studies to viewings of *One Flew Over the Cuckoo's Nest.* His hopes depend on Harbour, who loves him, tries to save him from himself, and brings him home to live with him.

Harbour (Adrian Rawlins) runs the used book store left him by his father. It is a shabby but inviting place, its windows following the curve of the road, its stock in a jumble. There seems to be only one customer, a man who visits almost daily, demanding Kipling, and is invariably told that there must be some Kipling around here somewhere, but Harbour can't put his hands on it.

Another frequent visitor wants to sell, not buy. This is Alice, played by Shirley Henderson, that luminous actress from *Trainspotting, Bridget Jones's Diary, Topsy-Turvy,* and half a dozen others; do not be put off that she played Moaning Myrtle in *Harry Potter and the Chamber of Secrets.* She brings in books that were left behind by patients at the hospital where she works, but the books are really an excuse for seeing Harbour, with whom she feels a strange affinity; perhaps they met in earlier lives, since Rawlins played Harry Potter's father.

In no time at all Alice and Harbour have fallen in love. Alice and her daughter, Mary (Lisa McKinlay), bring order to the store, so that Kipling can easily be found, and then Alice and Harbour are married. That leads to rather cramped living conditions in the small flat above the store, where Wilbur is also established.

This doesn't add up to a lot of incident, but it occupies more than half the movie, because the director and cowriter, Lone Scherfig, loves human nature and would rather enjoy it than hurry it along with a plot. The pleasure of the movie is in spending time in the company of her characters, who are quirky and odd and very definite about themselves. There is also a certain amount of escapism involved, at least for somebody like me, who would rather run a used book store than do just about anything else except spend all my time in them.

Now then. The real heart of the movie involves events I do not want to even hint about. That's because they creep up on the characters so naturally, so gradually, that we should be as surprised as they are by how it all turns out. Let me say that the bleak comedy of Wilbur's early suicide attempts is replaced by the deepening of all of the characters, who are revealed as warm and kind and rather noble. The movie's ending is almost unreasonably happy, despite being technically sad, and the affection we feel for these characters is remarkable.

The filmmaker, Lone Scherfig, is a Danish woman whose first film, *Italian for Beginners,* was a Dogma comedy. That she was able to make a Dogma comedy tells you a great deal about her. Here she does away with the Dogma rules and makes a movie in the tradition of the Ealing comedies produced in England in the 1950s and early 1960s: modest slices of life about people who are very peculiar and yet lovable, and who do things we approve of in ways that appall us. The title may put you off, but don't let it. Here is a movie that appeals to the heart while not insulting the mind or forgetting how delightful its characters are.

The Wild Parrots of Telegraph Hill ★ ★ ★
G, 83 m., 2005

A documentary about Mark Bittner, directed and produced by Judy Irving.

Mark Bittner is calm, intelligent, confiding, wise, and well spoken. You would be happy to count him as your friend. He has not worked in thirty years, has lived on the street for fifteen of them, and in recent years has devoted his life to getting to know forty-five wild parrots who formed a flock in San Francisco. It takes a lot of time to get to know forty-five wild parrots as individuals, but as he points out, "I have all the time in the world."

The Wild Parrots of Telegraph Hill, a documentary about Bittner and his birds by Judy Irving, is not the film you think it is going to be. You walk in expecting some kind of North Beach weirdo and his wild-eyed parrot theories, and you walk out still feeling a little melancholy over the plight of Connor, the only blue-crowned conure in a flock of red-crowned conures.

Connor had a mate, Bittner tells us, but the mate died. Now Connor hangs around with the other parrots but seems lonely and depressed, a blue-crowned widower who can sometimes get nasty with the other birds, but comes to the defense of weak or sick birds when the flock picks on them. Picasso and Sophie, both red-crowned parrots, are a couple until Picasso disappears; Bittner begins to hope that maybe Connor and Sophie will start to date and produce some purple-headed babies.

Nobody knows how the parrots, all born in the wild and imported from South America, escaped captivity, found each other, and started their flock. Irving has several North Beach residents recite the usual urban legends (they were released by an eccentric old lady, a bird truck overturned, etc.). No matter. They live and thrive.

You would think it might get too cold in the winter for these tropical birds, but no: They can withstand cold fairly well, and the big problem for them is getting enough to eat. Indeed, flocks of wild parrots and parakeets exist in colder climates; the famous colony of parakeets in Chicago's Hyde Park was evicted from some of their nests in 2005, after fifteen or twenty years, because they were interfering with utility lines.

Oddly, some bird lovers seem to resent trespassers such as wild parrots on the grounds that they are outside their native range. That they are here through no fault of their own, that they survive and thrive and are intelligent and beautiful birds, is enough for Mark Bitt-

ner, and by the end of the film that's enough for us, too.

He gives us brief biographies of some of the birds. Sometimes he takes them into his home when they're sick or injured, but after they recover they all want to return to the wild—except for Mingus, who keeps trying to get back into the house. Their biggest enemies are viruses and hawks. The flock always has a hawk lookout posted, and has devised other hawk-avoidance tactics, of which the most ingenious is to fly *behind* a hawk, which can only attack straight ahead and has a wider turning radius than parrots.

Bittner originally came to San Francisco, he tells us, seeking work as a singer. That didn't work out. He lived on the streets, did odd jobs, read a lot, met some of the original hippies (Ginsberg, Ferlinghetti, Gary Snyder). For the three years before the film begins, he has lived rent-free in a cottage below the house of a wealthy couple who live near the parrots on Telegraph Hill. Now he is about to be homeless again, while the cottage is renovated into an expensive rental property. The parrots are threatened with homelessness, too, and Bittner testifies on their behalf before the city council. San Francisco mayor Gavin Newsom vows nothing bad will happen to the parrots; would that we had such statesmen in Illinois.

As Bittner tends and feeds his flock, visitors to the wooded area on Telegraph Hill want to categorize him. Is he a scientist? Paid by the city? What's his story? His story is, he finds the parrots fascinating and lovable. He quotes Gary Snyder: "If you want to study nature, start right where you are." Can he live like this forever? He is about fifty, in good health, with a long red ponytail. He says he decided not to cut his hair until he gets a girlfriend. Whether either Connor the blue-crowned conure or Bittner the red-headed birdman find girlfriends, I will leave for you to discover.

Willard ★ ★ ½
PG-13, 100 m., 2003

Crispin Glover (Willard Stiles), R. Lee Ermey (Mr. Martin), Laura Elena Harring (Cathryn), Jackie Burroughs (Henrietta Stiles). Directed by Glen Morgan and produced by Morgan and

James Wong. Screenplay by Morgan, based on a book by Gilbert Ralston.

You never know what a rat is going to do next, which is one of the big problems with rats. In *Willard*, you mostly do know what the rats are going to do next, which is a big problem with the film. That's because Willard is able to marshal his rats into disciplined groups that scurry off on missions on his behalf; he is the Dr. Dolittle of pest control.

Willard is a remake of the 1971 film, which was a surprise hit at the box office. My explanation at the time: People had been waiting a long time to see Ernest Borgnine eaten by rats and weren't about to miss the opportunity. This version looks better, moves faster, and is more artistic than the original film, but it doesn't work as a horror film—and since it is a horror film, that's fatal. It has attitude and a look, but the rats aren't scary.

Consider an early scene where Willard (Crispin Glover) goes down in the cellar after his mother complains of rat infestation. The fuse box blows and he's down to a flashlight, and this should be a formula for a scary scene (remember Ellen Burstyn in the attic with a candle in *The Exorcist*). But the scene isn't frightening—ever. The blowing of the fuse is scarier than anything else that happens in the basement.

The plot is essentially a remake of the earlier *Willard*, but with elements suggesting it is a sequel. A portrait that hangs in the family home, for example, shows Bruce Davison as Willard's father—and Davison, of course, was the original Willard. So hold on. If that Willard was this Willard's father, then that means that this Willard's mother (Jackie Burroughs) was that Willard's wife, and has become a shrew just like her mother-in-law, and young Willard still works for an evil man named Mr. Martin (R. Lee Ermey), which was the Borgnine character's name, so he must be Martin Jr. In the new movie, Willard's mom complains about rats in the cellar and Mr. Martin insults Willard and threatens his job, and the sins of the parents are visited on the sequel.

The best thing in the movie is Crispin Glover's performance. He affects dark, sunken eyes and a slight stoop, is very pale, and has one of those haircuts that shouts out: Look how

gothic and miserable I am. There is real wit in the performance. And wit, too, in R. Lee Ermey's performance as the boss, which draws heavily on Ermey's real-life experience as a drill sergeant.

The human actors are okay, but the rodent actors (some real, some special effects) are like a prop that turns up on demand and behaves (or misbehaves) flawlessly. A few of the rats pop out: Socrates, Willard's choice for leader, and Ben, who is Ben's choice for leader. Ben is a very big rat (played, according to ominous information I found on the Web, "by an animal that is not a rat").

Laura Elena Harring, the brunette sex bomb from *Mulholland Dr.*, turns up as a worker in Willard's office who worries about him and even comes to his home to see if he's all right. My theory about why she likes him: He is the only man in a 100-mile radius who has never tried to pick her up. Willard is too morose and inward and Anthony Perkinsy. If they'd reinvented the movie as a character study, not so much about the rats as about Willard, they might have come up with something. Here the rats simply sweep across the screen in an animated tide, and instead of thinking, "Eek! Rats!" we're thinking about how it was done. That's not what you're supposed to be thinking about during a horror movie.

Wimbledon ★ ★ ★
PG-13, 98 m., 2004

Kirsten Dunst (Lizzie Bradbury), Paul Bettany (Peter Colt), Sam Neill (Dennis Bradbury), Jon Favreau (Ron Roth), Austin Nichols (Jake Hammond), Bernard Hill (Edward Colt), Eleanor Bron (Augusta Colt). Directed by Richard Loncraine and produced by Eric Fellner, Liza Chasin, and Mary Richards. Screenplay by Adam Brooks, Jennifer Flackett, and Mark Levin.

Wimbledon is a well-behaved movie about nice people who have good things happen to them. That's kind of startling, in a world where movie characters, especially in sports movies, occupy the edge of human experience. What a surprise to hear conversation instead of dialogue, and to realize that the villain may actually be right some of the time.

The movie stars Paul Bettany and Kirsten

Dunst as tennis pros—she a rising star, he a fading one. Lizzie Bradbury's greatness is ahead of her, but Peter Colt fears his is all behind. He was once ranked 11th in the world, is now down around 113 and falling. He gets a wild card berth at Wimbledon and vows that, win or lose, he'll retire from the pro circuit after this tournament.

The two players have parents representative of their respective civilizations. Lizzie's dad, Dennis (Sam Neill), is a hard-driving American control freak who has managed Lizzie's career since she was a child. Peter's parents (Bernard Hill and Eleanor Bron) are rich British eccentrics; his mother potters in the garden, and his father moves into the tree house after a fight with his wife. Stop to consider how few movie sports heroes even have parents (some do not even seem of woman born).

Lizzie and Peter have a Meet Cute early in the film, when he is mistakenly given the key to her suite at the Dorchester. She is nude in the shower, but handles the situation with such composure that we wonder if she arranged for him to get the key, especially after, with admirable frankness, she asks him, "Where do you come down on the whole fooling-around-before-a-match issue?"

She comes down in favor of it, and soon they're snuggling and holding hands. Her father, of course, believes sex before a match is a drain of precious bodily fluids, and warns Peter away. Peter tries to reassure him, but the father says, "This time it's different. She's falling for you."

And so she is, in a movie where the lovers keep late hours for finalists at Wimbledon. His nightly workouts seem to inspire Peter, who scores one upset after another over highly seeded players. But Lizzie's father is afraid she's tiring herself, tries to hide her, and even tracks the lovers to Brighton in a scene embarrassingly captured on live television.

All of this is told in a movie more realistic about tennis than about love. The tennis scenes are well choreographed and acted (Bettany looks to me like a competent player). They make sense visually and dramatically, and they evoke the loneliness of a sport where everything depends on one person at one moment in time. Interior monologues allow us to

hear Peter talking to himself, psyching himself out, quieting his fears. Is it ridiculous to believe he plays better because he's in love? Of course not.

But what kind of love is it? On Peter's part, it seems to be old-fashioned over-the-moon romance. But Lizzie is rather alarmingly direct in the way she originally recruits Peter, and later she seems too willing to give him up. Does she use lovers like a convenience? We've seen male characters like this in the movies, but a woman with such a casual attitude is unusual. For that matter, is she really casual? There's a stretch of the movie when we're not sure.

We're also not so sure we like Ron (Jon Favreau), Peter's once and future agent. He's a little too much of a caricature, and the movie uses his cell phone for easy laughs. Sam Neill, as Lizzie's father, could also be a caricature, but I liked the way the movie backed off toward the end, and showed a certain common sense beneath his decisions.

What I mostly liked was the warmth between the two leads. Lizzie and Peter like each other, and because they share the same profession they have more to talk about than their feelings. We get a sense for what it's like to be all alone on a court with everything depending on you and no possible excuses. This is not a great movie and you will be able to live quite happily without seeing it, but what it does, it does with a certain welcome warmth.

Win a Date with Tad Hamilton! ★ ★ ★
PG-13, 95 m., 2004

Kate Bosworth (Rosalee Futch), Topher Grace (Pete Monash), Josh Duhamel (Tad Hamilton), Gary Cole (Henry Futch), Ginnifer Goodwin (Cathy Feely), Nathan Lane (Richard Levy), Sean Hayes (Richard Levy). Directed by Robert Luketic and produced by Lucy Fisher and Douglas Wick. Screenplay by Victor Levin.

Here is a movie for people who haunt the aisles of the video stores searching for 1950s romances. I could have seen it at the Princess Theater in Urbana in 1959. Maybe I did. It's retro in every respect, a romantic comedy in a world so innocent that a lifetime is settled with a kiss. And because it embraces its innocence like a lucky charm, it works, for those willing to allow it. Others will respond with a horse laugh, and although I cannot quarrel with them, I do not share their sentiments.

Maybe it's something to do with Kate Bosworth's smile. She plays Rosalee Futch, a checkout clerk at the Piggly Wiggly in Fraser's Bottom, West Virginia. Her manager, whom she has known since they were children, is Pete Monash (Topher Grace). He loves her, but can't bring himself to tell her so. Then she wins a contest to have a date with Tad Hamilton (Josh Duhamel), a Hollywood star whose agent thinks his image could use a little touch-up after a supermarket tabloid photographs him speeding, drinking, letching, and littering all at the same time.

Well, of course Rosalee is ecstatic about the trip to L.A., the stretch limo, the suite at the W hotel, the expensive dinner date, and the moment when she teeters on the brink when Tad invites her to his home, and then says, gee ... you know, it's late and I have to fly home tomorrow. That she is a virgin goes without saying. What she can't anticipate is that Tad will follow her back to Fraser's Bottom, because there was something in her innocence, her freshness, her honesty, that appealed to an empty place deep inside him.

Within days he has purchased a house in West Virginia, taken her to dinner several times at the local diner, and made friends with her father, Henry (Gary Cole), who starts surfing Variety.com and wearing a Project Greenlight T-shirt.

As it happens, I'm reading *Anna Karenina* right now, and for some foolish reason Rosalee started to remind me of Kitty, the ingenue in the novel. She and a good man named Levin have long been in love, but she's swept off her feet by the sudden admiration of a snake named Vronsky, and rejects Levin when in fact her fate is to be his wife, and Vronsky's love is a mirage. Just today I read the charming pages where Levin and Kitty, too shy to speak their hearts, play a word game in order to find out if they have survived Vronsky with their love still intact. I was startled by how happy it made me when they got their answers right.

Win a Date with Tad Hamilton! could have had a similar effect, since there is a real possibility that Rosalee will wed the slick Tad instead of the steady Pete. But it doesn't have that kind

of impact because of a crucial misjudgment in the screenplay and casting.

To begin with, Josh Duhamel is more appealing than Topher Grace—maybe not in life, but certainly in this movie, where he seems sincere within the limits of his ability, while the store manager always seems to have a pebble in his shoe.

And then the movie devotes much more screen time to Rosalee and Tad than to Rosalee and Pete—so much more that even though we know the requirements of the formula, we expect it to be broken with a marriage to Tad. And yet—what is the function of Pete, within the closed economy of a screenplay, except to be the hometown boy she should marry?

You can guess for yourself (very easily) what decision she finally comes to, but let me observe that the courtship between Rosalee and Tad is charming, warm, cute, and applaudable, and that Pete spends a great deal of time grumping about in the store office and making plans to go off to Richmond and become a business major. In 1959, or any other year, a movie like this would have known enough to make Tad into more of a slickster. There is the strangest feeling at the end of the film that Rosalee might have made the wrong choice.

That imbalance at least has the benefit of giving a formula movie more suspense than it deserves. And I liked it, too, for the way it played Tad and Hollywood more or less straight, instead of diving into wretched excess. The dream date is handled with lots of little touches that will warm the innards of PG-13 females in the audience, and the movie wants to be gentle, not raucous in its comedy. Kate Bosworth holds it all together with a sweetness that is beyond calculation.

Note: That leaves just one other elbow sticking out of the sack. Tad's agent and manager, played by Nathan Lane and Sean Hayes and both named Richard Levy, are so over the top that they break the mood in their scenes. For Lane, Win a Date represents yet another peculiar career choice in the movies, a medium where he is successful mostly when heard but not seen, as voice-over talent. To be sure, this isn't the suicidal career move of his decision to play Jacqueline Susann's husband in Isn't She Great, but as roles go, it's thankless. Here's the highest-priced Broadway star of his generation, and what's he doing in this little role, anyway?

Winged Migration ★ ★ ★
G, 89 m., 2003

A documentary directed by Jacques Perrin and produced by Christophe Barratier and Perrin. Screenplay by Stéphane Durand and Perrin.

Jacques Perrin's Oscar-nominated *Winged Migration* does for birds what the 1996 documentary *Microcosmos* did for insects: It looks at them intimately, very close up, in shots that seem impossible to explain. That the two plots intersect (birds eat insects) is just one of those things.

The movie, which is awesome to regard, is not particularly informative; it tells us that birds fly south in the winter (unless they live in the Southern Hemisphere, in which case they fly north), that they fly many hundreds or thousands of miles, and that they navigate by the stars, the sun, Earth's gravitational field, and familiar landmarks. These facts are widely known, and the movie's sparse narration tells us little else.

But facts are not the purpose of *Winged Migration.* It wants to allow us to look, simply look, at birds—and that goal it achieves magnificently. There are sights here I will not easily forget. The film opens and closes with long aerial tracking shots showing birds in long-distance flight into the wind, and we realize how very hard it is to fly a thousand miles or more. We see birds stopping to eat (one slides a whole fish down its long neck). We see them feeding their young. We see them courting and mating, and going through chest-thumping rituals that are serious business, if you are a bird. We see cranes locking bills in what looks like play. We see birds trapped in industrial waste. And in a horrifying scene, a bird with a broken wing tries to escape on a sandy beach, but cannot elude the crabs that catch it and pile onto the still-living body, all eager for a bite. In nature, as the film reminds us, life is all about getting enough to eat.

How in the world did they get this footage? Lisa Nesselson, *Variety*'s correspondent in Paris, supplies helpful information. To begin with, 225 feet of film were exposed for every foot that got into the movie. And some of the birds were raised to be the stars of the film; they were exposed to the sounds of airplanes and movie cameras while still in the shell, and greeted upon their arrival in the world by crew members. (We remember from *Fly Away Home* that newborn birds assume that whoever they see upon emerging must be a parent.)

Some footage was made with cameras in ultralight aircraft. Other shots were taken from hot air balloons. There are shots in which the birds seem to have been scripted—they move toward the camera as it pulls back. And some scenes, I'm afraid, that were manufactured entirely in the editing room, as when we see snowbirds growing alarmed, we hear an avalanche, and then cut to long shots of the avalanche and matching shots of the birds in flight. Somehow we know the camera was not in the path of the avalanche.

I am pleased, actually, that the film has such a tilt toward the visual and away from information. I wouldn't have wanted the narrator to drone away in my ear, reading me encyclopedia articles and making sentimental comments about the beauty of it all. Life is a hard business, and birds work full-time at it. I was shocked by a sequence showing ducks in magnificent flight against the sky, and then dropping one by one as hunters kill them. The birds have flown exhaustingly for days to arrive at this end. It's not so much that I blame the hunters as that I wish the ducks could shoot back.

Winter Solstice ★ ★ ★
R, 89 m., 2005

Anthony LaPaglia (Jim Winters), Allison Janney (Molly Ripken), Aaron Stanford (Gabe Winters), Mark Webber (Pete Winters), Ron Livingston (Mr. Bricker), Michelle Monaghan (Stacey), Brendan Sexton III (Robbie). Directed by Josh Sternfeld and produced by Doug Bernheim and John Limotte. Screenplay by Sternfeld.

Oh, what a sad movie this is: Sad not with the details of tragedy, but with the details of life that must go on after the tragedy. *Winter Solstice* is about a family living in emptiness that threatens to become hopelessness. Jim Winters, the father, is a landscape gardener. His boys Gabe and Peter are in high school. Five years ago, Pete was in the car with his mother when there was an accident and she was killed. The family has been broken ever since.

It's conventional in such stories to assign blame to the father, who is seen as distant or bitter. Not here. Jim (Anthony LaPaglia) is filled with desperation as he tries to reach out to his sons. But he doesn't have the tone or the gift, or perhaps they're at that maddening stage in adolescence when they just clam up, taking it out on everybody else that they're angry with themselves.

The movie is not plot-driven, for which we must be thankful, because to force their feelings into a plot would be a form of cruelty. The whole point is that these lives have no plot. The characters and their situation are on stage and waiting for something to happen, but Josh Sternfeld, the writer-director, isn't going to let them off that easily. If this movie ended in hugs it would be an abomination.

Gabe (Aaron Stanford) thinks he will leave town and move to Tampa. He has no firm plans for what he will do in Tampa and only vague reasons for choosing Tampa instead of any other place on the face of the Earth. "What about Stacey?" his father asks. Stacey (Michelle Monaghan) is Gabe's girlfriend, welcome in the house, well liked. "That's my problem and I'm dealing with it," Gabe says. He's dealing with it the way a lot of teenage boys deal with girls: He's dropping her, and letting her figure it out. Stacey isn't a weeper; she wisely doesn't answer his phone calls and leaves him without the opportunity for justification, blame, closure, or anything else except a feeling of being lonely on his own.

Pete (Mark Webber) is in trouble at school. His teacher, Mr. Bricker (Ron Livingston) knows he's smart and can do better and rather bravely tries to get around his defenses, but Pete is miserable and punishes himself. The worse he does, the worse he can feel, which is fine with him.

A woman named Molly (Allison Janney) moves in down the street. Jim helps her shift some boxes. She invites them to dinner. Jim has not looked at another woman in five years, and maybe isn't really looking at Molly when he accepts; maybe he just knows it's time to break the pattern. Gabe and Pete fail to turn up for the dinner, and Jim throws their mattresses out into the lawn and lets them sleep under the stars; this is perceived not as tough love but as anger, which is probably just as well, since these boys are well defended against love.

Josh Sternfeld, like his character Stacey, knows he will have more effect on us if he denies us closure. It would be simple to give this movie a happy ending, but why does the happiness have to come at the end of this particular winter? Maybe it will come five years down the road, with Gabe returning from Tampa with a wife and a kid, and Pete safely in college, and Jim and Molly living together. Or maybe it won't end that way.

The movie knows that life is sometimes very discouraging, and keeps on being discouraging, and sometimes you can't save everybody and have to try to save yourself. Who is to say that it's a bad idea for Gabe to move to Tampa? Sure, his father thinks it is, but is Gabe making any progress in New Jersey? Would it be an answer to marry Stacey? Marrying somebody to solve a problem is never the answer to the problem, just a way to share it. LaPaglia, who often stars in crime movies and comedies, has a sad, resigned tone that is just right for this movie, as it was for the overlooked *Lantana* (2001).

When *Winter Solstice* is over, we sit and look at the screen and wonder what will happen to them all. We don't expect dramatic developments; these lives don't seem on a course for tragedy or happiness, but for a gradual kind of acceptance. Maybe the movies do us no service by solving so many problems, in a world with so few solutions.

With All Deliberate Speed ★ ★ ★
NO MPAA RATING, 110 m., 2004

As themselves: Julian Bond, Rev. Joe DeLaine, Barbara Johns, Vernon Jordan, Thurgood Marshall Jr., E. Barrett Prettyman. Re-creating the words of historical figures: Alicia Keys, Mekhi Pfifer, Larenz Tate, Joe Morton, and Terry Kinney. Directed by Peter Gilbert and produced by Gilbert.

On May 17, 1954, the Supreme Court ruled unanimously that "separate but equal" could no longer be the rule of the land. Its decision in the case of *Brown vs. Board of Education* ended segregated schools and opened the door for a wide range of reforms guaranteeing equal rights not only to African-Americans but also, in the years to come, to women, the handicapped, and (more slowly) homosexuals. The decision was a heroic milestone in American history, but it was marred, this new documentary says, by four fateful words: "with all deliberate speed."

Those words were a loophole that allowed some southern communities to delay equal rights for years and even decades; the last county to integrate finally did so only in 1970. And there was the notorious case of Prince Edward County, Virginia, which closed its schools for five years rather than integrate them. Most people alive today were born after *Brown* and take its reforms for granted. But *With All Deliberate Speed,* the documentary by *Hoop Dreams* producer Peter Gilbert, doesn't end on May 17, 1954. It continues on to the present day, noting that many of America's grade and secondary schools are as segregated now as they were fifty years ago.

The most valuable task of the film is to re-create the historic legal struggles that led to *Brown,* and to remember heroes who have been almost forgotten by history. Chief among them is Charles Houston, who was the first African-American on the editorial board of the *Harvard Law Review.* As dean of the Howard University law school, he was the mentor for a generation of black legal scholars and activists who would transform their society. Although he died in 1950, before *Brown* became law, it was his protégé Thurgood Marshall who argued the case before the Supreme Court, and later became the first African-American on the court.

It was Houston, the film says, who shaped the legal groundwork for *Brown,* arguing in the 1930s and 1940s that "separate but equal" could not, by its very nature, be equal. He helped convince the NAACP to mount legal challenges against segregation, and Marshall led the organization's legal efforts from 1940 onward. The film talks with the descendants of Houston and Marshall, and with many of the law clerks, now elderly, who as young men served the justices who handed down the landmark decision.

It also recalls the crucial role of Chief Justice Earl Warren in guiding his fellow justices toward what he felt had to be a unanimous decision. The previous chief justice, Fred Vincent, had little enthusiasm for such a controversial ruling. When he died, President Dwight Eisenhower appointed the former California governor Warren as chief justice; Justice Felix Frankfurter famously told his clerk that the death of Vincent "showed there is a God." So hated was *Brown* in some right-wing circles that an Impeach Earl Warren campaign continued throughout his term.

The film also tracks down some of the children involved in the first crucial cases, such as Barbara Johns of Prince Edward County. And it brings belated recognition to another hero of the time, the Reverend Joe DeLaine of Summerton County, South Carolina, who led the legal struggle against a system that required many black students to walk seven miles each way to school. His church was burned, his home was fired on, he was forced to flee the South, and only in October 2000, twenty-six years after his death, were charges against him cleared by the state.

Gilbert, of course, has no audio or video footage of the arguments before the Supreme Court, but he uses an interesting technique: He employs actors to read from the words of Thurgood Marshall and his chief opponent, the patrician John W. Davis. And he does a good job of recapturing the 1954 impact of the decision—with which, he notes, Eisenhower at first privately disagreed, although Ike later came around, and sent federal troops to enforce integration in the late 1950s.

What is the legacy of *Brown*? It's here that Gilbert's film is most challenging. It observes that while many communities have truly integrated schools, patterns of residential segregation in many areas have resulted in schools where the students are almost entirely of one race. He talks with blacks and whites who are in a tiny minority in their schools, and listens to discussions of race by today's high school students. And in reunions held today, he gathers students, now grown, who were at the center of the original case, and hears their memories of what it was like then and what it is like now. America moves imperfectly toward the goal of equality, but because of *Brown,* it moves.

A Woman Is a Woman ★ ★
NO MPAA RATING, 84 m., 1961 (rereleased 2003)

Anna Karina (Angela Recamier), Jean-Paul Belmondo (Alfred Lubitsch), Jean-Claude Brialy (Émile Récamier), Marie Dubois (Angela's Friend), Jeanne Moreau (Woman in Bar). Directed by Jean-Luc Godard and produced by Georges de Beauregard and Carlo Ponti. Screenplay by Godard.

A Woman Is a Woman was Jean-Luc Godard's second feature, made in 1961 close on the heels of *Breathless* (1960). "It was my first real film," he has said, but a statement by Godard is always suspect and in this case is plain wrong: *Breathless* was his first real film, a masterpiece, and *A Woman Is a Woman* is slight and sometimes wearisome.

The movie stars Godard's wife, Anna Karina, who was to achieve her own greatness in his next film, the wonderful *My Life to Live*. Here she plays a completely improbable character, a stripper who comes home to her yuppie boyfriend and tells him she wants a baby. Surely no strip club in movie history has been more genteel and less sleazy than the one she works in, where the women walk idly up and down between rows of tables where clients smoke, and look, and nurse their drinks. Their five-minute stint over, the girls say good-bye all around and return to the street, free spirits.

Angela Récamier is her name, and Jean-Claude Brialy plays Émile Récamier, but the movie strongly suggests they are not married. Nor does Émile want a baby, although his friend Alfred Lubitsch (Jean-Paul Belmondo) would be happy to impregnate her. Naming the Belmondo character after Lubitsch is one of the movie's countless cinematic in-jokes; there is even a moment when Belmondo runs into Jeanne Moreau and asks her, "How is *Jules and Jim* coming along?" And another where he smiles broadly at the camera, in tribute both to Burt Lancaster and to the fact that he did the same thing in *Breathless*.

The movie, which comes advertised as Godard's tribute to the Hollywood musical, is not a musical, and indeed treats music with some contempt, filling the sound track with brief bursts of music that resemble traditional movie scoring, but then interrupting them arbitrarily. It contains other moments designed to suggest the director calling attention to his control of his materials, including the device of having the same couple kissing in a street alcove in shot after shot.

There is, although, one sequence, showing the mastery of technique by Godard and his editor, Agnes Guillemot. Angela is shown a photograph that Alfred claims Émile shows with another woman. As she studies the photo, the movie cuts from her face to his face to the photo, and then again and again. Sometimes there is a little dialogue. The photo keeps reappearing on the screen. The effect is to suggest the way she becomes obsessed with the hurtful image and can't stop thinking about it, and as a visual evocation of jealousy, it's kind of brilliant.

But the film itself, at eighty-four minutes, is overlong, a minor chapter in an early career. It has been carefully restored for this theatrical rerelease. The print showcases the wide-screen cinematography of Raoul Coutard, and we can see here stylistic choices that would become omnipresent in the films to come: the use of big printed words on the screen, the use of bold basic colors, and the use of books as objects that embody their titles (in one cute moment, Angela and Émile aren't speaking, and hold up books with titles that indicate what they want to say). The movie is bright and lively, but too precious, and Godard would soon make much better ones.

Wonderland ★ ★
R, 99 m., 2003

Val Kilmer (John Holmes), Lisa Kudrow (Sharon Holmes), Kate Bosworth (Dawn Schiller), Dylan McDermott (David Lind), Josh Lucas (Ron Launius), Franky G (Louis Cruz), Tim Blake Nelson (Billy Deverell), Carrie Fisher (Sallie Hansen), Eric Bogosian (Eddie Nash). Directed by James Cox and produced by Michael Paseornek and Holly Wiersma. Screenplay by Cox, Captain Mauzner, Todd Samovitz, and D. Loriston Scott.

One of the things that make police work in Los Angeles tricky, Vincent Bugliosi says, is that anyone is likely to know anyone else. In other cities social connections are more predictable.

A cop who knows who you are, where you live, and how you work has a pretty good idea who you are likely to know. But drugs, sex, and showbiz act like L.A. wormholes, connecting the famous with the obscure. John Holmes, for example, was a porn star who became addicted to cocaine, and told his dopehead friends that Eddie Nash, a nightclub owner, kept a lot of money in his house. The dopeheads broke into Nash's house and took money and jewelry. Not long after, Holmes unwisely arrived at Nash's house and was beaten until he told Nash about the dopeheads. Holmes then allegedly helped Nash's bodyguards enter the house at 8763 Wonderland Avenue in the Hollywood Hills, where the dopeheads lived. Four of them were murdered, leaving the most horrifying crime scene one of the arriving cops had ever witnessed. The police eventually linked Holmes to the murders through the testimony of Scott Thorson, Liberace's lover, who saw Holmes being beaten.

And just to complete the circle, I got this information from charliemanson.com, no relation to the cult leader. I was looking it up because at the end of *Wonderland* I had no clear idea of what had happened, except that Holmes was apparently the connection. Perhaps because Eddie Nash is still alive and was acquitted on the murder charges after two trials, the movie never comes right out and says that he sent his men to commit the murders. The interior logic of the movie says he must have, but that's not actionable. To obscure a possible libel, or for artistic reasons, or both, the movie tells the story in the style of *Rashomon,* moving back and forth through time and using contradictory stories so that we think first one version and then another is the truth.

Rashomon was told with great clarity; we were always sure whose version we were seeing, and why. *Wonderland* is told through a bewildering tap dance on the time line, with lots of subtitles that say things like "four months earlier" or "July 1, 1981." There are so many of these titles, and the movie's chronology is so shuffled, that they become more frustrating than helpful. The titles, of course, reflect the version of the facts they introduce, so that a given event might or might not have happened "three weeks later."

Actors separated from chronology have their work cut out for them. A performance can't build if it starts at the end and circles in both directions toward the beginning. Yet Val Kilmer is convincing as John Holmes, especially when he pinballs from one emotion to another; we see him charming, ugly, self-pitying, paranoid, and above all in need of a fix. Holmes, acting under the name "Johnny Wadd," made a thousand hard-core pornos (according to this movie) or more than 2,500 (according to the Website). But by the time of the action, drugs have replaced sex as his obsession and occupation, and Kilmer does a good job of showing how an addict is always really thinking about only one thing.

Holmes is essentially just a case study: not interesting, not significant, not evocative. Nash (Eric Bogosian) is even less dimensional, existing completely in terms of his function in the plot. The human interest in the movie centers entirely on two women: Dawn Schiller (Kate Bosworth), Holmes's teenybopper girlfriend, and Sharon Holmes (Lisa Kudrow), his wife. Why either of these women wants to have anything to do with Holmes is a mystery, although Dawn perhaps somewhere in her confused reverie thinks of him as a star, and Sharon still cares for him despite having moved on to a settled, respectable lifestyle. Maybe she remembers a boy she was trying to save.

The movie is tantalizing in the way it denies us more information about the Dawn-Sharon-Holmes triangle. The two women are on good terms with each other (and are friends to this day, I learn); sexual jealousy seems beside the point when your man is the busiest porn star in history. At one point Holmes actually informs incredulous cops that he wants to go into the witness protection program with *both* women. Kudrow's performance is the most intriguing in the movie, and when she goes face-to-face with Holmes and coldly rejects his appeals for help, we guess maybe he needs her because she's the only adult in his life.

Parts of this story, much altered, have been told already in Paul Thomas Anderson's incomparably better film *Boogie Nights* (1997). Dirk Diggler (Mark Wahlberg) was the Holmes character there, and Heather Graham's Rollergirl is, I guess, something like Dawn. True crime procedurals can have a certain fascination, but not when they're jumbled glimpses of what might or might not have happened involving a lot of empty people whose main claim to fame is that they're dead.

The Woodsman ★ ★ ★ ½
R, 87m., 2005

Kevin Bacon (Walter), Kyra Sedgwick (Vickie), Mos Def (Sergeant Lucas), Benjamin Bratt (Carlos), David Alan Grier (Bob), Eve (Mary-Kay), Kevin Rice (Candy), Michael Shannon (Rosen), Hannah Pilkes (Robin). Directed by Nicole Kassell and produced by Lee Daniels. Screenplay by Steven Fechter and Kassell.

For the first several scenes of *The Woodsman*, we know that Walter has recently been released from prison, but we don't know the nature of his crime. Seeing the film at Cannes, I walked in without advance knowledge and was grateful that I had an opportunity to see Kevin Bacon establish the character before that information was supplied. His crime has now been clearly named in virtually everything written about the film, and possibly changes the way it affects a viewer.

Walter is a pedophile. The film doesn't make him a case study or an object for our sympathy, but carefully and honestly observes his attempt to reenter society after twelve years behind bars. Maybe he will make it and maybe he will not. He has a deep compulsion that is probably innate, and a belief that his behavior is wrong. That belief will not necessarily keep him from repeating it. Most of us have sexual desires within the areas accepted by society, and so never reflect that we did not choose them, but simply grew up and found that they were there.

Bacon is a strong and subtle actor, something that is often said but insufficiently appreciated. Here he employs all of his art. He seems to have no theory about Walter and no emotional tilt toward his problems, and that is correct, because we do not act out of theories about ourselves, but out of our hopes and desires. Bacon plays the character day by day, hour by hour, detail by detail, simply showing us this man trying to deal with his daily life. Larger conclusions are left to the audience.

He gets an apartment across from a grade school playground. He did not choose the lo-cation; he found a landlord who would rent to an ex-con. He gets a job in a lumberyard. No one there knows about his crime, but a coworker named Mary-Kay (Eve) doesn't like him and senses something is wrong. Lucas, his parole officer (Mos Def), visits regularly and is hostile, convinced it is only a matter of time until Walter lapses.

There is a woman at work named Vickie (Kyra Sedgwick), who is tough-talking but has an instinctive sympathy for the newcomer. She's a fork-lift operator, a realist. They start to date. We know, but she doesn't, that this may be the first normal sexual relationship Walter has had. She is not only his girlfriend but, in a way, an unknowing sex therapist. He eventually feels he has to tell her about his past. How she deals with this, how she goes through a series of emotions, is handled in a way I felt was convincing.

Mary-Kay finds out the truth about Walter and posts a Web site at work. His privacy is gone. There are other developments. Watching the playground through his window, for example, he becomes aware of a pedophile who is obviously hoping to find prey there.

The film has a crucial scene involving Walter and a young girl named Robin (Hannah Pilkes). Without suggesting how the scene develops, I will say that it is so observant, so truthful, that in a sense the whole film revolves around it. There is nothing sensational in this film, nothing exploitative, nothing used for "entertainment value" unless we believe, as I do, that the close observation of the lives of other people can be—well, since entertaining is the wrong word, then helpful. It is easy to present a pedophile as a monster, less easy to suggest the emotional devastation that led into, and leads out of, his behavior. The real question in *The Woodsman* is whether Walter will be able to break the chain of transmission.

The movie is the first film by Nicole Kassell, a recent graduate of the NYU film school, who wrote the screenplay with Steven Fechter, based on his play. It is a remarkably confident work. It knows who Walter is, and to an extent why he is that way, and it knows that the film's real drama exists inside his mind and conscience. This is not a morality play but a study of character—of Walter's character, and of those who instinctively detest him, and of a few, including Vickie and his brother-in-law Carlos (Benjamin Bratt), who are willing to withhold judgment long enough to see if he can find redemption.

The reason we cannot accept pedophilia as we accept many other sexual practices is that it requires an innocent partner whose life could be irreparably harmed. We do not have the right to do that. If there is no other way to achieve sexual satisfaction, that is a misfortune, but not an excuse. It is not the pedophile that is evil, but the pedophilia. That is true of all sins and crimes and those tempted to perform them: It is not that we are capable of transgression that condemns us, but that we are willing.

The Woodsman understands this at the very heart of its being, and that is why it succeeds as more than just the story of this character. It has relevance for members of the audience who would never in any way be even remotely capable of Walter's crime. We are quick to forgive our own trespasses, slower to forgive those of others. The challenge of a moral life is to do nothing that needs forgiveness. In that sense, we're all out on parole.

Word Wars ★ ★ ★
NO MPAA RATING, 80 m., 2004

A documentary directed by Eric Chaikin and Julian Petrillo and produced by Chaikin.

Spelling bees and Scrabble begin with the same skill: the ability to remember the correct spellings of a bewildering number of words, many of them obscure, illogical, and of slight everyday utility. Spelling bees end in sudden death, with one winner left standing. Professional Scrabble tournaments, to judge by the documentary Word Wars, are more like a living hell, a vortex into which its addicts disappear.

The movie uses the same structure as Spellbound, the charming doc about the national spelling bee. The difference is, Scrabble players are not charming. Both movies introduce us to leading contenders for the national championship, watch them train, worry, and obsess, and follow them to the national finals. For Word Wars, the end of the rainbow is in San Diego, which also spells "diagnose"; the movie

has cute graphics rearranging one word into another, illustrating the Scrabble skill of looking at tiles that seem to spell nothing and willing then to spell something, anything.

We meet four players who are famous within the world of Scrabble, a world not of cute kids hoping for college scholarships but of desperate men and a few women with tunnel vision, who have chosen a sport as narrow and obsessive as championship poker, but without the big pots. The top prize in the tournament, if I recall correctly, is $25,000, and there are no cable stations paying to look over your shoulder while you play Scrabble with Ben Affleck.

Of finalists who are all unhappy in one way or another, the most miserable may be Joel Sherman, known in Scrabbleland as "G.I. Joel" because of his gastrointestinal tract, a battlefield of churning acids. He chugs drugstore remedies. Then there's Marlon Hill, an African-American who likes to come across as an angry militant, even if angry black militancy finds little opportunity to express itself in Scrabble. Oh, I forgot: Scrabble is an example of the way the world colonizes his mind by forcing him to use standard English since there is no Ebonics version of the game.

Matt Graham specializes in demanding goals with low chances of success: He wants to be not only a Scrabble champion but also a successful standup comic. If he played the lottery, he'd have a trifecta. He consumes mysterious pills that are allegedly not illegal. I believe him, but I also believe, based on their effect on him, that they should be.

Among the four contenders, the one who is relatively centered is Joe Edley, who has won the national championship three times, and thus would be a household name and the idol of millions if his sport were only professional tennis. Edley practices the entire New Age routine, with meditation, mantras, chants, Tai Chi, and various weird behaviors designed to intimidate his opponents by how much more together he is than they are. Ozzy Osborne is more together than they are.

We meet professional Scrabble hustlers in Washington Square Park, not far from the professional chess hustlers. The difference is, chess is an exercise in applied logic in which the better player always wins (if he loses, he is by definition not the better player). Poker is also a game where the better player usually wins, or has an edge, although something depends on the luck of the cards. Scrabble requires the most masochistic traits of both chess and poker. To some degree, you win because you know how to spell more words and are better at teasing them out from the alphabet soup on your rack. To some degree, you lose because you drew lousy tiles. There is a shot in *Word Wars* of the tiles a player draws at a crucial moment in a game, and the audience groans. They may be the worst tiles in history.

Word Wars is compellingly watchable because (a) we all know how to play Scrabble, (b) the characters are such authentic oddballs, (c) their world seems more arcane and peculiar the longer we spend in it, and (d) there is suspense approaching desperation at the end; some of the players almost need to win in order to buy their next meal.

Scrabble is one way to kill time. I can think of better ways to pass obsessive, lonely, antisocial lives; a documentary named *Cinemania* is about people who literally attempt to spend every waking hour watching movies, seven days a week. At least they get to see the movies. After a Scrabble player has triumphantly played a word that contains Q without U, where does he go from there? How long can you treasure that memory?

X

X2: X-Men United ★ ★ ★
PG-13, 124 m., 2003

Patrick Stewart (Charles Xavier), Hugh Jackman (Wolverine), Ian McKellen (Magneto), Halle Berry (Storm), Famke Janssen (Dr. Jean Grey), James Marsden (Cyclops), Rebecca Romijn-Stamos (Mystique), Brian Cox (General William Stryker), Alan Cumming (Nightcrawler), Shawn Ashmore (Iceman), Aaron Stanford (Pyro), Kelly Hu (Yuriko Oyama), Anna Paquin (Rogue). Directed by Bryan Singer and produced by Lauren Shuler Donner and Ralph Winter. Screenplay by Michael Dougherty and Daniel P. Harris, based on the story by David Hayter, Zak Penn, and Singer and the comic books and characters by Stan Lee.

X2: X-Men United is the kind of movie you enjoy for its moments, even though they never add up. Made for (and possibly by) those with short attention spans, it lives in the present, providing one amazing spectacle after another, and not even trying to develop a story arc. Having trained on the original *X-Men* (2000), I tried to experience the film entirely in the present, and the fact is, I had a good time. Dumb, but good.

Like the comic books that inspired it, *X2* begins with the premise that mutant heroes with specialized superpowers exist among us. Name the heroes, assign the powers, and you're ready for perfunctory dialogue leading up to a big two-page spread in which sleek and muscular beings hurtle through dramatic showdowns.

Like all the characters in the Marvel Comics stable, the X-Men have psychological or political problems; in the first movie, they were faced with genocide, and in this one their right to privacy is violated with the Mutant Registration Act. Of course, there will be audience members who believe mutants should have no rights, and so *X2* provides a valuable civics lesson. (How you register a mutant who can teleport or shape-shift is not explained.)

Perhaps not coincidentally, the movie has a president who looks remarkably like George W. Bush. The film opens with one of its best scenes, as a creature with a forked tail attacks the White House and whooshes down corridors and ca-

reens off walls while the Secret Service fires blindly. The creature's purpose is apparently to give mutants a bad name, inspiring still more laws undermining their rights.

Despite all of the havoc and carnage of the first film, just about everybody is back for the sequel. Amazing that they weren't all killed. Charles Xavier (Patrick Stewart) still runs his private school for young mutants, Magneto (Ian McKellen) still plots against him, and there is a new villain named General William Stryker (Brian Cox), who is assigned by the government to deal with the mutant threat and uses the turncoat mutant Yuriko (Kelly Hu) on his team.

The principal mutants are, in credits order, Wolverine (Hugh Jackman), who has blades that extend from his knuckles; Storm (Halle Berry), who can control the weather; Dr. Jean Grey (Famke Janssen), whose power of telekinesis is growing stronger; Cyclops (James Marsden), whose eyes shoot laser beams; Mystique (Rebecca Romijn-Stamos), a shape shifter whose shapes are mostly delightful; Nightcrawler (Alan Cumming), the teleporter who attacked the White House; Iceman (Shawn Ashmore), who can cool your drink and lots of other things; Pyro (Aaron Stanford), who can hurl flames but needs a pilot light; and Rogue (Anna Paquin), who can take on aspects of the personalities around her.

These superpowers are so oddly assorted that an X-Man adventure is like a game of chess where every piece has a different move. Some of the powers are awesome; Storm stops an aerial pursuit by generating tornadoes with her mental powers, and Dr. Jean Grey is able to restart an airplane in midair.

Odd, then, that Wolverine is one of the dominant characters even though his X-Acto knuckles seem pretty insignificant compared to the powers of Pyro or Cyclops. In a convention borrowed from martial arts movies, *X2* pairs up characters with matching powers, so that when Wolverine has his titanic battle, it's with an enemy also equipped with blades. What would happen if Pyro and Iceman went head to head? I visualize the two of them in a pool of hot water.

One might reasonably ask what threat could possibly be meaningful to mutants with such remarkable powers, but Magneto, who has serious personal issues with mutants, has devised an invention that I will not describe, except to say that it provides some of the movie's best visuals. I also admired the scene where Dr. Jean Grey saves the X-Men's airplane, and the way Famke Janssen brings drama to the exercise of Grey's power instead of just switching it on and off.

Since the earliest days of *Spider-Man,* Marvel heroes have had personal problems to deal with, and there's a classic Stan Lee moment here in the scene where Iceman breaks the news to his parents that he is a mutant. The movie treats the dialogue as a coming-out scene, half-seriously, as if providing inspiration for real-life parents and their children with secrets.

Other possibilities are left for future installments. There's a romance in the movie between Rogue and Iceman, but it doesn't exploit the possibilities of love between mutants with incompatible powers. How inconvenient if during sex your partner was accidentally teleported, frozen, slashed, etc. Does Cyclops wear his dark glasses to bed?

X2: X-Men United lacks a beginning, a middle, and an end, and exists more as a self-renewing loop. In that, it is faithful to comic books themselves, which month after month and year after year seem frozen in the same fictional universe. Yes, there are comics in which the characters age and their worlds change, but the X-Men seem likely to continue forever, demonstrating their superpowers in one showcase scene after another. Perhaps in the next generation a mutant will appear named Scribbler, who can write a better screenplay for them.

XXX: State of the Union ★ ★ ½
PG-13, 94 m., 2005

Ice Cube (Darius Stone), Willem Dafoe (George Deckert), Samuel L. Jackson (Agent Augustus Gibbons), Peter Strauss (President), Xzibit (Zeke), Robert Alonzo (Guard), Rich Bryant (Man in Trench Coat), Steve Carson (Prisoner). Directed by Lee Tamahori and produced by Gillian Libbert, Neal H. Moritz, and Arne Schmidt. Screenplay by Rich Wilkes and Simon Kinberg.

XXX: State of the Union is theater of the absurd, masquerading as an action thriller. Consider. The president of the United States is giving his State of the Union message, unaware that outside the U.S. Capitol building, storm troopers in black body armor, with little red pin-points for eyes, are attempting to break in and assassinate him, as well as the vice president and everyone else in the chain of command, until they get to the secretary of defense, who has hired them for his attempted coup.

Opposing them—well, we have an ex-con named Darius (Ice Cube), who has recruited a gang of black street warriors from an up-market chop shop and outfitted them with supercharged dragsters and heavy-duty weapons. These men have been put into play by a national security agent named Gibbons (Samuel L. Jackson), who is temporarily a prisoner of the secretary of defense (Willem Dafoe), although he will be freed in time to participate in a high-speed chase after the president (Peter Strauss) is spirited out of the Capitol on a secret bullet train.

In the climax of the movie, Darius (now known as XXX) will pursue the bullet train in his 220 mph car, shredding its tires so that it can run on the rails, and so that Darius can leap from his car onto the back of the train, enter it, grab the president, and attempt to swing him to safety via a helicopter before . . . well, before other stuff happens.

How strange to see this movie on the very day when a bullet train in Japan jumped the rails and crashed into a building. And in the very week when Amtrak appealed once again for rescue from its permanent fiscal crisis, caused in part by the lack of adequate rails for bullet trains. As the president's escape train was rocketing along, did he reflect that the tracks were only safe up to about 60 mph? Should have signed that transportation bill! Or was he too busy wondering why he was being rescued from his own secretary of defense by a black dude?

I showed Mario Van Peebles's *Baadasssss* at my Overlooked Film Festival. It is a movie about the making of a 1970 movie by his father, Melvin, about a black man who defies society and yet does not die at the end of the movie. It suggests that there may be corrupt police officers. This movie was very controversial thirty-five years ago. Now we have a movie in which the entire defense establishment is corrupt, and the president is rescued by a posse of baadasssssses, who capture a tank and use it to blast their way into the Capitol, at which point I assume but cannot be sure that the media finally notice that all hell is breaking loose.

I am not sure because *XXX: State of the Union* has such a breakneck pace that it doesn't pause for the customary news updates in which the State of the Union Address is interrupted with the information that a war is raging on Capitol Hill. No, there's not even a crawl across the bottom of the screen: *Snows blanket New England . . . Armored vehicles attacking U.S. Capitol . . . Illinois 98, Michigan 91* . . . Just wondering: Are there any kind of security arrangements around the Capitol Building? You know, TV cameras or security guards who might notice when heavily armed bands of warriors dressed like Darth Vader are using rocket launchers?

The premise of the movie is apparently that within the nation's security apparatus there is a deeper, more lethal level of countersecurity agents whose job it is to defeat the regular security guys should they turn traitor. This force is always led by a superwarrior code-named XXX, and now that the original XXX (Vin Diesel) has been killed, Sam Jackson springs Ice Cube from prison to take over the assignment. (Diesel does not appear in the sequel after a salary dispute, which may explain why a Diesel lookalike plays a cameo role as a dead businessman.)

You are eager to know if any of the characters resemble current or former presidents or vice presidents or defense secretaries of the United States. No, they do not. They barely resemble fictional presidents, and so on. The president in the movie believes we must make our enemies our allies. The secretary of defense disagrees, which is why he wants to assassinate the president and half his administration. No political parties are named. There is a moment when the president says something in his speech and everybody on the Republican side of the chamber stands up to applaud, and I thought, a-ha, he's a Republican!—until I saw that all the Democrats

stood up, too, and I realized they were all probably applauding praise for themselves.

Did I enjoy this movie? Only in a dumb, mindless way. It has whatever made the original *XXX* entertaining, but a little less of it. Does it make the slightest sense? Of course not. Its significance has nothing to do with current politics and politicians, the threat of terrorism, and the efficiency of bullet trains. It has everything to do with a seismic shift in popular culture.

Once all action heroes were white. Then they got a black chief of police, who had a big scene where he fired them. Then they got a black partner. Then they were black and had a white partner. Now they are the heroes and don't even need a white guy around, although there is one nerdy white guy in *XXX* who steps in when the plot requires the ineffectual delivery of a wimpy speech. So drastically have things changed that when Ice Cube offers to grab the president and jump off a train and grab a helicopter, all the president can do is look grateful.

Oh, and later, in his new State of the Union speech, our nation's leader quotes Tupac, although he doesn't know he does. Well, you can't expect him to know everything.

XX/XY ★ ★ ★ ½
R, 91 m., 2003

Mark Ruffalo (Coles Burroughs), Kathleen Robertson (Thea), Maya Stange (Sam), Petra Wright (Claire), David Thornton (Miles). Directed by Austin Chick and produced by Isen Robbins and Aimee Schoof. Screenplay by Chick.

XX/XY portrays a man that many women will recognize on sight. Coles is like a social climber at a party, always looking past the woman he's with to see if a more perfect woman has just appeared. Women know his type, and sometimes, because he is smart and charming, they go along with the routine. But they're not fooled. Late in the film, when Coles finally tries to commit himself, a woman tells him, "You still haven't chosen me. You're settling for me."

As the film opens in the autumn of 1993, Coles (Mark Ruffalo) is studying film at Sarah Lawrence College. One night at a party he meets

Sam (Maya Stange), and asks her, "Would you think I was being too forward if I said, 'Let's go back to your room?'" Her reply: "What would you say if I said, 'Let's go back to my room, but let's bring Thea?'" This was not what he had in mind, but openness to experimentation is obligatory for all Sarah Lawrence students, and besides, Thea (Kathleen Robertson) is intriguing in her outsider rebel way.

What follows is a kinduva sortuva ménage à trois; the possibility hovers that the real reason for including Thea is that she is Sam's roommate and so it seemed like good manners. The next day, as Sam and Coles discuss it on the phone, they both try to backtrack and Coles concludes, "So we're all sorry—but we all had fun." This is, if only Sam could intuit it, an analysis that Coles will be making frequently in the years to come.

Sam likes him. Coles likes her, but he cheats on her anyway, "meaninglessly," with a one-night stand. When he confesses, something breaks between them. When a man tells a woman he loves that he has cheated but "it didn't mean anything," this translates to the woman as, "It is meaningless to me that I cheated on you." Coles doesn't quite grasp this.

As undergraduates the three form the kinds of bonds that do not find closure with graduation. Ten years pass. Coles is now working in the advertising business in Manhattan, and has been living for five years with Claire (Petra Wright). He runs into Sam one day, and finds that she has returned to America after breaking off an engagement in London. She tells him that Thea, who was once so wild, is the first of the three to be married; she runs a restaurant with Miles (David Thornton).

Coles, of course, is attracted to Sam, who looks all the more desirable because she is now the woman he would be cheating with, instead of cheating on. She's on the rebound, and they share a heedless passionate heat. The victim now is Claire, who of all the characters is the wisest about human nature. She is trim, elegant, a little older than Coles, and knows ex-actly who he is and what he is. When she walks in on Coles and Sam, she walks out again, and conceals what she has seen because she is prepared to accept Coles, up to a point.

All of these lines of sexual intrigue come to a head in a weekend at the Hamptons house of Thea and Miles. To describe what happens would be wrong, but let's suggest it would be a comedy if written by Noel Coward but is not a comedy here. Much depends upon poor Coles, who is addicted to infatuation, and finds fidelity a painful deprivation in a world filled, he thinks, with perfect love that is almost within his grasp.

Mark Ruffalo plays the character with that elusive charm he also revealed in *You Can Count on Me*. In that film he was the unreliable brother of Laura Linney, who loved him but despaired of his irresponsibility. He has a way of smiling at a joke only he can understand. He isn't really a villain (there are no bad people in the movie), but more of a victim of his own inability to commit; he ends up unhappier than any of the people he disappoints.

Maya Stange and Kathleen Robertson find the right notes for their undergraduates who seem to trade places as adults—the reliable one becoming rootless while the daring one settles down. But it is Petra Wright who does the best and most difficult job among the women, finding a painful balance between Claire's self-respect and her desire to hang on to Coles. She is hurt not so much by his sexual infidelity as by his failure to value her seriously enough. "I feel a little like a consolation prize," she says at one point.

One review of this film complains that all of the characters are jerks, and asks why we should care about them. Well, jerks are often the most interesting characters in the movies, and sometimes the ones most like ourselves. *XX/XY* would be dismal if the characters all behaved admirably, but the writer and director, Austin Chick, knows too much about human nature to permit that. The film has a rare insight into the mechanism by which some men would rather pursue happiness than obtain it.

Y

The Yes Men ★ ★ ★
R, 80 m., 2004

A documentary directed by Dan Ollman, Sarah Price, and Chris Smith and produced by Price and Smith.

From an economic point of view, the Civil War was the least profitable of all our wars, because the destruction of lives and property involved Americans on both sides. In our other wars, most of the lives and property belonged to foreigners. The war was fought to abolish slavery, but slavery would soon have faded away on its own because it made no economic sense. Think how much it costs to support a slave.

The involuntary servitude of imported labor, which is what slavery amounts to, has been replaced in our times by the much more efficient system of exporting jobs to countries that are poor to begin with, and thus have lower maintenance costs for labor. This "remote labor" is the natural alternative to slavery, and, as a bonus, there is no reason for the worker not to be free. Thus he is responsible for his own housing, feeding, and medical care—which can be at a cost level much lower than a slave owner could safely provide.

The new "remote labor system," enforced by the World Trade Organization through its system of loans and regulations for poor countries, is much more efficient for First World capitalism. It exports manufacturing and assembly jobs to Third World countries where athletic shoes, clothing, home appliances, tools, computers, and toys are assembled by labor forces paid only pennies an hour. The use of child labor further reduces the cost, and by removing the children from school, diminishes the threat of educated opposition to the system.

On the statements above we can all agree, right? Or was there a point at which you realized I was making an outrageous and immoral argument, and you were offended? I ask because when a fake "spokesman" for the World Trade Organization made the same argument before a WTO trade forum in Finland, the audience listened politely, applauded, and had no questions.

The Yes Men is a disturbing documentary in which a couple of tricksters named Mike Bonanno and Andy Bichlbaum create a fictional WTO spokesman named Hank Hardy Unruh, and a fake WTO Web site where he can be contacted. Real-world groups contact Hank Hardy, and he flies out to their meetings to deliver a speech at which he summarizes the anti-WTO argument in terms the audience, incredibly, absorbs and passively accepts. Apparently (a) no one is really listening, (b) no one is thinking, or (c) the immorality of the WTO's exploitation of cheap foreign labor becomes invisible when it is described in purely economic terms. Answer: All three, which is why the United States and the other nations controlling the WTO can live with the inhuman cost of its policies, and why so many people simply don't understand what the demonstrators at world trade forums are so mad about.

What is incredible in the film is the lengths to which a trade audience can be pushed without realizing it is the butt of a joke. At the meeting in Finland, which is about "Textiles of the Future," Hank Hardy Unruh concludes his speech, has an assistant rip off his "business suit," and reveals beneath it a gold lamé body suit. It has an inflatable appendage that pops up to allow him to view a computer screen at eye level. This appendage looks uncannily like a large phallus. Do the audience members laugh uproariously or walk out in anger? No, *they just sit there.* They have lost all ability to apply reality to the ideological construction they inhabit.

The film shows another fake lecture, before a group of New York students. At this one, McDonald's hamburgers are passed out, and the students chow down as the fake speaker laments the fact that the human body is inefficient in processing food. In fact, 90 percent of all the calories we eat are eliminated by the body. The challenge, they're told, "is to recycle postconsumer waste into fast food. A single hamburger can be eaten ten times!"

The students, thank God, don't just sit there. They are outraged—which means, however, that they took the speech seriously. "Do you think you guys are lacking kind of, like, a human element?" one student asks. And a cynic shouts: "How much did McDonald's pay you guys to come here today?"

Yeah, like McDonald's is really going to recycle excrement into Cheese McCraps. I watched the movie in astonishment and dismay. Have we lost all balance, all critical ability, all the instincts that should warn an intelligent person that a joke is being played? Is satire possible in a world where nobody gets it? Have modern forms of corporatespeak so depersonalized language that no one expects it to mean anything?

No one with a feeling for literature and poetry can read the typical best-selling business or self-help book with a straight face, because their six rules or nine plans or twelve formulas are so manifestly idiotic, and couched in prose of such insulting simplicity. If I were a boss, I would fire any employee reading such a book, on the grounds that he was not smart enough to be working for me. If I were the employee of a company that hired one of those motivational gurus, I would quit on the grounds that management had been taken over by pod people.

But I am a film critic, and must report that *The Yes Men* is amazing in what it shows, but underwhelming in what it does with it. The film seems a little hasty and disorganized, as if available footage is being stretched further than it wants to go. The filmmakers are Dan Ollman, Sarah Price, and Chris Smith; Price and Smith made *American Movie* (2000), without a doubt the funniest documentary I have ever seen, and one of the best.

This time, they have such colorful characters and such an alarming story to tell that the film works in spite of its imperfections. Yes, we'd like to know more about the infrastructure that supports the Yes Men, and have more objective information about the WTO. Or maybe the blank looks on the faces of the audience regarding the inflatable phallic "Employee Visualization Appendage" tells us everything we need to know.

Young Adam ★ ★ ★ ½
NC-17, 93 m., 2004

Ewan McGregor (Joe Taylor), Tilda Swinton (Ella Gault), Peter Mullan (Les Gault), Emily Mortimer (Cathie Dimly). Directed by David Mackenzie and produced by Jeremy Thomas. Screenplay by Mackenzie, based on a novel by Alexander Trocchi.

Two men and a woman on a barge. No one who has seen Jean Vigo's famous film *L'Atalante* (1932) can watch *Young Adam* without feeling its resonance. There cannot be peace unless the woman or one of the men leaves. In the Vigo film, newlyweds make the barge their occupation and home, and the bride feels pushed aside by the crusty old deckhand (the immortal Michel Simon). In *Young Adam,* the chemistry is more lethal. The barge is owned by Ella Gault (Tilda Swinton), who has a loveless marriage with her husband, Les (Peter Mullan). Les has hired the young and cocky Joe Taylor (Ewan McGregor), who fancies himself a writer.

It is a foregone conclusion that Joe will eventually have sex with Ella, as the barge *Atlantic Eve* trades on the dank canals between Glasgow and Edinburgh, circa 1960. But that's really not the movie's subject, even though it provides rich opportunities for Peter Mullan, that intense and inward Scotsman, to underplay his rage and suppress his feelings. (At one point, as Joe and Ella linger in bed, they hear Les's boots on the deck overhead and decide, "He's letting us know he's back.") No, the *Atlantic Eve* is not the setting for adultery so much as for guilt and long silences.

As the film opens, Joe sees the body of a young woman floating in the canal, dressed only in lingerie. He uses a hook to pull it closer, and Les helps him haul her on board. The police are summoned. It is a drowning, perhaps a suicide. No foul play, apparently.

But Joe knows more about the body than he reveals—more, much more, than anybody would ever be able to discover, and he reads the papers with interest as it is learned the woman was pregnant, and that her boyfriend, a plumber, has been charged with the murder.

Joe is a hard case. Opaque. Not tender, not good with the small talk. Around women he has a certain intensity that informs them he plans to have sex with them and it is up to them to agree, or go away. He is not a rapist, but he has only one purpose in his mind, and some women find that intensity of focus to be exciting. It's as if, at the same time, he cares nothing for them and can think only of them. No amount of sweet talk would conquer them, but his eyes penetrate to their souls and rummage around.

As the murder case goes to trial, Joe finds himself attending the court sessions. He becomes fascinated by the defendant. Flashbacks fill in chapters of Joe's earlier life, episodes known only to him, including a moment when he could have acted, and did not act, and does not even begin to understand why he didn't. He is not a murderer, but a man unwilling to intervene, a man so detached, so cold, so willing to sacrifice others to his own convenience, that perhaps in his mind it occurs that he would feel better about the young woman's death if he had actually, actively, killed her. Then at least he would know what he had done, and would not find such emptiness when he looks inside himself. This is an almost Dostoyevskian study of a man brooding upon evil until it paralyzes him.

Although Britain and Ireland now enjoy growing prosperity, any working class person thirty or older was raised in a different, harder society. That's why actors like Ewan McGregor and Colin Farrell, not to mention Tim Roth and Gary Oldman, can slip so easily into these hard-edged, dirty-handed roles. With American actors you have the feeling they bought work clothes at Sears and roughed them up; with these guys, you figure they got their old gear out of their dad's closet, or borrowed their brother's. Peter Mullan, who is older, is a sublime actor, too much overlooked, who can play a working man with a direct honesty that doesn't involve a single extra note. Look at his movie *My Name Is Joe*, where he plays a recovering alcoholic who tries to help a friend and to risk a romance. As for Tilda Swinton, here is directness so forceful you want to look away; she doesn't cave in to Joe because of his look, but because he can match hers.

A movie like *Young Adam* is above all about the ground-level lives of its characters. The death of the girl and the plot surrounding it is handled not as a crime or a mystery, but as an event that jars characters out of their fixed orbits. When you have a policy of behavior, a pose toward the world, that has hardened like concrete into who you are, it takes more than guilt to break you loose. It takes the sudden realization that the person you created continues to function, but you are now standing outside of him. He carries on regardless, and you are stranded, alone and frightened.

Z

Zatoichi ★ ★ ★ ½
R, 116 m., 2004

Beat Takeshi (Zatoichi), Michiyo Ookusu (Aunt O-Ume), Gadarukanaru Taka (Shinkichi), Daigoro Tachibana (Geisha O-Sei), Yuuko Daike (Geisha O-Kinu), Tadanobu Asano (Gennosuke Hattori), Yui Natsukawa (O-Shino), Ittoku Kishibe (Ginzo). Directed by Takeshi Kitano and produced by Tsunehisa Saito. Screenplay by Kitano, based on novels by Kan Shimozawa.

Zatoichi embodies the kinds of contradictory elements that make Takeshi Kitano Japan's most intriguing contemporary actor-director. He plays, as usual, a man with an impassive face, few words, and sudden bursts of action that end in a few seconds. He is vastly amused at private jokes. He has a code, but enforces it according to his own rules. And then there is the style of the movie, and what can only be called its musical numbers.

Kitano, who acts under the name Beat Takeshi, has played mostly modern tough guys, but here he ventures back to the nineteenth century to step into the shoes of Zatoichi, a blind swordsman who was the hero in one of the two most popular movie series in Japanese history. Zatoichi, always played by Shintaro Katsu, appeared in twenty-six Zatoichi films before his death in 1997. (Tora-san, a sort of Japanese Jerry Lewis, was played by Kiyoshi Atsumi in no less than forty-eight films between 1969 and 1995.)

Kitano playing Zatoichi is a little like Clint Eastwood playing Hopalong Cassidy; the star brings along a powerful persona that redefines the pop superficiality of his character. He poses as a humble, wandering, blind masseur whose hearing and instinct are so razor-sharp that he knows better what is going on around him than those who are limited to sight. He walks with a slight stoop, sometimes smiles or laughs to himself, carries his head cocked to one side, never seems tense or coiled, and then in an instant his cane-sword has found its target.

In its broadest outlines, *Zatoichi* is a revenge drama. The blind swordsman encounters on his travels two sisters (one actually a transvestite) who work as geishas at a wayside rest station. They were orphaned when their parents were killed by the merciless Ginzo gang, which shakes down small merchants. Zatoichi learns about their story, and although he never declares his intention to do anything, eventually the gang's retainers begin to die while trying to kill him. Finally all comes down to a duel between Zatoichi and the crime boss's high-priced bodyguard Hattori (Tadanobu Asano), a warrior of fierce talents.

This plot, however conventional it may sound, plays quite differently in Kitano's hands because of his acute and distinctive style of pace and timing. Not for him the ten-minute Hong Kong–style martial arts extravaganzas. In one scene set in a stony wasteland, Zatoichi is attacked by eight enemies, kills them one after another with almost blinding speed, and leaves the gray stones splashed with red blood, in what is, apart from anything else, a rather effective abstract color pattern.

Zatoichi is hardly on screen every moment, or even in every scene. The movie devotes full time to the Ginzo boss (Ittoko Kishibe) and his auditions for a bodyguard, and establishes Aunt O-Ume (Michiyo Ookusu), who befriends the two geishas, O-Kinu (Yuuko Daike) and O-Sei (the transvestite Daigoro Tachibana). We get a sense of village life, of gossip and speculation, of keen interest in this curious blind masseur.

And then there is the matter of the music of syncopation. Kitano often combines violence with artistic excursions of the most unexpected sorts, and here he weaves a thread of percussive rhythm through the film. In an early scene, we see four men with hoes, breaking up the earth in a field, and their tools strike the ground in a rhythm that the sound track subtly syncopates with music. Later, there is a duet for music and raindrops. Still later, the men with hoes are stomping in their field, again in rhythm. There is a scene of house-building where the hammers of all the workmen are timed to create a suite for iron against wood. And the final curtain call, worthy of *42nd Street*, begins with a boldly choreographed stomp dance—and then all of the actors come on from the wings and join in the dance, including actors who played some of the characters at younger ages.

This element of the film is almost unreasonably delightful, because it's completely irrelevant and uncalled-for; Kitano allows fanciful playfulness into what might have been a formula action picture. Remarkably, some of the people I saw the movie with (at two different viewings) came out complaining, as if there were a rigid template for action movies and Kitano had broken the rules. I was surprised and grateful.

Takeshi Kitano, born in 1947, has directed eleven films, written thirteen, and acted in thirty-two (there are some overlaps). An expert entry in the online encyclopedia Wikipedia says he has also published more than fifty books of poetry, film criticism, and fiction, and is also a game show host (one of his shows, retitled *MXC*, plays on Spike TV). He also hosts a weekly talk show of Japanese-speaking foreigners, who comment on Japan from their foreign perspectives.

Like many artists of long experience and consistent success, he gives himself permission to work outside the box. *Zatoichi* is not a continuation of the original series (itself available on DVD), but a transformation. It's the kind of film I more and more find myself seeking out, a film that seems alive in the sense that it appears to have free will; if, in the middle of a revenge tragedy, it feels like adding a suite for hoes and percussion, it does. Kitano is deadpan most of the time on the screen, but I have a feeling he smiles a lot in the editing room.

Zhou Yu's Train ★ ★
NO MPAA RATING, 97 m., 2004

Gong Li (Zhou Yu/Xiu), Tony Leung Ka Fai (Chen Qing), Honglei Sun (Zhang Qiang). Directed by Sun Zhou and produced by Huang Jianxin, Zhou, and Bill Kong. Screenplay by Zhou, Bei Cun, and Zhang Mei.

Zhou Yu's Train tells a pointlessly convoluted version of a love story that would really be very simple, if anyone in the movie possessed common sense. We know love is blind, but need it be obtuse? The three lovers in Sun Zhou's film, controversial in China for sex scenes that are more fond than fervent, make life miserable for themselves and, to a lesser degree, for us.

Our misery is leavened by the visual qualities of the film, which like most recent work from China is spectacularly good to look at. There's also the central presence of the Chinese superstar Gong Li, who plays a dual role so confusingly written that it might as well be one person, but plays it well.

Her character is a painter of porcelain pottery named Zhou Yu, who is secretive, with an active romantic imagination. A teacher and poet named Chen Qing (Tony Leung Ka Fai) falls in love with her, and gives her a poem comparing her to a mystical lake named Xan Hu. That this poem to her also appears in the district newspaper makes a deep impression, and soon she is taking a long train ride twice a week from her city to his.

The movie backs into this straightforward narrative by beginning in the middle of one of the journeys, as a veterinarian named Zhang Qiang (Honglei Sun) flirts with her and asks to buy the painted porcelain vase she is taking as a present to Chen Qing. Zhang is so insistent that she finally ends the conversation with a bold dramatic gesture. She dislikes Zhang as much as she loves Chen Qing—she thinks.

But Chen Qing is a case rewarding further study. He seems to be a squatter in a kind of forgotten library, where his simple bachelor existence suits him well. He is happy enough to make love two afternoons a week, but a little frightened of Zhou Yu's fervor. Mention is made of a teaching position he could take in Tibet.

It occurs to us, long before it occurs to Zhou Yu, that the vet would make a better partner than the poet. This would be even more obvious if the film weren't needlessly fragmented, so that we jump around in time and have to piece together the actual chronology of her relationships with the two men. The vet at one point actually follows her on one of her train journeys, discovering a secret about Chen Qing that is well known to Zhou Yu but will not be mentioned here.

In my notes, I wrote: "Who is the short-haired girl? Looks like Gong Li." Reader, it was

Gong Li, in the dual role, playing a character named Xiu. She is apparently a former lover of Chen Qing's who is now a narrator telling us about his affair with Zhou. All very well, except by casting the same actress the movie led me to assume I was seeing Zhou herself at two stages of her life, or at least at two stages of her hairstyling history. Xiu works mostly as an unnecessary diversion.

The qualities of the movie come during small, well-observed moments. Zhou covering her lover's face with hungry kisses. The train conductor reminding the vet, "That's the same girl who fainted one day, and you refused to treat her." The vet pointing out he has been trained to work with animals. Above all, the loneliness of the long-distance journeys, which seem to take on an existence of their own, as if Zhou prefers faithfully traveling to and from her lover to actually being with him, or apart from him.

The film is impeccably photographed, and the characters become convincing as themselves, if not always in their relationships. The story, once the complex telling is unraveled, invests these people with more romantic significance than they deserve. And if it is true, as I suspect, that Zhou Yu's train journeys have an importance for her apart from their alleged purpose—if, to put it simply, she just plain likes to take the train—the movie could have been a little more amused, and amusing, about that. Does she get frequent traveler miles?

The Best Films of 2004

December 19, 2004—As we entered December I had a shortlist of candidates for my choice of the best films of the year, but no obvious first-place entry. *Kill Bill: Vol. 2* came close, and *Vera Drake* had a sombre perfection and a great performance, but I hadn't seen a film that simply stepped forward and announced itself as, clearly, the year's best.

Then I saw Clint Eastwood's *Million Dollar Baby*. I don't know what I expected. Actually, I expected nothing, as I'd heard so little about the film in advance. But as it played I realized it never steps wrong. Never a false note. It has a purity of narrative line and a strength of performance that is classical in its perfection. I had my winner.

1. *Million Dollar Baby*

Classical filmmaking by Clint Eastwood, pure, simple, and true. Great because of what it puts in, and great because of what it leaves out: no flash, nothing much in the way of special effects, no pandering to the audience, but a story that gains in power with every scene, about characters we believe in and care for.

Hilary Swank stars as Maggie, a waitress who dreams of becoming a boxer. She's thirty-one, too old to start professional training. That's what Frankie (Eastwood) tells her. Besides, he doesn't approve of women boxers. He owns a run-down gym and runs it with the help of his oldest friend, Eddie (Morgan Freeman). Maggie will not listen to discouragement. She comes back every day, and finally Eddie takes mercy and shows her a few moves, and finally Frankie breaks down and agrees to train her.

So now you think you know where the movie is going, but you are wrong. It's not a boxing movie; it's the story of these people and what happens to them, and it goes deeper and deeper, never taking a wrong step, never hitting a false note. It touched me like no other film this year.

2. *Kill Bill: Vol. 2*

The second half of Quentin Tarantino's *Kill Bill* is not only better than the first, but makes the earlier movie better by providing it with a context; now we can see the entire story, and it has exuberance and passion, comedy and violence, bold self-satire and action scenes with the precision of ballet. Tarantino is the most idiosyncratic and influential director of the decade, taking the materials of pop art and transforming them into audacious epic fantasies.

Uma Thurman stars as The Bride, whose fiancé and entire wedding party are massacred by Bill; seeking revenge, she did battle with the Deadly Viper Assassination Squad in *Vol. 1*. Now we see her early training under a legendary warrior master, and her deadly conflicts with Elle Driver (Daryl Hannah), one-eyed expert of martial arts, and Bill's beer-swilling brother Budd (Michael Madsen), who buries her alive. Her final confrontation with the legendary Bill (David Carradine) is great filmmaking, illustrating how Tarantino's dialogue uses graphic description to set up scenes so that the action isn't the point, but the payoff.

3. *Vera Drake*

Another brilliant performance by a woman: Hilary Swank, Uma Thurman, now Imelda Staunton, as three characters who could not be more unlike. Staunton plays a London cleaning lady in the London of the early 1950s, where wartime rationing is still in effect and poverty is the general reality. Vera Drake has another, secret existence, "helping out girls who get in trouble." She is an abortionist, but doesn't think of it that way, accepts no payment, is a melodious plum pudding of a woman whose thoughts are entirely pragmatic.

Abortion is illegal, although Mike Leigh's film shows how easily one can be obtained by the wealthy, whose doctors sign them into private clinics. For poor and desperate women, there is Vera. Leigh creates the woman and her family with gentle perception and an eye for small details that build up the larger reality; the scene where the police come to call has an urgency in which silence, shame, grief, and love struggle for space in the small lives of these people.

4. Spider-Man 2

The best superhero movie ever made. The genre does not lend itself to greatness, although the first *Superman* movie had considerable artistry and *Blade II* and *The Hulk* had their qualities. Director Sam Raimi's first Spider-Man movie was thin and the special effects too cartoony, but the sequel is a transformation. Tobey Maguire and Kirsten Dunst bring unusual emotional complexity to comic-book characters, Alfred Molina's Doc Ock is one of the great movie villains, and the special effects, while understandably not "realistic," bring a presence and a sense of (literal) gravity to the film; Spider-Man now seems like a human and not a drawing as he swings from the skyscrapers, and his personal problems—always the strong point of the Marvel comics—are given full weight and importance. A great entertainment.

5. Moolaade

From Senegal, the story of a strong woman who stands up to the men in her tribe when four girls come to her for protection. The custom in the land from time immemorial has required women to be circumcised, their genitals mutilated so they feel no sexual sensation. Men will not marry them otherwise. But Colle (Fatoumata Coulibaly) has refused to let her own daughter be cut, and now she evokes the tribal rule of "moolaade," or "protection," to shield the other four. This story no doubt sounds grim, and will not prepare you for the life, humor, and energy of the film, by the African master director Ousmane Sembene. He creates a sure sense of the village life, of local characters, of men and women using tribal law like the pieces in a chess game. An important film, since ritual circumcision is common in Muslim lands, although most Islamic teaching forbids it.

6. The Aviator

Martin Scorsese's hugely enjoyable biopic tells the story of a man whose risks, victories, and losses were all outsize. Howard Hughes was a golden boy with a Texas tool-making fortune who conquered Hollywood, made spectacular epics, loved spectacular women, built airplanes including the largest in history, bought an airline, and went bankrupt several times in the process of becoming the world's richest man.

Leonardo DiCaprio embodies this mercurial legend, and Scorsese re-creates a lavish Hollywood world of glamour and power. At the same time, they show Hughes battling obsessions that finally overcome him; the king of the world becomes the captive of his own fears. DiCaprio doesn't look much like Hughes, but we forget that as he embodies the character's obsessions. He leads a lonely life, playing a public role as a successful winner while knowing, deep inside, that he is going mad. There is a scene at the height of his glory when he stands inside the door of a men's room, afraid to touch the doorknob because of a panic attack about germs. Against this dark side, Scorsese balances a glorious portrait of a fabled era, and Cate Blanchett does an impersonation of Katharine Hepburn that's just a smile this side of wicked.

7. Baadasssss!

Not your usual movie about the making of a movie, but history remembered with humor, passion, and a blunt regard for the truth. Mario Van Peebles' film tells the story of how his father, Melvin, all but created modern independent black filmmaking with *Sweet Sweetback's Baadassss Song*, a 1971 exploitation film that won critical praise and unexpectedly grossed millions. Made by, for, and about African-Americans, it contained harsh truth and gritty irony that hadn't been seen on the screen before.

The production was fly-by-night on a shoestring, and Mario, who was present for most of the original film and played Sweetback as a boy, doesn't sugarcoat his memories. Melvin did what was necessary to get the film made, and never has there been such a knowledgeable portrayal of how money, personalities, compromise, idealism, and harsh reality are all part of any movie—but especially those that cost the least.

8. *Sideways*

A joy from beginning to end, with occasional side trips into sadness, slapstick, and truth. Paul Giamatti stars as a 40ish sad-sack loser, an alcoholic whose best friend (Thomas Haden Church) is getting married in a week. As best man, Giamatti treats Church to a vacation in California wine country, where they meet two friends (Virginia Madsen and Sandra Oh) and many delightful bottles of wine. Church shamelessly cheats on his fiancée and deceives Oh; Giamatti and Madsen find a gentle, tender tentative romance, describing grapes in the way they might describe themselves. Alexander Payne's film moves easily from broad to subtle comedy, from emotional upheaval to small moments of romance. The kind of movie you want to go see again, taking along some friends.

9. *Hotel Rwanda*

In 1994 in Rwanda, a million members of the Tutsi tribe were massacred by members of the Hutu tribe, in an insane upheaval of their ancient rivalry. Based on a true story, Terry George's film shows how the manager of a luxury hotel (Don Cheadle) saved the lives of his family and 1,200 guests, essentially by using all of his management skills, including bribery, flattery, apology, deception, blackmail, freebies, and calling in favors. His character intuitively understands that only by continuing to act as a hotel manager can he achieve anything. As the nation descends into anarchy, he puts on his suit and tie every morning and fakes business as usual, dealing with a murderous Hutu general not as a criminal, but as a valued client; a man who yesterday orchestrated mass murder might today want to show that he knows how to behave appropriately in the hotel lobby. With Nick Nolte as a UN peacekeeper who ignores his orders in order to help Cheadle and the lives that have come into their care.

10. *Undertow*

The third film by David Gordon Green, at twenty-nine the most poetically gifted director of his generation. Jamie Bell and Devon Alan play two brothers in rural Georgia, one a rebel, one a sweet, odd loner. Their father mourns for their dead mother and chooses for them to live in virtual isolation; then their ex-con uncle arrives, and everything changes. There is a family legend about gold coins that leads to jealousy and bloodshed, and the boys escape the uncle and try to survive during a journey both harrowing and strangely romantic; the film has the form of an action picture but the feel of a lyrical fable, and Green's eye for his backwoods locations and rusty urban hideaways creates a world immediately distinctive as his own.

His style has been categorized as "Southern Gothic," but that's too narrow. There is a poetic merging of realism and surrealism; every detail is founded on accurate observation, but the effect is somehow mythological. Listen to his dialogue; his characters say things that sound exactly like the sort of thing they would really say, and yet are like nothing anyone has ever said before.

Special Jury Prize

At every film festival, the jury creates a special prize for a film that did not win their first award, and yet is somehow too good for second place. As a jury of one, I usually award my Special Prize to ten splendid films, but this year I have chosen fifteen, because there is not one I can do without. Alphabetically:

The Assassination of Richard Nixon, stars Sean Penn as a man whose demons have destroyed his marriage and now threaten his job as an office supplies salesman. Whatever his problem, his symptom is to decide what is absolutely right, and then to absolutely insist upon it; he doesn't know when to shut up, and has little idea of his effect on other people. Under unbearable psychological pressure, he marches steadfastly toward madness.

Closer is Mike Nichols' story of four characters who fall in and out of love and betrayal in various combinations, complicated by their tendency to tell the truth when it doesn't exactly help anyone to know it. Natalie Portman is luminous in her first grown-up role, as a New York stripper who comes to London and falls in love with Jude Law, a journalist who writes a novel about their affair and then falls in love with Julia Roberts, as his publicity photographer. She in turn meets Clive Owen, a doctor who, in his turn, meets Portman. These four people richly deserve one another; seduced by seduction itself, they play at relationships that are lies in almost every respect except their desire to sleep with each other. Based on the play by Patrick Marber.

The Dreamers is Bernardo Bertolucci's love song to a vanished era, the film-worshiping, politically radical, sexually liberated Paris of the late 1960s. A naive American student (Michael Pitt) meets twins (Eva Green and Louis Garrel) and is absorbed into their world of obsession with movies, politics, and sex. It all seems wonderful, for a time, in a movie that places their story against a backdrop of a brief season when it did seem as if cinema could change the world.

House of Flying Daggers, by Zhang Yimou, is an audaciously beautiful, improbable, exuberant martial arts romance set in Chinese medieval times, as an undercover cop falls in love with a beautiful woman who leads a band of revolutionaries. There are extraordinary feats of combat and marksmanship, in a film not so much about action as about transcending the laws of physics. There are passages of remarkable beauty and grace, including a battle in a bamboo forest that combines conflict, choreography, and syncopation. With Zhang Ziyi (from *Crouching Tiger, Hidden Dragon*), Takeshi Kaneshiro, and Andy Lau.

Kinsey stars Liam Neeson in a bravura performance as a scientist who studies human sexuality while discovering almost nothing about human nature. Kinsey's best-selling books revised conventional thinking about what people do sexually, how they do it, how often they do it, and with whom. Neeson plays Kinsey as a man who takes pure logic perhaps further than it needs to go in personal relationships; Laura Linney is wonderful as perhaps the only woman in the world who could both understand and love this impossible man. Directed by Bill Condon.

The Merchant of Venice is yet another reminder of what a versatile and powerful actor Al Pacino is, and how he continues to grow. Shakespeare's play is classified as a "comedy," and indeed the farce of Portia's courtship is funny, but the story of Shylock, which it contains, is a tragedy. The film, directed by Michael Radford, creates a Shylock who is strangely, perversely sympathetic; Pacino's readings of the famous speeches vibrate with fierce, wounded pride, and the cinematography creates a Venice of night, shadow, decadence, and deceit, to set beside Portia's sunny world.

The Passion of the Christ is accurately titled; Mel Gibson's movie is not about the teachings of Jesus, not about theology, miracles, or parables, but about how he suffered and died. One of the most violent films I have ever seen, but what would be the purpose of softening the anguish? Christians believe Christ died for our sins; this is above all the story of what happens to the man, to the physical body. The film was divisive and controversial. How you related to it depended on what you brought into the theater, on your own beliefs and background. Some found it anti-Semitic. I did not and tried to explain that in my review.

The Polar Express was decisively defeated at the box office by *The Incredibles* when the two films opened almost simultaneously, but it didn't fold up and go away. Instead, week by week, it discovered its audience, and its 3-D screenings at IMAX theaters were always sold out. Tom Hanks voices five of the characters, and provides a model for their body movement, in the story of a boy who boards a train to the North Pole and witnesses great wonderments there. Creepy in that teasing way that lets you know eerie things could happen; a shivery tone, instead of the mindless jolliness of the usual Christmas movie.

Ray stars Jamie Foxx in a virtuoso performance as Ray Charles, the blind musical legend who largely created soul music and embraced all the pop genres. The movie doesn't sugarcoat his womanizing and drug usage, but shows him emerging from addiction to become a supremely creative force; Foxx is uncanny in his ability to evoke

Charles's body language, which seemed to reflect and even conduct the music.

The Saddest Music in the World is a film beyond strange, by the quirky Canadian genius Guy Maddin. Isabella Rossellini plays a glass-legged brewery heiress who summons entries for a depression-era contest to find the saddest song. Not silent and not entirely in black and white, but it looks like a long-lost classic from decades ago, grainy and sometimes faded; Maddin shoots on 8mm film and video, and creates images that look like a memory from cinema's distant past. The effect is peculiar and delightful.

Sky Captain and the World of Tomorrow. Jude Law, Gwyneth Paltrow, and Angelina Jolie star in a tour de force by Kerry Conran, who uses real actors and creates almost everything else on the screen with digital effects that look like Flash Gordon's daydreams. If Tom Corbett, Space Cadet, had gone to film school, this would have been his first movie.

The Terminal, by Steven Spielberg, starred Tom Hanks as a man without a country—or at least, without a visa. His nation ceases to exist just as he lands in America, and a customs and immigration officer (Stanley Tucci) tells him he's free to remain in the terminal, but forbidden to step outside. Hanks creates a man of boundless optimism and great lovability, who makes friends, fashions a life, and even begins a romance in the terminal; inspired by the French comedies of Jacques Tati, Spielberg and Hanks find comedy not only in characters but in places and things and the oddness with which they fit together.

Touching the Void was as unsettling and disturbing a film as I saw all year, telling the story of two men who set out to climb a mountain. One falls and shatters his leg, the other tries to help him down, they find themselves in an impossible situation, the rope must be cut, and the injured man falls into a deep crevice and incredibly, agonizingly, despairingly, fights for his survival.

The Twilight Samurai stars Hiroyuki Sanada as a samurai in the dying days of the samurai era, who works as a bookkeeper and then is assigned to perform a murder, to his immense reluctance. Intercut with a poignant love story, and involving an extraordinary conversation between the samurai and his intended victim, it is a bittersweet masterpiece.

When Will I Be Loved, perhaps the best film by the mercurial James Toback, stars Neve Campbell as a rich girl with a scruffy boyfriend who essentially tries to sell her favors to an Italian millionaire. The catch is, she doesn't need the money—something not known by the Italian (Dominic Chianese) as they enter into a financial and psychological negotiation involving some of the smartest and most agile dialogue of the year.

Best Documentaries

It was a year when political documentaries made news, and Michael Moore's *Fahrenheit 9/11* made headlines, both with its political controversy and by setting a box office record for docs. These I especially admired, alphabetically:

The Agronomist, by Jonathan Demme, was about the life and death of Jean Dominique, a courageous Haitian reformer who continued to broadcast attacks on corruption over his radio station, despite death threats that eventually came true.

Aileen: Life and Death of a Serial Killer, by Nick Broomfield and Joan Churchill, was a painful, unblinking portrait of the real Aileen Wuornos, bringing depth and context to the fictional version of her life in *Monster* and illuminating how brilliantly on-target Charlize Theron's performance was in that movie.

Fahrenheit 9/11 was, apart from everything else that has been said about it (and a lot has been said), surprisingly entertaining; Michael Moore is a reformer with the soul of a stand-up comic. The movie became a rallying point for pro-Kerry forces and a lightning rod for anti-Kerry critics, and will be remembered for a sequence in which Bush, told of the attack on the World Trade Center, remains immobile in a primary school classroom for long strange minutes.

My Architect, by Nathaniel Kahn, is about his relationship (or lack of one) with his father, the architect Louis I. Kahn, who built wonderful buildings while leading an untidy and deceptive private life; he secretly supported three families at the same time.

Riding Giants was Stacy Peralta's extraordinary doc about the world of obsessive championship surfing, with archival footage showing each generation of surfers out-daring the last in their quest for near-suicidal challenges. Unlike the inane "surf's up" docs of the past, this one suggests the sport's dark and deadly undertow.

And *Tarnation* was Jonathan Caouette's autobiographical memory of a boy growing up gay and dealing with a mother whose mental health was destroyed by shock treatments. The film was excellent on any terms, and all the more remarkable since it was made for $218 on a borrowed Macintosh, and won an invitation to Cannes.

Interviews

Joan Allen and Sally Potter

June 28, 2005—When I interviewed Joan Allen and Sally Potter about their new film, *Yes,* I assumed everyone who saw it would love it as I do. I was mistaken. Although it has many supporters, it has opened to some savage reviews ("ideas of almost staggering banality"—A. O. Scott, the *New York Times*).

I find this opposition hard to understand. The movie finds an elegant and original way of telling its story, it is erotic beyond description, it contains politics that are provocative even if you find them wrongheaded, and has ever a movie loved an actress more than this one loves Joan Allen? It also boldly contains its own running critique in the form of minor characters who observe the romantic leading characters and sniff that they, too, sweat, excrete, shed dead cells, and are destined to rejoin the dust.

This is a movie so daring in its approach that it should be applauded even if it didn't also work on the level of a story about two people who find that sex is simple but life is baffling. The central characters are named She and He (Joan Allen and Simon Abkarian), and even this has offended some critics; would they have been placated by Betty and Mustafa? Angie and Ali?

She is the unhappy wife of a cold and distant man (Sam Neill). He was once a surgeon in Lebanon, is now a cook in London. Their eyes meet during a boring dinner where she is a guest and he is a server. They do not look away, but begin a dance of curiosity and complicity that leads, soon enough, to sudden and needful sex. After the novelty of their ecstasy runs thin, they are faced with the facts that she is Western, rich, and married, and he is Arabic, poor, and has Muslim ideas about women that do not correspond to her behavior. What to do?

To this outline I must now add something that has caused consternation to a few critics: The characters speak in rhyming iambic pentameter. That is the rhythm scheme of Shakespeare, who found it the vehicle for the most supple prose ever written. Because the actors are so skilled and because the dialogue is phrased and rhymed so subtly, many viewers of the film may never even much notice the poetry.

"My intention," Potter said, "was to naturalize the dialogue completely. When it was written it was tightly structured. Most of it is iambic pentameter: ten syllables a line with rhymes at the end of the line; sometimes two in a row, sometimes first and fourth, sometimes the rhyme halfway through the line as well, for double rhymes. From a writing perspective, it was a great discipline, but strangely, incredibly freeing to work within that discipline, to go deep into the ideas.

"But once it got to the performing state, it was about—okay, now let's throw it away. We don't respect the lines; we ignore them. We concentrate on the meaning and emotion. And so we went deeply into the emotions, and I think Joan was a genius in the way she naturalized the verse."

"And yet," Joan Allen said, "I've never done Shakespeare. Can you believe that? Ever?"

This was at the Toronto Film Festival, after I saw the movie at Telluride. We talked again after a screening of the movie in Chicago. I was aware of two professionals in the full flower of their talents. For Allen, a founder of the Steppenwolf Theater in Chicago and a three-time Oscar nominee, this has been a year of wonders, with her work in *Off the Map* (as an earth-woman living off the land in New Mexico with a dreamy daughter and a depressed husband); *The Upside of Anger* (as an alcoholic suburban housewife who has an affair with a boozy ex–baseball hero); and now *Yes,* as an elegant woman catapulted by eroticism out of her dead life and into dangerous opportunities.

As for Potter, have you seen *The Tango Lesson* (1997), in which she plays an ordinary British woman who impulsively goes to Argentina and gives herself over to the tango? Or her *Orlando* (1992), starring Tilda Swinton in Virginia Woolf's story of a very long-lived person who is sometimes male and sometimes female, doing a sort of gender-optional tour of British history?

Allen pointed out that the first character to speak in the film is the woman's maid, played by Shirley Henderson. She mops and dusts and speculates on the tiny dust mites and infinitesimal creatures that occupy our space and munch away on our debris.

"She launches the film," Allen said, "and she has an extraordinary ability to make the dialogue style seem incredibly conversational; because of the way she delivers it, she sets the stage for all of us to come afterward."

Did it take a lot of work before filming began?

"There were so many layers to explore and discover," Allen said. "In films, you know, you don't get much rehearsal time, but we had probably altogether maybe six or seven weeks."

When you first saw the screenplay, I asked her, were you flummoxed?

"I was a little intimidated, but then as soon as I met Sally, it all sort of made sense—especially the rhyming."

"I've had the hope," Potter said, "that people might come out of the film just wishing that we always talked that way. That it was natural, that the long song form or verse is actually a natural, rhythmic way of speaking. When we go to Shakespeare we're aware and we're not aware—which iambic pentameter makes possible because it gives you a long leg to go with, a long verbal stride."

But enough about the poetry, how about the sex? There is a scene in the movie where He and She are in a restaurant. There is no nudity. Nothing is explicitly shown. We understand but cannot see what is happening. She has an orgasm all the more thrilling for being suppressed and concealed. Nobody at another table tells a waiter, "I'll have whatever she's having." This scene is extended and subtle—bold, but boldness concealed.

"The secret there was to get to the point where the actors were having fun," Potter said. "Most sex scenes in the movies have actors who are so deadly serious, and self-conscious, and uptight. We rehearsed it until we could laugh about it, enjoy it—not the sex, the acting—and then when we filmed, everyone was relaxed and there was a joy instead of all that tension."

I don't know, I told Allen, when I've seen a more voluptuous character on the screen, glowing within her own skin, particularly in scenes where you have no makeup on, or you're dripping wet, and you lack the safeguards that actresses use; you're saying, here I am, I'm healthy, I'm in good shape, I'm loved, and I feel great.

"Sally has an incredible balance of emotional and psychological content," Allen said. "I felt well taken care of, and Aleksei Rodionov, the cinematographer, was that way as well. I felt so protected that I could relax and go to places because I knew it was going to be fine."

Sally Potter said Allen has a beauty that "brings out intelligence. It's a beauty that shows first in the eyes. When I'm working with somebody, whether it's Tilda Swinton or Joan Allen, I really study that person a lot. I look all the time. Joan, you must have felt my eyes on you. I'm trying to figure out how this person's face works, and what happens here, and what happens there. It's a joyful process."

I'm taking it for granted, I said, that there is an echo of Molly Bloom in the title—Molly Bloom, whose monologue ends James Joyce's *Ulysses.*

"Yes," Joan Allen said.

"Yes," said Sally Potter. "Which is the word Molly Bloom says. Over and over. Yes yes yes."

Kevin Bacon

January 2, 2005—"I wanted to do something more mainstream," Kevin Bacon said. "I wanted to do something where I actually got paid, you know. I was just coming off of *Mystic River* and I didn't want to do anything dark." He certainly didn't want to play a child molester who is released from prison and tries to control his obsession, lead a normal life, even have a normal relationship.

He read Nicole Kassell's screenplay for *The Woodsman,* and, "I felt the movie chose me, in a way. I couldn't say no. And when I met Nicole I found her to be young, yes, and really almost shy. But she seemed to be such a compassionate kind of person that I just felt like she could do it."

Together they made the film. Bacon plays a pedophile who precariously reenters society.

Bacon's wife, Kyra Sedgwick, plays a woman he meets at work and starts to date. It is a hazardous subject and a difficult role, the kind many actors would avoid.

"I've heard people say you have to love the characters you play," he told me during an interview at the Toronto Film Festival. "I don't feel that way. I've played a lot of people that I don't love at all. What's important to me is to try to make them real. That was especially important with this guy. I wanted him to be an everyman, the guy who has lived next door to you for twenty years and you had no idea he has this problem."

The character, named Walter, is released after twelve years in prison and moves into an apartment that is close to a grade school. Well, many apartments are. He gets a job in a lumberyard and meets a fork-lift operator named Vickie (Sedgwick), and knows she will have to learn about his past sooner or later. *The Woodsman* is the first film by Nicole Kassell, a recent graduate of the New York University film school. She saw the stage play by Stephen Fechter, optioned it, and wrote the screenplay with Fechter. It was invited to the Directors' Fortnight at Cannes 2004, where she told me, "I wanted to show that such men cannot be dismissed as simply evil, but must be understood in more complex terms, dealing with childhoods in which something usually went very wrong."

Not that the terms are ever explained in detail. "I didn't want this to be a movie where a guy talks a lot about why he is the way he is," Bacon told me. "What I wanted to do was take his sadness, shame, history, his twelve years in prison, all that kind of stuff, and put it in my belly and then find ways to let it out, through the eyes or voice or whatever."

He does, in a performance of subtle modulation, so that we watch intently, trying to read his emotions. Bacon avoids any strategy to make Walter likable, but we become sympathetic with his struggle. We hope he makes it.

"There was a sparse quality to the writing that I really responded to," Bacon said. "I felt horror and revolt and then sort of compassionate, and then I would hate myself for feeling that way. I went through this whole series of emotions, and finally I knew how I was going to play Walter. He may be saying something and simultaneously hating himself for saying it, and trying to pull back and knowing that it's wrong and knowing that it's going to ruin his life and the life of his victim and yet, something is taking over and he can't stop himself. It's like the alcoholic reaching for that drink."

It takes a certain courage for an actor to go with a character like this; I suggested to Bacon that most agents would recommend against it.

"I don't have people who would advise me against this based on some sort of 'image.' At some point you have to decide if you're going to be a personality or you're going to be an actor. If playing this kind of a role could have a negative effect on my public personality, I don't care. I'll play anything, if I think there's something compelling, or there's a director I'm dying to work with, or a part I hadn't done before, or a costar I think is great."

That philosophy has taken him from overnight stardom as a sex symbol in *Footloose* to the dark roles in *Mystic River,* by Clint Eastwood, and now in *The Woodsman.*

"A long time ago, when I was a kid, I wanted to be a pop star. Then I started taking acting classes. I moved to New York when I was a teenager, and really wanted to be a serious actor. I wanted to do off-Broadway, I wanted to do Chekhov, Shakespeare. I wanted to have a Meryl Streep kind of career.

"When *Footloose* came out, I became a pop star, but by then that's not what I wanted. I wasn't being taken seriously. I wasn't smart about the industry and the ways that you can parlay pop stardom into a serious acting career if you make the right choices.

"I spun my wheels for a while, and then I got this part in Oliver Stone's *JFK*. It's a small part, but very character-driven: gay, fascist, I mean, it was extreme. That turned things around for me. I didn't even read for it. Oliver just looked at me and said, 'Will you transform yourself for me?' And I said, 'yes.' Off-Broadway, I'd been doing that, but that doesn't mean anybody in the movie industry is going to see you that way."

Bacon said that for him, being an actor means becoming different people, wearing different masks.

"But that's a hard thing to work toward, because people want to see you do the same thing you did before, especially if it made money or they liked you in it. It's hard, really hard, to get what Tom Hanks has, where he truly can go into completely different sorts of roles. You have to fight like crazy to have that kind of career. And you have to be willing to take some risks and not do leads all the time."

On his next film, he said, he will be the director. It's called *Lover Boy,* and Kyra Sedgwick stars as a woman who wants to get pregnant, and does.

"It's sort of lighthearted in the beginning, and then you slowly find out that her obsession with this kid is strange. She believes that the two of them are going to create a utopian existence, and it's about that moment when kids start to break away and want to see the world outside. She's incapable of letting that happen. It's dark."

Bacon says he has a role in the film, and so do Sandra Bullock, Oliver Platt, Marisa Tomei, Campbell Scott, and Matt Dillon. "It's one of those movies where I could get people to come in for a couple of days here and a couple of days there, and we shot it in New York for next to nothing. I'm hoping to take it to Sundance."

Is he, like Eastwood, increasingly interested in directing?

Bacon thought about that. "You know," he said, " I think of being an actor as kind of a young man's gig. It's emasculating, in a way, people messing with you and putting makeup on you and telling you when to wake up and when to go to sleep, holding your hand to cross the street. I can do it up to a certain point and then I start to feel like a puppet.

"You can sit around and complain that Hollywood doesn't make any good movies. But you can generate your own material. So I read books. I come up with ideas. I was the producer on *The Woodsman* to help get that off the ground. Sometimes that extends itself to directing."

His wife feels the same way?

"She takes it very seriously. They say that traditionally it doesn't work when a husband and wife act together. So right before we were about to start shooting *The Woodsman,* there was a big article in the *New York Times* about why couples in movies don't work. Kyra is like, 'That's it; I'm outta here.' And I said, 'This is not a $40 million romantic comedy, where

we're trying to trade somehow on our relationship. People don't really care about us that much in terms of our marriage. It's not something that's in the gossip columns.'"

You talked about having lived most of your life on a movie set, I said. In *The Woodsman* you were directed by someone who was stepping onto a set for the first time on her first day of filming. Was she intimidated, working with veterans like you? How did you deal with that?

"By giving her respect, by collaborating, by showing up on time, and by demanding that the crew give her respect. But Nicole was amazing. There's nothing cocky about her. She's not some kid that's made a bunch of rock videos and dresses cool and thinks she knows it all. She is a very, very smart woman who is a compassionate human being and has strong vision that she had been living with for a long time. So I felt ready to put myself in her hands.

"She'd never directed a movie before," he said, and smiled, "but she'd also never directed a bad movie."

Frank Cottrell Boyce

March 20, 2005—There was this guy from Liverpool named Francis Boyce who hung out on the old Ebert Forum at Compuserve in the early 1990s. It was only belatedly that I realized that Francis was the gifted British screenwriter Frank Cottrell Boyce.

In 1990 he had already written his first screenplay, which was made into Michael Winterbottom's first film, and in the years to come he wrote four more for Winterbottom, and others for Alex Cox, Julien Temple, Anand Tucker, and Danny Boyle. He was working with a group of cutting-edge British filmmakers, and becoming arguably the most original and versatile screenwriter in the land. Who else could show the range represented by *Butterfly Kiss, Welcome to Saravejo, Hilary and Jackie, The Claim,* and *24 Hour Party People*?

Perhaps you haven't heard of those movies, except *Hilary and Jackie.* But I gave them an average review of 3.62 stars, if you don't count the two-star review for *Sarajevo* ("a film you hated," Boyce reminds me). Now Boyce and Danny Boyle *(Trainspotting, 28 Days Later)* have worked together for the first time on an extraordinary new film named *Millions,* which I rated at four stars, bringing his non-Sarajevo average up to 3.7 stars. It is a magical film, and what is perhaps more amazing, coming from Boyle and Boyce, is that it's a family film.

I am obsessing about the average star rating because that's the kind of discussion we had back in the old Compuserve days. So after I saw *Millions* and loved it, I thought it would be appropriate to interview Boyce via e-mail.

Roger Ebert: What led a professional to an Internet forum?

Frank Cottrell Boyce: Well, I don't regard myself as a professional. I think I'm more like a fan who's too enthusiastic to confine himself to spectating. In *24 Hour Party People* there's a man called John the Postman who got so excited during every gig that he jumped onstage and sang "Louie Louie." That's me. Do you know that I help run a small independent cinema? I do popcorn duty and stand at the back to keep things in good order. I'm famous for stopping a screening of *The Others* on the grounds that the audience were making too much noise. I sent them all home!

RE: You've worked with Michael Winterbottom right from the beginning, with *Forget About Me* (1990), when he was twenty-nine.

FCB: Michael and I are contemporaries. We met when he was working for a London television broadcaster as a trainee editor. In order to become a proper editor you had to wait for the present editor to die. I'm not sure whether the training included killing techniques or not. Anyway, he was frustrated. And I was working on a script about the dangers of smoking, so I was even more frustrated. We met in the canteen and plotted our escape route. It involved me writing a spec script for Michael to shoot. It never got made, but it was good enough to get us some meetings.

RE: *Millions* is a complete departure in subject and tone for Danny Boyle. How did you come together on the project?

FCB: I wrote it way back—straight after *Welcome to Sarajevo* (a film you hated!), but people were understandably nervous about making a family film like *Millions.* If you make *24 Hour Party People,* you're competing with Mike Leigh or Ken Loach. But if you make a family film you're supposedly competing with Pixar, for which you need more firepower. So

no one was interested until Danny came along. I don't know what made him want to do it. I didn't ask, in case he started to question it himself. It did feel like winning the lottery the day he said, "This is a great script," even though he did go on to say, "Well, the first thirty pages are great anyway." It might seem like a departure, but to me it's the destination I've been trying to get to for a long time.

RE: In the film, your young hero has perfectly reasonable conversations with several saints and is an expert on their lives and histories. How did the saints make their way into a movie about two small boys who find the loot from a train robbery?

FCB: You already know the answer and you're being coy! I read an interview that you did with Martin Scorsese in which Scorsese said he'd been influenced by a book called *The Six O'Clock Saints,* about the lives of the saints.

People think of saints as vaguely nice and virtuous, but in fact, they were often difficult, mad, driven by a different energy. Buñuel made a film about "Simon of the Desert," who avoided temptation by living on top of a marble column. Even St. Francis—who was one of the two or three greatest human beings ever to walk the Earth—could be a bit weird.

Your interview with Scorsese sent me scuttling back to a dictionary of saints I'd had as a child, and opening it up was like opening my own mysterious bag of cash—endless mad, gigantic stories. Narrative cash. The thing about the saints is that for nearly 2,000 years they were the popular culture. Those gory, erotic statues you see in old churches are like early cinema, aren't they?

RE: The films you've done with Winterbottom are so various in subject matter. Comment, please, on these titles:

Butterfly Kiss (1995), with its amazing Amanda Plummer performance as a disturbed drifter driven by self-destruction and violence.

FCB: I still love this film, though I haven't watched it since then. It was written and made very quickly, and I still don't really understand where it came from.

Welcome to Sarajevo (1997), a rough-edged docudrama about reporters in the war zone.

FCB: You hated this, but I was very happy making it. It was made with great spirit.

Michael insisted on shooting it in Sarajevo in the face of incredible difficulties. It was a Herzogian thing to do. The script was rough and ready and not that well informed because we wanted to make it quickly.

Michael has since made *In This World* with the same kind of heroic lack of finesse. I think that's his best film. My sister's ex-boyfriend was a journalist who was killed in Sarajevo, and the news coverage of the war was so slight that we didn't know he was dead for about a year.

The Claim (2000), about a man who sells his wife and daughter for a claim to a gold mine.

FCB: Ohhhhmygod. What might have been. Unlike the other two, we worked for years on the script of this. Obviously, it was a higher budget. I had such ambitions for it, but I completely lost control during the development process. It's so nearly good.

Pathe were obsessed with the idea that we would lose sympathy for the hero if he sold his wife at the beginning, which is the whole point of the story and which is where the Thomas Hardy novel starts. So they tried to sneak his terrible crime in halfway through in a flashback. As a result the film is fuzzy and unfocused, and dare I say it, pointless. Michael did amazing things in it—the house moving, the landscape, the town—but without the story, it was just a magic lantern show. I fought for it for a while and then gave up.

24 Hour Party People (2002), about Tony Wilson, a man who is transformed by a Sex Pistols concert and becomes a one-man recording and club industry who transforms the British music scene.

FCB: I utterly love this film. It's a hymn to Manchester, and to Tony Wilson, who is reviled and laughed at in Manchester for being pretentious and pompous. I think in these times being pretentious is sort of heroic, and I hope the film makes that case for him. His career seems to have had a lift from it.

I was amazed that anyone who lived outside the northwest of England could begin to understand it. It was particularly weird watching it in Cannes with a stoned and bewildered Tony on one side and some bejeweled and well-groomed Riviera bourgeois on the other (they didn't really get it). I've met people in Brazil and Germany and Croatia who love this film, and that always makes me go gooey about

the generosity of the human heart—that people would care about something so parochial.

Also, people generally believe that it was largely improvised, which it wasn't at all (you try and get Steve Coogan to improvise about Boethius or DNA!). But I do think that's the greatest compliment a script could have. I remember the first time I saw *Spinal Tap* I didn't twig that they weren't a real band! I wasn't sure you were supposed to be laughing.

Code 46 (2003), about a future world in which personal freedom and relationships are governed by genetic information.

FCB: Ohhh. Don't let's go there. By the way, four of the above films contain sequences shot in Formby Woods—a pinewoods on the beach near my house. *Hilary and Jackie* opens on the same beach. I do try to bring investment into my poor benighted hometown.

Tristam Shandy, based on the classic Sterne novel, which, being the autobiography of a man who begins before he was born and never quite gets to his birth, seems to have anticipated the recent screenwriting adventures of Charlie Kaufman.

FCB: This was the first film idea I ever pitched to Michael. It's now become a film about making a film, which sounds a bit Kaufmanny but it's actually more like Truffaut's *Day for Night*, I think—quite a warm film about the fun of the film set. Steve Coogan, who is always brilliant, stars again. The book is about the birth of a baby, and about how all your hopes for the baby are dashed but somehow it doesn't matter. That seems very human and straightforward and true to me. At least true of *some* of my children anyway.

RE: You also wrote Anand Tucker's *Hilary and Jackie* (1998), the story of cellist Jacqueline du Pre, her sister, and her disordered life. Both Emily Watson and Rachel Griffiths won Oscar nominations; were you surprised that this risky, intimate story won the attention of the Academy?

FCB: Flabbergasted. Although I thought Emily's performance was amazing—more like necromancy than acting. We'd seen her in *Breaking the Waves*, and we took her out and told her the story. We didn't have a script, and we said we wouldn't write one unless she said yes because there was no point as she was the only one who could play it. I didn't appreciate at the time how unusual it was for a distinguished actress (she got a nomination for *Breaking the Waves* too) to respond to a pitch like that. She has a season ticket for the Arsenal Football Club and so does Anand, so maybe football played its part.

RE: You've worked for fifteen years at the cutting edge of the British film industry, which is famously described as an invalid. Despite its precarious health, despite living outside Liverpool, you work with great success at projects of your own choosing. Is that a miracle to equal what your saints provide in *Millions*?

FCB: I think I've been very, very lucky in that I've never had an actual hit. If you have a hit, then anything you do after it has to be a hit too; otherwise it's a failure. I've never done anything that I had to live up to!

RE: You were the TV critic for the magazine *Living Marxism*. In *Millions*, your young hero Damian distributes handfuls of cash, possibly illustrating Marx's *From each according to his abilities, to each according to his needs.* Comment?

FCB: Well, I think *24 Hour Party People* was also a film about reckless generosity. Maybe it comes from working in the film industry where money is like an actual physical force acting on you all the time—like gravity or something. Reckless generosity—that's my philosophy of life. That's what unites Tony Wilson and St. Francis.

RE: Your *Saint-Ex*, about Antoine de Saint-Exupéry, stars another kind of saint, who wrote about a Little Prince who was somewhat saintly. Am I reaching here? The two boys in *Saint-Ex* are your sons?

FCB: Yes, they are! And very cute they looked too. I wouldn't normally let my kids near the set, but it was a low-budget film and the restrictions on children's hours were putting weeks on the shoot, so I used my own kids and worked them half to death. Poor Aidan—who was about five at the time—had to fall backward off a gantry into my arms at one point. He did it about five times and the fifth time, when I looked down he was asleep. They put me in a cab back to Euston, and I got on the train and made it all the way back to Liverpool without him waking up. I turned up at the door and he was still in his costume.

RE: How do you function as a successful screenwriter with six children in the house?

FCB: Blimey. Well, I'm not sure that I'm that successful! I think I've probably let others do all the moving and shaking for me. Living far away from London may have something to do with it. People hesitate about calling you down to meetings, so you never get sacked. Maybe people don't want to sack someone who's got so many mouths to feed! By the way, it's now seven children, not six. I'm working on an adaptation of *The Odyssey* (!) at the moment, and my eight-year-old is massively excited and contributes hugely to it. They're just particularly wonderful children, I suppose.

RE: Just like the kids in *Millions*.

Neve Campbell

Toronto, Canada, September 19, 2004—*When Will I Be Loved* is about a young woman who accepts a million dollars from a rich man who wants to have sex with her. What the man doesn't know is that she's rich too.

"Had she been poor this would have been a completely different film," Neve Campbell was telling me. "It would have been about the money. We've seen that in a lot of films. But for her it's not about the money, so it becomes this psychological game."

She plays the woman, named Vera, in a movie that is deceptive, intriguing, erotic, and intelligent; it gives Campbell scenes where her character responds in the moment, improvising poetic justice for one man who wants to sell her and another who wants to buy her. This film and Robert Altman's *The Company* are breakthrough roles for Campbell, moving her out of the *Scream*-queen category and allowing her to grow in unconventional roles. She makes intelligence sexy.

The movie's psychological game involves three characters trying to con one another. Fred Weller plays Ford, a motormouth street kid, brilliant in a sleazy way, who is the girl's lover. Neve Campbell's Vera enjoys the sex with him, responds to the excitement of his outlaw personality, even really likes him—until she realizes that he not only wants to sell her to an Italian billionaire, but cheat her on the payoff. Dominic Chianese plays the rich count, whom Ford is trying to con. The count sees Ford with Vera and asks Ford to arrange a meeting.

The film was written and directed by James Toback, a director who operates at the intersection of sex, money, crime, and verbal persuasion. His characters often think they can enforce their will through the sheer weight and rush of words. That's true of Toback too; the late *Spy* magazine once ran a four-page foldout charting his attempts to pick up a dozen Manhattan women, and the lines he used, the names he dropped, the compliments he paid, and the strategies he employed. He is not shy about this aspect of his character, as his film *The Pick-Up Artist* acknowledged.

When Will I Be Loved operates in an entirely different arena, however. It's the best film yet by Toback, who was the screenwriter of *Bugsy,* a movie about a man who essentially talked Las Vegas into existence. The film centers on an extraordinary scene in which Campbell and Chianese negotiate how much will be paid, how it will be paid, and what it will be paid for. This is not a crass scene. Vera and the count recognize each other as intelligent sophisticates, and as they negotiate for her body, they both take pleasure in the sheer audacity of what they are doing, and the verbal elegance with which they're doing it.

"He's not just a chump," I said to Campbell. This was at the Toronto Film Festival.

"Right," she said. "He has self-respect and intelligence."

"So," I said, "it's not just the obvious angle where you would be twisting him . . ."

". . . around my finger . . ."

". . . sexually and so forth . . ."

"That's why I loved it. Neither one is a victim. They're two equals. The count is excited to find that the woman challenges him from a position of strength."

"It must have been amazing when you read the script," I said.

"Well, there were only thirty-five pages of the script originally," Campbell said. "A lot of it was improvised. And Jim was writing in the evenings and bringing it to us in the morning. When he originally called me there was the scene with Dominic and there was the scene with Fred Weller when he was trying to manipulate me. But I was really impressed by those pages. It's a rare thing to find someone in Hollywood who is able to have that knowledge of human nature and put it on paper without unnecessary words. I think he's incredibly daring, and explores things to an extreme that most directors aren't willing to go to. That first day we were supposed to meet for an hour; we met for twelve hours."

I believed that, because Toback says he wrote the film for Campbell because he was obsessed with her. Well, of course he was. He's obsessed as a way of life, and the movie opens with a scene where he plays a professor interviewing Vera for a job as his assistant. As they walk near the campus, she talks to a couple of guys and he suggests that she is thinking of picking them up. In response, she suggests that the whole interview was a device to get her to sleep with him. This not only establishes her character's negotiating abilities before she meets the count, but also, I suspect, gives us an insight into their twelve-hour meeting.

I talked to Toback right after talking to Campbell. I'd been offered the chance to talk to them together, but no, I've interviewed Toback many times over the years, and if there's one thing I've noticed, it's that nobody else gets to talk. Since he is brilliant, funny, and a little mad, this is not a problem, unless you want to hear what the other person has to say.

Toback gave me an example of his improvisational method. There is an early scene where Vera and a girlfriend spontaneously make love. It's not that they're lesbians so much as that they're sexual beings able to talk themselves into unexpected developments.

"When it came time to shoot that scene," he said, "I told them to go into another room: 'Take as long as you want. When you're ready to shoot the scene come out, we'll shoot it.' They came out, and I didn't even want to hear what they were going to do. They just planted themselves by the window and we shot the scene. And if you'd given me ten weeks to come up with a list of thirty different scenes, I wouldn't have been able to come up with one as good. And they would never have been able to do it as well because on some level, even though Neve and I had incredible harmony, she and certainly the other girl would have been asking, 'Exactly why did he feel it was necessary to tell us what he wanted, instead of preferring to see what we wanted to do?' And it never would have been the same thing."

Improvisation sometimes leads Toback's films into meandering byways. *When Will I Be Loved* is notable for the clockwork precision of the crucial scenes, in which Vera decides from moment to moment what she will do and how she will do it, and then, when there is an unexpected development, is able to turn on a dime and improvise a radical development that neatly turns the tables.

"A lot of people are saying she's a femme fatale or a black widow," Campbell said, "but I think she's quite the opposite in a lot of ways. She's not a woman who decides to take revenge, plots it out, and accomplishes it. She's a woman who is fascinated by human beings, fascinated by what makes them tick, fascinated by power, fascinated by how far people will go with their darkness to get what they want. She's testing herself and she's testing the others. And it's moment to moment and she's improvising every step of the way."

"That's what I love about it," I said. "Usually when you see a con movie, at the end you wonder how they could have planned it all in advance and counted on everything happening according to schedule."

"Yeah," she said. "She doesn't have a plan at the beginning and you can see it being created as she goes along."

Campbell, who is still only thirty, was born in Guelph, Ontario, and trained with the Royal Ballet of Canada before switching to acting at twenty with the TV series *Party of Five.* She had the good luck to play the victim in *Scream* (1996), an enormous box office hit that led, as such things do, to *Scream 2* (1997), and *Scream 3* (2000). But she was electrifying in the little-seen *Wild Things* (1998), a sexually charged thriller, and in the overlooked *Panic* (2000) she played a lesbian who becomes the confidant of a Mafia hit man (William H. Macy) after they meet in the waiting room of their shrink.

She had a personal triumph in Robert Altman's *The Company* (2003), playing a member of the Joffrey Ballet of Chicago in a film she cowrote and coproduced. And now *When Will I Be Loved* is a calling card for roles of great emotional complexity.

"It's been funny," she said, "because people think I *chose* to be a horror film actress. *Scream* was the first movie I got as lead, so that's what I did, and it ended up becoming huge. But that was not the genre I chose. I don't watch horror movies. I used to be really concerned about what the industry would think of me. When you first start out you have a lot of agents and managers and publicists giving you their opinion of what the next step should be. At some point I realized there's no controlling it, that I should just go with my instincts. I think I have good instincts, and so I'm finding people and scripts that I'll be challenged by, where I feel I can grow as an actress."

"Which you certainly did on *Company.*"

"I loved Robert Altman. I'm so passionate about that man, and with James and Robert, their egos don't get in the way of the art. There are so many directors in Hollywood who want to think it was all their idea. They don't invite their artists to bring their art to the table. But Robert and James want you to argue with them and suggest the new concepts and ideas. Altman creates worlds, you know. Robert to me is more a choreographer than a film director. He told me, 'I'd rather direct eighty people than three,' because eighty people give him more room to breathe."

I'd read that Campbell insisted on a clause in all her contracts that specified no nude scenes. That clause must have been missing from the Toback contract.

"Yeah," she said, "I've had issues with nudity when I feel that the scenes have nothing to do with the film itself—when it's solely for box office draw or for the titillation of the audience. But in this film, the power of this woman's sexuality is what the story's about, in a way. So it wouldn't make sense to not see her in that way."

Campbell smiled. "You know, I've had a lot of men say she's twisted and she's really dark. They don't mention the fact that she was being manipulated by these terrible people. I've had a lot of women say they felt sorry for her and were grateful for the outcome."

"Well," I said, "she's responding to the fact that the man she loves is willing to sell her, and this other man wants to buy her, and that's how they both think of her."

"Absolutely," she said. "And the fact that a million dollars is not that important to the count is even more insulting."

"In his mind," I said, "he's getting you for a cheap price."

"Or he thinks he is," she said.

Clint Eastwood

December 19, 2004—"I'm going to make the movie regardless of whether you want to or not," Clint Eastwood told the suits at Warner Bros. when they balked at financing *Million Dollar Baby*. They'd read the screenplay, Eastwood recalls, and they said, "We don't think boxing movies are very popular right now." You can imagine Eastwood's eyes narrowing as he responded, "This to me is not a boxing movie. It's about hopes and dreams, and a love story."

His agent shopped the project in three or four places, Eastwood told me. "They all passed. Then Tom Rosenberg in Chicago, Lake Shore Entertainment, called up and said he was bullish on the film; he wanted to finance half of it, and take the foreign rights. I didn't know Tom that well, but he understood the film."

With half the money on board, Eastwood said, "Warners finally called up and said, 'You've been here a long time, so we'll finance the other half.'"

He has been there a long time. Twenty-five years, on and off, making millions for the studio as a star and director. "I can't promise you you'll make a zillion dollars, like on one of your sequels or remakes," Eastwood told them, "but if everything goes well, I think it'll be a film you'll be proud to have your name on."

Well, it's that, all right. In a season of enormous publicity campaigns, *Million Dollar Baby* was almost a stealth opening. It was screened for critics. They liked it so much, "people are leaving the screenings stunned," wrote industry pundit David Poland. The film took on a life of its own, shouldering its way into the front of the Oscar ranks just on word

of mouth. It opened in New York, Chicago, and Los Angeles.

Eastwood said he took a low-key approach in preparing the movie. "I just wanted to make it. I don't want publicists hanging about. We stayed under the radar. With all the big $150, $200 million films out there, they thought this film was at a different importance level. I had about $25 million to make it with. They had their *Alexanders* and *Polar Expresses* they were working on, and I figured my movie was going to have to live or die on its own terms.

"So, we went and made it, they didn't know anything about it, and after we showed it to them," Eastwood recalled, "they said, 'Jesus, it's not too bad.' Some people in the organization started getting enthusiastic. Eddie Feldman, the distribution guy, says, 'How shall we open it?' 'Why don't we just put it out sometime after Thanksgiving,' I said. He said we had to mount a campaign. 'No mounting a campaign, no mounting anything,' I said. 'Just see where it goes.'"

Eastwood was speaking by phone from Los Angeles, where, at seventy-four and fresh from last year's success with *Mystic River*, he's at the top of his game.

If boxing movies weren't supposed to be popular, I asked, what were? Sword-and-sandal movies?

"I asked the same question, believe me. Bill Goldman, the writer, was right when he said, 'Nobody knows nothin'.' At the major studios you see people wanting to remake a TV series, wanting to make a sequel. I guess I've done it in my career, three different sets of sequels, but I'm too old for that now. I kind of try to advocate that maybe they should just concentrate on writers and original scripts and go back like the old days and have writers in the building.

"I made this movie for the story and the relationships. No computer special effects, nothing to slow things down. We shot it in thirty-nine days, the same as *Mystic River*. When I look back at the pictures I grew up on, like *The Grapes of Wrath*, it was made in thirty-nine days. Everybody accuses me of moving fast when I direct a picture. I don't move fast, but I just keep moving. I come to work ready to make films. I love it. I've been doing it a long time, and every time I think I'll quit, something good comes along."

Vincent Gallo

August 29, 2004—Vincent Gallo and I have a history. In May 2003, I called his *The Brown Bunny* the worst film in the history of the Cannes Film Festival. Then he put a hex on me to give me colon cancer. Now we're about to meet for the first time.

It was a little tense in the Lake Street Screening Room, following the screening of the reedited, shorter version of *The Brown Bunny*. I heard Gallo was in the elevator. I heard he was in the hallway. I heard he was around the corner. Then there he was. The atmosphere lightened after he explained he had never wished colon cancer on me in the first place. He was misquoted. He actually specified prostate cancer.

"You know how that happened?" he asked. "I have prostatitis. I go to this guy doctor in California. He doesn't want to put me on antibiotics or whatever. But I get these things called a prostate massage."

"Are you taking flaxseed?" I asked him.

"I know all my nutritional things," he said. "I had been battling this prostatitis and a reporter who I didn't know said, 'I'm doing a story on Cannes and I want to know if you read what Roger Ebert said about your film.' I said, yeah, I read all about it. 'Well, do you have any comment?' And I said something like, 'Tell him I curse his prostate.' I said it in a joking way. And she converted it into a curse on your colon. At that point, I had become the captain of black magic."

"I don't believe in hexes," I said. "Besides, if I can't take it, I shouldn't dish it out."

"Right."

"Maybe by saying you made the worst film in Cannes history, I was asking for it."

"But I thought your response was funny when you responded with the colonoscopy line."

That was when I said the film of my colonoscopy was more entertaining than *The Brown Bunny.*

"I felt we were now on a humorous level," he said, "so I apologized. To tell you the weirdest story, I started getting these letters from cultist people criticizing me for going back on what they thought was like a genius thing I did. There was this guy in L.A. who approached me in a club and he was like, 'We're really disappointed in you.' And I asked why. And he said, 'Because we heard that you removed the curse from Roger Ebert.' I took one look at him and I thought, well, I did the right thing."

"Anyway, your aim was bad," I said, "because I had salivary cancer."

We had not yet actually discussed the Worst Film in the History of the Cannes Film Festival, so I broke the ice: "I've got to tell you, it's a different film now. I have to start over in the process of reviewing it because it's not the film I saw at Cannes. I think it's a better film."

The Brown Bunny involves several days in the life of a motorcycle racer named Bud Clay, who loses a race and drives his van cross-country while bugs collect on the windshield and he has sad, elusive encounters with lonely women. At the end of his odyssey, he seeks out his great former love, Daisy (Chloe Sevigny), and, like Gatsby, discovers that the light is out at the end of Daisy's pier.

"Did you know the lead-up to Cannes?" Gallo asked. "Did you know why it was shown at Cannes? Did you know what state it was in?"

I said I'd heard he let it be shown even though he wasn't finished with it.

That was the tip of the iceberg. Gallo's explanation of the pre-Cannes adventures of *The Brown Bunny* ran to 1,487 words (I know because I transcribed the interview). The highlights include:

—"I got involved in the film in a sacrificial way, beyond my normal self-abuse—like not eating, not sleeping, freaking out about unimportant things. Like, I had to use these Mitchell lenses, these Bausch & Lomb lenses, but I had to have them converted and it took a year. I was bringing all my good and bad habits into this project."

—"I had to postpone the racing sequences because I couldn't train in time and I was having problems with the motorcycles and I wasn't riding well."

—"Chloe had to shift her schedule a month and a half and I wanted to film her scene first because I wanted to sense the vibe of that scene and play off that vibe for the rest of the film. So the postponements cost me three months."

—"Curtis Clayton, who edited *Buffalo '66* with me, calls me every day—'It's the greatest, you've covered everything, the film looks great.' I just wanted him to look at the footage, tell me if anything was scratched or not usable, and then we would edit together. I finish shooting and he works one day with me, and he makes an odd face and says, 'You know, I've told you if I ever get my film financed I might not be able to finish this film.' I'm like, oh yeah, no problem, we should be done anyway. He says, 'Well, Ed Pressman called me while you were at lunch and said my film is green-lit.'"

"Curtis is a beautiful person with a lot of integrity, but he has a sort of smugness. He went, 'So I can work ten more days with you if you want, but that's it.' I said, 'Listen, if you felt you were even coming close, you should have brought me in on that. You cost me $150 grand just to look at my footage.' He goes, 'Well, I have the footage all arranged.'

"I said, 'You don't know the geography of America; I can't go by your things; I'm just gonna wipe the discs clean and I'll reload myself and I'll have it batch-digitized and I'll arrange everything in my way because I don't know if you had a foolproof system where you batch-digitized every frame of the film; you made so many mistakes in *Buffalo '66*—not intentional, but those things happen. I'm a fanatic and I wanna be sure that I have every frame of my picture.'

"And we had a little tension, but he's not the kind of person you really have ordinary tension with so he just sort of left in a smug way. And I was freaked out because I could control everything else but I needed Curtis not even so much for his talent but for his voice of reason, his maturity, and his ability to keep me balanced, you know, allowing me to have a point of view and to take radical chances but with balance, you know.

"He leaves and for about two weeks I don't do anything; I'm nervous, very nervous. And I find an assistant who would be one of at least ten assistants, each of them leaving on a bad note because I was extremely unpleasant to work with."

What with one thing and another, the film seemed destined to be finished in September 2003. But then Thierry Fremaux, the artistic director of the Cannes Film Festival, asked to see it.

"I hadn't even cut the motel scene at this point, so not only is the film in rough cut, I haven't even got to the Chloe scene."

The Chloe scene. That would be the scene of graphic oral sex, which contrasts with the earlier scenes in the way pornography might contrast with a travelogue.

"I showed Thierry everything up until the motel scene; he asks if I will be able to finish the film in time for the festival. I say I don't know. I negotiate with the Japanese financiers that I'll rough through the motel scene—which will be good for me, because I've been stuck on it—and I'll make some fake ending because I was supposed to shoot the ending in April, which should have a motorcycle crash at the end."

Where you die?

"Yeah, where I die. A deliberate suicide. Not thinking clearly if I would use it because I had the same dilemma in *Buffalo '66*. I always write the film with the suicide and then I find a way out of it. The guy was gonna have a negative fantasy for a second of the van crashing. There were some shots of bunnies, there was the shot of him on the side of the road. I sort of clipped it together with the song."

The result was one of the most disastrous screenings in Cannes history. I refer to the press screening; at the public screening, reaction was more evenly divided between applause and boos, but the press hated the film. The impression got around that I led the boos, perhaps because the hex on my colon drew untoward attention toward me, but the British trade magazine *Screen International,* which convenes a panel of critics to score each entry, reported that *The Brown Bunny* got the lowest score in the history of its ratings.

Did I sing "Raindrops Keep Fallin' on My Head" at one point? To my shame, I did, but softly and briefly, before my wife dug her elbow into my side. By that point the screening was out of control anyway, with audience members hooting, whistling, and honking at the screen.

As it turns out, the French director Gaspar Noe was seated near me.

"He's not a great pal," Gallo said, "but I do

know him, and he sort of twerks me on all the time. He loves to wind me up. And he came out of the screening and left like six messages on my voice mail. And he pinned it all on you, because he was sitting close to you and he presented it to me that you were orchestrating..."

But there were 3,000 seats in that theater, I said. It got pretty demonstrative.

"Well," said Gallo, "because you asked and it needs to be answered clearly: Did I feel the film was finished at Cannes? No, of course not."

The next day at a press conference, I said, there was the impression you apologized for the film.

"*Screen International* falsely said I apologized for the film. What I said was this: Film has a purpose. It's not art. Real art is an esoteric thing done by somebody without purpose in mind. I've done that in my life and I'm not doing that making movies. I'm an entertainer. I love all movies. I don't divide them up into art films, independent films. *The Brown Bunny* was my idea of what a good movie would be.

"I'm not a marginal person. I don't pretend to be a cult figure. I'm just making a movie and I think the film is beautiful and I think, wow, everybody's gonna see how beautiful it is and when they don't agree with me, then in a sense I failed. I didn't fail myself because I made what I think is beautiful and I stand behind thinking that it's beautiful. I've only failed in this commercial way because I haven't entertained the crowd. If people don't like my movie, then I'm sorry they didn't like my movie. But I wasn't apologizing for it."

This new version, I said, is a lot shorter and in my opinion a lot better. It has a rhythm and tone that the Cannes version lacked.

"Seeing my film for the first time at Cannes," he said, "I was able to see what was wrong. It was clear that the Colorado and Utah piece was too long. There was also a dissolve where the film turned black for a minute. That was a mistake in the lab. Now if that mistake happened in a hundred other movies at Cannes, the audience would have been prepared to look past it. But because the film was so extreme and so untightened at that time, it really stood out."

What did you take out?

"What changed was the opening sequence. I shortened the race, which was a good four and a half minutes longer. The whole film at Cannes was exactly twenty-six minutes longer. The credits were three and a half minutes longer at the end, and one minute longer in the beginning. So that's about nine, ten minutes there. So there's sixteen more minutes of changes, and here's where the biggest chunk came. When he comes out of the Kansas motel, he does not wash the car, he does not change his sweater, and he does not go on that sequence through Colorado and Utah. Eight minutes and thirty seconds came out of that driving sequence.

"The other cuts were in the motel scene.... I rambled on maybe another two or three minutes. And those road shots at the end were about another minute leading up to the closing sequence, and then I cut out the end, which was three and a half or four minutes. That's what I cut. There's no tightening or tweaking anywhere else."

Now about the motel scene. That's where the hero imagines a reunion with his onetime lover and she performs oral sex in a graphic scene that gained even greater notoriety after a soft-focus shot of it appeared on a Sunset Strip billboard for three or four days before it was abruptly removed.

"I wanted to show what people do every day all over the world," Gallo said. "In sexualized behavior, your mind fills up with the intimacy of sexual thoughts, but in my character it stays locked in resentment, fear, anger, guilt. When you juxtapose that against images you're used to seeing for the purpose of enhancing pleasure, I felt it could create a disturbing effect. It's metaphysical. You're seeing how he visualizes his own sexuality.

"Never in my life have I had sexual or violent images as components in any of my work and this was not the inspiration of a provocateur; that was not the goal. Some people respond to it deeply in the way that it was intended."

I know what he means. But to explain why the scene works that way, you have to know something it would be unfair to reveal at this point—something about how the scene enters the realm of the character's disturbed mind.

We talked a lot longer. Gallo grew confessional: "When I modeled for some ads, people started saying, oh, you've done modeling. I mean, I know what I look like. My mother knows what I look like, and when you call a person like me a model, I'm aware of people sort of snickering at that comment, so it embarrasses me."

Apart from the news that he is a Republican, that was the most astonishing revelation he made: He doesn't like the way he looks. I disagree; I find him a striking screen presence. His comment provided me with an insight into his character in *The Brown Bunny*, a lonely, solitary wanderer whose life traverses a great emptiness punctuated by unsuccessful, incomplete, or imaginary respites with women.

That's related to something else he said:

"The inspiration for the film was, I was at a discotheque once and I noticed a pretty gal, but it was during a period in my life where I could never talk to a girl that I thought was smart or pretty or interesting in any way. I would just stare at them. And I stared at her and at 11 P.M. she was having fun, she was drinking a little. Three in the morning she was hammered. She was on the floor and the guys in the room were sort of moving around her. They noticed this sort of broken-winged bird or wounded animal. They were like hyena. It was one of the ugliest things I've ever seen. I saw them eventually leave with her. And it upset me conceptually. I felt the ugliness of mankind's basic nature can be avoided. That's what *The Brown Bunny* is about."

Liam Neeson

November 14, 2004—Alfred Kinsey has been dead for forty-eight years, and he still makes people angry. Even before it opened, *Kinsey*, a movie inspired by the life of the sex researcher, inspired an AP story about "indignant conservative groups" who think it is propaganda for the sexual revolution.

Kinsey is partly responsible for her generation "being forced to deal face-to-face with the devastating consequences of sexually transmitted diseases, pornography, and abortion," Brandi Swindell, head of Generation Life, told the wire service. And here is Robert Knight, director of Concerned Women of America's Culture and Family Institute: "Instead of being lionized, Kinsey's proper place

is with Nazi Dr. Josef Mengele or your average Hollywood horror flick mad scientist."

Strong words about a man who never advocated anything, and specialized in research that simply attempted to discover what people actually do in their sex lives. Before Kinsey, it was generally believed that hardly anyone was homosexual, that masturbation could cause madness, that American married couples seldom strayed from the missionary position, and that people rarely had sex before or outside of marriage. Kinsey found that most people masturbated, that a third of men reported at least one homosexual experience, and that oral sex and sex outside marriage were commonplace.

Those who don't want to believe those findings, or think they shouldn't have been revealed even if true, find Kinsey's statistics devastating, and blame them on Kinsey, as if he made them up.

"The forces of prudery come back in waves every other generation or so," Liam Neeson thinks. He plays Kinsey in the movie. "In Kinsey's time, America was confused sexually, and it's still confused. We have a situation where millions of people bemoan the fact that a wonderful show like *Sex and the City* goes off the air; it's about four women talking about sex in a very indelicate fashion, to put it very mildly. And yet images of two gays kissing after they get married provoke outrage."

Neeson's performance, which seems likely to win an Oscar nomination, shows Kinsey as a scientist obsessed by his work. Before he began cataloging human sexual behavior, he collected and studied a million gall wasps, and in both cases he observed, recorded, and reported what he found. Nobody got mad about the wasps.

"He had an extraordinary manner when he conducted interviews," Neeson told me. This was one night when we had dinner after he introduced *Kinsey* at the Chicago Film Festival. "He devised his questions over two or three years, and it took his research assistants a year to learn them; there was a minimum of 288 questions and a maximum of 800, and they had to memorize them all. I gather he could be brusque and cold, but in his interviews he exuded warmth, and he was absolutely nonjudgmental when asking people the most personal questions about sexuality. Apparently people came out of the room feeling charged in some way, having gone through some extraordinary spiritual process by being honest about themselves. Kinsey did nearly 8,000 interviews, and the whole team did 18,000 over a period of eighteen or twenty years."

For Neeson, *Kinsey* was a chance to play another character like his famous Michael Collins or Oskar Schindler: "I love people with so much energy and commitment that sleep gets in the way of their destiny."

The fascinating thing about Kinsey, he said, was that "he asked people the most intimate, probing questions without any sense he might be offending or even bothering them. That actually allowed some of his subjects to relax, because he seemed so dispassionate."

He was bull-headed, Neeson said, and he upset people: "They were looking for a way to shut him down. The McCarthy era was starting, and after they finished with the Communists of course they went for Kinsey."

In the movie, Kinsey is so focused as to seem monomaniacal. He got into trouble with congressional critics and lost his funding from the Rockefeller Foundation because he bluntly said what he believed without the slightest regard for public relations.

"Kinsey was intent on separating science from morality," Bill Condon told me during the same dinner. He wrote and directed the picture, his first since directing *Gods and Monsters* and writing *Chicago.* "You have to do that when you study sex, because it's so connected to religion, culture, and people's idea of morality. If you look around today, whether it's sex education or the stem cell debate, people are trying to impose an agenda on something that should be entirely scientific."

Condon said he gets unhappy when people say that Kinsey "believed" or "thought" something: "He drew his conclusions from actual research. It wasn't an opinion."

Although Kinsey's critics blame him for changes in the sexual climate, "he would have been horrified by the gay movement or the women's movement. These were movements that in some ways he created, but he didn't believe in people defining themselves simply by sexual activity."

He felt sexual definitions were "pretty fluid,

anyway," Condon said, with most people falling somewhere along Kinsey's famous 0-to-6 graph from gay to straight.

The AP story quotes Tom Neven of Focus on the Family, a Colorado ministry: "To say that (the movie) is rank propaganda for the sexual revolution and the homosexual agenda would be beyond stating the obvious."

Condon's opinion: "I think it's nice to remind people that he was first and foremost a scientist. He's become such a hot-button figure and a demon for some. Certain groups think if they can somehow discredit the man, the science will be discredited, and therefore everything that's come as a result of that science will be undone. That's a fool's errand."

Gwyneth Paltrow and Jude Law

September 12, 2004—So this guy named Kerry Conran goes into his garage and sits down at his Macintosh and creates six minutes of images to show what he's thinking about, and the next thing you know he's directing a movie starring Gwyneth Paltrow, Jude Law, and Angelina Jolie. He must have been a good salesman.

"He's a terrible salesman," Gwyneth Paltrow said. "He's shy and quiet."

"We didn't meet him for nearly a month," Jude Law said. "Jon Avnet, who was producing the project, was the salesman."

It must have been an amazing six minutes, I said.

"The six minutes looked so extraordinary," Paltrow said, "that you just thought, if I'm ever going to do an action adventure, this is it. It's unique. There's nothing rehashed about it, nothing formulaic. And like, wow, I can be a part of something that's actually new and redefining the genre."

And she could, and she was, and it did. *Sky Captain and the World of Tomorrow* is a movie of astonishing skill and heedless joy. And it is a seamless marriage between human actors and computer-generated images. Paltrow and Law and the other cast members acted their more sensational scenes in front of blue screens, which were later replaced with CGI. They couldn't see the robots or the skyscrapers or the airplanes or the fearsome weapons of mass destruction. They had to imagine them.

"There were days," Paltrow said, "when we were surrounded by the blue screen. Nothing was real. There were no props and no sets, and Jude was saying, 'The robots!' and we were looking at nothing and I was wondering, are we going to have egg on our faces? Or is this going to work?"

I said I loved the Fay Wray scene where Paltrow is dodging the feet of the giant mechanical men and always seems about to get squashed.

"That was Gwyneth running through a blue room," Law said.

"With big heels on," Paltrow said. "Because you couldn't see the robots, you were always wondering if you were overdoing it. You didn't want to look like a complete fool."

"You'd want to know where you were supposed to be looking," Law said. "You'd ask how big the robot was. This big? Even bigger? Way up there?"

"There were orange dots we were supposed to look at to line up perfectly with the effects," Paltrow said.

Paltrow and Law were visiting Chicago to do the *Oprah* show, and we talked later the same morning at the Peninsula Hotel. They had only recently seen the completed movie, so now they knew what was happening behind them on the blue screen, and it was not your ordinary sci-fi thriller, but a kind of poetry of images.

"I was completely gobsmacked when I finally saw it," Paltrow said. "I thought it looked exquisite. We had spent all this time in front of a big blue screen, having no idea what it would look like, and then to see how beautifully it was illustrated, and how it had such visual sophistication. Wow."

"It harkens back to a style of serials and a world that was the norm fifty or sixty years ago, and has slowly been lost," Law said.

"There's a sweetness," said Paltrow. "An innocence, when the world was simpler and a dame was a dame."

In the movie, which is set in a decade vaguely like the 1930s, the villain of course wants world conquest, and only Sky Captain (Law) can defeat him. Polly Perkins is a newspaper reporter, played by Paltrow, who used to date the Captain and climbs into the second seat of his airplane for death-defying scoops.

The story hurtles fearlessly through awesome scenes, but what's magical about the movie is its look and tone; Kerry Conran, the first-time director from Flint, Michigan, has created a visual feast that looks like every old *Buck Rogers* movie you've ever seen while at the same time it looks like nothing you've ever seen before.

What a leap of faith it must have taken, I said, to commit to this on the basis of an untried director's home movie. You're both always being pitched stuff that maybe has a better pedigree.

"It's a matter of just going with your instincts sometimes," Paltrow said. "If you saw his short film and you read his script, you thought, I'll be surprised if this isn't something special."

Do you have trouble with agents or advisers who want you to go with safer projects?

"Jude and I have always kind of cut our own path and done things that were not the most obvious," Paltrow said. "It took us forever to get him to be the star of a movie! He was forever hiding in character roles and supporting parts and playing baddies. All of Hollywood was clamoring for him to be the star of a movie for about seven years."

As a director, was Kerry Conran intimidated to be working with such high-profile actors?

"He evolved," Law said. "I remember watching him on the first day. Can you imagine this poor guy? Angelina Jolie and Gwyneth Paltrow came out and he was sort of speechless. I remember thinking, I've got to watch and see how this guy changes. And there was an evolution. He became more vocal and precise. Underneath his modesty and shyness was a real clarity of thought and a real sense of what he wanted and what he could get from this."

Another famous actor who appears in the movie is Sir Laurence Olivier, who died in 1989, and appears in a computer-manipulated performance. At the first word of this posthumous performance, eyebrows were raised, including mine. But when you see the movie, you see that using Olivier makes—well, a certain sense.

"I'd like to think that Gwyneth and I would not use an idea like that as a gimmick," Law said. "Without giving anything away, it was because of the end of the film that it made absolute sense to use someone of great stature who is actually deceased."

I have one more question, I said to Paltrow. You have a new baby girl named Apple. Any relationship to the fact that *Sky Captain* started life on a Macintosh?

"That would make a good story," she said, "but her daddy (composer Chris Martin, leader of the rock group Coldplay) picked the name. He just liked it."

Martin Scorsese

Los Angeles, December 12, 2004—Martin Scorsese is not a creature of the sound bite. In an age when directors and stars are trained by their publicists to stay on message and repeat glowing mantras about their movies, Scorsese is all over the map.

He loves his movie, *The Aviator,* you can tell that, but he's finished with it. It's in the can. He's straining at the bit. He's talking out loud about ideas for his next movie. He'll make a Boston police picture, starring DiCaprio for the third time in a row. Then maybe he'll adapt Endo's *The Silence,* about a Jesuit missionary in Japan in the sixteenth century. Or maybe Boswell's *London Journal*—he loves that book, about a young man from Scotland, on the make in the big city: "I love it when he gets the clap from that actress and after he's treated he goes around and presents her with the doctor's bill."

We are having lunch in the Beverly Wilshire Hotel. He is eating a piece of chicken that has been prepared to his specifications. Flattened. Seasoned. Breaded. His mother was a great cook. He once included her recipe for tomato sauce in the credits of a movie. He knows how he wants his chicken.

His hair is gray now. His face is lined. I met him when we were in our twenties. He had a mane of hippie hair and a beard, wore the jeans and the beads, was editing *Woodstock* in a loft in SoHo. We went down to Little Italy on the Feast of San Gennaro and ate pasta, and he told me about a project that would become, a few years later, *Mean Streets.* I cannot look at Martin Scorsese and see a man who is sixty-two. I see the kid. Certainly I hear the kid.

"I've never been that interested in Howard

Hughes's life, beginning to end," he said, talking about the subject of *The Aviator.* He was interested in the middle. Warren Beatty worked for years on a Howard Hughes project, but it never got made; maybe he couldn't get the right screenplay. Then Scorsese saw a screenplay by John Logan, who is good at finding the story line in an epic life; he wrote *Gladiator* and *The Last Samurai.*

"What Logan chose not to show, that's what interested me," Scorsese said. "You can't do the whole life. The last twenty years, it's a guy locked in a room watching movies. I went through a phase like that myself, movies all day long, all night long, my friends would say I was walking around with the Kleenex boxes on my feet again. Just like Howard Hughes.

"What I liked was the young Howard Hughes who came to Hollywood with the money his dad made on drill bits, and bet the store. He had energy and lust. I saw him walking into the Coconut Grove, beautiful girls on swings above the dance floor, L. B. Mayer standing there with his flunkies, asking Mayer if he could borrow a couple of cameras. 'Cause he's got twenty-four cameras for this scene, but he needs two more. He needed twenty-six cameras to film the aerial fights in *Hell's Angels.*

"Mayer gave him excellent advice. 'Go back to Houston. You'll go broke here.' But even *Hell's Angels,* the most expensive picture ever produced, eventually made its money back. He was a genius at getting rich, he had a visionary sense, but always there was that fatal flaw eating away at him, consuming him."

Hughes spent his last decades as a mad recluse, but Scorsese's film takes him only to the point where he is about to shut the door on the world. There are episodes of madness, but also flashes of triumph. We know Hughes is falling to pieces, but the world doesn't guess; he faces down a congressional hearing that tries to paint him as a war profiteer but fails.

"Most of the Senate stuff, that's what he really said, verbatim," Scorsese said. "He won. He really did say if the *Spruce Goose* didn't fly he would leave the country and never come back again. And it flew."

It flew, in one of several special effects scenes that Scorsese integrates with eerie realism into the film; another is a scene where Hughes crash-lands in Beverly Hills, the wing of his plane slicing through the wall of a house.

"You want my guess?" Scorsese said. "Ultimately, when he looks in the mirror at what he has become, he would do it all again. It was worth it."

And the girls. Jean Harlow, Katharine Hepburn, Jane Russell, and the pneumatic brassiere he personally designed to assist her bosom in its heaving.

"Breasts!" Scorsese said. "He embraced them so passionately. I am appreciative of that part of the female form, but it's not my point of view. But he loved them!"

There came a time when Scorsese had to decide between two projects: Alexander the Great or Howard Hughes. "Alexander or Howard? But Alexander would take years of preproduction, and I'm not getting any younger. And Oliver Stone told me it was the passion of his life. And the John Logan screenplay about Hughes was so attractive."

And you worked again with Harvey Weinstein and Miramax, I said, despite all those stories about how you were at each other's throats during *Gangs of New York.*

"Harvey? A difference of opinions. Issues of taste. No bloodletting. And ultimately, it came down to a hard, cold case of production costs and how much we could spend." Scorsese hinted, almost under his breath, that *Gangs of New York* had fallen a little short of what he had dreamed, but in the real world of production money and how much it can buy, Scorsese made the best movie it was possible to make.

More to the point, I thought, was the movie before that, *Bringing Out the Dead* (1999), with Nicolas Cage as an ambulance driver in Hell's Kitchen. This I thought was a brilliant film, a descent into the underworld. "But it failed at the box office," Scorsese said, "and was rejected by a lot of the critics."

I was astonished by its energy and dark vision, by its portrait of a man venturing nightly into hell to rescue the dying and the damned.

"I had ten years of ambulances," Scorsese said. "My parents, in and out of hospitals. Calls in the middle of the night. I was exorcising all of that. Those city paramedics are heroes—and saints, they're saints. I grew up next to the Bowery, watching the people who worked

there, the Salvation Army, Dorothy Day's Catholic Worker movement, all helping the lost souls. They're the same sort of people."

Saints, I said. A lot of saints in your films.

"Despite everything, I keep thinking I can find a way to lead the spiritual life," he said. "When I made *The Last Temptation of Christ,* when I made *Kundun,* I was looking for that. *Bringing Out the Dead* was the next step. Time is moving by. I'm aware of that."

Do you still read all the time, and watch movies all the time?

"Both of them, all of the time. On our top floor, I have a projection room, a big screen. I'm always watching something, and my daughter's bedroom is at the other end of the hall. She knocks on the door: 'Daddy, turn the movie down'!" He laughed. "It's supposed to be the daddy who tells the kid to turn down the noise. And reading. George Eliot. All of Melville—everything he wrote. I'm fascinated by whale boats, but I'm afraid of a picture on the water, so many technical problems. Then got sidetracked by Ovid, and he took me back to Propertius." He spells "Propertius" for me. "You gotta read Propertius."

The movies? He sighed. "It's almost like I've seen enough of some of the old films. *Citizen Kane,* it's a masterpiece, I'm in awe of it, but I know it. I know it. It comes up on TV, I don't stop. Now *The Trial,* by Welles, *Touch of Evil,* I'll stop and watch. And music. Leadbelly. If you sit through all the credits after *The Aviator,* at the end we play a song written and performed by Leadbelly: 'Get up in the morning, Put on your shoes, Read about Howard Hughes.' He wrote that. Leadbelly wrote that."

Oliver Stone

November 21, 2004—Oliver Stone seems at the end of his rope, but then he always seems at the end of his rope. Here is a man who needs sleep. He has flown in from Paris, he's jet-lagged, he's talking in that rapid-fire way we use when we're so tired we don't have the strength to talk slowly.

He is talking about *Alexander,* his 173-minute epic about "the most amazing life in history," and he describes him: "Already, at twenty-six, he had the political leadership of the world." Switching thoughts: "We used to think young people could rule the world.

Today, young people are a demographic, a market."

There is so much that is wrong, so much to fight against. "If we had to do things the American PG way, then we were screwed. This had to be an R picture. If you work in Hollywood, you have to get past the studio development committees. The thousands of demands. The previews where they dumb it down for the audience. The system wears you down. It's a monster—demanding, uncompromising. Marty Scorsese and Spike Lee have been through hell."

The lesson being that the German financial backers of *Alexander* allowed the director to make his epic his way, as a film that juxtaposed violent battle scenes with scarcely less violent sex scenes between Alexander (Colin Farrell) and his barbarian bride Roxane (Rosario Dawson)—and also encompassed Alexander's love for a man, Hephaestion (Jared Leto). There were rumors that Stone would show Alexander and Hephaestion making love, although in the event they just hug a lot, and kiss once. There is a passionate nude scene involving Roxane, despite the distinct possibility that Alexander prefers his lifelong friend to the Asian woman he marries to consolidate his empire.

"When it came to love and friendship," Stone said, "I think Alexander felt more with a man. A woman was for bearing sons. And Roxane bore him no children for more than three years. She is one of the least-covered, least-known characters in history. If I could talk to Alexander, I'd ask him why he married her. But the Greeks did have a regard for women: Six of the twelve gods are women, after all. Marrying her pissed off all of his men, but he didn't care; he was making a point."

Actually, five of the Greek gods are women, but never mind: There is also Alexander's closeness to his mother, Olympias (Angelina Jolie). "I think maybe he married his mother in Roxane," Stone speculated. You might think Jolie is too young to play a king's wife and a conqueror's mother, but let it be observed they married early in those days, and that in any event Olympias denies that her husband, Philip of Macedonia, is Alexander's father. Her son's father, she insists, is Zeus.

"Did she really believe Zeus was the father?" I asked Stone. "I mean he's a god, so did he, uh-well, what did he do?"

"It wasn't until 1630 that the Dutch discovered ovaries," Stone explains. While I'm writing that down, he explains that in early days there was more mystery about conception: "In her mind, Zeus was the father."

Stone said he fell under Alexander's spell as a child, reading the biography of him in a Children's Classics series. "This was the golden boy of all history. I've been trying to make the movie for a long time. In 1989 with Val Kilmer, in 1996 with Tom Cruise. Then Colin Farrell came along and he was perfect. He was a tough, Tyrone Power, barstool-looking boy from Dublin. We made him a blond, which was perfect for him, and he became Alexander."

How did Farrell feel about the homosexual side of the character?

"Alexander wanted to find the end of the world. Aristotle said the Eastern Sea was the end of the world, but Alexander went there, and the world did not end. So he kept on going, conquering everything in his path, year after year. For him, sexuality was also part of knowing the end of the world. And conquering the fear of death, that was knowing the end of the world. Colin Farrell understood that.

"Alexander was the first king in history ever to be seen weeping over his troops. He knew their names; he knew their families. He lost as few troops as possible, and he never left enemies behind. If an insurrection broke out behind him, he went back and cleaned it up. When the Greeks rose up, he wiped out Thebes. Wiped it out. It was a terrible thing to do, but the other Greek city-states got the message, and so he saved lives. He went for the head. Kill the king, and your enemy folds. Alexander would have gone after Osama bin Laden. I'm sorry, but Kerry was right. It all worked for Alexander, until he was overwhelmed by India."

All of this came tumbling out as urgent news. Stone sat on a sofa in the Four Seasons Hotel and spoke as if it was important to get it all said immediately. It was hot in the room, he said. A window was opened. He asked for a cup of coffee. He apologized for losing his train of thought because of jet lag. He seemed as if he might have been overwhelmed by travel too.

Stone filmed on four continents, he said: Morocco, Thailand, England, America.

"If this had been a Hollywood production, everything would have had to be done digitally. We had real soldiers."

There are shots, I said, where it does look real, as the troops march through a mountain pass, and not like all the little digital ants in *Troy* and *The Lord of the Rings*.

"We used *some* digital," he said. "I've been using digital for years, before you ever heard of it, in *JFK, The Doors, Nixon* . . . but the shots you're talking about, most of them, many of them, were real."

Stone said Alexander didn't destroy the peoples he conquered. "He included their customs, their clothes, their languages, he wanted to assemble the entire world under one leader. He married an Oriental woman to show how he included them, instead of a Greek princess. He had a mobile empire that moved with him. The Romans used his empire as the basis for their empire. And then the Vandals, the Huns, the Crusades . . . by 2050, they say Europe will have a Muslim majority."

Was it a struggle to get *Alexander* made at its longer running time?

"We got it done. I don't believe in this business of chopping up a film and then releasing a 'director's cut' on DVD. What you see should be the director's cut. *This* is the director's cut. If you can spend four hours killing Bill, Alexander deserves some space."

Hilary Swank

December 15, 2004—Hilary Swank will quite possibly win the Oscar as Best Actress this year, for a role in a movie nobody had heard of. The movie is Clint Eastwood's *Million Dollar Baby,* which wasn't in any of those stories we were all reading about Oscar "front-runners," because crafty old Clint doesn't believe in a lot of foolish publicity before he has a movie to show you. Oh, and the movie will be a contender for Best Picture, Actor, Supporting Actor, and Director, too, and Cinematography, Editing, all those categories. It is the best film of the year.

What happened was, Eastwood showed it to Warner Bros., which had no plans for an Oscar campaign until studio executives realized they had an amazing movie on their hands. Word began to spread: Tear up your Oscar predictions and start over again.

The movie stars Hilary Swank as Maggie Fitzgerald, a girl "who has always been told she is trash," who grew up in a welfare family in a trailer park, who has been waitressing since she was thirteen, and who at the age of thirty-one wants to become a boxer. Eastwood plays Frankie, the veteran trainer who doesn't approve of "girlies" who want to box, and Morgan Freeman is Scrap, his oldest friend and resident manager of his run-down gym.

"I'm a girl who grew up in a trailer park," Hilary Swank told me quietly. "Maggie Fitzgerald is the closest I've felt to any character I've ever played. We're both girls who had a dream, worked hard, and were diligent and driven and focused. I was lucky I had someone who believed in me."

That was her mother, Judy. "She said to me, 'Hilary, you can do anything you dream in life as long as you work hard.'" Her dream was to be an actress. Perhaps even her mother did not dream Hilary would win an Oscar, but she did, as Best Actress, for *Boys Don't Cry* (1999). She played a girl who tries to live as a boy, and who is killed when her secret is discovered.

That was a great performance. Her Maggie Fitzgerald is, I think, probably even greater, because she takes us on an even longer journey. Maggie is direct, sympathetic, and believable. You care about this woman. You feel protective. *Million Dollar Baby* is the kind of movie where people look you in the eye and tell you to see it, and their voices have a curious intensity.

How did you get from the trailer park to the Oscars? I asked Swank.

"My mom got fired from her job. My parents were separated. She said, 'Okay, let's go to Hollywood,' and we drove to Hollywood in our broken-down Olds Cutlass Supreme. We had 75 bucks and we drove there from Washington State, and we lived off our Mobil card. We'd buy food in the gas station minimart, and my mom would slowly pay it off.

"There were a few weeks when we lived out of that car. People say, oh, that's so intense and difficult and sad. It wasn't any of that to me. I was in Hollywood and for me every single minute of it was ecstatic."

You sense stability and thoughtfulness as she speaks, and you see that in the character of Maggie too. There's not a lot of behavior and acting-out going on; she's not nodding and smiling and looking for feedback.

"What we'd do is, we'd find a friend who was moving out and their house was for sale. There'd be nothing in the house. We'd blow up air mattresses and sleep on those at night and roll them up in the car. My mom got a job after about a month of that, and we rented a room for $500, lived there for a year, and things slowly built up."

Many such stories, most of them, end in disappointment. But there was a plucky quality about Swank that had attracted the Seattle casting director Suzy Sachs, who worked with her and put her in local productions from the age of nine.

"In Hollywood," said Swank, "my first movie was *Buffy the Vampire Slayer* in 1992, and then came *The Next Karate Kid*."

That was in 1994, when she was twenty. She played a troubled teenage girl whom Mr. Miyagi heals through the lessons of karate. Swank has worked more or less steadily ever since, sometimes forgettably (*The Affair of the Necklace*) sometimes not (*Insomnia*). She said her marriage to actor Chad Lowe "comes first," and acting is the rest.

Seeing her in *Million Dollar Baby* and *Boys Don't Cry*, you realize that the right role is crucial. Frances McDormand was great but unsung before *Fargo*. Halle Berry and Charlize Theron were skilled professionals before *Monster's Ball* and *Monster*, but those roles transformed them. Swank has had two roles like that in five years. Meryl Streep knows what that feels like, but most actresses can only wonder.

Of course, somebody has to make it happen. Do people realize how good Clint Eastwood is as a director? He's been a movie star so long, it obscures the view.

"I would work for the rest of my life with Clint, if I could," Swank told me in Chicago, on a press tour that became necessary when the movie went from obscurity to contender in a few days. Eastwood's strategy of no advance publicity had been brilliant. Why tell people your movie is going to be great, when you can just show it to them and let them see for themselves? There was another reason to keep it under wraps: You don't want to know too much about the plot before you see it. It's not really a boxing movie; it's about Maggie as a person.

"The early reviews that have appeared in the trade papers have avoided revealing too much," Swank said. "Thank God for that."

As for Eastwood: "There is a quiet presence about him that's not arrogant or egotistical, it's just that he's been around and knows what he wants. His belief in you makes you believe in yourself, which makes you follow your instincts. Then you watch the finished film and you realize his fingerprints are all over it. You were being guided so subtly and simply, you never felt like anything was being forced on you. You felt like everything was your idea. It was the best experience I've had in my career so far."

What she saw in Eastwood and Morgan Freeman as actors, she said, was an unadorned and effortless approach, with everything unnecessary stripped away: "You don't know where the acting starts and stops. Morgan will just be talking to you and you'll realize, oh, we're rolling, and he's saying his lines! I was all the time just trying to observe Morgan and Clint. All I did was stare and gawk. I was on the set even when I wasn't in the scene. I just wanted to sponge it up."

Tom Rosenberg, the Chicago-based producer of the film, told me that working with Eastwood was a revelation: "Always under budget, always ahead of schedule, and he makes great movies. How many directors can you say that about?"

Hilary Swank nodded. "Tom was around all the time. He's hands-on. He was involved in my training. He was concerned we only had two months to build me up to look more like a boxer. Well, finally we had three. I put on twenty pounds of muscle."

She talked about her training, six days a week, two and a half hours of boxing, two hours of weights, then the endurance training and protein, protein, protein: "I just plugged my nose and downed these egg whites, flax oil, raw fish, cooked fish, green vegetables."

She agreed with Rosenberg about Eastwood's discipline as a director. "He gets everything he wants, and doesn't waste one additional moment. Our longest day was twelve hours, and that included moving the company to another location. Sometimes we would finish the day's shots before lunch and he'd tell us to go home and he'd see us tomorrow. He was like one of the crew. He stood in line for lunch like everybody else. He'd never think of cutting in, which is the director's right. He was always on the set, never in his trailer.

"Every day that went by, it was a day I was sad, because it was a day less that I had to spend with them. I would joke around at the end that I might not know my lines tomorrow, just so that we wouldn't finish early. I just didn't want it to be over."

The Weavers

Toronto, Canada, September 20, 2004—Pete Seeger was standing in the corner of the big dressing room, playing a tune on his recorder. Fred Hellerman was planted on a chair, listening to him.

"It's an old Japanese air," Seeger said, putting down his recorder.

"I've heard you play a whole opera on that thing," Hellerman said.

This was at the Toronto Film Festival, where the Weavers were going to sing that evening for probably the last time. Three of them—Seeger, Hellerman, and Ronnie Gilbert—go back more than fifty-five years together, and their songs are like the national sound track. Think of "Goodnight, Irene" and "Wimoweh" and "This Land Is Your Land" and "If I Had a Hammer" and "Midnight Special" and "Rock Island Line," and it's their voices you hear in your memory.

Pete Seeger is eighty-five now. Ronnie Gilbert and Fred Hellerman are pushing eighty. Lee Hays, the fourth member of the original group, died in 1981. Erik Darling and Eric Weissberg have joined the group for reunions since then, and now all five gathered for a conversation before their rehearsal.

The occasion was the premiere that evening of Jim Brown's *Isn't This a Time,* a documentary about a Carnegie Hall concert in honor of Harold Leventhal's fiftieth anniversary as an impresario. It was Leventhal

who booked them into Carnegie Hall the first time in the late 1940s, and Leventhal who reunited them a few years later at the height of McCarthyism, when the group's left-wing politics had made them victims of a show business blacklist. In between, they'd had a No. 1 hit with Leadbelly's song "Goodnight, Irene," become the most popular singing group in the country, and then faced oblivion because of the blacklist.

Seeger, heir to his friend Woody Guthrie as the nation's folk troubadour, retired from touring a few years ago, claiming his voice was gone. He agreed to the Carnegie Hall concert because it honored Leventhal. "Because of Harold," Hellerman said, "we became the Weavers."

The film shows Seeger and the others in joyous voice at a concert also featuring Arlo Guthrie, Theo Bikel, Leon Bibb, and Peter, Paul, and Mary. "But we didn't feel we were necessarily at our best," Hellerman said. So the Weavers were a little apprehensive about how it would go in Toronto after the movie, when they planned "not a concert—more of a nightcap, three or four songs."

"They claim they only have four songs they've rehearsed enough to play publicly," Michael Cohl grinned. He's the coproducer of the film and a concert promoter whose acts include the Rolling Stones—and, when he can persuade them, the Weavers. "Rehearsal means they sing each of the four songs twice, and then they sit around for hours singing every other song they know, and they all sound great."

"The empty seat is for Lee Hays," Seeger said as the group settled down to talk. Hays died shortly after the filming of *The Weavers: Wasn't That a Time* (1982), also directed by Brown, the great musical documentary about their farewell concert at Carnegie Hall. This time, it looked like farewell for good.

They started out talking about the origins of "people's songs," which came from folk, labor, spiritual, and country roots. No, they never played the Grand Ol' Opry as a group, but they listened. "I remember," said Ronnie Gilbert, "a song called 'What Kind of Fool Would Steal 29 Books of Green Stamps?' It was a woman complaining about her man. I didn't believe it, because no country woman would ever turn her guy in to the police."

"Remember the old joke," said Hellerman,

"about when you play the country record backwards, he gets his wife back and repossesses the truck?"

I said my friend Studs Terkel tells a story about how Seeger and Woody Guthrie and some other singers needed a place to stay for a few nights in Chicago, and Studs sent them home to his wife, Ida, with a note saying they were good guys and could sleep on the floor.

"That was in 1940," Seeger said. "We slept there for three nights. There were two rooms including a kitchen. It got a little crowded. Not long ago my wife, Toshi, and I had our twelve-year-old grandchild in a taxi with Studs, and in fifteen minutes Studs had the taxi driver's entire life story."

Seeger said the beginning of the Weavers was probably in 1940, when he and Lee Hays and Woody Guthrie formed the Almanac Singers to perform union songs. "We rehearsed right on the stage," he said, "arguing about who was going to sing the next verse. After the war, Lee said, 'Let's get another group and actually rehearse.'"

The 1982 documentary tells the story of the Weavers's rise and fall and rise, and how they overcame McCarthyism to become one of the best-selling groups of the decade. They were the key inspiration for the 1960s folk singers who fueled the civil rights and antiwar movements, including Peter, Paul, and Mary, whose hit "If I Had a Hammer" was cowritten by Seeger and Hays.

"Yesterday," Ronnie Gilbert said, "somebody asked us, 'Did you change the world?' Maybe you can't change the world. But you can keep trying."

"Why don't you do one last concert tour?" I asked them.

"In 1980, it was very easy for us, like riding a bicycle," Hellerman said. "That's not true today. We live all over the country, and we all have our own causes and interests."

Do you know what songs you're going to sing tonight?

He laughed. "We've known them for forty years."

That night the movie electrified the huge Elgin theater; the audience sang along, clapped in rhythm, and applauded each song as if it had been live.

Then the Weavers came onstage and opened with "When the Saints Go Marching In," and I looked over the audience and saw people cheering and crying at the same time. They were in great voice—"a lot better than Carnegie Hall," Eric Weissberg told me later.

They sang "My Mother's House Was Filled With Music" and "Wimoweh," and for an encore they sang "Goodnight, Irene." And Ronnie Gilbert stepped up to the mike and urged the Americans in the audience to vote for John Kerry, and told them, "You can change the world."

Maybe songs can change things. Seeger explains "Wimoweh" in the movie: It's a South African song from the 1940s, and the lion that sleeps in the jungle represents the Africans of South Africa, who would rise up and overthrow apartheid. Around the edge of Seeger's banjo are written these words: "This machine surrounds hate and forces it to surrender."

The next morning I joined Michael Cohl and his cousin Dusty, the founder of the film festival, at their Saturday morning coffee ritual.

"The Weavers have sung together for the last time," said Michael. "Unless—one thing. Unless John Kerry would like them to do some concerts for his campaign. They've agreed they would do that."

So perhaps it is too soon to envision the Weavers going their separate ways, singing perhaps Guthrie's "So Long, It's Been Good to Know You." Perhaps they will walk onto a stage yet once again to remind us, also in Guthrie's words, that this land is our land.

"There's a kind of eerie moment in the movie," I said to Seeger before the rehearsal, "when Arlo Guthrie observes that he has now performed with you twice as long as his father did."

"Time," said Pete Seeger. "Time, time. A beautiful mystery."

Fred Hellerman smiled. "At least it keeps everything from happening at once," he said.

Essays

Robert Altman Directs an Opera

December 5, 2004—Does anyone ever really think about the director of an opera? I'm not talking about opera professionals or music critics, who know all about such things. I'm thinking of ordinary ticket-holders. We think about the singers above all, and then, in descending order, about the composer, the sets, the costumes, the plot, and the conductor. There's a libretto, which we think of primarily as a framework for the music. There's lighting, which we notice, and the person in front of us, who we notice even more if our view is blocked. Directors? Don't operas direct themselves?

One Saturday afternoon in November, Robert Altman was presiding over a rehearsal of *A Wedding,* the Chicago Lyric Opera production. He wrote the libretto with Arnold Weinstein and David Levin; the composer is William Bolcom. Robert Altman is a director, all right—one of the three or four best movie directors in the world, if you ask me. I've seen him at work on a lot of sets, including, for that matter, the set of his movie *A Wedding,* which was filmed in 1977 in Lake Forest, Illinois, and inspired this opera.

He has a kind of conspiratorial style, as if he and the actors are putting something over on absent enemies. There may not be a director who likes actors more. He has a temper, and I have seen him angry with cinematographers and teamsters and prop men and lighting guys and critics and people making noise during a shot, but actors are his darlings and can do no wrong. When he asks for another take, there is the implication that he enjoyed the last one so much he wants to see the actors do it again simply for his personal pleasure.

On this afternoon, he is working with the famed soprano Lauren Flanigan, who will play a leading role, Tulip, the mother of the bride. Altman sits in a high-backed director's chair with the libretto open on a music stand in front of him. Standing at a podium next to him is James Johnson, the Lyric's associate conductor. Beyond him are the rehearsal pianists, Alan Darling and assistant conductor

William Billingham. The opera's actual conductor, Dennis Russell Davies, is still in New York, but his wife, Linda Kim Davies, is an observer. On Altman's left, seated at the sort of long table you see in school lunch rooms, is Pat Birch, the choreographer. Next to her, stage directors Amy Hutchison and Greg Fortner, and stage manager John Coleman. William Bolcom, the composer, is conducting a workshop elsewhere in the Civic Opera House, but will arrive later. It takes a lot of people to stage an opera, and the attention of all of these people is focused on Tulip (Miss Flanigan), who is dressed in a loose-fitting scoop-necked white blouse that is ideal for what Pat Birch cheerfully calls "the Russ Meyer scene."

What surprised me was how much care and detail they were putting into one brief episode. In the scene, Tulip enters the bathroom of a Lake Forest mansion, all in a bother. Behind her is a wall of mirrored doors, two leading to the mansion, the others to toilet cubicles. Tulip is up from Louisville for her daughter's wedding, and has astonishingly just been propositioned by Jules Goddard (Jake Gardner), who is the bride's uncle by marriage. As a sensible Kentucky woman she is uneasy anyway with the Sloans of Lake Forest. To have an affair? At her age!

She is flabbergasted, and says so in song, until she is interrupted by Goddard, who enters and passionately pursues his courtship while burying his nose warmly in her cleavage (the Meyer homage). She flees to a bench that circles a pillar, and he chases her around it until his nose finds its cradle again. It is all too much for Tulip, who begs him to give her a break. As he leaves, he hands her a single red rose. Overcome with emotion, she sings of her distress, and flings the rose to the ground. As she exits, her door closes precisely as another door opens and Buffy (Lauren Carter) enters. She is a bridesmaid, has overheard the whole exchange, picks up the rose, and inhales.

A fairly simple scene, you would think. Not really.

First there is the matter of the choreography. Tulip and Goddard have to carefully coordinate their chase around the bathroom and the business with the bench and the pillar. Done correctly, it will be high physical comedy. If the timing is off even a little, they'll look ungainly and will be wrongly positioned for their big exits. Then there is the business of the rose. To fling it to the ground and exit with split-second timing as the other door opens is not as easy as it sounds, particularly since Tulip is in an emotional turmoil and must fling it without looking, and yet aim it so well that it's the very first thing Buffy sees when she enters.

There are questions about the music. Miss Flanigan thinks perhaps one lyric can be abbreviated so that it coordinates better with a laugh. Altman agrees. Pencils are applied to the libretto. They try the revised version with new blocking, and it works better, but not perfectly. She thinks perhaps if she rushes forward in terror before she circles in indecision, that will fit the music. Pat Birch has a conference with her, and they try it that way. It works.

Then Jake Gardner enters as Goddard, and the choreography of their chase is worked on. It must seem reckless and impulsive, yet every step must be planned or the timing will be wrong. And there is the problem of a cushioned stool, which moves on four little wheels, and the circular bench around the pillar. Neither seems to be functioning well.

Miss Flanigan tries the stool, which seems dangerously ready to slip out from under her. The bench is precariously attached to the pillar, which is allegedly a structural element of the mansion but can quite clearly be seen to move.

This is where Altman employs one of his favorite directorial strategies. No one in the room can do any wrong (indeed, no one has). But absent villains must be blamed. He fulminates about the props. Can the mirrored doors be made to close decisively? (They will be improved, he is told.) Can additional wheels be attached to the stool, so it balances better, or is such a simple task beyond the resources of the Lyric? (The stool disappears and returns with more wheels.) Can the pillar somehow be anchored? (Well, no; a cable steadying it from the top would be visible, and you can't exactly bolt it to the stage.) The Lyric

is in fact well supplied with resources; stagehand Glenn Haack unobtrusively came to the rescue by adding additional wheels to the stool, and thinks he knows how to steady the candelabra.

All very well, but now the rose causes a crisis. There is almost no way that Tulip can convincingly erupt with emotional turmoil and yet precisely aim the rose so that Buffy will see it. Tulip's body language must not suggest the slightest calculation in her rose-throwing. There are three or four run-throughs, the rose lands in three or four places, and when Buffy enters she clearly has to seek it out, even though, of course, she isn't supposed to know it's there—which is why it must be exactly in her line of sight.

The way Altman handles this is a study. Other directors would no doubt get up out of their chairs and conduct rose-throwing demonstrations. Altman's response is to seem intensely interested in the problem, and curious about how it will be resolved. Another rehearsal. The doctor exits, Tulip sings passionately about the tempest in her heart, she darts about the stage, and then ...

"I know what to do!" Miss Flanigan says, interrupting herself in midlyric. "Go back to the beginning." Johnson nods, the pianists backtrack, she sings, she darts, and then she flings the rose entirely over the top of the set and out of sight. A moment later, as Tulip exits, enter Buffy, bearing a rose.

Brilliant, don't you think? Lateral thinking. In midaria, Flanigan realized that the toilet cubicles don't have ceilings. So Tulip flings the rose over the top, the offstage Buffy presumably sees it land in front of her, and can already be armed with a standby rose for her split-second entrance.

The rehearsal is now in its third hour. Altman calls for one more run-through, and I am amazed by how well everything now fits together, how it works as music, as action, as comedy. The chase around the bathroom meshes perfectly with the music and the laugh points. The nose in the bosom is hilarious slapstick. Tulip's emotions veer from shock to curiosity to fear to remorse to perhaps something like lust. And the red rose turns up with perfect timing in the hands of the young lady, where it works as all red roses do, as a symbol of love. If the whole opera is as lovingly crafted as this scene, it will be wonderful.

There is a coffee break. Altman looks pleased. Pat Birch comes over and they decide to lock in the scene. "I don't have anything to do with the music," he tells me. "I leave that to the experts." Altman's wife, Kathryn, who entered quietly an hour earlier, joins him. She is a redhead, smart and sassy, who has copiloted him through thirty-three major films and countless television and stage productions.

He was a journeyman for many years, directing episodic TV like *Peter Gunn* and *Combat!* between sporadic feature forays, before, in 1970, when he was already forty-five, he emerged as a major director with *M*A*S*H* and never looked back. Altman works all the time, averaging a film a year, and tells time by the films; when we were trying to remember what year he directed the Bolcom-Weinstein-Altman opera *McTeague* for the Lyric (it was 1992), he asked Kathryn, "What films did that come between?"

In 2000, on the set of *Gosford Park* outside London, he told me: "When I'm not making a film, I don't know how to live. I don't know what to do with the time. I don't have an assistant director taking me to this little restaurant around the corner, and a production manager telling me about my hotel, and a driver to take me where I have to go."

You get the sense that he invents his life as he goes along, improvising it, spurred by happy chances. Consider his great film *Three Women* (1977), which was inspired, right down to the dialogue and the casting, by a dream he had one night. While he was making it, the original idea for *A Wedding* came to him quite strangely. He told me about it in 1977 at Cannes, where *Three Women* was an official entry. It was a month before he was scheduled to start filming *A Wedding* in Lake Forest:

"We were shooting *Three Women* out in the desert and it was a really hot day and we were in a hotel room that was like a furnace, and I wasn't feeling too well on account of having felt *too* well the night before, and this girl was down from L.A. to do some in-depth gossip and asked me what my next movie was going to be. At that moment I didn't even feel like doing *this* movie, so I told her I was gonna shoot a wedding next. A *wedding*? Yeah, a wed-ding. So a few moments later my production assistant comes up and she says, 'Bob, did you hear yourself just then?' Yeah, I say, I did. 'That's not a bad idea, is it?' she says. Not a bad idea at all, I said, and that night we started on the outline."

Altman's laid-back directorial style is all the more confounding because he imposes such a distinctive personal mark on his films. Sixty seconds of an Altman film, and you know who directed it, and yet there is such democracy in the way he works. He loves big casts with a lot of speaking roles (*A Wedding*, both as movie and opera, has a long list of family and guests), and his famous overlapping dialogue doesn't insist on listening to the star all the time (he'll try some overlapping singing in the opera).

He's always up for something new; his film, *The Company*, was about a year in the life of a ballerina with the Joffrey Ballet of Chicago, and he filmed it like a kid aiming for Sundance, using a handheld digital camera and staying open to improvisation. He's collaborating with Garrison Keillor on *A Prairie Home Companion*, and his casting is as free-ranging as usual, with roles for Keillor, Lyle Lovett, Meryl Streep, Lily Tomlin, and Tom Waits. (Apparently, not all the men in his Lake Wobegon are good-looking, although the women are no doubt strong and the children above average.)

"I used to plan on another decade," he told me at the end of the day. "Now I'll settle for a few more years." I advise him to keep on telling time by making films and he will never die, because it won't be in the production schedule.

National Society of Film Critics Awards

January 10, 2005—Not all movie awards are created equal. Countless groups bestow their praise on each year's movies, no doubt stirred by honorable motives, as well as a desire to influence the Oscars and get publicity. The Golden Globes are no doubt the best known of the pre-Oscars, but not necessarily the most respected. For respect, the top of the field is occupied, I think, by the National Society of Film Critics and the American Film Institute.

The AFI lists the year's top ten films alphabetically. They're picked by a jury of professionals from various areas of the movie world, which debates for a day in Los Angeles; I was the chairman this year, and our choices were *The Aviator, Collateral, Eternal Sunshine of the Spotless Mind, Friday Night Lights, The Incredibles, Kinsey, Maria Full of Grace, Million Dollar Baby, Sideways,* and *Spider-Man 2.*

The National Society, the group originally identified with such giants as Pauline Kael, Stanley Kauffmann, and Andrew Sarris, meets every January in New York, and has been chaired for fifteen years by Peter Rainer of *New York* magazine. To become a member, you have to be voted in by the existing members, so the membership arguably represents the best of American film criticism.

Unlike the AFI, the Oscars, the Globes, or any other group, the NSFC actually releases the results of its voting, naming the winning film and the first two runners-up. The numbers do not represent vote totals, however, but point totals, in which each member awards five points to a first-place vote, three to a second and one to a third.

The key result of this year's awards, is that Clint Eastwood's *Million Dollar Baby* outpointed Alexander Payne's *Sideways,* which has won awards from a number of critic's groups. That reflects the year-end groundswell for *Baby,* which Eastwood didn't screen until the second week in December, avoiding the usual prerelease hoopla. The Seattle and Dallas–Fort Worth critics also recently named it the year's best. It goes into wide release, just prior to no doubt making many headlines when the Oscar nominations are announced on January 25. (The Chicago critics, I am unhappy to report, voted for *Sideways,* which is a wonderful film—but I've seen *Million Dollar Baby,* and critics, *Sideways* is no *Million Dollar Baby.*)

The NSFC results may reflect East Coast support for Eastwood against Los Angeles support for Payne; two *New York Times* film critics, A. O. Scott and Manohla Dargis, picked *Baby* as the year's best film; Dargis put *Sideways* third on her list, but Scott attacked it as "the most overrated film of the year," leading industry pundit David Poland to wonder if he was trying to sink its chances (answer: yes).

Other NSFC awards may help leading Oscar contenders. That Imelda Staunton *(Vera Drake)* and Hilary Swank *(Million Dollar Baby)* tied for best actress is good for them both; Staunton may edge into the final five because of notice like this. Virginia Madsen seems to have a lock on a supporting actress nomination for *Sideways,* and the NSFC agrees. Jamie Foxx's nod for both *Ray* and *Collateral* help nail down his best actor nomination. And Paul Giamatti of *Sideways,* edged out 31-29 by Foxx, also seems to have good Oscar prospects.

The NSFC winner least likely to be helped—because it's a critical favorite but has not attracted attention in the industry—is Richard Linklater's *Before Sunset,* a virtuoso sequel to his *Before Sunrise* (1994); in both films, Julie Delpy and Ethan Hawke are strangers who talk for hours about the direction of their lives. The NSFC put *Before Sunset* third on its list of best films, and also mentioned Delpy's performance and the screenplay by Hawke, Delpy, and Linklater.

The complete results, so you can see the vote totals and the runners-up:

PICTURE
1. *Million Dollar Baby* (Clint Eastwood)—50
2. *Sideways* (Alexander Payne)—44
3. *Before Sunset* (Richard Linklater)—28

FOREIGN-LANGUAGE PICTURE
1. *Moolaade* (Ousmane Sembene)—29
2. *House of Flying Daggers* (Zhang Yimou)—27
3. *Notre Musique* (Jean-Luc Godard)—15

DIRECTOR
1. Zhang Yimou *(House of Flying Daggers and Hero)*—33
2. Alexander Payne *(Sideways)*—31
3. Clint Eastwood *(Million Dollar Baby)*—30

NONFICTION FILM
1. *Tarnation* (Jonathan Caouette)—27
2. *Story of the Weeping Camel* (Byambasuren Davaa and Luigi Falorni)—25
3. *Bright Leaves* (Ross McElwee)—16

SCREENPLAY
1. *Sideways* (Alexander Payne and Jim Taylor)—60
2. *Eternal Sunshine of the Spotless Mind* (Charlie Kaufman)—55

3. *Before Sunset* (Richard Linklater, Julie Delpy, and Ethan Hawke)—29

CINEMATOGRAPHY
1. *House of Flying Daggers* (Xiaoding Zhao)—39
2. *Hero* (Christopher Doyle)—31
3. *Collateral* (Dion Beebe and Paul Cameron)—18

ACTRESS—tie
1. Imelda Staunton *(Vera Drake)*—52
1. Hilary Swank *(Million Dollar Baby)*—52
3. Julie Delpy *(Before Sunset)*—40

SUPPORTING ACTRESS
1. Virginia Madsen *(Sideways)*—58
2. Cate Blanchett *(The Aviator* and *Coffee and Cigarettes)*—37
3. Laura Linney *(Kinsey)*—18

ACTOR
1. Jamie Fox *(Ray* and *Collateral)*—31
2. Paul Giamatti *(Sideways)*—29
3. Clint Eastwood *(Million Dollar Baby)*—26

SUPPORTING ACTOR
1. Thomas Haden Church *(Sideways)*—55
2. Morgan Freeman *(Million Dollar Baby)*—54
3. Peter Sarsgaard *(Kinsey)*—19

Million Dollar Baby Gains Oscar Momentum

January 11, 2005—In an era of multimillion-dollar Oscar campaigns, Clint Eastwood's *Million Dollar Baby* may be heading for success with an old-fashioned formula: Keep a poker face until you reveal your winning hand. Although Alexander Payne's *Sideways*, itself a wonderful picture, seemed on track to burst out of the indie ranks and lead the Oscar parade, now the momentum seems to be shifting to *Million Dollar Baby.*

Eastwood's strategy for the film was the opposite of Hollywood's conventional wisdom. There were no on-set interviews, no trailers, no advance ads, no hoopla. He made the movie quietly and efficiently, on a budget of about $25 million, which is peanuts these days. Then he held a handful of quiet screenings around the country; in Chicago, his editor Joel Cox flew in with a print shown to a few critics.

Those screenings generated astonished pre-release reviews. I walked out convinced I had seen a masterpiece, certainly the best film of the year, and said so on the *Ebert & Roeper* program.

Eastwood opened *Baby* in just seven theaters, where it led the nation in its per-screen box-office average. Although many critics' groups already had their awards in motion and gave top honors to *Sideways,* Eastwood began to pick up important trophies: Both A. O. Scott and Manohla Dargis of the *New York Times* thought it was the best film of the year, as did the National Society of Film Critics.

Most Academy voters live in Los Angeles and New York, where the early theatrical runs were supplemented by Academy screenings. Now the movie opens, perfectly timed to take advantage of the Oscar nominations, which will be announced on January 25. As Oscar voters get their ballots, the nation's moviegoers will have the power of *Million Dollar Baby* fresh in their minds.

It's a well-known Oscar phenomenon that movies opening late in the year dominate the awards. One year, all five best picture nominees opened in December. That may be because the emotional currents stirred up by a movie lose strength over time. *Sideways* opened in October, which means that its delights may not be as fresh in the minds of Academy voters. (To be sure, some will see it on those free videos we hear so much about.)

Not only did A. O. Scott pick *Million Dollar Baby* as the best film of the year, he also took the extraordinary step of writing a *Times* piece in January, nine weeks after *Sideways* opened, calling that the "most overrated" film of the year. He concedes that the "funny-sad" movie is praiseworthy, but as he ponders the year-end compilations that add up all the awards and reviews, he arrives at an intriguing notion:

"(T)he near-unanimous praise of [*Sideways*] reveals something about the psychology of critics, as distinct from our taste. Miles, the movie's hero, has been variously described as a drunk, a wine snob, a sad sack, and a loser, but it has seldom been mentioned that he is also, by temperament if not by profession, a critic."

I don't think that fact influenced my own review of the movie, because I thought of Miles as a drunk, yes, but not a critic—not that the two groups don't sometimes overlap. "He's an oenophile," I wrote, "which means he can continue to pronounce French wines long after most people would be unconscious."

I have no doubt Eastwood set his sights on the Oscar from the moment he read the screenplay by Paul Haggis, based on stories by F. X. Toole. It is, I think, a nearly perfect screenplay, in that it contains everything necessary to accomplish what it sets out to do, and not one thing more.

Eastwood must have felt the same way. The movie's star, Hilary Swank, told me this was the only movie she's ever made with "no colored pages." As screenplays go through drafts and rewrites, the changed pages are reproduced on different colors of paper to distinguish them; Eastwood, therefore, was filming the first draft without a single change.

Famed in Hollywood as a quick, efficient director who films under budget and ahead of schedule, Eastwood assembled a team of longtime collaborators. Joel Cox has edited twenty-three of Eastwood's films, and won an Oscar for *Unforgiven;* production designer Henry Bumstead, who is ninety and won the first of his two Oscars for *To Kill a Mockingbird* in 1962, has designed Eastwood's most recent nine films. ("They built a room for Henry on the sound stage," Swank told me, "and he had all his models and sketches in there.")

Although Eastwood has a long association with Warner Bros., the studio was not thrilled about the project. Eastwood had to raise half the money from Chicago-based producer Tom Rosenberg before Warner kicked in the rest.

"With all the big $150 and $200 million films out there, they thought this film was at a different importance level," Eastwood told me. "I had about $25 million to make it with. They had their *Alexanders* and *Polar Expresses* they were working on, and I figured my movie was going to have to live or die on its own terms."

I think that suited him just fine. Suspecting his film had the potential for greatness, Eastwood wanted to go off in a quiet corner and make it unobserved.

"We went and made it, they didn't know anything about it, and after we showed it to them," Eastwood told me in an interview, "they said, 'Jesus, it's not too bad.' Some people in the organization started getting enthusiastic."

Considering its Oscar chances, a studio executive discussed "mounting a campaign." Eastwood says he replied: "No mounting a campaign, no mounting anything. Just see where it goes."

It was his idea to open it in a handful of showcase theaters and depend on word of mouth—a strategy that last worked for an Oscar winner with *Chariots of Fire* (1981). These days important movies open on thousands of screens on the same day, partly to take advantage of national media buys, partly because, well, the word of mouth may not be all that good (consider the case of *Alexander*).

Writing in the *Sunday Independent* of London, the paper's California-based film critic David Thomson flatly states Eastwood's film "is going to win Best Picture," and adds that his tears at the end "were not just for its story but for the movies. Because at long last someone has said, 'Look, this is how you do it.'"

Thomson is the author of the long-respected *Biographical Dictionary of Film.* That adds weight to his observation: "At the age of sixty or so, (Eastwood) began to improve, no matter that he was rich and successful enough to do whatever he wanted. This is a very rare phenomenon in today's world of film where people of Eastwood's age (seventy-five) either turn impossibly childish or senile, or stop. Instead, Eastwood has begun to search for better and better material, and in the process has enlarged himself as an actor and an artist."

All true, but I am still running into people who say, "I hear it's good, but I don't like boxing movies." To which all I can say is, "It's not a boxing movie. It's a movie about a boxer. Trust me on this."

Independent Spirit Awards

Santa Monica, California, February 28, 2005—*Sideways,* the story of two buddies who make a prewedding tour of California's wine country, swept the twentieth annual Independent Spirit Awards, winning for best feature, best male lead (Paul Giamatti), best supporting female (Virginia Madsen), best supporting male (Thomas Haden Church), best director (Alexander Payne), and best screenplay (Payne and Jim Taylor).

Madsen, an especially popular winner, brought her young son, Jack, onstage, and observed she had been making independent films for "about seventeen years," alluding directly to career struggles before her current stardom with *Sideways*.

The Indies, a luncheon ceremony held under a huge tent on the beach in Santa Monica, were founded to provide a showcase for independent films at a time when the Oscars were dominated by mainstream commercial films. Now the categories sometimes overlap.

Sideways, for example, was nominated for Oscars in all the same categories it won Indies for, except best actor, where Paul Giamatti, passed over by the Academy, got a huge ovation even though he confessed onstage, "I'm neither spirited nor particularly independent."

Other major Indie winners included *Maria Full of Grace*, the story of a young Colombian who is a "mule" carrying drugs to New York, which won for best female lead (Catalina Sandino Moreno, an Oscar nominee) and best first screenplay (Joshua Marston). *The Motorcycle Diaries*, the story of a youthful trip by future revolutionary Che Guevera, won Indies for best debut performance (Rodrigo de la Serna) and best cinematography (Eric Gautier).

Other winners were eventual Oscar winner *The Sea Inside*, directed by Alejandro Amenabar of Spain, as best foreign film; *Metallica: Some Kind of Monster*, by Joe Berlinger and Bruce Sinofsky, as best documentary; and *Garden State*, by Zach Braff, as best first feature.

"Four years ago," Braff said, holding his award onstage, "I rented a bike so I could pedal down here and watch all of you guys coming out of the tent."

Although the winners were worthy, there was a trend that some found disturbing: In almost every major category, the winner was the most successful, visible, or largest film. At a ceremony founded to honor outsiders and independents, the prizes went to films that already had box office success and, in most cases, Oscar nominations.

Some veterans of the awards, sponsored by the Independent Feature Project, have noted in recent years that voters are not required to see all of the nominees in order to vote, and the totals seem to indicate a tilt toward estab-lished box office winners. The Academy, in its documentary and foreign categories, demands members prove they have seen all five films before they can vote, and some members of the Indie Spirits community think it's time to make a rule like that for their awards.

Three $20,000 prizes were given for extraordinary work. The Bravo/American Express Award went to producer Gina Kwon, of *You and Me and Everyone We Know*. The DirectTV/IFC "Truer Than Fiction" award went to Zana Briski and Ross Kauffman, producers of the documentary *Born Into Brothels*. And the Turning Leaf Wineries "Someone to Watch" award went to Jem Cohen, director of *Chain*.

Mean Creek, a film about young people on a river trip that ends in tragedy, won the John Cassavetes Award, named in honor of the godfather of independent filmmaking, for its director, Jacob Aaron Estes; the film's ensemble cast won an award for "special distinction."

Samuel L. Jackson emceed the event, declaring each of the best film nominees "my personal favorite." Presenters included Robin Williams, Kevin Bacon, John Waters, Quentin Tarantino, and Kyra Sedgwick.

Million Dollar Baby Takes Top Honors at Oscars

Hollywood, California, February 28, 2005— *Million Dollar Baby* scored a late-round rally at the seventy-seventh annual Academy Awards as Clint Eastwood's movie about a determined female boxer won for Best Picture and took Oscars for Actress (Hilary Swank), Supporting Actor (Morgan Freeman), and Director (Eastwood).

It was another bitter disappointment for legendary director Martin Scorsese, who was passed over by the academy for the fifth time in the directing category. To be sure, Scorsese's *The Aviator* led the evening with five Oscars to four for *Baby*, but it won only one major award, for Cate Blanchett as Supporting Actress.

As the evening began, it looked like it might be an *Aviator* night, as the Howard Hughes biopic dominated the early going with awards for art direction, costume design, cinematography, and editing. But academy members are said to vote with their heads in the technical categories, and with their hearts in the top categories, and *Million Dollar Baby* was a much more emotional film than *The Aviator*, with its distant, enigmatic hero.

No surprise, but the audience was joyous when Jamie Foxx won as Best Actor for *Ray*, a biopic based on the life of music legend Ray Charles. After thanking the usual suspects, Foxx said: "I see Oprah (Winfrey) and I see Halle (Berry), and I just want to say your names." He thanked Winfrey for introducing him to Sidney Poitier, an inspiration, and then, in an extraordinary moment that brought a hush to the house, Foxx thanked his grandmother, Marie.

"She was my first acting teacher," he said. "'Stand up straight. Put your shoulders back. Act like you got some sense.' We would go somewhere, and she would say, 'Act like you been somewhere.' And she would whup me, but then she would talk to me, and she still talks to me now, only now, she talks to me in my dreams. And I can't wait to go to sleep tonight, because we got a lot to talk about. I love you."

Accepting his director prize, the seventy-four-year-old Eastwood also thanked a relative, his ninety-six-year-old mother, "who is here with me tonight." He also singled out legendary production designer Henry Bumstead, ninety, as "the head of our crack geriatrics team." When he saw eighty-year-old Sidney Lumet on the stage, accepting his honorary Oscar earlier in the evening, Eastwood said he realized, "I'm just a kid." (In any case, Eastwood is now the oldest person ever to win Best Director honors.)

As widely predicted, Swank won her second Oscar for Best Actress, for the title role of *Million Dollar Baby*. "I don't know what I did in this life to deserve all this," said Swank, in a reference to her previous Oscar win for *Boys Don't Cry* (1999). "I'm just a girl from a trailer park who had a dream."

As the music swelled to cut off her speech, Swank said, "Wait! I saved Clint for the end. Thank you, Clint Eastwood, for allowing me to go on this journey with you. You're my 'Mo Chuisle,'" referring to her character's nickname ("My Darling") in *Million Dollar Baby*.

It was one of the shorter modern Oscar ceremonies, clocking in at a little over three hours and ten minutes, as opposed to a recent four-hour extravaganza. That was partly because host Chris Rock opened on a high-energy note, partly because most of the winners this year avoided reciting laundry lists of their agents, lawyers, relatives, publicists, and accountants.

Until Swank's victory, the ceremony had been dominated by *The Aviator*, with wins for Supporting Actress, Editing, and Cinematography. The evening's first upset came when Alexander Payne and Jim Taylor won for screenplay adaptation for *Sideways*. Paul Haggis was thought to be the front-runner for *Million Dollar Baby*.

In another upset, the telecast's scene-stealer was Jorge Drexler, Best Song winner for "Al Otro Lado del Rio," from *The Motorcycle Diaries*. He sang his thank-you speech—the chorus of the song—in Spanish.

Another Spanish-language movie took a major prize: Alejandro Amenabar's *The Sea Inside*, from Spain, won as Best Foreign Film. It stars Javier Bardem as a man long-paralyzed, who chooses to die and must persuade others to help him. The film shared with *Million Dollar Baby* a subject that generated protest from advocacy groups who believe life is very much worth living despite such disabilities. Picketers outside the Kodak Theatre held large banners denouncing Eastwood and his film, but did not single out *The Sea Inside* as a target.

As expected, *The Incredibles*, won as Best Animated Feature. Director Brad Bird took the Oscar home to Pixar, a center of change in the transition of animated films from children's entertainment to mainstream audiences.

"I don't know what's more frightening, being watched by millions of people, or the hundreds of people that are going to be annoyed with me tomorrow for not mentioning them," said writer-director Bird.

The Aviator surge continued with Cate Blanchett's Oscar for Supporting Actress. The elegant Australian thespian, who took a considerable risk in playing a Hollywood legend, Katharine Hepburn, thanked director Scorsese and other collaborators, but didn't show much, or any, emotion.

Had Chicago hometown favorite Virginia Madsen won, it would have been a different story; her nomination was a dramatic turn in a career that has seen its discouraging moments. But Madsen and her mom, Elaine, were upbeat on the red carpet, and Elaine said she told her daughter before the ceremony that being nominated was the real honor, that it allowed her to stand with pride before the industry, and opened up opportunities for many more roles.

Another major *Aviator* award came in the crucial category of editing: Thelma Schoonmaker, Scorsese's longtime collaborator since the dawn of their careers. She had won once before, for Scorsese's *Raging Bull*, and said, "This belongs to you, Marty, as much as to me, not only because you helped me edit the picture, but because you think like an editor."

"This was a labor of love," said Morgan Freeman, accepting his first Oscar after four nominations. His was the first of the major wins for *Million Dollar Baby*, and his speech was short and to the point: "I want to thank everybody and anybody who ever had anything at all to do with the making of this picture." He mentioned director and costar Eastwood, costar Swank, and left the stage, cool and composed. No histrionics for the man about whom film critic Pauline Kael once asked, "Is there a better actor in America?"

If Freeman was reserved, others were more animated. "Boy, am I glad there wasn't a fourth episode of *Lord of the Rings*," quipped John Dykstra, who shared with three collaborators the visual effects Oscar for *Spider-Man 2*.

Another director loomed large, honorary winner Sidney Lumet. Presenter Al Pacino said Lumet's stage production of Eugene O'Neill's *The Iceman Cometh* inspired him to become an actor. He would later work with Lumet in *Dog Day Afternoon*. Lumet, whose work also includes *12 Angry Men, Network, The Verdict*, and *Running on Empty*, received his Oscar for lifetime achievement.

"I was lucky enough to be nominated for my first picture, and started fantasizing about my speech," Lumet said. "I was a real smart aleck and thought I'd say, "I don't want to thank anyone; I did it all on my own." Now, at the other end of his career, he had an endless list of people to thank, and listed directors and writers and great screen moments, and said, "What it comes down to is, I'd like to thank

the movies." In its understatement and simplicity, it was the model of a perfect Oscar acceptance speech.

Another industry veteran, Roger Mayer, picked up the Jean Hersholt Humanitarian Award, presented by Scorsese, for his preservation efforts of classic movies—one of Scorsese's own favorite causes. When Mayer and others, including Scorsese, began to organize their preservation work, many movies were being trashed or allowed to disintegrate.

What did Oscar producer Gil Cates slip into the coffee of the winners this year? Speeches were short and to the point, and the ceremony moved with an unaccustomed zip. Let's hope it's a trend for future telecasts.

Diary Review Sparks E-Mail Flurry

March 1, 2005—Well, now I know who Tyler Perry is. I published a negative one-star review of *Diary of a Mad Black Woman*, and since then I have received more e-mails about it than about any review I have ever written, outnumbering *Fahrenheit 9/11* and *The Passion of the Christ* put together. And they were not all the same message, generated by some Website or its followers. Each manifestly came from an individual reader who felt moved to write.

Some sent references to a recent National Public Radio report on Perry, "America's most successful unknown playwright." Others referred me to the movie's extraordinary message board at Yahoo—where, after more than two months in release, *Being Julia* has generated fifty-two messages and an average grade of C-plus, and *Diary of a Mad Black Woman*, after four days in release, has more than 2,100 messages and a grade of A-minus.

Many of the messages say versions of the same thing: White critics don't get it. We don't know who Tyler Perry is, we have never heard of the millions of dollars his plays have grossed all over America, in theaters, churches, school halls, and on DVD, and—most of all—we don't know that characters like his Madea are based on strong black women the writers are all familiar with.

To back up a second: *Diary of a Mad Black Woman*, which will win the weekend box office contest with an estimated gross over $25 million, is a movie starring Kimberly Elise as Helen, the wife of a rich African-American attorney (Steve Harris). After eighteen years of marriage and verbal abuse, he dumps her for another woman (Lisa Marcos) who has two kids—all the more painful because Helen's miscarriages were caused by his mistreatment.

The movie, up to this point, is a strong family drama that had engaged my sympathy. Then Helen flees into the arms of her grandmother, Madea, played in drag by playwright Tyler Perry, who (I quote myself) "is built along the lines of a linebacker . . . a tall, lantern-jawed, smooth-skinned, balloon-breasted gargoyle with a bad wig, who likes to wave a loaded gun and shoot test rounds into the ceiling." Madea visits the cheating husband's house to destroy his furniture with a chainsaw. I ended: "I've been reviewing movies for a long time, and I can't think of one that more dramatically shoots itself in the foot."

Other critics agreed with me. At rottentomatoes.com, where only twenty-three of seventy-eight critics liked the film, we read:

"This isn't a situation in which the right hand doesn't know what the left is doing. It's more like they're not even part of the same body."—Robert Denerstein, *Rocky Mountain News*

"A crudely made hodgepodge of rank clichés that veers between shrill melodrama, glossy soap opera, and broad, sitcom-level comedy."—Timothy Knight, Reel.com

"Stay clear of this mess."—Lou Lumenick, *New York Post*

"Sure, I laughed. Yes, I cried. But mostly I just wanted to throw up."—Michael O'Sullivan, *Washington Post*

"Blows to the head are delivered with more subtlety than the message of *Diary of a Mad Black Woman*."—Wesley Morris, *Boston Globe*

All clueless white critics? No, Morris is an African-American who knows who Tyler Perry is and compares Madea to Martin Lawrence's character in *Big Momma's House*. He adds: "Perry's brand of touring 'urban' theater has made him a star in black America. I've seen a couple of his shows on DVD while waiting to get my hair cut at the barbershop. On the stage, their overall hamminess wears down your resistance, and the frisky interplay with the live audience makes them passable

fun. A precise double take is always good for a big laugh. But there's nothing precise about the movie that director Darren Grant has made of *Diary*."

The e-mails I've received are more direct: As a white man, I'm told, I am clueless to understand that strong older black women, who have had to be tough to survive in hard times, are familiar in all African-American families, and do not conform to the genteel manners of the art-house crowd. More than one writer, especially on the Yahoo message boards, calls me and other critics of the film racist. "Y U B Hating?" is one headline. Demon2002 writes: "Look some of you really need to stop (white people) especially those of you with your racist comments about all blacks in the ghetto. I'm willing to bet my entire direct deposit pay, which is probably substantially more than many of you will see in three months, that you didn't see this movie . . . I hate that home computers have been made so accessible in price that the lower class and closed-minded whites are spewing foolishness across the net."

Deborah Young of Overland Park, Kansas, was friendlier and more helpful in a message direct to my Answer Man column: "Sure, Madea is an exaggeration. At the same time, there's a lot about Madea that rings true for me. As an African-American woman, I've seen many tamer versions of Madea, women who refused to settle for anything less than their birthrights (respect, consideration, and fair treatment). Sometimes these women can get a little rough, knock some heads together, so to speak, but they can be endearing as well. It's clear that other black viewers share my views. Tyler Perry's touring stage plays and DVDs have grossed millions. Why? Because black audiences can identify with Madea. They recognize her as a larger-than-life version of some of the no-nonsense, good-hearted aunts, mamas, or grannies they've known and loved."

At a pre-Oscar party honoring Ebony's sixtieth anniversary, I talked with *Diary* producer Reuben Cannon, whose credits include the wonderful *Down in the Delta* and *The Women of Brewster Place*. At the Indie Spirits, I talked with Kimberly Elise. They also worked together on *Woman, Thou Art Loosed* (2004), based on a screenplay and costarring Bishop T. D. Jakes, another icon of the black community not widely known to whites. That was a much better movie, proving (as *Diary* and *Beloved* do) that Elise is a gifted actress. But it has no Madea, and grossed $6.7 million domestically, a figure *Diary* passed on its opening day.

Cannon and Elise were awfully nice to me, under the circumstances. Perhaps the fact that their movie was No. 1 at the box office helped. Cannon knew about my review but wasn't angry. He said *Diary* was *intended* as a mixture of genres, a movie that would defy convention. They were aware when they made it that Madea was on a different reality level than the other characters, but the formula had been wildly popular in productions of Perry's plays, and they wanted the film to capitalize on the enormous popularity of Perry and (especially) Madea.

I have reread my original review, and see no need to change a word. It expresses what I think about *Diary,* and a critic is worthless if he starts writing what he thinks his readers want to read. He becomes the dummy and his readers become ventriloquists.

But the outpouring of dissent about *Diary* has me thinking in another direction. The assumption beneath my review was that a movie should discover the correct tone for its material and stick to it. I was grabbed at the outset by the plight of the Kimberly Elise character, was moved by her despair, was touched by the character of her mother, played by Cicely Tyson, and I recoiled every time Madea came charging in like a train wreck.

Yet the most successful film industry on Earth, India's Bollywood, deliberately mixes genres. "You get everything in one film," my Mumbai friend Uma de Cuhna told me. *Diary of a Mad Black Woman* provides melodrama, romance, scandal, the escapism of a lavish lifestyle, a message of forgiveness, and the larger-than-life Madea, whose pot-smoking doesn't seem to bother the Christian church audiences who make up a large part of Perry's fan base. It's not supposed to be all of a piece, told with a consistent tone. It's more like a variety show. And Madea is

no more supposed to be a "real" African-American grandmother than Dame Edna Everage is supposed to be a "real" Australian housewife.

Okay, I get it. I refuse to accept the theory that I am racist because I disliked the film (many of the Yahoo messages attack the notion that racism belongs in the discussion). But I do realize that Tyler Perry is under the radar of the white-dominated media, and that the loss of Elvis Mitchell at the *New York Times* leaves us with only a handful of black critics (Morris, Desson Thomson at the *Washington Post,* Armand White at the *New York Press,* and 3BlackChicks.com, for example). Doesn't it seem like there ought to be more mainstream black film critics than Oscar nominees?

Unfortunately, White, Thomson, and all three black chicks have not reviewed the film. It's by no means certain that Mitchell would have praised it, although he would have put it in context. In the *New York Press,* White's stablemate, Matt Zoller Seitz, writes: "This may prove to be a slow-building cult phenomenon that endures withering pans but lingers in theaters for weeks, eventually forcing the same critics who dismissed it to write think-pieces explaining its success."

The ink is scarcely dry on his review, and here I am, doing just that. Do I think I failed *Diary of a Mad Black Woman* in my duty as a critic? No, because (1) I told you honestly what I thought about it, and (2) I provided a good idea of what's in the movie, so that readers can decide they'd like it even if I didn't. My crime seems to have been disliking Madea. But I don't dislike her—I simply can't stand her in this movie. I would like to see Kimberly Elise in a serious drama that gives range to her considerable gifts, and Madea in a comedy in the genre of *Big Momma's House.* But not in the same movie, please.

Q&A for Kevin Smith's Website "Movie Poop Shoot"

Q. The Internet's lack of word counts seems to encourage reviews that ramble on and on. To prove that reviews can be effective without being verbose, for the two contests we've run for the *Great Movies* books, I've asked entrants to submit a movie review in fifty words or less, which has proven a good challenge. What sort of advice can you give Net reviewers about economizing their words and making their point as briefly as possible?

A. Jeez. This is like writing the haiku of film criticism! But you make a good point: Space is unlimited on the Web, but users' time is limited, and the wise critic would follow the immortal advice of Strunk and White, in *The Elements of Style* (a book that should be at every writer's elbow):

"A sentence should contain no unnecessary words, a paragraph no unnecessary sentences."

If you can follow that, no matter how long your piece is, by definition it is not too long.

Q. A follow-up to that question would be, do you think reviews that discuss a reviewer's mind-set and details of their day leading up to a screening are effective or detract from the review of the film itself?

A. Depends. I can do without some of Harry Knowles's reviews that begin with his breakfast. On the other hand, the fact that I first saw *The Third Man* as a college kid on my first visit to Paris, in a smoky Left Bank revival house, is absolutely bound to my feelings about that film.

Q. Internet reviews often cite the immediacy of the Internet and the ability to post a review almost as soon as a screening ends as proof that it's a more effective communication tool than print. You work in both—agree or disagree with this thinking? Do you feel a reviewer is more insightful by writing up a review as soon as possible while a film is still fresh in their heads, or do better movie reviews benefit from reflection for a time before writing the review?

A. I don't like to let long periods of time elapse, because while factual memory is durable, emotional memory tends to fade. When I see a film at a festival and it opens months afterwards, I always ask for another screening. The fresher the film is in the mind, the better.

Q. Many new reviewers spend more time laying out a movie's plot points than they do critiquing what they've seen. What're some tips that would help reviewers focus more on the critique of a film than simply summarizing its story?

A. When Mary Knoblauch was film critic of the late, lamented *Chicago Today,* she held herself to a rule of: One paragraph only for the plot summary. I would find that draconian. Sometimes my reviews may essentially be a description of the plot (tilted and opinionated and with asides and digs of the elbow), and that is all right, but other times I get bogged down in the plot, and try to be briefer. In my review of *Million Dollar Baby* I think I found a good balance between plot (less the surprise development) and specific comments on particular scenes. I was amused that John Simon's review of *Beyond the Valley of the Dolls* was the longest one in one of his collections, because he unwisely got into the plot.

Q. New movie reviewers typically have only their own film background as their film education and don't have film school backing their opinions. Is it important to know the difference between, say, *film noir* and *film soleil,* or to recognize echoes of John Ford in a movie to write an effective review? Is the lack of a comprehensive movie education a problem for upcoming reviewers?

A. You learn on the job. The movies teach you. There were no film classes at the University of Illinois when I was a student. But I read books, learned by visiting sets and interviewing film people, taught film classes, and taught myself. So did the film critics who inspired me like Pauline Kael, Manny Farber, James Agee, Dwight Macdonald, Stanley Kauffmann, and Andrew Sarris.

For the basics, in plain English without theoretical hoop-jumping, I recommend David Bordwell and Kristin Thompson's books *Film Art, Film History,* and, more advanced, the brilliant, *On the History of Film Style.* Also Louis Gianetti's *Understanding Movies,* now in its tenth edition. I bought the first edition the day I was named film critic.

Q. If so, how would you suggest they add to their knowledge? Reading *The Great Movies I* and *II* is a perfect source, but are there other ways? Just watching as many movies from as many eras as possible?

A. Yeah, go to the movies. Rent movies. Break out of the present and plunder the past. Taking one of the Great Movies books and working your way through it is one idea, since there will be some titles you're not familiar with and others you disagree with.

Q. Many reviewers write reviews as though they're only looking to provide quote-ready sound bites for newspapers. Is it more important to focus on the craft of writing a good review than it is getting a quote pulled and seen by a wide number of people?

A. Publicists have complained to me that some of my reviews contain *no* blurblike comments. On the other hand, when I wrote "One of the greatest performances in the history of the cinema" about Charlize Theron in *Monster,* I knew it read like a blurb and that was fine with me. The movie came within a whisker of going straight to video. By reviewing it three weeks early on *Ebert & Roeper,* I think we were able to attract crucial attention to it.

Q. Which reviewers who write primarily for the Internet—that is, people who don't have their printed reviews run at a paper's Website or some such—have you noticed who do a good job at covering movies? Or do you even read others' critiques of movies?

A. Of the Web-based critics, I like Charles Taylor, David Edelstein, James Berardinelli, Stephanie Zacharek, JoBlo, Emanuel Levy, Ray Pride, and several others (this is not a complete list). I like what Jim Emerson, the editor of rogerebert.com, is writing for our site. I do not usually read critics before writing my own review, because when I am writing they are also writing and the movie has not opened yet. My reviews appear on opening day, or from festivals before the movie opens. But I feel no particular fetish about keeping myself pure by reading no reviews before writing. As a graduate student of English, I was taught to survey the critical literature in preparation for my own writing. I think I probably mention other critics more frequently than most current critics, because I believe in credit where due.

Here is my favorite recent use of the Web in one of my own reviews. It is from my review of *Ong Bak:*

* * *

The movie stars Tony Jaa, a young actor who is already an accomplished stunt man and expert in Muay Thai boxing, a sentence I have typed just as if I had the slightest idea what Muay Thai boxing is. Thank you, Website.

* * *

Q. In *The Great Movies II,* which reviews do you feel you particularly nailed? I'm looking for examples people can read and benefit from, reviews that you really feel stated your opinion perfectly.

A. Hmmm. I think I successfully defended *Bring Me the Head of Alfredo Garcia.* I hit the right note on *Touchez Pas Au Grisbi.* Also, happening to look under the letter m: *My Neighbor Totoro, Mon Oncle,* and *Moonstruck.*

Q. Do you have any other words of advice for upcoming reviewers? Remember, these are people who would love to take your job someday!

A. Whether or not you write in the first person, criticism is all opinion, and your review is your opinion. I am very comfortable with first person.

Remember that not all movies have the same audience, and therefore not all reviews have the same readers. Write in a way that seems appropriate to each film. That doesn't mean writing up or writing down, but writing in a way relevant to the film.

Feel free to place a film in context with other films and other works by the same director. Films are not born in a void.

Remember that your readers are not being paid to go to the movies, and you are. Do not give a movie the equivalent of a 4-star or 3.5-star review unless you personally believe that if you were not a film critic, it would have been worth your own time and money to leave the house, go to the theater, and buy a ticket.

Evil in Film: To What End?

On August 12, 2005, I published two zero-star reviews, of *Deuce Bigalow: European Gigolo* and *Chaos*. The first was a moronic comedy, and its review will appear in next year's edition of this book. The review for the second appears below. In it, I wrote:

"*Chaos* is ugly, nihilistic, and cruel—a film I regret having seen. I urge you to avoid it. Don't make the mistake of thinking it's 'only' a horror film or a slasher film. It is an exercise in heartless cruelty and it ends with careless brutality. The movie denies not only the value of life, but the possibility of hope."

The *Deuce Bigalow* review speaks for itself. The review of *Chaos*, which at the time of the review had not yet received a wide national release, deserves some discussion. I received a provocative letter from Steven Jay Bernheim, its producer, and David DeFalco, its director, that was printed in an advertisement in the Weekend section of the *Chicago Sun-Times*. I reprint their letter here, followed by my response (which reveals important plot details).

* * *

Dear Mr. Ebert:

Thank you for reviewing our film, *Chaos*, and for your thoughtful comments. However, there are some issues you raised that we strongly feel we need to address. First, it is obvious that our film greatly upset you. In your own words, "it affected [you] strongly," and filled you "with sadness and disquiet." You admitted that the film "works." Nevertheless, you urged the public "to avoid it," and you went so far as to resort to expletives: "Why do we need this s—t?," you asked.

As your colleague at the *Chicago Daily Herald* commented, *Chaos* "marks the first real post-9/11 horror film," and "the horror reality has long ago surpassed the horror of Japanese movies and PG-13 films." Simply put, the *Herald* gets it and you do not.

Natalee Holloway. Kidnappings and beheadings in Iraq shown on the Internet. Wives blasting jail guards with shotguns to free their husbands. The confessions of the BTK killer—these are events of the last few months. How else should filmmakers address this "ugly, nihilistic, and cruel" reality—other than with scenes that are "ugly, nihilistic, and cruel," to use the words you used to describe *Chaos*?

Mr. Ebert, would you prefer it if instead we exploit these ugly, nihilistic, and cruel events by sanitizing them, like the PG-13 horror films do, or like the cable networks do, to titillate and attract audiences without exposing the real truth, the real evil?

Mr. Ebert, how do you want twenty-first century evil to be portrayed in film and in the media? Tame and sanitized? Titillating and exploitive? Or do you want evil portrayed as it really is? "Ugly, nihilistic, and cruel," as you say our film does it?

We tried to give you and the public something real. Real evil exists and cannot be ignored, sanitized, or exploited. It needs to be shown just as it is, which is why we need this s—t, to use your own coarse words. And if this upsets you, or "disquiets" you, or leaves you "saddened," that's the point. So instead of telling the public to avoid this film, shouldn't you let them make their own decision?

Respectfully,

Steven Jay Bernheim
Producer, *Chaos*

David DeFalco
Director, *Chaos*

* * *

Here is my response (which reveals important plot details):

Dear Mr. Bernheim and Mr. DeFalco:

Your film does "work," and as filmmakers you have undeniable skills and gifts. The question is, did you put them to a defensible purpose? I believed you did not. I urged my readers to avoid seeing the film. I have also urged them to see many films.

Moviegoers make up their own minds. Like many at the screening I attended, I left saddened and disgusted. Michael Mirasol, a fellow critic, asked me why I even wrote a review, and I answered: "It will get about the audience it would have gotten anyway, but it deserves to be dealt with and replied to."

Yes, you got a slightly better review from the *Daily Herald,* but every other major critic who has seen the movie shares my view. Maybe we do "get it." As Michael Wilmington wrote in his zero-star review in the *Chicago Tribune,* the movie "definitely gave me the worst time I've had at a movie in years—and I wouldn't recommend it to anyone but my worst enemies." And from Laura Kern at the *New York Times:* "Stay far, far away from this one." The line "Why do we need this s—t" was not original with me; I quoted it from Ed Gonzalez at slantmagazine.com, who did not use any dashes in his version. I find it ironic that the makers of *Chaos* would scold me for using "coarse" language and "resorting to expletives."

But there is a larger question here. In a time of dismay and dread, is it admirable for filmmakers to depict pure evil? Have 9/11, suicide bombers, serial killers, and kidnappings created a world in which the response of the artist must be nihilistic and hopeless? At the end of your film, after the other characters have been killed in sadistic and gruesome ways, the only survivor is the one who is evil incarnate, and we hear his cold laughter under a screen that has gone dark.

I believe art can certainly be nihilistic and express hopelessness; the powerful movie *Open Water,* about two scuba divers left behind by a tourist boat, is an example. I believe evil can win in fiction, as it often does in real life. But I prefer that the artist express an attitude toward that evil. It is not enough to record it; what do you think and feel about it? Your attitude is as detached as your hero's. If *Chaos* has a message, it is that evil reigns and will triumph. I don't believe so.

While it is true, as you argue, that evil cannot be ignored or sanitized, it can certainly be exploited, as *Chaos* demonstrates. You begin the film with one of those sanctimonious messages depicting the movie as a "warning" that will educate its viewers and possibly save their lives. But what are they to learn? That evil people will torture and murder them if they take any chances, go to parties, or walk in the woods? We can't live our lives in hiding.

Your real purpose in making *Chaos,* I suspect, was not to educate, but to create a scandal that would draw an audience. There's always money to be made by going further and being more shocking. Sometimes there is also art to be found in that direction, but not this time.

That's because your film creates a closed system in which any alternative outcome is excluded; it is like a movie of a man falling to his death, which can have no developments except that he continues to fall, and no ending except that he dies. Predestination may be useful in theology, but as a narrative strategy, it is self-defeating.

I call your attention to two movies you have not mentioned: Ingmar Bergman's *The Virgin Spring* (1960) and Wes Craven's *The Last House on the Left* (1972). As Gonzalez, despite his "coarse" language, points out, your film follows *Last House* so closely "that Wes Craven could probably sue DeFalco for a dual screenwriting credit and win." Craven, also indebted to Bergman, did a modern horror-film version of the Bergman film, which was set in medieval times. In it, a girl goes into the woods and is raped and murdered. Her killers later happen to stay overnight as guests of the grieving parents. When they discover who they are, the father exacts his revenge.

In the Craven version, there is also revenge; I gave the movie a four-star rating, because I felt it was uncommonly effective, even though it got many reviews as negative as my review of *Chaos.* Craven, and to a greater degree Bergman, used the material as a way of dealing with tragedy, human loss, and human nature.

You use the material without pity, to look unblinkingly at a monster and his victims. The monster is given no responsibility, no motive, no context, no depth. Like a shark, he exists to kill. I am reminded of a great movie about a serial killer, actually named *Monster* (2003). In it, innocent people were murdered, but we were not invited to simply stare. The killer was allowed her humanity, which I believe all of us have, even the worst of us. It was possible to see her first as victim, then as murderer. The film did not excuse her behavior, but understood that it proceeded from evil done to her. If the film contained a "warning" to "educate" us, it was not that evil will destroy us, but that others will do unto us as we have done unto them. If we do not want monsters like Aileen Wuornos in our world, we should not allow them to have the childhoods that she had.

What I miss in your film is any sense of hope. Sometimes it is all that keeps us going. The message of futility and despair in *Chaos* is unrelieved, and while I do not require a "happy ending," I do appreciate some kind of catharsis. As the Greeks understood tragedy, it exists not to bury us in death and dismay, but to help us to deal with it, to accept it as a part of life, to learn about our own humanity from it. That is why the Greek tragedies were poems: The language ennobled the material.

Animals do not know they are going to die and require no way to deal with that implacable fact. Humans, who know we will die, have been given the consolations of art, myth, hope, science, religion, philosophy, denial, and even movies, to help us reconcile with that final fact. What I object to most of all in *Chaos* is not the sadism, the brutality, the torture, the nihilism, but the absence of any alternative to them. If the world has indeed become as evil as you think, then we need the redemptive power of artists, poets, philosophers, and theologians more than ever.

Your answer, that the world is evil and therefore it is your responsibility to reflect it, is no answer at all, but a surrender.

Sincerely,

Roger Ebert

* * *

Chaos   no stars
NO MPAA RATING ,78 m., 2005

Kevin Gage (Chaos), Stephen Wozniak (Frankie), Kelly K.C. Quann (Sadie), Sage Stallone (Swan), Chantal Degroat (Angelica), Maya Barovich (Emily), Ken Medlock (Sheriff). Directed by David DeFalco and produced by Steven Jay Bernheim. Screenplay by DeFalco.

Chaos is ugly, nihilistic, and cruel—a film I regret having seen. I urge you to avoid it. Don't make the mistake of thinking it's "only" a hor-

ror film or a slasher film. It is an exercise in heartless cruelty and it ends with careless brutality. The movie denies not only the value of life, but the possibility of hope.

The movie premiered in late July at Flashback Weekend, a Chicago convention devoted to horror and exploitation films. As I write, it remains unreviewed in *Variety,* unlisted on Rotten Tomatoes. As an unabashed retread of *The Last House on the Left* (itself inspired by Bergman's *The Virgin Spring*), it may develop a certain notoriety, but you don't judge a book by its cover or a remake by its inspiration. A few Web writers have seen it, and try to deal with their feelings:

"What is inflicted upon these women is degrading, humiliating, and terrible on every level."
—Capone, Ain't It Cool News

"Disgusting, shocking, and laced with humiliation, nudity, profanity, and limit-shoving tastelessness."
—John Gray, pitofhorror.com

"What's the point of this s—t anyway?"
—Ed Gonzalez, slantmagazine.com

But Capone finds the film "highly effective" if "painful and difficult to watch." And Gray looks on the bright side: DeFalco "manages to shock and disturb as well as give fans a glimpse of hope that some people are still trying to make good, sleazy, exploitation films." Gonzalez finds no redeeming features, adding, "DeFalco directs the whole thing with all the finesse of someone who has been hit on the head one too many times (is this a good time to say he was a wrestler?)."

I quote these reviews because I'm fascinated by their strategies for dealing with a film that transcends all barriers of decency. There are two scenes so gruesome I cannot describe them in a newspaper, no matter what words I use. Having seen it, I cannot ignore it, nor can I deny that it affected me strongly: I recoiled during some of the most cruel moments, and when the film was over I was filled with sadness and disquiet.

The plot: Angelica and Emily (Chantal Degroat and Maya Barovich) are UCLA students, visiting the country cabin of Emily's parents, an interracial couple. They hear about a rave in the woods, drive off to party, meet a lout named Swan (Sage Stallone), and ask him where they can find some Ecstasy. He leads them to a cabin occupied by Chaos (Kevin Gage), already wanted for serial killing, Frankie (Stephen Wozniak), and Sadie (Kelly K.C. Quann). They're a Manson family in microcosm. By the end of the film, they will have raped and murdered the girls, not always in that order. Nor does the bloodshed stop there. The violence is sadistic, graphic, savage, and heartless. Much of the action involves the girls weeping and pleading for their lives. When the film pauses for dialogue, it is often racist.

So that's it. DeFalco directs with a crude, efficient gusto, as a man with an ax makes short work of firewood. Kevin Gage makes Chaos repulsive and cruel, Quann is effective as a pathetic, dim-witted sex slave, and the young victims are played with relentless sincerity; to the degree that we are repelled by the killers and feel pity for the victims, the movie "works." It works, all right, but I'm with Ed Gonzalez: Why do we need this s—t?

In Memoriam

Anne Bancroft

And here's to you, Mrs. Robinson, Jesus loves you more than you will know.
    —*Mrs. Robinson* by Simon and Garfunkel

Anne Bancroft, who won an Academy Award for one performance and everlasting fame for another, died June 6, 2005, in New York. She was seventy-three. Her Oscar came for *The Miracle Worker* (1962), in which she played Annie Sullivan, the teacher who used touch to reach into the world of the blind and deaf Helen Keller. Her fame came for *The Graduate* (1967), in which she played Mrs. Robinson, a married woman who used her worldly sexuality to seduce a young college graduate (Dustin Hoffman). The name "Mrs. Robinson" became synonymous with sexy older women, not least because of the famous Simon and Garfunkel song that celebrated the character.

Miss Bancroft, who was married for more than forty years to the writer, director, and comedian Mel Brooks, died in Mount Sinai Medical Center. A family spokesman said the cause of death was uterine cancer.

After *The Miracle Worker,* Bancroft was nominated for four more Oscars, playing an emotionally tormented wife in *The Pumpkin Eater* (1964), Mrs. Robinson in *The Graduate,* a ballet dancer who chose her career over a personal life in *The Turning Point* (1977), and a mother superior in *Agnes of God* (1985). She also had great success on the stage, where she won Tony Awards for her work in *Two for the Seesaw* and *The Miracle Worker.*

Arthur Penn, who directed her in both of those plays and in the film *The Miracle Worker,* told the *New York Times:* "More happens in her face in ten seconds than happens in most women's faces in ten years."

That was certainly the case in *The Graduate,* where as the bored wife of a profoundly conventional suburbanite, she boldly seduces Benjamin Braddock, the Hoffman character. The plot grows emotionally hazardous when he later falls in love with her daughter (Katharine Ross). A still photo of Benjamin regarding Mrs. Robinson's leg in a nylon stocking became an icon of movie imagery.

Although much was made of the generation gap, Bancroft was only thirty-six when the movie was made, and Hoffman was thirty. Revisiting the movie in 1997, I realized that it played completely differently for me than it had thirty years earlier. Then I had found Mrs. Robinson "magnificently sexy, shrewish, and self-possessed enough to make the seduction convincing."

After the 1997 viewing I wrote: "Well, here *is* to you, Mrs. Robinson: You've survived your defeat at the hands of that insufferable creep, Benjamin, and emerged as the most sympathetic and intelligent character in *The Graduate.*"

I added: "Mrs. Robinson is the only person in the movie who is not playing old tapes. She is bored by a drone of a husband, she drinks too much, she seduces Benjamin not out of lust but out of kindness or desperation. Makeup and lighting are used to make Anne Bancroft look older. . . . But there is a scene where she is drenched in a rainstorm; we can see her face clearly and without artifice, and she is a great beauty. She is also sardonic, satirical, and articulate—the only person in the movie you would want to have a conversation with."

I ran into Bancroft and Brooks not long after writing that rereview, and told her of my conviction that Mrs. Robinson was the most intriguing character in the movie.

"Of course she is," Bancroft smiled. "Why do you think I took the role?"

Her long-running marriage with Brooks was a high-wire act between two quick-witted, verbal acrobats. Brooks cast her in cameos in his *Blazing Saddles* (1974) and *Silent Movie* (1976), they costarred in Alan Johnson's *To Be or Not to Be* (1983), and Brooks cast her as a psychic seer in *Dracula: Dead and Loving It* (1995).

In *Silent Movie,* her brief but scene-stealing

moment comes when she crosses her eyes. In an interview with Brooks, I observed that she seemed able to cross either eye separately.

"How did you get that effect?" I asked.

"*Effect?*" said Brooks. "That was no effect, that was *Annie!* She can really do that! That's why I married her. Twelve years ago, we're sitting in 21, I'm in love with her, I ask, 'Come on, how am I doin'?' And in reply, she crosses her eyes like that. Now I *know* it's love. For twelve years, I've been searching for the right role for Annie. Not *The Miracle Worker.* Not *The Pumpkin Eater.* Not Mrs. Robinson. The *right* role, where she can cross her eyes!"

George Anthony, chief of entertainment programming for the CBC, remembers that Bancroft and Brooks were a "genuine, bona fide love match, in the early years almost as famous for their public battles as Elizabeth Taylor and Michael Todd." He recalls one of their fights when he grabbed her arm and she pulled away from him. Anthony's story:

"'Don't you dare touch my instrument!' she raged, in her highest Actors Studio dudgeon.

"'Oh, so this is your instrument?'

"'Yes. This is my instrument!'

"'OK. Play 'Melancholy Baby.'"

She was Italian, he was Jewish, together they were electric. In person, she was as funny as he was, but he was always on and she sometimes took a break. Their careers had their ups and downs. Brooks had a box-office slump with such later films as *Space Balls* (1987), *Life Stinks* (1991), and then came back with a Broadway musical version of his 1968 comedy *The Producers* that became one of the biggest hits in Broadway history. Filming has just been completed on the film musical version.

She started in the movies, as she was fond of observing, at the bottom of the ladder, claiming to have played the title role in *Gorilla at Large* (1954). After more forgettable roles, she moved to Broadway for her two Tony-winning performances and other successes, and returned to Hollywood much further up the ladder. She appeared in some sixty-five films and made-for-TV movies and miniseries, notably as Jenny Churchill in *Young Winston* (1972), Greta Garbo's biggest fan in *Garbo Talks!* (1984), a book lover in *84 Charing Cross Road* (1987), the title role at age 100 in *The*

Oldest Living Confederate Widow Tells All (made for TV, 1994), and a rich Italian principessa in *Up at the Villa* (2000).

When the stage version of *The Producers* opened in Chicago before moving onto Broadway, it was clear on opening night that the musical would be a huge hit. At the party afterward, I asked her what she was doing. "I keep retiring," she said. "Then I get offered something. Then I retire again."

She was born Anna Maria Italiano in 1931 in the Bronx, and retained a Bronx accent as an option in her acting arsenal. Beneath her glamorous appearance, Arthur Penn said, "she's heavy-duty Bronx." She acted for a brief time as Anne Marno before choosing the stage name Bancroft, the AP reported, "because it sounded dignified." She met Brooks in 1964 during the taping of a Perry Como TV special; he was a writer who had worked for Sid Caesar and would soon team with Buck Henry to create the *Get Smart* TV series.

Johnny Carson

Gene Siskel dreamed of getting into one of the legendary poker games Johnny Carson held in his house in Malibu. He thought Carson would be a masterful poker player, able to send signals and conceal them with such facility that to watch him would be an entertainment and an education.

It was that way on *The Tonight Show* too. Carson was always completely and serenely at home on the show, night after night and year after year, and he was a superb interviewer: sympathetic, a good listener, quick with zingers, putting himself down rather than his guests. And yet when you watched for years, as I did, you could read his mind, or you thought you could, and the signals he was sending told you whether he thought his guest was holding a good hand or not.

The first time Siskel and I were invited to appear on *The Tonight Show,* the evening began badly.

"We do not belong here," Gene told me in the dressing room as we heard Doc Severinsen and the orchestra playing the show's theme. "We are Midwest boys from Chicago and we belong in Chicago right now, this very moment, watching this show on television."

A writer popped his head into the dressing

room with a last-minute thought: "Johnny might ask you about some of your favorite films this year." The writer left. Siskel and I looked at each other in horror. We were terrified. Our minds went blank. At that moment I could not think of a single title.

"Name a film," Gene said. "*Gone With the Wind*," I said. "Me, too," Gene said. He called our office in Chicago and said, "Quick, tell me the names of some movies we like."

Then the moment of truth arrived. We marched out onto the stage just as if we were real *Tonight Show* guests and not pathetic imposters, and you know what? It was okay, because Johnny made it okay. He projected an aura of welcome and calm. There is no other way to describe it. We were not pinned like butterflies to a corkboard, being watched by millions, but simply sitting there on the couch talking to Johnny, who was talking to us as if it were the simplest thing in the world.

Carson's gifts were limitless. His skits and his characters, his slapstick and gags and funny hats and costumes came from inexhaustible comic energy, but he never overplayed his hand. He was cool beyond cool. He made Sinatra seem to be trying too hard.

On one show, an awkward moment took place. Chevy Chase had been the first guest, promoting his holiday movie *Three Amigos*. Now Gene was in the chair and I was on the sofa, and Chevy had moved down one, next to me. After five or six minutes that went smoothly, Johnny looked straight at me and asked, "Roger, which of the new Christmas movies do you like the least?"

In one heart-stopping moment I knew that the only honest answer was *Three Amigos*. I should have found a way around that answer, but I could not. *Three Amigos*, I said, looking, I hope, as miserable as I felt. A strange energy enveloped all four of us.

"Looking forward to *your* next film," Chevy said, which broke the ice, and then Johnny said, "I wish I hadn't asked you that," and I said, "I wish you hadn't too."

After the show, Chase told me he disliked the movie, too, but that wasn't the point. Then Johnny popped his head around the door. "I asked you, and I got my answer," he said. "Good television."

Off-camera, Carson was cordial to his guests, but kept a certain distance. By comparison, Jay Leno walks into the dressing room, sits down, and tests his monologue on you. David Letterman believes everything should happen for the first time on the air, so he avoids even seeing his guests before they come onstage.

Carson was affable, amused, welcoming, but a little detached, because we were not his personal friends, and he wasn't one of those showbiz types who treated everyone like an old buddy. That was the job for Freddie DeCordova, his longtime producer, who sat just out of camera range beyond the sofa and communicated with Johnny in the telepathic way a catcher works with a pitcher.

I watched Carson for hundreds and hundreds of hours of my life. He was a performer born for the medium of television. When he retired, nobody really believed he was gone for good. Everyone thought he'd be back, as a guest, or in a movie, or hosting the Oscars, or somewhere, somehow. But he wasn't. He retired, and enjoyed his private life, and that was that. A great poker player knows that you lose if you stay in the game too long. There is a right time to walk away with your winnings, and your memories.

Ossie Davis

Ossie Davis, an actor and activist beloved and revered for his contributions to theater, film, television, and the civil rights movement, died February 4, 2005, at eighty-seven. The legendary figure, who combined militancy with grace and humor, was found dead in a Miami Beach hotel room. He had been on location, filming *Retirement*, a comedy also starring Peter Falk and Rip Torn.

Davis and his wife of fifty-seven years, the actress Ruby Dee, who survives, were one of the leading couples of the American stage and screen; the AP compared them to Alfred Lunt and Lynn Fontaine, and Hume Cronyn and Jessica Tandy. They appeared together for the first time in *Jeb* and *Anna Lucasta* during the 1946–1947 Broadway season, and were married in 1948 on their one day off from rehearsing for their next play. They jointly received Kennedy Center Honors in 2004.

Davis's first Hollywood role was in *No Way Out* (1950), which was also Sidney Poitier's first film. Together they went on to create roles that broke the stereotypes of black actors in American movies. Among his major early roles was the title character in a TV production of Eugene O'Neill's *The Emperor Jones* (1955), the lead in *Gone Are the Days!* (1963), based on his play *Purlie Victorious,* and Sidney Lumet's *The Hill* (1965).

The same year, he delivered a poetic eulogy at the funeral of the murdered black leader Malcolm X, saying "what we place in the ground is no more now a man but a seed which, after the winter of our discontent, will come forth again to meet us." Three years later, he delivered another dramatic eulogy at the funeral of Dr. Martin Luther King Jr. It was Mr. Davis's, voice heard saying, "A mind is a terrible thing to waste" on the ads for the United Negro College Fund. Mr. Davis repeated the 1965 eulogy as a voice-over in Spike Lee's *Malcolm X* (1992), and had notable roles in five other Lee films: *School Daze* (1988), *Do the Right Thing* (1989), *Jungle Fever* (1991), *Get on the Bus* (1996), and *She Hate Me* (2004).

"The great thing I got from Ruby and Ossie," Spike Lee told me, "is that you could be an activist and an artist too. They were strong and brave at a time when many Negro entertainers stood on the sidelines. Ruby and Ossie were by Malcolm's side, they were with Dr. King in Birmingham, Selma, and the March on Washington, and never worried about the negative impact it might have on their careers."

Lee said that Davis told him the hardest role he ever had to do was the reverend in *Jungle Fever*. "He didn't know if he could play that scene where the father has to shoot his son. It's a great performance by Samuel Jackson, in a crack-crazed euphoria, and Ossie shoots him, and he dies in the arms of his mother, played by Ruby Dee."

In his earlier years, one of Davis's biggest roles was as Burt Lancaster's costar in *The Scalphunters* (1968), a film that opened with him playing an escaped slave stumbling behind Lancaster's horse. His character is the most educated person in the movie, but gets a different kind of education in rough-and-ready frontier life.

The film was made at a time when Davis and Dee were vocal leaders of the civil rights movement, and during an interview, I observed that the role was not in the emerging tradition of Sidney Poitier heroes. "It's a pre–Civil War version of the back of the bus," he told me with his infectious grin. "But this is the way it is. Sometimes Burt Lancaster is on the horse, and sometimes you're on the horse, but there's only one horse."

Other important roles came on TV, where he played Martin Luther King Sr. in *King* (1978) and appeared in *Roots: The Next Generations* (1979). In 1980 he and his wife starred in *Ossie and Ruby!* a TV series, and in 1990–1994 he was in the cast of *Evening Shade*. His other major film roles included *Grumpy Old Men* (1993), where he ran the bait shop frequented by Walter Matthau and Jack Lemmon; *I'm Not Rappaport* (1996), in which he and Matthau engage in a philosophical park bench conversation; and the cult comedy success *Bubba Ho-tep* (2002), in which he and Bruce Campbell costar as John F. Kennedy and Elvis Presley, both still alive in a nursing home. ("But Jack," says Elvis, "you're black." JFK nods: "When my assassination was faked by Lyndon B. Johnson, they dyed me.")

One of Davis's final roles was as Mario Van Peebles's grandfather in *Baadasssss!* (2004), the story of the director's father, Melvin Van Peebles, another African-American filmmaking pioneer, whose *Sweet Sweetback's Baadasssss Song* (1970) gave momentum to the black independent film movement.

Davis himself was central to that movement. He directed five films, including *Cotton Comes to Harlem* (1970), a box office hit. In the same year he also went to Nigeria to direct *Kongi's Harvest*, based on the play by the leading African author Wole Soyinka, who starred. In 1972 he directed *Black Girl*, about a seventeen-year-old who dreams of being a ballet dancer but is discouraged by her family. His *Gordon's War* (1973) starred Paul Winfield in the story of Vietnam vets at war against Harlem drug dealers. And he directed and costarred with Ruby Dee in *Countdown at Kusini* (1976), about an African nation moving into independence.

Davis was born in 1917 in the hamlet of Cogdell, Georgia, and grew up in Waycross and Valdosta. In 1935 he hitchhiked to Washington, D.C., to talk his way into Howard University, where he entered the theater school.

By 1939 he was appearing in his first roles on Broadway. In World War II he was a surgical technician in an army hospital in Liberia, and when he returned to New York in 1946 he met Dee in the cast of his first play.

Davis was found dead by his grandson after he failed to answer knocks on his hotel room door. He had a history of heart disease. He is survived by Dee; in 1998 they coauthored the book *With Ossie and Ruby: In This Life Together*. They had three children, Nora, Hasna, and Guy, who survive, along with seven grandchildren.

Janet Leigh

Janet Leigh, who starred in one of the most famous scenes in movie history, is dead at seventy-seven. Miss Leigh, a top Hollywood star in the 1950s and 1960s and an intelligent and funny woman offscreen, "died peacefully at her home" on October 3, 2004, a family spokeswoman said. At her side were her husband, Robert Brandt, and her daughters Jamie Lee Curtis and Kelly Curtis, who both followed her into acting.

"I will always be remembered for that one scene," she told me one afternoon in 1998, as we shared a seat on the ski lift at the Telluride Film Festival. "That scene," of course, was the scene in Alfred Hitchcock's *Psycho* (1960) where she is stabbed to death in a shower by a madman played by Tony Perkins. It was considered at the time the most violent scene to ever appear in a major movie, and Hitchcock's friends feared it would harm his career; instead, the film was a box office triumph, hailed as a classic.

I asked her how it felt to *always* be asked about one scene, after a career that eventually included some sixty movies made between 1947 and 2000.

"Better to be remembered for one great scene than no great scenes," she smiled. "If we fall out of this ski lift, they'll mention the shower scene before they mention you."

She was good company, having survived the Hollywood studio system and an eventful life that began when she eloped for her first marriage at fourteen, and for her third husband married the star Tony Curtis. Her fourth marriage, to Brandt in 1962, was long and happy.

She was "discovered" by Hollywood in such an improbable way that it equals Lana Turner's discovery at the counter of a soda fountain. The star Norma Shearer, once married to the powerful producer Irving Thalberg and still with influence at MGM, saw her photo on the hotel counter where Miss Leigh's father worked, and told the studio to test her. They did.

Some thought *Psycho* a classic, some called it a scandal, but Miss Leigh appeared in at least two movies that rank among the best American films of all time: Orson Welles's *Touch of Evil* (1958) and John Frankenheimer's *The Manchurian Candidate* (1962). Restored versions of both films played theaters before being released in DVD versions.

She was at Telluride to celebrate the restoration of *Touch of Evil*, which the studio took away from Welles and recut. It was returned to its intended form on the basis of a long memo Welles dictated about the studio's changes.

"My husband asked me why in the world I was coming up here for this screening," Leigh said at Telluride. "I said that this was something we had started forty years ago, and it was time to finish it. They cheated Orson. And they cheated us. This is vindication."

In *The Manchurian Candidate*, she plays a woman who meets Frank Sinatra, a brainwashed Korean War veteran, on a train. She breaks off her engagement and quickly marries him. Their conversation on the train is beyond peculiar.

"Maryland's a beautiful state," she tells him. "This is Delaware," Sinatra says, and she replies: "I know. I was one of the original Chinese workmen who laid the track on this stretch. But nonetheless, Maryland is a beautiful state. So is Ohio, for that matter."

What does this mean? Is it some kind of a coded message, triggering responses that were hypnotically implanted in his mind by the Chinese Communists? Why does she end her engagement with another man even before their first date and marry him in such haste? Is she his handler? Is there a subterranean level of conspiracy below the surface of *The Manchurian Candidate*? Miss Leigh said it was possible, but she preferred to take the film at face value.

The shower scene in *Psycho* has been analyzed shot-by-shot as a masterpiece of editing. Although the viewer has the impression of Miss Leigh's nudity, the editing avoids actual nudity, in keeping with the Hollywood production code at the time. The final shot, of her blood curling down the drain, was the reason Hitchcock filmed in black and white: He felt if the blood were red, it would seem so real that audiences would be offended.

Many years later, Saul Bass, who designed the film's titles, claimed that Hitchcock let him direct the shower scene. Miss Leigh was outraged: "Absolutely not! I was in that shower for seven days, and believe you me, Alfred Hitchcock was right next to his camera for every one of those seventy-odd shots."

Her daughter, Jamie Lee, later starred in the famous series of *Halloween* horror films, and Miss Leigh appeared in one of them, *Halloween H2o: 20 Years Later* (1998). She never won an Oscar, but was nominated for *Psycho*, and won the Golden Globe that year. Among her many other films, some of the best included *Scaramouche* (1952); Anthony Mann's *The Naked Spur* (1953), opposite James Stewart; *Harper* (1966), with Paul Newman; and *Houdini* (1953), playing the magician's wife, opposite Curtis in the title role.

She had been in good health until she fell victim to vasculitis, an inflammation of the blood vessels.

After filming the shower scene, she often said, she refused to take another shower, and took only baths. She liked the story Hitchcock told, about a woman who wrote him complaining that after seeing his shower scene, and a drowning in a bathtub in *Diabolique*, her daughter refused both to shower and to bathe. "What should I do with her?" she asked the Master of Suspense, who suggested: "Send her to the dry cleaners."

Ismail Merchant

The news of Ismail Merchant's death on May 25, 2005, arrived here in the countryside near Toulouse. We are visiting friends in a hilltop house overlooking vineyards and forests, and fields that will soon be blanketed with sunflowers. "It's like a Merchant-Ivory film," we said when we arrived.

Not many filmmakers have given their names to lifestyles. Although Mr. Merchant and his partner, the director James Ivory, made films on many subjects, they were best known for stories about intelligent and complicated characters of the middle and upper classes, living more often than not in an elegant setting—an English country house, a Tuscan villa.

Mr. Merchant died in a London hospital of complications following surgery for abdominal ulcers.

The producer of nearly fifty films and television productions and the director of five films of his own, he formed a lifelong professional and personal partnership with Mr. Ivory after they met at the 1961 Cannes Film Festival. They were key figures in the development of independent filmmaking, often finding financing and distribution outside conventional channels.

Unlike independents who specialized in outsider and fringe subject matter, they often turned to important novels for their inspiration, including works by E. M. Forster *(Howards End, A Room With a View, Maurice)* and Henry James *(The Europeans, The Bostonians, The Golden Bowl).* Merchant also adapted modern novels, including Kazuo Ishiguro's *The Remains of the Day,* Kaylie Jones's *A Soldier's Daughter Never Cries,* Edward Albee's play of Carson McCullers's *The Ballad of the Sad Café,* and Evan S. Connell's *Mr. and Mrs. Bridge.* As a director, he adapted V. S. Naipaul's novel *The Mystic Masseur,* about a young Trinidadian of Indian heritage.

On almost every Merchant-Ivory film, the screenplay was by Ruth Prawer Jhabvala, born in Germany, raised in Britain, a novelist whose collaboration with Merchant and Ivory began with their first film, an adaptation of her novel *The Householder* (1963), and continued with *Shakespeare Wallah* (1965), about a troupe of Shakespearean actors traveling in India.

When she told Mr. Merchant on their first meeting that she had never written a screenplay, she recalled, he advised her to relax, since he had never produced one and Mr. Ivory had never directed one.

"He was the one and truly great maverick producer, a law to himself," said Sir Anthony Hopkins, who starred in *The Remains of the Day.* In a statement to the BBC, he explained: "He could charm the birds out of the trees, which had its very positive side (most of the time) and sometimes he could get you to work for nothing."

Merchant-Ivory films were not made cheaply, but they were made for far less than standard Hollywood budgets, and their look of elegance or luxury was often because of Mr. Merchant's ability to obtain locations for little or nothing. Warren Hoge, writing in the *New York Times*, recalled that the producer was able to film inside the Trianon Palace Hotel in Versailles "by draping himself in robes and posing as the Maharajah of Jodhpur. His crew masqueraded as his entourage and, once inside, set up the shoot."

Mr. Merchant was born in Bombay, India, in 1936. As a young man he enrolled in the MBA program at New York University, always with an eye toward the film industry, and made a short subject, which got him invited to Cannes. Although his skills as a businessman kept Merchant-Ivory Productions afloat and successful through many weathers for forty-five years, his personal style was relaxed and genial. I remember a Cannes festival in the 1970s when they promoted one of their films, perhaps *The Europeans* (1979), by hosting small dinner parties every night in a villa they rented in the hills above town. Mr. Merchant was a celebrated chef who supervised and helped prepare every meal, a fusion of Indian and French cuisine.

I met him again in 1999 at the Calcutta Film Festival, where he was presenting a retrospective of the great Indian cinematographer Subrata Mitra, who worked with the director Satyajit Ray from the first day of both of their careers. Mr. Merchant had helped to sponsor and underwrite a restoration of Mitra's and Ray's films, and every afternoon in the festival's common room he presided over tea, biscuits, and conversation. He had the ability to summon vast amusement and share it with his listeners.

Merchant productions earned thirty-one Academy Award nominations, including "Best Picture" mentions for *Howards End* (1992), *The Remains of the Day* (1993), and *A Room With a View* (1985). *The Creation of Woman* (1960), the short film that began his career when he took it to Cannes, was also an Oscar

nominee. *Howards End* and *A Room With a View* both won as best picture at the BAFTA awards, the "British Oscars."

His death came after he had supervised the restoration of the complete Merchant-Ivory catalog for release on DVD, a project that is currently under way and has provided many filmgoers with their first opportunity to see not only their better-known films (also including *Quartet, Heat and Dust,* and *Jefferson in Paris*) but also more obscure documentaries and made-for-TV features. At the time of his death, he was producing *The White Countess,* directed by Ivory, starring Ralph Fiennes and Natasha Richardson, and set for autumn release.

Mr. Merchant is survived by Mr. Ivory and by his sisters, Saherbanu Kabadia, Sahida Retiwala, Ruksana Khan, and Rashida Bootwala. His brother-in-law, Waheed Chauhan, told an Indian Website, "His body will be taken to Mumbai, his birthplace, in a couple of days for burial."

Russ Meyer

Russ Meyer is dead. The legendary independent director, who made exploitation films but was honored as an auteur, died September 18, 2004, at his home in the Hollywood Hills. He was eighty-two, and had been suffering from dementia. The immediate cause of death was pneumonia, said Janice Cowart, a friend who supervised his care during his last years. She announced his death.

Such bare facts hardly capture the zest of a colorful man who became a Hollywood icon. Meyer's *The Immoral Mr. Teas* (1959), hailed by the highbrow critic Leslie Fiedler as the funniest comedy of the year, created the skin flick genre, and after the box office success of his *Vixen* (1968), he was crowned King of the Nudies in a front-page profile in the *Wall Street Journal*. His *Beyond the Valley of the Dolls* (1970), for which I wrote the screenplay, represented the first foray into sexplitation by a major studio (20th Century Fox).

His films were X-rated, but not pornographic. Meyer told me he had two reasons for avoiding hard-core: (1) "I want to play in regular theaters and keep the profits, instead of playing in porn theaters and doing business with the mob." (2) "Frankly, what goes on below the waist is visually not that entertaining." For Meyer, what went on above the waist was a lifelong fascination; he cheerfully affirmed his obsession with big breasts.

Meyer was the ultimate auteur. He not only directed his films, but could and often did write, photograph, edit, and distribute them, and carried his own camera. In a genre known for sleazy sets and murky photography, Meyer's films were often shot outdoors in scenic desert and mountain locations, and his images were bright and crisp. He said his inspiration was Al Capp's *L'il Abner* comic strip, and his films were not erotic so much as funny, combining slapstick and parody. He once told me there was no such thing as a sex scene that couldn't be improved by cutaways to Demolition Derby or rocket launches.

Meyer was born March 21, 1922, in San Leandro, California, and raised in the Oakland area by a mother who gave him his first 8mm movie camera. He enlisted at eighteen in the U.S. Army Signal Corps, learned motion picture photography in an army school at MGM, and found World War II "the greatest experience of my life."

He was often assigned to General George Patton, and told of being taken along one night late in the war to shoot the newsreel footage when Patton assembled a strike force to dart across the lines and capture Hitler—who was believed to be visiting the front. The report was false, Hitler was not captured, Patton issued dire warnings to anyone who spoke of the raid, and Meyer was denied the greatest newsreel scoop in history.

On another assignment, he filmed the original Dirty Dozen before they were parachuted into France, and E. M. Nathanson's best-selling novel credits Meyer as its source. "In the real story," Meyer said, "they disappeared and were never heard of again."

In peacetime Meyer and other Signal Corps cameramen found themselves frozen out of the cinematographer's union. He made industrial and educational films, and then drifted into cheesecake. More than half of the first year's Playboy Playmates were photographed by Meyer. Observing Hugh Hefner's success at retailing nude images of young, wholesome-looking women, Meyer tried the same approach in *Mr. Teas*. Films exploiting nudity had been consigned to marginal theaters and burlesque houses, but *Teas* won mainstream distribution, played for a year in some of its first engagements, and defined the rest of Meyer's career.

He made one film after another, all of them involving unlikely plots, incongruous settings, and abundantly voluptuous actresses. "Where do you find those women?" I asked him. "After they reach a certain bra size," he said, "they find me." He disapproved of silicone implants: "They miss the whole point."

Meyer's titles were entertaining in themselves: *Faster, Pussycat! Kill! Kill!* and *Mud Honey*, both made in 1965, were taken as names by 1990s rock bands, and director John Waters said *Pussycat* was the greatest film of all time. Other directors who praised his work included Jonathan Demme, who always uses Meyer's favorite actor, Charles Napier, in his movies, and John Landis. Mike Myers used music and dialogue from *Beyond the Valley of the Dolls* in his *Austin Powers* pictures.

Other titles included *Motor Psycho* (1965—a busy year), *Common Law Cabin* and *Good Morning... and Goodbye!* (both 1967), *Finders Keepers, Lovers Weepers!* (1968), *Vixen!* (1968), *Cherry, Harry and Raquel!* (1970), *Blacksnake!* (1973), *Supervixens* (1975), *Up!* (1976), and *Beneath the Valley of the Ultra-Vixens* (1979), which I cowrote.

In the 1980s he announced an epic film to be called *The Breast of Russ Meyer*, but it was never completed. He did publish a massive three-volume, seventeen-pound, 1,210-page, $199 autobiography, *A Clean Breast* (2000). "It keeps you turning the pages even when you can't lift the book," wrote *Time* magazine film critic Richard Corliss, who called *Beyond the Valley of the Dolls* one of the ten best films of the 1970s.

After I wrote a letter to the *Wall Street Journal* praising Meyer's work, we met and became friends, and when he was summoned by Fox to make *Beyond the Valley of the Dolls* he asked me to write the screenplay. We produced it in six weeks, making it up as we went along, laughing aloud, although in directing it Meyer urged the actors to perform with complete seriousness. The film cost $900,000, grossed $40 million, and became a cult favorite; the Sex Pistols punk rock band saw it in

London in the late 1970s and hired Meyer to direct and me to write a film for them. *Who Killed Bambi?* (1978) shot for only one day before the Pistols's production company went bankrupt.

Russ Meyer made X-rated movies, but he was not a dirty old man. He didn't use the casting couch, prohibited sex on his sets ("save it for the camera"), and was a serial monogamist. He married Eve Meyer in 1955, and later photographed her as a Playmate; they had a friendly divorce in 1970 and continued to work together until her death in an airplane crash. His 1970 marriage to starlet Edy Williams was not so happy, and inspired a scene in *Supervixens* where the hero's wife attacks his pickup with an ax. In later years his most frequent companion was Kitten Natividad, who starred in *Ultra-Vixens*.

He was a loyal friend. He stayed in lifelong contact with his Signal Corps comrades, organizing local and national reunions and sending tickets to those who needed them. He worked with the same crew members again and again. In a field known for devaluing women, he treated the actresses in his movies with affection and respect. Haji, Uschi Digard, Tura Satana, Kitten Natividad, and the *BVD* stars Dolly Read, Cynthia Myers, Marcia Mc-Broom, and Erica Gavin stayed in contact and attended reunions.

His films were unique in that the women were always the strong characters, and men were the mindless sex objects. The film critic B. Ruby Rich called him "the first feminist American director." Meyer took praise with a grain of salt. After *The Seven Minutes* (1971), an attempt at a serious, mainstream, big-studio picture, flopped at the box office, he told me: "I made the mistake of reading my reviews. What the public wants are big laughs and big tits and lots of 'em. Lucky for me, that's what I like too."

Christopher Reeve

Christopher Reeve, who became famous playing a character who could fly around the world, and as a man whose wheelchair did not limit his flights of idealism, died October 9, 2004, at fifty-two. In the years since he was paralyzed in a riding accident in 1995, he became the nation's most influential spokesman for research on spinal cord injuries, and never lost the hope that he would someday walk again.

Only a week before his death, Reeve was in Chicago to help observe the fiftieth anniversary of the Rehabilitation Institute. Talking to the *Sun-Times*'s Bill Zwecker, he said "little miracles are happening every day" at the institute, and hailed recent advances in physical therapy for those with paralysis.

Reeve died in Northern Westchester Hospital in Mount Kisco, New York, his publicist Wesley Combs said, after he had a heart attack while being treated at home for an infected bedsore. He went into a coma from which he never emerged. At his side was his wife, Dana.

Reeve became famous after starring in *Superman* (1978), which began the current cycle of movies about superheroes; with *Spider-Man 2*, it is one of the two best films in the genre. When he took the role, he told me at the time, it looked like possible career suicide, because previous Superman movies had been cheesy B features. But director Richard Donner, working from a screenplay by Mario Puzo *(The Godfather)*, and David Newman and Robert Benton *(Bonnie and Clyde)*, assembled an A-list cast including Marlon Brando, Gene Hackman, Margot Kidder, and Trevor Howard.

Reeve turned out to be perfectly cast as the Man of Steel. After a highly publicized talent search, the producers "found the right guy," I wrote in my 1978 review. "He is Christopher Reeve. He looks like the Superman in the comic books (a fate I would not wish on anybody), but he's also an engaging actor, open and funny in his big love scene with Lois Lane, and then correctly awesome in his showdown with the arch villain Lex Luthor."

He starred again in *Superman II* (1981), which I liked as much as the original, and in *Superman III* (1983) and *Superman IV* (1987), where the franchise began to run out of gas. Like all actors who are associated with an archetypal role, Reeve found it hard to shake the Superman image, but he was a skilled classical actor, at home on the stage. He was impressive in mainstream roles in *Street Smart* (1987), as a writer whose research in street life gets him in deep trouble; *The Re-*

mains of the Day (1993), as a U.S. congressman with strong words during a dinner with a British lord who supports the Nazis; and *The Bostonians* (1984), based on the Henry James novel, with Reeve as a lawyer thrown into the middle of the suffragette movement. One of his most popular movies was *Somewhere in Time* (1980), where he plays a modern playwright who visits the Grand Hotel on Mackinac Island, sees a photograph of an actress who played there in 1912, and travels through time (or perhaps only thinks he does) to meet her.

His riding accident left him unable to move from the neck down or even breathe for himself. Yet he kept up a busy schedule, traveled, gave interviews, and worked as an actor and filmmaker. Before his death he completed directing *The Brooke Ellison Story*. Lacey Chabert stars as a woman with injuries like Reeve's, unable to breathe on her own since the age of eleven, and Mary Elizabeth Mastrantonio plays the mother who supports her in a journey that leads to her graduation from Harvard in 2000.

Reeve was an activist in favor of stem cell research, which might someday be able to regenerate damaged spinal cells, and was outspoken in his testimony before Congress after President Bush set limits on the research. During the presidential debate, Senator John Kerry said Reeve was "a friend of mine . . . (who) exercises every single day to keep those muscles alive for the day when he can walk again." He said it is "respecting human life to reach for that cure," but the president's policy "makes it impossible for our scientists to do that."

Reeve told Zwecker that opponents "don't understand the stem cells that scientists want to work on are taken from the 400 in vitro fertilization clinics across the country where— on a daily basis—35 to 40 percent of excess embryos (unneeded after couples conceive) are thrown away as medical waste. Those discarded cells could be used to cure and treat millions of people."

Reeve had two children, Matthew, twenty-five, and Alexandra, twenty-one, from a long-term relationship with Gae Exton, and had joint custody. He married Dana Morosini, a cabaret performer, in 1992, and their son, Will, is eleven. Reeve was born in 1952, the son of two writers, and attended Cornell before winning an invitation to spend his senior year at the Julliard School for the Performing Arts. His stage work included roles opposite Katharine Hepburn and Celeste Holm, and as a young man he worked backstage as a "dogsbody" at the Old Vic in London and the Comedie Francaise in Paris.

Reeve told friends that when he first learned the extent of his injuries, he considered suicide. Then he determined to do all he could despite his limitations, and to work for recovery. He was cheered by the fact that he regained some sensation over 70 percent of his body, although he could not move below the neck. The best thing about regaining some feeling, he said, is that he could feel it when his family hugged him.

Film Festivals

Telluride Film Festival
Telluride Report No. 1:
A Mystery Solved

Telluride, Colorado, September 3, 2004—After years of controversy, one of the most persistent questions in the world of film has finally been settled: Yes, Annette Bening's face was used as the model for the torch-bearing woman on the logo that opens every Columbia Picture.*

I know this because Annette Bening told me so herself. We were clutching our water bottles at the opening-day brunch of the Telluride Film Festival, and despite the uncounted intelligent questions I might have devised, I just plain asked her if she was the Columbia Woman, "because she looks just like you."

"Oh, sure," she said, with a smile you will never see on the very serious Columbia Woman. "The artists told me it was me. But just the face. Not the body."

The body is covered in such flowing robes, however, that the question is academic, and soon Bening was saying that she hardly ever attends film festivals, but that this one seemed kind of special. It is wonderful, I agreed, especially after you grow accustomed to the 10,000-foot altitude and can stop panting.

Telluride may be the only film festival without an angle. Audiences come here to see films, not to buy, sell, or hype them. Well, maybe a little hype. Far from trying to publicize its films, Telluride never even announces them in advance; you have to attend on faith.

The programming is ingenious in the connections it makes. This year, for example, Bening is here because she appears in Istvan Szabo's *Being Julia*, rumored to be an Oscar contender. The movie is based on the novel *Theater*, by W. Somerset Maugham, and set in the London theater world of the 1930s. Bening's character shocks her circle and betrays her husband (Jeremy Irons) by having an affair with a young American.

Starting with *Being Julia*, the festival programs sideways by adding a special screening of a restored print of Alfred Hitchcock's *Secret Agent* (1936), based on a novel by Maugham, and also showing one of the four sequences in *Quartet* (1949), based on Maugham stories. Jeffrey Meyers, Maugham's biographer, will speak before and after the screenings. And then another sideways move, to *Blackmail* (1929), Hitchcock's last silent film, not connected to Maugham, but connected to the Alloy Orchestra of Cambridge, Massachusetts, which every year performs a score for a silent film here.

So you see how the audience wanders from one venue to another, led by Telluride's belief that a festival should celebrate all kinds of films.

The Telluride Medal will be presented to three honorees: Theo Angelopoulos, the Greek director; Laura Linney, the American actress (and star of two festival selections, *P.S.* and *Kinsey*); and Jean-Claude Carriere, greatest of modern French screenwriters (and then you can slip out of the Sheridan Opera House and go down the street to the Mason's Hall and admire Carriere's screenplay for Buñuel's *Belle de Jour*, and remember that its star, Catherine Deneuve, was awarded the Telluride Medal a few years ago).

Telluride follows the careers of those it has discovered, including the director Lodge Kerrigan, whose *Clean, Shaven* and *Claire Dolan* played here. Both brilliant, both hard to take. Now he's back with *Keane*, starring Damian Lewis as a deranged homeless man. And the festival salutes the careers of those it loves; Rip Torn will be here for a revival of his great performance in *Payday* (1973), directed by Daryl Duke and inspired by the last days of Hank Williams Sr. *Payday* will be introduced by Buck Henry, this year's guest programmer, who has also brought along *Hunger*, the 1966 Henning Carlsen film about an artist starving to death; and *Million Dollar Legs* (1932), starring W. C. Fields. Talk about eclectic.

I eagerly anticipate *Yes*, directed by Sally Potter *(The Tango Lesson)* and starring Joan Allen as a scientist having an affair with a Lebanese immigrant worker. And *Palindromes*, the Todd Solondz film, starring Ellen

Barkin in a story about a young runaway. And *Unforgivable Blackness*, Ken Burns' new documentary about heavyweight champ Jack Johnson. And Johnny Depp is rumored to be coming for a sneak preview of his new film *Finding Neverland*, but it's not on the schedule; the festival says it knows nothing about it, which is always a good sign.

American audiences will get their first looks at several Cannes 2004 hits: *Moolaade*, by Ousmane Sembene of Senegal, a drama about the ritual genital mutilation of young women; *Bad Education*, by Spain's Pedro Almodovar, about a man deceived by a story of an old school friend (well, that's sort of what it's about), and *House of Flying Daggers*, by Zhang Yimou, whose *Hero* is the current box-office champ. Zhang Ziyi, the great beauty who stars in both films and in *Crouching Tiger, Hidden Dragon*, will be here in person.

We have been invited to dinner every night, and have declined. To sit down in a restaurant is to miss a movie, maybe two movies, and the interlocking Telluride schedule operates according to the domino principle; miss one, and your whole lovingly devised festival plan goes to pieces. We have stocked up on sliced turkey, peanut butter, and corn flakes, know where the best bran muffins are to be had, and will even turn to popcorn before losing two hours in a restaurant. We have three days to see fifteen films. More, if we're lucky. Of course, some of these films will also play at the Toronto Film Festival, which differs from Telluride in several ways, including the availability of oxygen.

*Not necessarily. See "Columbia Lady" in the Answer Man section.

Telluride Report No. 2: Regarding Sex

September 7, 2004—Three of the best films at this year's Telluride festival deal with unusual frankness with sex. Sally Potter's *Yes* stars Joan Allen as a scientist trapped in a loveless marriage, who begins a passionately physical affair with a Lebanese cook. Bill Condon's *Kinsey* stars Liam Neeson as Dr. Alfred C. Kinsey, whose research revolutionized conventional ideas about human sexual behavior. And Todd Solondz's *Palindromes* is a story of messy, sad teenage sexual experiences.

The Solondz film has sharply divided audiences; some hate it, some think it is the best work yet from the director of *Welcome to the Dollhouse* and *Happiness*. No one seems indifferent. I thought it was brilliant and bold, especially in the way Solondz uses many different actresses to play his heroine, a young girl who, in various versions of the story, seeks sexual experience, wants to get pregnant, seeks or avoids abortion, runs away, and is involved in the murder of an abortion doctor.

Solondz uses actresses of different sizes, ages, and races to play versions of the same character, in a device that makes the film not simply the story of one young woman's experiences, but a meditation on various possible scenarios and how the same personality might respond to them. His use of many actresses makes the material universal. There are no rapes in the film, although the men are singularly unskilled or uncaring; his heroine in all of her manifestations is naive and unprepared for the emotional anguish that sex causes for her.

What a contrast *Yes* is. Has a movie ever loved a woman more? Sally Potter celebrates the classic beauty of Joan Allen not by making her look glamorous, but simply by observing her private moments as she falls into love with a Lebanese man who picks her up at a party. He was once a surgeon, is now an exile working as a cook; they fall helplessly in love, but there are issues caused by her wealth and his poverty, and by her Western values and his Muslim background. The film's dialogue is all in rhyming verse, which sounds so natural and flows so smoothly it deepens rather than distracts.

In many scenes Allen wears no makeup, and Potter's camera sees her pure, unadorned, and breathtakingly beautiful. The film is willing to be quiet with her, to observe her, to allow us to empathize. Then it has a curious counterpoint: Several maids and housecleaners, led by the film's narrator (Shirley Henderson), provide a variant, starkly realistic view of the same world, about the debris we leave behind—how the world never rids itself of anything, but simply moves it around. This quasi-Marxist running commentary puts the romance in stark relief.

Kinsey is likely to be the best-received biopic since *A Beautiful Mind*. Liam Neeson gives an Oscar-worthy performance as the sex researcher who began by collecting a million wasps and then moved from etymology to the bedroom and became obsessed with collecting sexual histories. Laura Linney plays the student who becomes his wife and calm, wise companion as his monomania grows.

When Kinsey came on the scene, sexual misinformation was epidemic; the list of alleged results of masturbation sounds like a catalog of medical catastrophes. Kinsey, a virgin on his wedding night, began to provide more realistic advice to students at Indiana University, but as a scientist realized no data existed on real people and what they actually do. His best-sellers in the 1950s revealed that most people have more sexual partners and forms of sexual expression than anyone had guessed. Neeson plays Kinsey as a man obsessed with his message, who had little sense of how he affected other people and whose findings were attacked in Congress as a Communist plot.

Director Bill Condon (*Gods and Monsters*, the screensplay for *Chicago*) says he was surprised when *Kinsey* got an R rating from the MPAA, with no cuts. "We thought it might get the NC-17 and be an ideal test case for challenging that rating," he told me, "but they thought it was a serious and informative film, and they passed it with no cuts." How *Yes* and *Palindromes* will be rated is a good question; neither has explicit sex, but both deal so directly with the subject that the MPAA may be roiled.

Lots of other good films have unreeled, in a festival that combines premieres with revivals. I especially enjoyed screenings of two Hitchcock classics, *Secret Agent*, based on a novel by W. Somerset Maugham and introduced by the author's biographer, Jeffrey Meyers, and *Blackmail*, Hitchcock's final silent film, with a live score performed by the Alloy Orchestra, an institution at Telluride.

There were two surprise sneak previews. *Finding Neverland* stars Johnny Depp in the story of J. M. Barrie, whose fixation on a young widow (Kate Winslet) and her four boys provides the inspiration for his play *Peter Pan*. It's a poetic, gentle film that faces and disposes with the possibility that Barrie was in some sense a pedophile; it sees him as a romantic fantasist, led helplessly by his idealism. The other sneak was one of the festival's great word-of-mouth successes, *Up and Down*, by Jan Hrebejk, about two Czech families, one affluent, one poor, and how their lives intersect because of a stolen baby. It's a busy comedy involving issues of race, immigration, soccer hooliganism, and emotional need; maybe he tries to cover too many topics for one movie, but there's quite a payoff.

I saw five movies on Saturday. What else could I do? It was raining most of the day, and then for a change it snowed. As I was standing in a tent waiting to get into the screening of *Yes*, a young woman appeared out of the downpour, her coat drenched, wet hair in her eyes, and said, "I *hate* it how I love movies so much that I put myself through this!"

Telluride Report No. 3: *Overlord*

September 7, 2004—The most remarkable discovery at this year's Telluride Film Festival is *Overlord*, an elegiac 1975 film that follows the journey of one young British soldier to the beaches of Normandy. The film, directed by Stuart Cooper, won the Silver Bear at Berlin—but sank quickly from view after a limited release, and was all but forgotten until this Telluride revival.

Unlike *Saving Private Ryan* and other dramatizations based on D-day, *Overlord* is an intimate film, one that focuses closely on Tom Beddoes (Brian Stirner), who enters the British army, goes through basic training, and is one of the first ashore on D-day. Beddoes is not a macho hero but a quiet, nice boy, who worries about his cocker spaniel and takes along *David Copperfield* when he goes off to war.

The movie tells his story through a remarkable combination of new and archival footage. It was produced by the Imperial War Museum in London, where Cooper spent three years looking at documentary and newsreel footage from World War II. About 27 percent of the film is archival, and awesomely real—for example, a scene where soldiers and their landing boat are thrown against rocks by furious waves. There are sights I had never seen before, including monstrous mechanical wheels that propel themselves across the beach to explode land mines and flatten barbed wire. One of these machines is driven by a ring of rockets around its rim, and as it rolls forward, belching fire and smoke, it looks like a creature of hell.

Overlord, whose title comes from the code word for one of the invasion plans, uses archival footage to show the devastation of bombing raids from above and below. Cooper's cinematographer, the Kubrick favorite John Alcott, used lenses and film stock that matched the texture of this footage, so the black-and-white film seems all of a piece. Tom's story is not extraordinary; he says good-bye to his parents, survives some hazing during basic training, makes a few close friends, and becomes convinced he will die in the landing. This prospect does not terrify him, and he writes a letter to his parents, consoling them in advance.

He meets a local girl (Julie Neesam) at a dance, in a club filled with soldiers on leave. All of the clichés of such scenes are abandoned. She is a nice girl, he is a nice boy, they are kind to each other, tender and polite, and agree to meet again on Monday. But on Monday he is part of the early stages of the invasion, which seems, he writes his parents, like an entity that is growing to unimaginable proportions while he becomes a smaller and smaller speck of it. He has a fantasy in which he meets the girl again; to describe it would reveal too much about this film, which is a rare rediscovery.

* * *

Lodge Kerrigan, who makes films about lonely and isolated people, is back at Telluride for the third time with *Keane,* starring Damian Lewis as a schizophrenic man who drifts between being calm and functional, and raving in the streets. He is obsessed with a daughter he thinks was abducted.

The first half of the film follows him from bars to cocaine dealers to quick sex in a truck stop; at one point, he attacks a man in the street. Then, at his transient hotel, he meets a woman and her young daughter. He seems calm and sane to the mother, who entrusts him to pick up the girl after school and bring her home; a few days later, she's gone overnight, trying to track down her husband.

Suspense grows organically out of this material. How long will Keane's period of functionality endure? Will he confuse this girl with his lost daughter? Is the child in danger? Lewis's performance is intense and inward;

Kerrigan's camera stays close to him as he drifts in and out of illness, showing him sometimes desperately trying to head off a dangerous episode. Like his first two films, *Clean, Shaven* and *Claire Dolan,* this new film is observant and sympathetic to a character tortured by inner demons.

* * *

Sometimes you overhear extraordinary things on your way out of a theater. After the Telluride screening of Michael Radford's jolting *The Merchant of Venice,* I heard a woman behind me saying to her friend, "Gee, I thought the poor Jew really got the shaft." So Shakespeare's message got through.

The movie stars Al Pacino as Shylock, the Venetian money lender who loans 3,000 ducats to Antonio (Jeremy Irons), a merchant. When the loan defaults, he demands the payment of a pound of flesh. There is a romantic parallel plot involving young lovers, mistaken identities, exchanged rings, and so on, but Radford focuses on Shylock and Antonio, and I do not recall any other production of the play that underlines so vividly Shylock's bitterness about his treatment at the hands of Antonio and other gentiles.

Antonio has called him a dog, spit at him, cursed him, condemned the practice of money lending. Yet now he guarantees the loan to his young friend Bassanio (Joseph Fiennes), who needs it to marry the fair Portia (Lynn Collins). Shylock asks Antonio if he is not opposed to usury. Yes, Antonio says, but he will not be using the money himself. Soon after, Shylock is betrayed when his daughter Jessica (Zuleikha Robinson) elopes with a gentile, taking along part of his fortune.

The trial scene in the Ducal Palace, where Shylock demands his repayment, is treated by Radford's screenplay as a courtroom drama, and Pacino is uncompromising as a Shylock single-mindedly focusing on revenge. Pacino plays a fierce, proud man throughout the movie, and his delivery of the famous speech including "does not a Jew bleed?" is barked out as a savage appeal for simple justice. Pacino is not a tall man, but camera angles and staging make him appear ever shorter as his enemies loom over him and he fights against his fate.

Toronto Film Festival
Toronto Report No. 1:
Oscar Preview

Toronto, Canada, September 10, 2004—Oscar season starts this weekend. The Toronto International Film Festival has become the showcase for ambitious autumn releases by studios hoping for Academy Awards, or at least for good reviews of movies that adults can enjoy without resorting to their child within.

This year, I'm going into the festival having already seen twenty-three of the films—at Cannes, Telluride, or at advance screenings. Before I plunge into ten days of three to five movies a day, here's what I know now.

—Neve Campbell deserves an Oscar nomination for her fascinating performance as a sexually alive, unforgivingly vengeful rich girl in *When Will I Be Loved.* This is the best film in the career of writer-director James Toback, starring Campbell as Vera, the child of millionaires, who has a romance with a streetwise con man named Ford (Fred Weller). Her boyfriend meets an Italian count (Dominic Chianese) who is fascinated by Campbell and offers $1 million to meet her ("no strings—we'll see what happens"). When Ford tells Vera about the deal, she agrees to meet the count, and then there's a brilliant scene of astonishingly frank dialogue as these two smart and self-confident people discuss exactly what is being negotiated. It is crucial that Campbell's character doesn't need the money.

The film develops as a series of surprises; it doesn't start out as a con, but in responding to a developing situation it improvises into one, and then into another. All three roles are tricky and difficult, and all three actors are perfectly aimed, but Campbell is the catalyst. In the way she deals with her character's sexuality, curiosity, intelligence, and feelings about being sold, she creates one of the year's most spellbinding characters.

—While we're handing out Oscar nominations, what about one for Liam Neeson, in the title role of *Kinsey?* This is a biopic about a difficult, even monomaniacal man, who knew almost everything about human sexuality, and almost nothing about human nature.

Neeson plays Dr. Alfred C. Kinsey as an obsessive fact-gatherer, who collects a million moths and then vows to collect a million human sexual histories. Heedless of the effect his theories and findings have on ordinary people (and on politicians, and on the foundations who support his research), he makes shocking and controversial statements as if he is simply imparting common sense—which he is, of course, but tell that to heterosexual North Americans unable to imagine sex outside marriage or beyond the missionary position. Neeson makes Kinsey a very particular man, exasperating, brilliant, driven, and finally maybe a little mad.

—Joan Allen is amazing in Sally Potter's *Yes.* And director Sally Potter is amazing in the way she makes her amazing. Has ever a film looked more clearly and with more love at an actress? Allen, playing most of her key scenes without makeup, sometimes sleepy-eyed, sometimes dripping wet, quite simply becomes an object of carnal embodiment. Who would have thought it of the actress who played Pat Nixon? In the movie, she escapes from a sterile marriage to a rich man and begins an affair with a lusty Lebanese cook (a surgeon, before he immigrated). They're forced to confront how their private lives conflict with their public lives, their different ethnicities and religions, and the fact that she has all the money. That's interesting, but what's fascinating is the way Joan Allen conveys her character's discovery of sexual abandon. Maybe she's your third Oscar nominee from Toronto this year.

—An Oscar nomination in the documentary category may find its way to *Tell Them Who You Are,* Mark Wexler's touching and truthful documentary about his father, the great cinematographer and political activist Haskell Wexler. Listing his father's triumphs, including two Oscars, Mark adds: "I am not his fan. I am his son." Like many sons of strong and famous fathers, he found it difficult to make his way out of the parental shadow. When he moves from photojournalism into documentary filmmaking, Mark is invading the old man's turf, but Haskell agrees, reluctantly, to be filmed.

Haskell says in the film that he believes he could have directed most of the films he shot better than their directors, and he certainly believes it of this one; he advises, corrects, criticizes, expresses doubts, suggests shots, finds problems with the lighting, and lectures his son on the principles of documentaries. There's a scene where he has something important he wants to say on camera, and Mark wants him to say it on a balcony at sunset, and this clash between form and content dramatizes all their differences.

The movie, seen entirely from Mark's point of view, is critical at times, but is told with love and respect, and I'm glad Haskell agreed to it. He comes across as a remarkable man, an idealist and a perfectionist—proud, brave, and complicated. One can imagine a boring documentary about career highlights and showbiz memories. Instead, Haskell Wexler is honored with a movie which, with its honesty and sympathy, shows the father taught the son better than either one of them realizes.

—I've got a possible winner in the Best Foreign Film category: Ousmane Sembene's *Moolaade,* a film of great urgency and rich beauty, from the father of African cinema. The word "moolaade" means "protection," which is what a powerful woman in a village extends to four girls who do not want to undergo ritual circumcision. Under tribal custom, she can shield them as long as they don't stray outside her compound.

This isn't a solemn social problems picture, but one that resonates with life and sometimes with humor; the costumes bring visual joy into the frame. The story has immediate relevance because female genital mutilation is still practiced in parts of more than thirty African nations. One wonders what Alfred C. Kinsey would have to say about this film. Or, for that matter, the characters played by Neve Campbell and Joan Allen.

Toronto Report No. 2: *Undertow* Premiere

September 13, 2004—This kid David Gordon Green is twenty-nine years old, and he is a great filmmaker. He walked onto the stage at the Toronto Film Festival wearing jeans, a T-shirt, and flip-flops, and said he'd gotten worked up over the premiere of his new film and stubbed his little toe on his coffee table and broken it. "It's twice the size it was an hour ago," he said morosely, peering down at the injured digit. And then he showed us *Undertow,* and this film is a masterpiece.

Green has his own voice, his own tone, his own world. He tells stories of wandering and disaffected young people—not rebels, not outcasts, just somehow lost—who live in an American South of empty fields and marginal homes and rusted-out remnants of bankrupt manufacturing enterprises. They yearn to love and belong, spend moments of peace and gentleness, live in a world where terrible things can happen. He photographs them with the attention of an artist. He gives them things to say that you have never heard anyone say before, and yet it always sounds as if they would say them.

His first film, *George Washington,* made in 2001, was an astonishing debut in which a young character dies and his death is concealed and no one is really to blame and a great sadness grows. Then at Sundance 2003 came *All the Real Girls* (2003), about a boy who has made meaningless love to many girls but now meets a girl he really loves, and hesitates to touch her because it would reduce her to being like all of the others. Those films had a distinctive, assured voice, unlike any I had heard before; they were unique in story and style while still somehow seeming familiar, as if their world was not new but simply forgotten.

Now here is *Undertow,* about two boys being raised in a rural district by their father, who mourns the death of his wife. The older boy gets in trouble, runs a nail through his foot, loves his little brother. One day their father's brother turns up fresh from prison, and moves in. He is not a nice man. He wants the gold coins left by the boys' grandfather. His greed leads to death and danger, and an odyssey by the two boys across the worn-out local landscape. They meet homeless kids their age, get close to trouble but not in it, build a shelter in a junkyard. All the time the younger brother eats strange things and they make him sick.

I pause in frustration at such a bald plot outline. Nothing I have written can convey the poetry and beauty of the film. The plot never really engages as it would in a traditional film; it's more like a surface the characters can skate over on their way to growing up. Green said he was inspired by the fairy tales of the Brothers Grimm, the adventure stories of Poe, Twain, and Robert Louis Stevenson, and modern crime stories like *In Cold Blood.* That seems like an unlikely list, until you see the film and realize it really does contain all of those inspirations. And lives up to them too.

* * *

Kevin Spacey absolutely can sing. He could quit the day job. In his new film, *Beyond the Sea,* he plays Bobby Darin, a singer he has said he was born to portray. He does look a lot like him. The movie has many songs in it, and Spacey sings them himself, and he sings them damned well. It takes nerve to put yourself on the line like that, but he knew what he was doing.

The movie, which premiered at a Toronto gala, follows a fairly familiar biopic formula: rags to riches, romance that grows stale, early death looming on the horizon. Kate Bosworth plays Sandra Dee, Darin's wife. They love each other but they are an odd fit and ill-suited, and at one point he unkindly complains, "Warren Beatty is there with Leslie Caron who was nominated for an Oscar, and I'm there with Gidget." In a fresh touch, they *both* throw clothes into suitcases and move out of the house simultaneously. The movie has some problems, including a strange structure involving Darin as a child commenting on his own adult life, but it also has real qualities, including musical numbers that really deliver.

* * *

That Nick Nolte, what a card. He shambled onstage before the Toronto premiere of his *Clean,* wearing a long frock coat that made him look like the landlord of the House of the Seven Gables. In *Clean,* he plays a man raising his young grandson while the boy's mother (Cannes best actress winner Maggie Cheung) tries to get off drugs.

"I love Canada," Nolte told the Toronto audience in that hoarse, rough voice of his. Applause. "And of all the cities—not just in Canada, but in the world—the one I love the most is—Montreal."

* * *

Paris and Nicky Hilton, get out of town. The Dahl sisters are here. Lolo, Melinda, and Caitlin Dahl, dressed for a walk on the wild side, were among the celebrities at the twentieth annual luncheon sponsored by Hollywood gossip legend George Christy. All three have movies coming out: *Slave to Love* (Lolo), *The Mogols* (Melinda), and *504* (Caitlin). I sat near Lolo at the Christy lunch, and observed that she skipped dessert, perhaps not because she was dieting, but simply because there was no room for anything more inside the clothes she was wearing. I gotta say those Dahl girls really brighten up a room.

Toronto Report No. 3: Cheadle Outstanding in *Hotel Rwanda*

September 13, 2004—Moviegoers at this festival who have seen *Hotel Rwanda* talk about it in a hushed tone, and their eyes turn away as if remembering the images. One person I know walked out of the theater, skipped her next movie, and went back to her hotel room and cried. Here is a film about a brave and good man, but it is also a howl of rage against the crimes of men against men.

The movie takes place in Rwanda during the 1994 "civil war" that amounted to genocide by the majority Hutu against members of the Tutsi tribe and their Hutu sympathizers. More than a million people died, while the United Nations and the rest of the world failed to intervene. This tragedy is seen through the eyes of Paul Rusesabagina, the house manager of a five-star hotel run by Sabena airlines in Kigali, the nation's capital.

Don Cheadle's performance as Paul is magnificent on both the large scale and the small. His character, based on the life of the real Rusesabagina, finds himself as the protector of some 1,000 refugees, most of them Tutsi, who have come to his hotel for shelter. Calling in favors after many years of paying off the locals, in a nation where bribery is not a crime so much as a parallel economy, he tries to buy protection from corrupt army officers by handing out bottles of whiskey and fistfuls of cash. His situation is hazardous because, although he is a Hutu, his wife, Tatiana (Sophie

Okonedo), is a Tutsi, and that means she and their three children are under death sentence.

Paul takes pride in his job and his hotel, and that helps inspire his survival strategy. He knows how to impress, how to intimidate, how to shame, how to bribe, how to flatter. He fights not just with bravery but with intelligence and his insight into human nature, in a movie at once intimate and horrifying. *Hotel Rwanda,* directed by Terry George (*Some Mother's Son* and the screenplay for *In the Name of the Father*), is powerful and important, and finds scope for the full range of Don Cheadle's gifts as an actor.

* * *

Jamie Foxx is another actor who will emerge from this year's Toronto Film Festival trailing clouds of glory. He won a standing ovation for his virtuoso performance in Taylor Hackford's 152-minute epic *Ray,* based on the formative years of Ray Charles—the man who created soul music by merging gospel with rhythm and blues, and then, always looking for something new, moved into lush orchestrations like "Georgia on My Mind" and even, to initial opposition and eventual applause, into country music.

The film has its emotional base in Charles's childhood, where he felt guilt after the drowning of a younger brother, and where his mother (Sharon Warren) gave him strength and courage to take on the world despite his blindness after the age of seven. The movie, developed with Charles's participation and incorporating his performances, shows his dark side, including many years of heroin addiction and womanizing, but it also shows him clean of drugs for the last forty years of his life, a period during which he was beloved as a genius and innovator.

Hackford's film is rich with Ray Charles songs. It may be a little simplistic in the way it shows songs being inspired by specific events, but that allows the music to interlace easily with the life story. *Ray* is forthright about the way Charles faced prejudice both as a black man and as a blind one, and dramatizes the historic moment when he became the first major performer to refuse to play a segregated concert in Georgia. It's a nice touch that Julian Bond, the African-American politician from Georgia, is seen in a ceremony giving Ray the keys to the state and making "Georgia on My Mind" as the official state song.

* * *

Alexander Payne's *Sideways* is the best guy movie of recent years, and a lot more than that. It's a comedy, it contains a lot of sex, and yet underlying everything is a sadness and a loneliness and a hopefulness that make it quite surprisingly moving. Paul Giamatti, that actor who looks like he should be playing Kevin Spacey's morose or doubtful brother-in-law, gives a performance that's the equal of his conflicted character in *American Splendor.* He's Miles, a recently divorced man who is gradually crossing the line from being a connoisseur of wine to being an alcoholic.

His old college roommate Jack (Thomas Haden Church) is getting married in a week, and so these two forty-five-year-olds head to California wine country for a final seven days of buddyhood. Once there, they hook up with two local women. The bold Jack, who wants a fling before marriage, connects with Sandra Oh, while the shy Miles, still mourning the loss of his marriage, is dubious about a sunny waitress and would-be horticulturist played by Virginia Madsen.

The film could have been a formula buddy/road picture, but despite the underlying structure it feels fresh and original. The characters are allowed quirks and complexities, and the situations they get themselves into, however bizarre, seem just barely possible. I loved a scene where Miles and the waitress essentially fall in love after Miles explains why he feels tenderness, sympathy, and love for the pinot noir grape, and she realizes he's talking about himself.

Toronto Report No. 4:
Midnight Movies and Todd Solondz

September 15, 2005—I went to be interviewed for Stuart Samuels's new documentary, *Midnight Movies,* and it started me thinking. His film will be about the transgressive movies that started appearing in the 1970s—titles like *Eraserhead, El Topo,* and *The Rocky Horror Picture Show.* He wanted to know who went to see them, and why, and what it all meant, and his questions started me thinking.

Midnight movies need not, of course, play at midnight, but I know what he means. As a social pastime they've been threatened by home video, although they survive in big cities and near college campuses. But midnight movies as a liberated genre survive and prosper, for example, at the Toronto Film Festival. Consider Todd Solondz's *Palindromes*, which some audiences will embrace passionately while others are left puzzled or angry.

His movie, which I saw at Telluride and which is creating a stir in Toronto, is about a twelve-year-old girl who wants to get pregnant—and succeeds, while remaining in more or less complete ignorance of sex. Her mother (Ellen Barkin) argues strongly for an abortion. The girl encounters the prolife Sunshine Family, which provides her with a haven. But it's not as simple as that. The father of the Sunshine Family is an activist who plans to kill an abortionist. And as for the girl—well, this isn't a tidy narrative that arrives at a comfortable conclusion, but instead it's a series of versions of her story with different outcomes. The character is played by several actresses, some young teenagers, one (Jennifer Jason Leigh) in her forties, another (Sharon Williams), a tall, large black woman in her twenties.

"In all of the actresses playing the role," Solondz told me, "I was looking for fragility, innocence, vulnerability. By showing the character played by several actresses in several possible scenarios, I think I was suggesting that we do not change. We're palindromes; instead of developing, we fold in on ourselves. We can lose weight, gain weight, get older, even have a sex change, and still the inner core remains constant. I see that as somewhat liberating."

The device of using several actors in several possible versions of the story is bold and original, and yet I heard grumbles from some audience members after the screening I attended. One man uttered those words immediately identifying the speaker as a case of arrested development: "I go to the movies to be entertained." We all go to the movies to be entertained, but some of us do not require to be entertained within narrow, predictable limits. To be challenged by an audacious concept like Solondz's is, for me, entertaining.

Still, in the real world, Todd Solondz and his films *(Welcome to the Dollhouse, Happiness, Storytelling,* and now *Palindromes)* are transgressive, offensive, opaque, and maddening. They are about strange people having odd, sometimes distasteful experiences, often in the privacy of their secret lives.

"I don't set out to deliberately disturb the peace," he told me, "but what gives me a certain charge is not appealing to some audiences, and to the people who finance movies. Most movies have handsome and heroic protagonists, and we feel better about ourselves after seeing them. My movies, you'd be disappointed if you expected to walk out with that."

What, for example, is the message of *Palindromes*? Is it prochoice or prolife? With Solondz, you don't get a simple answer. Because he leans toward prochoice, he said, he wanted to give a break to the prolife Sunshine Family. That leads to a connection we may not notice the first time around. When the Ellen Barkin character recommends abortion to her daughter, she lists the birth defects that are more common among very young mothers. When we see the adopted children of the Sunshine Family, we realize each one is an example of one of the defects she mentioned. The Sunshine Family consists of children the girl's mother would have aborted.

All well and good, until we balance that against the sad or even horrifying experiences the twelve-year-old undergoes in getting pregnant, sometimes at the hands of ignorant older boys, once as the victim of a truck driver. Even then Solondz refuses to categorize. Is the truck driver a pedophile? In a moment of chilling insight, the girl herself tells him, "You're not a pedophile, because pedophiles love children."

Will *Palindromes* find an audience? Yes, because Solondz has informed us with his previous films how his universe works and who lives in it. That's why he's always the hottest ticket at a festival. Will it gross millions? Unlikely.

Consider the experience of Alexander Payne, another director at this year's festival. He made the challenging, off-putting *Citizen Ruth* (1996), starring Laura Dern as a glue-sniffing loser who gets pregnant and becomes the object of a tug-of-war between prolife and prochoice groups that are equally nasty. A lot of people disliked that one because it didn't tell them how they should feel. No matter what their position, it didn't congratulate them and attack the other side, but argued that there was much to be said against both sides. That made for a fascinating movie that most people found deeply unsatisfying, unless they were evolved enough to appreciate its refusal to simplify. This year Payne is at Toronto with *Sideways*, a warm human comedy about two buddies. I loved it. But it's a safe movie, right down the middle, without ambiguities.

Another film at Toronto this year is *The Woodsman*, written and directed by Nicole Kassell and starring Kevin Bacon as a pedophile who is released from prison after twelve years, moves to an apartment near a playground, notices the children—and also notices a pedophile who may be a danger to them. So, for that matter, might he be; the movie doesn't make it easy for us.

Bacon told me he wasn't exactly looking to play such a character, especially after the dark side of his great performance in Clint Eastwood's *Mystic River*. But he read the screenplay and was drawn in by curiosity about the man, his weakness, his dilemma. So was I when I saw the film. I leaned forward with attention, observing small moments that might be clues to the strength or weakness of this man, and the direction of his intentions.

What intrigued him, Bacon said, was that the character gets into a grown-up sexual relationship with a woman coworker (played by Kyra Sedgwick, his real-life wife). "I could work out how he could be a pedophile and how he might be dealing with that," he said, "but how did that fit with adult sexuality? I didn't know, and to play the character I had to find out."

Movies like these are why people at film festivals are always talking, talking, talking. What should they think about them, and why? What have they learned about human nature from movie characters set free from the rigid requirements of genre? Some directors choose to work outside the safe area favored by that man who goes to the movies to be entertained. No wonder they end up making Midnight Movies. I've always thought the most interesting people stay up late.

Toronto Report No. 5: South Africa at Toronto

September 15, 2004—Anant Singh opened his first video store in Durban, South Africa,

when it was still illegal for a nonwhite to own a store in a whites-only area. Mark Bamford and Suzanne Kay moved from Los Angeles to South Africa four years ago to make movies. For many years, their interracial marriage would have been against the law there.

Darrell James Roodt started making anti-apartheid films in the early 1980s, when he had to work in secret. His producer was Anant Singh, who used profits from his video stores to back films he could not legally make. Leleti Khumalo, who is thirty-three, spent the first twenty-three years of her life living under apartheid. Her father died when she was three. Her mother worked as a domestic, raising her four children in a home with a bed as its single piece of furniture.

All of these people grew up to become major players in the emerging South African film industry—which, ten years after the fall of apartheid and the election of Nelson Mandela as president, is being showcased at this year's Toronto International Film Festival. It's a measure of the maturing South African film scene that there were enough new titles of festival stature to justify the recognition. A few years ago there would have been only one or two, such as *Sarafina!* (1992) and *Cry, the Beloved Country* (1995), both made by the pioneers Singh and Roodt, both starring Leleti Khumalo.

I've seen four of the films with South Africa connections, and they are among the best films at Toronto this year. Like Australia in the early 1970s, the nation is finding its voice on the screen. Sometimes that voice expresses pain and courage, as in *Yesterday*, starring Khumalo as a Zulu woman who lives in an isolated village while her husband works in the mines of Johannesburg. Sometimes it expresses the joys and sorrows of human nature, as in Bamford and Kay's *Cape of Good Hope*, about the everyday lives of Cape Town characters of African, European, and Indian descent. Sometimes it explains extraordinary political events, as in Tom Hooper's *Red Dust*, which is about the Truth and Reconciliation Commission, which gave amnesty to South Africans willing to tell the truth about crimes they committed under apartheid. Sometimes it looks north on the continent, as in Terry George's *Hotel Rwanda*, which is about genocide against the Tutsi minority by the ruling Hutu.

These films express a new freedom for South African cinema, where every single film no longer has to carry the burden of representing the entire nation to the world. *Cape of Good Hope* shows interlocking Cape Town lives not unlike those in the Los Angeles movie *Grand Canyon. Yesterday* is the first film shot in the Zulu language. *Red Dust* explores a paradox: To be pardoned, the defendants in Truth and Reconciliation hearings had to confess, not deny, their crimes. *Hotel Rwanda* is a glimpse of what might have happened in South Africa if the wounds, injustices, and hatreds of the past had been allowed to fester after apartheid fell.

The four films are wonderful in different ways. The most universal in its impact is the one that might seem most provincial, *Yesterday*. Directed by Roodt, produced by Singh and his associate Helena Spring, it stars Khumalo as Yesterday, a farm woman who raises her daughter, Beauty (Lihle Mvelase), in a Zulu village "in the middle of nowhere." Her husband sends money from his labor in the mines, but is away for months at a time.

Yesterday develops a cough, and walks two hours to a rural clinic, where the doctor appears on Tuesdays and can't get to most of the patients. When she finally gets an appointment, Yesterday discovers she is HIV-positive. She has to cope with her illness, with her dying husband, with her little daughter for whom she has such dreams. The movie is about Yesterday's hope and her courage, and it is powerful and moving, conveying information about AIDS in a country where it is widely misunderstood. It was crucial to film in Zulu, Khumalo says, so the message could go where it was most needed.

Yesterday tells "a simple story," says Singh, "but it is stronger for its simplicity." It's simple not because it is simplified (its emotional complexity runs deep), but because by containing not a single unnecessary shot, word, or character, it achieves a kind of purity and universality, like *Bicycle Thief* or *Salaam Bombay* or *Pixote*. It will be this year's South African contender for an Oscar nomination.

Cape of Good Hope follows several lives: a white woman (Debbie Brown) who runs an animal shelter, a white veterinarian (Morne Visser), an Indian woman (Quanita Adams) who cannot conceive a child, a black domestic, her son, and a Nigerian refugee who has a Ph.D. in astronomy but finds work only as a handyman at the shelter. (He volunteers at the planetarium on his day off, but is fired even though he is not paid, because "the board wants your position reserved for a South African, not an immigrant.") Nthati Moshesh is riveting as the domestic worker, who is assaulted by her employer and then accused of theft, and whose son finds a surrogate father in the Nigerian (Eriq Ebouaney, who played the title role in *Lumumba* (2000)).

"We made it a point to cast all of the roles with South Africans," Bamford said after a screening. "There was a lot of interest from Hollywood in this screenplay, but they wanted to plug in American stars." He and his wife, Kay, were Hollywood screenwriters unable to tell the stories they wanted. "We moved to Cape Town for one year," Kay said, "and four years later we're still there. South Africa has problems, but it also has great people and great hope. It's an exciting place to live."

Red Dust, also produced by Singh and Spring, stars the London-born Chiwetel Ejiofor as an antiapartheid activist, now a member of Parliament. He returns to the rural area of his birth for the Truth and Reconciliation hearing of a white policeman (Jamie Bartlett), who tortured him for a month and may have been responsible for the murder of a friend. Hilary Swank plays a white woman raised in the district, who immigrated to America but returns to act as his attorney.

Red Dust deals with a difficult reality: Both blacks and whites may have reasons why it is convenient for the truth to remain obscure. Does the policeman know more than he wants to admit? Did his prisoner crack under torture? The movie shows how the truth is liberating for all sides, clearing the future so the country can move on, instead of endlessly picking at old wounds, as in Northern Ireland, Bosnia, Chechen, and Rwanda.

I wrote about the South African-coproduced

Hotel Rwanda in an earlier Toronto report. These films, like the urgent *Moolaade* from Senegal, announce that Africa is no longer a far-away location for exotic adventure stories, but a continent speaking for itself on the screen.

A few years ago when my wife and I were in Durban, Anant Singh showed us the storefront where he opened his first video store. He had a white friend who acted as the owner of record. He also illegally exhibited films that the apartheid government had banned for nonwhite audiences. "We showed them in people's houses," he said. "The word got around." Now he is South Africa's leading producer, and he owns a chain of multiplexes and video stores, which are all in his name.

Toronto Winners

September 20, 2004—*Hotel Rwanda,* a film that left its audiences shaken with its portrait of genocide in Africa, won the People's Choice Award as the audience favorite at the twenty-nineth Toronto International Film Festival.

The movie, directed by Terry George, stars Don Cheadle as the manager of a luxury hotel in Rwanda, who bribes, lies, and deceives in a desperate effort to protect refugees who have taken shelter in his hotel. Many of them, including his wife and children, are members of the Tutsi tribe, which was targeted for extermination by the ruling Hutu tribe; some 800,000 Tutsis and others died, while a United Nations peace-keeping force stood by ineffectually.

Nick Nolte costars in the film as a character based on General Romeo Dallaire, a Canadian UN commander who does all he can to bend the rules and save lives. The Cheadle character is based on a real man, Paul Rusesabagina, who now lives in Brussels and attended the Toronto festival.

Hotel Rwanda made an overwhelming impact during the festival's opening weekend, and was a favorite all week to win as People's Choice—which, at a festival without juries, is the top prize. Also winning an important award was *Omagh,* the story of families of bombing victims in Northern Ireland. It won the Discovery Award, voted on by some 800 critics and journalists who cover the festival. Firpresci, the international film critics' organization, appoints its own jury at all major festivals, and awarded its best-of-the-fest award to *In My Father's Den,* from New Zealand, about a war correspondent who returns home.

The City Award, given to the best Canadian film, was won by Michael Dowse's *It's All Gone Pete Tong,* about a rave deejay and party animal. City TV and the city of Toronto donated a $30,000 prize to the award winner. The City TV $15,000 award for best first Canadian feature went to *La Peau Blanche,* by Daniel Roby.

The awards wrapped up what many, me included, thought was the strongest Toronto fest in years. The award to *Hotel Rwanda,* which was coproduced by a South African company, was appropriate in a year when South African films were showcased in a special section of the festival. *Red Dust,* another strong South African film, was about a hearing of the Truth and Reconciliation Commission, which sought to discover and air the truth about crimes during the apartheid years—to head off the kinds of festering resentments and endless reprisals that both *Hotel Rwanda* and *Omagh* were about.

Savannah Film Festival

Savannah, Georgia, November 1, 2004—The chair moves. It truly does. It may not seem like a big deal to you, because you are a reasonable person who is not obsessed with *Citizen Kane,* but I have seen the movie perhaps 100 times, and analyzed it shot-by-shot in at least thirty sessions at festivals and in class, and I thought it contained no more surprises for me. The beauty of the shot-by-shot approach is that the theater is filled with other eyes watching the screen.

Here at the Savannah Film Festival, we

were analyzing the scene where young Charles Foster Kane's parents sign the papers that will send him east with Mr. Thatcher. There is an unbroken camera movement that begins with Charles playing in the snow, tracks back inside a window to show the three adults looking at him, and then precedes them as they walk deep into the room so Mrs. Kane can sit down at a table and sign the document. Question: Since we can see the ceiling, the camera is clearly not mounted on an overhead rail. How, then, does it arrive on the other side of the table without going through it?

Answer: The table is moved into position below the frame a second after the camera has passed. It's in place by the time we see it—but a top hat on the table is still jiggling.

This is a well-known *Kane* artifact, delightful for those who seek hints of artists at their work, monumentally insignificant for just about everyone else. We appreciated it one afternoon at the Trustee's Theater of the Savannah College of Art and Design, which sponsors the festival, and then we moved on. The scene ends as the three adults walk back toward the window, the camera again moving "through" the table, which is whisked away out of view.

"Stop! The chair moved!" somebody shouted. The rules of the shot-by-shot approach are simple. When you see something you want to talk about, you shout "stop!" I freeze the frame, and we talk about it. Because the lights are out in the theater, there is a protective anonymity.

"Just as the camera tracks past the chair on the lower right," the voice said, "the chair moves out of the way."

We reversed the shot and looked at it again. The voice was right. The chair movement isn't even subtle. An unseen hand clearly yanks the chair away from the path of the camera. But because our attention is naturally on the three moving actors and not on an obscure chair in the corner, we miss it. We miss it so completely that in thirty years of *Kane* shot-by-shots nobody had ever spotted it.

Until now. "Thank you for the chair," I told the audience, quite sincerely. I love *Citizen Kane*, and was touched by the discovery that it still keeps some secrets.

The Savannah Film Festival, now in its seventh year, benefits from being in a city a lot of people have always wanted to visit, especially since the publication of John Berendt's *Midnight in the Garden of Good and Evil*. So notorious are the book and movie of that title that in Savannah, I was told, they are simply referred to as "The Book" and "The Movie." There's a store called "The Book Store" that deals only in The Book and related items.

The college, universally called SCAD, also puts Savannah on the map. It has become the largest art and design school in the nation, supplying the city with the most artistic waiters and Starbucks employees in the world.

This year's festival featured a lot of new shorts by SCAD film students, and the premieres of new features such as Bill Condon's *Kinsey* and *Undertow*, by David Gordon Green, who found many of his crew members at SCAD. In addition to the three-day *Citizen Kane* workshop, I did a Q&A with the actor Jason Patric after a screening of James Foley's *After Dark, My Sweet* (1990), a modern *film noir* that made both of the Best 10 lists on *Siskel & Ebert*, but sank so quickly at the box office that it never played Chicago and grossed less than $2 million.

Patric, an intense and gifted actor who works rarely because he appears only in films he thinks will be good, gives a haunting performance as an ex-boxer and current mental patient who drifts into the life of a sexy widow (Rachel Ward) and "Uncle Bud" (Bruce Dern), who has a plan to kidnap a local rich kid. They involve the boxer, in a story that does not pay off like a typical crime drama, but descends through *film noir* into the darkest shadows of tragedy and bleak redemption. A new print has been made of the nearly lost film; now it is time for it to be rediscovered.

The godfather of the Savannah festival is Bobby Zarem, a local boy who became one of New York's most famous publicists (*People I Know* stars Al Pacino in a role inspired by Bobby). Zarem is everywhere, in his off-the-rack duds from the Savannah Big Man store and his New Balance running shoes. He knows everybody—all the stars, and also the waiters, the ushers, the kids at the next table at the boiled-shrimp dive. He is a moving force behind the festival's Lifetime Achievement Awards—which went this year to Kathleen Turner, director Norman Jewison, Peter O'Toole, and me. I would like to think my award was indeed for lifetime achievement and not for my achievement in inviting *People I Know* and Zarem to my own Overlooked Film Festival at the University of Illinois. Either way, I'm keeping it.

Sundance Film Festival
Sundance Report No. 1:
Opening Night

Park City, Utah, January 21, 2005—For ten days, Robert Redford was observing, the population here swells from 7,500 to 45,000. That's a gain (I'm guesstimating here) of 37,499 cell phones, 15,000 SUVs, 400,000 cups of designer coffee, 100,000 postcards advertising a movie that forty-seven people will see, and 170 restaurant hosts and hostesses fed up with people asking them, "Don't you know who I am?" This last complaint has grown so common that a T-shirt has emerged with the message: "No, I don't know who you are, and I don't f—— care."

Oh, the rudeness, it is epidemic. Last year one of the biggest pains in the butt, according to a Canadian journalist, was me. This is not likely because (a) I am the gentlest and most grateful of individuals, and (b) I did not attend last year's festival, and can prove it with a note from my doctor.

But enough about me. What about my festival? Some kind of a new record was set on board the American Airlines flight to Salt Lake City, when I was given a DVD of one of the films by its director while the plane was still at the gate. At the SLC airport, I met a charming woman who had the name of her son's film emblazoned on the back of her jacket, and was handing out postcards for its screening.

Postcards. There are thousands of them. I turn instead to the official program, which lists, I dunno, 180 films, and I look for (a) directors I like, (b) actors I like, and (c) subjects that sound interesting. Then I feed all the screenings into my computer, and find I can see everything if I am only willing to view four films at once.

So I race off to the Eccles Center for opening night, a film by Don Roos named *Happy Endings*. It stars a roll call of indie gods, including Lisa Kudrow, Maggie Gyllenhaal, Laura Dern, Bobby Cannavale, and Tom Arnold (some are born indie; others have it thrust upon them).

I am told my press pass, which is good for everything up to and including, I hear, free cappuccinos, will not get me into the screening: I need an actual ticket for opening night. I am not rude and indignant, because this seems reasonable enough—and besides, the Canadian may be lurking about. I say I will attend a later screening, and then an angelic woman I have never seen before in my life simply says "here," and hands me a ticket.

Inside, I find that Howie Movshovitz of Denver's Starz Film Center and Rob Denerstein of the *Rocky Mountain News* have saved me a seat in the back row on the left. This is where we always sit every year, and they figured I'd turn up.

"But where is Ken Turan?" I ask, because the *Los Angeles Times* critic invariably lurks back there in the shadows with us. He has not been sighted, but Debbie, the babe, who always sits right in front of us, is here again this year. We like her because she's not tall and we can see over her. Also for other reasons, but at Sundance that's the most important one.

The screening is delayed for half an hour by a locustlike horde of photographers, who are jammed into the lower right-hand corner of

843

the vast room, which is why we always choose the upper left. They are all trying to repair the tragic shortage of photos of Robert Redford. Eventually Bob climbs onstage and observes that he is here because he did not get invited to another event on Thursday night. That would be the Inaugural Gala—ho, ho.

The movie is … but that can wait until I file a roundup of several of the first movies I have seen. I am too agog just to be here. My wife, Chaz, who arrives tomorrow, sent me an item from Page Six. Just think how many reporter-hours went into compiling the following information:

"At the Motorola Lodge, celebs get free phones, Escada dresses, Kiehl's products and Mercedes loaners. On Main Street, Hewlett-Packard is giving out iPods, cameras, computers and printers. Nearby is the Levi's ranch where jeans, Xboxes and Ray-Bans are doled out. Seven jeans, Swarovski crystal and Cake makeup have a celebrity dressing suite at the Goldener Hirsch Inn. The Park City satellite of Marquee will be pouring Crown Royale for celebs, while Fred Segal has set up a spa at the Village at the Lift right next to the Yahoo! Cafe and the Timberland suite. One lucky winner at the Hewlett-Packard & Entertainment Weekly party tomorrow night will go home with a $25,000 gift bag including an all-expense-paid trip to South Beach, Adam + Eve intimate apparel, AG Jeans, a spa weekend in Arizona and goodies from MAC Cosmetics."

Me again. News items like this make my heart glow. I remember when Sundance was so scrawny it wasn't even called Sundance. It was called the U.S. Film and Video Festival, and so few people attended that the awards banquet was held in a meeting room of the Holiday Inn. Now there are 37,500 people here, and one of us is going home with a $25,000 gift bag.

Sundance Report No. 2:
Brosnan Is Superb in *Matador*

January 22, 2004—*The Matador* sounds on paper like a formula film, the kind of generic dreariness you expect Sundance to avoid. On the screen, it's another matter altogether—funny, quirky, and sad, and wonderfully well acted. The Sundance premiere audience walked out astonished by a film so much better than they'd expected.

Well, what did we expect? The movie stars Pierce Brosnan as a professional hit man, and Greg Kinnear as an unemployed Denver executive. They meet in a bar in Mexico City, become unlikely friends, and find themselves sort of in business together. When Kinnear's wife (Hope Davis) gets the chance to meet this assassin she's heard so much about, she gets right to the point: "Did you bring your gun?"

Everything I have described could perfectly well add up to a mediocre comedy destined for the video shelves. It adds up to so much more. Writer-director Richard Shepard finds an eerie balance of the macabre, the delightful, and the sentimental; the movie is so nimble it sometimes switches tones in the middle of a sentence.

Everything centers on the best performance Pierce Brosnan has ever given. A loner with no home and no friends, a man who uses booze and prostitutes to distract himself from killing people for a living, he wears a series of shirts that look as if they've been through way too many hotel laundries. He's coming to pieces when he meets Kinnear in a hotel bar. They have a series of conversations so pitch-perfect, even in the way they can't agree on the same pitch, that just to listen to them is a delight entirely apart from what it leads to.

Kinnear can hardly believe Brosnan actually kills people, and there is a virtuoso sequence at a bullfight when Brosnan demonstrates how easy it would be to kill—well, almost anyone. But he's beginning to fall apart, and botched a job in the Philippines. Now his employers are planning to kill him. The problem with *The Matador* is that no description can do it justice, because its elements sound routine, but its direction, writing, and acting elevate it into something very special. It's *Sideways* with death instead of wine, someone said after the screening. I think it was me.

Of the other films I've seen, one I particularly admired was *Rory O'Shea Was Here,* an Irish film by Damien O'Donnell, with James McAvoy and Steven Robertson as young roommates in a care home for the physically handicapped. McAvoy plays Rory, paralyzed from the neck down, except for two fingers, by muscular dystrophy. Robertson is Michael Cunningham, whose cerebral palsy makes him almost impossible to understand—except for Rory, who acts as his translator.

Rory hates institutional life. Michael is okay with it, but agrees it would be good to move into an apartment. They wage a campaign against a well-meaning supervisory board and win the right to move out on their own, recruiting a pretty young blonde (Romola Garai) as their caregiver. The strength of the film is in the way it neither sidesteps the severity of the heroes' disabilities nor allows itself to be depressed by them. Rory O'Shea is a cheeky rebel, and Michael's life is changed by him.

Two other films—the opening night film *Happy Endings* and the British crime drama *Layer Cake*—are both accomplished exercises in interlocking plots and intersecting characters. Don Roos's *Happy Endings* tells a labyrinthine story about several couples, some of them gay or lesbian, and a tangled web of adoption and sperm donation. Lisa Kudrow is especially effective as a girl without visible means of support, who successfully seduces a kid she is pretty sure is gay, and uses him as a springboard to his rich dad (Tom Arnold). Sounds cynical until you see the film and realize all these people basically mean well, in their own sometimes very specialized ways.

Matthew Vaughn's *Layer Cake* is another in the recent genre of hard-boiled British movies about gangsters who are too clever by half, or not half clever enough; it amounts to the same thing. Daniel Craig stars as a man who thinks he can run a sane and rational drug distribution business; Colm Meaney once again shows a disconcerting ability to be the most likable and hateful of characters.

We shuttle from one of these Sundance screenings to another on the tirelessly circulating Park City buses, which function as an instant buzz network. You get on board, and by the time you reach the next stop you may have been talked out of the film you were going to see, and into a film you hadn't even heard about. I now know, for example, that I absolutely must see *Murderball*, a documentary about wheelchair rugby players. How do

I know that? I heard it on two different shuttle buses. That constitutes a quorum.

Sundance Report No. 3: *Murderball* Earns Festival Buzz

January 23, 2004—I knew you needed leather balls to play rugby, but I didn't know you could also use steel ball bearings. *Murderball*, probably the most talked-about documentary at Sundance this year, is about the extreme sport of wheelchair rugby, played in reinforced and armored chairs by quadriplegics with various degrees of disability. It is a full-contact sport.

The film follows the fortunes of Team USA, undefeated for eleven years in the annual tournaments, and one of its stars, Mark Zuban, who intimidates opponents with a fierce goatee and bold tattoos. Another player, Joe Soares, was all-American for years, but has been dropped from the team. In revenge, he becomes coach of the Canadian team, setting up fierce duels at a tournament and also at the 2004 Athens Paralympics.

The movie works first of all as an astonishing sports documentary. The rules are simple: When you have the ball, you have to dribble or pass within ten seconds. Cross the goal line with the ball, and you score. Degrees of disability are rated from 0.5 to 3.5, and a team is allowed to field players totaling eight points. One of the best American players has no lower arms or legs.

The players are strapped into their customized chairs, and a good thing, too, because one of the ways you play the game is to crash into an opponent and try to knock his chair over. That happens a lot. Before their injuries these guys were jocks. They still are.

But the heart of *Murderball*, directed by Dana Adam Shapiro and Henry Alex Rubin and produced by Shapiro and Jeff Mandel, is the story of overcoming injuries and despair, and learning through rehabilitation and training not only to function in the everyday world, but to become Olympians. The movie is very frank about details of quadriplegia, including questions about sexuality (yes, many quads can). Most people think all quads are paralyzed from the neck down, like Christopher Reeve, but we find there are degrees of paralysis and many retain various degrees of control of their limbs.

They talk about how people are awkward around them and don't know what to say, and Zuban says: "Hey, I'm shorter than you because I'm in this chair. That's about it." During a school visit, an eight-year-old displays the openness of children when he asks the player without forearms: "How do you eat your pizza?" He finds out. Also how he cooks, drives, and plays quad rugby.

There is controversy here this year about two recent films in which paralyzed characters decide that they want to die. Listen to Mark Zuban, who is attending Sundance with his buddy, Christopher Igor. In high school, it was Chris who crashed his pickup, not realizing Mark was asleep in the truck bed. Mark was thrown into a canal where he awaited rescue for thirteen hours.

They went through a period of blame and guilt, they said, before finally accepting that it was an accident. They're best friends again. An audience member asked, "If you could, would you turn back the clock on that day?" Zuban, whose full-time job is as a civil engineer, answered slowly and seriously: "No, I don't think so. My injury has led me to opportunities and experiences and friendships I would never have had before. And it has taught me about myself." A pause. "In some ways, it's the best thing that ever happened to me."

Another Sundance doc is also a wonderful portrait of an unexpected lifetime. Steve James, who directed *Hoop Dreams*, is here with *Reel Paradise*, the story of a New Yorker named John Pierson who distributed and represented the films of Spike Lee, Kevin Smith, and many other indie directors, and hosted *Split Screen*, an IFC program on independent films.

He grew tired of doing the same job day after day, he said, and decided to move with his wife, Janet, his teenage daughter, and middle-school son to—well, to Taveuni, one of the smaller and more obscure of the Fiji Islands. There they would reopen the local movie theater and show movies for a year, most of them free.

Steve James joined the Pierson family for the last month of their year to shoot this film.

You might wonder if there is much of a film to shoot: Movie nut goes tropical, shows Buster Keaton, *Matrix*, and *Jackass* to cheering local audiences. But James has a knack, a gift, or a curse of turning up when dramatic things are happening. The closing scenes of *Hoop Dreams* outrival fiction, for example.

Here what happens is such intriguing human drama that we realize: This is what reality TV could be like if it had a brain and a soul. Pierson's experiment in Fiji is a great success, despite travails with unpredictable projectionists. The theater is jammed with audiences who scream with delight more or less nonstop through everything, which is why Buster Keaton is so popular; with a silent film, you don't need to hear the dialogue. He also shows *Apocalypse Now*, over the objections of his son, Wyatt, an uncommonly smart and realistic kid who predicts no one will come, and observes that "most indie films are boring."

Meanwhile, Georgia the daughter has made best friends with Miriama, a girl her age, and goes through a period of wanting to stay out later than her mother thinks is wise. It's the usual teenage rebellion stuff, made simpler because her Fijian friends are good kids. But then there are two thefts, including John and Janet's laptop computers, and suspicion descends—not on Miriama, but in general. It feels like betrayal.

Still, the family loves their decision to spend a year on the other side of the world, and Wyatt observes that in New York he might have five kids in his house in a week, but in Fiji he never had less than five friends in the house at any given time. The movie is about families, cultural differences, ideas of raising children—and about movies. If I had seen *Jackass* in John Pierson's theater with those 300 uproariously happy kids, I might have liked it. I certainly would have understood it better.

Sundance Report No. 4: Herzog Debates Nature

January 25, 2004—I took a day off to cover the Oscars, and I'm nine films behind. That's nine I've seen, not nine I've missed. They are so various and in many cases so good that the problem is to write about them without sounding like a crazed cinemaniac.

Grizzly Man is the best place to start. This new documentary by Werner Herzog is an astonishing portrait of Tim Treadwell, who like many of Herzog's subjects is possessed of a serene ecstasy that forces him to go too far, try too much, risk his life in his search for the sublime.

You read about Treadwell in the papers, or maybe you saw him on *Letterman*. He's the guy with the Prince Valiant haircut who spent thirteen summers in Alaska living with grizzly bears. He spoke their language, he said, and knew their moods, and survived unarmed among them. But in the autumn of 2003 the communication broke down, and Treadwell and his girlfriend were killed and eaten by a bear—a bear he didn't much like.

Herzog, a great filmmaker, doesn't simply tell this story but transcends it, engaging in a debate with the dead man over the nature of Nature. Treadwell thinks Nature is harmonious. Herzog says he thinks it is made of "chaos, hostility, and murder." When Treadwell looks into a bear's eyes, he sees a friend. Herzog sees a wild animal, curious and possibly hungry.

Treadwell got a video camera in 1999, and left behind ninety hours of extraordinary footage taken in the wilderness. The footage includes shots taken hours before his death, at the place where his bones were found, and shots of the bear that would eat him. He comes across as an engaging, exuberantly childish man who talks to the animals as if they were children, and dramatizes his own mission and the constant danger he says (accurately) surrounds him. Herzog talks to his friends, former lovers, and partners, to the pilot who dropped him off and found his remains, and the coroner who opened up the bear. *Grizzly Man* is chaotic, hostile, deadly, harmonious, and brilliant.

I also greatly admired *Nine Lives*, by Rodrigo Garcia, which has a large cast including many famous names, and uses them in a series of nine vignettes, each one filmed in a single shot of ten to twelve minutes. Some of the segments have the impact of great short stories. For example, a scene in which Robin Wright

Penn plays a pregnant woman who is in the supermarket when she meets a former lover, also now married. It becomes clear to them that their old attraction is still powerful. In another lovely scene, Aidan Quinn and Sissy Spacek meet in a motel for illicit love, but the arrest of a woman in another room changes the dynamic. Glenn Close stars in a bittersweet closing segment in a cemetery. The film's mood is elegiac but hopeful, as needy people uncertainly reach out to one another.

Rebecca Miller's *The Ballad of Jack and Rose* stars her husband, Daniel Day-Lewis, as the last survivor of a 1960s hippie commune. He lives on in his wind-powered island house with his teenage daughter (Camilla Belle), in a relationship too close to be healthy. After a heart attack, concerned about the future, he promises marriage to his mainland girlfriend (Catherine Keener), and she arrives with her two sons. Miller, who also wrote, develops the story not as a standard relationship crisis but as a series of tenderly observed and sharply emotional surprises.

Steve Buscemi's *Lonesome Jim* is a little masterpiece of mood, starring Casey Affleck as an Indiana boy who fails to make it in New York and returns home to a relentlessly cheerful mother (Mary Kay Place), a distant father (Seymour Cassel), and a brother (Kevin Corrigan) who soon enough is in the hospital. There Affleck meets a nurse (Liv Tyler), and they begin a relationship filled with apprehension, caution, and the frightening possibility of love. It's not what happens so much as how it feels, and sometimes it's funnier than I make it sound.

Michael Hoffman's *Game 6* is a *written* picture, by which I mean that the dialogue must be attended to as in a stage play. It's the first and only screenplay by the novelist Don DeLillo, with Michael Keaton as a successful playwright, Griffin Dunne as a writer who is falling to pieces, and Robert Downey Jr. as a critic of great eccentricity. Because the principal characters are writers, they talk like writers, with specific and evocative word choices. Mostly what they talk about is the collapse of the Boston Red Sox in 1986. Game 6 of that famous World Series unfolds during the movie, as the men find a metaphysical connection between themselves and their team. DeLillo's dialogue allows for a complexity and richness of speech that is refreshing compared to the subject-verb-object recitation in many movies.

There are other good films I will write about, and I must not neglect Stephen Chow's *Kung Fu Hustle*, which is—what? Imagine a film in which Jackie Chan and Buster Keaton meet Quentin Tarantino and Bugs Bunny. Yes. That describes it nicely.

Oh, and I met a man named Dave Gebroe here, who says I must see his film *Zombie Honeymoon,* which he describes as his response to my call for a truly romantic horror film. I cannot quite remember issuing that call, but no doubt he is right, and certainly there is a tragic lack of such films.

Sundance Report No. 5: Rosario Dawson

January 26, 2004—Rosario Dawson should be on those Sunday morning political talk shows, as a guest or a host, either way. She is so intelligent and fiercely opinionated that I forgot, for a moment, I was talking with a movie actress, and got into my Problems of the World mode.

Most people know her as The Rock's tough, muscular costar in *The Return,* or as a woman in black in *Men in Black II,* or as the fiery Roxanne, who takes the lead with Colin Farrell in *Alexander* and turns their wedding night into a form of martial arts. They haven't seen the Rosario Dawson who reads a poem in Ethan Hawke's *Chelsea Walls,* or plays the possessive girlfriend in Spike Lee's *He Got Game,* or is the competitive journalist in *Shattered Glass.*

Now here she is at Sundance in Stephen Marshall's *This Revolution,* starring as a New York woman whose husband was killed in Iraq, and who has joined a group organizing protests at the 2004 Republican National Convention. Movies are wonderful in the way they can take us from Roxanne the sensuous dancer and voluptuous bedmate of Alexander the Great, to Tina Santiago, with blond cornrows and a wardrobe from the Gap.

"You're not at all protective of yourself in this role," I said. "You're a beautiful woman, but here you don't do anything much with

hair or makeup or clothes; you look kind of scruffy sometimes."

"I like to play lots of different characters, not just the same thing again and again," she said, "and I follow the character to who she is."

The movie is a deliberate homage to Haskell Wexler's *Medium Cool,* the famous blend of fact and fiction set during the protests at the 1968 Democratic National Convention in Chicago. Again this time, the central relationship is between a news cameraman (Nathan Crooker) and a woman he meets on a story. Tina (Dawson) has lost her husband, is raising the outspoken young Richie (Brett Del-Buono), and has become radicalized by what she sees as her husband's needless death in Iraq. The cameraman is having an affair with his boss, played by Amy Redford, daughter of festival founder Robert; they differ on politics, and he finds himself attracted to the angry, grieving widow and her lovable son.

Even small details are parallels from the earlier film, including the pigeons the boy raises on the roof of his tenement. And Marshall repeats one of Wexler's most daring gambits, which was to plug his fictional actors directly into real events. In *Medium Cool,* the cameraman (Robert Forster) and the woman (Verna Bloom) are in Grant Park when police fire tear gas at demonstrators. We can hear the famous offscreen line, "Look out, Haskell, it's real!"

Here Dawson and her costars joined the real protests during the RNC, followed by cameramen who looked, of course, just like the real news cameramen. (Crooker in real life makes documentaries, so could shoot his character's own footage.) So effectively did this work that Dawson was actually arrested, handcuffed, and held in jail for nine hours before convincing the police she was an actress playing an activist.

"It wasn't that bad for me, compared to the real people I was locked up with," she said. "You got the idea that the city and the Republicans equated dissent with treason. That's not the American way."

The story of Dawson's discovery rivals the story about Lana Turner on the stool in the soda fountain. Dawson was sitting on the front stoop of her house one day when Larry Clark and Harmony Korine, the director and writer of *Kids* (1995) saw her. "I wrote this part just for you!" Korine said, "although I didn't know that until I saw you!" Many careers were started by that film, including Chloe Sevigny's, but Dawson has achieved the most.

"I never set out to be in the movies," she said. "One thing just followed another. My parents were very supportive. I never took any acting lessons or anything like that; I learned by doing it."

Although she could work exclusively as a toned and sexy action heroine, she chooses her roles all over the map, and is as quick to work for almost nothing in *This Revolution* as for millions in *Alexander.*

"I was all set to be in Spike Lee's *She Hate Me,* and then the start date was pushed back," she said. "Oliver Stone offered me the role in *Alexander,* and I took it. Spike was sooooo mad! He said, 'You can be in a movie like that any day!' I said, no, I couldn't. How many epics are there? We shot for six months, in Morocco, England, all over. It was a great professional experience."

Her character in *This Revolution* differs from the Verna Bloom character in *Medium Cool* in being political, radical, and vocal. She delivers one of the movie's key speeches, articulating the argument against Bush and the war in Iraq. Apart from what she says, we sense that she understands and believes it, and is generating it. Some actors are hopeless with political speeches, obviously only delivering the dialogue. With Dawson's Tina, we feel she's speaking spontaneously. Given that the movie was shot in eleven days on a budget of approximately zero, that may even have been the case.

The movie is outspoken about manipulation of the media; the cameraman discovers that his raw footage of street demonstrators is being turned over to Homeland Security investigators, which is a breach of journalistic ethics. His form of revenge is unlikely but dramatic.

Rosario Dawson flew in to Sundance and was back to the preparations for her current movie, Chris Columbus's Rent, where she plays the lead, Mimi. "I sing and dance," she said. "I like physical stuff. I don't work out a lot per se, but I'm very active physically—running, scuba diving, climbing."

I began by saying she could work as a political commentator. As we spoke, she developed a sophisticated vision of the connection between movies and politics, between image and policy. I have it all on tape. There's not room for it in this festival report, but I'm going to get back to Rosario Dawson and her ideas. If it doesn't work in the paper, maybe I can submit it to the *Nation.*

Overlooked Film Festival
Selections in the 2005
Overlooked Film Festival

Chicago, March 16, 2005—A 70mm French comedy by Jacques Tati will open my seventh annual Overlooked Film Festival, and a Bollywood musical starring "the most beautiful woman in the world" will close it.

The festival, held from April 20 through April 24 at the University of Illinois at Urbana-Champaign, showcases overlooked films, formats, and genres, and is held in the 1,600-seat Virginia Theater, a restored movie palace in downtown Champaign.

The twelve selections, in alphabetical order, will be:

After Dark, My Sweet (1990), a moody *film noir* directed by James Foley and starring Jason Patric, Rachel Ward, and Bruce Dern as three loners who conspire in a foolhardy kidnap scheme. Jason Patric will appear in person.

Baadasssss! (2004), the story of how Melvin Van Peebles's 1969 film *Sweet Sweetback's Baadasssss Song* gave a crucial impetus to the independent black film movement. His son, Mario Van Peebles, who directed the film and stars as his own father, will appear in person.

Map of the Human Heart (1993), Vincent Ward's visionary romance about a love between a young Eskimo boy and an Indian girl he meets in a Montreal hospital. Jason Scott Lee and Anne Parillaud star in a story that takes them, when they are adults, from Canada to the center of World War II. Invitations are pending with Ward and Lee.

Me and You and Everyone We Know, my favorite feature at Sundance 2005, starring Miranda July as a would-be artist who falls in love with a shoe salesman (John Hawkes). That hardly suggests the originality and complexity of the story, which is about the mysteries of sex and the enchantments of the heart. Miranda July, a performance artist who also wrote and directed, will appear in person.

Murderball, winner of the Audience Award for best documentary at Sundance 2005, is about the sport of full-contact wheelchair rugby, and is especially appropriate for the Urbana campus, one of the birthplaces of wheelchair sports. In person: star player Mark Zupan, famed coach Joe Soares, directors Dana Adam Shapiro and Henry Alex Rubin, and producer Jeff Mandel.

The Phantom of the Opera, the 1925 silent classic starring Lon Chaney, "The Man of 1,000 Faces," who keeps his well-hidden for most of the film. Live in the orchestra pit: the Alloy Orchestra of Cambridge, Massachusetts, performing its original score for the film.

Playtime (1967), by the great French director and actor Jacques Tati. A recently restored 70mm print will continue the Overlooked custom of opening with a 70mm film. The movie, which features Tati's famous M. Hulot bemused and bewildered by a series of modern architectural spaces, was Steven Spielberg's inspiration for his comedy *The Terminal.* In person: *Chicago Reader* critic Jonathan Rosenbaum, who considers *Playtime* perhaps the greatest film ever made.

Primer (2004), a brilliant sci-fi film about techheads who construct a device in the garage that turns out to be a time machine. The movie's charm is its ability to observe its heroes combining cybertheory with venture capitalism. Made for a reported $7,000, but looking professional and accomplished, the film won the 2004 Grand Jury Prize at Sundance. In person: the writer, director, and star, Shane Carruth.

The Saddest Music in the World (2003), by the famed Canadian independent filmmaker Guy Maddin, whose comedy, in the form of a 1930s documentary, is about a Winnepeg contest to find the saddest song of all. Presiding is Isabella Rossellini, as a glass-legged beer baroness who invites musicians from all over the world. Also on the program: Maddin's *The Heart of the World* (2000), arguably the most-hailed short subject of the last five years. In person: Guy Maddin.

The Secret of Roan Inish (1994), by John Sayles, a hero of the independent film movement, will be our free family matinee. Photographed in Donegal, Ireland, by former festival guest Haskell Wexler, the film tells of a ten-year-old who learns the local legend of Selkies, who are sometimes human, sometimes seals. In person: John Sayles and his producer throughout his career, Maggie Renzi.

Taal (1999), a glorious Bollywood extravaganza, will be the matinee musical. The movie stars "Miss Bollywood," Aishwarya Rai, often called the most beautiful woman in the world, as a singer who falls in love with the son of a rich neighbor—until his parents insult hers, and she seems about to marry a famous music video director. In person: the director, Subhash Ghai, and Uma da Cunha, publisher of a Mumbai trade journal and expert on Indian films.

Yesterday, one of this year's Academy Award nominees for Best Foreign Film, and the first feature shot in the Zulu language. A beautiful and deeply moving film, it stars Leleti Khumalo *(Sarafina! Cry, the Beloved Country, Hotel Rwanda)* as a village woman whose husband works in the mines of Johannesburg while she raises their young daughter. In person: two pioneers of the independent South African film movement, producer Anant Singh and his longtime colleague, director Darrell Roodt. Miss Khumalo will attend if her filming schedule permits.

The festival will also offer free panel discussions. I will lead a panel of the visiting filmmakers. Professor Andrea Press of the Institute of Communications Research will chair a panel on "Women in Film." I will have a discussion with our special guest, Jean Picker Firstenberg, director of the American Film Institute.

All guest film artists receive the Golden Thumb Award, which will also be given to Ms. Firstenberg, Brenda Sexton of the Illinois Film Office, Rosenbaum, Gerson, and Uma da Cunha, Roger and Joanne Plummer, and Betsy Hendrick.

Films are selected by me, with the invaluable advice and counsel of Professor Nate Kohn of the University of Georgia, who is the festival director. The executive producer is Nancy Casey, the assistant director is Mary Susan Britt, the festival manager is Nickie Dalton, and Chaz Hammelsmith Ebert is the special adviser. The festival is a special event of the College of Communications of the University of Illinois, which produces it.

Cannes Film Festival
Cannes Report No. 1:
Allen Serves *Match Point*

Cannes, France, May 12, 2005—Woody Allen is back. He hasn't exactly been away, but not many of his recent films have stirred up the kind of excitement inspired here by *Match Point,* which is a thriller involving tennis, shotguns, and adultery.

"Would you say this is the sexiest movie you've ever made?" he was asked after the film's first screening at Cannes. He replied in pure Woodyese: "Well, it was very discreetly done, without a lot of, a lot of *overt* sex and violence, and so, ah, it may have been sexy for one of *my* movies, but, ah . . ."

Oh, it was sexy all right, and violent. It was also literate, hard-edged, and seductive in its story of an Irish tennis pro who settles in London, marries the boss's daughter, impregnates the former girlfriend of his new brother-in-law, and then grows desperate at the thought of losing his big job and chauffeured car and the weekends in the country.

The movie represents a break for Allen from his routine of filming a movie every year in or near Manhattan. He shot it in London, with a mostly British cast: Jonathan Rhys Meyers as Chris, a poor Irish boy who has some success on the tennis tour, becomes a pro at a London club, lucks into friendship with a rich young man (Matthew Goode), catches the eye of his rich sister (Emily Mortimer), and is taken under the wing of his rich father (Brian Cox). What bad luck when Chris meets the rich boy's

American girlfriend (Scarlett Johansson) and falls very seriously into lust.

"Men think I may be something special," she tells him, in one of their first flirtatious conversations.

"Well, are you?"

"No one has ever asked for their money back."

The movie is rich in humor and irony, like a literate Hitchcock story. Tension coils tightly under the surface as the pleasant young man becomes a liar, an adulterer, a betrayer of trust, and finally a man who thinks it might be convenient to commit murder. Allen toys with the audience in scenes where Chris seems about to be discovered, exposed, trapped, or disgraced.

Allen's press conference was one of those typical Cannes seances in which impenetrable questions inspire inscrutable answers. As usual, almost all the questions went to the director, while Johansson, Mortimer, and Rhys Meyers smiled and smiled and were possibly thinking that this, then, was what it was like to be Prince Philip.

"I'm hard of hearing," Allen explained, when he seemed to misunderstand some of the questions, although never the ones he wanted to answer. Consider this exchange:

Q: This is your thirty-sixth film. At this point in your career, how much is passion, and how much is force of habit?

A: "Making films is a distraction for me. If I didn't have them, if I had nothing to distract me, I would be fighting depression, anxiety, terror. I'm like a mental patient doing finger painting. It's therapeutic. Even if nobody comes to see my film, I've still had the benefit of living in another world for a year, and I've kept myself from having to live in the real world. I, uh, don't know if that answers your little question."

Allen said he is able to get his movies financed in America, but increasingly the studios "want to read the script, watch the dailies, and make their little suggestions. I can't work that way. I just want them to give me the money in a brown paper bag and go away." His working method is "very democratic: Everyone is paid nothing and billed in alphabetical order." Working in England is a pleasure, "especially because the English actors speak so wonderfully; even with the smallest parts, you could understand every word." Rhys Meyers cleared his throat: "Just for the record, I'm Irish."

For years it was said that a Woody Allen picture cost $3 million and grossed $9 million, and then he got to make another one. "Some of my films have never played south of the Mason-Dixon line," he once told me.

Match Point has a good chance, I suspect, of being his biggest box office success since *Annie Hall* and *Hannah and Her Sisters*. It's commercial, it will wrap audiences in its grip, and yet it's a Woody Allen picture.

"The film seems very cynical," one critic said during the press conference.

Allen replied, "Cynicism is reality with maybe an alternate spelling."

Allen's triumph was a good start for my first morning at Cannes. Then it was directly downhill. Along with a few dozen other critics, I journeyed to the Olympia cinema on a side street for a 2 P.M. screening of *Kiss Kiss Bang Bang,* a satirical murder mystery, part Raymond Chandler, part David Lynch, all starring Val Kilmer and Robert Downey Jr. My review of the film can wait, because I am too eager to review the screening.

All of us in the lobby, including the film's publicist, agreed the screening was to start at 2 P.M. But the theater management insisted it had been screened at noon, as agreed. Perhaps there was a noon screening, we argued, but

that did not in itself make a 2 P.M. screening impossible. The publicist asked a theater employee, a grandmotherly type with considerable oomph, if there was a screening room available.

"Theatre neuf," the grandmother meditated, shrugging as if to suggest that anyone who saw a movie in "theater neuf" would have to be responsible for the consequences. The Olympia has nine screens of various sizes, which during the festival are all devoted to screenings of films that their makers earnestly hope will be opening soon at a theater near you.

"Theater nine!" the publicist said cheerfully, but then a gloomy presence materialized from the depths of the theater and was identified as "le manager."

"Impossible!" he said, or something similar. In such situations all French words sound like "impossible!" to me.

But . . . we argued. The theater is empty! The print is here! The audience is standing by! And, viola!—here is the publicist to make all the arrangements.

The manager thought deeply and announced that he would allow the screening on condition that he speak on the telephone to someone from Warner Bros. But not just anyone from Warner Bros. would do. He specified one person and one person only from Warner Bros. whom he would consent to speak with.

The publicist raced out into the alley where her cell phone worked better, and in five minutes or less she was gesturing wildly to the manager: "Monsieur le Warner Bros!"

The manager walked outside and paced back and forth dubiously, waving his free arm as he consulted with the one and only man to whom he would consent to talk.

"Who is he talking to?" I asked a colleague who had become involved as a negotiator.

"The senior international vice president of Warner Bros. Or he thinks he is."

Cannes Report No. 2:
Van Sant Explores Lonely Death

May 13, 2005—If you're going to make a movie about a rock star who drifts into drugged oblivion and death, you basically have two choices. You could make one of those lurid biopics filled with flashbacks to a tortured childhood and lots of concert scenes and sex, while the star savors success before it destroys him.

Or you could do it the Gus Van Sant way. His new film, *Last Days,* is a dark, lonely portrait of a man leaving this world almost obliviously. A closing credit acknowledges that the film is inspired by the life and death of Kurt Cobain, and adds, in the most precisely worded disclaimer I can imagine, "the characters are, in part, fictional."

Last Days, an official festival entry here at Cannes, is a film I admire enormously while wondering if anyone will want to see it. The more you know about filmmaking the more you will appreciate it; the more you know about Kurt Cobain, the less. Van Sant refuses to romanticize the material or analyze the personality or motivation of his subject, named Blake (Michael Pitt). He doesn't even show him using drugs. Sometimes he doesn't even show him at all.

The film is wonderfully photographed by Harris Savides, who captures a damp, chilly world of cold stone houses isolated in a dark, gloomy forest. Blake is first seen wandering in the woods, mumbling to himself, sliding down a hill, splashing in a stream, and sitting beside a campfire defiantly shouting "Home on the Range" into the indifferent night.

The film watches, mostly in long shot, as he drifts in and out of a cabin on the grounds of one of the houses. Visitors arrive and leave. Band members talk vaguely of songs they're working on. A private detective (Ricky Jay) arrives to have a look at him and can't find him. A woman, not identified, appears and asks, "Do you talk to your daughter? Do you say, 'I'm sorry that I'm a rock-and-roll cliché?'" She wants him to leave with her. He will not.

There are disconnected passages from a suicide note, which he reads aloud to himself. Long shots of him at a distance, moving aimlessly inside the cabin. Events unfold around him without his notice or participation. One night as some friends are driving away, one stops and looks for a long time at his figure, wandering alone in a window. The next day he is found dead.

This is the third of Van Sant's death trilogy. *Gerry* was about two friends who go for a walk in the desert and get lost, and never get found.

Elephant, which won the Palme d'Or here two years ago, was inspired by Columbine and followed two students as they methodically went about the process of murder. Now this bleak death of a man so wiped out by drugs that he is not really present for his own exit.

The distinguishing thing about all three films, the courageous thing, is that Van Sant refuses to manufacture drama to "explain" the events. In the world of these films, death comes without motive or meaning. The characters are already doomed when we meet them, but not for reasons he supplies in a simple-minded docudrama way. When Jim Morrison checks out in *The Doors,* it's Wagner crossed with *Entertainment Tonight.* When the "in part, fictional" character in *Last Days* dies, it is like the slow flickering out of a lamp. This, Van Sant suggests, is what it is really like to die of numbing drug abuse: not sensational, not dramatic, just the mind wandering away and leaving the body to stumble into its grave.

* * *

What are the odds the film will win another Palme for Van Sant? Derek Malcolm doesn't have a clue. Faithful readers will recall that Malcolm, a former jockey who became the film critic of the *Guardian* of London, is the festival's unofficial bookie. He offers odds, takes bets, pays off on winners. Really. This is not a joke.

I ran into him right after the screening of *Last Days.* I asked him what odds he was quoting. "No odds as yet," he mused. "This is a very difficult festival to handicap." The problem, it is said, is the jury president, Emir Kusturica. "He's such an a–hole. You never know what he's going to back. He's very competitive with other directors."

Another problem: The legendary French director Agnes Varda, who is also on the jury. "Varda and Kusturica will be at each other's throats. God knows what the winners will turn out to be." Other jurors, including author Toni Morrison, actress Salma Hayek, actor Javier Bardem, and director John Woo, are likely to be hiding under the table.

Malcolm said, however, he hopes to be quoting odds in a day or two. "I could make a lot of money on this festival," he said, "since people will, as always, make the mistake of betting on the movie they like the most."

That movie so far is Woody Allen's *Match Point*, which is playing out of competition but has scored a genuine triumph. It's a diabolical story, set in London, about tennis, snobbery, adultery, and murder, shot through with guilt and sweaty palms. I wrote about it with much enthusiasm.

"I wonder if even Woody himself knows what a good film he has made," the critic Peter Brunette mused, after consulting Derek Malcolm on the odds. Todd McCarthy, the influential chief critic of *Variety,* the showbiz bible, says in his review: "Well-observed and superbly cast picture is the filmmaker's best in quite a long time." A French newspaper headline translates as "The day of glory for Woody Allen."

Allen's recent films have not set the box office on fire. *Match Point* currently doesn't have a U.S. distributor, but a bidding war is under way and rights may sell for more than any Allen picture in years.

* * *

Faithful readers will recall Billy (Silver Dollar) Baxter, the Damon Runyonesque character who in the 1970s and early 1980s added color, excitement, and a great deal of noise to the festival. His policy was that all waiters everywhere in the world are named "Irving." His war cry in the Majestic Bar was always the same: "Irving! Brang 'em on! Johnny Walker! Black Label! Big glass! Pas de soda! Pas de ice! And clean up this mess! And bring me some peanuts and those little olives like I like!"

Silver Dollar Baxter brought along a bag of silver dollars to use as tips, and they got him service that a $50 bill could not have purchased. He starred in two of my books, the factual *Two Weeks in the Midday Sun* and the fictional *Behind the Phantom's Mask.*

Billy retired from the Cannes scene twenty years ago. But he is not forgotten. Today I wandered into the Majestic Bar, sadly refurbished from its former shabby glory, and ran into the New York film distributor Ben Barenholtz, who was beaming with joy.

"There's still one Irving left," he said. "I walked in last night and shouted 'Irving!' and this guy came running out from behind the bar vibrating with excitement. But it was only

me. He reached in his pocket, and showed me his silver dollar."

Cannes Report No. 3: Egoyan Film Opens to Raves

May 14, 2005—Because the party was being given for Atom Egoyan and because he has made a terrific new film and is a nice guy, I went to it. People have been known to shed blood to attend the parties every night in the beachfront restaurants, but I would pay good money to get out of most of them. The parties are always the same: Too many people, too much smoke, not enough food, music to rupture your eardrums, and weird lights in your eyes. The caterers here must have trained on *The Manchurian Candidate.* I've never been able to understand why hosts allow music so loud they have to go out on the beach and talk to their guests on cell phones.

Egoyan, however, was in a rare mood, because his movie *Where the Truth Lies* is one of the big successes of the first weekend at Cannes, which is off to its best start in years. His film stars Kevin Bacon and Colin Firth as a showbiz team in the 1950s who will remind all sentient viewers of Martin and Lewis, although everyone connected with the film swears they were the last two people on their minds. When the naked body of a dead blonde is found in the bathtub of a casino suite in Atlantic City, a scandal is created that echoes through the years, until in the 1970s a young blond investigative journalist (Alison Lohman) tries to solve the mystery. Although the movie has a magnificently convoluted *noir* plot, its strongest quality is the nature of the film's human relationships; I was blindsided by a crime movie where the journalist's reason for *not* revealing the solution is inspired by kindness.

Bacon is on a roll right now, after *Mystic River, The Woodsman,* and now *Where the Truth Lies.* Along the way, something intriguing has happened to his face, which used to be clean-cut and without complications, and has deepened into character and mystery; everyone eventually grows into the correct age for their face, and Bacon is right now able to do more with a close-up than some actors can accomplish with a soliloquy.

Egoyan is the Canadian director of films

that deal powerfully with eroticism, not as a subject, but more as a problem. His credits include *Exotica* (1994) and *The Sweet Hereafter* (1997), for which he won Oscar nominations for writing and directing.

Egoyan introduced me to his father and said that his father does not like this film, but his mother does. The last time he had a film at Cannes, *Ararat*, about the Turkish massacre of Armenians, he invited his mother to attend. She didn't like it, but his father did.

"My father is more political about Armenia; my mother is more assimilationist," he said. Yes, but the fact that he has two parents who tell their son what they really think about his films may help explain why he makes such good ones.

"Dad immigrated from Armenia to Canada, studied for three years at the Art Institute of Chicago and became an abstract expressionist painter," Atom told me, "but then he had a show in Paris that didn't sell and so he went into the furniture business." Someone says one sentence to you, and it's a short story.

If the Egoyan film has a labyrinthine plot, you should see *Hidden*, an official French entry by Michael Haneke. The critics spent all day standing in lines and debating the plots of the two films. For that matter, Woody Allen's *Match Point*, also has a plot that snakes around and nibbles its own tail. With Allen and Egoyan, you can at last arrive at a reasonable understanding of what has happened. The whole point of the Haneke is that you can't.

His films stars Daniel Auteuil as the host of a TV talk show, and Juliette Binoche as his wife. They live in contentment with their young son in a book-filled house until someone starts sending them videos. The videos make no threat and state no purpose; they simply make it clear that someone knows where they live and work, and is watching them. This leads eventually to the disintegration of Auteuil's personality and his marriage, and to an onscreen death as surprising as any I have ever seen.

Throughout the movie, many shots have backed off to regard the action objectively from a distance. That's also the strategy of the videos. Then comes the film's last shot, also from a distance. It is composed in such a way that our attention is drawn to a character who

turns out to be unimportant. Only observant audience members (such as myself) noticed that on the left side of the screen, a conversation is taking place between two people who should have no way of knowing each other. What does it mean that they do, and does that explain the plot? Knowing the answers to those questions would not be nearly as interesting as standing in line debating them.

Cannes Report No. 4: George Lucas Receives Festival Medal

May 15, 2005—The Force was with us at the Cannes Film Festival. So was the Queen. The *Queen Mary 2* was anchored in the Cannes harbor, making the yachts of the millionaires look like bathtub toys. Sunday we were piped aboard to celebrate the Cannes premiere of *Star Wars*, and George Lucas was presented with the Medal of the Festival.

Lucas is here for the world premiere of *Star Wars: Episode III—Revenge of the Sith*, which played twice on the vast screen of the Theater Lumiere in the Palais des Festivals. There is no larger screen in the world, no better sound, no hipper audience, and the ticket scalpers in front of the Palais ("Invitation, monsieur?") were so eager they could have eaten Sith for breakfast.

The event on the *QM2* was more elegant on the part of the ship than on the part of its guests, a ravenous mob of paparazzi who descended on the buffet in the Queen's Room as if they had not seen a decent meal since moving out from under the roofs of their parents many years ago. Two dozen or more chefs presided over buffet tables groaning with the fruits of the sea, the creatures of the forest, the fowls of the air, the eggs of the fish, the legs of the crabs, and the cheese of the cows. Gigantic ice sculptures immortalized Yoda, Luke Skywalker, and Princess Leia, and the immaculately groomed ship's officers stood at attention about the room like a field test of starch.

After the press corps had gorged itself on caviar, we staggered down to the ship's theater, wiping sour cream off our Nikon straps and elbowing each other for front-row seats at the presentation ceremony. Alas, all of the front-row seats were reserved for "Official Cunard Photographers," of whom they appeared to be expecting eight. Photographers condemned to the third row were bitter and gloomy until supermodel Eva Herzigova came in and sat down in the fourth row. Then they were so ecstatic you would have thought she was Chewbacca.

George Lucas entered only twenty minutes late, which is so early at Cannes it is gauche. He was wearing blue jeans, a plaid shirt, a sports coat, and a silver-tipped cowboy belt, and looked every inch the master of Skywalker Ranch. He was called onstage by the commodore of the QM2 and by Thierry Fremaux, the "delegue artistique" of the festival, and Veronique Cayla, the "directrice generale."

They introduced a film in which Gilles Jacob, the president of the festival, stood atop the Palais with the QM2 in the background and remembered the first time he met Lucas, in San Francisco in 1972. Jacob said he did not remember which of the two of them had been the most shy, but it reminded him that Stanley Kubrick sometimes drove up in front of the houses of his friends, talked to them on his cell phone, and then drove away "without seeing a single person." I was not sure about the purpose of this anecdote, but I was happy to hear it.

Lucas was then given the Medal of the Festival, which in the past has gone to a select few, including Max Von Sydow, Jeanne Moreau, Sean Penn, Alain Resnais, Gong Li, Gregory Peck, and Melanie Griffith. One would love to see them gathered for Scrabble. He made a speech recalling that when he was at Cannes in 1971 with his *THX 1138* he signed a contract for the first *Star Wars*, and so it was appropriate that he had returned here for the sixth and final film.

Back ashore, I turned to view the magnificent ship one final time. It was a thrilling sight, although yesterday I saw a triple-length bright red Mini Cooper stretch limousine, and that was not only thrilling but hilarious. You should have seen all those big spenders in tuxedos, hunched defiantly inside.

Cannes Report No. 5

May 17, 2005—A midterm report from the Cannes Film Festival: Regulars are beginning to cautiously murmur that this may be one of the best Cannes Film Festivals in recent years. Even Lars von Trier's sequel to *Dogville* is a success. One strong film has followed another, and every day the buzz about possible festival winners gets revised.

The big audience success on Monday was *A History of Violence,* by David Cronenberg, the Canadian who sometimes makes oblique studies of madness like *Spider,* and sometimes makes inspired audience thrillers like this one. Not that it's only a thriller; it's more of a family drama in which violence is an unwelcome guest.

Viggo Mortensen stars, in one of the best performances of his career, as a man named Tom Stall, who runs a diner in a small Indiana town and lives peacefully with his wife (Maria Bello), teenage son (Ashton Holmes), and tiny daughter. One day two serial killers walk into the diner thinking to kill and steal, and Tom hurls a pot of coffee, jumps over the counter, grabs a gun, and kills them both. He becomes a media hero, which attracts unwelcome attention, and three tough guys in a big black car arrive in town. One of them, played by Ed Harris, has a horribly scarred face. Somebody blinded him with some barbed wire. Who could that have been?

How the movie unfolds I will leave for you to discover, along with a brief but indelible performance by William Hurt. None of the violence in the film is gratuitous, and all of it is necessary from Tom's point of view and even from our own.

There may be an acting award for Mortensen from this film, but then again Daniel Auteuil could win that prize for his work in Michael Haneke's *Hidden,* which is also being mentioned for the Palme d'Or. He plays a Paris TV host whose happy family (teenage son, wife played by Juliette Binoche) is also disturbed by unwelcome visitors—in this case, videos indicating the family is under surveillance. Who is sending these, and why? Answering the mystery has become a festival obsession and Manohla Dargis of the *New York Times* brilliantly writes: "My guess is that the videotapes were not shot or sent by anyone; rather, they simply exist, ontologically, as evidence." Yes, but if they were not shot or sent by anyone, how do they exist? Is ontological evidence visible to physical characters? In this movie, maybe.

When Lars von Trier's *Dogville* played

here, it was not precisely a popular favorite, although it found defenders among some critics. It was a deliberately artificial period melodrama set in the Rockies in the 1930s and filmed on a bare set where streets, buildings, and props were marked off with chalk and decorated with a few props. Gangsters arrive in the town and institute a reign of terror designed to show the underlying violence of U.S. society. It was said that the film's critics disliked it because it was anti-American. I disliked it because I thought it was very, very bad.

Now comes *Manderlay,* a sequel and also an official entry. Once again, a bare sound stage, chalk outlines, a few props. Once again, a plot that strains or perhaps even ruptures credulity. Bryce Dallas Howard steps into the role played by Nicole Kidman in the last film, as a gangster's daughter. Her father and his gang drive from Colorado to Alabama, where they happen upon a cotton farm where slavery still exists, sixty-five years after it was abolished.

Howard sizes up the situation, makes patriotic speeches, and idealistically decides to stay. Her dad lends her a few gangsters as helpers, and she frees the slaves and tries to institute a system of democracy. Some of the freed slaves are dubious about her methods, including an old and wise man played by Danny Glover.

The film uses language and descriptions few American films would dare to use—both for matters of taste, and because nobody talks that way. But somehow this time von Trier's story and characters take over and upstage the artificiality of the plot. His America is like a nightmare inspired by left-wing (and, for that matter, right-wing) paranoia, but a curious reality creeps into the situation and there are moments that are genuinely powerful.

Other major successes: The South African film *U-Carmen Ekhayelitsha,* which won the top award at Berlin, is playing here out of competition, and is wonderful. It's a vivid version, bursting with life, of the Bizet opera, translated into the Khosa language and sung by the magnificent Pauline Malefane and directed by Mark Dornford-May.

Does the transition to a township near Cape Town work? The opera seems almost to have been written for its new location. Miss Malefane and the other cast members are not only gifted singers but are better actors than many opera singers; no wonder the film was embraced at Berlin.

Miranda July's *Me and You and Everyone We Know* was my favorite film at Sundance, and I invited it to Ebertfest. Now it is having a big success here in the Critics' Week; it's eligible for the Camera d'Or award, for best first film. The critic of the *London Guardian* wrote that people mention two or three big films they admire, and then add that they saw this wonderful little film they're afraid will get overlooked. It has not been.

Another much-admired film is *Factotum,* by Bent Hamer, in the Director's Fortnight. It stars Matt Dillon as Charles Bukowski, the poet of Skid Row, and watches as he negotiates a series of brief employments, long hangovers, and troubled but passionate romances. Lili Taylor and Marisa Tomei are two of the barflies who pass through his life. Dillon has an uncanny feel for the character, and sometimes even looks like Bukowski, minus the acne. I recall his audio book recording of Kerouac's *On the Road,* and again this time admire how he captures the rhythm of a natural, untutored writer and outlaw.

And now I will sign off and turn to the dictionary and study the word "ontological," which I have a feeling will become increasingly useful as we approach the awards.

Cannes Report No. 6: Murray Impresses in *Broken Flowers*

May 17, 2005—Although *Star Wars: Episode III* was wall-to-wall action, some of the best films at Cannes this year have been very, very quiet. Consider *Broken Flowers,* by Jim Jarmusch, starring Bill Murray as a man who "made some money in computers" and now finds himself sitting in perfect stillness in the middle of his sofa, listening to music and not really listening to it. His hand reaches out to pick up a glass of white wine, and then he thinks better of it. Better just to sit.

Murray plays Don, and he is well named; as his latest girlfriend, Sherry (Julie Delpy), leaves, she tells him he's a Don Juan, always has been, always will be, is incapable of marriage. He receives an anonymous letter. It informs him that about twenty years ago, he had a son he was never told about. Now, the letter says, the son wants to find his father, and may come knocking on the door.

Who could the mother be? Don's next-door neighbor is Winston (Jeffrey Wright), who holds down three jobs to support his wife and five kids, but has time to be a Sherlock Holmes on the computer. Starting with a list of every lover Don can recall from twenty years ago, Winston plots out a journey for Don to take: airline tickets, MapQuest directions to their homes, everything. Don sets out stoically to visit each of the candidates: A widow (Sharon Stone) whose husband died in a car race "in a wall of flame." A Realtor (Frances Conroy), who sells prefabricated midlevel luxury. An "animal communicator" (Jessica Lange), who discovered she could hear animals talking. ("Is he saying something?" Don asks about her cat. "He's saying you have a hidden agenda.") And a tough broad (Tilda Swinton) whose lawn is decorated with rusting cars and motorcycles in various stages of repair.

Does he find the mother of his son? Is there a mother? Is there a son? Not really the point. The point is the Bill Murray performance, and the six kinds of counterpoint provided by the women and Winston the neighbor. Murray has often worked by withholding emotion, by inviting us to imagine what he's thinking behind a protective facade. Curiously, his technique can be more emotionally effective than any degree of emoting. In *Lost in Translation,* his loneliness and emotional need were communicated in the silences between the words. In *Broken Flowers,* he communicates with even less apparent effort, all the more difficult because, as I neglected to mention, the movie is a comedy—or in any event a serious personal quest during which the audience finds itself laughing a lot.

Some actors give the kinds of performances where we want to get out of the room, stand on the lawn, and watch them through a window. Murray has the uncanny ability to invite us into his performance, into his stillness and sadness. I don't know how he does it. A Bill Murray imitation would be a pitiful sight:

Passive immobility, small gestures of the eyes, enigmatic comments, yes, those would be easy, but how does he suggest the low tones of crashing chaotic uncertainty?

* * *

More quiet films and journeys. Cyndi Williams is at the center of Kyle Henry's *Room,* in the Directors' Fortnight, as a dumpy but sweet-faced Houston woman who begins to have blackouts and strange visions of over-lit warehouses and abstract patterns. She's a hard worker, always on the run: Working at a bingo parlor, delivering Yellow Pages, anything. Money is short and there are no presents for Christmas. For no reason she can understand, she steals some money, gets on a plane, flies to New York, and wanders the streets, an innocent compelled to search for—what?

Henry describes the movie as "sort of science fiction." Maybe it's about alien abduction, without the aliens or the abduction. Maybe it's about a mental state that causes people to believe they are receiving messages and summonses, even when they're not. What distinguished the deliberately aimless plot is the performance by Williams, who looks every inch and ounce a real person. She is so earnest, so focused, so worried.

And another quiet film and a journey. Francois Ozon, who made the art-house hit *Swimming Pool,* is back in the official competition with *The Time That Remains,* starring Melvil Poupaud as a gay photographer who discovers he has three months to live. He, too, goes on a solitary quest that involves parents who understand him better than he deserves, a sister he fights with for no good reason, and finally the grandmother he feels closer to than anyone else in his life. Jeanne Moreau plays the grandmother, with such tact, depth, and tenderness she distinguishes the whole film by her attention to it.

Two films I've written about from other festivals are having considerable success here. Werner Herzog's *Grizzly Man,* from Sundance 2005, is about Tim Treadwell, a man who spent his summers wandering unarmed among the grizzly bears of Alaska, thinking of them as his friends. All except for the one who ate him. Herzog employs ninety hours of

Treadwell's own video footage to create a portrait of a strange and trusting man.

And Lodge Kerrigan's *Keane,* from Telluride 2004, stars Damian Lewis as a schizophrenic who is sometimes functional and logical, sometimes torn with anguish. He believes his daughter has been abducted. Perhaps he is right. It is true enough in his own mind. There is one astonishing sequence during which, while he seems rational, he is entrusted with the care of a small girl. He wants to protect her and does not want to harm her, and wages a fearful struggle with the demons who might make him a danger to her.

All of these films have something in common: They are nourishing to the human spirit. They challenge the intelligence, they engage the emotions in a worthy way, they are curious about this business of being alive. When you come to Cannes you feel like the animal communicator. You can hear the movies talking to you.

Cannes Report No. 7: Tommy Lee Jones Directs *Three Burials*

May 20, 2005—In this festival of smooth, mannered style, what a jolt to encounter *The Three Burials of Melquiades Estrada,* directed by Tommy Lee Jones. Here is a film as direct as a haymaker, a morality play where you don't need a dictionary.

Hidden, one of the favorites for the Palme d'Or, involves a video that no one seems to have made and a crucial onscreen meeting that half the audience doesn't notice, and then here's Jones with *The Head of Alfredo Garcia Meets the Treasure of the Sierra Madre.* Desson Thomson of the *Washington Post,* who like me is an admirer of the film, calls it "old-fashioned," which he means as a compliment.

The story is simply told. Tommy Lee Jones plays a ranch hand in Texas who makes a friend of a cowboy from Mexico who is an illegal alien. Barry Pepper is a reckless young border patrolman who shoots the cowboy dead in a stupid mistake. Nobody much seems to care about one Mexican cowboy more or less; certainly not the local sheriff (Dwight Yoakam). So Jones kidnaps the border patrolman, handcuffs him, and sets him

to work digging up Melquiades' body and taking it by horseback to the little town in Mexico where Mel said he was born. "I don't want to be buried among these billboards," Mel once said.

Flash floods and mud nearly wiped out the production, Jones told me during a public Q&A session at the American Pavilion. There were some close calls with horses on dangerous terrain. But, no, that wasn't a real horse falling off a 900-foot cliff. It just looked like one. And how did they get the shot that seems to show the horse falling directly onto the camera?

"I had my guys drop a bag of sand over the edge," Jones said, "and where it landed, I said, that's where we put the camera. Then we pushed over a prosthetic horse. We used some animation to make it look alive on the way down." When the artificial horse hit, the camera got smashed and they lost a few hundred feet of film. But it's quite a shot.

And in a festival where subtle notes in final scenes can shift a film's whole emotional center, *Three Burials* has two lines of dialogue that reveal what has happened to the two men during their long, painful, and undoubtedly smelly journey.

* * *

Three Burials is one of twenty-one films in the official competition. I checked in with Derek Malcolm, film critic of the *Guardian* of London, to get the latest favorites. Malcolm, you will recall, is the former jockey who sets odds and takes bets for the Palme d'Or. He's still complaining that jury president Emir Kusturica of Serbia-Montenegro is clouding the crystal ball.

"I heard that he asked the jury to meet every day," Malcolm said, "and then he didn't turn up for any of the meetings." He did, on the other hand, sing with his band at a party on the beach. Meanwhile, Malcolm quotes these odds:

9-4: *Hidden,* by Michael Haneke, the film about a family traumatized when someone sends them videos that indicate they are being secretly observed.

5-1: *Manderlay,* by Lars von Trier, with Bryce Dallas Howard as a gangster's daughter who frees slaves still in bondage on an Alabama plantation sixty-five years after the Emancipation, and tries to establish democracy.

6-1: A tie between *Broken Flowers,* the Jim Jarmusch film starring Bill Murray as a man looking for a son he might have fathered twenty years ago, and *L'Enfant,* by Jean-Pierre and Luc Dardenne, about a homeless young couple trying to raise their baby when what they really require is someone to raise them.

10-1: *A History of Violence,* by David Cronenberg, starring Viggo Mortensen, Maria Bello, and William Hurt in the story of a small-town family where the father's heroism attracts dangerous attention.

15-1: *Kilometre Zero,* by Hiner Saleem, the story of a Kurdish draftee into Saddam Hussein's war against Iran.

"Remember," Malcolm told me, "these are not my predictions or my favorites. They are simply the odds established in the betting."

* * *

People are still agreed that Woody Allen's story of guilt and murder, *Match Point,* would have been a front-runner for the Palme if it had not played out of competition. In the rankings by panels of film critics who vote in the daily festival papers, Allen is close behind the Haneke and Jarmusch films. The critics don't seem to share the enthusiasm of Malcolm's punters for the von Trier film.

I talked to the actress Emily Mortimer at the screening of the lovely Critics' Week film *Junebug,* which stars her husband, Alessandro Nivola. She stars in Woody's picture, and said: "He's always so sort of down on himself. When the audience was cheering him after the screening, he was waving and happy, and then he whispered, 'Remember, tomorrow we go back to real life.'"

* * *

Morgan Freeman is here to receive the Medal of the Festival at a formal dinner, and to present the Palme d'Or at the ceremonies. He's also in meetings with South African producer Anant Singh to star in *Long Walk to Freedom,* the biography of Nelson Mandela, which has been on again, off again for four years. Now it's on, with Darrell James Roodt, director of *Yesterday,* South Africa's first Oscar nominee, set to direct.

Freeman and his associate Lori McCreary

are also talking up their company, Revelations Entertainment, which is in partnership with Intel to market a device that will combine the functions of a DVD player, an Internet terminal, and TiVo. The idea is to find a legal way to deliver and sell movies over the Web, at a time when piracy threatens to cripple the movie business. He paints a stark picture: Now that high-speed distribution is widely available, the day may come when Internet thieves can download any movie they want, for free. All of the movies will be ten years old, however, because the industry will no longer be able to afford to make new ones.

The Palme d'Or awards, preceded by the traditional arrival of the stars on the famous red-carpeted staircase of the Palais des Festivals, will be carried both live and on tape by the Independent Film Channel, hosted by Annette Insdorf and me. IFC coverage from Cannes will play during the following two weeks.

Cannes Report No. 8:
24 Hours at Cannes

May 21, 2005—Suddenly calm has descended on Cannes, like a movie without sound. The traffic has returned to sanity. Housewives stroll through the market, filling their wicker baskets with artichokes and lettuces. The awards will be announced, but most of the buyers and sellers and big shots have already flown out of the Nice airport, and the festival is left in the custody of its most faithful guests: the press, the cineastes, the paparazzi, and the fans.

I have just had twenty-four hours I want to tell you all about. These hours explain why I come to Cannes, why all the confusion, expense, and hassle, the staying up too late, the getting up too early, the computer meltdowns, the intestinal emergencies, the three or four movies a day, the endless debates about impenetrable plots, are all worth it. Why I love it.

Every morning we awake at seven and have café au lait in the little dining room of the Hotel Splendid, which has been owned for thirty years by Madame Annick Cagnet, who is so loyal to her customers that they must die before their rooms can be given away. We have pastry and fruit and then we hurry across the street to the Palais des Festivals for the 8:30 A.M. press screening of that night's official entry.

Yesterday the film was *Three Times* by the Taiwanese master Hou Hsiao Hsien. You may not have heard of him, but forgive yourself; the entire movie distribution system of North America is devoted to maintaining a wall between you and Hou Hsiao Hsien.

His film was magnificent. Like Clint Eastwood's *Million Dollar Baby*, which opened without a breath of advance notice and won the Oscar, *Three Times* has appeared at the end of the festival just in time to win the Palme d'Or. Or maybe not. It is just as great a film either way.

Three short stories. Each one starring the actress Qi Shu and the actor Chang Chen. In each, she is May and he is Chen. All three are about emotional lives and missed connections. In the first, set in 1966, May runs a billiard parlor and Chen is her admirer. In the second, set in 1911, May is a prostitute and Chen is an idealistic journalist who is her customer. In the third, set in 2005, they are confused modern young people, she with health problems, involved in two or three parallel romances that exist mostly on cell phones and text messages.

The film uses exquisite visual and tonal strategy. The 1911 story is told as a silent film, with a sad, distant piano on the sound track. The 2005 story is all noise. The 1966 film is all waiting. None brings the subject of romance up to the level of a plot; it is handled in terms of longing, loneliness, secret feelings, or the brutal carelessness of life. The film is wise, and heartbreaking.

There is a lunch at the Carlton Hotel's beach restaurant to promote two movies: Wim Wenders's *Don't Come Knocking* and Phil Morrison's *Junebug*. The first is an official selection about a broken-down cowboy star in search of a lost son; it stars Sam Shepard (who wrote it), Gabriel Mann as the son, Jessica Lange as his mother, Fairuza Balk as his girlfriend, and Sarah Polley as a waif with a secret. The second is . . . well, I slept through it.

"I'm not going to BS you," I told Phil Morrison. "I fell asleep during the opening titles. It wasn't the film's fault. I got food poisoning the night before and I was feeling like hell, and then my computer crashed and I was up all night trying to get it to work, and all I can say is, my wife, Chaz, thinks your film is lovely and I felt safe enough to slip that word into an article, because I did wake up once, and saw Scott Wilson saying, 'Now if I was a screwdriver, where would I be?' And he said it as only Scott Wilson could say it, as if he wanted to know with all of his heart and soul where that screwdriver was."

"I slept through the first film I saw here after I got off the plane," Morrison said. And in a moment we were deep in conversation about the redemptive power of film, and Morrison's belief that good ones can make you a better person and touch you spiritually, and my feeling that they can be a form of prayer. Without having even seen his film, I can tell you, because I feel it, that Phil Morrison has the heart of a great director.

"I was asked by a TV crew for my favorite moment in the cinema," he said, "and I mentioned a shot in Vincente Minnelli's *The Clock*. An hour later, I walked into the Carlton and there was Liza Minnelli, who may even have been conceived while her father and Judy Garland were making that movie."

The Carlton beach buffet was thrown open, and we loaded our plates with enormous piles of known and unknown foodstuffs. I sat down next to Wim Wenders and Sam Shepard, who lit up little cigars and talked about how Jessica Lange (Shepard's love of many years) would not rehearse her big angry scene because she wanted it to be fresh, and so it was quite a surprise for both of them when she slapped Shepard. "I was so amazed, I forgot to walk away," Shepard said, "and then she kicked me."

Wenders said he has been in the official competition at Cannes seven times, winning with *Paris, Texas*. Some veteran directors enter their films out of competition, but we agreed that's the same as using birth control: It can be a lot of fun, but you don't have any babies. "Something should be at stake," he said. He added that Cannes was still "the great festival." Not Venice: "Every screening starts an hour late, they mix up the reels, it's a mess."

Fairuza Balk and Gabriel Mann joined the table. She can look so fierce and so often plays characters on the edge that it was a surprise to learn not only that her career began in *Return to Oz,* but that she is warm and funny. She said she saw *Paris, Texas* when she was a child, and became obsessed with it; after *Wings of Desire,* she dreamed of working with Wenders. Mann said his parents took him to art movies and gave him great books to read, and he grew up "like any teenager, idolizing Wenders." Not like every teenager, I suggested.

You realize, talking with young professionals like these, that although Paris Hilton can grab all the headlines at Cannes, it takes intelligence and substance to stay alive as an actor. "You don't set out to be in a Wim Wenders film," Mann said, "but if you get there, wow." Balk said she tries as a strategy to work with good directors: "I've been in a couple of doozies, but mostly I've been lucky."

After lunch, I walked down to the Bazin screening room in the Palais for a preview of *Chromophobia,* an official selection directed by Martha Fiennes, in which the characters deal with government fraud, bulimia, cancer, breast augmentation, adultery, illegal stock transactions, children out of wedlock, journalistic sensationalism, killing animals as a sport, and personal betrayal, and the stories all somehow resolve themselves in an ending that can be scored by Beethoven's "Ode to Joy." It's not a boring film.

Soon it was time to put on our formal clothing and walk down the Croisette to the official dinner honoring Morgan Freeman, who was being given the Medal of the Cannes Film Festival. Gilles Jacob, the president of the festival, hosts an official dinner every night at the Carlton, and we have been to more than a few, including the one where we discovered that a trick of the room's architectural dome allowed us to hear every word being said at a table across the room, all of it sounding like malicious gossip, although unfortunately not in a language we understood.

Morgan Freeman is some kind of a man. Tall and courtly, and filled with an appreciation of the moment. He introduced us to his wife, Myrna, and they sat down next to Toni Morrison, the Nobel Prize–winning journalist, who is on the official jury.

Over at our table we were with another jury member, the great John Woo, whose work has forever changed the way action films look. He was with his daughter Angeles, who has worked with him for four years and will be a great director, he said. She was named for the city of Los Angeles. I told him that both children of the director Ang Lee were born in my hometown of Champaign-Urbana, but that perhaps it is best they were not named after it.

On my right, Michael Barker, copresident of Sony Classics, told me that Harvey Weinstein has apologized to him "for all the terrible things I've done to you in the past." His anger, Harvey explained, was caused by undiagnosed diabetes and a daylong diet of M&M's. Now that he has his disease under control, he has been able to lose weight and be a nicer person.

Seated on the left of my wife was the famous William Morris agent, Cassian Elwes, who told Chaz that Harvey Weinstein had called him up and apologized for his bad behavior in the past, explaining about the M&M's and saying that he was going to be a better person from now on. "What I *really* want to know," Barker said, "is *what* terrible things Harvey has done to me. I couldn't think of anything. If I ever find out, I'll probably be really mad at him."

We walked home along the Croisette, running into the director Alexander Payne *(Sideways),* the head of the jury for the category named Un Certain Regard; only the French would consider it a compliment to hold a film in "a certain regard." He told us his jury had selected *The Death of Mr. Lazarescu,* by Cristi Puiu of Romania, as its prize winner. Payne's next stop: the jury at Karlovy Vary, in the Czech Republic. "Then back to making movies."

We could sleep as late as we wanted. I woke up at 7 A.M. and was definitely up for good. You know the feeling. I walked down through the Cannes marketplace, past the onions and radishes, the baskets of flowers and groaning boards of cheese, the sausage man and the herb lady, and then I strolled down around the harbor until I found a restaurant serving breakfast.

Tom Luddy was already at a table. He is the cofounder of the Telluride Film Festival and knows everyone and everything about film. Soon the next table was occupied by the French film critic Michel Ciment, who also knows everyone and everything, and holds strong opinions about them.

"The Hou Hsiao Hsien has changed everything," Ciment said. "It is a great film, and this morning it has the top score in the critics' voting. It just might win. I love the way he has such a delicate touch, knowing just how to place everything without ever being obvious or doing one unnecessary thing." He mentioned seven or eight of his other favorite films by Hou Hsiao Hsien. Ciment knows everything, but he is so nice about it, and he always talks as if he assumes you know it all too.

Luddy said his friend Werner Herzog has left for Thailand to scout locations for a fiction film based on his documentary *Little Dieter Needs to Fly*, about a German who joined the American army, was taken captive by the Viet Cong, escaped, and walked to freedom through hundreds of miles of jungles filled with tigers, snakes, fevers, and chills. We agreed that the Herzogs are the nobility of the film world, the Quixotes who never lose faith. His latest doc, *Grizzly Man*, is a big success here and may be a box office winner; it incorporates video footage taken by a man who lived every summer with the grizzly bears of Alaska, coming to no harm for years, until he was eaten.

Then I walked back around the harbor to the Hotel Splendid, the sun bright now in the eastern sky, the flags flying brilliantly on top of the Palais. I joined Chaz in the breakfast room and we chatted with Madame Cagnet, who introduced her new puppy. "I thought I was finished with dogs," she says, "until I saw this one." We made friends with the puppy. Richard Pena, the director of the New York Film Festival, was at the next table. "Didn't you love the Hou Hsiao Hsien?" he said.

Cannes Winners

May 21, 2005—Tommy Lee Jones walked away from the fifty-eighth Cannes Film Festival here Saturday night as a double winner, after his film *The Three Burials of Melquaides Estrada* won him the award as best actor, and the screenplay by Guillermo Arriaga was also honored. The movie stars Jones as a Texas cowboy who kidnaps the border patrolman (Barry Pepper) who has murdered his Mexican friend, and forces him to join on a long horseback journey to rebury the corpse in the man's hometown.

Another double winner was Miranda July, whose *Me, You and Everyone We Know*, the story of several dreamy, goofy, unlikely romances and sexual adventures, won the Camera d'Or as the best first film in any of the festival's categories. July, who wrote, directed, and starred, also won the Critics' Prize. Her Camera d'Or was shared with the Sri Lankan film *The Forsaken Land*, by Vimukthi Jayasundara, about a soldier tormented by a mistaken killing.

The top prize, the Palme d'Or, went to *L'Enfant*, by the Dardenne brothers, Jean-Pierre and Luc, whose film is about a twenty-year-old and his eighteen-year-old girlfriend who have a child and try to raise it while still essentially children themselves. It's the subtle story of how responsibility imposes itself on them almost despite themselves.

The Grand Jury Prize, or runner-up, went to the veteran American indie director Jim Jarmusch for *Broken Flowers*, which stars Bill Murray in one of his best performances, as a lonely retired millionaire who learns he might have had a child twenty years earlier, and goes on a solemn but comic search through his past, visiting four women who could plausibly have been the mother. Both the Jarmusch and July films have the potential to be *Sideways*-style breakthrough hits.

The prize for best actress went to Hanna Laslo, an Israeli comedienne in her first dramatic role, in *Free Zone*, by Israel's Amos Gitai. She plays a cab driver who drives an American (Natalie Portman) to Jordan, on a journey during which they both make unexpected discoveries.

A Special Jury Prize went to *Shanghai Dreams*, by Wang Xiaoshuai of China; it's the story of a family relocated to the provinces during the social experiments of the 1960s, and a father who wants them to return to the city.

The award for best director went to Michael Haneke for the French film *The Hidden*, starring Daniel Auteuil and Juliette Binoche in the story of a family torn apart by the arrival of anonymous videos showing someone has them under ominous surveillance.

The Palme d'Or ceremony is held with admirable brevity; the arrival of guests on the

863

famous red-carpeted staircase lasts longer than the awards, which this year included the surprise appearance of Oscar winner Hilary Swank to join her *Million Dollar Baby* costar and fellow Oscar winner Morgan Freeman in presenting the Palme d'Or. Other presenters included Fanny Ardant, Penelope Cruz, and Lambert Wilson.

The jury, headed by Emir Kusturica of Serbia-Montenegro, included the actresses Nandita Das of India and Salma Hayek of Mexico, the American author Toni Morrison, the French directors Agnes Varda and Benoit Jacquot, the Spanish actor Javier Bardem, the German director Fatih Akin, and the director John Woo, of Hong Kong and Hollywood.

Backstage after the awards there was a jumble of celebration, with the Americans perhaps realizing that only at Cannes would Tommy Lee Jones meet Jim Jarmusch, and Miranda July bond with Hilary Swank. When I interviewed Jones during an American Pavilion presentation, he said *Three Burials* began when he was on a Texas deer-hunting trip with the writer Arriaga and the producer Michael Fitzgerald. "We said, hell, we got enough talent in the cab of this pickup truck to make us a movie," he said, "and that's when we started."

Reminded of this story after the ceremony, Fitzgerald smiled and said, "That's how we started, all right, but it took a long time to get this movie made, and it wasn't exactly easy."

Cannes Report No. 9: Jury Press Conference

May 22, 2005—Emir Kusturica, the jolly Serbian who headed this year's Cannes jury, stayed up late at the beach party after the awards. He loved the fireworks, the Fellini music, and his new green shirt. He also sang with the band, as Salma Hayek and Penelope Cruz danced "very savagely," he said, with, of all people, the festival president, Thierry Fremont. "Many girls told me they loved the green shirt," he said, as he joined the eight other jury members in their annual press conference.

Kusturica, whose opinions are forcefully expressed, was expected to be the dictator of this year's jury. Rumors were that he clashed particularly with Agnes Varda, the French di-

rector, and Toni Morrison, the American author, who each headed factions backing a different film. Asked during the press conference if that was true, Kusturica said, no, it was a question of "four or five" films they all admired. This was later amended to "five or six" and then to "six or seven," before Kusturica decided there were "two or three" that covered both the "artistic and the public" aspects. "Most of the films were a little bit less good than I expected," he said, and for the main prize, there were different opinions about what could have won.

Those three were apparently *L'Enfant,* by the Dardenne brothers of Belgium, which won the Palme d'Or, *Broken Flowers,* by Jim Jarmusch, which won the Grand Jury Prize and was known to be Kusturica's favorite, and *The Hidden,* by Michael Haneke, which won for best director and was said to be Varda's choice.

"One might think that Fidel Castro was president of the jury," Kusturica said, "but I am trying to reduce my reputation of dictatorship." Others on the jury decided he was "a sweet dictator."

The jury press conference is an innovation at Cannes, held for the first time last year. The nine jurors defended their choices, hinted at their negotiations, and fielded tough questions. One involved their award to Guillermo Arriaga for his screenplay of Tommy Lee Jones's *The Three Burials of Melquaides Estrada.* The movie tells the story of a border patrolman who kills an illegal Mexican immigrant, and then is forced by an American ranch hand (Jones) to dig up the corpse and travel with it deep into Mexico for reburial.

Doesn't this story, a woman asked, describe the kind of "vigilante simplistic macho ethic" that Toni Morrison and Salma Hayek have particularly decried?

"Not at all," said Morrison. "The film is always on the side of the people who suffer. It is about an ethical relationship and the last wish of his friend."

And Hayek said, "In this film, only one man dies and the weight of his death takes over the entire film."

That caused Kusturica to recall the role of Mexico in his life, as he grew up in Yugoslavia. "Rock and roll was dangerous and could get you in trouble, because it was Western. Russian music was out because we had broken with Russia. So for us Mexican music was a sign of freedom. We grew up with the sound of mariachis."

Critics asked why such films as *A History of Violence,* by David Cronenberg, and *Don't Come Knocking,* by Wim Wenders, were passed over by the jury. "Last year," Kusturica said, "I came here and my film won nothing, and I went home very sad, and the next day went back to work. Both of those films I would go to the theater and see again." He added enigmatically: "Our convention was to rediscover modernity of language very close to the content," which would seem to describe the Cronenberg movie perfectly, but apparently not.

Kusturica was poetic about the role of Cannes in providing an alternative "door into the cinema." When he came here twenty years ago with his first entry, he said, that door opened for him and launched his life as a filmmaker. "This place kills uniformity. To be global, to make a film that plays everywhere, you have to be slightly stupid."

That was the obvious moment to ask him about the Cannes premiere of *Star Wars,* but alas, the hour was up and the jury was on its feet, signing autographs, and edging toward the exit.

Questions for the Movie Answer Man

Ad Problems

Q. The Canadian release of the *Finding Neverland* DVD contains an advertisement for an American automobile manufacturer. It is bad enough that we must watch ads in the theaters, but now on DVD? I've registered a complaint with the film company and the manufacturer but am not naive enough to believe it will have any effect. It would not be as bad if there were an ability to fast-forward or skip the ad, but that option is not available on this disc.

—J. W. Leman, Edmonton, Alberta

A. This is a new low. Advertising supports programming that I receive for free, on radio and television, and that's fine with me. But when I pay, I expect to see only what I have paid for. Ads in theaters are an abomination, hated by most of the moviegoers I talk to. To be locked into a compulsory viewing of an ad on a DVD, on top of the useless FBI warning that also cannot be skipped, is a new species of outrage. And years after that car is off the market, you'll *still* have to look at the ad, as it breeds continuing ill-will for the manufacturer.

Q. Regarding the Answer Man item about ads on DVDs: I own the special edition of *Le Fabuleux destin d'Amélie Poulain,* or *Amélie,* as it's known in the U.S. This is a box set designed for the Québec market that cost me about sixty dollars. Before the main menu even appears on the screen, you have to sit through an FBI warning, the Macrovision trailer, the movie distributor's logo, a Bordeaux wine commercial, and finally instructions on how to navigate the DVD. And *none* of it is skippable! Whenever I try to watch the movie I feel as if I've paid sixty bucks to watch a wine commercial. And I don't even drink!

—François Caron, Montréal, Québec

A. You'd think for sixty bucks the Québec edition could at least give you a warning from the Mounties.

Peter Becker is president of the Criterion Collection, the class act of the DVD market. He responds: "I've never seen discs like the one your reader mentions, but we like our editions to start as straightforwardly as possible. You buy a DVD to play the movie, so animations, warnings, and ads shouldn't get in your way. As for making that stuff unskippable, I think locking out viewer input is never a good idea."

Q. Either someone at your Website has a great sense of humor or the automated Google ads are programmed to create creepy coincidences from time to time. In your review of *House of Wax,* you wrote, "There is also an eerie sequence in which a living victim is sprayed with hot wax and ends up with a finish you'd have to pay an extra four bucks for at the car wash." Below your review, one of the ads offered wholesale candle wax."

—Joel Meza, Mexicali, Mexico

A. I searched other promising titles for strange ad combos, but the Google software seems to do a fairly good job of matching appropriate ads to the reviews. Below *Beyond the Valley of the Dolls,* however, was an ad asking, "Was *Apollo 11* real?"

Aishwarya Rai

Q. According to an article I read about Bollywood in the *New York Times Magazine,* you consider Indian actress Aishwarya Rai, who stars in *Bride and Prejudice,* to be the world's second-most beautiful woman. After seeing her film *Kyun . . . ! Ho Gaya Na,* I find it hard to argue with that statement. The question is: Who's your No. 1?

—Matt Sandler, New York City, New York

A. Aishwarya Rai is also the world's first-most beautiful woman.

Q. In response to Matt Sandler's query asking you who is the world's first-most beautiful woman, you foolishly answered Aishwarya Rai instead of "my wife." I hope you bought a huge bouquet and a box of chocolates for Mrs. Ebert after you realized your mistake.

—Vicente Salazar, Española, New Mexico

A. Matt Sandler asked about women, not goddesses.

Q. Finally I have read in the American media about Aishwarya Rai. I agree with you, she truly is the most beautiful woman in the world, but what are the chances of her ever being mentioned on *People* magazine's list?

—Scott Hunter, Toronto, Ontario

A. Only a matter of time. The British celeb mag *Hello!* did an online poll and the results were: 1. Aishwarya Rai. 2. Keira Knightley. 3. Nicole Kidman. 4. Catherine Zeta-Jones. 5. Kate Winslet. 6. Angelina Jolie. 5. Shakira. 8. Queen Rania of Jordan. 9. Gwyneth Paltrow. 10. Cindy Crawford.

However, Reuters reports, when Amitabh Bachchan won the BBC's online poll to discover the greatest superstar of all time, he explained, "This proves Indians do nothing else but surf the Web."

Amityville Horror

Q. Upon picking up the new *Amityville Horror* DVD box set, I was puzzled to read the following disclaimer on the bottom of the packaging: *Amityville 3-D* is not a sequel to the pictures *The Amityville Horror* or *Amitville [sic] II: The Possession.* From the story synopsis, *3-D* sounds like a sequel to me, given that it takes place in the same Amityville house and occurs after the previous two films. Further research has shown that this disclaimer was also on past releases of *Amityville 3-D*, both on VHS and laser disc. So I must ask, if *Amityville 3-D* is not a sequel to *The Amityville Horror,* then what is it (other than an awful movie)?

—Rhett Miller, Calgary, Alberta

A. According to the Internet Movie Database, it is not a sequel because . . . because . . . are you ready for this? The events in the first two films were "real," while *Amityville 3-D* was (gasp!) made up! One way or the other, it remains unseen by me. This tradition continues with the 2005 *Amityville Horror,* which was not previewed for Chicago critics, an infallible sign that the studio has good reason to believe it will not, in the words of *Variety,* draw fave raves from the scribes. Because of my forthcoming Overlooked Film Festival, I may not have time to see it in a theater. I can live with that.

Auteurs

Q. A recent question about George Lucas's revisions on the *Star Wars* DVDs has me wondering: What would Andrew Sarris say? Lucas's constant tinkering (or tampering) with the original trilogy prompts some interesting questions about the auteur theory: Can an auteur be faulted for violating his own work? If a director claims authorship of a film as stridently as Lucas has, why shouldn't he be allowed to refine it? I don't mean to champion Lucas's changes to episodes IV through VI, some of which I find harmless and others distracting, but I see in his continuing changes an exciting example of the auteur theory being put to the test. How much of the film can Lucas still claim as his own after the original release? Many fans scorn his updated versions as travesties, and although I sympathize I think they tread a fine line.

—Michael McGinnis, Warren, Michigan

A. I forwarded your question to Andrew Sarris of the *New York Observer,* who is America's foremost advocate of the auteur theory. He replies: "I have not yet seen the latest *Star Wars,* but I doubt that it will shake the auteurist credit George Lucas deserves for the entire series. The idea that an auteur can be disqualified by the changes that are made in his work, whatever that means, strikes me as bizarre. My own feeling—and this I have felt from the beginning of the *Star Wars* series— is that the genre itself leaves something to be desired. I have never been taken with Mr. Lucas's later conceits, but I did have a favorable reaction to *American Graffiti.* I simply haven't thought about the *Star Wars* phenomenon for a long time. It's a fact of life and business, and I don't see any point in arguing with the man, who's made billions in the industry. I just find so many more things in the cinema more interesting."

Barmy and *Rumpy-pumpy*

Q. I just wanted to thank you for bringing to my attention the word *barmy* by using it twice (in the reviews of *Anacondas* and *Danny Deckchair*). It has joined *meretricious, lubricious,* and several other wonderful-sounding words I might not have run across outside your reviews. Another is *fragrant,* used as a quick way to communicate that a character is a beautiful woman.

—Jake Cremins, New York City, New York

A. *Fragrant* was first used in that sense by a British judge smitten with the wife of a defendant charged with adultery. How could the husband possibly cheat on such a woman? asked the judge: "Is she not fragrant?" I am working to popularize *labyrinthine, tumescent,* and *rumpy-pumpy.*

Be Cool

Q. In your review of *Be Cool,* you mention that the Rock plays a character named Elliot Wilhelm, which is the name of a friend of yours who runs the Detroit Film Theatre. You guessed that author Elmore Leonard knows this and used the name since he also lives in Detroit. Here's the actual story: Wilhelm, who's run the DFT for the past thirty years as the film curator of the Detroit Institute of Arts, made the top bid of $2,700 at a 1998 DFT fund-raiser to have Leonard use his name in an upcoming book. The book was *Be Cool* and moviemakers kept the name for the Rock's character. The real Wilhelm also turns up as an extra in the bar scene where John Travolta meets the Rock, which is a great inside joke for those of us who are fans of the DFT and Elliot.

—Robert Musial, Grosse Pointe Woods, Michigan

A. Elliot Wilhelm is a brilliant programmer and critic, and a heck of a nice guy. On the basis of his cameo, I think he has a promising future ahead of him as a programmer, critic, and nice guy.

Before Sunset

Q. I just saw *Before Sunset* and thought it was one of the best movies I've seen in a while. While I enjoyed *Before Sunrise* very much when I saw it nine years ago, it seems to me that the first film was really a setup to this encounter—that this is the real payoff of the story. My question is about the ending. I thought it was perfect in its own ambiguity. It seemed to me while walking out of the theater that Jesse had made up his mind to stay with Celine. But after thinking about it some more, I'm not so sure. Maybe he was still indecisive and too overwhelmed by the circumstances to

know what to do. What do you think he meant by his last response?

—John Cochrane, Tempe, Arizona

A. I think he's going to choose to miss his plane, but that doesn't mean he won't take a later flight. By the way, Richard Linklater's brilliant animated film *Waking Life* (2001) apparently exists in an alternate Jesse-and-Celine universe, where they're waking up in bed together, something they never do in *Before Sunrise* or *Before Sunset,* which presumably chronicle every moment they've spent together.

Best 10 Lists

Q. Last March, you rated *Spartan* as one of the best and gave it four stars, but it didn't make your Best 10 or your honorable mention list. Oversight or intentional?

—Dennis Hussey, Mountain View, California

A. Stupid oversight. I reviewed 274 movies last year, gave four stars to twenty-six, did a search for "four-star reviews" to compile a working list, and *Spartan* failed to show. My admiration for it remains undiminished. My enthusiasm for Best 10 lists remains muted. I absolutely refuse all invitations to compile additional lists of the Best 10 Horror Films, Best 10 Date Movies, Best 10 Movies to Watch on TV, Best 10 this, and Best 10 that.

Beyond the Sea

Q. I know to be politically correct you had to backpedal on your statement that Kevin Spacey is a better singer than Bobby Darin. I don't agree. I was a big fan of Bobby Darin music and sent all my friends his greatest hits. I got the sound track to *Beyond the Sea* and thought Spacey was great, maybe even better than Darin—albeit he had Phil Ramone and Abbey Lane Studios. Then I got tickets to see Spacey at House of Blues. You should have been there. Then you wouldn't have had to make your apples-and-oranges statement. You were correct in your initial judgment. Spacey is better.

—Nancy Kranzberg, Highland Park, Illinois

A. With all due respect, I think I was wrong to compare them in the first place. Pop singing is a subjective art form, and the good and great singers are in some sense literally incomparable. But I remain surprised by how good Spacey was—not that he should give up the day job.

Birth of a Nation

Q. What do you think about the NAACP's basically preventing a recent screening of *Birth of a Nation*? This amounts to censorship in my book.

—Jeff Robinson, Los Angeles, California

A. Charlie Lustman, owner of the Silent Movie Theater in Los Angeles, planned to show D. W. Griffith's *The Birth of a Nation* (1915) for one night but canceled the screening. The Associated Press reported: "The NAACP, which had protested the planned showing, said the movie 'poisoned racial relationships in America for nearly a century.' The group called the cancellation a victory for it and other community organizations."

I delayed writing about *The Birth of a Nation* in my Great Movies series because I was conflicted between the film's historical and artistic importance and its vile racism. I eventually did confront it, saying it was "an unavoidable fact of American movie history and must be dealt with." To screen it for one night in a historical context with a discussion before or after, as Lustman planned, seems a useful approach. By preventing the screening, the NAACP places itself in opposition to free speech and draws greater attention to the film by enhancing it with the aura of the forbidden.

Here is how my article ended: "As slavery is the great sin of America, so *The Birth of a Nation* is Griffith's sin, for which he tried to atone all the rest of his life. So instinctive were the prejudices he was raised with as a 19th-century Southerner that the offenses in his film actually had to be explained to him. To his credit, his next film, *Intolerance*, was an attempt at apology. He also once edited a version of the film that cut out all of the Klan material, but that is not the answer. If we are to see this film, we must see it all, and deal with it all."

The complete article is online at suntimes.com/ebert/great.

Q. I was perusing a Website that gives estimates on when DVDs will be released, and I noticed with puzzlement what it claims is your position on Disney's decision to not release the controversial film *Song of the South*. It claims you are in favor of keeping it shelved. Is that true? You've spoken of the value of *Birth of a Nation* despite its distasteful overtones; what is the difference between that film and *Song of the South*?

—Alex Mayo, Cincinnati, Ohio

A. Well, one difference is that *Birth of a Nation* is incomparably more vile and blatant in its racism. Disney has made a corporate decision to hold *Song of the South* from release because of its stereotyping of some of the African-American characters, and I have expressed sympathy with that position because the film is directed primarily toward children who see films literally. I would not want to be an African-American child at a screening of the film, but I would support its screening for mature audiences.

Bob & Ray

Q. In your *Sahara* review, you refer to Bob & Ray's *Blake Dent, Boy Spotwelder*. Bob & Ray fans near and far are, I'm sure, letting you know that it's *Matt Neffer, Boy Spotwelder* ("Over here behind the duck press, Todd"). With hundreds of hours of B & R indelibly etched in my brain, I cannot recall a Blake Dent in any context.

—Art Scott, Livermore, California

A. You are absolutely correct, and you win a year's supply of Parker House rolls with rich creamery butter from nearby farms. I was delighted to learn that virtually the entire Bob & Ray archive is available at bobandray.com. Not many people know that when you solve *The Da Vinci Code*, that's where it leads you, right there to the archive's friendly front parlor, where on a good day you might meet Kent Lyle Birdley, Wally Ballou, Charles the Poet, Dean Archer Armstead, and Mary Backstayge. Just the other day I dropped in and overheard a scintillating conversation:

"Golly gee whillikers, Mr. Science! What's that long brown object?!?"

"That's known as a board, Jimmy."

The Brown Bunny

Q. You've gotten some harsh reactions from people in Hollywood due to your negative reviews of their films. Vincent Gallo and Rob Schneider have publicly insulted you. If this type of person made a film you absolutely loved, would you be able to do the film justice in your review, or would you hold a grudge based on the relationship with the filmmaker?

—Andrew Shuster, Merrick, New York

A. I would say I absolutely loved it. If you can't take it, you shouldn't dish it out. Oddly enough, just today I had a long conversation with Vincent Gallo and will write about it when *The Brown Bunny* opens in September.

Q. Your interview with Vincent Gallo and his recent film was enlightening. Thank you for not holding grudges before taking the time to find out the truth, and for giving second chances to films and to people. I was going to see the film anyway but now am able to be excited rather than lower my expectations.

—Phillip Kelly, Studio City, California

A. The difference between the film that played at Cannes and *The Brown Bunny* after twenty-six minutes of cuts is astonishing and could be used in film classes as an example of editing being used to find the good film within a bad one.

Canadian Crime Rate

Q. In your *Ebert & Roeper* review of Michael Wilson's *Michael Moore Hates America,* you blurted out an erroneous opinion, expressing your doubts about the film's claim that the Canadian crime rate is double the U.S. rate. I checked with www.statcan.ca, listed as "the official source for Canadian social and economic statistics and products," and with the U.S. Department of Justice Bureau of Justice Statistics. The bottom line: These sites agree with Wilson's assertion that crime in Canada is much worse than in the USA.

—James Elias, Highland Ranch, Colorado

A. Astonishing. For the year 2003, per 100,000 population, Canada had 8,530 crimes, and the United States 4,267. For crimes of violence, 958 vs. 523. For property crimes, 4,275 vs. 3,744. Michael Wilson, director of the film, tells me, "There was originally a comedic segment in the film that attributed this to the proliferation of Tim Horton's doughnut franchises, but I couldn't make it work."

Q. Re. the Answer Man discussion about the claim in *Michael Moore Hates America* that Canada's crime rates are twice as high as the United States: You questioned that figure in your review but printed a letter from a reader who cited official statistics indicating it was true. Actually, your original instinct was entirely correct. At www.statcan.ca/Daily/English/011218/d011218b.htm, the Canadian and American rates for 2001 are compared, and the U.S. rates are more than double for violent crime. The rates of theft were similar in the two countries and the arson rate was 40 percent higher in Canada than in the United States. I suspect that the erroneous information in the movie comes from the fact that the U.S. Bureau of Justice Statistics uses different methodology and definitions than Statistics Canada. As an example, in the article linked above, it is mentioned that the American definition of aggravated assault includes the Canadian crimes of attempted murder, assault with a weapon, and aggravated assault. It is always dangerous to compare statistics from two sources without delving into methodology and terms.

—Louise Malloch, Halifax, Nova Scotia

A. I received countless similar messages, including one from Kevin Beckett of Ottawa, Ontario, who studies the statistics as part of his job. He says, "We have an apple-and-orange situation. The numbers reported by the U.S. Bureau of Justice Statistics are for rates per 1,000 'charged.' The Statistics Canada rates quoted are for 'incidents.' 'Incidents' in Canada refer to every instance where the police are called or notified, even if they then find no evidence or never lay charges."

Catwoman

Q. In your recent *Catwoman* review you stated, "Her eyes have vertical pupils instead of horizontal ones." I don't know about you, but most of my friends have round pupils—unless you're hiding the shameful truth that you are indeed Goat Boy's father.

—Bob Bailin, Hamden, Connecticut

A. The little dickens starts his freshman year at Connecticut in September.

Citizen Kane

Q. Re. your AM item about the moving chair in *Citizen Kane:* I carefully reviewed the famous tracking shot that goes from a young Charles outdoors to his parents indoors. You claim a chair wiggles in this shot because it has just been put down, having been offscreen to make way for the camera's backward movement. The chair does indeed move, but not for that reason at all. If you watch carefully (as I'm sure you do), the chair is visible in the corner of the screen. It is not moving at all. It only wiggles when Mrs. Kane walks by it, suggesting that she has brushed it with her skirt. Why would the chair sit still and then suddenly start wiggling unless Mrs. Kane had touched it?

—Matt Johnson, Chicago, Illinois

A. It's not the chair but the top hat that jiggles because the table has just been moved into position. The chair movement I'm referring to takes place toward the end of the scene, as the three adults walk back toward the window, and the camera again moves "through" the table. You can clearly see the chair being pulled away.

Q. On snopes.com, an urban-legends Website, a message talks about a possible rape in *Citizen Kane.* It goes on to discuss the recycling of sound effects. Apparently these sound effects are from another movie and include sounds like screams.

—Lem Smalley, Fayetteville, North Carolina

A. The scene in question is when Kane and Susan take their guests on a picnic. Tents are pitched, a band plays, and in the background, between trees, if we look closely we can see pterodactyls, the prehistoric flying reptiles. The back-projection footage for these shots was borrowed from *Son of Kong* (1933). When Kane and Susan have an argument inside their tent, a loud woman's shriek is heard on the sound track. It's not a rape, in my opinion, but rather simply provides a counterpoint to the emotional shriek in Susan's mind.

Q. I work for the online division of the University of Colorado at Denver and am creating some cheating-prevention resources for fellow faculty. I was using as an example this line from your *Citizen Kane* review: "The structure of *Citizen Kane* is circular, adding more depth every time it passes over the life." When I Googled the quote, I found two links that were not yours. In both cases, these were paper mills promising to sell completed essays to students.

—David Thomas, Denver, Colorado

A. The sites, which I checked out for myself, were www.allfreeessays.com and a pay site, www.exampleessays.com. There is a certain consistency, don't you think, in a site that sells plagiarism and practices it?

Color and Black & White

Q. I am insulted by Columbia TriStar Home Entertainment's "innovative process" called "Color+B&W," intended "to broaden the appeal of classic black-and-white films and introduce them to a new generation of viewers." This egregious process, which makes its debut on two *Three Stooges* DVDs released August 10, also includes a "ChromaChoice" feature, which "allows viewers to toggle between the original black-and-white version of a film and its colorized version in a seamless manner using the DVD remote." Supposedly this newfangled attempt at colorization is further authenticated through research involving original film elements, props, cloth swatches, etc., found in Columbia's archives. "Finally," states the press release, "through collaboration with West Wing Studios, whose talented artists have years of experience in color designing, the highest level of historical accuracy is achieved in the images." When will these idiots in charge of precious studio libraries ever learn that any kind of colorization—even optional—is an insult to the legacy of black-and-white film? Did anyone learn a lesson from Ted Turner's dubious precedent?

—Jeff Shannon, Lynnwood, Washington

A. Colorization is a form of vandalism. A b&w movie isn't lacking something, it's adding something: The world is in color, so we get that for free, but b&w is a stylistic alternative, more dreamlike, more timeless. Fred Astaire hated color because it distracted from the pure form of his dancing. One could make the same argument about the Stooges, who in their own way are as pure and classic as Astaire. The Columbia TriStar claim of "re-searching" the original colors of the costumes, props, etc., is hilarious, since colors were selected for how they photographed in b&w, not for how they really looked. If they wanted to be consistent, all of the actors' faces would be light green, since greenish makeup was used because it photographed better.

Q. Your column noted that Columbia TriStar says its upcoming *Three Stooges* DVDs will be released in color and b&w to "broaden the appeal of classic black-and-white films and introduce them to a new generation of viewers." The obvious implication there is that classic b&w films do not appeal to today's younger generation. I'm in my late thirties and enjoy older films, but I find myself in the minority among my age group. My parents are in their late fifties. It seems that those in that age range constitute the last generation to have a sincere desire to watch older b&w films, or older color ones, for that matter. In the next twenty to twenty-five years, will we face the virtual extinction of old classic films, with the exception of such films as *The Wizard of Oz* and *Casablanca*? With profit being the bottom line, and with the likely decline in the demand for these older movies, will scrounging around for used VHS/DVDs on eBay be the primary avenue for the classic movie fan of the future to find these great films?
—Tim Dubois, Bedford, Texas

A. There will always be those who love old movies. I meet teenagers who are astonishingly well-informed about the classics. But you are right that many moviegoers and video viewers say they do not "like" black-and-white films. In my opinion, they are cutting themselves off from much of the mystery and beauty of the movies. Black and white is an artistic choice, a medium that has strengths and traditions, especially in its use of light and shadow. Moviegoers of course have the right to dislike b&w, but it is not something they should be proud of. It reveals them, frankly, as cinematically illiterate. I have been described as a snob on this issue. But snobs exclude; they do not include. To exclude b&w from your choices is an admission that you have a closed mind, possess a limited imagination, or are lacking in taste.

Columbia Lady

Q. Much as Annette Bening may like to take credit for being the model for the Columbia Pictures logo, as you reported in quoting her recently, it simply isn't true. A story about the "Columbia Pictures lady" portrait by Doug McCash, art critic for the *New Orleans Times-Picayune,* reports that Bening's claim "was interesting news to the French Quarter artist who painted it and the former New Orleanian who modeled for it." A retraction would be appreciated.
—Brian Flores, New Orleans, Louisiana

A. Quite so. But in fairness to Annette Bening, she didn't volunteer the information; I asked her, and she said that so she had been told.

Doug McCash put me in touch with artist Michael Deas, then of New Orleans, now of New York, who sent me a photograph of his actual model. He wrote: "I am the illustrator who in 1992 painted the latest version the Columbia Pictures logo. I am troubled by recent claims by the actress Annette Bening that she was the inspiration for my painting. I have never met Annette Bening, nor have I ever spoken to her. While Ms. Bening is a talented actress, she was not the model for my Columbia Pictures lady. The actual model is Jenny Joseph, a homemaker and mother of two children now living in the Houston area. She was an exceptionally gracious and unassuming model, and received very little compensation for her work in 1992. The face of the Columbia lady is perhaps one of the most famous in the world . . . and it happens to belong to Ms. Jenny Joseph."

Doug McCash's story quotes the model: "These days, Jenny Joseph is a Houston muralist and mother of two. She is bemused by Bening's recent appropriation of her moment in the sun. 'When I go to the movies, I get my fifteen minutes of fame,' she said. 'The kids get a kick out of it.'"

Confederacy of Dunces

Q. I recently found out that David Gordon Green's film *Confederacy of Dunces,* with Will Ferrell and Drew Barrymore, has been canceled. Green is one of my favorite directors, and I have high hopes for his career. What is the story behind the cancellation and what will this do to his career?

—Jonathan Warner, Evanston, Illinois

A. At thirty, David Gordon Green is one of the brightest talents of his generation and has made three wonderful films. *Confederacy of Dunces* would have been based on the cult novel by John Kennedy Toole about a quixotic New Orleans character. Green responds:

"To the disappointment of many of us, *Dunces* was put on hold last year. We had assembled the cast of my dreams (Will Ferrell, Lily Tomlin, Mos Def, Drew Barrymore, Olympia Dukakis, etc.) and I adopted New Orleans as my new home, but politics over the property rights—torn between Miramax, Paramount, and various camps of producers—put a weight on the project that wasn't creatively healthy to work within.

"The draft of the script by Scott Kramer and Steven Soderbergh did the novel justice and provided a healthy cinematic spotlight for these eccentric characters, but it didn't cater to a lot of the clichés or conditioning of contemporary American studio sensibilities. So I suppose the difficulty was even beyond the political baggage and paperwork and stemmed in many ways from the manner in which I wanted the film to be executed. I believe in the dramatic foundation and comedic highlights of these characters and am not interested in the cartoon version of obvious comedy that has often been pushed for. I have yet to develop a project within the studio system that has been made, for whatever stubborn resistance to compromise on my part with the machine.

"That being said, many of the rights issues have since expired, and from what I am told, Paramount holds all consideration on their own shoulders. That at least simplifies the objective. I am hopeful, with the new names and faces over there under Brad Grey, that Kramer, Soderbergh, and I can again arm-wrestle some enthusiasm. Scott Kramer is the die-hard producer who has been with the project since before the book's publication. The history of the book and various efforts for a filmed version make an epic of their own. (I would have loved to see the Harold Ramis–directed early '80s take with John Belushi, Ruth Gordon, and

Richard Pryor.) My hope is that we get our paws on the flick and Kramer writes his memoirs of the whole deal."

Daryl Elfield Saga

Q. When you reviewed *Before Sunrise* in 1995, you got a response from a man named Daryl who, inspired by the film, went out and had a similar experience and met a woman named Jessica. Now, nine years later, we have a sequel named *Before Sunset.* Have you heard what happened to them?

—Rob Kelly, Marlton, New Jersey

A. In May 1995, Daryl Elfield wrote me this heart-rending letter:

"I recently saw the movie *Before Sunrise,* where Ethan Hawke and Julie Delpy meet each other on a train, start talking, and end up spending the night walking around Vienna, Austria. Caught up in the romance of it all, I boarded a train from Philly to Charlottesville, Va. (I had to go there anyway.) On the train I met a woman dressed exactly like Julie Delpy and about as beautiful. So began a rather romantic trip that began with her asking me to come to Atlanta with her and ended with my return to law school two days later. But now the story takes an interesting twist and could probably be called *After Sunrise.* Since I had missed some school, I felt the need to explain to a professor where I had been. Unfortunately, I was too embarrassed to relate the full details, so I informed him I was sick. Two weeks later I was asked to leave the school for lying to a professor. My legal career is probably now over."

At the time, I talked with Elfield, with the woman, named Jessica; and with Alison Kitch, one of his law professors at Washington and Lee University, who told me: "I am quite sympathetic with what happened to him. But he indeed broke the rules. He got thrown out for doing what the honors book says you will be thrown out for: He lied. If he had only told his professor he missed class because he met a young woman on a train and spent two days with her in Atlanta, he might have gotten a bad grade, but he wouldn't have been thrown out of school."

In 2004, I Googled the hapless Elfield but found no trace of him.

Q. I was touched to read your recent column on Daryl Elfield and his *Before Sunrise* story. Since then, I've had a few *Before Sunrise* experiences myself. It's amazing how much I can open up in an encounter in a foreign land with a woman I've never met before. It may be that you feel no inhibitions about baring your soul, because you are fairly sure you won't ever meet this person again. I applaud the quest to find out what happened to Daryl. As for me, I ended up marrying my *Before Sunrise* gal, whom I met in China. You can see pictures from our wedding at www.geocities.com/bryanlchan.geo/webpage/brian_dream.html.
—Brian Nomi, Camarillo, California

A. Daryl Elfield has been found! The subject of the best-remembered exchange in Answer Man history is alive and well and living in London. Before I tell you his current story, here are highlights from his saga:

In 1995, Elfield wrote me a letter describing his romantic encounter on a train. At the time the Answer Man made some calls. The woman Elfield met on the train was Jessica Turner, a Spanish teacher from Fryeburg, Maine, who said: "I hadn't seen the movie when we met, but we saw it together after we got off the train in Atlanta. I really was wearing one of those black dresses, like the woman in the movie. We started talking, he told me all about the movie, and when we got to Charlottesville, I asked him if he wanted to stay on the train and spend some time in Atlanta. I feel really awful about what happened."

Then I spoke with Alison Kitch, Daryl's law professor at Washington and Lee University in Lexington, Va., who explained why Elfield was thrown out of school.

I also talked with Eric Chaffin, who represented Elfield before the honors committee. He told me, "It's made me really want to see that movie."

In July 2004, *Before Sunset*, a sequel to *Before Sunrise*, opened, again directed by Richard Linklater, again starring Ethan Hawke and Julie Delpy. They run into each other in Paris, where he is signing copies of a novel he wrote about their day and night together. They have not seen each other in the intervening years, but they pick up their conversation almost where it left off.

Rob Kelly of Marlton, New Jersey, wrote me asking if there was also a sequel to Daryl Elfield's story. I asked readers to help track him down. Aaron Honn of Houston, Texas, was the first of several readers to find an item from a University of California at Santa Cruz Website reporting "Daryl Elfield obtained a law degree in England in 1999 and is now working for a dot-com company near London." Then reader Rich Gallagher of Fishkill, New York, narrowed the search until he came up with a possible address and e-mail. I wrote to Daryl Elfield, and it was the right man. The following is my Q & A with him:

R.E. What happened in your life after leaving law school?

D.E. I moved back to live with my father in California for a few months. I started working in IT, but within six months I had moved to New Zealand—another romance! I stayed there for a year and set up my own Website design company, but sadly things didn't work out with the girl, so I moved back to England, which is where I had been brought up (although my parents are American). Since then I've been living in London, working as a managing consultant during the day and studying to be a lawyer at night. I should qualify as a barrister next year.

R.E. Did you ever see Jessica again?

D.E. Just once more. When we parted in Atlanta we decided that since chance had played such a large part in our meeting, we shouldn't tempt fate by making any concrete plans to meet again. (It made sense at the time!) Within a few days of my getting back to college, however, she called, and whatever connection we'd made that weekend seemed to still exist. Sadly within a week my life fell apart and I think, reasonably enough, Jessica was freaked out by the whole thing. I did fly up to Boston to see her about two weeks later and we had another weekend together—but I was in no state to enjoy it. When I moved to California we stayed in touch for a few months by phone and by e-mail but then lost contact. In terms of tracking her down, do you even have her last name? I thought of her quite a lot this year and imagined, in the wake of the sequel, that she must be thinking about me. However, I have no way to find her. . . .

R.E. Have you found romantic happiness?

D.E. Yes and no! I've certainly had my fair share of relationships and I think they've frequently been characterized by the sort of romantic/insane spontaneity I discovered with Jessica. However, I have managed to avoid getting fired! Have I been in love? For sure. Have I found lasting happiness? Not yet . . .

R.E. Was it all for the better—or maybe not?

D.E. I get asked this question a lot. It took me about eighteen months to realize I had a good story to tell. I was in Prague and I met a couple guys in a bar, and we just started talking. They were just gobsmacked. It made me realize that it was time to move on and stop being resentful about being kicked out of college. I'm obviously sorry things happened the way they did, but I can't regret that it happened. I can remember even now the feeling I had when I made the decision to stay on the train rather than go back to college—it was like stepping off a cliff without having any idea what lay beneath. I'm sure if I'd had any idea of the consequences of my actions I would never have done it, but in the end that's the point: You only have one life to live, and sometimes you have to take chances.

R.E. Anything else?

D.E. My friends got *far* too excited about your getting in touch with me, and I thought you'd be amused to know I now have volunteers for media-relations handler, manager, and trophy wife, just in case someone decides to make the film of my life.

*   *   *

Q. Someone asked the Answer Man what happened to Daryl Elfield, the reader who got in trouble because he was too inspired by *Before Sunrise.* That reminded me of another young man you wrote about–an enterprising young director at Sundance who went to great lengths to get you to see his short movie, called something like *Bobby Loves Mangos.* Anyway, you said it was a good short and I've always

wondered if the short is available anywhere, and whatever happened to the director?
—David Zobel, Atlanta, Georgia

A. That was a wonderful short by Stuart Acher, who bribed the café manager at Park City's Yarrow Inn to put it on the big TV so he could nudge me to see it. You can view the film for free at atomfilms.shockwave.com/af/content/atom_81.

The short won Acher an agent, talks with studios, and lots of work directing commercials for such clients as Porsche. He made a music video named "Powder: Up Here," featuring the band Powder, which is also free at Atom Films, and he is preparing his first feature.

Documentaries

Q. The Motion Picture Academy has named the twelve finalists for the Best Documentary category. Two of the titles jumped off the list for me: *The Story of the Weeping Camel,* and *Touching the Void.* Since both of these films were fictionalized versions of their stories and employed actors to play many of the roles, how do they qualify as documentaries?
—Greg Nelson, Chicago, Illinois

A. Bruce Davis, executive director of the Motion Picture Academy, replies: "The questions about the eligibility of *The Story of the Weeping Camel* and *Touching the Void* in this year's Feature Documentary field are fair ones to ask, since both films contain substantial amounts of 're-created' material. *Camel* was the easier call. It's not the kind of documentary usually seen these days, though, where events are captured on film as they actually happen. This is more of an ethnographic study; the filmmakers clearly observed life in a Mongol community in the Gobi Desert and then asked its inhabitants to re-create various aspects of their lives for the camera, imposing a wisp of a story on the material for structure. To say that *Camel* isn't a documentary would be to rule most of Robert Flaherty's body of work (like *Nanook of the North*) outside the documentary pale, and most documentarians would be slow to do that. *Void* consists of pure documentary material—interviews with the participants in the ill-fated climb in the Peruvian Andes—intermixed with footage in which actors re-create parts of the adventure. At some point in a film of this kind, the ratio of staged to doc material becomes problematic (we wouldn't have accepted *Reds* as a documentary, for example), but after taking a careful look at *Void,* our documentarians welcomed it into this year's competition."

Q. One of the finalists for 2004 Best Documentary Feature is *Tupac: Resurrection* which was released in 2003. Call me crazy, but I thought to be eligible for a documentary Oscar this year, a film must have been released between January 1 and December 31 of this year. How did a film that came out November 2003 get nominated in 2004?

—Dennis Earl, Hamilton, Ontario

A. Bruce Davis, executive director of the Motion Picture Academy, replies: "The Feature and Short Documentary categories, along with a couple of others that involve heavy viewing loads for the groups determining the nominations, have always had a different eligibility year from the 'standard' categories. With last year's shift of our show date into February, the difference has become even greater: Though the calendar year remains the eligibility period for dramatic features, the year for documentaries runs from September 1 to August 31. *Tupac* didn't become eligible until the current (seventy-seventh) Awards year."

Down and Derby

Q. In your televised review of *Down and Derby,* [a movie about the Pinewood Derby, where children race little cars carved from pine], you said the movie makes the fathers seem obnoxious and over-involved in the competition. I can testify to the derby's sheer lunacy, both as son and father. When I was a young man living in Carbondale, Illinois, my entry was paltry. It was set against items, I later learned, that had been tested in wind tunnels and engineered by the fathers of my competitors. Twenty-five years later I coaxed my son to develop his own entry, believing in my heart that Carbondale was an anomaly. I was wrong. We were living in Rhode Island, and the difference was significant. Where in Carbondale some fathers used the wind tunnel as a resource to ensure victory for their

pasty and distemperate children, in Rhode Island you had the General Dynamics and Sikorsky laboratories at the disposal of the parents of similarly dyspeptic children. I took the Pinewood Derby as an opportunity for fathers to show sons how to use simple carpentry and build self-confidence. Others cast this notion aside.

—John W. Womick, Ballwin, Missouri

A. I think we need a sequel: *Down and Derby 2: This Time, It's Personal.* All of the child actors should be pasty, distemperate, and dyspeptic.

Q. Re. the discussion of *Down and Derby*: When my son was a Scout, the local organization had two divisions, one for the Scouts, and one for the parents. That way, the Scouts could learn the value of competition and the fun of building the car, and the dads (myself included) could have some fun, too. One dad designed his car in the local Lockheed wind tunnel, but the winner of the division was a car with a plastic Kermit sticking up out of the cockpit. It was built by one of the moms.

—Ralph Burkey, Fort Worth, Texas

A. Case closed.

Dwarfs and the M-word

Q. I am an actor you have reviewed neither favorably nor unfavorably in two movies: *Death to Smoochy,* and *Things You Can Tell Just by Looking at Her.* I have absolutely no objection to your trashing a film or lauding it. I do object to the use of the word *midgets* in your review of *Death to Smoochy.* As a writer you are aware of the power of words. The use of the word *midget,* for little people, is equated with any other hate word someone might use to describe a minority group. I simply ask you: If you were to see little people children, would you take away their humanity in the same way with the use of such a hate word? I can respect a yes answer but I cannot respect the person who answers yes.

—Danny Woodburn

A. I had no idea the word *midget* was considered offensive, and you are the only person who has ever written to me about it. In my mind it is a descriptive term, like *dwarf.* Now that I am informed that *midget* is offensive, I will no longer use it.

In doing some research, I found a fascinating essay titled "What Offends Us," by Leonard Sawisch, Ph.D., a dwarf who shares your dislike of the M-word. He writes: "Ironically, *midget* is the newest term for people like us. It was coined by P. T. Barnum in the mid 1800s to describe members of the dwarf community who were the most socially acceptable, i.e., 'well-proportioned' little people who could entertain on the front stage for polite society. The rest of the dwarf community, those of us whose bodies are shaped differently enough to look more than just 'really short,' were relegated to the back stage or freak shows."

Sawisch has a great deal more to say, and so did you as we exchanged messages. I am posting our full exchange, and Sawisch's essay, at rogerebert.com.

Enduring Love

Q. Just a comment about your review of *Enduring Love*. You said that if all the people who grabbed hold of the ropes attached to the hot-air balloon had held on, they might have been able to keep the balloon from rising again, and that whoever was the first person to let go of the balloon was probably responsible for the death of the man who held on until he was so high that letting go caused him to fall and die. I'm not a licensed balloon pilot, but I have friends who are involved as crew of the Goodyear blimp. One of the first rules of handling lighter-than-air craft is that if you are holding on to the craft in any way, the moment your feet lift off the ground, you let go—no ifs, ands, or buts about it. I have to say that every single person I know of with lighter-than-air experience would take the view that the guy who held on and was lifted skyward was responsible for his own death.

—Karin Cozzolino

A. Invaluable advice. Readers: Clip and save!

Etiquette at the Movies

Q. What is the etiquette for handling a request to move over to the next seat in the movie theater? Recently my wife and I were sitting in the same row as a couple who had an empty seat on either side of them. As the theater filled up, two couples separately requested that the couple already sitting there move over one seat so that they could sit together. The couple in the seats refused to move. Each time, the reaction by the requesting couple was shock. My wife and I felt that the couple sitting there had every right to refuse to move since they had arrived early enough to choose their seats. Your thoughts?

—Kevin C. Rung, New Orleans, Louisiana

A. The Answer Man refers all questions of etiquette to his lifelong friend Dear Prudence, who writes the advice column for Slate.com. Prudie replies: "This is a judgment call—or, to be more precise, a 'feeling call,' as in, how one is feeling at the moment. People are not impolite to ask, and often they will be accommodated. But by the same token, those who've chosen particular seats and wish to keep them have every right to do so. Sometimes a curmudgeon will say no just to say no. Regarding absorbing shock at a negative response, Prudie's inner snarky self thinks, Well, so? You do not know these people, ergo, what's momentary discomfort compared to sitting exactly where you please?"

Q. In response to last week's etiquette question: I believe that a couple who refuse to move over one measly seat so you can sit with the person with whom you came is extremely rude. Next time that scenario occurs, you and your friend or wife should sit on each side of the couple. Then, during the movie, feel free to lean over them and discuss the film. You still get to enjoy the movie with the person you came with, and you get to ruin the moviegoing experience of two rude people.

—Daniel Brody, North Woodmere, New York

A. Of course, it is also rude to discuss a film in an audible tone. On the earlier question, the Answer Man consulted his friend Dear Prudence, of Slate.com, who said that the couple who sit down first need not feel obligated to move to let another couple sit together. Several readers were outraged by Prudie. Here is Sean Blythe, of Los Angeles: "How petty and mean-spirited does one have to be to refuse to move two feet to allow a couple to sit together at the movies? I mean, what's the rationale? Sound and picture quality? It's a movie theater, kids, not the freaking promised land. Lighten up, come to grips with the idea that you're not the only people in the world, and move the hell over. Geez."

On the other hand, I get really unhappy when somebody with dozens of seats to choose from sits directly in front of me.

Q. What's proper behavior for sharing the armrest with a stranger next to you? Some people tend to commandeer the armrest, and in those cases, I subtly assert myself by gradually reclaiming half of it back. Should people really be keeping their arms within the confines of their seats as defined by the armrests?

—Tom Clark, Columbia, Maryland

A. Once again I turned to my friend Dear Prudence, and once again Prudie offered counsel:

"Prudie is amused by the vision of reclaiming half an arm rest—leaving both parties with the equivalent of a very narrow ledge on which to prop up an arm and assert territorial rights. This is one of those situations involving strangers where nonverbal communication comes into play. Your default position, no pun intended, is of course the way it's going to work out for the less aggressive armrester: arms within the confines of the seat. Perhaps being a nonconfrontational wimp, whenever Prudie feels the neighbor's arm she immediately retreats. Often the other person will do the same thing. Sometimes there will be a silent agreement to alternate. Should the person be obstinate, you have no choice but to let it go . . . either that or take it out into the alley."

Q. So I'm watching *Million Dollar Baby* for the second time. Fine. Then, during the last time we see Frankie talking to the priest (arguably the best scene in the film) somebody's cell phone rings. It rings and rings and rings some more. The audience member frantically searches and finally yanks it out of her bag— only to answer it! Someone makes a comment, and then someone makes a comment about that comment. The scene finishes and is ruined for the whole audience. My question:

What is being done to prevent people from using cell phones in theaters?!

—Michael Armstrong, Toronto, Ontario

A. A special circle of hell is being reserved for them. And on a more pragmatic level, Anant Singh, a leading producer and exhibitor in South Africa, tells me of devices that can block cell phone signals in theaters. Meanwhile, we face the prospect of cell phones being legalized on airplanes, which may force us to undergo the unspeakable experience of watching the in-flight movie to block the chatter.

Evolution at the Movies

Q. I just read your article regarding *Volcanoes of the Deep,* the IMAX movie that several theaters in the South have chosen not to run, most likely because the movie dares to mention the *E* word (*evolution*). My own local Fernbank Natural History Museum has chosen not to run it on its screen, not because there was a problem with the film's content, but because it was "slow moving and a little dry." The film's maker, Stephen Low, says this is a cop-out, and these museums and science centers don't want to admit they're kowtowing to religious pressure.

—Steven Stewart, Atlanta, Georgia

A. Now that the film has become the center of controversy, of course any self-respecting science museum will insist on showing it, to demonstrate its support for sound mainstream science and its refusal to cave in to pressure groups. Right? Uh-huh.

I have not seen the film, although I did see and admire James Cameron's *Aliens of the Deep,* another recent IMAX film that shows life under incredible conditions on the seabed. Confusingly, Cameron was also executive producer of *Volcanoes.* Although different directors and crew members are listed for the two films, the *Variety* review of *Volcanoes* suggests it has much the same material, even including speculation about life on Jupiter's moon, Europa. *Volcanoes* was first released in September 2003, *Aliens* in January 2005.

It is important to make clear that the IMAX theaters that have declined to show *Volcanoes of the Deep* did not do so because of protests from anti-Darwinists, but simply because they *feared* such protests. Any administrator of a mainstream science facility allowing decisions to be made on that basis is a disgrace to the profession.

Fahrenheit 9/11

Q. I read your review of *Fahrenheit 9/11* and I was very disappointed that at *no point* did you question Michael Moore's political agenda and the reality of the film's claims. This seems to be promoting Moore's agenda, rather than providing an objective review of the film. I personally hate films that are obviously motivated by a political agenda; it causes me to question how much is reality and how much is exaggerated or fabricated. I don't have the time to review every fact and determine which is real and which is a lie or exaggeration. Moore is obviously a brilliant filmmaker, but I wish he could just do a documentary that focuses on an event, rather than taking an event to promote his political opinions.
—Bill Meyers, White Lake, Michigan

A. Moore's film comes labeled as partisan and subjective. Were you equally inspired to ask, "How much is reality and how much is exaggerated or fabricated," when the Bush administration presented Saddam's WMDs as fact? I declared my own political opinion in the review and made it clear I was writing from that viewpoint. It's opinion. I have mine, you have yours, and the theory is that we toss them both into the open marketplace of ideas.

Fever Pitch

Q. You mentioned it's difficult to imagine anyone other than Jimmy Fallon as the Red Sox baseball fan in *Fever Pitch* (2005). I'm having a hard time imagining anyone other than Colin Firth as the long-suffering Arsenal soccer fan in *Fever Pitch* (1997). Both movies are based on the same memoir by Nick Hornby. I enjoy the older movie so much that I'm having a hard time deciding whether I can see the new one. As an added factor, I don't really like the Red Sox. How can I best approach this dilemma?
—Billy Guinigundo, Hamilton, Ohio

A. The 1997 movie, unseen by me, was a North American box office flop, making less than $250,000 and on one weekend actually grossing only $170. But quite frankly, I'm so depressed that Illinois lost the final game of the NCAA basketball tournament, after coming back from 13 down to tie it up, that I wouldn't pay for a ticket if the Red Sox played Arsenal. To you and your dilemma, I say, "Oskee wow-wow."

Film Critics

Q. Do you have any idea why, after finally tottering into the black, Salon.com's new editors would fire Charles Taylor, whose thoughtful, beautifully articulated film reviews have been the gold standard for online magazines since 1998? I have to admit, my heart sank after reading editor Joan Walsh's "welcome" letter. She described the new music download column; promised an innovative new guide to political Weblogs; swore they'd continue "the best television coverage around"; and said she wouldn't "apologize for loving *America's Next Top Model*." Not a word about their film coverage.
—Sheila Benson, Seattle, Washington

A. Ms. Benson, like Charles Taylor and me, is a member of the National Society of Film Critics, which has sent e-mails racing around its membership expressing concern about the loss of Taylor and the trend toward de-emphasizing criticism in favor of inane pop "news." I spoke with new Salon editor Joan Walsh, who said Salon has only twenty-two editorial employees and could not justify three film critics. (The others are Stephanie Zacharek and Andrew O'Hehir.)

Film criticism is being swamped these days, not so much on Salon as everywhere else, by idiotic celebrity coverage, gossip, hype, and any possible way to discuss a movie without actually saying whether it is any good. Most of the entertainment-oriented TV shows are all foreplay: weeks of gushing and hype, "exclusive" interviews, "first looks" at trailers, and then, when the movie comes out, no critical opinion at all—just a box-office report.

Walsh said Salon does not plan to go that route, and I hope she's right. I know I didn't subscribe to the site to read about *America's Next Top Model*. (Editorial tip: Given the nature of the modeling business, a much more interesting article could probably be written about "America's Former Top Model.")

Friday Night Lights

Q. I had to laugh at elements of your review of *Friday Night Lights*. You wrote: "Certainly there are countless citizens in that Texas town who lead happy and productive lives and are fulfilled without depending on high school football." Obviously you've never lived in Texas. I've lived here for five years now and I can attest that in a small town like Odessa, high school football *is* everything. You mention that the Odessa "stadium is larger than those at many colleges." True. Our high school north of Austin recently completed a $20 million, 11,000-seat stadium complete with AstroPlay synthetic turf and a Daktronics ProStar scoreboard. In Texas, the school funding debate rages on like it does everywhere, but they can't let the kids play on a shabby field, can they?

—Doug Matheson, Austin, Texas

A. And Glen Gummess of Joliet, Illinois, writes: "I lived in Odessa's sphere of influence for nearly twenty years; in Hobbs, New Mexico, where I lived as a newsman, I covered our team's basketball games against Odessa Permian and others. Basketball is to Hobbs what football is to Odessa. You are absolutely right about the 'nationalistic' loyalty of local fans and their indignation when teams go sour. About Odessa, you're right. To be sure there are citizens who live happy and fulfilling lives without football, but I've seen the all-consuming mania when the season rolls around. I don't know if it's morally right or wrong that whole towns get so soaked up in the success or failure of their teams. I do know it's highly dysfunctional, and it leads to emotionally charged situations and plenty of grief."

Getting Too Soft

Q. I have noticed lately that you have been getting softer on bad movies (compared to the general critical consensus and my tastes, too). These movies include *Garfield: The Movie, The Stepford Wives,* and *The Day After Tomorrow.* I had the displeasure of seeing the former and the latter, and they did not deserve even one of your precious stars. Of course, I could be imagining things, but it just seems like lately you have been more sympathetic to bad movies. If this is true, why?

—Daniel Mills, Alameda, California

A. In my reviews I tried to give specific reasons why I enjoyed those movies: Bill Murray's voice-over work as Garfield, the witty *Stepford* dialogue, and the remarkable special effects in *Day After Tomorrow.* All three movies were flawed. In the case of *Stepford,* I probably should have praised the dialogue but cranked down the stars. *Garfield* we can debate. I was absolutely right about *Day After Tomorrow.* I was also right to dislike *I, Robot,* despite the "general critical consensus," etc.

Q. Do you hold different genres to different standards? It would seem so. You gave *The Stepford Wives* three stars, most likely just because it wasn't the *worst* remake you'd ever seen, but you gave *The Life Aquatic* two and a half stars, probably because to you it was not on par with *The Royal Tenenbaums.* Would you honestly rather sit through *The Stepford Wives* again than *The Life Aquatic?* I know I'd sooner have a Charles Nelson Reilly movie marathon.

—Jeff Robinson, Los Angeles, California

A. Stars are relative, not absolute, and analyzing them represents a waste of valuable time that could be profitably spent watching aquarium fish or memorizing the sayings of Dr. Johnson. I am compelled to award them because of market pressures. I, too, would rather see *The Life Aquatic* again than *The Stepford Wives,* but within the context of the two films, I think *The Life Aquatic* falls farther short of what it was trying to do—even though what it does is better than anything in *The Stepford Wives.* I realize my logic is impenetrable. I recommend just reading the reviews and ignoring the stars.

Q. I have finally figured out how to read your reviews. A review isn't about what it says; it's about how it goes about saying it:

• If you are stimulated to eloquence by the movie, then the movie is a must-see. It doesn't matter if you rate it well or poorly; it is the fact that you reacted strongly to the movie and worked hard at clarity that tells me what I need to know.

• If the review looks like it "wrote itself," then you enjoyed the film and I may or may not like it based on personal preference.

• If the review seems to lack punch, or seems

confused, then I know the film was a stinker no matter which way you look at it, and should be avoided for mental health reasons.

—Ron Wodaski, Cloudcroft, New Mexico

A. By following these rules, one would not always see good movies, but one would usually see interesting ones.

Q. I am a liberal Democrat but am bothered by what appears to be a bias in your reviews of some films by African-Americans. I think you are being more generous because the filmmaker is black. Spike Lee's *She Hate Me* is an example. Very few reviewers liked it, you had tons of criticisms of it in your quite negative review, yet in the end you gave it a positive rating. Now I find myself prone to looking at additional reviews of movies by African-Americans to judge whether you appear to be demonstrating this bias.

—Ward Reynolds, Mount Pleasant, South Carolina

A. My review of *She Hate Me* is not negative at all, although it predicted most other reviews would be and listed the reasons why. I am proud of that review because I wasn't content with level-one criticism of obvious "faults," but I assumed that Spike Lee made the film he wanted to make and tried to figure out what that film was, and why. Most critics just dismissed it as implausible or idiotic; I anticipated it would get a 20 on the Tomatometer, and I was right on the money. But the movie was also provocative and deliberately non-PC. I believe Lee made his points in an indirect and daring way. As for whether I'm too easy on African-American films, may I forward your words to those who accused me of being a racist after my review of *Diary of a Mad Black Woman*?

Gloomy Sunday

Q. 1) *Gloomy Sunday* is still playing at a local art theater after sixty weeks! 2) In Krzysztof Kieslowski's *White,* one of the tunes that Karol plays on his comb in the subway is called "The Last Sunday." I believe it is the title song from the film *Gloomy Sunday.*

—Robert Sprich, Waban, Massachusetts

A. I have just listened to the comb performance by Zbigniew Zamachowski in *White,* and I agree with you: It is the same song.

Gloomy Sunday played for more than a year in Australia and New Zealand. In June 2003, it opened in only one American theater, the Wilmette, north of Chicago, and ran for weeks. It had a "limited" national release in November 2003 and is still playing here and there. It's one of those films that inspires enormous interest while keeping a curiously low profile. The movie is set in Budapest before and during the Nazi occupation, and the plot centers on "Gloomy Sunday," a song said to drive its listeners to suicide. Recorded by artists as diverse as Artie Shaw, Billie Holiday, Björk, and Elvis Costello, it was at one point actually banned by the BBC because of its supposed effect.

Godzilla

Q. I take exception with your disparaging review of the original *Godzilla.* The film is technically not on a par with the works of Ray Harryhausen, but unlike the typical Hollywood monster-on-a-rampage flick, it has considerable dramatic substance. Director Ishiro Honda and virtually all others involved with the film were actual witnesses to the mass destruction of WWII, not only of Hiroshima and Nagasaki, but also the firebombing of Tokyo and so many other Japanese cities. As a result its emotions are intense and authentic, and its sense of awe, sorrow, and existential terror are palpable.

After reading your dismissive review, I find myself agreeing with a Japanese director who said, "[Honda's] mind was full of hope that no one would have as sad a war experience as his. His films are full of his sincere humanity and his tender personality—films like *Godzilla.* I like it very much. His films have remained popular because they were shot honestly and sincerely—they're naturally good." That director's name? Akira Kurosawa.

—David Wise, Los Angeles, California

A. Humanity, a tender personality, honesty, and sincerity are also attributes of the cinema of Joe Camp. You can't do better than his latest, *Benji Off the Leash.*

Godzilla has historical importance, both as the founder of a genre and as a reflection of the post-bomb Japanese state of mind, but as a film it's pretty shabby.

Harry Potter and the Prisoner of Azkaban

Q. In response to Corey Slack's complaint in a recent Answer Man that you should not have tipped off the identity of the werewolf in your review of *Harry Potter and the Prisoner of Azkaban:* You missed the point. We are not masters of Latin, nor are we as schooled in Latin roots. But when you connected the word *lupus* to the werewolf, there isn't a moron (or child) alive who wouldn't realize you were talking about Professor Lupin, mentioned a few lines before. You ruined the surprise with a comment about as cryptic as an exit sign.
—Fiji Hebden, Rutgers University, New Brunswick, New Jersey

A. But ... but ... the movie gives itself away, by calling him Professor Lupin! You are at Rutgers but have never heard the word *lupine*?

Hoop Dreams

Q. *Hoop Dreams,* the 1994 documentary about two Chicago inner-city kids who dream of playing in the NBA, is one of my all-time favorite films. I was saddened to learn of the death of Arthur Agee's father, Arthur "Bo" Agee Sr. The film showed Arthur Sr. going through a transformation: He escaped the drug life and became a minister. It is good to know he was interviewed for the forthcoming *Hoop Dreams* DVD. My heart goes out to the Agee family.
—Justin Rielly, Lawton, Oklahoma

A. His family has the consolation of knowing he died clean and sober, and making a contribution to society. I was fortunate to meet his wife, Sheila Agee, a warm and brave woman, and I recall a comment Gene Siskel made: "There are thousands in the crowd for the basketball games, but when she graduates as a nurse's aide, the room is almost empty. She's the movie's real heroine."

House of D

Q. In your review of *House of D,* you made fun of a conversation taking place at the Women's House of Detention in Greenwich Village between an inmate and someone on the sidewalk. When I arrived in the Village in 1963, I was surprised to see conversations regularly taking place between inmates on upper floors and, usually, husbands and children on the street. It is unlikely I will ever see this film, but I think on this score you owe the writer-director an apology.
—Michael Levin, New Mexico

A. So I do, although the distance from the upper floor to the street looks too far for voices to carry.

House of Flying Daggers

Q. I was happy to see your mention of Fred Astaire in your review of *House of Flying Daggers.* For years now I've told friends they should watch a Jackie Chan movie the same way they would watch a Fred Astaire film. The fight scenes and dance numbers are the bits you've come to see; the plot is just a framework. The fights/dances were carefully planned and blocked out, and Astaire and Chan both make great use of "found props" in their numbers. If I were a director, my dream project would be to get Jackie Chan and Michelle Yeo to star in a musical together. Absolutely no fight scenes—I'd want them to be Fred and Ginger for the twenty-first century.
—Siobhan Doran, Chicago, Illinois

A. There is a distinction between the elegant choreography of many Asian martial arts movies, most recently *House of Flying Daggers,* and the ugly, chopped-up martial arts sequences in routine action movies, where so many cuts and close-ups are used that we get no sense of the characters' movements through space and time.

Q. The first battle scene in *House of Flying Daggers* involves the death of several horses during the melee. In this sequence I noticed that when a horse was injured, its front legs would give way, and the horse would fall forward, onto its head or neck. The end credits do not contain a disclaimer that "no animals were harmed." This made me think that perhaps trip wires were used to cause the horses to fall. If this is true, do you feel that our obligation as movie lovers is to attend wonderful films like this one, or that as believers in animal rights we should avoid such a movie?
—Richard Shore, Longmont, Colorado

A. It is a question you do not need to answer for *House of Flying Daggers,* since reportedly no animals were injured. Michael Barker, co-president of Sony Classics, tells me, "We have been assured by both the producer and director that no animals were harmed during the shooting of this movie."

I, Robot

Q. In your review of *I, Robot* you stated that the movie should have credited Isaac Asimov as the creator of the famous three laws of robotics. However, within the fictional universe of *I, Robot* the three laws would have been created by a fictional someone. Much like Shakespeare was the one who wrote "But Brutus says he was ambitious / And Brutus is an honorable man," but, within the fictional universe of *Julius Caesar* it was Antony who said it. If Brutus were to refer to that quote, he would cite Antony as saying it, not Shakespeare. In the same way, since the fictional Dr. Lanning wrote Asimov's Three Laws within Asimov's fictional universe, it is accurate to say Dr. Lanning wrote the three laws.

—Brian Valentine, Lake Wales, Florida

A. I got lots of complaints about that. Here is what I wrote: "The dead man is Dr. Alfred Lanning (James Cromwell), who, we are told, wrote the Three Laws. Every schoolchild knows the laws were set down by the good doctor Isaac Asimov, after a conversation he had on December 23, 1940, with John W. Campbell, the legendary editor of *Astounding Science Fiction.* It is peculiar that no one in the film knows that, especially since the film is 'based on the book by Isaac Asimov.' Would it have killed the filmmakers to credit Asimov?"

From a logical point of view, you are absolutely right. From my point of view, my tongue was in my cheek. Not everybody appreciates irony. Several readers helpfully informed me that every schoolchild does not, in fact, know about Asimov's December 23, 1940, conversation with Campbell.

Ice Princess

Q. In *Ice Princess,* Casey (Michelle Trachtenberg) discusses the science of skating by saying ". . . by tucking in my arms this will increase my moment of inertia and so I will spin faster." This is incorrect. Tucking in her arms

decreases her moment of inertia and by conservation of angular momentum she spins faster. All the fourth-grade students I have explained this phenomenon to will become horribly confused.

—Dave Kupperman, Oak Park, Illinois

A. They're studying moments of inertia and conservation of angular momentum in fourth grade? When I was in grade school, we didn't even have them as spelling words.

Q. In your review of *Ice Princess,* you wrote, ". . . the surprise is that Michelle Trachtenberg seems able to skate too. That didn't look like a double on the ice, although *Variety,* the showbiz bible, reports, 'Four different skaters sub for Trachtenberg in the more difficult performances.'" As you probably have heard by now, there *were* doubles, although I agree it really looked like the actress herself. How do you feel about the visual trickery?

—Susan Lake, Urbana, Illinois

A. I would have been fooled if not for the information from *Variety.* Dennis Berardi of Mr. X Inc. in Toronto produced the visual effects for the film. He writes: "As one of the effects studios responsible for face replacement on the film, we're taking your words as a compliment. Miss Trachtenberg indeed demonstrated considerable natural skating ability during filming, and her talents provided the foundation for our studio's effects work. But *Variety* was correct. There were four different skaters who took the ice for Trachtenberg (Jennifer Robinson, Sandra Jean Rucker, Cassandre Van Bakel, and Lauren Wilson), as well as extensive if invisible visual effects. Our studio was responsible for seamlessly replacing the faces of the stunt skaters with that of Miss Trachtenberg. Ultimately, the best effects are those that look so real that they cannot be seen. So, you actually paid our digital artists the ultimate compliment, by not recognizing their work."

The Incredibles

Q. In your review of *The Incredibles* you mentioned that the character Edna Mode was inspired by Q from the Bond movies. I'm pretty sure she was based more on the facial features and occupation of Edith Head, the Oscar-winning costume designer.

—Mohsen Ghofrani, North Canton, Ohio

A. J. Oyen of San Mateo, California, adds: "Edna's uncanny resemblance to Hitchcock's favorite costume designer and the fact that Edna is a world-famous clothes designer in the movie seem to support the Edith Head connection." I am persuaded that Edith Head is the inspiration for the character but that her role has been enriched by Q behavior.

Ingmar Bergman

Q. You are a fan of the work of Ingmar Bergman. According to his biography on imdb.com, he retired from directing in May 2004. How did this make you feel?

—Joey Laura, New Orleans, Louisiana

A. Grateful for his work, and aware that he is one of those rare people who can retire knowing he achieved what he set out to achieve, and did it brilliantly, and it will endure.

Footnote: Bergman was not quite retired, and his masterful Saraband, *a sequel to* Scenes from a Marriage *(1973) was released in the summer of 2005. It starred the same two actors, Liv Ullmann and Erland Josephson, giving us a unique opportunity to follow characters over decades.*

Inside Deep Throat

Q. Your review says *Deep Throat* grossed $600 million, "making it the most profitable movie of all time." According to the-numbers.com, it grossed $4,600,000. How do you explain such a tremendous difference?

—Don Pruitt, Golden, Colorado

A. That $600 million figure looked fishy to me, and I should have queried it more severely in my review. I did point out, "Since the mob owned most of the porn theaters in the pre-video days and inflated box-office receipts as a way of laundering income from drugs and prostitution, it is likely, in fact, that *Deep Throat* did not really gross $600 million, although that might have been the box-office tally."

Actually, I doubt that was even the post-laundering tally. *Variety's* list of all-time box-office champs doesn't have *Deep Throat* in the top 250 (where the 250th film is *Star Trek 4*, at

$109 million). However, on leesmovieinfo.net, it is indeed listed as the twenty-sixth largest grossing film of all time, with a worldwide gross of $600 million. Less than 7 percent of that is said to be from the U.S. box-office; however, is it possible that 93 percent of the movie's gross was international? *Screen Daily*, from the UK, says $600 million was the "FBI estimate," and the FBI is not known for its box-office scorecards. The bottom line is from the *Hollywood Reporter:* "No one was really counting."

Q. I always thought the most profitable movie of all time (based on percentage of return) was *The Blair Witch Project*. However, the movie poster for *Inside Deep Throat* claims that *Deep Throat* is the most profitable movie ever. Is there an authority who can settle this once and for all?

—Andrew Woodhouse, Tempe, Arizona

A. Startled by the claim in *Inside Deep Throat* that the original movie grossed $600 million in circa 1970 dollars, Michael Hiltzik of the *Los Angeles Times* ran the numbers and wrote an article suggesting that figure was a fantasy that has been repeated for years without any fact-checking.

Hiltzik writes me: "The Website the-numbers.com says $40.8 million. That could be in the ballpark, keeping in mind that given the cash nature of the distribution it's a pretty muddy ballpark. At the time of the Memphis verdicts, the standard newspaper estimate seemed to be $30 million to $50 million, and then it abruptly jumped up to $600 million and no one ever looked back. When Linda Lovelace appeared before a congressional committee in the mid-'80s, the chair, Arlen Specter, said something like, "So it grossed $600 million and you got a lot of bruises?" and she replied, in effect, "Yeah."

The Interpreter

Q. You have a right to complain about casting decisions. But in the case of *The Interpreter*, a different screenplay would have had to be written to accommodate your objections, and you damn well know it. I've been watching you slide off the left side of the page for the past few years. It diminishes you as a reviewer. You seem to want to be elevated to the position of supreme arbiter. It isn't going to happen. And, yes, I agree that your recommended substitute probably would have been effective in the role. So would a number of other black actresses. But as you have often suggested, why don't you review the movie you saw, not the movie you wanted them to make?

—Tim Monroe, Delavan, Wisconsin

A. *The Interpreter* stars Nicole Kidman as a white woman born and raised in Africa, working at the United Nations as an interpreter. She supported her nation's black ruler in his fight against white colonialism, but now he has become a despot whose population is starving. (The fictional character is obviously based on Robert Mugabe of Zimbabwe.) In a footnote to my review, I wrote: "I don't want to get politically correct, I know there are many white Africans, and I admire Kidman's performance. But I couldn't help wondering why her character had to be white. I imagined someone like Angela Bassett in the role and wondered how that would have played. If you see the movie, run that through your mind."

Yes, I advise reviewing the movie that has been made, not the one I would have made. In this case, Sydney Pollack has made a good movie, and I said so. But it occurred to me that a different dynamic would have occurred if the woman had been a black African protesting black misrule. I do not see this as a suggestion from the left or right, but simply a reflection on the African reality.

Interspecies Cartoon Romance

Q. In *The Three Musketeers,* the new made-for-DVD animated feature from Walt Disney Productions starring Mickey Mouse, Goofy, and Donald Duck, Goofy falls in love with Clarabelle the Cow. This leads me to wonder: Is this the first interspecies romance depicted in a Disney cartoon?

—Joe Leydon, Houston, Texas

A. Few people know more about animated characters and even their sex lives than my friend and colleague Leonard Maltin, who responds: "The first thing that comes to mind is Donald Duck's aggressive flirting with human bathing beauties in *The Three Caballeros.* For the most part, Disney kept the animal species together, as nature intended, but the very same Clarabelle Cow kept company for years with Horace Horsecollar—a horse—which no one ever seemed to question!"

Q. Regarding your recent Answer Man item on interspecies dating in Disney cartoons: I'm sure I won't be the first to point out that while Disney tends to keep things pretty strict, over at Warner Bros., it's "Toons Gone Wild." Consider Bugs Bunny's transvestite dalliances with the all-too-human Elmer Fudd—not only interspecies, but same sex! They even got married, for the sake of opera. And of course, there's the great Pepé Le Pew, a skunk who more than once danced off with a feline female at the end of the short (of course, she usually had a bad head cold at the time). It may not have been as family friendly, but it was a lot more fun, in my book.

—Ken Bearden, Wyandotte, Michigan

A. In turning to Leonard Maltin for an expert answer, I specified only Disney films. At Warner Bros., as the late and great Chuck Jones used to say, they got away with murder.

Q. You and Leonard Maltin both neglected to mention that in a series of Goofy shorts from the 1950s, Goof lived in blissful domesticity with a human wife. I suppose you could argue that Goofy is exempt from discussions of interspecies romance considering that we still don't know what species he is, but I think he qualifies, and your reader thought so, too. Also, don't forget about the most famous interspecies couple in American history, Kermit the Frog and Miss Piggy.

—Stephen Silver, New York City, New York

A. I've always thought of Kermit and Miss Piggy as just very, very good friends.

Q. Regarding your recent column on interspecies dating, specifically the relationship of Kermit the Frog and Miss Piggy: I had the good fortune in June 1999 to interview Mr. Frog around the release of *Muppets from Space.* Kermit said that the public has been terribly misinformed concerning his relationship with Miss Piggy. "This whole romance thing is just a figment of the pig's imagination. It's not true. There is nothing going on there whatsoever," he said. "I don't know whether she knows it but she certainly should be aware by now. She tends to still be out there telling people that we're married or we're dating or all that stuff, but it's just not true." Kermit went on to say, "The pig is crazy," but I sadly had to cut that quote due to space constraints.

—Robert Bishop, Prairie Village, Kansas

A. So there you have it, straight from the frog's mouth.

Kill Bill: Vol. 2

Q. I was a little surprised when you named *Kill Bill: Vol. 2* as the best film of the year so far on the *Tonight Show.* I thought it was exemplary in lots of ways, but I'm not sure that it really taught me anything about real life or real people. Also, I wonder if you owe Michael Moore an apology. He's probably not the thin-skinned type, but it seems you could have been a little more tactful than in not naming his film as the best of the year, since he was sitting on-stage right there with you.

—Steve Replogle, Denver, Colorado

A. The curse of the critic is that we are required to tell the truth. Years ago Chevy Chase appeared on the *Tonight Show with Johnny Carson,* promoting *The Three Amigos.* Then Siskel and I came out, I sat down next to Chevy, and Carson asked me which holiday movie I liked the least. "Uh, *The Three Amigos*," I said. "I wish I hadn't asked you that," Johnny said. "So do I," I said.

Kung Fu Hustle

Q. I just finished reading your review of *Kung Fu Hustle* and I have to know, what is Jack Lemmon's story about seeing Klaus Kinski buying a hatchet at Ace Hardware?

—Barnaby Thieme, San Francisco, California

A. Jack Lemmon told me that he was in line at Ace Hardware in Beverly Hills, and the salesclerk kept looking past him. "I may not be the biggest star in the world," he said, "but, jeez, usually when I stand in line the clerk will notice me. I turned around, and there was Klaus Kinski with an ax."

Lemony Snicket

Q. In your review of *Lemony Snicket's A Series of Unfortunate Events,* you described Meryl Streep's character as being "literally afraid of everything, a condition I believe is called phobiaphobia." This is not the correct term. I am not a psychologist, but I have watched *A Charlie Brown Christmas Special* many times, and "pantophobia" is the diagnosis Lucy gives to Charlie Brown at her ten-cent psychiatry stand.

—Dain Fagerholm, Seattle, Washington

A. I was afraid of that.

The Life and Death of Peter Sellers

Q. I saw *The Life and Death of Peter Sellers* on HBO. On countless Websites, people are praising Geoffrey Rush's performance and bemoaning the fact that he will not be eligible for an Oscar since this film has not been released theatrically in the States. Rumor has it HBO felt Peter Sellers was not "famous" enough in the United States. Is there any truth to this absurd explanation?

—Sid Wagner, New York City, New York

A. It may be that the film simply did not appeal to test audiences. I saw it at Cannes and wrote: "Of the official entry *The Life and Death of Peter Sellers,* directed by Stephen Hopkins, starring Geoffrey Rush as the great comedian and Emily Watson and Charlize Theron as two of his wives, what can be said is that Sellers was one miserable SOB. 'I have no personality, except for what I get from my characters,' he said. Not quite true. The film sees him as a neurotic, cruel, selfish, immature monster even whose charming moments have a cloying insincerity. Rush brilliantly embodies these qualities, which may not be what Sellers fans are hoping for. Here is a good film about a very unpleasant man."

The Life Aquatic with Steve Zissou

Q. In your review of *The Life Aquatic,* you wrote, "Steve Zissou is very tired. I suggest for his epitaph: 'Life for him was but a dreary play; he came, saw, dislik'd, and passed away.'" I was initially taken with your poetic elegance but then realized that this is from Southwark Cathedral in London, from the headstone of the young Mary Buford. Is this an incredible coincidence, or have you been south of the Thames lately?

—Steven Dagdigian, London, formerly Chicago, Illinois

A. I was hoping someone would spot that. Yes, Southwark and its cathedral are two of my favorite places in London.

M Is for *Best*

Q. Your best film of the year has started with an *M* for four years in a row: *Monster's Ball, Minority Report, Monster,* and *Million Dollar Baby.* Just a coincidence?

—Kabir O., Chicago, Illinois

A. If time is hanging heavy on your hands, my friend Carol invites you to join her ukulele club.

The Manchurian Candidate

Q. In your obituary of Janet Leigh, you write that her character's conversation with the Frank Sinatra character in *The Manchurian Candidate,* when they meet on the train, is "beyond peculiar," and you wonder if they are exchanging coded messages, and if she is perhaps his controlling agent. What you and several other critics don't seem to realize is that this dialogue wasn't written especially for the movie—it's in the book! Why didn't you all go and ask author Richard Condon himself while he was alive?

—Mel Narunsky

A. Because it hadn't occurred to me. I've just listened to director John Frankenheimer's commentary track, in which he notes it's "very weird dialogue—very strange." But instead of speculating about the dialogue, he discusses how quickly the scene was shot. Looking at the scene again, I'm struck by the moment when Sinatra's character says, "I'm in the railroad business," and Leigh replies; "If you'll permit me to point out—when you ask that question, you really should say, 'I'm in the railroad line.'" I'm convinced they are both on a hypnotically induced script and that in some way she plays another of his controllers.

Q. I have a question about a moment in *The Manchurian Candidate.* It's in the scene where

Janet Leigh's character comes to the police station to pick up Maj. Ben Marco (Sinatra). Just before Leigh enters, at the far left of the frame, deep in the background, there is a policeman who has his pants down, and is . . . well, I'm not sure *what* he's doing. As Leigh enters, the camera moves right, following her, and the pantsless policeman appears to hitch his pants up and shuffle behind a door. What do you think this character is doing? Is it just a sort of sight gag, designed to slip past pre-freeze-frame audiences? Did Frankenheimer ever comment on it?

—Chris Labarthe, San Francisco, California

A. The scene is exactly as you describe it. Frankenheimer doesn't mention it in his commentary. My best guess: The cop is getting into uniform and is standing outside a locker room; when a woman enters the station, he moves out of sight. What's nice about the moment is that it is entirely gratuitous, put in for no better reason than the amusement of Frankenheimer—and us.

Marlon Brando

Q. I couldn't let Marlon Brando's passing go by without telling this story. Over twenty years ago when I was just starting out as a teacher in Chicago, I had a student who loved Brando. For a writing assignment, I'd promised to find addresses for the stars the kids liked so they could write to them and see who answered. The kid was overjoyed. She told Brando they shared a birthday and that she wanted to become a writer, but couldn't convince her parents she had the goods. The Brando fan received a handwritten letter— one of the sweetest, most encouraging letters a teen could ever receive—about dreams and what really matters in life. And a year later, she received, on her birthday, a hand-signed card, asking her if she was still writing, and for a sample of something she'd written. I've never forgotten it. Brando was and will always be one of my idols, too, and that's how I'll remember him: as I saw him in the eyes of that teenage girl, so many years ago.

—Cynthia Dagnal Myron, Tucson, Arizona

A. One of the reasons Brando was a great star was that he never followed the form book, but lived his life spontaneously, personally, and sincerely.

Melinda and Melinda

Q. I took a few friends—none of whom had ever seen a Woody Allen film—to see *Melinda and Melinda*. They loved it. They said it was the best movie they had seen in 2005. They wondered why no one was talking about the film. Radha Mitchell was brilliant, they said. Goes to show, if this were the first Woody Allen film to be released, we'd be throwing bouquets at his feet. I think of Allen films as a great jazz piece—say, "Kind of Blue." All the movies share a melody, but each is its own instrument putting down a harmony. I am hopeful that Americans will learn again to appreciate one of our great artists, Woody Allen.

—Tim Varner, Toledo, Ohio

A. Oddly enough, much the same thing was said at Cannes about Allen's newest film, *Match Point*. Had it been signed with another name and entered in the competition, some thought, it might have won. Woody has made so many films over so many years that, as A. O. Scott observed a few months ago in the *New York Times*, we have come to take him for granted and even resent his productivity. The challenge in marketing *Match Point* will be to tell potential customers: You think you know all about Woody Allen and you think the returns are in, and has he got a surprise for you.

Million Dollar Baby

Q. I read your review of *Million Dollar Baby*. As a huge Clint Eastwood fan I thought I might take my children even though they are a little young. So I consulted another critic, Movie Mom, and was quite upset when the plot was revealed. I've been robbed!

—Tom Brandenburger, Madison State, South Dakota

A. Movie Mom is Nell Minow, who probably felt the information was useful for parents, but there should have been a "spoiler" warning. Don't let anyone spoil this great film for you.

Q. Billie "The Blue Bear," who is Hilary Swank's most fearsome boxing opponent in

Million Dollar Baby, made a real impression on me. What's her story?

—Greg Nelson, Chicago, Illinois

A. Lucia Rijker is a Dutch African who is a four-time world kickboxing champion and an undefeated junior welterweight champion. Hilary Swank tells me: "Physically she's this incredible powerhouse, and yet she needed to balance out boxing, so she became a Buddhist. 'The boxing Buddha,' I called her."

Q. Unfortunately, I heard Michael Medved review *Million Dollar Baby* on the right-wing Christian show *700 Club* the very day I was going to see it. Ouch. Medved did not really review the film. What he did was deliberately give away vital secrets and surprises, then label the movie as an "issue" piece. I imagine that his intention was to drum up a Red State "moral issue" boycott of the film. I believe most *700 Club* viewers would be moved, entertained, and inspired by this movie and would engage in provocative, "think for themselves" discussions about its story after seeing it. While I'm aware of the subjectivity that is required for film reviews, I found Mr. Medved's technique really disgusting—especially after seeing the movie, which is a masterful piece of work, a sobering, powerful, and moving examination of the human condition. I won't ever forget the characters in *Million Dollar Baby*, and I doubt I'll ever forgive Michael Medved.

—Peter Crooks, Walnut Creek, California

A. Revealing key plot points of a movie very early in its release amounts to a desire to damage the movie. Medved knows better, so what he did was deliberate and unforgivable. Some film critics on the Christian right use their reviews to advance their political agenda (which is their privilege, so I am only observing this). For example, because *The Polar Express* was seen in those circles as being offensive, for reasons I cannot imagine, they obliquely attacked it by pushing *Christmas with the Kranks*, urging their followers to "support" it. The Kranks movie is totally secular—no Jesus in the manger, no hymns, the priest skips midnight Mass to be at the party—but it does contain the message that people who do not celebrate

Christmas are somehow antisocial, anti-American, or haters of the holiday.

Q. In your review of *Virgin* you stated; "The priest in *Million Dollar Baby* is the first good priest I can remember in a film in a long time." I would also like to point out the priest in the film *You Can Count on Me*. As someone who felt a close affinity to the siblings in that film, I was apprehensive when the sister sought the advice of her priest. The scenes between them ended up being my favorites. So often religion is used as a crutch, target, or burden in movies, but the priest in Kenneth Lonergan's film (played by Lonergan himself) was a welcome surprise.

—Mack Lewis, Boise, Idaho

A. Quite true. What I liked about Father Horvak in *Million Dollar Baby* (played by Brian F. O'Byrne) was that he was having an ongoing discussion with the Eastwood character, rather than simply dropping into the plot as a convenience.

Warning: The following letters discuss plot details of Million Dollar Baby.

Q. You think that guarding the secrets of *Million Dollar Baby* to preserve a "key plot point" (as you put it) is of the highest importance. In my opinion, it is the teaching of *Million Dollar Baby* that should have been the focus of your review. Why? Eastwood and all motion picture directors and writers are teachers. They teach us how to dress. How to express ourselves. Whether to smoke. Movies teach the public about acceptable and unacceptable behavior. Movies usually are not propaganda. They do, however, express a moral point of view, a teaching. There is no such thing as a morally neutral movie.

Million Dollar Baby forces us to think, as you wrote. But it does far more. In *Baby*, Eastwood teaches us in a powerful and highly emotional way that sometimes it is morally good to kill a paralyzed person. This teaching is false and the reasons it is false, should be published. You wrote: "A movie is not good or bad because of its content." I write: A movie is good or bad because of many elements. One

of these elements is its content. It's not the ending or any "key plot point"—it's the teaching.

—James A. Colleran, Pastor,
St. Mary of the Lake, Chicago, Illinois

A. Thank you for your eloquent letter. I wrote a little more specifically, "A movie is not good or bad because of its content, but because of how it handles its content." There is a difference. The movies do teach us, as you observe, but in this case do they teach us to agree with what Frankie does, or to question it? I thought it was a great movie about a man who, given who and what he is, does what he thinks is right, but what I think is wrong. I was struck by the positive portrait of the priest in the movie. I believe he is correct when he warns Frankie that his decision will haunt him for the rest of his days. It's interesting that a point of view opposed to Frankie's receives an eloquent voice in the film.

In all the mail I've received regarding this movie, the most moving message came from someone I have quoted before, film critic Jeff Shannon of Seattle, a quadriplegic. He writes:

"Would a viewing of *Million Dollar Baby* necessarily be harmful if the viewers truly value life? My personal feelings about the first year (or years) of paralysis are that you are, essentially, held in a kind of limbo. You don't want to live, but you don't want to die (at least, I didn't), and so you are stuck in a state of spiritual and philosophical stasis, and it is during this crucial time that options begin to come into focus. For every moment of every day for the past twenty-six years, I have had solid, justifiable reasons for hating my life and wanting to die, but by the same token, I got through that 'stasis' period, as the vast majority of paralyzed people do, and despite all the daily pain and hassles of being quadriplegic I do not hate my life and I do not wish to die. I have found, as many people do, a certain grace and benefit from living with the cards I've been dealt. I do not say this out of any kind of personal nobility, because I didn't choose this life and, contrary to many disabled folks, I would prefer to be able-bodied because I am painfully aware, on a daily basis, of all the things that I have lost to paralysis. But as I know, there are options besides death and self-pity, and we forge ahead, leading lives that will, in the long run, reveal the benefits of choosing to stay alive.

"Maggie Fitzgerald, in *Million Dollar Baby*, doesn't feel that way, and for all the reasons you state in your think-piece about the movie, she is entitled to her decision."

Q. Re. your column about the effort to sabotage *Million Dollar Baby*. Not only do the spoiler guys disrespect the audience, but they also profoundly misunderstand the movie. There is nothing "pro-euthanasia" about it. As a man who goes to Mass every day and kneels down to say his prayers every night, Frankie would believe the priest's admonition that he will be "lost forever" if he helps Maggie die. I saw his action as a stunning self-sacrifice. He literally gave up his soul because he loved her and could not refuse her. It seemed to me that he never talked himself out of his moral repugnance; he just took the consequences. It reminded me of the sacrifice that Karl makes in *Sling Blade*, deliberately sending himself back to a psychiatric prison to save a little boy.

—Margaret A. McGurk,
film critic, *Cincinnati Enquirer*

A. You help explain his action despite the remarkable impact of the priest's warning. Tracy Brown of Marina del Rey, California, also writes about Frankie's motivation: "You omitted two important elements in his decision-making process: 1) The trainer resists Maggie's entreaties until after her leg is amputated. For this athlete, her entire identity is tied into her body. 2) After the amputation, Maggie tries to kill herself by biting her tongue to drown in her own blood. She is determined. In the end, Frankie's assistance comes across as an act of mercy, love, and the weakness of a man who can't bear to watch her struggle so hard to die. It is sad and disappointing that people with an agenda insist the movie is taking a stand on an issue, when you are entirely correct that it's a story about these characters, their choices, and pain that doesn't

discriminate between action and no action in the face of tragedy."

Q. Left completely unresolved in *Million Dollar Baby* was what happened to Maggie's opponent after delivering the illegal sucker punch. It is vaguely suggested that the opponent was allowed to retain the contested title. This is ludicrous. After such conduct, no legitimate sanctioning body would simply award a championship to the offending fighter. Even though the conduct occurred in a boxing ring, there would probably be public outcry for criminal charges. I'm not objecting to the presentation of Maggie's story, but I feel there should have been some resolution to the boxing-related issues.

—Alan C. Douglas, Chicago, Illinois

A. Tom Rosenberg of Chicago's Lakeshore Entertainment, one of the film's producers, replies: "The referee did not see the late punches in either bout. Often fighters are hit after the bell without disqualification. This ties in to Frankie's constant advice to Maggie: 'Protect yourself at all times.' Maggie did not win the fight but her mother is incorrect, highlighting her meanness, when she tells Maggie, 'You lost.'"

Q. I have never felt so bad watching a movie as I felt during *Million Dollar Baby*. Eastwood has simply made us love the character, to great emotional effect. Now I can't even think about gathering the courage to watch the movie again. I don't think I can stand the emotional overload once more. My question is, am I overreacting? Are there any movies that you can't bear to watch, too?

—Aydin Çıl, Istanbul, Turkey

A. I edited your message to preserve a plot secret. Yes, I know what you mean. There have been movies that affected me deeply, such as *Do the Right Thing* and *Leaving Las Vegas*, but none so deeply I could not watch them again. However, Mitzi Thomas of Fort Wayne, Indiana writes:

"My husband and I went to *Million Dollar Baby* last Saturday. Unfortunately, we didn't get to see the final fifteen minutes of the film because something happened that still has me puzzled: I passed out. Since fainting is something I've never done under any circumstance, I can only attribute this to the power of the film. My episode came immediately upon the heels of Maggie's final fight. I think I must have been so emotionally invested in the characters that I had a very real and embarrassing reaction. Thankfully, the theater manager and other people I inconvenienced were very kind. The manager even gave my husband two free passes."

Spoiler alert: The following exchange reveals a plot point from Million Dollar Baby.

Q. Michael Medved misled a TV audience when he claimed you said his negative review of *Million Dollar Baby* was "unforgivable." You said it was unforgivable for him to reveal a key plot point in his review. You're right. This is akin to telling everyone that Darth Vader was Luke's father and revealing that Bruce Willis is a ghost in *The Sixth Sense.* (These movies are no longer in release, as opposed to *MDB*.) Medved has every right to disagree with you. I'm not debating that. He has every right to point out what he perceives to be the lack of a moral compass in Hollywood, but he has a responsibility to review the film without divulging its secrets.
—J. David Van Dyke, Buchanan, Michigan

A. Medved actually claims he did not divulge secrets! In an article in the *Washington Times,* he wrote: "Initially, the condemnation centered on my alleged role as a 'spoiler,' suggesting that I had maliciously damaged the commercial prospects for *Million Dollar Baby* by 'describing its plot in great detail' (according to Roger Ebert). As a matter of fact, I never disclosed specifics on the movie's dark surprise, nor indicated which of its endearing characters chose to exercise 'the right to die.'"
Me again. Uh, hello, Michael. Revealing that one of the movie's characters exercises the right to die is specifically revealing an enormous surprise. What if I told you one of the characters in *The Crying Game* was passing as a woman but was really male? Or that one of the characters in *The Sixth Sense* was a ghost?
The movie is about a female boxer. How many intelligent moviegoers would read your comments and ask: "Gee, I wonder which character dies?" At least your article admits, tacitly, that you think it would be wrong to reveal the surprise, even though it is hilarious that you claim you didn't.

Narcissistic and Self-absorbed Characters

Q. I saw both *Closer* and *Sideways* recently. I know that both of these films got rave reviews, but I left both feeling disappointed and wondering "what am I missing?" I didn't like any of the characters in *Closer* and just saw a narcissistic emptiness. I had no idea why they did what they did. In *Sideways* it felt like when I go to a museum—I know I should like it, but I don't. Again I found the characters to be narcissistic and self-absorbed. There was nothing about them I liked, so the movie felt flat to me.
—Stew Frimer, Forest Hills, New York

A. Your doubt is based on the assumption that to be good, a movie must be about characters you like. Both *Closer* and *Sideways* were indeed about characters who were narcissistic and self-absorbed—and brilliantly acted and seen. I believe that a movie is good (or bad) not because of what it is about, but because of how it is about it. I didn't like the heroine of last year's best movie, *Monster,* but I wasn't supposed to. I was deeply touched by its power of observation and its attempt to see into a tortured soul.

National Treasure

Q. You imply in your review of *National Treasure* that it was a rip-off of *The Da Vinci Code.* But *National Treasure* has been in development since 1999, a good four years before Brown's book was published. So what is the true rip-off?
—Jack Brown, Grand Rapids, Michigan

A. Stories with similar themes often come up simultaneously in Hollywood, although by the time *National Treasure* was finally filming, *The Da Vinci Code* was certainly a best-seller. Mainstream historians agree that both stories are balderdash, but I have received more than two hundred e-mails accounting for the differences between the two movies, most of them convinced that one or the other, or both, are based on truth.

For example, Carmen M. Rodero-Scardelis of Redmond, Washington, whose husband is a 32nd degree Master Mason, writes: "There have to be similarities between *The Da Vinci Code* and *National Treasure,* as both of them are based on Freemason stories and the Knights Templar whose stories are centuries old." She recommends two books to me and continues, "There are many versions of what the treasure was. The one that Dan Brown mentions is about Mary Magdalene carrying Jesus's bloodline and His descendants forming one of the royal lines of Europe. A totally different version involves the physical treasures as mentioned in *National Treasure,* and perhaps the most credible one is that the Knights Templar found some secret under King Solomon's temple and used it to blackmail the Catholic Church for many centuries, becoming the second-richest organization in the world until they were successfully persecuted by king and pope in the 1300s. It appears that you are taking Brown's book as an invention of his imagination, when in reality it is based on one of the theories about the Knights Templar—a completely different one than *National Treasure* is based on."

New Directors

Q. Who are some of your favorite new directors from the '80s up? Some of mine are Paul Thomas Anderson, Quentin Tarantino, Christopher Nolan, Joel Coen, Kevin Smith, Tim Burton, Spike Jonze, and Martin Scorsese ... whoops, Scorsese isn't new.
—Jeff Paxton, Chicago, Illinois

A. Scorsese will always be new for me. At the Toronto Film Festival I was reminded of some of the most creative directors of very recent years, including David Gordon Green, whose *Undertow* is as good as his great *George Washington;* Todd Solondz, whose *Palindromes* is likely to be one of the year's most contentious films; Alexander Payne, whose *Sideways* takes the buddy movie and rotates it into a funny, touching consideration of the loneliness of single men; and Lodge Kerrigan, whose *Keane* is another of his films about

people living at the edge of sanity and hanging on for dear life.

Oscars 2005

Q. I remember reading in one of your reviews of the late '90s that you felt Chris Rock should be considered as a host for the Oscars. It seems that you have prophetic insight! What do you think of the news that Rock will host the upcoming awards ceremony?
—Ben McMaster, Sunshine Coast, Australia

A. I feel vindicated. I've been suggesting him for years. He's quick, he has an instinct for the comic angle, and like Billy Crystal he can think on his feet.

Q. Why is it that only very recent movies (i.e., less than four months old) usually get nominated for Academy Awards, especially for Best Picture? The oldest movie this year is *Ray,* released in October. In 2001, all five Best Picture nominees were released in December. Do the members of the Academy really have short memories?
—Robert Karwacki, Coral Springs, Florida

A. It's an intersection of two things: 1) Hollywood actually has an "Oscar season," which opens the weekend after Labor Day at the Toronto Film Festival, where last year such nominees as *Ray, Hotel Rwanda, Finding Neverland, Being Julia, Sideways, Yesterday,* and *The Sea Inside* all premiered. 2) The Oscars are regarded by the studios at least partly as a marketing tool. They naturally prefer to promote films that are still in theaters, or about to be released on DVD, rather than films that have already played out in the marketplace.

Q. How important is it when an actor or actress gets an Academy Award nomination? We are longtime admirers of the actress Virginia Madsen. Will being nominated as Best Supporting Actress have an effect on her career?
—Susan Lake, Urbana, Illinois

A. Elaine Madsen, mother of Virginia and her brother Michael (who played Bill's brother Budd in *Kill Bill: Vol. 2*), was once a Chicago movie critic. She tells me: "We got the happy news a few days ago. And although you have said so kindly 'if there's any justice' Virginia will win, as far as we're concerned, justice happened with that nomination. This puts Virginia on the A-list. She starts a movie with Harrison Ford on February 9 in Vancouver, and another movie really dear to her heart is telling her they'll wait for her to finish the Harrison one so she can do theirs. Only time will tell where all this will take her—but if there is something beyond the nomination, we will name that 'Grace.'"

Q. I found out that award presenters, nominees, and winners receive gift baskets worth a staggering amount of money. This disappoints me because these people do not need these things. The money spent on the gift baskets could feed many starving families, or it could buy medical supplies for doctors in third-world countries.

—Alison Danes, Winfield, Illinois

A. Bruce Davis, executive director of the Motion Picture Academy, replies:

"We don't give baskets to Academy Award nominees, or even to recipients. The baskets are called 'presenter baskets' because they go to the presenters on our show (some of whom, on a given evening, are also nominees, which may have led to your reader's misapprehension). The presenters on the Academy Awards are nearly always prominent actors. Most of them command breathtaking salaries, and if the thirty or so who handle the presenting of the statuettes were to demand even a small fraction of their usual fees, the show wouldn't happen. We couldn't afford them.

"Every presenter on the Oscar show is working for free—not even for Guild minimum. They do it as a contribution to the Academy and to their art form. The baskets are our way of thanking them for that, and for making our shows possible. For many years we gave our thank-you gifts without the world's knowledge, but in recent years the gossip world has learned about the baskets. They've made extravagant guesses about what is in them and, of course, translated all gifts into dollar amounts. The

wilder the estimated cash valuation, the better the story.

"Your questioner may be relieved to know that 'the money spent on [them]' doesn't exist, because the contents of the baskets are donated. I hope she'll find further comfort in the fact that most if not all of the presenters on the Academy Awards are already vigorous supporters of various charitable causes and tend to put their money where their mouths are.

Footnote: There is evidently a recent trend of companies directly bestowing gifts on the individuals nominated for awards of various kinds. The Academy has no role in any such promotions.

Q. As you mention in your "Outguess Ebert" Oscars column, Jamie Foxx was actually the lead in *Collateral*, but was nominated for Best Supporting Actor. I can't help but be reminded of Samuel L. Jackson's getting a mere Best Supporting Actor nomination for *Pulp Fiction* while John Travolta, who did not have a larger part, received a Best Actor nomination. I suppose with *Ray* it was impossible not to give Foxx the Best Actor nomination. Is the mere presence of a white actor in a role of similar size enough to cause a black actor not to be nominated for Best Actor?

—Justin Young, Syracuse, New York

A. Foxx was obviously a leading contender for best actor for *Ray*, so it made sense to position him as supporting actor for *Collateral*, instead of running him against himself. This year's twenty acting nominations include four African-Americans (Don Cheadle, Morgan Freeman, and Foxx twice), a Brit of African descent (Sophie Okonedo), and a Latina, Catalina Sandino Moreno, from Colombia. I thought the Academy showed imagination in reaching beyond the obvious front-runners, especially in naming Okonedo and Moreno.

Q: Martin Scorsese, arguably the greatest living American director, lost the Oscar for Best Director to Clint Eastwood's *Million Dollar Baby*. It was the third time Scorsese has lost to an actor-turned-director (Robert Redford and Kevin Costner were debut directors in 1980 and 1990, respectively). A disappointed Scorsese was quoted as saying, "I got the message," upon losing to Eastwood, joining the ranks of other five-time losers like Robert Altman and Alfred Hitchcock. Is it just me, or will Martin Scorsese be relegated (like the great Sidney Lumet) to the dreaded Lifetime Achievement Award?

—Eric Robert Wilkinson, Oregon City, Oregon

A: There is nothing to dread about the Lifetime Achievement Award, which is harder to win than an actual Oscar. And after directing twenty-five films, Eastwood cannot be described merely as an "actor-turned-director." If he had never acted at all, he would be a major filmmaker.

Yes, Scorsese obviously deserves an Oscar. But I had mixed feelings during the ceremony. I was hoping for Scorsese to win, yet I chose *Million Dollar Baby* as the year's best film, and logic would suggest that its director should be honored. Still, Oscars come and go. Scorsese's reputation is assured, his work will be seen and treasured as long as there are movies, as will Hitchcock's and Altman's, and that is the truest honor the art form can confer upon its practitioners.

The Passion of the Christ

Q. Mel Gibson's *The Passion of the Christ* is to be re-released this week as *The Passion: Recut*. In the ads, Gibson is quoted as saying, "By softening some of its more wrenching aspects, I hope to make my film and its message of love available to a wider audience." Gibson says he will cut about six minutes of his 126-minute film (mostly from the flogging section). I'm not sure that "softening" (his word, not mine) Christ's Crucifixion is really the answer to getting a "wider audience." If Gibson wanted to make an unrelenting film about Christ's passion, that's what has happened with this film, and I'm not sure any editing will do it justice.

—Eric Robert Wilkinson, Oregon City, Oregon

A. Avoiding the usual press-release clichés, Gibson says many people felt the film was too strong for their "Aunt Martha," and he listened to their feelings and has made a version that might be more to their liking. This is his right as the director, and I think it's refreshing that he flatly and without adornment says what he has done and why he has done it.

Phantom Scene Phenomenon

Q. I received Frank Capra's *Mr. Deeds Goes to Town* on DVD. I eagerly put the disc in for viewing but was disappointed. There appear to be a number of scenes missing from the original: 1) an altercation during his society/opera gala, 2) the scheme between the lawyer, the nose-twitching Semple, and his wife, and 3) possibly another scene leading up to Mr. Deeds's giving away plots of land to folks willing to become self-sufficient through farming. Am I crazy, or were these scenes lost in the years before many of these old gems were preserved?

—Sabrina Martin, Batavia, Illinois

A. You may be a victim of the Phantom Scene Phenomenon, in which we "remember" scenes that are described, implied, or happen offscreen. It has been so long since I saw *Mr. Deeds* that I turned for a definitive opinion to Tim Dirks, whose awesome Website (www.filmsite.org) contains detailed descriptions of three hundred great American films, along with many other riches. He writes:

"There is always the possibility that the original theatrical release of *Mr. Deeds Goes to Town* contained some scenes that were edited out or have since been lost. Secondly, the question raises the bigger question of people's memories after viewing a film. I find that when filmgoers try to recollect various scenes from films, their memories invariably play tricks on them, and they cannot recollect accurately. I believe that this person has falsely remembered what the 'original' film contained.

"Regarding the three scenes in question: 1) This scene does exist in my DVD copy of the film. 2) This scene also exists in my DVD copy. The 'altercation' is merely an off-screen action, however. There is no on-screen altercation in the screenplay, either. 3) This is an unclear description, so I can't tell what scene(s) she is remembering. Amazon.com is currently selling a DVD version with a different cover. Whether it is different from my version is something I can't compare."

Playtime

Q. In your recent "Great Movies" review of Jacques Tati's *Playtime*, you cited Noel Burch as observing, "the film has to be seen not only several times, but from several different points in the theater, to be appreciated fully." At the Seattle International Film Festival screening of *Playtime* recently, the presenter told this anecdote: Upon *Playtime's* release, Tati wanted the audience to experience the film as a community and to bring all of their viewpoints (both mental and geographical from within the theater) to the table. So he encouraged audience members to shout out curious visual details and actions as they saw them.

—Erik Hustad, Issaquah, Washington

A. American audiences have been doing that for years.

Polar Express

Q. In *The Polar Express*, is the 113th and Edbrooke Avenue address in the movie actually that of Bob Zemeckis when he was a child?

—Albert R. Croarkin, Wilmington, Illinois

A. Zemeckis was born on the South Side of Chicago, where there is indeed an intersection of 113th and Edbrooke Avenue near Palmer Park in the Pullman district.

Politics and Movies

Q. Re. the Bush campaign's TV ad, "Kerry's Coalition of the Wild-eyed": I linked to a script of the spot and noticed that they are using what's described as a "video clip" from the 2003 Oscars, when Michael Moore berated George W. Bush. I've always understood that the Academy is extremely vigilant about protecting its copyright and permits clips from the Oscars to be rebroadcast only in very special cases (for example, when a presenter or recipient dies). If the Oscar clip really is in the Bush ad, does this mean AMPAS has relaxed its licensing/usage policy? If not, will its leaders demand that Bush and co. cease and desist?

—Stuart Cleland, Evanston, Illinois

A. Bruce Davis, executive director of the Oscars, replies: "Your correspondent is correct that the Academy prefers that the copyrighted footage from its shows be reused—following the brief grace period immediately after each broadcast—only in the context of obituaries or definitive biographies. We are not enthusiastic about clips from our broad-

cast being used in political ads, whether they're blue, red, green, or any other hue, but we've been advised by our attorneys that the clip in the Bush ad is short enough, and oddly enough political enough, to be protected under the fair-use doctrine. Fair use trumps copyright infringement. So while we're not happy about what we regard as a misappropriation of our material, there doesn't seem to be much that we can do about it beyond grousing in the columns of movie critics when we get the chance."

Q. You once said that movies must not be judged by the politics behind them, and you mentioned *The Birth of a Nation* and *The Triumph of the Will* as examples. I don't think that any human being can apply that concept 100 percent. Let's imagine a masterpiece directed by a radical terrorist (a modern issue that we can relate to, unlike racism in the first half of the twentieth century). Now, can you really be fully neutral? I'd love to say yes, I'd love to play the role of fair critic, but I don't think it's in our nature even if we say it is.

—Hazim Ibrahim, Riyadh, Saudi Arabia

A. I do in fact sometimes judge movies by the politics behind them, but I try to make my politics clear when I do so—as in my review of *Fahrenheit 9/11*. Remaining neutral is not the task of a critic, who is expected to take a position. I think what I was trying to say is that a work of art can express artistic greatness even if it is in the service of a cause one despises. *Triumph of the Will* exalts Nazism, but it also helps us to understand how Hitler rose to power through the exploitation of nationalistic propaganda. And it helps show us how documentary films can involve events that were staged for the screen, or exist only on the screen.

Q. I greatly enjoy your reviews and the thoughtful observations they contain. However, I get a little worried about the strength of your argument in your review of *Unleashed* when you make the case for women being able to stir a man's humanity by using Ann Coulter as your example. That is the same person who claimed women should bear arms but not be able to vote.

—C. Perla, Miami, Florida

A. Wouldn't you sleep more soundly at night knowing Ann Coulter was in the Army and not in a voting booth?

President Dann Gire

Q. You ended your recent review of *Harold & Kumar* by quoting advice you got from Dann Gire, president of the Chicago Film Critics' Association, then writing: "Still another reason our leader's photograph should be displayed in every government office and classroom." I just didn't get this joke. Was this a reference to a) Dubya, or b) Dann Gire? If there's a laugh there, I'd like to laugh, too.

—Miguel E. Rodriguez, Tampa, Florida

A. There is only one leader mentioned in the review, and that is President Gire.

Princess Diaries 2

Q. I often get your jokes, but today you threw me for a loop. In your *Princess Diaries 2* review you wrote of the possible romance between the queen and chief of security as "a loving couple kept asunder, when they should be sundering." Since *asunder* means into parts or apart from each other and *sunder* means to break apart or separate, are you trying to say they are "a loving couple kept apart from each other, when they should be breaking apart"?

—Troylene Ladner, Jersey City, New Jersey

A. I wasn't just trying; I actually said it. Just part of my lonely crusade to free *sunder* from its negative connotations.

Product Placement

Q. Just watched the new trailer for the re-release of Jean Luc Godard's *Masculine-Feminine,* the movie that makes the famous statement "We are the children of Marx and Coca-Cola." The new trailer says it's a movie about Paris, sex, and "the Pepsi generation." No children of Marx and Coca-Cola here. Then, at the end of the trailer there's a copyright notice for Pepsi—followed by the statement that *Paris* and *sex* are still in the public domain. What is going on here? Did Coke forbid the mention of its product? If not, why would they substitute Pepsi?

—Jim Emerson, Seattle, Washington

A. Bruce Goldstein, of Film Forum and Rialto Pictures, replies: "The Pepsi disclaimer at the end of the trailer was a little joke of mine. No one asked us to add the copyright notice, nor does Pepsico even know about it (maybe they will after reading your column). And there was no interference by the Coca-Cola Company. Originally I tried working 'the children of Coca-Cola' into the trailer but felt it was too academic and a little off-putting. However, in the movie Chantal Goya is asked if she's a member of 'the Pepsi generation,' so it's a fair reference. (Her answer: 'J'adore Pepsi.')"

Quentin vs. Spike

Q. After thoroughly enjoying *Kill Bill: Vol. 2* and reading your review of *She Hate Me,* I was reminded of the feud between Tarantino and Spike Lee. Who do you think is a better filmmaker, the man who can take an idea with no substance and still make the audience hang off the edge of its seat, or the man who incessantly crams his own social message into every frame and disregards the opinions of anyone else?

—Eric James, Enfield, Connecticut

A. Do I have to choose? Your first example would include a director like Hitchcock, who even invented a name—the MacGuffin—for the "idea with no substance." Your second example would include filmmakers as diverse as Lars von Trier, Andrei Tarkovsky, Robert Bresson, Yasujiro Ozu, Ingmar Bergman, Spike Lee, and Michael Moore. I gather you think the director in the second example is doing something all wrong, but of course it all depends on whether the film is any good. Remember Ebert's First Law, which admirably encompasses both categories: "A movie is not about what it is about, but about how it is about it."

Quotes in Ads

Q. I read in a Reuters news article that you, Richard Roeper, MPAA President Jack Valenti, and executives from Lion's Gate and IFC Films had a conference call debating the use in *Fahrenheit 9/11* ads of Roeper's quote "Everyone in the country should see this film." Valenti upheld the MPAA ruling against the quote because the film was rated R, meaning not everyone *can* see it. Why couldn't Roeper have just contributed a new quote, right then and there, such as, "Everyone who can should see this film"? Wouldn't that have satisfied all parties?

—Chris Tong, Kelseyville, California

A. Maybe, but it wasn't what Roeper said, and we don't supply quotes for ads; they must come from words actually used in our reviews. I had a similar experience after my *Whale Rider* review, which said, "Take the kids and they'll see a movie that will touch their hearts and minds." The MPAA objected to that quote in the ads. They said a film with a PG-13 rating can't be marketed to children—even though I said *take* the kids, not send them in alone. As Valenti explained the *Fahrenheit 9/11* ruling to the rest of us on the conference call, I realized he would win the argument, because the studios have indeed signed an agreement to follow the MPAA's rules and regulations, which clearly say that films rated PG-13 or older cannot be advertised for the whole family. The MPAA cannot be blamed for enforcing the rules, but perhaps the studios should re-evaluate the guidelines.

Racing Stripes

Q. In your review of *Racing Stripes* you wrote about the love affair between a horse and a zebra: ". . . the movie wisely avoids the question of what would happen should they decide to begin a family." Their offspring would be called a zebroid, a cross between a zebra and a horse.

—Bennett Haselton, Seattle, Washington

A. As Michael Caine likes to say, "A lot of people don't know that."

Ripley's Game

Q. I just rented the excellent John Malkovich-Dougray Scott thriller *Ripley's Game,* and my question is, why didn't this ever show up in theaters? It's riveting and the performances are brilliant. It's one thing for something awful to be relegated to video shelves, but this is a fine film featuring an Oscar-worthy turn by Malkovich that earned a lengthy write-up in the *New Yorker.* It's the kind of class act that deserves a late-year

Oscar run, not a quick turn onto the Blockbuster rack.

—J. D. Frankfort, Los Angeles, California

A. Richard Roeper and I admired *Ripley's Game* and reviewed it on the show, despite its straight-to-DVD status. A week ago, my wife and I hosted a benefit for Chicago's Steppenwolf Theater at which the movie was shown and John Malkovich and producer Russell Smith discussed it. This is a movie that would have made my Best 10 list, had it been released. Directed by Liliana Cavani (*The Night Porter*), it is a masterful evocation of Patricia Highsmith's Ripley character, more true to her vision than *The Talented Mr. Ripley* (1999) and the equal of René Clément's great *Purple Noon* (1960). Smith said he thought the film fell through the cracks because at the time New Line was obsessed with *Lord of the Rings.* Internal studio politics may also have been involved.

Rodney Dangerfield

Q. I wrote you once before about the Motion Picture Academy's refusing to admit Rodney Dangerfield to membership. Now that Rodney has died, does he still get no respect?

—Charlene Smith, Dubuque, Iowa

A. Dangerfield told me in 1995 he had applied for membership in the actor's branch of the Academy. "I got a letter from Roddy McDowell, the head of the actor's branch. He wrote that I should 'improve my craft' and apply again later. Hey, I'm seventy-three years old. What am I gonna do? Apply again when I'm 104?" Certainly he qualified, with pictures ranging from *Caddyshack* to *Natural Born Killers.*

Q. Re Rodney Dangerfield and the Academy. I heard that the dipsticks at the Academy later decided that Mr. Dangerfield was in fact amusing and offered him a membership. Mr. Dangerfield declined, being the dignified class act he was (not counting *Meet Wally Sparks*).

Another thing: In your review of *Hijacking Catastrophe,* you drew an analogy of Larry punching Curly, who retaliates by punching Moe. Ignoring any comments on the aptness of your observation, even the most casual

Stooge observer knows that Moe initiated the punches, pokes, slaps, and eye gouges. To the extent that punches traveled down the line, it would be Moe punching Larry, who then punched Curly (or Shemp—nobody cares about Curly Jo). May you forget to place your open hand against your forehead on the next two-finger eye poke.

—Bill Abendroth, Portland, Oregon

A. You are right about the Stooges, whom I may not have studied as carefully as I should have.

As for Rodney Dangerfield's not becoming a member of the Academy, Bruce Davis, executive director of the Motion Picture Academy, tells me:

"Dangerfield was proposed at one point for membership but was not one of the candidates accepted that year by the committee of actors who make the decisions for the actor's branch. It's not at all unusual for candidates not to be accepted on their first trip to the plate, but Mr. Dangerfield evidently took the news badly, a somewhat surprising reaction for a man who built a career out of the lack of respect the world paid him. In any case, he was reproposed at the next meeting and accepted. He never responded to the invitation, though, so he was never on our roster."

Russ Meyer

Q. I was saddened to hear about the passing of Russ Meyer, who should be credited with getting sexually explicit (but not hard-porn) films into the mainstream. I recently watched his *Good Morning . . . and Goodbye* (1967) and noted a very young Don Johnson in the cast. Is this the same Don Johnson who later became a star in the 1980s with *Miami Vice* and film? It sure looks like him.

—Scott Favareille, Pinole, California

A. Janice Cowart of RM Films says no, not the same Don Johnson.

The Sea Inside

Q. In your review of *The Sea Inside*, about Ramón Sampedro, a quadriplegic who wants to die, you said: "If a man is of sound mind and not in pain, how in the world can he decide he no longer wants to read tomorrow's newspaper?" I say: What is the point of living a life where one is always going to be dependent on others? That is the kind of life that is useless and is, therefore, not worth living.

—Hans Bottenberg, Waterloo, Iowa

A. We are all dependent on others every moment of every day, and few of us would live for long if dropped into the wilderness. Nor would we be useful there, except to ourselves. Most of the contributions we make to each other are created with our minds. The greatest physicist since Einstein is physically helpless. Heather Rose could move one finger of one hand, and she wrote and starred in *Dance Me to My Song*, a great film. Seattle writer and film critic Jeff Shannon recently wrote me: "Despite considerable pain and anguish for a variety of quad-related reasons, I agree with Ramón Sampedro's cause but I cannot share his attitude for one simple reason: I look at life the way I look at a good movie—I can't wait to see what happens next."

Schrader's *Exorcist*

Q. *Taxi Driver* scribe Paul Schrader's long-shelved version of *The Exorcist: The Beginning* is finally seeing the light of day at the International Festival of Fantastic Film in Brussels. Given the lukewarm reception toward Renny Harlin's version, is there any chance for success for Schrader's more restrained, theologically terrifying film here in the States?

—Chris Lettera, Youngstown, Ohio

A. The Brussels festival says, "When the financial backers of *Exorcist: The Beginning* saw that Paul Schrader had directed a psychological horror film and not the expected special-effects extravaganza, they hired Renny Harlin to reshoot the entire picture." The Harlin version opened in August 2004 to bad reviews (89 percent unfavorable on the Tomatometer, a 30 score at Metacritic) and moderate business ($41 million in the United States, against an estimated budget of $80 million for the two versions).

Schrader writes me: "The first print was struck last night and sent directly to Brussels for the premiere March 18. The first time I'll see it on screen is then. I'm working on getting a video copy for myself. Warner Bros. has apparently reversed its position and will now give the film a limited release in April or May, albeit only if it is positioned as a 'new' film. But that can change."

Q. I noticed that you did not review the prequel *The Exorcist: The Beginning* which came out last year. Do you have something against the movies that continue the story of the original *Exorcist*?

—Dan Harris, Brookings, South Dakota

A. It was not previewed for critics, and I never caught up with it. I have, however, just seen Paul Schrader's original *Dominion: Prequel to the Exorcist,* which was shelved by the studio, reportedly because it was "too serious." Renny Harlin was hired to make a version that replaced three of the four leads, spent $50 million on top of Schrader's $30 million, and scored only 11 percent on the Tomatometer. The Schrader version is a very good film, strong and true. It is intelligent about spiritual matters, is sensitive to the complexities of its characters, and does something risky and daring in this time of jaded horror movies: It takes evil seriously.

Sean and Chris and Jude

Q. Having heard of what Sean Penn said in defense of Jude Law, but missing what Chris Rock had to say about Law during his opening monologue at this year's Oscars . . . what happened, and how did the audience take it?

—Meursalt Mann, Los Angeles, California

A. Rock's monologue poked fun at actors and casting choices, and accused Law of being in every movie last year (he was in six). Rock then advised filmmakers to always go for their first choice, ending a string of examples with, "You want Denzel and all you can get is me? Wait!"

Sean Penn, who later made *All the King's Men* with Jude Law, came onstage as a presenter and defended Law as a fine actor. Backstage, asked if he and Penn had spoken afterward, Rock told reporters, "I just hugged Sean. He said because he's working with Jude Law in a movie right now, that's why he felt the need to say something." Rock was asked, "How did you feel when he said it?" He said, "Oh, boy, I got another joke."

Yes, but Rock missed the obvious zinger. He should have come onstage and said, "I really, really feel bad and want to apologize for what I said about Jude Law. Producers—you want Jude Law and all you can get is Sean Penn? Wait!"

Sex and Violence

Q. A recent news item reported, "Violence, sex, and profanity in movies increased significantly between 1992 and 2003, while ratings became more lenient, according to a new Harvard study." They seem to be examining two related phenomena (lax ratings and graphic content). I see two possible scenarios, the first being that movies are indeed increasing in graphic quality/quantity. The second is that movie content has not changed, relatively, but instead films are not being rated appropriately (e.g., what was appropriate for R is now okay for PG-13). I guess I'm wary of this study's possible politics and underlying agenda. Do you really feel that films are becoming more violent, or do you see the increase in violence as a misperception based on a crappy rating system?

—Shawne Malik, St. John's, Newfoundland, Canada

A. There is less "real" violence (as opposed to CGI fantasy violence) in movies today than in the 1970s—and a lot less sex and nudity. At the same time, I have the subjective sense that the ratings system has become more permissive or porous. The studios put enormous pressure on the MPAA to give them ratings that maximize their audiences. The NC-17 rating was the first victim, and now the studios are avoiding the R. I agree with the Harvard study that there is more violence and profanity in PG-13 movies. A long-term result of this trend may be a loss of serious content for adults, as more movies position themselves for the desirable teenage-boy market.

Q. I watched *Metropolis* (1926) recently. In the second scene, where the sons and daughters of the powerful are frolicking in the garden, we see the bare back of a woman. I immediately thought of the recent flap over seeing very much the same thing during an opening for Monday Night Football. What was acceptable in a silent film of 1926 is not acceptable in 2004 America?

—Tim Stack, Westminster, Colorado

A. You know, I'll bet *any* scene from *Metropolis* would have drawn protests from football fans.

She Hate Me

Q. In your review of Spike Lee's *She Hate Me* you predicted that your quasi-positive review wouldn't match the general consensus of your fellow critics. Your review seemed to believe that to evaluate a film you must first evaluate the director. This is a huge miscalculation. A work should not be viewed with the director in mind but should stand alone. If you're going to use preposterous material, make it clear within the film that this material is being approached as such (e.g., *Kill Bill*). Is it actually your suggestion that we view movies through the eyes of the director?

—Jayel Labe, Hershey, Pennsylvania

A. Not at all. We should view them through our own eyes. The real problem is with directors who try to view movies through our eyes, instead of their own. They make disposable multiplex fodder that grinds down the intelligence of the audience, teaching it to be the passive receiver of formula dreck. Directors like Lee and Tarantino may have varying degrees of success with their films, but they're always trying to engage all of their intelligence; they challenge us with the form of their work as well as its content. Better a movie that tries and fails but leaves us with something to think about, than a movie without a thought in its empty little head.

Sin City

Q. Can you shed some light on the conflict between the Directors Guild and Robert Rodriguez? More specifically, why does the DGA have its "one director, one film" policy—and why could it not be relaxed for *Sin City*, when it has been waived in other seemingly similar situations (Coen brothers and other siblings; collaborative projects like *Four Rooms*)?

—Laurie Morgan, Sacramento, California

A. Rodriguez wanted to share directing credit with Frank Miller, author of the *Sin City* comic books, and with Quentin Tarantino, who directed one scene in the film. Told by the DGA he couldn't do that, he indeed asked about other teams, such as the Farrellys, the Hugheses, and the Wachowskis, and was told they always worked as a team, and joined the guild as a team. Exceptions could not be made for individual films. At that point, he resigned from the DGA.

Q. Lately some people have been complaining that *Sin City* was the No. 1 movie in the country the same weekend the pope passed away. I'm guessing they are referring to the violence and sexual content of the picture, which could be mistaken for anti-Catholicism, even though it is a great film. My question is, where do you stand on this issue and why?

—Ryan Graham, Yellowknife, Northwest Territories, Canada

A. I think it is more of a coincidence than an issue. I did get a lot of messages saying my review should have underlined the level of violence in the movie. They were correct: I became absorbed in my discussion of the film's visual style and its roots in film noir and comic books. The violence did not seem real to me, as it did, for example, in *Monster*. It had no psychological depth or realistic meaning but was simply the medium that the genre swims in. Still, my review should have given a better idea of the film's content. Readers might also have been well advised to note the MPAA rating ("Rated R for sustained strong stylized violence, nudity, and sexual content including dialogue").

Sky Captain and the World of Tomorrow

Q. As a freelancer for the *Seattle Times*, I recently interviewed Kerry Conran, the writer-director of *Sky Captain and the World of Tomorrow*. When we discussed the film's budget, he quoted a figure—off the record—that was far below the $70 million that's been quoted in dozens of reviews and articles. While I'm familiar with the ego-soothing spin strategies that studios use to inflate a film's budget, in the case of *Sky Captain* wouldn't it make more sense if Paramount had actually boasted about the film's relatively modest budget, since it represents a digital milestone?

—Jeff Shannon, Lynnwood, Washington

A. I heard the budget was not a million miles away from $38 million, which is the advertising budget for some films in that genre. So *Sky Captain* will win back its cost and turn a profit despite a relatively tame reception at the box office. Many readers tell me I liked it more than they did, and they accuse me of being blinded by its style, as if there's a surplus of style in today's movies.

Q. I am surprised by your acceptance of director Kerry Conran's grave-robbing use of archival footage of Laurence Olivier in *Sky Captain.* As someone who (like me) objected to the use of footage of Fred Astaire in TV ads, how can you possibly countenance the cheap and disrespectful depiction Olivier receives in this film? Your assertion that "surely every actor on his deathbed, entering the great unknown, hopes he has not given his last performance" is cheap and unworthy. Olivier did not choose to give this performance. And surely as a mark of respect to a man who is generally considered to be the greatest actor of his generation, we can let his amazing body of work stand. In a film that has demonstrated that we don't actually need sets or location shots, can we at least allow that we need actors? Or at the very least the consent of the actors to use their talents?

—Matthew Weedman, Van Nuys, California

A. We are in deep philosophical waters here. I disapprove of the unworthy use of the images of dead actors, as when Fred Astaire was shown dancing with a Dust-Buster and John Wayne was shilling for a savings and loan. But certain kinds of reuse make artistic sense, as in the case of *Sky Captain,* where (spoiler warning!) the whole point is that the character had been dead for years, and to use a dead actor to portray him underlines the point. I presume they had the permission of the Olivier estate, which must have agreed.

Q. I really enjoyed *Sky Captain,* but I think I know why it failed at the box office. The sepia tone was fatal to the movie's success. Sometimes people who appreciate movies love a new style. Yet for the vast majority of people, a new innovative style distracts from the story line.

—Cal Ford, Corsicana, Texas

A. I wonder if you're correct. I thought the color was the perfect choice for the material, evoking as it did the rotogravure newspaper sections of the period, but of course no one under forty has seen rotogravure, and wit and style can turn off slack-jawed action fans. I've been saying for years that black-and-white is more mysterious and evocative than color, but lots of people continue to "hate" it, little realizing how much that reveals about their taste.

Spider-Man 2

Q. In your review of *Spider-Man 2* you noted: "One of the keys to the movie's success must be the contribution of novelist Michael Chabon to the screenplay; Chabon understands in his bones what comic books are, and why." While this may be true, and Chabon contributed a draft, the story that was used should be credited to Alfred Gough and Miles Millar. As they stated in an interview: "All the writers contributed something, but to us there were three versions of this movie: the one that we wrote, one that David Koepp wrote, and one that Michael Chabon wrote. If you look at all three, ours was absolutely the one they went with. Michael Chabon, whom we'd never met, called us and told us that he was outraged. He thought we deserved credit." I don't mean to write off Chabon's contributions to the story, but rather to raise notice for two writers who also elevated the superhero genre on TV, with *Smallville.*

—Adam Lenhardt, Slingerlands, New York

A. Screenplay credits often conceal and obscure where the real credit should go. Knowing Chabon's wonderful novel, I singled him out, and I am pleased to have your input about Gough and Millar.

Spoilers

Q. I see your point in disagreeing with Michael Medved for revealing the plot of *Million Dollar Baby.* But didn't you basically do the same thing in your review of *The Girl Next Door?*

—John Fitch, Lake in the Hills, Illinois

A. Yes, I did. Right there in the first two sentences of my review, I wrote: "The studio should be ashamed of itself for advertising *The Girl Next Door* as a teenage comedy. It's a nasty piece of business, involving a romance between a teenage porn actress and a high school senior." It was supposed to come as a surprise that she was a porn actress.

On the other hand, in the movie's trailer we hear the line, "Matt, she's a porn star, okay, dude?" And on the film's Website, we read, "When Matthew discovers this perfect 'girl next door' is a one-time porn star, his sheltered existence begins to spin out of control." So the cat was already out of the bag.

With *Million Dollar Baby,* the plot was not revealed in the advertising, but was a closely held secret, and Medved and Rush Limbaugh went out of their way to reveal the details long before the movie was in general release. I think they were deliberately trying to harm it.

Star Wars Episode III

Q. I've been revisiting the original *Star Wars* trilogy in preparation for *Episode III.* I was shocked to see at the end of *Return of the Jedi* the ethereal image of the older Anakin Skywalker replaced by Hayden Christensen's younger version. The change didn't make any sense, any more than if George Lucas had replaced Sir Alec Guinness with Ewan McGregor. I didn't mind all the other little tweaks, but this left me feeling cheated. More than that, don't you think it's disrespectful to Sebastian Shaw?

—Jimmy Jacobs, Columbia, South Carolina

A. I turn to a modern Jedi Master, *Sun-Times* tech columnist Andy Ihnatko, who replies:

"Well, if it's disrespectful to Sebastian Shaw—who played the role for exactly one scene in the entire double-trilogy—then it must be n times more disrespectful to David Prowse and James Earl Jones, who portrayed Vader's body and soul in every other scene of the Middle Trilogy, except for that one. I think it's actually a little poetic that Anakin goes off to Jedi Valhalla in the form he had before he 'turned.'

"I encourage the questioner to transfer his outrage to places where Lucas's revisionism merits no lesser reaction. Mr. Lucas, I'm sorry, but look: Apparently, I know more about these characters than you do because I know you got it right the first time. Han Solo *didn't* shoot Greedo after being fired upon. He knew he was about to be hauled back to Jabba the Hutt and certain death, so he just shot him while the idiot was talking (see Tucco's advice in *The Good, The Bad, and The Ugly*). Boba Fett isn't just some flunky in the service of a crime lord on a dirtwater planet. He got involved in the Solo affair for the reward, he hung around for a while afterward because hey, cool, there were dancing girls and free drinks on the sand barge, and if he hadn't gotten eaten by the Sarlacc, he'd have been outta there, kicking the sand off his boots and pursuing his next bounty somewhere in the next star system."

Q. How you can give the new *Star Wars* movie three and a half stars when you write, "The dialogue throughout the movie is once again its weakest point: The characters talk in what sounds like basic English, without color, wit, or verbal delight, as if they were channeling Berlitz." Doesn't this make it a movie deserving no more than two stars? Just because a fabulously wealthy producer can afford the best in special effects, does that warrant a rating close to perfection?

—Robert Cavanaugh, Wheaton, Illinois

A. I got a lot of messages saying there was a disconnect between my star rating and my review. Perhaps there was. Star ratings are the bane of my existence, because I consider them to be relative and yet by their nature they seem to be absolute. *Star Wars: Episode III* returned to the space-opera roots of the original film and succeeded on that level, and for that I wanted to honor it, while regretting that it did not succeed at the levels of intelligence and wit as it did on the levels of craftsmanship and entertainment.

Q. In your review of *Star Wars: Revenge of the Sith,* you wrote that the voice of Gen. Grievous "sounds curiously wheezy considering the general seems to use replacement

parts." I would like to clarify why he wheezes. Cartoon Network within the past year ran a series of short cartoons called *Star Wars: Clone Wars*. It was set in the time period leading up to *Episode III*. In the final chapter (No. 25), as Grievous makes his escape with Palpatine, he encounters Mace Windu. Windu uses the Force to crush Grievous' chest cavity, causing the "wheezing." So by the time Palpatine is secure aboard the starship, *Episode III* has begun and, realistically, only a few hours have passed.
—Leonard Blackman, Las Vegas, Nevada

A. I have received countless explanations of Grievous' condition from readers who go into almost theological detail in their analysis. If they are now expected to incorporate information from the Cartoon Network series into their interpretations, I fear their heads may explode. Continuity is not everything. I grew up watching Captain Video, on which three rocks were rearranged to indicate they had left one planet and were now on another.

Q. In your review of *Star Wars: Revenge of the Sith*, you said it is not explained why Darth Vader is several inches taller. Obi Wan cut off Anakin's legs at the knee during their battle. Vader's legs in the suit are appendages.
—Brian Killian, Berwyn, Illinois

A. We should send Gen. Grievous the name of his surgeon.

Q. There is a pants/no-pants continuity error in Padme's maternity getup when she arrives on the lava planet. How do such errors creep into movies made with such budgets and so many eyes checking and approving things?
—Mark Suszko, Springfield, Illinois

A. I cannot recall this detail, but as you describe it, it certainly sounds like the kind of detail that should be noticed.

Q. Is George Lucas a knowing economic terrorist? Lucas *knew* the effect releasing the last *Star Wars* movie would have on the United States economy. The movie was released on a working day. The effect was a $627 million loss in American productivity. The box-office take was $158.5 million. That leaves

a $468.5 million cost to the U.S. economy. But that's not the end of the loss. Each day Lucas is losing $1.5 million to pirates—a capital cost to his investors of $6 million in four days and climbing. The loss could and should have been avoided by release on a Saturday or Sunday, and simultaneous distribution to television, sales, and rentals. The question becomes: would George Lucas really damage the economy to make a point of his hatred for the Republican Party and President George Bush?
—D. L. Graham, San Diego, California

A. And what happened to Padme's pants?

Stephen King

Q. Stephen King has a column in *Entertainment Weekly* where he basically rants how critics pan average films like *Troy* and overpraise good films like *Spider-Man 2*. He makes a pointed reference at you and your thumbs, claiming that one thumb is tucked away where the sun don't shine. Kind of a cheap shot, if you ask me.
—Paul West, Seattle, Washington

A. There is a much greater distance between *Troy* and *Spider-Man 2* than between "average" and "good," but when it comes to areas where the sun don't shine, I bow to King's superior expertise.

King's *On Writing*, by the way, is one of the most intelligent, engaging, and useful books ever written by a writer about his craft. In his *EW* article, he says the four-star rating should be reserved for classics like *The Godfather*, and criticizes me for putting it on a par with *Spider-Man 2*. I consider stars to be relative to genre, not absolute; since *Spider-Man 2* was one of the best movies ever made about a comic book superhero, I gave it four stars. If stars were absolute and four stars were calibrated at the level of *The Godfather* or *Citizen Kane*, there might be years without a single four-star movie.

Theo van Gogh

Q. A terrible thing has happened. You've probably heard that Theo van Gogh, a fine and most courageous filmmaker, was murdered by a Muslim extremist in Holland. I worked closely with him throughout the years. I saw him the night before I left Holland and we laughed about his bodyguards! Theo dared to speak out, dared to face the truth as he felt and perceived it. His aim was not to entertain or to reap success and glory for himself, but to transmit a message of purpose through our medium. What a tragedy that he could not escape the fate of all great humanitarians—to be sacrificed. I'm devastated by this blow. It doesn't happen—filmmakers being killed because they have something to say and dare to speak! But it did and the world has moved one step closer to the abyss. May he rest in peace.

> —Paul Cox, Melbourne, Australia

A. Van Gogh's film, named *Submission,* is online at ifilm.com. The list of living directors who honor the cinema by remaining true to themselves in their work has been tragically shortened by one more name. But it still contains your name, Paul, and I am pleased that I wrote about your *A Woman's Tale* last Sunday as my Great Movie.

Turn Up the Lights!

Q. I recently saw a film at a drive-in theater in Tucson that I had already seen in a "regular" theater. Okay, I'll admit it was *Alien vs. Predator.* At the drive-in, I noticed that the film was a *lot* darker than it had been previously. Since it takes place two thousand feet underground in an abandoned pyramid, it is already a dark film, and the added darkness made it incomprehensible at certain points. You've discussed the problem of under-lit films before. Could this problem be even worse at drive-ins? After all, with fewer tickets being sold, the theater managers have less incentive to provide quality cinematic displays.

> —David O'Brien, Redwood City, California

A. It's not a problem limited to any kind of theater, but caused by shortsighted, greedy, stupid management. Many theater owners continue to believe that if they turn down the power of the expensive projector bulb, the bulb's life span will be lengthened. As the AM has tirelessly explained, this is not true. The only result is that moviegoers see a dim and washed-out picture, and they have little rea-

son to return to that theater. Martin Scorsese has been especially active in sending assistants with light meters to theaters, to measure the actual strength of the light falling on the screen. Some films are legitimately dark, such as his own classic *Taxi Driver,* but you cannot appreciate the play of light and shadow if a dimmed bulb obscures everything.

Q. I know well your well-deserved attacks on theater managers who don't have bulbs at full brightness. So when I was hired as the general manager of the Grand Cinema, a non-profit movie theater in Tacoma, Washington, I resolved not to be one of those managers. One of my first questions to my projectionist was whether we have the bulbs of our three screens at full power. We don't. And five months later we still don't. As he tells me, our theaters are so small (no more than fifty or sixty feet from projector to screen) that having our bulbs at full power would burn our screens and wash out a picture. I've relied on his judgment, but I think it's time to check this. Is there any evidence to suggest that a bulb should be dimmed slightly or significantly if playing in a very small theater?

> —Erik Hanberg, Tacoma, Washington

A. Steve Kraus of the Lake Street Screening Room in Chicago, who is a scholar of film projection, tells me: "Yes, it is possible to be too bright. Of course you can't literally burn the screen, but the picture could be washed out and uncomfortable to watch. There are many factors in picture brightness, but there is no reason for guessing. A technician with a light meter can read the reflected brightness of the screen with the projector running without film. It should be 16 footlamberts. I would recommend the forum section at film-tech.com, where he can get detailed advice about his particular equipment."

Q. You noted that when you saw *Seed of Chucky* the film looked dim and murky because there was not enough light on the screen. I would like to clear up why many theaters have bulbs turned far too low and seem to be lacking ambition to fix the problem. Simply put, for the most part the projectionists don't know any better. As a theater manager of four years and a certified projector tech, I can assure you of this: Most individual theaters do not even have an actual projectionist on hand. Most of the time they train managers and sometimes ushers. Outside of that, general maintenance is a complete mystery to them. They must rely on their appointed projector tech, who lives up to fifty miles away and is responsible for upward of twenty theaters. Most of the time these techs are under the misguided notion that turning the wattage down will somehow extend the life of the bulb (if it does, I have yet to see any improvement). Blame the corporate mentality that says, "You don't need to be fully trained, as long as people keep paying."

—Mitch Ehrhardt, Norfolk, Virginia

A. What amazes me is that audiences will sit like sheep through a movie with lousy projection. If the picture is not bright and sharp and a pleasure to watch, chances are the fault is in the projector booth. Although some scenes in some movies are intended to be dim or murky, the test is with the Coming Attractions, which are intended to look terrific. In the past I have quoted projection expert Steve Kraus, who says there is *no evidence* that turning down the bulb lengthens its life. Theaters that charge in the region of ten dollars for admission owe it to their customers to show them a good-looking movie.

TV-to-Movies

Q. In your review of *Thunderbirds*, you wrote: "I had never heard of the series and, let's face it, neither have you." This is one of those situations where there is a clear pop-cultural disconnect between the United States and other parts of the world, because the Thunderbirds are quite iconic in Britain, Australia, Japan, and a few other places. In Australia, when I grew up the original television episodes were shown and reshown endlessly, and Thunderbirds merchandising items have been sold in huge quantities for forty years now and are extremely lucrative.

—Michael Jennings, London, England

A. I was wrong to imply the series never played in America. Jim Carey of Aurora, Illinois, writes: "I was born in '63 and I remember Thunderbirds from WGN or WFLD. I think they played the series a couple of years after it first aired. But . . . will Hollywood revisit Clutch Cargo?"

The Village

Q. M. Night Shyamalan's affection for *The Twilight Zone* is well documented, so I can't help but wonder if the so-called "surprise" in *The Village* wasn't at least partially borrowed from "A Hundred Yards Over the Rim," a *Twilight Zone* episode written by Rod Serling that starred Cliff Robertson and originally aired on April 7, 1961. The exact nature of the surprise and the way it's presented (also prompted by a medical emergency, by the way) are nearly identical to what Shyamalan serves up so unconvincingly in *The Village*. You could argue that there are no new ideas, only new ways of presenting them, and of course filmmakers borrow from their pop-cultural inspirations all the time. But it seems rather sad that someone of Shyamalan's proven talent would borrow so obviously, then turn a good idea (like Serling's) into—let's face it—a really bad one that collapses under scrutiny.

—Jeff Shannon, Lynnwood, Washington

A. *The Village* stirred up a lot of activity in the Answer Man's world, with 162 readers passionately defending or attacking it in about equal numbers. Some of its defenders argued that the "surprise ending" was beside the point. Ben Angstadt of Irmo, South Carolina, wrote: "So did you totally miss the point that *The Village* was about the politics of terror and George W. Bush, or did you just not care?" And Erik Goodwyn of Cincinnati wrote (spoiler warning): "What I mean is that even though the creatures aren't scary, once their secret is revealed—that's the point! Shyamalan is saying something very pointed about the peculiar nature of fear." Several other readers saw the film as an allegory for terror used as an excuse for political repression. That didn't occur to me, but as a theory it doesn't make the film any more entertaining, in my opinion.

Q. I was disappointed when I read in your review of *The Village* that you agreed to "avoid

905

revealing the plot secrets." Not a big deal, I thought, until I read a review empty of all but the most basic facts. Some restraint is necessary for the sake of your readers, but not for the sake of the producers. Next time, why not refuse such "enjoinings" and reveal what you—not they—want you to reveal?

—James Holter, Aurora, Illinois

A. Your exhortation is fascinating to me because of the angry communications I got from readers accusing me of giving away too much—the whole plot, said one, while another said that I had spoiled everything by even hinting there was a surprise. Scott Robinson of Pierrefonds, Québec, on the other hand, wrote: "What I find strange is that the marketing of this movie promises a surprise that is not really there. Shyamalan's first couple of films deliver a surprise that you are not expecting, but *Signs* and *The Village* seem to promise a surprise or at least an answer that never appears. While I must agree that no amount of marketing, however honest or creative, could save this film, I do believe that promising a little less would certainly allow the movie to deliver a little more."

Q. Given your lambasting of *The Village*, I was surprised to see a TV ad for the movie displaying a quote attributed to "Ebert & Roeper" that proclaimed it to be "one of the best movies of the year." I guess your partner in crime must have really liked *The Village*, but isn't it frustrating that your name was associated with a positive review of a film you so obviously disliked? Does this type of misleading marketing happen often?

—John Frank, Madison, Wisconsin

A. Beneath the large letters saying "Ebert & Roeper," they ran the name "Richard Roeper" in very small type—so small that I heard from more than thirty readers who had missed it and felt the ad misrepresented my opinion, as it probably was intended to do; studios use a similar strategy in using large fonts for words of praise from quote whores, whose names are microscopic. The guidelines for quotes from our show suggest that when only one of us is being quoted, the name come first in a similar type size: "Richard Roeper, Ebert & Roeper." After we pointed this out, the ad was changed.

What the #$*! Do We Know?

Q. I've read your review of *What the #$*! Do We Know?*, a film that attempts to explain some of the more interesting aspects of quantum physics. These explanations are given by what you describe as "experts" in the field. I am a professor of physics at the University of Massachusetts, doing research in the field of experimental particle physics. I glanced at the cast and didn't recognize any of them as leading names in the field of theoretical particle physics or cosmology. I even searched for their names using the search engine of the high-energy physics database, which references authors of papers appearing in the leading journals of the field. Nothing came up. I suspect that the people in the film are not physicists who have a rigorous training in the very mathematical and non-metaphysical theory of quantum mechanics. If this is indeed the case, then I warn you that the content of the film may have little or nothing to do with the actual theory of quantum mechanics.

—Carlo Dallapiccola, Amherst, Massachusetts

A. Since the expert who made the most sense to me was JZ Knight, who claims to be channeling Ramtha, a 35,000-year-old mystical sage from the lost continent of Atlantis, this does not come as a shock to me.

Q. While the film *What the #$*! Do We Know?* parades itself as a tell-all about quantum physics, it turns out that it's actually a 111-minute infomercial for . . . that's right, the Ramtha School of Enlightenment (RSE). In fact, the three filmmakers, William Arntz, Betsy Chasse, and Mark Vicente, are all devotees of Ramtha (aka JZ Knight). There's little or no accurate science in the film, and, as a physicist pointed out recently in your Answer Man, the individuals quoted are pretty far from qualified experts in the field of quantum mechanics. Case in point: One of the people expounding on causality and quantum physics (Dispenza) is a chiropractor. The film's sole purpose appears to be to promote the ideology of the Ramtha School of Enlightenment. A quick browse through its Website clearly demonstrates that the film's pseudoscientific nonsense comes straight from the teachings of the RSE.

—Rubin Safaya, Edina, Minnesota

A. Several other readers also unmasked the documentary as a hoax. I knew there had to be something fishy when the expert who made the most sense was channeling a 35,000-year-old seer from Atlantis.

Q. Re. your Answer Man item about *What the #$*! Do We Know* being a hoax perpetrated by the Ramtha School of Enlightenment: Did you or your readers go out and sign up for Ramtha's school? No, and neither did I. Instead I walked away absolutely astounded by the insights into my own life experience and the direction that I needed to go in order to affect my life in a positive way. Whether the scientists in the film are "experts" or not (who defines these terms, anyway?) I found their insights and perspectives extremely helpful. The filmmakers encourage us to begin to understand the theory of quantum physics and start to ask ourselves questions that will lead us to a mindful life.

—Kiara Lee, Berkeley, California

A. I also received a sharply worded letter from Mark Vicente, Betsy Chasse, and William Arntz, the co-directors, defending the stature of their experts and the integrity of the film.

What the #$*@! has turned into a sleeper hit around the country, drawing repeat audiences and generating strong word of mouth. I felt a certain affection for the film, although as my original review indicated, the "movie attempts to explain quantum physics in terms anyone can understand. It succeeds, up to a point. I understood every single term. Only the explanation eluded me."

Among the experts on the screen, I wrote, "only one seemed to make perfect sense to me. This was a pretty, plumpish blonde woman with clear blue eyes who looked the camera straight in the eye, seemed wise and sane, and said that although the questions might be physical, the answers were likely to be metaphysical. Since we can't by definition understand life and the world, we might as well choose a useful way of pretending to."

This woman, I later learned, was the psychic JZ Knight. Still later, a letter to the Answer Man from an actual physicist, Rubin Safaya, informed me the people quoted were far from experts in the field.

The film is what it is, a group of people trying to explain the nature of reality. The confusion comes if you think they are discussing physics, when in fact they are discussing metaphysics. There is nothing wrong with having a belief system and using it to fashion your worldview; the error comes in ascribing scientific truth to what is by definition a matter of faith. The argument between Darwinians and Creationists is similar: Darwinians use science, Creationists use faith. "Creationist science" is laughed at by reputable scientists because it tries to use its easily refuted "science" to explain a belief that grows from and depends entirely on faith. By the same token, although the Ramtha School may indeed have valuable insights into the nature of reality, it is misleading to present them as science.

Ziyi Zhang

Q. I'm curious to know what you think about Chinese actress Ziyi Zhang being chosen to play the lead role in *Memoirs of a Geisha*. Zhang is a lovely and talented actress, but don't you think that in all of Japan there is an equally talented and lovely Japanese actress who could play the part? I wonder if the selection of a Chinese actress to play a Japanese woman will sit well with Japanese fans of the book.

—Rosanne O'Toole, San Antonio, Texas

A. Ziyi Zhang at twenty-six has become an important international star, after such films as *Crouching Tiger, Hidden Dragon, Rush Hour 2, Hero, House of Flying Daggers,* and *2046.* No other Asian actress has the same international fame, and star power is crucial in a project where the title character is central to every scene.

Ebert's Little Movie Glossary

These are the year's new contributions to my glossary project. Hundreds of entries were collected in *Ebert's Bigger Little Movie Glossary,* published in 1999. Contributions are always welcome.

* * *

Answering-Machine Pickup Rule. If the plot requires that an injured or incapacitated character answer a phone, it will ring an infinite number of times until the character can crawl to the phone. The caller will not hang up and the answering machine will not pick up. If the plot requires only that the audience hear what the caller has to say, the answering machine will pick up after one ring.

—Mike Zobel, Rochester, New York

Arbitrary Ramp Rule. Every stunt that involves a vehicle flying through the air requires a conveniently located ramp that has absolutely no business being there in the first place. (See the ramp at the pier for *Starsky & Hutch* and the one at the end of the freeway in *Speed.*)

—Gerardo Valero, Mexico City, Mexico

Bald Beanstalk Boss in Blue Bad-Boy Rule. Any supervisor who happens to be tall and balding will usually end up having some dirty secret and may even turn out to be the villain, especially if he's in law enforcement. Actors cast in this role include James Cromwell, John Lithgow, and J. T. Walsh.

—Wei-Hwa Huang, Mountain View, California

Bartlett's Law. Whenever one character recites a quote from memory to another, the second person already knows it and tells him or her the origin. If it is from the Bible, the second person always knows which chapter and verse.

—Mike Pearl, Orange, California

Big Slow Spaceship Shot Syndrome. Since the first *Star Wars,* every science-fiction movie set in space has had at least one shot of an enormous spaceship appearing from out of frame and moving slowly past the camera. It is usually seen from beneath. Low bass rumbles are used on the sound track.

—Geraldo Valero, Mexico City, Mexico

Candles at Wholesale Rule. In any movie scene involving candles, there will be hundreds or even thousands of them, even if the characters live in poverty. We are left to wonder how one person, or even everyone in the cast, could light them all before the scene began. See *Because of Winn-Dixie.*

—R.E.

The Exploding Blender. With the exception of *Cocktail,* anyone in the history of the cinema who has ever tried to use an ordinary household blender has managed to have the lid fly off and the contents spray into the air, covering everything within a six-foot radius with soup, smoothie, etc.

—Chris Hardie, Melbourne, Victoria, Australia

Fallacy of the Snarling Beast. A variation on the Fallacy of the Talking Killer. Any ferocious animal, monster, etc., upon cornering its prey, will slow to a menacing creep and begin to snarl, growl, or otherwise attempt to terrify. Unfortunately for the beast, this always gives his quarry time to escape.

—Mike Pearl, Orange, California

The "Get Off the %^&* Bus" Rule. Whenever a group of people get off a bus, the passenger who lingers for several seconds on the last step, leering from left to right (while holding up the remaining passengers in the bus), is the bad guy.

—Sam Comer, Atlanta, Georgia

Ghostly Communication Rule. Ghosts come in two types in movies. If it's a comedy or drama, the ghost is chatty, easygoing, and/or likes to crack jokes (*Ghost Dad, The Sixth Man, Always*) and appears as a normal human. If it's a horror or thriller, the ghost has a dark purpose and doesn't talk. Although it can open and close doors and walk through walls, the ghost prefers to leave cryptic messages written in blood or vapor, or carved in the wall (see *Gothika, What Lies Beneath, The Haunting*).

—Sebastian Tabany, Buenos Aires, Argentina

The Important-Question Rule. When a man looks deeply into the eyes of the woman he's been dating and says, softly and importantly, "There's a very important question I want to ask you, but I could never find the right moment—until now," the question is never "Will you marry me?"

—R.E.

Law of Asynchronous Sleep. If two people are sleeping in the same bed, they will never arise at the same time. Instead, we will see a) Person A getting up and leaving while Person B is still asleep; b) Person B waking up to see Person A finishing getting dressed (if Person A is male, he is guaranteed to be putting on a tie); or c) Person B waking up to discover that Person A is already long gone (see Futile Hug Syndrome).

—Adam Fromm, Glens Falls, New York

Lukewarm Latte Rule. When characters are handed a cup of coffee at a coffee shop, the cup is not treated as if it is full and scalding hot. Characters take long, thoughtful sips from the cup without noticing the mouthful of seared flesh that would necessarily ensue.

—Bill Maselunas, Dallas, Texas

Morse Code Rules I and II. Rule I: Characters are able to decipher entire sentences by listening to a few dit-dit-dahs on the telegraph, or watching a few flashes of light. In *The Hunt for Red October* Sam Neill looks at the signal lamp of an approaching warship and in a few seconds makes out "Red October, Red October. Halt and stay where you are. Do not attempt to submerge or you will be fired upon." For an accurate example of how long it takes to communicate Morse code, see the brig scene in *Star Trek V*. Rule II: Expert Morse operators verbally repeat the message they are sending, for the audience's benefit.

—Brian Henley, Norristown, Pennsylvania

The One-Hit-Wonder Broadway Show. In movie bios involving musicals, the curtain rises, the star performs a single number, and the curtain drops to a standing ovation. No

one seems to want their money back after such a short show. See Susan Hayward's (dubbed) "I'll Plant My Own Tree" in *Valley of the Dolls* or any of the Broadway numbers in *De-Lovely*.

—Howard Gollop, Cleveland, Ohio

The Orlok Scale. Reflects the tendency of movie vampires to seem less like the ghoulish vampires of folklore and more like well-dressed superheroes. Old-school vampire traits (can turn into mist or a bat or a wolf; fears garlic; doesn't drink . . . wine) are replaced by super speed, rock music, and a tendency to "turn good" and renounce human blood. Also, the newer vampires are easier to kill; a simple arrow through the heart replaces the much more labor-intensive method of having to hammer a stake through the heart, then cut off the head. Count Orlock of *Nosferatu* rates 10 (highest) on the Orlok Scale; the vamps in *Underworld* rate a pathetic 3.

—Rav Schazten, Long Island, New York

Pets for Ethical Treatment of Actors. Hundreds of people can be killed in a trailer, but any endangered dog or cat must be shown alive and unharmed by the end of the trailer. This is also true of the full film. Recent example is *Meet the Fockers,* where the dog emerges unharmed from the toilet, but my favorite is the opening of *Armageddon,* where New York City is devastated, but the dog survives uninjured.

—Bob Hawks, Carpentersville, Illinois

Rule of Length of Death. All superfluous characters die quickly, but the central villain or hero will endure a prolonged death while the camera lingers for maximum effect.

—Steve Kaszycki, Pittsburgh, Pennsylvania

Self-Ringing Steel. In any recent movie involving sword fighting, sound editors make sure that every motion of a blade is accompanied by the familiar steel-on-steel ringing sound regardless of whether it touches other metal: when being drawn from its nonmetal scabbard, when piercing human flesh, sometimes even just slicing through the air. This is most obvious in the *Lord of the Rings* movies, but see also *The Last Samurai, Gladiator,* etc.

—Dan Knight, Oak Park, Illinois

The Van Winkle Isn't RIP Principle. All elderly characters found slumped in a chair in front of the fire, if upper class, or in front of the TV, if not, are never dead no matter how corpselike they appear or how tenuous we've been told their hold on life is. They always sputter back to life as soon as the consequences of their demise have been reviewed. See *Bad Santa* and any physical comedy from Bob Hope to Adam Sandler.

—Gary F. Phelps, Niantic, Connecticut

The What About Bob? Rule. In any movie set in the future, characters have names that sound nothing like today's names and contain lots of *Zs* and *Ks*.

—Michael McCluskey, Halifax, Nova Scotia

The "Yeah!" Guy. In a Mission Control Syndrome scene, the camera focuses on an individual whose "Yeah!" reaction is louder than the general applause and cheering on the soundtrack. Sometimes more than one "Yeah!" guy is employed; occasionally he says "Woo!" Not to be confused with a lesser character, the "Yes!" guy, who pumps his fist in the air.

—Nate Bailie, Huntsville, Alabama

Your Escape Should Be Up to Your Room in Less than Thirty Minutes, or It's on Us. All hotel room security precautions made by heroes, villains, or cops or bodyguards watching heroes or villains can in one way or another be overcome by a deftly deployed room service cart.

—Jon Myers, Chicago, Illinois

Index

A